Concise Oxford Companion to
# The English Language

The most authoritative and up-to-date reference books for both students and the general reader.

## Oxford Paperback Reference

Concise Oxford Companion to

# The English Language

*Editor*

**TOM McARTHUR**

*Assistant Editor*

**ROSHAN McARTHUR**

Oxford   New York

**OXFORD UNIVERSITY PRESS**

1998

Oxford University Press, Great Clarendon Street, Oxford OX2 6DP

Oxford  New York

Athens  Auckland  Bangkok  Bogotá  Bombay  Buenos Aires
Calcutta  Cape Town  Dar es Salaam  Delhi  Florence  Hong Kong  Istanbul
Karachi  Kuala Lumpur  Madras  Madrid  Melbourne  Mexico City
Nairobi  Paris  Singapore  Taipei  Tokyo  Toronto  Warsaw

and associated companies in
Berlin  Ibadan

Oxford is a trade mark of Oxford University Press

British Library Cataloguing in Publication Data
Data available

Library of Congress Cataloging in Publication Data
The concise Oxford companion to the English language / edited by Tom
McArthur.
Includes bibliographical references (p.   ) and index.
1. English philology—Encyclopedias.   2. Language and languages—
Encyclopedias.   I. McArthur, Tom (Thomas Burns)
PE31.C66  1998      420'.3—dc21      98–6736
ISBN 0–19–280061–2

10  9  8  7  6  5  4  3  2  1

Typeset by Best-set Typesetter Ltd., Hong Kong
Printed in Great Britain by
Cox & Wyman, Reading, Berkshire

# Contents

# Contents

# Introduction

*The Concise Oxford Companion to the English Language* provides compact, comprehensive, up-to-date, and easily accessible information about key aspects of ENGLISH at the end of the twentieth century. Among other things, it covers: the distribution and varieties of ENGLISH; its cultural, political, and educational impact worldwide; its nature, origins, and prospects; and its PRONUNCIATION, GRAMMAR, VOCABULARY, WORD-FORMATION, and USAGE. The aim has been to do this dispassionately without being bland, and in a scholarly fashion without being opaque, drawing on and distilling the unique international range of expertise that went into the original full-size *Oxford Companion to the English Language* (1992) and its abridged version (1996). The distinctive features of this edition include:

- The highlighting of key articles both at the beginning and in the body of the book, for easy reference
- Information panels throughout the text, for example giving thumbnail accounts of the PLACE-NAMES of major English-speaking countries, as a means of highlighting particular topics
- Selective cross-referencing in small capitals in the body of the text (as in this introduction), as well as at the ends of entries
- A chronology of English from 55 BC to AD 1997 (Appendix 1)
- An extensive thematic bibliography (Appendix 2)

The *Concise Companion* rests on the view that, in recent years, STANDARD ENGLISH has become a global resource that does not owe its existence, or the protection of its essence, to any one nation or group. Inasmuch as a particular LANGUAGE belongs to any individual or community, English is the possession of every individual and every community that uses it, regardless of what any other individual or community may think or feel about the matter. It is therefore intended as a resource for any person anywhere who is in any way involved with English.

There has been considerable discussion over the last two decades regarding the nature and use of English, and especially what Robert W. Burchfield has called 'its innumerable clearly distinguishable varieties' (Introduction, vol. iv, *A Supplement to the Oxford English Dictionary*, 1986). Scholars have discussed both its usage (local, regional, and international) and its varieties (STANDARD and NON-STANDARD), while in broader public debate many people have—sometimes anxiously—wondered whether the language might be 'going to the dogs', and be so over-extended around the world that it might break up into mutually unintelligible forms: that is, into a range of ENGLISH LANGUAGES.

The English language complex can however be viewed in several ways. Depending on the perspective we choose, it can be a single language or an aggregate of languages. The oneness of English is obvious in its standard worldwide printed form, but the manyness becomes equally clear when we compare and contrast that standard with 'the guid SCOTS tongue' in Lowland Scotland and Northern Ireland, or with TOK PISIN ('Talk Pidgin'), one of the three official language of Papua-New Guinea, alongside English and Hiri Motu. To these we can add such traditional dialects as YORKSHIRE and NEWFOUNDLAND, such recently acknowledged NEW ENGLISHes as INDIAN ENGLISH and the varieties used in NIGERIA and SINGAPORE, and the many controversial ANGLO-HYBRIDS, such as SPANGLISH in the United States (blending SPANISH and English) and TAGLISH in the PHILIPPINES (blending TAGALOG and English).

At the close of the fifth millennium since recorded history began, English is unique. No other WORLD LANGUAGE has ever been put to so many uses by so many people in so many places or on such a scale—on land, by sea, in the air, and in space; in the mind, in the mouth, and by hand (in WRITING or SIGN); through PRINTING on paper and increasingly on screen; on tape and film; and through radio, television, telephone, electronic networks, and multimedia. It is used as a mother tongue or other tongue (fluently, adequately, or haltingly; constantly, intermittently, or seldom; happily, unhappily, or ambivalently) by about a fifth of the human race—something over a billion people.

At the same time, the academic study of English is a global industry. Thousands of university scholars, in addition to teaching a huge student population, produce year on year an unquantifiable number of books, journals, dissertations, articles, reports, conference proceedings, course books, class notes, newsletters, and (increasingly) contributions to INTERNET newsgroups. Their total output is far more than any one of them can digest, and few if any will see—or even learn about—every document relating even to their areas of special interest.

The day-to-day language acts of users of English around the world are so vast and varied that no person, group, or system could ever catch and catalogue them all. Even the most extensive, flexible, and subtle computer CORPUS that we can currently imagine cannot encompass all the usages of the STANDARD LANGUAGE alone. Total knowledge of the subject is therefore impossible, and because of this our efforts in describing, prescribing for, and TEACHING ENGLISH—however effective and influential they might be—are incomplete and indirect. In GRAMMARS, DICTIONARIES, and other publications there has often been an impressive match (as far as we can tell) between what scholars think goes on and what is actually happening, resulting in many highly practical achievements. But all the models and descriptions of English ever made—and certainly this one—are exercises of the imagination, not God's truth.

I am grateful to all who have been involved in the creation of the mother book, the abridged edition, and now this concise edition: for the work they have done and the patience they have shown, and most particularly to my daughter Roshan, whose diligence, perseverance, and intuition have made the abridged and the concise editions possible.

Although all three Companions are complex works, they remain interim reports. No book that seeks to describe a living language can ever be complete, and no printed product can directly exhibit the diversity of SPEECH, or hope to cover every feature and nuance of written, printed, and electronic expression. Because of this, and the on-going nature of the work, constructive comment and suggestions are welcomed by The Editor, *The Oxford Companion to the English Language*, Oxford University Press, Great Clarendon Street, Oxford OX2 6DP, England.

TOM MCARTHUR

*Cambridge, 1997*

# Contributors and consultants

## Contributors

Jean Aitchison
A. J. Aitken
John Algeo
Robert E. Allen
Jon Amastae
Tony Augarde
Richard W. Bailey
William W. Barker
Dennis E. Baron
Laurie Bauer
John Baugh
Paul Beale
David Blair
Eyamba G. Bokamba
Whitney F. Bolton
Jean Branford
William Branford
Lawrence B. Breitborde
Christopher J. Brumfit
Robert W. Burchfield
Garland Cannon
Lawrence D. Carrington
Frederic G. Cassidy
Sylvia Chalker
Raymond Chapman
Paul Christophersen
Isagani R. Cruz
David Crystal

W. D. Wimal Dissanayake
Connie C. Eble
John Edwards
Stanley Ellis
Margery Fee
Jean-Marc Gachelin
Charles Gilman
Andrew Gonzales
Sidney Greenbaum
Anjum R. Haque
Reinhard Hartmann
Mohamed H. Heliel
Geoffrey Hughes
Robert F. Ilson
Braj B. Kachru
Yamuna Kachru
Gillian S. Kay
Francis E. Knowles
Gerald Knowles
Margot Lawrence
Sangsup Lee
Michael Lesk
Peter H. Lowenberg
William D. Lutz
Iseabail C. McLeod
Rejend Mesthrie
Salikoko S. Mufwene
Walter Nash

Cecil L. Nelson
Noel E. Osselton
Frank R. Palmer
Rajeshwari Pandharipande
John Platt
René James Quinault
William S. Ramson
Suzanne Romaine
Adrian Room
William Shephard
Larry E. Smith
S. N. Sridhar
James Stanlaw
Sol Steinmetz
Peter Strevens
Mary Tay
Loreto Todd
Barry Tomalin
Peter Trudgill
Christopher Upward
Laurence Urdang
Katie Wales
Heidi Weber
Edmund Weiner
Lise S. Winer
Margaret E. Winters.

## Consultants

Richard Allwright
Jacqueline Anderson
Lourdes B. Bautista
Ben Benedikz
Roger Bowers
J. K. Chambers
Sandra Clarke
Rachel Davis
Agnes Drever
Robert A. Dunbar
Anna Dunlop
Barbara Goldsmid
David Gough
Barbara Harris

Tom Hecht
Joan Hughes
Sally Hunt
Fadilah Jasmani
S. Johansson
Damian J. Kelly
Virginia LaCastro
Leonhard Lipka
Louise McIvor
Kevin McNamee
David I. Masson
Dhun Mehta
Godfrey Meintjes
Tatsuo Miyajima

Diarmaid Ó hAirt
Maria-Grazia Pederzani
Mary Penrith
Frederick H. G. Percy
Peter Pitman
Arnold D. N. Pitt
Graham Pointon
Velma Pollard
Camilla Raab
F. Gordon Rohlehr
A. O. Sanved
Sybil Sarel
Donald Scragg
John Singler

Brian Smith
K. Sørenson
Mats-Peter Sundström
Paul Thompson

Ronald Threadgall
Hamish Todd
Junko Uozu
Henry Warkentyne

Henry Widdowson
David Williamson
Carol Winkelmann.

# Abbreviations

Only those abbreviations are listed that are not explained in the entries in which they occur.

| | | | |
|---|---|---|---|
| AfrE | African English | NZE | New Zealand English |
| AmE | American English | *OED* | *Oxford English Dictionary* |
| AusE | Australian English | PakE | Pakistani English |
| AV | Authorized Version of the Bible | RP | Received Pronunciation |
| | | SAfrE | South African English |
| BrE | British English | ScoE | Scottish English |
| c | century/centuries | TEFL/EFL | (Teaching) English as a Foreign Language |
| CanE | Canadian English | | |
| CarE | Caribbean English | TEIL/EIL | (Teaching) English as an International Language |
| ELT | English Language Teaching | | |
| EngE | English in England | TESL/ESL | (Teaching) English as a Second Language |
| ESP | English for Special/Specific Purposes | | |
| | | TESOL | Teaching of English to Speakers of Other Languages |
| IE | Indo-European | | |
| IndE | Indian English | U. | University |
| IPA | International Phonetic Alphabet/Association | UCLES | University of Cambridge Local Examination Syndicate |
| IrE | Irish English | | |
| MLA | Modern Language Association | WAE | West African English |
| | | WelshE | Welsh English |

The asterisk symbol (\*) has two uses in the body of the *Companion*: it marks either a grammatically unacceptable form (as in \**has went*) or an unattested or hypothetical form (as in \**ultraticum*).

# Values of phonetic symbols used in the *Companion*

a  *a* as in ScoE *pat* and Parisian French *patte*

aɪ  *y* and *i–e* as in RP and AmE *try, write*

aʊ  *ou* and *ow* as in RP and AmE *noun, now*

ɑ  *a* as in RP *father*; *a* and *o* as in AmE *father, bother*

ɒ  *a* and *o* as in RP *wash, odd*

æ  *a* as in traditional RP and in AmE *cat, trap*

b  *b* as in *back*; *bb* as in *rubber*

ç  *ch* as in German *ich*; *h* as in Japanese *hito*; occasionally, *h* as in *hue*

d  *d* as in *day*; *dd* as in *rudder*

dʒ  *j* and *dge* as in *judge*, and *ge* as in *George*; *j* as in Hindi *raj*

ð  *th* as in *this, other*; *d* as in Spanish *nada*

e  *ay* as in ScoE *day*; *é* as in French *thé*; *e* as in Italian *pesca* (fishing)

eɪ  *ay*, *a–e*, and *ea* as in RP and AmE *day, face, steak*

ə  [the schwa or neutral vowel] *a* as in *about, sofa*, *e* as in *hyphen*, *o* as in *reckon* (ect.)

əʊ  *o* and *oa* as in RP *go, goat*

ɛ  *e* as in *get*, German *Bett*, and Italian *pesca* (peach)

ɛə  *ai* and *a–e* as in RP *fair, square*

ɜ  *e, i, o, u* as in RP and AmE *her, stir, word, nurse*

f  *f* as in *few*; *ff* as in *puff*

g  *g* as in *got*; *gg* as in *bigger*

h  *h* as in *hot*

i  *e* as in *he*, *ee* as in *see*; *i* as in Spanish and French *si*; *ie* as in German *sie*

ɪ  *i* as in *ship* and in German *Schiff*

ɪə  *ea* and *e–e* as in RP *hear, here*

j  *y* as in *yet*; *j* as in German *ja*

k  *c* as in *car*; *k* as in *key*; *ck* as in *clock*; *kk* as in *trekked*; *qu* as in *quay*

l  [clear 1] *l* as in RP *lip*

ɫ  [dark 1] *l* as in RP *all*; as commonly in ScoE *all, lip, hilly*

ɬ  *ll* as in Welsh *Llanelli*

m  *m* as in *much*; *mm* as in *hammer*

n  *n* as in *now*; *nn* as in *runner*

ŋ  *ng* as in RP and AmE *sing*; *n* as in Spanish *cinco*

o  *o* as in ScoE *no*, in advanced RP *force*, and in Italian *dove*; *eau* as in French *beau*; *oh* as in German *wohl*

oʊ  *o* and *oa* as in AmE *go, goat*

ø  *eu* as in French *peu*; *ö* as in German *schön*

œ  *eu* as in French *veuve*; *ö* as in German *zwölf*

ɔ  *o* as in *north* and in German *Sonne*; *a* as in *war*

ɔɪ  *oi* and *oy* as in *noise, toy*

p  *p* as in *pen*; *pp* as in *pepper*

r  generally, *r* as in *round* and *rr* as in *sorry* (however pronounced); strictly, the rolled *r* of traditional ScoE, and of Spanish and Italian

ʀ  uvular *r* as in Parisian French *rue* and the Northumbrian burr s     *s* as in *see*; *ss* as in *missed*

ʃ     *sh* as in *ship*; *ssi* as in *mission*; *ti* as in *motion*; *ch* as in French *chose*; *sch* as in German *Schiff*

t     *t* as in *ten*; *tt* as in RP *written*

tʃ     *ch* as in *church*; *tch* as in *latch*; *c* as in Italian *cello*, *ciao*; *tsch* as in German *Deutsch*

θ     *th* as in *three*, *heath*, and Greek *thésis*; *c* and *z* as in Castilian Spanish *cerveza*

u     *u* as in *lunar* and *oo* as in RP *pool*; *u* as in Italian *subito* and German *gut*; *ou* as in French *tout*

ʉ     *ui*, *ou* (etc.) in Scots *puir* (poor) and *doun/doon* (down), and as in Norwegian *hus*

ʊ     *oo* and *u* as in RP and AmE *foot* and *put*

ʊə     *u* and *u–e* as in RP *pure*

v     *v* as in *very* and in French *vrai*; *w* as in German *wohl*

ʌ     *u*, *oo*, and *o–e* as in RP and ScoE *bud*, *blood*, *love*

w     *w* as in *will*; *ou* as in French *oui*

hw     *wh* as in ScoE and IrE *when*, *white*

x     *ch* as in ScoE and German *ach*; *j* and *g* as in Spanish *jabón* and *gente*

y     *u–e* as in French *lune*; *ü* as in German *über*

ɣ     *g* as in Spanish *luego*

z     *z* as in *zeal* and French *zèle*; *s* as in *position*; *ss* as in *scissors*

ʒ     *s* as in *decision* and *measure*; *j* and *g* as in French *Jacques* and *rouge*

ʔ     [glottal stop] *tt* as in Cockney and Glasgow pronunciations of *better butter*, and as a phoneme in Arabic and Hawaiian

:     [the length mark] used to indicate a long vowel, as in /u:/, in RP *loose*, *truce*

~     [the tilde] set over a symbol to indicate nasality

# World map

## English throughout the world

A numbered list and map of territories for
which English is a significant language

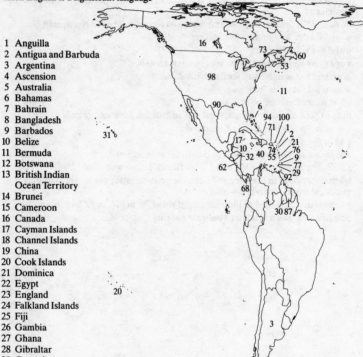

1 Anguilla
2 Antigua and Barbuda
3 Argentina
4 Ascension
5 Australia
6 Bahamas
7 Bahrain
8 Bangladesh
9 Barbados
10 Belize
11 Bermuda
12 Botswana
13 British Indian
   Ocean Territory
14 Brunei
15 Cameroon
16 Canada
17 Cayman Islands
18 Channel Islands
19 China
20 Cook Islands
21 Dominica
22 Egypt
23 England
24 Falkland Islands
25 Fiji
26 Gambia
27 Ghana
28 Gibraltar
29 Grenada
30 Guyana
31 Hawaii
32 Honduras
33 Hong Kong
34 India
35 Indonesia
36 Iraq
37 Irish Republic
38 Isle of Man
39 Israel
40 Jamaica
41 Japan
42 Jordan
43 Kenya
44 Kiribati
45 Korea

46 Kuwait
47 Lesotho
48 Liberia
49 Malawi
50 Malaysia
51 Maldives
52 Malta
53 Maritime Provinces
54 Mauritius
55 Montserrat
56 Namibia
57 Nauru
58 Nepal

59 New England
60 Newfoundland
61 New Zealand
62 Nicaragua
63 Nigeria
64 Northern Ireland
65 Oman
66 Orkney
67 Pakistan
68 Panama
69 Papua New Guinea
70 Philippines
71 Puerto Rico

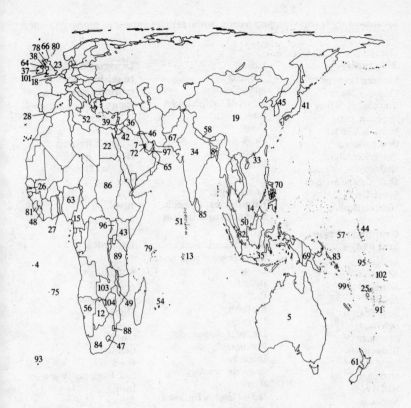

# A thematic list of key entries

Because of their wide-ranging nature, some articles appear in more than one theme.

## Biography

Chaucer, Geoffrey
Chomsky, Noam
Greenbaum, Sidney
Jespersen, Otto
Johnson, Samuel
Orwell, George
Quirk, Randolph
Shakespeare, William
Shaw, George Bernard
Sweet, Henry
Webster, Noah

## Grammar, style, and usage

Adjective
Adverb
Adverbial
Article
Basic English
Determiner
Grammar
House style
Logic
Metaphor
Modal verb
Negation
Nonsense
Noun
Number
Participle
Phrasal verb
Plain English
Plural
Preposition
Pronoun
Question
Relative clause
Rhetoric
Sentence
Standard
Style
Subject
Subjunctive
Subordination
Survey of English Usage
Tense
Usage
Usage guidance and criticism
Verb

## Language, linguistics, speech, and pronunciation

Accent
BBC Pronunciation Unit
Child language acquisition
Creole
Dialect
Dictionary
Etymology
Language
Language change
Lexicography
Linguistics
Linguistic typology
Name
Oxford English Dictionary
Philology
Pidgin
Progress and decay in language
Psycholinguistics
Received Pronunciation
Rhythm
Semantics
Sociolinguistics
Speech
Stress
Tone
Variety
Vowel

## Language learning, teaching, and translation

ELT (English Language Teaching)
Examining in English
Language learning
Language teaching
Teaching English
TEFL
TEIL
TESD
TESL
TESOL
Translation

## Languages

Arabic
Celtic languages
China
French
Gaelic
German
Greek
Indo-European languages
Irish
Italian
Japan
Latin
Hawaiian
Maori
Norse
Romance languages
Russian
Sanskrit
Scandinavian languages
Scots
Slavonic/Slavic languages
Spanish
Tok Pisin
Welsh

## The Evolution of the Alphabet

| THE CAPITAL LETTER | | | | | | THE SMALL LETTER | | | | |
|---|---|---|---|---|---|---|---|---|---|---|
| EARLY FORMS | | | | CURRENT FORMS | | EARLY FORMS | | | CURRENT FORMS | |
| Phoenician | Greek | Etruscan | Roman (Latin) | roman | italic | Roman cursive | Roman uncial | Carolingian minuscule | roman | italic |
| K | ΔA | A | A | A | A | λ | ᴀ | ᴀ | a | a |
| 9 | ᴀB | 8 | B | B | B | ᴀ | B | b | b | b |
| 1 | ΠΓ | ᴧ | C | C | C | < | C | C | c | c |
| △ | ◁Δ | ᴅ | D | D | D | ᴅ | δ | d | d | d |
| ᴣ | ƎE | ᴣ | E | E | E | ᴇ | ᴇ | ᴇ | e | e |
| Y | ᴦF | � | F | F | F | F | F | ſ | f | f |
| | | | G | G | G | ᴝ | G | g | g | g |
| ᴴ | ᴮH | ᴼ | H | H | H | ᴴ | h | h | h | h |
| ᴣ | ᴸ| I | I | I | I | I | J | ᴌ | i | i |
| ᴣ | ᴸ| I | I | J | J | J | J | ᴌ | j | j |
| ↓K | ᴈK | ᴋ | K | K | K | | K | ᴋ | k | k |
| ᴸ | ᴦᴧ | ᴧ | ᴸL | L | L | ᴌ | L | l | l | l |
| ᴢ | MM | ᴍ | M | M | M | ᴍ | ᴍ | ᴍ | m | m |

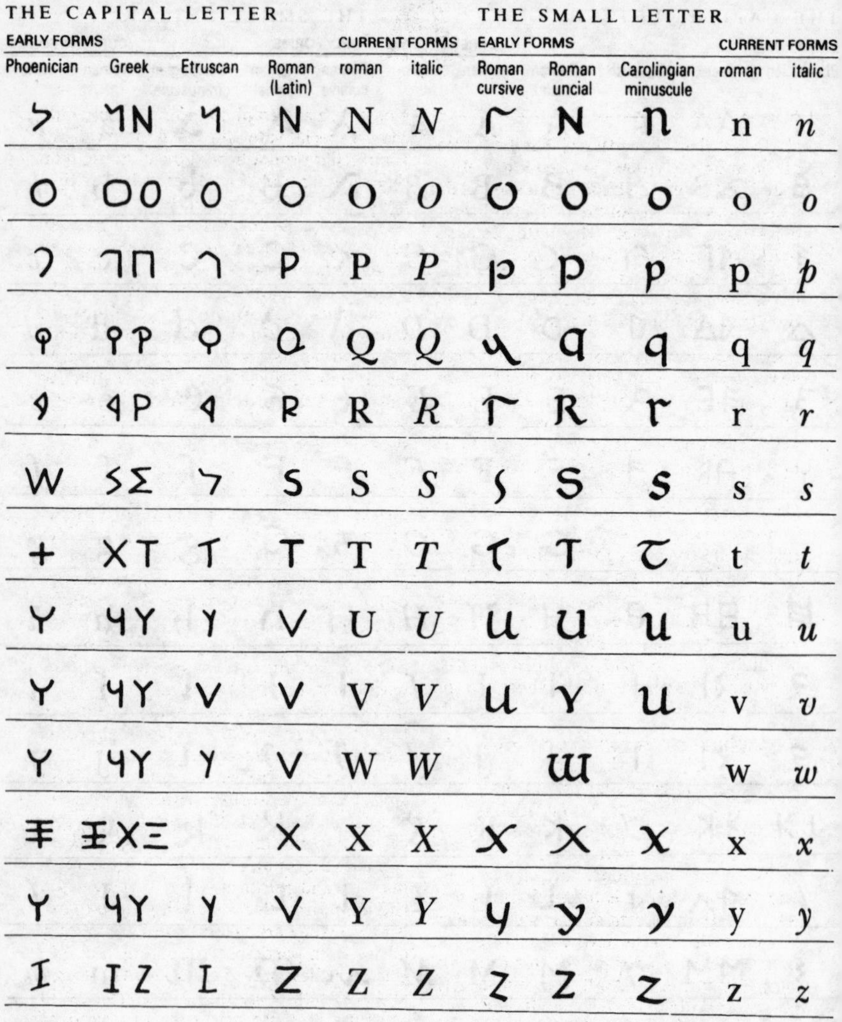

| THE CAPITAL LETTER | | | | | | THE SMALL LETTER | | | | |
|---|---|---|---|---|---|---|---|---|---|---|
| EARLY FORMS | | | | CURRENT FORMS | | EARLY FORMS | | | CURRENT FORMS | |
| Phoenician | Greek | Etruscan | Roman (Latin) | roman | italic | Roman cursive | Roman uncial | Carolingian minuscule | roman | italic |
| 5 | ᛉN | Ч | N | N | *N* | ⌐ | N | �na | n | *n* |
| O | ◻O | O | O | O | *O* | O | O | o | o | *o* |
| ꓶ | ꓶΠ | ꓶ | P | P | *P* | ꓷ | ꓷ | p | p | *p* |
| φ | φφ | Ҩ | Q | Q | *Q* | ʮ | q | q | q | *q* |
| ꓒ | ꓒP | ꓒ | R | R | *R* | ⌐ | ꓘ | ꓨ | r | *r* |
| W | ꟻΣ | ꟽ | S | S | *S* | ʂ | S | *s* | s | *s* |
| + | XT | ꓔ | T | T | *T* | ꓔ | T | ꓔ | t | *t* |
| Y | ꓩY | Y | V | U | *U* | u | u | u | u | *u* |
| Y | ꓩY | Ʌ | V | V | *V* | u | Y | u | v | *v* |
| Y | ꓩY | Y | V | W | *W* | | ɯ | | w | *w* |
| � | ꓱX三 | | X | X | *X* | ꓫ | X | ꓫ | x | *x* |
| Y | ꓩY | Y | V | Y | *Y* | ꓳ | ꓬ | ꓬ | y | *y* |
| I | IZ | I | Z | Z | *Z* | Z | Z | ꓜ | z | *z* |

# A

■ **A, a** ─────────── ■

[Called *ay*, rhyming with *say*]. The 1st LETTER of the Roman ALPHABET as used for English. It descends from the Phoenician symbol for a GLOTTAL STOP, the sound at the beginning of its name, *'aleph* ('ox'). This letter, a consonant in Phoenician, was adopted by the Greeks as a vowel, A, to which they gave the name *alpha*. It was later adopted as *A* first by the Etruscans, then the Romans.

**Sound values**. (1) Short, as in *hat, lack, apple*. (2) Long, as in *hate, lake, maple, chaos*. In many accents of English, this sound is a diphthong, /eɪ/, often in RP with a special value before *r*, /eə/, as in *vary, scarce*. (3) In RP and related accents, phonetically long and open, /ɑ:/, in such words as *clam, dance, far, father*. (4) SCHWA in weak syllables, as in *avoid, prevalent, viable, vital, relevant, vicar, villa*. In RP, the weak form sometimes has the value of short *i*, /ɪ/, as in *private, village*. (5) After /w/ and before /l/, a phonetically long, open value of *o*, /ɔ:/, as in *wall, war, water, quarter, tall*; in RP, after *w*, a short *o*-sound, /ɒ/, as in *swamp, swastika*; likewise in *yacht*. (6) In *any, many*, the short *e*-sound in *hen*.

**Digraphs and other combinations**. With the value of long *a* in cases 1–3. (1) *a–e*, where one or more consonants separate *a* and *e*: *hate, pale, waste*. (2) *ai*, initially and medially: *aid, pail, maintain*. The value of short *e* is often heard in *again, against, said*. (3) *ay*, in final positions: *day, dismay, relay*. The value of short *e* is often heard in *says*. (4) *au*, initially and medially: *sauce, author, because, laurel*. These have values of *o* that tend to be accent-dependent: for example, /ɔ/ in RP, and /ɒ/ in AmE, sometimes with length variation. (5) *aw*, in all positions, but especially finally: *awful, drawl, saw* (with various values, many comparable to those of *au*). (6) *aa*, only in loans, such as: names from Hebrew, with the long-*a* value in *Aaron, Canaan*, and schwa in *Isaac*; from Afrikaans, with the value of phonetically long, open *a* (*aardvark, kraal*). (7) *ae*, in diverse loans, usually with the value of long *a*: *maelstrom*, from Dutch; *Gael*, from Celtic; *Ishmael, Israel*, from Hebrew. (8) As second

element in a digraph (*ea, oa*), *a* usually indicates a special value for the first vowel, but is not itself pronounced: long *e* in *east, beat, cheated*, long *o* in *oats, boat, soaked*, with a glide effect before *r* in non-rhotic accents, as in *fear, boar*. (9) In four words, *ea* has the value of long *a*: *break, great, steak, yea*. (10) In many common words, the digraph *ea* is pronounced as short *e*: *bread, meadow, ready, sweat, zealous*. (11) The letter *a* combines in unusual, sometimes unique ways with other vowel letters in: *aisle, aunt, beauty, broad, guinea, laugh, quay*. (12) Distinctive values in loanwords are usually preserved: *bureau, gauche, gaucho, naive/naïve*. For the symbol æ, see DIGRAPH.

**Variations**. (1) In some pairs of derivationally associated words, *a* has been replaced or has disappeared in unstressed syllables (*abstain/abstinence, maintain/maintenance, float/flotation*); in others, it alternates with other letters (*appearance/apparent, comparative/comparison, message/messenger*). (2) There is variation in the endings *-ant/ent, -ance/ence, -ancy/ency*, producing such forms as *assistant, concomitant, consistent, insistent, persistent, resistant*. These differences relate to the historical derivation of the words in question: whether they were acquired directly from Latin or through French. If taken straight from Latin, the words derive from the participles of verbs that have either an *a*-stem (as with *concomitant*, from *concomitans* accompanying) or an *e*-stem (as with *consistent, insistent*, and *persistent*, from variations on the base form *-sistens* standing, setting). If, however, they are taken from French, they derive from participles all of which end in *-ant*, regardless of verb class (as with *assistant* and *resistant*). Sometimes, a distinction in meaning and use arises, as in *dependant/ dependent*, but in *ambiance/ambience* there is no such distinction.

■ **ABBREVIATION** ─────── ■

The shortening of words and phrases (*kilogram* to *kg*, *Imperial Chemical Industries* to *ICI*) and a result of such shortening (*MA* for *Master of Arts*, *sitcom* for *situation comedy*).

**History**. Alphabetic abbreviation became possible around 1000 BC and was common in the classical world: the Greek letters *ΙΧΘΥΣ* (making up the word for 'fish') stood for *Ἰησοῦς Χριστὸς Θεοῦ Υἱὸς Σωτήρ* (Jesus Christ Son of God Saviour), and as a result of their use the fish became a Christian symbol; the Latin letters *SPQR* stood for *Senatus Populusque Romanus* (the Senate and the Roman people). In addition, short forms such as *IMP CAES* (*Imperator Caesar* Emperor Caesar) were common on inscriptions and coins.

Although present-day abbreviation in English descends from such forms, its more immediate origin was in the practices of medieval scribes, among whom short forms were mnemonic and a means of economizing on parchment, effort, and time. As writing extended from Latin into the European vernacular languages, short forms went with it, first as loans (such as *AD* for *Anno Domini*: from the year of the Lord), then as native creations (such as *BC* for *Before Christ*). All such devices combine economy (of effort, space, and reference) with repetition (of the familiar and formulaic); although some are casual or temporary creations, others have become over the centuries so institutionalized that their origins and natures are seldom considered: as for example *AD* and *BC*, when used for everyday secular purposes.

**Nature**. Although abbreviations usually need to be concise, convenient, and easy to remember, they do not need to be fully understood to serve their purpose. People literate in English can work successfully with such formulas as *e.g.* and *q.v.* whether or not they know their full Latin forms *exempli gratia* (for the sake of example) and *quod vide* (which see). The more familiar and successful the short form, the less need for the full form, which may in course of time be forgotten. The full forms of *mob* (Latin *mobile vulgus* the fickle crowd) and *radar* (radio detection and ranging) have no functional value in the 1990s, and many are entirely unaware that these words are (or were) abbreviations. The members of organizations usually have little difficulty with the abbreviations they use, because of sheer familiarity, but people who are not part of the in-group may regard their use as (sometimes frustrating and provocative) jargon.

**Orthography**. There are six conventions for writing and printing abbreviations: (1) Capital letters and points: *I.N.S.E.A.* for 'International Society for Education through Art'. (2) Capital letters without points: *BBC* for 'British Broadcasting Corporation'; *NATO* for 'North Atlantic Treaty Organization'. (3) Lower-case letters with points for formulas such as *e.g.* and *q.v.*, and without points for items then that have become everyday words, such as *laser*, *radar*. (4) Mixed capitals and lower case, without points, capitals usually for lexical words, lower case for grammatical words: *DoWLT* for 'Dictionary of World Literary Terms'; *MoMA* for 'Museum of Modern Art'; *mRNA* for 'messenger ribonucleic acid'; *WiB* the organization 'Women in Business'. (5) Internal capitals, as in *CompuSex* for 'Computer Sex', and *DigiPulse* for 'Digital Pulse'. (6) Hybrid forms: *B.Com.* for 'Bachelor of Commerce'.

**Typology**. There are three types of abbreviation: (1) Letter-based, such as *AAA*. (2) Syllable-based, such as *con*. (3) Hybrid, such as *B.Com.* All may have a symbolic or a lexical function: symbolic abbreviations serve as formulas, as with *c.c.* or *cc* (cubic centimetres/meters), *Fe* (iron, from Latin *ferrum*); lexical abbreviations are generally word-like, some less so because they are spoken as letter sequences, as with *BBC*, some more so because they are spoken as words and often cannot be usefully distinguished from them, as with *NATO*, *radar*.

***Symbolic abbreviations***. Abbreviations that serve as symbols are usually pronounced as letter sequences or as their full originating words, as with *c.c.* ('cee-cee', 'cubic centimetres'). Some are spoken very differently from anything suggested by etymology or appearance: for example, the former British symbol *£.s.d.* is pronounced either 'ell-ess-dee' or 'pounds, shillings, and pence', not *\*Librae, solidi, et denarii* (the Latin for which the signs stand). In some instances, where abbreviations start with a vowel, the use of *a* or *an* indicates whether a writer is thinking of them as letters or words: *a MP* 'a Member of Parliament'; *an MP* 'an em-pee'.

***Lexical abbreviations***. Abbreviations that serve as words fall into three types that shade into a fourth less clear-cut type: (1) *INITIALISM*. A letter group that cannot be pronounced as a word, and must therefore be spoken as letters: *BBC* spoken as 'bee-bee-cee'. (2) *ACRONYM*. A letter group that can be, and is, pronounced as a word: *NATO* spoken as 'Nay-toe'. (3) CLIPPING. A part of a word standing for the whole: *pro* for *professional* and *phone* for *telephone*. (4) BLEND, also *portmanteau word*. A word made from two or more other words, by fusion (*brunch* from *breakfast* and *lunch*) or by putting together syllabic elements from other words (*Oxbridge* from *Oxford* and *Cambridge*). There are at least five variations and hybrids of these basic types: (1) Both initialisms and acronyms: *VAT* (Value Added Tax) is referred to as both 'vat' and 'vee-ay-tee'. (2) Forms that look like one type but behave like another: *WHO* (World Health Organization) is 'double-you-aitch-oh', not 'hoo'; *POW* (prisoner of war) is 'pee-oh-double-you', not 'pow'. (3) Part-initialism, part-acronym: *VTOL* (vertical take-off and landing) is pronounced 'vee-tall'; *CD-ROM* (compact disc read-only memory) is 'cee-dee-rom'. (4) Combinations of letter groups and clippings: *ARPAnet* (Advanced Research Projects Agency computer network). (5) Initialisms adapted as acronyms: 'GLCMs (ground-launched cruise missiles) and SLCMs (sea-launched cruise missiles) are called Glickems and Slickems by those in the know' (from *Time*, 18 Feb. 1985).

**Occurrence in texts**. When abbreviations are familiar, they are used without explanation but, because they cannot always be presented without a gloss, there are at least six ways of bringing them into a text:

**1. Indirect association**. 'The Art Gallery of Nova Scotia is now touring three other national exhibitions . . . In the last fiscal year AGNS sent 23 exhibitions to 63 centres' (Halifax *Chronicle Herald*, 11 Nov. 1982).

**2. Full form, bracketed abbreviation**. 'Britain may ban imports [of blood] that could be spreading the killer disease Acquired Immune Deficiency Syndrome (AIDS)' (Montreal *Gazette*, 3 May 1983).

**3. Abbreviation, bracketed full form**. 'The uncertainty surrounding SERPS (State earnings related pension scheme) deepens' (*Times*, 11 May 1985).

**4. Using '(stands) for'**. 'Here's an acronym you should know: MEGO. It stands for "My Eyes Glaze Over"' (William Safire, *New York Times*, Jan. 1988).

**5. Using 'or'**. 'Ethylene dibromide, or EDB, has been described as the most powerful cancer-causing agent the Environmental Protection Agency has tested' (*International Herald Tribune*, 4/5 Feb. 1984).

**6. Using 'as it is known'**. 'The failure may explain the absence so far of any announcement about "Initial Operating Capability," due to have been achieved at Greenham Common on Thursday. IOC, as it is known, means that one flight of missiles is declared officially capable of being launched on a "mission"' (*Observer*, 18 Dec. 1983).

Occasionally, an abbreviation is glossed not by the word or words it shortens but by others with which it has semantic links: 'Paris imposed the ban [on British beef] . . . because of concern over BSE, or "mad cow" disease' (*The European*, 1–3 June 1990). *BSE* in fact stands for *bovine spongiform encephalopathy*.

**Word-formation**. Because they are word-like, abbreviations play a part in WORD-FORMATION, as follows:

**1. Conversion**. The word *overdose* is used as a noun and a verb. So also is its medical abbreviation *OD*: '*ODing* on aspirin' (overdosing on aspirin).

**2. Derivation**. (1) With prefixes: an *ex-PoC* is someone no longer a prisoner of conscience (Amnesty International); *pro-JLP* means in favour of the Jamaican Labour Party. (2) With suffixes: *Rabisms* are noteworthy sayings of the British politician R. A. Butler; *WASPy* means like a White Anglo-Saxon Protestant. (3) With both: an *ex-CFL-er* is a former member of the Canadian Football League.

**3. Attribution**. Like *steel* in *steel bridge*: an *AI gambit* is a gambit relating to artificial intelligence; an *IRA gunman* is a gunman belonging to the Irish Republican Army. Abbreviations occur attributively before other abbreviations: a *BBC micro* is a British Broadcasting Corporation microcomputer; an *IBM PC* is an International Business Machines personal computer. Abbreviations may occur in a string in which precise attribution is not easily determined: *NYS ESOL BEA* refers to the composite New York State English to Speakers of Other Languages Bilingual Educators Association.

**4. Compounding**. With the same stress patterns as *teapot* and *blackbird*: *A-bomb*, *AIDS cure*. Composites containing abbreviations are common and often intricate, mixing compounding and attribution: *NY kiddie* *porn, an AIDS-Africa link, Metro-Montreal QPF contingent patrols* (Metropolitan Montreal Quebec Police Force contingent patrols). Combining forms may precede or follow abbreviations: *pseudo-* in a *pseudo-BBC accent*; *-logy* in *UFOlogy*, the study of Unidentified Flying Objects. In some classical compounds, a syllable is dropped for ease of expression: *symbology* from *symbol* and *-ology*.

**5. Blending**. Because blending is associated with abbreviation, the analysis of formations is particularly complex. A blend may be created for stunt purposes or convenience and bring together an abbreviation and part of a word: for example, *IBMulation* is the emulation of International Business Machines.

**Ad hoc usage**. The use of abbreviations has long been part of note-taking, file-making, cataloguing, and the making of inventories. In such activities, short forms are often created for ad hoc purposes, used for a time, then dispensed with and forgotten. In such restricted systems, *LA* may mean not *Los Angeles* but *late arrivals*. Ad hoc abbreviation is a major feature of computer use, especially in the creation of filenames: for example, *Vocab-doc* 'Vocabulary document'.

**Special effects**. Abbreviations may be ironic, humorous, or whimsical: for example, the rail link between the town of *Bed*ford and the London station of St *Pan*cras is locally known as *the Bedpan Line*. Comments on life may be telescoped into such sardonic packages as: *BOGSAT* a Bunch Of Guys Sitting Around a Table (making decisions about other people); *TGIF* Thank God It's Friday (after a particularly hard working week). In addition, some institutionalized abbreviations have more than one interpretation. This double meaning may be intentional, as with *ATI*, whose primary meaning is *American Tours International* and secondary sense, as a kind of business motto, is *Attitude, Teamwork, Initiative*. More commonly, however, secondary meanings are ironic: for example, in the British honours system, the form *CMG* (Commander of St Michael and St George) often glossed as *Call Me God*.

See ABRIDG(E)MENT, CONTRACTION, DIACRITIC, JEWISH ENGLISH, LETTER WORD, NUMBER[1], SYLLABLE WORD, TELESCOPING.

**ABLAUT**. A term used in PHILOLOGY for both the diachronic shifting of vowels (also known as *VOWEL SHIFT*) and the synchronic grading of vowels (also known as *vowel gradation*), especially in the INDO-EUROPEAN languages. Vowel gradation occurs in English in the formation of some irregular noun plurals (*man, men; goose, geese*) and some irregular verbs (*sing, sang, sung; swim, swam, swum*). Compare STRONG VERB.

**ABORIGINAL ENGLISH**. The technical name given to a continuum of varieties of English, ranging between standard AusE and creoles, acquired and used by Aboriginal Australians and often referred to by their speakers as *blackfella English* or *blackfella talk*. In some parts of Australia, the transition from a traditional language to Aboriginal English has occurred within four generations in the 20c. It is used by Aborigines both among themselves and with non-Aborigines. Most varieties are intelligible to speakers of standard AusE, though certain norms for the use of language are very different (for example, direct questions are not typically used to elicit information), and there are considerable differences in grammar and phonology. Some of the features of Aboriginal English are shared by nonstandard varieties around the world, such as the use of past and participial forms of certain verbs (*brang*, not *brought*), and double negatives (*He hasn't got no toys*). Others are more characteristic of creoles, such as the nonoccurrence of the copula (*His name John*, not *His name is John*) and lack of plural marking with *-s* (*two bird*, not *two birds*). Although the variety is generally stigmatized by white Australian society, it often functions as a symbol of Aboriginal identity. See AUSTRALIAN PIDGIN, KRIOL.

**ABRIDGEMENT**, also **abridgment**. **1.** The act, process, or result of shortening or condensing a text, usually to a given length such as half or one-third, or to a required number of words. **2.** A work produced in this way: an abridgement of Thomas Hardy's novel *Far from the Madding Crowd*. In most abridgements, the intention is to keep the main sense and substance of a work, such as the main plot and characters in a novel. Abridgements are undertaken because: (1) A text may be longer than a given group (such as younger readers) is willing to attempt, but nonetheless of intrinsic interest to them: for example, by current standards, 19c novels like those of Hardy are too long and leisurely in their development, but nevertheless have plots and motifs of wide appeal. (2) Foreign learners of a language like English might benefit from a simplified abridgement of a novel that retains the human interest but replaces more difficult and longer passages with easier vocabulary and syntax and less bulk. See ABSTRACT, PRÉCIS.

**ABSOLUTE**. A term indicating that a word, phrase, or clause stands apart from the usual relations with other elements in a sentence: *This being so* in *This being so, we'll have to make new plans*. Traditionally, such a combination is an *absolute phrase*, but it is now widely referred to as an *ABSOLUTE CLAUSE*.

**ABSOLUTE CLAUSE**. An adverbial CLAUSE that has its own subject, and has a participle as its verb or no verb at all: 'The *dinner having been prepared*, I had time to take a nap before the guests arrived'. Here, the verb is the participle phrase *having been prepared* and the subject is *the dinner*. Contrast the adverbial participle clause in 'Having *prepared the dinner*, I had time to take a nap', where the subject of *having prepared the dinner* is understood to be identical with the main subject *I*. An absolute clause is not introduced by a *subordinating conjunction*: *after having prepared the dinner* and *while preparing the dinner* are not absolute clauses. The participle may end in *-ing* (*trembling* in 'His *voice trembling*, he described what had happened') or *-ed* (*wasted* in 'Their *money wasted on imprudent schemes*, they could not expect any further help'). With some irregular verbs, the participle may not end in *-ed*: *spent* in 'Their *money spent on imprudent schemes*, they could expect no further help.' Absolute clauses may be without a verb, as in 'The soldiers emerged from their hiding places, *their hands high above their heads*', a corresponding participle clause being *their hands held high above their heads*. (The end of the previous sentence itself contains an absolute clause with the participle *being* as its verb.) Outside a few set phrases such as *all being/going well*, *weather permitting*, *present company excluded/excepted*, absolute clauses are infrequent and usually confined to formal written English.

**ABSOLUTE DEGREE**. See POSITIVE DEGREE.

**ABSTRACT**. A summary of a statement,

thesis, paper, or other document, usually providing its *gist* (essential elements and argument). See ABRIDG(E)MENT.

**ABSTRACT AND CONCRETE**. Contrasting terms in traditional philosophy and grammar, *concrete* referring to the material and specific, *abstract* to the ideal and general. Abstraction as a mental process starts with many particular things or events and moves to a single generality within or behind them, such as the concept *time* abstracted from such changes as day and night, the seasons, and ageing. In grammar, an *abstract noun* refers to an action, concept, event, quality, or state (*love, conversation*), whereas a *concrete noun* refers to a touchable, observable person or thing (*child, tree*). This semantic classification cuts across the syntactic division countable/uncountable NOUN. Although abstract nouns tend to be uncountable (*courage, happiness, news, tennis, training*), many are countable (*an hour, a joke, a quantity*). Others can be both, often with shifts of meaning from general to particular (*great kindness/many kindnesses; not much industry/a major industry*).

**ABUSAGE**. An archaic term for misuse and defilement, revived in 1942 by Eric Partridge in the title *Usage and Abusage: A Guide to Good English* (1942). It is currently used only in his sense of improper, unidiomatic, and ungrammatical language. Compare CONFUSAGE.

**ABUSE**. **1.** Wrong or improper use of anyone or anything. The term is often (usually emotively) applied to language:

Some native speakers claim that the *use* of the language is deteriorating. One charge is ethical: people are said to be abusing the language, more so than in the past, with intent to conceal, mislead, or deceive, generally through euphemism or obscure language. Usually, the accusation is directed principally against politicians, bureaucrats, and advertisers, but the abuse is felt to have an adverse effect on the language as such. Certainly, the contemporary mass media facilitate the rapid and widespread dissemination of such language abuses. The other charge is aesthetic or functional: people are said to be using the language less elegantly or less efficiently than in the recent past, a charge that is commonly directed against young people. The charge may or may not have some justification, but in any case is impossible to substantiate. ('Standards of English', section 1.11 in Quirk *et al.*, *A Comprehensive Grammar of the English Language*, 1985).

**2.** Harsh or coarsely insulting language: *to hurl abuse at people*. See STYLE, SWEARING.

**ACADEMIC USAGE**, also **academic English**. The REGISTER of English used by scholars and scientists: an elevated and often complex style associated with concern for accuracy, objectivity, and dispassionate comment, and characterized by: (1) Qualifying expressions such as *at least, may, probably, under such conditions, usually*. (2) Parenthetical asides, intended to modify, support, or otherwise affect statements: *according to the date, apparently, as far as we can tell at this stage*. (3) Passive constructions serving to minimize or remove personality: *It was found that . . . , The data were analysed, When completed, the experiment was discussed*. (4) Impersonal and non-dramatic ('dry') speech that may consist of reading a prepared paper (with or without extempore comments) or making extempore remarks supported by notes. Replies to comments and questions are often marked by pauses to rephrase a statement for the sake of precision and self-defence. Speakers may announce such rephrasing as they engage in it, using such formulas as *that is (to say), . . . , or, more precisely . . . , Let me rephrase that so as to . . .* Concern for precision sometimes leads to statements framed so as to cover every possible aspect of a topic, with detailed annotation full of supporting documentation in written work.

Academic writing generally makes use of such *scholarly apparatus* as introductions, provisos, disclaimers, acknowledgements, NOTES AND REFERENCES, BIBLIOGRAPHIES, and indexes. Such apparatus descends from the Middle Ages and the Renaissance and became more easily organized with the PRINTING of books and papers. For many lay people, academic usage is often rarefied and pedantic. It can intimidate and appear to be at odds with plain English. As a result, many regard it as acceptable in the ivory tower but impractical elsewhere. Many academics, however, see such a style as the proper and perhaps sole medium of rational expression, and dislike the implication

that it can be used as a shield against the world. Extreme styles are pejoratively referred to as *academese*, such as: 'Chieftaincy as a sanctional source, a symbolic referent, an integrational integer, and for ethnic and sub-ethnic definition, represents an orientational base for the charismatic persona' (from a 1960s sociology paper). See SOCIOLOGESE.

**ACADEMY**. **1.** A school, college, or other educational institution. **2.** A cultural institution for the maintenance or raising of standards in art, science, or language, such as the *Académie française*, founded in 1634. It made such a profound impression in 17c England that the issue of whether English should also have such an institution was discussed for many years. Nothing came of this discussion. When from time to time the question of the 'missing' English Academy is raised, authoritarians deplore and libertarians applaud its absence. See DEFOE, FRENCH, JOHNSON.

■ **ACCENT** ─────────── ■

**1.** A way of speaking that indicates a person's place of origin and/or social class: *a working-class accent, a London accent, a working-class London accent; a regional accent; an American accent; an American regional accent*. In phonetic terms, an accent is a set of habits that make up someone's PRONUNCIATION of a language or language variety. **2.** In poetics and PHONETICS, the prominence of a syllable: in *dogmatic*, the accent (or stress) is on the second syllable, *dogMAtic*. **3.** A diacritical mark, as over the first *e* in *élite* (an ACUTE ACCENT). Acute accents are often used over vowels to mark prominent syllables, as in *This is the wáy it's dóne*. When so used, they are called *accent marks. Accent* in this sense is also used figuratively for emphasis (*The accent is on entertainment*) or special detail (*a dress with vivid blue accents*).

**Accent as way of speaking**. In everyday USAGE, *accent* means 'way of speaking', a sense that may have developed in the Middle Ages in reference to the distinctive 'tunes' of SPEECH. Since the 16c, the term has been used in English for styles of speech that mark people off from each other, principally by region. Most people can identify the main accent types in their language and those of some groups of foreigners speaking that language, and may have feelings and opinions about them. Even so, however, it is not easy to say just what an accent is. Phoneticians and linguists do not know why particular features come together to form accents, although they can list such features and show how they cluster as aspects of particular accents.

**Accent and dialect**. It is also not easy to separate *accent* from DIALECT. The terms have long been used together and certain accents are considered to belong 'naturally' to certain dialects: in the North of England, the GEORDIE accent of Tyneside is part of Geordie dialect; in New York, a Brooklyn accent is part of Brooklyn dialect. Most individuals, however, have personal ways of speaking (their *idiolects*), and may conform more or less to particular kinds of accent and dialect. Britons who live for a time in the US may incorporate accentual Americanisms into their speech; Americans may take on local linguistic colour in Britain. For many people, especially if they belong to a privileged group or to a community that has little contact with outsiders, an accent is someone else's way of speaking. In such cases, the group's speech is often thought of as *accentless*: only outsiders 'speak with an accent'. Certain words, some dismissive and pejorative, are used to describe speech, including *adenoidal, barbarous*, BROAD, *cute, distinct*, EDUCATED, FLAT, *foreign, funny*, GUTTURAL, *harsh, heavy, lilting*, NASAL, *posh, provincial, quaint, rough, rustic*, SINGSONG, *strong, uneducated*. By means of such words, people can be marked out as having, for example, *a distinct New England accent, a strong Scottish accent, a broad Yorkshire accent, a posh public-school accent*, and so forth. All such informal accentual labels have social implications, some of which are strong and long-lasting, both in social and personal terms.

Some phoneticians and linguists treat accent as part of dialect; others treat it as separate or separable from dialect, especially with regard to use of the standard variety of a language. Many argue that standard English can be spoken with a range of more or less 'educated' accents. Others consider that it can only be spoken with one accent (such as RECEIVED PRONUNCIATION in England) or a small group of accents (such as those which have social and educational prestige in the major English-speaking countries). Others again consider that there is a continuum of possibilities, some

accents being 'modified' more, some less, towards a perceived regional or other standard, with the result that people may be speaking more or less 'standardly', or may come closer to a standard in some contexts and move further from it in others. The matter is controversial, especially when applied linguists and others seek to use the theories and findings of phonetics and linguistics to influence policies for the teaching of English either as a mother tongue or as a second or foreign language. However, all phoneticians and linguists agree that the widely held view that many accents are corruptions of a pure pronunciation has no scientific basis whatsoever.

**Defining an accent**. Two features commonly characterize accents: (1) Their 'tunes' (melodies and tones), usually described in evaluative terms, such as *flat*, used of such urban accents as Scouse (Liverpool), *lilting*, used of Irish and Scottish accents associated with Gaelic, and of Caribbean accents associated with Creole, and *singsong*, used of Welsh, Anglo-Indian, and Filipino accents. (2) Kinds of articulation and voice quality, often identified with anatomical features, such as *adenoidal*, used of Scouse, and *nasal*, used of many North American accents. More or less precise non-technical names are often given to voice qualities, such as DRAWL, BROGUE, BURR, TWANG. Some names figure frequently in the informal description of particular accents: for example, *a distinct Dublin brogue, a soft Highland lilt, a guttural Northumberland burr, a laid-back Southern drawl, a sharp Yankee twang*. Although voice quality is often a part of accent, people with the same accents may have different voice qualities, so that not all Highland voices softly lilt, and not all Liverpool voices are flatly adenoidal. Even where accents are thought to be well delineated, features that contribute to them are unevenly distributed, so that there are more or less American, Brooklyn, British, Cockney, and other accents. In addition, the accents of people who have lived for long periods in various places lay down a kind of 'vocal geology', with strata from the different times and places in their lives.

See ADVANCED, CLIPPED, DIACRITIC, ELOCUTION, ENGLISH IN ENGLAND, GLOTTAL STOP, INTONATION, *L*-SOUNDS, ORTHOEPY, PROPER, PUBLIC SCHOOL ENGLISH, RECEIVED PRONUNCIATION (RP), RECEIVED STANDARD AND MODIFIED STANDARD, RHOTIC AND NON-

RHOTIC, RHYTHM, *R*-SOUNDS, STRESS, TONE, VOICE.

**ACCEPTABILITY**. A term in LINGUISTICS relating to whether a phrase or sentence is grammatically or semantically acceptable to a native speaker. Compare CORRECT, GRAMMATICALITY.

**ACCIDENCE**. The part of traditional GRAMMAR dealing with INFLECTION (changes in the forms of words to express such grammatical meanings as case, number, and tense). In English, the differences between *work, works, worked, working*, and between *worker, workers, worker's, workers'* would be described and explained under accidence. Nowadays, these differences are usually handled in *inflectional morphology*, a division of *MORPHOLOGY* (the study of word form) that deals with the formation and uses of inflections.

**ACROLECT**. **1.** The variety of LANGUAGE in a POST-CREOLE CONTINUUM closest to the standard or SUPERSTRATE language: for example, in Jamaica a local variety of standard English. **2.** The most prestigious variety of a language, such as standard BrE with an RP accent in England.

■ **ACRONYM** ─────────────── ■

Also **protogram**. An ABBREVIATION formed from the first letters of a series of words and pronounced as one word: *NATO* from *North Atlantic Treaty Organization*, pronounced 'Nay-toe': *radar* from *radio detection and ranging*, pronounced 'ray-dar'. Some lexicologists regard the acronym as a kind of initialism; others see it as contrasting with the initialism, in which case that term is restricted to abbreviations that are pronounced only as sequences of letters: for example, *BBC* as 'bee-bee-cee'. In this entry, acronyms and initialisms are treated as distinct. Informally, it is not unusual for both kinds of abbreviation to be lumped together as *letter words*, and there are many grey areas between them. In structural terms, there are three kinds of acronym: (1) Letter acronyms, such as *NATO, radar*. (2) Syllabic acronyms, such as *Asda* (Associated Dairies) and *sitcom* (situation comedy). (3) Hybrids of these, such as *CoSIRA* (Council for Small Industries in Rural Areas) and *MATCON* (microwave aerospace terminal control).

**Pronunciation and orthography**. The pronunciation of letter acronyms has encouraged two tendencies in abbreviation: to omit points (*NATO* rather than *N.A.T.O.*); to use lower-case letters (*radar* rather than *RADAR*). As a result, an acronym may become so fully a word that its letter-based origin ceases to signify or be remembered, as with *radar*. Occasionally, contrasts occur, such as lower-case *radar* and upper-case *RADAR* (Royal Association for Disability and Rehabilitation). There are variations, inconsistencies, and idiosyncratic practices in the presentation of letter acronyms: the United Nations Educational, Scientific, and Cultural Organization is conservatively contracted to *U.N.E.S.C.O.*, but commonly contracted to *UNESCO* and sometimes *Unesco*. In the house styles of some publications, common acronyms are presented as if they were proper nouns: 'When the Vice-President explicitly links European concessions on Gatt [General Agreement on Tariffs and Trade] to the continuance of Nato, he bangs a crude drum' (editorial, *Guardian*, 11 Feb. 1992). Syllabic and hybrid acronyms do not have points (*Asda, sitcom*), may be lower-case, upper-case, or mixed, and sometimes have internal capitals: for example, *HoJo*, short for the US hotel-and-restaurant group *Howard Johnson*.

**The effects of pronounceability**. Because acronyms are pronounceable and easy to create, they make convenient shorthand labels, mnemonic aids, and activist slogans. A typical *shorthand acronym* is Disney's *EPCOT* or *Epcot*: Experimental Prototype Community of Tomorrow (in Florida). *Mnemonic acronyms* are often homonyms of existing words that help fix events and ideas in people's minds: *SALT*, which is not connected with sodium chloride and means 'Strategic Arms Limitation Talks'; *SQUID*, which has nothing to do with the sea and means 'superconducting quantum interference device'. *Slogan acronyms* are parasitic on existing words, coined to label a cause and send a message at the same time: *ASH* for 'Action on Smoking and Health'; *DUMP* for 'Disposal of Unused Medicines and Pills'; *NOW* for 'National Organization of Women'. Mnemonic and slogan acronyms are particularly subject to word-play, especially in headlines: *Can START be stopped?* refers to Strategic Arms Reduction Talks; *A ConCERNed Pope* refers to the Vatican's interest in radiation and in CERN, the

## A SPECTRUM OF ACRONYMS

There is no sharp dividing line between initialisms and acronyms, and among acronyms the dividing line is not sharp between the pronounceable but meaningless and forms that have been chosen because they give 'added value'. The five stages below represent the continuum from initialisms to slogan acronyms.

**Unpronounceable initialisms**

| | |
|---|---|
| Amateur Athletic Association | AAA |
| Graduate of the Royal School of Music | G.R.S.M. |

**Semi-acronyms**

| | |
|---|---|
| British Broadcasting Corporation (informal usage, omitting the C) | BBC (Beeb) |
| Cambridge College of Arts and Technology | CCAT (See-cat) |

**Shorthand acronyms**

| | |
|---|---|
| Experimental Prototype Community of Tomorrow | EPCOT/Epcot |
| Roll-on, roll-off (ferries) | RO-RO/ro-ro |

**Mnemonic acronyms**

| | |
|---|---|
| Strategic Arms Limitation Talks | SALT |
| Superconducting quantum interference device | SQUID |

**Slogan acronyms**

| | |
|---|---|
| Aboriginal Lands of Hawaiian Ancestry | ALOHA |
| National Organization of Women | NOW |

In addition, because acronyms are so much like words, they can become part of further acronyms, as when *AIDS* (Acquired Immune Deficiency Syndrome) contributes the *A* in both *ARC* (AIDS-related complex) and *DIFA* (Design Industries Foundations for AIDS).

---

Centre européen pour la recherche nucléaire.

**Syllabic acronyms**. Syllabic acronyms, currently fashionable in many languages, are related to word blends such as *brunch* and *electrocute*. Some two-syllable and three-syllable forms are: *Amoco* American Oil Company; *Asda* Associated Dairies; *Con Ed* Consolidated Edison; *Fedeco* Federal Electoral Commission (Nigeria); *HoJo* Howard Johnson [Motor Lodges] (US); *op-ed* opposite the editorial page (journalese); *sitcom* situation comedy (television drama). The factors that have encouraged their spread include computer usage, telex addresses, the naming of scientific and technical devices and activities, and the often flamboyant labelling of commercial products.

**Creativity**. Acronyms are numerous and more are constantly being coined. As a re-

sult, they are often gathered, with other abbreviations, in such collections as *Elsevier's Foreign-Language Teacher's Dictionary of Acronyms and Abbreviations* (Udo O. H. Jung, 1985), which contains more than 3,500 items like *Flint* (Foreign Language Instructional Technology) and *Team* (Teachers of English Arabic Monthly). Although many acronyms are soberly functional, others have a touch of whimsy about them, such as *BOMFOG* (Brotherhood of Man, Fatherhood of God), a term used by US journalists for pious and platitudinous speeches, evidently an abbreviation of phrases with which Nelson Rockefeller like to end his speeches. The informal BrE term *bumf* (unnecessary papers and paperwork) is comparable; it derives from public-school and Armed Forces slang for toilet paper, which in turn descends from *bum fodder*, a 17c expression for trashy printed matter. See Q, -ONYM, SYLLA-BLE WORD.

**ACTIVE (VOICE)**. See PASSIVE (VOICE), VERB, VOICE.

**ACUTE ACCENT**. A right-inclined oblique stroke over a letter, as in French *é* (*café*, *é lite*, *née*), transliterated Sanskrit *ś* (*śastra*, *Siva*), Spanish (to mark the vowels of stressed syllables, as in *nación*), and the rising tonal ACCENT of classical Greek (*logikós*, *prótasis*). In English, the acute accents present in loans from other languages are often dropped (*cafe*, *elite*, *nee*) or replaced by some other device (such as *h* in *shastra*, *Shiva*), except when the use of foreign conventions is necessary for accuracy or effect.

■ **ADJECTIVE** ───────────────── ■

A PART OF SPEECH or word class chiefly used to premodify NOUNS (*romantic* in *romantic story*) and as a complement to copular verbs such as *be* and *seem* (*happy* and *healthy* in *Jeremy is happy*, *Mervyn seems healthy*).

**Form**. (1) Simple adjectives such as *good*, *sad*, *old*, *yellow*, *bitter*. (2) Derived adjectives, formed through adding suffixes to nouns and verbs, such as *-able* adorable, *-ful* careful, *-ic* heroic, *-ish* foolish, *-ive* attractive, *-ous* (famous), *-y* (tasty).

**Function**. Adjectives function attributively as pre-modifiers (*my forgetful parents*) and predicatively as complements to the subject (*My parents are forgetful*) and the object (*They found my parents forgetful*). Many adjectives have only one of these functions, at least as used in a particular sense. In the following phrases, *utter*, *certain*, and *former* are attributive only: *an utter lie*, *a certain person*, *our former friends*. Some adjectives are predicative only, as with *afraid*, *loath*, and *aware* in: *Your brother is afraid of them*, *My friends seem loath to interfere*, *The manager became aware of her attitude*. Adjectives that occur predicatively can also post-modify certain pronouns, usually when the adjectives are part of a larger adjective phrase: (*those*) *forgetful* (*of their duties*), (*somebody*) *afraid* (*of me*). Adjectives ending in *-able* or *-ible* can function as post-modifiers in certain circumstances: *the best treatment available*, *the only teacher suitable*. There are also some fixed phrases (mostly legal terms derived from French) that have an adjective following the noun: *heir apparent*, *court martial*, *attorney general*, with the formal plurals *heirs apparent*, *courts martial*, *attorneys general*.

Adjectives that refer to people are sometimes introduced by the definite article *the* or by a possessive pronoun. They can function in the same way as nouns, namely as subject, object, etc.: *The poor require our help*, *We should look after our young*, *The British are coming*. The adjective phrases *the poor*, *our young*, and *the British* are plural and refer to a group of people. A few adjectives are used in the same way as singular abstract nouns, mainly in set phrases: *for good*, *in private*, *in common*. The semantic distinction between *restrictive* and *non-restrictive modification* applies to adjectives that modify nouns as well as to *relative clauses*. The adjective *clever* in *my clever daughter* is restrictive if its function is to distinguish one daughter from the others; it is non-restrictive if there is only one daughter in question and the adjective is conveying a characteristic of that daughter rather than defining which daughter is being referred to.

**Comparison**. The comparative and superlative degrees in adjectives are shown in two ways: (1) For shorter, usually monosyllabic, words, through a comparative inflection *-er* as in *older* and a superlative inflection *-est* as in *oldest*. (2) For longer words, through the addition of premodifiers, the comparative *more* in *more hostile* and superlative *most* in *most hostile*. Some adjectives may take both constructions: *common* with *commoner/more common* and *commonest/most common*, *friendly* with *friendlier/more friendly* and *friendliest/most friendly*. Sometimes, for emphasis, shorter adjectives may take *more* and *most*: *Could you be more clear so that we all understand?* There are also some irregular forms: *good*, *well* (that is, healthy) with *better/best*, *bad* with *worse/worst*, and *far* with *farther/farthest* or *further/furthest*. Comparison applies only to adjectives that are *gradable*, that is, that can be viewed as on a scale of intensity, such as those illustrated above. Adjectives that are not gradable, such as *utter* and *atomic*, cannot be compared or modified by an INTENSIFIER such as *very*. There are differences in usage with a few adjectives, such as *perfect*, *complete*, *unique*, since some people but not others will use *more perfect*, *very complete*, *really unique*, etc. See DEGREE.

**Modification**. Gradable adjectives are premodified by intensifying adverbs such as *very*, *extremely*, and *completely*: *very young*, *extremely cold*, *completely unfriendly*. Examples of phrases where the adjective is postmodified are: *trustworthy indeed*, *clever enough to help*, *fond of you*, *glad that you could make it*.

**ADJECTIVE CLAUSE**, also **adjectival clause**. The traditional name for a RELATIVE CLAUSE, because such clauses modify nouns. The term is also used for constructions in which an adjective phrase is felt to function as a CLAUSE: *Aware of his difficulties* (Since she was aware of his difficulties), *she did not press for an immediate answer*.

**ADJUNCT**. See ADVERBIAL.

**ADNOMINAL**. In contemporary GRAMMAR, a word or phrase that modifies a NOUN and forms part of a noun phrase. Adnominals may precede or follow their nouns: '*her new* house', '*the little red* book', '*a library* book', '*the manager's* book', 'a book *about dinosaurs*', 'a book *to read*', 'a book *(that) I've been meaning to read*'. See RELATIVE CLAUSE.

**ADVANCED**. **1.** In PHONETICS, said of a sound articulated with a tongue position closer to the front of the mouth. **2.** In phonetics and LINGUISTICS, said of an ACCENT or elements of an accent that are further along certain lines of change than others, to which the term *conservative* is given. Some linguists dislike the term because it may be taken to mean that the form in question reflects social progress or importance, as for example in the phrase *advanced RP*, a term used for the RECEIVED PRONUNCIATION of some members of the upper class and royal family in Britain. **3.** In language teaching and applied linguistics, said of a student whose competence in a foreign language has passed beyond the intermediate stage.

■ **ADVERB** ──────────── ■

A PART OF SPEECH or word class chiefly used to modify VERBS, ADJECTIVES, or other adverbs.

**Form**. (1) Most adverbs are formed from adjectives by the addition of the ending -ly as in *suddenly*, *playfully*, *interestingly*, or -ally after -ic as in *automatically*, *spasmodically* (with the exception *publicly*). (2) Some are formed from NOUNS in combination with other suffixes: -wise as in *clockwise*, *lengthwise*, and -ward(s) as in *northwards*, *skyward*. (3) A set of common adverbs have no suffixes (*here*, *there*, *now*, *just*, *well*), though some are compounds (*therefore*, *nevertheless*). (4) A set of common adverbs, also known as *adverbial particles*, are used along with verbs: *in*, *out*, *on*, *off*, *up*, *down*, etc. See PHRASAL VERB.

**Function**. The class is heterogeneous, and some grammarians have attempted to establish separate classes for some sets of words that are traditionally regarded as adverbs, such as INTENSIFIERS. Within the traditional adverb class, a distinction is made between adverbs that modify adjectives or other adverbs (the most frequent being *very* as in *very quick*), and adverbs that modify verbs or verbs together with some other part of the sentence (such as *competently* in *She handled the matter competently*). Adverbs in the second group are sometimes said to have an ADVERBIAL function, a function also performed by such constructions as prepositional phrases and clauses. The adverb *competently* is an adverbial in *She handled the matter competently*, as are the prepositional phrase *in a competent manner* in *She handled the matter in a competent manner* and the clause *as everybody expected her to do* in *She handled the matter as everybody expected her to do*.

**Sentence adverbs**. Adverbials that modify the sentence as a whole are *sentence adverbials*, and adverbs that function as sentence adverbials are *sentence adverbs*. In the following examples, *fortunately* and *however* are both sentence adverbs: *Fortunately, she handled the matter competently*; *The task was formidable*; *however* (that is, despite the task being formidable), *she handled the matter competently*.

**Wh-adverbs**. There is a subclass of so-called *wh*-adverbs: *how*, *when*, *where*, *why*, and combinations such as *whenever* and *wherever*. The four simple adverbs introduce *wh*-questions (*When did they come?*), and they and the others introduce certain types of subordinate clauses (*He told us when they had come*).

**Comparison and modification**. (1) Apart from modifying adjectives and adverbs, some adverbs may modify prepositions (*well* in *He kicked the ball well past the line*), certain pronouns and determiners (*virtually* in *They admitted virtually everybody*), noun phrases (*quite* in *It was quite a quarrel*), and nouns of time and place (*afterwards* in *the week afterwards*). (2) Some adverbs may also function as the complement of certain prepositions (*now* in the phrase *by now*). (3) Like gradable adjectives, *gradable adverbs* allow comparison and modification by intensifying adverbs: *more humbly*, *very humbly*. Only a small number of gradable adverbs take comparative and superlative inflections, many of them having the same forms as the corresponding adjective: *work hard/harder/ hardest; drive fast/faster/fastest*. There are also some irregular forms: *plays well/better/best* (compare *good/better/best plays*), *sings badly/ worse/worst* (compare *bad/worse/worst songs*). See DEGREE, PERIPHRASIS.

■ **ADVERBIAL** ──────────── ■

**1.** Relating to an ADVERB: *an adverbial clause*. **2.** A WORD, PHRASE, or CLAUSE that modifies a VERB or a verb plus other words: *usually* and *on the terrace* in 'Breakfast is *usually* served *on the terrace*'; *more quietly* in 'You must close the door *more quietly*'. Unlike subjects, verbs, and objects, most adverbials are optional and may be omitted without making a sentence ungrammatical: '*At this time of the year* they *usually* serve cider *with the meal*, *if the guests don't object*'. Some verbs, however, require an adverbial: *put* needs a place adverbial ('Put the dog *outside*'), *last* an adverbial of duration ('The meeting lasted *nearly two hours*'). Grammarians usually distinguish between *sentence adverbials* (adverbials that modify the sentence as a whole) and *adjuncts* (all other adverbials).

**Sentence adverbials**. There is no agreement on the adverbials to be counted as *sentence adverbials* (sometimes also called *sentence adverbs*). Such an item, however, modifies either a sentence as a whole (*unfortunately* in *Unfortunately, the bank will not give me a large enough mortgage*) or a clause within a sentence (*unfortunately* in *I wanted to buy the house, but unfortunately the bank will not give me a large enough mortgage*). The two major classes of sentence adverbs are *conjuncts* and *disjuncts*. Conjuncts indicate a connection between the unit in which they appear and another usually preceding unit: *for example, accordingly*. Disjuncts are a comment on the content or manner of what is being said or written: *frankly, surprisingly*. Most adverbs that function as conjuncts or disjuncts may have other functions.

***Conjuncts***. Most conjuncts are adverbs (also known as *conjunctive adverbs*) and prepositional phrases. Their role can be demonstrated through paraphrases. In the sentence *The shop ran out of liver before my turn came, so I raced to another shop, so* can be paraphrased as 'because the shop ran out of liver before my turn came', giving the reason for what is said in the sentence or clause that it introduces. Conjuncts are grammatically

distinct from *coordinating conjunctions* such as *and*, because the two types can occur together: in . . . *and so I raced to another shop*. Furthermore, unlike such conjunctions, most conjuncts are not restricted to initial position, as when *so* is replaced by *therefore*. The units linked by conjuncts vary in size, though typically they are sentences or clauses. The example with *so* demonstrates a link between two possibly independent sentences, but the connection may be between smaller units: *yet* in *She was over ninety and yet in full possession of her mental faculties*. Conjuncts can also link paragraphs or sequences of paragraphs. They signal a variety of connective meanings, such as: listing (*first, firstly, first of all, second, secondly, next, finally, also, furthermore*); summarizing (*overall*); apposition (*for example, for instance, namely, in other words*); result (*so, therefore, consequently*); inference (*then*); contrast (*on the one hand/on the other hand, rather, however, nevertheless*); transition (*incidentally*). On the whole, conjuncts are a closed class of items that can be listed, with the exception of enumerative adverbs (*first, second,* etc.) which make up a potentially infinite list.

***Disjuncts***. There are two kinds of disjuncts: *style disjuncts* and *content disjuncts*. Style disjuncts express comments by speakers on the style or manner in which they are speaking: *frankly*, as in *Frankly, you have no chance of winning* (= I am telling you this frankly); *personally* in *Personally, I'd have nothing to do with them*; *with respect to* in *With respect, it is not up to you to decide*; *if I may say so* in *They are rather rude, if I may say so*; *because she told me so* in *She won't be there, because she told me so* (= I know that because she told me so). Content disjuncts comment on the content of what is being said. The most common express degrees of certainty and doubt as to what is being said: *perhaps* in *Perhaps you can help me*; *undoubtedly* in *Undoubtedly, she is the winner*; *obviously* in *Obviously, she had no wish to help us*. Others evaluate the content of the utterance, conveying some attitude towards it: that it is surprising (*Unexpectedly, he arrived home and found them*; *To my surprise, nobody came*) or not surprising (*Naturally, I wanted to help*; *Understandably, she was annoyed*); that it is fortunate (*Happily, they came to me first*; *Luckily, we already knew about it*) or unfortunate (*Sadly, he died in an air crash*; *Tragically, we heard about it too late*). Some pass judgement on the topic raised or indicate an emotional position:

*Rightly, she objected to what they were doing; Foolishly, he asked for more money; To my annoyance, nobody came.*

Adverbs that typically have other functions also serve as disjuncts. Such a use occasionally arouses objections, as when *hopefully*, usually a manner adverb as in *He waited hopefully for his results*, is used as a content disjunct, as in *Hopefully, we won't have to wait much longer.* The use of an adverb as a disjunct can be unusual, as in: '*Awkwardly*, President Reagan's most forceful and innovative cabinet officer is in charge of a department that has marginal responsibility . . .' (*The Economist*, 23 Nov. 1985); 'Borges signed manifestos against the dictator and the dictator *famously* took his job away . . .' (*London Review of Books*, 7 Aug. 1986). The functions of conjuncts and disjuncts are found in units other than adverbs: like *finally* are *in conclusion* and *to sum up*; like *frankly* are *frankly speaking* and *if I may be frank*; like *probably* are *in all probability*.

**Adjuncts.** Adverbials integrated within the structure of the sentence are *adjuncts*. Among the features indicating that an adverbial is an adjunct is the ability to be questioned and negated. The *because*-clause in *She took off her jacket because she felt hot* can be questioned (Why did she take off her jacket?—Because she felt hot) and negated (She didn't take off her jacket because she felt hot, but for some other reason). Another common feature is that the *because*-clause can become the focus of a cleft sentence: *It was because she felt hot that she took off her jacket.* See PART OF SPEECH.

**ADVERBIAL CLAUSE.** A subordinate CLAUSE with an adverbial function: the *when*-clause in 'He got angry *when I started to beat him at table-tennis.*' Adverbial clauses express such meanings as time, place, condition, concession, reason, purpose, and result. See ADVERB, SUBORDINATION.

**ADVERBIAL PARTICLE.** A PARTICLE with an adverbial function, as in PHRASAL VERBS: for example, *out* in *I've turned out the light*, and *up* in *We gave up.* See ADVERB.

**AELFRIC OF EYNSHAM.** [*c.*955–*c.*1020], also **Ælfric** (pronounced 'Elfritch'). West Saxon monk, teacher, and writer, Abbot of Eynsham from 1005. He wrote homilies, saints' lives, translations from the Old Testament, treatises, and letters, and for learners of Latin a grammar, glossary, and teaching dialogue. He used LATIN literary devices in his English works, alliteration and verse rhythm from poetry in his prose, and was influential until long after the Norman Conquest of 1066. See BIBLE.

**AESTHETICS**, AmE also **esthetics**. A branch of philosophy concerned with the understanding of beauty and taste and the appreciation of art, LITERATURE, and STYLE. It seeks to answer the question: is beauty or ugliness inherent in the object in question, or is it 'in the eye of the beholder'? The term *aesthetic* often refers to responses, judgements, and statements that are subjective and emotive rather than objective, clinical, and detached. These have social power, and serve a variety of rhetorical ends, such as asserting a point of view (*What thrilling words!*; *That accent is ugly*), presenting opinion as fact (*Shakespeare is the greatest writer in the world*), seeking to persuade (*Don't you think he speaks very coarsely? Doesn't she have a delightful voice!*), seeking to coerce (*You really must learn to appreciate the classics*), dismissing the unacceptable (*Can't they write better than that?*), and asserting or maintaining stock responses, especially of a social, ethnic, or linguistic kind (*BBC English is the best English; I really like her soft Irish lilt; I don't like her Irish brogue*).

The ability to appreciate and produce language that is considered aesthetically pleasing (or at least adequate) has been associated with such concepts as 'refinement', 'culture', and 'cultivation'. A refined or cultured person is widely taken to be able to distinguish the good from the bad, the beautiful from the ugly, and to know when it is not right to make such judgements at all; it is also often considered that the less cultured or the uncultured should learn, gladly or grudgingly, from such a person. Ability with language has been ascribed to divine inspiration or grace, to good breeding or the right social background, to the right kind of teacher, to proper observance of the rulings of a group with privilege and authority, or to a mix of these. By and large, good taste has traditionally been considered to have an absolute form: some people have it or approximate to it; others do not have it or are deficient in it. Sometimes, creative speakers and writers may be seen as having great skill but deplorable taste in how they use that skill.

Sociologists of language generally consider that a sense of the correctness, goodness, or beauty of something results from exposure to the norms and expectations of a community: the individual learns or fails to learn how to respond in terms of the values of the group. Aesthetics, from this point of view, is relative, and good taste varies from community to community. A sense of the acceptable may be more fully reinforced in the centre or heartland of a society than at its periphery, where other societies may exert an influence. When distinct groups (tribes, nations, classes, religions, and speakers of certain languages or varieties of a language) are neighbours, become mixed, or are in competition, uncertainties about aesthetic and other values arise, along with problems of choice. These may lead to a search for security in terms of fundamentals (good religion, good grammar), may prompt an eclectic pragmatism (a certain thing is good in one place but not in another; is sometimes good and sometimes not), or may offer greater or less confusion (with no clear conception of what is good or bad, or with uneasily shifting conceptions). Whatever the case, however, people constantly make aesthetic judgements and often institutionalize them in terms of praise or abuse, compliments or insults, affectionate or dismissive names, and a wide range of judgemental expressions such as (for language) the adjectives *bad*, *good*, *harsh*, *lovely*, PLAIN, and PURE. See ACCENT, DESCRIPTIVISM AND PRESCRIPTIVISM, EDUCATED AND UNEDUCATED, HARD AND SOFT, STYLE, USAGE.

**AFFECTATION**. Behaviour that does not come easily or naturally and therefore seems stilted, false, and often exaggerated. People 'affecting' the STYLE or ACCENT of an élite may be dismissed or condemned as *putting on airs* or *getting above themselves*. Élites affecting particular usages, however, may be regarded as leaders of fashion. In the 18c, 'polite' society in England affected fashionable French expressions, while in Scotland it affected both fashionable French and English expressions. In some parts of the world in the late 20c, affectation may include adding words and phrases of English to a local language or using English instead of that language. See GENTEELISM, HYPERCORRECTION, KENSINGTON, MORNINGSIDE AND KELVINSIDE, OXFORD ENGLISH, USAGE.

**AFFIX**. An element added to a WORD, BASE,

or ROOT to produce an inflected or derived form, such as *-s* added to *house* to form *houses* and *re*-added to *write* to form *re-write*. Affixed elements include the PREFIX (*anti-* in *anti-war*), the SUFFIX (*-ity* in *formality*), the INFIX (*-m-* in *recumbent* but not *cubicle*, a relic from Latin), and the INTERFIX (reduced *and* in *sun 'n' sand*). See DERIVATION, ENDING, WORD-FORMATION.

**AFFRICATE**. In PHONETICS, a stop CONSONANT that is released slowly into a period of FRICATIVE noise: for example, the *ch*-sounds in *church* and *j*-sounds in *judge*.

## ■ AFRICAN-AMERICAN VERNACULAR ENGLISH ──── ■

Short form **AAVE**; also **African-American English**, **Afro-American English**, **Afro-American**, **(American) Black English**, **black English**, **Black English Vernacular (BEV)**, **Ebonics**. Terms in SOCIOLINGUISTICS for English as used by a majority of US citizens of Black African background, consisting of a range of socially stratified urban and rural dialects. The most non-standard varieties are used by poor blacks with limited education, who have restricted social contact beyond their native communities. Standard varieties are influenced by regional norms: black standard English in the South is different from the African-American standard in the North, and each in turn reflects colloquial usage among educated whites in the same areas. Considerable style-shifting occurs between blacks talking to non-blacks and especially on less formal occasions when blacks prefer to use vernacular speech among themselves. The corresponding variation is pervasive, occurring with phonology, intonation, morphology, syntax, African-American slang, idioms, and ritualized verbal confrontations.

**Origins**. American BLACK ENGLISH was born of slavery between the late 16c and mid-19c, and followed black migration from the southern states to racially isolated ghettos throughout the US. According to J. L. Dillard (*Black English*, 1972), some 80% of black Americans speak the vernacular, and he and several other commentators stress its African origins. The pidginization and creolization that resulted from slavery linger on the tongues of Americans of African descent. Slave labour in the South gave birth to diverse linguistic norms; former indentured servants from all parts of the British Isles, who often became overseers on plantations, variously influenced the foundations of AAVE. See GULLAH. First the industrial revolution then the Civil War disrupted slavery and promoted African-American migration within the US, as a result of which slave dialects were transplanted from Southern plantations to the factories of the North and Midwest. When 'smokestack' industries grew, so too did urban employment for blacks, but racial segregation, rigorous in the South, was maintained in various forms throughout the entire US, and has not yet come to an end.

**Pronunciation**. (1) Like the English of the Southern states in general, AAVE is non-rhotic: 'ca' for *car*, 'pahty' for *party*. Comparably, /l/ is absent in word-final consonant clusters with labials ('hep' for *help*, 'sef' for *self*), and both /r/ and /l/ are absent in such usages as 'We comin' for *We're coming* and 'We be here' for *We'll be here*. (2) A syllabic /n/ commonly replaces /ŋ/ in *-ing* forms: 'comin' and 'runnin' for *coming* and *running*. (3) Word-final consonant clusters are reduced: 'des' for *desk*, 'tes' for *test*, 'col' for *cold*. (4) Past-tense endings are also absent in such clusters: 'look' for *looked*, 'talk' for *talked*. (5) Word-initial /d/ often takes the place of /ð/, as in 'dat day' for *that day* and 'dis house' for *this house*. (6) Word-final /f/ often replaces /θ/, as in 'boof' for *booth* and 'souf' for *south*. (7) There is often heavy initial stress in disyllabic words: *pólice* for *políce*, *défine* for *defíne*.

**Grammar**. (1) Multiple negation is common, as with many non-standard English dialects: *No way no girl can't wear no platform shoes to no amusement park* There is no way that any girl can wear platform shoes to an amusement park. (2) Existential *it* replaces *there*: *It ain't no food here* There is no food here. (3) Inflected forms such as plural, possessive, and singular *-s* and past *-ed* are variably omitted (as illustrated for pronunciation, points 3 and 4, above): *He got three cent*; *That's my brother book*; *She like new clothes*; *They talk* (= talked) *all night*. (4) Some inversion occurs with questions: *What it is?*, *How you are?* (5) Auxiliary *do* can replace *be* in a negative statement: *It don't all be her fault* It isn't always her fault. (6) Auxiliary *be* is often used to indicate habitual occurrence:

*They be fightin* They are always fighting, *He be laughin* He laughs all the time. (7) Stressed *been* conveys long-standing events with remote pasts: *I been see dat movie* I saw that movie long ago; *She been had dat hat* She has had that hat for some time. (8) Intention is sometimes expressed by the particle *a*: *I'm a shoot you* I'm going to shoot you: compare Appalachian English *I'm a gonna* for 'I am going to'. (9) Aspectual usage with *steady* occurs before progressive verbs or with heavy stress in sentence-final position; greater emphasis occurs when sentences conclude with *steady*: *We be steady rappin*, *We steady be rappin*, *We be rappin stéady* We are always talking; *They steady be high*, *They be steady high*, *They be high stéady* They are always intoxicated (from drugs or alcohol). In such cases, *steady* indicates that the activity is persistent, consistent, and intense. (10) *Come* sometimes functions as a semiauxiliary: *He come tellin me some story* He told me a lie; *They come comin in here like they own de place* They came in here like they owned the place. (11) Adverbial use of *like to* meaning 'almost': *I like to die(d)* I almost died; *He like to hit his head on that branch* He almost hit his head on that branch.

**Vocabulary**. (1) Such terms as *goober* (peanut), *yam* (sweet potato), *tote* (to carry), and *buckra* (white man) trace their history to West Africa, as do the grammatical functions of habitual *be* and aspectual *steady* (above). (2) Several ingroup terms are used to refer to intimates or to other African Americans in general. For example, *homeboy* was coined by convicts who served prison terms with other 'boys from home': that is, other convicts from the same neighbourhood. The bond between *homeboys* is stronger than that between other *brothers* or *bloods* (other blacks) who have had no relationship prior to imprisonment. This term moved from prisons to the black communities where most (ex)convicts live(d). *Homies* is the plural form and *homegirl* the feminine equivalent of *homeboy*. (3) Pejorative ethnic terms for whites include *honkie* and *whitey* for all whites, and *redneck* and *peckerwood* for poor and/or rural and/or Southern whites, especially such overt racists as members of the Ku Klux Klan.

**Slang**. (1) Established slang includes significant changes in the senses and applications of words: *bad* is used to mean 'good' (*Hey, that's a bad car, man!*); *cool* and *hot* are used with equal intensity to mean 'very good' (*That car is real cool/hot*); *crib*, usually associated with infants, can mean any home, apartment, or place where one lives, including a federal housing project; *short* and *ride* can refer to an automobile: *Homeboy be steady driving that short/ride*. (2) Everyday idioms include: *stepped-to* (subject to a physical advance by an opponent before a possible exchange of blows), as in *So I said, 'What's up?' and I got stepped-to*; *upside the head* (against the head), as in *He got hit upside the head*; *ashy*, in reference to a dry skin condition that appears as a slight discoloration: *His skin always be so ashy*. (3) Many expressions used in AAVE have 'crossed over' into mainstream colloquial AMERICAN ENGLISH: *hip* or *hep*, referring to someone who is very knowledgeable about popular (especially inner-city African-American) culture; *dude* as a generic reference for any male: *That dude be crazy*.

**Usage**. Many kinds of African-American speech acts go back to African oral traditions: *the dozens* verbal insults towards an opponent's mother; *rapping* a voluble, rhythmic eloquence that includes both the language of seduction and the lyrics of popular music; *shucking, jiving* deceiving whites through verbal trickery without their knowledge; *sounding* engaging in verbal duels. The 'men and women of words' who embody these traditions are common in most black communities; preachers, poets, musicians, and political radicals tend to be consummate practitioners of a rhetoric derived from Africa and often influenced by the Bible. Although men are perceived as dominating these traditions, women have played a significant role in the oral traditions of African America. Such music as Negro spirituals and jazz, as well as dance, poetry, rap, and even elaborate handshakes have substantially 'crossed over' and become part of popular culture in the US and elsewhere.

**Literary AAVE**. The implementation of AAVE in AmE literature is comparable to that of literary Cockney in England. J. L. Dillard (*Black English*, 1972) observed that the earliest literary renditions appeared before 1790: 'Attestation (recorded literary examples) from Crèvecoeur, Cotton Mather, Benjamin Franklin, the court records of Salem, Massachusetts, and several other sources may be found before the 1790's—

and all without any recourse to fictional sources. The wealth of material after that date is simply astonishing. There is, in fact, a very great deal of pre-Civil War literary Negro dialect'. Contemporary African-American writers, including Maya Angelou, Langston Hughes, Toni Morrison, Alice Walker, and Richard Wright, have provided literary versions of Black English that continue to have an impact on broader interpretations of English usage and American literature.

**Conclusion**. African-American varieties of English vary considerably, tending to reflect the social background and personal aspirations of individual speakers as well as the social circumstances in which different dialects thrive. The historical evidence confirms a combination of African, English, Scots, and Irish influences that have evolved through complex processes of pidginization and creolization.

See AFRICAN ENGLISH, AMERICAN ENGLISH, BRITISH BLACK ENGLISH, CARIBBEAN ENGLISH, CARIBBEAN ENGLISH CREOLE, DIALECT IN AMERICA, EBONICS, JIVE, NEW ORLEANS, PIDGIN, RAP, SOUTHERN ENGLISH.

# ■ AFRICAN ENGLISH ──────── ■

Short form *AfrE*. The English language as used in Africa. In principle, the term can refer to English used anywhere from the Mediterranean to the Cape of Good Hope, including in Egypt by speakers of Arabic, in Nigeria by speakers of Hausa, Igbo, and Yoruba, and in the Republic of South Africa by speakers of Afrikaans, Xhosa, Zulu, and other regional languages, as well as by settlers of British origin. In practice, however, the term is usually restricted to Black Africa, especially to ex-British colonies, with three subcategories: *WEST AFRICAN ENGLISH* (Cameroon, Gambia, Ghana, Nigeria, Sierra Leone, with Liberia as a special case because of its American associations), *EAST AFRICAN ENGLISH* (Kenya, Tanzania, Uganda, and perhaps Sudan), and *Southern African English* (Botswana, Lesotho, Malawi, Namibia, Swaziland, Zambia, Zimbabwe, with South Africa as a special case because of its history and ethnic diversity).

In the second sense, the term is open to two further interpretations: as either all forms of English since the establishment of trading posts in the 17c, including pidgins and creoles, or only the forms spoken and written by educated Black Africans after some territories were administered by the British (such as Ghana and Nigeria) and/or settled by the British (such as Kenya and Zimbabwe). If the first sense is adopted, English has been in Africa for nearly 400 years. If the second sense is adopted, English in Africa dates from the mid-19c. However the term is interpreted, the reality and worth of an indigenized *African English* (with subvarieties such as *Kenyan English* and *Nigerian English*) are controversial matters, asserted by some, denied by others, advocated by some and denounced by others. English is in daily use for many purposes in 18 sub-Saharan countries (including as a lingua franca between speakers of different indigenous languages), and reflects all manner of local and regional influences. It is also taught as a second language in francophone countries. To discuss such matters, the term *African English* seems inescapable.

**History**. The English pidgins and creoles of West Africa have been the product of contacts between Africans and Europeans who were concerned at first with trade and later with colonialism. These varieties were significant not only in West Africa but also in the development of creoles elsewhere, particularly in the New World. Educated AfrE, however, evolved out of the formal teaching of English as a second language during the colonial era, when the grammar–translation method was the dominant approach to language learning and the teaching of English literature was central to all advanced work. Most teachers were British, with little or no knowledge of indigenous languages. During this period, the language was taught to multilingual Africans by multidialectal Britons, so that two kinds of variation were present from the start. Multilingualism and the difficulty of establishing a single national African language in each of the countries concerned made it easy to impose and then continue the use of English as the language for education, administration, and panregional communication.

Like French, Portuguese, and Spanish in other colonies, English became the medium of communication between the administration and its educated subjects as well as the prized vehicle of upward mobility. Formal education was a primary agent in its spread to the relatively few Africans admitted to the school system. As a result, English became the shared language of the colonial establishment and a Western-educated élite, while such African lingua francas as Hausa and Swahili continued to serve the everyday needs of the masses. Contact between standard English and these lingua francas (including the pidgin and creole Englishes of West Africa) has added to the complexity of AfrE and provided it with a range of situations in which diglossia, code-switching, and borrowing have been common.

**Creative writing**. As in other former colonial societies, creative writing has contributed to the emergence and recognition of AfrE as a distinct variety or group of varieties. In attempting to transcreate African cultures through their literary works in English, African writers have found it necessary to adapt and indigenize certain aspects of the language, including both lexicon and narrative style. The work of the Nigerian novelist Chinua Achebe is an example of such creative indigenization. He has observed:

> My answer to the question, can an African ever learn English well enough to be able to use it effectively in creative writing? is certainly yes. If on the other hand you ask: Can he ever learn to use it like a native speaker? I should say: I hope not. It is neither necessary nor desirable for him to be able to do so. The price a world language must be prepared to pay is submission to many different kinds of use. The African writer should aim to use English in a way that brings out his message best without altering the language to the extent that its value as a medium of international exchange will be lost (*Transition* 18, 1965).

This adaptation of the language to accommodate the African cultural experience, combined with the unconscious structural adjustments attendant on language contact and foreign-language learning, accounts for the development of an English that is distinctively African.

**The contemporary situation**. English is an official language of 16 countries: in *West Africa* Cameroon (with French), Gambia, Ghana, Liberia, Nigeria, and Sierra Leone; in *East Africa* Sudan (with Arabic), Uganda; in *Southern Africa* Botswana, Lesotho (with Sesotho), Malawi (with

Chichewa), Namibia, South Africa (with Afrikaans and nine indigenous languages), Swaziland, Zambia, and Zimbabwe. In Kenya and Tanzania, Swahili is the official language, English the second language and medium of higher education. Because of its official role and use by the media, standard English occupies a privileged place in the stratification of languages in these regions, but is by and large a minority language learned mainly through formal education. Depending on situation, the choice of code to be used in a conversation is generally a local language, a national language or lingua franca, or English. Other elements in such a range of choices are the pidgins and creoles of English in West Africa and of Afrikaans in South Africa and Namibia. Because of the large number of countries and the vast distances and considerable cultural differences involved, it is not easy to list examples of usages that are true for AfrE as a whole, but some generalizations are possible.

**Pronunciation**. (1) Non-rhotic and generally syllable-timed. (2) West African speakers tend to have antepenultimate word stress as in 'condition, East and Southern African speakers to have penultimate word stress as in main'tenance, reflecting that of the Bantu languages. (3) By and large, there is a reduced system of five to seven vowels /i, e, a, o, u/ and perhaps /ɔ, ɛ/, with such homophones as bit/beat (sometimes distinguished by length), had/hard as /had/, full/fool as /ful/, and cut/court/caught as /kɔt/. Individual items may be variously realized: bed as /bed/ or /bɛd/, bird as /bed/ or /bɔd/. (4) The consonants /θ, ð/, are usually realized in West Africa as /t/ and /d/ ('tree of dem' for three of them), in East and Southern Africa as /s/ and /z/ ('sree of zem' for three of them). Useful/youthful and breeze/breathe may be homophones, having the first pronunciation for both members of each pair. (5) The nasal /ŋ/ is often pronounced as /n/ or /ŋg/ ('singin' for singing). (6) The consonants /l/ and /r/ are often exchanged ('load' for road, 'rolly' for lorry, 'fright' for flight), but this is becoming rare in West Africa. In parts of Nigeria, there is an exchange of /l/ and /n/, as in lomba wan for number one. (7) Word-final consonant clusters are often simplified: 'nest' for next, 'nees' for needs.

**Grammar**. The discussion of syntax tends to centre on deviation from standard

English rather than a consideration of distinctively AfrE forms. Features include: (1) Sporadic countable use of usually uncountable nouns: firewoods for bits of firewood, furnitures for pieces of furniture, correspondences for letters. (2) The inconsistent omission of the plural in some contexts: Madam X gave birth to triplet. (3) A tendency to repeat words for emphasis and rhetorical purposes: Do it small small Do it slowly, bit by bit; What you say, you say; My boy, I see what I see; They blamed them, they blamed them for all the troubles that have befallen our land. (4) A common use of resumptive pronoun subjects: My daughter she is attending that school; My father he is very tall. (5) Yes–no questions typically answered to accord with form rather than meaning: Hasn't he left yet?—Yes, He hasn't; Didn't you break that?—Yes, I didn't. (6) Simple verbs often used instead of their phrasal-verb derivatives: crop crop up, pick pick up, leave leave out, leave in.

**Vocabulary**. (1) Words and phrases borrowed from local languages: West African oga master, boss (Yoruba); South African madumbi tubers (Zulu), East African pombe local traditional beer (Swahili). (2) Hybrids from English and local languages: Southern African lobola-beast, from Nguni ukolobola (to give dowry), an enemy who uses a bride price as a means of exploitation while feigning friendship, kwela music, from Xhosa kwela (to get moving), penny-whistle music; East African mabenzi people and wabenzi, from Swahili, people who own Mercedes-Benz cars, the rich. (3) Loan translations from local languages: West African chewing stick a piece of wood used as a toothbrush, cornstick a corncob, tight friend a close friend, intimate, mami water a female water spirit, enstool to enthrone, destool to overthrow (a chief), with derivatives enstoolment, destoolment. (4) Semantic shift in the use of everyday words: Nigerian and Cameroonian in state pregnant, Nigerian to have long legs to wield power and influence, West African high life local music similar to jazz, Kenyan thank you reply to 'goodbye', East African beat me a picture take my photograph, and It's/that's porridge It's/that's a piece of cake.

**Style**. (1) AfrE, especially in works of fiction and the media, is marked by the use of African proverbs and figurative usage, and by a narrative style characteristic of African rhetoric, using titles, praise words, and special epithets: My brother, son of my fathers, *you have failed*; *You are mighty, my brother, mighty and dangerous*; *Do you blame a vulture for perching over a carcass?*; *Father, isn't it true that a wise man becomes wiser by borrowing from other people's heads? Isn't it true that a rich man becomes richer through the toils of those he exploits?* (2) It is frequently marked by code-mixing involving various lingua francas: 'He paraded me to the world, I'ogolonto' (Igbo 'stark-naked', in Wole Soyinka's *Kongi's Harvest*, 1967); 'Each feared onwana wa rikutene—a bastard child' (in Abel Mwanga's *Nyangeta: The Name from the Calabash*, 1976). This mixing may also include the use of pidgin: ' "He no be like dat," said Joseph. "Him no gentleman. Not fit take bribe" ' (Chinua Achebe, *No Longer at Ease*, 1960).

**English influence**. The influence of English on African languages varies considerably, depending on the extent of contact in an area. In some languages, such as those in the francophone zones, English has supplied very few words: for example, forms of *kitchen*, *matches*, and *school*. In others, such as Hausa, Shona, and Swahili, because of bilingualism and code-mixing, the influence may have affected not only vocabulary but also structure. Anglicisms typically occur in such registers as administration, education, finance, and technology, such as: Hausa *cijjoji* chief judge, *satifiket* certificate, *dala* dollar, *injin* engine; Shona *inispekita* inspector, *chikoro* school, *cheki* cheque, *rori* lorry; and Swahili *meneja* manager, *jiografia* geography, *pensheni* pension, *beteri* battery.

**Conclusion**. As English continues to spread, through education, the media, and administrative institutions, with Africans serving as models for Africans, the distinctness of the varieties subsumed under the term *African English* is likely to become more evident and the varieties are more likely to be recognized as legitimate by both their own users and the rest of the English-speaking world. See SOUTH AFRICAN ENGLISH.

**AFRICANISM**. An African usage, style, or way of thought; a word or phrase from an African language, such as *juju* a charm or fetish (probably from Hausa *djudju* evil spirit, fetish). The term is sometimes modified to refer to parts of the continent: *South Africanism*, *West Africanism*. See AFRICAN ENGLISH.

**AFRIKAANS**. A LANGUAGE related to DUTCH, the mother tongue of about 6m people in Southern Africa and a second language for millions of South Africans and Namibians. It is the source of many hundreds of loanwords in SOUTH AFRICAN ENGLISH, including such internationally known words as *apartheid*, *boer*, *laager*, *trek*, *veld*, and has in turn borrowed extensively from English.

**AFRIKAANS ENGLISH**. English used as a second language in South Africa and Namibia by speakers of AFRIKAANS. It is generally rhotic, characterized by a trilled or rolled *r*. It also has schwa where RP has the vowel /ɪ/ in such words as *pin* and *sit* (/pən/ and /sət/), a sound regarded as the characteristic South African vowel, with a varying influence on SOUTH AFRICAN ENGLISH. Initial and medial /h/ is often voiced, and gives the impression of being dropped, so that *red hair* may be heard as 'red air'. Conversely, there is often an intrusive aspirate between vowels, as in 'cre-haytion' for *creation* and 'hi-haytus' for *hiatus*. Before /ju/, as in *you*, the intrusive /h/ is palatalized as in English *huge*, while *huge* is often rendered as 'yoodge'. Final voiced consonants tend to be devoiced: 'dok' for *dog*, 'piecess' for *pieces*. Because Afrikaans verbs are not marked for third-person singular, confusion of concord is common, including in the media, particularly with *is/are*, *has/have*, *does/do*. Use of prepositions is also influenced by Afrikaans: *He's by the house* (at the house), *She's not here on the moment* (at the moment), *They're waiting on their results* (for their results). Many expressions are carried over from Afrikaans: 'I *rode* (drove) all over town looking for my shoes but didn't find it (compare *dit*, the Afrikaans inanimate pronoun for 'them'). Most frequently heard is the phrase *Is it?*, from Afrikaans *Is dit?* (Really? Is that so? Are they?, etc.). Some Afrikaans-derived expressions have been assimilated into South African English, such as *He's lazy to get up* He's too lazy to get up, *The tree is capable to withstand frost* The tree is capable of withstanding frost, *He farms with wine grapes* He grows grapes for wine, and *The village boasts with beautiful vineyards* The village boasts beautiful vineyards.

**AGENT**. In grammar, the person or other being that instigates the happening denoted by the verb: *Jenny* in the sentences

*Jenny has written me a letter* and *Jenny made Henry angry* refers to the doer of the action or the causer of the event. In English, the semantic role of the subject in active constructions is typically agentive, but not exclusively so: *books* in *These books sell well* is not the agent but the affected. In a passive construction, the agent may be represented in an optional *by*-phrase: *Anita and Michael were mugged (by some louts) on their way home last night*. The term *agent* or *agentive* is used in case grammar for one of the sematic cases.

**AGENTLESS PASSIVE**. A common type of PASSIVE construction in English, in which the role of the AGENT is not represented, as in *Michael was mugged on his way home*. Here, such a *by*-phrase as *by some louts*, the agents of the mugging, has been omitted. The agentless passive is common in formal reports: *Although insufficient funds had been allocated, the decision was taken to continue for another six months in the hope that more money would be made available*. See VOICE.

**AGGLUTINATING**, also **agglutinative**. A term in LINGUISTICS for a language whose words are mostly made up of units (morphemes) that are easily distinguishable, as in: Turkish *evlerde* (*ev-ler-de*, house-*plural*-in, 'in the houses'); SWAHILI *ninakupenda* (*ni-na-ku-penda*, I-*present*-you-love, 'I love you'). Most languages have some agglutination, as in English *cows* (cow-s), *goodness* (good-ness), *distasteful* (distaste-ful), but in some languages such as Turkish or Swahili, it predominates. See LINGUISTIC TYPOLOGY.

**AGREEMENT**. See CONCORD.

**AIRSPEAK**, also **air traffic control English**, **Aviation English**. The English of international civil aviation, a RESTRICTED LANGUAGE established after the Second World War by the *International Civil Aviation Organization (ICAO)*. Although in some conditions aircraft may use a local language, commercial flying is universally conducted in English. When speech is necessary, it is as concise and unambiguous as possible, uses only accepted conventions for procedures and message types, is not too dense (that is, does not contain too many propositions before allowing the interlocutor to speak), and has checkbacks so that speakers can be sure that what was said is what was heard. Everything used for these purposes

is English in grammar, vocabulary, or pronunciation, but some of the vocabulary is technical and specialized. Radio conversation not relevant to a flight is forbidden. International agreements ensure that all pilots are trained in this English, and cockpit conversations as monitored to ensure that rules are adhered to. The following extract, for an aircraft descending from cruise height towards its destination airport, is typical:

> *Control*. BA six zero six Alfa: squawk ident.
> *Pilot*. Identing, BA six zero six Alfa.
> *Control*. BA six zero six Alfa, radar contact. Descend to flight level three one zero.
> *Pilot*. Leaving flight level three nine zero. Descending to level three one zero. BA six zero six Alfa.

[Glossary: *ident* identity, *identing* identifying, *squawk* reveal, make known.] See ESP, SEASPEAK.

**AITCH**. The name for the letter *H*, often used disparagingly in such expressions as *an aitch-dropper*, *aitch-free*, and *aitchless*. In phonetics, the term *aitch-dropping* refers to the absence of initial /h/ in such words as *harm* and *here* (usually shown in writing as *'arm* and *'ere*), common in working-class and lower middle-class SPEECH in much of England; the use of the term, however, is controversial because one cannot 'drop' a sound that one has not first 'held'. Absence of initial /h/, though widespread, is nonstandard in BrE. On its absence from COCKNEY speech, Robert Barltrop and Jim Wolveridge make the following comment in *The Muvver Tongue* (1980, pp. 6 and 101):

> Cockneys drop h's. So do the French. . . . The teacher's case is that 'h' should be sounded on English words because this is the established practice. So it is—but not among Cockneys. They know that h's are there and put them in in writing; but to use them in speech is 'talking posh'. Their omission does not lead to misunderstandings, except by non-Cockneys. . . . One Sunday morning some years ago I sat in a bus behind a man who had his little boy of about four on his lap. The child had a picture-alphabet book, and the father was explaining it carefully; when they came to h, the picture was of a hedgehog. The

man said: 'that's an edgeog. It's really two words, edge and og. They both start with h.'

Many upwardly mobile non-aitch-using people in England have sought to 'restore' (that is, acquire) initial /h/, with varying success. Some socialists, however, have made a political point of its absence from their speech or, if brought up 'aitch-fully', have sought to drop their aitches as a token of working-class solidarity. In 1903, Shaw observed in *Man and Superman*: 'This man takes more trouble to drop his aitches than ever his father did to pick them up.' See ARTICLE, ASPIRATE, DIALECT IN ENGLAND, GEORDIE, STRESS.

**AKU**, also **Aku Talk, Gambian Krio**. An English-based creole spoken in GAMBIA and closely related to KRIO in SIERRA LEONE. See WEST AFRICAN PIDGIN ENGLISH.

**ALFRED** [849–99]. Old English *Ælfred*. Scholar king of the West Saxons (871–99), often called *Alfred the Great*, who prevented the Danes from conquering all of England, and promoted learning and literacy in ENGLISH and LATIN. In the preface to his translation of Gregory the Great's *Pastoral Care*, he reasoned that GREEK and Latin translations of the Old Testament were a precedent for translating some Latin classics into English for the children of free men to read. Although he lacked a profound knowledge of Latin, his translations initiated OLD ENGLISH prose writing. The ANGLO-SAXON CHRONICLE probably began during his reign (c.890) and may reflect his influence. At the time when the Vikings were destroying the celebrated Latin culture of Northumbria, Alfred's programme of translations gave English an important place in early medieval culture, an unparalleled development among European vernaculars of the time. His books continued to be copied in Norman England. See BIBLE, ENGLISH LITERATURE, HISTORY OF ENGLISH, INDIAN ENGLISH.

**ALLEGORY**. A story, such as George ORWELL's *Animal Farm* (1945), that can be read on two levels: as a surface narrative that may or may not be realistic and at a deeper level that is often didactic and moralistic, and sometimes satirical. Characters and episodes are intended to represent some elements in human life: Orwell's farm is a nation state and his pigs are Marxist revolutionaries. Allegory may occur in any genre, does not constitute a literary form, and is in effect an extended METAPHOR. See ANALOGY.

**ALLITERATION**, also **head rhyme**, **initial rhyme**. Terms in RHETORIC, poetics, and general usage for the repetition of the same sound, usually an initial CONSONANT such as the *f* in 'Fixed fate, free will, foreknowledge absolute' (Milton). Alliteration can serve both a mnemonic and an ornamental purpose, and is common in: *verse* O Wild West Wind, thou breath of autumn's being (Shelley); *story-telling prose* the great grey-green, greasy Limpopo River (Kipling); *speech-making* Do not let us speak of darker days; let us rather speak of sterner days (Churchill); *advertising* Guinness is good for you, You can be sure of Shell; *TONGUE-TWISTERS* Peter Piper picked a peck of pickled peppers, She sells sea-shells on the seashore; *similes* cool as a cucumber, dead as a doornail; *reduplicative words* flimflam, tittle-tattle; *collocations, idiomatic phrases, PROVERBS* bed and breakfast, footloose and fancy-free, Look before you leap; *nicknames and epithets* Battling Bill, Tiny Tim, the Broadway Butcher; *tabloid newspaper headlines* Saucy Sue brings home the bacon.

**Alliterative verse**. Verse that depends for its effect on alliteration. Such verse was unknown in classical Greek but common in Latin and the Celtic and Germanic languages. Old English verse such as the epic poem BEOWULF was alliterative, as in: 'Hwæt, we gardena in geardagum, / þeodcyninga þrym gefrunon, / hu ða æþelingas ellen fremedon'. These lines have been translated into modern alliterative verse in 1973 by Michael Alexander as: 'Attend! We have heard of the thriving of the throne of Denmark, / how the folk-kings flourished in former days'. Such verse died out with the coming of the Normans and consequent French influence, but was revived in the 13c. The best-known poems are Langland's *Piers Plowman* and the anonymous *Sir Gawain and the Green Knight* (both 14c). Two lines from Langland run: 'In a somer seson whan soft was the sonne, / I shope me in shroudes, as I a shepe were' (*shope* dressed, *shepe* ship). See ASSONANCE, ENGLISH LITERATURE, REDUPLICATION, REPETITION.

**ALLOPHONE**. See **1.** ANGLOPHONE, **2.** PHONEME.

**ALLUSION**. An indirect reference. The term formerly included metaphors, parables, and puns, but now generally means implicit use of someone else's words. Whereas quotations usually come with acknowledged sources, allusions are indirect, even cryptic, sometimes dropped in passing, with little thought, sometimes used with care, so that a speaker or writer can share an understanding with certain listeners or readers. Allusions often adapt their originals to new ends, the audience making or failing to make the connections, as when the US journalist William Safire cries out in his column: 'Ah, Fowler! Thou shouldst be living at this hour; usage hath need of thee' (*New York Times*, July 1989). Here, Safire addresses the master of his craft much as Wordsworth once opened a sonnet: 'Milton! Thou shouldst be living at this hour, / England hath need of thee.' Similarly, Wordsworth's paradoxical statement 'The Child is father of the Man' is embroidered by the British television critic John Naughton when saying of Richard Burton, 'the abandoned, motherless child was father to the volatile, generous, self-hating man' (*Observer*, Sept. 1988). Newspaper headlines are often allusive: *Amid the Alien Porn*; *Brontë village fears wuthering blight*; *A Chase That Stopped a Thousand Trips*; *The Laser's Edge*; *Comedy of Terrors*. See ANALOGY, BIBLE, ECHOISM, QUOTATION, SHAKESPEARE.

■ **ALPHABET** ───────────── ■

A system of written and printed LANGUAGE in which each symbol generally represents one sound, as with *b* for the voiced bilabial stop at the beginning of the word *boat* in the ROMAN alphabet as used for English.

**Nature**. In most alphabetic systems, such as the Roman alphabet as used for Spanish, the correlation of symbol to sound is close, representing with considerable success a language's inventory of *phonemes* (smallest identifiable units of speech). The system used for English, however, falls well short of ideal *phonographic* (SOUND/SPELLING) equivalence: for example, the LETTER *f* conventionally represents the voiceless labio-dental fricative sound /f/, as in *fast*, but in some words this sound is represented by *gh* as in *tough*, and in others by *ph* as in *phone*. Again, in French, the letter *d* generally represents the voiced alveolar plosive sound /d/ in *dans*, but has no phonetic value in, for example, *canard* (where the *d* is said to be 'silent').

*Alphabets and syllabaries*. A clear-cut distinction cannot always be made between alphabets proper and *syllabaries*, sets of syllabic symbols as in the Japanese *kana* systems. Syllabic signs, like letters, represent small units of pronunciation, typically a spoken consonant followed by a spoken vowel, as in the four signs for the syllables *yo, ko, ha, ma* in the place-name *Yokohama*. Single alphabetic letters may represent a double sound, as with the letter *x*, which in Roman-derived alphabets generally stands for the two sounds /ks/, and sometimes a representation is syllabic, as with the letter *m* in the English word *spasm*, which consists of the 'ordinary' syllable *spas* and the syllabic consonant *m*. In addition, alphabets are commonly part of a graphic inventory that includes non-alphabetic signs, such as *punctuation marks* (?, !, " ", etc.), *diacritics* (ˆ, ´, ¯, etc.), *ideograms* (representing such concepts as the numbers 1, 2, 3), and *logograms* (standing for specific words, as with &, $, £).

*Phonography and ideography*. Probably the most fundamental distinction among writing systems, however, is between the *phonographic principle* (in which writing is done by means of sound symbols organized in alphabets and syllabaries) and the *ideographic* or *logographic principle* (in which writing is done by means of symbols that directly represent ideas or words). Traditional Chinese writing is typically ideographic, its thousands of characters generally representing meanings and not sounds, whereas the symbols of phonographic systems represent sounds and not meanings. There are, however, few if any pure phonographic or ideographic systems: the English writing system, for example, employs such ideograms as numeral signs and such logograms as the ampersand and dollar sign (as indicated above), and is part of a general system that adds iconic forms such as a pointing hand indicating a direction to take or male and female figures for toilet facilities, often part of an international system reminiscent of the hieroglyphs of ancient Egypt.

**The Phoenicians and Greeks**. Scholars who study the world's writing systems generally agree that the alphabetic principle was invented only once, in West Asia. The original set of some 30 signs, known as the *North Semitic alphabet*, was used in and around Canaan and Phoenicia from *c*.1700–1500 BC onwards. It was the ultimate ancestor of all later alphabets, such as those used for Phoenician, Hebrew, Greek, Arabic, Latin, English, French, Russian, the languages of the Indian subcontinent, and those of Ethiopia.

From the 11c BC, Phoenicians using a 22-sign variant of the North Semitic alphabet traded throughout the Mediterranean littoral, sometimes setting up colonies. In Carthage, a colony established in present-day Tunisia, the Punic version of their alphabet continued in use until the 3c AD. Like all early Semitic systems, the Phoenician scripts were written from right to left and consisted only of signs for consonants, because of the pre-eminence of consonants in the formation of Semitic word forms. The Greeks, *c*.1000–900 BC, developed a script heavily influenced by this alphabet, in which, however, they reassigned certain symbols that had no spoken equivalents in their own language to represent vowel sounds, which were central to their system of word-formation and word use.

Initially, Greek was written from right to left like Phoenician, but later changed from left to right. The reason for this development is unknown.

The pre-classical Greek alphabet contained several symbols that did not survive into classical times but nonetheless had an influence beyond Greek. They included the letters *digamma* and *koppa*, the ancestors of Roman F and Q (see F, Q) and a modification of P written with a tail, which served as an early model for Roman R (see P, R). These forms gradually disappeared from the writing of the classical language, but were adopted by other Mediterranean peoples into their own Greek-derived alphabets. The mature Greek alphabet of *c*.400 BC contained several new letters, such as *phi* (Φ), *chi* (X), *psi* (Ψ), *omega* (Ω), all added at the end of the traditional alphabetic list.

**The Etruscans and Romans**. Among the Mediterranean peoples who developed their own versions of the Greek alphabet were the Etruscans in Italy *c*.800 BC. Their alphabet was in turn adopted and adapted by their neighbours the Romans, and the Roman alphabet as used for classical Latin can be related as follows to that of classical Greek: (1) The capital forms (but often not the later small forms) of the letters *A, B, E, I,*

*K, M, N, O, T, Y, Z*, and their sound values, remained broadly the same as in Greek. (2) Earlier Greek letters, abandoned in the classical alphabet, were retained in Roman F, Q. (3) Earlier Greek sound values were retained for Roman H, X. (4) Changes in form occurred in *D, L, P, R, S, V*. (5) A change of form and sound value occurred in *C*, and the letter *G* was invented for Latin. (6) The original Roman alphabet comprised 23 letters, but the germs of the future *J* and *U* were contained in the letters *I* and *V*, although the graphic distinction between the vowel and consonant letters in the pairs *I, J* and *U, V* was not universally accepted until the 17–19c. The letter *W* emerged in the Middle Ages from the doubling of *U/V*.

Many languages that use variants of the Roman alphabet employ *diacritics* to enable a given letter to represent more than one sound unambiguously, as when German writes *ö* to indicate a different value from *o*. Sometimes a letter with a diacritic may be listed separately from its plain form, as with *å* in Danish, Norwegian, and Swedish, which is added at the end of the alphabet list. Sometimes a language that uses a digraph (double-letter combination) to represent a distinct phoneme will list the digraph separately in the alphabet too: in Welsh *ch, dd, ff, ll, ph, rh* are listed after their first letter, while *ng* occurs between *g* and *h*. Conversely, a language that does not use certain of the conventional 26 letters to spell its native vocabulary may not include them in its alphabet: in Welsh, *j, k, q, v, x, z* are not used, and *w* generally represents a vowel. Variants of the Roman alphabet are used throughout Europe and the Americas, in most of sub-Saharan Africa, in Australasia, in parts of South-East Asia, and as a secondary system in most of the rest of the world.

**The English alphabet**. Old English was first written in the runic alphabet known as *futhork*, and isolated runic inscriptions continued to be made in Britain until the 12c. With the advent of Christianity, the Roman alphabet was applied to the language with fairly regular sound-symbol correspondence but sometimes with different spoken realizations in different dialects. Because Old English had phonemes not present in Latin, however, a number of new symbols were introduced: æ (ASH), þ (THORN), ð (ETH), and ƿ (WYNN), thorn and wynn being taken from futhork. The letter *g* was modified as ʒ (YOGH), which existed alongside continental g for some centuries after the Norman Conquest in 1066. The use of these symbols was discontinued after the introduction of printing in the 15c, partly because printers' sets of continental typefaces lacked them. By that time, the sound of æ had merged with that of short *a*, the sound of thorn and eth was already spelt *th* in words transliterated from Greek into Latin, and wynn had been largely superseded by *w*. The loss of these letters left an alphabet of 24 letters, in which *i/j* and *u/v* were not clearly distinguished. From about 1600, however, they were gradually separated over a period of more than two centuries into the vowel letters *i*, *u* and the consonant letters *j*, *v*. Graphic variation was long preserved with the two forms of lower-case *s*, written either as *s* or *ʃ* (long s), the latter normally in medial position, as in *poʃʃeʃs* (roman: poʃʃeʃs) possess. The greater typographical simplicity of using only one form of *s* led to the rapid abandonment of the long form by printers after 1800, and by the general public soon after. The Roman alphabet as currently used for English consists of the 26 large and small letters *Aa, Bb, Cc, Dd, Ee, Ff, Gg, Hh, Ii, Jj, Kk, Ll, Mm, Nn, Oo, Pp, Qq, Rr, Ss, Tt, Uu, Vv, Ww, Xx, Yy, Zz*. No diacritic marks are normally used for native English words, unless the apostrophe and the diaeresis sign are counted as such.

See ASCII, HISTORY OF ENGLISH, WRITING, and the letter entries A to Z.

**ALPHABETICAL ORDER**, also **alphabetic order**, **ABC order**, **alphabetic(al) arrangement**. The order used for presenting, teaching, memorizing, or otherwise using the letters of an ALPHABET. It is particularly favoured as an invariant series by which information can be organized in catalogues, concordances, dictionaries, directories, encyclopedias, indexes, and the like. Thoroughgoing alphabetization did not establish itself fully until printing had become widespread and printers had become used to manipulating letters first physically (as bits of metal in alphabetized trays), then conceptually.

Conventionally, alphabetical ordering must be consistent through words, word groups, names, name groups, etc., so that, for example, *access* precedes *accessibility* which precedes *accessible* which precedes *accessibly*. Word groups may be ordered strictly by letter throughout the group, ignoring spaces (as are the headwords in this book); alternatively, they may be ordered word by word, a shorter word then preceding all longer words that begin with the same sequence of letters. Compare the following:

| *Letter-by-letter order* | *Word-by-word order* |
|---|---|
| American | American |
| American English | American English |
| Americanese | American language |
| Americanism | Americanese |
| American language | Americanism |

Difficulties may arise in English over certain placings, such as *Mac* and *Mc* names and the names of saints. Further complications include ordering according to personal names that follow surnames in a directory, as with *Macleod, John; McLeod, Margaret; MacLeod, Morag; McLeod, Murdo*, etc.

**ALVEOLAR** [Stress: 'al-VEE-o-lar']. **1.** Relating to either of the bony ridges in the mouth that contain the teeth, but especially in phonetics to the ridge behind the upper teeth (*the alveolar ridge*), and to any sounds made when the TONGUE touches or comes close to it: for example, the CONSONANTS /t, d/ are alveolar stops, while /s, z/ are alveolar fricatives. **2.** A sound made in this way: /d/ is a voiced alveolar. See *L*-SOUNDS, PALATE, *R*-SOUNDS, SPEECH.

**AMBIGUITY.** Actual or potential uncertainty of meaning, especially if a word, phrase, or sentence can be understood in two ways: for example, the written statement *They can fish*, which could mean *They may or are able to fish* and *They put fish in cans*. Many statements are ambiguous in isolation but clear in context or are amenable to logical analysis: although there are scores of meanings of *run*, someone who speaks of *running the marathon* is not likely to be using the word in the sense of *running a company*, although that is possible and may in some circumstances be so. In conversation, ambiguity can usually be resolved by asking, 'What do you mean, X or Y?', but in reading there is no one to ask and, unless the term is marked so as to designate the meaning intended, it may be impossible to distinguish one meaning from another but in such sentences as *They can fish* some distinction can be made in speech through stress and intonation. Because of their compactness, newspaper HEADLINES are particularly prone to peculiar elliptical effects, as in *MACARTHUR*

*FLIES BACK TO FRONT*, referring to US general Douglas MacArthur during the Korean War. See DOUBLE MEANING, DOUBLE TALK, JANUS WORD, PUN, PUNCTUATION.

**AMELIORATION**. See MELIORATION.

**AMERICAN**. An occasional term for English as used in the US, often in contrast with *English* (sometimes *British*), and seriously or facetiously implying a distinct language: 'The American I have heard up to the present, is a tongue as distinct from English as Patagonian' (Kipling, *From Sea to Sea*, 1889); 'Too often are spoken English and spoken American criticized as though it were impossible for them to have any laws of their own' (Partridge, *Usage and Abusage*, 1947/57); 'Brandon has a beaut: the transmission from American to English of *cost-effective*' (Safire, *New York Times*, Oct. 1988).

**AMERICAN BLACK ENGLISH**. See AFRICAN-AMERICAN VERNACULAR ENGLISH.

# ■ AMERICAN ENGLISH ■

[Short forms *AmE*, *AE*. Also **United States English**, short form *USE*.] The English language as used in the United States of America. The speakers of AmE outnumber all native speakers of English outside the US by about two to one and those of BrE by nearly four to one. This advantage, strengthened by US involvement with world affairs, has given AmE a global importance in the late 20c comparable to that of BrE in the late 19c. The history of the variety falls into three periods, whose dates correspond to political and social events with important consequences for the language: (1) *The Colonial Period*, during which a distinctive AmE was gestating. (2) *The National Period*, which saw its birth, establishment, and consolidation. (3) *The International Period*, during which it has come increasingly under foreign influence and has exerted influence on other varieties of English and on other languages.

**The Colonial Period** (1607–1776). English colonization of the Americas came relatively late, as compared for example with Spanish settlement in Central and South America. In 1497, John Cabot explored the coast of what became the Canadian province of Nova Scotia, but no effort was made to establish a colony for nearly

another century, when Humphrey Gilbert claimed the island of Newfoundland (1583) and Walter Raleigh attempted his ill-fated settlement at Roanoke, Virginia (1584). Raleigh's 'lost colony' did not survive, so the first permanent English settlement on the mainland was at Jamestown in 1607. Both religious and commercial motives prompted the founding of the Plymouth colony of 1620 and the Maryland colony of 1634. Colonization of the Carolinas began in 1663. The Dutch settled Manhattan Island in 1624, but were brought under English rule in 1664. European settlement of Pennsylvania, partly by the Dutch and Swedes, preceded the English chartering of a Quaker colony there in 1681 under William Penn. From the beginning, the colonies were of mixed origin. Because settlers came from a variety of locations, there was no simple transplanting of British dialects, but rather a combination of features in a single colony, resulting in the levelling of divergent features and the apparently random survival of features from disparate sources. The result was more uniform speech in the colonies than in the motherland. The barrier of the Atlantic began the process of divergence of American from British usage almost immediately. Changes in the motherland were slow to reach the colonies, the colonists adapted old uses to new purposes, and borrowed from other groups, especially the Amerindians, Dutch, and French. Although still depending on England for authority and a standard, the colonies were forced to develop their own resources.

**The National Period** (1776–1898). The War of Independence (1775–83) brought the Colonial Period to a close. Several of the Founding Fathers of the new republic recognized that political independence would require cultural independence as well. Linguistically, this period faced two related challenges: the evolution and recognition of a separate standard English for the US and the extension of that standard over the whole nation as it expanded westward. Noah WEBSTER is most closely associated with linguistic nationalism in promoting what he called Federal English, but others contributed to it. The Civil War (1861–5) disrupted the fabric of the Union in politics, culture, and language. By the time it began, US sovereignty extended to the Pacific, fulfilling a sense of a mission (the 'Manifest

Destiny' of the US) which motivated national policy during this period. The assimilation of foreign influences continued, including large numbers of immigrants from Europe and contacts with speakers of Spanish in Florida and the West. Developments which moulded the language of Americans during the 19c included the settlement of the West, the extension of the railroads, the growth of industry, the labour movement, the invention of the telegraph and telephone, the burgeoning of journalism, the expansion of education at all levels, and the publication of textbooks and dictionaries. The establishment of a national identity and its domestic elaboration were the preoccupation of this period, but by the end of the century new directions in national policy began to affect the language. By the 1890s the domestic frontier was exhausted, and expansionism took Americans into territories overseas. The Spanish-American War (1898) lasted barely four months, but was a turning-point in foreign policy. During the 120 years since the founding of the nation, the US had generally observed George Washington's counsel to avoid foreign alliances and followed an isolationist policy concentrating on domestic matters. With this war, however, the US and its English became internationally significant.

**The International Period** (from 1898). The Hawaiian Islands were annexed during the course of the Spanish-American War, the island of Puerto Rico was ceded to the US, and the Philippines were bought for $20m. In the following years, the US extended its overseas interests: an Open Door policy was affirmed for China; the US mediated the Russo-Japanese war of 1905; the Panamanian revolution against Colombia was supported (if not actually fomented), so that the US could build a canal across the isthmus of Panama; intervention in Latin American affairs became frequent, to prevent European involvement and secure American interests; the Virgin Islands in the Caribbean were purchased from Denmark; and in 1917 the US entered World War I. Thereafter, Americans played an increasing role in world politics and economics with a consequent effect on AmE usage. In turn, such US institutions as the movie industry in Hollywood, jazz and popular music from the South, participation in World War II, post-war technological devel-

opments such as the computer, and the activities and products of major US corporations and publications, from Coca-Cola to *Time* magazine, have helped disseminate Americanisms throughout the world.

**Variation**. Variation within AmE is far less than within many other national languages. Although Americans are conscious of the odd way their fellow citizens in other communities talk, considering the size and population of the US, its language is relatively homogeneous. Yet there are distinctive speechways in particular communities: the BOSTON Brahmins, the old families of New England who pride themselves on their culture and conservative attitudes and are noted for their haughtiness; the Gullah, who live on the islands off the shore of South Carolina and Georgia and talk with heavy West African influence; the Cajuns of Louisiana, descended from Acadian French immigrants, with folkways, cuisine, and speechways that blend influences from several traditions; the Appalachian mountain people; the TEX-MEX bronco-busters; the laid-back life-stylers of Marin County, California; the Charlestonian Old South aristocracy; the inner-city African Americans; the Minnesota Swedes; the Chicanos of the Southwest; and many others. Beneath the relative uniformity of its standard, edited variety, American English is a rich gallimaufry of exotic and native stuffs.

**Pronunciation**. Underlying the regional accents of the US are some widespread features that are typical of AmE: (1) With the exception of the Southern states, eastern NEW ENGLAND, and NEW YORK City, pronunciation is rhotic, postvocalic /r/ being pronounced in such words as *part, four, motor*. (2) The AmE /r/ is retroflex, and is often lost after an unstressed vowel if another /r/ follows: the r in *govern* is pronounced but is dropped in *governor*. (3) The vowels of words like *hoarse* and *horse* are increasingly merged in favour of a vowel of the quality in *haw* or *hoe*. (4) In words like *path, can't, dance*, AmE generally has the vowel of *pat* and *cant*. (5) The vowels of the stressed syllables in such words as *father* and *fodder* are generally identical. (6) The o-sound of *go, note, soap* begins with a rounded vowel, while the o-sound in *not* is unrounded. (7) Generally there is no /j/ glide before a stressed u-vowel in words like *tune, duke, new, sue, thews, lute* ('toon', 'dook', 'noo', etc.), in which a dental consonant precedes, but the glide is retained in un-stressed syllables (the second syllables of *menu, value*), when the vowel is initial (*ewe*), and when it is preceded by a labial or velar sound (*pew, cute*). (8) Among changes already under way and likely to become general is a merger of the vowel sounds in words like *caught, cot*. The resulting vowel is sometimes lightly rounded but more often unrounded, like the stressed vowel of *father*. (9) A /d/ typically occurs where the spelling has *t* or *tt* in words like *latter, atom, metal, bitty* which are homophonous with *ladder, Adam, medal, biddy*. (10) Similarly, /t/ is often lost from /nt/ in *winter* ('winner'), *anti* ('annie', though retained when the second vowel has full value and some stress, 'an-tie'), *international* ('innernational'). The *t* of words like *eaten* is usually glottalized and is followed by a syllabic *n*. (11) The *l* at the end of words and between vowels (*bill, pillow*) is typically dark: pronounced with the back of the tongue lifted toward the soft roof of the mouth. (12) Secondary stress is normal on the penultimate syllables of words like *laboratory* and *secretary*, so that these words end like *Tory* and *Terry*. At the same time, syncope is common in words like *fam'ly, fed'ral, happ'ning*.

**Grammar**. (1) For the verb *get*, the old past participle *gotten* occurs alongside the newer *got*. Americans use both, but differently. *Gotten* generally occurs when a process rather than a state or condition is intended: *I've gotten it* means 'acquired', whereas *I've got it* means 'possess'. Similarly, *I've gotten to go* means 'received permission or opportunity', whereas *I've got to go* means 'am obliged'. (2) *I will, you will, he will*, etc., are usual. *Shall* is rare in AmE, being largely restricted to formal invitation (*Shall we dance?*) and emphasis (*I shall return*). (3) A simple preterite rather than a perfect form is sometimes used for action leading up to the present time, even with adverbs: *Did you ever hear that?*; *I already did it*. (4) In formal mandative constructions, with clauses following verbs, adjectives, and nouns of requiring and urging, AmE prefers the present subjunctive form: *They insisted that he go with them*, *It is imperative that you be here on time*. (5) When the subject of a clause is a collective noun, there is generally a singular verb, in concord with the form rather than the sense of the subject: *The airline insists . . .* ; *The government is . . .* (6) The use of prepositions is often distinctive:

Americans live *on* a street (BrE *in*), cater *to* people (BrE *for*), do things *on* the weekend (BrE *at*), are *of* two minds about something (BrE *in*), have a new lease *on* life (BrE *of*), and when mentioning dates when things happen, may use or omit *on* (*Jack went home on Monday and came back Thursday*).

**Vocabulary**. A distinctive vocabulary developed from the Colonial Period until the present, including: (1) Old words put to new uses: *creek* for a small stream (compare AusE) rather than an estuary (as in BrE). This use probably arose because the term was first applied to the mouths of streams along coasts settled by the colonists then extended to the whole watercourse. (2) New words made up from old resources: *lengthy* from *length* and *-y* for the marked sense of *long* (of greater length than usual) as distinct from the unmarked sense (How long is it?), which does not imply great length; *Briticism* an expression peculiar to Britain; *complected* in combinations like *dark-complected* (having a dark complexion). (3) Borrowing from Amerindian languages: *chipmunk, hickory, moccasin, pecan, skunk, squash, totem, wigwam*. Sometimes such words came through French: *caribou, toboggan*. (4) Borrowing from other colonial languages: French *chowder, prairie*; Dutch *boss, coleslaw, cookie, Santa Claus, sleigh, snoop, waffle*, and probably *Yankee*; SPANISH *corral, lasso, ranch*. (5) Borrowing from later immigrant languages: African *goober, gumbo, juke, voodoo, zombie*; German (especially through Pennsylvania Dutch) *dumb* stupid, *noodle, sauerkraut, snorkel*, and the *-fest* and *-burger* endings in *bookfest, cheeseburger*, etc. Among food terms are Mexican Spanish *chili* (*con carne*), Chinese *chop suey*, Czech *kolach* a kind of sweet bun, Italian *pizza*, Swedish *smorgasbord*, Japanese *sukiyaki*, Nahuatl-Spanish *tamale*, German *wiener*. (6) Some typically AmE words with complex histories: *lagniappe*, a term for a small present given by merchants to their customers, extended to any little extra benefit. Associated with the South, it is from Louisiana French, borrowed from Spanish *la ñapa* the gift, from Quechua *yapa*.

A selection of words of American origin indicates the variety and significance of the AmE contribution to English at large: *airline, boondoggle, checklist, disco, expense account, flowchart, geewhiz, halfbreed, inner city, junk food, kangaroo court, laser, mass meeting, nifty, ouch, pants, quasar, radio, soap opera,*

## THE STORY OF OK

The best-known and most exported item in AmE, *OK* or *okay*, has a particularly complex history tracked down by Allen Walker Read to two fads of the 1830s in the city of Boston. In the first, the initials of the words in a phrase were used instead of the phrase itself: *OFM* for *our first men*; *ng* for *no go/no good*. In the second, comic misspellings of words were favoured; *oll wright* for all right. The two came together to produce initialisms like *OW* ('oll wright), *KY* ('know yuse': no use), and *OK* ('oll korrect': all correct). *OK* would probably have gone the way of *OFM* and *OW* into the graveyard of forgotten usage, except that it was taken up as a pun on the nickname of the politician Martin Van Buren: *Old Kinderhook* (after the town in New York state in which he was born). A political organization, the OK Club, was formed to support his political fortunes, and its use of the term in the election campaign of 1840 spread knowledge of the word. Van Buren lost the election, but his catchword endured. (Other etymologies for *OK* have been proposed, tracing it to French, Finnish, Norwegian, Greek, German, Scots, Cockney, Choctaw, and several African languages, as well as to a number of personal names. All are imaginative, but lack documentary support.)

---

*teddy bear, UFO, vigilante, wholehearted, xerox, yuppie, zipper*.

**Social issues**. Through the closing years of the 19c and throughout the 20c, the American concern over correct usage seems to have been more intense than the British. Questions of language engineering have generally been more vigorously considered in the US than in other English-speaking countries. Three issues in particular have powerful and volatile social repercussions: feminist concern for sexist language; the relationship between Black English and the standard language; and the relationship between English and other languages in the US, particularly Spanish:

**Sexism**. The question of sexism in language arouses violent partisanship. One of its simpler manifestations is the use of words with masculine implications (*man, he*) when both sexes are intended or appropriate. Occupational terms like *chairman, foreman, policeman, mail man,* and *airline stewardess,* with real or perceived sexual reference, are now being replaced by sexually neutral terms like *chair, supervisor, police officer, letter carrier,* and *flight attendant*. A brief fad for the use of *person* instead of *man* in such forms seems to have run its course, leaving some words, such as *chairperson,* in widespread use and others, such as *foreperson,* as curiosities. Another sore point is the requirement that a woman's social title (*Mrs* or *Miss*) specify her marital status, whereas a man's (*Mr*) does not; as a consequence, the female title *Ms* has become very widely used, partly because it is handy when the marital status of a woman is unknown even for those who are otherwise indifferent to the problem. A subtler form of SEXISM in language is the use of *girls* and *ladies* with reference to mature women; both are thought to be condescending, the first because it labels women as immature and the second because it isolates them socially. In this, as in other matters, however, much depends on one's age and social status. Among many middle-aged clubby women, *the girls* is the normal way of referring to one's intimates (just as *the boys* is among men), and *ladies* is the preferred general term, *women* sounding abrupt and rude. In general, consciousness of sexism in language is a younger-generation, urban, and politically liberal concern.

**Black English**. The terms used for Americans descended from African slaves continue to fluctuate as members of the group change the name by which they prefer to be known. At one time, *colored person* was the preferred term, enshrined in the National Association for the Advancement of Colored People (NAACP). It was replaced by *Negro* (with a first vowel like *league*, as opposed to the sound in the variant *nigra*), then by *Black,* and more recently *African American*

## AMERICAN PLACE-NAMES

The place-names of the United States reflect mixed linguistic origins over some 500 years, and fall into three broad types:

**1. *Adoptions from indigenous languages*** The state name *Alaska* is from Aleut 'mainland' (as viewed from the islands), *Hawaii* is a Polynesian name whose meaning is unknown, and *Manhattan* is Amerindian, probably meaning 'island mountain'.

**2. *Transfers and inventions by British settlers*** Transfers from the original homeland include *Birmingham* Alabama, from Birmingham in the English Midlands, and *New York* from old York (replacing the Dutch *Nieuw Amsterdam* 'New Amsterdam'). Inventions include *Pikes Peak* (named for the explorer Zebulon *Peak*) and *Cedar Rapids* (identifying a place by its fast-flowing water and trees). There are at least six categories of such names (with some overlap among them): (1) *Commemorative names*: either nostalgically transferring a name without adaptation (as in *Boston, Burlington, Montgomery, Swansea*) or incorporating *new* to suggest a kind of re-creation (as in *New England, New London, New Orleans, New York*). (2) *Classical names*, transferred for purposes of inspiration and aggrandizement, as in *Athens, Cicero, Olympia, Parnassus, Rome, Syracuse*. (3) *Pseudo-classical names*, intended to give a place dignity and grace, as in the Anglo-Latin *Georgia* (named for King George II) and *Indiana* (from the Indiana Company of land developers), suggesting the opening up and civilizing of untamed lands (applied to a territory that in due course became a state). (4) *Names commemorating people*: *Jamestown* (for James I) and *Washington* (both city and state: for George Washington). The classical-style *Atlanta*, Georgia may have been named after either the Western Atlantic Railroad, of which it was the terminus, or Martha Atalanta Lumpkin, daughter of a Georgia governor (an earlier local settlement being called *Marthasville*). (5) *Descriptive names*: *The Black Hills*, Dakota; *Long Island*, New York; *the Blue Ridge Mountains* of the Appalachians; *Long Island*, New York; *the Red River*, Texas; *the Rocky Mountains/the Rockies*. (6) *Associative names*: *Hog Island*, Michigan; *Paper Mill Creek*, California; *Newspaper Rock*, Arizona (so named because the Amerindian petroglyphs found there were wryly regarded as the journalism of their day).

**3. *Names from other European settler languages*** Mainly Spanish, French, and Dutch: (1) Spanish names include saints' names in the West and South-West,

*Continued opposite*

has been favoured. Considerable controversy has existed about AFRICAN-AMERICAN VERNACULAR ENGLISH or *AAVE*, the language associated with African Americans. There has been argument about whether such usage should be a medium of instruction as an alternative to standard English. Among the strongest opponents of such a development have been older members of the group. The origin and history of BLACK ENGLISH has also been a subject of controversy among scholars, and the very existence of such a discrete dialect has been questioned.

***English and Spanish***. There is a similar controversy about the official use of any non-English languages, but particularly of Spanish, as a medium of instruction in public schools, for voting in elections, and for other governmental and official functions. Pressure for such use of other languages comes from immigrant communities desirous of maintaining their identity within US society and has generated a counter-pressure to declare English the official language of the US. Several communities and states have passed laws or resolutions to that effect. The *English for US, English First*, or *Official English* movement has been called xenophobic, but can be seen as an

## AMERICAN PLACE-NAMES *continued*

such as *San Luis Obispo* ('Saint Louis the Bishop'), *San Francisco* ('Saint Francis'), and *Nuestra Señora de Los Angeles* ('Our Lady of the Angels'), now simply *Los Angeles* (and *L.A.*), and such descriptive names as *Boca Raton* 'rat's mouth' and *Rio Grande* 'great river'. (2) French names of settlements and landmarks include *St Louis* (a city) and *Grand Teton* ('great teat', a mountain). (3) Dutch names, concentrated in the North-East, include *Brooklyn*, an anglicization of *Breukelyn*, and the *Catskill* mountains (from *Kats kill* 'cat's stream'), both in New York State.

***The names of states***. Of the 50 states of the Union, 25 have Amerindian names (adopted directly or through various European languages), 9 are from French, Spanish, or another language, and 16 are English or Anglo-Latin. Names taken directly from Amerindian include *Connecticut* ('at the long river'), *Massachusetts* ('at the big hills'), *Kentucky* ('meadowland'), Michigan ('big lake'), *Missouri* ('people of the big canoes'), and *Oklahoma* ('red people'). Names from Amerindian through French include: *Arkansas* (a tribal name) and *Illinois* ('men', a tribal name). Names from Amerindian through Spanish include *Arizona* ('place of the small spring') and *Texas* ('friends/allies'). State names from English or Anglo-Latin or a hybrid of the two include *New Hampshire* and *New York* (after old Hampshire and old York in England), *Carolina* ('Charlesland', North and South, after Charles I), *Maryland* (associated with both the Virgin Mary and Henrietta Maria, Charles I's queen), *Pennsylvania* (named for the Quaker William Penn, adding *sylvania*, 'forest land' in Latin), and *Virginia* (named for Elizabeth I, the Virgin Queen).

***Misapplications***. The misunderstanding and displacement of names have often occurred, as for example in: (1) The Amerindian *Meche-weami-ing* ('at the big flats'), originally the name of a valley in Pennsylvania. A condensed Anglicized version of the name was popularized in 1809 in Thomas Campbell's poem 'Gertrude of Wyoming'. Because of its romantic associations, the name was given to a territory (which later became a state) far to the west of the region where the original words were used. (2) An early name for the Wisconsin River was *Wisconsink*, which a French map of 1715 misspelt as two words, printing them on separate lines as *Ouaricon sint*. Various forms of the first element, including *Ourigan* and *Ouragon*, were used for a legendary river flowing into the Pacific. When the Columbia River was found and named, it was linked with this legend, as a result of which the surrounding territory (and later state) was called *Oregon*.

extension of the 'Federal English' campaign of the early Republic, whose aim was the establishment of a uniform national language.

**Conclusion**. Regardless of the constitutional or other status of English in the US, the future of AmE is hardly in doubt. The international use of English seems assured for the foreseeable future. The extent to which international English reflects the standards of BrE or AmE, or a mid-Atlantic compromise, is open to speculation, but the question is of no great practical consequence: all national standards of English are close to one another. The growth of 'New Englishes' in the nations that have emerged since World War II may diversify the total range of the language, but international use is closely tied to the relatively uniform American–British complex.

See AMERICANISM, AMERICAN LANGUAGE, AMERICAN LANGUAGE (THE), AMERINDIAN PIDGIN ENGLISH, BROOKLYNESE, CANADIAN ENGLISH, CHICANO ENGLISH, DIALECT IN AMERICA, ENGLISH LANGUAGE AMENDMENT, GENERAL AMERICAN, GULLAH, JEWISH ENGLISH, MENCKEN, NASAL, NETWORK STANDARD, NEW ORLEANS, NEW YORK, SOUTHERN ENGLISH, TEXAS.

# ■ AMERICAN ENGLISH AND BRITISH ENGLISH ──────── ■

Because BRITISH ENGLISH and AMERICAN ENGLISH are the foremost varieties of the ENGLISH language and serve as reference norms for other varieties, they have often been compared and contrasted. Such comparison and contrast are complex matters, made even more complex by the ambiguity and vagueness of the terms themselves. They are ambiguous in that each has more than one meaning; they are vague in that the boundaries between them are often fuzzy. For example, to say that the spelling *colour* is BrE means that it is used widely in the UK, is not used, or not widely used, or no longer used, in the US, may or may not be used in Canada, and may also be widely used in other parts of the English-speaking world. To say that the spelling *color* is AmE means that it is used widely in the US, is not used, or not widely used, or no longer used, in Britain, is probably used widely in Canada, and may or may not be used in other parts of the English-speaking world.

**General ambiguity and vagueness**. The terms *British English* and *American English* are used in different ways by different people for different purposes. They may refer to: (1) Two national varieties, each subsuming regional and other subvarieties, STANDARD and NON-STANDARD. They do not extend beyond the frontiers of their states, but within those frontiers everything is included. (2) Two national standard varieties, each excluding the national non-standard varieties, but to some extent merging with at least some of these. Each is only part of the range of English within its own state, but the most prestigious part. (3) Two international varieties, focused on particular nations, but each subsuming other varieties in a more or less ill-defined way. Each is more than a national variety of English. (4) Two international standard varieties that may or may not each subsume other standard varieties. Each serves in a more or less ill-defined way as a reference norm for users of the language elsewhere. Furthermore, whether BrE and AmE are understood as national or international varieties, there is so much communication between them that items of language pass easily and quickly from one to the other, often without clear identification as primarily belonging to one or the other, or to some other variety.

**Lexicographical ambiguity and vagueness**. The ambiguity of the terms is reflected in dictionaries. When a dictionary labels something *BrE*, users can safely assume that it has more currency in Britain than in the US, but cannot be sure whether it is restricted to Britain or is used elsewhere, as for example in Australia or New Zealand. Often enough, the lexicographer using the label does not know either. The vagueness due to the easy passage between the two varieties is also reflected in dictionaries, by the tendency to qualify the labels with some such word as *chiefly* or *especially*, a tendency that appears to be increasing as communication between AmE and BrE increases: the 1st edition of the *American Heritage Dictionary* (1969) used both *British* and *Chiefly British* as labels, but the 2nd (1982) uses *Chiefly British* only. The use of qualifiers with BrE and AmE is in sharp contrast to their non-use with labels of certain other types: an item may be labelled *Slang* or *Archaic*, but not *\*Chiefly slang* or *\*esp archaic*. An item labelled *Chiefly BrE* or *esp BrE* is not more likely to be used in, say, Australia: it is more likely to be used in the US. Similarly, an item labelled *Chiefly AmE* or *esp AmE* is not more likely to be used in, say, Canada: it is more likely to be used in Britain. In this respect, qualifiers like *Chiefly* and *esp* loosen the national restrictions on BrE and AmE, but do not affect their international range, which is already rather ill defined.

**National standards**. In the following discussion, the emphasis is first on AmE and BrE as two national standard varieties and then on their differences rather than their similarities. Paradoxically, the desire for a discussion of British/American differences reflects an underlying confidence that the similarities between them are greater: even if Americans and Britons are said to be 'divided by a common language', the language remains essentially common, especially in terms of standard usage. The two standard varieties are contrasted below in terms of spelling, pronunciation, grammar, vocabulary, and idioms.

**Spelling**. Most spelling differences between BrE and AmE do not signal differences in pronunciation. Rather, they serve as emblems or shibboleths of linguistic nationalism. It is primarily spelling that indicates whether a text is British or American in origin. By and large, the adoption of certain spellings in AmE has impeded their use in BrE or hastened their decline if they were used in that variety: such AmE *-or* spellings as *color* were once freely available alternatives to *-our* in BrE. However, when spelling is 'normalized' to one or other print standard, it may no longer be possible to identify the source of a text. It was once common to change the spelling of American books published in Britain, but in recent years the practice has been less common. This may mean that British linguistic nationalism is waning, or simply that the practice costs less, but since it also makes American texts easier to identify in British editions, it may slow down the adoption of expressions and constructions identified as AmE in those texts. There are two ways in which the orthographic differences can be classified: systemic or non-systemic; exclusive or non-exclusive.

**1. Systemic or non-systemic differences.** If a difference is systemic, it affects large classes of words; if non-systemic, it affects only one word or a small group of words. By and large, the difference between BrE *colour*, AmE *color* is systemic, affecting such words as *hono(u)r*, *favo(u)r*, *neighbo(u)r*, *vigo(u)r* (but note *languor*, *stupor*, *torpor*, etc., in both varieties). The BrE variant *gaol* (by contrast with the common *jail*) is non-systemic, affecting only one word and its inflections (*gaols*), derivatives (*gaoler*), and compounds (*gaolbird*). Occasionally, variants exist in both varieties: the optional *e* in *abridg(e)ment*, *acknowledg(e)ment*, *judg(e)ment* can be found in both AmE and BrE.

**2. Exclusive or non-exclusive differences.** When writing *colo(u)r*, either a BrE or an AmE spelling must be chosen; there is no international alternative. In the case of *gaol/jail*, however, there is a choice between local *gaol* and international *jail*. In the case of *ax(e)*, an international variant *axe* coexists with an *ax* that is now AmE, though it was once used in BrE: in 1884, the *Oxford English Dictionary* favoured this spelling, but in 1989 the 2nd edition has changed to *axe*. There seem to be no cases of an international spelling variant coexisting with a marked BrE variant on one side and a marked AmE variant on the other.

All permutations and combinations of the two categories are possible: *colour/color*, sys-

temic exclusive variants; the suffixes *-ise/-ize*, systemic non-exclusive variants in BrE; *gaol/jail*, *axe/ax*, non-systemic, non-exclusive variants in BrE and AmE respectively; in banking, *cheque/check*, non-systemic exclusive variants. Among the principal systemic variants are:

**1. The colo(u)r group.** Most words of the type *color/colour* are from Latin or French: *arbo(u)r*, *armo(u)r*, *endeavo(u)r*, *favo(u)r*, *flavo(u)r*, *hono(u)r*, *humo(u)r*, *labo(u)r*, *odo(u)r*, *rigo(u)r*, *savo(u)r*, *tumo(u)r*, *valo(u)r*, *vigo(u)r*. In Latin, their forms are uniformly *-or* (*arbor*, *odor*) and in Modern French their cognates may have *-eur* (*couleur*, *honneur*). Some, however, are Germanic in origin (*harbo(u)r*, *neighbo(u)r*) and seem to have picked up their *u* by analogy. The BrE *u* is not used in words, other than *neighbo(u)r*, that readily refer to people: *actor*, *author*, *emperor*, *governor*, *survivor*, *tenor* are the same in both varieties, though especially during the 16–17c such spellings as *emperour*, *governour* occurred. In such cases, the *-or* is generally interpreted as an agent suffix like the vernacular *-er*: *author* is as invariable in its spelling as *writer*. There are, however, a number of anomalies: such words as *error*, *mirror*, *pallor*, *terror*, *tremor* have no *u* in BrE, and in AmE the spellings *glamor*, *savior*, *savor* are nonexclusive variants, coexisting with the international *glamour*, *saviour*, *savour*. *Saviour* appears to be the last surviving *-our* agent suffix referring to a person. In AmE, the *colo(u)r* group has *-or-* in its inflections (*coloring*), derivatives (*colorful*, *coloration*), and compounds (*color-blind*). BrE derivatives are more complex. Before vernacular suffixes, the *u* is retained: *armourer*, *colourful*, *flavoursome*, *savoury*. It is also kept before the French suffix *-able*: *honourable*. Before Latinate suffixes, however, it is dropped: *honorary*, *honorific*, *humorous*, *humorist*, *coloration*, *deodorize*, *invigorate*. In such cases, AmE and BrE spellings are the same. Even so, there are some residual anomalies: BrE keeps the *u* in *colourist* and AmE can have the *u* in *savoury* and appears to be more likely than BrE to have a *u* in *glamo(u)rize* and *glamo(u)rous*.

**2. The centre/center group.** In words of this type, BrE has *-re* and AmE *-er*, and the difference is exclusive. The chief members are of non-Germanic origin and are: *centre/center*, *fibre/fiber*, *goitre/goiter*, *litre/liter*, *meagre/meager*, *mitre/miter*, *sabre/saber*, *sombre/somber*, *spectre/specter*, *theatre/theater*.

The agent suffix *-er* (as in *writer*) and comparative ending *-er* (as in *colder*) are unaffected. Many words in both varieties have *-er* (*banter, canter*) and *-re* (*acre, lucre, massacre, mediocre, ogre*). In the case of the second group, an *-er* spelling would suggest a misleading pronunciation (therefore no *\*acer, \*lucer*, etc.). BrE distinguishes *metre* (unit of measurement) from *meter* (instrument for measuring; prosody), but AmE uses *meter* for both. Though *theater* is the preferred AmE spelling, *theatre* is common as a part of a name. Generally, the differences are preserved in inflections (*centred/centered*) and compounds (*centrefold/centerfold*), but usually vanish in derivatives through the loss of the *e*, which is no longer pronounced (*central, fibrous, metric/metrical, theatrical*).

**3. The (o)estrogen group.** In words of Greek origin (in which an original *oi* became a Latin ligature *æ*), BrE has *oe* in exclusive variants, AmE *e* or less commonly *oe*, typically in non-exclusive variants: *am(o)eba, diarrh(o)ea, hom(o)eopathy, (o)esophagus, (o)estrogen, (o)estrous*. The differences are maintained in all inflections, derivatives, and compounds. Two words of Latin origin have been assimilated into this class, *f(o)etus* and *f(o)etid*. In both varieties, all trace of the earlier *oeconomy, oeconomical, oecumenical* has gone (in *economy, economic/economical, ecumenical*, etc.). Within a word, (*o*)*e* is pronounced /iː/ in both varieties; at the beginning it is pronounced /iː/ in BrE and may be so pronounced in AmE, though *e* tends to be pronounced /ɛ/. The pronunciation of BrE *oestrogen* is therefore 'ees-', of AmE *estrogen* is generally 'ess-'.

**4. The (a)esthete group.** In words of classical (ultimately Greek) origin in which a Neo-Latin *æ* passed into English as *æ* then *ae*, BrE has tended to keep *ae* as an exclusive variant and AmE has had *e* and *ae* as non-exclusive variants: (*a*)*eon, arch(a)eology, gyn(a)ecology, (a)esthetics, an(a)emia, encyclop(a)edia, h(a)emophilia, h(a)emorrhage, medi(a)eval, pal(a)eontology*. The spelling differences are maintained in inflections, derivatives, and compounds. In the case of (*a*)*esthete* and its derivatives, the spelling can signal a difference in pronunciation: beginning in BrE with /iː/, /i/, or /ɛ/ and in AmE with /ɛ/. Elsewhere in this class, however, (*a*)*e* is pronounced /iː/ in both varieties. One classical form keeps *ae* in both varieties: *aer-* as in *aerate, aerobics, aerodynamics, aerosol*. In both varieties, *encyclopedia* and *medieval* are commoner than *encyclopaedia* and *mediaeval*, but where BrE pronunciation typically begins 'meddy', AmE pronunciation often begins 'meedy'. There is now a tendency for *e* and *ae* to become non-exclusive variants in BrE in such words as *co-eval, primeval* and *archeology, gynecology*.

**5. The instil(l) group.** In such words, BrE has a single written vowel plus *-l* and AmE has a single written vowel plus *-ll*, the exclusive variants are all disyllabic verbs stressed on the second syllable: *distil(l), enrol(l), fulfil(l), instil(l)*. Exceptionally, *extol* prevails in AmE over *extoll*. Verbs like this but with *a* in the second syllable belong to this class in AmE: *appall, enthrall, install*. In BrE, however, the preferences vary: *appal, befall, enthral, install*. The verb *annul* has *-l* in both varieties.

**6. The final -l(l) group.** In BrE, verbs that end in a single written vowel plus *-l* or *-ll* keep them before *-s* (*travels, fulfills*), have *-l* before *-ment* (*instalment, fulfilment*), and have *-ll* before a suffix beginning with a vowel (*travelling, fulfilling*). In AmE, verbs that end with a single written vowel plus *-l* or *-ll* keep them before *-s* and *-ment* (*fulfillment, installment*); before a suffix beginning with a vowel, the verbs ending with *-ll* keep both letters (*fulfilling*), but the verbs ending with *-l* either have *-ll* as in BrE (*compelling, cavilling*) or more usually follow the general rules for doubling final consonants (*compelling, caviling*). Sometimes the result is the same for both varieties: *compel, compels, compelled*. Sometimes it is different: *travel, travels, travelled, traveller* shared by both, but AmE generally *travels, traveled, traveler*. *Parallel* does not usually double its final *-l* in either variety.

**7. The -ize and -ise group.** Some verbs can only have *-ize*: *capsize, seize*. In some, only *-ise* is possible: *advise, surprise*. In many, both *-ise* and *-ize* are possible, as in *civilise/civilize, organise/organize*, and the *-s-* or *-z-* is preserved in derivatives: *civilisation/civilization*. For such verbs, AmE has systemic, exclusive *-ize*, and BrE has both *-ise* and *-ize*. In AusE, *-ise* is preferred. British publishers generally have their own house styles: among dictionary publishers, *-ize* is preferred by Cassell, Collins, Longman, Oxford, *-ise* by the Reader's Digest (UK). Chambers has *-ise* for its native-speaker dictionaries, *-ize* for its EFL learners' dictionary, intended for an international public. There is no infallible rule identifying the verbs that take both, but they generally form nouns in *-tion*. With the exception of *improvise/improvisation*, verbs that take only *-ise* do not generally have a noun in *-tion*: *revise/revision*, *advise/advice*. However, some verbs that allow both forms do not form nouns in *-tion*: *apologise/ize*, *apology*; *aggrandise/ize*, *aggrandisement*, *aggrandizement*.

**8. The -lyse and -lyze group.** In such verbs as *analyse/analyze* and *paralyse/paralyze*, BrE prefers *-lyse* and AmE *-lyze*. The variants are systemic and have been mutually exclusive, but recently *analyze* has begun to appear in BrE. The difference disappears in corresponding nouns: *analysis*, *paralysis* are international, as the /z/ of the verbs becomes /s/ in the nouns.

**9. The -og(ue) group.** Although in words like *catalog(ue)*, *dialog(ue)*, *monolog(ue)*, *pedagog(ue)*, *prolog(ue)*, AmE sometimes drops *-ue*, only *catalog* is a widely used AmE variant. Thus, such spellings are systemic, non-exclusive variants in AmE. *Analog(ue)* is a special case: the spelling *analog* prevails in contrast with *digital* when referring to such things as computers, but that is true not only in AmE but also in BrE, where AmE spellings are generally used in the register of computing.

***Conclusion.*** **1.** Where differences exist, AmE spellings tend to be shorter than BrE spellings: *catalog*, *color*; AmE *jewelry*, *jeweler*, BrE *jewellery*, *jeweller*; AmE *councilor*, *counselor*, BrE *councillor*, *counsellor*. Exceptions include: AmE *instill* and *installment*, BrE *instil* and *instalment*; AmE *skillful* and *thralldom*, BrE *skilful* and *thraldom*. **2.** In general terms, a spelling used in Britain is more likely to be acceptable in America than is an American spelling in Britain. BrE seems sometimes to use spelling to distinguish items with the same pronunciation: *tyre* and *tire*, *cheque* and *check*, the *kerb* in a street and *curb* restrain/restraint. AmE seems to do this rarely: moral *vice* and *vise* the tool.

**Pronunciation.** Because BrE and AmE spelling can be seen in printed and edited texts, comparing and contrasting them is more or less straightforward, but because of the diversity of speech forms within AmE and BrE, there is no analogous basis for comparing BrE and AmE pronunciation. What follows is a comparison of two major features in the pronunciations shown in British dictionaries, typically based on the

accent called *RECEIVED PRONUNCIATION* or *RP*, with those in American dictionaries, typically clustering round a set of pronunciations often called *GENERAL AMERICAN* or *GA*.

**1. The treatment of R.** GA is RHOTIC and RP non-rhotic: that is, in GA, /r/ is pronounced in all positions in words like *rare*, *rarer*, but in RP it is not pronounced unless a vowel follows. In RP, therefore, /r/ does not occur finally in *rare* and *rarer* unless followed by a word beginning with a vowel: *a rare article*, *a rarer article*. Generally, /r/ is a retroflex consonant in GA and an alveolar consonant in RP: see R-SOUNDS.

**2. The treatment of A.** In about 150 words where the sound represented by the letter *a* precedes a fricative (such as /s, f, θ/) or a nasal (such as /n, m/) followed by another consonant, GA has /a/ and RP /ɑ/, as in: *after*, *can't*, *dance*, *fast*, *half*, *pass*, *past*. Other cases of /a/ versus /ɑ/ include *aunt*, *example*, *laugh*, *draught*, *sample*, and the second *a* of *banana*. The RP pronunciation is widely known as the 'broad *a*', and is considered 'posh' in Britain and 'tony' or affected in America. It is in fact a phonological bone of contention throughout the English-speaking world. In RP, in the pronunciation of the broad *a*, there are many traps for the unwary: *grant*, *slant* have the broad *a*, but *cant*, *grand*, *hand*, *pant* do not. Words such as *translate* and *telegraph* may or may not have it, and *telegraphic* does not.

**Grammar.** A discussion of grammatical differences is closer to a discussion of spelling than of pronunciation, because it can be based on textual evidence. The following are significant contrasts:

**1. Shall/will.** Though *shall* is even less common in AmE than in BrE, the only significant differences concern two of the least common BrE uses: second-person questions and the contraction *shan't*, as in *Shall you be at the embassy reception?—No, I'm afraid I shan't*. Both are virtually unknown in AmE. As for *will*, two of its BrE uses are much less likely in AmE: inference *will*, roughly equivalent to *must* (*That will be the postman at the door*); stressed *will* indicating a disagreeable habit or practice (*He WILL keep telling us about his operation!*).

**2. Should/would.** In polite first-person statements (*We should be happy to comply with your request*), *should* is rarer in AmE than in BrE, particularly in advice-giving formulas

(*I should dress warmly if I were you*). *Should* is also rarer in AmE in its putative use: *I demand that they should leave*; *It is astonishing that they should have left without telling me*. *Would* is primarily BrE in uses that parallel *will* above: *That would have been the postman at the door*; *He WOULD keep telling us about his operation!* However, it seems to be primarily AmE as an initial equivalent of *used to*: *When I was young, I would get up early*, though as a subsequent substitute for *used to* it is shared: *I used to get up early and before breakfast I would go jogging*.

**3. Can/may**. Both varieties use *can* freely for permission as well as ability, a usage formerly discouraged on both sides of the Atlantic: *You can see him now* (You are permitted to see him). In a negative inferential sentence like *If you got wet you can't have taken your umbrella*, *can't* is more likely in BrE than AmE, which allows *mustn't* (see following).

**4. Must/have (got) to**. An affirmative inferential sentence like *This has to be/This has got to be the best novel this year* is more likely to be AmE than BrE, though it is becoming an alternative in BrE to the shared *This must be the best novel this year*. A negative inferential sentence like *If you got wet you mustn't have taken your umbrella* is AmE rather than standard BrE, which uses *can't* (see preceding).

**5. Have (got)**. There have been differences between BrE and AmE in the use of *have*, but in the last decade they have become largely of historical interest only. The major surviving difference is the past form *had got*: *She left because she'd got a lot to do/she'd got to do a lot* is a largely BrE alternative to the shared *She left because she had a lot to do/she had to do a lot*.

**6. Let's**. The negative form *let's not (argue)* is shared, coexisting with the chiefly BrE variant *don't let's (argue)* and the AmE variant *let's don't (argue)*, often reproved as nonstandard.

**7. Subjunctive forms**. After words like *demand*, several constructions are possible: *I demanded that he should (not) leave* (more BrE than AmE), *I demanded that he (not) leave* (somewhat more AmE than BrE, especially with *not*), *I demanded that he left/didn't leave* (far more BrE than AmE).

**8. Perfective forms**. With *yet* and *already*, such perfective sentences as *Have you eaten yet?* and *They've already left* are shared usages. Such alternatives as *Did you eat yet?* and *They left already* are virtually exclusive to AmE, but may be regarded as non-standard.

**9. Tag forms**. Such sentences as *They're here, aren't they?* combine positive and negative verb forms and are shared. Such sentences as *So they're/They're here, are they?* combine positive with positive and are somewhat more BrE than AmE. Such sentences as *So they/They didn't do it, didn't they?* combine negative with negative, are virtually exclusive to BrE, and are not used freely even by all BrE speakers. Tags used otherwise than to elicit or confirm information tend to be more BrE than AmE, in particular peremptory and aggressive tags such as *You'll just have to wait and see, won't you?* and *I don't know the answer, do I?*

**10. Give**. The form *Give me it* is shared, while *Give it me* is BrE.

**11. Provide**. The form *That provided us with an excuse* is shared, while *That provided us an excuse* is AmE.

**12. Enough**. The form *They're rich enough to retire* is shared, while *They're rich enough that they can retire* is chiefly AmE.

**13. Agree, approximate, protest**. The forms *They agreed to the plan* and *They agreed on the plan* are shared, while *They agreed the plan* is BrE. *That approximates to the truth* is chiefly AmE, while *That approximates the truth* is AmE. *They protested their innocence* and *They protested against/at the verdict* are shared; *They protested the verdict* is AmE.

**14. Time expressions**. The form *Monday to Friday inclusive* is shared, while the synonymous *Monday through Friday* is AmE. *Monday through to Friday* is BrE, and may be ambiguous as to whether Friday itself is included. The forms *a week from today* and *a week from Friday* are shared, while *a week today*, *a week on Friday*, *Friday week* are BrE. The form *half past six* is shared, and coexists with the informal BrE *half six*. The use of *past* in time expressions (*10 past 6*, (*a*) *quarter past 6*) is shared; the corresponding use of *after* (*10 after 6*, (*a*) *quarter after 6*) is chiefly AmE. The form *ten* (*minutes*) *to six* is shared, while *ten* (*minutes*) *of six* is AmE.

**15. Go, come**. The forms *Go and see/Come and see what you have done* are shared, while *Go see/Come see what you have done* are AmE.

**16. One**. The form *If one does one's best, one will succeed* is shared and tends to be formal in both varieties, while *If one does his best, he will succeed* is AmE (and under attack by feminists and others as sexist usage).

**17. *Group nouns*.** Such a collective usage as *The government is divided* is shared, while *The government are divided*, emphasizing the members of the group, is chiefly BrE.

**18. *Collocations*.** There are many differences of idiom. The collocations *go to church/school/college* and *be at church/school/college* are shared, but *go to university/be at university* and *go to hospital/be in hospital* are BrE, AmE requiring the *the* as in *go to the university*. Forms like *in a jubilant mood* are shared, but *in jubilant mood* is BrE. The expressions *on offer* and *in future* are BrE, the former the equivalent of the shared *being offered*, the latter of the shared *from now on/from then on*. The form *in the future* is shared. The form *do a deal* is BrE and *make a deal* is AmE. *Take a decision* is chiefly BrE, though *make a decision* is shared. *Seems/Looks like a good deal* is shared, but *Seems/Looks a good deal* is chiefly BrE. *Members of* is shared; *membership of* is BrE; *membership in* is AmE.

**Vocabulary and idioms**. As with differences in spelling, lexical differences can be divided into the exclusive (such as BrE *windscreen*, AmE *windshield*), and the non-exclusive. The non-exclusive differences subdivide into those in which the shared variant coexists with an exclusive usage (such as shared *editorial*, BrE *leader*; shared *autumn*, AmE *fall*), and those in which a shared variant coexists with both a BrE variant and an AmE variant (shared *socket*, BrE *power point*, AmE *outlet*). Systemic differences in vocabulary are due to two factors: source and subject. AmE and BrE draw on different sources for certain words, especially in informal styles, AmE drawing for example on Spanish because of its associations with Latin America, BrE drawing for example on Hindustani because of its long connection with India (see COCKNEY). They have also developed differences in some subjects more than others. In areas of technology that developed before the European settlement of America, such as sailing, differences are small; in those developed in the 19c, such as rail and automotive transport, they are much greater, but in 20c technology, such as aviation, they are few. In the vocabulary of computing, AmE spellings are used in BrE, such as *program*, *disk*, while BrE *programming* is used in AmE. See AMERICANISM, BRITICISM.

AmE and BrE sometimes have slightly different idioms, such as: BrE *a home from home*, *leave well alone*, *a storm in a teacup*, *blow one's own trumpet*, *sweep under the carpet*, AmE *a home away from home*, *leave well enough alone*, *a tempest in a teacup/teapot*, *blow one's own horn*, *sweep under the rug*. The use of prepositions is often different: for example, Americans live *on* a street while Britons live *in* a street; they cater *to* people where Britons cater *for* them; they do something *on* the weekend where Britons do it *at* the weekend; are *of* two minds about something while Britons are *in* two minds; have a new lease *on* life where Britons have a new lease *of* life. American students are *in* a course and British students *on* a course. Americans can leave Monday while Britons must leave *on* Monday. See letter entries E, L, O, R, Z.

**AMERICANISM**. A usage or custom peculiar to, or common in, the US. The term refers primarily to English words and phrases that acquired a new sense (*bluff*, *corn*, *lumber*) or entered the language (*OK*, *raccoon*, *squash*) in what is now the US, but also to features of pronunciation, grammar, and sentence structure. The term has often been used contrastively, especially in the US, with BRITICISM. 'Bilingual' lists, drawn up for both academic and popular purposes, commonly contrast items in pairs, one being identified as the American usage, the other as the British equivalent (or vice versa). The following list contains a number of pairs of words and phrases (Briticisms first, Americanisms second) widely regarded as distinguishing AmE from BrE: *accommodation* (uncountable), *accommodations* (countable plural), with regard to rooms in hotels, etc.; *aluminium*, *aluminum*; *anticlockwise*, *counter-clockwise*; *biscuit*, *cookie*; *bonnet*, *hood* (of a car); *boot*, *trunk* (of a car); *candy floss*, *cotton candy*; *caravan*, *trailer* (pulled by a car); *cornflour*, *cornstarch*; *cot*, *crib*; *drawing pin*, *thumbtack*; *fanlight*, *transom*; *founder member*, *charter member*; *goods train*, *freight train*; *high street*, *main street* (of a town); *hoarding*, *billboard*; *jumble sale*, *rummage sale*; *lift*, *elevator*; the abbreviations *maths* and *math*; *nappy*, *diaper*; *noticeboard*, *bulletin board*; *noughts and crosses*, *tick-tack-toe*; *number plate*, *licence plate* (for a road vehicle); *pavement*, *sidewalk*; *petrol*, *gas(oline)*; *post code*, *zip code*; *return ticket*, *round trip ticket*; *right-angled triangle*, *right triangle*; a *rise*, *raise* (in salary); *rowing boat*, *rowboat*; *sailing boat*, *sailboat*; *silencer*, *muffler* (on a car); *single ticket*, *one way ticket*; *skirting board*, *baseboard*; *sledge*, *sled*; *sweets*, (*hard*) *candy*; *torch*, *flashlight* (powered by batteries); *windscreen*, *windshield* (on a vehicle); *zip*, *zipper*. See AMERICAN ENGLISH AND BRITISH ENGLISH.

**AMERICAN LANGUAGE**. A term that presents AMERICAN ENGLISH as a national language, sometimes as an aggressive assertion of independence from the standard language of England: 'This occasional tolerance for things American was never extended to the American language' (H. L. MENCKEN, *The American Language*, 4th edition, 1936); 'George Bush is hardly known for his rhetorical gifts. But his speech at last summer's Republican Convention has already left its mark on the American language' (Laurence Zuckerman, 'Read My Cliché', *Time*, 16 Jan. 1989). Compare AMERICAN.

***AMERICAN LANGUAGE, The***, short form *AL*. An encyclopedic study of English in the US by Henry Louis MENCKEN (New York: Alfred A. Knopf, 1919), which demonstrates the distinctness of AmE, chronicles the contributions of each of the nation's major ethnic groups to the language, and stresses American linguistic creativity and independence. Revised and enlarged editions of the *AL* appeared in 1921, 1923, and 1936, and two large supplements to the 4th edition in 1945 and 1948. The later editions used anecdotal contributions from readers as well as contemporary AmE scholarship. Mencken ignored 20c developments in linguistics. A 1963 abridgement and conflation of the 4th edition and its supplements (which remain in print as a three-volume set) was edited with additions by Raven I. McDavid Jr.

**AMERICAN STYLE GUIDES**. See HOUSE STYLE.

**AMERINDIAN PIDGIN ENGLISH**. A general term for PIDGIN languages based on the indigenous languages of the Americas, such as *Chinook Jargon*, *Delaware Jargon*, *Mobilian Jargon*, *Trader Navajo/Navaho*. Amerindian varieties of English descend from a makeshift language used between Indians and white settlers, especially in the US. Each variety retains features of its ancestral languages, but a shared feature is the transitivizing suffix *-um* after verbs (*Squaw makum bed*), also found in Melanesian Pidgin English and Kriol in Australia. Loanwords (*chipmunk*, *moose*, *squash*) and loan translations (*firewater*, *peacepipe*, *warpath*) have come into conventional English from this pidgin.

**AMPERSAND**. A printer's term for the characters & and æ, originally forms of Latin *et* (and), as in *Gilbert & Sullivan*. Both & and £ (short for *libra* pound) survive from the system of ABBREVIATION used by medieval scribes. Once a common replacement for *and*, it is now largely a flourish on business cards and letter-heads. It also occurs in *&c*, a variant of *etc*. It is short for *and per se and*: 'and by itself (means) and'.

**ANACHRONISM**. [Stress: 'a-NA-kronizm'.] In RHETORIC, the appearance of a person or thing in the wrong epoch, such as the clock in Shakespeare's *Julius Caesar*. Linguistic anachronisms are generally a matter of awareness, context, and expectation: for example, the archaism *wight* (person, man) may be appropriate at a seminar on the Elizabethan poet Spenser, but is incongruous and probably unintelligible elsewhere. Similarly, a character in a period novel who says *OK* long before the phrase was current rings false for anyone who knows (or senses) that its time is out of joint. Compare ARCHAISM.

**ANACOLUTHON**. [Stress: 'a-na-ko-L(Y)OO-thon']. Also **anacoluthia**. In RHETORIC, a break or change of direction in a speech: 'I will have such revenges on you both, / That all the world shall—I will do such things, / What they are, yet I know not' (Shakespeare, *King Lear*, 2.4). In texts, the break is often signalled by a DASH: 'I was listening to the news—this man, he's a company director in London—the police arrested him.' See APOSIOPESIS.

**ANADIPLOSIS**. [Stress: 'a-na-di-PLO-sis']. In RHETORIC, a word repeated for effect: 'Victory at all costs, victory in spite of all terror, victory however long and hard the road may be' (Winston Churchill, House of Commons, 4 June 1940). Compare ANAPHORA, REDUNDANCY, REPETITION.

**ANAGRAM**. A word or phrase made by rearranging the letters of another word or phrase: *mad policy* from *diplomacy*. Anagrams are used mainly in games and puzzles, especially cross-words, where a clue like 'a confused tailor in Venice' leads to *Rialto*, an anagram of *tailor*.

**ANALOGY**. A comparison or correspondence between two things because of a third element that they are considered to share. An analogy is usually framed in order to describe or explain the nature of something: for example, *time* in 'Let me give you an analogy. Time is like a river. Just as the river flows from higher to lower ground, so time flows from the past into the future.' Once the time/river analogy has been drawn, people can talk about *the flow of time* and *the currents of history*. When such usages are established, their users may forget the analogy and come to think of them as statements of fact: what else can time do but flow? Because analogies depend on the concept *as if*, they often take the form of METAPHORS and SIMILES.

**Grammar**. In traditional language teaching, such PARADIGMS as the conjugations of Latin and French display inflections in a fixed order, using a REGULAR form of the verb for each class of inflections. In French, *j'aime* (I love) is to *tu aimes* (thou lovest) as *j'adore* (I adore) is to *tu adores* (thou adorest). Students learn to apply the basic example to all words of the same type and in this way can form *nous adorons* (we adore) from *nous aimons* (we love). In learning a language, children and students constantly make such analogies, both on their own and under guidance. Sometimes, however, they engage in *false analogy*. Here, the child or student uses such known relationships as *cat*:*cats* and *dog*:*dogs* to produce *sheep*: *\*sheeps*. The analogy has been correctly applied but is false because languages are not completely logical or analogical.

**Word-formation**. In LEXICOLOGY, many words are described as created by analogy with other words: that is, new forms are modelled on older forms, as when *cavalcade* (a procession of horses and riders) prompted the formation of *camelcade* (a procession of camels) and *motorcade* (a procession of cars). In addition to the semantics of processions, important factors here appear to be a pattern of three syllables in which sole or primary stress falls on the first. The phonologically suitable *\*beavercade* is semantically unlikely, however, while the semantically suitable *\*elephantcade* is

phonologically unlikely. Through such analogizing, the suffix *-cade* (meaning 'procession of') is added to the language, its use subject to certain constraints. This kind of analogy is fundamental to the formation of compound and derived words.

**Rhetoric**. Analogies are commonly employed for rhetorical, stylistic, or dramatic effect, often in the service of a social or political position:

> Planet Earth is 4,600 million years old. If we condense this inconceivable time-span into an understandable concept, we can liken Earth to a person of 46 years of age. Nothing is known about the first 7 years of this person's life, and whilst only scattered information exists about the middle span, we know that only at the age 42 did the Earth begin to flower. Dinosaurs and great reptiles did not appear until one year ago, when the planet was 45. Mammals arrived only 8 months ago; in the middle of last week man-like apes evolved into ape-like men, and at the weekend the last ice age enveloped the Earth. Modern man has been around for four hours. During the last hour, Man discovered agriculture. The industrial revolution began a minute ago. During those sixty seconds of biological time, Modern Man has made a rubbish tip of Paradise (from a Greenpeace recruiting and fund-raising pamphlet, 1989).

See ALLUSION, FIGURATIVE LANGUAGE, USAGE, WORD-FORMATION.

**ANALYTIC**, also **isolating**. A term in linguistics for a language in which each basic grammatical unit (MORPHEME) tends to form a separate word, as in Vietnamese: *tôi sẽ làm cho ông* (I *future* do benefit man, 'I'll do it for you'). English is a mildly analytic language, seen mainly in vocabulary from sources other than Latin and Greek: *Pick it up and put it in the bag*; *The dog can sleep on the floor*. See LINGUISTIC TYPOLOGY.

**ANAPHORA**. [Stress 'a-NA-fo-ra']. **1.** Also *anaphoric reference*. A term in GRAMMAR and LINGUISTICS for referring back in a stretch of language, as with *it* in: 'Although *the aircraft* had been damaged, *it* could still fly.' Here, the pronoun *it* substitutes for its antecedent *the aircraft*. In the next example, the definite article *the* in *the conference* is anaphoric, referring back to *a conference*: 'The EC leaders agreed to hold *a conference* on economic and monetary union, and have now fixed a date for *the conference*.' Anaphoric reference may be achieved through ellipsis, as in 'We asked them to join us, but they wouldn't', where *they wouldn't* means *they wouldn't join us*. The term is sometimes extended to include CATAPHORA (forward reference to a following part of the text). **2.** Also *epanaphora*. A term in rhetoric for the repetition of the same word or phrase at the beginning of successive phrases, clauses, sentences, and stanzas: 'He shows us a country where a man can be denied the right to know of what and by whom he is accused. A country where some police shoot first and ask questions later' (*Christian Science Monitor*, international edition, 11 Apr. 1988). Compare ANADIPLOSIS.

**ANGLICISM** [with or without an initial capital]. **1.** An expression from English used in another language, such as *le fairplay* in French. **2.** A characteristic, quality, fashion, or fad deriving from England, such as cricket or afternoon tea in Pakistan. **3.** A feature of the English language that is peculiar to England, such as the working-class phrase *feelin' proper poorly* feeling really ill. See BRITICISM.

**ANGLICIST**. **1.** Someone who favours the use of English. See INDIAN ENGLISH. **2.** Also *Anglist*. A scholar who specializes in English, especially in continental Europe (compare French *Angliciste*, German *Anglist*).

**ANGLICIZE** AmE & BrE, **Anglicise** AusE & BrE [with and without an initial capital]. **1.** To make (someone or something) English in nationality, culture, or language: 'What a strange character is Tennyson's Arthur in *Idylls of the King* . . . the most rigorously de-Celticised and Anglicised figure since Layamon's' (Tom Shippey, *London Review of Books*, 26 July 1990). **2.** To adopt the English language: 'Are they allowed to *Anglicise* if they like, as the Scottish Highlanders were?' (P. Thompson, 1857, cited in *OED*). **3.** To turn into an English form: 'Fort Ross—an anglicized abbreviation of *Fuerte de los Rusos*' (*Harper's Magazine*, Jan. 1883). Compare ANGLIFY, ENGLISHIZE.

**ANGLIFY** [with or without an initial capital]. A usually informal and sometimes

pejorative alternative to ANGLICIZE: 'The greatest American linguistic investment by far has been the Anglification of the millions of immigrant and indigenous speakers of other languages' (Joshua A. Fishman, in Ferguson & Heath (eds.), *Language in the USA*, 1981).

**ANGLO**. **1.** In and around the US Southwest, a clipping of Spanish *anglo-americano* and English *Anglo-American* standing, sometimes pejoratively, for a (white) speaker of English: 'Chicano norms always seem to be somewhat less formal than Anglo norms' (Fernando Peñalosa, *Chicano Sociolinguistics*, 1980). **2.** In Canada and especially Quebec, a clipping of ANGLOPHONE, standing for a speaker of English: *anglo rights*. It does not usually have a capital and may contrast with *franco*. **3.** In Scotland, a clipping of *Anglo-Scot*, standing for someone who is half-English, half-Scottish, a Scot who has been influenced by English ideas, mannerisms, etc.

**ANGLO-**. A combining form relating to: the Angles (*Anglo-Saxon culture*), England and the English (*Anglo-Welsh relations*) or Britain and the British (*the Anglo-Irish agreement*), location in England (*Anglo-Jewry* the Jews of England), and the English language (*Anglo-Danish pidgin*). In Northern Ireland, Scotland, and Wales, the use of the term to mean *Britain/British* is widely disliked. In Scotland, newspapers tend to avoid this sense of *Anglo-*, using instead such phrases as *the British-Irish agreement*.

**ANGLO-AMERICAN**. **1.** Relating to England or Britain and the US: *Anglo-American trade talks*. **2.** A citizen of the US born in England or of English origin. **3.** An American who speaks English: compare ANGLO. **4.** A term for the English language proposed by the British zoologist and amateur linguist Lancelot Hogben in *The Mother Tongue* (1964). **5.** American English: 'Since the Second World War, the Nordic languages have taken over not only direct loans, but also calques and grammatical constructions from Anglo-American' (*Language International* 2: 2, 1990).

**ANGLOCENTRIC**. Centred on England and the English (or Britain and the British), or on the English language.

**ANGLO-ENGLISH**. An occasional term

for the (standard) English language as used in England: 'I have chosen one accent for Scottish Standard English and one for "Anglo-English"' (David Abercrombie, in *Languages of Scotland*, 1979). See ENGLISH ENGLISH, ENGLISH IN ENGLAND.

**ANGLO-HYBRID**. A recent term for a relatively informal mix of English and another language: 'Although the various Anglohybrids are currently unstable, the hybridity itself is stable enough . . . If past situations are anything to go by, those languages affected today will undergo irreversible change, as English did after the Danish invasions and the Norman Conquest' (Tom McArthur, 'The Coming Hybrids', *Verbatim: The Language Quarterly* 29: 3, Winter 1993). The phenomenon has been particularly noted in the 20c, giving rise to such often facetious but troubled terms as *Spanglish*, for English mixed with SPANISH, especially in the US, and *Taglish*, for English mixed with TAGALOG in the Philippines. See CODE-MIXING AND CODE-SWITCHING.

**ANGLO-INDIAN**. **1.** Now rare: relating to England or Britain, and India: *Anglo-Indian ties*. **2.** Of English or British people and their activities in India during the Raj: *Anglo-Indian words and phrases*. **3.** Of the community of Eurasians in India descended from European fathers and Indian mothers. The mother tongue of the Anglo-Indian community is English. In present-day India, an *Anglo-Indian school* is an English-medium private school associated with the community and a Christian denomination, but open to students of all backgrounds. *Anglo-Indian English* is a subvariety of INDIAN ENGLISH. **4.** Relating to the body of writing in English centred on the Indian subcontinent and written by such non-Indians as Rudyard Kipling, E. M. Forster, and John Masters, making use of forms of language appropriate to the cultural, sociolinguistic, and political contexts of the region: *Anglo-Indian literature*.

**ANGLO-IRISH**. **1.** Relating to England or Britain and Ireland: *the Anglo-Irish agreement*, *Anglo-Irish tensions*. **2.** Relating to the English in Ireland and the Protestant Ascendancy: 'PAT. He was an Anglo-Irishman. / MEG. In the blessed name of God, what's that? / PAT. A Protestant with a horse' (Brendan Behan, *The Hostage*, 1958, Act I). The

term is disliked by many Irish nationalists when used to refer to Irish literature in English or when it obtrusively recalls the centuries of English/British rule over Ireland. **3.** A term, especially in linguistics, for a variety of English spoken over most of Ireland. It derives mainly from the English brought to Ireland by 17c *Planters* (settlers) from England, modified by contacts with Irish Gaelic, Ulster Scots, and Hiberno-English. It is a continuum of usage influenced by the level of education of its speakers, their regional origin, and the area of original settlement. The usage of more educated speakers approximates to Irish broadcasting norms, whereas less educated speakers have more distinctive accents and non-standard usages.

**Pronunciation**. The middle-class Anglo-Irish accent has been influenced by and continues to be close to RP. However, it is rhotic (with a retroflex *r*) and the /t, d/ in words like *true* and *drew* tend to be dental rather than alveolar, suggesting 'thrue' and 'dhrew'. In working-class speech, the following features are common: (1) Words such as *leave* and *tea* sound like 'lave' and 'tay', *cold* and *old* sound like 'cowl' and 'owl', *bull* and *could* can rhyme with 'cull' and 'bud', and *which* and *whether* are distinguished from *witch* and *weather* (beginning with /hw/, not /w/). (2) In such words as *arm* and *film*, a vowel often opens up the consonant clusters: 'aram' and 'fillim'. (3) In the South, words such as *pence* are often pronounced 'pensh' (an /ʃ/ in word-final position) and *story* and *small* are often pronounced 'shtory' and 'shmall' (an /ʃ/ in consonant clusters). Less often, such words as *fizzed* and *puzzle* sound like 'fizhd' and 'puzhl' (a /ʒ/ in consonant clusters). Also in Southern Anglo-Irish, words such as *thin* and *then* sound like 'tin ' and 'den' (/ð, θ/ replaced by /t, d/). Words such as *try, dry, butter*, and *under* sound like *thry, dhry, butther*, and *undher* (with interdental rather than alveolar plosives).

**Grammar**. Standard Anglo-Irish is close to the standard BrE varieties. Non-standard Anglo-Irish syntax has six features also found outside Ireland: (1) *Done* and *seen* in the past tense: *She done it because she seen me do it*. (2) Special past participles: *He has div* He has dived; *They have went* They have gone. (3) Auxiliary *have* reduced to *a*: *You should a knew* You should have known; *They would a* *helped you*. (4) *Them* as a demonstrative plural adjective and pronoun: *Them shoes is lovely yet. Them's the ones I wanted.* (5) A plural form of *you*. In the South, it tends to be *ye* (rhyming with *he*: *Ye'll all get what's comin to ye*) or *youse* (rhyming with *whose*: *Youse childher will get a good beatin' when your father gets in!*). In the North, it is *yiz* (rhyming with *his*: *Yiz'll all get what's comin to yiz, Yiz childher will get . . .*). (6) Singular *be* with plural subjects: *Me and Mick's fed up, Mary and the daughter's out shopping, Yiz is late, Themins* (those ones) *is no use.* Such features are probably tolerated higher up the social ladder than in Britain.

**Vocabulary**. 1. Distinctive words never current in the standard language: *atomy* a small, insignificant person, as in *Did you ever see such a wee atomy of a man?*; *cog* to cheat, for example by copying, as in *I wouldn't let just anybody cog my exercise*; *thole* to endure, as in *There was nothin for it but to thole* (shared with ScoE). 2. General words with distinctive senses: *backward* shy, *bold* naughty, *doubt* strongly believe, as in *I doubt he's coming* (shared with ScoE). Most regionally marked words occur in the speech of older, often rural people; it is unlikely that *biddable* obedient, *feasant* affable, *pishmire/pismire* ant, occur in the natural usage of people under 40. See BELFAST, DUBLIN, IRISH ENGLISH, NEWFOUNDLAND ENGLISH, NORTHERN IRISH ENGLISH.

**ANGLO-NORMAN**. 1. Of the Normans in England or both the Normans and the indigenous English: *Anglo-Norman culture*. 2. Of NORMAN FRENCH as used in England or a contact language mixing French and English, used between the Normans and their subjects: 'The Anglo-Norman jargon was only employed in the commercial intercourse between the conquerors and the conquered' (George Ellis, *Specimens of the Early English Poets*, 1801).

**ANGLOPHILE**. 1. Admiring or loving England and the English and/or the English language: *the Anglophile party in Scotland*. 2. Someone with such an attitude: *unrepentant Anglophiles*. The term may or may not include Britain as a whole, and non-English Britons may experience *Anglophilia*.

**ANGLOPHOBE**. 1. Also *Anglophobic*. Fearing or hating England and the English and/or the English language: *Anglophobe reaction*. 2. Someone with such an attitude: *an inveterate Anglophobe*. The term may or may not include Britain as a whole, and non-English Britons may experience *Anglophobia*.

**ANGLOPHONE**. [Often used without an initial capital]. 1. A speaker of English: (Africa) *locally born anglophone whites*; (Quebec) *certified anglophones*, permitted by law to send their children to English-medium schools. 2. Of speakers of English: *an anglophone school*. The term occurs mainly where French is also used. It contrasts with *francophone* (French-speaking), *allophone* (speaking a language other than French or English), *arabophone* (speaking Arabic), *hispanophone* (speaking Spanish), and *lusophone* (speaking Portuguese), etc.

**ANGLO-SAXON**. Originally a name for the Saxons who with the Angles invaded and settled in Britain (5–7c), to contrast them with the *Old Saxons* of Germany. The name was later given both to the Angles and Saxons, also known as *the Old English* (*Anglo-Saxon law*) and to their language, also known as *Old English* (*Anglo-Saxon grammar*). More broadly and recently, it has served to identify a culture, spirit, style, heritage, or ethnic type associated with England, Britain, the British Empire, and/or the US: *Anglo-Saxon civilization*. It is also used to label vernacular English, especially when considered plain, monosyllabic, crude, and vulgar: *Anglo-Saxon words*.

**History**. For many centuries there was no agreed collective name for the Germanic peoples who settled in Britain. By the time of the Norman Conquest (1066), *English* had emerged for the peoples and their language, but when the Normans began to call themselves English the older sense of the word was obscured and the identification of *English* with post-Conquest England was strengthened. The mass of the people were classed by their overlords as SAXON. Medieval Latin chroniclers used *Anglo-Saxones* and *Angli Saxones* to refer to both Angles and Saxons, a practice that became universal after 1600 for anything before the Conquest. In 1884, James Murray noted in the *OED* entry *Anglo-Saxon* that this practice had led 'to an erroneous analysis of the word, which has been taken as = *Angle* + *Saxon*, a union of Angle and Saxon; and in accordance with this mistaken view, modern combinations have been profusely formed in which *Anglo-* is meant to express "English and . . .", "English in connexion with . . .", as "the Anglo-Russian war"; whence, on the same analogy, Franco-German, Turko-Russian, etc.'

**Culture**. An extension of the term to mean the people of England and (loosely) Britain developed in the 19c, for example when the journalist Walter Bagehot referred in a speech to wealth as 'the obvious and national idol of the Anglo-Saxon'. In 1956, the novelist Angus Wilson revived a phrase of Lewis Carroll's as the title of his satirical novel *Anglo-Saxon Attitudes*. The term *Anglo-Saxon* now refers to anyone in any way linked with England, the English language, and their traditions: in France, *anglo-saxon* has been used, often negatively, for shared 'Anglo-American' attitudes and culture, while in 1975 the Tanzanian writer Ali Mazrui coined *Afro-Saxon* to describe Black Africans who adopt English as the language of the home and with it cultural attitudes and values which in effect make them Black Englishmen.

**Plain usage**. In Victorian times, the term was associated with the Germanic element in English vocabulary, especially by such purists as William Barnes. Its use as a label for direct and often coarse language marks a perception of OLD ENGLISH[1] as a medium that called a spade a spade. This view contrasts a simple, vigorous vernacular with an effete Latinate style little understood and seldom used by the people at large. For those who hold this view, *smell* and *sweat* are plainer, briefer, and better than *odour* and *perspiration*. More pointedly still, the term is used for vulgar expressions. Webster's *Third New International Dictionary* (1966) gives *Anglo-Saxon word* as a synonym of *four-letter word*, and Charles Berlitz has observed: 'In general, almost all the polysyllabic words in English are of French-Latin origin while the one-syllable words come from Anglo-Saxon' (*Native Tongues*, 1982). There are, however, many Anglo-Saxon polysyllables, such as *bloodthirstily* and *righthandedness*. See PLAIN, RUNE.

**ANGLO-SAXON CHRONICLE** [c.891–1154], also *Old English Annals, Old English Chronicle*. A set of annals, the first extended original composition in English, probably begun in the court of King ALFRED and continued in monasteries, in which the seven surviving manuscripts were written. The last, for 1154, is also the last known document in OLD ENGLISH[1]. The Chronicle includes six poems amidst the prose entries, starting with the 937 annal on the battle of Brunanburh. The chroniclers used many sources, including Bede's history, other annals and records, and popular stories. The use of the vernacular rather than Latin for chronicles was rare at that time.

**ANIMATE NOUN**. A semantic category of NOUN, referring to a person, animal, or other creature (*boy, sheep, worm*), in contrast to an *inanimate noun*, which refers to a thing or concept (*corn, boyhood, sleep*). In general, animate nouns correlate with the pronouns *he, she, who* and inanimate nouns with *it, which*.

**ANTECEDENT**. **1.** The words in a text, usually a noun phrase, to which a pronoun or other grammatical unit refers back. *Cook* is the antecedent of *him* in: 'In 1772, Cook began his second voyage, which took *him* further south than he had ever been.' Similarly, *his second voyage* is the antecedent of *which*. With impersonal *it, this, that, which*, the antecedent may be a whole clause or paragraph, as in: '*Might not the coast of New South Wales provide an armed haven?* To some people *this* looked good on paper, but there is no hard evidence that *it* did so to William Pitt or his ministers.' Despite the implications of the name, an antecedent can follow rather than precede: 'For *his* first Pacific voyage, *Cook* had no chronometer.' **2.** In logic, the conditional element in a proposition. In *If they did that, they deserve our respect*, the antecedent is *they did that*.

**ANTICLIMAX**. **1.** In RHETORIC, a descent from the elevated and important to the low and trivial: 'Here thou, Great Anna! whom three realms obey, / Dost sometimes counsel take—and sometimes Tea' (Pope, *The Rape of the Lock*, 1712). **2.** In drama, the lowered state after a CLIMAX; in life, an outcome that fails to live up to expectation. See BATHOS, FIGURE OF SPEECH.

**ANTITHESIS** [Stress: 'an-TI-the-sis']. **1.** In RHETORIC, a construction in which words are opposed but balanced: 'For many are called, but few are chosen' (Matthew 22: 14); 'To err is human, to forgive, divine' (Pope, 1711). Technically, the first part of such constructions is the *thesis* ('for many are called'), the second the antithesis ('but few are chosen'). **2.** In general usage, opposite: *This policy is the antithesis of everything we believe in.* See CHIASMUS.

**ANTONOMASIA** [Stress: 'an-to-no-MAY-zy-a']. **1.** In RHETORIC, the use of an EPITHET to acknowledge a quality in one person or place by using the name of another person or place already known for that quality: *Henry is the local Casanova; Cambridge is England's Silicon Valley.* **2.** The use of an epithet instead of the name of a person or thing: *the Swan of Avon* William Shakespeare.

**ANTONYM.** One of two WORDS or other expressions that have opposite meanings: *fast* and *slow, hot* and *cold.* Some words are antonymous in some contexts but not others: *straight* is generally the opposite of *bent/curved,* but is the antonym of *gay* in the context of homosexuality. Linguists identify three types of antonymy: (1) *Gradable antonyms,* which operate on a continuum: (*very*) *big,* (*very*) *small.* Such pairs often occur in binomial phrases with *and:* (*blow*) *hot* and *cold,* (*search*) *high* and *low.* (2) *Complementary antonyms,* which express an either/or relationship: *dead* or *alive, male* or *female.* (3) *Converse* or *relational antonyms,* expressing reciprocity: *borrow* or *lend, buy* or *sell, wife* or *husband.* See SEMANTICS, SYNONYM.

**APHAERESIS** BrE, **apheresis** AmE [Stress: 'a-FER-e-sis']. The removal of an element from the beginning of a WORD, usually for informal economy of expression: *copter* and *gator* from *helicopter* and *alligator.* Sometimes aphaeresis and APOCOPE occur together: *tec* from *detective, flu* from *influenza.* The use of an APOSTROPHE to mark aphaeresis ('*gator,* '*phone,* '*plane*) is now rare, expect when used to mark novel or unusual forms, as in '*kyou* for 'thank you'. See APHESIS, CLIPPING, ELISION.

**APHESIS** [Stress: 'AH-fe-sis']. The loss of an unstressed vowel at the beginning of a WORD, as in *prentice* from *apprentice,* sometimes leading to a word with a new meaning and use: *lone* from *alone, slant* from *aslant, squire* from *esquire.* Younger children often speak aphetically, a style that Rudyard Kipling imitates in *Just So Stories* (1902), marking the loss with an apostrophe: '*Stute*

*Fish,* '*scruciating idle,* '*sclusively bare,* '*satiable curiosity.* See APH(A)ERESIS, ELISION.

**APOCOPE** [Stress: 'a-POK-o-py']. **1.** The removal of an element at the end of a WORD, usually for informal economy of expression, as in: *kit* and *marge,* formed from *kitten* and *margarine.* Sometimes a suffix is added to the apocopated form, as in *kitty* from *kitten* and AusE *journo* from *journalist.* Apocope is common in especially affectionate nicknames: *Margery* becomes *Marge, William* becomes *Will.* Sometimes APHAERESIS and apocope occur together: *Elizabeth* cut to *Liz, detective* to *tec.* **2.** The loss of the inflectional endings of Old English, as when *singan* became *sing.* See CLIPPING, ELISION.

■ **APOSTROPHE**[1] ──────────── ■
[Pronunciation and stress: 'a-POS-tro-fy']. The sign ('), sometimes regarded as a PUNCTUATION MARK, sometimes as a DIACRITIC. The apostrophe has three uses: (1) To mark the omission or ELISION of letters and sounds, as in *didn't* for *did not* and *fo'c'sle* or *fo'c's'le* for *forecastle.* (2) To indicate a plural form, especially in abbreviations, as in *V.I.P.'s* (short for *very important persons*). (3) To mark POSSESSION in nouns, as in *Jack's house* (the house belonging to Jack), but not in possessive pronouns (*hers, ours,* etc., not \**her's,* \**ours'*), with the exception of *one's.* Each of the functions is discussed in detail below.

**Omission and elision**. The apostrophe was introduced into English in the 16c from Latin and Greek, in which it served to mark the loss of letters, as in the systematic dropping of *er* in Latin writing: for example, the word *tercius* ('third': classical form *tertius*) was commonly reduced in manuscripts to *t'cius.* Printers used the mark in the same way in English: for example, in *o'er,* a short form of *over,* and '*tis,* a short form of *it is.* By the end of the 16c, the sign was commonly used in this role. Since the 19c, the convention has stabilized in four related areas: (1) The representation of colloquial or informal elisions, such as the reduced *not* in *couldn't, hadn't, wasn't* and the reduced *-ing* in *huntin', shootin',* and *fishin'.* (2) The marking of initial word CLIPPINGS, as in '*fraid so* for *afraid so* and '*gator* for *alligator.* (3) the omission of prefixed numbers, as with *the '80s* for *the 1980s.* (4) The representation of nonstandard speech and dialect, as in *reg'lar, fr'en's o' mine,* and *fa' doun* (Scots: fall down).

Increasingly, however, 20c writers of dialect have regarded this use of the apostrophe as a patronizing convention marking dialect as deviant from, and subordinate to, standard usage. Many have therefore dispensed with it in their work. Bernard Shaw disliked the use of the apostrophe of omission in such forms as *didn't*, which he changed to *didnt*, a convention that continues to be followed when his works are printed.

**Plurality**. There was formerly a respectable tradition (17–19c) of using the apostrophe for noun plurals, especially in loanwords ending in a vowel (as in *We doe confess Errata's*, Leonard Lichfield, 1641, and *Comma's are used*, Phillip Luckcombe, 1771) and in the consonants *s, z, ch, sh* (as in *waltz's and cotillions*, Washington Irving, 1804). Although this practice is rare in 20c standard usage, the apostrophe of plurality continues in at least five areas: (1) With abbreviations such as *V.I.P.'s* or *VIP's*, although forms such as *VIPs* are now widespread. (2) With letters of the alphabet, as in *His i's are just like his a's* and *Dot your i's and cross your t's*. In the phrase *do's and don'ts*, the apostrophe of plurality occurs in the first word but not the second, which has the apostrophe of omission: by and large, the use of two apostrophes close together (as in *don't's*) is avoided. (3) In decade dates, such as *the 1980's*, although such apostrophe-free forms as *the 1980s* are widespread, as are such truncations as *the '80s*, the form *the '80's* being unlikely. (4) In family names, especially if they end in -*s*, as in *keeping up with the Jones's*, as opposed to *the Joneses*, a form that is also common. (5) In the non-standard ('illiterate') use often called in BrE the *greengrocer's apostrophe*, as in *apple's* 55p per 1b and *We sell the original shepherds pie's* (notice in a shop window, Canterbury, England).

**Possession**. Although apostrophes began to be used to mark possession in the late 16c, only 4% of the possessives in the First Folio edition of Shakespeare (1623) had them. Most of the nouns using such apostrophes were loanwords ending in -*o*, such as *Romeo's*. The device proved useful, however, as a means of visibly distinguishing the possessive case, so that the Fourth Folio of Shakespeare (1685) made fairly consistent use of it in the singular. Scholars have generally regarded this use of the apostrophe as arising from the omission of the letter *e* in Old and Middle English -*es* GENITIVE

singular endings (such as *mannes* man's, *scipes* ship's), spreading in due course to all genitives, with or without an *e* and plural as well as singular. Others have cited a noun-and-pronoun pattern of possession common in the 16–17c, as in *Charles his name*, where noun and pronoun came together as *Charles's name* and then spread to all possessives, male or female, singular or plural. However, it is the Old English inflection that more directly accounts for the use of the apostrophe in Modern English.

Variations in the use of the possessive marker continued for a long time, however; 'As late as 1794 Washington Irving used apostrophes in only 38% of the possessives in his personal correspondence' (Greta D. Little, 'The Ambivalent Apostrophe', *English Today*, 8 Oct. 1986). By the mid-18c, however, the convention had extended to the possessive use of irregular noun plurals (*children's, men's, and women's clothing*), but the treatment of regular *s*-plurals posed problems. Some grammarians of the period, for example, saw no need for the mark in such phrases as *the soldiers hats*, because nothing was omitted; indeed, there was debate as to whether a distinct plural genitive existed in Modern English. By the middle of the 19c, however, such forms as *the soldiers' hats* were more or less established, but even so it appears from the evidence that there was never a golden age in which the rules for the use of the possessive apostrophe in English were clear-cut and known, understood, and followed by most educated people.

The conventions for the use of the possessive apostrophe in late 20c standard English are: singular nouns add '*s* (known as *apostrophe s*), as in *John's new suit* and *Your mother's job*. Plural nouns have *s*' (known as *s apostrophe*), as in *the Smiths' cat* and *my parents' house* (the house belonging to my parents). If a plural does not end in *s*, an apostrophe *s* is added: *the children's food*. Such a phrase as *the sheep's behaviour* is ambiguous out of context: it can be singular or plural. Beyond this point difficulties and inconsistencies are as common in the 1990s as in earlier times, especially with proper nouns. Singular use varies with place-names (*St John's, Newfoundland*, but *St Albans, England* and *St Andrews, Scotland*). There has been an accelerating tendency since the turn of the century to drop the apostrophe in the names of organizations and publications as well as place-names, as in: *Barclays Bank, Collins English Dictionary, Crows Nest, Debenhams, Harrods, Marks and Spencer, McMahons Point, Pikes Peak*. There is also widespread difficulty with *its* and *it's. Its* is the genitive or possessive of the personal pronoun *it*, as in *The cat licked its paws*, where it is possessive but does not have an apostrophe. *It's* is a contraction of *it is*, as in *It's too late* (It is too late), or *it has*, as in *It's made a mess* (It has made a mess); it is not possessive, but does have an apostrophe, because letters have been omitted.

There is widespread inconsistency and uncertainty in the use of the apostrophe when a singular noun already ends in *-s*. Traditional usage adds the apostrophe *s* if it is pronounced: *the boss's explanation*. With names of classical origin, a second *s* is not usually added, especially when the end sound of a word is /z/ rather than /s/: *Xerxes' battle, Socrates' pupils*. In speaking, a further syllable is less likely with such names as *Xerxes'*, where the last syllable already has two sibilant sounds, but might or might not be pronounced with *Socrates'*. With non-classical names ending in *-s*, again spoken and written forms may or may not have the same number of syllables. With short names, an extra syllable is generally pronounced, although the possessive can be written either way: *Mr Harris' job, Mr Harris's job; Keats' poetry, Keats's poetry*. The extra syllable for *Jesus* is optional in both writing and speech: *in Jesus' name, in Jesus's name*. The possessive plural of a singular name ending in *-s* (*Jones*) may be written either *'s* or *s'*: *the Jones's house, the Jones' house*. The tendency seems to be towards simplification and omitting the apostrophe: a century ago, *Chambers English Dictionary* was *Chambers's English Dictionary*.

**Instability**. Some observers consider that the general use of the apostrophe, especially for possession and plurality, is in decline, because it bears little relation to the spoken word and is a source of confusion in writing and print. Others urge that it be abandoned in some or all of its roles, a position that, if carried to the extreme, would make homographs of *he'll* and *hell*. Still others prefer a middle option that keeps the apostrophe for omission and elision but drops it for plurality and possession. Greta Little (above) sees the following forms (all authentic) as typifying many present-day public signs: *Dads Favorite Shop, Chelsea Mans Shop, Men's and Ladies Wear, Ladies and Mens Hair Styling, Childrens section, First 200 Mom's Get a Free Rose, Knoxville Welcome's Big John Tate, Violators will be towed at owners expense, Joe's Joke Book, Poes Kiddie Komics*. Because such conflicting forms occur close to each other in prominent places such as shopping malls in the US, she notes:

> In and of itself the diversity can be confusing to youngsters on their way to achieving literacy. But what are these learners to make of direct contradictions like *Vella's Deli* and *Vellas Deli* or *Richie's Lounge* and *Richies Lounge*? They are very likely to conclude that the apostrophe means nothing, that it plays some non-significant, decorative role. And there is often evidence which would support that hypothesis: Kelly's with a shamrock 'apostrophe', Moma's Restaurant with a heart, and Patricia's Toy Closet where the apostrophe is a claw on the paw of a tiger that is stretched out atop the sign.

It is likely, however, that the many and varied uses of the apostrophe will remain part of the language for a long time to come, despite some reduction in range, and accompanied by a great deal of inconsistency and error in practice. See APH(A)ERESIS, APHESIS, SAXON GENITIVE.

**APOSTROPHE**[2] [Stress: 'a-POS-tro-fy']. **1.** In RHETORIC, addressing someone or something that cannot respond, such as: a dead person ('Milton! thou shouldst be living at this hour': Wordsworth), a place ('Sweet Auburn! loveliest village of the plain': Goldsmith), or an idea ('O liberty! O liberty! what crimes are committed in thy name!': translating Mme Roland). Originally, the term referred to the invocation opening such epics as Homer's *Iliad*: 'Sing, Goddess, of the deadly wrath of Achilles, son of Peleus.' **2.** A deliberate interruption, as when a lawyer breaks off from an argument to address a judge or turn on an opponent, usually for rhetorical effect or to divert attention from a tricky issue or a weak argument.

**APPALACHIAN ENGLISH**. The English of the mountain region of Appalachia in the south-eastern US: in parts of Kentucky, North Carolina, Tennessee, Virginia, and all of West Virginia. The most influential settlers in these areas were the SCOTS-IRISH, who began arriving in the British American colonies *c.*1640 and moved to the south and west. Because of the relative isolation in which it has developed and the continuance of forms regarded elsewhere as archaisms, Appalachian English has been regarded (popularly but incorrectly) as a kind of Elizabethan or Shakespearian English. However, it shares features with other kinds of non-standard English, particularly in the South: absence of the copula (*That alright*); the use of *right* and *plumb* as intensifying adverbs (*I hollered right loud, The house burnt plumb down*). Phonological features include: initial /h/ in such words as *hit* for *it*, *hain't* for *ain't*; -er for -ow as in *feller/tobaccer/yeller* (fellow/tobacco/yellow). Grammatical features include: *a*-prefixing with -*ing* participial forms (*He just kept a-beggin' an' a-cryin'*) and the use of *done* as a perfective marker (*He done sold his house*: He has sold his house). *A*-prefixing is a relic of a construction containing the OLD ENGLISH preposition *on* in unstressed positions before certain participles: *He was on hunting* (He was engaged in hunting). Currently, Appalachian English is often socially stigmatized because it is spoken in its most distinctive form by poor, often uneducated, mountain people. See DIALECT IN AMERICA, SOUTHERN ENGLISH.

**APPLIED LINGUISTICS**. The application of LINGUISTICS to the study and improvement of LANGUAGE TEACHING, LANGUAGE LEARNING, LANGUAGE PLANNING, communication between groups, speech therapy and the management of language handicap, systems of communications, translating and interpreting, and lexicography. The bulk of the work of applied linguists to date has related to language teaching and language learning and especially English as a foreign or second language. The term owes its origin to US language-teaching programmes during and after the Second World War, largely based on Leonard Bloomfield's *Outline Guide for the Practical Study of Foreign Languages* (1942), which was influenced by the early, mainly European, advocates of the Direct Method, in particular Henry Sweet. In 1948, *Language Learning: A Quarterly Journal of Applied Linguistics* was started at the U. of Michigan by Charles C. Fries, supported among others by Kenneth L. Pike and W. Freeman Twaddell, to disseminate information about work at Fries's English Language Institute (founded 1941). In Britain, a *School of Applied Linguistics* was established by J. C. Catford at the U. of Edinburgh in 1956, and the *Center for Applied Linguistics* was set up in Washington, DC, under Charles Ferguson in 1959. Similar institutes have since been set up in various parts of the world. National associations of applied linguists came together in 1964 to form the *Association internationale de la linguistique appliquée* (*AILA*), which holds a four-yearly international congress with published proceedings. See HALLIDAY.

**APPOSITION**. Two consecutive, juxtaposed NOUNS or noun phrases are in apposition when they refer to the same person or thing, and when either can be omitted without seriously changing the meaning or the grammar of a sentence. *Mrs Thatcher* and *the British Prime Minister* are in apposition in *Mrs Thatcher, the British Prime Minister, became leader of the Tory party in 1975*. Here, both *Mrs Thatcher became leader* . . . and *The British Prime Minister became leader* . . . could serve equally well alone. The term is often used when these criteria only partly apply, some grammarians using terms like *partial* or *weak apposition* to distinguish various types of lesser acceptability: '*The heir to the throne* arrived, *Prince Charles*' (where only the second noun phrase can be omitted).

**APPOSITIVE CLAUSE**. See RELATIVE CLAUSE.

**APPROPRIATENESS**, also **appropriacy**. A term in LINGUISTICS for the intuitive expectation that styles of language vary between situations. It provides a theoretical alternative to the traditional notion of *correctness*, which is an absolute standard against which all usage must be judged, and which invariably reflects the formal and written norms of language, especially as institutionalized in grammars, dictionaries, and manuals of style. The difference in approach can be illustrated by such sentences as *There's the man Mary spoke to*. Traditionally, this sentence would be considered incorrect, as it breaks the prescriptive rule that sentences in English should not end with a preposition; the recommended alternative would be *There is the man to whom Mary spoke*. In terms of appropriateness, each sentence has its own validity: the former in informal settings, the latter in formal settings. See CORRECT, REGISTER.

**APPROXIMANT**, also **continuant**. In PHONETICS, a sound, usually a CONSONANT, with a manner of articulation more open than a stop or fricative, as in the /r/ of *rink* compared with the /z/ of *zinc*. Approximants are normally voiced (/r/ after /d/ as in *drink*), but are often devoiced after a voiceless stop or a fricative (/r/ after /t/ as in *trinket*). The increased flow of air that results from the devoicing produces noise similar to that of a fricative. The set of approximants includes LIQUIDS, NASALS, and GLIDES.

# ■ ARABIC ─────────────────── ■

A Semitic language of West Asia and North Africa that originated in the Arabian peninsula in the early first millennium AD. It is the mother tongue of *c*.150 m people in Algeria, Bahrain, Chad, Egypt, Iraq, Jordan, Kuwait, Lebanon, Libya, Mali, Mauritania, Morocco, Oman, Qatar, Saudi Arabia, Sudan, Syria, Tunisia, the United Arab Emirates, and Yemen, as well as communities elsewhere in Asia and Africa, and immigrant communities in Europe (especially France) and the Americas. Because of its role as the scriptural language of Islam, it has cultural significance and linguistic influence in Bangladesh, India, Indonesia, Iran, Malaysia, Nigeria, Pakistan, the Philippines, Somalia, Turkey, various Central Asian republics and other countries where there are Muslim communities. Arabic has influenced such languages of southern Europe as Italian, Portuguese, and Spanish. It was formerly a language of Europe, being spoken for some 400 years in the Iberian peninsula, and is still represented by its offshoot *Maltese*, which has been strongly influenced by both Italian and English.

**Classical and colloquial Arabic**. The Arabic language is generally described as having two forms: *classical Arabic* and *colloquial Arabic*. The classical or literary language includes and is based on the Arabic of the *Qur'ān* (Recitation), the text of the teachings of the Prophet Muhammad in the 7c. The colloquial form consists of many vatieties that may or may not be mutually intelligible and fall into several groups: those of Arabia, Egypt, the Maghreb (North Africa west of Egypt), Iraq, and Syria. Classical usage is uniform throughout the Arab world, and all colloquial varieties have been influenced by it. Classical Arabic has immense prestige and liturgical significance wherever Muslims live, but, just as there are Muslims who do not speak Arabic, so there are speakers of Arabic who are not Muslim.

**Speech and script**. (1) Arabic has a series of velarized consonants, pronounced with constriction of the PHARYNX and raising of the tongue, and a group of uvular and pharyngeal fricatives that give the language a characteristic throaty sound. (2) The GLOTTAL STOP is a consonantal phoneme, represented in Arabic script by the letter *alif* and in ROMAN transliteration by the lenis symbol ' (or the apostrophe '): *'ana* I, *sa'al* he asked. The sign *hamza* also represents a glottal stop and is transliterated in the same way. In the TRANSLITERATION of the letter *ain*, a voiced pharyngeal fricative, the asper symbol '(or the turned comma ') is used, as in *ʿāmiyya* colloquial, *sharīʿa* Islamic law. (3) There are three short and three long vowels, transliterated as *a, i, u, ā, ī, ū*. (4) Words start with a consonant followed by a vowel. Clusters of more than two consonants do not occur. (5) Arabic script, which probably developed in the 4c, is the next most widely used writing system after the Roman alphabet. It has been adapted as a medium for such non-Semitic languages as Malay, Persian, SPANISH, SWAHILI, Turkish, and URDU. It has 28 letters, all representing consonants, and runs from right to left. (6) A set of diacritics, developed in the 8c, can be used for short vowels and some otherwise unmarked grammatical endings.

**Grammar and word-formation**. Arabic syntax and word-formation centre on a system of *tri-consonantal roots* that provide the basic lexical content of words: for example, the root *k–t–b* underlies words relating to writing and books, and *s–l–m* underlies words relating to submission, resignation, peace, and religion. Such roots are developed in patterns of vowels and affixes: words formed from *k–t–b* include the nouns *kitāb* (book) and *kātib* (one who writes, a clerk or scribe); words formed from *s–l–m* include *'aslama* (he submitted), *islām* (submission to the will of God), *muslim* (one who so submits), and *salām* (peace, safety, security).

**Arabic in English**. Contacts between Arabic and English date from the Crusades (11–13c). BORROWINGS, though often individually significant, have never been numerous: for example, in the 14c *admiral*, *alchemy*, *alkali*, *bedouin*, *nadir*, *syrup*; 16c *alcohol*, *algebra*, *magazine*, *monsoon*, *sheikh*, *sultan*; 17c *albatross*, *alcove*, *assassin*, *ghoul*, *harem*, *jinn*, *mullah*, *sofa*, *zenith*; 19c *alfalfa*, *jihad/jehad*, *majlis*, *safari*, *yashmak*; 20c *ayatol-*

*lah*, *intifada*, *mujahedin*. Arabic words in English tend to relate to Islam (*ayatollah*, *mullah*), Arab society and culture past or present (*alcove*, *bedouin*, *sultan*), and learning (*alchemy*, *alkali*), including mathematics and astronomy (*algebra*, *nadir*, *zenith*). Many have come into English through a third language: *admiral* through French, *albatross* through Portuguese and Spanish, *safari* through Swahili, *ayatollah* through Persian. One set of loanwords incorporates the Arabic definite article *al*, and includes *albatross*, *alchemy*, *alchol*, *alcove*, *alembic*, *alfalfa*, *algebra*, *alhambra*, *alkali*, *almanac*.

**Variations in spelling**. Some Arabic words have more than one spelling in English. Of these, the more traditional forms, usually because of rivalry and animosity between Christians and Muslims, have taken little account of Muslim sensibilities. Vernacular and academic orthography are therefore often sharply contrasted, the latter having strict conventions for transliterating Arabic into Roman script. Forms of the name of the Prophet include the obsolete and highly pejorative *Mahound* (equating him with a devil, false god, or idol), the archaic *Mahomet* (disliked by Muslims because *ma-* is a negative Arabic prefix), *Mohammed* and *Mohamed* (currently common among Muslims and others), and *Muhammad* (used principally by scholars). Similarly, a believer in Islam has been a *Mahometan* or *Mohammedan* (on the analogy of *Christian*, terms disliked by Muslims because they emphasize the Prophet and not God), *Moslem* (widely used), and *Muslim* (used especially by scholars, but increasingly in general writing). Names for Islam have included the obsolete and offensive *Mahometry* and *Maumetry* (meaning 'false religion') and the more recent *Mahometanism* and *Mohammedanism*, neither of which is acceptable to Muslims. The name for the Islamic scriptures has been *the Alcoran* (archaic: redundantly incorporating the definite article), *the Koran* (in general use), and *the Qur'ān* (especially among scholars). In the following excerpt, the Arabic words are transliterated using current scholarly conventions:

The Shāfi'ī school traces its founding to Abū 'Abdallah Muhammad ibn Idrīs al-Shāfi'ī, a Meccan of the Quraysh, who taught in Egypt in Fustāt (now part of Cairo). He died there A.H. 204/AD 920 (J. E. Williams, *Islam*, 1962).

**English in Arabic**. Because of increasing contacts between the Arab world and English, many words have been borrowed into both spoken and written Arabic: for example, in Egypt, where the British had a colonial presence for 72 years (1882–1954), loans span many spheres and include the colloquial, such as: general *aftershave*, *ceramic*, *shampoo*, *spray*; architectural *motel*, *roof garden*, *shopping centre*, *supermarket*; clothing *cap*, *overall*, *shorts*; foodstuffs *grapefruit*, *ice cream*; sport *football*, *half-time*, *match*, *tennis*. The question of how to transfer foreign terms into the written language, especially scientific and technical terms, has long been hotly debated; innovators advocate borrowing terms where there are gaps, while purists urge the use of equivalents coined for the purpose. By and large, the Arabiciation of such words takes three forms: loan concepts that use the language's own system of roots and derivatives (*adā'a* to broadcast, *idā'a* broadcasting, *mūdī'* broadcaster); loan translations that create new Arabic forms (*semiotics* becoming *'ilm al-rumūz*); loan adaptations that give an Arabic look to foreign borrowings (*philosophy* becoming *al-falsafa*, *morpheme* becoming *al-murf īm*).

**English in the Arab world**. In the late 20c, English is a significant additional language in most Arab countries. Four European languages of empire have affected the Arab world, especially in the 19–20c: English especially in Bahrain, Egypt, Iraq, Jordan, Kuwait, Oman, Qatar, Saudi Arabia, Sudan, the United Arab Emirates, and Yemen; French especially in Algeria, Egypt, Lebanon, Morocco, Syria, and Tunisia; Spanish in Morocco; and Italian in Libya. Although the age of European colonial power passed in the 1950s/1960s, the English and French spheres of linguistic influence in particular are still clear-cut. Currently, English is extensively used for business, technical, and other purposes, especially in and around the Arabian peninsula and the Gulf, and is an increasingly important technical and educational resource in countries formerly closely associated with French.

See DIGLOSSIA, EUROPEAN LANGUAGES, GUTTURAL, HEBREW, HINDI-URDU, LINGUISTIC TYPOLOGY, Q. Compare SANSKRIT.

**ARCHAISM**. In RHETORIC, literary criticism, and PHILOLOGY, a style that reflects the usage of an earlier period (*literary archaism*) and an out-of-date or old-fashioned word or phrase (*a lexical archaism*). *Literary archaism* occurs when a style is modelled on older works, so as to revive earlier practices or achieve a desired effect. *Lexical archaisms* are a common feature of such a style and of such registers as religion and law. Archaism is often a consequence of purism and may rest on the belief that language and life in days of yore were plainer, more democratic, and more natural. Such archaisms as *ere* before, *prithee* I pray you, are often used for effect, especially in the dialogue of historical novels: 'Dear father, prithee add thyself to that venerable company ere the soup cools' (Margaret in Charles Reade's *The Cloister and the Hearth*, 1861). See ANACHRONISM, JOURNALESE, SAXONISM.

**ARGOT**. The SLANG of a restricted, often suspect, social group: 'They have their own argot: they bimble, yomp, or tab across the peat and couth a shirt in readiness for a Saturday night bop with the Bennies (locals)' (Colin Smith, *Observer*, 26 May 1985, writing about British soldiers in the Falkland Islands). See CANT, JARGON, POLARI, ROMANI.

## ■ ARTICLE ──────── ■

A traditional PART OF SPEECH, in contemporary grammar often included in the word class *determiner*. Some languages, such as classical Greek, have complex systems of articles varying according to person, gender, number, and case, but in English there are only two: *the*, the *definite article*, and *a/an*, the *indefinite article*.

**Functions**. The definite article marks a phrase as uniquely identifiable and can be used with any common noun: singular (*the house*), plural (*the houses*), uncountable (*the bread*). It also forms an essential part of some proper names: *The Hague*, *the Pennines*, *the Vatican*. *A/an* is used with singular countable nouns: *Give me a bag*, not *\*Give me bag*. The form *a* is used before consonant sounds (*a book, a house*) and the semi-vowel/j/ (*a European, a UN official, a year*). The form *an* is used before vowel sounds, however spelled: *an American, an honour, an MP, an uncle*. There is some uncertainty about words beginning with a pronounced *h* and an unstressed first syllable, and practices vary: *a/an hotel, a/an historical event*. For more detail see the entry

for *H*. Exceptionally and for emphasis, *a/an* is used before an uncountable noun with the meaning 'an example of', as in: *They displayed a breathtaking indifference to my problems*.

**Zero article and ellipsis**. Some grammarians use the term *zero* for the absence of an article before uncountable and plural nouns, such as *wine* and *bottles* in *He puts wine in bottles*. They argue that a zero article has the same sort of indefinite meaning as *a/an* before singular nouns. This convention and the usage it describes is distinct from the suppression of articles in certain kinds of writing and speaking, such as note-taking (*have suitcase, will travel*: I have a suitcase and I am willing to travel) and elliptical instructions (as in dramatic scripts, *leaves room*: the actor leaves the room).

**Specific versus generic**. The distinction of specific and generic cuts across the distinction between definite and indefinite. Specific reference is to particular people or things: *The Browns live next door to me*; *Shut the door*; *I went to a marvellous party last night*; *Help yourself to coffee*; *Biscuits are on the table*. In the last two examples, with the zero article, *some* could be added to the uncountable noun *coffee* and the plural noun *biscuits* without an appreciable change of meaning. Generic reference is to people or things as examples of a class in general: *The kangaroo is an Australian animal*, *A kangaroo is an Australian animal*, *Kangaroos are Australian animals*. As these examples illustrate, if the nouns are countable generic reference can be shown by the singular with the definite or indefinite article and the plural with the zero article. However, *the* with the plural has generic reference in two cases: nationality nouns (*The Afghans are engaged in a civil war*) and adjectives denoting a class of people (*The poor are always with us*).

A further distinction is sometimes made between specific reference (where particular people or things are intended) and nonspecific reference (where instances of the kind of people or things are intended): for example, *I want to buy a secondhand car* or *Sue is looking for a partner*, where *a secondhand car* and *a partner* do not have reference to a specific car or partner. For non-specific relations, the indefinite article is used with singular countable nouns (as in the two examples above) and the zero article or *some* is used with plural and uncountable nouns: *I want to buy (some) secondhand cars; She is looking for (some) partners.*

**ARTICULATION. 1.** In general usage, the act or process of speaking, especially so that every element can be clearly heard. See DICTION, ELOCUTION, ORTHOEPY. **2.** In phonetics, the production of SPEECH sounds, especially that part of the process taking place above the LARYNX. See DOUBLE ARTICULATION.

**ARTIFICIAL LANGUAGE. 1.** An invented language, such as Zamenhof's *Esperanto*, formed by blending elements of various Indo-European languages, or an adapted language, such as Ogden's *Basic English*, formed by radically reducing standard English. Hundreds of artefacts of this type have been created and many promoted over the last 150 years, mostly without success. Esperanto is, however, well known and its name serves virtually as a generic term for all kinds of artificial communication. Such languages are discussed in detail by Andrew Large in *The Artificial Language Movement* (Blackwell, 1985). **2.** A system of symbols constructed for a particular purpose, such as a computer language or a system of symbolic logic. Such 'languages' originated in the 17c, as part of a search for a universal logical system that would transcend all natural language. An early form was *Real Character*, a codelike writing system invented by Bishop John Wilkins, a member of the Royal Society. See AIRSPEAK, BASIC ENGLISH, CORNISH, INTERLANGUAGE, JESPERSEN, NEWSPEAK, RESTRICTED LANGUAGE, SEASPEAK.

**ARYAN.** [Pronounced both 'AY-rian' and 'AH-rian']. A term used by 19c philologists for the common ancestor of many European and INDIAN LANGUAGES. When the terms *Indo-Germanic* and *Indo-European* were adopted as more accurate, *Aryan* was restricted to the Indo-Iranian branch of the Indo-European language family. In Nazi terminology, the word was used to mean white and especially Nordic by race. Because of the disrepute of this third sense and confusion about the earlier senses, the term is now used in linguistics and ethnology only in the combination *Indo-Aryan*, referring to the INDO-EUROPEAN LANGUAGES of India.

**ASCII** [Pronounced 'Askee'; The abbreviation of, and the common term for, the *American Standard Code for Information Interchange*]. Also **ASCII code**. A set of computer codes devised in 1968 and standardized in 1982 as a means of storing and transmitting (American) English texts. The standard code covers 32 non-displayed control characters (such as 'start of text' and 'carriage return') and 96 displayed alphanumeric and other characters, every letter or other symbol having a number from 0 to 128: for example, 33 for *!*, 36 for *$*, 65 for *A*, 66 for *B*, 97 for *a*, and 98 for *b*. An *ASCII keyboard* contains all and only such symbols and enables them to be directly coded; *ASCII files* are text files set in ASCII only. The prime purpose of the code is compatibility among electronic networks, texts being composed in, or converted to, ASCII in order to be transmitted and received successfully. The system, at first used only in North America, has been rapidly adopted worldwide; however, because the standard code is inadequate for complex texts and for languages with writing conventions different from English, an *Extended ASCII* has been developed, containing letters with diacritical marks, some vulgar fractions, monetary symbols such as for the pound and yen, and a range of graphic symbols (255 in all). See CHARACTER SET, COMPUTING.

**ASEAN** [Pronounced 'Ah-SEE-an' or 'AY-sian']. The abbreviation of, and common name for, the *Association of South-East Asian Nations*, a regional organization for economic, social, and cultural cooperation formed in 1967 by INDONESIA, Malaysia, the PHILIPPINES, Singapore, and Thailand. BRUNEI joined in 1984, Vietnam in 1995, and BURMA/Myanmar and Laos in 1997. The working language of ASEAN is English.

**ASH**, also **æsc**, **aesc**. The scholarly name for the LIGATURE (upper case Æ, lower case æ or *æ*) of *a* and *e*, used in Old English orthography for a sound related to but distinct from the sound represented by each LETTER separately. The form æ is used in IPA for a not quite open, front unrounded vowel, higher than Cardinal 4 and lower than Cardinal 3, as in many pronunciations of *cat* /kæt/. This was probably the sound represented by the Old English symbol. See ALPHABET, RUNE.

**ASIAN ENGLISH**. See EAST ASIAN ENGLISH, SOUTH ASIAN ENGLISH, SOUTH-EAST ASIAN ENGLISH.

**ASPECT**. The grammatical category (expressed in verb forms) that refers to a way of looking at the time of a situation: for example, its duration, repetition, completion. Aspect contrasts with *TENSE*, the category that refers to the time of the situation with respect to some other time: for example, the moment of speaking or writing. There are two aspects in English: *the progressive aspect* ('We *are eating* lunch') and the *perfect aspect* ('We *have eaten* lunch').

**ASPIRATE**. A term in PHONETICS for the *h*-sound, as in *hope*. *Aspiration* is a delay in voicing: for example, the release of the voiceless stops /p, t, k/ is often followed by further voicelessness like a brief *h*-sound, as in *tick* /tʰɪk/. Such stops are not aspirated after an *s*-sound, as in *stick* /stɪk/. See AITCH, ARTICLE, H, HIBERNO-ENGLISH.

**ASSIMILATION**. **1.** In PHONETICS, a process of connected speech in which one sound becomes similar to another, neighbouring sound, as for example with the phrase *one man*, in which the /n/ of *one* is assimilated to the /m/ of *man* ('wum man'). **2.** The same process exhibited orthographically: for example, in the Latin-derived word *aggression* (originally *adgressio*), the *d* of the prefix *ad-* has been assimilated to the *g* of the base *-gress-*; in the informal English word *wanna* ('want to'), the *t* of both *want* and *to* have been assimilated to the preceding *n*. **3.** In LEXICOLOGY, the adaptation of items into one language from another, such as into English from French. The degree of assimilation of loanwords generally depends on the length of time since the borrowing took place and on the frequency of use. Compare the degree of spoken and written assimilation of *honour* (c.1400), *salon* (c.1700), *sabotage* (c.1900): see BORROWING, LOAN. **4.** In SOCIOLINGUISTICS, the absorption of speakers of one language or dialect into another. Immigrants into the English-speaking world experience pressure to adapt and different metaphors are sometimes used to discuss and even euphemize the processes involved: immigrants to the US are said to enter a *melting pot*, while immigrants to Canada become part of a *mosaic*.

**ASSONANCE** [Stress: 'ASS-o-nanss']. In RHETORIC and poetics, a resemblance or correspondence of sound between syllables or words, such as the repeated vowel in *easy to*

*please* and the repeated consonant pattern *b–t–d* in *bright-eyed and bushy-tailed*. Traditionally, the term has been reserved for vowel REPETITION alone and *consonance* has been reserved for consonants, but this distinction is now rare. Assonance has been described as both a kind of rhyme and an alternative to rhyme. The terms *ALLITERATION, assonance*, and *RHYME* identify kinds of recurring sound that in practice are often freely mixed together. In considering a poem, it may not be easy or useful to decide where one stops and another starts.

**ASTERISK**. A star-shaped mark (*), used in writing and printing: (1) To indicate a reference or annotation, especially a first footnote, in which case it follows the word, phrase, or sentence being marked in a text, and precedes the footnote or reference. (2) To mark a cross-reference in an encyclopedia or similar work: *\*Darwin* or *Darwin\**, meaning 'Darwin (see entry under that name)'. (3) To mark the omission of a letter, especially in four-letter words: *f\*\*k* for *fuck*. (4) In philology, to mark a reconstructed form not (yet) attested in a text or inscription: for example, the hypothetical Latin word *\*ultraticum* proposed as the source of English *outrage* and Italian *ultraggio*. (5) In linguistics, to mark a word, phrase, sentence, or utterance as unacceptable for grammatical, semantic, or other reasons: for example, *\*I went for to do it* discounted as a sentence of standard English. See ELLIPSIS.

**ATTRIBUTIVE**. A grammatical term contrasting with *predicative*. The attributive position is in front of a noun: the position of *new* in *a new house* and *steel* in *steel bridge*. It may imply a permanent attribute, as a result of which some adjectives and most nouns can only be attributive: *an atomic scientist* but not *\*the scientist was atomic*; *the greenhouse effect* but not *\*the effect is greenhouse*. Some attributive-only adjectives refer to relationships (a *former* chairman), intensify a noun (It's a *downright* swindle), or limit it (the *only* time, the *main* idea). Some adjectives that are both attributive and predicative can have a special meaning when attributive (my *late* uncle, a *certain* person, a *perfect* nuisance, a *good* listener, *poor old* you). Some phrases that are otherwise not hyphenated are hyphenated when attributive: *well known* in *a well-known politician*, *round the clock* in *a round-the-clock vigil*, right to life in the right-to-life movement, but hyphens are not usual after an adverb ending in -ly (contrast a carefully written report with a well-written report). See JOURNALESE, PARTICIPLE, PHRASE WORD, PREDICATIVE ADJECTIVE, SENTENCE WORD.

**ATTRIBUTIVE NOUN**. A noun that modifies another noun: steel in steel bridge; London in London house. Nouns used in this way are sometimes said to be adjectives or to behave like adjectives. They are generally not used predicatively: the bridge is steel is possible, *the house is London impossible. Phrases with attributive nouns are common, and are similar to COMPOUND NOUNS like teapot and coffee jug. However, such phrases have the same stress patterns as adjectival phrases (equal stress: a bíg hóuse, a Lóndon hóuse), but compounds take contrastive stress, emphasizing the first element in a pair: the WHITE Hóuse in Wáshington, rather than the white hóuse next dóor; COFfee pót as opposed to stéel brídge. In answer to questions or for emphasis, however, phrases with ATTRIBUTIVE nouns are contrastively stressed and sound like compounds: What kind of bridge is it?—A STEEL brídge. Noun compounds and phrases with attributive nouns can usually be paraphrased in the same way: A steel brídge a bridge made of steel; a coffee pot a pot for (making) coffee (in). An attributive noun can modify a compound (china in a chína téapot) and one compound can modify another attributively (STRIKE committee modifying POLicy decísion in a STRIKE committee POLicy decísion). Such phrases are numerous and unpredictably creative, especially when they incorporate one or more loanword: alfresco staircase, glissando laugh, goy Zionist, Uzbek mafia. See EPONYM.

**AUREATE DICTION**, also **aureate language**, **aureation**. An ornate style fashionable among such 15c poets as John Lydgate in England and William Dunbar in Scotland, whose aim was to gild or 'illumine' the vernacular with classicisms, such as superne and eterne in 'Hale, Sterne Superne! Hale, in eterne, In Godis Sicht to schyne!' (Dunbar, Ballad of Our Lady). Later critics have generally regarded the results as florid and overdone. See DICTION, EUPHUISM, INKHORN TERM.

**AUSTRALASIAN ENGLISH**, sometimes **Antipodean English**, **Austral English**.

AUSTRALIAN ENGLISH and NEW ZEALAND ENGLISH taken together; all three terms have been popular in the past as a reflection of the similarities between the two varieties, but have fallen into disuse. Similar histories led to near-identity of the varieties: both are non-rhotic and based on late 18c southern BrE, and the lexicon of each has been heavily influenced by immigration from rural Britain. It is arguable that elements of ScoE are evident in New Zealand, as are elements of IrE in Australia, but the differences between two countries were never substantial enough to distinguish speakers with any certainty. As late as 1970, Australians could only volunteer that the speech of New Zealanders was more 'English', while some New Zealanders saw AusE as more 'broad'. Speakers of BrE and AmE could normally do no more than distinguish the two from the English of South Africa. Linguists commonly treated the varieties together in the same publications, under such headings as 'Australia and New Zealand'.

Since c.1970, however, AusE and NZE have begun to show a publicly noted divergence in phonology almost entirely due to a shift in the NZ short front vowels, which have been raised and retracted. One effect of this shift has been the merging of /ɪ/ with /ə/. Australians now characterize New Zealanders as eating 'fush and chups', while New Zealanders return the compliment by hearing Australian 'feesh and cheeps'. Phonologically inspired graffiti near Bondi Beach in Sydney run: NEW ZEALAND SUCKS, AUSTRALIA SEVEN. The merging of /ɪ + ə/ with /ɛ + ə/ in most speakers, so that ear and air become homophones, further reduces the phonemic inventory of NZE. The rapidity of these changes has produced a distinctive age-grading in NZE phonology. Speakers over 50 cannot often be identified as New Zealanders or Australians, except by a degree of /ɪ/ retraction. Those under 30, however, show that the notion of a uniform spoken 'Australasian English' is out of date. Observations suggest that some Australians may be following the NZ lead in the vowel shift, but the pattern appears to be increasing divergence from the old near-identity. Younger speakers of AusE and NZE appear on the whole to respond readily to the opposing linguistic stereotypes.

**AUSTRALIAN**. **1**. Australian English: 'English and French spoken; Australian understood' (O. Hogue, *Trooper Bluegum at the Dardanelles*, 1916). **2.** Australian bad language: 'Then he began to speak some pure Australian, and the language that came out of the hole in that driver's face heated the air for yards around' (*Honk*, France, 1915).

# ■ AUSTRALIAN ENGLISH ——— ■

Short form *AusE*. The English language as used in Australia. It has a short history, reflecting some 200 years of European settlement, and an even shorter period of recognition as a national variety, the term being first recorded in 1940. It is only since then that features of AusE have been regarded as distinctively and respectably Australian, instead of as evidence of colonial decline from the norms of the STANDARD ENGLISH of England.

**Background**. Initially, and uniquely, a majority of the British colonies in Australia were penal. As they expanded and as free colonies were developed, immigrants using languages other than English were insignificant. Relations with the Aborigines were generally poor and after an initial intake of words from their languages (such as *boomerang, dingo, kangaroo, koala, kookaburra, wombat*) were not conducive to extensive borrowing. The settlers were almost all Anglo-Celtic and geographical isolation was of great importance. The preoccupations of the colonists were the discovery and exploration of a new land, rich in exotic flora and fauna, and pastoral occupations such as raising sheep and cattle under circumstances vastly different from 'the Old Country'. In the late 20c, however, Australians are predominantly urban and increasingly multicultural. The major areas of lexical growth are international, as in computing and surfing. In the 19c, the situation was the reverse.

**Pronunciation**. The most marked feature of the Australian accent is its homogeneity, with no regional differences as marked as those in BrE and AmE, though recent studies have associated particular phonological characteristics with state capitals. There is, however, a social continuum in which three varieties are generally recognized: *Broad Australian, General Australian*, and *Cultivated Australian*. Of these, Cultivated Australian most closely approaches British RP and Broad Australian most vigorously exhibits distinctive regional features. It is generally assumed that the Australian accent derives from the mixing of British and Irish accents in the early years of settlement. However, although most convicts and other settlers came from London, the Midlands, and Ireland, the influence of the original accents cannot be conclusively quantified. The present spectrum was probably established by the early 19c.

The major features of AusE pronunciation are: (1) It is non-rhotic. (2) Its intonation is flatter than that of RP. (3) Speech rhythms are slow, stress being more evenly spaced than in RP. (4) Consonants do not differ significantly from those in RP. (5) Vowels are in general closer and more frontal than in RP, with /i/ and /u/ as in *tea, two* diphthongized to /əɪ/ and /əʊ/ respectively. (6) The vowel in *can't dance* may be /æ/ or /a/. (7) The schwa is busier than in RP, frequently replacing /ɪ/ in unaccented positions, as in *boxes, dances, darkest, velvet, acid.* (8) Some diphthongs shift, RP /eɪ/ towards /ʌɪ/, as in *Australia, day, mate*, and /aɪ/ towards /ɒɪ/, as in *high, wide.* (9) Speakers whose first language is not English or who have a bilingual background (Aboriginal, immigrant) often use sounds and a delivery influenced by the patterns of the first or other language. (10) The name of the letter *h* is often pronounced 'haitch' by speakers wholly or partly of Irish-Catholic background.

**Grammar and vocabulary**. There are no syntactic features that distinguish standard AusE from standard BrE, or indeed any major non-standard features not also found in Britain, but there are many distinctive words and phrases. However, although AusE has added some 10,000 items to the language, few have become internationally active. The largest demand for new words has concerned flora and fauna, and predominant occupations like stock-raising have also required new terms. Because of this, AUSTRALIANISMS are predominantly naming words: single nouns (*mulga* an acacia, *mullock* mining refuse, *muster* a round-up of livestock), compounds (*black camp* an Aboriginal settlement, *black tracker* an Aboriginal employed by the police to track down missing persons, *black velvet* Aboriginal women as sexual objects, *red-back* a spider, *redfin* a fish, *red gum* a eucalypt), nouns used attributively (*convict colony* a penal colony, *convict servant* or *convict slave* a convict assigned as a servant).

***The penal settlements***. The first settlements were penal colonies and until 1868, when transportation ceased, a vocabulary similar to that in a slave society described the life of the convicts. A major distinction was maintained between *bond* and *free*, as in *free emigrant*, *free native*, *free labourer*, *free servant*, and the distinction between *free* and *freed*. The settlements were populated in part by convicts and the attendant military forces, in part by free settlers. Though convicts who had served their sentences or obtained pardons (known from 1822 as *emancipists*) became *free* in their own eyes and those of the law, they often had difficulty escaping the stigma of servitude and obtained only a measure of freedom, being known by the *exclusives* or *exclusionists* as *free convicts* or *freed men*.

***Stock-raising***. Concomitantly, the land was explored and opened up for settlement and the stock-raising industry was developing. *Squatters* (stock-raisers or *graziers* occupying large tracts of Crown land under lease or licence) moved inland from the *limits of location* (the frontier of settlement) into the *back country* or *back of beyond* in search of land suitable for *runs* (tracts of grazing land) or *stations* (ranches). They looked for *open* land (free from forest or undergrowth), seeking *open forest* or *open plains*, and using words like *brush* (dense natural vegetation), *bush* (the distinctive Australian natural vegetation), *mallee* or *mulga* (forms of natural vegetation giving their name to their habitat), and *scrub* (generally, poor vegetation) to describe features of an unfamiliar environment. The stock industry employed *overseers* or *superintendents* (both convict terms), *stockmen*, and *rouseabouts* (general hands). *Drovers* travelled stock long distances *overland*, the original *overlanders* driving stock from New South Wales to South Australia. The importance of sheep in opening up the country and establishing a frontier society was such that the occupational vocabularies of droving and shearing figure largely in Australian literature.

***The goldfields***. Gold was discovered in the 1850s, leading to movement between the Californian, Australian, and New Zealand goldfields. *Rushes* (first used of the sudden escape of a number of convicts and then of the sudden movement of a number of miners to a particular place or *goldfield*) followed when a *prospector* (*gold-finder*, *gold-hunter*, *gold-seeker*) made a *find* and established a *claim*. A number of mining terms originated in Australia, but many are shared with other varieties of English, and the importance of the discovery of gold, and of the rushes that followed, lies in the mobility it encouraged and the effect of this on the homogeneity of the accent.

***Colloquialisms***. A growing sense of national identity was fostered by involvement in the First World War. The line between formal and informal usage is perhaps less rigidly drawn in Australia than elsewhere, colloquialisms being more generally admissible than in Britain. In informal usage, the suffixes *-ie* or *-y* and *-o* or *-oh* are freely attached to short base words (*roughie* a trick, *tinnie* a can of beer, *bottle-oh* a bottle merchant, *plonko* an addict of *plonk* or cheap wine, *smoko* a work break) and clippings (*Aussie* an Australian, *arvo* an afternoon, *barbie* a barbecue, *Chrissy* Christmas, *compo* workers' compensation, *derro* a derelict or down-and-out, *reffo* a refugee).

**Kinds of Australianism**. In terms of origin and structure, Australianisms fall into six categories: (1) Words from Aboriginal languages: *boomerang* a throwing weapon, *corroboree* a ceremonial dance, *jackeroo* a trainee farm manager, *kangaroo* a large hopping marsupial, *kookaburra* a kind of bird, *wombat* a burrowing marsupial. (2) Extensions of pre-existing senses: *bush* natural vegetation, or rural as opposed to urban life, *station* a garrison, colonial outpost, tract of grazing land, ranch. (3) Novel compounds: *bushman* someone skilled in traversing the bush, *bushranger* an armed bandit; *convict overseer* a convict appointed to supervise other convicts, *convict police* convicts appointed as police; *cattle/sheep station* station for raising cattle or sheep, *station black* an Aboriginal employed on a station; *stock agent* someone buying and selling livestock, *stockman* someone employed to tend livestock. (4) Novel fixed phrases: *black bream*, *black swan*; *colonial ale*, *colonial tobacco*; *native plum*, *native potato*; *red ash*, *red cedar*; *white box*, *white cockatoo*; *wild banana*, *wild spinach*. (5) Coinage: *emancipist* a freed convict, *go slow* a form of industrial protest in which employees work to rule (now international), *woop-woops* remote country. (6) Words with greater currency in Australia than elsewhere include new applications of words from British regional dialects: *dinkum* reliable, genuine, *dunny* a privy, *larrikin* a hooligan, *wowser* a killjoy.

**Style and usage**. By and large, printed English is much the same as elsewhere. The authoritative style guide is the Australian Government Printing Service's *Style Manual for Authors, Editors and Printers*, first published in 1966 and in its 4th edition. The manual was intended to set standards for government publications, but is widely used and has received input from the community at large through the Macquarie *Style Councils*. An informal guide is Stephen Murray-Smith's *Right Words: A Guide to Usage in Australia* (Viking, 1987, revised edition 1989). Where BrE and AmE spelling norms differ, BrE is preferred: *honour*, but *Labor* the name of the political party, *centre*, *licence*. The *-ise* spelling, as in *realise*, is generally preferred to *-ize*.

**Strine and stereotyping**. Australian usage has attracted comic stereotyping. The term *STRINE* refers to a kind of stage Australian in which vowels are distorted and syllables reduced, as in *strine* itself, collapsing the four syllables of *Australian* to one, and in *Emma Chisit*, a joke name derived from *How much is it?* The usage of the comedian Barry Humphries (b.1934), created by exaggerating certain features of pronunciation, delivery, or vocabulary, reflects a longstanding deference to BrE models combined with a new-found and exuberant recognition of national identity. Humphries' use of English has contributed both to colloquial idiom and a widespread perception of AusE as casual and vulgar. His characters include Dame Edna Everage (Average), a suburban Melbourne housewife turned megastar, Sir Les Patterson, an Australian 'cultural ambassador', and Barry McKenzie, an *ocker* (uncultured Australian male) in a comic strip in the British satirical magazine *Private Eye*.

**Social issues**. Until recently, Australia was determinedly assimilationist. Although immigrant languages such as Greek and Italian are now accorded the status of *community languages*, and bilingualism is actively encouraged by the government, the impact of these languages on AusE has been negligible. Two issues currently dominate the linguistic scene:

*Multiculturalism*. The arrival of immigrants (locally known as *migrants*) is slowly converting a homogeneous Anglo-Celtic society into a multilingual, multicultural society that is more or less tolerant of difference. A recent development has been the publication of a *National Policy on Languages* (J. Lo Bianco, 1987), a report commissioned by the Commonwealth Department of Education in 1986, a key document for federal and state initiatives to improve the teaching of English as a first and a second language, promote bilingualism, especially in those whose only language is English, and preserve and foster the teaching of community languages, including Aboriginal languages. Important also has been the increased prominence of ABORIGINAL ENGLISH within the spectrum accessible to the average Australian.

*American, British, and New Zealand influence*. Despite a new-found sense of independence (including the export of Australian films and television series), AusE is subject to the media-borne influences of BrE and AmE. By and large, because of traditional ties, there is less resistance to BrE than to AmE, particularly in pronunciation and spelling. Although it is 1,200 miles away, New Zealand is considered to be a close geographical, cultural, and linguistic neighbour. The constant movement of labour between the two countries ensures continuing exchange and sharing of features with NZE. See AUSTRALASIAN ENGLISH, DIALECT IN AUSTRALIA, NEW ZEALAND ENGLISH.

**AUSTRALIANISM**. A word, phrase, pronunciation, idiom, or other usage peculiar to, or particularly common in, Australia. Australianisms include loans from Aboriginal languages, such as *kangaroo*, *wombat* names of kinds of marsupial, and 'national treasures' such as *cobber* a companion, friend, *ocker* a rough and uncultivated Australian male. See AUSTRALIAN ENGLISH.

**AUSTRALIAN LANGUAGE**. **1.** An Australian aboriginal language: 'In no Australian language is there any word for "five"' (J. Fraser, *The Aborigines of Australia*, 1888). **2.** AUSTRALIAN ENGLISH: 'The Australian language developed during the 19th century, first mainly in the penal settlements' (Richard D. Lewis, 'Let's Talk Strine', in *The Linguist*, Vol. 30 No. 2, 1991). **3.** Especially formerly, foul language used by Australians: 'I tried to back the bullocks, but they scorned me utterly, in spite of the Australian language I used' (M. Roberts, *Land Travel and Sea-Faring*, 1891). See AUSTRALIAN.

# AUSTRALIAN PLACE-NAMES

The place-names of Australia reflect mixed linguistic origins over some 300 years, and fall into three broad types:

**1. *Adoptions from Aboriginal languages*** Recorded by European explorers, especially from the 1820s onward, or borrowed and somewhat Anglicized by settlers, such names are usually polysyllabic, often with sets of double letters, as in *Boggabri, Gunnedah, Indooroopilly, Murrumbidgee, Tantanoola, Wollongong,* and *Wooloongabba.* A number are reduplicative, as in *Tilba Tilba, Wagga Wagga,* and *Woy Woy.* The meanings of Aboriginal names are often uncertain: for example, the name of the Australian capital, *Canberra,* may mean either 'meeting place' or 'woman's breasts' (after a pair of hills).

**2. *Transfers and inventions by British settlers*** These relate mainly to place-names in the British Isles, notable individuals, and geographical descriptions. Transferred place-names include *Morpeth, Newcastle, Perth,* and *Windsor.* Names commemorating people related either to those in Britain in earlier colonial times (who may never have seen or wanted to see Australia) such as *Adelaide* (after William IV's queen), *Hobart* (after a Secretary of State for War and the Colonies), *Melbourne* (after a prime minister), and *Wellington* (after the Duke of Wellington), or people prominent in Australia, as with *Brisbane* (after a governor), *Lake Eyre* (after an explorer), *Ayers Rock* (after a premier of South Australia), and *Reynella* (after John Reynell, who established a vineyard there).

**3. *Survivals from Dutch and French explorations*** These include *Grotte Eylandt* and *Rottnest* straight from Dutch, and the Dutch/English hybrids *Arnhem Land* (after the name of a ship in turn named after a city in the Netherlands), and *Van Diemen's Land* (after Anthony van Diemen, a governor of the Dutch East Indies, a name duly replaced by the Anglo-Latin *Tasmania,* for the Dutchman explorer Abel Tasman, the first European to visit the island). Hybrid names arising out of those given by French explorers include *Huon River* and *D'Entrecasteaux Channel,* while such names as *Freycinet Peninsula* and *La Perouse* (a Sydney suburb) commemorate explorers themselves.

***Terra Australis.*** The name *Australia* is an adaptation of Latin *Terra Australis,* from the original *terra australis incognita* ('unknown southern land'), the name for a continent that some geographers reckoned should exist to the south of Asia and Africa. Exploration established that there were in fact two distinct land masses, now known as *Australia* and *Antarctica* ('place opposite the Arctic'). In the mid-17c, the Dutch charted the western coastline of a land mass they called *New Holland,* and in 1707 Captain James Cook charted what was later recognised as the eastern coastline of the same mass, to which he gave the name *New South Wales.* The explorer Matthew Flinders favoured the name *Australia* for what came to be seen as a distinct 'new' continent; promoted by Lachlan Macquarie, it became from the 1820s the cover term for all the British colonies throughout the continent. The wider term *Australasia* ('southern Asia'), which was sometimes used for the same area, currently refers to Australia, New Zealand, and the adjacent islands of the Pacific.

***AUSTRALIAN LANGUAGE, The***. The title of a book on Australian English by Sidney James Baker (1912–76), a New-Zealand-born journalist working in Sydney (1945, Angus & Robertson; 1966, revised, Currawong). Baker attempted to do what H. L. Mencken had done for AmE: establish the independence of the variety and find in it the fullness of an Australian cultural identity. Always tendentious, often idiosyncratic, frequently exasperating because assertive and undocumented, the work has none the less been popular and influential. Baker was interested primarily in the colloquial and in slang. Drawing on written and oral sources, he compiled lists of words from all walks of life, many subsequently shown not to be exclusively Australian. However, his division of local vocabulary into such subject areas as the bush, the road, and the city was influential in shaping the perception of AusE.

**AUSTRALIAN LANGUAGES**. Some 200 Aboriginal languages were spoken in Australia when British settlers arrived in the later 18c. About 50 are now extinct, 100 are dying, and some 50 are in active first-language use, especially along the north coast of western and central Australia, on Cape York, and in the western and central interior: that is, in places remote from major population centres. There are several thousand speakers of dialects of the *Western Desert Language* (the best-known of which is Pitjantjatjara) and of Aranda, around Alice Springs. There are many more speakers of Kriol and Torres Strait Creole. English is the first and only language of some 83 per cent of Australia's 16 m people. Minority languages during the 19c included Chinese in goldfield communities, German in a Lutheran settlement in South Australia, and Gaelic and Welsh in rural families. Non-British immigration increased greatly after the Second World War and multilingualism has been encouraged since the 1970s. Immigrant languages spoken by more than 100,000 people are (in decreasing order) Italian, Greek, Chinese. Arabic, and German. See AUSTRALIAN ENGLISH

**AUSTRALIAN PIDGIN**. A general name for contact varieties of English, used especially between Aborigines and European settlers from the late 18c, which spread from Sydney to other settlements. One of the most important, pidgin English in Queensland (also known as *Queensland Canefields English* and *Queensland Kanaka English*) was used on the sugar plantations *c.*1860–1910. It appears to be descended from *New South Wales pidgin*, an early CONTACT LANGUAGE taken north by explorers, convicts, and settlers, and spoken mainly by Melanesian indentured labourers rather than by Aborigines. Most returned to their home islands by 1910 and the pidgin currently exists only in fragmentary form among the elderly. However, it had a great influence on the subsequent development of *MELANESIAN PIDGIN ENGLISH*. Other varieties include *KRIOL*, in the Northern Territory and parts of Western Australia, and *Torres Strait BROKEN*, in the Torres Strait Islands. See ABORIGINAL ENGLISH, PACIFIC JARGON ENGLISH.

**AUXILIARY VERB**, also **helping verb**. A category of VERB that regularly accompanies full verbs such as *write, run, shoot, is* in *is writing, has* in *has run, may be* in *may be shooting*. In English, auxiliary verbs are customarily divided into: (1) The primary auxiliaries *be, have, do*. (2) The modal auxiliaries or MODAL VERBS *can, could, may, might, shall, should, will would, must*. The marginal modal auxiliaries, also called *semi-modals*, are *dare, need, ought to, used to*. They are marginal because they do not share all the properties of the others or do not do so regularly. Auxiliaries have four properties: (1) They are used with the negative *not* to make a sentence negative: *Frank may buy me a sweater/may not buy me a sweater*. Most have reduced negative forms: *isn't, hasn't, doesn't, can't, won't*, but not usually \**mayn't*. (2) They form questions by changing positions with the subject: *Wendy has invited me/Has Wendy invited me?* (3) To avoid repetition, they can occur without a full verb: *Has Jonathan written to you yet?—Yes, he has*. (4) They can emphasize the positive, in which case they carry the accent: *David* *may not be there.—His mother told me he WILL be there*. The same properties apply to *be* as a full verb (*Jonathan isn't tired*) and particularly in BrE as an alternative to *have* as a full verb (*I haven't a headache*). In the absence of any other auxiliary, *do* is introduced for these functions: *Leslie didn't tell Doreen*; *Did Leslie tell Doreen?*; *Yes, he did*; *He DID tell her*.

The auxiliary *be* is used to form, with a following *-ing* participle, the progressive (*is employing, may have been proving*) and with a following *-ed* participle the passive (*is employed, may have been proved*). The auxiliary *have* is used with a following *-ed* participle to form the perfect (*has employed, may have*

*proved*). The modal auxiliaries convey notions such as possibility, obligation, and permission. They are the only verbs not to have a distinctive third-person form in the present: *He can/They can* contrasts with *He is/They are, He has/They have, He sees/They see*. Like auxiliary *do*, they are always the first verb in the verb phrase (*should have apologized, could be making, did tell*) and are followed by the bare infinitive. In standard English, two modal auxiliaries cannot co-occur, but they can in some non-standard varieties, such as Appalachian English *They might could come*. See MODALITY.

# B

[Called 'bee']. The 2nd LETTER of the modern Roman ALPHABET as used for English. It descends from the Phoenician symbol *bēth* ('house'), which was adopted by the Greeks as *beta*, B, then by the Romans as *B*.

**Sound values**. In English, *b* normally represents the voiced bilabial stop, with *p* as its voiceless equivalent: *bad/pad*. Word-final *b* is rare, occurring mainly in monosyllables (*hub*, *rib*, *scab*), but occasionally in longer words (*superb*, *disturb*, *cherub*).

**Double B.** (1) The doubling of *b* occurs when monosyllables with a short vowel are followed by *-er*, *-ed*, and *-ing*: *rob/robber/robbed/ robbing* (contrast the phonetically long vowel in *daub/dauber/daubed/daubing*). (2) Many disyllables contain double *b* after a stressed short vowel (*abbey*, *rabbit*, *ribbon*, *rubber*, *rubble*), but many others do not (*cabin*, *debit*, *double*, *habit*, *robin*).

**Silent B.** *B* is silent after syllable-final *m* (*dumb*, *numb*, *tomb*), including in some words of Germanic origin in which it was formerly pronounced (*climb*, *comb*, *dumb*, *lamb*, *womb*) and in French-derived words with final *mb* (*aplomb*, *bomb*, *jamb*, *plumb*, *succumb*, *tomb*). In a number of words, a silent *b* has been added by analogy: *crumb*, *limb*, *numb*, *thumb*. In some of these, it was created by back-formation from words of the type *crumble*, *thimble* (formerly without *b*). *Crum* began to be written with *b* in the 16c, but occurs without it in Johnson's dictionary (1755) and in some 19c dictionaries. Derivatives from *mb*-words mostly keep the silent *b*, as in *climber*, *lambing*, *thumbing*, but *b* is pronounced in such non-derivative polysyllables as *cucumber*, *encumber*, *Humber*, *slumber*. There is no *b* in *dummy*, derived from *dumb*, or *crummy*, derived from *crumb*, and although *b* is not pronounced finally in *bomb*, medial *b* is pronounced in *bombard*.

**Epenthetic B.** *B* is epenthetic in *debt*, *doubt*, and *subtle*, which entered English from French as *dette*, *doute*, and *soutil*. As in French, these words were given a *b* in deference to their Latin etymons *debitum*, *dubitum*, and *subtilis*. However, while French

shed *b* in *dette* and *doute* in the 18c and came to pronounce the *b* in *subtil*, English has kept a silent *b* in all three. EPENTHESIS also occurs after medial *m* in some words: for example, Latin *camera* and *numerus* became French *chambre* and *nombre*, English *chamber* and *number*. Compare German *fummeln* and *rummeln* with English *fumble* and *rumble*.

**BABY TALK**. Kinds of speech used by small children. When used by adults, it is sometimes known technically as MOTHERESE, *caretaker language*, *caregiver language*. In the utterances of young children there is little grammar, vocabulary is idiosyncratic, and pronunciation immature, such as *Dada gone car* (Daddy has gone in the car). Adults speaking to small children adopt simplified grammar, special vocabulary, and exaggerated intonations: *All gone*, *doggie* The dog has gone. The appropriateness of 'adult baby talk' is sometimes questioned on the grounds that to provide a child with such a distortion of normal speech hinders the process of language learning. However, many researchers consider that the simplified grammar and marked stress patterns have an important role in making the structure of speech more accessible to the child. Forms of baby talk are also used in jocular, intimate conversation. See CHILD LANGUAGE ACQUISITION.

**BACK-FORMATION**. The creation of one WORD from another by removing rather than adding an element: *laze* from *lazy*; *gruntled* from *disgruntled*. Such words are usually coined for effect or because people think they exist or ought to exist. Some offend for aesthetic or conservative reasons, such as *enthuse* from *enthusiasm* (1820s AmE), *intuit* from *intuition* (1770s BrE), *liaise* from *liaison* (1920s BrE). Some usages may be denounced as back-formations when they are in fact long-established words: for example, the verbs *aggress* and *resile* are attested from the 16c, but are often taken to be back-formed from *aggression* and *resilient*. To *back-form* is itself a back-formation. Back-formations may fill structural as well as semantic gaps: aircraft *formate* when flying in formation, commentators *commentate* when reporting on games. Stunt and nonce forms are common: 'Do your leching away from the office!' (Maurice West, *Backlash*, 1958). See NOUN-INCORPORATION, WORD-FORMATION.

**BACK SLANG**. A form of slang used especially in Britain, in which words are spoken or spelt backwards: *yob* boy (originally to disguise the word, now used to mean a 'backward' boy or lout); *ecilop* police, often modified to *slop* (*The slops are after you*). See COCKNEY, PRIVATE LANGUAGE, REVERSAL, SHELTA.

**BACK-SLASH**. See OBLIQUE.

**BAD ENGLISH**. An informal term for English that does not measure up to approved norms, because it is ungrammatical, poorly spelt, or uses expletives: 'What is called "bad English" in the usual sense may be highly effective in the appropriate context' (W. Nelson Francis, *The English Language*, 1967). See (A)ESTHETICS, GOOD ENGLISH, STANDARD ENGLISH.

**BADIAN**. See BAJAN.

**BAD LANGUAGE**. An informal term for expressions that offend against taste. Although often a weaker synonym of *foul language*, it is more likely to include obscene expressions and those that are blasphemous or abusive. The term does not usually include language considered stylistically bad, situationally inappropriate, or difficult to understand. See (A)ESTHETICS, SWEARING.

**BAFFLEGAB**. An informal pejorative term for fluent language that sounds impressive but confuses and confounds, and is often associated with politicians. In 1988, Senator J. Danforth Quayle, then a candidate for US Vice-President, explained his position on the need for a strategic defence initiative by saying, 'Why wouldn't an enhanced deterrent, a more stable peace, a better prospect to denying the ones who enter conflict in the first place to have a reduction of offensive systems and an introduction to defensive capability?' See JARGON.

**BAHAMAS, The.** Official title *Commonwealth of the Bahamas*. A Caribbean country and member of the COMMONWEALTH, consisting of 700 islands and 2,000 cays. The islands have a mixture of English, Amerindian, Spanish, and Greek names, as in *Grand Bahama*, *Great Abaco*, *Bimini*, *Andros*, *Eleuthera*, *Cat Island*, *San Salvador*, *Great Exuma*, *Long Island*, *Acklins Island*, *Mayaguana*, *Great Inagua*. Columbus visited the islands 1492. First European settlement 1647, by religious refugees from Bermuda. British colony 1717. Independence 1973. The term *Bahamian English* refers to a continuum of usage from creole to standard. It has been influenced by migration between the Bahamas and the US and by a tourist industry that caters mainly for Americans. Of all CARIBBEAN ENGLISH varieties, Bahamian English most closely follows AmE.

**BAHASA INDONESIA, BAHASA MALAYSIA**. See MALAYSIAN ENGLISH.

**BAJAN**, also **Badian, Bajun**. An abbreviation of *Barbadian* and the informal name for Barbadian Creole. Because British colonization started in 1627, Bajan is one of the earliest English-based CREOLES. The function of BARBADOS as a slavers' entrepôt for the Caribbean and North America made Bajan a contributor to the characteristics of such other creoles as GULLAH, JAMAICAN, and SRANAN. It has been so eroded by the spread of English that some scholars consider it better classified as a DIALECT than a creole. However, the presence of features similar to those of such conservative creoles as Jamaican allows its continued classification as a creole. See CARIBBEAN ENGLISH CREOLE.

**BAMBOO ENGLISH**. See EAST ASIAN ENGLISH, JAPANESE PIDGIN ENGLISH.

**BANGLADESH**. A country of South Asia and member of the COMMONWEALTH. Languages: Bengali (official), English for higher education, indigenous languages. Local links with English date from the 17c; from the 18c till 1947, Bengal was part of British India. In 1947, East Bengal became *East Pakistan*. In 1971, the territory seceded from Pakistan during a short war and became independent. During the Pakistani period, Urdu was the national language, and English was the official second language (used for administration, higher education, and as a link language between educated speakers of Bengali and Urdu).

Bengali came third. Resentment of Urdu led to a prolonged and violent language movement. When in 1987 the *Bangla Procolon Ain/Bengali Implementation Act* was passed, Bengali became the main language of education and English ceased to be the official second language. It continues, however, to be used as the language of the higher law courts and of South Asian communication, and has a place in radio and television. A number of newspapers and magazines are published in English. In 1989, English was made a compulsory language for primary and secondary education: a pass in Bengali and English is mandatory for the Secondary Certificate. At university level, English is a popular optional subject. English as used in Bangladesh is similar to that in West Bengal in India. See SOUTH ASIAN ENGLISH.

**BANTU**. A term with a neutral, scholarly use throughout the world and, especially formerly, a sociopolitical use in SOUTH AFRICA that, in the context of apartheid, was largely pejorative and is therefore disliked by black South Africans. The international sense relates to a group of over 300 widely distributed and closely related languages of Black Africa south of a line from CAMEROON to KENYA, and by extension to c.60m people of various ethnic backgrounds who speak these languages. The *Bantu languages* belong to the Niger–Congo family and include: Douala in Cameroon, Ganda in UGANDA, Kongo in Zaïre, Nyanja in MALAWI, Shona and Ndebele in ZIMBABWE, Sotho in LESOTHO and South Africa, Tsonga in Mozambique and South Africa, Tswana in BOTSWANA and South Africa, Siswati in SWAZILAND, and Xhosa and Zulu in South Africa. The most widely used Bantu language is SWAHILI, a LINGUA FRANCA of East and Central Africa that has been strongly influenced by ARABIC. The original Bantu-speaking peoples appear to have originated in the region of Cameroon. In the structure of their languages, bases and affixes play a pre-eminent role: for example, from the base *Tswana* are formed *Batswana* the Tswana people (formerly rendered in English as *Bechuana*), *Motswana* an individual Tswana, *Botswana* land of the Tswana, and *Setswana* the Tswana language. Bantu loanwords in English are relatively few. Among them are: the animal names *impala*, *zebra*; *boma* a thorn-bush enclosure; (Zulu) *impi* regiment,

*indaba* gathering, conference; (Swahili) *uhuru* freedom. English words associated with the Bantu-speaking peoples can be etymologically deceptive: Swahili *bwana* (master, boss) is from Arabic *abuna* (our father); *assegai* (spear, lance) has passed from Berber into Arabic and thence to Southern Africa; *kraal* is from PORTUGUESE through AFRIKAANS, and is a doublet of *corral*. Bantu languages have borrowed extensively from English, especially in South Africa: for example, Zulu *ikhalenda* calendar, *ukheroti* carrot, *ukholiflawa* cauliflower; Xhosa *ibhentshi* bench, *ikati* cat, *ukubhaptiza* to baptise. See AFRICAN LANGUAGES, BORROWING.

**BARBADOS**, informal **B'bados**. A Caribbean country and member of the COMMONWEALTH. British colony 1627. Independence 1961. The Barbadian variety of English is rhotic with stronger nasalization than in other CARIBBEAN ENGLISH varieties. Word-final /t/ as in *about*, *but* is glotalized and /aɪ/ as in *mine*, *try* is narrowed to /əɪ/. See BAJAN.

**BARBARISM**. A non-technical term for a WORD considered to offend against good taste by combining elements from different languages, especially classical with vernacular, or being used in an unsatisfactory way. The following words were widely considered to be barbarisms when first used: *escalate*, back-formed from *escalator*; *finalize*, GREEK *-ize* added to LATIN *final*; *mob* a clipping of Latin *mobile vulgus*; *television* a HYBRID of Greek *tele-* and Latin *vision*. In *Modern English Usage*, FOWLER pointed to two problems: one might lack the information to decide whether an item is a barbarism or not; even if a philologist were consulted and a barbarism identified, people would not necessarily stop using it. In present-day usage, despite Fowler's strictures, concern for classical and linguistic purity is minimal and the coining of etymological hybrids is casual and massive. See CLASSICAL COMPOUND, CORRECT, SOLECISM, THEMATIC VOWEL.

**BARE INFINITIVE**. An INFINITIVE without *to* (*win* rather than *to win*), used: (1) After modal verbs: *I must go.* (2) In the pattern verb of perception plus object plus infinitive: *We heard the door bang.* (3) With some verbs: *Let go*; *Help me do this*; *Make them pay.* (4) After *rather than* and *sooner than*: *I'll go without* *rather than pay so much*. (5) In cleft sentences: *All I did was ask*.

**BARNES, William** [1801–86]. English schoolmaster, clergyman, dialectologist, and poet, born in Dorset of a farming family. In addition to textbooks, grammars, and articles on etymology, philology, archaeology, and local history, he produced a primer of OLD ENGLISH (*Se Gefylsta*, 1849) and collected dialect material. Most of his poetry was in DIALECT. He wrote two grammars and glossaries of the Dorset dialect, which, together with *Philological Grammar* (1854), compared features of STANDARD ENGLISH and the Dorset dialect with those of other languages. As a teacher and clergyman, he was distressed by the intricacies of English vocabulary, blaming its shortcomings, as he saw them, on its HYBRID nature. He set out therefore to counteract the classical influence. He revived Old English usages, such as *hearsomeness* and *forewit* to replace *obedience* and *caution*, drew on dialect, using *fore-elders* and *outstep* to replace *ancestors* and *remote*, made LOAN TRANSLATIONS from other Germanic languages, such as *birdlore* and *speechlore* to replace *ornithology* and *grammar*, and coined new words on VERNACULAR principles, such as *birdstow* and *beestow* to replace *aviary* and *apiary*. Although his PURISM had little impact, it was comparable to that in other parts of 19c Europe.

**BASE**, also **base form**. A WORD or LEXEME from which another is derived: the base of *sharpen* is *sharp*, of *dorsal* is *dors-*. Within a series, successive forms are bases: *sharp* for *sharpen*, *sharpen* for *sharpener*. Here, *sharp* is a primary base and *sharpen* a secondary base. A word that serves as a base is a *base word*; part of a word that serves as a base is a *BOUND base*. See MORPHOLOGY, ROOT, STEM.

■ **BASIC ENGLISH** ─────── ■

Also **Ogden's Basic English**, **Basic** [an acronym for British, American, Scientific, International, Commercial]. A reduced form of English devised in the 1920s by the writer and linguist C. K. Ogden, in cooperation with the critic I. A. Richards. It was favoured by the British Prime Minister Winston S. Churchill, with some support from the US President Franklin D. Roosevelt. Basic was an exercise in language planning, intended to extract from STANDARD ENGLISH the minimum grammar and vocabulary needed for everyday communication. Ogden saw it as serving three ends at the same time: an international medium in its own right, an introduction to 'full' English, and a kind of PLAIN ENGLISH. The name of the organization created to further Basic, the Orthological Institute, echoes such terms as *orthodoxy*, *orthography*, and *orthoepy*.

**Nature**. Ogden and Richards' *The Meaning of Meaning* (1923) contains in its chapter on definition the germ of Basic, which took final shape in 1928. Its minimal syntax has a fixed analytic word order (as in *I will put the record on the machine now*) and six affixes (*-s* for plurals and verbs, *un-* to negate adjectives, *-ed* and *-ing* to form participles, *-ly* for adverbs, and *-er* as an agent suffix). Ogden encouraged compounding such as *farmhouse* and *teapot*, *madman* and *blackbird*, and *get up*, *go out*, *put on*. The syntax was accompanied by a reduced vocabulary of 850 words in sets: 400 general words and 200 picturable words (600 nouns), 150 adjectives, 82 grammatical words, such as *across*, *all*, *can*, and 18 operators (such verbs as *get* and *put*). Operators had three roles: to replace more difficult words (*get* replacing *receive*, *obtain*, *become*), to form phrases that would obviate other verbs (*give money for* replacing *buy*, *give him a push* instead of *push him*), and to be part of a phrasal verb (*put together* replacing *assemble*). By such means, he considered that his operators could stand in for some 4,000 verbs. He accepted figurative extensions of meaning and supplemented the basic words with numbers, names, and lists of technical terminology according to need.

Ogden described the system in *Basic English* (1930) and *The System of Basic English* (1934). In 1940 he published *The General Basic English Dictionary*, which gave 'more than 40,000 senses of over 20,000 words, in basic English'. This work went into over 20 impressions until discontinued in the late 1980s, one of the first dictionaries for learners to use a defining vocabulary. In the introduction, Ogden stated:

> With its help, anyone who has had some training in the structure of English through Basic or any other system, will be able to make headway by himself with the English of Library, Radio, and Newspaper. . . . Words which are now come across only in the works of early writers and words which are the stamp

of the old learning based on Greek and Latin are looked on as no less the apparatus of the expert than the words of some branch of science, and have been given no more space. As far as possible a balance has been kept between the interests of the old education and the new, without overlooking the fact that, for the learner, what is current is more important than what is past.

This extract is composed entirely in Basic, which includes the word *apparatus*. The following passages compare Basic and standard English. The first is from 'Time in Philosophy and Physics' (Herbert Dingle, *Philosophy*, 54, 1979), the second its restatement in Basic:

*Original*. Let us look first at the question 'What is time?' Time is an inescapable—perhaps the most inescapable—fact of experience, but we cannot define it. The final word on this was said by St Augustine. 'What is time?' he asked, and replied 'If no one asks me I know: if I want to explain it to a questioner, I do not know.'

*Basic*. Let us give a look first at the question 'What is time?' Time is a fact of experience from which there is no getting away—possibly the only such fact of which this is completely true—, but we are unable to give any clear account of it. The statement which says the most it is possible to say about it was made by St. Augustine. His answer to the question 'what is time?' was: 'If no-one puts the question to me, I am certain about it; if I have a mind to give a questioner an account of it, I am uncertain.'

**Critical responses**. Most commentators have agreed that Basic is ingenious. Some have expressed sympathy for one or more of its aims, and enthusiasm for some or all of Ogden's principles and practices, but others have regarded it as pernicious. Basic was the subject of an acrimonious debate in the 1930s between Ogden and Michael West (see West *et al.*, *A Critical Examination of Basic English*, University of Toronto Press, 1934; Ogden, *Counter-offensive: An Exposure of Certain Misrepresentations of Basic English*, Cambridge, the Orthological Institute, 1935). West argued that Basic was a sort of PIDGIN English, and feared alike its success or failure: if successful, it would endanger such other forms

of simplified English as his own, and lead to a deterioration in usage; if a failure, it would cast doubt on the approach he endorsed. It was, he claimed, 'an incalculably grave disservice' to humanity. Ogden in turn accused West of 'grave errors' and 'ludicrous' views.

Both adverse and favourably disposed critics generally agree that Basic has three weaknesses: (1) It cannot be a world auxiliary language, an avenue into standard English, and a reminder of the virtues of plain usage at one and the same time. (2) Its dependence on operators and combinations produces circumlocutions at times unacceptable in standard English (as above, where Dingle's 'If no one asks me I know' becomes 'If no-one puts the question to me, I am certain about it'). (3) The Basic words, mainly common, short words like *get*, *make*, *do*, have some of the widest ranges of meaning in the language and may be among the most difficult to learn adequately. Charles C. Fries and A. Aileen Traver reported that for the 850 words the *OED* lists no fewer than 18,416 senses (*English World Lists*, Ann Arbor, 1950).

**Vernacular English**. Apart from a few items like *account*, *experience*, *machine*, *question*, and *apparatus*, Ogden's words are drawn from the vernacular stratum of English vocabulary. Like the 19c purist William Barnes, he appears to impute special merit to a core of words that were there before the majority of Latin and Greek 'big words' arrived. The syntax and word structures singled out for inclusion are Germanic, and the active-voice model for sentences rejects the passives common in academic and technical language, and originally based on Latin models. Like the early 17c lexicographer Robert Cawdrey, Ogden explains and replaces Latin-derived verbs like *impose* with vernacular verbs like *lay on*. However, as critics and many foreign learners have often pointed out, such vernacular forms as *lay on* can be harder to use than their Latinate partners.

**Conclusion**. In 1943, Churchill asked Harold Palmer to consider changes that would make Basic more flexible and useful as an international medium. Palmer suggested the addition of 'an adequate number of verbs' (so that, for example, *give him a push* could once again if necessary be *push him*), more grammatical words, and the replacement of non-standard compounds with their everyday equivalents. These recommendations were not adopted, but many word lists used in writing simplified readers and in introductory language courses, as well as defining vocabularies in learner's dictionaries, owe much to Ogden's pioneering efforts. Although the logical minimalism of Basic has few advocates and the system is now little used, its indirect influence has been considerable. See ARTIFICIAL LANGUAGE, RESTRICTED LANGUAGE.

**BASILECT**. **1.** The variety of language in a POST-CREOLE CONTINUUM most different from the STANDARD or SUPERSTRATE language: for example, Jamaican Creole as opposed to standard English. **2.** The least prestigious variety of a language, such as *Gutter Glasgow* in Scotland and *Brooklyn* in New York City. See DIALECT.

**BATHOS**. A term in RHETORIC for a ludicrous ANTICLIMAX: 'For God, for country, and for Acme Gasworks' (*Random House Dictionary*, 1987). Satire is often deliberately bathetic; in Swift's *Gulliver's Travels* (1726), the real-life disputes of Protestants and Catholics are presented as a Lilliputian war in which Big-Endians and Little-Endians fight over where to open a boiled egg.

**BAY ISLANDS**, Spanish *Islas de la Bahía*. A group of coastal islands in the western Caribbean, constituting a department of Honduras. Population: 18,744 (1983). The Bay Islanders speak a CREOLE descended from the English of British settlers, and of African and Carib slaves brought by them from the West Indies. The area was held by Britain between 1850 and 1858, then ceded to Honduras. See CARIBBEAN ENGLISH.

**BBC**, short form of *British Broadcasting Corporation*. A broadcasting organization, perhaps the best-known in the world: a non-commercial public service centred on London, with stations throughout the UK, providing radio and television services financed through licence fees paid annually by owners of TV receivers, as well as radio and television services throughout the world (the *BBC World Service*), financed by the Foreign and Commonwealth Office. The BBC broadcasts primarily in English, but its local services include Welsh and Gaelic and its world services are transmitted in 36 different languages.

## ■ BBC ENGLISH ■

A non-technical term for the speech of newsreaders and presenters of the national and international English-language programmes of the British Broadcasting Corporation. The phrase refers especially to the accent known to phoneticians as RECEIVED PRONUNCIATION (*RP*) and sometimes informally referred to as *a BBC accent*. The term is used in at least three ways: neutrally, in the sense of English as heard on BBC news; positively, as the exemplary English of BBC announcers; negatively, as the accent of privilege imposed on the nation by a monopolistic and allegedly patronizing state institution. In recent years, while RP and near-RP accents continue to dominate BBC newsreading and presentation, they are no longer exclusive for announcements and continuity on radio and television. Reasons include the limited numbers of RP speakers available for training as broadcasters, the rise of local radio and TV stations with a demotic style in which RP might be a handicap, a gradually increasing national use of speakers with other accents in tandem with a degree of social levelling, and changes in the nature of RP itself, including forms blending with some southern accents: see ESTUARY ENGLISH. The use of RP remains strong in the World Service, and for many overseas listeners the traditional BBC voice is equated with good English.

**The BBC and spoken English**. The BBC was founded in 1922 and in 1924 its managing director, John C. W. Reith, a Scottish engineer, published the book *Broadcast over Britain*. In a chapter devoted to 'The King's English', he observed:

> We have made a special effort to secure in our stations men who, in the presentation of programme items, the reading of news bulletins and so on, can be relied upon to employ the correct pronunciation of the English tongue.... I have frequently heard that disputes as to the right pronunciation of words have been settled by reference to the manner in which they have been spoken on the wireless. No one would deny the great advantage of a standard pronunciation of the language, not only in theory but in practice. Our responsibilities in this matter are obvious, since in talking to so vast a multitude, mistakes are likely to

be promulgated to a much greater extent than was ever possible before.

**The Advisory Committee**. To implement and supplement his language policy, Reith established in 1926 an *Advisory Committee on Spoken English*. Its chairman was Robert Bridges, the Poet Laureate and a founder of the Society for Pure English, and its honorary secretary Arthur Lloyd James, a Welsh phonetician at the School of Oriental and African Studies, U. of London. Its other original members were Daniel JONES, Professor of Phonetics at U. College London and compiler of the *English Pronouncing Dictionary* (1917), the actor Sir Johnston Forbes-Robertson, the naturalized American scholar Logan Pearsall Smith, and the Irish playwright and critic George Bernard SHAW. The committee's task was to make recommendations on policy and on the pronunciation of contentious words, both native and foreign, decisions being reached by majority vote.

***Recommended pronunciation***. Reith sought 'a style or quality of English that would not be laughed at in any part of the country'. It was generally agreed that the most appropriate medium was the accent which Jones at that time referred to as *Public School Pronunciation* and shortly afterwards began to call *Received Pronunciation*. The committee considered that PSP would convey a suitable sense of sobriety, impartiality, and impersonality. A necessary implication of the decision, however, was that posts as announcers would only be filled by men of a certain class and type. The committee's recommendations on the pronunciation of individual words were mandatory for announcers and newsreaders. To some extent, the presence of phoneticians on the committee ensured that the strict prescriptivism expressed by Reith in 1924 was to some extent mitigated. In the foreword to *Broadcast English I* (1928), the first booklet of recommendations (covering 332 words), Reith wrote: 'There has been no attempt to establish a uniform spoken language.... The policy might be described as that of seeking a common denominator of educated speech.' Lloyd James noted in the *BBC Handbook* (1929) that recommending certain pronunciations to announcers 'is *not* to be regarded as implying that all other pronunciations are wrong: the recommendations are made in order to ensure uniformity of practice, and to protect the Announcers from the criticism to which the very peculiar nature of their work renders them liable'. There was from the earliest years an element of tension and disagreement among those responsible for shaping language policy as well as among the listeners, some of whom took BBC usage to be authoritative while others did not.

***Recommended pronunciations.*** Pronunciations of individual words agreed by the committee were not written in IPA symbols but in a respelling system (with an acute accent marking stress) that would be more readily intelligible to the BBC's staff. Early recommendations that had no long-term effect include *allies* and *mishap* stressed on the second syllable, *immanent* as 'immáynent', to avoid confusion with *imminent*, *pejorative* as 'péejorativ', and *quandary* as 'kwondáiry'. The membership of the committee grew over the years, until it was over 20 strong. Bridges died in 1930 and Shaw became chairman; new members included Alistair Cooke because of his work with the American Dialect Society, the *OED* editor C. T. Onions, the dialectologist Harold Orton, and the lexicographer Henry Cecil Wyld. It was not easy to agree on the pronunciations of many words: in 1928 the committee recommended the pronunciation 'gárrazh' for *garage*, in 1931 changed to 'gárredge', then in 1935 returned to 'gárrazh'. In the same year, under the leadership of Lloyd James, it published its recommendations for place-names and family names in six volumes that served as an internal BBC standard for many years. Words whose recommended pronunciation has stood the test of time include *Auld Lang Syne* ('sign', not 'zine'), *centenary* ('sentéenäri', not '-tenn-'), *controversy* (stress on the first syllable), and *machination* ('mack-').

***Transition.*** In 1939, at the beginning of the Second World War, the committee was suspended. Lloyd James and Jones remained as advisers for the rest of their lives and day-to-day work was taken over by Miss G. M. Miller, assistant secretary to the committee, with the title of Pronunciation Assistant, and Miss E. D. Anderson, both Scots and graduates of London U. trained in phonetics. After the war, the committee was not reactivated and at an uncertain date in the 1940s the group became known as the BBC PRONUNCIATION UNIT, whose brief was to give guidance to newsreaders and announcers on the pronunciation of place and personal names.

**Reithian broadcasting**. From 1926, newsreaders and programme announcers were required to wear dinnerjackets when on duty in the evenings. In his memoirs, Stuart Hibberd observed:

> Personally, I have always thought it only right and proper that announcers should wear evening dress on duty. After all, announcing is a serious, if new, profession, and the wearing of evening dress is an act of courtesy to the artists, many of whom will almost certainly be similarly dressed if they are taking part in a programme from 8 p.m. onwards. There are, of course, certain disadvantages. It is not ideal kit in which to read the News—I myself hate having anything tight round my neck when broadcasting—and I remember that more than once the engineers said that my shirt-front creaked during the reading of the bulletin (*This—is London*, 1950).

Informality was forbidden, as were impromptu additions and statements of personal opinion. However, when the newsreader Frank Philips, after the late-night shipping forecast, said to sea captains, 'Good night, gentlemen, and good sailing', listeners approved of it as a pleasant and worthy departure from the norm.

**Changes in policy**. Although the official voice of the BBC continued after the war to be that of the public school and Oxbridge, in some kinds of broadcasting non-RP speakers were used, such as weather forecasting, sports commentating, discussions of gardening, and drama and entertainment. In the 1950s, the BBC's approach was challenged by the more demotic style of new Independent Television. The BBC began to use some announcers and commentators from regional stations on network current affairs, especially for sport. The new radio networks in the 1960s led to a further relaxation, and in 1979 the retired newsreader Alvar Lidell complained about declining standards in an article in *The Listener*. A committee was set up to monitor the situation, one of whose members was Robert Burchfield, editor of the *OED Supplement*. In a booklet called *The Spoken Word* (1981), he stated that although standards had in some

respects become more relaxed, there had been no decline. Radio 3 and the BBC World Service continued the RP tradition, but in 1989 the World Service announced a new policy of using announcers and newsreaders with a more representative range of accents. The process of relaxation continues and is especially noticeable in local BBC services throughout Britain.

## ■ BBC PRONUNCIATION UNIT – ■

A body of 'assessors and interpreters of educated usage' (*BBC Pronunciation Policy and Practice*, leaflet, 1974/9), set up in the 1940s as part of the BBC Presentation Department to replace the Advisory Committee on Spoken English, and now part of the BBC's Corporate Library Services: see BBC ENGLISH for preceding events. The Unit does not promote a standard BBC accent, but decides on the PRONUNCIATION of individual words and names. Its decisions are mandatory only for announcers and newsreaders, not for other BBC broadcasters, professional or casual. Any influence it may have on BrE is therefore indirect and limited. Where names are concerned, the Unit's policy covers two areas: those used in English-speaking countries and those from other languages.

**Names in the English-speaking world**. (1) *The United Kingdom*. For personal names and titles, the BBC uses the pronunciation preferred by the person(s) concerned. To check such usage, the Unit consults them or near relations or colleagues. Some names are perennial problems, because of different preferences in vowel quality and stress: *Burnett, Izard, Jervis, Laing, Powell, Symon(d)s*. For place-names, local educated usage is followed, established when necessary by consulting local clergy, councillors, or police. Special policies have been developed for such bilingual regions as Wales, the treatment of place-names generally requiring English pronunciations for English-based names (*Bridgend, Newport*) and Welsh pronunciations for Welsh-based names (*Ystrad Mynach, Llanfair*). Because Wales is only partly bilingual, Welsh-language names in English-dominant areas are given local Anglicized pronunciations. (2) *Elsewhere*. For such countries as Australia, Canada, New Zealand, and the US, the Unit seeks to follow personal and local usage, consulting appropriate government offices, the works of reference of local broadcasting organizations, established gazetteers, and resident BBC colleagues.

**Names elsewhere**. (1) Where a well-established pronunciation and perhaps written form already exist, such as *Florence* for *Firenze* and *Munich* for *München*, they are used. Some pronunciations, however, change over time: where once *Calais* and *Cadiz* were 'káliss' (like *chalice*) and 'káydiz' (like *sadist*), they are now pronounced more or less as in French and Spanish. *Seville* no longer rhymes with *Greville*, but is stressed on the second syllable. In difficult cases, the Unit assesses the situation and makes its decision: for example, that *Majorca* remains Anglicized with a *y*-sound ('mi-yórkă'), while *Marbella* has a Castilian-like pronunciation ('maarbélyă'). (2) When there is no established usage, an Anglicization is recommended, based on the native pronunciation or the usage of long-term English-speaking residents. Thus, *Chernobyl* in the Ukraine becomes 'chĕrnóbbil'. From time to time, adjustments are necessary: *Kenya*, once 'kéenyă', is now 'kén-yă', after a request from the Kenyan government.

**English-language usage**. The BBC policy leaflet notes that the Unit 'normally does not step outside its advisory role to lay down the law on the pronunciation of individual words from the general vocabulary stock; but occasionally after pressure from outside, it issues reminders about this or that "desirable" pronunciation. Some modern phoneticians might be inclined to consider even this misguided.' The aim is not to lead the way in language change, but to keep 'an ear to the ground for the moment when a new pronunciation begins to displace an old one'. The leaflet notes: 'The Pronunciation Unit is equipped to advise good speakers, indeed any speaker, on the finer or more controversial points of educated usage. It cannot eradicate overnight the habits of a lifetime from the speech of a bad speaker.'

In recent years, the Unit has found it 'less useful to make rulings on English vocabulary words, as educated usage now accommodates far more variation than formerly, but certain words of more than one pronunciation have one which causes less annoyance than the others, and in these cases we do make recommendations which we like broadcasters to follow: *controversy* (first syllable stress), *dispute* (second syllable stress for both noun and verb), *kilometre* (first syllable stress), *soviet* (*-o* as in *no* rather than in *not*), *cervical* (first syllable stress, *-i* as in *pin*, not as in *nine*)' (Graham Pointon, Director of the BBC Pronunciation Unit, in *English Today*, 15, July 1988). The seven published pre-war *Broadcast English* booklets have long been out of print, but in 1971 Oxford University Press published the *BBC Pronouncing Dictionary of British Names*, ed. G. M. Miller (2nd edition, enlarged, 1983). This work incorporates information from most of the booklets. The Unit publishes a series of Pronunciation Guides which it has compiled: lists of names of musicians, British politicians, and others, as well as Chinese syllables in their Pinyin and Wade-Giles transliterations, with BBC recommendations. It also publishes update bulletins for subscribers. The Unit is not perceived by the BBC as a guardian of the language but as a reflection of the preferred usage of the British public.

**BEACH LA MAR**. Also **Sandalwood English**. An English-based contact language used from the 1840s in parts of the New Hebrides (now VANUATU), New Caledonia, and the Loyalty Islands, and the ancestor of *BISLAMA*. The names derive from trade in sea slugs and sandalwood, the main products of the islands. See MELANESIAN PIDGIN ENGLISH.

**BELFAST**. The capital of Northern Ireland, settled in the early 17c with *planters* (settlers) mainly from England. The numbers of Scottish Protestants increased in the 18c and of Irish Catholics in the 19c, the often mutually hostile communities tending to live in different parts of the city. There is a range of usage varying according to level of education, with some homogeneity in working-class speech. Such words as *true* and *drew* sound like 'thrue' and 'dhrew' (an interdental pronunciation), *good* and *cap* sound like 'gyood' and 'kyap' (addition of the semi-vowel /j/), *cheap* and *speak* sound like 'chape' and 'spake' (with the vowel sound /e/), *push* and *took* rhyme with 'rush' and 'luck', *ever* and *yet* sound like 'ivver' and 'yit', *deck* and *penny* sound a little like 'dack' and 'panny' (having a close /a/ vowel), *board* and *course* sound like 'boored' and 'koors' (the /oʉ/ diphthong), *cold* and *hold* sound like 'cowl' and 'howl', *berry*/*bury* and *cherry* sound like 'barry' and 'charry', *bag* and *can* sounding like 'beg' and 'ken', *off* and *shop* sound like 'aff' and 'shap'. *Y'are not* is commoner than *you're not*. None of the above features are exclusive to Belfast, but their co-occurrence and the rapidity of informal speech distinguish Belfast speakers from other speakers of IrE. These features of pronunciation are associated with the vocabulary and the grammatical patterns described for non-standard ANGLO-IRISH, but lexical influence from ULSTER SCOTS also occurs, especially in the north and east. See NORTHERN IRISH ENGLISH.

**BELIZE** [Pronounced 'Be-LEEZ']. A country of the Central American Caribbean and member of the COMMONWEALTH. Languages: English (official), CREOLE, Spanish, Mayan, Carib. Colonized in the 17c by shipwrecked British sailors and disbanded soldiers known as *baymen*. After the Treaty of Paris in 1763, they became loggers. Supported by the Royal Navy, they defeated the Spanish in 1798. The colony of *British Honduras* was established in 1862, changed its name to Belize in 1973, and became independent in 1981. See CARIBBEAN ENGLISH.

**BEOWULF.** The longest of the known poems in OLD ENGLISH and the first major recorded poem in a European VERNACULAR language. Its 3,182 lines survive in one manuscript (BL Cotton Vitellius A. 15) of *c.*1000, which was damaged in a fire in 1731, first transcribed in 1787, and first published in 1815. The poem tells the story of its Geatish hero Beowulf in two parts: ridding the Danes of the monster Grendel and his mother, and a fatal struggle against a fire dragon after he became king of the Geats.

**BERLITZ, Maximilian Delphinus** (later **David**) [1852–1921]. German-American language teacher and organizer of the Berlitz Method. Born in Württemberg, Germany, he emigrated to the US in the 1870s and opened a language school in Providence, Rhode Island (1878), the first of many in the US and elsewhere. Among the languages taught by conversational means was English as a foreign language. From the first lesson, only the target language was used in class, and no translation was allowed. The teachers were native speakers of the language, and the materials used were so systematized and the directions so precise that it was possible to employ quite

young and relatively untried people as teachers. The Berlitz Method has often been referred to as the DIRECT METHOD, with the result that it has become associated with the method of the Reform Movement initiated by Wilhelm Viëtor and other scholars from the 1880s onwards. This, however, differed in using phonetic texts and phonetically trained teachers who were usually the same nationality as the learners, in using translation sparingly, and in having broader educational aims.

**BERMUDA**, formerly *Somers Islands*. A self-governing British dependency in the Western Atlantic, comprising 138 islands. Language: English. The islands were settled in 1612 by the Virginia Company, became a colony in 1684, and gained internal self-government in 1968. Bermudian English mixes BrE and AmE influences.

## ■ BIBLE ────────────── ■

A collection of sacred texts usually regarded as a unified whole and published as a book consisting of a number of books. For Christians these are in two groups, an Old Testament (OT), whose original texts are HEBREW (and some Aramaic), and a New Testament (NT), whose original texts are GREEK. The first five OT books are known in Hebrew as the *Torah* (instruction, law) and in Greek as the *Pentateuch* (five scrolls). Tradition ascribes them to Moses. The first seven make up the *Heptateuch* (seven scrolls). The TRANSLATION of all OT writings into Greek, including the Apocrypha or non-canonical texts, is known by the Latinate name *Septuagint* (seventy), after the number of scholars believed to have engaged in their translation in Alexandria (3–2c BC). The term *testament* (from LATIN *testamentum* a witnessed contract) reflects the Christian belief that God made two covenants with humanity, the first with the Hebrews as a chosen people, the second with the followers of Jesus Christ. When, in the 4–5c, St Jerome translated OT Hebrew and NT Greek into one language, Latin, the Christian scriptures in the West acquired a linguistic homogeneity that strengthened perceptions of the Bible as a single text providing an unbroken account of events and prophecies. Although generally aware of the heterogeneous origins of the Bible, Christians in recent centuries have tended not to dwell on them.

**The Bible as scripture**. The books of the Bible were accumulated over some 1,300 years and are not set out in the order in which they appear to have been written. Although there are names attached to most of them (such as the OT *Book of Job*, the NT *Gospel according to Mark*), there is no firm evidence of authorship for most of them and little indication of how they were edited into their present forms. Since the 18c, however, there has been close scholarly scrutiny of the texts and their sources. The Bible is a miscellany of genres: story, history, law, prophecy, song, poetry, and letters, making up a sacred 'encyclopedia' which has for centuries been a prime source of reading throughout the world. For Christians, it is the foundation document of their faith; some admit no other authority, while others respect or insist on certain pastoral traditions and later documents. The books of the OT and NT have reached their present number and arrangement by a process of adjustment and elimination over centuries. As a selection from a larger number of texts, they constitute the Christian canon and stand in contrast with the deuterocanonical (secondary) or non-canonical works known as the *Apocrypha* (Greek: hidden), which may or may not appear as an appendix to the OT in Protestant Bibles. Following a longstanding tradition, *The New English Bible* (1970, Oxford and Cambridge University Presses) appends the 15 traditional apocryphal works to the 39 canonical books of the OT, but excludes the various apocryphal gospels from the NT, which are regarded as non-canonical by all mainstream Christian groups. Its successor, *The Revised English Bible* of 1989, excludes both.

**The Bible as social archetype**. For cultures with their roots in medieval Western Christendom, the word *bible* is both symbolic and archetypal. The symbolism is explicit when the *Longman Dictionary of Geography* is reviewed as 'the geographer's bible' and Plain English campaigners describe Ernest Gowers's *Complete Plain Words* as 'the bible of techniques for clear writing'. It is implicit in the use of the definite article in such expressions as *the Dictionary* and *the telephone directory*, as if such works were as fundamental as *the Bible*. Both name and object are associated in many places with the Christian missions that often paralleled European colonial and commercial expansion. The ties between missionaries and colonialism were lightly touched on by Archbishop Desmond Tutu of South Africa on a visit to the US in 1984: 'When the missionaries first came to Africa they had the Bible and we had the land. They said, "Let us pray." We closed our eyes. When we opened them again we had the Bible and they had the land.'

**The Bible as literature**. The Bible, whether in the original or in translation, both in itself and because of its influence, is among the great literary achievements of the world. As such, it can be considered in terms of both its genres (poetry, prose, prophecy, gospels, and epistles) and its many translations. In recent decades, a sense of the uniqueness and inviolability of the Bible has given way to scholarly inquiry and an interest in content for its own sake, and the study of the Bible as a text, apart from and/or in addition to its significance as a religious document, has increased. In addition, interest in its language and rhetoric has been stimulated by scholarly study of how this work relates to and has influenced the culture of the peoples who were once part of Western Christendom. As the Canadian critic Northrop Frye has put it:

> My interest in the subject began when I found myself teaching Milton and writing about Blake, two authors who were exceptionally Biblical even by the standards of English literature. I soon realized that a student of English literature who does not know the Bible does not understand a great deal of what is going on in what he reads: the most conscientious student will be continually misconstruing the implications, even the meaning (*The Great Code: The Bible and Literature*, 1981).

**Biblical poetry**. The Bible's poetic aspect is most obvious in the Psalms, an anthology of pieces which have for centuries formed part of Jewish and Christian liturgies. There is also poetry in the prophetic books, the *Book of Job*, and elsewhere, but it has often been concealed by the prose form of the older English translations. The *Song of Solomon* is a cycle of love poems to which allegorical meaning was given by the early Church, and in the Authorized Version (AV) has the intensity of medieval and Tudor love lyrics (original spelling):

13 A bundle of myrrhe is my welbeloued
vnto me; he shall lie all night
betwixt my breasts.

14 My beloued is vnto me, as a cluster of
Camphire in the vineyards of Engedi.

15 behold, thou art faire, my loue:
behold, thou art faire, thou hast
doues eyes.

16 Behold, thou art faire, my beloued;
yea pleasant: also our bedde is
greene.

17 The beames of our house are Cedar,
and our rafters of firre.

Classical Hebrew poetry depends not on
rhyme and metre but on parallelism. The
phonetic pattern is almost impossible to reproduce in English, but the parallelisms of
thought can be seen in familiar versions
(modern spelling):

**Synonymous**. The second half-line emphasizes the first: 'The heavens declare the
glory of God: and the firmament showeth
his handywork' (Psalms 19: 1).

**Antithetical**. The second half-line contrasts
with the first: 'I see that all things come to
an end: but thy commandment is exceeding
broad' (Psalms 119: 96).

**Synthetic**. The second half-line supplements the first with a consequence or example: 'I did call upon the Lord with my
voice: and he heard me out of his holy hill'
(Psalms 3: 4).

**Progressive**. Building to a climax by repetition: 'Hear the right, O Lord, consider my
complaint: and hearken onto my prayer,
that goeth not out of feigned lips' (Psalms
17: 1).

**Stepped**. Each statement reinforced by a re-
frain, similar to many Border ballads: 'O
give thanks unto the God of all gods: for his
mercy endureth for ever. / O thank the Lord
of all lords: for his mercy endureth for ever'
(Psalms 136: 2–3).

The poetry of the Bible is expressed not only
in formal structure. There is much use of
imagery, usually direct and simple in keeping with the concrete thought and limited
lexical range of OT Hebrew. It reflects the
life of a people close to the wilderness, exposed to extremes of climate, and the constant threat of enemies. NT Greek imagery,
however, shows a more settled life of agriculture. Much of the linguistic power of
the Bible lies in the archetypal nature of its
imagery: fire and water, night and day,

wind and sun. Similes and metaphors are
common and animals and birds are frequent sources of analogy: 'He is like a
refiner's fire, and like fullers' soap' (Malachi
3: 2); 'His truth shall be thy shield and buck-
ler' (Psalms 91: 4); 'They were swifter than
eagles, they were stronger than lions' (2
Samuel 1: 23).

**Biblical prose**. Much of the Bible is narrative and its style immediate, like unadorned
speech:

OT. And Cain talked with Abel his
brother: and it came to pass, when they
were in the field, that Cain rose up
against Abel his brother, and slew him.
And the Lord said unto Cain, Where is
Abel thy brother? And he said, I know
not (Genesis 4).

NT. And all the city was gathered
together at the door. And he healed
many that were sick of divers diseases,
and cast out many devils; and suffered
not the devils to speak, because they
knew him (Mark 1).

The force of the stories lies not in em-
bellishment or subtle plotting but in
sequential events moving to a climax. They
can be exciting and dynamic, often moving
to a violent or tragic end like the sacrifice
of Jephthah's daughter or the death of
Absalom, or to rescue by divine intervention like the story of Abraham and
Isaac. There is little detail of characterization; people are described mainly in brief
physical terms. The good and the bad,
Moses, David, Jezebel, Elijah, Jonah, and
the rest come to life as they are seen acting
and responding to the consequences of
action.

There are some more sophisticated compositions: the *Book of Ruth* is a compelling
and well-knit novella, with a few interacting
characters and the finale of a fruitful marriage after tribulation. The *Book of Job* has
the qualities of epic drama as Job (with a
background chorus of friends) wrestles
with disaster and his changing attitude to
God, who at the end intervenes like a classical *deus ex machina*. Even the historical books
have tragic attributes: David is punished for
his hubris in numbering the people; Samson wins great victories but a fatal weakness
exposes him to the wiles of a false woman
and the catastrophe of blindness and cap-
tivity, followed by triumph in death. The
constant wars and feuds of the ancient

world have the grim vigour of the heroic sagas.

The books of the NT were written with urgency and immediacy, to spread the good news (gospel) of recent events and in expectation of the end of the world. The parables of Jesus, based on a tradition of moral tales, contain many vignettes of contemporary life: the sower, the shepherd and his flock, the woman seeking a lost coin, the farmer hiring labourers. The Gospels (Matthew, Mark, Luke, John) are a genre without counterparts in the ancient world, written not so much as biography but as to awake belief. Much of the NT is in the form of pastoral letters (the Epistles), written with conviction rather than in the forms of strict classical RHETORIC.

**Literary and popular impact**. In addition to its literary quality, the Bible has been an influence on ENGLISH LITERATURE and culture. Stories and characters from the Bible have been treated imaginatively by writers ranging from John Milton (*Paradise Lost* 1667, *Paradise Regained* 1671, *Samson Agonistes* 1671), to Christopher Smart (*A Song to David* 1763), Lord Byron (*Cain* 1821), and in the 20c James Bridie (*Jonah and the Whale* 1932) and Christopher Fry (*A Sleep of Prisoners* 1951). The style of the AV has influenced many, most noticeably John Bunyan's use of a Biblical style of narrative in *The Pilgrim's Progress* (1678–84). Swift praised the simplicity of Biblical English in *A Proposal for Correcting the English Tongue* (1712). The complex and eclectic style of Thomas Carlyle has the Bible as one of its strands. John Ruskin acknowledged the effect of frequent Bible reading in his early life and his prose sometimes echoes its more sonorous and stately passages. The language of hymnology has often been strongly biblical, especially in the compositions of John and Charles Wesley and Isaac Watts.

Because the Bible was for so long a part of the common cultural heritage of English-speaking people, ALLUSIONS and direct quotations are frequent in all literary genres. The speech of fictional characters includes many such references, often incidentally and naturally, but sometimes satirically exaggerated, as in Dickens's *Bleak House* (1853) and the Evangelical Cambridge group in Samuel Butler's *The Way of All Flesh* (1903).

Popular usage continues to incorporate biblical allusions such as *coals of fire, a soft answer, a broken reed, the root of all evil, a word in season, the eleventh hour, a thorn in the flesh, cover a multitude of sins, the old Adam, riotous living*. Page headings in the AV have contributed *the Prodigal Son* and *the Good Samaritan*, the latter adopted in part by the helping organization, the Samaritans. Many English forenames are derived from the Bible: the continuingly popular *John, Mary, Peter, James, Elizabeth, Thomas, David*, and the less frequent or once fashionable *Abraham, Isaac, Daniel, Rebecca, Enoch, Nathaniel, Martha*. The less virtuous characters of the Bible, like Jezebel, Herod, and Judas, have not been adopted, but Thomas Hardy introduces a character christened *Cain* in *Far from the Madding Crowd* (1874), because his mother got confused and thought that it was Abel who killed Cain.

**Translation**. Much of the literary quality of the Bible is lost in translation, even in the 'biblical' prose of the King James Version. English cannot reproduce the cadence of Hebrew poetry, such puns as the comparison of Peter to a rock (Greek *Pétros/pétra*), or the acrostic in the closing verses of *Proverbs*. However, in the 1611 version and other translations, writers have created a Bible tradition native to English, in which such themes as conflict and triumph, suffering and joy, can seize the imagination of readers with no knowledge of Hebrew or Greek, just as translation has served, in secular terms, to pass on through English the epics of Homer. The vigour and simplicity of OT Hebrew and NT Greek have to a great extent been successfully conveyed in biblical English, especially in narrative. Both often had a direct paratactic style, with strong, concrete images and vivid, physical metaphors. There is often repetitive and incremental emphasis, as in: 'Hast thou not knowen? hast thou not heard, that the euerlasting God, the Lord, the Creatour of the ends of the earth, fainteth not, neither is wearie?' (Isaiah 40: 28), and balanced antithesis, as in: 'The Lord will not suffer the soule of the righteous to famish: but he casteth away the substance of the wicked. Hee becommeth poore that dealeth with a slack hand: but the hand of the diligent maketh rich' (Proverbs 10: 3–4).

**Translators**. The early translations were made at a time of change, as the language moved from its 'Middle' to its 'Modern' phases, when printing and standardizing were becoming central elements in the spread of literacy, and when religious protest then reformation inspired the translators. They preferred the vernacular to a high Latinate style, because they wished their work to reach, and be understood by, the mass of the people. In the view of the martyred 16c translator William TYNDALE, ordinary English was better suited to translate both Hebrew and Greek than Latin and German, because: 'In a thousand places thou needest but to translate it into English word for word' (in 'Obedience of a Christian Man', 1528). Like the originals, Tyndale's style was paratactic and immediate. His frequent use of 'and' (following the Hebrew) may have influenced later generations of writers of English prose (compare the AV rendering of Mark, on p. 70). The early translators also influenced general vocabulary: the common word *nowadays* goes back to WYCLIFFE, and Tyndale's use of *beautiful* rather than the earlier and commoner *belle* and *fair* helped establish the word. *Peacemaker*, *long-suffering*, and *scapegoat* are other examples of his inventiveness. The vocabulary of the AV is relatively small, some 6,000 words of which a high proportion are vernacular.

**Quotation and allusion**. For centuries, the Bible was read both aloud and silently, and people were used to hearing long excerpts from it in sermons and speeches. After the establishment of lectern Bibles in all churches in 1538 and then the publication of the AV in 1611, the Bible was so well known that even unattributed quotations and allusions were instantly recognized. When Sir Richard Grenville said, 'Let me fall into the hand of God not the hand of Spain' (1591), he was adapting David's words in 2 Samuel (24: 14). The style of the AV directly influenced many writers, most prominently John Bunyan in *The Pilgrim's Progress* (1678), which opens:

As I walked through the wilderness of this world I lighted on a certain place where was a den, and laid me down in that place to sleep; and, as I slept, I dreamed a dream. I dreamed, and behold I saw a man clothed with rags standing in a certain place, with his face from his own house, a book in his hand, and a great burden upon his back.

**The early translations**. The translations of the Bible in the 15–17c have been a powerful influence on the development of English. The entire corpus of Modern English prose has grown up since, and been influenced by, the works of Tyndale and Coverdale, and during the formative period of the early translations there was little other widely available reading matter. Through private and public reading, the successive early translations introduced the general population to a range of genres, styles, and subjects distinct from song, folktale, and popular romance. The 16c Bible in particular provided a model of expression which was the chief written source of formal English for many people well into the 19c. There were translations of parts of the Bible in Anglo-Saxon times, associated with ALFRED and AELFRIC. Between the 11c and 13c, when Norman French was the dominant language and Latin the language of religious authority, translation into English lapsed, and though copies of earlier translations appear to have circulated, they have not survived. The translation into the 14c dialect of the East Midlands and London by John Wycliffe and such helpers as Nicholas Hereford and John Purvey was the first attempt to produce the complete Bible in English. It was hugely popular and widely circulated by itinerant *bible-men*, with manuscript copies of the NT selling for six months' wages; one copy of a few chapters sold for a load of hay. This translation was also important in helping to fix the dialect used as standard and spread it through England. Wycliffe's Bible was more often heard and listened to than read privately, and so influenced both those who could and those who could not read. Despite its being proscribed with severe penalties, some 170 manuscripts have survived.

**Sixteenth-century Bibles**. Wycliffe's translation was from the Vulgate and was not printed until after it had been superseded by the translations of Tyndale and Coverdale. These were made under the influence of the 'new learning' from Greek and Hebrew; Coverdale's was the first published translation into English and both translations had to be printed abroad, being at first smuggled into England as 'waste paper'. The first translation printed in England, in 1536, was a reprint of Tyndale's NT of 1534. Once Bible printing in England was legalized in 1537, publishing enterprise resulted in fresh editions such as *Matthew's Bible* (a synthesis of Tyndale and Coverdale with a commentary) and *Taverner's Bible*, a revised printed version of Matthew's.

The *Great Bible* of 1539 was the first officially authorized version, produced by a group headed by Coverdale and based on Matthew's. Largely printed abroad, where the technology was more advanced, this work went into seven editions in two years, because it was required in all churches and other versions were proscribed by law. The division of the Bible into chapters dates from the 13c, attributed both to Stephen Langton, Archbishop of Canterbury (d. 1228), and Hugo de Sancto Caro, who produced a concordance of the Vulgate in 1244. OT verses were numbered in the early 16c in Hebrew and in Latin, and Robert Estienne numbered the verses in his French NT in 1551. The numbering of verses was adopted in the English NT of 1557, the work of refugees in Geneva who undertook the revision of the entire English Bible, culminating in the *Geneva Bible* of 1560, which had both chapter and verse numbered. This work was also known as the *Breeches Bible*, because it described Adam and Eve as sewing themselves breeches. It included marginal notes which commended it to the Puritans, who wished to study it without need of priestly interpretation.

**The King James Bible** (also *The Authorized Version*; short forms *KJB, AV*). The popularity of the Geneva Bible prompted Archbishop Parker to revive a long-discussed project for an authorized revision approved by the English bishops. The Bishops' Bible was first published in 1568, a revision of Coverdale's Great Bible of 1539. One of the first acts of James VI King of Scots, on accession to the throne of England in 1603 as James I, was to approve a suggestion for a new translation, 'as consonant as can be to the original Hebrew and Greek . . . and only to be used in all churches of England'. He apparently appointed 54 'learned men' to work on the project, 50 of whom have been identified. They included scholars from Oxford, Cambridge, and Westminster (prominent among them Lancelot Andrewes, John Hardinge, John Harmer, John Reynolds, Henry Saville, Miles Smith, and Robert Spalding), working in five committees which invited comment and observations from the clergy in general as the work progressed. The rules for the project included: (1) Following the 1572 edition of the Bishops' Bible so far as fidelity to the origi-

nal sources would allow. (2) The division into chapters to be altered only where strictly necessary. (3) Where specially difficult passages occurred, consultation to follow with 'any Learned Man in the Land, for his Judgement of such a place' (*Rules to be Observed in the Translation of the Bible*). (4) Where a Hebrew or Greek word admitted of more than one possible meaning, one to be in the text, the other in the margin. (5) Any words that had to be inserted for colloquial reasons to be printed in italics. The new work appeared in 1611.

**Bible publication**. In England, the publishing rights of the AV are vested in the Crown and in practice limited to the printing house holding the royal appointment, together with the universities of Oxford and Cambridge, whose privilege under their 16c charters allowed them to publish bibles. This exclusive right of printing the Bible had earlier come into being in the reign of Elizabeth I. Since 1769, the Royal Printers have been Eyre and Spottiswoode, in London. In Scotland, the Lord Advocate, representing the Crown, holds the patent and approves the choice of publishers, in practice the Glasgow publisher William Collins (now part of HarperCollins). In the US, no such restrictions have been placed on the publishing of the Bible; many publishers have brought out editions of the AV, amending it on their own initiative and responsibility.

**Later translations**. The publication of the AV, though intended to be definitive, did not put an end to Bible translation, especially by Protestant nonconformists and would-be popularizers: for example, John Wesley, founder of Methodism, who in 1755 published his own NT for 'unlettered men who understand only their mother tongue'. Subsequent translations, from the *Revised Version* (1884) through to late 20c versions, have not had the aim of producing work in an improved literary style, but of claiming greater fidelity to the original Hebrew or Greek as understood by the most recent scholarship. Some of these claims have been contested and the translations have made no special impact on the language. The *Revised Version* was the result of over ten years' work by Protestant scholars in the UK and US, following a decision in the Church of England in 1870 to set up a group of its members to work with others, irrespective

## WELL-KNOWN QUOTATIONS FROM THE KING JAMES BIBLE

The AV has been acclaimed as a landmark in both religious literature and the evolution of the English language, an achievement that comprises all earlier Bible translation and that has served for many as a standard against which all subsequent Bible translation must be judged. Many also consider that its verbal beauty is unsurpassed in the whole of English literature. It has provided many quotations and allusions which have become proverbial, and has been quoted, knowingly and unknowingly, in literature and in conversation at every level for centuries, from pubs to Parliament. Well-known quotations include:

**Genesis**. And the evening and the morning were the first day; Be fruitful, and multiply, and replenish the earth; bone of my bones and flesh of my flesh.

**Exodus**. Let my people go; the burning bush; the golden calf; Eye for eye, tooth for tooth.

**Ruth**. For whither thou goest I will go.

**Job**. Man is born unto trouble, as the sparks fly upward.

**Proverbs**. Go to the ant thou sluggard; consider her ways, and be wise.

**Ecclesiastes**. Vanity of vanities; all is vanity.

**Isaiah**. For unto us a child is born, unto us a son is given.

**Jeremiah**. Is there no balm in Gilead?

**Matthew**. Repent ye: for the kingdom of heaven is at hand; The voice of one crying in the wilderness, Prepare ye the way of the Lord (quoting Isaiah).

**Mark**. My name is Legion; Suffer the little children to come unto me.

**Luke**. Judge not, and ye shall not be judged; For the labourer is worthy of his hire.

**John**. In the beginning was the Word; I am the way, the truth, and the life.

**Paul** (I Corinthians). Though I speak with the tongues of men and of angels; For now we see through a glass darkly.

**Revelation**. And I saw a new heaven and a new earth: for the first heaven and the first earth were passed away.

---

of nation or religious affiliation. The revised OT was based on virtually the same Hebrew text as the AV, but the NT translators worked on a considerably reconstructed Greek text (itself the subject of controversy) and adopted the plan (rejected by the 1611 translators) of always translating the same Greek word by the same English word, which it was claimed preserved the meaning more faithfully. This version was less well received than had been hoped.

The Presbyterian scholar James Moffat brought out a colloquial translation in 1913 and the Anglican priest J. B. Phillips produced a NT in contemporary English in 1958. By contrast, *The New English Bible* (1961), *The Good News Bible* (1976), and the *New International Version* (1978) were produced by panels of scholars, each with the aim of a Bible in the language of the present day. NEB resulted from an interdenominational conference initiated by the Church of Scotland and had the aim of aiding private study and scholarship rather than reading aloud. GNB was produced by William Collins and the United Bible Societies, based on the latter's simplified and colloquial versions originally aimed at the mission field, where users were mostly not speakers of English as a first language. NIV was intended to attract readers without prior religious commitment. All three fol-

## THE STRATA OF BIBLICAL TRANSLATION INTO ENGLISH

The following translations of the Gospel of Matthew (25: 14–15) show how language, style, and interpretation have changed over six centuries of translation from Greek into English.

῞Ωσπερ γὰρ ἄνθρωπος ἀποδημῶν ἐκάλεσε τοὺς ἰδίους δούλους, καὶ παρέδωκεν αὐτοῖς τὰ ὑπάρχοντα αὐτοῦ καὶ ᾧ μὲν ἔδωκε πέντε τάλαντα ᾧ δὲ δύο, ᾧ δὲ ἕν, ἑκάστῳ κατὰ τὴν ἰδίαν δύναμιν κοὰ ἀπεδήμησεν εὐθέως.

**1380**. Sothely as a man goynge fer in pilgrimage, clepide his seruauntis, and bitoke to hem his goodis; And to oon he ȝaue fyue talentis, forsothe to an other two, but to an other oon, to eche after his owne vertu; and went forth anoon. (Wycliffe)

**1526**. Lykewise as a certeyne man redy to take his iorney to a straunge countre, called hys seruantes to hym, and delyvered to them hys gooddes; And vnto won he gave v. talentes, to another ij, and to another one, to every man after his abilite; and streyght waye departed. (Tyndale)

**1611**. 14 For *the kingdome of heauen is* as a man trauailing into a farre countrey, who called his owne seruants, and deliuered vnto them his goods. 15 And vnto one he gaue fiue talents, to another two, and to another one, to euery man according to his seuerall ability, & straightway tooke his iourney. (King James)

**1913**. For the case is that of a man going abroad, who summoned his servants and handed over his property to them; to one he gave twelve hundred pounds, to another five hundred, and to another two hundred and fifty; each got according to his capacity. Then the man went abroad. (Moffat)

**1941**. 14. For it is as when a man, about to take a journey, got his servants together, and gave them his property. 15. And to one he gave five pounds, to another two, to another one; to everyone as he was able; and he went on his journey. (Basic English)

**1983**. Or again, it is like this. A man at wis gaein out o the kintra ca's up his servans an haundit his haudin owre tae them tae gyde. He lippent ane wi five talents, anither wi twa, an a third wi ane—ilkane wi the soum confeirin til his capacitie. Syne he gaed his waas out o the kintra. (William L. Lorimer, *The New Testament in Scots*)

**1989**. [14]'It is like a man going abroad, who called his servants and entrusted his capital to them; [15]to one he gave five bags of gold, to another two, to another one, each according to his ability. Then he left the country.' (The Revised English Bible)

**1958**. It is just like a man going abroad who called his household servants together before he went and handed his property over to them to manage. He gave one five thousand pounds, another two thousand and another one thousand—according to their respective abilities. Then he went away. (Phillips)

**1970**. 'It is like a man going abroad, who called his servants and put his capital in their hands; to one he gave five bags of gold, to another two, to another one, each according to his capacity. Then he left the country.' (New English Bible)

**1982**. 'For it will be as when a man going on a journey called his servants and entrusted to them his property; to one he gave five talents, to another two, to another one, to each according to his ability. Then he went away.' (Reader's Digest Bible) lowed the precedent of the RV in relying to an increasing extent on reconstructed or rediscovered texts unavailable to, or rejected by, the translators of the KJB.

**Inclusive language**. In the last two decades, efforts have been made to produce 'non-sexist' versions of the Bible in English, to meet the theological and social contention of feminists and others that male terms for the Deity are inadequate and inappropriate, for example *Give thanks unto the Lord; call upon his name: make known his deeds* (Psalm 105: 1), because they attribute maleness to a being believed to be above considerations of gender. The problems of reconciling fidelity to the original Hebrew and Greek with inclusive late 20c usage have proved considerable and controversial, relating not only to specific biblical texts but also to general assumptions in Christianity and other religions about the nature and naming of Divinity.

**Conclusion**. The existence of vernacular Bibles was important for the growth, enrichment, and even preservation of many of the languages of Europe, and the early translations into English were profoundly important for the development of the language. In English, both the established churches and nonconformists in 17–18c Britain, Ireland, and North America emphasized Bible study and reading aloud, and so encouraged a culture focused on the printed word. Bible translation in its most active stage coincided with both the development of printing and the need for STAN-DARD LANGUAGES in the nation-states of late medieval and Renaissance Europe. Because the Protestant nonconformists took the Bible (Geneva or AV) as their standard, it strongly influenced such writers as John Milton, George Fox, John Bunyan, and Richard Baxter, and through them later polemical and political writers in the UK, USA, and elsewhere. Its influence is also evident in the works of 19–20c writers as diverse as John Betjeman, George Eliot, T. S. Eliot, Thomas Hardy, Rudyard Kipling, Sean O'Casey, Dylan Thomas, Mark Twain, Evelyn Waugh, and P. G. Wodehouse. At least three factors contributed to the vast influence of the Bible on English from the 16c to the 20c century: the 16–17c legal requirement that all should attend the parish church, later transmuted into a widely respected social custom; the use of the Bible in legally re-

quired school assemblies till well after the Second World War; and compulsory church parades in the armed services of the British Empire until the 1950s. These ensured that vast numbers of people for generation after generation were exposed to the English of the King James Bible as a living variety. It is to these factors, as much as to studies and use by scholars and writers, that the widespread survival of biblical usage and allusion can be attributed.

See AMERICAN ENGLISH, ARCHAISM, BOOK OF COMMON PRAYER, CHAUCER, EUPHUISM, INCLUSIVE LANGUAGE, KRIO, LETTER[2], PROSE, PROVERB, PUN, RASTA TALK, SAXONISM, SHIBBOLETH.

## ■ BIBLICAL ENGLISH ─────── ■

The register of English based on the Authorized Version (AV) of the BIBLE (1611), as in: 'And Jesus entered and passed through Jericho. And, behold, there was a man named Zacchaeus, which was the chief among the publicans, and he was rich. And he sought to see Jesus who he was; and could not for the press, because he was little of stature' (Luke 19: 1–3, modern spelling). Since the AV, translations have to a greater or lesser degree departed from this style, and so, paradoxically, many English-language Bibles are not in biblical English. The New English Bible (1961) translates the same passage of Luke as: 'Entering Jericho he made his way through the city. There was a man there named Zacchaeus; he was superintendent of taxes and very rich. He was eager to see what Jesus looked like; but, being a little man, he could not see him for the crowd.'

**Elevated Jacobean English**. By and large, biblical English is elevated Jacobean English, comparable to the style of Shakespeare and Thomas Browne. The AV, however, had a tradition of its own, evolving from or related to earlier works whose style is also recognizably biblical: for example, the *Great Bible* of 1539 and the *First Prayer Book* of 1549 (later the *Book of Common Prayer* of the Anglican communion). Biblical English, therefore, is not a variety which appeared suddenly in the early 17c, but evolved from the Wycliffite translations of the 14c, and in various forms has continued into the 20c. Two main factors have shaped it: the style of the original texts and the ideology and situation of the early translators. In addition, English literature is full of quotations in which Bible sentences or phrases are worked into an author's own language: Shakespeare, 'come *the four corners of the world in arms*' (*King John*, *c.*1595); Trollope, 'Vavasour's friends knew that *his goings-out and his comings-in* were seldom accounted for openly' (*Can You Forgive Her?* 1864); Kipling, a book title, *Thy Servant a Dog* (1930); Wodehouse: 'I was one of the idle rich. I *toiled not, neither did I*—except for a bump supper at Cambridge—*spin*' (*Leave it to Psmith*, 1923).

The AV had a lasting effect on people's passive vocabulary, and more than any other text (apart from the Book of Common Prayer) has been responsible for the ongoing capacity to recognize and interpret *thou* and *-est* (*whither thou goest I will go*), *-eth* (*I say to this man, Go, and he goeth; and to another, Come, and he cometh*), and inverted negation and interrogation (*I think not*; *What say you?*). In addition, preachers, writers, and others grew accustomed to inserting elements from the AV into everyday language: (1) Words: *beget*, *apostle*, *parable*, *talent*. (2) Names: personal like *Ruth*, *Rebecca*, *Samuel*, *Simon*, such names serving as the baptismal names of millions; place-names like *Bethesda*, *Bethlehem*, *Eden*, *Salem*, such names often being given to settlements established by Bible-reading colonists. (3) Noun phrases: *broken reed*, *burnt offering*, *fatted calf*, *stony ground*. (4) Linking statements: *and it came to pass*; *I looked, and behold*; *then he answered and said*. (5) Proverb-like phrases: *a word in season*, *don't hide your light under a bushel*, *gird up your loins*, *not my brother's keeper*, *a multitude of sins*.

A whole European culture of Bible-influenced languages spread to every continent in the world, its members sharing an appreciation of allusions to an enormous range of topics such as *Noah's Ark*, *the Tower of Babel*, *the waters of Babylon*, *the writing on the wall*, and *the money-changers in the Temple*. A symbol system from the Bible in the language of the AV has tended, at least as much as that of classical Greek and Latin, to dominate writers' minds; as C. S. Lewis has pointed out, English authors in elevated contexts have tended to use the symbols *corn and wine* rather than 'beef and beer', *sword* rather than 'gun' or 'pike', *bread* rather than 'potatoes', *trumpet* rather than 'bugle', and *stone* rather than 'brick' (Ethel M. Wood Lecture, 1950). Samuel Taylor Coleridge contended that intense study of the Bible would elevate the style of any writer (*Table Talk*, 1830).

**Modern developments**. Biblical English is, however, most immediately recognized as extended discourse rather than as words, phrases, and styles. Many late 20c users of English recognize the vocabulary, the grammar, and the cadences of biblical English without supposing that it has a living presence beyond church services, or that it is a resource on which various groups draw. In the 19c and 20c, however, at least three movements have adopted biblical styles:

1. The US civil rights movement, as exemplified in the language of preachers such as Martin Luther King Jr. The following is from a speech by Martin Luther King Sr., when his son received the Nobel Prize: 'I always wanted to make a contribution. And all you got to do if you want to contribute, you got to ask the Lord, and let Him know, and the Lord heard me and in some kind of way I don't even know he laid His hand on me and my wife and He gave us Martin Luther King and our prayers were answered.'

2. The Church of Latter-Day Saints, especially in *The Book of Mormon: Another Testament of Jesus Christ* (as published by Joseph Smith in 1830): 'For behold, it came to pass that the Lord spake unto my father, yea, even in a dream, and said unto him: Blessed art thou Lehi, because of the things which thou hast done; and because thou hast been faithful and declared unto this people the things which I commanded thee, behold, they seek to take away thy life' (First Book of Nephi, 2: 1).

3. The Baha'i World Faith, in a policy adopted in the early 20c of translating the writings of the founder Bahá'u'lláh and his son 'Abdu'l Bahá, as in: 'Ye are but vassals, O Kings of the earth! He Who is the King of Kings hath appeared, arrayed in His most wondrous glory, and is summoning you unto Himself, the Help in Peril, the Self-Subsisting' (Bahá'u'lláh, 'Proclamation to the Kings and Leaders of Religion', *c.*1860).

**BIBLIOGRAPHY**. **1.** A branch of library science dealing with the description, history, comparison, and classification of documents. **2.** A list of documents compiled according to a particular need and/or principle of classification, such as 20c books on gardening published in Britain or the printed sources used in a piece of research or a published work. Most bibliographies are relatively straightforward lists organized alphabetically, but may otherwise vary greatly. Usually keyed to authors' names, they may also be organized according to subject, place of publication, publisher, or some other criterion; in an electronic database, a bibliography may be variously tagged, to make its information accessible according to authors, topics in titles, publishers, etc. Bibliographies ordered according to surname take many forms, according to rules laid down by academic and other institutions, practices favoured in publishers' house styles, or authors' preferences. Such lists may be long enough to be documents in their own right or published as works of reference, but most are appendices to books, articles, and dissertations. Below are three possible formats for the same title:

Watson, James, & Hill, Anne (eds.). 1984. *A Dictionary of Communication and Media Studies.* London: Edward Arnold.

Watson, J., and Hill, A. (eds.). *A Dictionary of Communication and Media Studies* (London: Edward Arnold, 1984).

Watson, J., and Hill, A., eds., *A Dictionary of Communication and Media Studies,* London, 1984.

See NOTES AND REFERENCES.

**BILABIAL**. A term in PHONETICS for a sound made with both lips: for example, /m/ as in *move*. See SPEECH.

**BILINGUALISM**. The capacity to make alternate (and sometimes mixed) use of two languages, in contrast to *monolingualism* or *unilingualism* and *MULTILINGUALISM*. In the social context of languages like English, especially in England and the US, the traditional tendency has been to consider the possession and use of one language the norm. Bilingualism, however, is at least as common as monolingualism; about half the world's population (some 2.5 bn people) is bilingual and kinds of bilingualism are probably present in every country in the world. See CANADIAN LANGUAGES, CODE-MIXING AND CODE-SWITCHING, HIGHLAND ENGLISH, IRISH ENGLISH, MAORI ENGLISH, WELSH ENGLISH.

**BIRMINGHAM**. A large industrial city in the West MIDLANDS of ENGLAND, often referred to as *Brum*, an abbreviation of the METATHESIS *Brummagem*. The city's inhabitants are *Brummies*, and their speech is known as *Brummie*, *Birmingham*, and *Brummagem*. Accents vary according to such factors as age, education, locality, region of origin, and social aspirations.

**Pronunciation**. Middle-class speech in the city is RP or near-RP. The following points apply mainly to working-class speech: (1) It is non-rhotic and generally aitchless. (2) The vowel /a/ tends to be used in both *bat* and *bath*. The pronunciation of *Edgbaston* (the name of a better-off part of the city) is a class SHIBBOLETH: the *a* is short among the working class, who stress the first syllable ('EDGE-biston'), and long in 'posh' usage, with stress on the second syllable ('Edge-BAHston'). (3) There is a tendency towards /ʊ/ in both *but* and *boot*, although the /ʌ/ pronunciation in words such as *but*, *cut*, and *shut* is spreading. (4) Words such as *course* and *force* are sometimes realized with a triphthong /ʌʊə/, especially among older speakers. (5) The monophthong /ɪ/ is close, so that *it* often sounds like *eat* and *did* like *deed*. (6) The *-y* ending of words such as *happy* is often pronounced /əi/ or /ʌi/. (7) The diphthongs in *gate* and *goat* tend to vary as between /aɪ~ʌɪ/ and /aʊ~ʌʊ/ rather than the /eɪ/ and /əʊ/ of RP. (8) The diphthong of *house* and *mouth* is /æʊ/. (9) The diphthongs in *tie* and *toy* have merged in /ɒɪ/, producing homophones and uncertainty in such sentences as *Where's your tie/toy?* (10) Words and syllables ending in *-ng* tend to close with a voiced velar plosive: for example, /sɪŋgɪŋg/ for *singing* and /kɪŋglʊɪ/ for *kingly*. This feature has been criticized so often that many Birmingham speakers tend to overcompensate in the attempt to avoid it, using /ŋ/ where /ŋg/ is standard, as in /fɪŋə/ for *finger*.

**Grammar and vocabulary**. Especially among older speakers, the following grammatical features occur: *up* instead of *to*, as in *He went up the pub half an hour ago* and *We'll go up town tomorrow*; use of *her* instead of *she*, as in *What's 'er doing then?*; use of *as* as a relative pronoun, as in *It wasn't 'im as went*; use of /dai/ for *did not*, especially with *know*, as in *They dai know where they was*. Most people use the standard vocabulary, but older speakers may continue to use such words as *brewins* an outhouse, *closet* a toilet, *miskin* BrE dustbin, AmE trashcan, and *suff* a drain.

**BISLAMA**. A variety of Melanesian pidgin and the national language of VANUATU, sharing official status with English and French, which are the principal languages of education. Bislama, descended from BEACH LA MAR, is a LINGUA FRANCA for a population speaking some 100 distinct local languages, and is more or less evenly distributed throughout the country. It used to be learned mainly in adulthood by men, usually through work on plantations, in town, or on ships. Most adult males probably speak it, except in isolated parts of the islands. In towns today, most children speak their vernacular and Bislama. In the southern islands there has been an unbroken tradition of Bislama for almost 150 years. The constitution of Vanuatu states: *Lanwis blong Ripablik blong Vanuatu, hemia Bislama. Trifala lanwis blong mekem ol wok blong kantri ya, i gat Bislama mo Inglis mo Franis* 'The language of the Republic of Vanuatu is Bislama. There are three languages for conducting the business of the country, Bislama, English, and French.' See MELANESIAN PIDGIN ENGLISH.

**BISOCIATION**. The occurrence in a language of pairs of words with similar meanings, one member of each pair being native to that language (such as everyday English *sight*), the other being a loanword from an influential foreign source (such as *vision*, a loanword from Latin). In English, the vernacular members of such pairs are mainly Germanic (usually from Old English or Old Norse), while the loanwords are mainly classical (usually from Latin, often mediated by FRENCH), as in: *freedom/liberty*, *hearty/cordial*, *go up/ascend*, *go down/descend*. Bisociation in English has often been remarked on. Simeon Potter, for example, observes: 'We feel more at ease after getting a *hearty welcome* than after being granted a *cordial reception*' (*Our Language*, 1950/66). Similarly, Thomas Finkenstaedt has noted: 'Apparently the Elizabethans discovered the possibilities of etymological dissociation in language: *amatory* and *love*, *audition* and *hearing*, *hearty welcome* and *cordial reception*' (in *Ordered Profusion*, 1973). This kind of semantic parallelism has also occurred in Latin, which has absorbed many words from Greek, creating such pairs as Latin *compassio* and Greek *sympathia*. In many instances, such pairs have passed into English, leading to *trisociation*, as with Germanic *fellow feeling*, Latinate *compassion*, and Greek-derived *sympathy*. There are scores of such correspon-

dences in English, the Germanic material tending to be part of everyday usage (as with *newness*), the Latinate tending to be more formal and 'educated' (as with *innovate*), and the Greek tending to be highly technical and even arcane (as with *neophyte*). Compare CALQUE, DOUBLET. See BOOK OF COMMON PRAYER, ELYOT, INDO-EUROPEAN LANGUAGES, MIDDLE ENGLISH.

**BLACK ENGLISH**. A controversial term for the English of people of African origin or for English in Black Africa. In the US, the term generally refers to the VERNACULARS of descendants of slaves, some called dialects, some creoles. In the UK, the term generally refers to the usage of West Indian immigrant communities. The term *white English* has occasionally been used in contrast: 'local "white" English, BBC English' (David Sutcliffe, 'British Black English and West Indian Creoles', in P. Trudgill (ed.), *Language in the British Isles*, 1984). See AFRICAN-AMERICAN VERNACULAR ENGLISH.

**BLARNEY**. Extravagant eloquence that beguiles and flatters, impresses and deceives, often taken to be typically Irish. In 1602, Cormac Teige Macarthy unwillingly agreed to surrender Blarney Castle in County Cork, so as to have it returned to him as a loyal retainer of Elizabeth I. Afterwards he stalled and, tired of his glib equivocation, the queen is said to have shouted, 'This is all Blarney—he never means what he says, he never does what he promises.' In the wall of Blarney Castle is the *Blarney Stone*, said to bestow Macarthy's gift of eloquence on whoever kisses it. The ritual of kissing the stone appears to date from the 18c. Compare JIVE, PATTER.

**BLEND**, also **blend word, word blend, amalgam, fusion**. A word formed by fusing elements of two other words, such as Lewis CARROLL's *slithy* from *slimy* and *lithe*. He called such forms *portmanteau words*, because they were like a two-part portmanteau bag. Blending is related to ABBREVIATION, derivation, and compounding, but distinct from them all. In the making of *slithy* it is hard to identify the precise contributions of the source words, but some blends follow clear-cut boundaries, as in *Oxbridge*, formed from *Oxford* and *Cambridge*. Others serve as slogans: *Cocacolonization* asserting that a country has been taken over by American values. Although blending is distinct from derivation, it may affect it. Forms like *electrocute* (1880s) bring *electro-* and *execute* together so as to suggest a suffix *-cute* that means 'kill by means of'. This element has not been exploited, but *motorcade* (*c.*1913) blends *motor* and *cavalcade* and has prompted *aerocade*, *aquacade*, and *camelcade*.

**BLOOMFIELD, Leonard** [1887–1949]. American philologist and linguist, born in Chicago, Illinois, and educated at Harvard, Wisconsin, and Chicago. He taught at several universities (1909–27) before becoming Professor of Germanic Philology at Chicago (1927–40) and Professor of Linguistics at Yale (1940–9). Initially, he was interested in Indo-European, and particularly Germanic, speech sounds and word-formation. Later, he undertook pioneering studies in the Malayo-Polynesian languages, and made a detailed study of the North American Indian languages. His publications include: *An Introduction to the Study of Language* (1914), *Language* (1933), and *Outline Guide for the Practical Study of Foreign Languages* (1942). Influenced by European structuralism, Bloomfield is generally regarded as the founder of American STRUCTURAL LINGUISTICS. His definitions of the basic units of language were influential. He defined the PHONEME as 'a minimum same of vocal feature' (that is, as a physical piece of speech rather than as an abstract construct of the linguist) and believed (mistakenly, as it proved) that within a few decades it would be possible to establish the phonemes of a language in the laboratory. He defined the MORPHEME as the basic unit of grammatical arrangement, a 'minimal form which bears no partial phonetic-semantic resemblance to any other form' (*Language*, p. 161). The WORD was a 'minimum free form', the smallest unit that can occur in isolation, and might consist of one morpheme (*boy*, *but*) or more than one (*boyish*, *carelessness*).

**BOOK OF COMMON PRAYER**, short form *BCP*. The book used for public worship by Anglican Christians for over 400 years, and regarded as authoritative for doctrine. It originated with the First and Second Prayer Books of King Edward VI (1549, 1552), was mainly compiled by Thomas Cranmer, and drew on Latin, Orthodox, German, and Spanish liturgies. It underwent revisions, notably in 1662 when restored to use after being banned during the Commonwealth, but is recognizably Cranmer's original. A further revision in 1928, though not officially authorized, is in use in some places. *BCP* is the earliest source for many common words and phrases, such as *all one's worldly goods*, *at death's door*, *to have and to hold*, *in sickness and in health*, *land of the living*, *like lost sheep*, *tender mercy*, *to lead a new life*. Complex sentence structure with long subordinate clauses is a feature widely assimilated into the language: 'Almighty God, unto whom all hearts be open, all desires known, and from whom no secrets are hid; Cleanse the thoughts of our hearts by the inspiration of thy Holy Spirit, that we may perfectly love thee, and worthily magnify thy holy Name' (Collect at commencement of Holy Communion). *BCP* contains many pairs of synonyms, such as *praise and magnify*, *erred and strayed*, *prisoners and captives*, *prepare and make ready*, usually one word from Latin, the other Anglo-Saxon, the aim of which was comprehensibility among all levels of society. Because for 400 years a high degree of uniformity in worship was imposed by law, *BCP* has influenced vocabulary and syntax to an extent comparable to the BIBLE and SHAKESPEARE.

■ **BORROWING** ────────── ■

**1.** Taking a word or phrase from one language into another, or from one variety of a language into another. **2.** The item so taken, such as *arpeggio* from ITALIAN into English, and *schlock* from YIDDISH into AmE, then into BrE. Borrowing is a major aspect of language change, but the term itself is a misnomer: it presumes repayment, whereas there is no *quid pro quo* between languages. The item borrowed is not returned, because it never left the source language and in any case changes in the transfer. Compare LOAN, LOANWORD.

**Patterns of borrowing**. Any language, under appropriate circumstances, borrows lexical material from other languages, usually absorbing the exotic items or translating them into native equivalents. Some languages borrow more than others, and borrow more from some sources than others. English has borrowed massively from FRENCH, LATIN, and GREEK, significantly from Italian, SPANISH, GERMAN, DANISH, and

DUTCH, and to varying degrees from every other language with which it has come in contact. The Cannon corpus of 13,683 new English words shows that this process continues unabated; the 1,029 transfers listed in the corpus entered English from 84 languages (1987–9) as follows: French 25%, Spanish and Japanese both 8%, Italian 6.3%, Latin 6.1%, Greek 6%, German 5.5%, and 77 languages contributed 1–39 items each. Here, only the Japanese element breaks the traditional pattern, in which European languages predominate.

**Reasons for borrowing**. The preconditions for borrowing are: (1) Close contact in especially multilingual situations, making the mixing of elements from different languages more or less commonplace. (2) The domination of some languages by others (for cultural, economic, political, religious, or other reasons), so that material flows 'down' from those 'high' languages into 'lower' vernaculars. (3) A sense of need, users of one language drawing material from another for such purposes as education and technology. (4) Prestige associated with using words from another language. (5) A mix of some or all of these. Individuals may use an exotic expression because it seems to them to be the most suitable term available, the only possible term (with no equivalent in any other language), or the most impressive term. Much of the vocabulary of French entered English in the Middle Ages because French was the language of political and social power and the channel through which mainland European culture reached Britain. Much of the vocabulary of Latin entered English during the Renaissance (directly or via French) because Latin was the European language of religion, education, and learning. While so prestigious a language could provide time-hallowed resources, there was little encouragement to develop the resources of relatively insignificant vernaculars like English. In the late 20c, English sometimes serves in its turn as a kind of Latin in the main because both have been languages of empire. Thus, as part of the Malaysian Government's educational programme based on Malay (intended to unify the nation's ethnic groups), the already polyglot scientific and technical vocabulary of English has been massively adopted into Malay.

**Reasons for resisting borrowing**. Listeners and readers have their own responses to the use of an exotic term, and these responses affect their inclination to repeat it. Although such reactions are not properties of the item itself, the associations formed may affect its new use, so that it may remain in a limited field, such as French *œuvre* and *auteur* in English literary criticism. Such a term may not be understood outside its field or may be considered pretentious. However, some items are so universally apt that they swiftly occupy a niche in the language at large, such as French *garage* and *cliché*. In addition, there may be personal and communal reasons for resisting the influx of foreignisms: for example, a protectionist language policy (as in Iceland), on the grounds that the community is small and linguistically fragile; a sense of past oppression (as in such ex-colonial countries as Tanzania, where SWAHILI is promoted as a national medium rather than English); and pride in the home language and culture (as in Iran). All three factors were present in the Canadian province of Quebec in the 1970s, when official legislation militated against English influence on French.

**Diffusion and adaptation**. Borrowing is sometimes simple and limited (a few words taken from Language A into Language B), sometimes complex and extensive (much of the vocabulary of A becoming available for use in B, and perhaps C and D as well, as with SANSKRIT in India, ARABIC in West Asia, and Latin in Europe). What appears to be a single process affecting two languages may be multiple, in that an item may be diffused as a *pilgrim word* into a range of languages, usually adapting as it goes: (1) Greek *phantasía* has become French *fantaisie*, German *Fantasie*, Italian *fantasia*, PORTUGUESE *fantazia*, Spanish *fantasía*, and English *fancy*, along with *fantasy*, *fantasia*, and archaic *phantasy*. (2) Latin *planta* (sprout, offspring) passed into Italian as *pianta*, Old English and Old French as *plante*, Spanish *llanta*, Portuguese *chanta*, German *Pflanze*, WELSH *plant*, and Old Irish as *cland*, whence it became GAELIC *clann* (offspring, family, stock, race). Both *plant* and *clan* are now English words. (3) Sanskrit *dhyāna* (meditation) passed into Pali as *jhāna*, into Chinese as *ch'an*, then into Japanese as *zen*. Both *dhyana* and *Zen* are now English words.

There is a continuum in borrowing, from words that remain relatively alien and unassimilated in pronunciation and spelling (as with *blasé* and *soirée* from French), through those that become more or less acclimatized (as with *élite* rather than *élite*, while retaining a Frenchlike pronunciation, and *garage* with its various pronunciations) to forms that have been assimilated so fully that their exotic origin is entirely obscured (as with *cockroach*, from Spanish *cucaracha*, and *chocolate* through Spanish from Nahuatl *chocolatl*).

A word taken from a typologically or genetically related language would appear to be more easily assimilated than one taken from a very different kind of language. Like English, Spanish is an Indo-European language written in the Roman alphabet, and so the absorption of items like *armada* and *guerrilla* into English offers few problems. However, some elements may be too alien for convenient absorption: for example, although Mexican Spanish *chili* and *taco* have been easily absorbed, the phrase *frijoles refritos* has posed a problem, because the order of noun and adjective and the double plural are not native to English. As a result, the loan translation *refried beans* has become the choice for non-bilinguals. On the other hand, Chinese is a tone language usually written ideographically; in theory, this should deter transfer, but large-scale English–Chinese and Chinese–English borrowing has gone ahead without much difficulty, English for example acquiring *chow mein*, *ginseng*, *kaolin*, *taipan*, and *tea/char*.

**Linguistic effects of borrowing**. Transfers may have an influence on such basic aspects of a language as its pronunciation, spelling, syntax, and semantics. The local system usually overwhelms the acquisition; thus, when numbers of items with aspirated voiced stops came into English, spelled with *h*, the consonantal system remained unchanged, *bhang* being pronounced like *bang*, *dhow* like *dow*, *ghat* like *gat*. However, transfers into English from French may be pronounced as closely as possible to the French (as with *raison d'être*, *sabotage*), or with concessions to French and adaptations into English (the various pronunciations of *garage*). Morphological impact may introduce different plural forms: for example, such sets as Greek *criterion/criteria*, *thesis/theses*, Latin *appendix/appendices*, *stimulus/stimuli*, Italian *graffito/graffiti*, and Hebrew *cherub/cherubim*, *kibbutz/kibbutzim*. However, such adoptions are not always stable,

and conflict may occur between foreign and nativized forms, as with *cactus/cacti~cactuses*. See CLASSICAL ENDING. Perhaps the largest morphological impact on English has been the addition of French, Latin, and Greek affixes such as *dis-*, *pro-*, *anti-*, *-ity*, *-ism*, and such combining forms as *bio-*, *micro-*, *-metry*, *-logy*, which replaced many of the original Germanic affixes in English. Only rarely do affixes from other sources establish themselves to any degree in English: for example, the suffix *-nik*, from RUSSIAN, as in *kolkhoznik*, and Yiddish, as in *kibbutznik*, and nativized, as in *beatnik* and *peacenik*.

**Kinds of words borrowed**. Nouns make up the highest proportion of transfers, followed by adjectives. Verbs are usually few, with even fewer adverbs and grammatical words like pronouns. However, the replacement of the Old English third-person plural *hīe* by Old Danish *they* shows that such transfers sometimes occur. The 1,029 recent transfers in the Cannon corpus break down into 916 nouns (such as *art trouvé*, *honcho*, *pita*), 86 adjectives (such as *gauchesco*, *kitschy*, *Namibian*), 12 verbs (such as *francicize*, *nosh*, *vinify*), 3 interjections (*arigato* from Japanese, *ciao* from Italian, *inshallah* from Arabic), and 12 bound forms (including *atto-* from Danish/Norwegian, *-nik* from Russian, and *ur-* from German). This does not, however, mean that nouns are most and interjections least easily transferred; nouns in any case predominate in a language. In terms of such proportions, interjections are at least as easily borrowed, when the conditions are appropriate, as the worldwide spread of AmE *OK* testifies. Phrases are also commonly transferred, as with *drame à clef* and *roman à clef* from French into English, Sentences are less common, although English has a tradition of using short Latin and French sentences like *Tempus fugit* and *C'est la vie*.

See AFRIKAANS, BANTU, BISOCIATION, CALQUE, CHINA, CLASSICAL COMPOUND, CODE-MIXING AND CODE-SWITCHING, COMBINING FORM, DOUBLET, ETYMOLOGY, FOREIGNISM, INDO-EUROPEAN LANGUAGES, INTERNATIONAL SCIENTIFIC VOCABULARY, JAPAN, LANGUAGE CHANGE, MAORI, NEOLOGISM, NONCE WORD, NORSE, PHILOLOGY. ROMANI, TAGALOG.

**BOSTON**. The capital of the state of Massachusetts and cultural centre of NEW ENGLAND, one of the earliest areas of English settlement in what is now the US and a focal point from which English spread. Its social

## BORROWINGS INTO ENGLISH

In the following sections, arranged according to the world's major regions, is a wide selection of languages from which at various times and in various ways English has borrowed. The samples are organized so as to suggest the proportions in which material from other languages is present in English, but no section seeks to be exhaustive and the historical dimension (for example, the periods when particular words entered English) is not explored. In some cases, the intermediary languages through which material has passed are indicated.

***Oceania.*** **1.** Australian Aboriginal: *billabong, boomerang, corroboree, kangaroo, koala, kookaburra, murree, wallaby, wombat, yabber, yakka/yacker.* **2.** Polynesian, including: Hawaiian *aloha, heiau, hula, kapu, lanai, lei, muumuu, ukulele/ukelele, wahine;* MAORI *aroha, iwi, kauri, kiwi, Maoritanga, marae, moa, ngati, pakeha, pohutukawa, tangata whenua, tangi, toheroa, tuatara, whakapapa, whare;* Tahitian *tattoo;* Tongan *kava, taboo/tabu.*

***Africa.*** **1.** Afrikaans: *aardvaark, aardwolf, apartheid, Boer, commando, dorp, kop, kopje/koppie, outspan, spoor, springbok, trek.* **2.** BANTU languages, including Kongo, Swahili, Tswana, Xhosa, Zulu: *boma, bwana, chimpanzee, impala, impi, indaba, mamba, marimba, tsetse, zombie.* **3.** West African languages, including Ewe, Fanti, Hausa, Mandingo, mainly through the Atlantic creoles: *anansi, gumbo, harmattan, juju, juke(box), mumbo-jumbo, okra, voodoo, yam;* perhaps *banjo, jazz.* **4.** Malagasy: *raffia.* **5.** Khoisan languages: *gnu, quagga.*

***The Americas.*** **1.** Algonquian, including Abnaki, Cree, Micmac, Ojibway, Narragansett, Shawnee: *caucus, chipmunk, hickory, manitou, moccasin, moose, muskrat, opossum, papoose, pecan, pemmican, persimmon, pow-wow, rac(c)oon, skunk, squash, squaw, succotash, toboggan, tomahawk, wampum, wapiti, wigwam, woodchuck.* **2.** Aleut and Inuit: *anorak, igloo, kayak, parka.* **3.** Araucanian through Spanish: *coypu, poncho.* **4.** Arawakan, especially through Spanish: *barbecue, cacique, hammock, iguana, potato, tobacco, savanna(h).* **5.** Carib, especially through Spanish: *cannibal, canoe, hurricane, macaw, maize, manatee, papaya/pa(w)paw, peccary, tomalley, yucca.* **6.** Creek: *catalpa, tupelo.* **7.** Nahuatl through Spanish: *avocado, axolotl, cacao/cocoa, chili/chilli, chocolate, coyote, mescal, ocelot, peyote, teocalli, tomato.* **8.** Quechua through Spanish: *alpaca, charqui/jerky, coca(ine), condor, guanaco, guano, llama, pampas, puma, quinine, vicuna.* **9.** Tupi-Guaraní through French, Portuguese, Spanish: *buccaneer, cashew, cayenne, cougar, ipecac(uanha), jaguar, manioc, petunia, tapioca, tapir, toucan.*

***Asia: Western.*** **1.** Arabic, through European languages: *admiral, albatross, alchemy, alcohol, alcove, alembic, algebra, alkali, almanac, apricot, arsenal, assassin, assegai, attar, aubergine, azimuth, bedouin, caliph, cipher/cypher, emir, gazelle, genie/jinn, ghoul, giraffe, hazard, jasmine, kismet, Koran, lemon, magazine, minaret, mohair, monsoon, Moslem, nadir, saffron, sash, scarlet, sequin, sheik(h), sherbet, simoom/simoon, sirocco, sofa, syrup, talisman, tariff, zero;* direct or through Afro-Asian languages: *ayatollah, harem, hashish, henna, hooka(h), imam, Islam, jihad, kaffir, muezzin, mufti, mujahedin, mullah, Muslim, nadir, Qur'ān, safari, sahib, salaam, Sharia, shaykh, zenith.* **2.** Aramaic: *abbot, kaddish, pharisee.* **3.** Hebrew, especially through Greek, Latin, and Yiddish: *alphabet, amen, bedlam, camel, cherub, cinnamon, hosanna, Jehovah, manna, maudlin, nard, rabbi, seraph, shemozzle, simony, sodomy;* more or less direct: *behemoth, cabal, Cabala, chazan/haz(z)an, golem, hallelujah, leviathan, messiah, sabbath, shalom, shibboleth, Talmud, Torah, Yahweh.* **4.** Persian through European languages:

*Continued over*

## BORROWINGS INTO ENGLISH continued

*arsenic, azure, check, checkmate, magus/magic, paradise, peach, pilaf, pistachio, spinach, talc*; direct or through Asian languages: *bazaar, caravan/caravanserai, dervish, durbar, jackal, khaki, kiosk, lilac, maidan, mogul, pilau/pulao, pyjamas/pajamas, shah, shawl, sherbet, tiara, tulip, turban*. **5.** Turkish/Tatar: *bosh, caftan/kaftan, caique, coffee, cossack, divan, horde, kavass, khan, kumiss, mammoth, pasha, Tartar, turkey, turquoise, yoghurt/yogurt/(CanE) yoghourt*.

**Asia: Southern and South-Eastern**. **1.** Hindi/Urdu: *bungalow, crore, dacoit, deodar, dinghy, dungaree, ghee, gymkhana, lakh/lac, loot, paisa, pakora, Raj, samo(o)sa, shampoo, tandoori, tom-tom, wallah*. **2.** Javanese: *bantam, batik, gamelan, junk*. **3.** Malay: *amok/amuck, bamboo, caddy, camphor, cassowary, cockatoo, dugong, durian, gecko, gingham, gong, kampong/compound, kapok, kris, lory, mangosteen, organgutan/orang-outang, paddy, pangolin, rattan, sago, sarong*. **4.** Malayalam: *betel, coir, copra, singer, teak*. **5.** Marathi: *mongoose*. **6.** Sanskrit through various languages: *ashram, avatar, banya, banyan, beryl, brahmin, carmine, cheetah, chintz, chutney, crimson, juggernaut, jungle, jute, lacquer, mandarin, palanquin, pundit, sapphire, sugar, suttee*; more or less direct: *ahimsa, asana, ashrama, atman, avatara, bodhisattva, brahmana, Buddha, chakra, guru, hatha yoga, karma, lingam, maharaja(h), mahatma, mantra, Maya, nirvana, raja(h), rani/ranee, satyagraha, sutra, swastika, yantra, yoga, yogasana*. **7.** Sinhala: *anaconda, tourmaline*. **8.** TAGALOG: *boondock, ylang-ylang*. **9.** Tamil: *catamaran, cheroot, curry, mango, mulligatawny, pariah*. **10.** Telugu: *bandicoot*.

**Asia: Central and Eastern**. **1.** Chinese languages: *china, chin-chin, chopsticks, chopsuey, chow chow, chow mein, fan-tan, ginseng, gung-ho, kaolin, ketchup/catsup, kowtow, kung fu, litchi/lichee/lychee, loquat, mahjong, pekoe, sampan, tai chi, taipan, Tao, tea, yang, yen, yin*. **2.** Japanese: *aikido, banzai, bonsai, bushido, futon, geisha, haiku, harakiri, judo, jujitsu, Kabuki, kamikaze, kimono, koan, mikado, sake, samisen, samurai, sayonara, Shinto, shogun, soy(a), sushi, teriyaki, tofu, tycoon, yen, Zen*. **3.** Tibetan: *lama, yak, yeti*. **4.** Tungus: *shaman*.

**Europe: the Celtic languages**. **1.** Breton through French: *bijou, dolmen, menhir*. **2.** Celtic before Gaelic, Welsh, Breton, and Cornish, and through Latin, French, and Old English: *ambassador/embassy, bannock, bard, bracket, breeches, car/carry/career/carriage/cargo/carpenter/charge, crag, druid, minion, peat, piece, vassal/valet/varlet*. **3.** Cornish: *porbeagle, wrasse*. **4.** Gaelic: general: *bog, cairn, clarsach, coronach, crag, crannog, gab/gob, galore, skene, usquebaugh/whisk(e)y*; Irish: *banshee, blarney, brogue, colleen, hooligan, leprechaun, lough, macushla, mavourneen, poteen, shamrock, shebeen, shillelagh, smithereens, spalpeen, Tory*. **5.** Scottish: *caber, cailleach, cairngorm, clachan, clan, claymore, corrie, glen, loch, lochan, pibroch, plaid, ptarmigan, slogan, sporran, strath, trews, trousers*. **6.** Welsh: *bug, coracle, corgi, cromlech, cwm, eisteddfod, flannel, flummery*.

**Europe: the Germanic languages**. **1.** Danish: *smørrebrød/smorrebrod*. **2.** Dutch, including Flemish and Low German (but not Afrikaans): *bluff, boor, boss, brandy, bully, bumpkin, clamp, clipper, coleslaw, cookie, cruise, dapper, derrick, dope, drill, drum, easel, frolic, golf, grime, hunk, kink, landscape, loiter, poppycock, rant, runt, scow, skipper, sled, sledge, sleigh, slim, smack, smuggle, snap, snoop, splint, spook, stoop, yacht, yawl*. **3.** German: *blitz(krieg), dachshund, fahrenheit, flak, frankfurter, glockenspiel, gneiss, hamburger, hamster, kaffeeklatsch, kindergarten, kitsch, leberwurst, leitmotiv, nix, pretzel, quartz, realpolitik, sauerkraut, schadenfreude, schmaltz, schnitzel, schwa, strafe, waltz, weltanschauung, weltgeist, yodel, zeitgeist*. **4.** Icelandic: *auk, eider, geyser, saga*.

Continued opposite

BORROWINGS INTO ENGLISH *continued*

**5.** Norse: *anger, balderdash, bing, bleak, blether, blink, bloom, blunder, blur, call, clamber, creek, crook, die, dirt, dowdy, doze, dregs, egg, fellow, flat, flaunt, flaw, fleck, flimsy, gasp, gaunt, gaze, girth, glint, glitter, gloat, happen, harsh, inkling, kick, kilt, law, leg, loan, meek, midden, muck, muggy, nasty, nudge, oaf, odd, raise, root, scalp, scant, scowl, seat, skerry, skewer, skid, skill, skin, skull, sky, sniff, snub, squall, squeal, take, they, thrall, thrift, thrust, ugly, vole, want, weak, window.* **6.** Norwegian: *fjord/fiord, floe, kraken, krill, lemming, ski, slalom.* **7.** Scots, in English at large: *balmoral, burn, canny, carfuffle/kerfuffle, collie, cosy, eerie, eldritch, forebear, glamour, glengarry, gloaming, glower, gumption, guddle, lilt, pony, raid, rampage, uncanny, wee, weird, wizened, wraith*; mainly in Scotland: *ashet, bogle, bonnie, burn, cleg, dreich, dwam, fornent, furth of, glaikit, glaur, hochmagandy, howf, leal, lowp, outwith, scunner, speir, stot, thole, trauchle.* **8.** Swedish: *glogg, ombudsman, smörgåsbord/smorgasbord, tungsten.* **9.** Yiddish: *chutzpah, shlemiel, shlep, shlock, schmaltzy.*

***Europe: Greek***. **1.** Inflectional endings retained but spelt in the Latin style: *abiogenesis, aegis, analysis, anemone, antithesis, automaton, charisma, cinema, crisis, criterion, cytokinesis, diagnosis, dogma, drama, electron, enigma, genesis, gnosis, hoi polloi, kerygma, lalophobia, magma, osteoporosis, phenomenon, photon, rhinoceros, rhododendron, stigma, synthesis, thesis.* **2.** With Latin endings: *brontosaurus, chrysanthemum, diplodocus, hippopotamus, Pliohippus.* **3.** Endings dropped or adapted: *agnostic, agnosticism, alphabet, alphabetic, analyst, analytic, anthocyanin, astrobleme, atheism, automatic, biologist, biology, blasphemy, charismatic, chemotherapy, chronobiology, cinematography, critic, criticism, dinosaur, dogmatic, dogmatism, dramatic, dramatist, electric, electronic, enigmatic, epistemic, epistemology, gene, genetic, herpetology, narcolepsy, odyssey, oligarchy, patriarch, phenomenology, photograph, pterodactyl, sympathomimetic.* **4.** Modern: *bouzouki, moussaka, ouzo, rebetika, sirtaki, souvlaki.*

***Europe: Latin***. **1.** Inflectional endings retained: *addendum, albumen, apex, area, bacterium/bacteria, cactus, calix, camera, cancer, circus, colossus, complex, datum/data, discus, equilibrium, fauna, flora, formula, fungus, genius, genus, homunculus, honorarium, inertia, interim, latex, locus, medium/media, memorandum, momentum, onus, opera, ovum, pauper, pendulum, peninsula, propaganda, radium, referendum, series, simile, simplex, status, stimulus, terminus, vertigo, victor.* **2.** Actual inflected Latin verbs used as nouns: *audio, audit, caveat, exeunt, fiat, floruit, imprimatur, mandamus, video.* **3.** Fixed phrases: *ad hoc, a posteriori, de facto, de jure, extempore, (ex) post facto, post mortem, quid pro quo, sine die.* **4.** Binomials: *Homo sapiens, Pax Britannica, miles gloriosus, gluteus maximus.* **5.** Endings dropped or adapted, often through French: *add, addition, additive, agent, agentive, aqueduct, candle, colo(u)r, colossal, consider, contemplate, decide, decision, erupt, eruption, general, generic, hono(u)r, hono(u)rable, honorary, igneous, ignite, ignition, ignoble, illiteracy, illiterate, immoral, immortality, ingenious, ingenuity, literacy, literate, literature, meditate, meditation, meditative, memorable, memory, moment, momentary, momentous, moral, morality, nobility, noble, pendulous, peninsular, revise, revision, sex, similar, similarity, temple.*

***Europe: the Romance languages***. **1.** French, Old: *allow, bastard, beauty, beef, brush, castle, chivalry, choice, cloister, conquest, constraint, court, defeat, destroy, dinner, forest, frail, garden, govern, honest, hostel, interest, judge, loyal, marvel, mutton, paste, place, poison, pork, priest, push, quarter, quest, royal, stuff, sure, tempest, ticket, trick*; Modern: *aperitif/apértif, apresski/après-ski, avantgarde, bidet, bourgeois(ie), brasserie, brassiere/brassière, cafe/café, camouflage, canard, chateau/château, chef, chevalier, coup de grace/grâce, coup d'etat/état, croissant, cuisine, debacle/débacle/débâcle, debut/début,*

*Continued over*

BORROWINGS INTO ENGLISH *continued*

*dessert, elite/élite, esprit de corps, etiquette, fiance(e)/fiancé(e), fricasee/fricassée, frisson, garage, gourmand, gourmet, hors d'oeuvre, hotel, joie de vivre, liaison, limousine, lingerie, marionette, morale, nee/née, objet d'art. parole, pastiche, patisserie/pâtisserie, petite, pirouette, prestige, regime/régime, risque/risqué, silhouette, souvenir, toilette, vignette, voyeur,* **2.** Italian, through French: *balcony, battalion, brigade, charlatan, design, frigate, granite, squadron;* direct: *alto, arpeggio, bordello, broccoli, cameo, canto, confetti, contralto, cupola, ghetto, graffiti, grotto, imbroglio, lasagne, libretto, mozzarella, pasta, piano(forte), piazza, piccolo, pizza, pizzeria, pizzicato, ravioli, risotto, sonata, seraglio, soprano, spaghetti, staccato, stanza, studio, tagliatelle, vermicelli.* **3.** Occitan/Provençal, usually through French: *ballad, beret, cocoon, funnel, nutmeg, troubadour.* **4.** Portuguese: *albino, caste, marmalade, molasses, palaver.* **5.** Spanish, adapted: *alligator, anchovy, barricade, cask, cedilla, galleon, grenade, hoosegow, lariat, ranch, renegade, sherry, stampede, stevedore, vamoose;* direct: *adobe, armada, armadillo, borracho, bravado, chili, chinchilla, embargo, guerrilla, hacienda, mosquito, mulatto, negro, peccadillo, pinto, pronto, sarsaparilla, silo, sombrero, vigilante.*

***Europe: the Slavonic languages.*** **1.** Czech: *howitzer, pistol, robot.* **2.** Polish: *mazurka, polka.* **3.** Russian: *agitprop, borsch, cosmonaut, czar/tsar, dros(h)ky, glasnost, gulag, perestroika, pogrom, samizdat, samovar, steppe, troika, vodka.*

***Europe: the unique languages.*** **1.** Basque through Spanish: *chaparral, jai alai.* **2.** Finnish: *sauna.* **3.** Hungarian: *coach, czardas/csárdás, goulash, hussar, paprika, tokay.* **4.** ROMANI: *nark, pal.*

---

leaders are called *Boston Brahmins*, a wry allusion to the priestly caste of India. In the 19c, they included such literary figures as Oliver Wendell Holmes Sr., Henry Wadsworth Longfellow, and James Russell Lowell, whose tastes were European and unsympathetic to the majority of 19c US writers, such as Ralph Waldo Emerson, Edgar Allan Poe, Mark Twain, and Walt Whitman. Boston represented a 'genteel' tradition in literature and language that has not survived. Currently, Bostonian speech is most widely known from the usage of President John F. Kennedy and his brothers, as stereotyped for example by the long 'flat' vowel and *r*-lessness of expressions like *paak the caa* (park the car) and the intrusive *r* of *Cuba/r is a problem*. Bostonian speech ranges from low-prestige to Boston Brahmin, which, although educated and cultured, is not widely admired outside the city. Compare NEW YORK. See DIALECT IN AMERICA.

**BOTSWANA**. A country in southern AFRICA and member of the COMMONWEALTH. Languages: Setswana (national), English (official). In 1885, under threat of settlement by Boer farmers from the Transvaal, its lands came under British influence and were divided into a southern colony, now part of the Cape province, South Africa, and the northern protectorate of *Bechuanaland*, which became independent as Botswana in 1966. See BANTU.

**BOUND AND FREE**. Contrasting terms in LINGUISTICS, used to describe elements in WORDS. A *bound form* is part of a word and cannot stand alone: *un-* and *-ly* in *unhappily*, *bash-* in *bashful*, *tang-* in *tangible*. Affixes are bound, but sometimes break free as words: *ex, ism*. A BASE that cannot stand alone is a *bound base: vis-* in *visible*. A *free form* or *free word* can stand alone: *happy*. All such forms are known in linguistics as *bound* and *free MORPHEMES*.

**BOWDLERIZE**, also BrE & AusE **bowdlerise**. To censor or expurgate a text after the style of Thomas Bowdler (1754–1825), editor of an edition of Shakespeare's plays from which explicit sexual references and avowedly vulgar elements were removed: 'When *The Taming of the Shrew* was staged in New York's Shakespeare festival this summer, it was bowdlerised to dilute the bard's misogynist sentiments' ('Male, modern, macho', *The Times Saturday Review*, 10 Nov. 1990).

**BRACKETS**. The name for PUNCTUATION marks of various kinds that mark off (more strongly than pairs of COMMAS) certain matter as distinct, parenthetical, or interpolated. Material set between brackets is not grammatically essential to a sentence, which would be complete without it. Kinds of brackets include: *round brackets* BrE, *parentheses* AmE ( ); *square brackets* BrE, *brackets* AmE [ ]; *brace brackets* or less formally *curly brackets* { }; and *angle brackets* < >.

**Round brackets/parentheses**. Extra statements that provide an explanation, a comment, an aside, an afterthought, a reference, or more information may be placed between commas, but are often more clearly set apart from the main text by means of round brackets: *Bristol (and some other cities) were mentioned; Zimbabwe (formerly Rhodesia); We shall now discuss the ode (or lyric poem); They then decided (to everyone's dismay) to withdraw; their new house (an extremely smart one) is in London; there are many (apparent) difficulties; His next book (Fire Down Below) was well received; see the next chapter (pages 32–4); He is (as he always was) a rebel.* If overused, such parentheses can break up the flow of writing and become a distraction. The decision whether matter should be between commas, round brackets, or DASHES is made by author or editor, and may be a matter of personal, editorial, or house style.

**Square brackets/brackets**. Extra information attributable to someone other than the writer of the text is usually placed between square brackets: *Carol walked in, and her sister [Sarah] greeted her.* Such interpolations are usually made by an editor who wishes to add a comment (often information unknown to the original writer) to part of a text. The added item may replace a word or phrase in the original sentence: such a statement as *It is one of Shakespeare's less well-known plays* may become when cited *[Timon of Athens] is one of Shakespeare's less well-known plays.* In dictionaries, square brackets are often used to enclose etymological and other information at the beginning or end of entries. They are also often used in the texts of plays, to enclose stage directions (usually printed in italics), and in reports of meetings or proceedings, where they may be used to make asides, such as '[*shouts from audience*]', to indicate an occurrence or circumstance that is not an essential part of the reported information.

**Brace brackets**. Seldom used in ordinary writing, brace or curly brackets are common in mathematics and other formulaic usage, where they serve to enclose complex sets of symbols. A single brace is used to indicate displayed groupings and sets:

man
cats } carnivores
dogs

cattle
elephants } herbivores
giraffes

**Angle brackets**. Special words, phrases, and symbols may be highlighted by means of angle brackets when other parenthetical devices have already been assigned a use. In linguistics, *graphemes* or minimal elements in writing are often exhibited between angle brackets, as with the digraph <ou> in *shout*. Angle brackets are, however, rare in English and are generally used to enclose material that is not part of the text: for example, instructions to a printer typesetting a text.

**Nesting**. The nesting or embedding of brackets within brackets is not common in everyday print, but is not unusual in casual writing (especially handwritten letters), and is standard practice in some kinds of technical writing, such as grammatical analysis. When complex nesting occurs, the number of opening and closing brackets has to be the same, as in the analytical version of *Coventry car factory strike committee policy decision*: ((((Coventry) (car factory)) (strike committee)) (policy decision)). See PARENTHESIS.

**BREVE**. A cup-like DIACRITIC (˘) placed over a vowel letter to show that it is short. See MACRON.

**BRITICISM**. Also **Britishism**. A word or other expression typical of English as used in Britain, particularly after the late 18c, when varieties of the language were established beyond the British Isles and, especially in the case of AmE, began to develop their own standard and critical traditions. The term may or may not subsume ANGLICISM and SCOTTICISM, and contrasts with AMERICANISM in particular and also with AUSTRALIANISM, CANADIANISM, INDIANISM, IRISHISM, NEW ZEALANDISM, etc. Because AMERICAN ENGLISH AND BRITISH ENGLISH are the major forms of the language, are used by the largest number of native speakers, and are the most widely known of all national varieties, they tend to be defined and discussed in terms of each other. Scholars of English in the US are as inclined to point out Briticisms as their colleagues in the UK are to point out Americanisms. The term applies to all aspects of usage, but is most often applied to vocabulary: where *government* is often used in the UK in the sense of Prime Minister and Cabinet, the nearest US equivalent is *administration*; while in BrE *school* is generally restricted to pre-university education, in AmE it applies to any educational level. Technological fields that developed independently in the two nations have often had different terminologies, as in the automotive industry (BrE first in each pair): *bonnet/hood, boot/trunk, bumper/fender, dip switch/dimmer, dynamo/generator, fascia/dashboard, indicator/blinker, quarterlight/vent, silencer/muffler, windscreen/windshield, wing/fender.*

**BRITISH BLACK ENGLISH**, also known as **patois**. Any of several varieties of CREOLE English used in the UK by the children of immigrants from the Commonwealth Caribbean since the 1950s. While the older generation often retain their creoles, younger speakers have acquired local varieties of BrE and in some cases a modified variety of their parents' creole which may emerge during adolescence as an assertion of black identity. Its use is often associated with black youth culture, Rastafarianism, and reggae. Although speakers sometimes call it *Jamaican*, it is in many respects different from JAMAICAN CREOLE, which has no gender distinction, so that both male and female are referred to as *im*. In *London Jamaican*, *shi* is also used, probably under the influence of mainstream English. Linguists are not agreed whether there is a continuum of varieties linking English and the creole, as in Jamaica, or whether there are discrete, diglossic systems. Many speakers codeswitch between English and PATOIS and there are few intermediate forms. Most speakers live in the London area, with other concentrations in Birmingham and Leeds, where there is some influence from local speech. Patois is also used by some white children in black peer groups. There has been in recent years an increasing range of literature, especially poetry, in British Black English. See BLACK ENGLISH, DIGLOSSIA.

**BRITISH COUNCIL, The**, short forms *the Council, the BC*. An autonomous, non-political organization set up in the UK in 1934 to counter Fascist propaganda in Europe by promoting a wider knowledge of Britain and the English language, and developing cultural relations with other countries. It was incorporated by Royal Charter in 1940 and is run from London by a director general and a board with 17 advisory committees. Its first overseas offices were in Europe, Latin America, and West Asia; since the 1950s it has been involved with educational work in Commonwealth and other countries. In the 1980s, the Council merged with the *Inter-University Council*, a body that set up links between British and overseas universities. In matters of language scholarship and teaching, it is advised by an *English Teaching Advisory Committee*. In 1990, it had offices in 84 countries with 54 teaching centres in 35 countries. It organizes a wide range of educational, technical, and cultural activities, and Council Directors work closely with but separately from British embassies and high commissions.

**The BC and ELT**. During the 1960s, the Council through its advisory committee was instrumental in setting up the first departments of applied linguistics in British universities, to train, among others, those working overseas on Council and government contracts. Council-supported scholars remain a major source of students of applied linguistics and TEFL. The BC was the original publisher of *English Language Teaching* (now *English Language Teaching Journal*), *Language Teaching Abstracts* (now *Language Teaching*), and *ELT Documents*. Its management of the government-funded *Aid to Commonwealth English* (*ACE*) (1962–76) and *Key English Language Teaching* (*KELT*) (1977–89) schemes, now superseded, led to involvement in teacher education, curriculum development, and particularly *English for Special Purposes*. More recently, attention has turned to the promotion of British public- and private-sector services, and a Promotion Unit with its own representative steering group was set up in 1989.

**The BC and British English**. In 1985, the then director general Sir John Burgh noted in an interview that the Council does not 'actively propagate *British English* as a commodity or as the proper model for foreign users. It so happens that for all sorts of reasons—including, of course, that the very name *English* suggests to many foreign learners that we in this country speak the "purest", and, therefore, the best form of the language—British English is often the preferred model . . . The Council has no tradition or policy of preferring or propagating any one *accent* over another, and communicates with its many clients in standard written English. It occasionally happens that when recruiting staff for service with an overseas employer the Council will be asked for a speaker of Received Pronunciation or of BBC English' (*English Today*, 3, July 1985). In 1989, Sir Richard Francis, director general at that time, said in an interview: 'Britain's real black gold is not oil, but the English language' (to William Greaves, *The Times*, 24 Oct. 1989). He referred to the Council *as brokers* who assisted the British ELT *industry* to promote a *product* around the world, adding that 'it's difficult to quantify [English] as a national resource. The value, in the post-industrial age, of having people use the language of one's own culture is virtually inestimable. . . . I often refer to English as a linguistic continent, which isn't confined to the bounds of Africa or America or whatever.'

## ■ BRITISH ENGLISH ────── ■

Short from *BrE*. The English language as used in Britain. The phrase contrasts with kinds of ENGLISH used elsewhere, and especially with AmE. For many people, however, especially in England, the usage is tautologous. For example, the language-teaching organization Linguaphone has often made a distinction in advertising its courses between simply 'English' and 'American English'. In addition, the phrase *British English* has a monolithic quality, as if it were a homogeneous variety and a straightforward fact of life. The term, however, shares in the ambiguities and tensions associated with the term *BRITISH*, and can be used and interpreted in two ways, with some blurring between them:

**A broader interpretation**. Broadly understood, BrE is the English language as used in Great Britain (England, Scotland, and Wales) or the United Kingdom of Great Britain and Northern Ireland, depending on the use of *British* employed. In this sense, the term covers all varieties, STANDARD and NON-STANDARD, at all times, in all regions, and at all social levels. It is unlikely, however, to include the variety known as *SCOTS*, which in this context is usually treated, explicitly or implicitly, as a separate entity. In this interpretation, BrE is a heterogeneous range of ACCENTS and DIALECTS, including standard varieties used in several systems of education.

**A narrower interpretation**. Narrowly understood, BrE is the form of STANDARD ENGLISH used in Britain at large or more specifically in England, and more specifically still in south-eastern England. It is essentially the medium of the middle and upper classes. Although not confined to one accent, especially in recent decades, it has been associated since at least the late 19c with the accent known since the 1920s as RECEIVED PRONUNCIATION (*RP*), and with the phrases *the QUEEN'S ENGLISH*, OXFORD *ENGLISH*, and *BBC ENGLISH*. When BrE refers to a model of English taught to foreigners, it is an idealization of the south-eastern middle-class standard, as presented in dictionaries and other materials prepared for learners.

**Tensions and controversies**. The precise naming of the kind or kinds of English used in the UK, and in those parts of the English-speaking world which have been closely influenced by it (mainly in the Commonwealth), is affected by tensions and controversies that fall into three groups:

*Regional antagonism*. There are different perspectives and preferences in different parts of Britain. These include objections among the non-English to being categorized as English. While they object to this on grounds of ethnic reality, they also object to occasions when especially the southern English treat their use of English as quaint or inferior. Scots often argue that they exist in the worst of both worlds: they are called English when they are not English at the same time as their use of English is dismissed as not English. To a lesser degree, there are also within England tensions between in particular the North and the South, in which NORTHERN ENGLISH is often seen as secondary to Southern English, principally because it has no educated spoken standard to weigh against RP.

*Class antagonism*. Issues of class remain significant in Britain, often mixed with regional, ethnic, and linguistic issues. Many working-class people regard the standard language and RP as beyond their reach, as middle-class impositions, or both. Standard usage containing 'big words' is sometimes seen as a kind of social and educational conspiracy, while RP and near-RP accents, despite their general prestige, or perhaps because of it, are perceived as *posh, hoity-toity, put on,* or *toffee-nosed* (snobbish and affected).

***Precision of reference***. The issues relating to region and class become linguistic when their clarification depends on the preciseness or looseness of the terms used to discuss them. The scholarly debate includes both defences of and objections to the presentation of the traditional, standard, RP-linked variety as a single, prestige form when it is used by a small minority. The English sociolinguist Peter Trudgill has observed:

> My own preferred label for varieties of English from England is 'English English', by analogy with 'American English', 'Australian English' etc. . . . Note that, whatever label is used, we have been careful in this book to distinguish between the terms 'English English' and 'British English'. The latter is often used in literature, particularly, it seems, by Americans and writers on English as a foreign language, where it is really the former that is intended. (Introduction, *Language in the British Isles*, 1984)

**Kinds of British English**. It is not, however, surprising that the term *ENGLISH ENGLISH* is not widely used. To the English it seems as tautologous or as silly and inelegant as 'German German' and 'French French', whether or not there may be grounds for using those names, as for example to distinguish German in Germany from Austrian German and French in France from Quebec French. However, to many Scots, Irish, and Welsh people, and to others with comparable perspectives, some such term is essential to allow an explicit and productive contrast among the British varieties of English. Equally, however, the term *SCOTTISH ENGLISH* can seem odd to English and Scots alike, because of the ethnic sense of the word 'English': *Scottish English* seems to be a contradiction in terms. Similarly, the term *IRISH ENGLISH* may seem bizarre, both because of centuries-old connotations of illogic and whimsy acquired by the word *Irish* and because of the hostility of

many in Ireland towards anything that links them too closely with England.

Because they belong to groups with strong positions in the 'pecking order' of the language, English and American scholars have tended to find 'British English' and 'American English' convenient labels for their respective varieties and standards, without further qualification. However, in recent years interest in and action on behalf of other varieties has made it difficult for these labels to be used as sweepingly and uncritically as in the past. It has also become increasingly difficult to resist the use of such terms as *English English, Scottish English,* WELSH ENGLISH, HAWAIIAN ENGLISH, INDIAN ENGLISH, SINGAPORE ENGLISH on the grounds that they are tautologous, paradoxical, bizarre, or dubious.

See AMERICAN ENGLISH AND BRITISH ENGLISH, BRITICISM, BRITISH COUNCIL, ENGLISH IN ENGLAND, HISTORY, NORTHERN IRISH ENGLISH.

**BRITISH NATIONAL CORPUS**. Short form *BNC*. An electronic CORPUS of texts (compiled 1991–4) drawn principally from UK printed sources and intended in the main for researchers and publishers. The BNC consortium, which consists of academic institutions (the British Library, Oxford University Computing Service, and the University of Lancaster) and publishers (Chambers-Harrap, Longman, and Oxford University Press), has been supported by the UK Department of Trade and Industry. The corpus (sampling from 1960 onwards) consists of 100m running words of BrE, 90m of these from a wide selection of printed texts (technical and literary, books and periodicals, long-term and ephemeral, and including such unpublished material as postcards, tickets, and banknotes) and 10m from unscripted spoken text (at least half of it spontaneous conversation, and drawn from such sources as lectures, tutorials, sales demonstrations, legal proceedings, committee meetings, and broadcast chat shows).

**BROAD**. **1.** An often dismissive term for a DIALECT, ACCENT, or USAGE considered coarse, rustic, uneducated, and difficult to understand: 'I toke an olde boke, and the englysshe was so rude and brood that I could not wele vnderstande it' (Caxton, *Eneydos*, 1490); 'Broad Yorkshire talked all over the ship' (*Blackwood's Magazine*, 1859). **2.** In PHO-

NETICS, a term referring to a TRANSCRIPTION in which only significantly different sounds are marked, as opposed to a *narrow* transcription. See PHONETIC TRANSCRIPTION, SPEECH.

**BROAD SCOTS**, also **Broad Scotch**, **Braid Scots**. Traditional terms for SCOTS or for its more distinctive dialects. Unlike many other expressions involving *broad*, the terms are generally neutral or positive: 'In plain braid Scots hold forth a plain braid story' (Robert Burns, *Brigs of Ayr*, 1787). See BROAD.

**BROGUE**. An informal, non-technical term for an Irish and sometimes a Scottish or West Country ACCENT. In the 18c, the expression to *have the brogue on one's tongue* was common for an Irish accent and the word has been used at least since the 17c: '[They] had both their Education at the English Court, which something refin'd their Gibberish, yet not so much, but that there is still a Brogue' (James Farewell, *The Irish Hudibras*, London, 1689). The term is used humorously and facetiously in Ireland.

**BROKEN**. **1.** An informal, non-technical term for a foreigner's limited and ungrammatical use of a language: 'The skipper asked in broken English for his help' (*Observer*, 2 Sept. 1990). **2.** Also *TORRES STRAIT BROKEN*. The name given by its speakers to the English-based CREOLE of the Torres Strait islands between Cape York in Australia and Papua New Guinea, known technically as *Torres Strait Creole*.

**BROKEN ENGLISH**. An informal and usually dismissive term for English when considered badly spoken or imperfectly learned: 'Breake thy mind to me in broken English' (Shakespeare, *Henry V*, 5.2); 'English is the international language. Or, I should say, broken English is the international language' (Akira Nambara, quoted in the *International Herald Tribune*, 28 Sept. 1987). The term has often been used to describe the English used by foreigners, aboriginal peoples, refugees, street traders, servants, and slaves See BROKEN, FOREIGNER TALK, FRACTURED ENGLISH, JARGON, PATOIS, PIDGIN.

**BROOKLYN, BROOKLYNESE**. An informal name for the dialect of the people of Brooklyn, one of the five boroughs of NEW YORK City. Originally a Dutch settlement, Brooklyn is currently both residential and industrial, as well as a centre of transport. The dialect has been stereotyped as artificial, especially in films. A typical feature is the vowel of *earl*, pronounced /əɪl/, a pronunciation found also in New Orleans and other parts of the South. In some varieties, *oil* has the same vowel, a pronunciation once common in other forms of English, so that the two words are identical in sound. In stereotypical Brooklynese, the pronunciation of the words is reversed, so that *earl* is 'oil' and *oil* is 'earl'. See NEW ORLEANS.

**BROWN CORPUS, The**. A pioneering computer-based CORPUS of 1m running words of English developed in the US in 1963–4 by Henry Kucera and W. Nelson Francis at Brown University, Providence, Rhode Island, for the statistical analysis of words in texts. Representative extracts of 2,000 words each were taken from a selection of texts that sought to balance registers, styles, and genres, and included material from newspapers, scientific writing, romantic novels, and westerns.

**BRUNEI DARASSALAM**. A country in South-East Asia, in the island of Borneo (a variant of the same name). Member of the COMMONWEALTH. Languages: Malay, English (both official), Chinese. Brunei was a British protectorate from 1888 and gained its independence in 1984.

**BULLOCK REPORT**. A British report on TEACHING ENGLISH as a mother tongue, presented by the Committee of Inquiry set up by the Secretary of State for EDUCATION and Science, Margaret Thatcher, in 1972. The Committee was chaired by the historian Sir Alan Bullock, and reported in 1975. Its remit was 'to consider in relation to schools: (a) all aspects of teaching the use of English, including reading, writing, and speech; (b) how present practice might be improved and the role that initial and in-service training might play; (c) to what extent arrangements for monitoring the general level of attainment in these skills can be introduced or improved; and to make recommendations'. In a report of over 600 pages, with 333 recommendations, the Committee summarized much of the consensus of the 1970s on the nature of English teaching, particularly reflecting attitudes associated with the work of James N. Britton. Although sceptical about claims that literacy rates had fallen substantially, the Committee called for a major investment in training and development to improve linguistic skills and linguistic awareness among both teachers and learners, and drew attention to the number of English teachers whose training was not specifically for teaching in this area. The report has been criticized for its optimism, but reflects clearly the views on language which underlay the moves to a mass, comprehensive system of schooling through the 1960s–70s. See KINGMAN REPORT, LANGUAGE AWARENESS, NEWBOLT REPORT.

**BUREAUCRATESE**. A pejorative non-technical term for the language of bureaucrats. See -ESE.

**BURMA**. A country of South-East Asia. Languages: Burmese (official), and indigenous, such as Shan and Karen. Burma was annexed to India during three wars with the British between 1824 and 1886. It gained internal self-government in 1937, and became independent in 1948. Burma did not join the Commonwealth, and discontinued the use of English as a language of administration and education. See ASEAN.

**BURNS, Robert** [1759–96]. Scottish national poet, born in Alloway, Ayrshire, and educated by a tutor, by his father at home, and by his own wide reading. His childhood and youth were spent helping his father in unsuccessful farming ventures. His first volume of poems, the Kilmarnock Edition of 1786, aroused great enthusiasm and he was fêted in Edinburgh social circles. He had friends and patrons of high rank, despite his radical views, but it was not until 1789 that he obtained in Dumfries the excise appointment he sought, and not until 1791 that he gave up farming to become a full-time exciseman. In his earliest poems, Burns hesitates between SCOTS and ENGLISH, but the influence of Robert Fergusson confirmed his preference for Scots. Widely considered the supreme poet in that tongue, Burns draws on the registers of folksong, storytelling, preaching, social banter, and daily work, as well as the Bible and Augustan English poetry, and is noted for his ability to modulate between English and Scots for subtle effects:

But pleasures are like poppies spread;
You seize the flow'r, its bloom is shed;
Or like the snow falls in the river,
A moment white—then melts for ever;
Or like the Borealis race,
That flit ere you can point their place;
Or like the rainbow's lovely form
Evanishing amid the storm.
Nae man can tether time or tide;
The hour approaches Tam maun ride;
That hour, o' night's black arch the
    key-stane,
And sic a night he taks the road in,
As ne'er poor sinner was abroad in.
                    (from *Tam o' Shanter*, 1791)

The main achievement of his later years was a body of Scots songs, some 250 of them partly or wholly his own, contributed to the collections of James Johnson (six volumes, 1787–1803) and George Thomson (five volumes, 1793–1818).

**BURR**. An informal term for a pronunciation of *r* that is perceived as 'rough', like a burr (a flower head that sticks to one's clothes), especially the uvular trill once widespread in northeast England (the *Durham/Northumbrian/Northumberland burr*) and southeast Scotland (the *Berwick/Berwickshire burr*). This 'Parisian' *r* is prestigious in French (*r grasseyé*: GUTTURAL *r*) but often stigmatized in English, speech therapists traditionally treating it as a defect. Commentators on strong *r*-pronunciation do not, however, always distinguish uvular from alveolar; defining *burr* in the OED (1880s), James A. H. Murray noted: 'Writers ignorant of phonology often confuse the Northumberland *burr* with the entirely different Scotch *r*, which is a lingual trill.' The term is also used for an accent in which a burr is prominent: 'Miss Keith spoke with a Scotch burr' (Somerset Maugham, *The Razor's Edge*, 1967). See ACCENT, GEORDIE, NEW ZEALAND ENGLISH, RHOTACISM, *R*-SOUNDS, WEST COUNTRY.

**BUSINESS ENGLISH**. The REGISTER of English appropriate to commerce and industry, and the name for training courses in business usage, especially if offered to foreign learners: 'Much business English teaching concentrates on communication skills: meetings; presentation; telephoning, and social skills in a business context etc.' (*EFL Gazette*, Nov. 1990). Some observers regard international business English as a neutral, pragmatic means of communication among non-native users of the language. Andrew Fenner has labelled it *IBL* (*international business language*): 'In a European context, IBL is the sort of English a Norwegian would use when trying to communicate with an Italian in Belgium. In other words, it is a *lingua franca* used between those for whom English is not their native language, but the only common language in which any sort of communication is possible. Its grammar and syntax vary, being modelled on those of the language of the person speaking in each case' ('Lingua Anglica: The Emergence of International Business English', *Language International*, 2: 1, 1990). See COMMERCIALESE, ESP.

**BUZZWORD**, also **buzz word**. An informal term for a word that is fashionable and used more to impress than inform: for example, *power* with the sense 'pertaining to powerful persons, indicating political or economic power', which appeared in the US in the 1980s in such phrases as *power breakfast*, *power colour*, *power necktie*, *power suit*, *power writing*. Buzz words are particularly associated with the terminology and JARGON of corporate business, government, and the sciences. Compare KEYWORD, VOGUE.

# C

[Called 'cee']. The 3rd LETTER of the Roman ALPHABET as used for English. It descends from the hook-shaped Phoenician symbol *gimel* (a name probably related to *camel*), which represented the voiced velar stop /g/. This letter was altered by the Greeks to Γ (*gamma*), with the same sound value. Gamma was then adapted by the Etruscans to represent the voiceless velar stop /k/, a use taken over by the Romans. In Old English, *c* represented both the sound /k/ as in *cynn* ('kin') and the sound *ch* /tʃ/ axs in *cinn* ('chin'). In the Romance languages, and in English under the influence of Norman French, *c* acquired a second palatalized pronunciation /s/ before *e* and *i*: a 'soft' pronunciation, as in *cell* and *cite*, contrasting with the 'hard' *c* in *crown*. This development occurred after 1066 and resulted in a shift of spelling patterns and sound-symbol correspondences, Old English forms such as *cild, cyng, cwic, is* becoming *child, king, quick, ice*. In addition, such *c/k* pairs arose as *cat* and *kitten, cow* and *kine*.

**Sound values.** *C* has the greatest sound range of all English consonants, overlapping with the values of *k, q, s, t, x*: (1) It has the hard velar value /k/ before the vowels *a, o, u* (*cat, cot, cut*) and before consonants (*clip, creep, act, tics*). (2) It has the soft, palatalized value /s/ before *e, i, y*: *cell, city, cite, cycle, fancy*. (3) When *ce, ci* are followed by another vowel or vowels, usually pronounced as a schwa, soft *c* is often modified to a *sh*-sound: *ocean, herbaceous, special, efficient, suspicion*. (4) In some sets of derivationally associated words, *c* alternates between the above values: /k/ and /s/ in *electric/electricity*, /k/ anxd /ʃ/ in *logic/logician*. (5) Elsewhere, especially in some loans, *c* is soft before *ae, oe* in Latin *caesura* and Greek *coelacanth*, soft in French *façade* (often written without the cedilla, as *facade*), and generally hard in *Celt/Celtic*. It has a *ch*-sound as in *cheese*, in such loans from Italian as *cello, Medici*. (6) The *c* is silent in *indict, muscle* (but note *muscular*), and *victuals* ('vittles'), and may be regarded as silent before *q* in *acquaint, acquire*, etc., and after *x* in *excel, except*, etc. (7) The values of *cz* in

*Czech* (/tʃ/) and *czar* (/z/), also spelt *tsar*, are unique.

**Double C.** The following patterns for the pronunciation of double *c* are consistent with the basic hard and soft values of *c*: (1) Hard before *a, o, u*: *saccade, account, occult*. (2) Hard then soft before *e, i* (with the same value as *x*): *accept, accident* (but note the hard value in *soccer*).

**CH.** (1) *Vernacular.* Affricate /tʃ/ in word-initial position (*chase, cheese, choose*) and word-finally in *each, teach*. After single short vowels, *t* usually precedes *ch*: *match, fetch, kitchen, botch, hutch* (but note *t* after a long vowel in *aitch* and no *t* after short *ou* in *touch*). However, no *t* occurs in several grammatical words (*much, such, which*), in *rich*, after another consonant (*belch, lunch*), and in some longer words (*duchess*). (2) *Greek and Italian.* The value of /k/ in words derived from Greek (*chaos, technique, monarch*) and in loans from Italian before *e, i* (*scherzo, Chianti*). (3) *French.* Commonly, a *sh*-sound in loans from French: *Charlotte, chef, machine*. (4) *German.* The *ch* in *Bach, Aachen* is generally pronounced with /k/, but may have the German value /x/, especially in ScoE. (5) *Scottish.* A voiced velar fricative in many ScoE words (*loch, pibroch*) and in traditional Scots (*bricht, micht, nicht* = *bright, might, night*). Outside Scotland, such words as *loch, clarsach* are usually pronounced with /k/. (6) *Other values.* In *spinach, sandwich*, and a common local pronunciation for the English city of Norwich, the *ch* is often voiced ('spinnidge', 'san(g)widge', 'Norridge'). In *yacht* (from Dutch), and *fuchsia* (from German), the *ch* has probably never been sounded in English.

**CK.** (1) *CK* with the value /k/ is common after short vowels in short words: *cackle, peck, flicker, lock, suck*. The ending *-ic* was formerly spelt *-ick* in such words as *logic* (*logick*) and *magic* (*magick*), the shorter form becoming general first in AmE, then spreading to BrE in the 19c. Recent French loans like *bloc, chic, tic* have only *c*. (2) When suffixes are added to words ending in *c*, the hard value can be preserved by adding *k*: *panic/panicking, picnic/picnicker* (but note *arc/arced, arcing*).

An inhabitant of *Quebec* may be a *Quebecker* or a *Quebecer*, both pronounced with /k/.

**SC**. Before *e*, *i*, the value of *sc* is generally that of *s* alone: *scene*, *science*, *ascetic*, *descend*, *disciple*, *coalesce*. Some words containing *sc* acquired the *c* fairly late, sometimes by mistaken etymology: *scent*, *scissors*, and *scythe* were written *sent*, *sizars*, and *sithe* until the 17c. When followed by schwa, *sc* before *e* or *i* has the *sh*-sound of *c* alone in such a position: *conscience*, *conscious*, *luscious*. Loans from Italian also give *sc* the *sh*-sound before *e*, *i*: *crescendo*, *fascist*.

**SCH**. (1) Pronounced as /sk/ when it contains Greek *ch*: *scheme*, *schizoid*, *school*. (2) Pronounced as if *sh* in loans from German: *schadenfreude*, *Schubert*. *Schist* is usually pronounced as in German ('shist'), despite its ultimate Greek origin and its arrival in English through French. Greek-derived *schism* (spelt *scism* until the 15c) is either 'skism' or 'sism'.

**Variation**. (1) The use of *c* may depend on orthographic context. Word-finally, especially after long vowels, the hard value is normally represented by *k* (*take*, *speak*, *like*, *oak*, *rook*, *lurk*), but when such forms as *bicycle* and *Michael* are abbreviated, *c* becomes *k* (*bike* and *Mike*). If *l* or *r* follows, *c* may be found: *treacle*, *acre*. (2) A soft value in word-final position may be spelt *-ce* or *-se*: compare *mortice/mortise*, *fence/tense*, *fleece/geese* and BrE *licence/license*. (3) Sometimes, although there is no *c* in a base word, a secondary form has the letter: *louse/lice*, *mouse/mice*, *die/dice*, *penny/pence*, *despise/despicable*, *opaque/opacity*. (4) There is variation between *c* and *t* among some adjectives derived from nouns in *c*: *face/facial*, *palace/palatial*, *race/racial*, *space/spatial*, *finance/financial*, *substance/substantial*. (5) There has long been uncertainty about when to write *ct* and when to write *x* in such pairs as *connection/connexion* and *inflection/inflexion*, but not now in *complexion* (formerly also *complection*). (6) There is more or less free variation in the pairs *czar/tsar* and *disc/disk*, and a mild tendency for *cs* and *cks* to be replaced by *x*, as in *facsimile* shortened to *fax* and *Dickson* also spelt *Dixon*. (7) Common spelling errors include *supersede* spelt \**supercede* on the analogy of *precede*, and *consensus* spelt \**concensus* through the influence of *census*.

**American and British differences**. (1) AmE *defense*, *offense* (and optionally *pretense*) contrast with BrE *defence*, *offence*, *pretence*. (2) In BrE, there is a distinction between *practice* (noun) and *practise* (verb), but not in AmE, which has *practice* for both. (3) Only *vice* occurs in BrE, but AmE distinguishes *vice* (moral depravity) from *vise* (tool). (4) BrE has an anomalous hard *c* before *e* in *sceptic* (contrast *sceptre* and *septic*), but AmE has an unambiguous *k* in *skeptic*. (5) AmE prefers *mollusk* to *mollusc*, the only possible spelling in BrE. (6) AmE prefers *ck* in *check* to *que* in *cheque*, the only possible spelling in BrE. (7) *Sch* in *schedule* has the value *sh* in BrE, *sk* in AmE. Compare G, K, Q, X. See HARD AND SOFT.

**CAJUN**, sometimes **Cajan**. **1.** Also *Cajun French*. A dialect of French in southern Louisiana, developed from the regional French carried there in the 18c by immigrants expelled from Acadia in Canada. Cajun is one of three kinds of local French: Louisiana Standard French, Cajun, and CREOLE. All three are spoken varieties, although the now rare standard form is written for ceremonial occasions. *Creole* developed from the French-based creole brought by black slaves from the Caribbean. Cajun and Creole are spoken side by side and have been influenced by each other and by English. **2.** Also *Cajun English*. The English that has arisen in the 23 parishes of Louisiana called Acadiana, where about 16% of the population still speaks Cajun French. Several characteristics are borrowings or translations from French, such as *cher* as a term of endearment, *make* (compare French *faire*) as an auxiliary verb (*He made closed the door*), *hair* as a count noun (*I have to wash my hairs*: compare French *cheveux*), and the object pronoun used for emphasis at the beginning or end of a sentence (*Me, I'm going to the store*; *I was late, me*: compare *moi*). **3.** Someone descended from the original immigrants, especially if living in Acadiana and speaking Cajun French and English. Cajuns are known for devotion to family life, Roman Catholicism, hunting and fishing, and 'passing' a good time. Their cuisine and music enjoy widespread popularity in the US, as manifestations of the Cajun motto: *Laissez les bons temps rouler!* Let the good times roll! See AMERICAN ENGLISH.

**CALQUE**, also LOAN TRANSLATION. A word or other expression formed by translating from another language, such as Shaw's *superman* (1903), from German *Übermensch* (as used by Nietzsche in 1883). The Romans calqued freely from Greek; from *poiótēs* (suchness), *posótēs* (muchness), they formed *qualitas* and *quantitas*. Calques are often used for ad hoc glossing, as with 'suchness' and 'muchness' above. Sometimes, a Greek original and its Latin calque have both entered English: *apátheia* and its calque *indolentia* provide English with both *apathy* and *indolence*. Calques are often formed from compounds in a source language: for example, German *Weltanschauung* becoming English 'world-view'. They may also consist of entire translated phrases, such as 'Time flies' from Latin *Tempus fugit* and 'that goes without saying' from French *cela va sans dire*. See BORROWING, FOREIGNISM, LOAN.

## CAMBRIDGE CERTIFICATE OF PROFICIENCY IN ENGLISH, short form *CPE*.

Also referred to as *Cambridge Proficiency in English*, *Cambridge Proficiency*, *Proficiency*. A prestigious EFL examination introduced by UCLES in 1913 for foreign teachers of English, and taken throughout the world by advanced learners of English. It has no teacher-training content, but has an academic orientation and its standard is equivalent to GCE A Level (UK: General Certificate of Education Advanced Level).

## CAMBRIDGE ENGLISH. A name for

English literature as taught at the U. of Cambridge since the establishment in 1912 of the Edward VII Chair of English Literature, whose first incumbent was Arthur Quiller-Couch: 'Eventually an English Tripos [final honours degree examination] was proposed and agreed to in 1917, when, it was remarked, many of the dons who might have opposed it were away at the war. The ensuing Golden Age of Cambridge English has been widely commemorated in myth and memoir' (Bernard Bergonzi, *Exploding English*, 1990). Major figures of the 'golden age' (1920s–30s) included I. A. Richards, William Empson, and F. R. Leavis. Compare OXFORD ENGLISH.

## CAMBRIDGE SYNDICATE. See UCLES.

## CAMEROON. A country of West Africa

and member of the COMMONWEALTH. Languages: English, French (both official, but to be legally binding a document must be in French), KAMTOK or Cameroonian Pidgin, and indigenous languages. The first Europeans in the area were the Portuguese in the 15c, who established a trade in slaves that in the early 17c passed to the Dutch. The British declared this trade illegal in 1807 and policed the waters until it ended in the 1840s. Although the British established settlements, the territory became the German protectorate of *Kamerun* in 1884, which ceased to exist during the First World War. In 1919, the region was divided into French and British zones, which became League of Nations mandates in 1922 and United Nations trusteeships in 1946. French Cameroon became an independent republic in 1960. The southern part of British Cameroon voted to join it in 1961, while the remainder joined Nigeria.

The English of Cameroon is distinguished by its coexistence with French (for administration, commerce, and education) and with *Cameroonian Pidgin* or *Kamtok*, and English-based pidgin of relatively high prestige in many communities, but no official recognition. In anglophone Cameroon (former West Cameroon, under British administration 1919–60), English is the first language of local government and education. All Cameroonian post-primary students receive a bilingual education in French and English. The speech of educated Cameroonians is distinguished by local vocabulary for foods and cultural items and by phonological peculiarities shared with Kamtok. In the metropolitan varieties of English, BrE and AmE usages and informal local usages are melded into a variety that becomes more and more affected by Pidgin as situations become less formal and speakers are further from the highest social levels. Cameroonian English is part of a national network of linguistic repertoires, including at its maximum several indigenous languages, possibly pidginized varieties of such languages, Pidgin English, and a Cameroonian French that has the same relation to French elsewhere as Cameroonian English has to English elsewhere. See WEST AFRICAN ENGLISH, WEST AFRICAN PIDGIN ENGLISH.

## ■ CANADIAN ENGLISH ───── ■

Short form *CanE*. The English language as used in Canada, a country of North America and member of the Commonwealth: a constitutional monarchy and confederation of ten provinces and two territories. This national variety has coexisted for some 230 years with Canadian French, which is almost a century older, as well as with a range of indigenous languages such as Cree, Iroquois, and Inuktitut and a number of immigrant languages such as Italian and Ukrainian. However, only English and French are official. It has been marked by the now less significant influence of BrE and the enormous ongoing impact of AMERICAN ENGLISH. Because of the similarity of American and Canadian accents, English Canadians travelling abroad are virtually resigned to being taken for Americans. However, as Gerald Clark has noted, although Canadians seem 'indistinguishable from the Americans the surest way of telling the two apart is to make the observation to a Canadian' (*Canada: The Uneasy Neighbour*, 1965). Because CanE and AmE are so alike, some scholars have argued that in linguistic terms Canadian English is no more or less than a variety of (*Northern*) *American English*. In response to the dominance of AmE, some Canadians have tended to stress the indigenous or even British features in their variety while others have felt that to do so is pretentious. Studies of CanE of necessity compare it to BrE or AmE or both, and many do nothing else. Recently, however, the view that only highly distinctive varieties are 'true' national languages is changing. The US linguist Richard W. Bailey notes: 'What is distinctly Canadian about Canadian English is not its unique linguistic features (of which there are a handful) but its combination of tendencies that are uniquely distributed' ('The English Language in Canada', in Bailey & Görlach, eds., *English as a World Language*, 1982, p. 161). In addition, the environment of CanE differs significantly from that of other varieties in two ways:

**1. *The presence of French as co-official language*.** Spoken French is concentrated in QUEBEC, New Brunswick, and eastern Ontario, while written French is ubiquitous. It appears with English on everything from signs in post offices to boxes of cornflakes, which have long been the stereotypical example of how French was being 'rammed down' unwilling English throats. In English broadcasts, a simultaneous translation formerly drowned spoken French, but lately CBC news broadcasts allow the French speaker to be heard and rely on the commentator to make the message comprehensible to anglophones without a knowledge

of French. The first *Official Languages Act* (1969) confirmed the bilingual nature of Canada at the federal level and set up the *Office of the Commissioner of Official Languages*. The Commissioner deals with complaints concerning the infringement of language rights and oversees the implementation of the Act. The Office publishes a bilingual quarterly, *Language and Society/Langue et société*.

**2. *A preoccupation with the wilderness*.** An awareness of the great empty northern spaces exists even among urban Canadians. Much as Australians are preoccupied with their myth of 'mates in the Outback', contending against nature, many Canadians are conscious of the vast extent of Canada.

**Population**. The Canadian population is highly urbanized and mobile, 80% living in urban areas within 200 km of the US border. *Canadian Standard English* (*CSE*), the English spoken in cities from Ontario to British Columbia by the middle and upper classes, is remarkably homogeneous, but the nonstandard language varies, depending on which groups originally settled an area. The differences between the main regional varieties (such as in Newfoundland, the MARITIME PROVINCES, Quebec, and from Ontario westwards) can be accounted for primarily by settlement history. The history of Ontario, the province which currently has the largest number of English-speakers and dominates the country politically, economically, and linguistically, explains why CanE sounds very much more like AmE than like BrE.

**History**. English-speaking settlers began to enter mainland Canada in significant numbers after the Treaty of Paris ceded New France to Great Britain in 1762. Most were from the New England colonies and went to what are now the provinces of Nova Scotia and New Brunswick. During and immediately after the American Revolution (1776–83), a wave of some 50,000 settlers arrived from the US, usually called *Loyalists* or *United Empire Loyalists* (*UELs*). Some 10,000 went to Quebec, 2,500 settling in the Eastern Townships south-east of Montreal and 7,500 in western Quebec, which was named Upper Canada in 1791, Canada West in 1840, and Ontario in 1867. Government promotion of settlement resulted in the arrival from the US of at least 80,000 'late loyalists' after 1791. By 1812, Upper Canada's popula-

## CANADIAN PLACE-NAMES

The place-names of Canada reflect mixed linguistic origins over some 400 years, and fall into three broad types:

**1.** *Adoptions from Amerindian and Inuit languages* Such names have generally undergone a process of Anglicization or Gallicization, as in: *Canada* (from Iroquois *kanata* 'village'), *Manitoba* (from either Assiniboin *Mini Tobow* 'lake of the prairie' or Cree *Manito Wapow* 'strait of the spirit'), *Quebec/Québec* (from Algonkian *kebec* 'narrow passage, strait'), and *Saskatchewan* (from Cree *Kisiskatchewani Sipi* 'swift-flowing river'). Such adaptations may have an English spelling (as in *Shawinigan*), a French spelling (as in *Chicoutimi*), or a neutral form (as with *Ottawa* and *Winnipeg*). Combinations of names may perpetuate complex indigenous patterns, as in the city-and-province phrases *Saskatoon Saskatchewan* and *Winnipeg Manitoba*.

**2.** *Transfers and inventions by British and French settlers* Place-names of British origin fall into four broad categories: transferred British names such as *London*, *Hamilton*, and *Kingston* (all in Ontario); the commemoration of people in Britain and Canada, as with *the Queen Charlotte Islands*, *King Edward Island*, *Victoria*, *Prince Albert* (Saskatchewan), *Wolfe Island*, *Churchill Falls* (Labrador), and *Shakespeare* (Ontario); frontier coinages, such as *Hell's Gate* (rapids on the Fraser River in British Columbia), *Kicking Horse Pass*, and *Medicine Hat*; and descriptions, such as *Clear Lake* and *Thunder Bay*. Among place-names of French origin, whose pattern is similar, saints' names are particularly notable, especially in Quebec, as with *Saint-Chrysostome*, *Saint-Felix-de-Valois*, and even *Saint-Stanislas-de-Koska-de-la-Rivière-des-Envies*. Some predominantly French names have English equivalents, such as *Trois-Rivières* (Quebec), also known as *Three Rivers*. Many names have (more or less) the same spelling in both languages but different pronunciations, as for example *Montréal/Montreal*, *Ontario*, and *Québec/Quebec*. In addition, while the names of some provinces are more or less the same in both the official languages, some are distinctly different; for example, *British Columbia* is *Colombie-Britannique* in French, the Anglo-Latin *Nova Scotia* (New Scotland) is *Nouvelle-Ecosse*, and *Newfoundland* is *Terreneuve*.

**3.** *Native and Anglo-French hybrids and translations* The *Red River* which flows through Winnipeg, Manitoba translates French *Rivière Rouge* which in turn translates Cree *Miscousipi*. In Quebec, such forms as *Sainte-Hélène-de-Kamouraska* and *Saint-Prosper-de-Dorchester* result from French/Amerindian and French/English mixing. The now-extinct trading pidgin known as Chinook Jargon (blending Chinook, Nootka, French, and English) has provided the first elements in *Siwash Rock* (from French *sauvage* 'wild, savage', applied to Amerindians) and *Canim Lake* (from *canoe*), both in British Columbia. *Dauphin*, Manitoba and *Bienfait*, Saskatchewan are pronounced 'Doffin' and 'Bean Fate' respectively. And ironically, French *Baie D'Espoir* 'bay of hope', Newfoundland is locally pronounced 'Bay Despair'.

*In the North, an aboriginal revival*. Inuktitut (Eskimo) names are beginning to replace English-language place-names in the North: for example, *Frobisher Bay* has become *Iqaluit* and *Resolute Bay* is *Kaujuitoq*. In addition, the names for the proposed divisions of the Northwest Territories are *Nunavut* from Inuktitut for the Eastern Arctic and *Denendeh* from Dene for the Western Arctic.

tion of around 100,000 was 80% of American background. This population consolidated its values by fighting against American attack during the War of 1812. By 1871, the population of Ontario had risen to 1.6m.

Canadian linguists disagree about the reasons for the similarity between CanE and Northern AmE. Partly in reaction to American linguists' suggestions that CanE is simply derivative from AmE, M. H. Scargill (*A Short History of Canadian English*, 1988) has argued that the flood of immigrants that arrived after 1814 overwhelmed the dialect they found in Canada. In his view, CanE is the result of a mixture of northern British dialects. Its similarity to Northern AmE thus would be accounted for by common origins in the mix of British dialects. Walter S. Avis, however, has argued that by the time the first major wave of British immigrants arrived 'the course of Ontario speech had been set, American speech habits of the Northern variety having been entrenched from the beginning' ('The English Language in Canada: A Report', in *Current Trends in Linguistics*, 10: 1, 1973). Current opinion rests with Avis, although to call the UEL dialect 'American' invites debate. The Loyalists who arrived in Canada were far from homogeneous linguistically: some had been in the US for generations, others were recently arrived British soldiers, some were Gaelic- and others German-speaking. However, once the Loyalists did arrive, the process of dialect mix would have begun.

Although their descendants' tendency to overstate the loyalty and status of these settlers has been called 'the myth of the UEL', they had over a generation to establish themselves and their dialect before the first influx of British settlers. Since children generally adopt the usage of their peers rather than their parents, later British settlers had to accept the assimilation of their children's speech to an 'American' dialect:

> Listening to the children at any school, composed of the children of Englishmen, Scotchmen, Americans, and even of Germans, it is impossible to detect any marked difference in their accent, or way of expressing themselves (William Canniff, *The Settlement of Upper Canada*, 1869).

Indeed, the Irish and Scottish immigrants may well have embraced a patently non-English dialect as a sign of their rejection of England and its values. As Catharine Parr Traill observed:

> Persons who come to this country are very apt to confound the old settlers from Britain with the native Americans; and when they meet with people of rude, offensive manners, using certain Yankee words in their conversations, and making a display of independence not exactly suitable to their own aristocratic notions, they immediately suppose they must be genuine Yankees, while they are, in fact, only imitators. . . . You would be surprised to see how soon the newcomers fall into this disagreeable manner and affectation of quality, especially the inferior class of Irish and Scotch; the English less so (in *The Backwoods of Canada: Being Letters from the Wife of an Emigrant Officer*, 1836).

The English spoken in Ontario is the dominant urban form westwards because settlement west of Ontario was led by Ontario anglophones, who formed the middle and professional classes. It was deliberate government policy to ensure that non-English-speaking immigrants conformed culturally, not to their American immigrant neighbours, but to the values of the Ontario heartland, a policy accomplished primarily through the education systems.

**Pronunciation**. Generally, the standard forms of CanE and Northern AmE are alike whereas such regional varieties as the Maritimes and Newfoundland are more distinctive. The main features of standard CanE are: (1) *Canadian Raising*. There is a shibboleth that Canadians say such words as *house* and *out* differently from Americans, and by and large they do. *Canadian Raising* (a term coined by J. K. Chambers in 1973) is a convenient term for what is in fact a non-lowering of certain diphthongs that are lowered in most other dialects. The tongue is raised higher to produce the diphthong in *knife, house* than in *knives, houses*. In general terms, these diphthongs have a raised onset before voiceless consonants: /ai/ becomes /ʌi/ and /au/ becomes /ʌu/. In the following pairs, only the first word has the raised onset: *tripe/tribe, bite/bide, tyke/tiger, knife/knives, price/prizes, lout/loud, mouth (n)/mouth (v)*. Many Americans from western New England across the Great Lakes have the raised onset for /ai/, but far fewer have it for /aʊ/. These raised diphthongs appear to be an innovation resulting from dialect mix. Studies of the speech of Montreal, Ottawa, Toronto, Vancouver, and Victoria show that Canadian Raising is a majority usage (over 90% in Vancouver, over 60% in Ottawa), but that there is a trend away from raising toward standard AmE values, led by women under 40. (2) *The cot/caught distinction*. Many phonological features shared with Northern AmE are distributed distinctively in standard CanE: for example, the low back vowels have merged, so that Canadians pronounce *cot/caught*, *Don/Dawn*, *awful/offal*, *caller/collar* with the same vowel sound, although the quality of this sound varies. This merger is widespread in the US (in eastern New England and western Pennsylvania) and is spreading in the Midwest and West, but a distinction between *cot/caught*, etc. is maintained in all US areas bordering on Canada. (3) *T-flapping and T-deletion*. Especially in casual speech, many Canadians, like many Americans, pronounce /t/ as /d/ between vowels and after /r/, a feature known as *t-flapping*. Such pairs as *waiting/wading*, *metal/medal*, *latter/ladder*, *hearty/hardy* are therefore often homophones and the city of Ottawa is called 'Oddawa'. In addition, the /t/ is usually deleted after *n*, so that *Toronto* is pronounced 'Toronna' or 'Trawna' by most of the city's inhabitants. (4) *Use of WH*. Speakers of standard CanE tend more than speakers of standard Northern AmE to drop the distinction between initial /hw/ and /w/, making homophones out of *which/witch*. (5) Different regional and social groups vary the pronunciation of some words, such as *lever*, *schedule*, *aunt*, *route*, *hostile*. As with the lexical variants like *tap/faucet*, *pail/bucket*, *porch/verandah*, the differences are generally ascribed to the degree of influence from AmE.

**Grammar**. Where CanE differs grammatically from BrE it tends to agree with AmE. However, where such differences exist, Canadians are often more aware of both usages than Americans, either because they use both or have been exposed to both. Middle-class Canadians over 40 prefer *have you got* as in *Have you got a match?* to either the AmE *Do you have a match?* or the conservative BrE *Have you a match?*, but the younger generation and those with some post-secondary education are moving to the American form.

**Canadian EH**. The belief, especially among Americans, that Canadians frequently use *eh* (*It's nice, eh?*) is borne out by research, but until more comparative work can be done, the assertion of Walter Avis ('So *Eh?* is Canadian, eh?', in *Canadian Journal of Linguistics*, 17, 1972) that it is not uniquely a Canadianism must stand. As elsewhere, this interjection is used in Canada to mean *could you please repeat what you said*, but more commonly it is a tag question (*You do want to go, eh? = don't you?*) or serves to elicit agreement or confirmation (*It's nice, eh?*) and to intensify commands, questions, and exclamations (*Do it, eh?*). It is also common in anecdotes: *He's holding on to a firehose, eh? The thing is jumping all over the place, eh, and he can hardly hold on to it eh? Well, he finally loses control of it, eh, and the water knocks down half a dozen bystanders*. This last use, the anecdotal *eh*, is the most stigmatized.

**Vocabulary**. English Canadians have developed the vocabulary they have needed in their special environment by borrowing from indigenous languages and from French, by extending and adapting traditional English words, and by coining new words, in addition to which, CanE vocabulary has been affected by institutional bilingualism:

**1. *Borrowing from indigenous languages***. There are two sources of native borrowing: the Canadian Indian languages such as Cree, Dene, and Ojibwa, and Inuktitut, the language of the Inuit or Eskimo. Such words tend to relate to flora and fauna, early economic and social activities, travel, and survival. From the Indian languages come *chipmunk*, *mackinaw* (a bush jacket), *moose*, *muskeg* (boggy, mossy land), *muskrat*. From Inuktitut come *kayak*, *mukluk*, *anorak*, *parka*, *malemute*, *husky*. A productive borrowing from Micmac through French is *toboggan*, a runnerless wooden sled still used by children. The word produced the logging terms *bogan* and *logboggan*. A motorized sled was first called a *motor toboggan* and *autoboggan*, then *bombardier* (after the trade name of one such vehicle). Now a vehicle of this kind, widely used in the North instead of a dog team and in the South for sport, is a *skimobile*, *skidoo*, or *snowmobile*.

**2. *Borrowing from French***. In addition to the ancient legacy of French expressions in English, CanE has a range of usages which are distinctively North American:

*caboteur* (a ship engaged in coastal trade), *cache* (a place for storing supplies; a supply of goods kept for future use), *coureur du bois* (a French or MÉTIS trader or woodsman), *Métis* (a person or people of 'mixed' blood), *portage* (the carrying of canoes past rapids), *voyageur* (a French-Canadian canoeman in the service of the fur companies; someone travelling the northern wilderness), *mush* (from French *marcher*, used to order sled dogs to run), and *tuque* (a knitted cap). In addition, there are such technical terms as *anglophone* and *francophone* (without an initial capital, in the French style), *caisse populaire* (a credit union, a bank-like institution, especially in QUEBEC). The existence of two official languages has led to various usages, including the attributive use of *Canada* in the names of government departments, crown corporations, and national organizations, often with French word order, the attributive after the noun: *Canada Post, Revenue Canada, Air Canada, Loto Canada*. French and English often mix, as in names like the *Jeunesses Musicales of Canada* and on hybrid signs, especially those used for official purposes: *Postes Canada Post*. During the recent Canada games, some anglophone announcers referred to them as *the Jeux Canada Games* as if *Jeux* were an English word. In addition, the delicate relationship between English and French allows for originality: for example, the visual form of the name of the airline called *Canadian* in English and *Canadien* in French, in which the variable vowel is replaced by the company logo, a red arrow.

**3. *Extension and adaptation of traditional words*.** Many BrE words have had their meanings extended and adapted to conditions in North America. CanE shares with AmE many usages relating to landscape and social life, etc., but has a range of distinctive additional usages, such as: *Native* officially referring to the indigenous peoples of Canada (*the Native Peoples*); the distinction between *prime minister* (federal chief minister) and *premier* (provincial chief minister); *province, provincial* (referring to the major political divisions of the country, most of which were once distinct British colonies); *riding* (a political constituency); *status Indian* (someone officially registered as a Canadian Indian); CanE *reserve* as opposed to AmE *reservation* as a term describing land set aside for Native peoples.

**British influence**. The social institutions of Canada have been profoundly influenced by the British imperial connection: for example, Parliament in Ottawa, in which usage is comparable to that of the British Parliament in Westminster. The ties of blood are still strong in many places, but have been considerably weakened by the influx into Canada of immigrants from parts of the world where the British connection has been either minimal (as with China and Vietnam) or equivocal (as with India and the West Indies). In addition, the generation that fought alongside the British in the Second World War is growing old, the Queen's representative in Canada (the Governor-General) is no longer a British aristocrat but a Canadian, and where Britain's economic and military interests now lie with Europe, Canada's lie with the US. Nonetheless, some BrE forms are either holding their own or gaining. Younger Canadians of both sexes pronounce *been* to rhyme with *queen* and not *bin*, *anti-*, *semi-*, and *multi-* to rhyme with *me*, not with *my*; words ending in *-ile* to rhyme with *Nile* and not *ill*. These all run against the tide of AmE. It may not be clear to these speakers, however, that they are sustaining BrE forms.

**Social issues**. (1) Stigmatized usages include 'dropping the g' in the words ending *-ing*, especially in *going* ('goin'), dropping the *t* in words like *just* ('jus'), and the use of the contraction *had've*, sometimes written 'had of' (*We would've helped you if you had've asked us*). (2) The trend away from Canadian Raising led by young women seems to indicate that standard AmE rather than standard CanE or standard BrE is becoming the prestige dialect. Jennifer Coates notes, 'it seems as though women are more sensitive to status-giving prestige norms, . . . while men are more sensitive to vernacular norms, which represent solidarity and values traditionally associated with masculinity' (*Women, Men and Language*, 1986). English Canadians have said and written relatively little about linguistic nationalism and in this they are different from Americans, Australians, Brazilians, Argentinians, and French Canadians: '[T]he normal and natural development of linguistic nationalism has apparently been blighted by the peculiar condition of Anglo-Canadian culture, caught between the Scylla of England and the Charybdis of the United States' (David Haberley, 'The Search for a National Language', *Comparative Literature Studies*, 11,

1974, p. 87). However, it can be argued that linguistic nationalism is only 'normal' and 'natural' where its presence does not risk fragmenting the nation. CanE could be described as bland and Canadian attitudes to it as blighted, but CanE, like all varieties of English, is a practical response to a unique set of social, linguistic, and political pressures.

**Conclusion**. That Canada has had two official languages since its founding may explain why anglophone Canadians have by and large accepted bilingualism and multiculturalism as public policy. However, protest is mounting in New Brunswick and Ontario against this policy, especially by anglophone public servants who fear that their jobs will be classified as 'bilingual'. Heavy immigration (100,000 in 1985) is a commonplace of Canadian life and shows no sign of slowing. Immigrant varieties have developed, such as Toronto's *Italese*, an interlanguage resulting from three generations of contact between Italian and English. Currently, half the children in Vancouver schools and a quarter of those in Toronto schools speak English as a second language. This Canada has been described as a 'two-cultured, multi-ghettoed, plural community' (William Kilbourn, *Canada: A Guide to the Peaceable Kingdom*, 1970), where fascinating and unusual kinds of language change and accommodation are possible. See DIALECT IN CANADA, NEWFOUNDLAND ENGLISH, OTTAWA VALLEY, SOUTHERN ONTARIO.

**CANADIANISM**. A usage or custom special to or common in Canada, especially in language, such as the interjection *eh* in *He went into the store, eh, and saw this skidoo, eh*, and *riding* to mean 'political constituency'.

**CANT**. The JARGON of a class, group, or profession, often used to exclude or mislead others: a teenage gang member in Los Angeles saying that he was in his *hoopty* around *dimday* when some *mud duck* with a *trey-eight* tried to *take him out of the box* (he was in his car around dusk when a woman armed with a .38 calibre pistol tried to shoot him). Cant is a temporary form of language that changes quickly; when outsiders pick some of it up, the group evolves new usages. Expressions often move into the general language; cant terms that are now general SLANG include *moniker* name, *bilk* to

swindle, *beef* a complaint/to complain, and *hit* kill. See ARGOT, SHELTA.

**CAPITAL**, also **capital letter**. A large LETTER such as *A*, *B*, as opposed to a small letter, *a*, *b*, so named because it can appear at the 'head' of a text, chapter, page, paragraph, sentence, or word. The written and printed form of English has two interlocking systems of letters: large letters, known variously as *capitals*, *upper-case letters*, *majuscules*, and small letters, or *lower-case letters*, *minuscules*. Not all written languages have such a system; Arabic and Hebrew have only one set of letters. Lower-case letters are revisions of the forms of Latin capitals, developed in the minuscule script of the Carolingian period in France (8–9c).

**Capitalization**. The consistent use of capitals in Western European languages, to begin the first word of a sentence and for the first letter of a proper name (for example, *John*, *Mr Smith*, *New York*), began in the late Middle Ages, and was not fully systematized in English until the end of the 16c. During the 17c and 18c, common nouns and other words were often capitalized, much like (though less consistently than) the capitalizing of common nouns in present-day German. This practice is now largely restricted to abstract nouns like *Liberty*, *Equality*, *Fraternity*; even then the use is often ironic, *truth* being usually less absolute and grand than *Truth*. The practice of capitalizing content words in the titles of books, book chapters, articles, etc., is well established, but is not followed in all systems of reference, so that although *Gone with the Wind* is the dominant usage, *Gone with the wind* is also found. Despite the expectation that there are or should be rules for capitalization, above all for proper nouns, conventions remain unstable: should/Should the first word in a clause that follows a colon be capitalized? In BrE, the practice is generally not to capitalize in such cases, whereas AmE tends to favour a capital. Is it *the Earl of Essex* or *the earl of Essex*? There is no absolute rule, but there is a consensus in printing styles for *Earl* when designating an actual title.

**Additional uses**. (1) To identify a word more closely with a particular ethnic or other source: *the Arabic language* (contrast *arabic numbers*); *the Roman alphabet* (contrast *roman numerals*, *roman type*). (2) To identify a word more closely with a particular institution or highlight a particular term, usage, etc.: *the State* as opposed to *the state*; *the Church* as opposed to *the church*; *Last Will and Testament* as opposed to *last will and testament*. (3) To give prominence to such special temporal usages as days of the week, months of the year, and epochs (*Monday, September, the Middle Ages*), and such institutional usages as certain religious terms (*God, the Mass*) and trade names (*Coca-Cola, Kleenex*). (4) In a series of *block capitals* or *block letters*, to ensure that a handwritten word or name is clear. Serial capitals used to represent stressed speech are a largely 19c development: '"MISS JEMIMA!" exclaimed Miss Pinkerton, in the largest capitals' (W. M. Thackeray, *Vanity Fair*, 1847–8, ch. 1); Tweedledum, in Lewis Carroll's *Through the Looking-Glass* (1871, ch. 4), crying in a great fury, 'It's *new* . . . my nice NEW RATTLE!', where small capitals grow to full capitals, because his voice 'rose to a perfect scream'. (5) Initial capitals are widely used to highlight or dramatize certain words: 'The first rule of politics is Never Believe Anything Until It's Been Officially Denied' (Jonathan Lynn & Antony Jay, *Yes Prime Minister*, 1986). (6) 'Internal' capitals have become fashionable in recent years, especially in computing and commerce, to indicate that in a compound or blend the second element is as significant as the first, as in *CorrecText, DeskMate, VisiCalc, WordPerfect*. Related word- and letter-play may also occur, as in *VisiOn, CoRTeXT*. Such a convention allows an unlimited range of visual neologism. See ALPHABET, PUNCTUATION.

# ■ CARIBBEAN ENGLISH ———— ■

Short form *CarE*. A general term for the English language as used in the Caribbean archipelago and circum-Caribbean mainland. In a narrow sense, it covers English alone; in a broad sense, it covers English and CREOLE. The term is often imprecise, however, because of: (1) A long-standing popular classification of varieties of Creole as dialects of English, sometimes called *creole dialects* and *patois*. (2) The existence of a continuum of usage between English and Creole. (3) The use by scholars of the term *English* to cover both, as in the *Dictionary of Jamaican English* (1967, 1980) and the *Dictionary of Bahamian English* (1982). In order of decreasing specificity, the term embraces: (1) Regionally accented varieties of the standard language: standard JAMAICAN ENGLISH.

(2) Localized forms of English: Barbadian English. (3) Mesolects between English and Creole, as found in most communities. (4) Kinds of English used in countries where SPANISH is official or dominant, such as the Dominican Republic, Nicaragua, and PUERTO RICO. (5) Varieties of English-based Creole: CREOLESE in Guyana, JAMAICAN CREOLE, SRANAN in Surinam.

**Standard English.** Although English is the official language of the Commonwealth Caribbean, only a small proportion of the nationals of each country speaks regionally accented standard English as a native language. Many, however, acquire it through schooling and taking part in activities in which its use is common and accepted. For such people, standard English is the register of formal communication, complemented by vernacular usage for other purposes. Conservative varieties of regional English have BrE as their reference norm, especially for writing and print, but the influence of the US mass media and tourism has made AmE a powerful alternative. Equally influential has been the attainment of independence by most regional territories and the national consciousness associated with it.

**Localized English.** In each country of the Commonwealth Caribbean there is a localized non-standard form of English whose prosodic and phonemic systems differ. In like fashion, vocabulary related to flora, fauna, local phenomena, and sociocultural practices varies from country to country. Such vocabulary is drawn variously from Amerindian languages such as Arawak and Carib, West African languages such as Ewe and Yoruba, European languages such as DUTCH, FRENCH, PORTUGUESE, and Spanish, and, as in TRINIDAD AND TOBAGO, South Asian languages such as Bhojpuri and Hindi, as well as, predominantly, Creoles based on European lexicons and with African substrates. Differences among CarE varieties are to some extent determined by the nature of the vernaculars with which they come into contact. In addition, three forces (operating in different ways in different countries) affect the degree of standardization of these forms: internationalization, regionalization, and indigenization.

*Internationalization.* The acceptability of the norms of BrE depends on sensitivities related to the colonial experience of influential groups in individual countries. Degree of comfort with AmE norms also varies, depending on the perception of the US as a benevolent or malevolent force. At the same time, there is a body of pressure for the unequivocal adoption of an accessible and familiar internationally recognized standard variety as a reference norm.

*Regionalization*. Pressures towards regionalization are stimulated by intraregional travel, the spread of regional art forms (especially music), the sharing of a regional university (the U. of the West Indies), and the existence of a common examining council for secondary-level certification across the Commonwealth Caribbean. Procedures for marking scripts have exposed teachers to the written work of students in all parts of the region. Starting from 1977, the *Caribbean Examinations Council (CXC)* has been replacing the Cambridge Examination Syndicate as the certifying body for secondary education. Scripts are marked collectively by teachers from all parts of the region. The Council's guidelines have been established with significant sensitivity to localized forms of English, helping to modify teachers' perceptions of the acceptability of the forms with which they have become familiar. At the same time as they have recognized that no localized form merits greater respect than another, teachers have grown conscious of characteristics of English shared throughout the region. As a result, they have become more receptive to the idea of standards other than BrE and AmE.

*Indigenization*. Between 1962 and the early 1980s, most of the British Caribbean colonies became independent. This change has been associated with changes in the evaluation of local culture and institutions, including reassessment of Creole and other local speech forms. Positive evaluation of the vernaculars affects opinions about standardizing localized forms of English, and about the distinctness or 'purity' of a vernacular and the extent to which it should be preserved. It also increases the acceptability of code-switching and bidialectal expression, decreasing sensitivity to the limits of each variety. Generally, the result has been increasing indigenization of the localized form of English.

**Mesolects**. A *mesolectal* or *intermediate* variety is a form of speech lying between a localized English and a local Creole, arising from prolonged coexistence and the uneven penetration of English over several centuries of colonization. Such varieties are characterized by variation in the forms and structures used by the same speaker at different times and by different speakers on particular occasions. For example, in Trinidadian vernacular usage, the existential expression *it have* is equivalent to English *there is/are*, as in *It have plenty people in the park*. In the intermediate varieties of Trinidad, however, *they have* is used with the same meaning as both *it have* and *there is/are*, as in *They have plenty people in the park*. All three usages may occur in the speech of the same speaker depending on the level of formality or casualness of the context, or any one may be the preferred variant of different speakers.

**English and Spanish**. The term *Caribbean English* is also applied to varieties in the Latin countries of the region. There are two broad categories: (1) 'Foreigner' varieties, produced by people for whom Spanish is the primary language. This is especially the case in Puerto Rico, which, because of its close ties to the US, has AmE as the second language of the island. (2) Speakers of Creole in Colombia, Costa Rica, the Dominican Republic, Honduras, Nicaragua, and Panama, whose language is deemed English by opposition to Spanish rather than by congruence with English in its strict sense.

**Creole**. The final sense in which the term *Caribbean English* is used refers to the related English-based range of creoles throughout the region. These vernaculars are often referred to as variations of one form: CARIBBEAN ENGLISH CREOLE. They have traditionally been regarded as dialects of English, but are increasingly considered by scholars to be languages (*creoles*) or a single language with various forms (*Creole*) in their own right. There are close historical and linguistic links between the situation in and around the Commonwealth Caribbean and the PIDGINS and creoles of West Africa.

**Pronunciation**. (1) The varieties of JAMAICA, BARBADOS, and GUYANA are rhotic; the varieties of the BAHAMAS, BELIZE, Trinidad and Tobago, and the lesser Antilles are non-rhotic. (2) Rhythm tends to be syllable-timed. (3) There are fewer diphthongs than in RP: the distinction /iə/ versus /eə/ is neutralized in most varieties, so that *beer/bare*, *fear/fare* share the same vowels; in most acrolects, the equivalent of RP /eɪ/ in *face* is /e/, but in Jamaican and the varieties of the Leeward Islands it is /ie/; the vowel in such words as *goat* is generally /o/, but in Jamaican is /ʋo/. (4) Final consonant clusters tend to be reduced in all but the most careful speech, as in 'han' for *hand*. (5) There is a preference for a clear /l/ in such words as *milk*, *fill*, rather than the dark /l/ of RP.

**Grammar**. The syntax of CarE approximates fairly closely to general mainstream English. Special features include: (1) *Would* and *could* are common where BrE has *will* and *can*: *I could swim* I can swim; *I would do it tomorrow* I will do it tomorrow. (2) Where BrE has a simple past there is often a past historic: *The committee had decided* The committee decided. (3) *Yes–no* questions with a declarative word order and rising intonation are much commoner than the inversion of auxiliary and subject: *You are coming? Are you coming?*

**Vocabulary**. Regional usages include: (1) Local senses of general words: (Trinidad) *fatigue*, as used in to *give someone fatigue* to tease or taunt someone with a mixture of half-truths and imaginative fabrications; (general, as a noun) *galvanise* corrugated metal sheeting coated with zinc and used as roofing or fencing material; (Trinidad) *lime* to hang around, loiter without intent, be a casual observer of an event; (Trinidad and elsewhere) *miserable* mischievous; (Jamaica) *tall hair* long hair. (2) Local words: (Trinidad) *catspraddle* to send sprawling with a blow, to fall in an indecorous way; (Trinidad) *jort* a snack; (Trinidad) *touchous* touchy, short-tempered. (3) Loans from French Creole: *lagniappe* (shared with Southern AmE) something extra given by a vendor to a buyer for the sake of goodwill, a bonus; (Trinidad, SAINT LUCIA) *macafouchette* leftovers; (Trinidad) *ramajay* to warble, twitter, make an extravagant display. (4) Loans from local Spanish: (Trinidad, Barbados, and elsewhere) *alpargat(a)* a sandal with uppers made of woven rope-like material, canvas, or of intertwined leather thongs; (general) *parang* a term for a number of different musical rhythms, song types, and festivities associated with Christmas in Trinidad and parts of Venezuela (from *paranda*);

(Jamaican) *fruutapang* breadfruit (from *fruta* fruit, *pan* bread); (Jamaican) *mampala* an effeminate man (from *mampolón* a common cock, not a fighting cock); (Jamaican) *scaveeched fish* (from *escabeche* pickled fish). (5) Words from West African languages: (general) *bakra*, *bukra*, *buckra* a white person; (widespread) *cotta*, *kata* a head-pad used under a load carried on the head; (widespread) *fufu* a dish made by pounding boiled plantains, yams, or cassava in a mortar to form a smooth, firm mass that may be cut and served. (6) Loan translations from West African languages: *sweet mouth* flattery, a flatterer; *eye-water* tears; *hard-ears* stubborn; *door-mouth* doorway, entrance to a building.

See AFRICAN ENGLISH, AFRICAN-AMERICAN VERNACULAR ENGLISH, ATLANTIC CREOLES, BAJAN, BAY ISLANDS, BERMUDA, BLACK ENGLISH, BORROWING, BRITISH BLACK ENGLISH, BROKEN, CAYMAN ISLANDS, DUB, GRENADA, GULLAH, MISKITO COAST CREOLE, MONTSERRAT, NATION LANGUAGE, PANAMA, PATOIS, RAP, RASTA TALK, SAINT CHRISTOPHER AND NEVIS, SAINT LUCIA, SAINT VINCENT AND THE GRENADINES, TURKS AND CAICOS ISLANDS, VIRGIN ISLANDS, WEST AFRICAN PIDGIN ENGLISH.

**CARIBBEAN ENGLISH CREOLE**, also **Caribbean Creole English**, **Caribbean Creole**, **Creole English**, **West Indian Creole**, **Creole**. The technical term for an English-based CREOLE or group of creoles in the Commonwealth Caribbean, the Samaná peninsula of the Dominican Republic, the coastal areas of Nicaragua and Costa Rica, the Bay Islands of Honduras, the Colombian dependencies of San Andres and Providencia, parts of Panama, and Surinam. Two major forms can be identified in Surinam (*Ndjuka*, *Sranan*); only in that country do varieties have specific names used by both speakers and researchers. In all other cases, speakers generally call their varieties dialects, such as *Jamaican dialect*, while scholars label each variety by its territorial name followed by *English*, *English-based*, or *English-lexicon*, such as *Antiguan English Creole*, *Barbadian English-based Creole*, *Trinidadian English-lexicon Creole*. These varieties are also commonly referred to by location alone (*JAMAICAN CREOLE*) or, when the location is apparent, as *Creole* (both with and without an initial capital). The range of usage is referred to as both *Creole*, when looked at collectively, and *Creoles*, when regarded as a group of vernaculars. Since not all varieties have been researched to the same extent, the assumption that there are as many distinct forms as there are territories is convenient rather than definitive. The settlement patterns of the region and later migratory movement suggest that there are fewer distinct forms than locations. However, the absence of a regionally recognized standard reduces the perception of the unity of Creole, which is often currently discussed by scholars and others as a language in its own right, distinct from English. The unevenness of the research permits the continued use of a fragmentary and inconsistent labelling system.

**History and development**. Like most other such creoles, Caribbean English Creole is the outcome of contact among Europeans and West Africans in the course of European expansionism, the slave trade, and the colonization of the New World. The regional dialects of the English-speaking colonists were the dominant source of vocabulary for Creole before the 20c. More recently, standard varieties of English, propagated by contemporary mass media and the increased availability of schooling, have fed the expansion of the vocabulary. Large numbers of lexical items and phrases of West African provenance form part of the daily vocabulary. The grammatical structure of the group shows patterns that are characteristic of West African language families, patterns that are particular to creole languages as a whole, and features that appear to be restricted to the Caribbean Creole group.

**Effects of contact**. In most countries (excluding Surinam and the Latin American nations), the contact with English that produced Creole has persisted beyond its emergence, with a chain of associated results: (1) It has inhibited the evolution of widely recognized standard varieties within the group. (2) In its turn, the absence of one or more standards has made the language more permeable to influence from English than it might otherwise have been. (3) This permeability, combined with the prestige of English as a world language and its transmission through the official institutions of the societies concerned, has resulted in the evolution of varieties intermediate between the local variety of English and the prototypical variety of Creole. (4) The social

stratification of these varieties is such that language use involves some fluidity of movement among the intermediate varieties. (5) The effect is to exaggerate the variation that one might normally expect in a coherent language variety and further inhibit the evolution and identification of a standard. The layering of varieties between local standard English and a creole is commonly described as a *post-creole (dialect) continuum*. Three main strata are recognized: the *basilect*, which refers to the prototypical creole variety, the *acrolect*, which refers to the variety most like the official standard version of English, and the *mesolect*, which refers to the set of intermediate varieties.

**Features**. Despite differences among varieties, Caribbean English Creoles share several defining characteristics: (1) Expressing tense, mood, and aspect mainly by prepredicative particles: (Jamaican) *Im waak* He or she walked, He or she has walked, *Im a waak* He or she is walking, *Im bin waak* He or she walked, He or she had walked. (2) Marking noun plurals by postposed particles, not *-s*: (Jamaican, Guyanese) *di daagdem* the dogs, (Trinidad) *di dog-an-dem* the dogs. (3) Using front-focusing structures to disambiguate or emphasize: (Trinidad) *Iz mi mʌdʌ tel mi du it* My mother (and not someone else) told me to do it; (Jamaican) *A tief im tief di goot* He stole the goat (he didn't buy it). (4) Reduplication in word-formation and for emphasis: (Jamaican) *poto-poto* slimy, muddy, *fenky-fenky* slight, puny, cowardly, fussy, *batta-batta* to beat repeatedly; (Guyanese) *tukka-tukka* a kind of plantain. (5) Differentiation of singular and plural second person, like archaic *thou* and *you*: (Barbados) *yu* versus *wVnV*; (Trinidad) *yu* versus *all-yu*. (6) Possession shown by placing unmarked nouns side by side: (Trinidad) *mi fada kuzn hows* my father's cousin's house.

**Social status and use**. Creole is the preferred variety for informal and private communication, but yields to English in formal public settings. English, because of its strong association with educational systems and the official institutions of government and society, generally has higher prestige than Creole, but the latter enjoys increasing status as a sense of nationalism increases in various recently independent countries. The use of Creole for literature is increasingly common; it is the normal medium for popular drama and the lyrics of songs composed in local styles. The use of Creole in radio and television is most developed in Jamaica.

See ATLANTIC CREOLES, CARIBBEAN ENGLISH, NATION LANGUAGE, NEW ORLEANS, RASTA TALK, WEST AFRICAN PIDGIN ENGLISH.

**CARIBBEANISM**. A usage or custom special to, or common in, the Caribbean and any of the languages of the region, such as *sweetmouth* for 'flatterer' in general CARIBBEAN ENGLISH and *poto-poto* for 'slimy' or 'muddy' in Jamaican Creole.

**CARICOM** [Pronounced 'Carry-com']. The abbreviation of, and common name for, the *Caribbean Community and Common Market*. An organization for economic and social co-operation, and the co-ordination of foreign affairs, among former British territories in the Caribbean, formed in 1973 to replace the earlier Caribbean Free Trade Association (Carifta). Its members are: Antigua and Barbuda; the BAHAMAS; BARBADOS; BELIZE; Dominica; GRENADA; GUYANA; Jamaica; MONTSERRAT (a British colony); ST CHRISTOPHER AND NEVIS; ST LUCIA; ST VINCENT AND THE GRENADINES; and TRINIDAD AND TOBAGO. The secretariat is at Georgetown, Guyana, and the working language is English.

**CARROLL, Lewis** [1832–98]. Pen name of *Charles Lutwidge Dodgson*. English mathematician and writer, born at Daresbury, Cheshire, and educated at Rugby and Christ Church, Oxford, where he spent the rest of his life. His most famous book, *Alice's Adventures in Wonderland* (1865), developed from a story he told one afternoon to the three daughters of the Greek scholar H. G. Liddell, Dean of Christ Church. Alice, named after one of them, continued her adventures in *Through the Looking-Glass* (1871). Carroll wrote other books for children, including a long poem 'The Hunting of the Snark' (1876). He published several mathematical works, but was not distinguished academically. He never married, and found pleasure in the company of little girls, with whom he lost his shyness. He was also an inventor of puzzles, games, ciphers, and mnemonics, and an amateur pioneer in photography. Carroll was a master of fantasy and his stories have their own logic. Young readers seem untroubled by such tensions and anxieties as forgetting one's name and calls for beheading offenders, while the adult reader enjoys the commentary on human absurdities and the manipulation of language. Carroll used the PUN and coined NEOLOGISMS, including what he called 'portmanteau words' like *chortle* (combining *chuckle* and *snort*). See BLEND. He played games with idioms, using such expressions as 'beating time' (to music) in a literal sense. He reshaped such animals of fable or rhetoric as the *Gryphon*, *March Hare*, and *Cheshire Cat*, and invented such new ones as the *Bandersnatch* and the *Boojum*. As a parodist, he made NONSENSE poems out of well-known moral verses. His success as a children's author was aided by the illustrations of John Tenniel. Analysts of his works have made theological and psychoanalytical interpretations of his fantasies; students of language may find his genius more evident in Humpty-Dumpty's comment on people and words: 'The question is, which is to be master—that's all.' See BLEND, DOUBLET, HUMOUR, JOKE, NONSENSE.

**CASE**. A term for a set of forms for a NOUN, PRONOUN, or ADJECTIVE in an inflected language, the choice of form depending on syntactic function. In Latin, the noun form *dominus* (lord) is in the *nominative case*, used when the word is the subject of the sentence, whereas *dominum* is *accusative*, used when the word is the direct object. A set of cases constitutes a paradigm for the class to which a word belongs: *dominus* is a masculine noun of the second declension, whose paradigm consists of 12 forms for six cases (nominative, vocative, accusative, genitive, dative, and ablative, each with singular and plural forms) that were regarded in classical times as 'falling' away from an upright nominative.

**Case in Old English**. ANGLO-SAXON or OLD ENGLISH had the following cases for nouns, pronouns, and adjectives: *nominative, accusative, genitive, dative*, and to a limited extent *instrumental*. The equivalent of modern *stone* was masculine *stān* nominative and accusative cases (singular), *stānas* nominative and accusative (plural), *stānes* genitive singular (of a stone), *stāna* genitive plural (of stones), *stāne* dative singular (for a stone), *stānum* dative plural (for stones).

**Case in Modern English**. The contemporary language has cases for nouns and pronouns, mainly the *common case* (*Tom, anybody*) and the *genitive* or *possessive case* (*Tom's,* *anybody's*). Potentially, countable nouns have four case forms: two singular (*child*, *child's*), two plural (*children*, *children's*). In regular nouns, these manifest themselves only in writing, through the APOSTROPHE (*girl*, *girl's*, *girls*, *girls'*), since in speech three of the forms are identical. The genitive case is used in two contexts: dependently, before a noun (*This is Tom's/his bat*), and independently (*This bat is Tom's/his*). Most personal pronouns have different forms for the dependent and independent genitive: *This is your bat* and *This bat is yours*. The genitive case forms of personal pronouns are often called possessive pronouns. A few pronouns have three cases: subjective or nominative, objective or accusative, and genitive or possessive (see table).

| Subjective | Objective | Genitive (1) | Genitive (2) |
| --- | --- | --- | --- |
| *I* | *me* | *my* | *mine* |
| *we* | *us* | *our* | *ours* |
| *he* | *him* | *his* | *his* |
| *she* | *her* | *her* | *hers* |
| *they* | *them* | *their* | *theirs* |
| *who* | *whom* | *whose* | — |
| *whoever* | *whomever* | — | — |

The subjective is used when the pronoun is the SUBJECT of a finite verb: *I* in *I like strawberries*. The objective is used when the pronoun is the direct OBJECT (*me* in *The noise does not disturb me*), the indirect object (*me* in *She gave me her telephone number*), or the complement of a preposition (*The letters are for me*). When the pronoun is the subject complement, there is a divided usage: the objective is generally used (*It's only me*), but the subjective case occurs in formal style (*It is I who have the honour of introducing our guest speaker*). Except in formal style, *who* and *whoever* are generally used in place of *whom* and *whomever*. Compare the formal *Whom did you nominate?* and *For whom are you waiting?* with the more usual *Who did you nominate?* and *Who are you waiting for?* See DATIVE CASE, GENITIVE CASE, NOMINATIVE CASE.

**CATACHRESIS** [Stress: 'kata-KREE-sis']. A traditional term for the mistaken use of one word for another, as in *Royal Anglican Regiment* for *Royal Anglian Regiment*. An actual or assumed MISTAKE of this kind may cause confusion and resentment, and lead to controversy, as with the use of *disinterested* where *uninterested* might be more appropriate. Occasionally, catachresis can lead to the supplanting of one word by another: for example, *humble* for *umble* in the phrase *humble pie*. Such a pie was originally made from *umbles* (the innards of a deer) and was so recognized until the 19c. The *OED* records *humble pie* from 1648, and the figurative usage *eating humble pie* from 1830. In the 20c, only the figurative use occurs and there is therefore no confusion or resentment. By and large, catachresis arises when words are similar in form, as with *militate* and *mitigate* ('His book was always likely to be serious, which might have mitigated against a large sale,' *Sunday Times*, 17 Dec. 1989), or have a converse relationship, as with *learn* and *teach*, *imply* and *infer*, in which case one word may take over both senses (*Learn Yourself Scouse*: book title; *Are you inferring I don't know what I am doing?*). Confusion over such words can persist for centuries and is a popular topic in usage books and letters to editors. The term is neutral in PHILOLOGY but often pejorative in general use. See CONFUSIBLE, HOWLER, MALAPROPISM, SEMANTIC CHANGE.

**CATAPHORA** [Stress: 'ka-TA-fo-ra']. A forward reference in a text: the pronoun *she* is cataphoric in 'If *she* wants to, Nora can be charming.' Here, *she* substitutes for its antecedent *Nora*. The sentence exhibits *cataphoric ellipsis*, since *she wants to* is understood as *she wants to be charming*. Cataphora is less common than *anaphora*, in which the reference is backwards to a preceding part of the text. In broad terms, ANAPHORA subsumes cataphora.

**CATCHPHRASE**, also **catch phrase**, **catch-phrase**. A phrase that 'catches' one's attention, especially if often repeated and used as a slogan, as with 'Read my lips, no new taxes' (George Bush in his campaign for the US presidency, 1988). Some catchphrases are fashionable and ephemeral, others persist for years and may become idioms, such as *Follow that*, meaning 'Beat that' (dating from the 1950s), and *For my next trick* (followed by a pause, especially said by someone who has just botched something: dating from the 1930s patter of stage magicians). Advertisers and publicists try to create catchphrases, such as *Coke is it* and *the real thing* (advertising Coca-Cola). Sometimes they deliberately use special orthography, as in the British *Drinka pinta milka day* (advertising milk) and *Wotalotigot* (advertising the sweets called Smarties).

**CATCHWORD**. **1.** A memorable word or phrase, repeated by many people. **2.** Also *headword*, *guideword*, *flagword*, *running head*. A word printed at the top of the page of a work of reference to indicate the first or last entry or article on a page; part of a series of such words intended to help users find what they want. **3.** Also *KEYWORD*. In library science, a memorable or important term in the title, text, or abstract of an item being indexed and that is therefore used in the index entry.

**CAUSATIVE VERB**. A verb that denotes causing something to happen. Such verbs are often formed from adjectives or nouns by means of causative suffixes: *harden* (to cause to become hard; to make hard), *purify* (to cause to become pure; to make pure), *harmonize* (to cause or create harmony; to make harmonious). Some linguists use the term to describe a variety of verbs where there is an underlying meaning of causation: *kill* (cause to die); *put*, *bring*, *take*, *send* (cause to move somewhere else); *burn*, as in *Alfred burned/burnt the cakes* (cause to burn). The term is also applied to the verbs *let*, *make*, *have*, and *get*. The first three can be followed by an object plus a bare infinitive, but *get* needs a *to*-infinitive: *You should let/make/have the children tidy their own rooms; get them to tidy things up*. *Have* and *get* can be followed by an object and a participle: *We soon had the car going again; we got it repaired*. These patterns, however, may also have a non-causative meaning: *I had my wallet stolen*; *You'll get people pestering you*.

**CAWDREY, Robert**. English school-master (16–17c), from Oakham in Rutland, compiler of *The Table Alphabeticall* (1604), the first English dictionary, which briefly defined 2,560 'hard vsuall English wordes . . . gathered for the benefit & helpe of Ladies, Gentlewomen, or any other vnskilfull persons'. There were four editions to 1617.

**CAXTON, William** [*c*.1420–*c*.1491]. English printer, editor, and translator, who introduced PRINTING to England in 1476, and published the first printed editions of CHAUCER, Lydgate, Gower, and Malory. He was in Bruges in the Low Countries in 1450, where he became a leader of the English community and protégé of Margaret, Duchess of Burgundy. At her suggestion, he completed his first translation (from

French), *The Recuyell of the Historyes of Troye* (1471). Wearied by copying, he went to Cologne to learn the art of printing introduced at Mainz *c*.1450, and the *Recuyell*, the first book printed in English, was published in 1476 at his press in Bruges.

Caxton set up the first printing house in England near the court and Westminster Abbey, just outside London. He published about 100 works, mostly in English and rarely in fashionable French or revered Latin. His first dated book was *Dictes and Sayenges of the Phylosophers* (1477). His patrons included kings, nobles, and wealthy merchants, who sometimes commissioned books, but the religious works which he published were probably the most widely read. Many of his publications were his own translations, but many were by English authors, such as Chaucer's *Canterbury Tales* (?1478) and Malory's *Morte Darthur* (1485). He sometimes set out his views on language and style in prologues and epilogues added to his publications. Best-known is the prologue to his translation of the French *Eneydos* (1490), where he confronted the difficult choice among late 15c styles: native 'olde and homely termes', courtly 'fayr & straunge termes', and 'comyn termes that be dayli vsed'. He pondered the variation of English in time ('our langage now vsed varyeth ferre from that which was vsed and spoken whan I was borne') and space ('that comyn englysshe that is spoken in one shyre varyeth from a nother'), weighty considerations to the publisher who, unlike a scribe who supplies a unique copy for his patron, sold his books nationwide.

For Caxton, Chaucer 'for his ornate wrytyng in our tongue may wel have the name of a laureate poete. For to fore that he by hys labour enbelysshyd, ornated and made faire our Englisshe, in thys royame was had rude speche & incongrue, as yet it appiereth by olde bookes whyche at thys day ought not to have place ne be compared emong to hys beauteuous volumes and aournate writynges.' Such stylistic concerns influenced Caxton's practice as an editor-publisher: he altered the text of 'beauteuous' Chaucer little, producing a second edition when his first proved to rest on an untrustworthy manuscript; but he 'enbelysshyd' passages in Malory that showed the influence of their 'olde and homely' original. Though his introduction of printing was epochal for English language and literature, his own style, even with regard to choice of words, was variable: Germanic when he had a Dutch source, Romance when it was Latin or French. He was ramshackle when unguided by a source, ad-libbing his spelling (*wrytyng/writynge, ornate/aournate*) and doubling and tripling his terms (*vsed and spoken, enbelysshyd, ornated and made faire*). See CHANCERY STANDARD, EARLY MODERN ENGLISH, PROSE, PUNCTUATION, STANDARD.

**CAYMAN ISLANDS**. A British Caribbean dependency, consisting of the islands of Grand Cayman, Cayman Brac, and Little Cayman. Languages: English (official), Creole, and Spanish. Visited by Columbus in 1503 but never settled by Spain; ceded to Britain in 1670. Colonized from Jamaica, and chose to remain a dependency when Jamaica became independent in 1962. See CARIBBEAN ENGLISH.

**CEDILLA**. A DIACRITIC used in French under the letter *c* to indicate a soft pronunciation (/s/ not /k/): *Académie française, façade*. This use may or may not be carried over into English in a borrowed word: for example, both *façade* and *facade* occur. The cedilla is also used in Portuguese, Romanian, and Turkish.

**CELTIC**. [Pronounced 'Keltic' or 'Seltic'.] **1.** Of the Celts, their languages, and culture. **2.** An inclusive term for the CELTIC LANGUAGES, particularly the *Common Celtic* of ancient Europe and the British dialects of the first millennium AD. The term sometimes occurs in combinations: 'The Norman-Irish and the Celtic-Irish were drawn nearer to one another by common sorrows' (G. Bancroft, *History of the United States*, 1876).

**CELTICISM**. The way of life or special interests of the Celts; a custom or usage, including a CELTIC expression in a non-Celtic language, such as English *banshee*, from Irish Gaelic *bean sidhe* a fairy woman. See BORROWING.

■ **CELTIC LANGUAGES** ──────── ■

Sometimes **Keltic languages**, and **Celtic**, **Keltic** when taken as a unity. A group of INDO-EUROPEAN LANGUAGES, usually divided into: (1) *Continental Celtic*, a range of unwritten and now extinct languages spoken from around 500 BC to AD 500 from the Black Sea to Iberia, the best-known of which was *Gaulish*. (2) *Insular Celtic*, usually further divided into: *British* or *Brythonic* (from *Brython* a Briton) and *Irish* or *Goidelic* (from *Goidel* an Irishman: modern *Gael*). British and Gaulish were at one time a continuum of linked dialects. Philologists have referred to them as *P-Celtic* in contrast to Goidelic as *Q-Celtic*, on the basis of a sound shift of *q* to *p* which split an earlier tongue known as *Common Celtic*. The Gallo-British *p*-sound occurs in Old Welsh *map* son, *pen* head, and in Welsh *Prydain* Britain, while the Goidelic sound represented as *q* occurs in GAELIC *mac* son, *ceann* head, and in an ancient name for the Picts, *Cruithneach*, which may be a cousin of the name *British*. Currently, however, these terms are not generally used, Celticists arguing that a single sound shift, however important, should not serve as a label for such a complex division as that between British and Irish.

**The long decline**. In historical times, the British group has consisted of WELSH and Breton (which survive) and CORNISH, CUMBRIC, and perhaps Pictish (which are extinct). Breton, though a language of France, has no links with Continental Celtic; it was taken to Brittany in the 5–6c by migrating Britons. The Irish group consists of three languages or varieties of the same language: IRISH GAELIC and SCOTTISH GAELIC and the extinct Manx Gaelic. During the first millennium AD, there were speakers of the British varieties in Ireland and speakers of the Irish varieties in Britain, including by the 6c the Scots: settlers from Ireland who in due course gave their name to their adopted country. Cornish and Manx are in limited use among local revivalists, but show no sign of significant resuscitation. The Celtic languages have been in decline for nearly two thousand years and most have vanished without obvious trace. The Continental languages survive only in place-names and Greek and Roman records. The Apostle Paul wrote in Greek to Anatolian Celts in his *Epistle to the Galatians*; by the time of this letter (IC AD), the Galatians appear to have largely given up their own language. The languages of Iberia and Gaul were replaced in the early Middle Ages by Romance languages and British gave way to English from the 5c onwards. In medieval Ireland, Scotland, and Wales, the indigenous languages were not at risk from Norse,

Norman French, or English, but from the 16c Welsh and Gaelic have been in retreat before English and Breton before French. The last natural speaker of Cornish died in 1777 and of Manx in 1974. Welsh is the most viable of the survivors, with some half a million speakers (around 20% of the Welsh population). Irish Gaelic has some 100,000 speakers and Scottish Gaelic some 80,000 speakers.

**Reasons for decline**. The decline of these languages is a complex and often highly emotive issue. Efforts to slow or reverse their decline raise economic, educational, political, historical, and ethnic questions that relate to at least nine factors: (1) *Disunity* among the Celts in the face of colonization, cultural domination and assimilation, and the pressure of governments often regarded as alien and regarding Celts as alien. (2) *Loss of linguistic status* as English and French gained in strength and prestige. (3) *Shortage of reading material*, in tandem with the imposition of educational systems mediated by English and French. (4) *Lack of adequate instruction and backup*, even where a language has had official support, as in the Republic of Ireland and Wales. (5) *Loss of the language in religious life*, as in Scotland, under the influence of the Society for the Propagation of the Gospel (in English, with longterm Presbyterian resistance to translations of the Bible into Gaelic). (6) *Immigration* into Celtic areas by speakers of English and French, often to hold important posts and with little or no interest in the local language. (7) *Emigration*, often under pressure, as in the Irish famines and the Highland Clearances. (8) *The impact of the media*, especially in the 20c, with most or all newspapers, radio, cinema, and television in English or French. (9) *A sense of increasing irrelevance*, coupled with a general disdain for or indifference to Celtic speech, and assumptions of social and linguistic inferiority in the dominant culture that many Celts have slowly come to accept.

**The question of 'linguicide'**. These factors have promoted what some defenders of the Celtic languages see as a kind of linguistic murder. Although there has never been an official campaign to wipe out a Celtic language, Celtic communities have for centuries been officially and educationally neglected and their languages and literatures marginalized, especially in drives for national uniformity. Even where goodwill has existed, the positive results have been minimal, with the possible exception of Welsh. Even the backing of the government of the Irish Republic since the 1920s has failed to stop the decline of Gaelic, which has a belated co-official status with English. Welsh and Gaelic maintain only precarious holds as the circle of English continues to widen. In the process of that widening, however, Celtic SUBSTRATES have developed in varieties of BrE and IrE used alongside the original languages or in areas where they were once extensive.

**Celtic and Old English**. The influence of Celtic on OLD ENGLISH appears to have been slight: 'The small number of Celtic words which found their way into the English language in earlier times has always been a cause of surprise to philologists' (Bernard Groom, *A Short History of English Words*, 1934). This early impermeability of English can be accounted for in at least three ways: (1) *A familiar environment*. The old and new environments of the Anglo-Saxons were much the same and therefore the vocabulary they brought from mainland Europe served them well in Britain. Unlike the British in Australia a thousand years later, they had no need to adopt local words for novel flora, fauna, and experiences: for almost everything they encountered they already had serviceable words. (2) *Little or no hybridization*. There appear to have been no contact languages or CODE-MIXING between Celtic and Anglo-Saxon through which infiltration could occur, as happened later with Norse and with Norman French. Any hybridization in Western Europe at the time appears to have been between Popular LATIN and local languages, not among local languages. (3) *The attraction of Latin*. The major cultural and religious influence of the time was Latin, with an equal impact on Celtic and Germanic. Speakers of both went to Latin for cultural and religious loanwords. It is no more surprising therefore that Celtic did not influence Old English than that both Celtic and Germanic religion collapsed in the face of Christianization.

**Celtic in English**. In the course of the centuries, Celtic influence on English has been cumulative in four forms:

**1. *Loanwords***. Gaulish provided Latin with a number of loans, such as *carrus* a wagon, *carpentum* a light carriage, and *lancia* a long spear, from which are descended the English words *car, carry, carriage, chariot, charioteer, carpenter, carpentry, lance,* and *lancer*. From Insular Celtic there has built up over the centuries a set of words drawn from the main languages and linked with landscape and monuments, such as *ben, cairn, corrie, crag, crannog, cromlech, dolmen, glen, loch, menhir, strath, tor*: for further loans, see BORROWING.

**2. Literary themes, styles, and names.** After the Norman Conquest of England in the 11c, Breton and Welsh users of Latin, French, and English spread Celtic themes and stories in the courts and monasteries of Western Europe. A key element in this dissemination was the *Matter of Britain,* whose original French form, *Matière de Bretagne,* indicates the link with Brittany as well as Britain. Foremost in this material are the legends of Arthur and his knights in which characters have such Frenchified and Anglicized Celtic names as *Arthur, Gareth, Gawain, Guinevere, Lancelot, Merlin,* and *Morgan.* Intricate Celtic styles and themes became interwoven with Christian, classical, and Germanic styles and themes in both pseudo-histories of Britain and romances of chivalry and the Grail. Celtic creativity in English has continued ever since: for example, in the 18c in MacPherson's *Ossian,* in the 19c in Scott's poems and novels, and in the 20c in James Joyce's novels and Dylan Thomas's poetry.

**3. Place and personal names.** The foremost legacy of the Celts is names. Continental Celtic has left its place-names throughout Europe, most of them altered by other languages and many with such distinctive English forms as *Danube, Rhine, Rhone, Seine.* Some have regional connotations, such as the *-ac* names of France, several of which have uses in English: *Armagnac, Aurignac, Cadillac, Cognac.* Insular Celtic has provided such names as *Belfast, Cardiff, Dublin, Glasgow, London, York* for cities, *Avon, Clyde, Dee, Don, Forth, Severn, Thames, Usk* for rivers, and *Argyll, Cornwall, Cumbria, Devon, Dyfed, Glamorgan, Kent, Lothian* for regions. Personal names of Celtic origin or association are widely used, often without an awareness of their provenance: first names such as *Alan, Donald, Duncan, Eileen, Fiona, Gavin, Ronald, Sheila;* patronymic and ethnic surnames in *mac/mc* (*MacDonald, McDonald*) and *O* (*O'Donnell, O'Neill,* sometimes dropping the *O* as in *Sullivan*), and such others as *Cameron, Campbell, Colquhoun, Douglas, Evans, Griffiths, Jones, Morgan, Urquhart.* A common Celtic word for 'water' underlies such river-related names as *Aix-en-Provence, Axminster, Caerleon-on-Usk, Exmouth, Uxbridge.* It also underlies BrE *whisky* and IrE and AmE *whiskey.* These are shortenings of *whiskybae* or *usquebaugh,* from Gaelic *uisge beatha* (water of life, a calque of Latin *aqua vitae*).

**4. Celtic varieties of English.** In varieties of English used in Ireland, the ISLE OF MAN, Scotland, and Wales, there has been considerable influence from the local languages, which have served not only as sources of loans but also as substrates for the shaping of these varieties. In the case of IRISH ENGLISH, such influence travelled across the Atlantic from the 16c onward to provide a major element in the English of Newfoundland, England's (and in a sense Ireland's) oldest North American colony. See HIGHLAND ENGLISH, NEWFOUNDLAND ENGLISH, WELSH ENGLISH.

**CHANCERY STANDARD**, also **Chancery English**. Present-day terms for the 15c written usage of the clerks of Chancery in London, who prepared the king's documents. Before the 1430s, official records were mainly in Latin and French, but after that date mainly in an English based on the Central Midland dialect, with such usages as *gaf* (gave) not Chaucer's East Midland *yaf, such* not *swich,* and *theyre* (their) not *hir.* Until the end of the 15c, Chancery and the Exchequer built a foundation of written English that was developed by CAXTON when he set up his press in Westminster in 1476. Over the years, printers replaced some features of Chancery usage with London equivalents, such as third person *-s* instead of *-th* (*hopes,* not *hopeth*), and *are* instead of *be.* See STANDARD ENGLISH.

**CHANNEL ISLANDS, The,** French *Les Îles Anglo-Normandes* (the Anglo-Norman Islands). A group of British islands in the English Channel, closer to France than to England. The principal islands are Guernsey, Jersey, Alderney, and Sark. They are not part of the UK, but are an independent territory, the remnant of the English Crown's French possessions and the only part of the Duchy of Normandy to remain after 1204. Queen Elizabeth II is the islands' *Duke*, not Duchess. The island languages are ENGLISH (dialect and standard), and a variety of FRENCH related to the NORMAN FRENCH once used in England, now in limited use. See KING'S ENGLISH, LATIN.

**CHARACTER SET**. **1.** Also *character repertoire*. A set of print characters available in a particular type or font. **2.** A set of numbers, letters, punctuation marks, special symbols, and other representations formed from patterns of computer bits, such as *ASCII* (American Standard Code for Information Interchange: pronounced 'Askee') introduced in 1963, *EBCDIC* (Extended Binary Coded Decimal Interchange Code: pronounced 'Eb-see-dick'), used by IBM, and *ISO7* (International Standards Organization 7-bit Code). The most complex sets relate to East Asia: for example, the 256 possibilities in an 8-bit byte are inadequate for the characters of Chinese and Japanese, and so 16-bit representations are used instead. See COMPUTING.

■ **CHAUCER, Geoffrey** ───── ■

[1343?–1400] Poet of MIDDLE ENGLISH and one of the foremost figures in ENGLISH LITERATURE. No record remains of the education that gave Chaucer lifelong familiarity with Latin and several vernacular languages and literatures. However, as the son of a well-off London vintner, he had educational and social advantages that must have helped form his views. He may have attended the Inner Temple; by 1357, he was in the household of Edward III's daughter-in-law; in 1360, the king paid Chaucer's ransom after his capture by the French; by 1367, he had become a member of the king's household, and later he undertook many royal commissions to France, Spain, and Italy, some of them secret. In 1374, the king appointed him controller of the custom on wool, sheepskins, and leather in the Port of LONDON, the first of several increasingly important offices he held by royal appointment. From 1374 onwards, he also received various grants and annuities from the Crown. He was elected Member of Parliament for Kent in 1386.

**Works**. Chaucer's first important poem appears to have been the *Book of the Duchess*, a memorial to John of Gaunt's first wife, who died in 1368 (though the poem may be sev-

eral years later). Other major works were *The House of Fame* (1378–80), *The Parliament of Fowls* (1380–2), *Troilus and Criseyde* (1382–6), and *The Canterbury Tales*, some of them written earlier but assembled with others written *c*.1388–1400. In addition to these, Chaucer produced a great many translations, including a fragment of the *Romance of the Rose* (a version of the French *Roman de la Rose*), and a translation of Boethius's *De Consolatione Philosophiae* (On the Consolation of Philosophy). As a result, a French contemporary saluted him as a 'good translator', the earliest explicit literary response to him. Though his official duties left many records, in his lifetime only Thomas Usk mentioned Chaucer's 'manly speech' (1385), and John Gower his 'glad songs', remarks that do not account for his later reputation as the founder of literary English.

**Language**. The East Midland dialect of late 14c English, as Chaucer's works record it, differed from Modern English in structure, vocabulary, and especially spelling and pronunciation:

'So faren we, If I shal seye the sothe.'
'Now,' quod oure Hoost, 'yit lat me talke to the:
Why artow so discoloured of thy face?'
'Peter!' quod he, 'God yeve it harde grace,
I am so used in the fyr to blowe....'
              (*Canon's Yeoman's Prologue*)

Spelling poses the chief obstacles for a modern reader, for whom the second line would end 'yet let me talk to thee'. Aloud the passage is likely to be more difficult still. Because of the GREAT VOWEL SHIFT, which began *c*.1400, the second line included words that sounded like *noo* now, *may* me, *toe* to, and *they* thee, the third line words that sounded like *whee* why, *saw* so, and *fahce* face. Chaucer's English also pronounced almost all the consonants, including the *l* in *talke* and the *r* in *harde*. His *yeve* is akin to modern *give*, which however descends from a different variety of Middle English: see CHANCERY STANDARD. The quotation contains other clues to Chaucer's pronunciation: he must have said *sothe* like *SAWthuh*, so when it rhymes with *to the*, we have evidence that the second line had eleven syllables, stressing *Now*, *Hoost*, *lat*, the first syllable of *talke*, and *to*. The same evidence also shows that *the* in the second line was a form of *thee* with a spelling to reflect the unstressed pronunciation *thuh*. Modern personal pronouns also have unstressed forms, but conventional spelling does not represent the *y'see* or *have 'em sent* of more informal writing. The grammatical forms of Chaucer's English in these four lines are familiar, except for *the* thee, *artow* art thou, and *thy*, which are no longer part of English outside of special, usually religious, contexts. Chaucer had some verb endings that no longer remain, such as the *-en* in *faren we*. Nowadays, the subjunctive construction *God yeve it* would be *May God give it*, to indicate a wish for the action. Cast in modern spelling and grammatical forms, Chaucer's vocabulary is rarely strange. Here, only *fare* get along, *sothe* truth, and *quod* said, are obsolete, though all were current in Chaucer's time and continued to appear in much more recent works than his. *Discoloured* is familiar, but was probably not so to Chaucer's first readers: it came into English only in the decade when he wrote this passage, as did much of his poetic vocabulary.

**Style**. In pronunciation, grammar, and vocabulary, Chaucer was largely at one with his time and place, but in his use of these resources he was entirely singular. It was for his style that later centuries most admired him: William Dunbar called him 'rose of rethoris all' (the rose of all rhetoricians) and 'the noble Chaucer, of makaris flour' (flower of poets), William CAXTON praised his 'crafty and sugred eloquence', and Edmund Spenser deemed him 'the well of English undefiled'. Certainly his style varied, from the monosyllabism of the passage above to Criseyde's noble protest:

What, is this al the joye and al the feste?
Is this youre reed? Is this my blisful cas?
Is this the verray mede of youre
  byheeste?
Is al this paynted proces seyd—allas!—
Right for this fyn? O lady myn
      *(Troilus and Criseyde, Book 2)*

Like the earlier passage, these lines purport to be direct quotation of spontaneous speech, but here the poetry is marked with rhetorical figures: a repeated rhetorical question ('Is this . . . ?'), the anaphora varied at last with 'Is *al* this . . . ?', sarcasm ('my blisful cas'), alliteration ('paynted proces'), apostrophe ('O lady myn'), and more, just within these few lines. Chaucer's age respected and studied the 'arts of language': such rhetorical poetry was praiseworthy

and often poetically effective. So Chaucer drew not only on traditional rhetoric but on traditional views of language itself: 'Eke Plato seith, whoso kan hym rede, / The words moote ben cosyn to the dede'. Elsewhere, he conveyed his own observations of language, that it varied in time ('Ye knowe ek that in forme of speche is chaunge / Within a thousand yeer': *Troilus and Criseyde*, Book 2, cf. Horace, *Ars poetica*) and that it varied in space, for in *The Reeve's Tale* he used dialect to portray two students from the North of England, including features of their grammar, pronunciation, and vocabulary, such as *gas* for southern *goeth*. The evidence of his ear for language variety is consistent with everything else we know about Chaucer, whom John Dryden called 'the father of English poetry'. See COCKNEY, DICKENS, NORMAN FRENCH, PLAIN ENGLISH, PROSE, SATIRE, SLANG, STANDARD ENGLISH.

**CHIASMUS**, also **chiasm**. In RHETORIC, and INVERSION of word order that creates a counterbalancing effect in the second of two linked phrases: 'One must eat to live, not live to eat' (Cicero); 'This man I thought had been a Lord among wits; but, I find, he is only a wit among Lords' (Samuel Johnson, of Lord Chesterfield, 1754). See ANTITHESIS.

**CHICANO ENGLISH**, also **Mexican-American English**. English as used by Chicanos or Mexican-Americans. The term covers both English learned as a second language by people of Mexican-American heritage and the native English of speakers of Mexican-American background, both bilinguals and those who no longer speak SPANISH. Both lack definitive descriptions. Differences from other varieties are due to at least four factors operating over several generations: interference from Spanish, learning errors that have become established, contact with other dialects of English, and independent developments. It is difficult to distinguish between contemporary and historical interference of Spanish in a community that includes first-generation learners, bilinguals of varying competence, and near-monolingual English-speakers of Hispanic descent. Typical phonological features are: the vowel sound of 'sheep' for 'ship'; the use of *s* for *z*, the *s* of *present* pronounced like the *c* of *decent*; confusion over *ch* and *sh*, as in *chip* and *ship*, and 'shicken' for *chicken*; the devoicing

the learning of more subtle aspects of grammatical style and the building up of vocabulary.

**Other skills**. The task of language acquisition requires more than the learning of the structural skills of sounds, grammar, and vocabulary. Children must also learn to *use* these structures appropriately in everyday situations. They need to develop conversational skills, the rules of politeness (such as when to say *please* and *thank you*), the correct use of FORMS OF ADDRESS, and how to make requests in a direct or indirect manner ('I was wondering if you could . . .'). Older children need to be able to handle such 'manipulating' features of language as *well*, *you know*, and *actually*, to learn to decode and use more subtle interactional features (such as sarcasm), and to cope with such stylistic differences as formal and informal speech. School brings an encounter with learning to read and write, though for many children considerable awareness of written language has come from reading materials at home. Finally, children have to develop a set of *metalinguistic* skills (the ability to reflect on and talk about language), through the use of a range of popular, semi-technical, and technical notions, such as *sound*, *word*, *page*, *sentence*, *capital letter*. The task of language acquisition is complex. The fact that it is largely complete by puberty makes it one of the most remarkable (if not *the* most remarkable) of all learning achievements. See ANALOGY, HALLIDAY, LANGUAGE LEARNING, PSYCHOLINGUISTICS.

# ■ CHINA ——————————— ■

A country of East Asia. Languages: Putonghua (official: see below), various Chinese dialects (see below), and various minority languages, including Uighur, Tibetan, Manchu, Mongol, and Korean. No Western language has established itself in mainland China as such, but English is used in HONG KONG and Portuguese in Macao, and English is the principal foreign language taught in China.

**Chinese**. Although Chinese is generally treated as a single language of the Sino-Tibetan family, with many dialects, it may often be more accurately described as a group of mutually unintelligible (though grammatically similar) languages whose speakers employ the same non-phonetic writing system. This group is usually described as the mother tongue of some 1,000m Han Chinese, a number taken to show, often in comparison with English, that more people speak Chinese than any other language. The main varieties of 'Chinese' (Cantonese, Hakka, Hsiang, Kan, Mandarin, Min, and Wu) are as distinct from one another as English from Danish or German. Cantonese, though traditionally described as a 'dialect', is a major language spoken by millions in China, Hong Kong, Malaysia, Singapore, and elsewhere in South-East Asia. It is often contrasted with *Mandarin* (*Chinese*), the traditional governing language of the Chinese Empire. Difficulties encountered by the BBC World Service when broadcasting in Chinese illustrate significant differences between Mandarin and Cantonese associated with writing as much as with speech:

> Uniquely among the vernacular services, the BBC Chinese Section has to cope with two languages in one. In principle written standard Chinese is one language. In practice (quite apart from pronunciation problems), the differences between Cantonese and Mandarin can mean that scripts translated by Mandarin speakers may be difficult for Cantonese speakers to read for the microphone without recourse to the English original; and scripts translated by Cantonese speakers often present even more difficulty for speakers of Mandarin (Rodney Mantle, 'Speaking with One Voice in Thirty-Seven Languages', *The Linguist*, 29: 6, 1990).

The Chinese WRITING system is at least 2,000 years old. It consists of some 40,000 characters or ideograms, and is largely independent of sound, much as the numbers 1, 2, 3, 4, 5, etc., are language-independent and variously realized in different languages. Chinese characters have traditionally been written vertically and the columns read from right to left, but are often now written horizontally and read from left to right. In the People's Republic, a form of Mandarin has been developed as *Putonghua* (common speech), a unifying national standard and medium of instruction in schools that is written and printed in a simplified system of traditional characters (some 2,000 in number) and also, for certain purposes, in a system of romanization known as *Pinyin* ('phonetic spelling', from *pin* arrange, classify, *yin* sound, pronunciation).

**Pinyin and Wade–Giles**. The Pinyin system was introduced in 1958 and officially adopted in 1979. It differs significantly from the earlier system of romanization devised in the 19c by Sir Thomas Wade and adapted by Herbert Giles, and known as the *Wade–Giles system*. The following list has Wade–Giles first and Pinyin second in each pair: *Chou Enlai/Zhou Enlai, Mao Tse Tung/Mao Zedong, Nanking/Nanjing, Peking/Beijing, Sian/Xian, Soochow/Suzhou, Szechuan/Sichuan, t'ai chi ch'uan/tai ji quan, Teng Hsiao Ping/Deng Xiaoping*. The Beijing government prints all Chinese personal and placenames in the Pinyin style in its English-language publications and expects them to be used universally for diplomatic and official purposes and in the media. Pinyin is not, however, recognized as a replacement of Wade–Giles in Taiwan or by traditionalists outside the People's Republic, nor is it used in the People's Republic for everyday purposes. The use of Pinyin poses problems of distinguishing homographs, as in the 24 etymologically unrelated forms spelt *lian*. In traditional ideography, each of these has a distinct character. This problem may be circumvented with the use of the recently developed Monroe Keyboard for word-processing, which types most Chinese characters in a small number of keystrokes and may make the use of ROMAN symbols less necessary.

**Pidgin English**. Contact between the English and Chinese languages dates from the establishment of a British trading post in 1640 in Guangzhou (Kwangchow, Canton), where *PIDGIN English* developed in the 18c. This was a trade jargon of the ports, now known technically as *Chinese Pidgin English* and *China Coast Pidgin*. Influenced by an earlier *Cantonese Pidgin Portuguese* (used by and with the Portuguese traders who preceded the British), it developed into a lingua franca of the Pacific that influenced the pidgins of Papua New Guinea, the Solomon Islands, Vanuatu, Queensland, and elsewhere. With regard to its origin, the linguist Chin-Chuan Cheng notes: 'The Chinese held the British, like all "foreign devils," in low esteem, and would not stoop to learning the foreign tongue in its full form. The British, on the other hand,

regarded the "heathen Chinee" as beyond any possibility of learning, and so began to modify their own language for the natives' benefit' ('Chinese Varieties of English', in Braj. B. Kachru (ed.), *The Other Tongue*, 1982). Pidgin spread when the Treaty Ports were established in China in 1843, but declined towards the end of the 19c as standard English began to be systematically taught in schools and universities. It is now extinct in the People's Republic and marginal in Hong Kong. The jargon, though a practical and useful medium, was generally looked down on; a disparaging term for it was *coolie Esperanto*. An example from its heyday is: *Tailor, my have got one piece plenty hansom silk; my want you make one nice evening dress.*

**English in China**. In the first half of the 20c, English was based on the British model and taught largely through literature. After the Communist regime established itself in 1949, the BrE model continued, not because of trade or imperial connections, but because the new educational policy was influenced by that of the Soviet Union, for which BrE was also the model. For many years China and the US had limited relations, and AmE has only recently become a possible target for learners. Currently, there is enormous interest in English in the People's Republic, with an estimated 250m people at various stages in learning the language. For most Chinese, English is the international language *par excellence*, but as Cheng (above) observes, use often includes 'identical or very similar expressions used in various publications. This tendency towards fixed expressions is also noticeable in spoken English. To an outsider, both spoken and written varieties appear stilted.' He calls this politicized style *Sinicized English*. Its exponents, especially in such official organs as the English edition of the *Beijing Review/Beijing Zhoubao* (formerly the *Peking Review*), have tended to lace their English with such loan translations from Putonghua as *running dogs* for 'lackeys' (from *zou gou*) and *capitalist roaders* (from *zou zi pai*). English used by speakers of any Chinese dialect anywhere, regardless of their political persuasion, is often informally referred to as *Chinglish*.

**English and Chinese**. (1) *English in Chinese*. In the People's Republic, the influence of English on Chinese has been mainly lexical,

and in particular a large number of technical terms. English has had a mild effect on
the morphology of Mandarin/Putonghua,
in that the formation of loans and loan
translations (such as *modeng* modern, *moteer*
model, *shehui* society, and *yuanliang* excuse)
has meant an increase in polysyllables in a
mainly monosyllabic structure. In syntax,
translation from English and the study of
English grammar appears to have led to an
increase in passive usage entailing the
co-verb *bei*: compare KOREA. (2) *Chinese in
English*. The influence of Chinese on English
at large has been almost exclusively lexical,
with few items gaining additional senses beyond the originally borrowed meaning or
being transferred out of their Asian semantic contexts. A few, like *tea*, have become international forms borrowed into languages
around the world. Nearly 1,000 loans into
English have been tabulated, such as *chow
mein, ginseng, gung-ho, kaolin, kung fu, sampan,
taipan; typhoon*.

See BORROWING, CLASSICAL LANGUAGE,
DIALECT IN AMERICA, EAST ASIAN ENGLISH,
JAPAN, MALAYSIAN ENGLISH, Q, SINGAPORE
ENGLISH, SOUTH-EAST ASIAN ENGLISH,
TRANSLITERATION.

**CHOMSKY, (Avram) Noam** [b. 1928].
American linguist and political writer, born
in Philadelphia, Pennsylvania, and introduced to philology by his father, a scholar of
Hebrew. At the U. of Pennsylvania he studied under the structural linguist Zellig
Harris. After gaining his Ph.D. in 1955 (dis-
sertation: 'Transformational Analysis'), he
taught modern languages and LINGUISTICS
at Massachusetts Institute of Technology,
where he became full professor in 1961. He
was appointed Ferrari P. Ward Professor of
Foreign Languages and Linguistics in 1976.
During this period, he became a leading
figure in US linguistics, replacing a mechanistic and behaviouristic view of language
(based on the work of Bloomfield) with a
mentalistic and generative approach. His
linguistic publications include: *Syntactic
Structures* (1957), *Aspects of the Theory of Syntax*
(1965), *Cartesian Linguistics* (1966), *The Sound
Pattern of English* (with Morris Halle, 1968),
*Language and Mind* (1968, 1972), *The Logical
Structure of Linguistic Theory* (1975), *Reflections
on Language* (1975), *Lectures on Government and
Binding* (1981), *Barriers* (1986). His social,
political, and economic works include:
*American Power and the New Mandarins* (1969),

*The Political Economy of Human Rights* (two
volumes, 1979). *Language and Responsibility*
(1979) combines his linguistic and social
interests by exploring relationships among
language, science, ideas, and politics.

Chomsky originated such concepts as
TRANSFORMATIONAL-GENERATIVE GRAMMAR
(*TGG*), *transformational grammar* (*TG*), and *generative grammar*. His definition of GRAMMAR
differs from both traditional and structuralist theories, in that he is concerned not
only with a formal descriptive system but
also with the linguistic structures and
processes at work in the mind. He sees such
structures as universal and arising from a
genetic predisposition to language. Features drawn from mathematics include
*transformation* and *generation*. As proposed in
1957, *transformational rules* were a means by
which one kind of sentence (such as the passive *The work was done by local men*) could be
derived from another kind (such as the active *Local men did the work*). Any process governed by such rules was a *transformation* (in
the preceding case the *passivization transformation*) and any sentence resulting from
such rules was a *transform*. In Chomsky's
terms, previous grammars had only *phrase-
structure rules*, which specified how sentences are structured out of phrases and
phrases out of words, but had no way of relating sentences with different structures
(such as active and passive).

Such earlier grammars were also concerned only with *actual* attested sentences
and not with all the *potential* sentences in a
language. An adequate grammar, however,
in his view, should *generate* (that is, explicitly account for) the indefinite set of acceptable sentences of a language, rather than
the finite set to be found in a corpus of texts.
*Aspects* (1965) presented what is known as
his 'standard theory', which added the
concepts *deep structure* and *surface structure*:
deep or underlying forms which by transformation become surface or observable
sentences of a particular language. In this
theory, a passive was no longer to be derived
from an active sentence, but both from a
common deep structure which was neither
active nor passive. Comparably, sentences
with similar surface structures, such as *John
is easy to please* and *John is eager to please* were
shown to have different deep structures.
The standard theory distinguishes between
a speaker's *competence* (knowledge of a
language) and *performance* (actual use of a

language), Chomskyan grammar being concerned with competence, not performance.

Subsequent work has concentrated less on rules that specify what can be generated and more on *constraints* that determine what cannot be generated. A definitive statement of his recent views is *Lectures on Government and Binding*, in which the theory is *GB theory*. Government is an extension of the traditional term whereby a verb governs its object, but for Chomsky prepositions may govern and subjects may be governed. Binding is concerned with the type of anaphora found with pronouns and reflexives, but the notion is greatly extended. The traditional notion of case is similarly used, though modified in that it need not be morphological. Such devices can be used to rule out ungrammatical sentences that might otherwise be generated. *Barriers* (1986) extends GB theory.

Chomsky is widely considered to be the most influential figure in linguistics in the later 20c and is probably the linguist best-known outside the field. His views on language and grammar are controversial and responses to them have ranged from extreme enthusiasm, sometimes verging on fanaticism, through a sober and reflective interest, to fierce rejection by some traditionalist, structuralist, and other critics. See CHILD LANGUAGE ACQUISITION, COMMUNICATIVE COMPETENCE, LINGUISTIC TYPOLOGY, PSYCHOLINGUISTICS, STRUCTURAL LINGUISTICS.

**CHURCHILL, (Sir) Winston (Leonard Spencer)** [1874–1965]. British politician, statesman, writer, orator, historian, and painter; eldest son of Lord Randolph Churchill and his American wife, Jeannette ('Jennie') Jerome. He was born at Blenheim Palace and educated at Harrow School, of which he records that his weakness in Latin put him with the 'stupidest boys'. They learned 'to write mere English', and consequently 'I got into my bones the essential structure of the English sentence—which is a noble thing'. He served in the army, in several imperial campaigns, and was war correspondent for the London *Morning Post* during the Boer War. He became a Member of Parliament (1901) and in a long career served in many offices, including Home Secretary (1910–11) and Chancellor of the Exchequer (1924–9). After a period out of favour, he became Prime Minister (1940)

and war leader from crisis to victory. Defeated in the 1945 election, he was Prime Minister again (1951–5). Churchill had a reputation as a writer and speaker acknowledged even by his political opponents. His wartime speeches were rhetorical and passionate, inspired both country and Empire, and often drew on literary quotations, allusions, and cadences. He wrote one novel, a number of biographies, the autobiographical *My Early Life* (1930), and published two histories of his time, but his greatest literary achievement was *A History of the English-Speaking Peoples* (1956–8). He was awarded the Nobel Prize for Literature in 1953. Churchill's prose style is in the manner of Victorian historiography, notably that of Thomas Macaulay, and such a style is sometimes referred to as *Churchillian*. See BASIC ENGLISH.

**CIRCUMFLEX**. A DIACRITIC placed over vowel symbols. It has three possible forms: angled (^), rounded (⌐), or waved (~). In classical Greek, the circumflex marks a rise/fall in pitch; in French, it may indicate vowel quality (often due to the loss of a phoneme or syllable). It occurs in English only in unaltered loans from French: *gîte*; *dépôt* as opposed to *depot*. See ACCENT.

**CIRCUMLOCUTION**, also PERIPHRASIS. In RHETORIC, a wordy and indirect way of saying something, as when death in hospital is called *negative patient care outcome*. Such usage is often obscure, officious, pompous, authoritarian, and intimidating; the phrase *periphrastic usage* echoes the style it describes. See EUPHEMISM, JARGON, LITOTES, PLEONASM, POETIC DICTION, POETRY, REDUNDANCY, TAUTOLOGY.

**CLASSICAL COMPOUND**, also **learned compound**. A COMPOUND WORD whose elements and pattern derive from a classical language, as in *agriculture* from LATIN, *biography* from GREEK. Two features distinguish such words from most VERNACULAR compounds: further words can be derived from them, such as *agricultural(ly)*, *agricultur(al)ist* and *biographical(ly)*, *biographer*, and there are often SUFFIX-related stress shifts in their derivational patterns, such as *ágriculture/ agricúltural*, *biógraphy/biográphical*, caused in these instances by the addition of -(ic)al. Because they have long been an international resource, such compounds are both part of English and other than English; in form, they range from the entirely English *dinosaur* to the Neo-Latinate *Tyrannosaurus*.

**Origin**. Such compounds derive from word-forming systems absorbed to varying degrees by many modern European languages. They have been in English since the Middle Ages, but did not become common until the influx of Neo-Latinisms during the Renaissance: *mystagogue* 1550, *androgyne* 1552, *troglodyte* 1555, *geographical* and *hydrographer* 1559. In adopting such words, English followed French rather than German, which tended to resist NEO-LATIN compounds in favour of calques like *Landwirtschaft* for Latin *agricultura* and *Lebensbeschreibung* or *Lebensgeschichte* (description or history of life) for Greek *biographia* (although the term *Biographie* is widely used). In French, adoption was wholesale and adaptation minimal: *agricultura* and *biographia* became *agriculture* and *biographie*. From French, such items passed into English with little or no adaptation in spelling.

**Nature**. It is functionally unimportant whether a classical compound is first used in English, French, or any other language. The elements are international and the conventions for their adaptation well established. Greek elements are usually transmitted through Latin orthography. In this system, *k* usually becomes *c*: *cardiology*, not \**kardiology* (but note *leuk(a)emia*, not \**leuc(a)emia*, and both *leucocyte* and *leukocyte*). *R* with rough breathing becomes *rh* in French and English (*rhinocéros, rhinoceros*) or *r* in Italian and Spanish (*rinoceronte*). On occasion, a biological term may combine Greek and Latin: *Tyrannosaurus rex* (Greek 'tyrant lizard', Latin 'king') and *Oviraptor philoceratops* (Latin 'eggsnatcher', Greek 'lovable horned-face'). Some binomials contain information about people and places, such as *Albertosaurus sternbergi* Sternberg's Alberta lizard, and *Yangchuanosaurus shangyouensis* the Shanghai Yangchuan lizard. The classification for naturalists developed by such taxonomists as Carolus Linnaeus is an ad-hoc system that has its own fossils; it is as likely to mark ignorance as knowledge and to express subjective as objective comment. Linnaeus classified nonflowering plants as *Cryptogamia* (hidden marriage), because he did not know how they reproduced. When his successors discovered the processes

involved, they left the name unchanged. When the British anatomist Richard Owen coined the name *dinosaur* ('terrible lizard', 1841) for the extinct reptiles whose skeletons were found in rock strata, Romanticism contributed more than science.

**Uses and glosses**. The compounds are part of technical usage and include the names of many scientific studies: *biology, cardiology, meteorology*. Such labels are often opaque and intimidating to people not trained in their use, with the result that, although tools of technical description, they have some of the features of a secret language. They may be difficult to pronounce, because of their length and suffix-related shifts in stress. Someone attempting an unfamiliar form can mispronounce it and retreat in confusion: for example, 'Tonight we have someone interesting to talk to you, folks. He's an orni-, an ornitho-, a birdman' (BBC disc jockey, live, 1970). The switch from *ornithologist* to *birdman* is part of a practice of explaining classical compounds by translation into everyday terms. Such glossing ranges from formal etymologies to informal paraphrases, as in: 'The name "echinoderm" comes from the Greek *echînos*, a hedgehog, and *dérma*, the skin'; 'The *Archaeopteryx*, whose name means "ancient wing" . . .'; 'the reptile subclass *Archosauria* (ruling lizards)'; 'Cosmology, the science of the universe'; 'Coprolites or fossilized excrement'; 'Cryptozoology, the quest for animals that scientists have yet to discover'.

Although such terms as *neurology* and *Archaeopteryx* are scientific, classical compounding is not confined to the sciences, and pre-dates scientific method. In divination, compounds based on *-mancy* are numerous, including: *necromancy* divination through talking to the dead, *nephelomancy* through observing clouds, *ophiomancy* by inspecting snakes, *pyromancy* by watching flames, *tyromancy* by examining cheese. Sometimes compounds are used to impress and lend a cachet, as in *cosmetology* the art of applying cosmetics. They have also been coined for facetious and satirical purposes, as with *odontopedology*, the art of opening your mouth and putting your foot in it. Classical and vernacular elements combine to this end: *escapology* the carnival art of getting out of chains and cabinets, *kiddology* the art of kidding or conning people, *sudsology* the study of soap operas. See COMBINING

FORM, INTERFIX, INTERNATIONAL SCIENTIFIC VOCABULARY, WORD-FORMATION.

**CLASSICAL ENDING**. There are in English many nouns whose SINGULAR/PLURAL contrasts derive from LATIN and GREEK, such as *stimulus/stimuli* (Latin: masculine), *formula/formulae* (Latin: feminine), *memorandum/memoranda* (Latin: neuter), *phenomenon/phenomena* (Greek: neuter). During the 16–19c, when writing was largely the concern of the classically educated, many such endings were retained as a matter of course. Some are universally used (*radius/radii*), some have become restricted to certain registers (*formulae* to scientific discourse, *formulas* gaining ground generally; *indexes* in books, *indices* in mathematics), and some have been considerably adapted (the singular *agendum* has disappeared and the former plural *agenda* has become a singular, with the non-classical plural *agendas*). Asymmetry is common: *campus* and *ultimatum* have the plurals *campuses* and *ultimatums*, not *\*campi* and *\*ultimata*, while *desideratum* and *sanctum sanctorum* have the plurals *desiderata* and *sancta sanctorum*, not *\*desideratums* and *\*sanctum sanctorums*. Many would hesitate when choosing plurals for such words as *arboretum* and *thesaurus* (both classical and vernacular are possible).

Although contrasts such as Latin *addendum/addenda* and Greek *criterion/criteria* are maintained in academic and technical writing, *bacterium/bacteria* and *datum/data* pose problems. *Bacteria* is widely assumed to be collective, and *bacterium* and *datum* are so seldom used that they often raise doubts. *Data* is currently both plural ('The data are available') and collective ('How much data do you need?'), and is often therefore a controversial usage issue. *Curriculum* and *memorandum* have two plural forms: *curricula*, *curriculums* and *memoranda*, *memorandums*. The *medium/media* contrast is complex and extremely controversial. Among spiritualists, the plural of *medium* is *mediums*. In linguistics, it is both *media* and *mediums*. In the media, it is *media*, the singular *medium* often being overlooked, so that *media* is used as both plural ('the media are . . .') and singular ('the media is . . .'), with the occasional vernacular plural form *medias*; compare French *les médias*.

In the late 20c, traditional usage has declined as the number of people involved in technical and academic discourse has increased. Contrasting plurals are common: *cactus*, *formula*, *referendum* often have the technical plurals *cacti*, *formulae*, *referenda* and the popular plurals *cactuses*, *formulas*, *referendums*. Such usages as *a rock strata*, *a good criteria*, *this phenomena is widespread* all occur frequently, with the plurals *stratas*, *criterias*, *phenomenas*. They are disliked (often intensely) not only by purists but by many who consider themselves liberal in matters of usage. Purism, however, also has its barbarisms, such as the quasiclassical plurals *octopi* and *syllabi* for *octopus* and *syllabus*, competing with *octopuses* and *syllabuses*. (The Greek plurals for these words are, respectively, *octópoda* and *sullabóntes*.)

**CLASSICAL LANGUAGE**. A prestigious, often ancient language, such as LATIN or SANSKRIT, or a variety of a language, such as classical GREEK. Such a language is usually learned formally, is often a yardstick against which other languages are measured, and may be a norm in terms of which they are described. Classical languages are often contrasted with VERNACULAR languages, in a relationship of 'high' to 'low'. They have traditionally provided models for successor or dependent languages, especially for styles of verse and prose, literary genres, grammatical descriptions, pronouncements on usage, and philosophical and other texts. They have a body of literature, usually preserved in manuscript form and organized into a canon which may be scriptural (as with Sanskrit and Arabic), secular or secularized (as with classical Greek), or a mixture of these (as with Latin). The evaluation is often historical, made by later generations, and in many instances a certain period in the history of such a language has been regarded as a golden age.

**Classical strata in non-classical languages**. Generally, a classical language dominates a cultural area in which vernaculars are used. Because of this, elements of its vocabulary may be absorbed into a subordinate tongue, to form a more or less distinct 'high' stratum within it. Both learning the classical language and using its extension into a vernacular are often associated with prestigious systems of education in certain societies, such as Latinity in the public schools of England. After the invasion of the Persian Empire by Muslims from Arabia, Persian developed a learned stratum of Arabic, and in such languages as Hindi and Tamil there are Sanskrit strata. Both classical ARABIC and Sanskrit have been associated with traditional forms of education. The Neo-Latin stratum of English developed during and after the Renaissance, largely as a response to the need for a prose capable of handling scholarship and science, traditionally the domain of Latin.

**Dead language?** There is a widespread view that to be truly classical, a language should be 'dead': that is, not passed on from parent to child within a community. Some classical languages, such as Latin and Sanskrit, have not been mother tongues for centuries, but this is not a universal feature of such languages. At one and the same time, Greek in various forms was the mother tongue of the Greeks, a Mediterranean lingua franca, and for the Romans a classical source of literary and rhetorical inspiration. In such situations, there has been a tendency to look to one variety of such a language as 'the best': that is, the properly classical and normative. In the case of Greek this was the educated Attic or Athenian variety.

**A learned code.** Because of centuries of standardization and veneration of literary usage, a classical language or a classicized variety of a language may split off from everyday use. Classical Latin split off from the 'vulgar' varieties of the Republic and the Empire, and Sanskrit split off from the Prakrits of northern India. When such a division occurs, the classicized medium becomes progressively less and less available as a mother tongue. It is instead perpetuated in script, print, and formal instruction as the learned code of an élite, taught by accredited masters. Latin became a 'high' language first through its literary and rhetorical tradition, then its association with Christian learning. Sanskrit and classical Arabic became 'high' languages primarily as the vehicles of religion. Mandarin Chinese became such a language because, especially in writing, it served to hold the Chinese Empire together for centuries, was associated with Confucianism and public examinations, and influenced such other cultures as the Japanese and Korean.

**Classical English.** English has within it a double classical inheritance, from Latin and from Greek through Latin. The STANDARD LANGUAGE has two blended superstrates and is to some degree defined by their presence and use. After the Renaissance, English began to display classical tendencies of its own, when a 'refined' and 'elegant' standard was promoted by 17–18c writers who called themselves *Augustans* in imitation of the Augustan period in ancient Rome. Such writers and their associates set their own, especially literary usage above all other forms of the language and some campaigned for an academy and a dictionary that would enshrine classical norms. Samuel Johnson, however, found that he could not compile the kind of dictionary hoped for, and with the independence of the US a resistance to Augustan norms developed outside Britain. In 1828, the American writer John Neal observed:

> For my own part . . . I never shall write what is now worshipped under the name of *classical* English. It is no natural language—it never was—it never will be spoken alive on this earth: and therefore, ought never to be written. We have dead languages enough now; but the deadest language I ever met with, or heard of, was that in use among the writers of Queen Anne's day (unpublished preface to the novel *Rachel Dyer*).

Nevertheless, present-day STANDARD ENGLISH has received a double legacy from the Augustans: (1) The variety known as the *King's/Queen's English*, associated with the public schools and the universities of Oxford and Cambridge. (2) The *print standard*, which, despite minor differences in spelling and some other conventions in BrE and AmE, was largely systematized in the 18c. In the late 20c, Standard English has four quasi-classical features: it is a prestigious international medium; its literary canon is widely studied, including by many non-native speakers; its vocabulary is being drawn into 'vernaculars' throughout the world; and amid its varieties, the print standard serves as a canonical form, learned not at home but at school. It is not surprising, therefore, that for many people standard English is an object of some reverence, and that they wish to protect it from barbarians at its gates, as if it too were a classical language.

See BARBARISM, BIBLE, CHINA, INFLATED LANGUAGE, JAPAN, LATINATE, LATINISM, LATIN TAG, NEO-LATIN, POETIC DICTION, RECEIVED

PRONUNCIATION, RHETORIC, SOLECISM, THEMATIC VOWEL.

**CLAUSE**. In grammatical description, a SENTENCE or sentence-like construction included within another sentence, such as *because I wanted to* in *I did it because I wanted to*.

**Traditional kinds of clauses**. (1) *Main clause*. A simple sentence consists of one MAIN CLAUSE or principal clause: *I knew it. The computer industry is bursting with energy.* (2) *Coordinate clause*. In the following sentence, there are two main clauses, linked through COORDINATION by *and*. Each is therefore a COORDINATE CLAUSE: *They milked the animals and then they made yoghurt, butter, and cheese.* (3) *Subordinate clause*. In the following sentence, there are two clauses, linked through SUBORDINATION by *that*: *Some scientists argue that the earth's climate is changing.* In one contemporary analysis, the main clause includes the SUBORDINATE CLAUSE, and is the whole sentence, but in a traditional analysis the main clause is restricted to *Some scientists argue*. Two subordinate clauses may be coordinated (here with *and*): *We can see that the health of species is interconnected and that the human race is now in danger.* One subordinate clause may be subordinated to another, as in *I know that everybody believes that it is too late*. Both *that*-clauses are subordinate, but one of them (*that everybody believes that it is too late*) is superordinate to the *that*-clause within it (*that it is too late*). Some grammarians refer to a subordinate sentence or clause as being *embedded* within its *matrix sentence*.

**Non-finite clauses**. In some descriptions, the term *clause* is restricted to constructions whose verb is finite, as in the examples given so far. Other descriptions extend the term to sentence-like constructions that have a non-finite verb or no verb at all, both of which are PHRASES in traditional grammar. However, they are sentence-like because they can be analysed in terms of such elements as subject and object. In these more recent descriptions, the infinitive clause *to value two important pictures* in the sentence *She was asked to value two important pictures* can be analysed as having a verb *to value* and a direct object *two important pictures*, corresponding to the analysis of *She will value two important pictures*. Similarly, the verbless clause *obdurate as stone* in the sentence *Obdurate as stone, the man withstood all pleas* can be analysed as consisting of a subject complement, corresponding to the analysis of *The man was obdurate as stone*. In such a description, sentences are classified by form into three types: finite clauses; non-finite clauses (infinitive and participle clauses); verbless clauses.

**Clauses and functions**. The clause can also be classified into three major types: *nominal* or *noun clause*, *relative* or ADJECTIVE CLAUSE, and ADVERBIAL CLAUSE. Nominal clauses have functions similar to those of a noun or pronoun, such as subject or object; for example, the nominal clause *that the spacecraft were too big* is subject in *That the spacecraft were too big was maintained by many critics* (compare *That view was maintained by many critics*) and object in *The committee stated that the spacecraft were too big* (compare *The committee stated that*). Relative clauses have a function shared with that of most adjectives, that is, modifying a noun; for example *that she was angling for a hereditary peerage* modifies *rumours* in *She denied rumours that she was angling for a hereditary peerage* (compare *malicious rumours*). Adverbial clauses have functions shared with those of most adverbs, such as modifying a verb, alone or with some other parts of the sentence, or the sentence as a whole; for example, the clause *if the organization is run by an amiable nonentity* in the sentence *The problems will prove insoluble if the organization is run by an amiable nonentity* (compare *in the circumstances*) and the clause *when the museum moves into the new centre* in the sentence *When the museum moves into the new centre it will organize scholarly exhibitions* (compare *then*). See ABSOLUTE CLAUSE, PARTICIPLE, SUPERORDINATE CLAUSE.

**CLAUSE ANALYSIS**, also **general analysis**. A technique of formal grammatical analysis once common in schools in English-speaking countries and English-medium schools elsewhere. It involves the division of longer sentences into their constituent clauses: for example, the analysis of the complex sentence *When they arrived, they found that there was not enough food* into: *they found* (main or principal clause); *when they arrived* (subordinate adverbial CLAUSE of time, modifying the verb *found*); *that there was not enough food* (subordinate noun clause, object of the verb *found*). Such analysis was routine grammatical work in many secondary classrooms until the 1950s, but from the 1960s fell into disfavour. Most teachers and linguists currently present four arguments against such work: (1) It rests on a narrow theoretical base derived from the study of Latin, and ignores the range of types of clauses that can be identified in English. (2) It concentrates on only one aspect of grammar. (3) It is highly formal and remote from everyday language. (4) Most students did not respond well to it and many teachers did not like teaching it. As a result of the precipitous decline in teaching such analysis, students since the 1960s have generally had little organized instruction in sentence forms. Clause analysis continues to be favoured by many older, usually middle-class people, who argue that training in such analysis is useful in developing linguistic skills, especially in writing. See PARSING.

**CLEFT SENTENCE**. A construction in which a simple SENTENCE is divided into two clauses so as to give prominence to a particular linguistic item and the information it carries. The sentence *On Monday the players objected to the delay* can be restated as any of three cleft sentences: (1) With the focus on the players: *It was the players who/that objected on Monday to the delay*. (2) With the focus on the delay: *It was the delay that the players objected to on Monday*. (3) With the focus on Monday: *It was on Monday that the players objected to the delay*. The first clause of a cleft sentence consists of *It*, a form of the verb *be*, and the focused item. The rest is a relative clause. A similar device is found in the *pseudo-cleft sentence*, where the subject is generally a *nominal relative clause*, the verb is a form of the verb *be*, and the focused item follows at the end: *What I badly need is a good rest* (based on *I badly need a good rest*). Unlike the cleft sentence, the pseudo-cleft sentence can have a verb (and other elements that follow it) as the focused item: *What we did was replace all the carpets*. Similar are sentences in which a pronoun or noun phrase with general reference is used instead of the nominal relative clause: *Something I badly need is a good rest. The thing we did was replace the carpets*.

**CLICHÉ**, also **cliche**. A usually pejorative general term for a WORD or PHRASE regarded as having lost its freshness and vigour through overuse (and therefore suggesting insincerity, lack of thought, or laziness on the part of the user). Many IDIOMS and STOCK expressions are commonly called clichés: everyday phrases such as *all of a sudden, anything goes*; whole or part PROVERBS such as *there's no smoke without fire, don't count your chickens*; similes such as *dead as a doornail, avoid like the plague*; and fashionable usages such as *the name of the game, the bottom line*. In addition to its application to language, the term is widely used to refer to any social, artistic, literary, dramatic, cinematic, or other formula that through overexposure has, in the view of a commentator, become trite and commonplace. Critics of the media often castigate as clichés 'tired expressions' produced under pressure by journalists and others writing against a deadline, and language teachers commonly deplore HACKNEYED usages in the work of their students as marks of derivative ideas and sloppy presentation.

**The cliché and originality**. The use of the term *cliché* in the late 19c and throughout the 20c has been associated with a desire for originality of expression. Such a desire, however, is not much older than the term itself. Many stock expressions often currently described as clichés are part of a primarily oral process that facilitates fluency while speakers are thinking ahead to their next points or are wrestling with difficult ideas. Proverbs, because they are mnemonic formulas, help people pass on elements of oral tradition without needing or seeking to be novel or clever every time. Comparably, many common expressions derive from classical cultures (such as Greece and Rome) and much-admired texts (such as the Bible and Shakespeare's plays), and have become part of the language because they have long been highly valued, and acquire as a result a kind of proverbial status. Traditional approaches to education have also encouraged students to copy or quote the precise expressions of famous predecessors whenever possible rather than to seek to be original before they are ready. All such usages and formulas were admired precisely because they *were* unoriginal, and writers or speakers used them because they were familiar to their audiences. In such works as the Homeric epics, stock formulas served to maintain the rhythm of the verse and were mnemonically useful for performers and listeners alike. The phrase *rosy-fingered dawn* occurs so often in the *Odyssey* that a modern reader, accustomed to the idea of the cliché, might

conclude that Homer was sloppy and unoriginal where in reality he was following
the precise conventions of his craft. In making an assessment of various definitions of
and comments on the cliché, *Webster's Dictionary of English Usage* (ed. W. Ward Gilman,
1989) observes:

> We will offer only two suggestions. The
> first is that in all the use of *trite, overused,
> stale, outworn, threadbare* and such
> descriptors there is probably a con-
> necting thread of meaninglessness.
> You might, then, want to base your
> notion of the cliché not on the
> expression itself but on its use; if it
> seems to be used without much
> reference to a definite meaning, it is
> then perhaps a cliché. But even this line
> of attack fails to separate cliché from the
> common forms of polite social inter-
> course. A second and more work-
> able approach would be simply to call a
> cliché whatever word or expression you
> have heard or seen often enough to find
> annoying. Many writers, in fact, do seem
> to use some such rough-and-ready
> definition.

See JOURNALESE, METAPHOR, PLATITUDE,
POETIC DICTION, QUOTATION, SHIBBOLETH,
STEREOTYPE.

**CLIMAX**. **1.** In rhetoric, an ascending
series of words, ideas, or events, in which
intensity and significance increase step by
step: 'For want of a nail the shoe was lost;
for want of a shoe the horse was lost; and
for want of a horse the rider was lost'
(Benjamin Franklin, *Poor Richard's Almanack*,
1758). **2.** In drama, a crisis or moment of
decision. In a five-act play, such as Shakespeare's, the climax usually occurs near the
end of the third act. **3.** In general usage,
the highest or most intense point in an experience or series of events. By implication,
anything following a climax is anticlimac-
tic, but a work of literature, a drama, and
life itself may sustain a series of minor
and major climaxes. Generally, in the 20c, a
play, novel, or film ends after its main
climax. See ANTICLIMAX.

**CLIPPING**, also **clipped form, clipped
word, shortening**. An ABBREVIATION
formed by the loss of word elements, usually syllabic: *pro* from *professional, tec* from
*detective*. The process is attested from the 16c
(*coz* from *cousin* 1559, *gent* from *gentleman*

1564); in the early 18c, Swift objected to the
reduction of Latin *mobile vulgus* (the fickle
throng) to *mob*. Clippings can be either
selective, relating to one sense of a word
only (*condo* is short for *condominium* when it
refers to accommodation, not to joint sovereignty), or polysemic (*rev* stands for either
*revenue* or *revision*, and *revs* for the revolutions of wheels). There are three kinds of
clipping:

**1. *Back-clippings***, in which an element or
elements are taken from the end of a word:
*ad(vertisement)*, *chimp(anzee)*, *deli(catessen)*,
*hippo(potamus)*, *lab(oratory)*, *piano( forte)*,
*reg(ulation)s*. Backclipping is common with
DIMINUTIVES formed from personal names:
*Cath(erine)*, *Will(iam)*. Clippings of names
often undergo adaptations: *Catherine* to the
pet forms *Cathie, Kate, Katie, William* to *Willie,
Bill, Billy*. Sometimes, a clipped name can develop a new sense: *willie* a euphemism for
penis, *billy* a club or a male goat. Occasionally, the process can be humorously reversed: for example, offering in a British
restaurant to pay the william.

**2. *Fore-clippings***, in which an element or
elements are taken from the beginning of a
word: (*ham*)*burger*, (*omni*)*bus*, (*violon*)*cello*,
(*heli*)*copter*, (*alli*)*gator*, (*tele*)*phone*, (*earth*)*quake*.
They also occur with personal names,
sometimes with adaptations: *Becky* for *Rebecca, Drew* for *Andrew, Ginny* for *Virginia*. At
the turn of the century, a fore-clipped word
was usually given an opening APOSTROPHE,
to mark the loss: '*phone*, '*cello*, '*gator*. This
practice is now rare.

**3. *Fore-and-aft clippings***, in which elements are taken from the beginning and
end of a word: (*in*)*flu(enza)*, (*de*)*tec(tive)*. This is
commonest with longer personal names:
*Lex* from *Alexander, Liz* from *Elizabeth*. Such
names often demonstrate the versatility of
hypocoristic clipping: *Alex, Alec, Lex, Sandy,
Zander; Eliza, Liz, Liza, Lizzie, Bess, Betsy, Beth,
Betty*. Clippings are not necessarily uniform throughout a language: *mathematics*
becomes *maths* in BrE and *math* in AmE. *Reverend* as a title is usually shortened to *Rev* or
*Rev.*, but is *Revd* in the house style of Oxford
University Press. Back-clippings with -*ie*
and -*o* are common in AUSTRALIAN ENGLISH
and NZE: *arvo* afternoon, *journo* journalist.
Sometimes clippings become distinct words
far removed from the applications of the
original full forms: *fan* in *fan club* is from
*fanatic*; BrE *navvy*, a general labourer, is

from a 19c use of *navigator*, the digger of a 'navigation' or canal. See APHAERESIS, APOCOPE, COMPOUND WORD, EPONYM, WORD-FORMATION.

**COBUILD**. [An acronym for *Collins Birmingham University International Language Database*]. **1.** A British research facility set up at the U. of Birmingham in 1980 and funded by Collins publishers with the aim of compiling works of reference and course materials for the teaching of English. Its director was John Sinclair, Professor of Modern English Language. The primary work of COBUILD has been the creation and analysis of a CORPUS of contemporary, mainly BrE texts, some recorded from speech. By 1985, this corpus had reached 18m running words, representing 260,000 word types, over half of which occur only once, and 2% of the types (that is, 5,000 different spelling forms) account for 87% of the tokens. The implication is that 87% of all English texts comprises some 5,000 words, which could be presented in a basic dictionary as some 2,000 entries. **2.** An abbreviation and informal title for the *Collins COBUILD English Language Dictionary* (1987; 2nd edn 1995), a work derived from a study of the COBUILD corpus and primarily intended for foreign learners of English. It defines over 70,000 words, giving priority to the most frequent. Its definitions are generally supported by examples of usage taken from the corpus.

■ **COCKNEY** ─────────── ■

[Used with and without an initial capital]. A working-class Londoner, especially in the East End, and English as used by such a Londoner. Though often stigmatized as a gutter DIALECT, Cockney is a major element in the English of LONDON, the core of a diverse variety spoken by some 7m people in the Greater London area.

**Origins of the term**. In Langland's *Piers Plowman* (1362), *cokeneyes* means eggs, apparently small and misshapen, as if laid by a cock. In Chaucer's *Canterbury Tales* (c.1386), the Reeve uses *cokenay* in the sense of a mother's darling or milksop. By the early 16c, country people had extended the term to people brought up in cities and ignorant of real life: 'This cokneys and tytyllynges [*delicati pueri*] may abide no sorrow when they come to age. In this great citees as London, York the children be so nycely and

wantonly brought up that comonly they can little good' (Robert Whitinton, *Vulgaria*, 1520). By the early 17c, however, this expression of disdain for the city-bred young had narrowed to one place and one person: the 'Bow-bell Cockney' (1600) and 'our Cockney of London' (1611). In 1617, two definitions were written for the term in this sense:

> A *Cockney* or *Cockny*, applied only to one borne within the sound of Bow-bell, that is, within the City of London, which tearme came first out of this tale: That a Cittizens sonne riding with his father into the Country asked, when he heard a horse neigh, what the horse did his father answered, the horse doth neigh; riding farther he heard a cocke crow, and said doth the *cocke neigh* too? and therefore Cockney or Cocknie, by inuersion thus: *incock*, q. *incoctus* i. raw or vnripe in Country-mens affaires (John Minsheu, *Ductor in linguas: The guide into tongues*).

> Londiners, and all within the sound of Bowbell, are in reproch called Cocknies (Fynes Moryson, *An Itinerary*).

A succession of stigmas has therefore been associated with the name from the start: odd egg, milksop, young city slicker, and street-wise Londoner. At the same time, the reference of *Cockney* moved from something new or young (an egg, a child) to a spoiled adolescent (city youth) to anyone of any age born in London within the sound of the bells of St Mary-le-Bow Church. With 'our Cockney of London', the other usages were forgotten and a stereotype developed of a breed with no interest in life beyond the capital: 'That Synods Geography was as ridiculous as a Cockneys (to whom all is Barbary beyond Brainford; and Christendome endeth at Greenwitch)' (Richard Whitlock, *Zootomia, or observations on the present manners of the English*, 1654).

**Eighteenth-century Cockney**. Comments on the usage of London Cockneys date from the 18c. After setting out the faults of the Irish, the Scots, and the Welsh, the London elocutionist John Walker noted in 1791: 'There are dialects peculiar to Cornwall, Lancashire, Yorkshire, and every distant county in England; but as a consideration of these would lead to a detail too minute for the present occasion, I shall conclude these remarks with a few observations on the peculiarities of my countrymen, the Cockneys; who, as they are the models of pronunciation to the distant provinces, ought to be the more scrupulously correct' (*A Critical Pronouncing Dictionary of the English Language*).

Walker lists four faults: (1) A habit among Londoners of 'the lowest order' of pronouncing words like *fists*, *posts*, *wastes* as two syllables, as if there were an *e* between the *t* and the *s*. (2) Not confined to the lowest order, 'the pronunciation of *v* for *w*, and more frequently of *w* for *v*' ('vine and weal' for *wine and veal*), which he called 'a blemish of the first magnitude'. (3) Not pronouncing *h* after *w*, so that 'we do not find the least distinction between *while* and *wile*, *whet* and *wet*, *where* and *were*, &c.' (4) 'Sinking the *h* at the beginning of words where it ought to be sounded, and of sounding it, either where it is not seen, or where it ought to be sunk. Thus we not infrequently hear, especially among children, *heart* pronounced *art*, and *arm*, *harm*.' He also notes that words like *humour* are pronounced as if written 'yewmour'. Even so, he concludes: 'Thus I have endeavoured to correct some of the more glaring errors of my countrymen, who, with all their faults, are still upon the whole the best pronouncers of the English language.'

**Nineteenth-century Cockney**. Cockney and London usage seem to have been synonymous for Walker. He makes no distinction between refined and unrefined usage in the capital apart from his reference to the lowest social order. In the 19c, however, the term was limited to those whose usage never served as a model for anyone. By the time of SHAW's play *Pygmalion* (1913), Cockney was generally regarded as debased language ('gutter Cockney') and Shaw's flower-girl Eliza Doolittle received far more help from the phonetician Henry Higgins than Walker felt his fellows needed. The speech of all classes of Londoner has changed greatly since Walker's time. In the process, one of his 'faults' has by and large become a feature of the standard spoken English of England: the /w/ in such pairs as *while/wile*: see W and WH-SOUND. Of the others, one remains a stigma, one has only recently disappeared, and the third vanished long ago but remains controversial. The dropping of aitches is widespread beyond Cockneydom and is generally considered substandard. There is, however,

uncertainty about the extent to which aitches are sounded where they 'ought to be sunk': see AITCH, H. Pronunciations like 'fistiz' for *fists* continued into the 20c, but appear to have died out in the 1950s. The exchange of *v* and *w* has been the most controversial of Walker's SHIBBOLETHS, commentators who deny that it ever occurred sometimes blaming DICKENS for inventing it. He uses it copiously in *The Pickwick Papers* (1837), as part of the dialect of Samuel Weller, whose father calls him 'Samivel Veller':

> 'I had a reg'lar new fit o' clothes that mornin', gen'l'men of the jury,' said Sam, 'and that was a wery partickler and uncommon circumstance vith me in those days. . . . If they wos a pair o' patent double million magnifyin' gas microscopes of hextra power, p'raps I might be able to see through a flight o' stairs and a deal door; but bein' only eyes, you see, my wision's limited' (ch. 34).

Walker, however, provides the proof that Sam's style of speech existed well before Dickens created him, but it appears to have been in decline when Dickens made it a literary STEREOTYPE, and had virtually disappeared by the 1870s, as noted by Shaw in an appendix to *Captain Brassbound's Conversion* (1900):

> When I came to London in 1876, the Sam Weller dialect had passed away so completely that I should have given it up as a literary fiction if I had not discovered it surviving in a Middlesex village, and heard of it from an Essex one. Some time in the eighties the late Alexander Tuer called attention in the Pall Mall Gazette to several peculiarities of modern cockney, and to the obsolescence of the Dickens dialect that was still being copied from book to book by authors who never dreamt of using their ears, much less of training them to listen.

**Twentieth-century Cockney**. Currently, the term *Cockney* is applied to USAGE in the London area in a fairly free and easy way. There are, however, two broad perceptions: (1) That it is a range of usage centred on the East End of London, with fringe forms that shade out into the counties around the city, especially among the young. Here, the term refers to a widely diffused variety of working-class speech in south-eastern England. (2) That, in sociolinguistic terms, it is the BASILECT in a range of usages in which STANDARD ENGLISH with an RP accent is the ACROLECT. Here, Cockney is the core of working-class London speech and is not properly applied to the MESOLECTS of the area, which may however have Cockney-like features. Whichever viewpoint is taken, degrees of Cockneyhood are commonly perceived in the London area, according to such factors as class, social aspirations, locality, and education. The association with Bow bells is sometimes mentioned by inner Londoners with nostalgia. Few babies are now born near the Church of St Mary-le-Bow, and many who have in the past been born within the sound of its bells could never, because of their social class, have been Cockneys, except ironically. Cockney has long been associated with the East End and the inner suburbs of east London: Aldgate, Bethnal Green, Bow, Hackney, Limehouse, Mile End, Old Ford, Poplar, Shoreditch, Stepney, Wapping, and Whitechapel. Core Cockney is distinct from working-class usage south of the Thames in Bermondsey, Southwark, and Walworth. Like many varieties of English, it is most easily identified through its extreme forms. Like other stigmatized urban dialects, such as BROOKLYN (New York), GLASGOW, and SCOUSE (Liverpool), it is vigorous and influential, but generally viewed by both its speakers and outsiders as a liability for the upwardly mobile.

**Pronunciation**. The following features contribute to core Cockney speech: (1) *F and V*. Cockney differs from all other varieties of English in having /f/ for /θ/, as in 'firty fahsn' *thirty thousand*. This is matched medially by /v/ for /ð/, as in 'bovver' *bother*, 'muvver' *mother*. Initially, the sound is closer to /ð/ in such words as *this*, *these*, but pronunciations like 'vis' and 'vese' can be heard. *Everything, nothing, something* are pronounced 'evryfink', 'nuffink', 'sumfink'. A shibboleth for the *f/v* usage is *Firty fahsn fevvers on a frush's froat*. (2) *H-dropping*. Like many varieties of English in England, Cockney has no initial /h/ in words like *house* (*Nobody lives in them ouses now*), but sometimes adds /h/ for emphasis or as hypercorrection before initial vowels, as with 'hever' for *ever* (*Did you hever see the like?*). (3) *Diphthongs*. Cockney is well known for the elongation of its vowel sounds, often represented in print by

several vowels together, as in Shaw's 'daownt' for *don't*. Distinctive diphthongs include /əi/ for RP /iː/ in *beet/seat*, /ai/ for RP /eɪ/ in *fate/great*, /ɒɪ/ for RP /aɪ/ in *high/why*. Conversely, the monophthong /a/ serves where RP has the diphthong /aʊ/ in *about* 'abaht', *thousand* 'fahsn'. (4) *The glottal stop*. Use of the GLOTTAL STOP for medial and final /t/, /kt/, and /k/, as in *but*, *butter*, *hectic*, *technical* ('tetnical'), and a glottalized /tʃ/, as in *actually* ('atshelly'). (5) *Linking R*. There is no postvocalic /r/ in Cockney, which like RP is non-rhotic: 'cah' for *car*, 'cahd' for *card*. Cockney shares the linking *r* used generally in south-east England, as in 'draw/r/ing room' for *drawing room*, 'Shah/r of Persia' for *Shah of Persia*: see LINKING R. (6) Syllable-final /l/ is vocalized as /w/: 'tewwim' for *tell him*: see *L*-SOUNDS.

**Syntax and usage**. (1) The GRAMMAR of Cockney is by and large 'general nonstandard', with such usages as double negation (*There aint nuffink like it* There is nothing like it) and *done* and *seen* for *did* and *saw* (*I done it yesterday, I just seen er*). (2) Question tags are widely used to invite agreement or establish one's position: *I'm elpin you now, inneye?* I am helping you now, ain't I?—although I may not have helped you before or wanted in fact to help you at all; *Well, e knew all abaht it, dinnee?* Well, he knew all about it, didn't he?—Because he knew all about it, it's not surprising he did what he did. (3) The prepositions *to* and *at* are frequently dropped in relation to places: *I'm goin down the pub* I'm going down to the pub, *He's round is mate's* He is round at his friend's house, *They're over me mum's* They're over at my mother's.

**Literary and stage Cockney**. Since the time of Dickens, Cockney DIALOGUE has often been included in otherwise standard texts. A fairly consistent sub-orthography has developed for it, such as *abaht* about, *Gawd* God, *larf* laugh, *muvver* mother, *orful* awful, *orl* all, with the apostrophe used to mark absent *h* as in *'abit* and absent *g*, signalling the pronunciation of *-ing* as syllabic /n/, as in *cuttin'* and *shoutin'*. Writers generally use just enough for flavour, along with typical expressions and a cocky, cheeky, or cheerful style, as in Rudyard Kipling's *The 'Eathen* (1892):

> The 'eathen in 'is blindness bows down
> to wood an' stone;

'E don't obey no orders unless they is 'is
  own;
'E keeps 'is side-arms awful: 'e leaves 'em
  all about,
An' then comes up the Regiment an'
  pokes the 'eathen out.

Shaw employs a parallel stage Cockney for a
similar burst of chauvinism in *Captain Brassbound's Conversion*:

It gows agin us as Hinglishmen to see
these bloomin furriners settin ap their
Castoms Ahses and spheres o hinfluence
and sich lawk hall owver Arfricar.
Daownt Harfricar belong as much to
huz as to them? thets wot we sy
(Act I).

Allnutt, the mechanic in C. S. Forester's *The
African Queen* (1935: ch. 2) is less orthographically assertive, but remains unequivocally
a working-class Londoner:

'Why not?'
  'Rapids, miss. Rocks an' cataracts an'
gorges. You 'aven't been there, miss.
I'ave. There's a nundred miles of rapids
down there. Why, the river's got a
different nime where it comes out in the
Lake to what it's called up 'ere. It's the
Bora down there. That just shows you.
No one knew they was the same river
until that chap Spengler—'

Literary approaches to Cockney have generally been the work of middle-class non-
Cockneys. Their conventions have, however,
been both used and queried by Cockneys
writing about their own speech, as in
Barltrop and Wolveridge's *The Muvver Tongue*
(1980):

But the short ou of 'out' and 'about' is
the chronically misrepresented Cockney
vowel. For a hundred years there has
been a convention of writing it as 'ah'.
Shaw put 'baw ya flahr orf a pore gel'
into Eliza Doolittle's mouth: 'rahnd the
ahses' is the classic way of conveying
East London speech. It is painfully wide
of the mark. Whatever a Cockney's 'out'
may be thought to sound like, it is not
'art'—which is what 'aht' would make it.
The sound is a lengthened short u. It
might be written 'uht', the u as in 'cut'
but stretched out; more precisely, it is
'uh-ert'. The phonetic version of a
Cockney's 'buy a flower off a poor girl'
would be 'baheeya fluh-er orf a pore gel'.
Practically any Cockney does this when
he talks, but in a street vendor's chant it

would become a flourish and almost
musical.

**Tone and rhetoric**. A striking aspect of
Cockney, especially when compared with
RP, is its effusive range of tone and emotion.
Barltrop and Wolveridge comment:

The East Londoner likes his utterances to
be attention-catching whether they are
plaintive, indignant, gloomy or
humorous . . . Nagging, anecdote, giving
opinions and even greeting a friend in
the street are done with the same
mobility of voice, to squeeze the utmost
meaning out of them, and it is
noticeable in ordinary conversation.

The devices of vigorous delivery include a
wide range of tones, emphatic loudness,
strong facial expression, and vigorous body
language. There is in particular pitch
prominence on content words (nouns,
verbs, adjectives, adverbs) and their vowels
are often stretched, as in *You ought to ave
SEEEEN it—it was ever so GOOOOD*. In tandem,
Cockneys are generally more uninhibited
socially (laughing loudly, complaining vigorously) than middle-class Londoners, a
feature which may have been influenced by
Gypsies, Jews, and Irish in the East End.

**Slang**. Probably the best-known and most-
discussed usage is Cockney RHYMING SLANG,
as in *Would you Adam and Eve it?* Would you
believe it?, and *They had a bit of a bull and a
cow* a row. It may have originated in thieves'
CANT, but its history is unclear and there is
little evidence that it was ever widespread
or extensive enough to be a code in its own
right. If it was once so used by traders,
entertainers, thieves, and others, the secret
has been well kept. Such word-play was a
fashionable game in the West End of
London in the 1930s, and during and after
the Second World War was disseminated by
the media. Many of its usages have been
spread by television: *Brahms and Liszt* pissed,
drunk, in the 1970s TV comedy series *Steptoe
and Son*, which also used *berk*, a clipping of
*Berkeley/Berkshire Hunt* a cunt (whose first
*OED* citation is 1936). Several rhymes for the
same word may compete: *tea* is both *Rosy Lea*
and *you and me*. *Bristol Cities* (titties) may have
been media-inspired, traditional Cockney
being *Manchester Cities* or *threepenny bits* (tits).
Such slang has contributed to informal BrE
at large such usages as *cobblers*, as an expression of scepticism from *cobblers' awls* balls,
testicles, *butchers* from *butcher's hook* a look,

*Jimmy Riddle* a piddle (an act of urinating), *rabbit on* for talking all the time, from *rabbit and pork* talk, *raspberry* for a derisive blowing sound with the lips (apparently from *raspberry tart* fart).

Cockney SLANG includes: (1) Words from ROMANI: *chavvy* a child, *mush* a mate, buddy, *put the mockers on* to jinx. (2) Words from YIDDISH: *gezumph/gazump* to swindle, *schemozzle* a disturbance, *schlemiel* a fool. (3) MINCED OATHS and EUPHEMISMS, especially relating to *God*: *Blimey* God blind me, *Cor* God, as in *Cor stone the crows*, *Gordon Bennett* (the name of an early 20c car-racing promoter) God. (4) Forces slang picked up in Asia: *ackers* money (probably from ARABIC *fakka* small change), *bint* a girl (Arabic), *cushy* soft, easy, as in *a cushy billet* an easy job (from Hindi *khush* pleasure), *dekko* a look (from the HINDI imperative *dekho* look); *shufti* a look (Arabic), *doolally* (mad, from Deolali, a town in India where a British Forces mental hospital was located). (5) ABBREVIATIONS, sometimes with *-o* added (compare AusE slang): *aggro* aggravation (= aggression), *rarzo* a red nose (short for raspberry). (6) BACKSLANG: *yob* a boy, sometimes in the form *yobbo*. (7) Usage with run-together phrases that sound like, and are often written as, single words: *Gawdelpus* God help us, *Geddoudovit* Get out of it, *Gorblimey* originally 'God blind me', *Wotcha/Wotcher* What cheer (a once widespread greeting). Because of wartime contacts, National Service after the Second World War, and the media, many of these expressions are understood and often used throughout Britain.

**Social issues**. Core Cockney, fringe Cockney, and their neighbouring forms make up the most prominent and widely spoken urban dialect in Britain. It rests on an ancient working-class tradition and has had considerable media influence on BrE usage at large, especially in the London-based tabloid newspapers, and in radio and TV popular entertainment, such as the current BBC soap opera *EastEnders*. It remains, however, a stigmatized variety that attracts little academic attention and is often regarded as quaint and amusing. Barltrop and Wolveridge note:

> We wanted to write for Cockneys as much as about them. The language is constantly shown as picturesque or comic, and almost invariably as inferior; it is taken for granted as coming from a

people who do not know any better. We hope to persuade Cockneys as well as others that it is more than the equal of any other form of speech. . . . The Cockney does not have to define class—it defines him. While East Londoners are defined by the social system as are all other working people, they are resentful of it in a resigned sort of way and strongly conscious of 'Them and Us'. . . . Thus, speaking well—'talking posh'—does not make a great impression; it smacks of being the enemy's language.

The Cockneys share such sentiments with users of other working-class varieties that grew up with the Industrial Revolution. Like speakers of Scouse and Gutter Glasgow, they are embattled and often thumb a linguistic nose at the rest of the world. Cockneys have faced an extra stigma because they have often been seen as letting London down. Paradoxically, they are at the same time invoked with affection as a key element in defining the city. See ESTUARY ENGLISH, NEW ORLEANS.

**CODE.** 1. A system of WORDS, LETTERS, SIGNS, sounds, lights, etc., that conveys information. 2. A system of letters or other signs that makes sense only to someone who already knows its *key* or *cipher*, and because of this can *encode* or *decode* a message. 3. In SOCIOLINGUISTICS, a system of communication, spoken or written, such as a LANGUAGE, DIALECT, or VARIETY. See SEMIOTICS and next.

**CODE-MIXING AND CODE-SWITCHING**. Terms in SOCIOLINGUISTICS for language and especially speech that draws to differing extents on at least two languages combined in different ways, as when a Malay/English bilingual says: *This morning I hantar my baby tu dekat babysitter tu lah* (*hantar* took, *tu dekat* to the, *lah* a particle marking solidarity). A *code* may be a language or a variety or style of a language; the term *code-mixing* emphasizes hybridization, and the term *code-switching* emphasizes movement from one language to another. Mixing and switching probably occur to some extent in the speech of all bilinguals, so that there is a sense in which a person capable of using two languages, A and B, has three systems available for use: A, B, and C (a range of hybrid forms that can be used with comparable bilinguals but not with monolingual speakers of A or B). There are four major types of switching: (1) *Tag-switching*, in which tags and certain set phrases in one language are inserted into an utterance otherwise in another, as when a Panjabi/English bilingual says: *It's a nice day, hana?* (*hai nā* isn't it). (2) *Intra-sentential switching*, in which switches occur within a clause or sentence boundary, as when a Yoruba/English bilingual says: *Won o arrest a single person* (*won o* they did not). (3) *Intersentential switching*, in which a change of language occurs at a clause or sentence boundary, where each clause or sentence is in one language or the other, as when a Spanish/English bilingual says: *Sometimes I'll start a sentence in English y termino en español* (and finish it in Spanish). This last may also occur as speakers take turns. (4) *Intra-word switching*, in which a change occurs within a word boundary, such as in *shoppā* (English *shop* with the Panjabi plural ending) or *kuenjoy* (English *enjoy* with the Swahili prefix *ku*, meaning 'to').

**Names and attitudes: us and them**. Some communities have special names, often pejorative or facetious, or both, for a hybrid variety: in India, *Hindlish* and *Hinglish* are used for the widespread mixing of Hindi and English; in Nigeria, *amulumala* (verbal salad) is used for English and Yoruba mixing and switching; in the Philippines, the continuum of possibilities is covered by the terms *Tagalog—Engalog—Taglish—English*, in Quebec, by *français—franglais—Frenglish—English*. Despite the fact that mixing and switching are often stigmatized in the communities in which they occur, they often serve such important functions as marking ethnic and group boundaries. Among minorities, the home language (*the 'we' code*) is used to signify in-group, informal, and personalized activities, while the other language (*the 'they' code*) is used to mark out-group, more formal, and distant events. Speakers use a change of language to indicate their attitude to what is being said. In the following, Panjabi marks the in-group and English the out-group among immigrants to the UK: *Usi ingrezi sikhi e te why can't they learn?* ('We learn English, so why can't they learn [an Asian language]?'). The switch emphasizes the boundaries between 'them' and 'us'.

Other reasons for switching include the prestige of knowing the out-group or dominant language, often a language associated with a religion, empire, education, and a wide sphere of operation and interest: for example, social status has long been marked among Hindus in India by introducing elements of Sanskrit and Pali into vernacular use and among Muslims by bringing in Arabic and Persian. In Europe, the same effect has been achieved by introducing elements of Latin and Greek. Today, social status is marked in India and elsewhere by introducing elements of English. It is not always the case that borrowing or switching occurs because speakers do not know the words in one or the other language. Widespread code-switching often indicates greater or less shift towards the more dominant of the two languages. Currently, English is the most widely used language in the world for mixing and switching. See DIGLOSSIA, FRANGLAIS, INTERLANGUAGE, LANGUAGE SHIFT.

**COGNATE**. Related by descent; one of two or more words so related), especially across languages. English *mother*, German *Mutter* are cognate words; English *five*, Latin *quinque*, Greek *pénte* are all cognates, descended from the common Indo-European ancestor *penkwe*. Cognates are more or less like each other in form, but need not have much in common semantically: English *silly*, German *selig* holy, blessed. On the other hand, English *ma*, Chinese *mu* (mother) are known to be cognates; though similar in form and meaning, they cannot (at present at least) be traced to a common source. German *Standpunkt* and its English CALQUE *standpoint* are not usually called cognates, even when their elements are cognates: *Stand* and *stand*, *Punkt* and *point*. Pairs of cognates in a single language, such as English *regal* and *royal* (both ultimately from Latin) are called *DOUBLETS*. Cognates are easy to find in related (or cognate) languages such as English, German, Greek, and Latin, but unrelated languages may also have cognate items: the common ancestor of English *tea*, Malay *teh* appears to be *t'e*, from the Amoy dialect of Chinese. See LOAN.

**COINAGE**. An invented WORD or PHRASE and the process of inventing it. Like *loan* and *borrowing*, the term *coinage* is based on an ancient analogy between language and money. The creation of words without the use of earlier words is rare: for example, *googol*, the term for the number 1 followed by a hundred zeros, or $10^{100}$, introduced by the American mathematician Edward Kasner, whose 9-year-old nephew coined it when asked to think up a name for a very big number. See NEOLOGISM, ROOT-CREATION, WORD-FORMATION.

**COLLECTIVE NOUN**, also **collective**. A NOUN referring to a group of people, animals, or things, and occurring in the singular with a singular or plural verb: *army, couple, family, government, group*. The plural use (*The majority are in favour*) is commoner and more acceptable in BrE than AmE, where the singular form (*The majority is in favour*) is preferred. The choice of singular or plural verb depends on whether the group is seen as a unit or as a group of entities. Co-occurring possessives and pronouns differ accordingly: *I was impressed by the audience, which was a distinguished one. I was impressed by the audience, who were all in their seats by 7.30*. When plural, collectives follow normal rules of concord: *The audiences this week have been small but appreciative*. Names of countries can be used as collective nouns for sports teams, in such headlines as *Pakistan build up a substantial lead, England look in good shape for Santander*. See SYNECDOCHE. Collective nouns are sometimes called *group nouns* and the collective label is sometimes applied to plural-only words such as *cattle, clothes, people, police*, although these are not collective nouns as such. There are many collectives in popular and technical use for naming groups of people, animals, or things. Some are familiar to most people, such as a *bench* of magistrates, a *flight* of stairs, a *flock* of sheep, a *swarm* of bees; others are less well known (and of uncertain provenance), such as an *exaltation* of larks and an *unkindness* of ravens.

**COLLOCATION**. **1.** The act of putting two or more things together, especially words in a pattern, and the result of that act. **2.** In LINGUISTICS, a habitual association between particular words, such as *to* with *fro* in the phrase *to and fro*, and the uses of *to* after *answer* and before *me* in *You'll answer to me* (as opposed to *You'll answer me*). In the phrase *Let's draw up a list*, the phrasal verb *draw up* is said to collocate with the noun *list*; one can *draw up a list of legal terms* but not *\*draw up legal terms* (although one can *list legal terms*). Collocation is basic to language. Its subtleties must be learned, and failure to get the collocations of English

right is a major indicator of foreignness: for example, talking about *rotten* rather than *rancid butter*. IDIOMS are usually fixed in form and used without recourse to the meanings of their elements: it can rain *cats and dogs*, but never *\*dogs and cats* or *\*cats and cows*. Even with idioms, however, there can be some leeway: for example, at least the three verbs *banging, hitting*, and *knocking* can occupy the slot in the idiomatic sentence *It's like—your head against a (brick) wall*. Collocations are more loosely associated than idioms: contiguously (as with *tortoise* and *shell* in *tortoiseshell*) or proximately (as with *cat* and *purr* in *The cat was purring*). When the elements of compound words collocate, they form new lexical items: *house* and *boat* coming together in both *houseboat* and *boathouse*, each with a distinct meaning and use. An item that collocates with another is its *collocate*.

**COLLOQUIAL**. A semi-technical term for the VERNACULAR form of a language (*colloquial Arabic*) or, sometimes mildly pejorative, for informal, everyday speech, including SLANG (*colloquial usage*).

**COLLOQUIALISM**. A semi-technical term, sometimes mildly pejorative, for informal speech generally and any expression that is typical of it, especially if regarded as non- or substandard: *ain't* in *He ain't comin'* (He is not coming); *gonna* in *They're gonna do it* (They are going to do it).

**COLON**. The PUNCTUATION mark (:). It has an anticipatory effect, leading from what precedes to what follows. The following are the main uses: (1) To introduce a list of items: *You will need the following: a pen, pencil, rubber, piece of paper, and ruler*. (2) To introduce speech or quoted material, as a stronger alternative to the comma: *I told them last week: 'Do not in any circumstances open this door.'* (3) To lead or 'point' from one CLAUSE to another: from introduction to theme (*I want to say this: we are deeply grateful to all of you*); from statement to example (*It was not easy: to begin with, I had to find the right house*); from cause to effect (*The weather was bad: so we stayed at home*); from premiss to conclusion (*There are hundreds of wasps in the garden: there must be a nest there*); from statement to explanation (*I gave up: I had tried everything without success*). (4) To introduce an antithesis or highlight a contrast: *He died* *young: but he died rich; They spoke bitterly: and yet they were forgiving.* (5) To produce a staccato or paratactic effect, either by replacing a conjunction such as *but* (*I called: you did not answer*) or in a progression or sequence (*He arrived: he knocked at the door: we waited: he went away*). See SEMICOLON.

# ■ COMBINING FORM ─────── ■

In WORD-FORMATION, a BASE designed to combine with another, either also a combining form or a free word: *bio-* with *-graphy* to form *biography*, *mini-* with *skirt* to form *miniskirt*. A vowel usually facilitates the combination: in *biography*, the Greek THEMATIC VOWEL *-o-*, in *miniskirt*, the Latin thematic *-i-*. This vowel is usually regarded as attached to the initial base (*bio-*, *mini-*) rather than the final base (*-graphy*, *-skirt*), but in Greek-derived forms it is sometimes shown as attached to the final base (*-ography*, *-ology*). If, however, the final base begins with a vowel (for example, *-archy* as in *monarchy*), the mediating vowel has traditionally been avoided (no \**monoarchy*), but in recent coinages it is often kept and generally accompanied by a hyphen (*auto-analysis*, *bio-energy*, *hydro-electricity*, not \**autanalysis*, \**bienergy*, \**hydrelectricity*).

**Translation**. There are hundreds of combining forms in English and other European languages. As traditionally defined, they cannot stand alone as free words, but there are many exceptions to this rule, and in the late 20c such forms are increasingly used independently: *bio* as a clipping of *biography*, *telly* as a respelt clipping of *television*. Most combining forms translate readily into everyday language, especially nouns: *bio-* as 'life' *-graphy* as 'writing, description'. Because of this, the compounds of which they are part (usually *classical* or *learned compounds*) can be more or less straightforwardly paraphrased: *biography* as 'writing about a life', *neurology* as 'the study of the nervous system'. Many combining forms are designed to take initial or final position: *autobiography* has the two initial or preposed forms *auto-*, *bio-*, and one postposed form *-graphy*. Although most occupy one position or the other, some can occupy both: *-graph-* as in *graphology* and *monograph*; *-phil-* as in *philology* and *Anglophile*. Occasionally, the same base is repeated in one word: *logology* the study of words, *phobophobia* the fear of fear.

**Preposed and postposed**. Forms that come first include: *aero-* air, *crypto-* hidden, *demo-* people, *geo-* earth, *odonto-* tooth, *ornitho-* bird, *thalasso* sea. Many have both a traditional simple meaning and a modern telescopic meaning: in *biology*, *bio-* means 'life', but in *bio-degradable* it telescopes 'biologically'; although *hypno-* basically means 'sleep' (*hypnopaedia* learning through sleep), it also stands for 'hypnosis' (*hypnotherapy* cure through hypnosis). When a form stands alone as a present-day word, it is usually a telescopic abbreviation: *bio* biography, *chemo* chemotherapy, *hydro* hydroelectricity, *metro* metropolitan. Some telescoped forms can be shorter than the original combining forms: *gynie* is shorter than *gyneco-* and stands for both *gynecology* and *gynecologist*; *anthro* is shorter than *anthropo-* and stands for *anthropology*. Forms that come second include: *-ectomy* cutting out, *-graphy* writing, description, *-kinesis* motion, *-logy* study, *-mancy* divination, *-onym* name, *-phagy* eating, *-phony* sound, *-therapy* healing, *-tomy* cutting. They are generally listed in dictionaries without the interfixed vowel, which appears however in such casual phrases as 'ologies and isms'.

**Variants**. Some combining forms are variants of one base. The Greek base *-graph-* underlies three combining forms in English: *-gram* something written or shaped, etc. (*telegram*, *hologram*), *-graph* something written or a piece of equipment (*autograph*, *polygraph*), *-graphy* the activity or business of writing, shaping, etc. (*telegraphy*, *holography*). Some are also free words, such as *mania* in *dipsomania* and *phobia* in *claustrophobia*. Some are composites of other elements, such as *encephalo-* brain, from *en-* in, *-cephal-* head, and *-ectomy* cutting out, from *ec-* out, *-tom-* cut, *-y*, a noun-forming suffix.

**Origins**. In Greek and Latin grammar, combining bases usually require a thematic or stem-forming vowel. In *biography*, from Greek, the thematic is *-o-*; in *agriculture*, from Latin, it is *-i-*. In English, which does not inflect in this way and has no native thematic vowels, an element like *-o-* is an imported glue that holds bases together. Its presence helps to distinguish classical compounds like *biography* and *agriculture* from vernacular compounds like *teapot* and *blackbird*. Generally, English has acquired its classical compounds in three ways: through French from Latin and Greek, directly from

Latin and Greek, and by coinage in English on Greek and Latin patterns. An exception is *schizophrenia*, which came into English through German, and is therefore pronounced 'skitso', not 'skyzo'. The combining forms and the compounds built from them are as much a part of English as of Latin and Greek, and as much a part of French, Spanish, Italian, and any other language that cares to use them. They are an international resource.

**The conservative tradition**. From the Renaissance until the mid-20c, the concept of derivational purity has generally regulated the use of combining forms: Greek with Greek, Latin with Latin, and a minimum of hybridization. *Biography* is Greek, *agriculture* Latin, but *television* is a hybrid of Greek *tele-* and Latin *-vision* (probably so coined because the 'pure' form *telescope* had already been adopted for another purpose). *Kiddology* facetiously combines vernacular *kid* and *-ology* to produce 'the science of kidding people'. Most dictionaries follow the *OED* in using *combining form* (*comb. form*) to label such classical elements, but the name is not widely known. In appendices to dictionaries and grammar books, combining forms are often loosely referred to as roots or affixes: 'a logo . . . , properly speaking, is not a word at all but a prefix meaning word and short for logogram, a symbol, much as telly is short for television' (Montreal *Gazette*, 13 Apr. 1981). They are often referred to as affixes because some come first and some come last, but if they were affixes, a word like *biography* would have no base whatever. While affixes are grammatical (like prepositions), combining forms are lexical (like nouns, adjectives, and verbs): for example, *bio-* translates as a noun (life), *-graphy* as a verbal noun (writing). They are also often loosely called roots because they are ancient and have a basic role in word-formation, but functionally and often structurally they are distinct from roots: the *-graph* in *autograph* is both a root and a combining form, while the *-graphy* in *cryptography* consists of root *-graph-* and suffix *-y*, and is only a combining form.

**Contemporary developments**. By and large, combining forms were a closed system from the 16c to the earlier 20c: the people who used them were classically educated, their teachers and exemplars generally took a purist's view on their use,

contexts of use were mainly technical, and there was relatively little seepage into the language at large. However, with the decline of classical education and the spread of technical and quasi-technical jargon in the media, a continuum has evolved, with at least five stages:

***Pure classical usage***. In the older sciences, combining forms are generally used to form such strictly classical and usually Greek compounds as: *anthocyanin*, *astrobleme*, *chemotherapy*, *chronobiology*, *cytokinesis*, *glossolalia*, *lalophobia*, *narcolepsy*, *osteoporosis*, *Pliohippus*, *sympathomimetic*.

***Hybrid classical usage***. In technical, semi-technical, and quasi-technical usage at large, coiners of compounds increasingly treat Latin and Greek as one resource, to produce such forms as: *accelerometer*, *aero-generator*, *bioprospector*, *communicology*, *electroconductive*, *futurology*, *mammography*, *micro-gravity*, *neoliberal*, *Scientology*, *servo-mechanism*, *Suggestopedia*.

***Hybrid classical/vernacular usage***. In the later 20c, many forms have cut loose from ancient moorings: *crypto-* as in preposed *Crypto-Fascist* and *pseudo-* as in *pseudo-radical*; postposed *-meter* in *speedometer*, *clapometer*. Processes of analogy have created coinages like *petrodollar*, *psycho-warfare*, *microwave* on such models as *petrochemical*, *psychology*, *microscope*. Such stunt usages as *eco-doom*, *eco-fears*, *eco-freaks*, common in journalism, often employ combining forms telescopically: *eco-* standing for *ecology* and *ecological* and not as used in *economics*. In such matters, precision of meaning is secondary to compactness and vividness of expression.

***Combining forms as separate words***. In recent years, the orthography of many word forms has changed, usually without affecting pronunciation and stress. The same spoken usage may be written *micro-missile*, *micro missile*, *micromissile*, reflecting the same uncertainty or flexibility as in *businessman*, *business-man*, *business man*. When used in such ways, combining forms are often telescopic: *Hydro substation* Hydro-Electricity Board substation, *Metro highways* Metropolitan highways, *porno cult* pornography cult.

***New combining forms***. The mix of late 20c techno-commercial coinages includes three groups of post- and non-classical forms: (1) Established forms: *econo-* from 'economic', as in *econometric*, *Econo-Car*, *mini-* from 'miniature', as in *miniskirt, mini-boom, -matic* from 'automatic', as in *Adjustamatic, Instamatic, Stackomatic.* (2) Less established forms, often created by blending: *accu-* from 'accurate', as in *Accuvision*; *compu-* from 'computer', as in *Compucorp*; *docu-* from 'documentary', as in *docudrama*; *dura-* from 'durable', as in *Duramark*; *porta-* from 'portable', as in *Portacabin, Portaphone.* (3) Informal vernacular material in pseudo-classical form: *Easibird, Healthitone, Redi-pak, Relax-a-Cisor* (relax, exerciser). See BLEND, CLASSICAL COMPOUND, INTERFIX, INTERNATIONAL SCIENTIFIC VOCABULARY.

■ **COMMA** ━━━━━━━━━━━━━━ ■

The PUNCTUATION mark (,), which has many uses and is highly flexible. Essentially, it gives detail to (especially longer) sentences and helps clarify their meaning. The comma is used: (1) To mark off elements in a sequence of words and phrases when there are no conjunctions or there is only a final conjunction: *Cats, dogs, rabbits, hares, squirrels, and hedgehogs.* (2) In pairs, to indicate an aside or parenthesis: *She is, you know, one of my best friends.* (3) To separate clauses of sentences: *If you want him to come, ask him yourself.* (4) To introduce direct speech: *She said, 'I'd rather not do it.'* (5) To clarify meaning and prevent ambiguity: *Cereals, orange juice, milk, bacon, and eggs.* The following sections provide detailed comment on these uses.

**Commas with single words**. (1) Adjectives before nouns are separated by commas unless there is a strong association between a noun and the adjective immediately preceding it: compare *an enterprising, ambitious person* and *a distinguished foreign politician*. When a conjunction such as *and* or *but* separates the adjectives, a comma is not used, but a pair of commas suggests an aside or gives emphasis: compare *a great and generous leader* and *a great, and generous, leader* (with spoken emphasis on *generous*). (2) With nouns, adverbs, and adjectives more generally, commas are normally used only with three or more words in sequence: *They spoke slowly, deliberately, and softly; We found guns, ammunition, and grenades; The children were happy, noisy, and overexcited.* (For the comma before *and*, see *serial comma*, below.) A comma marking off two such words conveys emphasis, as would a dash: *They spoke slowly, and deliberately.* (3) The same considerations apply to a sequence of verbs

(*They arrived, shouted, and ran in*) and prepositions (*You will find it in, on, and under everything*). (4) *However* and *therefore* are often placed between parenthetical commas: *I do not, however, want you to go; We decided, therefore, to leave* (compare *We therefore decided to leave*). Parenthetical commas are optional with *moreover, nevertheless, unfortunately*, etc.

**Commas with phrases**. (1) Phrases such as *far and wide, by and large* are treated like single words: *They travelled far and wide through Spain; She was, by and large, very disappointed in the result.* (2) Parenthetical commas may be used to highlight a phrase in much the same way as dashes and brackets, but form a less distinct break: *The witness, a middle-aged woman, then stepped forward; Their new song, 'Singing through my tears', was published this year.* (3) Commas are used to separate items in a list or sequence, as in cases already given. Usage varies as to the inclusion of a comma before *and* in the last item (*bring a chair, a bottle of wine, and a good book*). This practice is controversial and is known as the *serial comma* or *Oxford comma*, because it is part of the house style of Oxford University Press. It is often superfluous, and there are occasions when the sense requires it to be omitted, but on many occasions it serves to avoid ambiguity: *These colours are available: red, green, yellow, and black and white* as opposed to *red, green, yellow and black and white*. (4) Practice varies regarding introductory phrases. A comma is often but not always helpful, and the important point is to achieve a consistent and clear approach: *In the meantime, we must wait; In the circumstances, I will agree to your request; In 1939, he joined the army.* When there is an implied verb, especially *be*, a comma is usual (*Although ill, she managed to finish the work; Whatever the difficulties, we must keep trying*).

**Commas with clauses**. Commas are used in longer stretches of writing in the following ways:

(1) To separate two main clauses when emphasis or contrast is needed: compare *He woke up and immediately got out of bed* and *He woke up, and immediately got out of bed*: in the second example, the emphasis of sense is on the second clause, whereas in the first there are two more or less equal statements.

(2) To mark off the main clause of a longer compound sentence when the two parts are not close enough in meaning or

content to form a continuous statement and are not distinct enough to warrant a semicolon. A conjunction such as *and*, *but*, *yet*, etc., is normally used: *The road runs through a beautiful wooded valley, and the railway line follows it closely*. It is usually considered incorrect to omit the conjunction: *\*I like swimming very much, I go to the pool every week* conventionally requires either the insertion of *and* before the second *I*, or the use of a colon or semicolon instead of the comma. However, there is no absolute rule: many writers place two short sentences together in this way (creating what is called a *comma splice*) when they wish to suggest a close tie between the sentences, are not subject to a publisher's house style, have a relaxed approach to punctuation, or are not certain about the use of commas and periods. The practice is often adopted to represent disjointed speech or thought, as in: 'We didn't stay long, it gave me the creeps' and 'I made myself some food, gosh, I was hungry' (Somerset Maugham, *The Razor's Edge*, 1967). See PARATAXIS.

(3) Sometimes, to separate a subordinate clause from a main clause, especially when the subordinate clause comes first or when the sentence is long: *I decided to wait because I thought you would soon arrive* (comma optional before *because*); *Because I wanted to see them, I decided to wait* (comma usual); *However much you try, you will find it difficult* (comma usual). Use of a comma is especially common after a conditional clause which is placed first (*If you want to come, you must hurry*) but less common in short sentences in which it is placed second (*You must hurry if you want to come*: a comma before *if* in this example would give extra emphasis to what follows, in the manner of other examples given above). A comma is normally required when the subordinate clause is participial: *Feeling unwell, they decided to stay at home*.

(4) To separate a RELATIVE CLAUSE from its antecedent when the clause is giving incidental information rather than identifying the antecedent: compare *the car, which was standing in the road, was stolen* and *the car which was standing in the road was stolen*. In the first example, the position of the car is extra information that is not essential to the main sense; in the second, it identifies the car being referred to.

(5) A comma is often used to introduce direct speech in place of a colon (*I then said, 'Why don't you come in?'*), and is usual in re-

suming direct speech after a break, if the direct speech continues a sentence ('*Go away,'* I said, '*and don't ever come back'*). See QUOTATION MARKS.

**The clarifying comma**. The comma is also used to prevent ambiguity or misunderstanding. If the comma is removed from the following examples difficulties may arise, at least for a moment: *With the police pursuing, the people shouted loudly*; *He did not want to leave, from a feeling of loyalty*; *However, much as I would like to, I cannot come*.

**Other uses**. The comma is also used in various ways not directly associated with punctuation, such as: (1) To indicate thousands in numerals, beginning from the right: *5,324,768*. (2) Traditionally, to separate a street number from the name of the road or street in addresses (a role that has diminished greatly in recent years): *24, High Street*, probably more commonly *24 High Street*. It has also traditionally been used to end each stage of an address, a practice that also appears to be obsolescent. (3) In letters, at the end of the initial greeting (*Dear James, . . .*; *Dear Mrs Taylor, . . .*), and at the end of the concluding formula (*Yours sincerely,*).

**COMMON**. **1.** Owned or shared by members of a community, general, public, free to be used by all: *common land, a common language*. **2.** Ordinary, familiar, everyday: *a common spelling mistake*. **3.** Cheap, inferior, low-class, unrefined, vulgar: *as common as muck, a common accent, very common English*. **4.** In GRAMMAR, not marked in any way: a *common noun* as opposed to a *PROPER noun*; *common GENDER* as opposed to masculine, feminine, or where applicable neuter.

**COMMON NOUN**. A NOUN referring to anything or anybody as an example of what the word in question denotes (*an actor, the town, cheerfulness*), in contrast with a *PROPER noun*, which uniquely identifies and NAMES, and begins with a capital letter (*London, China*). Grammatically, common nouns can be divided into countable and uncountable nouns. Semantically, common nouns can be classified as abstract and concrete nouns.

**COMMONWEALTH**. **1.** A term originally meaning 'the public good' (cf. the archaic phrase *the common weal*), variously used as part of the full official name of a territory or state, as in *the Commonwealth of*

*Massachusetts* (a constituent state of the USA), *the Commonwealth of Puerto Rico* (a territory part-integrated into the USA), and *the Commonwealth of Australia* and *Commonwealth of the Bahamas* (autonomous nation-states). **2.** (with *the*) also *Commonwealth of Nations*, formerly *British Commonwealth of Nations* (1931–46). An association of states and their dependencies, comprising Great Britain and a majority of the countries formerly in the British Empire, as constituted by the Declaration of London in 1949. The British monarch continues as symbolic head of the association. Its language is English and its aims are cooperation and understanding among nations. The organization has no constitution, no legal standing, and no legislative, executive, or judicial function. Every two years the heads of the Commonwealth meet for semi-formal discussions in a different venue. In 1965 a Commonwealth Secretariat headed by a Secretary-General was set up in London as a clearing-house for information and a source of advice on technical cooperation. The Commonwealth Institute, founded in 1959 and based in London and Edinburgh, promotes aspects of the culture and heritage of Commonwealth Nations. The Commonwealth Games are held every four years in different Commonwealth cities. The member states are: Antigua and Barbuda, Australia, Bahamas, Bangladesh, Barbados, Belize, Botswana, Brunei, Cameroon, Canada, Cyprus, Dominica, Fiji, The Gambia, Ghana, Great Britain, Grenada, Guyana, India, Jamaica, Kenya, Kiribati, Lesotho, Malawi, Malaysia, Maldives, Malta, Mauritius, Mozambique, Namibia, Nauru, New Zealand, Nigeria, Pakistan, Papua New Guinea, St Christopher and Nevis, St Lucia, St Vincent and the Grenadines, Samoa, Seychelles, Sierra Leone, Singapore, Solomon Islands, South Africa, Sri Lanka, Swaziland, Tanzania, Tonga, Trinidad and Tobago, Tuvalu, Uganda, Vanuatu, Zambia, Zimbabwe. See ENGLISH LITERATURE, EXAMINING IN ENGLISH.

**COMMUNICATION.** A fundamental concept in the study of behaviour, whether by humans, animals, or machines, that acts as a frame of reference for the concept of LANGUAGE. Communication refers to the transmission of information (a *message*) between a source and a receiver, using a signalling system. In linguistic studies, both source and receiver are human, the system involved is a language, and the idea of response to feedback (a message) holds a central place. In theory, communication is said to have taken place if the information received is the same as that sent. In practice, we have to allow for all kinds of interfering factors (technically known as *noise*), which reduce the efficiency of the transmission, such as poor articulation or hearing, extraneous noise, and unconscious personal associations for words. See AMBIGUITY, CHILD LANGUAGE ACQUISITION, CONVERSATION, DIALOG(UE), LANGUAGE SHIFT, LINGUA FRANCA, MEANING, SEMANTICS, SPEECH, WRITING.

**COMMUNICATIVE COMPETENCE.** [Coined by the US anthropologist Dell Hymes]. A term in SOCIOLINGUISTICS for a speaker's underlying knowledge of the rules of GRAMMAR (understood in its widest sense to include phonology, orthography, syntax, lexicon, and semantics) and rules for their use in socially appropriate circumstances. The notion is intended to replace Noam CHOMSKY's dichotomy of competence and performance. *Competence* is the knowledge of rules of grammar, *performance*, how the rules are used. Speakers draw on their competence in putting together grammatical sentences, but not all such sentences can be used in the same circumstances: *Close the window* and *Would you mind closing the window, please?* are both grammatical, but they differ in their appropriateness for use in particular situations. Speakers use their communicative competence to choose what to say, as well as how and when to say it. See COMPETENCE AND PERFORMANCE, LANGUAGE TEACHING.

**COMPARATIVE DEGREE**, also **degree of comparison**. The middle term in the three degrees of an ADJECTIVE or ADVERB. With some exceptions (*better*, *worse*, *farther/further*), the comparative is formed by adding -*er* to shorter words (*kinder*, *faster*) and *more* to longer words (*more beautiful*, *more nervously*). Many words that inflect can also be modified by *more*: *commoner/more common*. See SUPERLATIVE (DEGREE).

**COMPARATIVE PHILOLOGY.** The branch of PHILOLOGY that deals with the relations between languages descended from a common original, now generally known as *comparative linguistics*.

**COMPARATIVE SENTENCE**. A SEN-TENCE containing two clauses joined by a two-part comparative element: *as . . . as* (*It's as big as a house*); *not so/as . . . as* (*It's not so/as good as it used to be*); *the same . . . as* (*It's just the same as it used to be*); *less/more . . . than* (*It's a lot less/more than I wanted to pay*); (*nicer/faster*) *. . . than* (*The car's faster than we expected*).

**COMPETENCE AND PERFORMANCE**. In LINGUISTICS, the distinction between a person's knowledge of language (*competence*) and use of it (*performance*). Performance contains slips of the tongue and false starts, and represents only a small sample of possible utterances: *I own two-thirds of an emu* is a good English sentence, but is unlikely to occur in any collected sample. The terms were proposed by Noam CHOMSKY in *Aspects of the Theory of Syntax*, when he stressed the need for a GENERATIVE GRAMMAR that mirrors a speaker's competence and captures the creative aspect of linguistic ability. In *Knowledge of Language* (1986), Chomsky replaced the terms with *I-language* (internalized language) and *E-language* (externalized language). A similar dichotomy, *LANGUE* and *PAROLE*, was proposed by Ferdinand de Saussure (1915), who stressed the social aspects of *langue*, regarding it as shared knowledge, whereas Chomsky stressed the individual nature of competence. See COMMUNICATIVE COMPETENCE, MISTAKE.

**COMPLEMENT**. A constituent of GRAMMAR that completes the meaning of a word. Broadly, complements can be found for every major word class: VERBS (*in Canada* in *They live in Canada*); nouns (*of their debt* in the *payment of their debt*); ADJECTIVES (*that we're late* in *I'm aware that we're late*); ADVERBS (*for me* in *luckily for me*); PREPOSITIONS (*our place* in *at our place*). Some grammarians use the term *complementation* for the constituent or the process of complementing the word. More narrowly, complements refer to constituents that complete the meaning of the verb, including direct objects (*their debt* in *pay their debt*), indirect objects (*me* in *Show me the way*), and adverbial complements (*at them* in *Look at them*). In an even more restricted use, two kinds of complements are recognized for verbs: (1) *Subject complements*, which follow the verb *be* and other copular verbs, *my best friend* in *Tom is my best friend*. (2) *Object complements*, which follow a direct object and have a copular relationship with

the object: *I consider Tom my best friend*. *Complement clauses* are subordinate clauses that function as complements of a word: *that they were too noisy* in *She told them that they were too noisy*. The subordinator that introduces a complement clause is sometimes known as a *complementizer*: for example *that* in the sentence just cited.

**COMPLETE PLAIN WORDS, The**. A book written by Sir Ernest GOWERS, a senior British civil servant, the 1st edition published in 1954 by Her Majesty's Stationery Office. The book was based on two slimmer books that he wrote at the invitation of the British Treasury, *Plain Words* (1948) and *The ABC of Plain Words* (1951), which gave advice to civil servants on the writing of official English. *TCPW* became a classic guide to good writing and has been reprinted many times. There have been two subsequent editions. Both endeavoured to retain as much as possible of Gowers's original text, but revisions were needed to take account of changes in the language or in the practice of writers. The 2nd edition (1973) was by Sir Bruce Fraser and the 3rd edition (1986) by Sidney GREENBAUM and Janet Whitcut. See PLAIN, USAGE GUIDANCE AND CRITICISM.

**COMPLEX SENTENCE**. A SENTENCE consisting of one main CLAUSE in which are embedded one or more subordinate clauses: *I know where she lives*, in which *where she lives* is a subordinate clause. In *When I asked for his opinion, he said that he could not say anything at present*, there are two subordinate clauses: the *when*-clause and the *that*-clause. See SUBORDINATION.

**COMPLEX WORD**. A WORD consisting of a base and one or more derivational elements: *unlikely* (*un-*, *like*, *-ly*); *vitality* (*vit-*, *-al*, *-ity*). In origin and structural type, there are four kinds of complex word in English: (1) *Vernacular*. Formed on 'native' principles, but including some long-established words of LATIN, GREEK, and FRENCH background: *darkness*, *womanhood*, *beefy*, *priestly*. Such words may have equivalents in the GERMANIC LANGUAGES: English *unmanly*, German *unmännlich*. (2) *Romance*. Formed on Latinate principles. Many such words are structurally (though not phonologically) identical or similar in English and the Romance languages: English *impossible*, *discrimination*; French *impossible*, *discrimination*;

SPANISH *impossible, discriminación*. (3) *Greek*. Formed on principles adapted from classical Greek through NEO-LATIN. Many such words are structurally similar in English and Greek: English *dogmatic, magnetism*, Greek *dogmatikós, magnetismós*. (4) *Hybrid*. A mix of the above: *uncreative* mixes vernacular *un-* with Latin *cre-* and *-ative*; *ethically* mixes Greek *eth-* and *-ic* with Latin *-al* and vernacular *-ly*. See COMBINING FORM, COMPOUND-COMPLEX WORD, DERIVATION, PREFIX, SUFFIX, WORD-FORMATION.

**COMPOSITION. 1.** The action, process, or art of composing especially pieces of music and works of literature. **2.** An essay, usually short and written for training purposes, especially in school and usually in the English classroom. **3.** A course in WRITING in a school or other educational institution. **4.** The process of putting words and sentences together according to the traditional rules of GRAMMAR, STYLE, and RHETORIC. **5.** An obsolete term for WORD-FORMATION.

**COMPOUND-COMPLEX SENTENCE.** A compound SENTENCE in which at least one of the main CLAUSES contains one or more subordinate clause. In the following sentence, the second main clause (after *and*) contains a subordinate *since-clause*: *Road-building in those mountains is dangerous and, since work began in 1968, hundreds of labourers have been swept away by landslides*. See SUBORDINATION.

**COMPOUND-COMPLEX WORD.** A WORD whose structure is both COMPLEX and COMPOUND: *hot-bloodedness*, in which there are two base words, *hot* and *blood*, and two suffixes, *-ed* and *-ness*; *biographical*, in which there are two combining forms, *bio-* and *-graph* and a composite suffix *-ical*. Compare COMPLEX WORD, COMPOUND WORD.

**COMPOUND SENTENCE.** A SENTENCE consisting of two or more main CLAUSES. The clauses may be linked by a coordinating conjunction: *and* in *The power failed for the third time that day, and once again we sat in darkness*. There may be no connectives between them, as in *Smooth cotton sheets feel cold; fleecy blankets feel warm*; or they may be linked by a conjunct, as with *however* in *I telephoned at least ten times yesterday; however, the line was never free*. In SPEECH, such compounding goes unnoticed; in formal writing, a semicolon (as here) is used to unite the two clauses. In more relaxed styles, a comma is used. A period is generally used when a clear-cut division is required, in which case the clauses are taken to be separate sentences. See COORDINATION.

■ **COMPOUND WORD** ─────── ■

Also **compound**. A WORD made up of two or more other words: *teapot*, from *tea* and *pot*; *blackbird*, from *black* and *bird*. Compound words occur in many languages. In GERMAN, they are conventionally written in solid form: *Eisenbahn* ('ironway') railway; *Eisenbahnknotenpunkt* ('ironwayknotpoint') railway junction. In GREEK and LATIN, they are typically joined by thematic vowels, such as the *-i-* of Latin *agricultura*, the *-o-* of Greek *biographia*. In FRENCH, one kind of compound has the form of a prepositional phrase: *pomme de terre* ('apple of earth') potato; *arc-en-ciel* ('arch in sky') rainbow. Another consists of a verb–noun phrase: *gratte-ciel* ('scrape-sky') sky-scraper; *grille-pain* ('grill-bread') toaster. Such compounds occasionally occur in English; 'man of the church' matches *homme d'église*, and 'breakwater' matches *brise-lames*.

**Compounds in English.** The majority of English compounds fall into two types: (1) VERNACULAR compounds like *teapot* and *blackbird*, formed on principles typical of the Germanic languages. They are written in solid form, open form, or with hyphens. (2) CLASSICAL compounds like *agriculture* and *biography*, based on the compounding patterns of Greek and Latin. They are generally written in solid form. There are also some minor groups, such as those containing prepositions, in the French style: *commander-in-chief, man-at-arms, man of the church*. Grammarians generally treat the vernacular form as the compound proper. The classical compound belongs to a stratum of language which serves as an international resource on which many languages draw: see INTERNATIONAL SCIENTIFIC VOCABULARY. The status of vernacular compounds has traditionally been established through two criteria: how they sound and how they appear in writing and print. Because of this, they can be divided for practical purposes into *phonological compounds* and *orthographic compounds*.

**Phonological compounds**. In SPEECH, most two-word compounds have a falling intonation and are stressed on the first word (*TEApot*, *BLACKbird*) or primary stress falls on the stressed syllable of the first word (*eMERgency plan*, *RePUBlican Party*). This pattern of stress and intonation usually serves to distinguish compounds from expressions which typically have equal stress on both elements: such adjectival phrases as *the white house* (as opposed to *the WHITE House*) and nouns used attributively (*iron bridge*, as opposed to *IRONbridge*, the name of a town in England). Compound words, and phrases containing ATTRIBUTIVE NOUNS, generally have explanatory paraphrases: *teapot* a pot for tea; *iron bridge* a bridge made of iron. The following examples show differences in sound and meaning between compound and attributive usages (the compound first in each pair): *ORange juice* juice squeezed from oranges and *órange júice* juice that is orange in colour; *KEY position* the position of a key or keys and *kéy position* a posítion of great importance.

Adjective/noun combinations like *blackbird* are established as compounds both on the phonological criterion of stress and the semantic criteria of generic use and unique reference. *BLACKbird* has the stress pattern of *teapot* (distinct from the stress pattern of *a bláck bírd*) and serves as the unique generic name for all such birds. Colour adjectives often figure in such compounds (*blackboard*, *bluebird*, *brownstone*, *greenhouse*, *paleface*, *redcoat*, *redskin*, *whitecap*) as well as in place and personal names (*Blackburn, Greenland, Greystoke, Redpath, the White House, Whitehouse*).

Phonological and related factors become more intricate as structures containing compounds increase in length. In *car factory strike committee*, stress is placed on both *car* and *strike*. The group can be analysed as ((*CAR factory*) (*STRIKE committee*)), and paraphrased as a 'committee dealing with strikes in a factory that makes cars'. The compound *car factory* precedes the compound *strike committee*, and is therefore attributive. Such a combination is sometimes called a *double* or *multiple compound*. In principle, such groupings are indefinitely extensible: *Coventry car factory strike committee policy decision*, analysable as (((COventry) (CAR factory)) ((STRIKE committee) (POLicy decision))), and paraphrased as a 'decision about policy made by a committee dealing

with strikes in a factory that makes cars in Coventry'. In English, such expressions are not usually written as one word, as in German. Both languages, however, exploit very fully their capacity to form compounds and other multiple word groups.

**Orthographic compounds**. Traditionally, more attention has been paid to compounds on paper than to how they sound. In writing and print there are three forms: (1) *Solid compounds*, such as *teapot* and *blackbird*. (2) *Hyphenated compounds*, such as *body-blow, bridge-builder, mud-walled*. (3) *Open compounds*, such as *Army depot, coffee cup*. The conventions of solidity, hyphenation, and openness have tended to determine whether a word is considered a compound or not. Solidity and hyphenation endorse and reinforce compound status, visually distinguishing *a greenhouse* or *a green-house* from *a green house* (a house that is green). Although such distinctions can be valuable, they are not consistently applied: *Whitehouse* can be the name of a place or a family, but *the White House* in Washington is never *\*the Whitehouse* or *\*the White-house*.

In linguistics, the status of an item as a compound depends more on phonological than orthographic criteria, but in typography the orthographic forms have great importance. Even so, however, decisions about written compounds are more rule-of-thumb than rule, and fall into three groups: (1) Those made up of short words and therefore likely to be solid: *teapot, blackbird*. (2) Those made up of constituents which would look strange when combined and are therefore likely to be open (*coffee cup* rather than *coffee-cup* or *coffeecup*) or hyphenated (*body-blow* rather than *bodyblow*). (3) Compound-complex words are usually hyphenated: *bridge-builder, mud-walled*. However, many items freely vary: *businessman, business-man, business man; wine bottle, wine-bottle, winebottle*. As a further rule of thumb, the older and shorter a noun/noun or noun/adjective compound, the more likely it is to be solid: *rattlesnake*. The newer and longer it is, the more likely it is to be open: *population explosion*. Beyond that, the traditional practice appears to be, 'When in doubt, use a hyphen'. However, the writing and printing of many compound patterns remain uncertain and idiosyncratic, except where a house style is firmly applied. The same writer may make the same compound solid in one place (*worldview*), hyphenate it in another (*world-view*), and open it up in a third (*world view*), sometimes within a few pages of each other.

**Paraphrase patterns**. Next to phonology and orthography, the most distinctive aspect of compounds is susceptibility to paraphrase. This exhibits a kind of covert syntax based mainly on prepositional phrases: the compound *teapot* can be paraphrased only as 'a pot *for* tea', not a 'pot *of* tea'. Similarly, an *armchair* is 'a chair with arms', a *flower pot* 'a pot for (holding) flowers', a *goatskin* 'the skin of a goat', and a *bank clerk* 'a clerk in a bank'. Innumerable semantic relationships of this kind occur among compounds, some easy to interpret in isolation, others dependent on context. *London goods*, for example, may be 'goods in London', 'goods for London', 'goods from London'. Paraphrasing is not, however, always straightforward, even when the context is clear. What paraphrase is best for *steamboat*: 'a boat that uses steam', 'a boat using steam', 'a boat driven by steam', 'a boat with a steam engine in it', or 'steam drives this boat'? Precise paraphrase is impossible, but imprecise paraphrases still work adequately, because the relation between *steam* and *boat* is clear enough. It is the same with *sheepdog* 'a dog that? sheep', *silk merchant* a merchant who? silk, *car factory* a factory? cars, and *honey bee* a bee that? honey.

**Families of compounds**. There are many sets of compounds based on the same word, such as *gunboat*, *riverboat*, *rowboat*, *steamboat*. In such sets, the second element is generic, but its relationship with each member of its set is likely to be different. A *steamboat* is a boat propelled by steam, but a *riverboat* is not a boat propelled by a river. It is a boat used on a river. A *houseboat* is neither a boat propelled by a house nor a boat used on or in a house, but a floating house in the form of a boat, or a boat in the form of a house, usually moored in one place. Analogous forms are unlikely. There is no *\*bungalow boat* or *\*mansionboat*, except for nonce or stunt purposes. A *gunboat* is a boat with one or more large guns on it, a *rowboat* is AmE for a boat that can be rowed, BrE equivalent a *rowing boat*. Such forms and relationships are legion, but native speakers generally have little difficulty with them. Similarly, they have no difficulty in distinguishing a

*houseboat* from a *boathouse* or a *horse race* from a *racehorse*.

**Compound names**. Holistic compounds include proper names like *Sutton* (a reduced version of 'South Town') and *Shakespeare* (who shook no spears). Words like these have unique references and histories and their elements make no contribution to their everyday use. Historical association has produced various more or less opaque everyday compounds formed from names, such as *Wellington boot* (a British rubber boot named after the Duke of Wellington) and *Balaclava helmet* (a knitted cap associated with Balaclava, first used by British soldiers in the Crimean War). Such compounds are readily clipped, to become *wellingtons* (or *wellies*) and *balaclavas*.

**Compounds in context**. The coinage and use of compound words often follow a pattern of development in texts and social situations, usually a sequence that reinforces certain usages and may precipitate others. A character in a story may be introduced as *a man with a red beard*, brought in again as *a red-bearded man* and then called *Redbeard*. This might be his only name in a story for children or it could be an epithet, like *Eric Redbeard*, in a historical saga. In the flow of a narrative, new information is placed in focus in various ways. One such device is primary stress, already significant in compounds. It becomes particularly noticeable when texts containing patterns of compounding are read aloud, as in the following (each new focus italicized):

> Let's have a little talk about *tweetle* beetles—
> What do you *know* about tweetle beetles? Well . . .
> When tweetle beetles *fight*, it's called a tweetle beetle *battle*.
> And when they battle in a *puddle*, it's a tweetle beetle *puddle* battle.
> AND when tweetle beetles battle with *paddles* in a puddle, they call it a tweetle beetle puddle *paddle* battle.
> AND when beetles battle beetles in a puddle paddle battle and the beetle battle puddle is a puddle in a *bottle* . . .
> they call this a tweetle beetle *bottle* puddle paddle battle *muddle*.
> (from Dr Seuss, *Fox in Socks*, 1960)

**Creative paradigms**. Nonce and stunt compounds are often generated by social and linguistic circumstance. In the US television series *Hart to Hart* (1983), a character is asked: 'What's the matter, Max, you got heart-burn?' To which he replies, referring to a game of poker, 'Not only that—I got club-burn, diamond-burn, and spade-burn.' Comparably, *drug abuse* begets, as needs arise and similarities are recognized, such parallel forms as *alcohol abuse*, *child abuse*, *solvent abuse*, *spouse abuse*, *substance abuse*. Analogical paradigms of this kind are common.

**Conclusion**. Vernacular compounding is an open system. Users of English daily form and forget compounds in which words of vastly different pedigree and association come together. The following come from data collected in the 1980s: *ashram fashion*, *blimp patrol*, *energy vampire*, *karma debt*, *punctuality nut*, *Stupor Bowl*, *whale jazz*, *zombie powder*. See ABBREVIATION, ANALOGY, COMBINING FORM, EPONYM, FIXED PHRASE, NOUN-INCORPORATION, PHRASAL VERB, WORD-FORMATION.

**COMPUTERESE**, also **computerspeak**, **computer lingo**. Non-technical, often pejorative terms for usage associated with COMPUTING, such as: (1) Strings of letters and words used in programming and processing: the command *copy c: admı a:*, meaning 'copy from c-drive to a-drive the first administrative file' (where the c-drive is a built-in hard disk and the a-drive contains an inserted diskette). (2) Terms like *mainframe*, defined as either 'the combination of central processor and primary memory of a computer system' or 'any large computer system' (*Oxford Dictionary of Computing*, 1986). (3) Casual expressions used by computer enthusiasts: *Give me your input on this* Tell me what you think of this.

**COMPUTER USAGE**, sometimes **Computer English**. The REGISTER of English associated with computer technology and electronic communication, for both professional and other purposes, such as: the creation, use, and maintenance of equipment; recreation, such as video games and electronic bulletin boards; the writing and transmission of electronic mail; the promotion of products; word processing, desktop publishing and electronic publishing; and informal usage, including slang. Such usage has both lexical and syntactic aspects, including word-formation, semantic change, and distinctive prose styles.

**Word-formation**. (1) Compounds, such as *database* an organized store of information, *light pen* a light-sensitive rod for 'drawing' on screens or for reading data. (2) Fixed phrases such as *high-level language* an algebraic code with elements of natural language for operating computers, *mainframe* a very large computer system. (3) Abbreviations such as *ASCII* (pronounced 'Askee') for 'American Standard Code for Information Interchange', *CD-ROM* for 'compact disk read-only memory', *GIGO* for 'garbage in, garbage out', *WYSIWYG* or *wysiwyg* for 'what you see is what you get' (that is, a precise correspondence between what is on screen and what is printed out). (4) Blends, such as the programming languages *FORTRAN*, fusing 'formula' and 'translator', and *LISP*, fusing 'list' and 'processing'. (5) Eponyms, such as *non Von Neumann architecture*, any architecture basically different from the style of computer specified by the US mathematician John von Neumann, and *Turing machine*, an imaginary computer with characteristics as stated by the UK computing pioneer Alan Turing.

**Semantic change**. The adaptation of meanings and uses from the language at large into computer usage (new uses for old words), from computer usage to the language at large (public uses for private 'jargon'), and from one register to another (such as from medicine to computer usage):

*Specialization*. New uses for old words: *architecture* the arrangement of complex hardware and software, *chip* a tiny wafer of silicon on which is engraved a minute circuit, *compiler* a program which translates computer languages into machine language, *document* as a verb, meaning 'write', *interface* (noun) a connection between devices which cannot otherwise communicate with each other, (verb) to provide or have such a connection, *library* a set of programs for common tasks, *mouse* (plural sometimes *mouses*) an electrical pointing device like a remote control used to move elements on the screen of a personal computer.

*Generalization*. Extended uses for 'computer jargon': *input* and *output* as nouns, as in *I didn't like his input to the meeting*, and verbs, as in *Can you input that again?—I didn't understand*; *bug* as in *directions for home brewing have been debugged so thoroughly they are foolproof*; *interface* as in *the interface between government bureaucracy and the average citizen*; *mode* as in *I attended the meeting in sponge mode* (I listened but said nothing); and *network* as in *to network* (to call around one's friends and colleagues).

**Transfer**. The term *virus* has been transferred from medical to computer usage, to mean a planted program that copies itself from machine to machine, causing trouble along the way by using up memory or corrupting or deleting files. Before this term became established, such a program was briefly known as *a Trojan horse* or *Trojan*.

# ■ COMPUTING ─────── ■

The use of an electronic device that accepts data, performs mathematical and logical operations at speed on those data, and displays the results. Computers, although initially developed as calculating devices and open to a range of uses, have become central to communicative technology, and relate to language in at least three ways: (1) They require their own artificial languages in order to function. (2) Their use has adapted natural language to new ends, such as the processing of texts by computer. (3) Their users have developed their own styles and registers for working with them and talking about them. Since the 1950s, these factors have developed explosively and are major influences on late 20c English, the language most closely involved in computing.

**Nature**. The present-day computer derives from British work during the Second World War on cryptographic machines and is the most recent in a line of calculating devices that includes the abacus, the Jacquard loom, Babbage's Analytical Engine, and Hollerith's tab-sorter. Its primary purpose has been to compute, not to compile or converse. There are two kinds of computer: *analog* and *digital*. Analog computers, which are related to the slide rule and tables of logarithms (and virtually obsolete), use the strengths of voltages to represent the size of numbers, whereas digital computers use electrical signals only in the on/off form. Currently, digital computers consist of four major parts: (1) A *processor* or *central processing unit (CPU)*, which executes commands, performing arithmetical, logical, and manipulative operations on the data stored in the second part. (2) A *memory*, the information store. Most computers have at least two kinds of memory: primary and secondary.

Primary memory is usually silicon chips, typically DRAM (dynamic random access memory) chips. 'Random access' means that any part may be obtained immediately, as with a book that can be opened to any page. The process is fast, usually less than one microsecond to obtain an item of information. Secondary memory is usually magnetic disk, made of one or more platters rotating under a reading head. It is not random access: a particular part of the disk cannot be read until it rotates under the reading head, which usually takes several milliseconds. Storage is measured in *bytes*, one byte containing eight *bits*, and representing storage for one character in European alphabets. See ASCII. (3) *Input/output equipment*, which enables the user to get information into and out of the machine. The information is entered most commonly through a keyboard but also through removable disks, tapes, and other devices. Output goes to display screens, to printers (which produce text etc., usually known as *hard copy*), and also to disks and tapes. (4) *Communications equipment*, which permits a computer to 'talk' to other machines and to people located at a distance from it. The equipment includes a *modem* (an acronym for '*mo*dulator *dem*odulators'), which connect computers by telephone line, and networks to let machines talk at high speed to each other, as for example in using the INTERNET and the WORLD-WIDE WEB.

**Computer programs**. Since computers work very fast, they cannot be directed step by step. Instead, a script must first be written for the computer to follow. The script typically contains sequences to be repeated, so that the script is much shorter than the operation as executed. The computer responds to *machine language*, which is binary code (strings of 0s and 1s), in which the operations are very simple (such as elementary arithmetic or moving one piece of data from one place to another). Such scripts are written in *higher-level languages* called *computer programs* (BrE following AmE in this spelling, but AmE follows BrE in doubling the *m* in *programming*). A distinction is now universally made between the equipment as *hardware* and *software*, the latter now generally made available as commercial *software packages*.

**Computer languages**. Also *programming languages, high-level languages*. Digital computers can follow directions written in a great variety of artificial languages that provide precise specifications of operations to be done and the order in which they must be done. Although strings of letters are used to name commands in these languages, they are quite different from natural language. Among other things, they must be logical and unambiguous: unlike people, computers do not know that the *and* in *I like bread and jam* means 'both together', while the *and* in *I like cats and dogs* does not imply that both must be present at once (= 'I like cats and I like dogs'). Compared with natural language, high-level computer languages normally have: (1) *Very short words*: most programmers save effort by giving variables names such as *x*, one or two letters long, and by using many abbreviations, such as *del* for *delete*. (2) *Very short utterances*: written English sentences might average 20 words in length, but statements in programming language are typically only six items long. (3) *Little syntactic variety*: the typical computer language at present has a grammar of about 100 rules, compared with thousands in a formal grammatical description of English.

**Specific languages**. The many programming languages are divided into *business languages* (verbose, emphasizing simple operations on complex data) and *scientific languages* (terse, emphasizing complex operations on simple data). They often have distinctive histories and functions, and names of etymological interest. *ALGOL*, a language suitable for expressing algorithms, is the computational equivalent of Esperanto, created in 1960 by an international committee. Its name, a reduction of *Algorithm Language*, is a homonym of the star *Algol* (Arabic, 'the ghoul'). *BASIC* is short for *Beginner's All-Purpose Symbolic Instruction Code*, designed at Dartmouth College in New Hampshire in 1965 by J. Kemeny and T. Kurtz. It is often the first programming language learned and is similar to the *Basic* of BASIC ENGLISH, also an acronym. *ADA* was designed in a competition run by the US Department of Defense from 1974 to 1980, going through successive refinements with such names as *Strawman*, *Woodenman*, *Tinman*, *Ironman*. The French computer scientist Jean Ichbiah led the winning team. It was named after Lady Ada Lovelace, daughter of the poet Byron and a supporter of Charles Babbage, the inventor of the Analytical Engine, an early mechanical digital computer. She is often called the first programmer. For some years, the goal of 'programming in English' (that is, using a more or less unrestricted subset of the natural language) attracted attention, but it has so far proved unattainable.

**Processing text**. Computers, among other things, are extensions of writing and print systems, and have therefore been used with greater or less success to do such things as evaluate, index, parse, translate, correct, and 'understand' text. When a suitably programmed computer is fed English, it can process it at several levels, but with decreasing competence as the task becomes more complex. The following sequence is typical:

**1. *The character level***. Text can be entered into a computer by three means: *keying* it, typically into a word processor which will format the text (arranging the line lengths and character positions); *scanning* it, using a machine which transfers a paper version into an image followed by a program that seeks to recognize the characters in it; *transferring* it electronically, typically by diskette or telephone, from another compatible computer. Transfer is the fastest and most accurate method, but currently the least used. When a cleanly typed or printed original is available, without too many fonts or typographic complexities, scanning is faster and easier than rekeying. Once the text is entered, computers can print it in a wide variety of typefaces, sizes, and page formats, using either a printer or a desktop publishing system.

**2. *The word level***. A *spelling checker* can find some kinds of typing mistakes, usually by comparing words with a dictionary list and noting those that are not in that list. Programs can make *word lists* and *concordances* (lists of each word with some context before and after it). By noting the most frequent words in a document, and comparing the word frequencies in a particular text with the average word frequencies in English, a program can suggest words that might be used for *indexing* the document. The counting of relative *word frequencies* and comparison with word frequencies from a standard sample can also help in guessing the authorship of anonymous works or measuring the readability level of a text.

**3. *The sentence level***. On the level of syntax, PARSING programs can try to define the structure of sentences and relationships among words. This is typically done by applying grammar rules of the form 'a verb phrase may be a verb followed by an adverb'. Unfortunately many sentences are ambiguous. In the preceding sentence, a computer would not know whether *Unfortunately* modified the verb (implying that it is sad that ambiguous sentences occur) or the adjective *many* (suggesting disappointment that ambiguous sentences are so frequent). Adding a comma after *Unfortunately* could, however, serve as a means of disambiguation. However, some kinds of grammatical and stylistic errors can be diagnosed, and grammar checkers and style checkers have become available to help in the writing of business letters and the propagation of PLAIN ENGLISH.

**4. *The message level*.** At the level of word-and-sentence meaning, semantic analysis can map a sentence into a *knowledge-presentation language*. Some research projects have been able to take such sentences as *Which ships are in port?* and answer them by looking at a table of ship locations, but such systems currently operate in strictly limited subject areas. Other applications of semantics include machine translation and direct generation of language by computers (that is, the computer produces text without human input).

The above levels of activity depend on computational linguists writing rules of analysis, accumulating a GRAMMAR of syntactic and/or semantic rules for such a language as English. An alternative strategy for processing written language, however, uses reference books: the use of a MACHINE-READABLE dictionary or thesaurus may help a computer make reasonable guesses about which sense of an ambiguous word is intended in a particular context. Another strategy relies on the statistical properties of large corpora to determine word relationships. Such methods have allowed parsing without writing a grammar in advance, a higher quality of error correction in spelling, and the automatic recognition of phrases. However, they handle uncommon constructions less well than the grammar-based procedures handle them, and depend for their success on the fact that such constructions are uncommon. See COMPUTERESE, COMPUTER USAGE, CONCORDANCE, CORPUS, EMOTICON, ICON.

**CONCESSION.** In GRAMMAR, a relation-ship of contrast in which there is an implication of something unexpected. The relationship may be implicit in the content of two expressions that are juxtaposed: *The inhabitants were gentle, even friendly; underneath we sensed sadness*. The contrast may be made explicit by inserting the coordinating conjunction *but* before *underneath*: *The inhabitants were gentle, even friendly, but underneath we sensed sadness*. The unexpectedness may be made explicit by inserting concessive conjuncts (*yet, however, nevertheless*) or by subordinating the first clause and using a concessive subordinating conjunction to introduce it: *Although the inhabitants were gentle, even friendly, underneath we sensed sadness*. Clauses introduced by concessive subordinators such as *although, even though, though, while* are known as concessive clauses or adverbial clauses of concession.

**CONCORD**, also **agreement**. In GRAMMAR, the relationship between units in such matters as number, person, and gender: '*They* did the work *themselves*' (number and person concord between *they* and *themselves*); '*He* did the work *himself*' (number, person, and gender concord between *he* and *him*). Lack of standard concord occurs in sentences like *The books is on the table* and *I says do it but he don't do it*. Although ungrammatical in the standard language, such usage is consistent with the requirements of concord within some non-standard varieties.

**Number and person concord.** In standard English, number concord is most apparent between a singular or PLURAL subject and its verb in the third person of the simple present tense: *That book seems interesting* (singular: *book* agreeing with *seems*) and *Those books seem interesting* (plural: *books* agreeing with *seem*). The verb *be* involves concord for the first person singular (*I am*, etc.) and uniquely among English verbs has different forms for singular and plural in the past (*was, were*). Number concord, requiring that two related units should both be singular or both be plural, can involve complements and objects: *That animal is an elk, Those animals are elks, I consider him a spoilsport, I consider them spoilsports*. Both number and person concord are involved in the use of pronouns and possessives, as in '*I* hurt *myself*' and '*My* friends said *they* were coming in *their* car'.

**Singular *THEY*.** Controversy surrounds the use of *they* as a third-person singular pronoun, in defiance of number concord. It is common after indefinite pronouns: *If someone puts themselves forward in showbiz, they should be prepared for exposure if they err* (*Observer*, 18 Dec. 1988). The practice is popular as a way of avoiding the alleged sexism of the traditional use of masculine pronouns and the awkwardness that often attends *he* or *she* phrases. It has a long history: 'Here nobody hangs or drowns themselves' (Horace Walpole, 18c). It can occur where a masculine or feminine word could be used: 'He manages to think at least fifty years ahead, which for someone in their nineties is quite remarkable' (Prince Charles on the Earl of Stockton, *Daily Telegraph*, 22 Nov. 1985). Some grammarians claim that the usage is informal; others use it freely in their own formal writing: 'I have had a heart for years, but I would not know whether anyone else had a hole in theirs' (David Crystal, *Linguistics*, 1971).

**Gender concord**. This is an important part of the grammar of languages such as French or German, in which all nouns belong to a gender category, and articles and adjectives have to agree with them, as in the French *une petite plume* (a little pen), in which feminine agreement runs through the phrase, and *un petit livre* (a little book), in which the concord is masculine. In English, gender concord does not exist apart from personal and possessive pronouns, as in *Mary hurt herself badly in the accident but my father only broke his glasses*.

**Notional concord**. This stands in contrast to grammatical concord and means agreement by meaning rather than grammar, where the two are in conflict. In BrE, notional concord occurs when plural verbs are widely used with collective nouns: *The Opposition seem divided among themselves*; *The committee have decided to increase the annual subscription*. Some of the controversial uses of *they* can be accounted for in this way: *Everybody has left now, haven't they?* In both BrE and AmE, singular verbs are usual with apparently plural forms that are notionally felt to be singular, as in: *Fish and chips is no longer cheap*; *'The Grapes of Wrath' is a classic novel*; *$50 was a lot to pay*. Usage is divided in some areas. With various negative structures, some people favour grammatical, singular concord and others prefer notional, plural concord: *Neither John nor Mary knows about it* in contrast with *Neither John nor Mary know about it*, and *None of the bodies so far recovered was wearing a life-jacket* in contrast with *None of the bodies so far recovered were wearing life-jackets*.

**Proximity concord**. Clauses as subjects are usually treated as singular: *To err is human*; *That you don't agree upsets me*. With long noun phrases, the head word is relevant for number concord, as in *One of your friends is here*, not *\*One of your friends are here*, and *He is one of those people who always interfere*, not *\*He is one of those people who always interferes*, but in the heat of creation the concord in such constructions is often overlooked. In such cases, *proximity concord* operates, the verb agreeing with the nearest noun. It can also operate in awkward constructions like *\*Neither my sister nor I am going* and occurs in the traditional use of a singular verb after *More than one*, where both grammar and meaning require a plural verb: *More than one person has remarked on this strange fact*.

**CONCORDANCE**. **1.** Traditionally, an alphabetic index of the principal words in a book, such as the Bible or the complete works of Shakespeare, with a reference to the passage or passages in which each indexed word appears. **2.** In COMPUTING, a comparable list of the words in a text or CORPUS of texts, created by means of a *concordancing program*. The set of occurrences of any word in the text can then be displayed or printed out in alphabetical order, the word shown in the centre of the screen or page, each token of its occurrence being preceded and followed by its co-text. If more co-text or the original source is required, the program can provide it. Such concordances are now widely used by lexicographers to check and refine the MEANINGS, COLLOCATIONS, and CONTEXTS of words that already are or may be entered in a DICTIONARY.

**CONCRETE NOUN**. See ABSTRACT AND CONCRETE, NOUN.

**CONDITION**. In GRAMMAR, a relationship in which one situation is said to be dependent on another: in *He'll go if she goes*, his action is dependent on hers.

**Expressing condition**. There are various ways of expressing this relationship: (1) By a *conditional clause* introduced by the conditional subordinating conjunctions *if* and *unless*: 'Don't move *if it hurts*', where the prohibition depends on the fulfilment of the condition that it hurts. Other conditional subordinators include *as long as*, *assuming (that)*, *provided (that)*, *providing (that)*, *supposing (that)*, and (formal) *given that*. (2) Through the two clauses linked by *and* or *or*, where the first clause is generally a directive and the second clause describes the consequence of obeying or disobeying the directive: 'Have a glass of water *and you'll feel better*' (If you have a glass of water, you'll feel better); 'Don't say anything or you'll be sorry' (Don't say anything. If you do, you'll be sorry). (3) Through conditional conjuncts such as *then* and *in that case*: 'Don't move, *(and) then you won't get hurt*'. These conjuncts can also be used as correlatives after subordinators: '*If I see her tomorrow, then* I'll give her your regards.' (4) Through generic nouns modified by relative clauses: 'Employers *who do not consult their staff* cannot expect cooperation from them' (If employers do not consult their staff, they cannot expect cooperation from them).

**Kinds of condition**. Conditions may be open or hypothetical. *Open conditions* are neutral: they leave open the question of the fulfilment of the condition. *Hypothetical conditions* imply that the fulfilment is doubtful or has not taken place. They have a past or past perfect in the conditional clause and a modal (usually *would*) in the past or past perfect in the main clause: '*If he had recognized us*, he would have spoken to us' (but he didn't recognize us); '*If he apologized tomorrow*, I would forget the whole thing' (but the expectation is that he won't apologize). The past subjunctive *were* is used (as well as the simple past *was*) in the singular first and third persons of the verb *be* in hypothetical conditional clauses: '*If I were a rich man*, . . . (but I am not)'; '*If your sister were here*, . . . (but she is not)'; '*If it were to rain*, . . . (but it is unlikely that it will rain).' In formal style, the relationship may be expressed by bringing the auxiliary or the subjunctive *were* to the front of the conditional clause and omitting the subordinator: '*Had it rained*, we would have gone to the museum'; '*Were I your representative*, I would protest vigorously'; '*Should you be interested*, I could let you have a ticket.'

**CONFUSAGE**. An informal, non-technical term for usage that confuses, such as DOUBLESPEAK and GOBBLEDYGOOK, or results from confusion, such as *militate* used where *mitigate* was intended. See ABUSAGE, JARGON.

**CONFUSIBLE**, also **confusable**. A semi-technical term for one of two or more WORDS that are commonly or easily confused with one another: *luxuriant* with *luxurious*; *they're* with *there* and *their*. The British lexicographer Adrian Room (*Dictionary of Confusing Words and Meanings*, 1985) separates *confusibles* or 'lookalikes' such as *dominating* and *domineering* from *distinguishables* or 'meanalikes' such as *faun* and *satyr*. At least seven factors contribute to confusion: (1) Homophony, in which words have the same sound but different spellings and meanings: *slay*, *sleigh*. (2) Homography, in which words have the same spelling, but different sounds and meanings: *wind* moving air, *wind* to turn or twist. (3) Shared elements: *mitigate* and *militate* share the same number of syllables, the same stress pattern, and the same opening and closing syllables. (4) Transposable or exchangeable elements: *cavalry* and *Calvary*, *form* and *from*, *accept* and *except*. Factors 3 and 4 become more potent still when words have similar meanings and uses: *affect* and *effect*. (5) Words mistaken for phrases or vice versa: *already* and *all ready*. (6) Semantic proximity: *baroque* and *rococo*, *nadir* and *zenith*. Here, confusion may be encouraged by different but related applications of the same terms by different people: *acronym* and *initialism*, *subconscious* and *unconscious*. Some words are very different in meaning but sometimes displace one another because of close association: *acid* and *alkali*, *defendant* and *plaintiff*. (7) Uncertainty arising from different uses in different varieties of English: *biscuit* and *cookie* in BrE and AmE. See CATACHRESIS, DOUBLET, HOMONYM, MALAPROPISM, MISTAKE, SLIP OF THE TONGUE, SPOONERISM.

**CONJUGATION**. A PARADIGM, class, or table of VERB forms in such inflected languages as LATIN and FRENCH, where elements are distinguished from each other by patterns of INFLECTION, relating to tense, person, number. French has four regular conjugations, exemplified by *parler* to speak, *finir* to finish, *recevoir* to receive, *vendre* to sell. These verb classes conjugate differently, so that for example the perfect tense (for the first person singular) is respectively *j'ai parlé, j'ai fini, j'ai reçu, j'ai vendu*. The term is relevant to the grammar of Old English, in which there were seven conjugations of strong verbs, but not to Modern English, although irregular verbs can be divided into a number of pattern groups.

**CONJUNCT. 1.** A sentence ADVERBIAL that has a connective role: *therefore* in 'Our phone was out of order; we *therefore* had a period of uninterrupted peace.' **2.** A grammatical unit linked to other units through COORDINATION, that is, by means of *and, or,* or *but*: the phrase 'the children and their parents' contains two conjuncts: *the children* and *their parents*.

**CONJUNCTION**. A PART OF SPEECH or word class used to connect words or constructions. The two classes of conjunctions are *coordinating conjunction* or *coordinator* and *subordinating conjunction* or *subordinator*: (1) Coordinating conjunctions (chiefly *and, but, or*) connect units of equal status and function: the two equal clauses *They called me Ishmael, I didn't mind* in *They called me Ishmael, but I didn't mind*; the three equal adjectives *long, narrow, crooked* in *The street was long, narrow, and crooked*. (2) Subordinating conjunctions such as *because, if, although* connect a subordinate clause to its superordinate clause: *We did it because he told us to; Take it if you wish; Although it was late, they kept on working.*

Two or more subordinate clauses can be connected with a coordinator: *Take it if you wish and if no one else wants it*. The repeated subordinator may be omitted, if there is no danger of misinterpretation: *I know that she wants it and he doesn't*. The process of linking units by means of coordinators is known as *conjunction, conjoining*, and traditionally and most commonly *coordination*. The linked units that result are said to be coordinated or coordinate: for example, a coordinate clause. More recently, the units have been called *conjoins* or in generative grammar *conjuncts*. The process of linking units by means of subordinators is usually termed *subordination* or *embedding*. Both coordinators and subordinators may be reinforced by being combined with correlatives, a term used both for the reinforcing item and for that item and the conjunction it accompanies. The principal correlative coordinators are *both . . . and* (*Both Michael and Vivien were at my birthday party*), *either . . . or* (*You can discuss it either with me or with the manager*), *neither . . .*

*nor* (*Neither Jack nor Ava had the time to help me*). Correlative subordinators include *as . . . as* (*Derek is as fond of the grandchildren as Natalie is*), *whether . . . or* (*I'm not sure whether Ian or Carmel told me*), *the . . . the* (*The older I get, the less I worry*), and *if . . . then* (*If you tell Estelle, then she will tell Philip*). Although subordinators may consist of one word, as above, there are many complex subordinators of two or more words, such as *in order that, such that, as far as* (as in *as far as I know*), and *as if*.

**CONNOTATION AND DENOTATION**. Contrasting terms in LINGUISTICS. *Connotation*, also known as *affective meaning*, refers to the emotive and associational aspect of a term. *Denotation*, also known as *cognitive meaning*, refers to the direct relationship between a term and the object, idea, or action it designates. Connotation may be personal (stemming from experience, such as connotations of *swimming*, which one person may associate with recreation or training for competitions, another with fear of drowning) or common to a group (such as emotions raised by the name of a political leader). Denotation refers to the meaning of a word or expression in relation to everyday life and to other words and expressions: for example, colours can be described in terms either of wavelengths of reflected light or of such relationships as, in English, *red* with blood, *white* with snow, *green* with grass, *blue* with sea and sky. By virtue of their connotations, the same colours have further associations: *red* with anger or irritation, *white* with purity and innocence, *green* with inexperience or envy, *blue* with sadness and depression. See SENSE.

**CONSONANT**. A SPEECH sound distinct from a VOWEL (such as /b/ and /d/ in /bad/), and a LETTER of the ALPHABET that represents such a sound (such as *b* and *d* in *bad*). In general usage, a distinction between spoken consonants and written or printed consonants is not always made, but specialists seek to keep the two distinct. For some sounds and letters in English, the correspondence is straightforward and unequivocal, such as *d* and the alveolar PLOSIVE sound it represents. For others, correspondences are equivocal and can lead to uncertainty: for example, although the *c* in such words as *card, cord*, and *curd* has the 'hard' value /k/, and the *c* in such words as *cent* and *city* has the 'soft' value /s/, the *c* of

*Celt* is /s/ for some, /k/ for others. In ScoE, it is always /s/ in the name of the football team *Glasgow Celtic*, but generally /k/ in such expressions as *the Celtic languages*.

**Spoken consonants**. In PHONETICS, consonants are discussed in terms of three anatomical and physiological factors: the *state of the glottis* (whether or not there is VOICE or vibration in the larynx), the *place of articulation* (that part of the vocal apparatus with which the sound is most closely associated), and the *manner of articulation* (how the sound is produced). Following this order, the sound /k/ can be described as a 'voiceless velar plosive', where *voiceless* refers to the state of the glottis, *velar* to the velum as the place of articulation, and *plosive* to the manner of articulation (the release of a blocked stream of air). The consonant system of English is conventionally presented on a grid with manner of articulation shown horizontally and place of articulation vertically. Voiced and voiceless pairs are in the same cells of the grid, with the voiceless member of each pair to the left (see table).

| | Labial | Dental | Alveolar | Palatal | Velar |
|---|---|---|---|---|---|
| Plosive | p, b | | t, d | | k, g |
| Affricate | | | | tʃ, dʒ | |
| Fricative | f, v | θ, ð | s, z | ʃ, ʒ | |
| Nasal | m | | n | | ŋ |
| Lateral | | | l | | |
| R-sound | | | r | | |
| Glides | w | | | j | (w) |

Because of double articulation (pronunciation involving two places), /w/ occurs twice. The ASPIRATE /h/ is distinct from the other sounds because it is a FRICATIVE formed in the glottis. The grid shows that only *obstruents* (STOP and fricative consonants) enter into the voiced/voiceless distinction. Other sounds can be assumed to be voiced, so that /n/ for example can be described simply as an alveolar NASAL.

**Written and printed consonants**. In the Roman alphabet as adapted for English, 21 letters are commonly described as consonants: that is, all save *a*, *e*, *i*, *o*, *u*. Positionally, they precede and/or follow the vowel in most SYLLABLES: *to*, *ox*, *cup*, *fen*, *him*, *jab*, *keep*, *queer*, *wig*, *veil*, *yes*. Most may be doubled (*ebb*, *add*, *cuff*; *dabbed*, *runner*, *selling*), but dou-

bling of *k*, *v* is rare (*trekked*, *revved*), of *h*, *j*, *q*, *x* is abnormal (*Ahh*, *she sighed*), and none is doubled initially in native English words (but note *Lloyd* from Welsh, *llama* from Spanish). Many doubled consonants arise at the boundaries of affixes and roots, as with *abbreviation*, *accommodation*, *addition*, *affirmation*, *aggregation*, or before inflections, as in *fitted/fitting*, *redder/reddest*. Consonants regularly occur in strings or clusters without intervening vowels: initially, as in *stain* and *strip*, finally, as in *fetch* and *twelfth*, medially, as in *dodging*. Many clusters are digraphs, such as the *ch* in *chin*, *sh* as in *she*, *th* as in both *this* and *thin*, and *ng* as in *sing*. In addition, English uses numerous other consonant digraphs that do not represent a sound in any straightforward way; some, like *ph* in *photograph*, are borrowed from other languages, while others, like *gh* in *though*, *trough* are native to English but have lost their original sound value.

The distinction between vowel and consonant sounds and symbols is by no means always straightforward, as can be seen from looking at aspects of the letters *j*, *v*, *w*, *y*. Until at least the 18c, *j* and *v* (now established as consonants) were widely regarded as variants of the vowels *i* and *u*. In the 17c, the English alphabet was considered to have 24 letters, not 26: *j* and *v* were sometimes referred to as *tayl'd i* and *pointed u*. The consonants *w* and *y* have some of the characteristics of vowels: for example, compare *suite/sweet*, *laniard/lanyard*. Phonetic analysis may class such letters as either *semiconsonants* or *semi-vowels*. Many uses of *y* parallel those of *i*: *gypsy/gipsy*, *happy/Hopi*. The consonants *l*, *m*, *n*, *r* also often have some of the qualities of vowels when used syllabically: *l* in *apple*, *m* in *spasm*, *n* in *isn't*, *r* in *centre*. In such positions, they are often pronounced with a schwa preceding their consonant value. Most consonant letters are sometimes 'silent': that is, used with no sound value (some having lost it, others inserted but never pronounced); *b* in *numb*, *c* in *scythe*; comparably with *handsome*, *foreign*, *honest*, *knee*, *talk*, *mnemonic*, *damn*, *psychology*, *island*, *hutch*, *wrong*, *prix*, *key*, *laissez-faire*. In general, consonant letters in English have an uncertain relationship with speech sounds.

See AFFRICATE, AITCH, APPROXIMANT, CONSONANT CLUSTER, DIGRAPH, GLIDE, LIQUID, *L*-SOUNDS, *R*-SOUNDS, SIBILANT, SILENT LETTER, SPELLING, and letter entries for consonants.

the    owl  has   caught  a    mouse

**CONTACT LANGUAGE**. In SOCIOLINGUIS-
TICS, a simplified variety of language that
develops in situations where most speakers
have no common language, such as ports,
trading posts, plantations, and colonial garrison towns. It generally retains features of
the varieties that contribute to it, usually
local vernaculars and one or more languages brought by traders, settlers, soldiers,
and missionaries. It may also draw on universal strategies for communicating without a shared language. See FOREIGNER TALK,
LINGUA FRANCA, PIDGIN.

**CONTACT VARIETY**. In SOCIOLINGUIS-
TICS, a variety of a language, as for example
English, that results from contact with
other languages usually in multilingual
and multicultural contexts such as Africa
and India. With the passage of time, the
pronunciation, grammar, vocabulary, and
discourse of such a variety become stable,
but in forms that are not necessarily
amenable to the standards and assumptions about usage in traditional English-
speaking countries.

**CONTEXT**. **1.** Also *co-text*. The speech,
writing, or print that normally precedes
and follows a word or other element of language. The meaning of words may be affected by their context. If a phrase is quoted
*out of context*, its effect may be different from
what was originally intended. **2.** The linguistic, situational, social, and cultural environment of an element of language, an
action, behaviour, etc. Technically, the occurrence of a word in a linguistic context is
said to be determined by *collocational* or *se-
lectional restrictions*: the use of *rancid* with *butter* and *bacon*, of *flock* with *sheep* and *birds*, of
*pack* with *dogs*, *wolves*, and *cards*. Generally,
such association is largely or wholly determined by meaning (*drink milk/beer*, *eat
bread/meat*), but meaning can be affected by
collocation: *white* as in *white wine*, *white
coffee*, and *white people*. Non-linguistic context is often referred to as *situation*, and

meaning expressed in terms of context is
*reference* (in contrast with SENSE, which
exists in and among language elements
regardless of context). To illustrate the
meaning of *ram* by pointing to a picture or
an animal is to use context, but to define it
as *male sheep* in contrast with *ewe* is to do so
by means of sense. See SEMANTICS.

**CONTINUOUS**, also **progressive**. In
GRAMMAR, a VERB form that basically denotes duration. In English, the contrast is
between continuous (*They are repairing
computers*) and non-continuous (*They repair
computers*).

**CONTRACTION**. A reduction in FORM,
often marked in English in writing and
print by an apostrophe ('). There are five
major types: (1) Auxiliary contractions such
as *I've* I have, *he'll* he will, *somebody's* somebody is or has, *who'd* who had or would. (2)
Negative contraction such as *isn't* is not,
*don't* do not, *won't* will not. (3) Pronoun contraction of *us* in the first-person plural imperative *let's*, as in *Let's sit down awhile*. (4)
ELISIONS, such as *C'mon* Come on, *bo'sun*
boatswain. (5) Short forms used in note-
taking, such as *runng* running, *dept* department. When elements are removed from inside a word or phrase, but nothing is taken
from the end, a full point is often omitted.
There is inconsistency in the use of some
usually occupational titles, which may or
may not have a POINT, depending on individual preference or house style, such as *Dr*
or *Dr.* for *Doctor*. Although writers usually
follow a convention or are required to do so
by their publishers, the playwright George
Bernard SHAW defied the use of the APOS-
TROPHE for contractions, establishing a
unique norm for his texts with such forms
as *didnt*, *wouldnt*. Tradition favours the use
of apostrophes in writing dialect, so as to
mark deviation from the standard lan-
guage, as in *li'l ole me* (little old me) in colloquial AmE and *Ah'm no' comin'* (I am not
coming) in Scots. However, many late 20c
dialect writers reject this convention, arguing that it downgrades the medium they
have chosen to use and that for their purposes forms that may once have been contracted are not contractions at all. Writers
of Scots, for example, might use an apostrophe when two words come together, but not
for individual words, as in *Ah'm no comin*. See
ABBREVIATION, NEGATION.

**CONVERSATION**. The most basic and widespread linguistic means of conducting human affairs. Because of the pervasive, everyday nature of conversing, its scientific study has proved particularly complex. It has been difficult to obtain acoustically clear, natural samples of spontaneous conversation, especially of its more informal varieties. When samples have been obtained, the variety of topics, participants, and social situations which characterize conversation have made it difficult to determine which aspects of the behaviour are systematic and rule-governed.

**Conversational analysis**. In recent years, research in *conversation analysis* (an aspect of discourse analysis) has shown that conversation is a highly structured activity in which people tacitly follow a set of basic conventions. Occasionally, however, the rules are made explicit, as when someone says 'Can I get a word in?' or 'Don't interrupt'. To have a successful conversation in the English-speaking world, several criteria need to be satisfied: for example, everyone must have one or more turns (opportunities to speak), with no one monopolizing or constantly interrupting. People need to have a sense of when to speak and when to stay silent, and also need to make their roles clear: speaking as a parent, friend, employee, etc. There is a great deal of ritual in conversation, as when people wish to join in (*Excuse me, but . . .* , *Could I just say that . . .*) or leave (*Well, that about rounds things up . . .* , *Hey, is that the time?*), change the topic (*that reminds me . . .* , *Speaking of Mary . . .*), or check on listeners' attention or attitude (*Are you with me?*, *Don't get me wrong . . .*). The subject-matter is an important variable, with some topics being 'safe' in certain social groups (in Britain, the weather, pets, children, and the locality), others more or less 'unsafe' (religious and political beliefs, questions of personal income such as *How much do you earn?*)

**Turn-taking**. In conversation analysis, particular attention has been paid to the markers of conversational turns: how people know when it is their turn to speak. In formal DIALOGUE, there are often explicit markers, showing that a speaker is about to yield the floor; in debate, the person in the chair more or less closely controls speakers' turns. In conversation, however, the cues are more subtle, involving variations in the melody, rhythm, and speed of SPEECH, and in patterns of eye movement. When people talk in a group, they look at and away from their listeners in about equal proportions, but when approaching the end of what they have to say, they look at the listeners more steadily, and in particular maintain closer eye contact with those they expect to continue the conversation.

**Features of conversation**. There are several linguistic features that distinguish conversational style from other varieties of English. Speed of speech is relatively rapid: often over 400 syllables a minute, compared with a radio newsreading rate of around 200. There are many assimilations and elisions of consonants and vowels, such as the dropping of *t* in such words as *cyclists*, the reduction of *and* to *n*, or the compression of such auxiliary sequences as *gonna* and *wouldn'a'been*. It can be difficult to identify sentence boundaries in longer passages, because of the loosely structured narrative sequence (*. . . so I went out and got on a bus and found I'd left my purse in the house so I didn't know what to do and I hadn't any money and anyway . . .*). Informal DISCOURSE markers are common, such as *you know*, *I mean*, and *you see*. And there is a great deal of creativity in the choice of vocabulary, ranging from the unexpected coinage (*Don't be sad—be unsad*) and artificial accent (as in telling a joke about someone from a particular place not one's own) to the use of vague words (such as *thingummy* and *watchamacallit*). See PHATIC COMMUNION, REGISTER, REPETITION, SEXISM.

**CONVERSION** [BrE], **functional shift** [AmE], also **zero derivation**. The use of a WORD that is normally one part of speech or word class as another part of speech, without any change in form: *access*, usually a noun, as a verb in *You can access the information any time*; *author* in *They co-authored the book*. Such shifts are impossible in highly inflected languages like Latin, which require a formal change, but are common in analytic languages like English. English *love* is both noun and verb, but in Latin the noun is *amor*, the verb *amare*. Conversion has for centuries been a common means of extending the resources of English and creating dramatic effects: 'The hearts that spaniel'd me at heels' (SHAKESPEARE, *Antony and Cleopatra*, 4. 13). Etymologically, such words as *bang, crash, splash, thump* were once primarily nouns or verbs, but functionally they favour neither word class. The process has been described as derivation without a change of form (*zero derivation*), but because no new word is formed it can equally well be regarded as syntactic (many words are not tied to one grammatical role) or semantic (as a sense relation on a par with synonymy).

It is often said that 'there is no noun in English that can't be verbed': *bag* a prize, *doctor* a drink, *position* a picture with care, *soldier* on regardless. However, some factors appear to get in the way of complete freedom to convert: (1) *Morphology*. It is unlikely that such a verb as *organize* will shift, because of its verbal suffix: no *\*Let's have an organize*. (2) *Inertia*. Such a verb/noun contrast as *believe/belief* is unlikely to be overturned: no *\*This is one of my believes*. (3) *Utility*. In law, there may be no need for *jury* to be other than a noun: no *\*I've juried several times*. However, such a use cannot be ruled out. Striking one-off shifts often occur in fiction and journalism: 'I decided she looked like the vamp in those marvellous Hollywood westerns, the lady who goes hipping and thighing through the saloon' (Susan Howatch, *The Wheel of Fortune*, 1984); 'A formidable battery of legal grandees m'ludded and m'learned friended it out before Mr Justice Butt' (J. Keates, *Observer*, 18 June 1989). See JOURNALESE.

**COOK ISLANDS**. A self-governing dependency of New Zealand, which lies *c*.3,200 miles to the south-west of the 15 scattered islands. Languages: English (official) and local Polynesian languages. Between 1888 and 1901, the islands were a British protectorate; in 1901, they became a New Zealand dependency; in 1965, they became self-governing.

**COORDINATE CLAUSE**, also **coordinate clause**. A CLAUSE connected to one or more other clauses of equal status. In the sentence *I telephoned twice, but no one answered*, the two coordinate clauses are connected by the coordinating CONJUNCTION *but*. See COORDINATION.

**COORDINATION**, also **co-ordination**. In GRAMMAR, the process of connecting units of equal status and the resulting construction. Such units are usually connected by a coordinating CONJUNCTION (coordinator). *The houses and their occupants* is a noun phrase consisting of two coordinate noun phrases connected by *and*.

**COPULA**. A VERB that joins a SUBJECT to its COMPLEMENT. A term in the GRAMMAR of English for the verb *be*, but often extended to other verbs with a similar function. These *copular verbs* (also *linking verbs*) can be divided semantically into two types: (1) Those like *be* that refer to a current state: *appear, feel, remain, seem, sound*. (2) Those that indicate a result of some kind: *become, get* (wet); *go* (bad); *grow* (old); *turn* (nasty). *Be* is the copula that most often takes adverbial complements: *Maud was in the garden*; *Dinner is at seven*. All others take subject complements which characterize or identify the subject: *I felt cold*; *I felt a fool*.

**CORNISH**. **1.** The ancient Celtic language of Cornwall: 'In Cornwall is two speches: the one is naughty Englyshe, and the other is Cornyshe speche' (Andrew Boorde, *Introduction of Knowledge*, 1547). The language began to decline during the Reformation, and its last known fluent speaker, Dolly Pentreath of the village of Mousehole, died in 1777. **2.** Also *revived Cornish*. The partly ARTIFICIAL LANGUAGE administered by the *Kesva Tavas Kernewek* (Cornish Language Board), set up in 1967 'to promote the study and revival of the Cornish language'. This medium is sometimes referred to by scholars as *pseudo-Cornish*. The revival began with *A Handbook of the Cornish Language* (1904) by the Cornish nationalist Henry Jenner, followed by Robert Morton Nance's *Cornish for All: A Guide to Unified Cornish* (St Ives, 1929), Nance's dictionaries published by the Federation of Old Cornwall Societies, and A. S. D. Smith's grammar *Cornish Simplified* (1939). The revivalists claim that the traditional accent of English in Cornwall provides a key to Cornish pronunciation. The orthography was developed by Nance from the surviving texts, and vocabulary is extended by analogizing from Breton and Welsh and forming compounds from existing words. See CELTIC LANGUAGES.

**CORPUS** [From Latin *corpus* body, plural usually *corpora*, sometimes *corpuses*]. **1.** A collection of texts, especially if complete and self-contained: *the corpus of Anglo-Saxon verse*. **2.** In contemporary LINGUISTICS and LEXICOGRAPHY, a body of texts, utterances, or other specimens considered more or less representative of a language, a language area, a writer's work, etc., usually stored as an electronic database. Currently, computer corpora may store millions of running words whose features can be analysed by means of *tagging* (adding identifying and classifying tags to words and other formations) and *concordancing programs* (which draw up citations of words in context). Corpora of this kind can be created in three ways: (1) by keying texts into a computer and storing on disk; (2) by using optical equipment to scan text directly on to disk; (3) by acquiring MACHINE-READABLE texts directly from such sources as newspapers and publishers. In recent years, many print media have made their own corpora (for example, a year's issues of a newspaper), storing and marketing them on CD-ROMs which can be scanned and searched on screen. Such collections are of considerable interest to linguists, lexicographers, and others. *Corpus linguistics* is the study of corpora and the nature and use of the data in corpora. See BRITISH NATIONAL CORPUS, BROWN CORPUS, COBUILD, CONCORDANCE, GRAMMATICALITY, HYPERTEXT, INTERNATIONAL CORPUS OF ENGLISH, LONDON-LUND CORPUS, USAGE.

**CORRECT**. **1.** In accordance with a STANDARD, especially of artistic, literary, or linguistic style (and often synonymous with *proper*): *correct usage*. **2.** Of persons, adhering to an acknowledged standard of behaviour, speech, writing, etc.: 'The best and correctest authours' (Johnson, 1736, quoted in Boswell's *Life*). **3.** To set right, amend, mark or point out errors in (a text, essay, etc.); to rebuke, punish for faults of character or performance; to counteract and bring into line: 'I praye maister Iohn Skelton . . . poet laureate in the vnyuersite of oxenforde, to ouersee and correcte this sayd booke' (Caxton, *Eneydos*, 1490). See EDUCATION, ORTHOEPY, ORTHOGRAPHY, POLITICALLY CORRECT.

**CORRELATIVE**. In GRAMMAR, a term for words that are part of the same construction but do not occur side by side. In *correlative coordination*, a correlative CONJUNCTION is reinforced by a word or expression that introduces the first coordinate unit: *and* reinforced by *both* in *Both Geoffrey and Marion were at my party*. Pairs of correlatives and correlative conjunctions used in this way are *both . . . and*, *either . . . or*, *whether . . . or*, *not only . . . but*, *neither . . . nor*.

**COUNTABLE AND UNCOUNTABLE**. In GRAMMAR, contrasting categories of NOUN. A countable noun (also *count noun*, *unit noun*) can be both singular and plural, whether regular in form (*book/books*, *fox/foxes*) or irregular (*child/children*, *sheep/sheep*). In the singular, a countable noun cannot be used without a determiner or a possessive: *a book*, *one book*, *my book*, *that book*, *John's book*, but not \**book* alone. An uncountable noun (also *non-count noun*, *mass noun*) has no plural forms, takes only a singular verb, and can occur without a determiner: *furniture* as in *The furniture has arrived* is uncountable, but *chair* and *table* as in *They bought some chairs and a table* are countable. Some words can be used both countably and uncountably: *wine*, as in *This is a splendid wine* and *Have some more wine*. Some words are normally countable or uncountable, but in certain contexts may have special uses: *money* is normally uncountable, even though one can count the thing to which it refers: the forms *moneys*, *monies* occur only in limited financial contexts. Many abstract nouns are uncountable, but not all uncountable nouns are abstract. In general, countable and uncountable are subcategories of common noun, but not all common nouns fit the categories: *scissors*, *trousers*, and other words for things consisting of two parts; *cattle*, *clothes* and other words that are plural only. Compare COLLECTIVE NOUN.

**COX REPORT**. A report entitled *English for Ages 5 to 16*, published in 1989 in the UK for the Department of Education and Science on the teaching of English to pupils in England and Wales (but not Scotland and Northern Ireland) between the ages of 5 and 16, as part of the new National Curriculum. The committee which drafted the report was chaired by Professor Brian Cox of Manchester University, who had been a member of the committee that produced the KINGMAN REPORT (1988). However, whereas the Kingman Inquiry had to recommend a general model of the English language for teaching purposes, Cox was required to focus on how the teaching would be done. The Cox Report's recommendations reflected a compromise between concerns raised by the Kingman Inquiry regarding teaching a knowledge of language and the liberal consensus of many teachers of English. The recommendations were adjusted to the rigid format of the assessment model required by legislation relating to the National Curriculum established in 1987.

The report emphasized the subtlety of the process by which children acquire language and encouraged the use of English for a diversity of purposes. The role of wide reading and the centrality of LITERATURE in language development were also emphasized. At the same time, the report encouraged a sympathetic response to users of other languages in British society, but the successive levels of attainment proposed for the assessment of children's achievements reflected a monocultural rather than a multicultural view of English, with an expectation that the highest attainment would only be achieved by those using it for higher education, public speaking, or similar activities. The proposals were nonetheless widely reported as too liberal for the Secretary of State for Education. The National Curriculum Council, which was responsible for producing the version of the report to be used in schools (subject to parliamentary approval), attempted to add GRAMMAR in several places and make LITERACY more important than oracy, especially at the higher levels of schooling. Successive Secretaries of State also made pronouncements about the importance of SPELLING (associated with the view that READING should be taught primarily by the PHONIC method) in the assessment of all school subjects.

Because of concern about the level of knowledge of language on the part of teachers (who, at the secondary level, had mostly qualified with degrees in literature), the Cox recommendations were followed by a government-funded in-service training project known as *Language in the National Curriculum* or *LINC*, directed by Professor Ronald Carter of Nottingham University. However, the materials, due to be published by HMSO (Her Majesty's Stationery Office), were withdrawn in 1991 by ministerial order, and copyright was withheld for their commercial publication. Although precise reasons for these actions were not given, in the general view of the press they were a response to attempts by the writers to be sociopolitical about language and 'downgrade' STANDARD ENGLISH in relation to the use of DIALECT. The writers also rejected phonics as a technique for teaching spelling. In the opinion of many observers, the disagreements between Conservative politicians on the one hand and linguists

and educationists on the other had resulted in an act of direct official censorship. See MULTICULTURALISM.

■ CREOLE ────────────────── ■

A term relating to people and LANGUAGES especially in the erstwhile colonial tropics and subtropics, in the Americas, Africa, the Indian Ocean, and Oceania. In Portuguese, *crioulo* appears to have referred first to an animal or person born at home, then to a black African slave in Brazil who was born in his or her master's house. In the 17–18c, particularly in the West Indies, the term *creole* could mean both a descendant of European settlers (a *white creole*) or a descendant of African slaves (a *creole Negro* or *Negro creole*). Later, it came to apply also to life and culture in creole societies: for example, the (French) Creole cuisine of Louisiana. Since the later 19c, the term has extended to include a language spoken by creoles and has acquired a new sense in LINGUISTICS, associated with the development of PIDGIN languages.

**Creole languages.** In sociolinguistic terms, these languages have arisen through contact between speakers of different languages. This contact first produces a makeshift language called a *pidgin*; when this is nativized and becomes the language of a community, it is a creole. Such languages are often known locally as *pidgin* or *creole*, but may have such specific names as *AKU* in Gambia and *Papiamentu* in the Netherlands Antilles. They are usually given labels by sociolinguists that refer to location and principal *lexifier language* (the language from which they draw most of their vocabulary): for example, *JAMAICAN CREOLE*, in full *Jamaican Creole English* or *Jamaican English Creole*, the English-based creole spoken in Jamaica. *Haitian Creole French* is spoken in Haiti and is French-based. Creoles based on English, French, Spanish, and Portuguese occur in the Americas, Africa, and Asia.

**Creole English.** There are many English-based creoles. In West Africa, they include *Aku* in GAMBIA, *KRIO* in SIERRA LEONE, *Kru English* in LIBERIA, and *KAMTOK* in CAMEROON. In the Caribbean and the neighbouring mainland they include *BAJAN* in BARBADOS, *CREOLESE* in GUYANA, *MISKITO COAST CREOLE* in Nicaragua, *Sranan* in SURINAM, *Trinbagonian* in TRINIDAD AND TOBAGO, and the creoles of the Bay Islands of Honduras. In North America, they include *Afro-Seminole*, *Amerindian Pidgin English*, and *GULLAH*. In Oceania, they include *BISLAMA* in Vanuatu, *BROKEN* in the Torres Straits, *HAWAII CREOLE ENGLISH*, *KRIOL* in Northern Australia, *PIJIN* in the Solomon Islands, and *TOK PISIN* in Papua New Guinea. It has been argued that AFRICAN-AMERICAN VERNACULAR ENGLISH in the US has creole origins since it shares many features with English-based creoles in the Caribbean. In the UK, *British Black English*, spoken by immigrants from the Caribbean and their children, has features inherited from CARIBBEAN ENGLISH CREOLE.

**Shared features**. Typical grammatical features in European-based creoles include the use of preverbal negation and subject–verb–object word order: for example (from Sranan in Surinam) *A no koti a brede* He didn't cut the bread. Many use the same item for both existential statements and possession: for example, *get* in Guyanese Creole *Dem get wan uman we get gyal pikni* There is a woman who has a daughter. They lack a formal passive: for example, in Jamaican Creole no distinction is made in the verb forms in sentences such as *Dem plaan di tri* (They planted the tree) and *Di tri plaan* (The tree was planted). Creoles tend to have no copula and adjectives may function as verbs: for example, Jamaican Creole *Di pikni sik* The child is sick. Most creoles do not show any syntactic difference between questions and statements: for example, Guyanese Creole *I bai di eg dem* can mean 'He bought the eggs' or 'Did he buy the eggs?' (although there is a distinction in intonation). Question words in creoles tend to have two elements, the first generally from the lexifier language: for example, Haitian Creole *ki kote* (from *qui* and *côté*, 'which' and 'side') meaning *where*, and Kamtok *wetin* (from *what* and *thing*) meaning *what*. It has been claimed that many syntactic and semantic similarities among creoles are due to an innate 'bioprogram' for language, and that creoles provide the key to understanding the original evolution of human language.

**Creolization**. The process of becoming a creole may occur at any stage as a makeshift language develops from trade jargon to expanded pidgin, and can happen under drastic conditions, such as where a population of slaves speaking many languages has to develop a common language among slaves and with overseers. In due course, children grow up speaking the pidgin as their main language, and when this happens it must change to meet their needs. Depending on the stage at which creolization occurs, different types of structural expansion are necessary before the language can become adequate. In the case of Jamaican Creole, it is thought that a rudimentary pidgin creolized within a generation, then began to *de-creolize* towards general English. Tok Pisin, however, first stabilized and expanded as a pidgin before it became creolized; in such cases, the transition between the two stages is gradual rather than abrupt.

The term is also applied to cases where heavy borrowing disrupts the continuity of a language, turning it into a creole-like variety, but without a prior pidgin stage. Some researchers have argued that Middle English is a creole that arose from contact with Norse during the Scandinavian settlements (8–11c) and then with French after the Norman Conquest (11c). In addition to massive lexical borrowing, many changes led to such simplification of grammar as loss of the Old English inflectional endings. It is not, however, clear that these changes were due solely to language contact, since other languages have undergone similar restructurings in the absence of contact, as for example when Latin became Italian.

*De-creolization* is a further development in which a creole gradually converges with its superstrate or lexifier language: for example, in Hawaii and Jamaica, both creoles moving towards STANDARD ENGLISH. Following the creolization of a pidgin, a *POST-CREOLE CONTINUUM* may develop when, after a period of relatively independent linguistic development, a post-pidgin or post-creole variety comes under a period of renewed influence from the lexifier language. De-creolization may obscure the origins of a variety, as in the case of American Black English.

**Conclusion**. Pidgin and creole languages were long neglected by the academic world, because they were not regarded as 'real' or 'fully-fledged' languages, but their study is currently regarded as significant for general linguistics as well as the study of such languages as English. The study of pidgins and creoles has been rapidly expanding as linguists interested in language acquisition, language change, and universal grammar have taken more notice of them. Since pidgins and creoles are generally spoken in Third World countries, their role and function are intimately connected with a variety of political questions concerned with national, social, and economic development and transition into post-colonial societies. Some countries give official recognition to pidgin and creole languages, among them PAPUA NEW GUINEA, VANUATU, and Haiti. Pidgin and creole languages also function as symbols of solidarity in many parts of the world where their use is increasing.

See ABORIGINAL ENGLISH, ACROLECT, AFRICAN ENGLISH, ATLANTIC CREOLES, BAHAMAS, BASILECT, BELIZE, CAYMAN ISLANDS, GHANA, HAWAIIAN ENGLISH, JAMAICAN ENGLISH, MAURITIUS, MELANESIAN PIDGIN ENGLISH, MESOLECT, MONTSERRAT, NEW ORLEANS, NIGERIA, SAINT CHRISTOPHER AND NEVIS, SAINT LUCIA, SAINT VINCENT AND THE GRENADINES, SOLOMON ISLANDS PIDGIN ENGLISH, TALK, WEST AFRICAN ENGLISH, WEST AFRICAN PIDGIN ENGLISH.

**CUMBRIA**. A county of north-western England since 1974, formed from the former counties of Cumberland and Westmorland, and LANCASHIRE North of the Sands. It includes *the Lake District* or *Lakeland*, home of the poet Wordsworth. CUMBRIC was spoken there until the 11c, OLD ENGLISH from the 7c, and NORSE in the 9–11c. Local place-names reflect all three languages: Celtic as in *Culgaith* back wood, *Penrith* head of the ford, Old English as in *Broomfield* broom-covered field, *Rottington* farmstead of Rotta's people, Norse as in *Witherslack* wooded valley, *Haverthwaite* clearing where oats were grown. The DIALECT of Cumbria is closely related to SCOTS and to the dialects from North and East YORKSHIRE northward. Westmorland speech has features in common with the north-western Yorkshire Dales, such as 'skyool' for *school* and 'gaa' for *go*. The dialect around Howden in East York-

shire has more in common with that of Cumbria than with Wakefield, only 20 miles away in West Yorkshire.

The *Lakeland Dialect Society* was founded in 1939 to sustain interest in and use of the regional dialect. It publishes an annual journal whose poetry and prose attempts to display precise local usage with distinctive variants in spelling.

See DIALECT IN ENGLAND, NORSE, NORTHERN ENGLISH.

**CUMBRIC**. A Celtic language, akin to Old WELSH, spoken in southern Scotland and north-west England until early medieval times. Most relics of Cumbric are place-names such as *Pennersax* in Dumfriesshire, whose Welsh equivalent would be *Pen y Sais* Englishman's summit. Some commentators consider that garbled echoes of Cumbric survive in the *Cumbric Score* or *sheep-counting numerals*, numbers of a sort used in Cumberland and West Yorkshire by men counting sheep, women counting stitches, and children in games. A. J. Ellis published 53 versions of these in 1877–9, and Michael Barry 70 versions in 1969. In Borrowdale in Cumberland, 1–10 was *yan, tyan, tethera, methera, pimp, sethera, lethera, hevera, devera, dick* (Welsh is *un, dau, tri, pedwar, pump, chwech, saith, wyth, naw, deg*). 'Fifteen' was *bumfit* (Welsh *pymtheg*). The Score was acquired from informants at second hand; apparently, no one has ever been found actually using it. See CELTIC LANGUAGES.

**CYPRUS**. An island country in the Eastern Mediterranean, and member of the COMMONWEALTH. Languages: GREEK, Turkish (both official), and English widely used. From the 16c, Cyprus was part of the Turkish Empire, was ceded to Britain in 1878, and became independent in 1960. The UK retains sovereignty over the military bases of Akrotiri, Dhekalia, and Episkopi. Since 1974, the republic has been divided into Greek and Turkish areas that have little direct contact with each other.

# D

## ■ D, d ■

[Called 'dee']. The 4th LETTER of the Roman ALPHABET as used for English. It originated in the triangular Phoenician symbol called *daleth* (akin to Hebrew *dālāh*, 'door'), which ~~was altered by the Greeks to form their delta~~ (Δ), and later rounded to form Roman *D*.

**Sound values**. In English, *d* normally represents the voiced alveolar plosive. However: (1) The boundary between *d* and its close phonetic neighbours *t* and *th* is sometimes breached. Formerly, for example, there was variation between *d* and *th*: *father* and *mother* were until the 16c written *fader* and *moder*; *burden* and *murder* were until the 19c written *burthen* and *murther*. After voiceless consonants (with the exception of /t/), the past-tense inflection *d* is pronounced /t/: *sacked*, *touched*, *stuffed*, *sipped*, *hissed*, *wished*, *earthed*, *waxed*. (2) In AmE and AusE, intervocalic /t/ is typically voiced to /d/, making homophones of such pairs as *Adam/atom*, *ladder/later*, and *waded/waited*. (3) When the sound usually represented by *y* follows a *d*, the two sounds may merge to produce a *j*-sound /dʒ/: *grandeur*, *procedure*. This is acknowledged in the colloquial spellings of *Acadian*, *Barbadian*, *Indian*, *soldier* as *Cajun*, *Bajan*, *Injun*, *sojer*.

**Double D**. Two *d*s occur: (1) In monosyllables beginning with a vowel: *add*, *odd*. (2) In many disyllables after a stressed short vowel: *madden*, *meddle*, *midden*, *shoddy*, *muddy* (but contrast *shadow*, *medal*, *widow*, *modest*, *body*, *study*). (3) In monosyllables containing a short vowel when followed by suffixes: *bed*, *bedder*, *bedded*, *bedding*. (4) When the Latinate prefix *ad-* precedes a root beginning with *d*: *addition*, *address*, *adduce*.

**Variations on -ED**. The regular past-tense inflection adds *-ed* to the verb stem (*sail/sailed*, *stucco/stuccoed*), or *-d* if the stem already ends in *e* (*love/loved*, *hate/hated*, *free/freed*, *sue/sued*, *face/faced*, *rage/raged*). However, there is significant systematic variation in both spelling and pronunciation. There are also irregular past-tense forms, some using irregular *t* alongside regular forms with *d* (*costed/cost*, *smelled/smelt*) some

with *t* and without an *ed* equivalent (*caught*, *felt*, *left*, *lost*, *put*, *spent*), some using only the *d* of the base form (*fed*, *found*, *shed*, *slid*, *stood*, etc.), and some introducing *d* in an irregular way (*fled*, *had*, *heard*, *made*, *paid*, *said*, *shod*, *sold*, etc.).

After a single vowel letter pronounced short in a stressed syllable, a final consonant is normally doubled when *-ed* is added: *bat/batted*, *fit/fitted*, *commit/committed*, *refer/referred* (contrast *headed*, *hatched*, with multiple vowel or consonant letters). Final *-ic* becomes *-ick-* when *-ed* is added: *picknicked*, *trafficked*. Final consonant plus *y* changes *y* to *i*: *carry/carried*, *deny/denied*, *pity/pitied* (contrast *convey/conveyed*). This rule results in the single homographic past form *skied* from *to ski* and *to sky*. Words of more than one syllable, not stressed on the final syllable, do not normally double the final consonant (*offer/offered*), but there are exceptions. In BrE, for example, there is a subrule that unstressed final *-el* becomes *-elled* (*travel/travelled*), to which *paralleled* is an exception, whereas AmE follows the general rule (*travel/traveled*). Similarly, BrE writes *kidnapped* and *worshipped* (but *galloped* and *gossiped*), while AmE may have *kidnapped* or *kidnaped* and *worshipped* or *worshiped*. There is some uncertainty with verbs ending in *-s*, BrE tending to double (*bus/bussed*, *bias/biassed*, *focus/focussed*) and AmE tending to stay single (*bus/bused*, *focus/focused*). Publishing houses may have their own preferences: Oxford University Press in Britain favours *biased*, *focused*. In AmE *benefited* is the only form used; in BrE, although it is the dominant form, *benefitted* also occurs.

**Indicators of pronunciation**. (1) In the past tense of a regular verb whose stem ends in a /d/ or /t/, an unstressed (that is, centralized) vowel is heard before the final /d/: *needed*, *preceded*, *waited*, *hated*. The same is true of an adjective distinguished from a past participle: *an agèd man* as opposed to *aged 30*; *a learnèd professor* as opposed to *learned English quickly*. This distinction is sometimes required in poetry for metrical reasons, when the appropriate pronunciation can be shown by means of a GRAVE ACCENT or an APOSTROPHE. So, in Shake-

speare's *Hamlet*, *damned* has two full syllables in *smiling*, *damnèd villain* (1.5), but only
one in *A damn'd defeat* (2.2). (2) If pronounced
/t/, the inflection was formerly often written
t: in early editions of Shakespeare, the
phrase *untimely ripped* was spelt *vntimely ript*.
(3) In the 18c, especially in private writing,
the suffix -*d* was often preceded by an apostrophe to indicate an omitted silent *e* (*ask'd*,
*pass'd*, *shew'd*).

**Silent *D***. (1) In a few words, when *d* precedes or follows *n*, *d* is commonly no longer
pronounced: *handkerchief*, *handsome*, and
(with the exception of ScoE) *Wednesday*. (2)
The *d* of the Latinate prefix *ad*- is silent
before *j*: compare the pronunciations of
*ajar* and *adjacent*.

**Digraph *DG***. In the combination *dg*, the *d*
serves to mark or emphasize the soft *j*-value
of the following *g* (*badge*, *judge*: contrast *bag*,
*jug*), and is the equivalent of doubling a
single letter.

**Epenthetic *D***. (1) A number of words have
an epenthetic *d* after *n*: *thunder* (from Old
English *thunor*: compare German *Donner*),
and *jaundice*, *astound*, *sound*, from Old
French *jaunisse* (Modern *jaunise*), *estoné*
(Modern *étonné*), and *soner* (Modern *sonner*).
(2) The *d* in *admiral*, *advance*, *advice* was inserted in Early Modern English in the belief
that words like these were from Latin and
should therefore contain the prefix *ad*-, although the forms in which they had come
from French did not exhibit it: compare
French *amiral*, *avance*, *avis*. Quasi-Latinate
spellings with *d* became conventional, and
pronouncing the *d* followed, even where the
inserted letter was etymologically spurious:
for example, *admiral* derives from Arabic
*amir* (commander), and *advance* from Latin
*abante* (from before: compare Italian *avanti*).
*Advice* is from Old French *a vis* (abstracted
from the phrase *ce m'est a vis*: It seems to me),
which can ultimately be derived from Latin
*ad visum*. See EPENTHESIS, G, HARD AND SOFT.

**DANELAW**, also **Danelagh, Danelaga**.
The system of law in the part of England
ceded to Danish invaders in 878, and the
area itself, roughly north and east of a line
from London to Chester. In the mid-10c,
Scandinavian kings maintained a Norse-
speaking court at York, but the ordinary
population, English and Danish, seems to
have developed a simplified language for
use in their daily contact. In the later 10c,

the kings of Wessex established overlordship over the Danish settlers, who however
retained control of local affairs. William of
Malmesbury declared (*c*.1130) that the language north of the Humber and especially
at York 'sounds so harsh and grating that
we southerners cannot understand a word
of it' and blamed this on the presence of
'rough foreigners' (*De Gestis Pontificum
Anglorum*, Book 3, Prologue). See DANISH,
NORSE.

**DANISH**. A GERMANIC LANGUAGE spoken in
Denmark, in parts of Schleswig (North
Germany), and mostly as a second language
in Greenland and the Faroe Islands. It has
been historically influential on ENGLISH and
NORWEGIAN. In the 9–11c, Old Danish
(NORSE) was used extensively in England,
especially in the DANELAW. Danish influence
survives in the general vocabulary of
English (such as the *sk*- words *sky*, *skill*, *skin*,
*skirt*, *scrape*, *scrub*) and the dialect vocabulary of northern England and Scotland
(*gate/gait* a road, *sark* a shirt), as well as in the
unusual feature that the words *they*, *their*,
*them*, *though*, *both* are all Norse. Danish
place-names are common in the Danelaw,
especially those ending in -*by* (farm, town),
such as *Grimsby*, *Whitby*. See BORROWING,
SCANDINAVIAN LANGUAGES.

**DASH**. The PUNCTUATION mark (−), used to
indicate pauses and asides; it occurs singly,
or in parenthetical pairs when the main
sentence is resumed after the pause: compare commas and brackets. The main uses
are: (1) To indicate an additional statement
or fact, with more emphasis than is conveyed by commas or brackets: *She is a solicitor—and a very successful one as well*; *They say
that people in the north are more friendly—and
helpful—than people in the south*. (2) To indicate
a pause, especially for effect at the end of
a sentence: *There is only one outcome—
bankruptcy*. (3) To add an afterthought: *She
wore a red dress—a very bright red*. In print, the
dash is usually represented by an *em* RULE
(as in the preceding examples), although
some styles favour the shorter *en rule* with a
space on either side. An em rule is about
twice the width of an en rule, and about
three or four times the width of a HYPHEN.
An unspaced en rule is often used as a link
in cases such as *1944–80* and *the London–
Brighton line*, where it is equivalent to *to*. In
writing and typing, it is difficult to main-

tain any distinction in appearance between these three marks; few people attempt to do so in writing, but in typing some writers use a hyphen with spaces to left and right, or two hyphens together (with similar spaces). Dashes are also used non-punctuationally to stand for omitted letters, or for a whole word; for example a coarse word in reported speech: '*D—n you all*,' *he* said. The dash is sometimes used as a replacement for quotation marks (inverted commas) in printed DIALOGUE; for example, in the work of James Joyce, who disliked what he called 'perverted commas':

—Who is that? said the man, peering
 through the darkness.
—Me, pa.
—Who are you? Charlie?
—No, pa. Tom.

(*Dubliners*, 1914)

See ANACOLUTHON, PARENTHESIS.

**DECLARATIVE**. In GRAMMAR, a term for the MOOD through which statements are made, in contrast with *imperative*, *interrogative*, and *exclamative*. Although *declarative* is often used interchangeably with *statement*, it is useful as a means of distinguishing the syntactic form of a sentence from its function: for example, the sentence *You will do as I say* is declarative in form, but functions as a command See INDICATIVE.

**DECORATIVE ENGLISH**, also **atmosphere English, ornamental English**. Non-technical terms for English used as a visual token of modernity or a social accessory on items of clothing, writing paper, shopping bags, pencil boxes, etc., in advertising, and as notices in cafés, etc. The messages conveyed are 'atmospheric' rather than precise or grammatical, as in 'Let's sport violent all day long'. Use of decorative English appears to centre on JAPAN, but has spread widely in East Asia and elsewhere.

**DEFINITE ARTICLE**. In GRAMMAR, the technical term for the word *the* when introducing a noun phrase, as in *the telephone in my office*. *The* is also used, in a correlative pair, with a comparative adjective and adverb to introduce a clause: *The more I exercise, the healthier I feel*. For fuller discussion, see ARTICLE.

**DEFOE, Daniel** [1660?–1731]. Sometimes *De Foe*, English journalist and novelist, born in London of Flemish descent, son of a chandler, and best known for the novel *Robinson Crusoe* (1719). He sympathetically represented non-standard varieties of English in works like *Colonel Jack* (1722) and *A Tour thro' Somerset* (1724–7), but in *An Essay upon Several Projects* (1702) proposed that England emulate the Académie française with an ACADEMY appointed 'to encourage Polite Learning, to polish and refine the English Tongue, and advance the so much neglected Faculty of Correct Language. to establish Purity and Propriety of Stile, and to purge it from all the Irregular Additions that Ignorance and Affectation have introduc'd'. Like other proposals for such an academy, Defoe's concentrated on the literary language, and like them had no practical outcome. See JOURNALISM.

**DEGREE**. **1.** A grammatical category for items of language used to express relative intensity: *very much*, of a verb in *I admire them very much*; *highly*, of an adjective in *highly intelligent*; *very*, of an adverb in *very often*; *big*, of a noun in *a big fool*; *dead*, of a preposition in *They're dead against it*. Such intensifiers or words of degree are used with other words that are *gradable* (that is, on a scale of intensity). They may indicate a relatively high or low point: *slightly*, *somewhat*, *hardly*, *a bit*. **2.** Three types of comparison applied to gradable adjectives and adverbs: to a high degree (*bigger*, *biggest*); to the same degree (*as big as*), and with a preceding negative (*not so big as*); to a lower degree (*less big*, *least big*). Non-extreme forms may be followed by comparative clauses: 'Jeremy is taller *than his parents* (*are*)'; 'Naomi is less tall *than Ruth* (*is*)'; 'Doreen is as tall *as Leslie* (*is*).' Higher-degree comparisons may be expressed by inflections (the absolute or positive degree *happy*, the comparative degree *happier*, and the superlative degree *happiest*) or periphrastically, in combination with *more* for comparatives (*more happy*) and *most* for superlatives (*most happy*). Monosyllabic adjectives (*young*, *sad*, *small*) generally take inflections, polysyllabic adjectives (*beautiful*) periphrastic *more/most*. Many disyllabic adjectives take either form: *commoner/more common*, *commonest/most common*. Most adverbs allow only periphrastic comparison (*happily/more happily/most happily*), but a few are suppletive: *badly/worse/ worst*; *well/better/best*. See PERIPHRASIS, SUPPLETION.

**DEIXIS**. In LINGUISTICS, the function of an item or feature that refers to relative position or location (*here*, *there*) and point of reference (*me*, *you*, *them*). *I* and *you* are deictic because they refer respectively to speaker and person spoken to. The third-person pronouns may be deictic (as in *Look at her!*). *This* and *these* are deictic when pointing to objects in closer proximity to the speaker, in contrast to *that* and *those* for objects further away. Temporal deixis may be expressed through tense (*I speak the truth*, *I spoke the truth*) and through adverbs (*now*, *then*, *today*, *yesterday*, *tomorrow*). Interpreting deixis in utterances depends on the situation: the *I* in *I spoke the truth* varies according to speaker, but the *she* in *She spoke the truth* has normally been identified in a previous verbal CONTEXT. See DEMONSTRATIVE.

**DEMONSTRATIVE**. A term used in association with pronouns and DETERMINERS as an adjective and a noun: *a DEMONSTRATIVE PRONOUN*; *three demonstratives in one sentence*. A demonstrative usage indicates relationships and locations, such as between *this* (near the speaker and perhaps the listener) and *that* (not near the speaker, perhaps near the listener, or not near either). See DEIXIS.

**DEMONSTRATIVE PRONOUN**. A PRONOUN that shows where something is in relation to speaker and listener. STANDARD ENGLISH has four demonstratives, paired and with number contrast; *this/these* here, *that/those* there. Some dialects have three (*this*, *that*, *yon/yonder*) and SCOTS has *this*, *that*, *yon/yonder* and its variant *thon/thonder*. The sets of three are comparable to LATIN *hic* this near me, *iste* that near you, *ille* that over there. For some grammarians, the term covers the demonstratives however used; for others, demonstrative pronouns ('I like *that*', 'Give me some of *these*') are distinguished from *demonstrative determiners* ('I like *that* one', 'Who are *these* people?'). See DEIXIS.

**DENOTATION**. See CONNOTATION AND DENOTATION.

**DENTAL**. In PHONETICS, a term referring to sounds like /θ/ (the *th* in *thirty*) and /ð/ (the *th* in *those*), made with the tip of the tongue in the region of the upper front teeth. See ARTICULATION, LABIAL.

**DEPENDENT CLAUSE**. See SUBORDINATE CLAUSE.

**DERIVATION**. **1.** A process through which one WORD, PHRASE, or SENTENCE is formed from another: passive sentences (*They were met by a friend*) are often said to derive from active sentences (*A friend met them*). **2.** A process by which the forms and meanings of words change over centuries: English *nice* derives from Latin *nescius*. **3.** A process by which more complex words are formed from less complex words: *purification* from *purify* from *pure*. Although information about the history of words may help in analysing their current forms, there is no necessary link between a word's ETYMOLOGY and its current form and meaning: although *pure* has a close formal and semantic link with its ancestor, Latin *purus*, the tie makes no difference to how *pure* is used in English; present-day *nice* (meaning 'pleasant' and sometimes 'precise') has no obvious association in form, meaning, or function with its ancestor *nescius* (which meant 'ignorant').

**Etymological derivation**. The term *derivation* itself derives from an analogy between language and a river (Latin *rivus*), in which later forms flow from earlier forms: *pure* from *purus*, *nice* from *nescius*. It has traditionally been assumed that Modern English flows from Old English, that elements in English flow from languages which were earlier and more prestigious (Greek and Latin) or had power and prestige at the time when English was developing (Latin and French), that Latin, Greek, and the Germanic languages flowed from still earlier languages, and that studying the history of languages helps one appreciate this flow. Caution is often advisable when establishing the history of a word: although *outrage* seems to derive straightforwardly from *out* and *rage* (and mean anger beyond the normal), it actually comes from Old French *oultrage*: compare Italian *oltraggio*. The prior stage is however conjectural; philologists have reconstructed a Latin \**ultraticum* as the common ancestor of *outrage*, *oultrage*, *oltraggio*. It resembles comparable established usages, but has never been found in a text. In English, assumptions that *rage* is part of *outrage* have affected the use and meaning of the word, and as a result the reinterpretation of *outrage* as *out* and *rage* together has become a factor in the 'story' of the word. As a result, although the sound and look of *outrage* are not helpful in deciding its origin, they are relevant in a consideration of current meaning and use.

**Morphological derivation**. Time is different in everyday WORD-FORMATION. Derivational morphology has two aspects: static, when analysing internal arrangement, and dynamic, when considering how the more complex emerges from the less complex. In static terms, *transformation* can be analysed into three parts, *trans* + *form* + *ation* (PREFIX, BASE, SUFFIX). In dynamic terms, analysis can establish stages through which words develop: for example, from *form* to *transform* to *transformation*. How long the process takes (centuries or seconds) is a secondary matter; once such a flow or pattern exists, users do not usually concern themselves with how long any element in the pattern has existed, and once they have become accustomed to a new derivative like *transformational*, they do not usually think about the flow that produced it. Although many complex words are derived along only one flow or path (as with *pure–purify–purification*), more than one may exist. The path for *transformation* could be either *form–transform–transformation* or *form–formation–transformation*. Whatever path is followed, a new base for another possible derivative is formed: *pure* the base for *purify* which is the base for *purification* which then leads to *purificational* and if so desired to \**purificationalism*. Although there is no theoretical limit, in practice usefulness, comprehensibility, and pronounceability decide the cut-off points: \**antipurificationalistically* is well formed, but not very useful. See ANALOGY, EPONYM, INDO-EUROPEAN ROOTS, MORPHOLOGY, ROOT-CREATION.

**DERIVATIVE**. **1.** A WORD or other item of language that has been created according to a set of rules from a simpler word or item. **2.** A COMPLEX WORD: *girlhood* from *girl*, *legal* from *leg-* (law), *legalize* from *legal*. **3.** Of an essay, article, thesis, etc., and usually pejorative: depending for form and/or inspiration on an earlier and better piece of work.

**DEROGATORY**. Disparaging and offensive, a term often used in dictionaries (usually abbreviated to *derog*) to label expressions that intentionally offend or disparage: *skinny* when used instead of *thin*; AmE *ass-hole* for someone considered stupid, mean, or nasty. See ETHNIC NAME, PEJORATIVE.

**DESCRIPTIVE AND PRESCRIPTIVE GRAMMAR**. Contrasting terms in LINGUISTICS. A *descriptive grammar* is an account of a language that seeks to describe how it is used objectively, accurately, systematically, and comprehensively. A *prescriptive grammar* is an account of a language that sets out rules (*prescriptions*) for how it should be used and for what should not be used (*proscriptions*), based on norms derived from a particular model of grammar. For English, such a grammar may prescribe *I* as in *It is I* and proscribe *me* as in *It's me*. It may proscribe *like* used as a conjunction, as in *He behaved like he was in charge*, prescribing instead *He behaved as if he were in charge*. Prescriptive grammars have been criticized for not taking account of language change and stylistic variation, and for imposing the norms of some groups on all users of a language. They have been discussed by linguists as exemplifying specific attitudes to language and usage. Traditional grammar books have often, however, combined description and prescription. Since the late 1950s, it has become common in linguistics to contrast *descriptive grammars* with GENERATIVE GRAMMARS. The former involve a description of linguistic structures, usually based on utterances elicited from native-speaking informants. The latter, introduced by CHOMSKY, concentrate on providing an explicit account of an ideal native speaker's knowledge of language (*COMPETENCE*) rather than a description of samples (*performance*). Chomsky argued that generative grammars are more valuable, since they capture the creative aspect of human linguistic ability. Linguists generally regard both approaches as complementary. See DESCRIPTIVISM AND PRESCRIPTIVISM, STRUCTURAL LINGUISTICS.

**DESCRIPTIVISM AND PRESCRIPTIVISM**. Contrasting terms in LINGUISTICS. *Descriptivism* is an approach that proposes the objective and systematic description of language, in which investigators confine themselves to facts as they can be observed; particularly, the approach favoured by mid-20c US linguists known as *descriptivists*. *Prescriptivism* is an approach, especially to grammar, that sets out RULES for what is regarded as correct in language. In debates on language and education, enthusiasts for one side often use the label for the other side dismissively. See CORRECT.

**DETERIORATION**. **1.** An emotive term for LANGUAGE CHANGE seen as evidence of linguistic and social decline. **2.** Also *pejoration*. A category of SEMANTIC CHANGE, in which the meaning of a word or phrase depreciates with time: *crafty* once meant 'strong' and now means 'wily'; *cunning* once meant 'knowledgeable' and now means 'clever in a sly way'. See PROGRESS AND DECAY IN LANGUAGE.

# ■ DETERMINER ──────── ■

A PART OF SPEECH or word class that determines or limits a noun phrase, showing whether a phrase is definite (*the, this, my*), indefinite (*a, some, much*), or limiting it in some other way, such as through negation (*no* in *no hope*). Determiners include the articles and words traditionally classified as kinds of adjective or pronoun. They precede adjectives: *many clever people*, not *\*clever many people*; *my poor friend*, not *\*poor my friend*. Most words that function as determiners can be used alone as pronouns (*this* in *Look at this picture* and *Look at this*) or have related pronouns (*every/everyone/everything, my/mine, no/none*). Some grammarians regard as determiners such phrases as *plenty of . . .* in *We have plenty of money*.

Determiners can be subdivided into three groups according to their position in the noun phrase: (1) *Central determiners*. These may be articles (*a, the* in *a storm, the weather*), demonstratives (*this, those* in *this day, those clouds*), possessives (*my, your* in *my hat, your umbrella*), some quantifiers (*each, every, no, any, some* in *each moment, every day, no excuse, any help, some clouds*). Such determiners are mutually exclusive and contrast with adjectives, with which however they can co-occur: *the best weather, any possible help, no reliable news*. (2) *Post-determiners*. These are used after central determiners and including numbers (*two, first* in *those two problems, my first job*) and some quantifiers (*many, several* in *your many kindnesses, his several attempts*). (3) *Pre-determiners*. These are used before central determiners, mainly referring to quantity. They include: *all, both, half* (*all this time, both your houses, half a loaf*), *double, twice* and other multiplier expressions (*double the money, twice the man he was, once each day, six times a year*), fractions (*a*

*quarter of the price*), and *such* and *what* in exclamations (*Such a waste of money!, What a good time we had!*).

They can also be divided according to the countability of the nouns they co-occur with: (1) With singular countable nouns only: *a/an, each, every, either, neither.* (2) With singular countable and with uncountable nouns: *this, that.* (3) With uncountable nouns only: *much* and *little/a little,* and usually *less, least.* (4) With uncountable and with plural countable nouns: *all, enough, more, most, a lot, lots of,* and the primary meaning of *some, any.* (5) With countable plurals only: *a few, few, fewer, fewest, both, many, several, these, those,* and numbers. (6) with most common nouns: *the, no,* the possessives *my, your,* etc., and some *wh-* words (*whose roll/rolls/bread, by which date, whatever food you eat*).

**DEVIANT**. In LINGUISTICS, a unit of language is deviant if it does not conform to rules formulated in terms of data or native-speaker intuitions. A deviant unit is *ill-formed* and is generally marked by a preceding asterisk (*\*Dan does not be happy*). A form may be deviant in one variety of a language but *well-formed* in another: *sellt,* the past form of *sell* in SCOTS, as opposed to *sold* in STANDARD ENGLISH. A form can be acceptable to most users of a language but be deviant in a particular analysis because the rules cannot be formulated to include it. Similarly, an unacceptable form can be well-formed because the rules as formulated cannot exclude it. Some linguists consider the term socially loaded, especially in favour of standard usage, and do not use it. Compare ACCEPTABILITY, FIGURATIVE LANGUAGE, GRAMMATICALITY, NON-STANDARD, STYLE.

**DEVOICING**. In PHONETICS, the process by which SPEECH sounds that are normally voiced are made voiceless immediately after a voiceless obstruent: for example, the /r/ in *cream* /kri:m/ and the /w/ in *twin* /twɪn/. VOICE is slow to build up at the onset of speaking and fades at the end, so that voiced obstruents (stop and fricative consonants) are partly or wholly devoiced in initial and final position, as with the initial and final /d/ in *dead* /dɛd/ when spoken in isolation.

**DIACHRONIC AND SYNCHRONIC**. Contrasting terms in LINGUISTICS, which make a distinction between the study of the history of language (*diachronic linguistics*) and the study of a state of language at any given time (*synchronic linguistics*). Language study in the 19c was largely diachronic, but in the 20c emphasis has been on synchronic analysis. The terms were first employed by the Swiss linguist Ferdinand de Saussure, who used the analogy of a tree-trunk to describe them: a vertical cut was diachronic, a horizontal cut synchronic.

**DIACRITIC**, also **diacritical mark**. In alphabetic writing, a symbol that attaches to a letter so as to alter its value or provide some other information: in French, the acute and GRAVE ACCENTS over *e* (*é*, *è*); in GERMAN, the umlaut over *a*, *o*, *u* (*ä*, *ö*, *ü*); in SPANISH, the ACUTE ACCENT over *o* (*nación*) and the tilde over *n* (*mañana*). Some languages that have adopted and adapted the Roman alphabet use diacritics to represent values not covered by the basic letters: Czech, Polish, and Croat use them with both vowel and consonant letters to distinguish Slavonic phonemes not found in LATIN. Pinyin, the Romanized script for Chinese, uses them to represent distinctions in tone.

**Advantages and disadvantages**. Diacritics are economical, especially as alternatives to DIGRAPHS (two letters serving to represent a single sound). They can be written by hand, but are prone to distortion, misplacement, and omission in the heat of writing. In print, they have the disadvantage of requiring additional characters in a font: until the 1982 reforms, Modern GREEK required 13 varieties of the letter alpha to allow for all possible combinations of diacritics, but only two have been retained. This disadvantage is made worse by the limited number of characters on keyboards originally designed for English and may require a complex use of keys to add diacritics to letters.

**Uses**. (1) Diacritics were widely used by medieval scribes to form abbreviations by which savings could be made in the time needed for copying and the cost of parchment. An *m* or *n* might be represented by a macron above a preceding vowel (*poetā* for *poetam*, the accusative form of Latin *poeta*, poet). Omitted letters might be indicated by a suspension sign: the APOSTROPHE in M'ton, short for *Merton*. (2) In handwriting, diacrit-

ics may serve to distinguish letters, if the grouping into separate letters of several successive vertical strokes (*minims*) is unclear: for example, the 15 strokes of handwritten *minimum*. (3) A diacritic in one language and alphabet may sometimes be converted into a letter in another: for example, the Greek rough breathing or asper (') has been transcribed into Roman letters as *h* (Greek ῥυθμος becoming Latin as *rhythmus*, English as *rhythm*).

**Diacritics in English**. The use of diacritics is minimal in English. There is, however, a range of diacritical usage in or related to English, including two everyday marks with diacritical properties: the dot and the apostrophe. These are so much part of the writing system that they are seldom thought of as diacritical.

*The superscript dot*. The dot in lower-case *i* originally served to mark the stroke as a separate letter from adjacent strokes (*minims*). It was retained in *j* when that form became an independent letter. See I, J.

*The apostrophe*. Although it does not mark a particular letter, the APOSTROPHE has two diacritical functions: indicating the omission of a letter (*o* in *hadn't*) and possession (singular *boy's*, plural *boys'*).

*Foreign marks*. The use of non-native diacritics is generally kept to a minimum in English. It is optional in such FRENCH loans as *café* and *élite* (with acute accents), and is provided in others where the writer and publisher consider the provision necessary for accuracy or flavour: for example, GERMAN *Sprachgefühl* (with umlaut).

*Diaeresis*. In addition to use as the German umlaut, DIAERESIS marks are sometimes used on the second of two vowels to show that they are to be spoken separately and not as a digraph: *daïs*, *naïve*.

*Marks used in transliteration*. An internationally agreed set of diacritics is standard in the academic transliteration of texts from such sources as ARABIC and SANSKRIT script, in which the strict values of the original symbols must be shown.

*Stress marks*. Diacritics are widely used in dictionaries to mark STRESS. A stress mark is usually superscript vertical, but is sometimes oblique. Traditionally, such a mark has come after a stressed syllable (*demand'*), but currently, in conformity with the practice of the INTERNATIONAL PHONETIC ASSOCI-

ATION, the mark generally precedes the stressed syllable (*de'mand*). Frequently, two marks are used: a superscript for *primary stress*, a subscript for *secondary stress*: *'photo‚graph*. Such marks may be used in conjunction with standard spelling, in re-spelling systems, and with IPA symbols.

***Marks used in dictionaries***. In addition to stress marks, diacritics of various kinds are commonly used as aids to pronunciation and word-division in dictionaries: for example, to mark vowel quantity (the 'long' vowel ā marked with a MACRON, the 'short' vowel ă marked with a BREVE) and to indi-cate SYLLABICATION, as with the medial dot in *bath‚room*.

See CEDILLA, CIRCUMFLEX, PHONETIC TRAN-SCRIPTION, POINT, TRANSLITERATION.

**DIAERESIS**, BrE, **dieresis** AmE. A DIA-CRITIC consisting of two points set over a vowel, as in ä, ë. In English, it indicates that a vowel that might otherwise be silent is to be sounded (as in *Brontë*) or that the second vowel of a pair is to be sounded separately (*naïve*, *coöperate*). Forms of spelling that might once have had a diaeresis or a hyphen are currently often written and printed without either: *Bronte*, *naive*, *cooperate*.

■ **DIALECT** ─────────────── ■

A general and technical term for a form of a LANGUAGE: *a southern French dialect*; *the York-shire dialect*; *the dialects of the United States*; *Their teacher didn't let them speak dialect at school*, *but they spoke it at home*; *It's a dialect word—only the older people use it*. Although the term usually refers to regional speech, it can be extended to cover differences accord-ing to class and occupation; such terms as *regional dialect*, *social dialect*, *class dialect*, *occu-pational dialect*, *urban dialect*, and *rural dialect* are all used by linguists. In addition, the ex-tracted element LECT has become a term for any kind of distinct language variety spoken by an individual or group, with such derivatives as ACROLECT (a high or pres-tigious VARIETY), BASILECT (a low or socially stigmatized variety), MESOLECT (a lect in a socially intermediate position between these two). [see also EYE DIALECT.]

**Dialect, language, standard**. Most lan-guages have dialects, each with a distinctive ACCENT, GRAMMAR, VOCABULARY, and IDIOM. Traditionally, however, dialects have been regarded as socially lower than a 'proper'

form of the language (often represented as the language itself), such as *the King's* or *Queen's English* in Britain, and *le bon français* in France, or in general terms *the standard language*. Such a variety also has regional roots, but because it developed into the official and educated usage of a capital like London or Paris, it tends to be seen as non-regional, often as supra-regional, and there-fore not a dialect as such. Certain processes create a social and linguistic distance be-tween this variety and the dialects of a lan-guage: degrees of standardization in accent, grammar, orthography, and typography; its aggrandizement through the development of a literary canon and use as the medium of education and literacy; and social em-powerment through its use by the govern-ing, cultural, and scholarly élite. Many users of a STANDARD variety have tended to look down on dialect speakers as more or less 'illiterate' and teachers have often sought to impose the standard throughout a country and eliminate or greatly reduce all other 'deviant', 'low', or 'vulgar' forms, with the occasional exception of some limited 'good' dialect. Such dialect is usu-ally rural, seen as part of a romantic folk tradition or the vehicle of a favoured but unconventional writer (usually a poet, such as Robert Burns in Scotland). As a result of such factors, there is a long-standing ten-sion among such words as *dialect*, *standard*, and *language*.

**A dialect continuum**. During the 19–20c there has been considerable study of dialects in their own right and in relation to the standard variety of a language. As a re-sult of this study, philologists and dialec-tologists generally regard a dialect as a historical subtype of a language and a lan-guage as the aggregate of the features of its dialects. Within a language, there is usually a *dialect continuum*: speakers of Dialect A can understand and be understood by speakers of Dialect B, and C by B, and so on, but at the extremes of the continuum speakers of A and Z may be mutually unintelligible. The A and Z communities may therefore feel justified in supposing or arguing that A and Z are different languages. If politics inter-venes and the speakers of A and Z come to be citizens of different countries (as with Spanish and Portuguese, or Swedish and Danish), the dialects may well be socially revalued as 'languages' (in due course with their own dialects and standard variety).

Despite their differences, dialects have more shared than differing features, and those in which they agree (phonological, syntactic, lexical, idiomatic, etc.) serve as the defining core of a language, while the clusters of differences serve as the defining cores of the various dialects. Thus, a language X that has dialects A, B, C, D, E, may have 15 features, 12 of which are shared by A, B, C, 10 by B, C, D, 11 by B, D, E, and so forth. Perhaps only 8 features are common to all five. If they are, they form the core or common features of X, to which may be added additional features acquired through the conventions necessary for a standard language.

**The evolution of dialects**. Using a biological analogy, dialects can be described as the result of evolutionary speciation. The tendency of all languages to change in one detail or another and so develop dialects is restrained only by the need of communication between speakers, and so preserve a common core. Written forms, accompanied by the inculcation of a standard by the social and educational élites of a nation or group of nations, slow the process of change but cannot prevent it. Dialects are in fact often less changeable than the standard; their speakers tend to live in stable communities and to conserve forms of the language which are 'older' in terms of the development of the standard. Such a standard, however, is in origin also a dialect, and in the view of some linguists can and should be called the *standard dialect* (although for many this phrase is a contradiction in terms). Dialects prevail regionally while the standard is the usage of the nation at large, or at least of its most prominent and dominant representatives. As a consequence, many native speakers of a dialect may learn the standard as a secondary variety of their own language.

**The distribution of dialects**. Geographically, dialects are the result of settlement history. Dialect development can be understood to some extent in relation to topography: where populations can communicate easily, dialectal differences develop more slowly than where they lose immediate (or all) contact. An effective method of studying such matters is the science of LINGUISTIC GEOGRAPHY. Individual features (sounds, words, grammatical forms, etc.) can be displayed on maps showing where one or another feature prevails in use and where competing forms are found. Lines on a *dialect map* outline the area within which any form is regularly used. Alternatively, the differing features may be shown on maps with dots or other symbols, giving a visual dimension to the data. Certain features of dialect can also be seen in relation to social factors not necessarily connected with geography. The type of language one speaks (a *social dialect* or SOCIOLECT) depends on community, family background, occupation, degree of education, and the like. Where a standard form has become established, the tendency is to consider it 'right' and to denigrate other varieties, whose only fault may be that they are out of style in the mainstream of a language. Distinctive dialects are most fully preserved in isolated areas (along sea coasts, on islands, in mountain areas) where they are little influenced by outsiders and the population is relatively self-sustaining. The dialects of large cities, however, run the social gamut of the language, with outside features being brought in and new features being created more or less continuously. In terms of the distribution of the English Language worldwide, the traditional use of the term *dialect* works well with regard to the British Isles and North America, but not nearly so well for Australia, New Zealand, and South Africa, and not at all well in the Caribbean, West and East Africa, and Asia. The following dialect entries are restricted therefore to England, Scotland, Wales, Ireland, the United States, and Canada.

## Dialect in England

In its primordial form on the European mainland and in its early stages in Britain (5–7c), English was a continuum of dialects whose traces survive only in texts. Present-day terms do not serve well in discussing the period: 'English' and 'German' now have different meanings and 'language' and 'dialect' inadequately describe the condition of Germanic speech when the Roman Empire was in decline. Until *c*.600, apparently all the tribes could understand each other: for example, on their way to convert the English in 597, the missionary Augustine and his companions engaged Frankish interpreters to help them. However, polarization was already taking place between the continental and insular Germans. The settlers in Britain developed their own usages and those on the mainland were absorbed into other spheres of linguistic growth: the Angles into Danish, the Saxons into Low German.

**The Angelcynn**. Around 730, the historian Bede called the invaders Angles, Saxons, and Jutes, but other evidence indicates that they also included Frisians and probably Franks. Once established, they called themselves the *Angelcynn* ('Anglekin'), with *Englisc* as their common speech. The Angles settled in the MIDLANDS and along the east coast, from somewhere north of the Thames to the Forth. The Anglian or Anglic dialects were *Mercian*, associated with the kingdom of Mercia and spoken from the Thames to the Humber, and *Northumbrian*, associated with the kingdom of Northumbria, and spoken from the Humber to the Forth. The Jutes settled in and near Kent, but the dialect for the region is known as *Kentish*, not *Jutish*. The Saxons settled around the Thames, the south, and the south-west: East Saxons in *Essex*, Middle Saxons in *Middlesex*, South Saxons in *Sussex*, and West Saxons in *Wessex*. Each group had its own usages, but *West Saxon*, the dialect of Wessex, became dominant and for a time served as the literary language. The early dialects continued into the period of Middle English, many having undergone considerable change under the impact of the Danish settlements of the 8–9c.

**Middle English dialects**. By the 11c, the division of the island into the three domains of England, Scotland, and Wales had taken place and from that time forward the language developed with a border between the dialects of England and Scotland. The dialects of Middle English are generally classified as: *Northern*, both south and north of the border, the northern branch developing into Scots; *West Midland*, extending to the Welsh marches; *East Midland*, including EAST ANGLIA and the LONDON area; *Southern*, extending west to Celtic Cornwall; *Kentish*, stopping short of the Isle of Wight. The social and literary standard form of English which slowly emerged after the Norman Conquest in 1066 was based not on the Southern but the East Midland dialect, with an increasing Scandinavian overlay.

**Dialects and standard**. With the introduction by Caxton of the printing press in London in 1476 a great boost was given to the speech of the capital. As the standard language evolved, writing in the other dialects of England rapidly came to an end. Regional speech, increasingly commented on as harsh and difficult to understand, came to be seen as the language of the lower classes; the 16c diarist John Aubrey, for example, pointed out that Sir Walter Raleigh rather surprisingly remained all his life a speaker of Devon dialect. Despite the powerful influence of print and the prestige of London, however, letters, manuscripts, public comment, and representations of dialect in novels all show that local speech continued among the lesser gentry and the upper middle classes until well into the 18c, and among industrialists, politicians, and other public figures from lower middle-class and working-class backgrounds until the present day.

**Literary dialect and dialectology**. Dialect was used by Shakespeare and others to depict various provincial and rustic characters, and a distinctive form of south-western speech began to develop as a stage country-bumpkin dialect: see MUMMERSET. From the 18c onward, novelists have sought to represent dialect, especially in conversation; exponents of dialect writing in England include George Eliot in *Adam Bede* (1859) and Thomas Hardy in the Wessex novels. See DIALOG(UE). Interest by scholars in the varieties of English grew at the beginning of the 17c and an early mention by Alexander Gil in his *Polychronicon* (1619) began a tradition of examining and comparing dialect forms against standard English. Although scholars realized that there was a historical development behind the forms of their speech, dialect speakers became increasingly identified as lower class. Throughout the 17–18c, interest in both standard and dialect varieties of English continued to grow. Many clergymen recorded the grammar and vocabulary of their parishioners, and a number of word lists and monographs of various kinds, often linked to descriptions of local industrial processes, began to appear. The *English Dialect Society* often published these as part of its work towards an English dialect dictionary.

**The present day**. Currently, there is a widespread belief that local dialect is dying out and to a certain extent this is true of vocabulary, but strong local pronunciation continues to be heard, in London as well as in the regions, and from the 1970s began to be used increasingly widely on radio and television: for example, in such dramatic series as *Coronation Street* (Manchester), *Crossroads* (BIRMINGHAM), *Auf Wiedersehen Pet* (Newcastle), *Bread* (Liverpool), and *EastEnders* (London). In such large cities robust local forms of pronunciation and grammar, with their own social varieties within an area, show little sign of diminishment. These forms continue to change and develop over generations; pronunciations show the sporadic influence of RECEIVED PRONUNCIATION (a southern middle- and upper-class accent often described as the standard accent of England) but with considerable modification: for example, in Newcastle the traditionally developed /stiən/ and /stjen/ for *stone*, from a Middle English unrounded form /staːn/, can be heard alongside a loaned /støːn/ and /stəʊn/, developed from the more southerly Middle English /stoːn/.

See COCKNEY, CUMBRIA, DORSET, EAST MIDLAND DIALECT, ENGLISH DIALECT SOCIETY, ESTUARY ENGLISH, GEORDIE, LANCASHIRE, SCOUSE, SOMERSET, WEST COUNTRY, YORKSHIRE.

## Dialect in Scotland

The dialects of SCOTS fall into four main regional groups: (1) Those of the Northern Isles: see ORKNEY AND SHETLAND DIALECTS. (2) *Northern Scots*, from Caithness to Aberdeenshire and Angus. (3) *Southern Scots*, the Border districts of Roxburgh and Annandale, and Eskdale. (4) *Central Scots*, much of the rest of the Scots-speaking area, including the working-class dialects of EDINBURGH, GLASGOW, and other urban areas of Central Scotland. The working-class urban dialects are identified by both socially and regionally delimited features: see GUTTER SCOTS. The regional markers of the mainland dialects include:

**Pronunciation**. (1) The Northern use since the 15c of *f-* where other dialects have *wh-*, as in *Fa fuppit the fyte fulpie?* Who whipped the white whelp? (2) The different outcomes of the old front, rounded vowel *ui* /øː/ in such words as *guid* (good), *scuil* (school), *muin* (moon), *uise* (use: noun and verb), *puir* (poor), *shui* (shoe). In Angus and the Mearns in Northern Scots and in Southern Scots this pronunciation persists. In the

rest of Northern, however, the original vowel has since the 16c been unrounded to *ee* /i/: *meen* moon, *eese* use (noun), *eeze* use (verb), *shee* shoe. In the Grampian Region, however, after *g-* and *k-* the outcome is *-wee-*, with *gweed* good, and *skweel* school, but *geed* and *skeel* further north. In much of the Central dialect, the results of a different and more recent unrounding are conditioned by the *Scottish Vowel-Length Rule*. In these dialects. SVLR long environments yield *ai* /e/: *pair* poor, *shae* shoe, *yaize* use (verb), but in SVLR short environments the outcome is an *i*-like vowel /ɪ/: *min* moon, *bit* boot, *gid* good, *yis* use (noun). (3) South-Eastern and Southern dialects have *twae*, *whae*, *away*, *whare*, *waken*, *waiter* for Western and Northern *twaw/twaa*, *whaw/whaa/faa*, *awa/awaa*, *whaur/whaar/faar*, *wauken/waaken*, *wauter/waater* (two, who, away, where, waken, water) on either side of a swathe of country from Musselburgh on the Firth of Forth to Gatehouse-of-Fleet on the Solway Firth.

**Grammar**. The grammar of the dialects of the far north and far south is more archaic, in retaining the old opposition between the present participle and the verbal noun in *He's aye gutteran aboot* (participle, with *-an*) and *He's fond o gutterin aboot* (verbal noun, with *-in* or *-een*) and, though now almost obsolete, except in Orkney and Shetland, traces of the pronoun system with *thou/thee/thy* as well as *ye/you/your*. The use of *on-*, *ohn-* /on/ as a negative with participles is now confined to the North-East (Grampian Region): *to haud her ohn kent at she had tint it* (to keep her 'not known'/ignorant that she had lost it); *Fa could be on lauch'n at that?* (Who could keep from laughing at that?).

**Vocabulary**. Of the innumerable local items of vocabulary in the mainland dialects, some result from the influence of Scandinavian in Caithness, such as *aikle* a molar tooth, *gilt* a large haystack, *roog* a peat store, *scorrie* a young seagull, *scroo* a stack. For the much larger number surviving in the dialects of the Northern Isles, see ORKNEY AND SHETLAND DIALECTS. Caithness also displays local Gaelic influence with *ask* a chain for tethering cattle, *brotag* a caterpillar, *buckie-faulie* a rose-hip, primrose, *cairie* a breed of sheep, *coachie* soft, spongy, *cown* to weep, *crellag* a bluebottle, *cyowtach* smart in appearance, and many others. Similar, but individually different, lists of Gaelic-derived words can be cited for other parts of the

North, for the North-East, for Kintyre, and for the South-West, especially Galloway. Other variations result from the locally patchy effects of obsolescence and innovation, as with the words for 'soapy lather', for which the older *graith* is widely distributed in mainland Scotland, except the West (around Glasgow) and the South-West, where since the 18c it has been superseded by the newer *sapples*. The dialects also display numerous, seemingly random or inexplicable, variations in words for everyday notions, like such synonyms for *mud* around the country as *dubs, gutters, glabber, clabber, glaur*.

**Dialect literature**. Written representations of local forms of Scots began appearing in the late 17c in distinctive adaptations of the traditional 'mainstream' orthography of Scots. The North-East in particular established its own regional standard in the 18c, and this has provided many works of note, such as William Alexander's novel *Johnny Gibb of Gushetneuk* (1871), the dialogue of which is in a subtly modulated rendering of Aberdeenshire Scots, and today in the poetry of Flora Garry and the descriptive prose of David Ogston. See DORIC HIGHLAND ENGLISH, SCOTTISH ENGLISH, ULSTER SCOTS.

## Dialect in Wales

Dialect differences in the WELSH language are to a large extent limited to variation in accents, the vocabulary having been standardized by literature, education, and the media. Dialects of English in Wales are as diverse as elsewhere in Britain. They vary in terms of pronunciation, grammar, and vocabulary, but can be broadly categorized as: (1) The English of people who are bilingual, Welsh/English, and whose English is strongly influenced by Welsh. (2) Dialects of English similar to those in neighbouring countries of England, and often sharing features, especially at the syntactic level, with other working-class BrE dialects. (3) Standard English with a Welsh accent. (4) Standard English with an RP accent. See WELSH ENGLISH.

## Dialect in Ireland

Because of the spread of education and the influence of the media, it is becoming increasingly difficult to subdivide the continuum of English found in Ireland. However,

three main regional and several urban dialects can be distinguished. They are all rhotic, with a retroflex *r*, and share phonological features with AmE. The regional dialects are: (1) *Anglo-Irish*, used by the descendants of English settlers and found throughout the country with the exception of the most northerly counties. (2) ULSTER SCOTS, in the northernmost counties, the speech of the descendants of 17c Protestant Scots settlers. (3) *Hiberno-Irish*, spoken by usually Catholic people whose ancestral tongue was Gaelic. In any region, HIBERNO-ENGLISH approximates to the dominant dialect, whether ANGLO-IRISH or Ulster Scots but, in the Gaeltacht and in less educated, rural usage, it displays a strong Gaelic substrate. Ireland has fewer urban dwellers than most Western European countries, but each city, including Armagh, BELFAST, Cork, Derry, Donegal, DUBLIN, Galway, and Limerick, has its own forms and sphere of linguistic influence.

## Dialect in the United States

Americans tend to think that varieties of English are more determined by region than by any other factor that shapes usage, such as age, ethnicity, gender, and social class. Scholars who have investigated the matter have been influenced by the theory of dialect geography formulated in the 19c by A. J. Ellis for England, by Jules Gilliéron and Edmond Edmont for France, and by Georg Wenker for Germany. As a result, investigations have presumed the idea of long-settled and stable regions, an idea appropriate for Europe but less apt to the more recent and fluid settlement patterns of the US. Even so, AmE dialects are conventionally treated under four broad geographical headings: North, Coastal South, Midland, and West.

**The North**. The Northern dialect, stretching from NEW ENGLAND and NEW YORK westward to Oregon and Washington, was shaped by migration from the 17c colonial settlements in Boston and New York. While the population of the region was greatly enlarged by waves of migration (in the 1850s from northern Europe, especially Scandinavia and Germany, in the 1890s from eastern and southern Europe, and in the 1930s from the American South), the northern metropolitan areas are relatively uniform (Buffalo, Cleveland, Detroit, Chicago, and

Minneapolis). Both BOSTON and New York English have changed in ways not followed in their daughter cities to the west; despite their internal diversity, however, both Boston and New York remain distinctly Northern.

***Northern pronunciation***. (1) The most noticeable difference within the region is that New York and New England east of the Connecticut River are non-rhotic areas, while the western portion of the North is rhotic. Linking *r*, common in many non-rhotic dialects of English, occurs in New England in expressions like *the idea/r of it*. (2) The Northern dialect lags behind Midland and Western varieties in the vowel merger that makes homophones of *cot* and *caught*: in New England, where the merger is beginning to occur, speakers select the first vowel; in the Midland and West, the second vowel is used for both. (3) *Grease* tends to rhyme with *lease* in the North and West, rhyming with *freeze* elsewhere. (4) In Northern speech, *matter* and *madder* are often near-homophones.

***Northern grammar***. (1) A distinctive syntactic feature is *all the* + an adjective in the comparative degree: *That's all the farther I could go* (That's as far as I could go). (2) *Dove* as the past tense of *dive* is apparently a North American invention by analogy with *drive/drove* and *weave/wove*. Widely attested in Northern and in CanE, *dove* is holding its own in its historic territory and spreading in AmE. (3) *Had ought* and *hadn't ought*, while more common in less formal contexts, are Northernisms for *ought* and *ought not*, though the usage has spread elsewhere: 'If you don't like people, you hadn't ought to be in politics at all' (Harry S. Truman). (4) The Northern term *cellar* (basement) appears in a characteristic prepositional phrase *down cellar*: *Won't you go down cellar and get some potatoes?*

***Northern vocabulary***. Lexical usage provides the clearest evidence of the unity of the Northern region. In comparison to other varieties of AmE, Northern does not show many survivals of words or senses that have become archaic in BrE. The following terms are known elsewhere in the US and some are used for nationally distributed products, but they form a cluster that defines the Northern region: *American fries* boiled potatoes sliced and then fried in a pan, *bismark/danish* sweet pastry, *bitch* to complain, *bloodsucker* a leech, *cabbage salad* coleslaw, *comforter* a heavy quilt, *cowboy* a reckless driver, *grackle* a kind of blackbird, *ice-cream social* a gathering of people for refreshments, often to raise money for a worthy cause, *nightcrawler* a large earthworm, *pitch* the resin of coniferous trees, *sub(marine)* a sandwich prepared on a long roll, containing meat, cheese, and other ingredients, *sweet corn* maize grown for human consumption, *teeter-totter* a see-saw. Other languages have contributed to the Northern wordstock: *babushka* a head scarf (Polish and Russian), *cruller* a small fried sweet cake (Dutch), *frankfurter/forter, frankfurt/fort, frank* a cooked sausage, hot dog (German), *quahog* a thick-shelled edible clam (Narraganset), *schnozzle* nose (from Yiddish).

**The Coastal South**. Historically, the Coastal Southern dialect centres on the Atlantic port cities of the states of Virginia, the Carolinas, and Georgia, blending westward along the Gulf Coast into TEXAS. These areas are distinct both from the North and from their own hinterlands, whose dialect has conventionally been labelled *South Midland*. Coastal Southern was formed in a time of plantation and ranch agriculture, an economy that required large-scale operations, while the generally hillier interior regions were typified by villages and farms often close to the subsistence level. Plantation agriculture required an extensive labour force to grow rice, tobacco, and cotton, three early cash crops in America, and large numbers of Africans were enslaved to tend them. While the extent of African influence on Southern AmE remains a subject for debate, it is generally agreed that African influences remain in *Gullah*, a creole spoken on the offshore islands of South Carolina and Georgia. See AFRICAN-AMERICAN VERNACULAR ENGLISH, APPALACHIAN ENGLISH, CAJUN, GULLAH, NEW ORLEANS, SOUTHERN ENGLISH, SPANISH.

***Southern pronunciation***. (1) Coastal Southern is non-rhotic. While non-rhotic Northerners employ a vowel in place of historic r (in New England, seaboard New York, and New Jersey north of Philadelphia), many Southerners use the previous vowel alone, making *door* rhyme with *doe* and *torn* with *tone*. Linking r is rare. (2) The same tendency for diphthongs to become monophthongs is a related Southern feature, so that *hide* is a near rhyme of both *hod* and non-rhotic *hard*. On the other hand, Southern and Midland AmE add a vowel not used elsewhere in words like *loft* which results in a near rhyme with *lout*. (3) Some word-internal consonant clusters can be captured by such spellings as *bidness* (business) and *Babtist* (Baptist). (4) Merger of vowels in *pin* and *pen*, *since* and *cents* (to the vowel of the first in each pair) is a Southern feature that is spreading elsewhere.

**Southern grammar**. (1) A feature of the region is *all the* + adjective in the positive degree: *That's all the fast I can run* (That's as fast as I can run). (2) Though more common in Black than White speech (and more common among men and the young), the use of invariant *be* is especially Southern: *She be here tomorrow*; *I be pretty busy*; *That land don't be sandy*. (3) Coastal Southern and Upper South are typified by double modals: *She might can do it*; *Could you may go?* (4) These areas also share a tolerance for *ain't* in informal contexts, though *ain't* is the universal shibboleth in AmE and especially stigmatized in the North. In the Coastal and Upper South, degrees of stigma attach to *ain't* increasingly from the set phrase *ain't I?*, to its use for *are not* (*They ain't here*), to its use for *have not* (*You ain't told us yet*).

**Southern vocabulary**. The complex settlement history of the South is evident in cultural and linguistic differences between the coastal plains and the hill country. Much of the distinctive coastal vocabulary consists of expressions that have become archaic in other varieties of English: *all-overs* feelings of uneasiness, *antigoglin* askew, slantwise, *(ap)preciate it* thank you, *bank* a storage heap of potatoes, other vegetables, or coal, *branch* a brook, stream, *carry* escort, *firedogs* andirons, *gullywasher* a violent rainstorm, *hand* a farm worker, *hull* the shell of a nut, *kinfolk* relatives, *lick* a sharp blow, *Scat! Gesundheit!* Bless you!, *slouch* a lazy or incompetent person, *squinch* to squint. Other languages have contributed to Southern: *hominy* hulled kernels of corn/maize, *terrapin* a turtle (the Amerindian languages of Virginia and used more in the South than elsewhere); *cooter* a turtle, *gumbo* soup thickened with okra pods (the languages of West African slaves); *armoire* wardrobe, *bayou* small creek or river, *jambalaya* a stew made with rice and various meats, *lagniappe* a small gift given by a merchant to a customer (the French of Louisiana). Farther

west, there is Spanish influence: *arroyo* a brook or creek, *llano* an open, grassy plain, *riata* lariat, lasso, *vaquero* cowboy.

**The Midland**. Between Northern and Coastal Southern is a region that has been subject to much dispute. Some scholars have treated it as a unified area divided into North and South Midland; others emphasize its affiliation with its neighbours and describe it as *Lower North* and *Upper South*. The term *Midland* emphasizes the settlement pattern that flowed from Philadelphia in two directions: one, westward through Pennsylvania into Ohio, Indiana, and Illinois; the other, south-west into the hill country of Kentucky, Tennessee, the interior of the Southern coastal states, Missouri, and Arkansas. The south-western direction of migration brought settlers into contact with the transportation routes northward from New Orleans along the Mississippi, Arkansas, and Ohio rivers, and these contacts left enduring traces on the dialect.

**Midland pronunciation**. (1) In common with other AmE dialects west of the Atlantic coast, Midland is rhotic. (2) Philadelphia, the only rhotic city on the Atlantic seaboard, is the focal area for Midland, and its dialect has traditionally influenced the hinterland, including Pittsburgh, Columbus, Indianapolis, Springfield, and St Louis. Thus, the boundary between the now obsolescent Northern pronunciation of *creek* (rhyming with *trick*) meets the Midland *creek* (rhyming with *seek*) along an east–west line running parallel to the Pennsylvania migration routes. (3) The merger of vowels in *tot* and *taught* begins in a narrow band in central Pennsylvania and spreads north and south to influence the West, where the merger is universal. (4) In the Ohio River valley westward to Missouri, the vowel of *itch* makes a near rhyme with *each*, so that *fish* and *television* have the sound of the vowel in *meek*. (5) Another Midland vowel is found in *bit* and *hill*, with a diphthong resembling the non-rhotic pronunciation of *beer*. That pronunciation is beginning to spread among younger speakers in the inland North.

**Midland grammar**. (1) Though increasingly archaic, *a-* prefixation to verbs ending in *-ing* is a well-known Midland feature: *She went a-visiting yesterday*; *They were a-coming across the bridge*. (2) The use of *anymore* in the sense of 'nowadays' (and without the requirement of a prior negative) is spreading to other regions from a Midland base: *My aunt makes hats all the time anymore*; *We use a gas stove anymore*. (3) Regions of the Midland influenced by the German settlements of east-central Pennsylvania employ *all* to refer to a supply of food or drink that has run out: *The pot roast is all* (elsewhere *all gone*).

***Midland vocabulary***. (1) Distinctive terms for this region include: *blinds* roller window shade, *fishing worm* earthworm, *mango* sweet or bell pepper, *woolly worm* a caterpillar. (2) As with the other regions, some formerly limited usages have come into more general use: *bucket* pail, *hull* to remove the outer covering of a bean, *off* as in *I want off at the next bus stop*. (3) The isolation of the southern part of the Midland area, its poor soil and chronic poverty, made it inhospitable to further migrants after initial settlement by Scots-Irish and Germans. Hence, few influences from other languages are apparent in the vocabulary, which is typified by relic forms and archaisms no longer found elsewhere in AmE: for example, *brickle* brittle, *donsie* sickly, *poke* sack, bag, *redd* to tidy up (all from Scots).

**The West**. The West was first settled by English speakers after the gold rush of the 1850s. Southern migration along the Butterfield Stage Route brought settlers from Missouri and Arkansas through central Texas, New Mexico, and Arizona, to California; the Santa Fe trail also originated in Missouri and reached southern California by a somewhat more northerly route. Northern trails and subsequently the railroad took settlers into the central valley of California and San Francisco through Nebraska, Wyoming, and Utah. The Oregon Trail and its successor railroad connected the northern tier of states to the Pacific Northwest. For historically minded dialectologists, initial investigations of the Western dialect region dwelt on the continuity of migration westward on the presumption that Northerners preferred the northern Pacific coast while Southerners were mainly attracted to the more salubrious climate in southern California. Thus, it was no surprise that such studies emphasized continuity: for example, *curtains* (roller window shades), a Northern term, appears more commonly from San Francisco northward; *arroyo* can be traced from Texas westward to Los Angeles, but does not extend north to San Francisco. What is missed by this approach is the fact that the West became a source of linguistic innovation spreading back to the longer-settled dialect regions. While it may have been a 'mixed' region in the past, California and the Pacific Northwest are now coming to be seen as a coherent dialect region in their own right.

***Western pronunciation***. In some respects, the West brings to completion processes begun elsewhere. The merger of the vowels of *Don* and *Dawn*, noted above, is virtually universal in the West, and its influence is spreading eastward. The vowel in such words as *measure* and *fresh* (which has the value of *bet* in much of the East) is increasingly given the sound of *bait*, so that *edge* and *age* have come to resemble each other. Though Westerners distinguish *seal* from *sill*, Easterners hear these as nearly identical (with the vowel of *sill* in both); as a result, outsiders regard the Western pronunciation of *really* as identical to their own pronunciation of *rilly*.

***Western grammar***. The fact that Western is the least intensively studied of AmE dialects may contribute to the lack of evidence for a distinctive grammar of the region. Subgroups within the region employ marked syntax: *We all the time used to go outside* (Hispanic-influenced English, East Los Angeles); *I been tripping for three weeks* (1960s San Francisco drug usage); *Moray eel you can spear it* (HAWAIIAN ENGLISH); *Do you have any bets on?* (Las Vegas gambling talk); *Pete's wooding those trucks down* (logger usage, Pacific Northwest); *Here we shopping and went through the town to see things and places* (Apachean English of the Great Plains); *Like, no biggie* (San Fernando Valley teenage talk). All these examples suggest that grammatical variation in Western (as in other varieties of AmE) would profit from further study.

***Western vocabulary***. Some common Western terms are uncommon elsewhere except in reference to Western language or culture: *bar pit* a ditch by the side of an ungraded road, *bush pilot* a daring pilot of light aircraft used to reach remote Alaskan areas, *canyon* a steep-sided, narrow valley, *gunny sack* a burlap bag, *lug* a field crate for fruit and vegetables, *parking* (*strip*) a band of grass between sidewalk and curb on a city street, *sourdough bread* bread started with a piece of fermented dough.

The most important foreign-language

influence on Western is Mexican Spanish. Many borrowings are used mainly in southern California, Arizona, and New Mexico, but some are more widely known: *adios* goodbye, *adobe* sun-dried brick, *bronco* wild, mean, rough (from a wild or partly broken horse), *embarcadero* wharf, *hombre* guy, fellow, *Santa Ana* a seasonal hot, dry wind in southern California. Various terms for Mexican cookery were introduced into English elsewhere but are regarded as typical of the region and have widespread currency there: *carne seco* chipped beef, *frijoles* beans, *langosta* crayfish or spiny lobster, *tortilla* thin, round, unleavened bread. Other languages have contributed words to Western that have come to be known outside the region: *aloha* a greeting or farewell, *lei* a garland of flowers (Hawaiian); *chinook* a warm winter wind, *Sasquatch* (also called 'Bigfoot') a legendary hominid animal (Amerindian languages of the Pacific Northwest); *dim sum* meat-filled dumpling, *kung fu* a martial art (Chinese); *honcho* a strong leader, boss, *Nisei* a person of Japanese descent born or educated in the US (Japanese). See CHICANO ENGLISH.

**Influences on US dialects**. The usage of all Americans, regardless of dialect, is influenced by social networks that include gender, age and peer group, social class, ethnic background, occupations, and recreations. Some distinctive varieties have gained national prominence, such as JEWISH ENGLISH through its use by entertainers and others. People who are not Jewish are likely to have at least a passive knowledge of it and a sprinkling of such loanwords as *chutzpah, schmaltzy, schmooze*. Other varieties present stereotypes, such as *Country-Western*, originating in the Appalachian and Ozark regions of the Upper South, which has become well known in the 20c through country-and-western music, associated movies, and radio communication among airline pilots, truck drivers, and others who imitate them. *Hispanic English* has been increasingly disseminated through popular culture and the media, though outsiders may not appreciate that many who speak it have little or no competence in Spanish. Refined Southern speech has been made internationally familiar in the models presented by films and plays, and a Texas style has become popular through Western films and the TV soap opera *Dallas*. AFRICAN-AMERICAN VERNACULAR ENGLISH has long created social solidarity among African-

Americans and has been rendered (sometimes abusively) in popular entertainment. Such varieties, having national prominence, are available for imitation in dialect and ethnic jokes with enough shibboleths to identify the target group.

Other communities, though less widely known, exert similarly powerful constraints on their members and neighbours, for example the Finnish-flavoured English of northern Michigan; the German-influenced English spoken by the Amish and Mennonite communities of central Pennsylvania, Ohio, and Indiana; Native American or INDIAN ENGLISH, especially in Arizona and New Mexico; the *Polish English* of north-eastern industrial cities like Buffalo and Detroit; the *Cajun English* of Louisiana, with its French and Caribbean-creole traces. Even a single community can develop a distinctive linguistic identity: between 1880 and 1920, Boonville, a small town in northern California, developed a thoroughgoing transformation of English known as *Boontling*, a lingo that made members of the community at once unintelligible to outsiders when they so wished and conscious of the importance of being Boonters.

## Dialect in Canada.

In the traditional view, the English of Canada has four major regional dialects: *Atlantic* covering the MARITIME PROVINCES (New Brunswick, Nova Scotia, and Prince Edward Island) and the island of NEWFOUNDLAND as a distinctive sub-area; *QUEBEC*, with Montreal and the Eastern Townships as focal areas; the OTTAWA VALLEY, adjacent to the federal capital, Ottawa; and *General Canadian*, from Toronto westward to the Pacific. More recent scholarship, however, regards 'General Canadian' as a class-based urban dialect of broadcasting and educated speech, and closer scrutiny invites a description of regional differences that mark the *West* (British Columbia), the *Arctic North* (the Yukon, Northwest Territories, northern Quebec, and Labrador), the *Prairies* (Alberta, Saskatchewan, and Manitoba), and SOUTHERN ONTARIO. Variations from region to region include distinctive local words, many of which relate to local conditions and occupations: for example, in the West *boomsticks* 66-feet-long logs connected by *boom chains* to contain floating logs to be towed to a mill; in the Prairies *Calgary redeye* beer with tomato juice added, *stampede* a rodeo, *oil borer* (in contrast to *oil driller* in eastern CANADIAN ENGLISH and in AmE); in southern Ontario, *reeve* the principal officer of a township; Ottawa Valley *snye* a side channel, especially one bypassing rapids (from French *chenail*); Quebec *whisky blanc* a colourless alcoholic drink (compare AmE *white lightning*); and Newfoundland, *outport* a coastal settlement other than the capital St John's. Many distinctive words have been borrowed from indigenous regional languages, such as: (1) *The West*. Loans from local Amerindian languages in the *Lower Mainland* area of British Columbia (the city of Vancouver and its hinterlands) are virtually unknown elsewhere in Canada or in the US: for example, *cowichan* a vividly patterned sweater, *kokanee* land-locked salmon, *saltchuck* ocean, *skookum* big, strong, *tyee* chief, boss. (2) *The Arctic North*. Loanwords from Inuktitut: for example, *angakok* a shaman, *chimo* a greeting, toast before drinking, *kabloona* a non-Inuit, a White, *ouk* a command to a sleddog to turn right, *tupik* a tent of animal skins. (3) *The Prairies*. Loanwords from Cree, known only in the region: for example, *kinnikinik* a smoking mixture including sumac leaves and tobacco, *saskatoon* an edible berry and the shrub on which it grows, *wachee* a greeting (from Cree *wacheya*, from English *what cheer*).

**DIALECTOLOGY**. The study of DIALECTS, that is, of variant features within a language, their history, differences of form and meaning, interrelationships, distribution, and, more broadly, their spoken as distinct from their literary forms. The discipline recognizes all variations within the bounds of any given language; it classifies and interprets them according to historical origins, principles of development, characteristic features, areal distribution, and social correlates. The scientific study of dialects dates from the mid-19c, when philologists using data preserved in texts began to work out the historical or diachronic development of the Indo-European languages. Their interest was etymological and systematic. Scientific phonetics and the principle that sound change was not erratic but followed discoverable rules or laws, were a basic part of the growth of dialectology. Living dialects were seen to furnish a huge treasury of living data on phonology, lexicology, and other features of language that written texts could not furnish. The linguist's task was to gather, analyse, and interpret this living body of language. Dialectology is pursued through a number of methods; the American linguist W. Nelson Francis (*Dialectology*, 1983) describes the prevailing methods as traditional, structural, and generative.

In *traditional dialectology* the collection of data is the primary requirement. This entails fieldwork, the more detailed and massive the better, within the limits of practicability, and its presentation in the form of dictionaries, grammars, atlases, and monographs. This method Francis calls 'item-centered', emphasizing the individual datum and paying little attention to underlying system. In *structural dialectology*, the investigator seeks to find both the structure or system by which a dialect holds together or achieves synchronic identity and how it is changed by the introduction of any new feature. Since any change in the system affects every feature of it, it becomes in effect a different system, whose parts are, however, diachronically connected. There is a paradoxical element here which is partly due to difficulties of definition. In *generative dialectology*, the investigator holds that the language exists within the speaker as a competence which is never fully realized in performance. This competence, lying beneath actual language as it is produced (and as it is recorded by traditional dialectologists), works by a series of rules which transform it into actual speech. Thus, it is the dialectologist's task to find a basic system whose rules produce as economically as possible the surface structure of actual dialect. The complexities or variations within a language (its dialectal variants) may thus be traced back to a putative source form from which in the course of time they could by speciation have developed. However, without the mass of data which traditional dialectologists have furnished, theoretical systems could not have been either proposed or refined.

■ **DIALOGUE** ─────────── ■

AmE also **dialog**. A traditional semi-technical term for a CONVERSATION, especially if it is formal, or is presented in WRITING or print according to the conventions of drama and fiction.

**Dialogue in drama**. The playwrights of the Elizabethan and Jacobean periods (late

16c, early 17c) were the first to develop a full set of conventions for writing and presenting dialogue in English. Their use of dialogue, especially in blank verse, followed the classical tradition, in which speakers take turns to make lengthy, set-piece speeches, regardless of whether they are at ease in their homes or surrounded by enemies on the field of battle. Initial English attempts at dialogue did not therefore differ much from the stylized conversations of Homer's *Iliad*, except that at times the conversation of their characters could be short, sharp, and close to real life, as in Shakespeare's *Julius Caesar* (3. 2):

> 1st PLEBEIAN.
> Me thinkes there is much reason in his sayings.
> 4th PLEBEIAN.
> If thou consider rightly of the matter.
> Cæsar ha's had great wrong.
> 3rd PLEBEIAN.       Ha's hee not Masters?
> I feare there will a worse come in his place.

Prose dialogue was often reserved for less elevated moments and characters in a play, such as the comic exploitation of kinds of English that were remote from the London stage, as with the Irishman Mackmorrice in *Henry V* (3. 3):

> GOWER. How now, Captaine *Mackmorrice*, haue you quit the Mynes? haue the Pioners giuen o're?
> MACKMORRICE. By Chrish Law tish ill done: the work ish giue ouer, the Trumpet sound the Retreat. By my Hand I sweare, and my fathers Soule, the Worke ish ill done: it ish giue ouer: I would haue blowed vp the Towne, so Chrish saue me law, in an houre. O tish ill done, tish ill done: by my Hand tish ill done.

Prose was the common medium of drama by the end of the 17c, although Dryden and others wrote tragedies in heroic couplets. Prose was considered to be more realistic than verse and verse has never again been the principal medium of dramatic dialogue in English. In 18c prose drama, the presentation of turn-taking continued in much the same classical style as the longer speeches of Hamlet and Othello: for example, the following excerpt from Sheridan's comedy, *The Rivals* (1775):

> SIR ANTHONY. Why, Mrs. Malaprop, in moderation, now, what would you have a woman know?
> MRS. MALAPROP. Observe me, Sir Anthony.—I would by no means wish a daughter of mine to be a progeny of learning; I don't think so much learning becomes a young woman; for instance, I would never let her meddle with Greek, or Hebrew, or Algebra, or Simony, or Fluxions, or Paradoxes, or such inflammatory branches of learning neither would it be necessary for her to handle any of your mathematical, astronomical, diabolical instruments.

**Dialogue in novels**. The conventions of dramatic scripts required each speaker to have a separate section, for easy consultation. The conventions of prose, as seen in the novels of the 17–18c, did not follow the theatre, but used long, unbroken paragraphs within which entire conversations could be set, as in Henry Fielding's *The History of Tom Jones* (1749):

> "You don't imagine, I hope," cries the squire, "that I have taught her any such things." "Your ignorance, brother," returned she, "as the great Milton says, almost subdues my patience." "D—n Milton!" answered the squire: "if he had the impudence to say so to my face, I'd lent him a douse, thof he was never so great a man. Patience! An you come to that, sister, I have more occasion of patience, to be used like an overgrown schoolboy, as I am by you. Do you think no one hath any understanding, unless he hath been about at court?"

In this style, such formulas as *answered the squire* and *returned she* were well established and considerable flexibility was available, as with the dramatists, to capture special kinds of SPEECH. By the 19c, conversation was often still embedded in PARAGRAPHS, but a style similar to the dramatic script was beginning to open up these great blocks of print and speakers were often given paragraphs to themselves, turn for turn. Emily Brontë uses the 'open-plan' approach in *Wuthering Heights* (1847) in a passage that, like Shakespeare, uses dialogue to present dialect:

> "Have you found Heathcliff, you ass?" interrupted Catherine. "Have you been looking for him, as I ordered?"

"I sud more likker look for th' horse,"
he replied. "It 'ud be to more sense. Bud,
I can look for norther horse nur man of
a neeght loike this—as black as t'
chimbley! und Heathcliff's noan t' chap
to coom at *my* whistle—happen he'll be
less hard o' hearing wi' *ye*!"

By the end of the 19c, fictional dialogue
had become more or less stable. Writers
had become accustomed to paragraph-by-
paragraph turntaking and felt secure
enough in their own and their readers' ability to move down a page of short paragraphs
to dispense increasingly with such aids as *he
said* and *she answered* in every paragraph.
Novelists became more skilful in presenting
the registers and varieties of speech; dialect,
previously used mainly for comic or eccentric effect, was given by writers like Elizabeth Gaskell, George Eliot, and Thomas
Hardy to serious and even tragic characters.
From the late 19c to the present day,
fictional conversation has generally been
modelled closely on real life and used to exhibit characters' actions, styles, and attributes, as in this excerpt from Sir Arthur
Conan Doyle's short story 'The Five Orange
Pips' (in *The Adventures of Sherlock Holmes*,
1892):

> 'I have come for advice.'
> 'That is easily got.'
> 'And help.'
> 'That is not always so easy.'
> 'I have heard of you, Mr. Holmes. I
> heard from Major Prendergast how you
> saved him in the Tankerville Club
> Scandal.'
> 'Ah, of course. He was wrongfully
> accused of cheating at cards.'
> 'He said that you could solve
> anything.'
> 'He said too much.'
> 'That you are never beaten.'
> 'I have been beaten four times—
> three times by men and once by a
> woman.'

Once such a flexible set of conventions was
established, it became possible to experiment with other possibilities, in some cases
abandoning entirely the system of QUOTA-
TION MARKS built up in the tradition of
fiction and trying something closer to the
unadorned dramatic script, as in James
Joyce's *A Portrait of the Artist as a Young Man*
(1916: ch. 5):

> —Try to be one of us, repeated Davin.
> In your heart you are an Irishman but
> your pride is too powerful.
> —My ancestors threw off their
> language and took another, Stephen
> said. They allowed a handful of
> foreigners to subject them. Do you fancy
> I am going to pay in my own life and
> person debts they made? What for?
> —For our freedom, said Davin. . . .
> Ireland first, Stevie. You can be a poet or
> mystic after.
> —Do you know what Ireland is? asked
> Stephen with cold violence. Ireland is
> the old sow that eats her farrow.

By and large, however, the experimentation
has been less with quotation marks, turn-
taking devices, and white space, and more
with content: for example, in V. S. Naipaul's
*A Flag on the Island* (1967), 'outlandish' speakers of English, remote descendants of
Mackmorrice, turn up in a new guise. Fully
conforming to the conventions he learned
at school, Naipaul nonetheless uses the
time-honoured techniques of English literary dialogue to make a point of his own
about the trials of being a writer using a
language with conventions far removed
from everyday life:

> 'You know, I have been doing a lot of
> thinking. You know, Frankie, I begin to
> feel that what is wrong with my books is
> not me, but the language I use. You
> know, in English, black is a damn bad
> word. You talk of a black deed. How then
> can I write in this language?'
> 'I have told you already. You are
> getting too black for me.'
> 'What we want is our own language. I
> intend to write in our own language. You
> know this patois we have. Not English,
> not French, but something we have
> made up. This is our own. You were
> right. Damn those lords and ladies.
> Damn Jane Austen. This is ours, this is
> what we have to work with.'

Writers of dialogue will always have the
problem of accommodating the many
sounds of English to the 26 letters of the alphabet. Deviant spelling and typographical
contrivance are used to compensate for the
inadequate and inconsistent relationship
between the spoken and the written. Features of speech can sometimes be shown by
such means, but usually they continue to be
managed through such ad-hoc authorial

formulas as *he stated emphatically, she whispered, Sabina said huskily,* and *Drake answered, slurring his words.*

See ASIDE, COCKNEY, DIRECT AND INDIRECT SPEECH, LANGUAGE TEACHING, LITERATURE, PUNCTUATION, TALK.

## DICKENS, Charles (John Huffham)

[1812–70]. English writer. Born in Portsmouth and moved to Chatham, then London. He became deeply unhappy when his father was imprisoned for debt and he worked for a time in a blacking warehouse. He became a Parliamentary reporter for the *True Sun* (1832), then the *Morning Chronicle* (1834), acquiring the knowledge of London that underlies his novels. *Sketches by Boz,* a series of commentaries on London life, appeared in various periodicals. It was followed by *Pickwick Papers* (1836), a comic episodic novel that made his name, and *Oliver Twist* (1837), a melodramatic tale of criminal life that established his success. In *David Copperfield* (1849–50), written in the first person, he put into fiction some of the bitterness of his early life. Earlier novels like *Oliver Twist* dealt with such specific social abuses as the workhouse, but his later novels took a more generally critical view of society. His fame was by then widespread, but his relationship with his wife Catherine (married in 1836) had steadily deteriorated and ended in 1858 with a separation accompanied by her accusations of infidelity. He increased both his income and popularity by public readings in the UK and US, but the strain was great and he died suddenly, leaving the novel *Edwin Drood* unfinished.

**Characters and experiments**. The strength of Dickens is his characters, particularly the comics and eccentrics, who live largely through their speech and through catchphrases that helped fix them for readers who met them in monthly serials. Their names are notable and often say something about their bearers: Mr Bumble the Beadle, the benevolent brothers Cheeryble, Thomas Gradgrind the Utilitarian, the fawning clerk Uriah Heep, the convict Abel Magwitch, Mr McChoakumchild the teacher, the amiable nurse Clara Peggotty, the impostor Mr Pumblechook, the miserly Ebenezer Scrooge. His place-names are also often suggestive: Blunderstone, Coketown, Dotheboys Hall, Eatanswill. Like Scott, Dickens worked dialect into his novels,

particularly COCKNEY, for which he used idiosyncratic spelling that nonetheless conveyed the sounds and cadences of London, as for example the style, dialect, and accent of Mr Pickwick's servant Sam Weller:

> 'That a'nt the wost on it, neither. They puts things into old gen'lm'n's heads as they never dreamed of. My father, sir, wos a coachman. A widower he wos, and fat enough for anything—uncommon fat, to be sure. His missus dies, and leaves him four hundred pound. Down he goes to the Commons, to see the lawyer and draw the blunt—wery smart—top-boots on—nosegay in his button-hole—broad-brimmed tile—green shawl—quite the gen'lm'n. Goes through the archvay, thinking how he should inwest the money—up comes the touter, touches his hat—"Licence, sir, licence?"—"What's that?" says my father.—"Marriage licence," says the touter.—"Dash my veskit," says my father, "I never thought o' that."—"I think you wants one, sir," says the touter' (*The Pickwick Papers,* ch. 10).

Dickens learned shorthand for his work as a reporter and had a good ear for slang and colloquialism, and was accused of coarseness by contemporary critics. His experiments in the presentation of material included such non-traditional syntax and punctuation as:

> Thomas Gradgrind, Sir. A man of realities. A man of facts and calculations. A man who proceeds upon the principle that two and two are four, and nothing over. Thomas Gradgrind, Sir—peremptorily Thomas—Thomas Gradgrind. With a rule and a pair of scales, and the multiplication table always in his pocket, Sir, ready to weigh and measure any parcel of human nature, and tell you exactly what it comes to. (*Hard Times,* 1854, ch. 1).

**Poetic prose**. Dickens's general style is usually powerful and persuasive in direct narrative and description. He convinces the reader by an accumulation of detail that can be extravagant to the point of absurdity, but makes its effect in his imaginary world. His PROSE sometimes has an underlying rhythm close to blank verse, mimetic of sounds like the movement of coaches and trains. Some passages, with their non-classical punctuation, such as the opening of *Bleak House* (1852–3), have almost the quality of free verse:

LONDON. Michaelmas Term lately over, and the Lord Chancellor sitting in Lincoln's Inn Hall. Implacable November weather. As much mud in the streets, as if the waters had but newly retired from the face of the earth, and it would not be wonderful to meet a Megalosaurus, forty feet long or so, waddling like an elephantine lizard up Holborn Hill. Smoke lowering down from chimney pots, making a soft black drizzle with flakes of soot in it as big as full-grown snowflakes—gone into mourning, one might imagine, for the death of the sun.

**Stature**. Like Chaucer and Shakespeare, Dickens is a giant of ENGLISH LITERATURE, his work known as much through cinema and television as through his books themselves. On his contemporary significance, David Parker, Curator of the Dickens House Museum in London, has observed: 'For us Dickens stands where Homer did for earlier generations. We can no longer, without affectation, speak of the wisdom of Nestor, the beauty of Helen; we can, and we do, of a real Scrooge, a Micawberish attitude. Like Homer, Dickens gave us forms for the imagination, unconstrained by genre, affecting even the very language. Dramatizations of his novels were staged even before the final parts appeared, and the narratives he created now yield us, not only films and television serials, but also musicals, newspaper cartoons, Christmas cards, toby jugs, shop-window dressings, and annual festivals' (letter to the *Sunday Times*, 26 Feb. 1989). See CIRCUMLOCUTION, HUMOUR, SAXONISM.

**DICTION**. **1.** A way of speaking, usually assessed in terms of prevailing standards of PRONUNCIATION and ELOCUTION: *clear/slovenly diction*. **2.** A way or style of using words and phrases, especially in a literary tradition: *AUREATE DICTION, POETIC DICTION*. The range of vocabulary used by a particular writer: *Shakespearian diction; the diction of Robert Burns*. See ORTHOEPY, SPEECH.

■ **DICTIONARY** —————— ■

A generic name for a kind of reference book, usually devoted to the definition of words entered in alphabetic order, such as the *Collins English Dictionary*, but also including works of an encyclopedic nature, such as

*The Oxford Dictionary of Natural History*. Such books are so closely associated with alphabetized entries that the phrase *dictionary order* is synonymous with *alphabetic(al) order*, but in fact since the Middle Ages many works called 'dictionaries' have been differently arranged, and a wide range of reference books, including thesauruses and gazetteers, are referred to for convenience as 'dictionaries'. Among the many kinds of dictionary, the commonest contrast is between *monolingual* or *unilingual dictionaries* that list and define the words of one language and *bilingual dictionaries* that offer the equivalents of Language A in Language B, and vice versa. In computing, the term refers to both a list of codes, terms, keys, etc., and their meanings, as used in computer programs, and a list of words (often drawn from a conventional dictionary) against which spellings can be checked.

**Origins**. The earliest known prototypes of the dictionary were West Asian bilingual word lists of the second millennium BC. They were Sumerian and Akkadian words inscribed in parallel columns on clay tablets in cuneiform writing and were organized thematically. Even after the invention of the alphabet later in the same millennium many centuries passed before alphabetic ordering became a common tool for organizing information. The lists came into existence because the Akkadians (Babylonians) had inherited through conquest the culture and traditions of Sumer and used the sets of signs as a means by which their scribes could learn what was, in effect, the classical language of writing. Over two thousand years later in medieval Europe, the same principle was used when scribes who spoke vernacular languages learned to read and write in Latin; the first European dictionaries were bilingual lists of (difficult) words of Latin explained in the vernacular of the learners in question. A typical work that made Latin words accessible through English glosses was the *Promptorium parvulorum sive clericorum* (Storehouse for little ones or clerics) of Galfridus Grammaticus (Geoffrey the Grammarian), compiled around 1440.

**The hard-word dictionaries**. The need for a work in which harder English words were explained by easier English words arose in the late 16c. The first published dictionary of English was Robert Cawdrey's *Table Alpha-*

*beticall* (1604), which contained fewer than 3,000 'hard vsuall English wordes' listed alphabetically in roman type with the barest of explanations in black letter: *Dulcor*, sweetnesse; *Placable*, easie to be pleased. It was designed for quick consultation by 'Ladies, Gentlewomen, or any other vnskilfull persons', to help them understand and use foreign borrowings. It was followed by John Bullokar's *English Expositor* (1616), Henry Cockeram's *English Dictionarie* (1623), the first to be given that name, and Thomas Blount's *Glossographia* (1656), which had some 9,000 words, fuller definitions, and etymologies. Such works were concerned only with 'hard words', the classical vocabulary of Renaissance English: they bristled with 'Terms of Art', the technical and semitechnical words coined by geographers, mathematicians, doctors, and others. They were highly derivative, drawing in particular on the older Latin–English dictionaries, and answered a real need: Cockeram went through 12 editions to 1670 and the last of many printings of Bullokar was in 1775.

**The universal dictionaries**. The hardword tradition went on into the 18c in the work of John Kersey and Nathaniel Bailey, and traces survive in such traditional works as the *Chambers English Dictionary* (1988). A novel approach emerged, however, in the *New World of English Words* (1658) by Edward Phillips, a nephew of Milton and a miscellaneous hack writer. His folio volume had its hard words, but was altogether grander and more inclusive. By the 5th edition in 1696, it had grown to about 17,000 items and in 1706 was revised and further enlarged by John Kersey. Nathaniel Bailey's folio *Dictionarium Britannicum* (1730) is in the same tradition but with a new emphasis on scientific and industrial matters: for example, with a page on *orrery*, and 17 items on the metal *lead*. With the publication of special works such as John Harris's *Lexicon Technicum* (1704), the need for such encyclopedic material in general dictionaries was already decreasing; when Samuel Johnson set his face against extraneous matter, a British tradition of dictionaries for words and encyclopedias for facts was confirmed.

The notion that a dictionary should as far as possible be an inventory of all the words of the language became established with Kersey's *New English Dictionary* (1702), which gave the dictionary a place in competition with spelling books as a quick look-up source. To begin with, little information was given about common words ('To do, or act, &c.' is the whole of Kersey's entry for that verb), but from this time forward the monolingual dictionary was of greater value to foreign learners of English. Since Elisha Coles's *English Dictionary* (1676), a sprinkling of the commoner dialect words, as well as some cant and flash terms, had come to be included in general dictionaries. With these, the need arose for more systematic usage labels to warn the reader of the status of such a word. Some obsolete items had been given a distinctive mark by Bullokar in 1616 and the uptake of 'old words' increased in the 18c, including legal items and literary archaisms drawn especially from Spenser and Chaucer. Bailey's *Universal Etymological English Dictionary* (1721) gave English a one-volume reference dictionary of some 40,000 entries that was strong on bookish and technical vocabulary, weak in definition and semantic coverage, up-to-date in spelling, and provided the accepted etymologies of its day. It was the standard dictionary of the 18c and was gradually updated and enlarged to some 50,000 entries through successive editions and reprintings to the 28th and last edition in 1800.

**Johnson's dictionary**. The *Dictionary of the English Language* (1755) by Samuel JOHNSON differs from the works of his predecessors in both scale and intention. On the model of the dictionaries of the French and Italian academies, he sought to encapsulate the 'best' usage of his day, and did this on the basis of over 100,000 quotations from Sir Philip Sidney in the 16c to his own time. In definition and the internal arrangement of entries Johnson also went beyond his rivals. Benjamin Martin, in his *Lingua Britannica Reformata* (1749), had been the first English compiler to mark off the different senses of words; by arranging his senses chronologically, Johnson enabled his readers to follow the evolution of each word and provided the foundation for the historical lexicography of the 19–20c. Johnson gave little attention to collocation, idiom, and grammatical information, although he provided a brief grammar at the front. In cases of divided or uncertain usage he provided a prescriptive comment (*governant*: 'a lady who has the care of young girls of quality. The more general and proper word is *governess*'). His dictionary enjoyed unique authority among successive generations of users in the matter of word choice and word meaning. In spelling, it represented a strongly conservative tradition, compared with which Bailey was progressive: *horrour, inferiour*, etc., where Bailey has *horror, inferior*, etc.

**Pronouncing dictionaries**. The provision of information about pronunciation developed in the later 18c. Johnson, following Bailey's second volume (1727) and Thomas Dyche's and William Pardon's *New General English Dictionary* (1735), marked only word stress. With an increasing concern for *orthoepy* (proper pronunciation), however, *pronouncing dictionaries* became established in the latter half of the 18c, of which John Walker's *Critical Pronouncing Dictionary of the English Language* (1791) was the foremost. Walker provided his pronunciations immediately after each headword, dividing each italicized word into its syllables and placing a superscript number over each vowel to indicate its value as specified in a list at the beginning of the book. The Walker pronunciations were effectively married with Johnson's definitions in many of the abridged versions of Johnson's Dictionary, which lasted well into the 19c.

**A shift across the Atlantic**. In 1828, Noah WEBSTER, a publisher of school spelling books, created a new tradition and lent status to English as it was developing in North America with his *American Dictionary of the English Language*, which contained some 12,000 words not listed by Johnson and offered definitions of many words and concepts current in the New World. Webster rejected many of the more conservative spellings in Johnson and established for AmE forms like *honor, color* (not *honour, colour*), a different pattern for spelling inflected forms (*traveler, traveling, traveled*, not *traveller, travelling, travelled*, etc.), and *-ize* for *-ise*. Some reforms were based on etymology (Latin *color, honor*) and some were phonetic (*-ize* for *-ise*). One of Webster's employees, Joseph E. Worcester, established his own dictionary-publishing venture in Boston, and produced in 1830 his *Comprehensive Pronouncing and Explanatory Dictionary*, which went through several editions (1846, 1855, 1860) and was closer to the Johnsonian tradition. In his preface to *A Universal and Critical Dictionary of the English Language* (1846), Worcester wrote of Johnson's *Dictionary*: 'His dictionary, from the time of its

first publication, has been far more than any other, regarded as a standard for the language.' This view was shared by many in the US, especially by those who rejected Webster in favour of Worcester.

Other dictionaries by Worcester include *A Pronouncing, Explanatory, and Synonymous Dictionary of the English Language* (1855) and *A Dictionary of the English Language* (1860). Worcester died in 1865; although his heirs carried on, the competition from Webster's dictionaries proved too much, and the company failed. Webster died in 1843, but his son, William G. Webster, carried on, and in 1847, with Chauncey A. Goodrich of Yale, published a revised edition of the earlier work. Successive editions appeared in 1864 and 1890; in 1909 appeared a relatively large work, the 1st edition of *The New International Dictionary of the English Language*; a 2nd edition appeared in 1934, and a 3rd in 1961. The *Second Edition*, edited by William Allan Neilson, came to be regarded as the standard among dictionaries published in the US. Because of its descriptive approach (among other things), *Webster's Third* created even more consternation among conservatives in the mid-20c than Noah Webster's break with British tradition over a century earlier, and it failed to gain universal acceptance.

**Cross-fertilization**. During the 19c, US and UK publishers often produced new dictionaries by adapting established works, sometimes without acknowledgement but often through agreements with the publishers of the existing works. Such cooperation could lead to a succession of related works over many decades. For example, the Scottish publisher Blackie selected the 1841 edition of Webster's *American Dictionary of the English Language* as the basis for a dictionary to be prepared by the mathematician John Ogilvie. This work, the *Imperial Dictionary, English, Technological, & Scientific*, was published in parts between 1847 and 1850. It was more encyclopedic than the *Webster* and greatly expanded the use of illustrative engravings. When Ogilvie died in 1867, Charles Annandale began to edit a revision, which was published in 1882–3. The illustrations were augmented, and the entry and definition coverage expanded to include Americanisms, slang, and colloquialisms. This series of dictionaries was successful in Britain, and the Century Company, an American publisher of the periodical *The Country Magazine*, published an edition for sale in the US. In 1882, Century put forward a plan for *The Century Dictionary*, to be based on the Annandale edition of Ogilvie, to which they had acquired the rights. As that work had been based, originally, on a Webster dictionary, ironic intricacies emerged concerning the ultimate basis of *The Century*, which was prepared during 1884–9 under the direction of William Dwight Whitney. This work, available in several editions (1889–1911), occupied ten quarto volumes. Though out of date, it is still widely regarded as a paragon of clarity and accuracy for its definitions and etymologies and as a model of design, production, illustration, typography, paper, printing, and binding. Several dictionaries have been directly or indirectly based on it, including *The American College Dictionary* (Random House, 1947), *The Random House Dictionary of the English Language* (1966), and the *Collins English Dictionary* (1979).

**Popular and scholarly dictionaries**. By the late 19c, the making of dictionaries of English had fallen into two broad types: general, usually single-volume works for the expanding community of the literate, such as *Chambers's English Dictionary* (1872), and scholarly dictionaries on philological principles, often multi-volume, concerned either with cataloguing distinct varieties in great detail, such as the *English Dialect Dictionary* (1898–1905), or with covering the entire language, such as the *New English Dictionary on Historical Principles* that emerged from plans made by the Philological Society in 1858 and ultimately became the OXFORD ENGLISH DICTIONARY (1st edition, 12 volumes, 1928; 2nd edition, 20 volumes, 1989). The family of Oxford dictionaries is closely related to the *OED* and combines the two types. Its general list is relatively recent, beginning in 1911 with the 1st edition of *The Concise Oxford Dictionary*, edited by the brothers H. W. and F. G. Fowler.

**The dictionary industry**. The number of dictionaries of English published in the 19–20c in Britain, America, and increasingly elsewhere (especially Australia, Canada, the Caribbean, New Zealand, and South Africa) is vast and varied. In terms of the size of books and the markets for which they are intended, they range from the great multi-volume works through the large 'unabridged' dictionaries and the single-volume desk and family dictionaries to the mid-range collegiate and concise editions, various school and pocket editions, down to a plethora of minis and micros. Leading publishers of dictionaries aim at bringing out and keeping up to date volumes at all or most of these levels, often presented in a standard livery with a logo that seeks to catch the eye. Beyond these mainstream products are a multidue of specialities, such as products for the fiercely competitive ELT market that has developed since the Second World War, the complex range of bilingual publications for English and the world's significant languages, and special-interest works relating to etymology and word histories, dialects and regional varieties, technical subjects, controversial usage, slang, and the vocabulary of subcultures. See LEXICOGRAPHY.

**DICTIONARY OF MODERN ENGLISH USAGE**, short forms *Modern English Usage*, *MEU*. The best-known usage manual of the 20c, compiled by H. W. FOWLER and published by Oxford University Press in 1926, with a 2nd edition edited by Sir Ernest GOWERS in 1965. Every major hazard in English usage was subjected to reanalysis and, where necessary, provided with sage qualifications or 'Keep Off' signs. *MEU* is a collection of articles arranged under both ordinary headings (*this, thistle, thither, -th nouns, those, though*) and idiosyncratic ones (*battered ornaments, out of the frying pan, sturdy indefensibles, swapping horses*). This work in particular has made the name *Fowler* as well known among those interested in usage and the language as *Johnson* and *Webster*, a point of reference for both those who venerate and those who regret what he has had to say. In 1996, Oxford brought out *The New Fowler's Modern English Usage*, edited by R. W. Burchfield. Presented as the 3rd edition, this is effectively a new book that sets Fowler himself in historical perspective. Oxford currently publishes both the 2nd and 3rd editions. See USAGE GUIDANCE AND CRITICISM.

**DICTIONARY OF SLANG AND UNCONVENTIONAL ENGLISH**, short form *DSUE*. A work by Eric PARTRIDGE, published in 1937 in London by Routledge & Kegan Paul. The subtitle of the original work described its contents as: 'Slang, including the language of the underworld, Colloquialisms and Catchphrases, Solecisms and Catachreses, Nicknames, Vulgarisms, and such Americanisms as have been naturalized'. It built on more than 12 dictionaries of SLANG, beginning with Thomas Harman's *Caveat for Vagabones* (1567), and was based on Farmer and Henley's *Slang and Its Analogues* (seven volumes, 1890–1904). He added material from the *OED*, glossaries of contemporary slang from the 1930s onward, his observation of everyday common or specialized slang, and in due course notes from the worldwide network of correspondents that it brought into being. Its coverage was essentially the UK and Commonwealth. The *DSUE* was widely regarded as filling a lexicographical gap, because it treated four-letter words and sexual and scatological vulgarities that had previously been omitted by the *OED* and the general run of 'family' dictionaries. The obscenity laws of the time forbade the printing of such words in full; asterisks were therefore substituted for vowels in the two editions before the Second World War: 'c*nt. The female pudend'; 'f*ck. An act of sexual connexion'. Partridge noted in the preface: 'My rule, in the matter of unpleasant terms, has been to deal with them as briefly, as astringently, as aseptically as was consistent with clarity and adequacy; in a few instances, I had to force myself to overcome an instinctive repugnance.' By the 7th edition (1970), the book had become an institution and expanded to two (unstarred) volumes. In 1978, Partridge gave his notes for the 8th edition of *DSUE* to Paul Beale, who edited the two volumes back into one, as published in 1984.

**DIGLOSSIA**. A term in SOCIOLINGUISTICS for the use of two varieties of language for different purposes in the same community. The varieties are called *H* and *L*, the first being generally a standard variety used for 'high' purposes and the second often a 'low' spoken vernacular. In Egypt, classical ARABIC is H and local colloquial Arabic is L. The most important hallmark of diglossia is specialization, H being appropriate in one set of situations, L in another: reading a newspaper aloud in H, but discussing its contents in L. Functions generally reserved for H include sermons, political speeches, university lectures, and news broadcasts, while those reserved for L include everyday

conversations, instructions to servants, and folk literature.

The varieties differ not only in grammar, phonology, and vocabulary, but also with respect to function, prestige, literary heritage, acquisition, standardization, and stability. L is typically acquired at home as a mother tongue and continues to be so used throughout life. Its main uses are familial and familiar. H, on the other hand, is learned through schooling and never at home, and is related to institutions outside the home. The separate domains in which H and L are acquired provide them with separate systems of support. Diglossic societies are marked not only by this compartmentalization of varieties, but also by restriction of access, especially to H. Entry to formal institutions such as school and government requires knowledge of H. In England, from medieval times until the 18c, Latin played an H role while English was L. In some English-speaking Caribbean the H role is played by local standard English, the L role by English-based creoles.

The extent to which these functions are compartmentalized can be illustrated by the importance attached to community members to using the right variety in the appropriate context. An outsider who learns to speak L and then uses it in a formal speech risks being ridiculed. Members of a community generally regard H as superior to L in a number of respects; in some cases, H is regarded as the only 'real' version of a particular language, to the extent that people claim they do not speak L at all. Sometimes, the alleged superiority is avowed for religious and/or literary reasons: the fact that classical Arabic is the language of the Qur'ān endows it with special significance. There is also a strong tradition of formal grammatical study and standardization associated with H varieties: for example, Latin and 'school' English. See CODE-MIXING AND CODE-SWITCHING.

**DIGRAPH**. A term in ORTHOGRAPHY for two LETTERS that represent one sound, such as *th* in *this* and *sh* in *ashes*. If three letters together represent a single sound, they constitute a *trigraph*, such as *tch* in *catch* and *sch* in *schmaltz*. When letters form digraphs, they surrender their independent sound values so as to stand as a group for a single phoneme, usually because an alphabet has no letter to serve that purpose. In such cases, there may be some phonetic motivation in the combination (*sh*, *dg* roughly suggesting the sounds in *dash* and *dodge*), though this may have vanished as pronunciation has changed (for example, the *gh* in *tough* and *through*). Sometimes letters that happen to come together may look like (and be mistaken for) digraphs: for example, the *t*, *h* in *posthumous* being interpreted as the *th* in *asthma*. Because English has more phonemes than letters, digraphs are used to represent sounds for which no original Roman letter would serve: for example, the initial sounds in *three* and *this* and the final sounds in *rich* and *ridge*. There is a greater degree of consistency in English in the use of consonant digraphs and trigraphs than in vowel digraphs.

**Consonant digraphs**. Most English consonant digraphs consist of a single letter followed by *h*, modelled on the Latin digraphs *ch*, *ph*, *th* used to transcribe the Greek letters chi, phi, and theta. Consonant digraphs include: *ch* as in *chair*, *charisma*, and *loch*; *sh* as in *shout*; *th* as in *three* and *these*; *wh* as in *whale*; *ph* as in *philosophy*; *gh* as in *tough* and *daughter*; *ng* as in *longer* and *singer*; *ck* as in *track*; *dg* as in *judge*. Although *zh* is not a conventional digraph in English, occurring mainly in loans from Russian (*Brezhnev*), it is well understood and is sometimes used to give a spelling pronunciation of a word (*measure* as 'mezher').

**Vowel digraphs**. Because the vowel sounds of English greatly outnumber the symbols available, digraphs are widely used to represent them. A few are fairly regular, such as *ai* in *fail*, *pain*, *maintain*, but most can represent several vowels (as with *ea* in *bead*, *bread*, *break*, *hear*, *hearse*, *heart*) and many vowels can be represented by a variety of digraphs (especially if 'magic' *e* as in *fate*, *eve*, *wise*, *rote*, *mute* is counted as the second element in alternative digraphs to those in *wait*, *eat*, *flies*, *oat*, *root*). Most problematic is the spelling of the long *e* sound, as in the patterns *be*, *bee*, *eve*, *leave*, *sleeve*, *deceive*, *believe*, (BrE) *anaemia*, (BrE) *foetus*, *routine*. Some digraphs representing a vowel combine vowel and consonant letters (*sight*, *sign*, *indict*), while others vary within the same root (*speak/speech*, *high/height*). In addition, vowel digraphs are well known for their use in a number of highly irregular, sometimes unique spellings, such as *quay*, *key*, *people*, *leopard*, *broad*, *brooch*, *blood*, *build*.

**The digraphs Æ and Œ**. The LIGATURE digraph *æ* in *Ælfric*, *Cæsar*, *encyclopædia* was originally used in Latin and adopted by Old English for the vowel in *hat* (*hæt*), often referred to as *ASH*. It has been used in English, under the influence of Latin, to represent Greek *ai* as in *Æschylus*, *Æsop*, *anæmia*, *hæmorrhage*, now commonly *Aeschlus*, *Aesop*, and BrE *anaemia*, *haemorrhage*. The AmE practice of simplifying *ae* to *e* is becoming general, as in *anemia*, *hemorrhage*, *encyclopedia*, *medieval*, but not *\*Eschylus*, *\*Esop*. The Latin ligature digraph *œ* represents Greek *oi* as in *Œdipus*, *amœba*, now commonly *Oedipus* and BrE *amoeba*, *foetus*. The AmE practice of simplifying *oe* to *e* is becoming general, as in *ameba*, *fetus*, but not *\*Edipus*. In some words, the digraph (with or without the ligature) has long since vanished: for example, older *oeconomy* is now universally *economy*, and *ecology* has never been spelt *\*oecology*. See DIPHTHONG, SPELLING, WRITING, and A, C, E, G, H, I, K, O, P, R, S, T, W.

**DIMINUTIVE. 1.** An AFFIX, usually a SUFFIX, added to a WORD to suggest smallness (and, paradoxically, either affection or dismissal). In English, the diminutive suffix -*ling* is neutral in *duckling* little duck, affectionate in *darling* little dear, and dismissive in *princeling* little prince. Whereas the -*ette* in *cigarette* conveys smallness, in *usherette* it conveys femaleness and, generally, lesser status than *usher*. **2.** A NAME, usually a nickname or hypocorism, that suggests smallness, affection, dismissal, etc.: *Will*, *Willie*, *Willy* (and, in baby talk, the double diminutive *Willikins*) and *Bill*, *Billy* as short forms of *William*, and *willie* as a euphemism for the penis. See CLIPPING, *L*-SOUNDS, SCOTS, SEXISM.

**DIPHTHONG. 1.** In PHONETICS, a VOWEL that starts with one quality and moves in the direction of another quality, as in *toy*, which begins with the quality in *lawn* and moves towards the quality in *pin*. The combination is often described as a sequence of two vowels. There are several varieties of diphthong: wide and narrow; closing and opening; centring; falling and rising. A *wide diphthong* has a marked change in quality: in RP, the vowels in *high*, *how*, which move from open to close. A *narrow diphthong* has less movement: in RP, the vowel of *day*, which moves from half-close to close. The vowels of *weave*, *groove* are narrow diphthongs, because they move slightly within the close vowel area, but this movement is usually disregarded and they are treated as monophthongs. A *closing diphthong* ends closer than it begins, while an *opening diphthong* ends more open than it begins. The diphthongs of English tend to be of the closing type: in RP, *say, sigh, soy, so, sow*. A *centring diphthong* moves towards schwa: in RP, *here, there*. In rhotic varieties, this schwa is followed by an r-sound, but not in a non-rhotic variety like RP. A *falling diphthong* is stressed on the first element, and a *rising diphthong* is stressed on the second. The diphthongs of English tend to be of the falling type, with the exception of the vowel sound in *view*, which can be interpreted as rising. **2.** Two closely associated letters, such as *ai* and *oy*, whether or not they represent a diphthong. Technically these are more accurately known as DIGRAPHS. See MONOPHTHONG, SPEECH.

# ■ DIRECT AND INDIRECT SPEECH ─────── ■

Also **direct speech, reported speech**. Terms for kinds of grammatical construction in which reports are made of something said, written, or thought. Direct SPEECH gives the exact words in the report, and in writing and print uses QUOTATION MARKS, single as in *'I know the answer,' Jane said*, double as in *"I know the answer," Jane said*. Indirect speech conveys the report in the words of the reporter: for example, *Jane said that she knew the answer* (more formal), and *Jane said she knew the answer* (less formal). In direct speech, the reporting clause may appear initially (*He said, 'I'm finishing now and I'm going home'*), medially (*'I'm finishing now,' he said, 'and I'm going home'*), or finally (*'I'm finishing now and I'm going home,' he said*). The reporting verb is sometimes put before the subject, particularly when it is *said* and the subject is not a pronoun: *'I'm finishing now,' said Andrew*. A wide range of verbs can be used to indicate the type of utterance or the way in which something is said (such as *answer, ask, comment, cry, ejaculate, enquire/inquire, exclaim, groan, growl, moan, murmur, mutter, note, observe, reply, respond, retort, scream, screech, shout, shriek, smile, whine, yell*) and an adverb may be added to evaluate the speaker's manner (such as *angrily, demurely, happily, mysteriously, radiantly, sadly, sweetly*). Some writers use such variants and additions liberally, others with great restraint.

In indirect speech, verbs are generally 'backshifted' in tense to align them with the time of reporting, and other changes, such as in pronouns and adverbials of time and place, are made for the same reason: *Doris told Robert, 'You can now watch television'* would possibly be reported as *Doris told Robert that he could then watch television*. This backshift relationship of verb tenses in the reporting and reported clauses is known as the *sequence of tenses*. Backshift, however, is optional when what was said applies equally at the time of reporting: *Benjamin said that he is/was coming over to watch television tonight*. Such traditional shifts are not, however, used in certain kinds of relaxed, colloquial reporting and storytelling: *Then he says he's coming and she says that he could come or not for all she cared*.

Apart from direct and indirect statements, there are: (1) *Direct and indirect questions*, the latter normally following the statement order of subject and verb: direct *'Do you understand?' she asked* becoming indirect *She asked if he understood*; direct *'Where has he gone?' I wondered* becoming indirect *I wondered where he had gone*. (2) *Direct and indirect exclamations*, as when direct *'What a clever boy you are!' David told his son* becomes indirect *David told his son what a clever boy he was*. (3) *Direct and indirect instructions*, such as direct *Jane said to Jenny, 'Phone me if you need any help'* becoming indirect *Jane told Jenny to phone her if she needed any help*. In such reports, care may sometimes be necessary to ensure that pronoun reference does not become unclear. Two variants of reported speech occur mainly in fiction: free direct speech and free indirect speech:

***Free direct speech*** lacks a reporting clause to show the shift from narration to reporting; it is often used in fiction to represent the mental reactions of characters to what they see or experience. In the following extract from James Joyce's *Ulysses* (1922), Leopold Bloom reflects on what he sees as he walks along (italics not in the original have been added to mark the free direct speech):

> By Brady's cottages a boy for the skins lolled, his bucket of offal linked, smoking a chewed fag butt. A smaller girl with scars of eczema on her forehead eyed him, listlessly holding her battered caskhoop. *Tell him if he smokes he won't grow. O let him! His life isn't such a bed of roses! Waiting outside pubs to bring da*

*home. Come home to ma, da. Slack hour: won't be many there.* He crossed Townsend street, passed the frowning face of Bethel. *El, yes: house of: Aleph, Beth. At eleven it is. Time enough.*

**Free indirect speech** resembles indirect speech in shifting tenses and other references, but there is generally no reporting clause and it retains some features of direct speech (such as direct questions and vocatives). In this extract from the South African novelist Dan Jacobson's *A Dance in the Sun* (1956), Fletcher moves into free indirect speech in the course of a conversation with Frank (italics added):

He gave Frank the name of the house he had been in at school. He challenged Frank to look his name up in the school calendar, so that Frank would be able to see for himself the truth of what he was saying. *That was where he had learned what was right and what was not. It had not been his fault that his father had died and that the estate had been in disorder and that he had had to make his own way. But he had, and he had not done so badly either. But he was not a snob.* He repeated that he was not a snob, as though Frank had accused him of being a snob, as though Frank could see anything for him to be particularly snobbish about. *He was not a snob.* All he wanted was decency, decency, decency, he said.

See CONVERSATION, DIALOG(UE).

**DIRECT OBJECT**. In GRAMMAR, the person or thing affected by the action of a transitive verb. The direct OBJECT usually closely follows the verb ('I love *you*', 'Do *the work* now'), unless there is an *indirect object*, when the direct object comes second ('I've sent Audrey *a present*'). The expression 'affected by' has a range of meanings, referring also to things that only come into existence as a result of the action of the verb ('Then somebody invented *the wheel*') and objects of place ('She paced *the room*'). Although direct objects are typically nouns and pronouns, other structures can follow transitive verbs, and some grammarians analyse all the following constructions as direct object: *that*-clauses ('He said *that he loved her*'); clauses beginning with *wh*-question words ('She explained *why the idea was impossible*'); various *-ing* and infinitive structures with or

without subjects ('They both enjoy *dancing*', 'I can't bear (*you*) *to be unhappy*').

**DISCOURSE**. **1.** A general, often formal term for a talk, conversation, dialogue, lecture, sermon, or treatise, such as John Dryden's *Discourse concerning the Original and Progress of Satire* (1693). **2.** An occasional term for LANGUAGE and USAGE generally: *all human discourse; philosophical discourse.* **3.** In LINGUISTICS, a unit or piece of connected speech or writing that is longer than a conventional sentence. The analytical study of such sketches of language is known as *discourse analysis*. See PRAGMATICS, RHETORIC, TEXT.

**DORIC**. In 1721, the Scottish poet Allan Ramsay compared his use of SCOTTICISMS with the Doric dialect of the Sicilian Greek pastoral poet Theocritus (3–2c BC). In the 19c, British writers began applying the term (referring to the supposedly rustic and uncultivated dialect of the Dorians of the Peloponnese) to 'broad' rural dialects in England and especially the Scottish Lowlands. In recent times, the people of northeastern Scotland have adopted the term for their own dialect. Elsewhere in Scotland, the term is used for any form of vernacular SCOTS. Generally it is favourable, *the Doric* being seen as rich, expressive, and rooted in tradition, whereas the *gutter Scots* of the cities is widely taken to have degenerated from 'the genuine Doric'. See GUTTER SCOTS, SCOTTICISM.

**DORSET**. A county of southern England, regarded by many as the heart of the WEST COUNTRY, although others favour SOMERSET. Archaic DIALECT forms dating from Saxon times occur where the two counties meet: for example, the Old English first-person pronoun *ic* (pronounced 'itch': modern *I*) was heard in the 19c in what A. J. Ellis called 'the land of utch' (the area around Montacute in Somerset and stretching into Dorset). In the 1950s, fieldworkers for the *Survey of English Dialects* recorded *Udge am gwain* I am going. The Dorset dialect was made famous by the novelist Thomas HARDY, who usually portrayed the variety spoken by people who had received some schooling and were therefore influenced by the standard language. The philologist William BARNES wrote poetry in the dialect.

**DOUBLE GENITIVE**. A term taken from the GRAMMAR of LATIN and used in connection with a noun that is doubly possessed, using both *of* and either a possessive *s* or a possessive pronoun: '*Several neighbours of ours* were there', 'I've got an umbrella *of Rachel's*'. The first noun is normally indefinite (not *\*The neighbours of ours*) and the second is human and definite (not *\*an umbrella of a woman's*). The structure combines definiteness (*ours, Rachel's*) and indefiniteness (*several, an*) in a way not otherwise possible. The forms *\*several our neighbours* and *\*a Rachel's umbrella* are not possible. Compare also *a room of my own* but not *\*a my own room*. Exceptionally, the first noun can have definite *this/these* (etc.) in front of it, but does not refer to one or some out of several, as in *That extraordinary voice of hers* (She has an extraordinary voice) and *Those unfortunate mistakes of Neil's* (Neil made those mistakes).

**DOUBLE MEANING**. Often deliberate AMBIGUITY in a word or other expression, in which one sense is usually immediately apparent and relevant, while the other usually has a humorous, clever, cynical, or other implication: for example, British advertising slogans *Running water for you* (Thames Water Authority) and *London Weekend Television—the best shows*. When the implication is risqué, the obsolete French phrase *double entendre* is often used, as for example for the warning in a 1990 advertisement, showing a syringe and an arm: 'It only takes one prick to give you Aids.' See ABBREVIATION, PUN.

**DOUBLE NEGATIVE**. The use of two or more negatives in the same construction. There are two categories: (1) If the meaning is emphatically negative (*I never said nothing to nobody*), the construction is not part of STANDARD ENGLISH, though it is long-attested, and common in many varieties of the language. (2) If the meaning is rhetorically positive (*She is not unintelligent*: She is intelligent; *You can't not respect their decision*: You have to respect their decision; *Nobody has NO friends*: Everybody has some friends), the construction is part of standard English. Compare LITOTES. See NEGATION.

**DOUBLE PASSIVE**. The use of two PASSIVES together: *He was said to have been sacked; Their engagement is expected to be announced; Ten seamen are believed drowned.* The term is more commonly applied, however, to constructions considered clumsy: *A protest meeting is hoped to be held soon* (= *It is hoped to hold a protest meeting soon*).

**DOUBLESPEAK**. Language that diverts attention from, or conceals, a speaker's true meaning, or from what is on the speaker's mind, making the bad seem good, and the unpleasant attractive or at least tolerable. It seeks to avoid, shift, or deny responsibility, and ultimately prevents or limits thought. Doublespeak can be discussed in terms of euphemism, bureaucratese, JARGON, and inflated language. In 1984, the US State Department announced that in its annual reports on the status of human rights in countries around the world it would no longer use the word *killing* but instead the euphemism *unlawful or arbitrary deprivation of life*. When asked why US military forces lacked intelligence information on Grenada before they invaded the island in 1983, Admiral Wesley L. McDonald replied: 'We were not micromanaging Grenada intelligence-wise until about that time frame.' When a company 'initiates a career alternative enhancement program' it is laying off 5,000 workers. With global communication, doublespeak spreads quickly within countries and around the world. It gains a certain legitimacy when used by public figures, especially leading political figures, and spreads by imitation.

The Doublespeak Award, an ironic tribute established in 1974, is presented annually by the Committee on Public Doublespeak of the NCTE. It is given each year to a person or organization in the US that has used public language that is, in the committee's judgment, deceptive, evasive, euphemistic, or self-contradictory. The Award is restricted to those uses of public language which have pernicious social, political, or economic consequences. Winners of the Award have included the nuclear power industry for using such terminology as *rapid oxidation* for fire, *energetic disassembly* for explosion, and *abnormal evolution* for accident, and the Pentagon for calling the neutron bomb a *radiation enhancement weapon*. See DOUBLE TALK, -SPEAK.

**DOUBLET**. 1. One of two or more WORDS derived from one source: *fragile/frail*, from Latin *fragilis*, the first directly, the second through Old FRENCH *frele*. Three such words are *triplets*: *cattle/chattel/capital*, from LATIN *capitale*. Some doublets show little resemblance: *thesaurus/treasure*, from GREEK *thesaurós* (a store), the first directly through Latin, the second through Latin then Old French *trésor*. Doublets vary in closeness of meaning as well as form: *guarantee/warranty* are fairly close in form and have almost the same meaning; *abbreviate/abridge* are distant in form but close in meaning (though they serve distinct ends); *costume/custom* are fairly close in form but distant in meaning, but both relate to human activities. See COGNATE, NORSE. **2.** A game invented in the 1870s by Lewis CARROLL, in which a given word should be changed, letter by letter and always forming another word, into a second given word: for example, 'drive *pig* into *sty*' in the sequence *pig, wig, wag, way, say, sty*'. Carroll called the given words *doublets*, the interposed words *links*, and the complete series a *chain*.

**DOUBLE TALK**, also **double-talk**. **1.** PATTER that uses a mix of NONSENSE and real words. The US word buff Paul Dickson noted in 1982: 'Well done, it is a skilful blend of meaningful and meaningless words that when delivered leads the listener to think he is either hard of hearing or losing his mind. Or to be more to the point: a durnamic verbal juberance with clear mokus, flaysome, and rasorial overtones' (*Words*). **2.** Deliberately ambiguous and evasive language. Compare DOUBLESPEAK, JARGON, JIVE, STUNT WORD. See AMBIGUITY.

**DRAWL**. A non-technical term (verb and noun) for SPEECH in which words are drawn out, especially prolonging vowels and final syllables. The term is often pejorative, suggesting that a speaker is affected or lazy: 'I never heard such a drawling-affecting rogue' (Shakespeare, *The Merry Wives of Windsor*, 2. 1, 1598). Some accents are regarded as marked by drawling: *a southern drawl* (in the US). See ACCENT, STYLE.

**DUB**. A clipping of *double*. **1.** To alter a soundtrack, as in *dubbing a film*, especially to re-express dialogue in a different language, or to use a different voice, series of sounds, etc.: *dubbing 'Gone with the Wind' into German*; *His voice was often dubbed for special effect*. **2.** To alter a soundtrack by removing some parts and adding or changing others. To *dub in* means to add (music, speech, etc.) to a film or tape: *They'll dub the songs in later*. **3.** (Used especially of Afro-Caribbean disc jockeys speaking Creole) improvising against a soundtrack or a piece of recorded music. Dub is an especially Jamaican style of delivery that is associated with REGGAE and has spread in recent years to the UK, US, and West Africa. Performance poetry of this kind is called *dub poetry* and *toasting*; those who engage in it are *dub poets*. Compare RAP. See JAMAICAN CREOLE, RASTA TALK.

**DUBLIN**. The capital of the Irish Republic, Dublin pre-dates the 9c Scandinavian settlements and some parts of the city have been English-speaking for almost 800 years. It is the birthplace of among others Jonathan Swift, Oliver Goldsmith, Richard Sheridan, Oscar Wilde, George Bernard Shaw, James Joyce, Sean O'Casey, Iris Murdoch, and Samuel Beckett. The speech of middle-class Dubliners is closer to RP than is any other variety of Irish speech, but it differs from RP in four ways: (1) It is rhotic, with a retroflex *r*. (2) The realization of /t, d, n/ is more dental than alveolar. (3) There is more aspiration in words like *part, tart, cart* (syllable-initial /p, t, k/). (4) The sounds *wh* and *w* are distinguished, so that *which/witch* are not homophones. This speech is the norm for the middle class throughout the Republic. The speech of working-class Dubliners has the following features: words such as *thin* and *this* sound like 'tin' and 'dis' ('Dere was tirty-tree of dem'); words such as *tea* and *peacock* sound like 'tay' and 'paycock'; in words like *fat* and *fad* there is often an *s-* or *z*-like hiss (/fat$^s$/, /fad$^z$/: syllable-final affrication); in words such as *castle* and *glass* there is a front (short) /a/; in words such as *suit* and *school* there is a diphthong, so that for many people *suit/suet* are homophones; in words such as *but* and *hut* there is a centralized /u/; words such as *tie* and *buy* sound like 'toy' and 'boy'; the diphthong /æu/ occurs in such words as *how* and *mouse*, and in some pronunciations such words tend to be disyllabic; words such as *border* and *porter* tend to sound like 'bordar' and 'portar'. See EUROPEAN UNION, IRISH ENGLISH.

**DUMMY**. In GRAMMAR, an item that has little or no meaning but fills an obligatory position: (1) Prop *it*, which functions as subject with expressions of time (*It's late*), distance (*It's a long way to Tipperary*), and weather (*It's raining*); anticipatory *it*, which functions as subject (*It's a pity that you're not here*) or object (*I find it hard to understand what's meant*) when the subject or object of a clause is moved to a later position in the sentence, and is the subject in CLEFT SENTENCES (*It was Peter who had an accident*); (2) Existential *there*, which functions as subject in an *existential sentence* (*There's nobody at the door*). (3) The dummy auxiliary *do*, which is introduced, in the absence of any other auxiliary, to form questions (*Do you know them?*). See ANTICIPATORY IT.

**DURATION**. In PHONETICS, the time (measured in centiseconds or milliseconds) taken to produce a sample of speech. See QUANTITY.

**DUTCH**. The national language of the Netherlands, virtually identical with Flemish and ancestral to AFRIKAANS. Scholars use the term *Netherlandic* as a general and especially historical term for the varieties spoken in the Netherlands, Belgium, and north-western France. With English and FRISIAN, Dutch belongs to the Low German branch of the West Germanic group of INDO-EUROPEAN LANGUAGES; all are structurally similar. Such words as *lip*, *maken*, *open*, *water* show that Dutch is closer to English than is GERMAN, whose equivalents are *Lippe*, *machen*, *offen*, *Wasser*. It was a major language of commerce in the 17c, and was established in North America (especially in the colony first known as New Amsterdam, then New York), in southern Africa (where *Cape Dutch* became Afrikaans), in the Caribbean region, and in Indonesia (formerly the *Dutch East Indies*).

**Dutch and English**. (1) *Dutch in English*. There was a considerable influence on English from the later Middle Ages, through migration and commerce (especially the English wool trade with Flanders), as numerous Dutch nautical terms testify: *boom*, *deck*, *freebooter*, *sloop*, *smuggler*, *yacht*. Dutch was widely known in Europe in the 17c, when the first English–Dutch dictionaries appeared and such Dutch-derived artistic terms as *easel*, *etch*, *landscape*, *maulstick*, *sketch* were adopted into English. Later, many loans entered the language in the US: *boss*, *coleslaw*, *cookie*, *dope*, *poppycock*, *Santa Claus*, *snoop*, *spook*. (2) *English in Dutch*. Because of purist sentiment in the 16c and

17c, Dutch kept more of its Germanic character and resisted Latin more strongly than English did, but many Latinate words, such as *cruciaal*, *informatie*, and *educatie* (alongside Dutch *onderwijs*), are now entering Dutch from English, which has been the dominant foreign influence since the Second World War. English is now widely used for scholarly publishing in The Netherlands, is the first choice of foreign language in schools, and there is general exposure to it through the media, especially in TV from Britain. The effect is seen in BORROWINGS (*management*, *research*, *service*), loan translations (*diepvries* deep freeze, *gezichtsverlies* loss of face, *gouden handdruk* golden handshake), changes in the meanings of established words (*controle* in the English sense as well as earlier 'check, supervision'), and idioms (*je nek uitsteken* to stick your neck out).

See AMERICAN LANGUAGE, CANADIAN LANGUAGES, CARIBBEAN LANGUAGES, DIALECT IN THE UNITED STATES, EUROPEAN LANGUAGES, EUROPEAN UNION, FRISIAN, GERMANIC LANGUAGES, HISTORY OF ENGLISH, NORSE, OLD ENGLISH, ORKNEY AND SHETLAND DIALECTS, SCOTS, SOUTH AFRICAN ENGLISH, SPELLING REFORM.

**DYSLEXIA**, also **alexia**. A language disorder that primarily affects the ability to read and that can result in such written errors as 'saw' for *was* and 'dit' for *bit*. It may be *developmental*, occurring in young children with no clear cause, or *acquired*, occurring in previously literate adults as a result of brain damage. There are several types of acquired dyslexia, in which adults find themselves unable to read at all, or find difficulty with certain types of word, but most public attention has focused on children, where there has been considerable controversy over the nature of the problem. There are many children who, after only a short time at school, fail at the task of reading, writing, and spelling, despite normal intelligence, instruction, and opportunity to learn. Surveys of incidence vary greatly in their results, with the mean percentage of non-retarded children with reading difficulties often reaching 5%, and sometimes much larger. Boys outnumber girls in a ratio of at least 3 to 1.

The question of causation has prompted great controversy. Candidate causes have included medical, psychological, and social factors, including problems of visual perception, memory, eye movement, verbal processing, and hemispheric dominance. The two traditional camps are those who favour a medical explanation (such as unstable eye dominance), and those who consider that social and psychological factors (such as a poor short-term memory) are critical. No single explanation fits the various symptoms. Individual case studies show that there is a variety of dyslexic syndromes, reflecting several possible causes, and requiring careful behavioural assessment and individual methods of teaching.

**DYSPHEMISM** [Stress: 'DIS-fe-mizm']. In RHETORIC, the use of a negative or disparaging expression to describe something or someone, such as calling a Rolls-Royce a *jalopy*. A cruel or offensive dysphemism is a *cacophemism* (from Greek *kakós* bad: 'ka-KOFF-e-mizm'), such as using *it* for a person: *Is it coming again tonight?* See EUPHEMISM.

# E

## ■ E, e ───────────── ■

[Called 'ee']. The 5th LETTER of the Roman ALPHABET as used for English. It originated in the Phoenician consonant *hē*, which the Greeks adapted as E and called *epsilon* (that is, *E-psilón*, bare or simple E). The form was borrowed first by the Etruscans, then the Romans.

**Sound values**. The vowel letter *e* can represent a variety of sounds: (1) Short: *pet*, *very*, *herring*, *discretion*. (2) Long, as in stressed *be*, *he*, *me* and in *completion*, *region*. When unstressed, a shortened variant may be heard, as in *emit*, *acme*, and *the* before a vowel: *the apple*. (3) In RP, phonetically long and open, /ɛ/, before *r* in *there*, *where*. (4) In RP, long with a schwa glide before *r*: *hero*, *serious*. (5) In RP, often when stressed before *r* (unless followed by another vowel), the phonetically long, central sound in *her*: *infer*, *inferred*, *certain* (but not as in *peril*). (6) Schwa in unstressed syllables: *barrel*, *item*, *incident*, *robber*. In RP, there is sometimes a short *i*-sound, as in *emit*, *example*, *acme*; also (varying with schwa) in unstressed medial and final syllables (*packet*, *biggest*), especially in past participles (*admitted*, *waited*). (7) A long 'Continental' *e*, often with the sound of a long English *a*, in loans from French (*café/cafe*, *élite/elite*, *régime/regime*, *suède/suede*, *ballet*, *bouquet*), in Italian loans (*allegro*, *scherzo*), and in the Latin phrase *veni*, *vidi*, *vici* (I came, I saw, I conquered). (8) Exceptionally, *e* has the value of short *i* in *England*, *English*, *pretty*.

**Digraphs**. *E* the first element in the following digraphs:

***EA***. With the values: (1) Long *e* as in *be*: *eat*, *sea*, *meat*, *defeat*. (2) Long *a* as in *chaos* in four words: *break*, *great*, *steak*, *yea*, and some Irish names such as *Shea*, *Yeats*. (3) Short *e* as in *pet* in 50 base words and many derivatives: *breath*, *health*, *measure*, etc. (4) Phonetically long and open before *r* in: *bear*, *pear*, *swear*, *tear*, *wear*. (5) In RP, long *e* before *r*, with a schwa glide following: *ear*, *hear*, *near*. The same sound also arises when the *e* and *a* were formerly in separate syllables: *idea*, *real*, *theatre*, *European*. (6) In most accents, but not in ScoE, the vowel sound in *her*

before non-final *r* in over a dozen words, including *early*, *earth*, *learn*, *pearl*.

***EE***. With the values: (1) Long *e* as in *be*: *eel*, *see*, *meet*, *proceed*. (2) In a few words, short *i* as in *din*: especially in AmE, but sometimes in RP *been* ('bin'); especially in RP, but sometimes in AmE, *breeches* ('britches'), and widespread in BrE *coffee* ('koffy'). (3) In RP, when followed by *r*, phonetically long with a schwa glide: *beer*, *cheer*. (4) In loans, a 'Continental' long *e* as in *matinée/matinee* (from French) and *Beethoven* (from German).

***EI***. With the values: (1) Long *e* as in *be*: *conceive*, *receive*, AmE *leisure*. (2) Long *a* as in *chaos* in about 40 common words: *eight*, *neighbour*, *reign*, *rein*, *veil*, *weigh*. (3) In some loans, more or less as *y* in *my*: from Germanic languages (*eiderdown*, *gneiss*); from Greek (*kaleidoscope*, *seismograph*). (4) Short *e* as in *pet*: *heifer*, Leicester ('Lester'), BrE *leisure*. (5) Schwa or unstressed *i* as in the second syllable of *victim*: *foreign*, *sovereign*. (6) Variation in *either/neither* between a long *i* and a long *e* sound, and in *inveigle* between a long *e* and a long *a* sound.

*Note: EI and IE*. The digraphs *ei* and *ie* (as in *receive* and *believe*) cause confusion in spelling. The dictum '*i* before *e* except after c' holds good for nearly all words where the sound is long *e* ('ee' as in *seen*), as with *conceive*, *deceive*, *perceive*. There are some exceptions with *ie* after *c* (such as *species*), and some words with *ie* after *c* where the pronunciation is not 'ee' (as with *ancient* and *glacier*). There are some 30 words with *ei* not after *c* but pronounced 'ee', such as *protein*, *seize*, *weird*.

***EU***, ***EW***, ***EAU***. (1) The digraphs *eu* and *ew* generally have the value of *you*: *euphony*, *feud*, *queue*; *ewe*, *pewter*, *newt*. However, after alveolar and dental consonants, such as *n* in *new*, the vowel is often pronounced without the preceding *y*-sound in the US and in England in London and East Anglia ('noo'). After *j*, *l*, *r* (*jewel*, *lewd*, *rheumatism*), the *y*-sound has generally ceased to be pronounced. (2) In *sew*, the *ew* has the value of long *o*, as it did for the pre-20c spelling *shew* for *show*. (3) In *-eur*, in loans from French, *eu* may have the stressed value of the sound in

RP and AmE *her* (*connoisseur, saboteur*), but in RP the -*eur* of *amateur* may be schwa. (4) In loans from French, the trigraph *eau* typically has a long *o* value (*bureau, plateau*), but in *bureaucracy* it has the short *o* of *democracy*, and in *beauty* has the same 'you' value as *eu* and *ew*: but see EAST ANGLIA. (5) In loans from German, *eu* has the value 'oi': *Freudian, schadenfreude*.

**EY, EO**. (1) The digraph *ey* has the values: long *a* in *chaos* in *they, convey, survey*; long *e* in *key*; and long *i* in *eye*. See Y. (2) The rare digraph *eo* has no single dominant value: short *e* in *jeopardy, Leonard, leopard*; long *e* in *people*; long *o* in *yeoman*.

Note. The letter combinations of the above digraphs also occur with separate, non-digraph values, as in *react, create, pre-existing, deity, reinstate, reopen, reunite*.

**Following *E***. In addition to the above, a following *e* has special functions that alter the value of a preceding letter: (1) When it directly follows another vowel letter, that letter has its long value: after *a* as in *maelstrom*, after *e* as in digraph *ee* (*wheel*), after *i* as in *tie, fiery* (despite *fire, wiry*), after *o* as in *toe*, after *u* as in *Tuesday*. These patterns occur less often in mid-word position, where the *e* may disappear before a suffix (*argue/argument, true/truly*) or where the letters may be pronounced separately (*diet, poet, duet*). Occasionally a following *e* indicates an anomalous digraph value which confuses learners: *friend, shoe*. (2) A word-final following *e* may serve to mark the distinction between the hard and soft values of the consonants *c, g*: hard in *music, dig*, soft with following *e* in *convince, urge*. Sometimes, it indicates a preceding long vowel at the same time: *face, page*. The *e* may be retained in an inflected form to avoid ambiguity (contrast *singing/singeing*), as well as exceptionally in *ageing* (although *aging* also occurs, especially in AmE, in which it is the preferred form). (3) After final *s, e* sometimes distinguishes a word that ends in voiceless *s* from a plural *s* that is pronounced /z/: contrast *dense, dens*. (4) After final *th, e* may distinguish a verb with voiced *th* from a noun with voiceless *th*: *sheath/sheathe, teeth/teethe, wreath/wreathe*, but not in *a mouth/to mouth*. In *breath/breathe, cloth/clothe* the *e* may also mark a change in vowel quality.

**Magic *E***. After consonants, final silent *e* may give a long value to a vowel immediately before the consonant. This practice arose with the change in value of the preceding vowel at the time of the Great Vowel Shift, after which the final *e* fell silent. Examples for each vowel are *take, eve, quite, hope, lute*. This usage, often referred to as *magic e* (perhaps so called because it operates, as it were, at a distance), also sometimes occurs after two consonants: *waste, change*. When a suffix beginning with a vowel (such as -*ing*) is added, the final *e* disappears, but the preceding vowel remains long: *desirable, hoping*. As a counterpart to this convention, a word with a short vowel and a single final consonant is required to double its consonant, so as to avoid confusion in such pairs as *planning/planing, hopping/hoping*.

**Silent *E***. In many words, final *e* has no implications for pronunciation. It may silently mark a vowel that was once pronounced (as in *have*) or has been borrowed from French (as in *deplore, ignore*). In some combinations, it is a conventional device after certain consonants, especially *dg* and *v*, which do not usually occur in final positions in English: *judge, give*. In many words, a long *e* is indicated both by a digraph and by a final silent *e*: *receive, lease, needle*, BrE *meagre*. Some patterns with silent *e*: (1) After final /v/, particularly when the preceding vowel is short, in common monosyllables (*give, have, love*, contrast *shave, alive, move, rove*), in forms with -*lv*, -*rv* (*twelve, solve, carve, curve*, etc.), and with the suffix -*ive* (*active, motive*, etc.). (2) After *m, n* in some common monosyllables (*come, some, done, none, shone*, but contrast *company, home, son, on, tone*); similarly in some polysyllables (*cumbersome, destine, engine, discipline*, but contrast *random, mandolin, origin*). (3) In stressed vowel plus -*re* endings: *bore, core, more, restore* (contrast *abhor*); similarly in *are, were*. (4) After a short vowel and -*dg*: *badge, bridge, knowledge, porridge*. (5) In non-final position in *heart, hearth, hearken* (contrast *hark*), and *height* (not *\*hight*). (6) Medial *e* dropped is some words (*hindrance, disastrous*), but not in others (*preponderance, boisterous*). (7) In -*ate* endings of nouns and adjectives (all with a short vowel sound), but not verbs: contrast *a graduate/to graduate, moderate/to moderate*. (8) In -*ite*: *definite, favourite, opposite*. Contrast *calcite, Canaanite, Hittite* with *deposit, habit, benefit*. A similar contrast occurs between the unit of time *minute* ('minnit') and the adjective *minute* ('my-newt'). (9) After a consonant plus *l*, indicating that the *l*-sound is syllabic: *apple*, *steeple*. A similar convention once applied to such words as BrE *centre*, in which the sound is now schwa. (10) In unstressed final *-ure*: *brochure*, *figure* (contrast *murmur*, *mature*).

**Variations**. The use of *e* frequently alternates with other letters or in certain cases is optional:

***Latin and French prefixes***. (1) Historically, there has been some uncertainty in the spelling of words with the Latin prefixes *in-*, *dis-*, and their French equivalents *en-*, *des-*. Formerly, there was much free variation between *in-/en-* and *en-/des-*, as in *imploy/employ*, surviving in such pairs as *insure/ensure* (which are not strict synonyms), and BrE *dispatch/despatch* (AmE *dispatch* only), and *inquire/enquire* (in which there are slight differences in meaning in BrE, and AmE favours *inquire*). (2) A similar French/Latin variation is found between French-derived *letter*, *enemy*, *engineer* and Latin-derived *literal*, *inimical*, *ingenious*, and between *e* and *a* in the final syllable in pairs like *assistant/consistent*, *dependant/dependent*: see A.

***Vowel variation***. (1) *Agentives*. There is variation between *-er* and *-or* in the spelling of the agentive suffix in the words *adapter/adaptor*, *adviser/advisor*, *convener/convenor*, *imposter/impostor*: see O. Alternatives such as *briar/brier* also occur, as do such heterographs as *drier/dryer* and *friar/frier*. (2) *Endings in -y*. The endings *-ie*, *-(e)y* may occur as alternatives: *bogie/bog(e)y*, *curtsy/curtsey*. The adjectival suffix *-y* normally entails omission of a final *e* in the base word (*race/racy*), but *holey* ('holey socks') and *gluey* are exceptions. Alternatives such as *bony/boney* and *stony/stoney* also occur, but without variation for comparatives and superlatives: *bonier*, *stoniest*. There is grammatical variation in the use of *e* when words ending in *-y* inflect to *-ie* (*city/cities*, *pity/pitied*), but alternatives arise with *honey*, *money* (*honied*, *monies* or *honeyed*, *moneys*). (3) *Morphological variation*. Varying vowel values between grammatically or derivationally related words are often reflected in a switch from a digraph or magic *e* to simple *e*: *deep/depth*, *sleep/slept*, *succeed/success*, *lead/led*, *leave/left*, *reveal/revelation*, *receive/reception*, *thief/theft*, *serene/serenity*. Elsewhere, however, *e* may be replaced by a different vowel altogether: *clear/clarity*, *compel/compulsion*, *desperate/despair*. In addition, a spelling

change does not necessarily represent a change in sound (*height/high*, *proceed/procedure*, *speech/speak*), and sometimes a sound change is not reflected in a change of spelling: *deal/dealt*, *dream/dreamt*, *hear/heard*, *to read/he read*.

**Omitting or retaining E**. (1) The letter *e* may be optionally dropped or kept before the suffixes *-able*, *-age*, and *-ment*: *judgment/judgement*, *likable/likeable*, *lovable/loveable*, *milage/mileage*. (2) Adjectives ending in consonant plus *-le* lose the final *-e* when *-ly* is added: *able/ably*, *possible/possibly*, *probable/probably*, *simple/simply*. (3) While some nouns that end in *-o* add *-s* to form their plurals, others add *-es*, and others still vary, as with *pianos* (not \**pianoes*), *potatoes* (not \**potatos*), and both *ghettos* and *ghettoes*, often causing uncertainty. (4) The prefixes *for-/fore-*, *by-/bye-* are sometimes treated as interchangeable: *forego* is used with the meaning of both *to go before* and *to go without* (which strictly should be *forgo*); and both *by-law* and *bye-law* are found. (5) In some words initial *e* has been lost by aphaeresis: *squire* from *esquire*, *sample* from *example*, *state* from *estate*.

**American and British differences**. (1) BrE generally has *e* in *adze*, *axe*, *carcase*, *premise*, *programme*, *artefact*, and words of the type *analogue*, *catalogue*, while AmE commonly has *adz*, *ax*, *carcass*, *premiss*, *program*, *artifact*, and *analog*, *catalog*. BrE *to centre* has past tense *centred*, whereas AmE *to center* has *centered*. (2) In some words, where AmE follows a standard pronunciation for *e*, BrE gives it a value for *a*: *clerk*, *Derby*, *sergeant* (in which the pronunciation is the same as in the surnames *Clark*, *Darby*, *Sargent*). (3) Where AmE generally has *jewelry*, BrE generally has *jewellery*. (4) Where *e* in such words as *hostile*, *missile* has no value in AmE, in BrE it makes these words rhyme with *smile*. (5) BrE *whisky* contrasts with AmE and IrE *whiskey* as a generic name, but many people nonetheless keep the spelling *whisky* for the Scottish product and *whiskey* for the Irish and American products, regardless of the varieties of English they use. (6) In AmE, *story* and *stories* can mean both 'tales' and 'floors of a building', while in BrE they only refer to 'tales', the form for floors of buildings being *storey/storeys*. (7) Pronunciations differ for *lieutenant*: BrE 'leftenant', AmE 'lootenant'. (8) See also various points in the sections *Digraphs* (EE and EI), *Silent E*, and *Variations* above.

## ■ EARLY MODERN ENGLISH —— ■

Short forms *EModE*, *eModE*. From one point of view, the earlier part of the third stage of a single continuously developing English language; from another, the first stage of a distinct language, MODERN ENGLISH, that evolved from an earlier language, MIDDLE ENGLISH. Scholars differ in deciding the best approximate date for both the beginning of the period (*c.*1450, *c.*1475, or *c.*1500) and its end (1660, the year of the Restoration of Charles II, or *c.*1700, a convenient point during the Augustan Age). In this volume, the span is *c.*1450–*c.*1700. EModE was an unsettled language whose great variability can be seen in the following excerpts of prose texts from the beginning, middle, and end of the period.

*1490*. William CAXTON, printer. The opening words of the Prologue to his translation of *The Aeneid*:

After dyuerse werkes made / translated and achieued / hauyng noo werke in hande. I sittyng in my studye where as laye many dyuerse paunflettis and bookys. happened that to my hande cam a lytyl booke in frenshe. whiche late was translated oute of latyn by some noble clerke of fraunce whiche booke is named Eneydos / made in latyn by that noble poete & grete clerke vyrgyle / whiche booke I sawe ouer and redde therin. How after the generall destruccyon of the grete Troye. Eneas departed berynge his olde fader anchises vpon his sholdres / his lityl son yolus on his honde.

*1582*. Richard MULCASTER, headmaster. From ch. xiii of his textbook *The First Part of the Elementarie*, entitled 'That the English tung hath in it self sufficient matter to work her own artificial direction, for the right writing there of ':

As for the antiquitie of our speche, whether it be measured by the ancient *Almane*, whence it cummeth originallie, or euen but by the latest terms which it borroweth daielie from foren tungs, either of pure necessitie in new matters, or of mere brauerie, to garnish it self withall, it cannot be young. Onelesse the *Germane* himself be young, which claimeth a prerogatiue for the age of his speche, of an infinit prescription: Onelesse the *Latin* and *Greke* be young, whose words we enfranchise to our own vse, tho not allwaie immediatlie from

them selues, but mostwhat thorough the *Italian*, *French*, and *Spanish*: Onelesse other tungs [. . .] will for companie sake be content to be young, that ours maie not be old.

*1712*. Jonathan Swift, clergyman and writer. From 'A Proposal for Correcting, Improving and Ascertaining the English Tongue':

To examine into the several Circumstances by which the Language of a Country may be altered, would force me to enter into a wide Field. I shall only observe, That the *Latin*, the *French*, and the *English*, seem to have undergone the same Fortune. The first, from the days of *Romulus* to those of *Julius Caesar*, suffered perpetual Changes. and by what we meet in those Authors who occasionally speak on that Subject, as well as from certain Fragments of old Laws, it is manifest, that the *Latin*, Three hundred Years before *Tully* [Cicero], was as unintelligible in his Time, as the *English* and *French* of the same period are now; and these two have changed as much since *William the Conqueror*, (which is but little less than Seven hundred Years) as the *Latin* appears to have done in the like Term.

All three texts exhibit great differences in their written conventions. Sometimes these differences grew less over the centuries; for example, compare Caxton's spelling variants *lytyl* and *lityl* (little), Mulcaster's consistent *tung* and *young* (repeated in the same forms several times), and Swift's distinctly modern spelling. Where Caxton has *frenshe* and *destruccyon*, Mulcaster and Swift have *French* and Mulcaster has *prescription*. Sometimes, however, variability runs through the whole period: compare Caxton's nouns in lower-case roman letters (including most of his proper nouns such as *fraunce*, *vyrgyle*, *anchises*, but excluding *Eneydos*, *Eneas*, *Troye*), Mulcaster's lower-case roman for common nouns but initial capitals and italic for proper nouns, and Swift's nouns all with initial capitals, the proper names set in italic. Punctuation achieved relative standardization during the period: for example, contrast Caxton's unfamiliar use of virgule (slash) and full point with the familiar uses of comma and full point by Mulcaster and Swift. A grammatical change that took place mainly in the 17c is shown where Mulcaster uses *-th* for the third-person singular of the verb (*it cummeth*, *it boroweth*, *which claimeth*) but Swift uses *-s* (*the Latin appears*, not *\*appeareth*).

In general terms, EModE was marked by: (1) A major change in the vowel system of south-eastern English: see GREAT VOWEL SHIFT. (2) The development of a single literary and administrative variety of the language that was later to be called 'STANDARD ENGLISH'. (3) The spread of English throughout Britain and Ireland and the beginning of the retreat of the Celtic languages of Wales, Ireland, the Scottish Highlands and Western Isles, Cornwall, and the Isle of Man. (4) The further spread of English to colonies in North America and the Caribbean, and to trading stations in Africa and Asia. (5) Massive lexical borrowing from other languages during the Renaissance and Reformation, especially from LATIN and GREEK for scholarly purposes, from ITALIAN for literary and artistic purposes, and particularly through SPANISH and PORTUGUESE from sources beyond Europe. (6) The translation into English of many major foreign works, including a succession of versions of the BIBLE, classical Greek and Latin works, and contemporary writings from the European mainland. (7) The growth of a strong vernacular literature marked by the flowering of Elizabethan and Jacobean drama and the precursors of the novel.

See AUREATE DICTION, BOOK OF COMMON PRAYER, EUPHUISM, HISTORY OF ENGLISH, INKHORN TERM, PROSE, SHAKESPEARE.

**EAST AFRICAN ENGLISH**, short forms *EAE*, *EAfrE*. The English language as used in East Africa and associated parts of southern Africa, an outcome of European involvement since the 16c in KENYA, MALAWI, TANZANIA, UGANDA, ZAMBIA, and ZIMBABWE. In these countries, English is taking its place as an African language in the registers of politics, business, the media, and popular culture. It includes an expanding body of creative literature, by such writers as John Mbiti (b. 1931), Ngugi wa Thiong'o (b. 1938), Peter Palangyo (b. 1939), J. P. Okot p'Bitek (b. 1931), and David Rubadiri (b. 1930).

**Background**. When English was first used in East Africa, Swahili was already a regional lingua franca. Because of this, English came to be used as an additional language without any pidgin varieties. The contemporary choice of common language is most often between SWAHILI (with associations of informality) and English (with associations of formality and authority). The use of English, however, often depends on the attitudes of those being spoken to: there is a risk of causing offence by choosing English if the other people do not speak it, or Swahili, implying that they are uneducated. Linguistically mixed marriages (such as between a Luo and Kikuyu) may make English the first language of some families. EAE is greatly influenced by such languages as Swahili at large, Kikuyu in Kenya, Chichewa in Malawi, Luo in Kenya and Tanzania, and Shona in Zimbabwe. Since these are related BANTU languages, they contribute to a common Bantu substrate, but even so the ethnicity of a speaker can be identified on the basis of pronunciation and lexical choices.

**Pronunciation**. (1) EAE is non-rhotic. (2) It has a five-vowel system, /i, ɛ, a, ɔ, u/. As a result, there are more homonyms in EAE than in WAE and English at large: 'bead' for *bead/bid*; 'bed' for *bade/bed*; 'bad' for *bad/bard/bird/bud*; 'bod' for *bod/board/bode*; 'pool' for *pool/pull*. (3) A vowel, usually close to schwa, is often inserted in consonant clusters: 'konəfidens' for *confidence*, 'digənity' for *dignity*, 'maggənet' for *magnet*. (4) Consonants are often devoiced: 'laf' for *love*, 'sebra' for *zebra*. (5) Homorganic nasals are introduced before stop consonants: 'mblood' for *blood*, 'ndark' for *dark*. (6) A distinction is not always made between *l* and *r* for speakers of some mother tongues: speakers of Lozi often use 'long' for *wrong*; in Bemba, the name for *oranges* is (*ma*)*olanges*.

**Grammar**. (1) Because many people are multilingual, code-mixing is common, as in the mixed Swahili/English sentence: *Ile accident ilitokea alipolose control na akaoverturn and landed in a ditch* (The accident occurred when he lost control and overturned and landed in a ditch). (2) The omission of either the comparative adverb (*more*, *less*, *worse*, etc.) or the correlative *than* in comparative constructions, sometimes with the addition of *and*: *This university is successful in its training program than yours*; *They value children than their lives*; *They would have more powder on the hand and in their faces*. (3) Use of the all-purpose tags *isn't it?* and *not so?*: *He came here, isn't it?*; *She is a married lady, not so?*

**Vocabulary**. (1) Loans from local languages: Swahili *boma* enclosure, administrative quarters, *duka* store, shop, *ndugu* brother, friend, *piripiri/pilipili* red-pepper sauce. (2) Loan translations from local languages: Kenya *clean heart* pure, *elephant ears* big ears (often of someone who does not listen), *word to come into one's throat* to have a word on the tip of one's tongue. (3) Extensions in the senses and uses of general words, many well established, some more or less ad hoc: *come with* (bring), as in *I will come with the kitenge* (I will bring the women's cloth: Swahili); *medicine* (medical), as in *She is a medicine nun; duty* (work), as in *He is at his duty now*. (4) Hybrid compounds and fixed phrases such as *magendo whisky* black-market whisky (Swahili), *tea sieve* tea strainer. Occasionally, neologisms (some of them grandiloquent) are formed, such as *foodious* (gluttonous), *crudity* (to make crude), and *pedestrate* (to walk). See AFRICAN ENGLISH.

**EAST ANGLIA.** A region of England consisting of the counties of Norfolk and Suffolk, but also often taken to include Essex and parts of Cambridgeshire and Bedfordshire. It has two main urban areas, Norwich in Norfolk and Ipswich in Suffolk, which tend to influence the speech of the areas around them. The regional dialects belong to the MIDLANDS group, but are internally diverse: for example, Essex speech is closer to London varieties than are Norfolk and Suffolk speech. The so-called *singing Suffolk* accent has a wide pitch range and a high rising intonation at the ends of sentences. Many local accents are marked by a rhythm that tends to lengthen stressed vowels and to reduce or eliminate unstressed short vowels. Although many speakers are influenced by RP and media norms, some generalizations can be made of informal working-class speech: (1) It is non-rhotic. (2) Older, rural speakers tend to distinguish between the vowel sounds in words such as *game, grace*, and *tale* (with a long /e/) and words such as *bay, bait*, and *eight* (with /æɪ/ or /eɪ/). Younger speakers tend to use /æɪ/ or /eɪ/ for both. (3) Norfolk speakers in particular, especially older people, use two realizations for words that contain /əʊ/ in RP: words such as *bone* and *tone* have monophthongal /uː/ or a /ou/ diphthong, whereas words such as *bowl* and *tow* have /ʌu/. (4) Because of their use of /u/ for /əʊ/, some Norwich speakers have such homophones as *soap* sounding like *soup* and *boat* like *boot*.

(5) The vowel sounds in words such as *bare* and *beer* are merged into /ɛ/ or /ɛə/, producing additional homophones. (6) Throughout the region, there tends to be no /j/ in words such as *dew, dune*. *Do* and *dew* are therefore often homophones. The pronunciation 'bootiful' for *beautiful* (with the /t/ often glottalized) is a regional shibboleth. (7) Word-initial /h/ tends to be preserved in Norfolk and Suffolk but not in Cambridgeshire or Essex. (8) Glottal stops are common throughout the area, including the towns; /hæʔ/ is a common pronunciation of *hat*. (9) In older, rural Norfolk speech, /l/ tends to be clear; elsewhere, the clear/dark distinction is similar to RP. (10) In casual speech, the unmarked verb form is often used with all subjects in the present tense: *I go; He go*. (11) *That* is often used rather than *it* in such greetings as *That's a cold day!, That's nice now*. (12) A feature formerly widespread but now recessive is conditional *do: They don't go there; do, they'd have a surprise* They don't go there; if they did, they'd get a surprise. (13) Some distinctive rural words can be found, such as *hodmadod/dodman* a snail, *fourses* a light afternoon meal (compare *elevenses*), and *neathouse*, a shed for *neat* (cattle). Scandinavian influence was once strong and can still be found, especially in northern Suffolk, where streams continue to be called *becks*. See DIALECT IN ENGLAND, NEW ENGLAND.

**EAST ASIAN ENGLISH.** The English language as used in CHINA, HONG KONG, JAPAN, Macao, KOREA, and Taiwan. Its functions vary from place to place and in no country is there a significant indigenous community of English speakers. Contacts from the 17c led to a number of pidgins, particularly *Pidgin English* used by and with British traders on the China coast and *Bamboo English* used by and with US soldiers in Japan, Korea, and Vietnam. Such forms are now virtually extinct, having given way to a range of English usually learned, in part at least, in school. Because of a tradition of teaching English formally through grammar, translation, and literature, spoken usage is often stilted and bookish. In recent decades, EFL techniques have made an impact, but differences in language type and in writing systems currently impede progress. All varieties look elsewhere for their model of English (for example to BrE in Hong Kong and to AmE in South Korea and Taiwan) and display in varying degrees the influence of mother tongues, as for example difficulty with /l, r/ among speakers of Chinese and Japanese. Nonetheless, it is likely that in the next decade there will be an ever-increasing number of people (perhaps 300 m) with varying competence in English, because of its position as an international medium. Borrowing from English into local languages is high. See JAPANESE PIDGIN ENGLISH, JAPLISH.

**EAST MIDLAND DIALECT**. The dialect of the East MIDLANDS of England, especially the dialect of MIDDLE ENGLISH from which present-day STANDARD ENGLISH is generally agreed to have emerged. See CHANCERY STANDARD, DIALECT IN ENGLAND, WYCLIFFE.

**EBONICS**. [From *ebony* and *-ics* as in *phonics*]. An alternative name for AFRICAN-AMERICAN VERNACULAR ENGLISH, used by Robert L. Williams in his book *Ebonics: The True Language of Black Folks* (Institute of Black Studies, St Louis, Mo., 1975). It became internationally prominent for some months after 18 December 1996, when the board of Oakland Unified School District, California, formally resolved that Ebonics was the first language of most black American children in their area and English the second language, 'making [Oakland] the first district in the nation to give the dialect official status in programs targeting bilingual students' (Mary Curtius, 'California Educators Give Black English a Voice', *Los Angeles Times*, 20 December 1996). Reports of the resolution generated great media attention and public debate in the US, much of it hostile, as a result of which the board in mid-January 1997 issued a restatement from which the assertion that Black English was a distinct language was removed. The outraged response arose largely from a belief among many Americans of all backgrounds that the board wanted to focus on black rather than standard usage while at the same time seeking additional government funds by presenting English as the children's second language and not their mother tongue (in the same way that funds are provided to help many Hispanic children). It was assumed that the board would misuse tax dollars while also depriving the children of a solid grounding in the standard language, a primary tool for their social advancement. The board, however, wished to emphasize

that under-achieving black children need linguistic help to bridge the gap between vernacular and standard; one way of doing this is to highlight the differences between the two in the classroom, respecting both and constructively comparing them when teaching the standard.

**ECHOISM**. **1.** A WORD that echoes a sound: *splash*, echoing a liquid striking something or something striking liquid; *crunch* suggesting something brittle breaking into pieces. **2.** An expression that echoes or alludes to another: the statement 'Marking T. S. Eliot's centenary, not with a whimper but a bang' (*Time*, 26 Sept. 1988) echoes and inverts Eliot's own lines 'This is the way the world ends / Not with a bang but a whimper' (*The Hollow Men*, 1925). Compare ALLUSION, ASSONANCE, ONOMATOPOEIA. See -ISM, ROOT-CREATION, STYLE.

■ **EDINBURGH** ────────── ■

The capital of Scotland where local educated speech is more influenced by the norms of south-east England than elsewhere in Scotland. However, as part of the continuum of ScoE and SCOTS, vernacular speech is strong in working-class areas such as Leith and Gorgie and in the city's peripheral housing estates, showing variations due to dialect-mixing and nearby dialect boundaries.

**Pronunciation**. (1) Working-class Edinburgh speech shares features with GLASGOW and other Central Scots dialects: for example, only the /o/ vowel in such pairs as *cloak/clock* and *road/rod*; /e:/ in *dae* do, *pair* poor; /ɪ/ in *buit* boot, *guid* good; /e/ in *breath*, *death*, *meal*; /i/ in *dead*, *deaf*, *swear*; initial /j/ in *yae* (adjective) one, *yin* (noun) one, *yins* (rhymes with *rinse*) once, *yaise* (verb) use, *yis* (noun) use. There are also the stigmatized glottalization of medial and final /t/ and the epenthetic vowels in 'girrul' for *girl* and 'fillum' for *film*. (2) Although most people have a falling final intonation for statements, some working-class speakers have a Glasgow-like fall followed by a low rise. (3) The combination *wa* is /wɔ/ not /wa/ as in Glasgow: *want, warm, wash, water*. (4) The following both occur: *awaw* and *away* away, *twaw* and *tway* two, *whaur* and *whair* where (but only *whae*, *whase* who, whose). (5) *Make*, *take* also appear *as mak, tak*. (6) Where Glasgow has an unstressed word-final /ʌ/ as in *barra* barrow, Edinburgh has /e/, as in *barrie* barrow, *elbie* elbow, *fellie* fellow, *Glesgie/Gleskie* Glasgow, *lumbagie* lumbago, *awfie* awful, *carefie* careful, *moothfie* mouthful, *yisfie* useful. (7) The voiceless velar fricative /x/ may survive more strongly in Edinburgh than Glasgow, as in *richt* right, *strecht/strocht* straight. (8) Some speakers have 'terminal stress', whereby a normally unstressed final syllable is fully stressed, as in *Thát's áw-fíe, véry clé-vér, He had a sáir áir-rúm* He had a sore/painful arm.

**Grammar**. (1) Some features said to originate in Glasgow also occur in Edinburgh, such as *youse/yese* (plural) you, and *youse-yins* (formerly *you-yins*: 'you ones') you people. (2) The interrogative tags *eh?* and *Eh no?* are common, as in *Ye'll be wantin yer tea, eh?, Ye'll be wantin some tea, eh-no?* (3) The common pause-filler is *ken* (y'know), as in *Well, ken, ye dinny pey, ken, for ti just watch, ken* Well, y'know, you don't pay, y'know, just to watch, y'know. (4) The apologetic or depreciatory tag *like* is widely used, as in *Ah thocht ah heard ye greetin, like* I thought I maybe heard you crying, *Am ah gettin an invite, like?* Am I getting an invitation maybe?

**Vocabulary**. Local usages include *bairn* a child (where Glasgow has *wean*), *bunce* to share, *clipshear* an earwig, *dobbie/doobie* an idiot, *doddle* a lump of toffee, *guttie* a catapult/slingshot, *henner* a gymnastic feat, *hillan* a mound, hillock, *kip* a pointed hill, *lummie* a lum or chimney on fire, *mar oot* to score out, *poor-oot* a scattering of coins at a wedding, *swee* a swing.

**Literary dialect**. Much of Scotland's vernacular literature is by Edinburgh authors, mostly in literary Scots or in Lallans, but unlike Glasgow or Aberdeen, Edinburgh does not have a strong tradition of localized dialect writing. Among the sparse localized writings since the late 19c are pieces by the short-story writer Fred Urquhart (b. 1912) and the poet and critic Alan Bold (b. 1943), and the mixture of LALLANS and everyday Edinburgh Scots in the poetry of Robert Garioch (1909–81). An example from Bold under the pseudonym Jake Flower is:

> Ah havnae missed a day's work nigh on thirty year and ah've shifted some drink no danger. Ken? D'ye ken Bertie's Bar? D'ye no? Ye must ken Bertie's Bar, everybody kens Bertie's Bar. Ye cannae come fae Edinburgh if ye dinnae ken

Bertie's Bar ('Monologue', in *Scotia Review* 5, 1973).

See, GUTTER SCOTS, MORNINGSIDE AND KELVINSIDE, SCOTTISH ENGLISH.

**EDUCATED AND UNEDUCATED**. Contrastive terms especially in sociology and linguistics, used to refer to people who have or have not had formal schooling (usually to at least the end of secondary or high school), and to their usage. The contrast is often used to suggest a continuum (*more educated/less educated*), and there are three broad approaches to its use: (1) That the terms are self-evidently useful and do not risk either the self-esteem of the people discussed or the reputation of those engaged in the discussion. (2) That they can sometimes be helpful but should be used with care, because they are at least as much social as scientific judgements. A precaution often taken is to place the terms in quotation marks: *an 'educated' speaker of English*. (3) That they are best avoided unless they can be rigorously defined for certain purposes, because they risk oversimplifying or distorting complex issues and relationships and may in effect be euphemisms for distinctions of social class. The contrast appears in some contexts to be stereotypical and patronizing, implying that people are performing on an unusual level: *Educated Indian English* (compare *Cultivated Australian*). The phrase *an educated accent* is widely used to denote the ACCENT of someone educated to at least college level, often (for some of the time at least) at a private school, and implying (especially in Britain) that such an accent is not marked as regional, lower-class, or non-standard. See EDUCATED ENGLISH, STANDARD ENGLISH.

**EDUCATED ENGLISH**, also **educated usage**. The USAGE of speakers and writers of English who have been educated at least to the end of secondary level. The term is sometimes used as a synonym for *STANDARD ENGLISH*: 'Social levels of English shade gradually into one another. But we can recognize three main levels. At the top is *educated* or *standard English*; at the bottom is *uneducated English*, and between them comes what H. L. MENCKEN called the *VERNACULAR*' (W. Nelson Francis, *The English Language: An Introduction*, 1967). He adds: 'Uneducated English is that naturally used by people whose schooling is limited and who perform the unskilled labor in country and city. Certain grammatical features, such as the double or multiple negative are common to most regional varieties [of AmE].' See GEN-ERAL ENGLISH, STANDARD, VERNACULAR.

# ■ EDUCATION ─────── ■

Formal schooling of the young in preparation for life, usually as a passage through various institutions set up for that purpose and arranged in the levels *primary* (around the ages 5–7 to around 11), *secondary* (from around 12 to 15–18), and *tertiary* (from 16–18 onward). Formal education in the Western style acquired its present form only in the 19c, during which the concept and ideal of *universal education* has grown with the increasing complexity of society. With the development of institutions such as kindergartens and play groups for the early years, on the one hand, and further education and higher degrees for later adolescence and adulthood on the other, the concept of education has expanded so much as to be seen as virtually a lifelong process.

**Education and language**. In most systems of Western and Westernized education, the skills of READING, WRITING, and arithmetic (*the three Rs*) have been basic. Such systems were once dominated by LATIN, through which in addition GRAMMAR, LOGIC, and RHETORIC were taught. Until the late 19c, knowledge of contemporary foreign language was regarded as a social 'accomplishment' rather than an essential part of a school's curriculum; all LANGUAGE TEACHING was prescriptivist, assuming a grammar based on firm rules and concentrating on a relatively fixed CANON of literary texts both as source material and as models for composition. In the 20c, such assumptions have been increasingly disputed and greater language awareness has led to new, often experimental and controversial, approaches. Prescriptivism, however, is by no means dead. In contemporary educational practice, *oracy* as well as *LITERACY* is regarded as important, and a foundation of linguistic competence is taken to be essential for all subjects: that is, 'language across the curriculum', as recommended by the UK's Bullock Report in 1975.

Young people are currently introduced to many kinds of language material, including reports, advertisements, and technical in-structions, as well as literature of various kinds. Free expression is encouraged in writing, rather than composition on a set theme with assessment based largely on correct SYNTAX, SPELLING, and PUNCTUATION. Some educationists, however, consider that the processes of liberalism and liberation have gone far enough, and throughout the English-speaking world there appears to be an impulse towards basic knowledge and firmer standards (*back to the basics*). The teaching of foreign languages also looks to the living situation rather than a given literary CORPUS, with emphasis on the direct method and, wherever possible, complete immersion in the target language (especially by living among its speakers). Language in education has often been influenced by political factors: for example, WELSH was proscribed in the schools of Wales for a long time in the 19c, but is now part of their curriculum. In the many countries with substantial ethnic minorities, decisions have to be taken about the status of the mother tongue in relation to the national language or language variety, as a result of which it has often been necessary to introduce specific teaching of the national medium as a 'second' (sometimes in effect a 'foreign') language.

**Education and English**. Although a general recognition of English as a significant literary language developed in the second half of the 16c, it was long before it was equally honoured in the educational system. The principal aim of education was for centuries to inculcate skill in LATIN and to a lesser extent in GREEK. The *grammar* of 'Grammar Schools' was Latin grammar, and the use of Latin continued at the ancient universities. Richard MULCASTER, who offered guidance in the basic teaching of English in *The First Part of the Elementarie* (1582), was exceptional among schoolmasters; John Brinsley made a plea for English teaching in 1627, but these lone voices were virtually unheeded. Thomas Sheridan in 1763 advocated the study of English grammar at the universities, but classics continued to dominate their curricula until well into the 19c. However, more attention was given to English in the Dissenting Academies for sons of nonconformist families, such as the Northampton Academy founded in 1729. Where ENGLISH TEACHING developed, it was prescriptivist and based on formal grammars like those of Lowth and Murray.

The foundation of new universities in the 19c led to chairs and eventually whole departments of English. There was much concentration on OLD ENGLISH as giving a sound philological training; ENGLISH LITER-ATURE was taught largely in historical terms, with major authors and defined periods. The grammar schools and public schools of England began to give attention to English: for example, at Rugby, Thomas Arnold laid emphasis on essay-writing in English. In 1868, the Taunton Commission on the endowed grammar schools recom-mended the teaching of 'modern' subjects, including English, a view endorsed and strengthened by later official educational reports in Britain. As late as 1886, Winston CHURCHILL at Harrow was among those who 'were considered such dunces that we could only learn English' (*My Early Life*, 1930). The Victorian movement for popular education through Mechanics' Institutes and similar organizations gave some impetus to the study of English in circumstances where the traditional prestige of Latin and Greek did not come into the question.

By the beginning of the 20c, the teaching of English at all levels was established throughout the English-speaking world. A Board of Education report, *The Teaching of English in England* (1921), criticized the sur-vival of old-fashioned approaches in both schools and universities. Subsequently, the teaching of English has been influenced by wider understanding of the importance of language skills. In the schools, free compo-sition and oral practice have largely taken the place of formal exercises. University departments of English have proliferated worldwide, the historical approach being superseded by practical criticism and per-sonal response to texts. More recently, the abundance of rival theories of literary criti-cism has meant that a particular approach may be dominant in a department. Genre studies and work on writers outside the traditional canon are now almost universal. In addition, English is not always treated as a separate subject, but may be incorpo-rated into *media studies* or *communication studies*, with wider attention to other forms of expression.

See CHILD LANGUAGE ACQUISITION, EXAM-INING IN ENGLISH, FRIES, FUNCTIONAL LITERACY, GENERAL ENGLISH, HALLIDAY, HORNBY, JESPERSEN, KINGMAN REPORT, LAN-GUAGE AWARENESS, LANGUAGE LEARNING, LANGUAGE PLANNING, PITMAN (I.), PITMAN (J.), PUBLIC SCHOOL ENGLISH, PUBLIC SCHOOL PRONUNCIATION, SWEET, TEFL, TEIL, TESD, TESL, TESOL.

**EFFECTIVE WRITING**, also **good writing**. The ability to express oneself well in WRITING and PRINT. Many successful writ-ers have pointed out that writing well is a constant struggle ('the intolerable wrestle with words and meanings': T. S. Eliot, *East Coker*, 1940). There are no clear-cut, objec-tive criteria for establishing a scale of effec-tiveness in writing for all purposes and occasions, but teachers at both school and college level, and writers of writing manu-als, generally emphasize two levels of com-petence: (1) Ability with the basics of the written language: spelling, punctuation, grammar, and word use. (2) Awareness of the right STYLE and RHETORIC for the occasion and one's readership. The writers of four manuals that have been highly influential in the 20c offer their readers very similar 'core' advice on writing well:

Be direct, simple, brief, vigorous, and lucid . . . Prefer the familiar word to the far-fetched. Prefer the concrete word to the abstract. Prefer the single word to the circumlocution. Prefer the short word to the long. Prefer the Saxon word to the Romance (H. W. & F. G. Fowler, *The King's English: The Essential Guide to Written English*, Oxford University Press: 1st edition 1906, 3rd edition 1931, most recent reprint 1990).

But the secret of good writing is to strip every sentence to its cleanest components. Every word that serves no function, every long word that could be a short word, every adverb which carries the same meaning that is already in the verb, every passive construction that leaves the reader unsure of who is doing what—these are the thousand and one adulterants that weaken the strength of a sentence (William Zinsser, *On Writing Well: An Informal Guide to Writing Nonfiction*, New York: Harper & Row, 2nd edition, 1980).

The golden rule is to pick those words that convey to the reader the meaning of the writer and to use them and them only. This golden rule applies to all

prose, whatever its purpose, and indeed
to poetry too (Sir Ernest Gowers, *The
Complete Plain Words*, London: Her
Majesty's Stationery Office, first
published 1954, 3rd edition 1986;
written primarily for British
bureaucrats).

1. Place yourself in the background. 2.
Write in a way that comes naturally. 3.
Work from a suitable design. 4. Write
with nouns and verbs. 5. Revise and
rewrite. 6. Do not overwrite. 7. Do not
overstate. 8. Avoid the use of qualifiers. 9.
Do not affect a breezy manner. 10. Use
orthodox spelling. 11. Do not explain too
much. 12. Do not construct awkward
adverbs. 13. Make sure the reader knows
who is speaking. 14. Avoid fancy words.
15. Do not use dialect unless your ear is
good. 16. Be clear. 17. Do not inject
opinion. 18. Use figures of speech
sparingly. 19. Do not take shortcuts at
the cost of clarity. 20. Avoid foreign
languages. 21. Prefer the standard to the
offbeat (William Strunk & E. B. White,
*The ELEMENTS OF STYLE*, New York:
Macmillan, 3rd edition, 1979: a list of
the section-titles of ch. 5, 'An Approach
to Style').

Ability to write effectively is also commonly
associated with the following points: (1) The
habit of reading widely and a capacity to
respond to established writers in terms not
only of their surface messages but also their
styles, subtexts, and allusions. (2) A willingness to fit the writing to the reader: 'You
must give readers either the style or the
content they want, preferably both' (Peter
Elbow, *Writing With Power: Techniques for Mas-
tering the Writing Process*, New York: Oxford
University Press, 1981). (3) The capacity and
willingness to undertake planning and research that involve drawing up schedules
and agendas, making detailed notes,
preparing interim résumés, framing proposals for publishers, employers, or others,
and collating material in successive drafts.
(4) The willingness, however painful, to seek
and accept critical comment before the
publication or circulation of one's material,
and to live with adverse criticism afterwards. Established writers tend to be their
own first and severest editors, with the aim
of reducing the likelihood of changes imposed by their editors and negative comment from reviewers and readers.

See COMPLETE PLAIN WORDS, DICTIONARY
OF MODERN ENGLISH USAGE, ELEMENTS OF
STYLE, HOUSE STYLE, ORWELL, PLAIN ENGLISH,
USAGE, USAGE GUIDANCE AND CRITICISM.

**EFL.** See ENGLISH, TEACHING ENGLISH, EXAM-
INING IN ENGLISH, TEFL.

**EFL DICTIONARY.** See LEARNER'S
DICTIONARY.

**ELABORATED AND RESTRICTED
CODE.** Terms introduced by the British so-
ciologist Basil Bernstein in the 1960s, referring to two varieties (or *codes*) of language
use, seen as part of a general theory of the
nature of social systems and social rules.
The *elaborated code* was said to be used in
relatively formal, educated situations, permitting people to be reasonably creative in
their expression and to use a range of linguistic alternatives. It was thought to be
characterized by a fairly high proportion
of such features as subordinate clauses,
adjectives, the pronoun *I* and passives. By
contrast, the *restricted code* was thought to
be used in relatively informal situations,
stressing the speaker's membership of a
group, relying on context for its meaning-
fulness, and lacking stylistic range. Linguistically it is highly predictable, with a fairly
high proportion of pronouns, tag questions, and the use of gestures and intonation to convey meaning. The attempt to
correlate these codes with certain types of
social class background, and their role in
educational settings (such as whether children who are used to restricted code would
succeed in schools where elaborated code
is the norm) brought the theory considerable publicity and controversy. See
SOCIOLINGUISTICS.

***ELEMENTS OF STYLE, The***, known informally as *the little book*. A short (85-page)
prescriptive and proscriptive American
work on prose STYLE by William Strunk Jr.,
a professor at Cornell U. in New York State.
It is widely considered a classic of its kind.
Strunk used the text as teaching material
from at least 1919, first publishing it in
book form in 1935, with Edward A. Tenney.
The later, better-known editions (Macmillan, 1959, 1972, and 1979) were revised and
extended by E. B. White, a writer and former
student of Strunk's. In his introduction,
White refers to *Elements* as 'Bill Strunk's

*parvum opus'*. There are five chapters to the Strunk and White editions: *Elementary rules of usage*; *Elementary principles of composition*; *A few matters of form*; *Words and expressions commonly misused*; and *An approach to style*. See EFFECTIVE WRITING, USAGE GUIDANCE AND CRITICISM.

**ELICOS**, full form *English Language Intensive Courses for Overseas Students*. The common name in Australia for courses in English as a foreign language. The *ELICOS Association* was founded in the early 1980s.

**ELISION**. In SPEECH and WRITING, the omission or slurring (*eliding*) of one or more vowels, consonants, or syllables, as in *ol' man* old man, *gonna* going to, *wannabe* want to be, and the usual pronunciation of *parliament* ('parlement'). Although in speech there is no direct indication of elision, in writing it is often marked by an APOSTROPHE: *didn't* did not, *I'd've* I would have. Elision is common in everyday speech and may be specially marked in verse to ensure that readers keep the metre, as in *th'empire*. Foreign students often have difficulty coming to terms with elisions created by the stress-timed RHYTHM of English, which may make word sequences seem nonsensical, *It is no good at all* sounding like *Snow good a tall*. See APHAERESIS, APHESIS, APOCOPE, APOSIOPESIS, ELLIPSIS, SYNCOPE.

**ELLIPSIS**. The omission of an element of language for reasons associated with SPEECH, RHETORIC, GRAMMAR, and PUNCTUATION. The omitted element can usually be recovered by considering the context of what has been said or written. In speech and WRITING, sounds and letters are often left out of words: in the sentence *She said he'd come, he'd* is elliptical for either *he had* or *he would*. Such contractions are informal and usually arise from speed of delivery, economy of effort, and the RHYTHM of the language: see ELISION. At times, elliptical speech or writing is so concise that listeners and readers must supply missing elements through guesswork or special knowledge, and if they cannot, they fail to understand. Information can be left out or hinted at for reasons of style or discretion; in such areas as politics, diplomacy, and negotiation, remarks are often elliptical in nature and intent.

**In grammar**. Ellipsis is a common syntactic device in everyday language: for example, the full structure of the normal but elliptical sentence *Take another piece if you want to* is *Take another piece if you want to take another piece*. Here, the ellipsis depends on the words that precede it and is anaphoric: see ANAPHORA. In conversation, words may be omitted because they relate to what someone has just said: *When can I see you?—Tomorrow* (that is, *You can see me tomorrow*). In *Those who can should pay*, the elliptical *Those who can* depends for the interpretation *Those who can pay* on what follows and is cataphoric: see CATAPHORA. Anaphoric and cataphoric ellipsis are types of *textual ellipsis*, where the recoverability of the full structure depends on what occurs before or after. It contrasts with *situational ellipsis*, in which recoverability depends on knowledge of the situational context (*Got any money?* may be *Have you got any money?* or *Have they got any money?*), and *structural ellipsis*, in which recoverability depends on syntax (the headline *Poll shows labour 10 points ahead* corresponds to the full *A poll shows that the Labour Party is 10 points ahead*). Another type, often used in making notes or writing a diary, is the telegraphic *Went out. Had a meal. Came home and watched TV. Then bed.*

Grammarians tend to restrict the notion of ellipsis to instances where the missing part can be recovered uniquely. *The patient she examined was still unconscious* is not therefore strictly elliptical, since several items may be inserted: *The patient that/who/whom she examined was still unconscious*. Similarly, in *Being taller than his brother, John could see over the wall*, *Being taller* cannot be expanded to a full form, though it can be interpreted as *Since he is taller* or *As he is taller*. Grammatical ellipsis is a device for achieving economy by avoiding repetition. It contributes to clarity and emphasis, and enables attention to be focused on important information. It shares these characteristics with pronouns and other forms of substitution such as the auxiliary *do* in *Marion liked the play as much as I did*.

**In punctuation**. In writing and print, ellipsis is the formal convention, in the form of three *ellipsis points* (. . .), for leaving out parts of quoted sentences and texts, while at the same time indicating that an omission has occurred: for example, the sentence *There has been, as far as we can tell, no loss of life* can be reduced in quotation to *There has been . . . no loss of life*. When ellipsis follows the end of a sentence, there are sometimes four points, consisting of a period to close the sentence and then three ellipsis points: for example, the sentences *We mustn't give in. What would be the point? We must go on!* can be reduced to *We mustn't give in. . . . We must go on!* Ellipsis points often serve, as does a dash, to leave a statement dramatically 'hanging in the air' (*The enemy slowly came nearer, then . . .*), after which there may be a new paragraph, a change of topic, or no further text. When points are used to suggest not an omission but a pause (*They left . . . rather quickly*), they are known as *points of suspension* or *suspension points*, and are not elliptical. Asterisks (\*\*\*) are also sometimes used to mark omission, and a single asterisk is often used to replace a vowel in a taboo word (*c\*nt, f\*ck*); on such occasions, the asterisk serves as a kind of social ellipsis. See ARTICLE, USAGE.

**ELOCUTION**. The study and practice of oral delivery, including control of breath, VOICE, PRONUNCIATION, stance, and gesture (*Has he taken elocution lessons?*); the way in which someone speaks or reads aloud, especially in public (*flawless elocution*). An early meaning of the term was literary STYLE as distinct from content, and relates to the Latin meaning of *elocutio* ('speaking out'), one of the canons or departments of RHETORIC. Elocution as training in how to speak 'properly' (as in *taking elocution lessons*) was a feature of EDUCATION, particularly for girls, in the 18–19c. SHAW, who gave an extended dramatic treatment to elocution in *Pygmalion* (1912), added to his will in 1913 a clause giving some of the residue of his estate to 'The substitution of a scientific training in PHONETICS for the makeshifts of so-called elocution lessons by actors and others which have hitherto prevailed in the teaching of oratory'. See ORTHOEPY, PERIOD, PROSE.

**ELT**, short for *English Language Teaching*. A British term for TEACHING ENGLISH to non-native learners, often used in recent years either interchangeably with *EFL* (*English as a Foreign Language*) or as a cover term for EFL and *ESL* (*English as a Second Language*). Some commentators, such as Peter Strevens, have classified it as part of *FLT* (*Foreign Language Teaching*) in general. The term is not much used in North America, and tends not only to be the British term for the subject but

also to be the term for the British approach to the subject. The organized teaching of English to foreign learners in England dates from the 16c. During the 17–19c self-instruction manuals were published throughout Europe to meet the needs of travellers and traders, and while mother-tongue teaching in the schools was bound up with parsing, translation, and literature, there was more emphasis in such books on immediate results and on oral rather than written production. The reform movement of the late 19c slowly moved foreign-language teaching both within and outside the formal systems of education towards a greater emphasis on speech and spontaneous use. It also represented a systematic attempt to derive methods of LANGUAGE TEACHING from the precepts of the developing science of linguistics.

**Individuals and institutions**. As the language spread with general EDUCATION and the evolution of the British Empire into the COMMONWEALTH, ELT became a major element in the emerging post-colonial school systems. At first, syllabuses deriving from the teaching of English as a mother tongue predominated, with a strong literary emphasis, but the work of such 20c practitioners as Harold Palmer, Michael WEST, and A. S. HORNBY built on the reformers' *direct method* and moved techniques away from traditional literature-based approaches. West concentrated on the use of graded vocabulary in reading programmes and Palmer and Hornby developed syllabuses based on limited ranges of grammatical structures. The work of West in India and Palmer and Hornby in Japan continued through teacher trainers like John Bright and Lionel Billows in East Africa until well after independence from colonial rule.

The BRITISH COUNCIL, from its foundation in 1934–5, played a significant role in ELT research and development throughout the world. British publishers throughout the years after the Second World War expanded their ELT production, and a superstructure of teacher-training courses, research programmes, and professional associations developed. The Institute of Education at the U. of London trained EFL teachers from 1932, and had a chair in the subject from 1948 (its chair in teaching English in Britain being founded in 1976). The School (later Department) of Applied Linguistics at the U. of Edinburgh was founded in 1956, expressly to support high-level work in ELT, and the Association of Recognized English Language Schools (ARELS) was founded in 1960 to introduce professional controls on private English-language schools in UK.

**Methodologies**. Academically, the 1960s saw a swing away from work aimed at the COMMONWEALTH, to freelance and non-state-funded work throughout the world. The transfer of money to the Middle East resulting from the oil revolution of 1973 created a massive market for advanced education and thus indirectly for the English language that gave access to teachers and textbooks in major technical areas. English for specific purposes (ESP), providing access to academic English for education or job-specific English for training, became a major area of development. GENERAL ENGLISH, at lower levels in the educational systems, was neglected in the 1970s until the desire to humanize what was perceived as an aridly scientific emphasis brought back into consideration many traditional practices such as literature teaching and TRANSLATION. At the same time, approaches deriving from various psychological therapeutic models, such as the Silent Way, Counselling Learning, and Suggestopedia, became popular, particularly in the US, as another means of humanizing language teaching. While very different in the techniques and strategies adopted, these shared a concern to develop the full psychological potential of individual learners.

In the 1990s, the relationship between language and personal identity is a major issue for ELT theory, as the social and cultural implications of the role of English as an international language are assimilated. See EXAMINING IN ENGLISH, LANGUAGE LEARNING, TEFL, TEIL, TESD, TESL.

**ELYOT, (Sir) Thomas** [1499?–1546]. English statesman and scholar. In such works as *The boke named The gouernour* (1531), he held that though RHETORIC made LATIN and GREEK style more eloquent, the structure of English made meaning clearer. Elyot sought to increase English vocabulary by borrowing from Latin, Greek, and FRENCH, in order to correct 'the insufficiencie of our owne langage'. When introducing new words, he often used them in explanatory pairs: *education or bringing up of children*; *explicating or unfolding*. See BOOK OF COMMON PRAYER.

**E-MAIL**. Forms: **e-mail**, **E-mail**, **email**, **Email**; full form **electronic mail**. The transmission of a message by electronic digital code; a message sent in this way: *to receive news by e-mail*; *to get an e-mail message*; *to send someone an e-mail*. Such messages may be brief notes, communications like traditional letters, or electronic files. Some systems are limited to one computer network, others have *gateways* to further systems, and others still (the majority) use the full range of the INTERNET. E-mail began in the US in 1964, and it is estimated that currently some 25m users send 15b messages a year by this means. E-mail messages may be sent to individuals or to groups, in which case transmission is called *broadcasting*. E-mail systems store messages in mailboxes with electronic addresses, which receivers check from time to time. After a message has been read, it can be electronically filed, copied to others, deleted, and/or printed out on paper. It usually takes only seconds for an e-mail message to reach its destination if nearby, or a few minutes if on the other side of the world.

**EMBEDDING**. A term in generative GRAMMAR for the process by which one sentence is included by subordination within another (the *matrix* sentence). The sentence *John announced that they were engaged* is said to be derived from the matrix sentence *John announced (something)*, into which the COMPLEMENT clause *They were engaged* has been introduced by means of the complementizer *that*.

**-EME**. In LINGUISTICS, a noun-forming suffix used in naming certain theoretical units of language, such as the *PHONEME*, the minimal unit of phonology or speech sound, the *sememe*, a unit of meaning, the *prosodeme*, a unit of rhythm, and the *tagmeme*, a unit of structure. Of the many units created in recent decades, most are restricted to specific theories and works, and have little current use. See LEXEME, MORPHEME.

**EMOTICON**. [A blend of *emotion* and *icon*]. In COMPUTING, a small composite symbol, not unlike an ICON, formed from punctuation symbols and used by the sender of an E-MAIL message to indicate mood and attitude. The best-known emoticon is the *smiley* :-), indicating that whatever has been typed is a joke or well intended; others are :-( for 'sad' and ;-) for 'winking'. The term *smiley* is often used for all emoticons, even if they are not at all like smiling.

**EMPHASIS**. A use of language to mark importance or significance, through either intensity of expression or linguistic features such as STRESS and INTONATION. The classical sense of emphasis as something added to language survives in the phrases *add emphasis to* or *lay emphasis on*. It is generally achieved by any means that draws attention to a syllable, word, phrase, idea, event, or social situation, such as the increase of intensity and volume on *at once* when someone says 'Do it *at once!'* Here, print marks, by means of ITALICS and an EXCLAMATION MARK, what is achieved in SPEECH by an increase in the volume of sound (usually accompanied by a change of expression).

**In speech, writing, and print**. (1) Spoken emphasis is usually achieved by changing STYLE, PITCH, TONE, RHYTHM, STRESS, or any combination of these. Typically, people emphasize something by speaking more loudly or by shouting, but they can also be emphatic by speaking more quietly, intensely, clearly, quickly, or slowly. The normal rhythm of delivery can change so as to stress each word or syllable firmly and equally: DO—IT—AT—ONCE. Contrastive stress, involving rhythm and intonation, is commonly used to emphasize a word or point: *MARY should do it (not Joan), Mary SHOULD do it (and not avoid her responsibilities), Mary should DO it (rather than do nothing).* (2) Emphasis in WRITING is usually achieved by underlining or capitalizing words, and by using exclamation marks. In print, italics or other lettering are also used. The same word can therefore be emphasized as: 'Put the BOOK on the table', 'Put the *book* on the table', 'Put the <u>book</u> on the table.' A whole sentence can be emphasized as an order (*Put the book on the table!*), the exclamation mark implying anger, insistence, loudness, or any combination of these.

**In grammar and style**. (1) In its various emphatic uses the auxiliary verb is generally stressed. Prominent among them is contrastive emphasis on the positive or negative: *Why didn't you tell me?—I DID tell you; They say they've paid, but they HAVEn't.* The contrastive emphasis may be on tense (*Robert WAS—and still IS—a happy child*) or aspect (*She is living in Birmingham and HAS been for a long time*). The emphasis may, however, be non-contrastive, conveying emotion: *What HAVE you done?; Where ARE you going?; We ARE sorry; I DO like your hair.* The term *emphatic pronoun* refers to a reflexive pronoun used to emphasize a noun phrase, as in 'The town *itself* is very old' and 'Well, you said it *yourself.'* (2) A variety of devices alone or in combination serve to create emphases of style: a long sentence followed by a short sentence; a quiet tone followed by a loud tone; a dramatic pause; a change of direction; a deliberate omission; an unexpected silence; change in word order (*This I can do without* as opposed to *I can do without this*); REPETITION, especially towards a climax (*I want you to do it, I insist that you do it—and you'll do it NOW!*); figurative usage such as metaphor and rhetorical question (*Would you have believed he could design such a rhapsody in stone?*).

When a technique is overused or too many devices occur at the same time the result is *overemphasis*; when a technique is underused or too few devices occur the result is *underemphasis*. An intention to be emphatic is often introduced by such formulas as *I must emphasize that . . . , I cannot sufficiently emphasize that . . . , We lay emphasis here on . . . , I must stress that . . . , and This report underlines the fact that . . .* See ALLITERATION, CAPITAL, EXAGGERATION, HYPERBOLE, INVERSION, LITOTES, MEIOSIS.

**ENDING**. A grammatical or derivational element at the end of a WORD: *-s* added to *horse* to form the plural *horses*, added to *sell* to form the third-person singular *sells*; *-ity* added to *central* to form *centrality*. Elements like *-s* are often referred to as *inflectional endings*. Elements like *-ity* may be referred to as *derivational endings*, but are more commonly known as *suffixes*. Inflectional endings may or may not be classed as suffixes. See CLASSICAL ENDING, INFLECTION.

**ENG**, also less formally **tailed n, n with a tail**. The symbol ŋ, used in IPA and the pronunciation systems of some dictionaries for the voiced velar NASAL consonant represented in English by the digraph *ng* as in *sing* /sɪŋ/. The form appears to date from the 17c, and was used by Isaac PITMAN in 1845 with this value in his phonotypic alphabet. See LETTER[1], SPEECH.

# ■ ENGLISH ■

**1.** The name of a people (*the achievements of the English*); the adjective associated with that people and with its country, England, which occupies the southern part of the island of Britain (*English traditions*). **2.** Short forms *E*, *E.*, *Eng*. The name of a language originating in north-western Europe (*the history of English*); the adjective relating to it (*English dialects*). **3.** A course offered in schools, universities, and other institutions, whose aim is to provide students with knowledge about (and skills in relation to) the language, aspects of its literature, or both; *first-year English*; *English as a Foreign Language* (*EFL*); *English language teaching* (*ELT*); *English Language and Literature*; *Business English*; *remedial English*. **4.** The adjective and noun used in Canada for speakers of English as opposed to French, regardless of ethnic origin: *differences between the French and the English*; *English Canadians*. [In the article that follows, the first and second senses only are discussed. For the third sense, see TEACHING ENGLISH; for the fourth, see CANADIAN ENGLISH.]

**The English**. Early Germanic settlers in Britain were referred to in Latin as the *gens Anglorum*, which can be translated as both 'Angle race' and 'English people', and called themselves *Englisc/Ænglisc* or *Angelcynn* ('Angle-kin'). The name *Englisc* contrasted with the names of both Celtic and Scandinavian people in Britain: 'Nah naðer to farenne ne Wylisc man on Ænglisc lond ne Ænglisc on Wylisc' (Neither Welshman to go on English land, nor English on Welsh: ordinance); 'Gif Ænglisc man Deniscne ofslea' (If an Englishman kills a Dane: Laws of Aethelred, both citations from *c*.1000). However, by the time of the Norman Conquest, *English* was the name for all inhabitants of England, regardless of background. For many years after 1066, the Normans were commonly distinguished from their English subjects as *French*, a dichotomy sustained in state documents long after it ceased to mean much in social terms. By the 14c, *English* was again the name for all subjects of the king or queen of England, whatever their background, and has remained so ever since.

**Ambiguity**. A new uncertainty developed in the 16c. Wales was united with England in 1535 and the English and Scottish monarchies became one in 1603. The union of the parliaments of England and Scotland took place in London in 1707 and the state of Great Britain officially came into existence. Increasingly from these dates, the term *English* has been used in three ways: to refer to the people of England and matters concerning England alone; to refer to the people of England and Wales and matters concerning both; to refer to the people of Great Britain (England, Wales, Scotland, and varyingly all or part of Ireland), and matters concerning them all. Generally, the first usage prevails when Irish, Scots, Welsh, and English people are talking to or about each other, although English people are famous among the others for using their generic name to cover all four. When talking among themselves, through the media, and in international situations, many English people use *English* without specifying whether they are discussing themselves or all Britons and perhaps without being clear about the limits they intend. This is also often the case with Americans, mainland Europeans, and others:

'While Rafelson is a great admirer of Robert Redford, he did not think an American playing an aristocratic Englishman in "Out of Africa" worked. So he decided he wanted English actors and settled for two virtual unknowns. Patrick Bergin, like Burton, whom he plays, is Irish and the star of "Act of Betrayal," a recent mini-series about an Irish Republican Army informer. Iain Glen, a Scotsman, who plays Speke, was in the West End production of Tom Stoppard's "Hapgood" early last year' (in 'Quest for the Source of the Nile, on Film', *New York Times*, Feb. 1989).

**The language**. English is part of the Germanic branch of the Indo-European language family, along with, among others, Danish, Dutch, and German. Once confined to Britain, it is now used throughout the world. Its use and distribution can be discussed in various ways, including geographical distribution, status as an official or other language, and status as majority language or mother tongue (first language), alternative language, medium of education, second language, or foreign language.

In the later 20c, non-native users of English have come to outnumber native users, partly because of the accelerating

## THE WORLD DISTRIBUTION OF ENGLISH

The territories in which English is a significant everyday language, in alphabetic order according to regions of the world, are:

***Africa and the western Indian Ocean***. Botswana, British Indian Ocean Territory, Cameroon, Ethiopia, Gambia, Ghana, Kenya, Lesotho, Liberia, Malawi, Mauritius, Namibia, Nigeria, Seychelles, Sierra Leone, Somalia, South Africa, Sudan, Swaziland, Tanzania, Uganda, Zambia, Zimbabwe.

***The mainland Americas and the South Atlantic***. Argentina, Ascension (Island), Belize, Bermuda, Canada, the Falkland Islands, Guyana, Honduras, Nicaragua, Panama, St Helena, Surinam, Tristan da Cunha, the United States.

***Asia***. Bahrain, Bangladesh, Brunei, Cyprus, Hong Kong, India, Israel, Kuwait, Malaysia, the Maldives, Nepal, Oman, Pakistan, the Philippines, Qatar, Singapore, Sri Lanka, the United Arab Emirates, Vietnam.

***The Caribbean***. Anguilla, Antigua and Barbuda, Bahamas, Barbados, the Cayman Islands, Dominica, Grenada, Jamaica, Montserrat, Puerto Rico, St Christopher and Nevis, St Lucia, St Vincent and the Grenadines, Trinidad and Tobago, the Turks and Caicos Islands, the Virgin Islands (American and British).

***Europe***. The Channel Islands, Gibraltar, the Irish Republic, the Isle of Man, Malta, the United Kingdom (England, Scotland, Wales, Northern Ireland).

***Oceania***. Australia, the Cook Islands, Fiji, Hawaii (in the US), Kiribati, Nauru, New Zealand, Papua New Guinea, the Solomon Islands, Tonga, Tuvalu, Vanuatu, Western Samoa.

It is not always easy to establish whether English has a constitutionally endorsed status in the territories in which it plays a role. It might be expected to have such a status in the UK and the US, but does not; in both it is a *de facto* rather than a *de jure* official language, although in a number of US states it is formally endorsed as the official language: see ENGLISH LANGUAGE AMENDMENT. English has generally acquired legal status only when a government has concluded that explicit recognition is necessary, usually to establish it as a sole medium or a co-medium of administration and education. In the following countries, English has a statutory role: *Botswana* (with Setswana), *Cameroon* (with French), *Canada* (with French), *Gambia, Ghana, India* (with Hindi), *the Irish Republic* (with Irish Gaelic), *Lesotho* (with Sesotho), *Malawi* (with Chichewa), *Nigeria, Pakistan* (with Urdu), *Papua New Guinea* (with Hiri Motu and Tok Pisin), *the Philippines* (with Filipino), *Seychelles* (with Creole and French), *Sierra Leone, Singapore* (with Mandarin Chinese, Malay, and Tamil), *the Solomon Islands* (with Solomon Islands Pidgin English), *South Africa* (with Afrikaans, Ndebele, Pedi, Northern Sotho, Southern Sotho, Swati, Tsonga, Venda, Xhosa, Zulu), *Swaziland* (with Siswati), *Tanzania* (with Swahili), *Uganda, Vanuatu* (with French and Bislama), *Zambia, Zimbabwe.*

spread of the language, and partly because of increases in population and educational opportunities in many parts of the world. Estimates of the overall number of users of English relate to the three criteria of *English by birthright* (in the ENL territories in the 1970s estimated at *c.*300m people), *English through historical association* (in the ESL territories also *c.*300m), and *English through usually formal acquisition* (in the EFL territories *c.*100m). The total of *c.*700m was widely accepted in the early 1980s, but some linguists, for example David Crystal ('How Many Millions?—The Statistics of World English', *English Today* 1, Jan. 1985), have discussed doubling this total to *c.*1.4bn so as to

## ENL, ESL, AND EFL TERRITORIES

The global distribution of English is often currently described in terms of English as a Native Language (ENL), English as a Second Language (ESL), and English as a Foreign Language (EFL):

**1. *ENL territories*.** Most people in ENL territories have English as their first and often only language. There are two groups: (a) *English profoundly dominant*: Anguilla, Antigua and Barbuda, Ascension Island, Australia, the Bahamas, Barbados, Belize, Bermuda, Dominica, England, the Falkland Islands, Grenada, Guyana, the Isle of Man, Jamaica, Montserrat, Northern Ireland, St Christopher and Nevis, St Helena, St Vincent and the Grenadines, Trinidad and Tobago, the United States of America (but see next), the Virgin Islands (American and British). (b) *At least one other language significant*: Canada (French), Channel Islands (French), Gibraltar (Spanish), the Irish Republic (Irish Gaelic), Liberia (various Niger–Congo languages), New Zealand (Maori), St Lucia (Creole French), Scotland (Scottish Gaelic, and Scots if defined as a distinct language from English), South Africa (Afrikaans; various Bantu and Khoisan languages), Wales (Welsh). Some commentators argue that the US is, or will soon be, a member of this group, with Spanish as the other nationally significant language.

**2. *ESL territories*.** Many people in ESL territories use English for various purposes, and in some English has an official, educational, or other role. English may be generally accepted or more or less controversial. The territories are: Bangladesh, Botswana, Brunei, Cameroon, Cook Islands, Fiji, Gambia, Ghana, Hong Kong, India, Kenya, Kiribati, Lesotho, Malawi, Malaysia, Malta, Mauritius, Namibia, Nauru, Nepal, Nigeria, Pakistan, Papua New Guinea, Philippines, Puerto Rico, Seychelles, Sierra Leone, Singapore, Solomon Islands, Sri Lanka, Swaziland, Tanzania, Tuvalu, Uganda, Vanuatu, Western Samoa, Zambia, Zimbabwe.

**3. *EFL territories*.** The rest of the world. English may be more or less prestigious and more or less welcome in particular places. Many people learn it for occupational purposes and/or as part of education and recreation, at school or in college, or its acquisition may be casual and haphazard, in the family or the workplace, or on the street. Competence varies across a gamut from fluent to a smattering gleaned for limited purposes.

***Provisos*.** These categories need to be buttressed by certain provisos regarding, among other things, the varieties of English used in ENL territories, the existence and use of related English-based creoles in both ENL and ESL territories, and the presence of communities of native speakers in some EFL territories.

bring in anyone who uses any kind of English, extended or restricted, 'correct' or 'broken'. It is probably safe to assume that by 1990 some 10% of the inhabitants of the EFL nations were usefully familiar with English, and that around a billion people currently use it in varying degrees and for various purposes, in almost a 2-to-1 ratio of non-natives to natives.

**Variety**. The diversity of English has always been so great that efforts have often been made to distinguish between a 'proper' or 'correct' core, almost always a minority form associated with class and education, and other forms that are closer to or further away from that core, which is usually perceived as the standard language. There are four ways in which this kind of distinction has been made:

**Language and dialect**. The use of such terms as *LANGUAGE* and *DIALECT* for mutual definition is common to most European languages, but there is a paradox in how they are used and understood. Although a language is widely seen as being 'made up' of dialects, there is nonetheless in every language a single form held to be superior to all dialects: the social, literary, and educational standard. In this tradition, English paradoxically contains its dialects while standing apart from them. Linguists have sought to overcome the problem by treating STANDARD English as another dialect, the *standard dialect*, whose generally assumed superiority and prestige are not attributable to intrinsic merit but rather to social utility. Because of its status, this dialect has diversified in ways that make it the only one that can be used in discussing such matters as philosophy, economics, and literature. However, although a perception of the standard as also being a dialect may be helpful in social and educational terms (making it first, as it were, among equals), tensions persist between speakers whose usage is judged (more or less) non-standard and those whose usages (more or less) fit the norm.

***Language and lect***. Sociolinguists have created such terms as *acrolect*, *mesolect*, and *basilect* from the root element of *dialect*. At first the terms referred, respectively, to the high, middle, and low forms of CREOLE languages, when compared with the standard form of the language on which they are based: for example, the acrolectal form of Jamaican Creole is that form perceived by sociolinguists and others as closest to standard English, while its basilect is the form or forms farthest removed from standard English, its mesolects jostling for space somewhere between. The terms have, however, been extended in recent years to refer to positions on the continuum of all relationships in any language complex. From this viewpoint, standard English is an acrolect in a firmament of other assorted lects.

***Language and variety***. In order to avoid the social and class implications of such terms as *dialect* and *lect*, scholars have in recent years often preferred the neutral term *VARIETY*. Here standard English is one variety among others (whether it is first among equals or unequals), and in turn has its own (sub)varieties. The standard and its varieties are used for one range of purposes, Scots, Cockney, and their equivalents and all their varieties for other purposes, and Jamaican Creole, Krio, and their equivalents

and all their varieties for others still. By and large, this approach has proved useful and even emollient. *Variety* coexists with *dialect* and *lect* and enables diverse difficult issues to be examined and discussed in non-adversarial ways. It does not, however, change the general perception of one English that is, in effect, more equal than the others, an 'educated' variety that spreads into a vast periphery of other (usually 'uneducated') varieties.

***The Englishes and the English languages***. The most radical departure in recent years looks at English not as singular but plural: in effect, a family like the Germanic languages. In such a view, the term 'English' has always covered more than one language: Old English different from Modern English; Scots different from English (both being Germanic languages as distinct as Dutch and Frisian in the Netherlands, or Dano-Norwegian and Nynorsk in Norway). In addition, Krio in Sierra Leone, Kriol in Australia, and Tok Pisin in Papua New Guinea, etc., are so different from the core that they are 'English-based' rather than 'English'. The commonest term for the plurality of English, especially in Africa and Asia, is the *New Englishes*, referring to varieties that have grown up in territories once controlled or greatly influenced by the UK and the US. An even more controversial expression is the *English languages*, which places the main varieties of English on a par with such groups as the Romance languages and Slavonic languages.

Many kinds of more or less marginal usage occur every day. In code-switching, a mix of English and Hindi (or Spanish, or Tagalog, etc.) may be more English one moment, more Hindi the next; it is often hard to indicate precisely when speakers cross the border between two otherwise distinct languages, as for example English and French in Montreal, Quebec. One group of English-speakers may refuse to confer equivalent status on another ('They don't really speak English'), on weak grounds such as differences of accent or on strong grounds such as general unintelligibility. However, there is nothing new in this.

***Diversity***. Regardless of the terminology they might use, few scholars have supposed that there is only one monolithic English; rather, the problem has been how to reconcile one label with the many facets of the thing so labelled. English was diverse when it began and has continued to be diverse. Until the Union of the Parliaments (1707), the varieties used in England and Scotland were no less distinct than the different but closely related Spanish and Portuguese, but a consequence of the Union was the subordination of Scots (the English language of Scotland) to English (the English language of England) and a blurring of its ancient distinctness. In large part, the generic name *English* contributed to the assumption even among Scots that there was only one English language properly so called. In the same century, however, the American Declaration of Independence (1776) marked the creation of a new national and linguistic 'pole': a second national variety of the standard language that had been disconnected from London and the institutions of England. In the later 20c, Australia had begun to create the institutions of yet another national standard, while at the same time the concept of national standards has begun to spread: if there could be acknowledged varieties of the standard in two long-established autonomous nations, there could be further such varieties elsewhere.

**National standards**. The question has become: how many such standards are there (or can there be), and how do (or should) they relate to each other? In the last two decades, there has been a thoroughgoing reconsideration of the idea of a standard language or dialect or variety. Effectively, this is as much a political as a linguistic issue. In places once diffident about their English and accustomed to being patronized (such as Canada, India, Ireland, New Zealand, and Scotland), the possibility that they too either have or could have their own standard has led to such works as 'The Accents of Standard English in Scotland' (David Abercrombie, in *Languages of Scotland*, edited by A. J. Aitken and Tom McArthur, 1979) and *In Search of the Standard in Canadian English* (edited by W. C. Lougheed, 1985). Whereas few disagree that there is a national standard for the US and for England (or Britain), many are dubious about a standard Australian or an Irish standard, while others doubt that there is even such an entity as Indian English out of which a standard might grow. The debate proceeds, and institutions are emerging (linguistic surveys, dictionaries, publishers'

house styles, centres of language study) that increasingly serve to reinforce and even extend claims that once seemed both radical and slightly absurd.

See HISTORY OF ENGLISH, STANDARD ENGLISH.

**ENGLISH AS A FOREIGN LANGUAGE**. See TEFL.

**ENGLISH AS AN INTERNATIONAL LANGUAGE**. See TEIL.

**ENGLISH AS A SECOND DIALECT**. See TESD.

**ENGLISH AS A SECOND LANGUAGE**. See TESL.

**ENGLISH DIALECT SOCIETY**. A society for the study of DIALECT IN ENGLAND, formed in 1873 and dissolved in 1896. Its founder was Walter W. Skeat, Professor of Anglo-Saxon at Cambridge, who became its secretary and then its director. It published 80 works, mostly glossaries and grammars, and collected material for a dialect dictionary to complement the pronunciation work of A. J. Ellis. In 1886, Skeat launched a fund for such a dictionary, contributing a great deal of money himself to the project. In 1889, Joseph Wright began to edit the first collection for this work and appealed through newspapers and libraries for additional data. Over 600 people read material and collected and checked information. Helped by subscriptions, donations, and accommodation provided by Oxford University Press, Wright began in 1898 to publish in parts what became the *English Dialect Dictionary*. When the Society's aims had been achieved, it was dissolved. See AMERICAN DIALECT SOCIETY.

**ENGLISH ENGLISH**. English as used in England: 'Of the two hundred million people speaking English nearly seven-tenths live in the United States, and another tenth in the British dominions are as much influenced by American as English English' (*Spectator*, 5 Feb. 1943); 'Standard English English differs little from that used in Australia, New Zealand and South Africa' (Peter Trudgill, *Language in the British Isles*, 1984). The usage was rare until the 1980s, when it began to be used in professional discussion. See ANGLO-ENGLISH, BRITISH

## PLACE-NAMES IN ENGLAND

English place-names reflect mixed linguistic origins over more than 2,000 years, and fall compactly into seven chronological groups; Pre-Celtic, Celtic, Latin, Anglo-Saxon, Scandinavian, Norman French, and English. However, as a result of centuries of hybridization and adaptation, they are by no means neat and tidy: for example, the now unknown name of a Celtic town was turned by the Romans into *Eboracum*, which the Angles in turn called *Eforwic(ceaster)*, the Danes *Jorvik*, and the modern world calls *York*. Two examples of adaptation and hybridization together are: the Roman settlement called *Letoceto* (from a Celtic name meaning 'grey forest'), a reduced version of which combined with Anglo-Saxon *feld* 'open area' to become *Lichfield* (in Staffordshire); the city of *Lincoln* (pronounced 'Linken'), whose elements drive from Celtic *lin* 'pool' and Latin *colonia* 'colony'.

**1. Pre-Celtic and Celtic** Almost nothing is known about place-names before the Celts arrived in the British Isles, but traces of pre-Celtic usage appear to survive in such river names as *Itchen*, *Soar*, *Tamar*, and *Wey*. Many Celtic names survive in adapted forms, such as the river names *Avon* ('water') and *Thames* (perhaps 'dark'), such hills as *Malvern* ('bare hill'), and *Penkridge* ('chief ridge'), and such forests as *Arden* ('steep place'), as well as the hybrids *Chute Forest* and *Melchet Forest*, the first elements of which mean 'wood' and 'bare', and in *Dover* ('waters'), *Andover* ('ash waters'), and *Wendover* ('white waters').

**2. Latin** Although the Romans dominated the parts of Britain that became England and Wales, they added relatively few names of their own, all of which have been adapted and often hybridized. Among them are: *Catterick* in Yorkshire, from *Cataracta* 'waterfall', *Speen* in Berkshire from *Spinis* ('at the thorn bushes', ablative plural of *spina*), *Faversham* in Kent ('blacksmith's home', a hybrid of Latin *faber* 'smith' and Anglo-Saxon *ham* 'home'). Latinized Celtic has provided a large number of names, often hybridized with Anglo-Saxon, notably words ending in forms derived through Anglo-Saxon *ceaster* from Latin *castra* ('camp'): *Doncaster* ('camp on the Don', from Romano-British *Danum*, the name of a river), *Gloucester* ('bright camp', from *glevum*), and *Winchester* ('camp in a special place', from *Venta*). The city name *Chester* consists of the Anglo-Saxonized 'camp' element alone. In addition, Latin words appear in Anglo-Saxon names, such as *campus* ('field'), in *Warningcamp*, *portus* ('port'), in *Portsmouth*, and (*via*) *strata* ('paved way, street'), in *Stratford*.

**3. Anglo-Saxon (Old English)** Names in this group are either fully Germanic or adapted Romano-British. Common Anglo-Saxon elements include: *burh* ('fort'),

*Continued opposite*

---

ENGLISH, ENGLISH IN ENGLAND, STANDARD ENGLISH.

**ENGLISHES**. Varieties of ENGLISH collectively: 'Discourse analysis, non-native Englishes and second language acquisition' (title of a paper by Yamuna Kachru, in *World Englishes* 4: 2, 1985). The singular *an English* appears not (yet) to be common in the second sense, but comparable usage occur: 'There must . . . be provision for each English to have a distinctive lexical set that will express local cultural content' (Gerry Abbott, 'English across cultures', *English Today* 28, Oct. 1991). See ENGLISH LANGUAGES, -GLISH AND -LISH, NEW ENGLISH, TEIL, VARIETY.

**ENGLISH FIRST**. See AMERICAN ENGLISH, ENGLISH LANGUAGE AMENDMENT.

■ **ENGLISH IN ENGLAND** ──── ■

Also ANGLO-ENGLISH, England English,

## PLACE-NAMES IN ENGLAND *continued*

taking the later forms -*bury* (*Canterbury*, 'fort of the Kentish people'), -*borough* (*Peterborough*, 'St. Peter's fort'), and -*brough* (*Middlesbrough*, 'middle fort'); *dun* 'hill', as in both *the South Downs* and the -*don* of *Faringdon* ('fern hill') and *Swindon* ('swine hill'); *feld* ('open land'), as in *Macclesfield* ('Maccel's open land'), and *Petersfield* ('St. Peter's open land'); *ford* ('river crossing'), as in *Oxford* ('ford of the oxen'), *Stamford* ('stony ford'); *ham* ('settlement, homestead'), as in *Birmingham* ('settlement of Be-orma's people') and *Farnham* ('ferny homestead'); *stoc* ('place'), taking the later forms -*stoke* as in *Basingstoke* ('place of Basca's people'), and -*stock* as in *Woodstock* ('place in the wood'); *tun* ('farm, village, town'), as in *Eton* ('riverside farm'), and *Surbiton* ('southern barley farm').

**4. Scandinavian (Old Norse, Danish)** Danish names are found mainly in the east and north, and Norwegian in the north-west. The commonest elements are *by* ('village, fortified place'), as in *Corby* ('Kori's village'), *Formby* ('Forni's village'), and *Whitby* ('Hviti's village'), and *thorp* ('hamlet, outlying settlement'), as in *Scun-thorpe* ('Skuma's hamlet').

**5. Norman French** A notable consequence of Norman overlordship was mas-sive adaptation in the forms of place-names which they found difficult to pro-nounce: 'hard' *ch* became *c* as in *Worcester* (now pronounced 'Wooster'); *th* became *t* as in *Turville*; *r* became *l* as in *Salisbury* (earlier *Saresbury*) and in the adaptation of the county name *Salop* to the 'shrop' of *Shropshire*. In one instance, *n* became *r*, when *Dunholm* became *Durham*; in another, *Grontabricc* ('Grantabridge') was re-duced to *Cambridge* (compare the nearby village of *Grantchester*, whose name sur-vives more or less intact). The Normans also introduced French names which were in their turn adapted towards English, as with *Beaulieu* 'beautiful place' (now pronounced 'Bewley') and the name of Roger de Moubray, whose family originally came from *Montbray* but gave their name to the town of *Melton Mow-bray*, a typical hybrid form.

**(6) English** From *c.*1500 onward, place-names are generally more transparent to people today, their meanings no longer obscured by adaptation and hybridiza-tion. The same patterns found among English-speaking settlers in North Amer-ica, Australasia, and elsewhere are found in England itself, making full use of the traditional and often hybrid sources available there: for example, such descrip-tive names as *Coalville* ('coal town', combining English and French), *Devonport* ('port in/for Devon', originally called *Plymouth Dock*), *Newhaven* ('new harbour', using the older word *haven*), and names commemorating people, as with *Mary-port* (after the wife of its founder), *Nelson* (after Admiral Lord Nelson), *Peterlee* (for a local trade-union leader), and *Raynes Park* for a local land-owner.

---

ENGLISH ENGLISH. The English language as used in England. For many people in Eng-land and elsewhere, the terms *Anglo-English*, *England English*, and *English English* are tau-tologous and barbarous. It has seemed natural to them that, just as French is the language of France, so English is (and should be) the native language of the in-habitants of England. Other forms of the language have been used elsewhere, in some cases for many centuries, but they have been widely regarded in England as peripheral and in many cases deficient. In the late 20c, however, English in England is generally seen by scholars as one of many varieties that bear the name *English*, but because English English is, as it were, the parent stock it is often harder to discuss and describe than varieties that have added distinctive characteristics of their own. In the English of North America, parts of Africa, and South Asia, it is relatively easy to identify phonological, grammatical, and lexical features unique to certain varieties. It is less easy to say that a particular feature will be heard only or mainly in England.

**A language without competition**. Since the decline of French in the late Middle Ages, English in England has had no major competitor. English people have not shared the experience of the Celtic parts of Britain, where the presence of other vernaculars may affect the idiom even of those who do not speak them. Nor has there been resistance to the status of English, such as that which makes the Irish writer James Joyce's character Stephen Daedalus think after speaking to an Englishman, 'My soul frets in the shadow of his language.' The language has never been officially standardized, but a typically English nostalgia for the past is reflected in attempts to fix one period as definitive. In the 18c, the best English was widely supposed to have been used in the 'Augustan' reign of Queen Anne (1702–14). Writers and scholars like Swift and JOHNSON sought to fix it, but at the same time there was strong and successful resistance to suggestions for an Academy on the French model. There continues to be a feeling that a certain type of English is the best, phrases like *the Queen's English*, *BBC ENGLISH*, *OXFORD ENGLISH* suggesting that the ruling and cultural establishment has by right the correct usage.

**Standard and accent**. There is in England a degree of confusion between the terms *STANDARD ENGLISH* (SE) and *RECEIVED PRONUNCIATION* (RP). Although SE is generally defined by linguists and teachers in terms only of grammar and vocabulary, and RP only in terms of ACCENT, both are often used as virtual synonyms, and SE is often assumed to include (and require) RP. SE, however, can be and is spoken in many accents. RP emerged more slowly than SE; although regional accents were recognized and considered slightly comic or substandard as early as the 16c, generally dialect was not despised: Walter Raleigh spoke with a Devon accent and was an accomplished courtier and writer. It is not until the late 19c that the prestige of RP becomes apparent, with the desire to acquire it for the enhancement of status. SE is not a class usage, but RP is. Although it has considerable prestige value, RP is disliked and caricatured by many speakers with other

accents. It is accepted without comment from a BBC newsreader, but is liable to arouse mirth or hostility when used by anyone suspected of shedding the local speech and 'talking posh'.

The permutations of SE and RP are many. It is likely that an RP speaker will use SE in speech and writing. Most English people write SE, with occasional lapses in spelling and grammar. Many also speak SE, often with some mixture of regional words and idioms, ranging from an occasional item to full dialect. There has, however, been a steady decline in the degree of dialect differences from SE, accelerated over the last fifty years by media mainly purveying SE usage in RP voices. Dialect variation of lexis and syntax is less marked among younger people, but accents are still diverse. Some speakers in effect command two dialects, local for intimate uses and a version (among the many versions) of the national standard for more formal purposes. The increase of town populations has created marked differences between urban and rural dialects. In large conurbations, local forms which sometimes varied over even a small area have tended to lose their distinctiveness and merge into a more general and extensive type of speech. Pressures from the national educational system and the media have also acted to remove or reduce some of the more extreme variants. A large English town today will contain a variety of spoken English determined by social, educational, and generational factors, rather than the simpler division between educated speech and a fairly uniform local dialect which would until recently have been found in rural areas. The presence of immigrant groups has brought new forms of speech; the second generation usually acquires the local accent, but older speakers often keep distinctive features.

**Defending the language**. Strong feelings about the state of the language are made public in various ways. Among older middle-class users there is resistance to change and a freely expressed distrust of American and other influences. Resistance to an Academy has paradoxically resulted in unofficial watchdogs such as the *Society for Pure English*, founded in 1913, which carried on for many years a campaign against what it regarded as degenerate tendencies. Postwar exponents of 'U and non-U' (upper-class and non-upper-class usage) stigmatized certain words and idioms as 'common', and for a time in the 1950s the spotting of U and non-U terms was a kind of national game. The idea grew from an article by the linguist A. S. C. Ross, which suggested that the comparative levelling of outward signs of rank and wealth in post-war England had made linguistic usage a more important pointer. In 1979, taking a different tack, *Plain English Campaign* publicly destroyed government forms as the opening move in a crusade against officialese and obfuscation.

**Changes**. English in England appears to be losing many of its particularities. Traditionally, educated English people have separated *shall* for the first person and *will* for the second and third, and reversed them for special meaning or emphasis: *I shall come tomorrow; you shall go to the Ball!* The immediate 'Have you (got) a pen?' has been distinguished from the more habitual 'Do you have a pen?' Similarly, the present perfect tense has been used for past states within a continuing time period: 'Have you seen him today?' as against 'Did you see him yesterday?' Modal verbs such as *would* and *might* have been used to express hesitation or extra politeness. *Would you care for some more tea?—If I might.* These and other features are still found with older speakers but seem to be declining, perhaps through the influence of AmE. Because so much is shared with other parts of the UK, and because there has been so much AmE influence in recent decades, it is probably true to say that specifically English English is currently less distinctive within the British Isles than at any time in the past.

See AMERICAN ENGLISH AND BRITISH ENGLISH, ANGLO-, ANGLO-SAXON, BIRMINGHAM, BRITISH ENGLISH, BURR, CAXTON, CHAUCER, COCKNEY, CUMBRIA, DIALECT, DORSET, EAST ANGLIA, EAST MIDLAND DIALECT, GEORDIE, HISTORY OF ENGLISH, JUTES, KENTISH, KING'S ENGLISH, LANCASHIRE, LONDON, MIDDLE ENGLISH, MIDLANDS, MUMMERSET, NORTHERN ENGLISH, NORTHUMBRIA, OLD ENGLISH, OXFORD ACCENT, PUBLIC SCHOOL ENGLISH, SAXON, SAXONISM, SCOUSE, SHAKESPEARE, SOMERSET, VARIETY, WEST COUNTRY, YORKSHIRE.

**ENGLISHISM**. **1.** A habit or characteristic of the English; a policy pursued or favoured by, or typical of, the English: 'An Englishism which foreigners note' (*Indian Daily News*, 2 Oct. 1879). **2.** An English-

language WORD or other USAGE, occurring in another language: 'Whether in France or in French Canada, whether in Hebrew or in Yiddish, whether in Spain or in Spanish America, whether in Hindi, Indonesian, or Swahili—in every area and language the impact of English must be watched and regulated. At times the influence is disguised as "internationalisms," "Europeanisms," or "Westernisms," but in actuality it is more likely to be Englishisms than anything else' (Joshua A. Fishman, 'Sociology of English as an Additional Language', in Kachru (ed.), *The Other Tongue*, 1982). See ANGLICISM.

**ENGLISHIZE**, also especially AusE & BrE **Englishise**. **1.** To make English in manner or in language: 'the Englishised Indian' (*Blackwood's Magazine*, 1922). Compare ANGLICIZE, ANGLIFY. **2.** In LINGUISTICS, to adapt towards English, a recent term used to refer to the impact of English on other languages, especially in the noun form *Englishization*. The concept covers phonology, grammar, lexis, discourse, registers, styles, and genres, and relates to three major spheres of influence associated with the spread of the language: traditional areas of contact such as Europe, in which the languages are mainly cognate with English; areas in which English-speakers have settled or on which they have had a strong colonial influence, such as North America, the Caribbean, South Asia, South-East Asia, and parts of Africa; and such traditionally distinct areas as CHINA, JAPAN, and Latin America. The most noticeable influence is lexical, manifesting itself mainly through *loanwords* (such as *hardwarowy* and *softwarowy* in Polish, and *hardver* and *softver* in Hungarian), *loan translations* (such as FRENCH *gratte-ciel* as a response to 'sky-scraper' and *soucoupe volante* to 'flying saucer'), and *hybridizations* (such as Telugu *donga laysansu* illegal licence, and IndE *lathi charge* a charge, usually by policemen, in which *lathis* or metal-reinforced bamboo sticks are used). See CODE-MIXING AND CODE-SWITCHING, GAIRAIGO, GERMAN, -GLISH AND -LISH, ITALIAN, KOREA, LOAN, SPANISH, VARIETY.

## ■ ENGLISH LANGUAGE AMENDMENT ────────────── ■

Short form *ELA*. A proposed amendment to the constitution of the US that would make English the official language of the republic. The aim of the proponents of ELA is to ensure that English retains its leading role in US society, especially in the face of actual or potential competition from SPANISH. Despite a widespread assumption to the contrary, English has no official status in the US. For over two centuries, however, it has been the *de facto* national language which the vast majority of non-English-speaking immigrants have sought to adopt. In 1981, Senator Samuel Hayakawa, an American of Japanese background, introduced a constitutional amendment to make English the official language.

**US English**. Hayakawa did not succeed in his aim, but others have reintroduced the proposal, and following lack of action on his original measure he founded in 1983, with John Tanton, an organization called *US ENGLISH*, to support and promote the cause. This is a nationwide, non-profit-making, non-partisan organization, currently with some 350,000 members and a board of advisers that includes the writers Jacques Barzun, Saul Bellow, and Gore Vidal, and the journalist Alistair Cooke. It promotes English as a common bond (a 'blessing' that integrates America's diverse population) and often refers to official French/English bilingualism in Canada as a source of disharmony that Americans should seek to avoid. In addition to its concern that English be made official, *US English* holds that every effort should be made, particularly through education, to assist newcomers to acquire English. At the same time, it rejects linguistic chauvinism, nativism, and xenophobia, encourages foreign-language study, supports individual and private rights to use and maintain languages other than English, and does not propose to prohibit forms of bilingual education intended to ease children into English ability.

**Spanish**. Both John Tanton and Linda Chavez (a former president of the organization) have explained why *US English* was founded as it was: in the past, of the many languages in or brought to the US, none had the capacity to threaten English. This state of affairs has changed, however, with the influx of Spanish-speaking immigrants, especially in such areas as southern Florida, the Southwest, and such large cities as New York. Members do not favour a change in bilingual education from the transitional (in which English replaces the

mother tongue) to maintenance (in which a language like Spanish is retained alongside English). They also oppose the provision of bilingual Spanish/English ballots and comparable services.

**Support**. There appears to be considerable popular and political support for *OFFICIAL ENGLISH*, *English for US*, and *English First*, as the movement is variously called. A 'sense of the Senate' measure declaring English official has been passed three times in recent years as an attachment to immigration legislation. Such declarations do not, however, have the force of law. Seventeen states of the Union have made English their official language: Nebraska 1920, Illinois 1969, Virginia 1981, Indiana 1984, Kentucky 1984, Tennessee 1984, California 1986, Georgia 1986, Arkansas 1987, Mississippi 1987, North Carolina 1987, North Dakota 1987, Sorth Carolina 1987, Arizona 1988, Colorado 1988, Florida 1988, Alabama 1990, Montana 1995, New Hampshire 1995, South Dakota 1995, Wyoming 1996; in 1978, Hawaii made both English and Hawaiian official. Legislation is pending or planned in Maryland, Massachusetts, Missouri, New York, and West Virginia. Public-opinion polls in a variety of locations have also shown considerable support for English. Many have been relatively casual, often conducted by newspapers, radio, and television, but others have been taken by reputable survey organizations.

**Opposition**. *US English* has since the outset been subject to strong opposition. Many academics and ethnic leaders have seen it as a nativist organization that panders to the prejudices and entrenched attitudes of unilingual whites. Linda Chavez reports being called a fascist traitor to her own Hispanic heritage, and has been picketed at speaking engagements. A president of *La Raza* (a Hispanic political movement) compared *US English* to the Ku Klux Klan, and the journalist James Crawford has linked the group to allegedly racist funding agencies (through organizations called *US Inc.* and the *Federation for American Immigration Reform*, the latter also founded by John Tanton). These agencies include the Pioneer Fund, created in 1937 to promote 'racial betterment' through eugenics. Crawford has written about a leaked memorandum by Tanton which expresses fear of Hispanic control over America and lists such dangers as Roman Catholicism, large families, and a tradition of bribery. Linda Chavez resigned as president when she learned of this statement.

American organizations that have either explicitly or indirectly attacked *US English* and *Official English* include the *National Education Association* (a teacher's union), the *National Council of Teachers of English*, *Teachers of English to Speakers of Other Languages* (TESOL), the *Linguistic Society of America*, and the *Modern Language Association*. Many see it as promoting an English-only policy rather than simply *Official English*, despite claims to the contrary. Reaction has led to the *ENGLISH PLUS* pressure group (formed in 1987), which encourages Americans to be bilingual (English plus one or more other languages). It had its genesis in statements by the *Spanish-American League Against Discrimination* (*SALAD*: an acronym that implies disagreement with the traditional concept of the melting pot), and in 1987 established the *English Plus Information Clearinghouse* (*EPIC*), to canvass support and disseminate its views. Adherents to the idea of English Plus have proposed a constitutional amendment of their own: the *Cultural Rights Amendment*, which would give legal backing to the preservation and promotion of ethnic and linguistic diversity.

**Conclusion**. There is evidence that Hispanic immigrants tend, like others before them, to shed their original language so as to join the mainstream of American life. Such evidence of language shift does not, however, impress English-speakers in Miami or southern California who feel threatened by the powerful presence of an alternative language and culture. Similarly, despite disclaimers by *US English*, and its support for transitional bilingual programmes for adults, an impression of chauvinism among native speakers of English is being projected that arouses and reinforces old anxieties among non-English-speakers. Although the primacy of English in the US is hardly in doubt, people on both sides of the argument are likely to feel threatened for some time to come, whatever happens. See AMERICAN ENGLISH, AMERICAN LANGUAGE.

**ENGLISH LANGUAGES**. A phrase used by some linguists and other commentators to suggest that ENGLISH is a group of languages (comparable to the Romance languages) rather than one language: 'The European Society for the Study of English has been founded to encourage European understanding of English languages, literatures and cultures' (from a leaflet announcing the inaugural conference of the ESSE at the U. of East Anglia in England, Sept. 1991); *The English Languages* (book title), Tom McArthur, 1998. See ENGLISHES, VARIETY.

■ **ENGLISH LITERATURE** ———— ■

Short form **Eng lit**. An ambiguous term used and understood in at least five ways: as the LITERATURE of England, the literature of Great Britain (and Ireland) written in English, all literature in English (whatever the place of origin), a varying mix of all or any of these (depending on circumstance, preference, and emphasis), and any of these as a subject taught in schools and colleges.

**The literature of England**. In its first sense, English literature is on a par with other national literatures, such as Italian literature seen as the achievement and heritage of the people of Italy. This is the commonest sense of the term, widely used to contrast not only with Italian or French national literature but also with the national literature of the US, as in:

> When we think of modern literature, we almost invariably associate it with national groups. English literature does not include American, and there is even hesitation in including Austrian literature under German. In the Middle Ages such national groups either did not exist at all or existed only in a rudimentary form. We can speak only of works written in a particular language
> (W. T. H. Jackson, *Medieval Literature*, 1966).

**The literature of Great Britain**. In its second sense, the term refers to literature in English in the nation-state made up of England, Scotland, and Wales (and at certain times and in various ways all or part of Ireland), or of the British Isles:

> For coherence, I have focused on the literature of the British Isles, and specifically of England—although with many necessary side glances at Scotland and Ireland
> (Alastair Fowler, *A History of English Literature*, 1987).

This dimension is often inconsistently perceived and described: for example, Scottish writers like Walter Scott, John Buchan, and J. M. Barrie are included unreflectingly in lists, studies, and histories that do not precisely specify the 'Englishness' of the canon in question. This imprecision sometimes confuses the narrower heritage of England with the broader heritage of Britain and Ireland. The use of the term *British literature*, however, is complicated by the existence of literatures that are not in English (Gaelic, Welsh, and Cornish, and Scots when defined as distinct from English). The term is, however, sometimes used in contrast with literatures in English elsewhere.

**All literature in English**. The third, non-national or supra-national sense includes the preceding and such terms as *African literature in English*, *American literature*, *Australian literature in English*, *Canadian literature in English*, *Irish literature in English*. It may or may not have a capital L. The sense dates from the 19c, with changing emphases:

> Around 1900, not many literary historians in Europe or the United States would have been prepared to argue that there was such a thing as an American literature, or that the literature so far produced in America was worth an extensive analysis. Able American authors were conceded to exist. But they tended to be treated as men of individual merit—contributors (as Matthew Arnold saw it) to 'one great literature—English literature'
> (Marcus Cunliffe, *American Literature to 1900*, 1986).

This literature of English at large is sometimes referred to as *literature (written) in English*, as in *The Cambridge Guide to Literature in English* (ed. Ian Ousby, 1988). It includes not only the British and American traditions, but also COMMONWEALTH literature. The usage *world literature written in English* includes all literatures created in English and all literary works translated into English.

**A mixture of senses**. Because of the possible confusions and misunderstandings, resentment can arise among those interested in the literature and its description. Critics discussing such writers as Chinua Achebe, Robertson Davies, James Joyce, V. S. Naipaul, and Walter Scott, as part of 'mainstream' English literature with its supposedly 'universal' messages may or may not recall or appreciate that such writers have Nigerian, Canadian, Irish, Trinidadian, Scottish, or other dimensions as significant for their work as the English dimension of William Wordsworth and the American dimension of Mark Twain. Such problems arise partly from ambiguities inherent in the word 'English' itself and partly from distinctions and tensions among the peoples who use English, some of whom have no other language, some of whom are bi- or multilingual, and some of whom have seen English replace other languages important to them.

**The development of English literature**. Imaginative works have been written in English for over a thousand years, and, in historical terms, most of them are primarily the heritage of England. As with the language itself, such literature can be divided into Old, Middle, and Modern periods, the modern phase subdividing conveniently into compartments whose labels relate to monarchs (*Tudor, Elizabethan, Jacobean, Victorian*), cultural phases and assumptions (*Augustan, Romantic, Modernist*, etc.), centuries (*16c drama, the 18c novel*, etc.), and, most recently, varieties (*American literature, Indian English literature*, etc.).

**The language of literature**. Although English literature has not been so detached from everyday usage as some literatures, it is closer to everyday life in the 20c than previously. The concept and practice of a 'high style', to be kept apart from common usage, has been steadily eroded; the idiom of speech has thoroughly penetrated the literary text and become the norm for those genres of cinema and television which have inherited so much from literature. The tradition has been public and responsible; few writers have taken a position of total withdrawal and alienation from society. The language has in all periods been a literary medium; conversely, literature has enriched the language with neologisms, allusions, and quotations. People regularly use literary quotations, often without knowing their origins: *to the manner born, not wisely but too well, what's in a name?* (Shakespeare); *a little learning is a dangerous thing* (Pope); *God tempers the wind to the shorn lamb* (Sterne); *a sadder and a wiser man* (Coleridge); *the female of the species (is deadlier than the male)* (Kipling); *some animals are more equal than others* (Orwell).

**Literature in education**. The academic study and examinable subject known as *English Literature* (short form *Eng Lit*) is comparatively recent. Appreciation of English as a literary language began in the late 16c, but literary works in the vernacular were valued mainly for recreation and moral instruction, while the classical languages and literatures continued to dominate education at every level. However, knowledge of English writers was gradually encouraged as a social accomplishment and a mark of breeding, especially among women, for whom a classical education was not usually available.

**The dissenting academies**. The first movement away from the classical monopoly in education came in the 17c, among the English Protestant dissenters, for whom texts in English served as sources for exercises in grammar and rhetoric. When the Act of Uniformity (1662) excluded dissenters from the universities, a number of clergymen dispossessed of their livings opened schools in their own houses, and after the restrictions were slightly eased by the Act of Toleration (1689), some of these schools developed into the *dissenting academies*, offering an alternative to the ancient universities. Their curricula were usually similar to those of Oxford and Cambridge in the study of the classical languages, but gradually broadened to include history, science, modern languages, and English literature. The Northampton Academy, founded by Philip Doddridge in 1729, was one of the first to teach English authors, and John Aikin lectured on Milton and 18c English poets at Warrington Academy, founded in 1757. The influence of those academies was widespread, not only in the UK but in many other parts of the English-speaking world.

**The universities**. The first chair of English Literature was in Scotland, at the U. of Edinburgh (1762), and was known as the *Chair of Rhetoric and Belles Lettres*. Its first occupant was the rhetorician Hugh Blair. This was followed in the 19c by the first colleges of the U. of London: U. College (1828) and King's College (1831). Chairs of English Literature were then created at Owens College, Manchester (1850) and at the U. of Glasgow (1862), after which the practice extended widely. In 1848, Frederick Denison Maurice and others founded in London the Queen's College for Women. Here, in 1848, Charles Kingsley, in his inaugural lecture as Professor of English, spoke of literature as suitable preparation for women's lives. In the US, the academic study of English literature was established in the early 19c. The first Boylston Professor of Rhetoric and Oratory at Harvard, in 1806, was John Quincy Adams (later US president). In 1851, Francis J. Child occupied the same chair as Professor of English.

Oxford and Cambridge were slow in taking the subject up, but when they did their prestige helped establish it firmly in the English-using world. At Oxford, English literature was offered in the pass degree in 1873 and the Merton Chair of English Language and Literature was created in 1885. After much controversy, the Oxford honours school of English was founded in 1894, its growth owing much to the work of J. C. Collins and W. A. Raleigh. At Cambridge, the Edward VII Chair of English Literature was first held in 1912 by Arthur Quiller-Couch. In 1917, it became possible to take English with another subject, for a degree, but English did not rank as a sole honours subject until 1926. However, Cambridge made up for this late start by its influence on literary criticism, notably through the work of I. A. Richards (1893–1979) and F. R. Leavis (1895–1978). There was considerable controversy about the study of early forms of the language, especially Old English, in an honours school of English, although Old English had been studied by some Oxford scholars since the 17c. A chair of Anglo-Saxon had existed at Oxford since 1849 and at Cambridge since 1878.

**Canons and classics**. The literary texts of a language can be many things to many people; attitudes vary regarding the social and educational value or the appropriateness of certain texts and authors. Many people, whether or not they read acknowledged works of literature, regard them as a repository of 'good English' and as models for both the written and spoken language. The works form a canon (*the classics*), a greater or lesser knowledge of which is shared by the culturally literate. Historians, lexicographers, and other scholars, regardless of whether they share this view or gain aesthetic as well as academic satisfaction from their studies, find in the body of English literature a record of language usage over many centuries. Currently, many teachers and critics of English literature waver between a traditional aesthetic and value-laden approach to their subject and linguistic, Marxist, Freudian, postmodernist, feminist, or deconstructionist views of the inherited canon as texts to be dissected to provide proof of the rightness of a doctrine or reveal a writer's hidden agenda. They may seek at the same time to enlarge the canon by including overlooked writers (especially women) or adjust it by reassessing writers whom they see as overly revered, including Shakespeare.

**ENGLISH-ONLY MOVEMENT**. A name given, in the main by their opponents, to groups that since the early 1980s have aimed at an amendment to the US constitution, making English the official language of the republic. Proponents refer to the movements as *Official English* and deny that they wish to restrict people's options to English alone. See ENGLISH LANGUAGE AMENDMENT.

**ENGLISH PLUS**. A pressure group formed in the US in 1985 to promote bilingualism and counter the drive by *US English* for an amendment to the constitution, making English the official language of the republic. The name means 'English plus one or more other language(s)'. See ENGLISH LANGUAGE AMENDMENT.

**ENGLISH PRONOUNCING DICTIONARY**, short form *EPD*. A work of reference by the phonetician Daniel JONES, based on his *Phonetic Dictionary of the English Language* (1913). The *EPD* was published during the First World War by J. M. Dent (1917); it is one of the most influential ELT books ever published, is widely regarded as an institution, and is closely associated with the Department of Phonetics and Linguistics of U. College London, where Jones worked and where its revision was maintained for many years first by A. C. Gimson, then Susan Ramsaran. Their revisions appeared in 1924 (2nd edition: with supplement), 1926 (3rd: with revised introduction), 1937 (4th: enlarged and reset), 1940 (5th), 1944 (6th), 1945 (7th: with supplement), 1947 (8th), 1948 (9th), 1949 (10th), 1956 (11th: enlarged and reset), 1963 (12th: with supplement and phonetic glossary; with corrections and revisions by Gimson in the 1964 reprint), 1967 (13th: enlarged and reset), 1977 (14th: reset, with revisions and a supplement by Ramsaran in 1988). Cambridge University acquired the rights from Dent and in 1997 brought out the 15th edition, edited by Peter Roach and James Hartman. The dictionary is a pronouncing glossary that lists words and names in Roman letters followed by their equivalents (with variants, where appropriate) in a phonemic transcription that uses the International Phonetic Alphabet to represent RECEIVED PRONUNCIATION (in 1997, BBC Pronunciation) as a pronunciation model. There is an account in the introduction of the model and the notation. The 14th edition contains over 59,664 items, while the 15th has over 80,000. See PHONETIC TRANSCRIPTION, PUBLIC SCHOOL PRONUNCIATION.

**ENGLISH TEACHING**. See ELT, LANGUAGE TEACHING, TEACHING ENGLISH, TEFL, TESD, TESL, TESOL.

**EPENTHESIS** [Stress: 'e-PEN-the-sis']. The insertion of a sound or letter into a WORD or PHRASE. An epenthetic vowel can be added to break up a consonant cluster, as in Hiberno-Irish 'fillim' for *film*. Such a vowel often has the value of schwa. An epenthetic consonant can be added through being near another: /p/ close in articulation to both /m/ and /t/, as with *empty* (Old English *æmtig*); /b/ close in articulation to /m/, as with *b* in *nimble* (Middle English *nemel*). In RP, epenthetic /r/ is typically added between words that end and begin with certain vowels: *Shah/r of Persia*. Epenthetic vowels are common in non-native forms of English, to handle consonant clusters not found in the speaker's first language, as in 'sakool' for *school* among Punjabi speakers of English and 'iskool' among Kashmiris. See B, D, INTRUSIVE R, L, LINKING R, N, P, PARTICIPLE, SOMERSET, SPEECH, SYLLABLE, T.

**EPITHET**. **1.** An expression added to a NAME as a characterizing description, before it in *glorious Devon*, after it in *Richard Crookback*, with a definite article in *William the Conqueror, Scotland the Brave*. **2.** Also *Homeric epithet, poetic epithet*. A formulaic phrase containing an adjective and a noun, common in epic poetry: *grey-eyed Athene, rosy-fingered dawn, the wine-dark sea*. **3.** A word or phrase that substitutes for another: *man's best friend* for *dog, the water of life* for *whisky*. **4.** A word or phrase used to abuse and dismiss: *bastard*, *bugger*, *shit*, especially when used directly (*You shit!*, *You son of a bitch!*) or as a description (*The silly old cow!*). **5.** Such a phrase as *that idiot of a lawyer* and *a devil of a doctor*. **6.** An adjective or other descriptive word. See ANTONOMASIA, SWEARING.

**EPONYM. 1.** A personal NAME from which a WORD has been derived: *John B. Stetson*, the 19c US hatter after whom the *stetson* hat was named. **2.** The person whose name is so used: The Roman emperor *Constantine*, who gave his name to *Constantinople*. **3.** The word so derived: *stetson*, *Constantinople*. The process of *eponymy* results in many forms: (1) Such simple eponyms as *atlas*, which became popular after the 16c Flemish cartographer Gerardus Mercator put the figure of the titan Atlas on the cover of a book of maps. (2) COMPOUNDS and ATTRIBUTIVE constructions such as *loganberry* after the 19c US lawyer *James H. Logan*, and *Turing machine* after the 20c British mathematician *Alan Turing*. (3) Possessives such as *Parkinson's Law* after the 20c British economist C. Northcote Parkinson, and the *Islets of Langerhans* after the 19c German pathologist Paul Langerhans. (4) DERIVATIVES such as *Bowdlerize* and *gardenia*, after the 18c English expurgator of Shakespeare, Thomas Bowdler, and the 19c Scottish-American physician Alexander Garden. (5) CLIPPINGS, such as *dunce* from the middle name and first element of the last name of the learned 13c Scottish friar and theologian *John Duns Scotus*, whose rivals called him a fool. (6) BLENDS such as *gerrymander*, after the US politician Elbridge Gerry (b. 1744), whose redrawn map of the voting districts of Massachusetts in 1812 was said to look like a salamander, and was then declared a *gerrymander*. The word became a verb soon after. See -ONYM, WORD-FORMATION.

**-ESE**. A suffix added to nouns and adjectives. Its primary use is the identification of nationalities, languages, and the like, as in *Chinese*, *Congolese*, *Japanese*, *Javanese*, *Viennese*, *Vietnamese*, but a significant secondary use is the labelling of styles or registers of English. The primary use is neutral, but the secondary use is often pejorative, associated with individuals whose STYLE is distinctive and idiosyncratic (*Carlylese*, *Johnsonese*), groups whose stylistic tendencies are seen as undesirable (*academese*, BUREAUCRATESE),

language varieties considered deficient or peculiar (*BROOKLYNESE*, *Pentagonese*), and the media and technology (*cablese*, COMPUTERESE). Nonce and stunt creations are common, such as *UNese*, a diplomatic style said to be used in the United Nations Organization. See COMMERCIALESE, HEADLINE, JOURNALESE, LEGALESE, OFFICIALESE, SOCIOLOGESE. Compare -ISM, LINGO, -SPEAK.

**ESH**. In PHONETICS, an elongated form ʃ of the symbol *s*, that serves in IPA to represent the voiceless palato-alveolar central laminal fricative, a sound represented in English by the digraph *sh* as in *shape* and *rush*. The form was used by Isaac Pitman in 1845 with this value in his phonotypic ALPHABET. See LETTER[1], LONG *S*.

**ESL**. See EXAMINING IN ENGLISH, TEACHING ENGLISH, TESL.

**ESP**, short for *English for Specific/Special Purposes*. The English language taught for professional, vocational, and other specified purposes. Originating in courses of business English for foreign learners, ESP developed in the 1960s in response to demands for courses geared to practical and functional rather than educational and cultural ends. Whereas general EFL/ESL teaching offers courses to schoolchildren and to adults of mixed ages and backgrounds, ESP addresses learners with a common reason for learning, such as the English of air traffic control or of dyestuff chemistry. Planning an ESP course starts with a *needs analysis*, to establish the limits of the language learners' needs. Courses and materials are then designed to teach all and only that subset of English. Success appears to depend on the quality of the needs analysis, the authenticity of the materials used, and the sensitivity of the teacher to the maturity and status of the students. Although the development of such language teaching has been mainly in English, it is of growing importance for other languages as part of *languages for specific purposes* (*LSP*). Within ESP, there are further divisions: see EAP, TEFL.

**ESTUARY ENGLISH**, also **Estuary**. A term, coined in 1984 by the British phonetician David Rosewarne, a lecturer at Kingsway College, London, for a variety of English and in particular an accent common among younger people in and around LONDON. This appears to have been at first most noticeable in Essex and Kent, counties that lie immediately north and south of the Thames Estuary, hence the name. Not much discussed in the 1980s, the term and the phenomenon became hot media topics in London in the earlier 1990s, prompting among other things the laid-back pop-linguistic paperback *Do You Speak Estuary? The New Standard English: How to Spot it and Speak it* (Bloomsbury, 1993), written by Paul Coggle, a lecturer in German at the University of Kent. One result of the media and public interest has been the uncertain social status of the term and what it refers to; for some, Estuary is an intriguing and positive development; for others it is a deplorable departure from taste and tradition; for others still, whatever their outlook, it has immense social, linguistic, and educational implications for BrE at large.

Estuary is generally perceived as a compromise variety ranging between popular LONDON usage (especially COCKNEY) and RECEIVED PRONUNCIATION (RP); it is used by both upwardly mobile working-class south-easterners and younger people from public (that is, private) schools who wish to adapt away from the RP traditionally valued by their social class, perhaps, as both Rosewarne and Cottle suggest, in order to increase their 'street-cred' (slang abbreviation for *street credibility*, easy and confident familiarity with fashionable urban and especially youth culture). Rosewarne observes:

> The heartland of this variety still lies by the banks of the Thames and its estuary, but it seems to be the most influential accent in the south-east of England. In the decade since I started research into it, Estuary English has spread northwards to Norwich and westwards to Cornwall, with the result that it is now spoken south of a line from the Wash to the Avon. It is also to be heard on the front and back benches of the House of Commons and is used by some members of the Lords, whether life or hereditary peers. Ken Livingstone M.P. was given in the first article in *The Sunday Times* on 14 March 1993 as an example of an Estuary speaker. Interviewed a couple of days later in *The Daily Mail*, he said he was pleased with the label, adding 'I think it's true that

this kind of dialect is emerging'. Tony Banks M.P., interviewed on the B.B.C. radio programme 'Word of Mouth' on 29 June 1993 reported that Estuary English is now spoken by Conservative members of Parliament as well as Labour. Lord Tebbit, cited by *The Sunday Times* as an Estuary speaker, reports in his recent biography *Upwardly Mobile* that Conservative Prime Minister Harold Macmillan had referred to him as a Cockney speaker. ('Estuary English: tomorrow's RP?', in *English Today*, 37, January 1994).

Estuary English is most easily identified in terms of accent, located towards the middle of a continuum between traditional RP and Cockney usage, particularly noticeable in the following three features: (1) The use of /w/ where RP has /l/, especially in syllable-final positions: 'aw' for *all*, 'miwk' for *milk*, *St Paw's Cathedraw* for 'St Paul's Cathedral'. Such a pronunciation creates novel HOMO-PHONES and may lead to misunderstanding, as when Estuary 'fowty books' might be understood as either *forty books* or *faulty books*. In addition, in some words /l/ disappears entirely, as in 'vunnerable' for *vulnerable*. (2) Use of GLOTTAL STOPS instead of the stop consonants /k, p, t/ in syllable-final positions: 'te?nicaw' for *technical*, 'sto?' for *stop*, 'glo?aw' for *glottal*. (3) The use of /i/ instead of /l/ in word-final position: 'citee' for *city*, 'lovelee' for *lovely*, 'reallee' for *really*.

At least the following three factors appear to be at work in propagating Estuary so widely and swiftly: (1) Demographics, in that large numbers of Londoners have migrated since the Second World War into the surrounding counties, including such new towns Harlow in Essex and Slough in Berkshire, where their usage has had greater prestige than the traditional dialects. (2) Radio and television, in which a wide range of accents has in recent decades become common on the BBC and in independent broadcasting, locally and nationally. (3) A move towards greater linguistic comfort and compromise. Rosewarne notes: 'It is a shift to the middle ground of pronunciation. The R.P. speaker accommodates "downwards" and the local accent speaker accommodates "upwards", resulting in accent convergence. Consequently, in all social groups in the South-East of England it has been, for at least a decade, common for young people to speak a rather different accent from older members of their families.'

**ETH**, also **edh**. In OLD ENGLISH, the LETTER ð or ð, used to represent both a voiced and an unvoiced apico-dental fricative (the *th* in both *these* and *three* in Modern English); in Modern Icelandic and IPA, the letter ð, used to represent a voiced apico-dental fricative (as in *these*). It originated in Old English as a crossed *d*. Its upper-case form is Ð. See SPEECH, THORN.

**ETHNIC NAME**, also **ethnic label** and, when pejorative, **ethnic slur**. A nickname for someone from a particular nationality, race, community, or culture. The spectrum of ethnic names in English ranges from more or less affectionate nicknames (such as *Jock* for a Scotsman, as used in England) through relatively neutral terms (such as *Brit* for someone British) through the use in affectionate abuse of terms that can otherwise be offensive (such as *Limey* and *Yank* between American and British friends), to highly offensive racial and/or religious slurs used without restraint, such as *dago* for someone of Spanish, Portuguese, or Latin American background, and *Yid/yid* for someone Jewish.

**Social and etymological categories**. Ethnic names in English generally fall into three social categories: (1) For peoples (and their languages) outside the English-speaking world: *Frog/Froggie*, someone from France or who speaks French; *Kraut*, a German; *Polack*, a Pole; *Wop/wop*, an Italian. (2) For national and regional identities within the English-speaking world: *Limey*, especially in the US, for someone British; *Pom(mie)/pom(mie)*, in Australasia, for someone from England; *Newfie*, in Canada, for a Newfoundlander. (3) Groups marked as different by habitat, race, language, and/or religion: *Wog/wog* for an Arab, South Asian, or black African; *Yid/yid* a Jew. Such terms also generally fall into four etymological categories: (1) Taken from personal names already common in the group concerned: *Jock*, a common Scottish pet form of *John*; *dago*, from the common man's name *Diego* in Spanish. (2) Taken from names associated with the entire group: *Abo*, an abbreviation of *Aborigine*; *Newfie*, an abbreviation of *Newfoundlander*; *Yid*, a word already meaning 'Jew'. (3) Referring to something seen as characterizing the group in question, such

as complexion (*Coloured* and *Negro/nigger*), food (*Frog* from the eating of frogs' legs in France; *Kraut* from the eating of *sauerkraut* in Germany), or an emblem (*Kiwi*, the name of a flightless New Zealand bird; *bogwog*, in which the element *bog* is associated with Ireland: whence 'an Irish wog'). (4) Formed as plays on words associated with the target group: *Pommy*, an abbreviation of *pomegranate*, in turn a play on *immigrant* (see below).

Once established, however, a name's origin is often lost to its users, with the result that etymologists may have difficulty tracing its provenance. Many ethnic names have uncertain or disputed etymologies, among them folk etymologies that may have been created as jokes: for example, *wog* has been explained as a pseudo-abbreviation of 'Westernized Oriental Gentleman' and, in the plural, as originally an official British acronym for 'workers on government service' in the Suez Canal area, who are said to have worn armbands emblazoned WOGS. Probably, however, *wog* is a clipping of *golliwog/gollywog*, the name for a soft cloth doll with a black face and fuzzy hair, taken in turn from the name of a doll character in *The Adventures of Two Dutch Dolls—and a Golliwog* (1895), a children's book by the US writer Bertha Upton, and illustrated by her sister Florence.

Generally, ethnic names are restricted to informal and slang usage and ethnic slurs are associated with strong emotion and often unexamined bias on the part of the user. The degree of acceptability or unacceptability of such a name may change over the years, and from group to group. Sometimes, names that cease for a time to be used because of their derogatory associations are later revived with positive associations, as for example *Black/black* (see entry).

■ **ETYMOLOGY** ─────── ■

Both the study of the history of words and a statement of the origin and history of a WORD, including changes in its form and meaning.

**History**. Classical Greek interest in words owed much to the development of alphabetic writing, in which they were laid out for inspection like merchandise. Early investigators of words included the Stoics of the 4c BC, who held that all languages were in a slow state of decline from erstwhile perfection. They therefore looked for the *ETYMON* or true first form of a word. Their pessimistic view survives among those who insist that the best writers are long dead, and their belief in etyma continues among those who argue that the original meaning of a word has current as well as chronological priority over any later senses it may develop. In Spain in the 7c, St Isidore of Seville compiled a 20-part encyclopedia called *Originum sive etymologiarum libri* (Books of Origins or Etymologies), more commonly known as the *Etymologiae*. He took the view that the essence of a word could be found associatively: the Latin *homo* (man), adjective *humanus*, derived from *humo* (from the soil), because God made man from clay. This view served a didactic and mnemonic end, and was influenced by Hebrew precedents in the Old Testament, in which words were accounted for through homonymic comparisons (Hebrew *adam* being both man and clay). Isidore's students of Latin remembered *cadaver* as a kind of theological acronym of *CAro DAta VERmibus* (flesh given to worms). Isidore appears to have sought to formalize what is now called *FOLK ETYMOLOGY*, in which associative guessing dominates. His ideological approach was not unique. In the 20c, it has been used by feminists reinterpreting *history* and *boycott* for propaganda purposes as *his story* and *boy cott*, so as to be able to formulate *herstory* and *girlcott*.

Isidore's views on etymology were affected by his belief that Adam and Eve spoke Hebrew in Eden and that the story of the Tower of Babel was literally true. This continued to be the majority view among scholars through the Middle Ages and the Renaissance and conditioned the research of such 18–19c enthusiasts as the Englishman John Horne Tooke and the American Noah Webster. Both were convinced that language was the product of historical development, but lacked a non-biblical theory with which to transform traditional speculation into science. The study was transformed, however, by Sir William Jones and the comparative philologists, who depended on a painstaking analysis of textual evidence from many languages. As a consequence of their work, 20c etymology is part of historical linguistics.

**Nature**. Contemporary etymology is concerned with both fact and hypothesis. As with information in the fossil record of pa-leontology, what is known of the origin and development of a word or its elements is a matter of chance, since only the earliest recorded forms and meanings can be directly studied. Earlier forms reconstructed by means of this recorded evidence and the meanings assumed for such forms are hypothetical and need to be treated with caution. Where such forms are shown in writing or print, they are conventionally preceded by an asterisk (*) to mark their status. For English, such forms are usually those of INDO-EUROPEAN ROOTS and their derivatives, or Romanic and Germanic roots. Thus, the *-logy* part of the word *etymology* goes back to an IE ROOT *\*leg-* (collect). Many words, however, cannot be taken so far back; the recorded evidence does not suffice, and so etymologists may tag a word 'o.o.o.' (of obscure origin) or 'origin unknown'.

Historical changes in meaning are unpatterned, because DERIVATIONS are usually idiomatic; the meaning of the whole is not simply the sum of the meanings of the parts. The adjective *sedate* goes back to the Latin verb *sedare* (to settle: a person, a dispute, a war), which comes from the IE root *\*sed-* (sit); hence the basic meaning '(having been) settled'. The derived adjective *sedative* is then something that tends to settle someone. However, in Modern English, the adjective *sedate* means 'deliberately composed and dignified by one's own character or efforts', not (as *sedative* would suggest) 'stupefied by the effects of a drug'. The Modern English verb *sedate* is a backformation from *sedative* and therefore draws on the meaning of *sedative* and not on the meaning of the earlier adjective *sedate*. The homonymic adjective and verb *sedate* share a common origin in IE *\*sed-*, but have developed such divergent meanings that the ancient adjective cannot suitably describe someone who shows the effects of the recent verb. As the 19c German philologist Max Müller wrote: 'The etymology of a word can never give us its definition' (1880).

**Formal and semantic changes**. It is therefore not surprising that the etymology of some common words reveals origins very unlike their modern form, meanings, or both. Thus, the four words *dough*, *figure*, *lady*, and *paradise* all derive in part at least from the IE root *\*dheigh-* (to knead clay). Three of these words specialize or narrow the *knead* part of that meaning and ignore the *clay* part: (1) *Dough* is something that is kneaded like clay. (2) *Figure* derives from Latin *figura*, which comes in turn from IE *\*dhigh-ūrā*, something formed by kneading or manipulation. *Feign*, *fiction*, and *effigy* are from the same root. (3) *Lady* derives from OE *hlǣfdige*, composed of *hlāf* (loaf) and *\*digan* (knead). A lady was the member of the house who kneaded the loaf, and the *hlāford* (from which comes *lord*) was its guardian. Paradoxical developments of meaning attend the changes in *lady*. From one who kneads the dough it became both 'the chief female of the household' and hence the one least likely to deal with such chores. However, the fourth word specializes the *clay* part of the original meaning and ignores the *knead* part: *paradise*, originally an enclosed garden, from Indo-Iranian *pairi-daēza* (walled around), from *pairi* (around: compare *periscope*) and *daēza* (wall, originally made of clay). Few words escape such changes, because change of form and meaning is inherent in language. Etymological study works at the level of the individual word, but with reference to more general rules of LANGUAGE CHANGE, the basic fact of language.

See BORROWING, CALQUE, CATACHRESIS, FOLK ETYMOLOGY, INDO-EUROPEAN ROOTS, LOAN, LOANWORD, NAME, PARTRIDGE, PHILOLOGY, RADIATION, SEMANTIC CHANGE.

**ETYMON**. **1.** In the theory of LANGUAGE of the Stoic philosophers of ancient Greece, the true original form of which a current word is the degenerate descendant. **2.** In PHILOLOGY, the earliest traceable form from which a later WORD is derived: for example, *rex/regis* (king) is the Latin etymon of English *regal*, while the Indo-European verbal ROOT *\*reg-* (to move in a straight line, lead, rule) is the etymon of *rex/regis*, of Sanskrit *rājā*, and of the suffix *-ric* in *bishopric*. See ETYMOLOGY, INDO-EUROPEAN ROOTS, NOTATION, ROOTWORD.

**EUPHEMISM**. In RHETORIC, (the use of) a mild, comforting, or evasive expression that takes the place of one that is taboo, negative, offensive, or too direct: *Gosh* God, *terminate* kill, *sleep with* have sex with, *pass water*, *relieve oneself* urinate. Official euphemisms can be circuitous and formulaic, as in the British announcement *a man is helping the police with their inquiries*, meaning 'a man has been detained by the police and may soon be charged'.

Arbiters of usage are generally severe on euphemism. Ronald Ridout and Clifford Witting in the UK (*The Facts of English*, 1964) claim that people 'commit a euphemism' when trying to hide something unpleasant, or when using a mild and indirect term: 'It is prudery or a false sense of refinement that causes us to use *paying guest* for *boarder* or *lodger*.' Fowler (*Modern English Usage*, ed. Gowers, 1965) notes: 'Its value is notorious in totalitarian countries, where assassination and aggression can be made to look respectable by calling them *liquidation* and *liberation*.' The US critic Joseph T. Shipley (*Dictionary of World Literary Terms*, 1977) considers euphemism 'the bane of much writing in the 20th c., esp. in the jargon language of sociologists, educationists and bureaucrats'. The US journalist Hugh Rawson, however, responds to euphemism as 'society's basic *lingua non franca* . . . outward and visible signs of our inward anxieties, conflicts, fears, and shames', and adds:

> They cover up the facts of life—of sex and reproduction and excretion—which inevitably remind even the most refined people that they are made of clay, or worse. They are beloved by individuals and institutions (governments especially) who are anxious to present only the handsomest possible images of themselves to the world. And they are embedded so deeply in our language that few of us, even those who pride themselves on being plainspoken, ever get through a day without using them (*A Dictionary of Euphemisms & Other Doubletalk*, 1981).

Because of its genteel associations, the term has itself been used euphemistically. In Edward Albee's *Who's Afraid of Virginia Woolf?* (1964), a guest has said that she would like to *powder her nose*. George responds with: 'Martha, won't you show her where we keep the euphemism?' See, DYSPHEMISM, GENTEELISM, JARGON, MINCED OATH.

**EUPHONY**. A pleasant, harmonious quality in SPEECH. The perception of such a quality is partly physiological (soft, flowing, blending sounds are generally considered pleasanter than harsh, jangling, discordant sounds) and partly cultural (people tend to like sounds that they have been led to like). In English, euphony is often associated with long vowels, the semi-vowels or glides /j, w/, and the consonants /l, m, n, r/. All of these occur in the opening verse of Gray's 'Elegy Written in a Country Church-Yard' (1751):

> The Curfew tolls the knell of parting day,
> The lowing herd winds slowly o'er the lea,
> The plowman homeward plods his weary way,
> And leaves the world to darkness and to me.

Euphony can be achieved through the skilled use of a language's rhythms and patterns together with positive associations shared by performer and audience. These associations may relate to sound (preferred voice qualities and accents), allusion (oblique references to favoured or familiar poems, songs, etc.), and experience (bringing in positive images like spring, morning, youth, hope, love, and dreams). There may be agreement that X is *euphonious* and Y *cacophonous*, but people may differ as to just how and why this is so. Euphony in the sense of a greater ease in saying and hearing sounds has been cited as important in grammar and word-formation: as the reason for *an apple* rather than *\*a apple*, *Aren't I?* and not *\*Amn't I?*, *tobacconist* and not *\*tobaccoist*, *impossible* rather than *\*inpossible* or *\*unpossible*, and *calculable* rather than *\*calculatable*. In matters of this kind, however, analogy, convention, and phonology appear to be more significant factors.

**EUROPEAN UNION**, short form *EU*. An association of European countries, until the end of 1994 twelve in number: Belgium, Denmark, France, Germany, Greece, the Irish Republic, Italy, Luxembourg, the Netherlands, Portugal, Spain, and the United Kingdom. Membership now also includes Austria, Finland, and Sweden. In 1993, the EU subsumed the European Community (EC), previously known as the European Economic Community (EEC), which came into being in 1967 through the merger of several earlier associations formed after the Second World War. Its headquarters is in Brussels in Belgium, its Parliament mainly in Strasbourg, northern France, with some central institutions in Luxembourg. Its official working languages are ENGLISH and FRENCH, and its official languages DANISH, DUTCH, English, Finnish, French, GERMAN, GREEK, ITALIAN, PORTUGUESE, SPANISH, and Swedish. All eleven are used in EC meetings with simultaneous translation as a matter of course. Official documents must be published in all the official languages. In the period 1982–90, 40m ECUs (European Currency Units) were provided for EUROTRA automatic translation. There are between 30 and 40 minority languages, depending on definition, some of them varieties of official languages (such as Alsatian German in France), some unique (such as Breton in France and Basque in France and Spain). All member countries save Portugal have regional minority languages (such as GAELIC, SCOTS, and WELSH in the UK). The *European Bureau for Lesser-Used Languages*, set up in 1982 with its headquarters in DUBLIN, represents all such languages but not the 'trans-European' minority languages YIDDISH and ROMANY.

English is increasingly the LINGUA FRANCA of the EU. Representatives of smaller countries, such as Denmark and Greece, often give press conferences in English: 'The Danes are keener to speak English even than the British. . . . The Spanish on the other hand tend to talk French. On political subjects both languages are used in discussions. The French are very concerned to protect their language. But in more technical sectors—telecommunications or research for example—it is overwhelmingly English, as the technical vocabulary has developed on a more global basis' (Michael Berendt, *The Times*, 23 Oct. 1989). In Belgium, a country often disturbed by tensions between speakers of Flemish and French, English is a neutral medium. British television is widely watched along the north-western European coast, and in the Netherlands interviews in English on national television are often not translated. American TV is also widely available by satellite and cable.

While the aim of the Union is harmonization rather than homogenization, there is a strong EU-wide tendency towards greater use of English. Indeed, the results of any drive towards foreign-language learning may strengthen the already most prominent language: English is the first second language in all EU countries, including France.

**EUROSPEAK**, also **Eurolish**, **Minglish**. Generally pejorative or facetious terms for kinds of English used in Continental Europe and especially the European Union: 'And as more and more magazines and newspapers view Europe as home territory, neologisms and borrowed words will undoubtedly emerge—as long as newspapers and magazines don't resort to bland Eurospeak' (*Journalist's Week*, 22 June 1990). See -SPEAK.

# ■ EXAMINING IN ENGLISH ── ■

The formal testing of a student's command of English, usually in an educational institution or through a public system of evaluation and certification. Such testing dates from the mid-18c, when three necessary prior conditions had been fulfilled: (1) The standard language was increasingly widely taught in schools and had begun to be used as a vehicle for the testing of all school subjects. (2) A new educational tradition had developed, associated with the manufacturing and mercantile classes of Britain and America, an alternative to traditional LATIN-medium or Latin-based education. (3) A network of institutions and administrators had begun to spread: for example, in Britain the Dissenting Academies and the Royal Society of Arts, which was founded in 1754 and conducted examinations in English before 1800.

**British examinations**. By the mid-19c, public examinations had become necessary for the recruitment of officials and others at home and abroad. In 1858, the report of a Civil Service Commission (set up to consider inefficiencies in the Crimean War and the problems of directly governing India) called for recruitment 'by public competition and not by private patronage' and for the provision of tests by the universities of Oxford and Cambridge of 'the elements of a plain English education'. Two bodies were set up, the *Oxford Delegacy* and the *Cambridge Syndicate*, which remain central to the British tradition of examining by independent bodies. Their establishment lent weight to the existing external examinations of the *University of London*, administered for its own matriculating purposes. In 1903 the *Joint Matriculation Board* and in 1953 the *Associated Examining Board* were added, and the five boards became responsible for officially recognized school-leaving examinations in England. More directly government-sponsored bodies were set up for the same purpose in Ireland, Scotland, and Wales. By the end of the 19c a range of school examinations had been established in Britain and

parts of the Empire. These have been developed and refined throughout the 20c, under various names and with various emphases.

**Commonwealth examinations**. Within the Commonwealth there has been a process of devolution from British control, Australia, Canada, New Zealand, and South Africa having long had their own systems. In territories where English has second-language status the picture is complex. In some areas, links with UK examining boards have been retained, sometimes as the sole system of examination, sometimes alongside new indigenous systems. In India, there is a Council for the *Indian School Certificate Examination*, based on a grouping of English-medium schools and associated with the *Cambridge Overseas School Certificate*. A *West African Examinations Council* conducts school examinations in Ghana, Nigeria, Sierra Leone, and Gambia, in consultation with British boards (Cambridge and London) active in the area. London's influence continues to be strong for private candidates (adults seeking a second chance of education). An *East African Examinations Council* operates in Kenya, Uganda, Zambia, and Zimbabwe, associated with British boards (Cambridge and AEB). The Caribbean area has followed the same pattern, with the *Caribbean Examinations Council* established in consultation with British boards. Single-country examining authorities have been established, at first with British board sponsorship, in Hong Kong with London, and in Singapore and Malaysia with Cambridge. Smaller areas of UK influence, such as Malta, Cyprus, and the River Plate countries of South America, with their high level of second-language use, alternate between British or locally conducted school examinations and British-based EFL examinations such as Cambridge.

**American examinations**. State control of examining, closely linked to the systematic grading of classes, is a feature of US education that can be traced to the influence of the Enlightenment on the founders of the Republic. Each of the 50 states has its own educational system, of which testing is an integral part. In addition, decisions in many states are made by local school districts, as a result of which few useful generalizations can be made about examining in English for the whole country. Tests used for college admission in many parts of the nation are largely machine-graded, written and scored by such private bodies as the *College Entrance Examination Board* (with the *Scholastic Aptitude Test* or *SAT*), and the *American College Testing Program* (with the *American College Test* or *ACT*). Some students completing a first degree take the *Graduate Record Examination* (*GRE*) offered by *Educational Testing Service* (*ETS*) of Princeton, New Jersey, used by most US universities as one factor in admissions to postgraduate study. There is controversy over these standardized, multiple-choice tests of aptitude and the interpretation of their scores, and they are often said to be culturally biased or easier for those already accustomed to them. Despite such criticisms, they continue to be widely used, as one of a number of factors that include course grades, recommendations from teachers, application essays, and sometimes interviews: testing is less important as a determinant of the future of US students than in some other English-speaking countries.

**Other countries**. Local arrangements for the achievement and diagnostic testing of English in non-English-speaking countries follow the interests, needs, and resources of each country, varying from sophisticated provision for high levels of performance in northern Europe to more uncertain initiatives elsewhere, often linked with grammar-translation and literature-based approaches. Some countries have experimented in the teaching and testing of their own languages as foreign languages on EFL lines (for example, Swedish and Spanish), and have benefited from the resulting cross-fertilization in terms of local English teaching. Within Europe, the Cambridge examinations have achieved particular significance.

**English as a native language**. The broad target in examinations of English as a first language is a performance that meets the needs both of practical effectiveness and of conformity with agreed rules of syntax, vocabulary, and orthography, at a level associated with completion of a process of general education: that is, completion of an accredited school curriculum at 16, marked by a certificate that serves as a qualification for employment, vocational or other training, or higher education. The relevance of performance in public examinations to real-life social and communicative needs continues

to be a matter of controversy, along with the general role and procedures of examining boards. Public examining has been criticized for institutionalizing an interlocking and educationally sterile system of teaching and testing, for the discouragement of cultural development through wider reading and writing, and for its tendency to concentrate on testable minutiae of vocabulary and usage. For testers, the problem has been one of reconciling the relative importance of the holistic and atomistic elements in a syllabus.

Directly analytical testing of orthography, vocabulary, and syntax has been generally abandoned in the later 20c, on the grounds that it does not predict effective communicative performance. The usual pattern of testing combines a form of global assessment (with a communicative or functional basis) and an objective mode based on reading comprehension. Attempts to maintain a constant standard, though procedurally successful because of the long experience of the boards and the paramount importance of consistency, are deeply affected by such wider issues as the level of tolerance of 'error' in examination scripts and linguistic factors in the teaching of general school subjects: the presentation of information in note form or in a subject-specific register, or in the formal prose associated with the humanities. Such factors have made for considerable uncertainty of aim and procedure in language testing throughout the English-speaking world, with an associated tendency to deflect problems by emphasizing either objectivity (in the narrow fields of usage and the comprehension of texts) or creativity (of a personal kind or in terms of literary appreciation).

**English as a second language**. One legacy of empire is the problem of variation between locally accepted but not mutually or internationally intelligible forms of English. Such local forms are often assisted by long association with a British-based, or British-developed, school examination structure that has not systematically addressed problems of variation. Second-language users have widely varying aspirations towards quasi-first-language status, with varied effects on linguistic conservatism, first-language influence, and the teaching styles favoured as appropriate and practicable in each area. There is little systematic knowledge of the elements of difference and little motivation to build examination syllabuses on an agreed corpus of these; instead, the assessment of free composition by non-local examiners for a British board remains a standard though uncertain procedure. Organized examining has to date failed to take significantly into account such broad developments as archaism of vocabulary in India and Pakistan, syllable-timing in English as spoken in Africa, and the movement towards the 'legitimization' of Creoles and Black Englishes. Although the pattern of centralized non-local examining is especially British, the problem of integrating second-language pupils and examination candidates into general educational systems is shared by English-speaking countries as a whole, sometimes shading off into wider aspects of sociolinguistic development and sometimes into the more clear-cut area of EFL. Teaching shows the effects of this confusion, as do the availability and content of tests.

**English as a foreign language**. A number of factors emerged in the 1960s as the basis for improvement in the testing of English as an international language, with its built-in emphasis on efficient communication. The post-war, post-colonial demand for an equalizing lingua franca, serving the needs of an era of unprecedentedly heightened communication, had increased interest in examinations available internationally, with heavy increases in entries and a heightened sense of involvement among teachers. The Cambridge examinations in particular, introduced in 1913 as a small-scale extension of the board's British and overseas school examining, but greatly expanded since 1945, came under critical review, with special emphasis on problems of culture bias in content and assessment, the testing of oral performance, and the general validity and reliability of tests. The Syndicate's links with specialized teaching, through the BRITISH COUNCIL and newly established university schools of applied linguistics (notably Edinburgh), made possible a research programme that resulted in a remodelling (1975) of the Cambridge syllabus. In this, the relative weighting given to objective/analytical and holistic/impressionistic elements was computer-controlled in a five-paper examination covering reading, writing, listening, and speaking, with such features as task-based composition, active and specific testing (through conversion or transformation exercises) of the candidate's grasp of language patterns, a substantial but contained element of objective testing, and the exclusion of culture-based elements such as literature, translation, and Brito- or Eurocentric texts and situations. The immediate popularity of the new syllabus, available at two established levels (Certificate Proficiency in English and First Certificate English) showed its relevance to international needs and its predictive accuracy, particularly at the lower level. Cambridge's position was further consolidated by the introduction of similarly designed elementary level tests from 1980, a further streamlining of the main CPE and FCE syllabus in 1984, and the taking over of responsibility for both the British Council's *English Language Testing Service* and the Royal College of Arts' range of examination schemes for EFL teachers. A number of other British and non-British examining bodies, of varying status and operational scope, also currently offer English language tests for the foreign learner. In the US, the ETS offers the *Test of English as a Foreign Language* (*TOEFL*) to measure the English-language ability of foreign students seeking admission to American universities.

See CAMBRIDGE CERTIFICATE OF PROFICIENCY IN ENGLISH, EDUCATION, ELT, LANGUAGE LEARNING, LANGUAGE TEACHING, TEACHING ENGLISH, TEFL, TEIL, TESD, TESL, UCLES.

**EXCLAMATION. 1.** A cry; a sudden loud or emphatic utterance: *Hey! Ouch!* **2.** A SENTENCE that conveys a strong emotion: *Please leave me alone!* **3.** Also *exclamatory sentence.* A type of sentence, often verbless, that begins with *what* or *how* (followed by a noun phrase): *What courage! What a meal that was! How marvellous!* See EXCLAMATION MARK.

**EXCLAMATION MARK**, also AmE **exclamation point**. The PUNCTUATION MARK (!). Its primary use is to show that a preceding word, phrase, or sentence is an EXCLAMATION or strong assertion: *Of course!; No!; I won't do it!; Yes, you are!* It indicates various emotions conveyed in the substance of the statement, such as surprise, disbelief, or dismay (*You're joking!; What a silly way to behave!*), wonder or admiration (*What a good idea!; Aren't they beautiful!*), personal feeling (*I* love you!; *I hate them!*); and pain or suffering (*Ouch!*; *I'm so miserable!*). It also indicates an instruction or command (*Go away!*; *Left turn!*). It is sometimes repeated in informal usage to express a specially strong exclamation (*What nonsense!!*) or added to a question mark to indicate a mixture of questioning and surprise, anger, etc. (*Did you say the house was tidy?!*). It is also used in round brackets/parentheses, as a kind of aside, to denote surprise or reserve about, or dissent from, what is stated: *They told us about the beauty(!) of the place.*

**EXISTENTIAL SENTENCE**. A SENTENCE stating that something exists, usually consisting of *there*, the verb *be*, and an indefinite noun phrase: *There's a tavern in the town. There must be somebody we can ask.* Where more information follows (as in *There was an old woman who lived in a shoe, who had ...*), *there* can be dispensed with (*An old woman lived in a shoe, who had ...*). When *there* is used like this, as a prop subject, the newness of the information in the sentence is emphasized. That *there* is subject-like is shown by its use in question tags: *There's no problem, is there?* Existential *there*-sentences can also occur with some other verbs: *There came a big spider, and sat down beside her; There then began a time of great fear.* See GRAMMAR.

**EXPLETIVE**. **1.** Originally, an expression used to fill out a line of verse or a sentence, without adding anything to the sense. **2.** An interjected word, especially an oath or swearword. At the time of the Watergate hearings in the US in the 1970s, during the presidency of Richard Nixon, the phrase *expletive deleted* occurred frequently in the transcript of the White House tapes. See INFIX, SWEARING.

**EYE DIALECT**. A term first used by George P. Krapp in *The English Language in America* (1925) for how colloquial usage appears in print; spellings in which 'the convention violated is one of the eyes, not of the ear' (Krapp). Thus, spellings like *enuff* enough, *wimmin* women, *animulz* animals, indicate that those represented as using them are uneducated, youthful, rustic, or otherwise unlike the readership. In Krapp's definition, DIALECT writers use eye dialect not 'to indicate a genuine difference of pronunciation, but the SPELLING is merely a friendly nudge to the reader, a knowing look which establishes a sympathetic sense of superiority between the author and reader as contrasted with the humble speaker of dialect'. The term is sometimes extended to include both 'dialect' spellings and spellings based on pronunciation in a variety of English, as with *Kanajan* Canadian, *Murrican* American, *Strine* Australian. Eye dialect is an important element in humorous dictionaries and glossaries which poke fun at varieties of English: *Awreddy* already (*Eh, Goondu!*, Singapore, 1982), *Baked Necks* bacon and eggs (*Lets Stalk Strine*, Australia, 1965), *Fairy Nuff* fair enough (*Bristle with Pride*, Bristol, England, 1987), *pannyhos* pantihose (*More How to Speak Southern*, US, 1980), *yidownsay* you don't say (*Ah Big Yaws*, South Africa, 1973). See KING'S ENGLISH.

# F

[Called 'eff']. The 6th LETTER of the Roman ALPHABET as used for English. It originated in the Phoenician symbol *waw*, a vertical line forking at the top like Y, which was adapted by the Greeks into two letters: ϝ (digamma: 'double gamma'), which represented the sound /w/, and ϒ (upsilon), which represented /u/. *Waw* was also the ancestor of U, V, W. *Digamma* was lost in classical Greek, which used Φ (phi) first for aspirated /p/, later for /f/. The Etruscans, then the Romans, gave F the value it has today in English: the voiceless labio-dental fricative, which has V as its voiced equivalent. In Old English, however, *f* was used for both voiceless and voiced consonants. Formerly, *of* was not distinguished in spelling from *off*: the *f* was voiced when the syllable containing it was unstressed, and voiceless when stressed, until the two came to be distinguished (*c.*16c) in SPELLING and meaning as *off/of*, the latter retaining the sound /v/. In ScoE, *of* and *off* are often homophones, both pronounced with /f/.

**F/V alternation.** There is sometimes an alternation between *f* and *v* in grammatically or etymologically related words. For example, the following nouns have singular *-f(e)*, plural *-ves*: *calf, elf, half, knife, leaf, life, loaf, self, sheaf, shelf, thief, wife, wolf.* In some cases, the plural may be either *-fs* or *-ves*: *dwarfs/ dwarves, hoofs/hooves.* So engrained is the tendency to *f/v* alternation that *handkerchiefs, roofs* are often pronounced with /v/. Verbs from such nouns have *f* or *v*, but do not vary when inflected: *to knife/knifed, to halve/halved.* Other examples of *v/f* alternation include *believe/belief, leave/left, strive/strife, five/fifth, twelve/twelfth.* The *f/v* distinction in *fox/vixen* arises from the different dialects from which the words have been taken.

**Double F.** (1) Except in *if, of* and some loanwords, *f* is doubled in syllable-final position immediately after a single vowel letter that is pronounced short: *waffle, piffle, bailiff, cliff, scoff, stuff.* Single *f* occurs otherwise: *deaf, elf, beef, belief, dwarf, golf, loaf.* (2) There is doubling between vowels, especially to show the assimilation of the Latin prefixes *ad-*, *ob-*, *sub-*, as in *affair, offer, suffer.* An anomaly is single *f* in *afraid*, despite *ff* in the related *affray*.

**F, GH, and PH.** (1) In some common words, the digraph *gh* represents /f/: *cough, enough, laugh, rough, tough.* AmE does not make the BrE distinction between *draught/draft*, having *draft* for both. In BrE, a *draftsman* draws up the wording of documents and a *draughtsman* prepares technical drawings. See G. (2) The digraph *ph* represents /f/, generally in words of Greek origin: *photograph, philosophy.* See P. F has, however, varied historically with *ph* in some words: for example, with the revival of Greek learning in the 16c, *fantasy* began to be written *phantasy*, but in the 20c has reverted to *f*. Occasionally, words not derived from Greek have acquired *ph* in place of *f*: *nephew* was once written with both *f* and *v*. AmE *sulfur* retains the original Latin form, whereas BrE has *sulphur*; the AmE form is increasingly used internationally, as for example by pure and applied chemists. In commerce, a standard *ph* may be replaced by *f* in a trade name or for special effect, or both, as with *fotopost* and *freefone.* See WRITING.

**FALLACY.** In general usage, a false and often deceitful idea; in logic, a line of reasoning (also known as a *paralogism*) that may seem valid but is not. Fallacies of discourse were first described in Greek and Latin, and many therefore retain their classical names, either uniquely or alongside a vernacular label. They include: (1) *Argumentum ad baculum* [Latin: argument backed by a stick]. Resorting to threat in order to have a point accepted. (2) *Argumentum ad hominem* [Latin: argument directed at the person]. Often called an *ad hominem argument* or an *ad hominem attack.* Seeking to disprove a point by attacking the people making that point, either in terms of their character or by referring to their personal circumstances as an explanation of why a position has been adopted. (3) *Argumentum ad populum* [Latin: argument directed at the people]. An appeal to popular opinion, bias, and inclination. (4) *Non sequitur* [Latin: it does not follow]. A statement in which the premisses of an argument do not lead to the conclusion provided. (5) *Post hoc ergo propter hoc* [Latin: after this therefore because of this]. Asserting that because A came before B, A caused B.

**FAUX AMI**, also **false friend**. A term in LANGUAGE TEACHING for a word that has the same origin and general appearance as a word in another language, so that learners mistakenly assume that both have the same meanings and uses: English *deceive* to trick, French *décevoir* to disappoint. Compare CONFUSIBLE, DOUBLET. See QUEBEC.

**FEMININE**. A term relating to grammatical GENDER in nouns and related words. Words denoting female people and animals in such languages as FRENCH and LATIN are usually feminine, but grammatical gender is not about sex: in the French phrase *la plume de ma tante*, the pen is as feminine as its owner. In English, the term is largely confined to personal pronouns (*she/her/herself/hers*), some nouns (*mare* in contrast to *stallion*), and some suffixes (*-ess* as in *hostess*). See MASCULINE, SEXISM.

**FEMINISM**. A social philosophy concerned with the rights of women. Feminists generally consider women to be oppressed and in varying degrees alienated by a male-dominated society in which the use of language is anti-female. They argue that language favours men by helping to shape a society in which women are rendered subordinate and often taught to keep silent; when they speak, men often do not listen to them properly. In a radical feminist view, if society cannot change to accommodate both sexes equally, women will do their best to create their own society and their own kinds of language. This idea is explored by Suzette Haden Elgin in *Native Tongue* (Daw, 1984), which creates a world in which severely oppressed women rebel through an underground movement to make their own language, *Laadan*. In it, a distinction is made between *am* (love for blood kin) and *ashon* (love for kin of the heart), and prefixes at the start of sentences signal whether they are statements, promises, warnings, etc., making the language more explicit and avoiding possibly painful misunderstandings. See FORM OF ADDRESS, GENDER BIAS, SEXISM.

**FIGURATIVE EXTENSION**, also **extension**. A process of SEMANTIC CHANGE in which a word gains further senses figuratively, especially through metaphor or metonymy. For example, the reference of *crown* has extended from a usually royal head-dress to royalty itself, to (among others) a coin with this symbol on it, to the part of the head where a crown rests, to the top of a hill or other such place, to the crest of a bird, to a crown-like award or honour, to the enamel-covered part of a tooth above the gum, and to a standard size of printing paper.

■ **FIGURATIVE LANGUAGE** ──── ■

Also **figurative usage**. LANGUAGE in which FIGURES OF SPEECH such as METAPHORS and SIMILES freely occur. In classical RHETORIC and poetics there is an inherent contrast between *figurative* or ornamental usage on the one hand and *literal* or plain and conventional usage on the other; in this contrast, figures of speech are regarded as embellishments that deviate from the 'ordinary' uses of language. The 16c English rhetorician George Puttenham described the contrast as follows:

> As figures be the instruments of ornament in euery language, so be they also in a sort abuses or rather trespasses in speech, because they passe the ordinary limits of common vtterance, and be occupied of purpose to deceiue the eare and also the minde, drawing it from plainnesse and simplicitie to a certain doublenesse, whereby our talk is the more guileful and abusing, for what else is your Metaphore but an inuersion of sence by transport; your allegorie but a duplicitie of meaning or dissimulation vnder covert and dark intendments? (*The Arte of Poesie*, 1589).

Puttenham implies here that there is a core of simple, literal language that can be distinguished from ornate, figurative language (which engages in a kind of unnatural double-dealing). There is, however, a paradox at the heart of the classical argument that Puttenham presents. The 18c Scottish rhetorician Hugh Blair touched on it when he wrote:

> But, though Figures imply a deviation from what may be reckoned the most simple form of Speech, we are not thence to conclude, that they imply

anything uncommon, or unnatural (*Lectures on Rhetoric and Belles Lettres*, 1784).

In this paradox, figurative language succeeds, somehow, in being both natural and unnatural at the same time.

**From deviant to natural**. The classical view was dominant at the end of the 19c, when the American rhetorician John F. Genung described figurative language as an 'intentional deviation from the plain and ordinary mode of speaking, for the sake of greater effect' (*Practical Elements of Rhetoric*, 1893). In the late 20c however, a change of approach was under way: for example, while referring to 'an intentional deviation from the normal' (in the traditional way), the American critic Joseph T. Shipley observed: 'Figures are as old as language. They lie buried in many words of current use. They are the backbone of slang. They occur constantly in both prose and poetry' (*Dictionary of World Literary Terms*, 1970). Two recent dictionaries demonstrate more explicitly a shift in the perception of the term 'figure of speech' away from linguistic deviance towards stylistic creativity, defining it as: (1) 'a form of expression (e.g. a hyperbole or metaphor) used to convey meaning or heighten effect, often by comparing or identifying one thing with another that has a meaning or connotation familiar to the reader or listener' (UK: *Longman Dictionary of the English Language*, 1984); (2) 'An expression, such as a metaphor or hyperbole, in which a nonliteral and intensive sense of a word or words is used to create a forceful, dramatic, or illuminating image' (US: *American Heritage Dictionary*, 1985).

Deciding where the literal ends and the figurative begins is notoriously difficult. There is no irreducible core of 'literal' language from which 'figurative usage' diverges. Rather, there is an easy movement between the one pole and the other: for example, behind such an everyday word as *brand* (in the sense of 'product' or 'trademark') is a history of burning that includes what was done to animals and slaves to mark them as property. The modern use of *brand* as 'product' is in effect a literal usage, yet its origin in branding-irons and the like is distinctly metaphorical and figurative. Similarly, behind the various *fields* in which scholars work lie the patches of land where farmers have 'literally' worked for millen-

nia, and such a phrase as *electromagnetic field*, however mundanely literal it may be for physicists, depends for its creation on a comparable figurative shift: Puttenham's 'inuersion of sence by transport'.

**Defining figures of speech**. The precise definition of a figure of speech has proved to be as difficult as determining the limits of figurative usage. For centuries, rhetoricians have debated what each presumed figure refers to and how various figures relate to each other. As a result, *metaphor* in some approaches contains METONYMY, in others does not, and SYNECDOCHE may or may not be a kind of metaphor or metonymy. As a result, in recent years attempts to arrange the figures hierarchically have been abandoned in favour of lists in which the main devices are presented each more or less in isolation, as stylistic equals, but perhaps with notes on celebrated doubts and ambiguities about their precise natures and relationships. Classical rhetoric has tended to present figurative language as the concern primarily of poets, orators, critics, and language teachers, while conceding (usually in a brief aside) that everybody else uses it too and that the term therefore covers a universal practice in which sound, spelling, grammar, vocabulary, usage, and meaning are adapted to achieve special stylistic effects.

**Kinds of figurative language**. (1) Phonological figures include ALLITERATION, ASSONANCE, and ONOMATOPOEIA. In his poem 'The Pied Piper of Hamelin' (1842), Robert Browning repeats sibilants, nasals, and liquids as he shows how the children respond to the piper: 'There was a ru*stling*, that seemed like a bu*stling* / Of merry crowds ju*stling* at pitching and hu*stling*.' Something sinister has started. (2) Orthographic figures use visual forms created for effect: for example, *America* spelt *Amerika* (by left-wing radicals in the 1970s and as the name of a movie in the 1980s), to suggest a totalitarian state. (3) Syntactic figures may bring the non-standard into the standard language, as in US President Ronald Reagan's 'You ain't seen nothing yet' (1984), a nonstandard double negative to project a vigorous, folksy image. (4) Lexical figures extend the conventional so as to surprise or entertain, as when, instead of a phrase like *a year ago*, the Welsh poet Dylan Thomas wrote *a grief ago*. or when the Irish dramatist Oscar Wilde said at the New York Customs, 'I have nothing to declare but my genius.' When people say that 'you can't take' something 'literally', they are generally referring to usage that challenges everyday reality: for example, through exaggeration (the *HYPERBOLE* in 'loads of money'), comparison (the *simile* 'like death warmed up'; the *metaphor* 'life is an uphill struggle'), physical and other association (the *metonymy* 'Crown property' for something owned by royalty), and a part for a whole (the *synecdoche* 'All hands on deck!').

Puttenham divided figures into those that please the ear and the mind (or both), but to be effective, figurative usage does not need to please. The spelling *Amerikkka* has sometimes been used, especially in graffiti, to suggest that the Ku Klux Klan has great influence over how the US is governed. The usage is both imaginative and striking, but to many Americans it is very far from pleasing. The aim of all such usage is to make an impact: pleasing, shocking, political, social, etc. The ends of figurative language are achieved through repetitions, juxtapositions, contrasts, and associations, by violating expectations, by evoking echoes of other people, places, times, and contexts, and through novel, provocative imagery. When such usage succeeds, new expressions, concepts, and associations may be established in a language, as with *loads/tons of money*. When an expression succeeds so well that everyone adopts it, the result in due course is the opposite of what was first intended: a *CLICHÉ* from which the figurative power has drained away.

See ALLEGORY, ANACHRONISM, ANAPHORA, ANTICLIMAX, ANTITHESIS, ANTONOMASIA, APOSTROPHE[2], BATHOS, CHIASMUS, CLIMAX, DYSPHEMISM, ECHOISM, EMPHASIS, EUPHEMISM, EUPHONY, EUPHUISM, INVERSION, IRONY, LITERAL, LITOTES, MEIOSIS, MIXED METAPHOR, OXYMORON, PARADOX, PARALLELISM, PERSONIFICATION, PHRASAL VERB, PLAYING WITH WORDS, POETIC DICTION, PROLEPSIS, PUN, REPETITION, TROPE, ZEUGMA.

**FIGURE OF SPEECH**, also **figure**. In RHETORIC, a device that achieves a special effect by using words in distinctive ways, such as ALLITERATION, in which the same sound, especially an initial consonant, is repeated, as with /f/ in *life's fitful fever*, and HYPERBOLE, in which one engages, usually deliberately, in unrealistic exaggeration, as

in the informal phrase *tons of money* ('a great deal of money'). Here, a word usually associated with weights and measures has been moved out of context to refer to money, with which it is not normally associated. See FIGURATIVE LANGUAGE.

**FIJI**. A country in Oceania, consisting of some 330 islands. Languages: Fijian and English (both official), the Pacific languages Rotuman, Gilbertese, Tongan, and the Indian languages Gujarati, Hindi, Tamil, Telugu. Fiji was a British colony from 1874 to independence in 1970. Originally wholly Melanesian, the population became multiethnic through colonialism, especially the importing of plantation labourers from the Pacific islands and India. There are longstanding tensions between ethnic Fijians and the Indian community.

English in Fiji ranges from low-prestige varieties (the BASILECT) to a high-prestige variety (the ACROLECT). The language of education is STANDARD ENGLISH on a BrE model. A stable pidgin English did not develop, although some early plantation labourers knew MELANESIAN PIDGIN ENGLISH and later labourers arrived speaking a stable variety of the same PIDGIN, learned in Queensland. A pidginized Fijian was used on plantations. Features of local English include: (1) The focus marker *ga* (*You ga, you ga tell it* It's you who tells it) and the politeness marker *mada* (*Wait mada*). (2) Use of *one* as an indefinite article, as in varieties of IndE: *Tonight I'm going to one party*. (3) Use of *us two* as the first-person dual inclusive (myself and one other): *I can't give you us two's money because us two poor*. (4) The use of *fella* as the third-person pronoun with human reference: *Fella put that fella's hand in front* He put his hand in front. (5) Local words such as Fijian *tanoa* a bowl for making kava, and Hindi *roti* Indian flat bread. Such features as *us two* and *fella* are similar to those in Melanesian Pidgin English and indigenous languages; others are shared not only with pidgin and creole English but also with basilectal varieties of English as in Singapore, such as the use of *been* as a pre-verbal marker of past tense (*He been swear* He swore) and lack of copula (*That one nice house* That is a nice house).

**FILIPINISM**. A linguistic usage specific to or typical of the Philippines, such as *Open the light* Switch on the light, *captain-ball* basketball team captain, and *viand* any dish eaten with rice. See -ISM, PHILIPPINE ENGLISH.

**FILIPINO**. **1.** An inhabitant or citizen of the Philippines. The term is generic for all people in the Philippines, but *Filipina* is often used for women. **2.** Relating to the Philippines: *Filipino languages*. **3.** Also *Pilipino*. The co-official language (with English) of the Philippines, based on TAGA-LOG. See AMERICAN LANGUAGE, ASIAN LANGUAGES, HAWAII, TAGLISH.

**FILIPINO ENGLISH**. See PHILIPPINE ENGLISH.

**FINITE**. A term in GRAMMAR for any occurrence of a VERB inflected for features such as person, number, and tense. Compare FINITE VERB, INFINITIVE, NON-FINITE VERB.

**FINITE VERB**. A form of the VERB with a distinction in tense: *likes, like, liked* are finite verbs in *Justin likes strawberry ice cream, Anne and Robert like my story*, and *David liked his wife's cooking*. On the other hand, *like, liked* are non-finite in *Justin may like strawberry ice cream* and *David has always liked his wife's cooking*, since no tense contrast is possible in these sentences. Compare FINITE, INFINITIVE, NON-FINITE VERB.

**FIRST LANGUAGE, SECOND LANGUAGE**, short forms *L1, L2*. Terms in AP-PLIED LINGUISTICS and LANGUAGE TEACHING. The *first language* is the language in which learners are competent when starting a new language; the *second language* is another language that is being learned or has been learned to an adequate level. In many countries, a specific L2 is learned, usually at school, for national or international use. English is the second language for many purposes in such countries as India, Nigeria, and Singapore. An L1 may or may not be a learner's mother tongue, because a chronologically first language may not be the functionally first language of adulthood. Under certain conditions, such as migration, an original L2 may become a person's L1 or only language. See MOTHER TONGUE, TEACHING ENGLISH.

**FIXED PHRASE**. A PHRASE, often consisting of an ADJECTIVE and a NOUN, which functions as a WORD, either with unique reference (*Red Ensign, Red Indian, Red Sea*) or as an idiom (*red herring, red tape*). The usual stress is level (*Réd Séa, réd tápe*) as opposed to initial emphasis in compounds (*REDcap, REDcoat*). Fixed phrases are common in technical usage: *adaptive radiation, natural selection, solar nebula, spontaneous generation*. The dividing line between a widely used ordinary phrase and a fixed phrase is not easy to determine. There are degrees of fixedness, depending on frequency of occurrence and people's perception of the usage. Darwin's phrase *natural selection* did not become fixed in the language at large for many years, but for Darwin, it was probably fixed from the moment of coinage. The line between fixed phrases and compound words is also not easy to draw. Linguists disagree as to whether the following are fixed phrases or compounds: possessive eponyms (*Parkinson's Law, Tourette's syndrome*), words linked by preposition (*brother-in-law, actor-cum-manager*), and emphatic expressions (*brute of a man, hell of a time*). Fixed phrases are often incorporated into compounds: *red letter* in *red-letter day* (a *réd-LEtter dáy*), and phrases that have been incorporated into compound forms become fixed within them: *hot water* in a *hot-water system*; *quick action* in *quick-action glue*. See HOLOPHRASE, TECHNOSPEAK.

**FOLK ETYMOLOGY**, also **popular etymology**. A term in LINGUISTICS for 'folk' or 'popular' theories (that is, the thoughts of ordinary, non-academic people) about the origins, forms, and meanings of words, sometimes resulting in changes to the words in question: *plantar wart*, a wart on the sole of the foot (from Latin *planta*), reinterpreted as *planter's wart*. See ETYMOLOGY.

**FOREIGNER TALK**. A term in LINGUIS-TICS and language teaching for the conventionalized and simplified kind of language used by many native speakers with foreigners who cannot speak their language, such as (with exaggerated pointing gestures) *Me help you, Yes?* for *I am going to help you; is that all right?* It has a simple or non-existent morphology, more or less fixed word order, simple syntax, a small number of grammar words, and little or no use of the c̶ complex sentence such as *I have̶ man you're talking about could̶ and simplified as I no see mo̶* *man you talk I not see.* Compare BABY TALK, TEACHER TALK.

**FOREIGNISM**. A foreign WORD or expression, as in the headline 'No more *Antagonismo*' (*Time*, 15 Aug. 1988). Foreign expressions in English (as opposed to BORROWINGS or LOANWORDS proper) are generally used for special effect, for 'local colour', or to demonstrate special knowledge. In print, they typically appear in italics and are usually glossed:

> In the bazaars the shops were silently shuttered. In place of the turmoil of hawkers, scooters and vans pedestrians shrouded in the *phiran*, the long woollen winter coat, wandered or lounged in good humoured idleness, clutching under their wraps the *kongri*, a basket containing an earthenware bowl full of hot charcoal to keep them warm ('Letter from Srinagar', *The Times*, 23 Jan. 1984).

There tends to be a gradation in English from less to more foreign. French expressions range from the integrated (but variously pronounced) *garage* through *elite/élite* and *coup d'etat/état* to *fin de siècle* and *pâtisserie*. In such a spread, it is difficult to specify precisely where the 'properly' foreign begins: all the items are foreign, but some are more foreign than others, and more foreign for some than for others. Non-native words are used in English to a vast and unmeasurable extent. Many varieties of the language have everyday usages that in others would be foreignisms: Maori expressions in NZE, Hawaiian elements in AmE, and Gallicisms in the English of Quebec. See HARD WORD, LOAN, NATIVIZATION.

**FOREIGN USER**. A term in LANGUAGE TEACHING and APPLIED LINGUISTICS for a non-native user of a language, in either or both speech and writing, as opposed to both *foreign learner* and NATIVE SPEAKER and particularly in contrast to NATIVE USER. It is common in discussions of English as a foreign language: 'What most learners really want is to be competent foreign users of the language, not cheap imitation native speakers' (John Shepherd, *EFL Gazette*, Oct. 1990). See TEFL.

**FORM**. 1. In LOGIC, the abstract relations of terms in a proposition, and of propositions in a syllogism. 2. In LINGUISTICS, an in-ʔected variant of a word: *men* as the plural

form of *man*; *see*, *sees*, *saw*, *seen*, *seeing* as the forms of the verb *see*. 3. In linguistics, a category such as 'noun' when analysed in terms of structure (singular *man*, plural *men*) and FUNCTION (subject and object of sentence). Items that share characteristics belong to the same *form class*: the forms *happy* and *careful* belong to the adjective form class. Criteria of form are used to identify units and classes of units. Words such as *man* and *information* are identified as nouns by the formal criterion (among others) that they can be the main words in a phrase that functions as the subject of a sentence (*man* in *That man looks familiar*) or as the object of a preposition (*information* in *This is for your information only*). The criterion may be negative: nouns, unlike most adjectives, do not have comparative and superlative forms: there are adjective forms *happier* and *happiest* alongside *happy*, but no corresponding forms for *girl*. In contrast, notional or semantic criteria identify units and classes by meaning: a noun defined as the name of a person, thing, or place; a verb as a doing word. While such criteria may adequately characterize central members of a class, they are not comprehensive. The notional definition of a noun does not cover such words as *action*, *existence*, *happiness*, *temperature* that belong to the noun form class on formal criteria. See MORPHOLOGY, PARADIGM.

**FORMAL**. A term concerned with: (1) Structure and order: *a formal education*, *formal grammar*. (2) More or less elevated and stylized ceremonial: *a formal dinner*, *formal and informal meetings*. (3) Style and usage of a relatively elevated and impersonal kind: *a highly formal writing style*; '*receive*' a more formal word than '*get*'.

**FORMAL LANGUAGE**. 1. Language that is formal and ceremonial. 2. A language designed for use in situations in which natural language is considered unsuitable, such as logic, mathematics, and computer programming. Compare ARTIFICIAL LANGUAGE, NATURAL LANGUAGE.

**FORMATIVE**. 1. In PHILOLOGY, a derivational AFFIX, especially one that determines part of speech or WORD class: *-ness* in *darkness*, forming a noun from an adjective. 2. In structural LINGUISTICS, a word-forming element: the prefix *un-* and suffix *-ly* in *unkindly*. 3. In generative GRAMMAR, a minimal unit of syntax: in *The dancers performed gracefully*, the formatives (joined by plus signs) are *the + dance + er + s perform + ed grace + full + ly*. Compare BASE, MORPHEME.

## ■ FORM OF ADDRESS ─────── ■

Any WORD, such as a NAME, title, or PRONOUN, that designates someone who is being addressed in speech or writing. Such forms of address may be built into the grammar of a language used (as with the FRENCH pronouns *vous* and *tu*), or may evolve as a range of titles, names, kinship terms, terms of endearment, and nicknames, all usually with an initial capital in English.

**Pronouns**. Some languages, such as JAPANESE, have elaborate systems of pronouns to mark the relationship between addresser and addressee. Some European languages have systems in which one pronoun (French *vous*, SPANISH *Usted*) is used politely and formally among equals or by inferiors to superiors, and another (French *tu*, Spanish *tu*), used informally and intimately among equals or by superiors to inferiors. In French, the verbs *tutoyer* (to call *tu*; to be on familiar terms with) and *vousvoyer* (to call *vous*; to be on formal terms with) derive from and refer to this system. GENERAL ENGLISH once used pronouns in this way: in Shakespeare's *Tempest*, Prospero addresses his daughter Miranda with the intimate *th*-forms (*thou, thee, thy, thine*) and she addresses him with the respectful *y*-forms (*ye, you, your, yours*).

**A continuum of usage**. In addressing people, the two categories 'intimates/ children/social inferiors' and 'acquaintances/elders/social superiors, etc.' are the poles of a continuum. At the intimately personal end, actual names may not be used at all; forms of address tend instead to be terms of endearment (*baby, darling, honey*) or expressions of derision (*dickhead, idiot, stupid*), usually hostile and dismissive, but sometimes affectionate. At the impersonal end, such forms of address as *sir* and titles (bare or with surname) may be used: *Excuse me, sir/Sir; Doctor (Kildare), do you have a moment, please?; Follow your orders, Captain (Bligh)*. All the forms of address discussed below occur at various points on this continuum.

**Names and titles**. With the loss of its *th*-forms as living pronouns (except in North

of England and Northern Isles dialect) and the extension of the *y*-forms to all uses, English has come to rely primarily on forms of address to convey nuances of relationship. The broad rule for forms of address is that those who are intimates address each other with given names such as *George* and *Sue* (and are 'on first-name terms'), whereas those who are acquaintances use a title and family name such as *Mr Jones, Mrs/Ms/Miss Smith* (and are 'on last-name terms'). Strangers in more or less formal situations use titles only (*Sir, Madam*). This rule has, however, many refinements and exceptions. In Britain, in the public (that is, private) schools, socially prestigious clubs, the armed services, and other groups, it has been common for males to address each other by surname alone (*Good to see you, Brown!*, or, affectionately, *Brown, my dear chap, it's good to see you!*), but this practice appears to be on the wane. In casual situations, men of all classes and backgrounds may employ strong, even taboo expressions affectionately, with *you* as in *Come on, you old rascal/bugger, have another drink*.

Use of someone's given name (such as *Elizabeth*) when the person is commonly addressed by a diminutive (*Bess*) often signals formality, and, especially with a child, the possibility of a scolding. Between the unadorned given name and a title with a family name, a number of other uses are intermediate in formality but also restricted to certain groups. In the American South, the title *Miz* is spoken with a woman's first name as a respectful, but semi-familiar, form of address. The mother of US president Jimmy Carter, a Georgian, was affectionately called *Miz Lilian* by many journalists, and the matriarch of the 1980s television soap opera *Dallas*, set in Texas, is *Miz Ellie* (*Ewing*).

**Kinship usage**. Within families, kinship terms are often used: (1) Formally, *Father, Grandfather, Grandmother, Mother*. (2) Very formally, especially in the British upper classes, especially in the 19c, *Mama, Papa* (stress on second syllable) or the Latin *Mater, Pater* (with English pronunciations, 'mayter, pay-ter'). (3) Informally, with variations according to region and class, *Da/Dad/Daddy, Ma/Mam/Mom/Momma/Mum/Mammy/Mommy/ Mummy, Pa/Pop/Poppa*. *Father, mother, brother, sister* have been extended beyond the family for religious purposes and to express fellowship. Within the family, especially in AmE,

*Sister* has the short form *Sis*, *Brother* the occasional *Bro*, *bud(dy)* (extended into familiar use, mainly between men), and *brer*.

**Nicknames**. Used on an often close informal level, nicknames may be diminutives of given names that are relatively stable over years, or may be temporary monickers bestowed, changed, and dropped as the bearer moves from one group to another. Nicknames may be neutral (*Bill*, *Joanie*), admiring (*Refrigerator*, for a heavily built American football player), or stigmatizing (*Stinky*), and show a more intimate or immediate and often emotive relationship between addresser and addressee than if the bearer's ordinary name is used.

**Titles with last names**. At a markedly more formal and respectful level is the use of a title with the last name. The traditional set of such titles includes *Mr/Mr.* for men, *Mrs/Mrs.* for married women, *Miss* for girls and unmarried women, and *Master* for boys. The full form *Mister* (a variant of *Master*) is currently almost never used with the last name, but is a term of address to a stranger (*Mister, can you help me?*), usually considered a 'low' equivalent of *sir* (*Excuse me, sir, can you help me?*). Its short form in BrE is either *Mr* or more traditionally *Mr.*; in AmE, it is usually the latter. The conventions for *Mrs/Mrs.* are the same. Both *Mrs/Mrs.* and *Miss* are abbreviations of *Mistress*, a form once common (compare Shakespeare's *Mistress Quickly*, in *Henry V*), surviving into the late 20c in parts of Scotland, Northern England, and Ireland, and in the West Indies. The forms of address for married and unmarried women have been subjected to reassessment in recent years, especially by feminists, who have objected to the use of titles which announce a woman's marital status but not a man's. As an alternative, the form *Ms* (pronounced 'miz' like the Southern US form, but otherwise unrelated to it) has been adopted in recent years, first in the US, then elsewhere.

**Professional titles**. Certain professional titles may replace those just mentioned. In Britain, the academic title *Professor* (abbreviation *Prof.*) is restricted to holders of a professorial chair, while in North America generally any holder of a professorial rank (assistant, associate, or full professor) can use it. Consequently, most university-level teachers in the US and Canada are addressed and referred to as professors, while few in Britain and the Commonwealth are so addressed. In the military, titles for ranks are regularly used as forms of address: *Captain Bligh, some of the men would like to see you*. Similarly, titles for the clergy may be used in addressing them: *Father Brown, here is a mystery for you*; *Sister Bernadette, have you seen anything interesting lately?* In American law, judges are addressed as *Judge Bean* and lawyers as *Counsellor*, without surname (*Excuse me, Counsellor, but . . .*). In other branches of the US government, presidents, vice-presidents, senators, representatives (members of the House of Representatives, also called congressmen/women), governors, mayors, and assorted other office-holders are routinely addressed by their titles and surnames: *Senator/Mayor Smith, will you be running for office again?*

**Royalty and nobility**. In Britain, royal and noble titles have been in use since the Middle Ages, often involving complex conventions of address and precedence. A monarch is referred to as, for example, *King Edward* or *Queen Mary*, but is directly, formally, and traditionally addressed as *Your Majesty* (formerly also *Your Grace*); other royals are traditionally addressed as *Your Royal Highness*. At the present time, Queen Elizabeth and other royal ladies are addressed as *Ma'am*, male members of the royal household as *Sir*, without name. Members of the royal family are referred to as *His/Her Royal Highness*, often abbreviated to *H.R.H.*, especially in palace circles, without name (*H.R.H. would like . . .*). A lord is addressed either without name as *your lordship* (now restricted to use only by tradesmen or servants) or, in the case especially of a life peer in the House of Lords, as for example *Lord Bland*. The younger sons of dukes and marquesses are addressed as, for example, *Lord Henry*, distinguishing them by first name from relations with the same surname (*Lord Henry Barringby* from *Lord William Barringby*). A knight is addressed as, for example, *Sir Henry* (*Sherlock*). The wives of both lords and knights are addressed and referred to as *Lady Bland* (matching *Lord Bland*), and *Lady Sherlock* (matching *Sir Henry Sherlock*). The daughters of dukes, marquesses, and earls are addressed as *Lady Jane* (matching *Lord Henry*). When the highly formal *Your Majesty/Excellency/Holiness/Eminence*, etc., are used, the style is usually oblique: *Would Your Majesty care to honour us with a few words?*

**Bare titles**. Use of a title without any name spans the continuum of familiarity and respect, but is the only possibility between strangers. The titles normally so used are *Sir*, *Madam/Ma'am*, which tend, however, to be restricted to use in more up-market shops, restaurants, and hotels, and as salutations in business correspondence. In response, customers might use *Miss* to a (younger) woman waiting on them; there is no corresponding standard term for a male, the erstwhile use of *boy* in such circumstances in the US and parts of Africa and Asia being no longer generally acceptable. Certain occupational terms may be used without a name: *What do you recommend, Doctor? Nurse, could you get me an aspirin?; Yes, Sergeant; Father, bless me for I have sinned; It's so good of you to come, Vicar; Preacher, you had them in the aisles this Sunday.*

Informally, especially among working-class (BrE), blue-collar (AmE) groups, casual forms of address are common: (1) Male to male, *bud(dy)* in the US (especially to a stranger); *mac* in Scotland and parts of North America (to an equal, especially a stranger so perceived); *mate* in Britain, Australia, and New Zealand (to an equal, including a stranger so perceived); *pal* in North America and Scotland (to an equal, especially a stranger so perceived). (2) Female and male to female, *hen* (in Scotland, especially in Glasgow); *honey* (especially in North America, including to strangers), and its variant *hinny* in the North of England; *love* (especially in England, including to a male and a stranger, virtually regardless of social position).

Between strangers who are social equals, there are no polite forms of address in general use. Certain forms are used in limited circumstances, such as *Ladies and gentlemen*, the traditional opening of a formal speech, with less formal variants such as *Dearly beloved* (by clergymen), *Friends*, or such a formula as *My fellow citizens/Rotarians. Sir* and *Madam* (especially BrE) and *Ma'am* (especially AmE) are widely used as titles of respect, even for acquaintances, particularly those of more advanced years than the speaker, including in some traditional groups by children to any adult. In formal circumstances, in corresponding or with an audience, there are set forms for addressing royalty, titled persons, government office-holders, clergy, and others whose rank or function is deemed more important than their persons. The rules governing such forms of address are provided in guides to etiquette.

**FOUL LANGUAGE**. Indecent or obscene words and phrases, such as four-letter words, such sexual slurs as *poofter* and *whore*, especially when used directly to refer to or address someone, and swearwords referring to hell and damnation, but not usually ethnic slurs or simple abuse. *Dickhead* is foul language, but *blockhead* and *nigger* are not. Someone *foul-mouthed* regularly uses foul language. See OBSCENITY, SWEARING, USAGE.

**FOUR-LETTER WORD**. A word of four letters considered vulgar or obscene and referring to sex or excrement, such as (with varying degrees of offensive force) *arse*, *cock*, *crap*, *cunt*, *dick*, *fuck*, *piss*, *shit*, and probably *fart*. Such words are sometimes called 'Anglo-Saxon', although, of the above list, only *arse*, *cock*, and *shit* definitely derive from Old English. *Cunt*, *fart*, and *fuck* may, but firm evidence is lacking. *Dick* is a nickname for *Richard*, of uncertain age, while *crap* comes from Medieval Latin and *piss* from Old French. The phrase *four-letter* was first attested in print in 1923 and *four-letter word* in 1934. There are, in addition, some 'honorary' four-letter words, such as the five-letter but monosyllabic *prick*, *screw*. In English, there are no neutral terms for sex and excrement. Linguistic taboo makes four-letter words candidates for semantic extension and transfer: *Shit!* and *Fuck!* are interjections of disapproval or dismay. The form *fucking* often has an emphatic function in casual but 'coarse' conversation: *I got my fucking hand caught in the fucking machine!* Slurs used in referring to people's sexuality (such as four-letter *poof*, *dyke*) are often felt to be closer to ethnic slurs (such as four-letter *dago*, *kike*) than to typical 'four-letter words'. The meaning of the phrase can be wryly extended, as in 'Work is a four-letter word'. See SWEARING, TABOO.

**FOWLER, H(enry) W(atson)** [1858–1933]. English schoolmaster, lexicographer, and commentator on usage, born at Tonbridge, Kent, and educated at Rugby School and Balliol College, Oxford. He taught classics and English literature at Sedburgh School, then in north-west Yorkshire, now in Cumbria (1882–99). There followed a period in London as a freelance writer and journalist, before he moved to Guernsey to join his brother, Francis George Fowler. Their translation of the Greek writer Lucian of Samosata was published in 1905, and *The King's English* in 1906. The brothers went on to edit *The Concise Oxford Dictionary* (1911), one of the most successful of 20c dictionaries.

F.G.F. died from tuberculosis in 1918 and H.W.F. carried on alone, bringing out *The Pocket Oxford Dictionary* in 1924. H.W.F., as a member of the Society for Pure English, contributed numerous papers to its publications, including essays on *will/shall*, subjunctives, preposition at end, the split infinitive, *alright*, and nouns of multitude. His most famous work, *A DICTIONARY OF MODERN ENGLISH USAGE*, was published in 1926.

Fowler was a gifted amateur scholar. He remained essentially unaware of the linguistic controversies sweeping through the universities of Europe and the New World. He did not read the learned journals and books in which scholars like Ferdinand de Saussure, Leonard Bloomfield, Edward Sapir, and Otto Jespersen were propounding the doctrine of descriptive linguistics. His models were the classical languages of Greece and Rome, modified to suit the facts of the English language as he saw them. The responses of writers and scholars to his work have varied, journalists tending towards praise and even adulation, academic linguists towards caution and even reproof. See BARBARISM, EUPHEMISM, FIGURATIVE LANGUAGE, GENTEELISM, GOWERS, GREEK, HYBRID, INVERSION, PUN, SOCIOLOGESE, USAGE, USAGE GUIDANCE AND CRITICISM.

**FRACTURED ENGLISH**. A facetious term for inadequate and amusing English as used by non-native speakers: *Teeth extracted by latest Methodists*; *Because is big rush we will execute customers in strict rotation*. The amusement is prompted by incongruity, and may be innocent or disdainful. Raconteurs may report usages faithfully, embroider them, or invent examples of their own. The following widely quoted item appears to have been lovingly polished: *When a passenger of foot heave in sight, tootle the horn. Trumpet him melodiously at first, but if he still obstacles your passage then tootle him with vigor*. Not all such usage is treated as amusing; language professionals draw attention to it

from time to time to express their concern about the quality of English as a lingua france. See BROKEN ENGLISH.

**FRANGLAIS**. An often pejorative term for FRENCH (*français*) that contains many loans from English (*anglais*); it covers both the use of VOGUE words in the media and commerce and CODE-MIXING AND CODE-SWITCHING among bilinguals, especially in CANADA. It was popularized by the French writer René Etiemble in *Parlez-vous franglais?* (1964), in which he condemned the spread of ANGLO-SAXON culture and language since the Second World War. AmE rather than BrE was the target of Etiemble's criticism; imported US terms like *call-girl*, *coke*, *drugstore*, and *striptease* were seen as marks of Americanization. Etiemble's critique combines linguistic purism with a distaste for anything *yanqui* and hostility to Europe's becoming *un protectorat yanqui*. His views have been widely discussed, and among the solutions offered are the Gallicization of Anglicisms and the more extensive use of native resources, including those of French outside France. Orthographic adaptation could turn the patently English *meeting*, *ticket*, *rocket* into a Gallicized *métingue*, *tiquet*, *roquette*, and loan translation could turn *surfing*, *flashback*, *script-girl* into *rase-rouleaux*, *retour en arrière*, and *secrétaire de plateau*. See SPANGLISH.

**FREE VARIATION**. In LINGUISTICS, a relationship between the members of a pair of phonemes, words, etc., in which either can occur in the same position without causing a change of meaning: the initial vowels $/i/$ and $/\varepsilon/$ are in free variation in the pronunciation of *economics* ('eek-' or 'eck-') as are *up* and *down* in the phrasal verbs *slow up*, *slow down*.

■ **FRENCH** ────────────── ■

A ROMANCE LANGUAGE of Western Europe, the official language of France and an official language of Belgium (with Flemish) and Switzerland (with German, Italian, and Romansch); spoken in Luxembourg, Andorra, Aosta in Italy, and the CHANNEL ISLANDS; during the 11–13c widely spoken in the British Isles. In the Americas, French is an official language of Canada (with English), the official language of the French island department of St Pierre and

Miquelon (off Newfoundland), the French Caribbean island departments of Guadeloupe and Martinique, of French Guyana, and of Haiti, and is spoken in ST LUCIA, and TRINIDAD AND TOBAGO. It is spoken in the US in Maine and Louisiana and among immigrants from QUEBEC in Florida. In Africa, it is the official language of Benin, Burkina Faso, Burundi, Chad, Congo (Brazzaville), Congo (Kinshasa), Côte d'Ivoire, Gabon, Mali, Niger, Rwanda (with English), and Senegal, and is widely used in Algeria, Egypt, Morocco, and Tunisia. In the Indian Ocean, it is the official language of the Comoros Islands, the Malagasy Republic, and the French island of Réunion, and is spoken in MAURITIUS. In Asia, it is spoken in Lebanon, and, to a lesser extent, in Cambodia, Laos, and Vietnam. In the Pacific, it is the official language of the French island of New Caledonia and is spoken in Tahiti, VANUATU, and other islands. There are French pidgins and creoles in Africa, the Caribbean, and the Indian and Pacific oceans.

**Origins and nature**. Historically, the language is divided into Old, Middle, and Modern. Old French (OF) more or less coincides with OLD ENGLISH (OE) and early MIDDLE ENGLISH (ME). Middle French (MF) stretches from the 14c to c.1600. Geographically, French is traditionally divided into two areas: Northern French or the *Langue d'Oïl*, and Southern French or the *Langue d'Oc* (also *Occitan*). *Oïl* (from LATIN *ille* that) and *oc* (from Latin *hoc* this) are the words for *yes* in OF and Occitan. The northern tongue was influenced by Frankish, the Germanic language of the Franks, who gave their name to both France and French. The southern tongue is related to Catalan. Occitan (including Provençal) was a major medieval language, but declined after the annexation of the South by Paris and survives as a range of dialects. In medieval Europe, the northern language enjoyed great prestige, while in the 17–19c Modern French was a language of international standing, especially in diplomacy and culture. In 1637, the Académie française was founded with a view to fixing the standard language and keeping *le bon français* ('good French', based on court usage and 'the best writers') as pure as possible. See ACADEMY. The French Revolution in the late 18c promoted French as the language of national unity, the speaking of Basque, Breton, Alsatian, Flemish, and Corsican, etc., being considered unpatriotic. The Jacobin ideal of one standard national language was pursued by the founders of the modern educational system in the 19c, extended to French colonies around the world, and has continued into the 20c.

**Protective laws, activities, and groups**.

**1539** In the Ordinance of Villers-Cotterêts, King Francis I ordered the replacement of Latin by French as the language of law.

**1637** The Académie française was founded: see ACADEMY.

**1789** The Revolution linked the language to national unity and patriotism.

**1794** The Abbé Grégoire presented a report to the National Convention on the need and means to extirpate the patois and make standard French universal.

**1937** The *Office de la langue française* was formed by such linguists as A. Dauzat and F. Brunot. It disappeared after the German invasion, but was partially restored in 1957 as the *Office du vocabulaire français*, especially under pressure from Canadian francophones.

**1953** The *Défense de la langue française* was formed under the auspices of the Académie française.

**1964** René Etiemble published *Parlez-vous franglais?* (Paris: Gallimard): see FRANGLAIS.

**1966** The *Haut Comité pour la défense et l'expansion de la langue française* was formed, directly responsible to the Prime Minister of the Republic.

**1967** The *Association pour le bon usage du français dans l'administration* was formed, to regulate government language.

**1975** The Bas-Lauriol law was passed on the use of French only in advertising and commerce.

**1982** A government circular extended constraints to foreign exporters of goods destined for France.

**1977** *Loi 101/Bill 101* was passed in Quebec, Canada, making French the sole official language of the province, limiting access to English-medium schools, and banning public signs in other languages.

**1983** In France, a decree was passed requiring the use in teaching and research of terms made official by specialist committees.

**1984** The French *Haut Comité* was replaced by the *Commissariat général de la langue française*, to assist private groups and members of the public in the pursuit of violations of the Bas-Lauriol law.

**1994** In France, the Loi Toubon (named for Jacques Toubon, Minister of Culture and Francophonie in the Balladur government) stipulates: (1) that all documents relating to goods and services (including contracts and media commercials) should be in French (or, in special cases, accompanied by explanations in French); (2) that the medium of education and of all documents of an educational nature is French.

**Links with English**. The *Chanson de Roland*, an epic poem about the Emperor Charlemagne's army in Spain in the 8c, was the first major literary link between Britain and France. The poem was sung by the Normans at the Battle of Hastings (1066) and the oldest surviving copy was discovered in Oxford in 1834. The first grammar of French was written in England, John Palsgrave's *Lesclarcissement de la Langue Françoyse* (1530). Borrowing in both directions has been continuous from the earliest times: French *bateau* from OE *bat*, Modern English *navy* from OF *navie*. The two languages came into close association in the mid-11c, especially through the Norman Conquest, after which NORMAN FRENCH was the socially and politically dominant language of England and a considerable influence in Wales, Scotland, and Ireland. By the time French died out as a British language, it had greatly altered and enriched English, and the fashion of BORROWING from it continues to this day. Numerous conflicts, from the 14c Hundred Years War to the 18–19c colonial and revolutionary wars, did not prevent a mutual social and intellectual interest, accounting for Gallomania in Britain and Anglomania in France.

Because of its geographical position and cultural prestige, France has exported many words to its neighbours; of these, English has absorbed the highest proportion. As a result, hundreds of words have the same spellings in both languages, which also share a battery of Latin affixes. Before the Renaissance, prolonged contact with French had prepared English for an increased Latinization, just as French was itself re-Latinized. There is therefore a common NEO-LATIN technical vocabulary: French *homicide* (12c) antedates English *homicide* (14c), but English *suicide* is recorded earlier (1651) than French *suicide* (1739), and *insecticide* is recorded as almost simultaneous in both (French 1859, English 1866). However, the Latinization has gone further in English than re-Latinization in French: *pedestrian* and *tepid* are closer to Latin than *piéton* and *tiède*, and such words as *abduct*, *connubial*, *equanimity*, *fulcrum*, *impervious*, *odium*, and *victor* do not occur in French. On the other hand, many words borrowed into French from other Romance languages (especially ITALIAN) have entered English in a more or less French form: *artisan*, *caprice*, *frigate*, *orange*, *picturesque*, *stance*, *tirade*.

**French in English**. Medieval loans from French have given English much of the look of a Romance language. The movement of French words into English was eased by cognates already present in OE. Thus, OE *munt*, *nefa*, *prud*, *rice*, *warian* paved the way for *mount*, *nephew*, *proud*, *rich*, *beware* from OF.

**A hybrid vocabulary**. The ancient closeness of the two languages has had peculiar effects: a young English *hare* is a French *leveret*, a young English *swan* a French *cygnet*, and a small English *axe* is a French *hatchet*. An OE stem can be use with a French suffix (*eatable*, *hindrance*) or vice versa (*faithful*, *gentleness*). The English *stool*, originally a chair (OE *stol*), gave way to the Norman French *chair*, and was demoted in size and usage. The animals tended by the Saxon peasantry retained English names like *calf* and *sheep*, while their meat when eaten in the Norman castles became French *veal* and *mutton*. Because of the long presence of the language in England, many French fossils survive in the strata of English: for example, an *s* lost by French is preserved in *bastard*, *beast*, *cost*, *custom*, *escape*, *establish*, *(e)state*, *false*, *honest*, *hostage*, *interest*, *master*, *paste*, *priest*, *scout*, *tempest*. In addition, because of the French connection, English is sometimes a twofold language in which people can *answer* or *respond* and *begin* or *commence* to seek *freedom* or *liberty*. Such pairs are near-synonyms, sometimes expressing stylistic differences like *kingdom/realm*, *sight/vision*, and *snake/ serpent*. Others still are further apart in meaning, such as *ask/demand*, *bit/morsel*, *heel/talon*, and *illegible/unreadable*: see BISOCI-ATION, FAUX AMI.

**Calques and doublets**. French LOAN TRANSLATIONS often lie beneath English expressions, as in *flea-market/marché aux puces*, *ivory tower/tour d'ivoire*, and *third world/tiers monde*. Romance word structure is still noticeable in *centre of gravity, chief of state*, and *point of view*. The word order is French in such forms as *Governor-General, poet laureate*, and *treasure trove*. Some idiomatic calques go back to OF (*to bear ill will* to *porter male volonté*) while others are from Modern French, such as *in the last analysis* (*en dernière analyse*) and *it goes without saying* (*ça va sans dire*). English contains many DOUBLETS of French provenance: *constraint/constriction, custom/costume, frail/fragile, loyal/legal, marvel/miracle, poison/potion, sever/separate, straight/strict*. In some cases, one of the elements does not exist in French (here the second of each pair): *allow/allocate, count/compute, croissant/crescent, esteem/estimate, poor/pauper, royal/regal, sure/secure*. In other cases, the same word may have been borrowed more than once, with different meanings and forms: *catch/chase, chieftain/captain, corpse/corps, forge/fabricate, hostel/hospital/hotel, pocket/poke/pouch, ticket/etiquette, vanguard/avant-garde*.

**English in French**. Borrowing from English into French has been widespread for two centuries. However, when such borrowing takes place, special usages can develop. Thus, the role of a word may become specialized, a French *meeting* being political rather than general and an English *reunion* being for people who have not met for a long time (not general, like French *réunion*). Expressions may even swap roles, such as *savoir-faire* in English and *know-how* in French.

**Loanwords**. Waves of English words have been borrowed since the 18c, especially in: politics (*congrès, majorité, meeting, politicien, sinécure, vote*), horse-racing (*derby, outsider, steeplechase, sweepstake, turf*), sport (*baseball, basketball, football, goal, tennis*), railways (*bogie, condenseur, terminus, trolley, viaduc, wagon*), aviation (*cockpit, crash, jet, steward*), medicine (*catgut, pace-maker, scanner*), and social life (*bestseller, gangster, hot dog, leader, sandwich, strip-tease, western*). On occasion, English words can be Gallicized by adapting their forms and changing PRONUNCIATION and ORTHOGRAPHY: *boulingrin* bowling green, *contredanse* country dance, *paquebot* packet boat, and *redingote* riding-coat. Borrowing of additional senses for existing French words also occurs: *environnement* (in the ecological sense), 'conviction *viscérale*',

'*retourner* une lettre', '*delivrer* une carte d'identité', '*engagement* naval'. *Réaliser* and *ignorer* are now often used with their English meanings. Canadian French is especially open to such influences: 'la ligne est *engagée*'. Pseudo-Anglicisms have also arisen: *recordman* recordholder, *shake-hand* handshake, *tennisman* tennis player, and such forms in -ing as *footing* (recently replaced by *jogging*), and *lifting* (face-lift). French *dancing, parking, smoking* are reduced forms of *dancing hall, parking place, smoking jacket*, like *cargo, steeple, surf* (from cargo vessel, steeplechase, and surf-riding).

**Loan translations**. CALQUES conceal the English origin of certain French words: *cessez-le-feu* ceasefire, *franc-maçon* freemason, *gratte-ciel* skyscraper, *lavage de cerveau* brainwashing, *libre-service* self-service, *lune de miel* honeymoon, *prêt-à-porter* ready-to-wear, and *soucoupe volante* flying saucer. However, native coinages expressing resistance to Anglicisms include *baladeur* Walkman, *cadreur* cameraman, *logiciel* software, *ordinateur* computer, and *rentrée* comeback. French *lift* was replaced by *ascenseur*, but only after the production of *liftier* liftman. The spread of the -ing suffix, however, has prevented *doping, kidnapping*, and *parking* from replacement by *dopage, kidnappage*, and *parcage*, and only in Quebec has *weekend* been overshadowed by *fin de semaine*. Loan translations also involve whole idiomatic expressions (such as *donner le feu vert* give the green light), especially in Canadian French (such as *manquer le bateau* miss the boat). As such, they can affect syntax (infuriating purists), as when adjectives are placed before rather than after nouns (such as l'*actuel gouvernement, les éventuels problèmes, les possibles objections*), and the passive voice is used with an unexpected verb (such as *Il est supposé savoir*, 'He is supposed to know', rather than *Il est censé savoir*).

**The Anglo-Latinization of French**. Few speakers of French are aware that *faisabilité* and *indésirable* come from *feasibility* and *undesirable* because these words are felt to be the normal derivatives of *faisable* and *désirable*. *Deforestation* and *reforestation* look so French that few complain about their use instead of *deboisement* and *reboisement*. *Sentimental* was first used in French by the translator of Sterne's *A Sentimental Journey through France and Italy* (1768). It sounded as French as *international*, coined in 1780 by Jeremy

Bentham. 'Societé *permissive*' is easily associated by French-speakers with *permission*. Words coined in English from Latin in the 19c were absorbed into French (*exhaustif, sélectif, sélection, viaduc*) and the process continues. Thus, *crédible*, in competition with *croyable* as a recent LOANWORD (1965), easily crept in because of its closeness to *crédibilité*. Until *c*.1950, French *forum* referred only to Rome, but now has the English meaning 'meeting-place for discussion, especially on television'. In such ways, French, the Trojan horse through which Latin entered the citadel of English, is being Latinized in its turn through English.

See ANGLOPHONE, BEACH LA MAR, CAJUN, CANADIAN ENGLISH, CREOLE, DIALECT, DOUBLET, HISTORY OF ENGLISH, LAW FRENCH, NEW ORLEANS, PATOIS, PIDGIN.

**FREQUENCY COUNT**. An attempt to discover the number of occurrences of particular units in particular contexts of language use, principally WORDS in TEXTS. Such counts have usually been undertaken to provide a statistical basis for word lists used in the teaching of subjects like SHORTHAND and English as a foreign language (EFL). During the 20c there have been several large-scale frequency counts for English, particularly in the US under the inspiration of the psychologist Edward L. Thorndike, as in *The Teacher's Word Book* (1921). This was a list of 10,000 words that American children could expect to meet in their general reading. His list was derived from 41 different textual sources which provided 4m running words: 3m from the Bible and the English classics, 0.5m from letters, 0.3m from elementary school readers, 90,000 from newspapers, and 50,000 from general reading. The list was widely acclaimed as a breakthrough in the study and control of vocabulary and inspired many imitators and developers. It was considered a valuable objective measure of the appropriateness of vocabulary in schoolbooks and a basis for the construction of achievement tests in reading, spelling, and vocabulary. Although not so intended, it was also used as a basis for EFL word lists. One such list influenced by Thorndike was Michael WEST's *General Service List of English Words* (1953), which helped a generation of EFL lexicographers to develop the notion of a basic 'defining vocabulary'. The classic counts of the first half of the 20c were done with little or no me-

chanical assistance. More recently, the use of computers has made the gathering, analysis, and processing of data less laborious and time-consuming and has enlarged the body of texts (the CORPUS) which can be sampled in this way. Thus, the *Brown/Lancaster/Oslo/Bergen* corpus (started in 1967) has been used to confirm hunches about the predominance of certain features of WRITING, GRAMMAR, and SEMANTICS in particular varieties of English, and the Birmingham *COBUILD* corpus (started in 1980) has provided lexicographers with new information about COLLOCATION, grammar, and MEANING on which to base their decisions on how to structure DICTIONARY entries. See FREQUENCY OF OCCURRENCE, VOCABULARY CONTROL.

**FREQUENCY OF OCCURRENCE**. The number of times or the regularity with which something happens. Linguists and language teachers often take account of the frequency of occurrence of linguistic items and features. Geographic, socioeconomic, and ethnic varieties of a language generally differ in the frequency with which choices are made rather than in the presence or absence of an item or feature: for example, the use of negative *too* in spoken WELSH ENGLISH, as in *She won't do it, too* (as opposed to *either*). The same applies to stylistic variation in spoken and written language (ELLIPSIS and CONTRACTION are, for example, more frequent in SPEECH), such REGISTERS as legal language (which makes frequent use of compounds such as *hereinafter* and *thereof*), and religious language (with its use of *thou*-pronouns and corresponding verb forms), and in contrasts along the continuum from the most formal to the most casual (the choice of *furthermore* and *moreover* as opposed to *also* and *too*).

Language change commonly arises from the dominance of one variable over others and can often be observed through *FREQUENCY COUNTS*. The characteristics of a genre, author, or work may be identified through the relative frequency of items of VOCABULARY or of GRAMMAR features; this has been used to identify the disputed authorship of works and disputed passages in statements to the police. Information about frequency is commonly taken into account in selecting entries for dictionaries and ordering definitions within entries, as well as in grading material for learners of a language. Sociolinguists usually draw their evidence for relative frequencies from analyses of observed or elicited speech, sometimes incorporating the results in statements of probability. Some linguists have collected large corpora of written or spoken samples of a language, their frequency lists and studies of data made easier by computational processing. Recent experiments have obtained evidence of the perception of relative frequencies by eliciting judgements from native speakers: for example, of the relative frequencies of the subjunctive (*We urge that he give his reasons*), the *should*-construction (*We urge that he should give his reasons*), and the indicative (*We urge that he gives his reasons*). See CORPUS, VOCABULARY CONTROL.

**FREUDIAN SLIP**. A term known technically in psychoanalysis as *parapraxis*, an unintentional mistake, usually in speech, that is held to reveal an unconscious (especially sexual) inclination or motivation: She *What would you like: bread and butter or cake?* He *Bed and butter*. In general use, the term often refers to any unintentional verbal slip. Compare SLIP OF THE TONGUE.

**FRICATIVE**. In PHONETICS, a vocal sound made by bringing active and passive articulators close together, so that noise is generated as the airstream passes through the gap. The /f/ in *fee* is made by bringing the active lower lip close to the passive upper front teeth, and is a labiodental fricative CONSONANT. The /f/ and /v/ in *five* are the same kind of fricative; the first voiceless, the second voiced. Compare AFFRICATE. See SPEECH.

**FRIES, Charles C(arpenter)** [1887–1967]. American grammarian and lexicographer, born in Reading, Pennsylvania, and educated at Bucknell U., where he was appointed to the faculty in 1911 to teach RHETORIC and GREEK. In 1914, he shifted from classics to English, and he gained his Ph.D. in 1922 with a study of *shall* and *will* in Renaissance English. He joined the English department at the U. of Michigan in 1921 and worked there until his retirement in 1958. He became editor-in-chief in 1928 of the *Early Modern English Dictionary*, and was an adviser to the Random House *American College Dictionary* (1948). Fries sought to describe English as it was rather than as it

ought to be. In *American English Grammar* (1940), he investigated social-class differences through the study of letters written to a government agency. In defining the scope of this enquiry, he declared 'that there can be no "correctness" apart from USAGE'. A second descriptive work, *The Structure of English* (1925), drew on recorded telephone conversations; his innovative approach in that volume emphasized 'signals of structural meaning' that could be isolated and described from the stream of SPEECH rather than from the 'ideas' expressed. A conviction that English should be described and learned through speech rather than WRITING shaped *Teaching and Learning English as a Second Language* (1945) and *Foundations of English Teaching* (1961). The methods he developed at the *English Language Institute*, which he founded at Michigan in 1941, influenced ESL teaching around the world and his conception of *pattern practice* shaped ESL teaching for a generation. He was senior author of the *Fries American English Series* (1952–6), among other ESL textbooks. After retirement, he turned his attention to reading instruction for native speakers and published *Linguistics and Reading* (1963) and *A Basic Reading Series Developed upon Linguistic Principles* (1963–5). See APPLIED LINGUISTICS, BASIC ENGLISH, LITERACY.

**FRISIAN**. A GERMANIC LANGUAGE spoken in coastal regions and islands in the north of the Netherlands and in neighbouring western Germany to the Danish border; the most closely related of the Continental languages to English. Some scholars have supposed the existence of an *ANGLO-FRISIAN* language during the migratory period before the ANGLO-SAXON tribes reached Britain in the 5c. The languages share common phonological features, such as: the initial consonant in English *cheese*, *church*, *chaff*, Frisian *tsiis*, *tsjerke*, *tsjef* (compare DUTCH *kaas*, *kerk*, *kaf*, GERMAN *Käse*, *Kirche*, *Kaff*); a front vowel in English *sleep*, *sheep*, Frisian *sliepe*, *skiep* (compare Dutch *slapen*, *schaap*, German *schlafen*, *Schaf*); the loss of *n* in words such as English *goose*, *us*, Frisian *goes*, *ús* (compare Dutch *gans*, *ons*, German *Gans*, *uns*). The main variety is *Modern West Frisian*, spoken by some 400,000 people in and around the Netherlands province of Friesland. Since the 19c, Frisian has revived as a literary language. A movement seeking independence from the influence of the province of Holland has enhanced the legal status of Frisian and promoted its use alongside Dutch, especially in schools, where it was illegal until 1937. The *Frisian Academy* (founded in 1938) sponsors scholarly publications on Frisian history and culture, including a definitive historical dictionary.

**FUNCTIONAL LITERACY**. A term initially defined for UNESCO by William S. Gray (*The Teaching of Reading and Writing*, 1956, p. 21) as the training of adults to 'meet independently the reading and writing demands placed on them'. Currently, the phrase describes those approaches to LITER-ACY which stress the acquisition of appropriate verbal, cognitive, and computational skills to accomplish practical ends in culturally specific settings. Although also labelled *survival literacy* and *reductionist literacy* because of its emphasis on minimal levels of competency and the preparation of workers for jobs, functional literacy is defended by proponents as a way to help people negotiate successfully in their societies. The notion of literacy as a utilitarian tool arose in 1942 when the US Army had to defer 433,000 draftees because they could not understand 'the kinds of written instruction . . . needed for carrying out basic military functions or tasks'. In 1947, the US Bureau of the Census began defining literacy quantitatively, describing anyone with less than five years' schooling as *functionally illiterate*. With the passing of the Adult Education Act of 1966, 12 years of education became the literacy standard in the US, while in Britain, the right-to-read movements of the 1970s characterized functional literacy as the ability to: (1) read well enough to per-

form job activities successfully, and (2) understand printed messages. Over the decades, as societies have developed both technical innovations and new language formats and tasks, the definition of functional literacy has been modified to meet the changed demands. See ILLITERACY.

**FUSIONAL**. In LINGUISTICS, a term denoting a language in which the grammatical units within a word (its MORPHEMES) tend to be fused together, as in Latin *feminarum* of women, in which the ending *-arum* fuses the notions *possession*, *plural*, *feminine*. Many languages have some fusion: English *geese* ('goose' and *plural* together), *sat* ('sit' and *past* together), but in a language such as Latin this process predominates. See LINGUISTIC TYPOLOGY.

**FUTURE**. A TENSE contrasting with the present and the past. Traditionally, the *simple future* tense is *will* or *shall* followed by the infinitive: *will follow*. The *future continuous* or *future progressive* adds *be* followed by *-ing* participle: *will be following*. The *future perfect* adds *have* followed by the *-ed* participle: *will have followed*. The *future perfect continuous* combines the latter two: *will have been following*. Future time is also expressed by: *be going to* as in *Naomi is going to help Eliot*; the present progressive as in *I am playing next week*; the simple present as in *We leave for Paris tomorrow*; the use of *be to* as in *She is to be the next president of the company*; the use of *be about to* as in *It is about to rain*; the modal VERB *can* as in *I can see you on Tuesday morning*; the phrase *be sure to* as in *They are sure to help us*; such verbs as *intend* and *plan* as in *I intend to vote for you*.

# G

## G, g

[Called 'gee']. The 7th LETTER of the Roman ALPHABET as used for English. It primarily represents the voiced velar stop and was invented by the early Romans by adding a cross-bar to *C*, which represented the voiceless velar stop. In pre-Conquest England, a small *g* with a different shape from the Continental letter was used. This Insular *g* developed into ȝ, known as *yogh*. After the Norman Conquest (1066), both forms were used in English, *g* as it is today, ȝ either for the sound *y*, /j/, or for both a voiced and voiceless velar fricative. By the close of the Middle Ages, *yogh* was replaced by the digraph *gh*, as in *night* and *tough*: see GH (below).

**Hard and soft G**. In English, both *g* and *c* have inherited palatalized ('soft') values from the ROMANCE LANGUAGES, as in *cease*, *gem*, as opposed to the velar ('hard') values in *case*, *gun*. However, while the varied uses of *c* in English mostly derive from the Romance languages, many variations in the use of *g* are peculiar to English. It has three values: (1) The hard voiced velar stop: *got*, *gut*, *glut*, *grit*, *Gwen*, *argue*, *tug*. (2) The soft voiced palato-alveolar affricate /dʒ/, usually before *e*, *i*, *y* (*gem*, *gist*, *gymnast*, *rage*, *bilge*, *urge*). Especially in words of Germanic origin hard *g* can however also precede *e*, *i*, *y* (*begin*, *get*, *gig*), and very occasionally soft *g* precedes *a* or *o* (*gaol*, *margarine*, *mortgagor*). Rhyming words beginning with the sound of soft *g* are then commonly spelt unambiguously with *j* (*get/jet*, *gig/jig*), but *gill* remains ambiguous, having soft *g* when meaning 'liquid measure' and hard *g* for 'breathing organ of a fish' and NORTHERN ENGLISH 'stream'. (3) Some loans from FRENCH have kept the voiced palato-alveolar fricative value /ʒ/, as in *bourgeois*; this may be heard in *beige*, *genre*, *prestige*, *régime*, *rouge* and in some words ending in *-age* (*barrage*, *camouflage*, *fuselage*, *mirage*), including the AmE pronunciation of *garage*, with second-syllable stress.

**Hard/soft variation**. (1) One value of *g* may be replaced by another in derivatives, soft becoming hard in *allege/allegation*, purge/purgative, and hard becoming soft in *litigate/litigious* (but note *renege/renegade*, in which the *g* is always hard). The hard initial *g* of traditional BrE *gynaecology*, AmE *gynecology* is pronounced soft medially in *androgynous* and *misogyny*. (2) The hard–soft alternatives for *g* lead to uncertainty in its pronunciation in a number of words of classical origin: *hegemony* ('hedge-' or 'hegg-'?), *analogous* (hard as in *analogue* or soft as in *analogy*?), *pedagogical*, *longevity*, *longitude*.

**Double G**. (1) Normally hard as in *dagger* but exceptionally soft in *exaggerate* and BrE *suggest*. (2) Like many other consonants in monosyllabic words, *g* is doubled after an initial vowel (*egg*) but not after an initial consonant (*bag*, *leg*, *dig*, *fog*, *hug*), unless a suffix beginning with a vowel is added (*baggy*, *legged*, *digger*, *foggiest*, *hugging*). (3) Medial *g* in disyllables is commonly double after a short vowel: *haggis*, *trigger*, *nugget*. (4) The Latin prefixes *ad-* and *sub-* typically assimilate with roots beginning with *g*, causing *g* to double (*aggression*, *suggest*).

**DG**. The digraph *dg* is commonly a reinforced soft *g* (contrast *bad/bag/badge*, *bud/bug/budge*), but in unstressed final syllables the spelling of soft *g* has been uncertain: both *selvage/selvedge* are written today, and historically *colledge/knowledge*, *cabbach/spinach* could be spelt alike. The vowel preceding *g* in unstressed final syllables can vary as in *village*, *college*, *vestige*.

**GH**. The digraph *gh* causes difficulty. It is commonly a relic of a velar or palatal fricative that is preserved as a velar fricative /x/, as in SCOTS, in *bricht nicht* (bright night). (1) It is normally silent after *u* as in *taught*, *drought*, *naughty*, *thought*, *though*, *through*, *thorough*, *bough*, *drought*, and after *i* as in *straight*, *weight*, *height*, *high*, *light*, *night*. (2) It is pronounced /f/ in a few words such as *cough*, *enough*, *laugh*, *rough*, *tough*. (3) In the following place-names in England, each *gh* is different: *Slough* (rhymes with *how*), *Keighley* ('Keethley'), *Loughborough* ('Luff-'). (4) In *hiccough*, the *gh* was substituted for *p* (*hiccup*) in the mistaken belief that the word derived from *cough*. (5) It has disappeared in AmE *draft*, *plow* (formerly also used in

BrE) and in *dry, fly, sly,* although preserved in the related nouns *drought, flight, sleight.* (6) It sometimes alternates with *ch* in related words: *straight/stretch, taught/teach.* (7) Occasionally, *gh* has been inserted by analogy with rhyming words even where no fricative had previously been pronounced: in *delight* (from Old French *delit*), by analogy with *light*, and in *haughty* from French *haut*, perhaps by analogy with *high* and *naughty*. (8) In loans from Italian, hard *g* is indicated by *gh* before *e* and *i: ghetto, spaghetti, Malpighian*; the form *dinghy* is similarly distinguished from *dingy*, with its soft *g*. (9) William Caxton's Dutch printers may have introduced DUTCH *gh* in *ghastly* and *ghost*. (10) The *gh* in *ghoul* and *yoghurt* transliterates special ARABIC and Turkish consonants respectively.

**GU**. (1) The French and SPANISH practice of using *gu* to indicate hard *g* before *e* and *i* (*guerrilla, morgue, disguise, guy*) spread to some words of Germanic origin (*guess, guest, guilt*). The *u* in *fatigue*, however, no longer occurs in *indefatigable*. (2) BrE follows French in spelling Greek-derived final *-ogue* (*analogue, catalogue*), while AmE often removes the *-ue* (*analog, catalog*). (3) The *gu* in *guarantee, guard* was originally pronounced /gw/ in French, but as the *u* fell silent, it was dropped from the French spellings *garantie, garde* although preserved in English. The cognates *warranty, ward* derived from a different French dialect, and have kept the *w* in both SOUND and SPELLING. (4) The ambiguous sound value of *gu* is seen in its different pronunciations in *guide, languid* (contrast *languor*, often pronounced with a /w/), *ambiguity*, and especially word-finally, as in *ague* versus *plague*. (5) The form *tongue* is an isolated anomaly.

**NG**. (1) Commonly a velar nasal, as in *thing*. It occurs almost only after short vowels: *sang, length, sing, song, sung*. In such disyllabic base words as *anger, finger*, hard *g* is normally heard after the nasal ('angger', 'fingger'). *Finger/singer* do not rhyme in most accents, but may do in the accents of parts of Midland and Northern England (both like *finger*) and in Scots (both like *singer*). (2) The possibility of soft *g* in the digraph *ng* may give quite different pronunciations to parallel spellings: contrast *hanged/changed, singer/ginger*.

**Silent G**. In addition to silent *gh*, the letter *g* is silent: (1) Initially before *n* (*gnarl, gnash,*

*gnat, gnaw*) and in (usually GERMAN or GREEK) loans: *gneiss, gnome, gnostic*. (2) After a vowel before final *m*, in Greek forms (*diaphragm, paradigm, phlegm*), although the *g* is pronounced in derivatives (*paradigmatic, phlegmatic*). (3) Before final *n* in such Latinate forms as *assign, benign, design, malign, impugn*. This *g* effectively indicates a preceding long vowel (contrast *sign/sin*) and is sounded in some derivatives: *malignant, signal*. In such cases as *align, campaign*, the *g* has come from French, and is present in *deign*, though absent in cognate *disdain*. In *foreign, sovereign*, it has no etymological basis. In some French loans, *gn* is pronounced as *n* with a following *y: Armagnac* ('Armanyac'), *cognac, poignant, soigné*.

**Other features**. (1) There is variation between soft *g* and *j* in such names as *Geoffrey/Jeffrey, Gillian/Jillian, Sergeant/Sarjent. Jelly*, although cognate with *gelatine*, has become fixed with *j. Jest* and *jester* are etymologically related to *gesture* and *gesticulate*. The *jib* or projecting arm of a crane probably derives from *gibbet*, and *gibe* and *gybe* are often written *jibe*. The BrE alternatives *gaol/jail* exist for historical reasons: *gaol* from Norman French, *jail* from Central French. (2) Some words ending in *dge* in standard English (such as *bridge, ridge*) have Scots and Northern English variants in hard *g* (*brig, rig*). See HARD AND SOFT.

# ■ GAELIC ■

**1**. Of the Celts of Scotland, Ireland, and the Isle of Man, their languages, customs, etc.: *Gaelic coffee, a Gaelic phrase book*. **2**. The English name for the Celtic language of Ireland (*Gaeilge*), Scotland (*Gaidhlig*), and the Isle of Man (*Gaelg, Gailck*); commonly pronounced 'Gay-lik' in Ireland, 'Gallik' in Scotland, where it is often referred to, especially by its speakers, as *the Gaelic* (*Does she have the Gaelic? Does she speak Gaelic?*). In Ireland it is generally known as IRISH, and formerly in Scotland was referred to as both *Erse* and *Irish*. Gaelic was the principal language of Ireland before and after Norse settlement in the late 8c and remained so until the 18c, after which it went into decline under pressure from English. It was taken to Scotland in the 3–5c and was the foremost language of the kingdom during the early Middle Ages. It dominated the Highlands and Western Isles until the late 18c, after which it also went into decline under pressure from

English. It is the national language of the Irish Republic (co-official with English), spoken by some 100,000 and read by some 300,000 people; in Scotland it has some 80,000 speakers, mainly in the Hebrides and GLASGOW. It died out as a natural language on the ISLE OF MAN with the last native speaker, Ned Maddrell, in 1974, but revivalists sustain a version of it in an ORTHOGRAPHY distinct from the Irish and Scottish varieties. Gaelic was spoken widely in Canada and parts of the US in the 18–19c, but is now limited to a community of perhaps 5,000 in Nova Scotia, mainly on Cape Breton Island. See BORROWING, CANADIAN ENGLISH, CELTIC LANGUAGES, HIBERNO-ENGLISH, HIGHLAND ENGLISH, IRISH ENGLISH, SCOTTISH GAELIC, SHELTA.

**GAIRAIGO** [from Japanese, *gai* outside, *rai* come, *go* language]. Words or expressions of foreign, especially European, origin in the Japanese language, borrowed from the 16c onwards, such as *tabako* tobacco (from Portuguese), *kōhī* coffee (from Dutch). The reopening of JAPAN to the West during the 19c led to the absorption of an unprecedented number of foreign terms, mainly from GERMAN, FRENCH, and English. Attempts to exclude such words followed growing resistance to imported culture during the 1930s, but since 1945 thousands of terms have entered the language, mainly from English. Borrowing from different European languages can have etymologically complex outcomes: *karuta* a type of playing-card (from PORTUGUESE *carta*), *karute* a medical record (from German *Karte*), *arakaruto* à la carte (from French), and *kādo* identity, credit, greetings (etc.) card (from English *card*). Japanese use such terms freely in everyday conversation and writing, not always aware from which languages or expressions they derive. Non-Japanese may also fail to recognize LOANWORDS because of adaptations in pronunciation, meaning, and/or form.

**Writing, pronunciation, and meaning**. Foreign words are readily taken into the written language by means of the phonetic script *katakana*. As its signs represent native syllables (such as *sa* and *ke*), TRANSLITERATION almost invariably produces phonetic change. Most final consonants come to be followed by a vowel, and consonant clusters are often broken up: *erekutoronikkusu* electronics, *kurisumasu* Christmas. Sounds that

do not exist in Japanese are converted to the nearest Japanese syllables (*rajio* radio, *takushi* taxi, *chīmu* team), or are represented by special katakana combinations created to allow foreign words to be expressed in a form closer to their original pronunciation. The endings -*ar* and -*er*, and final SCHWA are usually expressed as long *a*, as in *hanbāgā* hamburger. Loanwords may undergo semantic as well as phonetic change, as with *manshon* high-class block of flats (from *mansion*), *konpanion* a female guide or hostess (from *companion*), *sumāto* slim (from *smart*).

**Abbreviation and combination**. (1) CLIPPINGS are common: *terebi* television, *apāto* apartment building, *masukomi* mass communication, *wāpuro* word processor: see ACRONYM. (2) Foreign words often combine with Japanese words: *haburashi* toothbrush (from Japanese *ha* tooth, English *brush*). (3) Words from different foreign languages can also come together: *rōrupan* bread roll (from English *roll* and Portuguese for 'bread'). (4) Two or more words from English are sometimes combined in new ways: *pureigaido* ('play guide') ticket agency, *bakkumirā* ('back mirror') rear-view mirror. Such usages are known in Japanese as *wasei eigo* ('made-in-Japan English').

**GALLICISM**. [From Latin *Gallicus* Gaulish, French, and -*ism*. Used with or without an initial capital]. A FRENCH word or phrase occurring in another language, such as *ancien régime*, *boutique*, and FAUX AMI in English. See FOREIGNISM, -ISM.

**GAMBIA**, sometimes **the Gambia**. A country in West Africa and member of the Commonwealth. Languages: English (official), Arabic (especially in Quranic schools), the English-based creole AKU, and such indigenous languages as Fula, Mandinka, and Wolof. Gambia became a British colony in 1807 and gained its independence in 1965. It occupies the banks of the Gambia River and, except for its short coast, is surrounded by Senegal, whose official language is FRENCH. In 1982, Gambia and Senegal formed the *Confederation of Senegambia*, bringing English, French, and the local languages into a relationship similar to that of CAMEROON. See WEST AFRICAN ENGLISH, WEST AFRICAN PIDGIN.

**GENDER**. A grammatical distinction, in which such PARTS OF SPEECH as nouns, adjectives, and determiners are marked as MASCULINE and FEMININE (as in French and Spanish), or masculine, feminine, and NEUTER (as in German, Latin, and Greek). In such languages, these parts of speech when being used together must agree in gender: the feminine endings in the LATIN phrases *illae feminae bonae* (nominative: those good women), masculine endings in *illi viri boni* (nominative: those good men) and neuter endings in *illa oppida bona* (nominative: those good towns). Distinctions in grammatical gender match some but not all natural gender distinctions and extend them to many items which have no natural gender: French *une pierre*, a stone (feminine). There can sometimes be considerable discrepancies between grammatical and natural gender: German *das Mädchen* (the girl) and *das Kind* (the child) are both neuter.

In English, grammatical distinctions of gender are mainly confined to the third-person singular PRONOUNS, *personal*, *reflexive*, and *possessive* (*she/her/hers/herself* versus *he/him/his/himself*). The terms *non-personal*, and *neuter* are used for *it/its/itself*. A contrast of personal and non-personal is also found with the relative pronouns *who/whom* versus *which*. *She/her* is widely used to refer to a ship or other means of transport (*She runs well before the wind*), to a country (*England will never forget those who gave up their lives for her*), and sometimes to machines (*She sounds rough; maybe the engine needs tuning*). A baby or young child (especially when the sex is not known) is sometimes referred to as *it*: 'You don't have to hit a child to abuse it' (charity advertisement). Plural *they/them* is genderless, being used for people and things. Its use with singular reference for people (*Ask anybody and they'll tell you*), a historically well-established usage which operates against the strict rules of concord, is common, especially in spoken language, but arouses controversy and is considered a solecism by purists.

Some natural-gender distinctions between pairs of nouns show a derivational relationship (*bride/bridegroom*, *hero/heroine*), but most have no morphological connection (*father/mother*, *uncle/aunt*, *mare/stallion*). Some feminine endings are criticized as pejorative and sexist, especially by feminists: *authoress*, *poetess*, *usherette*, *stewardess* appear to be more disliked than *actress*, *waitress*. In recent years, conscious attempts have been made to use the unmarked or masculine

term for both sexes: with little difficulty in such statements as *Emily Dickinson is a great poet*, more controversially in *She's a waiter/steward*. Such awkward usages are often avoided by neutral or unisex terms like *flight attendant*. Where terms exist that include *-man* (as in *chairman*), non-sexist alternatives like *chairperson*, *chair* are controversial and unstable, especially in the UK, although they are making some headway in the US. See GENDER BIAS, NOUN, SEXISM.

## ■ GENDER BIAS ■

A term in sociology and women's studies for bias associated with sexual roles in society and gender terms in LANGUAGE. It extends the grammatical term *GENDER* to cover language-related differences in the behaviour of women and men and in perceptions of that behaviour. Such perceptions are expressed through casual stereotyping, as in: 'Well, she's supposed to be back by now but she's probably stopped off somewhere to gossip. You know how women are.' There are many such generalizations: for example, that the tone of women's voices is or should be *soft* and *feminine*, while men's tones are or should be *deep* and *masculine*; that in female gatherings (*hen parties*), voices are *shrill* or *cackling*; that women's intonation is often (like that of children) *whining* or *nagging*. In contrast, many men are said to sound *gruff*, speak *roughly*, and have *hard*, even *harsh* voices, and at times *bark out* commands.

**Views of gender and language.** Women and men have been stereotyped as using language in the following ways, among others: (1) Women tend to use such words as *adorable*, *cute*, *lovely*, *sweet* in describing people and objects and such vocatives as *my dear*, *darling*, *sweetie*. (2) Men tend to be more direct, less inclined to show their feelings, and more likely 'to call a spade a spade'. Tradition also requires them to be laconic: *men of few words; the strong, silent type*. (3) Women have often engaged in an 'overflow' of adjectives and adverbs, found in an extreme form in the usage of society women between the world wars: *My dear, it's just too simply wonderful to see you!* (4) Women are often eager to talk about feelings and emotions in a way thought of as 'gushing', while many men are almost tongue-tied in such matters. (5) Women frequently use *so*, *such*, *quite*: as intensifiers (*It's been so nice to see you* *again, and such a pleasure to meet the children—I'm really quite thrilled*), or as qualifiers (*Well, he's so, you know, so helpful, and it's such a shame he can't be here—I'm well, quite upset about it*). (6) Women are considered to be more polite, using phrases such as *could you please*, and more concerned about 'correct' and 'proper' grammar and pronunciation. (7) In conversations, women are said to be by turn insecure and hedging (as shown by tags such as *do you?* or *isn't it?*, and qualifiers such as *I think*) and overbearing, talking and interrupting more than men do. (8) Women's 'delicate sensibilities', especially in the middle classes, have traditionally kept them from using obscene or blasphemous language, and restricted its use by men in their presence. (9) Women are more likely to use polite euphemisms for topics such as death and sex. (10) Men typically talk about 'important', 'worldly' topics such as politics, sports, and war, whereas women's talk is 'trivial' and usually 'gossip'.

**A masculine norm**. There appears to be some basis in fact for some of these assumptions, but sorting out fact from unsupported STEREOTYPE is complex and much work remains to be done in this area. Overall, such stereotypes associated with women's speech tend to be viewed negatively even by many women. This generally negative judgement of women's styles of speech appears to be linked to lower social status in relation to men, but it is a circular question whether lower status leads to negative opinions or certain speech characteristics lead to lower status. For example, although behaviour such as a high rate of tag questions such as *isn't it?* may be more typical of women than men, it is also common among lower-status men speaking to higher-status men. Indeed, much language that is currently characterized as female may be more general, and may represent the language that any lower-status person might use in the circumstances.

One problem in assessing gender-linked speech patterns is that men's speech is typically taken as the norm against which women's speech is measured; alternatively, women's speech is ignored. For example, the filters on older traditional spectrographs, used to analyse physical properties of speech such as pitch, were based on male voice ranges; consequently, women's

average higher-pitched voices (a result of generally smaller vocal cords) could not be clearly displayed and were not studied by most researchers. Related to gender-linked speech patterns is a variety of speech sometimes used for identification and communication by some homosexual men. It is characterized in part by higher pitch, elongation of words, increased nasality, and specialized vocabulary, such as *queen* (any male homosexual, or one considered 'flamboyant' or 'effeminate') and *butch* (stereotypically or exaggeratedly masculine in appearance or behaviour), and the use of female pronouns to refer to men.

**Social factors**. Recent studies suggest that in many situations, women seem to be more concerned than men about using educated language as a means of social mobility. The fact that so many teachers of especially younger children are women may also make their role as 'language correctors' more salient. This factor varies greatly with location, social class, and level of education: for example, many more British working-class men than women seem to use non-standard language as a badge of identity. Sometimes stereotyped behaviour appears to be gender-linked in terms of frequency, but other interpretations of its significance are possible: for example, tag questions such as *isn't it?* may indicate hesitancy, insecurity, or deference, but could also encourage conversation, in a non-aggressive way inviting the listener to respond. Such a strategy might be linked to women's greater use of minimal responses, such as *mmhm*, which indicate active listening, encouragement, or agreement. Both strategies can be characterized by hostile men as 'nagging' or 'pushing', if they are interpreted as inappropriate insertions in their conversation turn. Men's typically louder voices, less frequent uses of minimal responses, and greater use of obscenities can be seen as means of manipulating and dominating conversations. See FEMINISM, GENERIC PRONOUN, INCLUSIVE LANGUAGE, SEXISM.

**GENERAL AMERICAN**. [Introduced by George P. Krapp in *The English Language in America*, 1924]. Short forms *GA, GenAm*. A term sometimes employed to refer to 'a form of U.S. speech without marked dialectal or regional characteristics' (*OED Supplement*) but one 'no longer in technical use'

(*The Random House Dictionary of the English Language*, 1987). It was denounced by Hans Kurath in his review of Krapp's book, but has continued to be used in some scholarly and many popular treatments of AMERICAN ENGLISH, often subtractively to refer to whatever is left once various 'regions' have been described: usually NEW ENGLAND, NEW YORK, and SOUTHERN. Although there may have been some justification before 1945 for presuming uniformity elsewhere in the US, the term began to diminish in popularity once the complexity of AmE began to be understood. In revising MENCKEN's *The American Language*, Raven I. McDavid accounted for Mencken's use of the term by noting: 'In the last thirty years research for the L[inguistic] A[tlas] has shown that the so-called "General American" area is really made up of two major dialects' (1967). Some scholars outside the US continue to use the term, specifically to refer to a norm of PRONUNCIATION: for example, J. C. Wells, in both *Accents of English: Beyond the British Isles* (1982, p. 470) and the *Longman Pronunciation Dictionary* (1990). See NETWORK STANDARD.

**GENERAL AMERICAN ENGLISH**. A term for the STANDARD ENGLISH of the US, usually intended to include pronunciation, grammar, and vocabulary: 'The educational system in the Philippines uses General American English as the norm' (regional seminar report by Philippines linguists, 1981). Compare GENERAL AMERICAN.

**GENERAL AUSTRALIAN**. A term, especially in LINGUISTICS, for the pronunciation used by most Australians. See AUSTRALIAN ENGLISH.

**GENERAL BRITISH**. An occasional term in LINGUISTICS and LANGUAGE TEACHING for RECEIVED PRONUNCIATION as the accent that represents BrE, used especially to contrast with *GENERAL AMERICAN*: 'The British English form [in this dictionary] is that which has been called *Received Pronunciation or General British*' (*Oxford Advanced Learner's Dictionary of Current English*, 1974).

**GENERAL CANADIAN**. A term, especially in LINGUISTICS, for the usage of a majority of English-speaking Canadians (pronunciation, grammar, and vocabulary), especially from Ontario to the Pacific, traditionally considered one of four major dialects of Canada but increasingly regarded as a class-based urban dialect used for broadcasting and as an educational norm. See DIALECT IN CANADA.

**GENERAL ENGLISH**. **1.** A non-technical term for English when the language at large is contrasted with a usage, variety, dialect, or register: *That's Cockney; it isn't general English*. **2.** A semi-technical term for a course in English, usually as a mother tongue or in an English-medium school, within a framework of general education, usually teaching listening, speaking, reading, and writing. **3.** In LINGUISTICS, a range of English that includes the STANDARD but contrasts with specific accents and DIALECTS. The British phonetician John C. Wells contrasts *General English* (capitalized) and *traditional-dialect* (lower case): 'Within General English . . . there are non-standard varieties in which one says *I couldn't see no one* and *Peter done it* rather than the standard *I couldn't see anyone* and *Peter did it*' (*Accents of English*, volume 1, 1982). **4.** Also *English for General Purposes*. A term in language teaching for a broadly based, usually long-term EFL or ESL course, in contrast to *English for Specific Purposes* (Business English, English for Medical Purposes, etc.). Compare STANDARD ENGLISH.

**GENERAL INDIAN ENGLISH**. See INDIAN ENGLISH.

**GENERALIZATION**. A process of SEMANTIC CHANGE that widens the meaning of a WORD, PHRASE, or LEXEME. In Middle English, *pigeon* meant a young bird, especially a young dove, but from the late 15c has come to refer especially to the whole family Columbidae. *Dove* is now generally used for a smaller variety of pigeon. Such shifts in meaning are usually slow and tendential rather than rapid and absolute. Early usages continue indefinitely alongside later changes that have become dominant, as was true of *pigeon* and *dove* in the 16c. In the process of change, terms may acquire further meanings within a set of words: the pigeon is not a symbol of peace and no one *\*dove-holes* information. See COMPUTER USAGE, SLANG.

**GENERAL NEW ZEALAND**. A term, especially in LINGUISTICS, for the pronunciation used by most New Zealanders. See NEW ZEALAND ENGLISH.

**GENERAL SERVICE LIST**, short form *GSL*. Full title *A General Service of English Words with semantic frequencies and a supplementary word-list for the writing of popular science and technology*. A word list compiled and edited by Michael WEST for use by ELT teachers and writers, published in 1953 by Longmans, Green & Co., and based on earlier work done by West and others as a result of the Carnegie conference on vocabulary selection held in New York in 1934, whose purpose was the selection of vocabulary as a stage in the teaching of English. It incorporated material from *A Semantic Count of English Words* by Irving Lorge and Edward L. Thorndike (1938). The *GSL* greatly influenced the choice of vocabulary for EFL course materials, graded readers, and dictionaries until the mid-1970s. An entry lists a word with its part of speech, its frequency position in a count of 5m running words, and the percentages of its major sense divisions in that count: for example, *game* N., 638, fun and games 9%, with the idea of competition 38%, a particular contest 23%, games as an athletic contest 8%, and sundries. See FREQUENCY COUNT, VOCABULARY CONTROL.

**GENERATIVE**. A term borrowed in the 1960s from mathematics into LINGUISTICS by Noam CHOMSKY. If a GRAMMAR is generative, it accounts for or specifies the membership of the set of grammatical sentences in the language concerned by defining the precise rules for membership of the set. The use of the verb *generate* in this sense (*The grammar will generate the following set of sentences*) is distinct from its general sense 'produce'.

**GENERATIVE GRAMMAR**. A GRAMMAR which precisely specifies the membership of the set of all the grammatical sentences in the language in question and therefore excludes all the ungrammatical sentences. It takes the form of a set of rules that specifies the structure, interpretation, and pronunciation of sentences that native speakers of the language are considered to accept as belonging to the language; it is therefore regarded as representing native speakers' competence in or knowledge of their language. See CHOMSKY, COMPETENCE AND PERFORMANCE, GRAMMATICALITY, TRANSFORMATIONAL-GENERATIVE GRAMMAR.

**GENERIC. 1.** Belonging to or designating a genus (as opposed to a species) or a class, group, or kind. In SEMANTICS, a *generic term* includes other terms that belong in the same class: for example, *officer* includes *colonel, major, captain,* and *flower* includes *hyacinth, rose, tulip.* In law, a TRADEMARK ceases to be protected when it comes to be more widely used for, and understood as, a type rather than a brand: for example, the proprietary names *Hoover* for type of vacuum cleaner and *Xerox* for equipment that makes xerographic copies are, despite being trademarks, widely used for vacuum cleaners in general and xerographic copies of all kinds. When so used, especially as verbs, they are written without an initial capital (*to hoover; a xerox, to xerox*). When this happens, the mark is referred to as generic or *a generic.* **2.** In GRAMMAR, a word is generic if it applies to both men and women. *He* has traditionally been considered a *GENERIC PRONOUN*, but feminists, among others, object to both the classification and the usage. See SEXISM.

■ **GENERIC PRONOUN** —————— ■

Also **common-gender pronoun, epicene pronoun**. A PERSONAL PRONOUN that includes both masculine and feminine, such as *u* in Persian (which translates *he* and *she*) and *they* in English, which does not distinguish gender. English does not have a singular equivalent for *u*, but the *he*-group of pronouns has traditionally been called GENERIC, along with such words as *man* and *mankind*: 'Words importing the masculine gender shall be deemed and taken to include females' (from an Act of Parliament, London, 1850). The use of generic *he* is, however, often ambiguous, because it tends to identify masculine gender with the universally human and in the process appears to exclude or marginalize women. For these reasons, it has been challenged in recent years, especially by feminists. Generic *he* continues in use, but efforts have been made, with varying degrees of success, to circumvent it. These include: (1) The use of *he or she*, which serves in limited contexts but becomes awkward in longer texts. (2) The use of composite *s/he*, which cannot be spoken, and composite *he/she* and *she/he*, in effect compound pronouns. (3) The use of *she* alone, often to make a sociopolitical point. (4) The reversal *she and he*, for similar reasons. (5) Generic *she* in texts and contexts where women are in the majority, such as books about teaching and secretarial work. (6) The use of *he and she* and *she and he* alternately, which may become forced in longer texts. (7) General *you* and *one*, which may alter the message. In AmE, the tradition of *one . . . he* (*When one does this, he finds . . .*), as opposed to BrE *one . . . one* (*When one does this, one finds . . .*) returns the user to the problem of generic *he*. (8) Plurals rather than singulars wherever possible: *the doctor . . . he* changed to *doctors . . . they*. This appears to be a widespread strategy to avoid the problem. (9) Rephrasing sentences so as to avoid pronouns completely, especially by using the agentless passive.

**Singular *they***. The *they*-pronoun group is increasingly used in such singular constructions as: 'Anyone who wants to write non-sexist English will need to have their wits about them. They will need to be thick-skinned, too, for if they write sentences like my first one, they will hear criticism from those people who are upset by the use of the plural pronoun *them* with a singular pronoun like *anyone*' (Jenny Cheshire, 'A Question of Masculine Bias', *English Today* 1, Jan. 1985). The use of *they*-pronouns, as in *Everyone should bring their coats*, dates from the 16c, is widespread, is increasingly acceptable in informal BrE and AmE, and is increasingly common with 'dual gender' nouns such as *speaker*, *subscriber*. Singular usage increasingly includes *themself*, a form that dates from the 15c but has always been rare: 'I think somebody should immediately address themself to this problem' (A. Thomas Ellis, *The Times*, 9 Sept. 1987).

**Artificial pronouns**. In recent years, attempts to replace generic *he* have led to the invention of inclusive third person pronouns. As members of a syntactic system, pronouns are normally slow to change; the last great adaptation was the 17c replacement of the *thou*-group with singular *you*. The coining of such new pronouns has met with responses varying from sober consideration through wry amusement to open ridicule. The first such pronoun appears to have been *thon*, created by Charles Converse of Erie in 1884, who described it as a contraction of *that one* and appears not to have been aware that demonstrative *thon* (that one over there) has long been used in Scots and Northern English. In *On Writing Well*, William Zinsser may have spoken for

many when he commented: 'I very much doubt that thon wants that word in thons language or that thon would use it thonself. This is not how the language changes' (1980). Coinages (some serious, some tongue-in-cheek) include *co* (by the writer Mary Orovan), *et* (by Aline Hoffman of Sarnia, Ontario), *hey* (by Ronald Gill of Derby, England), *hesh/hirm/hizer* (by Professor Robert Longwell, U. of North Carolina), *hir* (in a 1979 supervisors' guide for the American Management Association), *per* (abbreviating *person*, by the writer Marge Pierce), and *ws/wself* (by Dr John B. Sykes, editor, *Concise Oxford Dictionary*, 7th edition). See GENDER BIAS, SEXISM.

**GENITIVE CASE**. A term in GRAMMAR marking possession and analogous relationships in the case system of LATIN and other inflected languages. In the phrase *dies irae* days of wrath, *irae* is the genitive of *ira* wrath, anger. The term has been carried over into English grammar, but is not so common as *possessive*. See DOUBLE GENITIVE, GROUP POSSESSIVE, SAXON GENITIVE.

**GENTEELISM**. A semi-technical term for both genteel behaviour in using language and a word or phrase used for genteel reasons: for example, the substitution of *tummy* for *belly*. Genteelisms are generally EUPHEMISMS used for evasive 'polite' purposes, such as *bathroom*, *lavatory*, *powder room*, *restroom*, *toilet* for a place for urinating, defecating, and washing. See -ISM, MINCED OATH.

■ **GEORDIE** ─────────── ■

**1.** A native of the North-East of ENGLAND in and around the city of Newcastle upon Tyne (Tyneside), an area often referred to informally as Geordieland. **2.** The variety of working-class speech in that area, deriving ultimately from NORTHUMBRIAN, one of the three divisions of OLD ENGLISH, and in many ways closer to SCOTS than to YORKSHIRE dialect. **3.** The term is often loosely applied to all people in the North-East of England and their speech. This can sometimes cause offence to non-Tynesiders, such as the people of Wearside and Middlesbrough.

**Pronunciation**. (1) Geordie is non-rhotic and the only urban accent of England in which initial *h* is not dropped. (2) The glottal stop occurs with /p, t, k/ in syllable-final position and sometimes initially before a weak vowel, as in *caper, city, local*. Phoneticians disagree as to whether the glottal stop precedes or follows the consonant. (3) There is a clear /l/ in all positions. (4) The uvular *r*, known as the *Durham* or *Northumberland BURR*, was once common but is now in decline, having been widely regarded and treated as a speech defect. The pronunciation of *r* is now generally dental, alveolar, or post-alveolar, but the burr has left a legacy in broad Geordie, in which certain vowels are pronounced as if still followed by the burr: *cure* as 'kyooah', *nurse* as 'noahss'. (5) Commonly, there is an /a:/ vowel in such words as *all, talk, walk, war*. Geordie *walk* sounds to non-Geordies like 'waak', and *work* like 'walk'. A joke recounts how a man went to his doctor because of a painful knee. The doctor bandaged it and asked: 'Do you think you can walk now?' The man replied: 'Work? I can hardly walk!' (6) There is an /o/ or /oə/ in such words as *don't, goat, know, told*. (7) The vowel in such words as *down, town* ranges from the /u/ of Scots *doun, toun* to its RP value. (8) The closing vowel in words like *bonny* and *happy* is /i/ ('bonnee', 'happee'). (9) There is often a low rising tone in statements, making them seem tentative or like questions to non-Geordies.

**Syntax, vocabulary, and usage**. (1) A traditional *Aa* where standard English has *I* (*Aa doan't know*), comparable to *Ah* in Scots. (2) A traditional but now sporadic use of negative *-na* rather than *not* or *-n't*, as in *Aa canna bide yon chap* I can't stand that chap, comparable to Scots and Ulster Scots -nae/-na/-ny. (3) The form *diven't* is a traditional alternative to *don't*: *I diven't do nothin'* I don't do anything. (4) Common forms of address include *bonny lad* (to a man or boy), *bonny lass* (to a woman or girl), *hinny* (honey: to a woman, girl, man, or boy): *How there, bonny lass?* How are you, dear? (5) Geordie shares many words with Scots and ScoE: *bairn* child, *bonny* fine, good-looking (used of women and men), *canny* steady and cautious (but with a local nuance of good, kind, and gentle). See DIALECT IN ENGLAND, *L*-SOUNDS, NORTHERN ENGLISH.

■ **GERMAN** ─────────────── ■

A GERMANIC LANGUAGE of Western Europe, the official language of Germany and Austria, and an official language of Switzerland (with FRENCH and ITALIAN) and Luxembourg (with French). It is also spoken by communities in Belgium, Denmark, France, Hungary, Italy, Liechtenstein, Poland, Romania, and parts of the former Soviet Union, is widely used as a second language in Turkey and in the former Yugoslavia, and is spoken in enclaves in North and South America, Africa, and Australia. With *c*.100m speakers, it ranks tenth among languages in world terms and first in Western Europe in numbers of native speakers. Because of close genetic links, German and English share many features, as seen in the sentence: *Für rund 95 (fünfundneunzig) bis 100 (hundert) Millionen Menschen ist Deutsch heute Muttersprache* (For around five and ninety to hundred million people is German today mother-speech: 'Today German is the mother tongue of about 95 to a 100 m people'). The difference in word order is great, but a close match can be made with *für/for, rund/around, fünf/five, neunzig/ninety, hundert/hundred, Mensch/man, ist/is, Mutter/mother, Sprache/speech* (with *million* as a shared Romance BORROWING). German is structurally more complex than English, having inflectional endings for number, case, gender, person, tense, etc., and in this it resembles OLD ENGLISH more closely than Modern English. In its orthography, German gives an initial capital letter to its nouns, a practice common in English until the mid-18c.

**Varieties**. Historically, German has been an amalgam of DIALECTS slow to develop a STANDARD language. The continuum ranges from the geographically 'low' German dialect of Westphalia in the north-west (mutually intelligible with DUTCH), through the dialects of Lower and Upper Saxony, the Rhineland, and Franconia, to the 'upper' German varieties spoken in Bavaria, Switzerland, and Austria. The term *Plattdeutsch* (sometimes translated as 'Low German') is used for the 'broad' dialects in the north and west. *Schwyzertüütsch* is the common spoken German in Switzerland, a dialect more than most others in diglossic contrast with the written and printed language. The linguistic distinction between *Niederdeutsch* (Lower German) and *Oberdeutsch* (Upper German) covers the same continuum. It is usually traced to the Second Sound Shift in the 8c, in which the Southern dialects became phonologically distinct from the Northern, producing such South/North contrasts as *machen/maken* (make) and *Schiff/skip* (ship). Confusingly, the geographical term *Hochdeutsch* or High German is applied to the result of this sound change, so that the term can refer both to all the Upper German (that is, geographically 'highland' and Southern) dialects and to an idealized STANDARD German language which is 'high' in the social sense.

Even then, however, the division into Lower and Upper/High German is not the whole story, as dialectologists and language historians generally recognize an intermediate variety: *Mitteldeutsch* (Central or Middle German) stretching from Cologne to Frankfurt and Leipzig. Observers can draw attention either to such Low/High contrasts as *Junge/Bub* a boy, and *Sonnabend/Samstag* Saturday, or such Low/Middle/Upper contrasts as *ik/ich/i* the pronoun *I*, and *Männeken/Männchen/Mandl* a little man. The contribution of the Central and Southern dialects to a common *Schriftsprache* (written or literary language) is often acknowledged, as is the fact that more recently a supra-regional *Umgangssprache* (colloquial semi-standard) has served to level out differences.

Tensions persist, however, between unifying and separatist tendencies. More than in English, orthographic conventions have been standardized, largely because of the influential *Duden* spelling dictionary (*Vollständiges orthographisches Wörterbuch der deutschen Sprache*, Konrad Duden, 1880; *Duden*, vol. 1, *Die Rechtschreibung*, 19th edition, Bibliographisches Institut Mannheim, 1986). Local differences in pronunciation occur at all social levels and are often deliberately asserted to establish people's backgrounds. A single, supranational norm for pronunciation does not exist in German-speaking countries any more than in English-speaking countries, although 19c *Bühnendeutsch* (stage German) and 20c media and social mobility have promoted compromises between Lower/North and Upper/South German speech forms. Distinct varieties have emerged in East and West Germany (prior to reunification in 1990), Austria, and Switzerland, especially in vocabulary, which have been partly codified in 'national' dictionaries.

Historically, (High) German is divided into Old High German from AD 750, Middle High German from 1150, Early New High German from 1350, and New High German from 1650.

**German in English**. Over the centuries, many German words have found their way into English: for example, Low German *brake*, *dote*, *tackle* and High German *blitz*, *dachshund*, *kindergarten*: see BORROWING. Cultural acquisitions have been significant in such fields as food (*frankfurter*, *hamburger*, *hock*, *pretzel*, *sauerkraut*), mineralogy (*cobalt*, *feldspar*, *gneiss*, *quartz*), music (*glockenspiel*, *leitmotiv*, *waltz*), philosophy (*weltanschauung*, *zeitgeist*), and politics (*diktat*, *realpolitik*). Two powerful sources of borrowing in AmE have been such German settlers as the Pennsylvania Dutch (that is, *Deutsch*) and YIDDISH-speaking Jewish immigrants.

**English in German**. Contacts between English and German have been on the increase since the early 18c, promoted by literary translation, diplomatic links, trade relations, language teaching, and the media. Loans have entered German from such fields as literature (*sentimental*, *Ballade*), sport (*boxen*, *Rally*), politics (*Hearing*; *Hochverrat*, from 'high treason'), and technology (*Lokomotive*, from locomotive engine; *Pipeline*). Resistance is no longer as vociferous as during the time of the *Sprachgesellschaften* (17c language societies) and the anti-foreigner propaganda of the Nazis in the 1930s. English usages are adopted and adapted as: loanwords (*babysitten* babysit), loan translations (*Beiprodukt* by-product), blends of LOANWORD and LOAN TRANSLATION (*Teamarbeit* team work), semantic transfer (*Schau* from 'show', in the sense of theatrical event), and loan creation (*Öffentlichkeitsarbeit*, 'work for the public', loosely based on 'public relations'). Most borrowing is at word level, but occasionally idioms or syntactic constructions are transferred, as in *grünes Licht geben* give the green light, *Ich fliege Lufthansa* I fly Lufthansa. The influence of English is strong in advertising (*High Life*, *Image*) and information science (*Compiler*, *Feedback*). In general, AmE has a greater influence than BrE.

See CAMEROON, DIALECT IN THE UNITED STATES, EUROPEAN UNION, GOTHIC, INDO-EUROPEAN LANGUAGES, INDO-GERMANIC, NAMIBIA, PAPUA NEW GUINEA, SPELLING REFORM, TANZANIA.

**GERMANIC LANGUAGES**. A group of related languages including ENGLISH, DUTCH, FRISIAN, GERMAN, the SCANDINAVIAN LANGUAGES (DANISH, Faroese, Icelandic,

Norwegian, Swedish), and a number of derived languages (YIDDISH from German, AFRIKAANS from Dutch) as well as the extinct Burgundian, GOTHIC, NORN, and Vandal. In spite of a scholarly tradition going back at least to Jacob Grimm in the early 19c, some basic questions regarding these languages still await convincing answers: At what point in history and in what ways did a common *Proto-Germanic* break away from Indo-European? Do the various Germanic languages form a DIALECT continuum? How can they best be classified into regional and typological groups? On these issues, linguistic speculation needs the support of more cultural and historical data. What is certain, however, is the common heritage of, and mutual contact between, the Germanic languages, as shown in the table.

| English | Dutch | German | Swedish |
|---|---|---|---|
| one | een | eins | en |
| two | twee | zwei | två |
| three | drie | drei | tre |
| come | komen | kommen | komma |
| day | dag | Tag | dag |
| earth | aarde | Erde | jord |
| hay | hooi | Heu | hö |
| live (verb) | leven | leben | leva |
| waterfall | waterval | Wasserfall | vattenfall |
| young | jong | jung | ung |

See ANGLO-SAXON, ARYAN, CAXTON, CLASSICAL COMPOUND, COMPOUND WORD, FRENCH, GRIMM'S LAW, INDO-EUROPEAN LANGUAGES, INDO-GERMANIC, NORSE, NORTHERN ENGLISH, NORTHUMBRIA, OLD ENGLISH, SCOTS.

**GERUND**. A traditional term for a VERBAL NOUN, in English a word ending in -*ing*: *visiting* in *They appreciate my visiting their parents regularly*. Like a noun, it can be introduced by the genitive *my* (compare *my visit to their parents*), but like a verb it takes the direct object *their parents* (compare *I visit their parents*). Some object to the non-genitive usage and avoid it, at least for names and pronouns, preferring *They appreciate Bill's visiting their parents* to *They appreciate Bill visiting their parents* and *They appreciate my visiting their parents* to *They appreciate me visiting their parents*.

**GESTURE**. A bodily movement, especially of the hands and arms, which conveys a meaning, such as the use of two fingers to convey 'V for victory' (in one orientation) or in British usage an insult (in a different ori-

entation). Gestures are a normal feature of COMMUNICATION, are relatively few in number, and are used to express a fairly constrained range of meanings. They should be distinguished from the more systematic and comprehensive use of hand movements in deaf SIGN LANGUAGE. See RHETORIC.

**GHANA**. A country in West Africa and member of the COMMONWEALTH. Languages: English (official), WEST AFRICAN PIDGIN ENGLISH, and indigenous languages such as Ashanti, Ewe, Fanti, and Ga. The region was under British influence from 1874, and present-day Ghana comprises the former British colonies of *the Gold Coast* and *Ashanti*, the protectorate of *the Northern Territories*, and the United Nations trusteeship of *British Togoland*. There is a cline of usage from English-based pidgin to the standard WEST AFRICAN ENGLISH of the media and such newspapers as the *Daily Graphic*, the *Ghanaian Times*, the *People's Evening News*, and *The Pioneer*. Ghanaian writers in English include C. Ama Ata Aidoo, Joseph W. Abruquah, Aye Kwei Armah, Kofi Awoonor, and J. Benibengor Blay.

Ghana has probably had more intimate and longer contact with English-speaking expatriates than any other West African country. The English established their first fort at Cormantine in 1631 and English seamen and merchants and their local wives appear to have formed a nucleus of English-speakers in Ghana more than a century before the settlements in LIBERIA and SIERRA LEONE. Ghanaians have always prided themselves on the quality of their English. Localisms include: (1) Words and phrases found in other parts of anglophone West Africa: *balance* change (as in *The balance you gave me is not correct*), *chop box* food box (as in *Put the yam in the chop box*), *themselves* each other (as in *Those two really love themselves*). (2) Distinctive local usage, such as *an airtight* a metal box, *a cover shoulder* a kind of blouse, *enskin* to enthrone (a chief), *an outdooring* a christening ceremony. (3) Uncountable nouns often used countably: *equipments*, *furnitures*. (4) Hybrids of English and local words: *kente cloth*, *donno drum*, *bodom bead*.

**GIBRALTAR**, also **the Rock of Gibraltar** or informally **the Rock**. A British colony and military base, a rugged peninsula on the south-west coast of Spain where Atlantic and Mediterranean meet as *the*

*Strait(s) of Gibraltar.* Languages: English (official), SPANISH widely spoken. The territory was ceded by Spain to Britain in 1713, and became a colony in 1830. Spain disputes right of possession, but Gibraltarians generally regard themselves as British. The local English is non-rhotic. Standard English with an RP accent is the prestigious norm, while the speech of manual workers is influenced by Spanish, including a parasitic vowel before a word-initial cluster beginning with /s/, such as 'espoon' for *spoon* and 'estreet' for *street*. Compare MALTA.

# ■ GLASGOW ────────────── ■

The largest city in Scotland and third largest in the UK. Like that of other Scottish regions, Glasgow speech is a continuum from the local accent of SCOTTISH ENGLISH to the working-class VERNACULAR. In origin a dialect of West Central SCOTS, the Glasgow vernacular has been modified by the mixing of population since the early 19c, resulting in particular in the introduction of several features from Ireland. Like other urban Scots dialects, it has suffered some erosion of traditional vocabulary. Partly as a result of this, working-class speech, known variously as *Glasgow English*, *Glasgow Scots*, *Glaswegian*, *Glesca*, *Glasgow*, *Gutter Glasgow*, has since the 19c been the archetypal stigmatized Scots speech, commonly described as 'debased', 'hopelessly corrupt', or 'the language of the gutter'. In addition to the more or less localized features below, Glaswegian shares stigmatized features of working-class Scots generally, such as glottal-stop realizations of non-initial voiceless stops, use of past participles of verbs for past tenses and conversely, and multiple NEGATION: see GUTTER SCOTS. For features shared with other Central Scots dialects, see EDINBURGH.

**Pronunciation**. The first three items are well-known SHIBBOLETHS. (1) Some speakers merge /er/ *air* with /ɛr/ *err*, as in *Merry Mary*, *ferr* fair. (2) Some speakers realize voiced *th* as /r/, as in *ra* for *the* (*ra polis* the police, *ramorra* tomorrow), *brurra* brother, *murra* mother. (3) In such words as *want*, *water*, *wash* the vowel is /a/, so that *patter* and *water* rhyme. (4) The words *away*, *two*, *who*, *whose*, *where* have an 'aw' sound: *awaw*, *twaw*, *whaw*, *whause*, *whaur*. (5) The /u/ of *blue*, *room* has a front, lowered realization, sometimes unrounded. (6) Unstressed final /ʌ/ appears

in such words as *barra* barrow, *fella* fellow, *Glesca* Glasgow, *morra* morrow, *awfa* awful, *yisfa* useful. (7) As in Edinburgh, the enclitic negative is *-nae*, *-ny*, as in *cannae* can't, *dinnae* don't, whereas other dialects have *-na*. (8) /d/ is lost after /l/ and /n/: *caul* cold, *staun* stand, *roon* round, *grun* ground, *win* wind. (9) The form *wan* one, and the adding of a /t/ to *once* and *twice* may be from Ireland. (10) Except in shibboleths like *It's a braw bricht munelicht nicht* traditional Scots forms in /x/ are rare, although the usual ScoE velar fricative prevails in such words as *clarsach*, *loch*, *pibroch*. (11) Intonation is characterized by a predominant pattern of a markedly lowered pitch on the final prominence of the tone group, followed by a low rise, and in this position the final stressed vowel may be prolonged:

> ahm thaht depehhhhndint
> hingoanti ma vowwwwulz
> hingoanti ma maaaammi
>
> (Tom Leonard, 'Tea Time', *Intimate Voices*, Newcastle: Galloping Dog Press, 1984)

**Grammar**. Well-known Glaswegianisms, some of which are spreading or have spread to Edinburgh, are: (1) *See* as a topic-defining word, as in *See me, see ma man, see kippers, we hate them.* (2) Of ULSTER origin, plural-marked forms of the second-person plural pronoun: *youse*, *yese*, *yiz* you, also *youse-yins* you ones. (3) A stressed form *Ah'm ur* I am, *Ah'm ur gaun* I am going, *Naw, Ah'm urnae* No, I am not. (4) Certain reinforcing sentence tags: *Ye're drunk, so ye ur*; *Ah'm right fed up, so Ah am/so Ah'm ur*; *Ah felt terrible, so Ah did*; *Ah didnae touch nuthin, neither Ah did.* (5) Other tags: *annat*, as in *Aw thae* (all those) *punters wi the wings an haloes annat* (and that); terminal *but*, as in *Ah dinnae waant it but.*

**Vocabulary**. (1) Localisms include: traditional *dunny* a basement, *ginger* a soft drink of any kind, *sherrickin* a public dressing down, *stank* a grating over a drain, *wallie close* the tiled entrance hall of a better-class tenement; more recent slang usages *bam*, *bampot*, *bamstick* idiot, *boggin*, *bowfin* smelly, *heidbanger/heidcase* a lunatic, *malky* a weapon. (2) Glasgow Scots is also receptive to slang expressions of wider currency like *chib* a weapon, *nooky* sexual intercourse, *stocious* drunk.

**Written dialect**. From the 1960s writings in and about Glaswegian have included, as well as caricature by stage comics and by authors of joke and cartoon collections, much poetry, drama, and prose fiction that treats the variety seriously and with concern or indignation at its status. Part of this writing, in poetry or prose, consists of representations of local speech, some of this in an ostentatiously untraditional 'phonetic' and quasi-illiterate orthography, intended to emphasize the demotic character of the speech. An exaggerated variant of this orthography has been favoured by or for the comedians Stanley Baxter and Billy Connolly. Both variants sometimes run words together to achieve an exotic or comically grotesque effect. In Scottish writing, this style, which apparently originated *c.*1960, is all but unique to Glasgow:

> Another interesting word heard in the discotheque is *jiwanni*. To a young lady a gentleman will make the request—*Jiwanni dance?* Should she find that he is overanxious to ply her with refreshments she will regard him with suspicion and inquire—*Jiwanniget mebevvid?* (Stanley Baxter, *Parliamo Glasgow*, 1982).

[*Jiwanni* Do you want to, *Jiwanniget* Do you want to get, *mebevvid* me bevvied (me drunk: from *bevvy*, a clipping of *beverage*)]

> ach sun
> jiss keepyir chin up
> dizny day gonabootlika hawf shut knife
> inaw jiss cozzy a burd.
>
> (Tom Leonard, from 'The Miracle of the Burd and the Fishes', *Poems*, 1973, Dublin: O'Brien)

[Ah, son. / Just keep your chin up. / Doesn't do going aboot like a half-shut knife. / And all just because of a bird (girl)]

See DIALECT IN SCOTLAND, MORNINGSIDE AND KELVINSIDE.

**GLIDE**. In PHONETICS, such APPROXIMANT sounds as the /w/ of *wet* and the /j/ of *yet*, which have no steady state even when pronounced in isolation. Whereas it is easy to say [s] and [m] and prolong them without a following VOWEL, [j, w] require a following vowel to glide into, such as schwa [wə, jə]. If they are artificially prolonged, they become vowels similar to the [u:] of *move* and the [i:] of *leave* respectively. The approximant *r* can also be regarded as a glide. Although they are vocalic, glides behave in a SYLLABLE as though they are CONSONANTS: the glides in *yak*, *wake*, *rake* belong to the syllable margin as do the consonants in *bake*, *sake*, *take*. In

view of their intermediate status, glides are sometimes known as *semi-vowels*, sometimes as *semi-consonants*. See R-SOUNDS, SPEECH.

**GLOBAL ENGLISH**. A term of the 1990s for English as the world's pre-eminent language: 'The future of global English' (title of the closing chapter of David Crystal, *English as a Global Language*, 1997); 'Technology . . . lies at the heart of the globalisation process, affecting the worlds of education, work and culture; it has helped to ensure that global English has become firmly entrenched as the lingua franca within such activities' ('English and the Internet', in *GEN: Global English Newsletter, Monitoring the Changing Role of English in the World*, 1, an electronic newsletter issued by BRITISH COUNCIL, November 1997). See GLOBAL LANGUAGE. Compare INTERNATIONAL ENGLISH, WORLD ENGLISH.

**GLOBAL LANGUAGE**. A late 20c term for a language used everywhere on earth (and usually linked with English): 'It has become *the* language of the planet, the first truly global language' (Robert McCrum *et al.*, *The Story of English*, 1986); 'What is a global language?—A language achieves a genuinely global status when it develops a special role that is recognized in every country' (David Crystal, *English as a Global Language*, 1997); 'The future of English as a global language therefore may depend, in large measure, on how the language is taken up and used by young adults in Asian countries' (David Graddol, *The Future of English?*, 1997); 'English is shockingly emerging as the only truly global language' (Michael Toolan, 'Recentering English', in *English Today*, 52, October 1997). See GLOBAL ENGLISH. Compare WORLD LANGUAGE.

**GLOTTAL STOP**. In PHONETICS, a stop sound made by bringing the VOCAL CORDS tightly together, blocking off the airstream and sealing the GLOTTIS, then releasing them suddenly. It occurs widely in the world's languages, including: (1) As an Arabic consonant, represented in script by the letter *alif* (and also by the sign *hamza*), and in Roman transliteration by the lenis symbol (or the apostrophe): *'akala* ate. (2) Comparably, as a consonant in Hawaiian: *a'o* to teach. (3) As a sharp 'attack' to an opening vowel in such languages as English and German, used by default when there is no consonant at the beginning of a syllable, as in forcefully saying *Anne, come here!* (4) In England and parts of Northern Ireland, as an accompaniment to the voiceless stops /p, t, k, tʃ/ in a stressed syllable. (5) Widely in BrE as an optional 'catch' between adjacent vowels, as in *co-opt, re-educate*. (6) As a substitute for post-vocalic /t/ in such accents as COCKNEY and GLASGOW, in words like *better, butter*, a process known technically as *T-glottaling*. In all but the last of the above functions, the glottal stop is socially neutral, but in the sixth it is stigmatized. Because many users of English know the term only in this sense, the concept of the glottal stop has long been associated in the English-speaking world with slovenly, SUBSTANDARD speech. In its stigmatized use, it has been shown orthographically in at least three ways: by means of an apostrophe (Glasgow, *be'ur bu'ur* better butter); in the 1950s by the Glasgow writer Cliff Hanley as a double colon (*be : : er bu : : er*); and in 1980 by the London writers Robert Barltrop and Jim Wolveridge by an exclamation mark (*be!er bu!er*). The IPA symbol is ʔ.

**GLOTTIS**. In anatomy and PHONETICS, the space in the LARYNX between the VOCAL CORDS or folds. Anything relating to the glottis is referred to as *glottal*, as in *GLOTTAL STOP*.

**GOBBLEDYGOOK**, also **gobbledegook**. A pejorative and facetious term for pretentious and opaque JARGON; inflated language: 'Just before Pearl Harbor, I got my baptism under "gobbledygook" . . . its definition: talk or writing which is long, pompous, vague, involved, usually with Latinized words' (Maury Maverick, *New York Times Magazine*, 21 May 1944). For examples of the kind of pretentious and opaque usage often classed as *gobbledygook*, see BAFFLEGAB, BUREAUCRATESE, DOUBLESPEAK, PLAIN, PLAIN ENGLISH.

**GOOD ENGLISH**. An informal term for English regarded as all or any of the following: well-spoken, well-written, well-constructed, fluent, effective, a mark of good breeding and social standing, a mark of good education. The term appears from time to time in the title of usage guides, in the sense of *good usage*: for example, Godfrey Howard's *A Guide to Good English in the 1980s* (London: Pelham Books, 1985). See BAD ENGLISH, GRAMMAR, STANDARD ENGLISH.

**GOVERNMENT**. In GRAMMAR, the way in which the use of one word requires another word to take a particular form, especially in highly inflected languages. In LATIN, prepositions govern nouns: *ad* is followed by an accusative of movement (*ad villam* towards the villa), *in* by either an accusative of movement (*in villam* into the villa) or an ablative of location (*in villa* in the villa). Though the concept is not strictly applicable to a mildly inflected language like English, prepositions require object pronouns where they exist: *of me* (not \**of I*), *to them* (not \**to they*), *for us* (not \**for we*). The term is usually contrasted with *agreement* or *concord*, a condition in which two words interact. Some grammarians extend the term to the way in which some verbs require a particular preposition before a following noun phrase, as in 'We insist *on* seeing you tomorrow' and 'I will not compromise *with* them *on* a matter like this.'

**GOWERS, (Sir) Ernest (Arthur)** [1880–1966]. English civil servant and writer on usage, born in London, and educated at Rugby and Clare College, Cambridge, where he studied classics. He entered the Civil Service in 1903 and rose to become chairman of the Board of Inland Revenue. On his retirement in 1930, he was chairman of numerous official bodies and committees of inquiry. At the invitation of the Treasury (concerned at the obscure or convoluted style of many civil servants), he wrote *Plain Words: A Guide to the Use of English* (1948) and *The ABC of Plain Words* (1951). These were combined, with revisions, in *The COMPLETE PLAIN WORDS* (1954). The books show his insistence on clarity, precision, and directness as essential for expository writing. Gowers's reputation as a sensible and sensitive authority on usage and style led to his being invited to revise FOWLER'S DICTIONARY OF *MODERN ENGLISH USAGE* (2nd edition, 1965). See EFFECTIVE WRITING, EUPHEMISM, HOUSE STYLE, PUN, USAGE GUIDANCE AND CRITICISM.

■ **GRAMMAR** ─────────── ■

**1.** The systematic study and description of a LANGUAGE, a group of languages, or language in general in terms of either SYNTAX and MORPHOLOGY alone or these together with aspects of PHONOLOGY, ORTHOGRAPHY, SEMANTICS, PRAGMATICS, and WORD-

FORMATION: *universal grammar, comparative Indo-European grammar, Spanish grammar, the grammar of American English*. The study of the grammar of a language may be restricted to the STANDARD variety or cover the standard and aspects of other varieties. Grammars of English have tended to deal mainly with either standard BrE or standard AmE, but in recent years have increasingly covered both main varieties, sometimes with notes on other varieties.

**2.** A set of rules and examples dealing with the syntax and morphology of a STAN-DARD LANGUAGE, usually intended as an aid to the learning and teaching of that language. A distinction is often drawn between *descriptive grammar*, which attempts to present an accurate description of the rules for actual usage, and *prescriptive grammar*, which prescribes certain rules for usage and often proscribes others: see DESCRIPTIVE AND PRESCRIPTIVE GRAMMAR. In practice, a *grammar book* or *grammar* may contain both kinds of rules. Prescriptive grammar is evaluative, distinguishing between *good grammar* (correct, approved usage) and *bad grammar* (incorrect, disapproved usage). A grammar may overtly or covertly downgrade regional and social dialects (implying that they either do not have 'proper' grammar or have no grammar at all). Such books have often been part of the equipment of formal education in Western countries and have tended to reflect (and endorse) middle-class values. As a result, reminders to offenders have often been couched in such terms as: *Mind your grammar—no double negatives!* A distinction is often made between a *reference grammar* (intended, like a dictionary, for individual reference) and a *pedagogical grammar* (intended chiefly for class use under the guidance of a teacher).

**3.** In LINGUISTICS, a term for the syntactic and morphological system which every unimpaired person acquires from infancy when learning a language: *a native-speaker's grammar*. In this sense, grammar is part of a Janus-faced psychological and neurological process: each person learns and uses a private system which blends into a social consensus. All speakers of a language like English 'know' this grammar in the sense that they use it to produce more or less viable utterances. Their knowledge is implicit, however, and it is not usually easy to think about and report on it. Formal education may help in some areas (especially in

relation to LITERACY) and higher education in language studies may extend this ability, but the use of this natural grammar does not depend on the acquisition of descriptive or prescriptive grammar. English, for example, was used for a thousand years before the first rudimentary grammar books were written, and no grammar book (however large) is ever fully comprehensive.

**Classical grammar**. The analytical study of language began in the second half of the first millennium BC in both Greece and India. In Greece, it began as the study of the written language, whereas in India it was concerned as much with the transmission of recited SANSKRIT as with its written forms. The present-day study of grammar descends from the Greek tradition, in which it was linked with LOGIC and RHETORIC. Both Plato and Aristotle took a close interest in language and, among other things, helped provide the foundation for the discussion of the PARTS OF SPEECH. Grammar was first developed as a formal system, however, by Greek scholars in Alexandria (Egypt). The foremost of these was Dionysius Thrax, author of *Hē grammátiké tékhnē* (The Art of Letters: *c*.100 BC), a brief discussion in 25 sections on the nature of LETTERS, SYLLABLES, WORDS (according to form, function, and meaning), and SENTENCES.

When Thrax wrote his treatise, students of reading and writing learned their letters in a strict order, aided by mnemonic hexameter verses. The letters were crucial for all learning, because each was simultaneously letter, number, and musical note. After their alpha-betas, students were taught syllables of increasing length, then simpler and more complex word forms, then specimen texts. In the texts of the period, there were no spaces between words, punctuation was meagre, and reading depended on a capacity to see patterns in the unbroken lines. Once this skill was acquired, an appreciation of the arrangement (*súntaxis*) of words was necessary, as well as their complex inflections, so as to see what was happening in a text. For this, the guidance in Thrax's treatise was crucial. It was in fact the prototype for grammars of all European and many other languages.

Thrax defined grammar as technical knowledge of the language of poets and writers. His interest did not extend to other kinds of GREEK, to any other language, to language as a general phenomenon, or to spoken language except insofar as it might help in learning to write. It was the job of the *grammatikós* to use brush and papyrus, to copy and to edit, and, if fortunate and able enough, to analyse and improve the texts of such works as the epics of Homer. Writing was a mystery to the population at large, which associated scrolls with knowledge and power. As a result, in classical and medieval times, grammarians were sometimes taken to be sorcerers, but the craft was so laborious that the sorcerers' apprentices were often frustrated by it. Ancient attitudes to grammar still survive: many people are in awe of it, know little about it, tend to fear or dislike it, often find it baffling and boring if exposed to it at school, and yet a minority is fascinated by it: a field in which precise scholarship and nit-picking pedantry have coexisted for centuries.

The Roman scholar Marcus Terentius Varro was a contemporary of Thrax's. Where the Alexandrian was brief, the Roman was copious, producing 25 volumes of *De lingua latina* (On the Latin Language). Of these, only Books 5–10 survive. Varro had studied the Greek debates on language, especially as to whether it was by nature regular or chaotic. He concluded that it is both regular *and* irregular, with a tilt towards the regular. He was the first comparative grammarian, looking at LATIN and Greek side by side and, although he focused on writing, moved the discussion beyond it. Grammarians such as Varro converted the technical terms of Greek into Latin, and adapted Greek-based rules to serve their own tongue. A great advantage in describing Latin more or less in terms of Greek was the similarity of the two languages: both are highly inflected, with complex verb and noun structures.

**Medieval and Renaissance grammar**. In the 4c, Aelius Donatus taught in Rome and wrote an elementary text known as the *Ars grammatica* (Art of Letters), the title a translation of Thrax's. He was the teacher of St Jerome, who translated the Bible into Latin, and was so influential that for a thousand years his name was given not only to a basic grammar book, but to any textbook or lesson. In Old FRENCH and MIDDLE ENGLISH, all of these were *donets*. In the 6c, a native of Mauretania, Priscianus Caesariensis

(Priscian), taught in Constantinople and wrote the *Institutiones grammaticae* (Grammatical Foundations), the only complete surviving grammar of Latin. The texts of Donatus and Priscian became the basis of medieval grammatical studies, Priscian's texts being integrated into the framework of Scholastic philosophy in the 13c and 14c. It is a testimony to his importance that around 1,000 manuscripts of parts or all of his *Institutiones* survive. Just as Thrax focused on Greek, so medieval grammarians such as Peter Helias (12c) and Petrus Hispanus (13c) focused on Latin. However, as the Middle Ages gave way to the Renaissance, as printing spread, and as new nation-states became more conscious of their languages, grammarians in the mould of Varro began in the 16–17c to write descriptions of their own mother tongues by comparing them with the grammatical descriptions of Latin.

The first grammar of a modern European language described SPANISH: Antonio de Nebrija's *Gramática de la lengua castellana* (Grammar of the Castilian language, 1492). The first grammar of FRENCH was written in England: John Palsgrave's *Lesclarcissement de la Langue Françoyse* (1530). An early grammar in one language but about another was in English: Richard Percivall's *Bibliotheca Hispanica, Containing a Grammar, with a Dictionarie in Spanish, English, and Latine* (1591). Like their predecessors, the creators of such works focused on the usage of the 'best' writers, establishing a tradition which lasted until the 19c and which still exerts considerable influence. Just as Thrax did not look beyond Greek and the medieval grammarians did not look beyond Latin, so the early modern grammarians hardly looked beyond a level of usage heavily influenced by Greek and Latin. On those occasions when they did so, they saw what seemed to be a barbarous mass of material lacking all grammatical order.

**Early grammars of English**. Most of the writers of grammars of English have been teachers, but some early grammars were written by men in other walks of life: in 1634, the playwright Ben Jonson wrote his *English Grammar*; in 1762, the Bishop of London, Robert Lowth, brought out *A Short Introduction to English Grammar*; in 1761 and 1762, the scientist Joseph Priestley, better known for discovering oxygen, published two grammars and a number of essays on language. James Harris, whose grammar appeared in 1751, was an amateur philosopher and a Member of Parliament. The American lawyer Lindley Murray grew rich outfitting the British troops who captured New York during the American Revolution, then retired to England and wrote a best-selling English grammar in 1795. In 1784, his compatriot Noah WEBSTER turned to spelling, grammar, and LEXICOGRAPHY as a last resort after failing to thrive as a lawyer or a teacher. Before 1800, at least 272 grammars of English were published and there have been countless since. From the 17c to the 19c, the vast majority of these works contained little more than Thrax's basic formula: lists of the letters and syllables of English, with comments on their pronunciation; definitions of the parts of speech illustrating their inflections; some elementary syntax, usually taught through the presentation of imprecise examples; and a section on punctuation and versification. Some grammars have been speculative and philosophical in nature, in the late medieval tradition: James Harris in *Hermes* (1751) took language as something to be discussed and analysed rather than outlined for rote learning. Few attempted an exhaustive description of English. Goold Brown, in his encyclopedic *Grammar of English Grammars* (1851), refers to almost every extant treatise on English grammar, well-known or obscure, establishing himself as the grammarian's grammarian.

**Latin and English**. In the main, the aims of the grammarians were pragmatic and educational rather than philosophic: to introduce foreigners to English, to teach students their own language, or to prepare them for Latin. The early textbooks were influenced by the Latin grammar of William Lily (1540), grandfather of the dramatist John Lyly. Lyly declined English nouns as if they were Latin. Just as a noun in Latin has a nominative (*dominus*), vocative (*domine*), genitive (*domini*), etc., so he had in English a nominative (*master*), vocative (*O master*), genitive (*of a master*), etc. Sometimes, even its indeclinable adjectives had their cases: nominative singular masculine *wise* and accusative feminine plural *wise*, etc. See CASE. For centuries, English remained in the shadow of Latin and Greek as a school subject and as a vehicle of learning. Samuel JOHNSON shared the common 18c opinion that English was a copious and disorderly tongue which had only recently come

under the sway of grammar. His own grammar fills 13 double-column folio pages in his two-volume dictionary. Of these pages, however, he devotes only 11 lines to syntax, explaining: 'Our language has so little inflection, or variety of terminations, that its construction neither requires nor admits many rules.' In his *Rudiments of English Grammar*, Joseph Priestley attributes this 'paucity of our inflections of words' to the barbarism of the Anglo-Saxons, from whom the language was inherited, 'the severity of whose climate, and difficulty of subsistence, left them little leisure for polishing, or indeed using, their language' (1761, p. v).

**The rules of good English**. So close-mouthed were the ancestors of English that, according to Johnson, the modern form of the language inherited only four syntactic rules: the VERB agrees with its SUBJECT; ADJECTIVES and PRONOUNS are invariable in form; the possessive NOUN is the GENITIVE CASE; transitive verbs and PREPOSITIONS take objects in the 'oblique' case. Priestley added four others: on pronoun agreement; on the concord of COLLECTIVE NOUNS (which may take a SINGULAR or PLURAL verb); on ELLIPSIS (most notably, deletion of the RELATIVE PRONOUN *that*); and on WORD ORDER (adjectives precede nouns; subjects precede verbs, and OBJECTS follow verbs). It would not have been easy for anyone to learn English from such a grammatical basis, even when expanded to 21 rules of syntax in Lindley Murray's *English Grammar* (7th US edition, 1837). Most 18c and 19c grammarians were prescriptive in their approach, presenting grammar as the art or science of correct speech and writing. Although many paid homage to the dictum of the Roman poet Horace that usage is the norm by which correctness is judged, few believed that the speech and writing of masses or élites should constitute standard English. For them, instruction in correct English consisted largely in having students memorize and recite definitions and rules. Many texts were arranged as dialogues or catechisms to facilitate this task. More advanced texts allowed students to parse a SENTENCE whose topic was morally uplifting. Examples from Murray include: *I learn*; *Thou art improved*; *The tutor is admonishing Charles*. Rosewell C. Smith, in his *English Grammar on the Productive System* (1843), emphasized the practical in his examples: *The* *business will be regulated; John is living within his income; He taught me grammar.*

**The unpopularity of grammar**. The grammarians' attitude toward language, combined with the mechanical instruction in grammar required by the texts, made the subject feared and despised by pupils and teachers alike. The 19c American commentator Richard Grant White, still smarting from a punishment he had received from his tutor many years previously for not knowing his grammar lesson, called grammar rules medieval. He preferred to criticize usage and particularly opposed the coining of new words. When grammar became a required subject in many US schools in the mid-19c, teachers objected that they knew no more about the subject than the students did. Since then, grammar has cycled in and out of favour in educational circles. In the early 1900s, progressive US educational groups called for an end to grammar instruction because it did not contribute to facility in writing. In Britain, the Newbolt Report (1921), which strongly favoured the teaching of English, advised against instruction in the science of language, because it interfered with the appreciation of literary art. In recent years, a conservative 'back-to-basics' movement in education, coinciding with a Conservative government, has encouraged a restoration of grammar drill as a way of solving the language problems of the schools in both the US and the UK.

Whether grammar has been in or out of favour, grammarians early on developed a negative image, both personally and professionally. Johnson called Harris a prig; Lowth was described as melancholy; and Lindley Murray was accused by his detractors of committing the errors he warned against. Although most dictionaries (with the exception of the *OED*) ignore this development, *grammarian* has come to mean someone whose concern for correctness in language is excessive or pedantic. According to Chambers' *Cyclopaedia* (1727–41, 1779–86), the formerly honourable title of *grammarian* had become a term of reproach: 'a person wholly attentive to the minutiae of language, industriously employed about words, and phrases; and incapable of perceiving the beauties, the delicacy, finesse, extent, &c of a sentiment'. Nowadays, not all students of grammar wish to be identified as grammarians. Serious academics who have produced comprehensive grammars of English, such as Otto JESPERSEN, formerly philologists, are now generally referred to as *linguists*.

**Scholarly grammars of English in the twentieth century**. There have been a number of 20c scholarly grammars of English characterized by a decidedly descriptive approach and a focus on syntax. The two largest works, both reference grammars, are by foreign speakers of the language. The Dutch grammarian Hendrik Poutsma published *A Grammar of Late Modern English* in five volumes at intervals (with revised versions of the first part) between 1904 and 1929. His grammar is historical (drawing on quotations from earlier periods) and comparative (contrasting the grammars of English and Dutch). The Danish grammarian Otto Jespersen produced his most important work, the seven-volume *Modern English Grammar on Historical Principles*, between 1909 and 1949. As the title indicates, Jespersen's grammar is also historical. This work continues to be consulted for its range of data and insights into grammatical phenomena.

The American structural linguist Charles C. FRIES published two works on English grammar that influenced the teaching of English in schools in the US and elsewhere: *American English Grammar* (1940) and *The Structure of English* (1952). In 1972 and 1985, two large reference grammars were published by a team associated with the SURVEY OF ENGLISH USAGE: the British scholars Randolph QUIRK, Sidney GREENBAUM, Geoffrey Leech, and the Swedish scholar Jan Svartvik: *A Grammar of Contemporary English* (1972) and *A Comprehensive Grammar of the English Language* (1985). Like the works of Fries, these are strictly synchronic. They take account of stylistic variation and the differences between BrE and AmE. Their derivatives are used in the teaching of English in universities and colleges throughout the world: *A University Grammar of English*, by Quirk and Greenbaum (1973), *A Communicative Grammar of English*, by Leech and Svartvik (1975), and *A Student's Grammar of the English Language*, by Greenbaum and Quirk (1990). In the last three decades there has been a noticeable increase in research publications (monographs and scholarly papers) on English grammar, stimulated by a ferment of ideas from competing theoretical approaches, the availability of several large corpora of English (now in computerized form, concordanced, and often grammatically coded), and the growth of importance of English as an international language. In 1996 Greenbaum brought out his *Oxford English Grammar*, in the breadth of its coverage perhaps the first grammar of international standard English.

See ADJECTIVE, ADVERB, ADVERBIAL, ANTECEDENT, APOSTROPHE[1], APPOSITION, ARTICLE[1], ASPECT, AUXILIARY VERB, CLAUSE, COLLOCATION, COMPLEMENT, CONCORD, CONDITION, CONJUNCTION, COORDINATION, COPULA, DEGREE, DESCRIPTIVISM AND PRESCRIPTIVISM, DETERMINER, DIRECT AND INDIRECT SPEECH, GENDER, GERUND, GOVERNMENT, GRAMMATICAL CATEGORY, GRAMMATICALITY, INFINITIVE, INTENSIFIER, INTERJECTION, IRREGULAR, MODALITY, MODAL VERB, MOOD, MORPHEME, NEGATION, NOMINALIZATION, NOUN, PARSING, PARTICIPLE, PARTICLE, PASSIVE (VOICE), PASSIVIZATION, PEDAGOGICAL GRAMMAR, PERIODIC SENTENCE, PERSON, PHRASAL VERB, PREDICATE, PREPOSITION, QUANTIFIER, QUESTION, QUESTION TAG, REFLEXIVE, REGULAR, RELATIVE CLAUSE, SENTENCE, SUBJUNCTIVE, SUBORDINATION, TENSE, TRANSFORMATIONAL-GENERATIVE GRAMMAR, USAGE, VERBAL NOUN, VOICE, WORD.

See also the grammar sections of entries for major varieties of English, such as CANADIAN ENGLISH.

**GRAMMATICAL CATEGORY**. In LINGUISTICS, a class of units such as *noun, verb, prepositional phrase, finite clause* and features such as *case, countability, gender, number*. These may in turn be subcategorized into kinds of noun, case, etc. Since nouns may be subclassified in various ways that do not coincide, they are said to be cross-classified in such pairs as *countable/uncountable, common/proper, animate/inanimate*. Grammatical units such as subject and object, which refer to functional relationships between the parts of a sentence or clause, are often termed *functional categories*. See PART OF SPEECH.

**GRAMMATICALITY**. In LINGUISTICS, conformity to the rules of a language as formulated by a GRAMMAR based on a theory of language description. The concept became prominent with the rise of GENERATIVE GRAMMAR in the 1960s, whose primary aim has been the construction of rules that would distinguish between the *grammatical*

or *well-formed* SENTENCES and the *ungrammatical*, DEVIANT, or *ill-formed* sentences of a language.

Grammaticality has been differentiated from *ACCEPTABILITY*, which is based on the judgements by native speakers as to whether they would use a sentence or would consider it correct if they met it. Judgements about what is acceptable may reflect views that a sentence is nonsensical, implausible, illogical, stylistically inappropriate, or socially objectionable. Many linguists believe that they can filter out such considerations in their investigations of the facts of language. Many also believe that they can rely on their own introspection to provide samples of clearly grammatical and clearly ungrammatical sentences that would be adequate for compiling and testing the rules. Others consider that the examination of large quantities of data stored and organized by means of computers can yield additional and more reliable information on what constructions are possible and which are central or peripheral to the language. See CORPUS.

A sensitive issue regarding grammaticality is variability within a language, for example the extent to which sentences are grammatical for one regional or social variety but not another, or indeed for one idiolect rather than another. Non-standard varieties of a language have their own grammars, which will resemble to a greater or less extent the grammar of the standard varieties, so that a sentence may be grammatical in one non-standard variety but ungrammatical in a standard variety, and vice versa. Some sociolinguists believe that linguists should have as their objective the compilation of *multilectal* grammar: a grammar that would take into account all variation within a given language.

**GRAPHEME**. In LINGUISTICS, a minimal unit in a writing system, consisting of one or more symbols serving to represent a *PHONEME*. Each grapheme is realized in writing or print by its *graphs*, such as the different ways of writing and printing an *a* or a *t*. An individual graph, when compared with another graph or representing a grapheme, is called an *allograph*. See -EME.

**GRAVE ACCENT** [Pronounced 'grahv']. A diacritical mark over a letter as in FRENCH *è: première, siècle*. It is not usually retained when a word containing it is borrowed into

English (*fin de siecle*, *premiere*), usually because it is not available on a keyboard or in type. Grave ACCENTS are, however, sometimes applied to English words to mark such distinctions as the pronounced *e* of the second item of the pairs *aged/agèd*, *learned/learnèd*. See D, DIACRITIC.

**GREAT VOWEL SHIFT**. A sound change that began *c*.1400 and ended *c*.1600, changing late MIDDLE ENGLISH long, stressed MONOPHTHONGS from something like the sounds of mainland European languages to those that they now have: for example, Middle English *fine* had an *i* like Italian *fino*. Words that entered English after the completion of the shift have often retained the original sound, as in *police*: compare *polite*, which entered earlier. In terms of articulation, the Middle English front VOWELS raised and fronted and the back vowels raised and backed; vowels already at the top became DIPHTHONGS with *ah* as the first element and the old vowel as the second, as in *fine* (see diagram). The shift marked a major change in the transition to EARLY MODERN ENGLISH, and is one reason the works of Geoffrey CHAUCER and his contemporaries sound so unlike present-day English. Chaucer's *a* in *fame* sounded much like the *a* in present-day *father*, his *e* in *see* like the *a* in *same*, the *i* in *fine* like the *ee* in *fee*, the *o* in *so* like the *aw* in *saw*, the *o* in *to* like the *oe* in *toe*, and the *ou* or *ow* in *crowd* like the *u* in *crude*. See E, LATIN, JESPERSEN, VOWEL SHIFT. Compare GRIMM'S LAW.

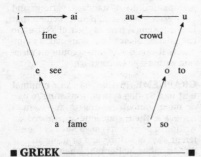

■ **GREEK** ───────────────────── ■

A LANGUAGE of south-eastern Europe, a classical LANGUAGE of the Western world, and a member of the INDO-EUROPEAN LANGUAGE family. It is commonly divided into *Ancient* or *Classical Greek* (often thought of as a dead language) and *Modern Greek*, the language of

Greece, Cyprus (with Turkish), enclaves in the Soviet Union and the eastern Mediterranean, and Greek and Cypriot immigrants in Australia, Britain, Canada, and the US.

**Greek in English**. The influence of classical Greek on English has been largely indirect, through LATIN and FRENCH, and largely lexical and conceptual, with some orthographic and other effects. For speakers of English, Greek has been traditionally perceived as remote, esoteric, and yet worth a certain respect: compare the idiom *It's Greek to me* (I can't understand it) and the saying *The Greeks had a word for it* (expressing a traditional view of the richness of the language). Greek word-forming patterns, words, and word elements were adopted and adapted into Latin over *c*.1,500 years, and passed through Latin into many European and other languages, being used in the main for scholarly and technical purposes. The flow into English was at first limited and largely religious, such as Old English *cirice* and its descendant *church* (from *kŭriakón dôma* the Lord's house). The significant influx was in the late Middle Ages and the Renaissance, as with *catalogue* 1460, *rhetorical* 1476, *stratagem* 1489, *psalmodize* 1513, *analytical* 1525.

**Greek in Latin dress**. The spelling of Greek words in English has been shaped by the orthographies of Latin and French: Greek *kalligraphia* becomes Latin *calligraphia*, French *calligraphie*, English *calligraphy*. Occasionally, however, a more Greek look survives: *kaleidoscope*, not *\*calidoscope*, *kinetic*, not *\*cinetic*. Synonymous variants sometimes occur: *ceratin*, *keratin*, both from *kéras* horn. Contrasts occur when a *k* survives in some usages but not in others: *ceratosaurus* horned lizard, *keratogenous* producing horny tissue; *cinematography* making moving pictures, *kinematograph* (obsolete) a film projector. Although most Greek personal and place-names have a Latinate look in English (*Achilles*, *Hercules*; *Athens*, *Crete*), they can, for literary and other purposes, take forms closer to the classical (*Akhilleus*, *Herakles*) or the modern (*Athinai*, *Kriti*). The use of *ph* as a marker of Greek words in Latin survives in English because it was favoured by French writers, the *ph* representing the Greek letter phi. English *philosophy* and French *philosophie* contrast with Italian *filosofia* and Spanish *filosofía*, which did not keep the Latinism: see F, P. English *neuralgia, neurosis* are closer to Greek than both French *névralgie, névrose* and Italian *nevralgia, nevrosi*, which have been influenced by the pronunciation of Modern Greek.

**Hybridized Greek**. Because it has been filtered into English through Neo-Latin, the Greek contribution has been liable to hybridization. However, because some loans (*diuretic, deontology, dogmatism*) are fairly close to their originals, and other forms are virtually identical with them (*diphtheria, dogma, drama*), the effects of Latinization and the easy creation of hybrids have tended to be overlooked. The words *rhetorical* and *analytical* are largely Greek, but they end with the suffix *-al*, an adaptation of Latin *-alis*. Scholars have tended to minimize such adaptations, because Latin and Greek were equally classical, sometimes discussing Greek as if it were a self-contained and pure source of technical vocabulary for English. Henry Bradley put it as follows:

> So well adapted is the structure of the Greek language for the formation of scientific terms, that when a word is wanted to denote some conception peculiar to modern science, the most convenient way of obtaining it usually is to frame a new Greek compound or derivative, such as Aristotle himself might have framed if he had found it needful to express the meaning (*The Making of English*, 1904).

This is only partly true. A new formation is likely to be more NEO-LATIN than classical Greek. It was circumstance rather than inherent worth that made Greek a prime source of terms for European academic discourse. Other classical languages, such as ARABIC and SANSKRIT, are comparably extensive in systems of WORD-FORMATION exploited in their own scholarly traditions, but have had little impact on English because no such channels as Latin and French were open to them. Elsewhere, however, they have had a comparable impact.

See BIBLE, BISOCIATION, BORROWING, CLASSICAL COMPOUND, CLASSICAL ENDING, CLASSICAL LANGUAGE, COMBINING FORM, COMPOUND WORD, EARLY MODERN ENGLISH, FIGURATIVE LANGUAGE, GRAMMAR, INTERFIX, PREFIX, RHETORIC, SUFFIX, WORD.

**GREENBAUM, Sidney** [1929–1996]. British linguist, internationally known not only for his work on the GRAMMAR of STANDARD ENGLISH but also for organizing computerized corpora of English texts and the grammatical tagging and analysis of their content. Born into a poor Yiddish-speaking family in the East End of London, he gained a BA and MA in Hebrew and Aramaic at Jews' College, U. of London, and trained (though he never practised) as a rabbi. After training as a teacher, he first worked in a primary school (1954–7) then taught English and Hebrew at the Hasmonean Boys' School in Hendon (1957–64), where he was head of English while also studying part-time for a BA in English at Birkbeck College, U. of London. In 1965 he became a research assistant on the SURVEY OF ENGLISH USAGE at University College London (UCL), working for Randolph QUIRK and gaining his Ph.D., following which he worked abroad, as: Assistant Professor of English at the U. of Oregon (1968–9), Associate Professor of English at the U. of Wisconsin-Milwaukee (1969–72), Visiting Professor in English at the Hebrew U. Jerusalem, 1972–3, and Professor of English at Milwaukee (1972–83). In 1983, he became Quain Professor of English Language and Literature, and director of the Survey of English, at UCL, in 1988 setting up the INTERNATIONAL CORPUS OF ENGLISH. In 1990, he retired from the Quain chair but continued as director of the Survey. His publications include: *Studies in English Adverbial Usage* (1969, based on his doctoral research), *A Grammar of Contemporary English* (with Randolph Quirk, Geoffrey Leech, and Jan Svartvik, 1972), *A University Grammar of English* (with Quirk, 1973); *The English Language Today* (editor, 1985); *A Comprehensive Grammar of the English Language* (with Quirk, Leech, and Svartvik, 1985); *Longman Guide to English Usage* (with Janet Whitcut, 1988); *An Introduction to English Grammar* (1991); and *The Oxford English Grammar* (1996). He was also an associate editor of *The Oxford Companion to the English Language* (1992), with particular responsibility for the grammar of the STANDARD LANGUAGE.

**GRENADA**. A country of the Caribbean, and member of the COMMONWEALTH. Head of state: the British monarch, represented by a governor-general. Languages: English (official), English Creole, French Creole. Columbus visited the island in 1498, in the mid-17c French settlers from Martinique ousted the Carib Indians, and the island

## GRIMM'S LAW

| | Sound shift | 'Before' | 'After' |
|---|---|---|---|
| Labials | p > f | *p*ed(al) | *f*oot |
| | b > p | la*b*(ial) | li*p* |
| | f > b | *f*und(ament) | bott(om) |
| Velars | k > h | *c*an(ine) | *h*ound |
| | g > k | *g*enu(flect) | *k*nee |
| | h > g | *h*ost(ile) | *g*uest |
| Dentals | t > th | *t*ri(ple) | *th*ree |
| | d > t | *d*uo | *t*wo |
| | th > d | *th*yr(oid) | *d*oor |

```
        p                           k
       / \                         / \
      /   \                       /   \
     /     \                     /     \
    b ----- f                   g ----- h


                    t
                   / \
                  /   \
                 d --- th
```

was ceded to Britain in 1783. It was administered as part of the Windward Islands in 1833, became a colony in 1877 and independent in 1974. See CARIBBEAN ENGLISH.

**GRIMM'S LAW**. The first Germanic sound shift, a statement of the relationship between certain consonants in GERMANIC LANGUAGES and their originals in Indo-European (IE), first described in 1818 by the Danish philologist Rasmus Rask (1787–1832) and set out in detail in 1822 by the German philologist Jacob Grimm (1785–1863). Greatly simplified, Grimm's Law states the regular changes in IE labials /p, b, f/, velars /k, g, h/, and dentals /t, d, θ/, as they developed in Germanic. Because English has words borrowed from Latin and Greek that retain the original IE sound, as well as words descended from Germanic that have the changed sound, it provides 'before and after' illustrations: see panel.

In general, Grimm's Law holds that unvoiced IE stops became Germanic unvoiced continuants, that voiced IE stops became Germanic unvoiced stops, and that un-

voiced IE continuants became Germanic voiced stops (see panel). In the triangles, the change from IE to Germanic runs clockwise, the derivation of Germanic from IE anticlockwise. See INDO-EUROPEAN LANGUAGES. Compare GREAT VOWEL SHIFT.

**GROUP POSSESSIVE**, also **group genitive**. Terms for those occasions when the possessive APOSTROPHE ('s) is added to a phrase rather than to the noun to which it logically relates: *The King of Thailand's visit* (not *\*The King's of Thailand visit*) or *the girl next door's bicycle.* See POSSESSION, SAXON GENITIVE.

**GULLAH**. The name of a member of a black community in the Sea Islands and coastal marshes of South Carolina, Georgia, and north-eastern Florida, and of the English-based CREOLE spoken by that community (also known as *Sea Island Creole*). Gullah is usually kept hidden from outsiders. It developed on 18c rice plantations after British colonists and their African slaves arrived in Charleston from Barbados in 1670, in an encounter among African languages such as Ewe, Hausa, Ibo, Mende, Twi, and Yoruba, the English of overseers from England, Ireland, and Scotland, and the maritime PIDGIN used in some West African forts and aboard slavers' ships. It shares many features with other Atlantic creoles, and is characterized by: (1) Distinctive words for tense and aspect: *He bin come* He came, He had come; *He go come* He will come, He would come; *He duh come* He is coming, He was coming; *He done come* He has come, He had come. *He come* may mean 'He came', 'He has come', 'He comes', but not 'He will come'. (2) Pronouns more inclusive than in general English: *He see um* He or she saw him/her/it; also *He see she* He saw her, and *He see we* He or she saw us. A pronoun usually has the same form whether subject or possessive: *He ain see he brother* He hasn't seen his brother, He didn't see his brother. (3) Subordinate clauses introduced by *say* (*Uh tell you say he done come* I told you that he has/had come), and by *fuh* (*Uh tell um fuh come* I told him/her to come). Both particles can be left out: *Uh tell you he done come*; *Uh tell um come*. There is a continuum between Gullah and local varieties of AmE: for example, from *He duh come* and *He duh comin* through *He comin* to *He's comin*. English words of African origin that may have come wholly or partly through Gullah include *goober* peanut (compare Kimbundu *nguba*), and *juke* bawdy and disorderly (compare Bambara *dzugu*, wicked), as in *juke house* brothel or cheap roadhouse, and *jukebox*. See BAJAN, WEST AFRICAN PIDGIN ENGLISH.

**GUTTER SCOTS**. A pejorative term for urban working-class speech in Scotland. Sometimes *SCOTS* is replaced by a local name, such as *Gutter GLASGOW*. It is identified by at least the following features, several of which are not confined to Scotland. (1) *The GLOTTAL STOP*, realizing /t/ and less regularly /p, k/ as glottal plosives after vowels and /l, n, r/: *better, bottle, try to, quarter, tryin'* to, *shelter, keeping, working*. (2) Disyllabic forms with an intrusive vowel: 'girrul' *girl*, 'wurruld' *world*, 'fillum' *film*. (3) 'H-' for *th-* in 'hink' *think*, 'hing' *thing*, 'sumhn' *something*, 'nuhn' *nothing*, 'everyhn' *everything*. (4) A realization of *thr-* as 'hr-': 'hree' for *three*, 'hred' for *thread*. (5) Generalizing past participle forms as past tenses and vice versa: *Ah never done that*; *Ah seen im*

*comin*; *Ah gien im aw Ah had* I gave him all I had; *Ah've swam further'n that*. (6) Other irregularities in verb morphology: *Ah seed im comin*; *Ah've brung ye some sangwidges*. (7) Multiple negation: *Ah dinna(e) waant nane* I don't want any. (8) *Never* used to negate one event: *Ah nivver done nothin* I didn't do that. (9) Double auxiliary *have*: *Ye'd've saw im if ye'd've came/If ye'd a came*. (10) *Here* as an exclamation of surprise: *And here! the shoap wis open efter aw*. (11) Repetition of reporting *say*: *He says tae me e says, 'Ah'm no comin'*; *Ah says tae him Ah says: 'Jis shut up!'* (12) MINCED OATHS as exclamations of surprise: *Jings* Jesus, *Crivvens* Christ, *Help ma Boab* (Help my Bob) Help me God. See SCOTS.

**GUTTURAL**. A general term for sounds made in or near the throat, such as the velar fricative in German *Achtung* and ScoE *loch*, the uvular *r* in Parisian French *derrière*, and the pharyngeal ARABIC sounds known as *'ayn* and *ghayn*. The term is imprecise and little used by phoneticians. It is often used loosely when describing English spoken with a 'throaty' foreign ACCENT: ' "I had some criticisms of my own education," he said in his slow guttural, uncompromised by 50 years of living and working in the USA' (referring to Bruno Bettelheim, *Observer*, 6 Sept. 1987). See BURR, PHARYNX, UVULA, VELUM.

**GUYANA**. A country of the Caribbean coast of South America and member of the COMMONWEALTH. Languages: English (official), English Creole, Bhojpuri, Hindi, Urdu, Amerindian languages. The region was sighted by Columbus in 1498 and settled by the Dutch in the 16c. The Dutch colonies of Essequibo, Demerara, and Berbice were ceded to the British in 1815, and consolidated as *British Guiana* in 1831, with independence in 1966. The term *Guyanese English* is used, in opposition to *Creolese* or *Guyanese Creole English*, to refer to educated local usage. Its vocabulary contains items from DUTCH (*paal* boundary mark, *stelling* wharf), Amerindian (*warishi* basket for heavy loads, *mashramani* celebration after cooperative work), and Indian languages (*sardar* field supervisor on a plantation, *dhan* rice paddy). See CARIBBEAN ENGLISH, CARIBBEAN ENGLISH CREOLE, SURINAM.

# H

[Generally called 'AITCH', and sometimes 'haitch' in IrE and AusE]. The 8th LETTER of the Roman ALPHABET as used for English. It derives from the Phoenician consonant *heth*, ancestor of the Greek letter *eta* (H). The Romans adopted *eta* to represent the ASPIRATE sound /h/.

**Sound Value**. In English, *h* represents a voiceless glottal fricative at the beginning of syllables before a vowel: *hat, behind, abhor, mishap*.

**Silent H.** (1) In syllable-final position, in exclamations such as *ah, eh, oh* and in such loans (usually Hebrew and West or South Asian) as *chutzpah, Jehovah, Messiah, Sara(h), howdah, veranda(h)*. (2) In words of Greek origin, after *r*: *catarrh, h(a)emorrhage, rhapsody, rhinoceros, rhododendron*. *Rhyme* (also *rime*) is so spelt by analogy with *rhythm*. (3) In *Thames, thyme*, and sometimes *Anthony*. (4) By elision after a stressed syllable (*annihilate, shepherd, Chatham*), and after *ex-* even at the onset of a stressed syllable (*exhaust, exhibit, exhort*). (5) In speech, commonly elided in *he, him, his, her* in unstressed positions, especially following a consonant: *What did 'e do; Tell us 'er name*. This elision affected the spelling and pronunciation of the Middle English pronoun *hit*, resulting in Modern English *it*. (6) After *c* in words of Greek and Italian origin, but indicating that the *c* is pronounced /k/: *archangel, archive, chemist, monarch, stomach, technical, chiaroscuro, scherzo*: and by analogy *ache*, modern spelling for earlier *ake*. (7) In words of Celtic origin, *ch* is generally pronounced /k/ (*clarsach, loch*), but in ScoE and often in IrE is a velar fricative /x/. English in England may have silent *h* in Irish names such as *Callaghan*, though in IrE and ScoE the *g* is generally silent. See *c*.

**French H.** Words derived from French vary in their use of *h*. Sometimes *h* has never been established in English: for example, *able* from Latin *habilis*, French *habile*. Sometimes *h* reached English, but has never been pronounced: *heir, honest, honour, hour*. Sometimes as silent French *h* has come to be pronounced in standard English: *horrible, hospital, host, hotel, human, humour, humble*. In some words *h* was introduced in English as in *hermit, hostage* (compare French *ermite, otage*), eventually coming to be pronounced. The *h* of *herb* is pronounced in standard BrE, but not in standard AmE.

**Initial H.** The uncertainty of initial *h* is shown in the controversy over the use of *an* before some words of French origin: *an heroic attempt* and *an historic occasion* as opposed to *a heroic attempt* and *a historic occasion*. Although it is now generally conventional to say *a hotel*, the form *an hotel* was once widespread and still occurs in England. In such cases, the *h* may or may not be pronounced in BrE (*an heroic attempt* or *an 'eroic attempt*) and is pronounced in AmE. This use of *an* before *h* is widely regarded as pretentious (especially when the *h* is pronounced), and has always been limited to words in which the first syllable is unstressed: no *\*an hopeless case* or *\*an hot day*.

***H*-dropping**. Also *aitch-dropping*. In England and Wales there are several *h*-less accents, such as Cockney and Brummie, where the pronunciations *an 'orrible 'appening* and *an 'opeless case* are normal. In written dialogue associated with such accents, unpronounced *h* is represented, as here, by an apostrophe.

**Digraphs**. (1) *H* following some consonants may represent special joint values, as in the digraphs *ch, gh, ph, sh, th, wh*. See C, G, P, S, T, W. (2) This use of *h* was first established in Latin, which used *ch, ph*, and *th* for the Greek letters *chi, phi*, and *theta*. The digraphs *ch, sh* developed in English after the Norman Conquest. *Wh* arose analogically by reversing Old English *hw*. *Gh* was introduced to represent the Old English palatal or velar fricative previously often spelt ʒ (YOGH), itself going back to an old English *h*-form (old English *liht* becoming *liʒt* then *light*), and *th* was substituted for the Old English letters ð (ETH) and þ (THORN). (3) *H* can be used in such digraphs because its usual value does not normally occur after consonants, except across syllable boundaries (see below).

**Other features**. (1) In some circumstances, ambiguity can arise regarding what may or may not be a digraph. Syllable boundaries may be unclear, so that the separate values of *sh* in *mishap* may be read together as in *bishop*. Uncertainty over syllable boundaries has influenced the spelling in *threshold* (contrast *withhold*). (2) The element *-ham* in place-names in England is often ambiguous in terms of pronunciation, the *h* being sometimes assimilated into a digraph (as in *Grantham*), sometimes not (as in *Clapham*). The spelling provides no guidance in such words. (3) In some languages, *h* can indicate aspiration of a preceding consonant (*bhakti, jodhpur, khaki*), but this use usually appears unmotivated to monolingual English speakers, who ignore it, especially in Indian usage (*bharat natyam, dharma, Jhabvala, Madhukar*) and often take aspirated *t* to be the conventional *th* digraph (*hatha yoga, Marathi*).

**HALLIDAY, Michael A. K.** [b. 1925]. English linguist and grammarian, born in Leeds, Yorkshire, into an academic family; his father, Wilfred J. Halliday (1889–1975), after retiring as a headmaster, played a major part in compiling material for the North of England in Harold Orton's *Survey of English Dialects*. The younger Halliday studied Chinese language and literature at the U. of London and LINGUISTICS at graduate level, first in Beijing and Guangzhou (Canton), then at Cambridge (Ph.D. 1955). In 1963, he was named to lead the *Communication Research Centre* at the U. of London, directing two influential projects: a description of scientific English, and a study of children's language that led eventually to *Breakthrough to Literacy*, his method of teaching children to read. In 1965 he became Professor of General Linguistics at London, in 1970 Professor of Linguistics at the U. of Illinois in Chicago, and in 1976 Professor in the Department of Linguistics at the U. of Sydney, where he remained until retirement in 1987.

Halliday's contributions to the study of English have been varied. For the past quarter-century he has set the agenda for applications of linguistics, as proposed with Peter Strevens and Angus McIntosh in *The Linguistic Sciences and Language Teaching* (1964). His interests include first- and second-language acquisition, poetics, artificial intelligence, linguistic disorders, discourse analysis, text linguistics, semiotics, speech, and English grammar. In the last of these fields, contributions include *Intonation and Grammar in British English* (1967), *Cohesion in English* (1976, with Ruqaiya Hasan), and *An Introduction to Functional Grammar* (1985). The theory he espouses, currently known as *systemic grammar* and *systemic linguistics*, has an orientation towards applications. 'The value of a theory,' he has declared, 'lies in the use that can be made of it.' The approach emphasizes the functions of language in use, particularly the ways in which social setting, mode of expression, and REGISTER influence selections from a language's *systems*: 'Meaning is a product of the relationship between the system and its environment.'

In his work on English texts, Halliday has asserted the unity of syntax and lexicon in a *lexicogrammar*, collapsing the usual distinction between GRAMMAR and DICTIONARY. Meanings are expressed through three interrelated functions: the *ideational*, the *interpersonal*, and the *textual*. Messages combine an organization of *content* deployed according to the *expressive* and *receptive* needs of speaker/authors and listener/readers within conventions of discourse organization. Language users make a series of choices drawn from the meaning potential of their language as they express themselves; it is the task of the linguist to describe those choices as they are shaped by individual minds and social context.

**HARD AND SOFT**. (1) Qualities of the letters *c* and *G* that depend on whether they are pronounced like *k* or *s* in the case of *c* or like the *g* in *get* or the *j* in *jet* in the case of *g*. When hard, *c* and *g* are pronounced as velar stops, as in *cap/gap*; when soft, *c* is pronounced as a sibilant, *g* as an affricate, as in *cell/gell*. (2) Popular terms used to describe VOICE quality, a *hard* voice being forceful and likely to be reinforced by stop consonants (*Damn well tell him to come back tomorrow!*), a *soft* voice being gentle, perhaps kind and compassionate, and likely to be reinforced by sibilants, affricates, fricatives, and liquids (*Hush now; just leave it all to me*). Male voices are often stereotyped as 'hard' and 'rough', female voices as 'soft' and 'gentle'. (3) In phonetics, in the description of consonants, *hard* is an older term for *fortis* (articulated with considerable muscular tension or force of breath or plosion, as with the voiceless consonants of English, such as /p, t, k, s/) and *soft* for *lenis* (articulated with little tension, as with the voiced consonants, such as /b, d, g, z/). See AESTHETICS, GENDER BIAS, HYPHEN, PALATE, SEXISM, SPEECH.

**HARD WORD**. A semi-technical term for a difficult WORD of foreign origin: for example, *azimuth, hierophant, munificence, perigee, Vedanta*. Early English dictionaries, especially in the 17c, that explained such exotic words by means of everyday words, came to be known as *hard-word dictionaries*. See CAWDREY, DICTIONARY, LONG WORD.

**HARDY, Thomas** [1840–1928]. English novelist and poet, born at Higher Bockhampton, Dorset, where his father was a stonemason and small builder, and educated in Dorchester and articled to a local architect. In 1862, he moved to London and worked with the fashionable architect Arthur Blomfield, but because of poor health he returned to Dorset in 1867. Continuing to work in architecture, he also began to write *Under the Greenwood Tree* (1872). He created the imaginary world of 'Wessex', based on Dorset and the surrounding counties, in which many of his locations are identifiable. His 14 novels include *The Mayor of Casterbridge* (1886), *Tess of the D'Urbervilles* (1891), and *Jude the Obscure* (1896).

More than simply a 'regional' writer, Hardy presented the life of the rural world in which he had grown up and preserved the image of a vanished way of life. A major achievement is the use of dialect. He could capture the tones of Dorset speech, without the elaborately deviant spellings which make the Dorset poems of William Barnes difficult to read, but conveying the distinctive sounds as well as the words and grammar:

' 'Tis not to married couples but to single sleepers that a ghost shows himself when a'do come. One has been seen lately, too. A very strange one.'

'No—don't talk about it if 'tis agreeable of ye not to! 'Twill make my skin crawl when I think of it in bed alone. But you will—ah, you will, I know, Timothy: and I shall dream all night o't! A very strange one? What sort of a spirit did ye mean when ye said a very strange one, Timothy?—no, no—don't tell me.'

'I don't half believe in spirits myself. But I think it ghostly enough—what I was told. 'Twas a little boy that zid it' (from *The Return of the Native*, 1878).

Hardy used dialect for both tragic and comic episodes and varied its intensity to suggest the status of the characters and the degree of their relationship. He valued and defended the dignity of Dorset usage, which he saw not as a deviation from the national standard, but as a survival of the ancient speech of Saxon Wessex.

■ **HAWAIIAN** ───────── ■

A Pacific language belonging to the Malayo-Polynesian family and cognate with Samoan and MAORI. It has eight consonants, /h, k, l, m, n, p, w/ and the GLOTTAL STOP, and ten vowels /a, e, i, ɔ, ʊ/ (each long and short). Hawaiian words end in vowels (*lei, kahuna*), consonants are separated by vowels (*Kalakaua, Lapakahi*), and many words have no consonants at all (*aia* there, *oiaio* truly) or more vowels than consonants (*heiau* temple). Among the differences between Hawaiian and some other Polynesian languages are: /k/ for /t/ (*kapu* for *tabu*), /l/ for /r/ (*kalo* for *taro*), a glottal stop where some have /k/, marked in technical writing by a reverse inverted apostrophe (ʻ) and in general usage by an ordinary apostrophe (') (*muʻumuʻu* or *muʻumuʻu* for *mukumuku* shapeless, a loose-fitting woman's dress). The glottal stop is phonemic and therefore contrastive: *kaʻu* mine, *kau* yours. The sound written as *l* may have been close to /r/. When missionary printers standardized the language in Roman after 1820, they voted six to two in favour of *l*; when the personal name of King Kamehameha II was set in type, he preferred *Liholiho* to *Rihoriho*. Repeating a word base usually has a special meaning: *lau* leaf, *laulau* a bundle of food baked in leaves; *pai* slap, *paipai* to drive fish by slapping the water. BORROWINGS into Hawaiian have generally been adapted to its phonology: *hokela* hotel, *kelepona* telephone, *kula* school, *nupepa* newspaper, *pipi* beef, *puke* book, and such biblical names as *Apikaila* Abigail, *Kaniela* Daniel, *Malia* Maria, *Kamaki* Thomas. borrowings from Hawaiian into English are common locally but few in the general language: *aʻa* and *pahoehoe* lava which cools rough and smooth respectively, *ukelele/ukulele* a jumping flea whose name was given to an adaptation of the Portuguese guitar.

**HAWAIIAN ENGLISH**. The English language as used in Hawaii, an archipelago in the Pacific, since 1959 the 50th state of the United States. Most ethnic Hawaiians now speak English or HAWAII CREOLE ENGLISH rather than HAWAIIAN, though there are attempts to revive the language. English has been the language of education for well over a century and is the administrative and general language of the state. The distinctive features of Hawaiian AMERICAN ENGLISH include words of indigenous origin, their combination with imported words, informal and slang expressions often incorporating elements of Hawaii English Pidgin/Creole, and unique expressions used in giving directions. Widely used words from Hawaiian include: *aloha* love, sympathy (a common form of greeting and farewell), *haole* originally any foreigner, now a Caucasian, *heiau* a traditional temple, *hula* a kind of dance (formerly usually sacred, now mainly performed for tourists), *kane* a man, *kapu* taboo, keep out, *lanai* a porch or patio, *lei* a garland of flowers, seeds, or shells (especially as a token of welcome), *mahalo* thank you, *mahimahi* a dolphin, *mahope* by and by, *pau* finished, *poi* a thick edible taro paste, *pupus* hors d'œuvres, *wahine* a girl, woman, wife, *wikiwiki* hurry up. Hybrid usages include: *the Ala Moana Center, an aloha party, Kalakaua Avenue, a lei-seller, the Kilauea Crater, the Kodak Hula Show, kukui nuts, the Waianae Coast, Waikiki Bar-B-Que House, the Waimea Arboretum.*

Hawaiian English mixes elements of AmE slang and informal usage with elements of Hawaiian, Hawaii English Pidgin/Creole, and other languages, as in: *ala-alas* balls (testicles), *brah* brother, *buddahead* (pejorative) someone from Japan or of Japanese background, *to cockaroach* to steal or sneak away with something, *da kine* that kind (*Wheah da kine?* Where's the whatsit?), *FOB* Fresh off the Boat, *haolefied* becoming like a haole, *JOJ* Just off the Jet, *kapakahi* mixed up (all from Douglas Simonson, *Pidgin to da Max*, Honolulu, 1981). Traditional terms of direction relate to geography, not points of the compass, as with *mauka* towards the mountains, *makai* towards the sea. On Oahu, these are combined with the names of two locations on the southern shore, *Ewa beach* and *Waikiki/Diamond Head*, as in: 'Go ewa one block, turn *makai* at the traffic light, go two blocks Diamond Head, and you'll find the place on the *mauka* side of the street' ('Which Way Oahu?', *National Geographic*, Nov. 1979); 'The ewa bound lanes of the H-1 Freeway airport viaduct were closed for hours' (*Honolulu Advertiser*, 27 Mar. 1990). Hawaiian journalists use localisms fairly freely; often with glosses: 'For 1,500 years, a member of the Mookini family has been the kahuna—priest—at an enormous heiau—temple—at Upolu Point in Kohala at the northern tip of the Big Island.' (*Honolulu Advertiser*, 4 May 1982). See MAORI ENGLISH.

**HAWAII CREOLE ENGLISH**, also **Hawaii English Creole.** An English-based CREOLE that developed for communication among a mixed population on plantations in Hawaii, a continuum from a low-status BASILECT to a high-status ACROLECT that has de-creolized. It retains features from the PIDGIN stage, such as the use of *bambai* (by and by: compare TOK PISIN *baimbai*) to mark future and hypothetical events: *Mai fada dem wen kam ova hia*; *bambai de wen muv tu Kawai* My father and the others came over here; then they moved to Kauai. The use of *wen* to mark the simple past is a more recent form taken from *went*. There is another, older form *bin* from *been* (compare Tok Pisin *bin*), as in *A bin go see mai fada* I went to see my father. Currently, many speakers use the English past tense auxiliary *had*. The use of *dem* (them) to mark plurals, as in *Stan-dem* Stan and the others, is found in other English-based creoles: for example, JAMAICAN CREOLE *Jan dem* John and the others.

**HAWAII PIDGIN ENGLISH**, also informally **Pidgin**. Although the term *Hawaiian pidgin* has been widely used to refer to the English-based PIDGIN and CREOLE varieties used in Hawaii, some people of ethnic Hawaiian descent have objected to it because it suggests that HAWAIIAN rather than English was pidginized. The term *Hawaii Pidgin English* is now generally preferred among scholars and teachers. It may have been a pidginized version of Hawaiian re-lexified with English words and used by the Chinese plantation labourers who took over the cultivation of taro from native Hawaiians. This pidgin was originally known as *olelo pa'i'ai* (pounded but undiluted taro language) and is partially related to one of the earliest forms of English in the islands, *Maritime*

*Pidgin Hawaiian*, which was used between Hawaiians and sailors and traders of various backgrounds, but principally from the US. During the development of a plantation economy in the later 19c, Hawaiians and English-speaking plantation owners communicated in so-called *hapa-haole* (half-foreign), probably foreigner talk rather than a pidgin. The crucial years for formation were 1890 to 1910, when most Chinese, Portuguese, and Japanese arrived. The initial pidgin was unstable and varied considerably, depending on the native language of the speaker. It became stable after the turn of the century, when pidgin-speaking immigrants married and brought up children using it as their primary language. At this stage, it was creolized and is now called HAWAII CREOLE ENGLISH.

## ■ HEADLINE ────────── ■

A heading, usually in large, heavy type, at the top of an article in a newspaper, magazine, or other publication, indicating the subject of the article. Constraints on space affect the language of headlines, sometimes known (in its more extreme forms) as *headlinese*. It has developed from more or less conventional syntax to increasingly brief, generalized, powerful, and cryptic units. Particularly in the *banner headlines* of the tabloid press, the VOCABULARY has tended to consist of short, emotive, and suggestive words, often metaphors of violence, such as *axe, clash, cut, hit, oust, slam, slate,* and 'broad-spectrum' words such as *ban, bid, boost, call, curb, link, probe, riddle, scare, swoop, vow.*

**Layout and punctuation**. Although, by and large, banner headlines continue to be popular, styles vary and many newspapers have sedate, largely lower-case styles: the *International Herald Tribune*, with initial capitals on main parts of speech (*For a Day, Pro Football Goes Global in Tokyo and London*); the *Independent*, with an opening initial capital, apart from proper names (*Sex abuse dispute children go home*). Punctuation, once the same as for prose, has been exploited in special conventions, notably among the tabloids: the exclamation mark used to generate interest (*MR K! DON'T BE SO BLOODY RUDE!*); the question mark implying speculation or doubt (*ELECTION PACT?*); both creating a visual shout (*Dogs! Dontcha hate 'em?!*). The comma is increasingly used for *and*: *PETROL, BUTTER PRICE HIKE*; *POUND'S FALL, PM*

*TO ACT.* Conventional punctuation marks may be ignored: *I'm innocent says blast jet woman* (*Observer*, 6 Apr. 1986). Within a headline, quotes mark a statement or allegation from which the newspaper distances itself: *Union opposed to 'liquor police'* (Montreal *Gazette*, 14 Apr. 1983).

**Style and syntax**. Whereas the quality press tends to be relatively sober and restrained, using 'high' register and less immediately emotive words (*Uzbekistan Shocked by the Socialist Heroes Who Lived Like Lords*: IHT, 8 Oct. 1988), the tabloids prefer 'low', colloquial, often pejorative usage (*The Floozy, Fatso and the Fall Guy*: *Daily Mirror*, 8 Feb. 1989). Present-day usage tends to string terms together in concentrated (often opaque) sequences: *Fodor, Ex-Violin Prodigy, Starts Paying the Piper* (IHT, 7 Aug. 1989); *Fox on up up up* (*Observer*, 14 Aug. 1988). Such strings often entail heavy pre-modification (*Deadlock over Anglo-Irish EEC cash bid*: *Independent*, 9 Oct. 1986) and the completely pre-modified *STRIKE BAN SHOCK PROBE*. Abbreviations are common: *Gandhi Assails U.S. on Pakistani N-Arms* (IHT, 13 Sept. 1986).

**Ambiguity and other effects**. Dense headlinese often demands a second reading, because of strange combinations and unintended sense relations: *Payphone revamp plan to cost BT £23 million* (*Guardian*, 11 Mar. 1987); *Blue jean robbery victim legs it after trouser thieves* (Montreal *Gazette*, 30 Nov. 1982). Some headlines are ambiguous until the text has been read: *SLAVE ENDANGERED TREASURE, SAY DAM CRITICS* (Montreal *Gazette*, 25 Aug. 1982) refers not to a bondsman but to the Slave River in Alberta, a stretch of which is regarded as a treasure. The AMBIGUITY can at times be funny: *WOMEN'S BODY SEEKS MEMBER* (Montreal *Gazette*, 30 July 1981). Two possible readings can also serve to embarrass a newspaper: *AMNESTY CHAMPIONS TORTURED GIRL* (*Observer*, 13 Oct. 1985). Word-play is common: *Basquing in glory* (*Independent*, 11 June 1988, about holidays in the Basque Country); *SAV-AGE DEFENCE* (*Guardian*, 20 Feb. 1986), with the text: 'Obstetrician Wendy Savage yesterday attacked male colleagues' intolerance of differing childbirth methods.' ALLUSIONS are also common (*US poaches our eggheads*: *Observer*, 19 July 1987), as well as MIXED METAPHORS (*Labour's last-ditch stand will go off with a bang*: *Independent*, 29 Nov. 1986). See ACRONYM, JOURNALESE, STYLE, TIMESPEAK.

# ■ HEBREW ■

The Semitic language of the ancient Israelites and modern ISRAEL, closely related to Aramaic and Phoenician, more distantly to ARABIC. Hebrew is one of the oldest living languages, best known as the language of the Hebrew or Jewish BIBLE. In biblical times, it was called *yehudit* (Jewish) and in post-biblical rabbinic literature *lashon kodesh* (Holy Tongue). Scholars divide it historically into four phases: *Biblical Hebrew* (*c.*12c BC–*c.*AD 70), *Mishnaic Hebrew* (*c.*AD 70–500), *Medieval Hebrew* (6–13c), and *Modern Hebrew* (from the late 19c). The fourth phase is known to its speakers as *ivrit*, a revived form developed chiefly in Palestine by European Jewish settlers, especially after 1880. It became the predominant language of the state of Israel after 1948 and with Arabic is one of its official languages. It is often referred to as *Israeli Hebrew*. The ALPHABET consists of 22 letters, all consonants. Hebrew is written from right to left with or without vowel signs above and below the consonants. Currently, it has about 4 m speakers, most of whom live in Israel.

**Hebrew in English**. (1) Because of the influence of Bible translations, there have been words and names of Hebrew origin in English since Anglo-Saxon times. They include *amen*, *babel*, *behemoth*, *camel*, *cherub*, *gehenna*, *leviathan*, *manna*, *rabbi*, *Sabbath*, *shekel*, *shibboleth*. (2) A number of religious and cultural terms were introduced during the Renaissance through the works of scholars, such as *Cabbala* 1521, *Talmud* 1532, *Sanhedrin* 1588, *Mishnah* 1610, *mezuzah* 1650. (3) Since the 19c, Yiddish has been an indirect source of Hebraisms, by and large colloquialisms such as *kosher* ritually fit, *all right*, satisfactory, legitimate, *mazuma* money, cash, *shamus* a policeman, detective, *chutzpah* impudence, gall, *goy* a gentile, *megillah* a long story. (4) During the 20c, terms from Modern Hebrew, used mainly by English-speaking Jews, include *kibbutz* a collective Israeli farming community, *hora* a Romanian and Israeli round dance, *moshav* a cooperative Israeli farming community, *sabra* a native-born Israeli.

**English in Hebrew**. The lexical and semantic influence of English on Israeli Hebrew has been considerable. During British rule in Palestine (1917–48), English was an official language. Following the establishment of Israel in 1948, the influence of English on Hebrew continued through American Jewish immigration, various English-language periodicals (notably the *Jerusalem Post*), and English-language motion pictures and television programmes (though most are subtitled in Hebrew). Generally, BrE is the dominant influence, as with *karavan* (a light mobile home) not AmE *trailer*, and *tships* (chips) not *french fries*, but AmE is becoming increasingly popular and includes such colloquialisms as *okey* OK and *hay* Hi. See JEWISH ENGLISH.

**HELPING VERB**. An informal term for AUXILIARY VERB, the class of verbs (such as *be*, *have*, *do*, *may*, *will*) that may combine with a following main verb to form a verb phrase, such as *is watching*, *has eaten*, *may have been playing*.

**HETERONYM**, also **heterograph**. A WORD that is spelt the same as another, but has a different meaning and often pronunciation. There are three heteronyms in the following passage: 'Heteronyms must incense foreign learners! I can't imagine a number feeling than if they spent hours learning a common English word, a minute little word, then found a second meaning and pronunciation!' (opening to 'Heteronyms', David Bergeron, *English Today* 24, Oct. 1990). See HOMONYM, -ONYM.

**HIBERNO-ENGLISH**. A VARIETY of English in Ireland, used mainly by less educated speakers whose ancestral tongue was IRISH GAELIC. It is strongest in and around the *Gaeltachts* (Irish-speaking regions) and in rural areas. It preserves certain Gaelic features in pronunciation, syntax, and vocabulary while at the same time many of its speakers approximate to the ANGLO-IRISH or ULSTER SCOTS norms of the area in which they live.

**Pronunciation**. (1) Such words as *cat* and *garden* sound like 'kyat' and 'gyarden': initial /k/ and /g/ with a following semivowel /j/. (2) Such names as *Hugh* and *Hughes* sound as if they began with a 'ky'. (3) Such words as *true*, *drew* sound like 'threw' and 'dhrew': dental rather than alveolar realizations of /t, d/. (4) In such words as *pine*, *time*, *come*, the opening consonant is aspirated, the /t/ in *time* sounding like a cross between *t* and the *th* in *three*: aspiration of syllable-initial /p, t, k/. (5) Some GAELIC rhythms include the use of an unstressed initial word in questions:

*An' do you like it?*; *An' was it nice?* The un-stressed word is usually *and*, but *well* and *sure* also occur. In Gaelic, questions normally begin with an unstressed element, which in the present tense is *an*: *An maith leat é?* Do you like it?

**Grammar**. Gaelic influence may be found in: (1) A preference for nominal structures: *Give her the full of it* Fill it; *He has a long finger on him* He steals. (2) Constructions with preposition and pronoun together: *His back's at him* He has a backache; *She stole my book on me* She stole my book; *I let a squeal out of me* I squealed. (3) Using *it* to foreground words and phrases: *It's a lovely girl she is now*; *It wasn't to make trouble I went.* (4) Foregrounding emphatic pronouns: *It's meself was the brave runner*; *It was himself I wanted.* (5) Differentiating singular and plural *you*: *You're dead bate, child*; *Yiz is dead bate, childer* You are dead beat (child/children). (6) Using forms of *be* to distinguish aspect: *She's a great wee help about the place*; *She biz a brave help when she comes*; *She doesn't be working all the time.* (7) Using *after* and *-ing* to indicate a recently performed action: *I'm after doing it this very minute.* (8) Using *a-* and *-ing* as a passive: *Where were you? You were a-looking* (being looked for) *this last hour and more.* (9) Using *and*, noun phrase, and *-ing* to show that two actions happen at the same time: *I went in and me trembling*; *In he walks and him whistling.* (10) Using traditional idioms: *She's as light on her foot as a cat at milking*; *There's a truth in the last drop in the bottle.* (11) Referring to God and religion: *In the name of God, did I rare an eejit?* (did I rear an idiot?). (12) Tending not to use *yes* and *no* in answering questions. Irish has no words for *yes/no* and many Irish people therefore tend to answer, for example, *Will you go?—I will*; *Is it yours?—It is not.* (13) Favouring emphatic forms such as *at all at all*, often rhythmic equivalents of Gaelic forms, such as *I'm not tired at all at all* (from *Níl mé tuirseach ar chor ar bith*). The emphatic *at all at all* also occurs in Highland English and the Canadian Atlantic provinces.

**Vocabulary**. Nouns retained from Irish often relate to food (*boxty* a potato dish, from *bacstaidh* mashed potato) and the supernatural (*banshee* a fairy woman, from *bean sídhe* a woman fairy). Others are: *kitter* a left-handed or clumsy person (from *citeóg*), *mass* respect (from *meas*), as in *I've no mass in them things now*, *smig* chin (from *smeig*), as in *It was a blow to the smig that felled him.* Gaelic

influence on meanings can be seen in words such as *destroy* and *drenched*. These have the semantic ranges of their Gaelic equivalents *mill* to injure, spoil (*He has the child destroyed with presents*) and *báite* drenched, drowned, very wet (*You're drowned child. Get all off you. There's not a dry inch to your clothes*). See HIGHLAND ENGLISH, IRISH ENGLISH, NEWFOUNDLAND ENGLISH.

## ■ HIGHLAND ENGLISH ────── ■

The English language as used in areas of the Scottish Highlands where GAELIC was spoken until the late 19c or later, and the Hebrides or Western Isles, where many still have Gaelic as their mother tongue. The varieties of these two areas have also been distinguished as *Highland English* and *Hebridean English* (sometimes *Island English*). Since the late 17c, the majority of the inhabitants of the Highlands and Islands have learned STANDARD ENGLISH by the book, mostly from Gaelic-speaking Highland or Hebridean teachers, only some of whom had studied in Inverness or the Lowlands. The consequent influence of Gaelic is widespread, but most strongly marked among the bilingual speakers of the Isles. It varies in detail with the underlying Gaelic dialect and is also variously influenced from Lowland SCOTS. Some features, of grammar especially, from the Gaelic substrate are shared with HIBERNO-ENGLISH.

**Pronunciation**. (1) Corresponding to the opposition between voiced and voiceless stops in English, Gaelic opposes voiceless unaspirated to voiceless aspirated stops, and lacks voiced consonants opposed to /s/ and /ʃ/. This has led to 'reversal of voicing', as in 'chust' for *just*, 'pleashure' for *pleasure*, 'whateffer' for *whatever*, 'pring' for *bring*, and more rarely the converse, as in 'baratice' for *paradise*. These usages are shibboleths of Gaelic-influenced speech. (2) 'Pre-aspiration' of voiceless stops is widespread: the insertion of an /h/ before certain consonants, as in 'weeʰk' for *week*, 'haʰpen' for *happen*, 'abouʰt' for *about*. (3) The same consonants are aspirated word-initially: 'pʰig' for *pig*, 'tʰake' for *take*, 'kʰeep' for *keep*. (4) In the Hebrides, /l/ is commonly clear. (5) Many speakers pronounce vowels long that are short in SCOTTISH ENGLISH generally: for example, in *bad, father, parlour, psalm, brainy, make, table, equal, heat, leak, weak, boat.* (6) As in the Lowlands and Ireland, some speakers realize such words as *film* and *worm* with epenthetic vowels: 'fillum' and 'wurrum'.

**Grammar**. The following features are characteristic: (1) Cleft sentences and other constructions with thematic fronting: *Isn't it her that's the smart one? Isn't she smart?; It's led astray you are by the keeping of bad company; From Liverpool he was writing*. (2) Simple verb tenses instead of perfect forms: *I'm a widow for ten years now; All my life I never went to the mainland*. (3) Progressive constructions: *Don't be learning bad English to the bairn; We were having plenty vegetables that year; If you can be waiting till the morning, our sale will be starting then*. (4) Distinctive modal usages in conditional and temporal clauses, including 'double *would*': *Try and get here before the rain will come; It's a poor crop we'll be having if there won't be more rain in it; If she would know about it, she would be over straight away*. (5) The formula *to be after doing (something)*, replacing the regular perfect or past: *I'm after taking the bus* I have just taken the bus; *That's me just after cleaning it up* I've just this minute cleaned it up. (6) *Doesn't* in all persons and numbers: *I doesn't know; They doesn't bother*. (7) Non-reflexive use of *-self*: *It's glad I am to be seeing yourself; I'll tell himself you are here; Herself will not be too pleased at that*. (8) Sentence-initial *sure*: *Sure, it'll spoil the taste of it*. (9) Double plurals, especially where the plural is irregular: *Many peoples are coming every year; Three womens did the work*. (10) Singular forms for normally plural words: *She had a trouser on; He cut it with the scissor*. (11) Anticipatory pronoun constructions, especially in questions: *Who is he, the man? Did you see him, the minister?* (12) Elliptical sentence responses replacing or supplementing *yes* and *no*: *Did Iain give you the letter?—He did; Is Morag coming?—She is not; Did you get the job finished?—Ay, we did/so we did*.

**Vocabulary and idiom**. In general, vocabulary is the same as in ScoE at large, and most people use such vernacular Scots words as *bairn* child, *brae* slope, *greet* weep, *oot* out, the negatives *no* (*He's no in*) and *-na* (*I canna say*), and *ay* yes. Many Gaelic words are freely used by Gaelic-speakers and some by non-Gaelic-speakers: *athair* father, *baile* village, *balach* lad, *bodach* old man, *bothan* shebeen, *caileag* young girl, *cailleach* old woman, wife, *duine bochd* poor fellow, *ropach* messy, *srùbag* a drink. Gaelic terms of address, vocatives, and salutations are common among Gaelic-speakers: *m'eudail, mo ghraid,* my

dear, *A Chaluim* Calum!, *A Mhammi* Mummy!, *beannachd leat/leibh* goodbye, *oidhche mhath* good night, *tapadh leat* thank you; *slàinte, slàinte mhath, slàinte mhór* health, good health, big health (all three known and used throughout Scotland as toasts). English and Gaelic may be casually mixed: *Geordie m'eudail, come oot till ye see the ronnags* (stars); *I have the cadaleunain* (pins and needles) *in my fingers*. The preposition *on* features in a number of idioms: *The minister has a terrible cold on him; That beast has a wild look on it; They're putting on him that he stole the sheep; It's on himself the stairn* (confidence) *is*.

**Literary usage**. In Lowland Scottish literature, a suspect tradition that dates from the mid-15c features such Highland shibboleths as the use of *she* and *her nain sell* (her own self) instead of the pronoun *I*: 'Her nainsell has eaten the town pread at the Cross o'Glasgow, and py her troth she'll fight for Bailie Sharvie at the Clachan of Aberfoil' (Walter Scott, *Rob Roy*, 1817, ch. 28). [Translation: I have eaten the town bread at Glasgow Cross and by my troth I'll fight for Bailie Jarvie at the Clachan of Aberfoyle.] Other representations display genuine Highland features, sometimes profusely, as in: 'I don't know what you'll get that you'll be foreffer in Iain Beag's shop. . . . The folk that will be gathering there on nights iss not the company I would be choossing for a son of mine' (Fionn MacColla, *The Albannach*, 1932; Reprographia, 1971). Compare HIBERNO-ENGLISH, ISLE OF MAN, WELSH ENGLISH. See SCOTTISH GAELIC.

**HINDI**. An Indo-Aryan language, spoken by over 250m people in India and by Indians in Britain, Canada, FIJI, GUYANA, South Africa, SURINAM, TRINIDAD AND TOBAGO, the US, and elsewhere. Hindi is the official language of India, with English as associate official language, the state language of Bihar, Haryana, Himachal Pradesh, Madhya Pradesh, Rajasthan, and Uttar Pradesh, and one of India's 15 national languages. It is written in a modified form of the Devanagari script, and its literary tradition dates from medieval times. Hindi proper has three stylistic varieties: a Sanskritized variety used in higher law courts, administration, legislation, journalism, literature, philosophy, and religion; a Persianized variety used in lower law courts, in certain genres of literature, and in films; an Anglicized variety in day-to-day administration, on college campuses, and in scientific and technical registers. See BORROWING, BRITISH LANGUAGES, COCKNEY, CODE-MIXING AN CODE-SWITCHING, INDIAN ENGLISH, SANSKRIT, SOUTH AFRICAN LANGUAGES.

**HINDI-URDU**. A composite name that emphasizes the common linguistic features of HINDI and URDU, languages that have the same general pronunciation, grammar, and vocabulary, but differ in their script, Hindi being written in Devanagari, Urdu in Perso-Arabic. They differ largely because of politics and religion in the Indian subcontinent: Hindi generally favoured by Hindus, Urdu by Muslims. Hindi is the official language of India, Urdu the national language of Pakistan. Both have been extensively influenced by other languages, but whereas Hindi looks especially to SANSKRIT for its technical vocabulary and literary conventions, Urdu looks especially to Persian and ARABIC. Both have borrowed extensively from English.

**HINDLISH**, also **Hinglish**. Informal terms for a mixture of HINDI and English that includes such HYBRID expressions as *city Kotwali* (city police station) and *relgari* (railway train), and complete sentences such as *Maĩ āp ko batātī hum̃, he is a very trusting person* I tell you, he is a very trusting person. See CODE-MIXING AND CODE-SWITCHING, INDIAN ENGLISH.

**HISTORICAL LINGUISTICS**, also **diachronic linguistics**. The branch of linguistics that deals with changes in language through time. Like PHILOLOGY, from whose later forms it is virtually indistinguishable, it studies language records, but may also include methods of synchronic linguistics in its approach to sounds, forms, meanings, or the social motivation of language change. See DIACHRONIC AND SYNCHRONIC LANGUAGE FAMILY.

■ **HISTORY OF ENGLISH** ──── ■

The history of a language can be an *internal history* (of linguistic categories such as sounds, structure, and vocabulary) and an *external history* (of geographical and social spread, attitudes toward the language, study of its features, and attempts at its regulation). Such a dual approach is useful so long as it does not ignore changes that overlap these categories, as when ENGLISH

borrowed heavily from FRENCH, in which attitudes (an external factor) influenced vocabulary (an internal feature.)

**Prehistory**. Almost all knowledge of English before *c.*600 is hypothetical, a reconstruction based on later documents in English and on earlier documents in related languages. Scholars agree, however, that the ultimate origins of English lie in INDO-EUROPEAN (IE), a postulated ancient language which may have been spoken in north-eastern Europe or near the Black Sea between *c.*3000 and *c.*2000 BC and can now only be reconstructed from its descendants. The incremental changes that produced the obviously related English *daughter*, GERMAN *Tochter*, Armenian *dushtr*, GREEK *thugátēr*, and SANSKRIT *duhitár* (etc.) from a common original are still at work; thus, the English spelling *daughter* masks a variety of pronunciations including *DAWtuh* and *DAHdur*, in which only the initial sound remains the same. IE ceased to exist sometime soon after 2000 BC, having diversified into a number of increasingly distinct offspring as a result of migration and natural linguistic changes. One of these offspring is known to scholars as *Primitive Germanic*, which like the original IE has left no written records. The Germanic-speaking peoples appear to have moved from the IE homeland to what is now Scandinavia and northern Germany, from which they later spread in several migrations, leaving a northern branch behind, creating a small eastern branch that included Gothic, and a much larger western branch, which was the source of German, DUTCH, and English, among others.

**Old English**. Several migrating tribes from northern Germany reached Britain in the early 5c speaking the mutually intelligible dialects which in their new home are now called *OLD ENGLISH (OE)* or *ANGLO-SAXON*. The first written form of the language was runic letters, replaced during the conversion to Christianity of the Anglo-Saxons after 597 by the LATIN alphabet, which was adapted to serve OE, making use of some runic letters and some letter shapes used by Irish scribes. Although OE was used as a literary medium and was the language of the ANGLO-SAXON CHRONICLE, it did not seriously rival Latin as an administrative or intellectual medium, and within a century of the Norman Conquest of 1066 it was dead. Like other early IE languages, it distinguished three grammatical persons, not only in the plural (as in modern English *we, you, they*) but in the singular (as in Early Modern English *I, thou, she/he/it*). It also distinguished three genders and five cases, categories that extended to the article, adjective, and noun. OE showed the effects of GRIMM'S LAW in its consonants, such as *p > f*, IE *\*peku* property (as in Latin *pecus*) becoming OE *feoh*, and *t > th*, IE *\*trei* three (as in Latin *tri-*) becoming OE *þrī*.

**Middle English.** Many linguistic changes occurred in late OE, and in MIDDLE ENGLISH (ME) almost every feature of OE changed radically, so that though late ME such as CHAUCER's usage remains intelligible now 600 years later, little or nothing of OE could have been intelligible to Chaucer only 300 years after the Norman Conquest. In structure, the elaborate system of cases, genders, and numbers vanished from the adjective and article, dwindled in the noun, and remained only in the personal pronouns. The form of verbs was less changed, though increasing numbers of 'strong' verbs like MODERN ENGLISH *drive* (past tense *drove*) joined the larger group of 'weak' verbs, like *climb* (past tense *climbed*); Chaucer has the strong past *clomb*. The modals *shall* and *will* (and their past tenses *should* and *would*) developed a use, almost unknown in OE, as expressions of the future.

ME DIALECTS are more numerous than OE dialects, and unregulated spelling often reflects the variations: in the late 14c, *church* appears in the North of England and in Scotland as *kirk(e)* or *kyrk(e)*, in the South-East as *cherch(e)* and *chirch(e)*, in the South-West as *church(e)*, and in the Midlands as a mixture of these forms plus *chyrch(e)*. There were more works of LITERATURE, especially in the EAST MIDLAND DIALECT, first largely through translation from LATIN and FRENCH. A variety of ME flourished as almost a separate language (at least in political terms) in Scotland. Also known as Middle SCOTS, it was dominant over GAELIC at the court of the kings of Scots and had a literature that included both epic and lyric poetry. In addition, varieties of ME and NORMAN FRENCH were being spoken in Wales and Ireland.

The most striking internal development is vocabulary. Some personal pronouns changed, the feminine from OE *hē* to *she*, the plural from OE *hīe* to *they*, with eventually *them* and *their*. More far-reaching,

however, were the borrowings, mostly from French, that transformed English from an almost wholly Germanic language to a language of mixed Germanic-Romance composition. See BISOCIATION.

**Early Modern English.** From the Renaissance onwards, as the structure of the STANDARD LANGUAGE stabilizes, comments about it become more frequent and external factors and influences become more marked and more important. In 1490, CAXTON observed the changes in English since he was born, and its variation in the several parts of England. He felt unsure about the correct literary mixture of old native words and their new borrowed and scholarly counterparts, and his spelling was inconsistent. His own introduction of PRINTING to England (1476), however, did much to spread the new features of English. Renaissance exploration added new words to the vocabulary. *Hurricano* appears in Shakespeare, but only in his last plays; the form shows that it came by way of Spanish, not directly from its West Indian origin, the Amerindian language Taino. Developments in the arts and sciences produced a huge influx of words, such as *sonnet* (from ITALIAN via French) and *sextant* (from NEO-LATIN). Exploration also enhanced the stature of English by establishing the language in new territories from Africa to the Americas. The Reformation provided a further impulse for TRANSLATION, not only in the sequence of English BIBLE translations from Tyndale (1526) to the Authorized Version (1611), but also in the translation of Greek and Roman classics.

With the accession of the Tudors to the English throne (1485), the increase of national pride promoted greater confidence in the VERNACULAR for original writing, often expressed with an exuberance of literary style, especially in the Elizabethan age. The range of the language was further enlarged when James VI King of Scots became James I of England in 1603. This event not only made possible the development of a standard language, especially in writing and print, throughout Britain and Ireland and later in North America and colonies elsewhere, but brought the King's English and the King's Scots together in one monarch. The outstanding symbol of this realignment into one variety of educated usage was the publication in 1611 of the Authorized Version of the Bible. The forms of

Renaissance English show the effects of the GREAT VOWEL SHIFT, though it was still incomplete. The development of some features of structure, such as -s for -th (hears instead of heareth), led for a time to competition: SHAKESPEARE used both, while the King James Bible used only -th. The preface to JOHNSON's Dictionary of the English Language (1755) and the American Declaration of Independence (1776) scarcely used the -th form, and both reveal that most other main features of Modern English structure were in place wherever English was used by the late 18c. However, pronunciation continued to change and diversify in the speech of all social classes and regional groups: Pope rhymed tea with obey, Johnson could find no certain authority for the sound of sea, and break still remains one of the few words with the old pronunciation of -ea-. The increasing uniformity of spelling, however, has tended to mask this diversity. See EARLY MODERN ENGLISH.

**(Late) Modern English**. In the 18c, the diaspora of English gained momentum. Not only was the language used almost everywhere in Britain and Ireland, to the increasing detriment of the CELTIC LANGUAGES, but the Crown gained Canada and India in competition with the French and supplanted the Dutch in colonizing Australia. In Britain and Ireland there had always been many subjects of the Crown for whom English was not the first or preferred language. Now, as English spread across the globe, large numbers began to use it as a second or learned it as a foreign language. In turn, English gained new vocabulary from languages throughout the world: words like Nahuatl tomato, Eskimo kayak, Hindi chintz, now so thoroughly assimilated that they retain no echoes of their exotic origins. With increasing scope and variety came increasing attempts at regulation. In 1664, a committee of the recently formed ROYAL SOCIETY of London sought to propound a set of rules for English, and in 1712 SWIFT proposed an ACADEMY comparable to the Académie française, 'for ascertaining and fixing our Language for ever'. Neither attempt succeeded. The English of Swift's day lacked the kind of reference books from which he had learned his Latin: the few GRAMMARS were sketchy and the dictionaries listed only the 'hard words' created by Renaissance borrowing and invention. In 1721, Bailey's DICTIONARY made an attempt at comprehensiveness,

and Johnson's dictionary in 1755 laid the foundation of modern LEXICOGRAPHY, though it recorded little but the literary vocabulary, and none from its own day. In 1762 appeared LOWTH's grammar, which set the tradition of concentration on 'errors' in usage, agreeing with Swift's opinions while finding fault with his grammar.

The growth of natural science after 1800 produced numberless new theories and products, along with knowledge of new substances, processes, and ailments, all nameless. Many received names composed by ANALOGY with their formulas (carbon monoxide); others were named for their discoverer (Hansen's Disease), by ACRONYM (AIDS), or by classical BORROWING (rabies, Latin for rage). The language of newer fields like computer science often gives technical meaning to familiar words: Apple Mac, dumb terminal, mouse. Among the new sciences was LINGUISTICS, the objective study of language. Emboldened by the achievements of philology in the first quarter of the 19c, scholars set aside such impressionistic views of language as Addison's that English was distinctively 'modest, thoughtful and sincere'. They also gave up culturally biased attempts to link HEBREW to Latin and Greek, and took account in their studies of non-Western languages such as Sanskrit. The publication of The OXFORD ENGLISH DICTIONARY under the leadership of J. A. H. MURRAY (1888–1933, with Supplements 1972–86, 2nd edition 1989) is a monument of late 19c linguistic science. See App. 1: CHRONOLOGY.

See AFRICAN ENGLISH, ALFRED, AMERICAN ENGLISH, AUSTRALIAN ENGLISH, BRITISH ENGLISH, CANADIAN ENGLISH, DANELAW, ETYMOLOGY, IRISH ENGLISH, NORSE, STANDARD ENGLISH.

**HOMOGRAPH**. A kind of HOMONYM: one of two or more words that are identical in SPELLING but different in origin, meaning, and PRONUNCIATION, such as entrance (noun: stress on first syllable) a door, gate, etc., and entrance (verb: stress on second syllable) to put in a trance; lead (verb: rhyming with 'deed') to take, conduct, guide, etc., and lead (noun: rhyming with 'dead') a metal.

**HOMONYM**. One of two or more words that are identical in sound or spelling but different in meaning. There are three kinds: those that sound and look alike (bank[1] a slope, bank[2] a place for money, and bank[3] a bench or row of switches); *HOMOPHONES*, that sound alike but do not look alike (*coarse*, *course*); and *HOMOGRAPHS*, that look alike but do not sound alike (the verb *lead* /liːd/, the metal *lead* /lɛd/). The occurrence of homographs is largely a matter of chance, although a tendency to assimilate the unfamiliar to the familiar is also a factor, as with *compound* (an enclosure, originally Malay *kampong*), and *pigeon* (as in 'not my pigeon', a variant of *pidgin*). Dictionaries distinguish homographs by means of superscript numbers preceding or following them, largely on the basis of etymology. The degree of separation in dictionaries usually depends on the extent to which variation in etymology is taken into account: for example, *bank* (slope) and *bank* (a place for money) are ultimately related, but have had sufficiently divergent routes on their way to English to warrant separate treatment. See CONFUSIBLE, HETERONYM, JANUS WORD, POLYSEMY.

**HOMOPHONE**. One of two or more words that are identical in sound but different in spelling and meaning: *beer/bier*, *there/their/they're*. The occurrence of homophones is largely a matter of historical chance, in which words with distinct meanings come to coincide phonologically: *byre* a cowshed, *buyer* one who buys. Words may be homophones in one variety of English but not another: *father/farther* and *for/four* are homophonous in RP, but not in AmE and ScoE; *wails/Wales* are general homophones; *wails/Wales/whales* are homophones for many, but not in IrE and ScoE. *Whether/whither* are homophones in Scotland, but not *whether/weather*, which are homophones in England. See HOMONYM.

**HONDURAS**. See BAY ISLANDS, BELIZE.

**HONG KONG**, also **Hongkong**. An autonomous region of CHINA, formerly a British colony. Languages: Cantonese, English, and Mandarin Chinese. In 1842, by the Treaty of Nanking, Hong Kong Island was ceded to Britain; in 1898, the mainland New Territories were leased to Britain for 99 years. The colony was restored to China in 1997. English is important in Hong Kong for written and printed communication, as a LINGUA FRANCA between Chinese and non-Chinese, and in international trade, but is not widely used as a spoken medium. Of

some 40 daily newspapers, two are in English: the *South China Morning Post* and the *Hongkong Standard*.

Hong Kong usage includes: (1) Words and phrases from Chinese: *dim sum* snacks served in Chinese restaurants, *fung shui* ('wind-water') geomancy used in deciding the sites, orientation, and design of buildings, *gweilo* ('ghost person') a European, *hong* a large usually long-established non-Chinese trading company, *pak choi* Chinese cabbage, *taipan* the head of a hong. (2) LOAN TRANSLATIONS from Chinese: *dragon boat* a long canoe-like boat raced at festivals, *snakehead* a smuggler of illegal immigrants. (3) Terms from other languages: *amah* (Portuguese) a maid, *godown* (Malay) a warehouse, *shroff* (Arabic through Persian and Anglo-Indian English) a cashier in a government office. (4) Local uses of general words: *the mainland* China proper; *triad* a secret criminal society. See EAST ASIAN ENGLISH.

**HORNBY, A(lbert) S(idney)** [1898–1978]. English grammarian and EFL teacher, born in Chester, and educated at U. College London. From 1923, he taught English in Tokyo, where he worked with Harold E. Palmer at the Institute for Research in English Teaching. In 1937, with E. V. Gatenby and H. Wakefield, he began work on an innovative DICTIONARY for foreign learners that would provide lexical, syntactic, and idiomatic information. It was completed in 1940 and published in 1942 in Tokyo by Kaitakusha, as *The Idiomatic and Syntactic English Dictionary*. When Hornby left Japan in 1939 he joined the BRITISH COUNCIL and after the war became editor of *English Language Teaching*. In 1948, the dictionary was reissued by Oxford University Press as *A Learner's Dictionary of Current English*. In 1963, its revision was retitled *The Advanced Learner's Dictionary of Current English*, the greatest commercial success in ELT publishing. See LEARNER'S DICTIONARY.

■ **HOUSE STYLE** ─────── ■

A term for rules adopted to bring uniformity and consistency to printed material coming from one source, such as a government department, publishing house, newspaper, professional association, or commercial company. Such organizations usually find it necessary to have a policy for points of STYLE and USAGE that arise in WRIT-

ING and PRINTING, and occasionally in SPEAKING. These include often delicate choices relating to: (1) SPELLING variants: *inquire* or *enquire*, *judgement* or *judgment*, *matins* or *mattins*, *publicize* or *publicise*. (2) The spelling and PRONUNCIATION of foreign names: *Beijing* or *Peking*, *Marseilles* or *Marseille*, *Moslem* or *Muslim*. (3) Style in ABBREVIATIONS, capitalization, etc.: *B.B.C.* or *BBC*; *the Company or the company*. (4) Contentious general usages: *the Arabian Gulf, the Persian Gulf*, or *the Gulf; Holland* or *The Netherlands; chair, chairman, chairperson*. (5) Contentious grammatical issues: *the management is/are; anyone . . . he* or *anyone . . . they*. (6) Use of double and single quotation marks: *He said, 'Tell us about it'* or *He said, "Tell us about it."* (7) Hyphenation or non-hyphenation: *dining room* or *dining-room; make-up* or *makeup*. (8) Compounding: *news letter* or *news-letter* or *newsletter*. (9) Inclusive language: *businessman* or *businesswoman*, or *businessperson*; generic *he* or *she* or *(s)he* or *he or she* or *she or he* or singular *they*.

In such matters, independent writers may find individual solutions on a longer- or shorter-term basis. Few such writers, however, are fully consistent in what they do and are often willing to alter their usages in relation to the expectations of publishers and tors. This means that the evidence of usage in printed material is not necessarily that of the authors, especially in such areas as spelling and pronunciation. Published material associated with an organization, especially in the media, almost always becomes subject to standardization, so as to create a consistent and even authoritative image. Rules are formulated so that people know where they are, creating in effect 'localized' versions of a standard language (established, as it were, by small-scale 'academies'). If writers do not for any reason follow the rules, editors, subeditors/copyeditors, printers, and proof-readers usually make the necessary changes (but even so some writers succeed in going their own way). Such rules make up a *house style*, often organized in a *style sheet, style guide*, or *style manual* for distribution and easy consultation. Such sheets, guides, and manuals usually become more consistent and detailed as time passes. They are usually available only within an organization, but may sometimes be more widely distributed or even published as commercial titles. This was the case with Ernest Gowers's *The Complete Plain Words* (1954), compiled for the benefit of British civil servants, and Keith Waterhouse's *Waterhouse on Newspaper Style* (1989), based on the house handbook for *Daily Mirror* journalists.

**Great Britain**. One of the most influential house styles in the UK is that of OXFORD UNIVERSITY PRESS, made publicly available in 1904 in the first published edition of *Hart's Rules* (see below), and in 1905 in the *Authors' and Printers' Dictionary*, ed. F. Howard Collins. Collins relied to a great extent on the *OED*, but often broke new ground where no previous guidance existed: for example, as to when to use initial capitals for words such as *Bible, Act of Parliament, New Year's Day, Squire*. Many of the rules that he formulated have since become widely accepted in BrE. 'Collins', as the handbook became known, influenced the house style of *The Times* and other newspapers, as well as publishing houses and learned societies. The 11th edition of the dictionary (1973) was extensively revised and rewritten, and published in 1981 as *The Oxford Dictionary for Writers and Editors (ODWE*, 448 pp.), ed. R. E. Allen, D. J. Edmonds, and J. B. Sykes. As a guide to usage, it is offered in conjunction with *Hart's Rules*, a work first compiled by Horace Hart in 1893, primarily for printers. The Press made the 15th edition available to the public in 1904, and the 39th was published in 1983 (182 pp.), revised and extended so as to complement *ODWE*. In 1986, the Press published a third work, *The Oxford Spelling Dictionary* (229 pp.), compiled by R. E. Allen, which also gives word divisions. Whereas the dictionaries provide information on individual items (*focused* not *focussed, tumour* not *tumor*), *Hart's Rules* has three sections: Rules for Setting English, Spellings, and Rules for Setting Foreign Languages.

**The United States**. American style manuals tend to be more detailed and to cover more topics than their British counterparts. The most influential is *The Chicago Manual of Style* (U. of Chicago Press, 13th edition, 1982, 738 pp.). It covers book formats, manuscript preparation and copy-editing, proofs, rights and permissions, design and typography, composition, printing, binding, general points of style, punctuation, numbers, illustrations and captions, tables, documentation styles, bibliographic forms, note forms, and indexes. Many publishing houses and university presses use it as their principal reference. Based on the *Chicago Manual*, Kate L. Turabian's *Manual for Writers of Term Papers, Theses, and Dissertations* (U. of Chicago Press, 5th edition, ed. Bonnie Birtwhistle Honigsblum, 1987) is a shortened, specialized 300-page version. Academic associations publish manuals geared to various disciplines, whose style (especially for documentation and citation) may vary greatly. In the humanities, *The MLA Style Manual* by Walter S. Achtert and Joseph Gibaldi (Modern Language Association of America, 1985, 271 pp.) is comprehensive and influential. It gives guidance in all matters of manuscript preparation and publication. The citation and documentation style it recommends (parenthetical documentation in the text keyed to a final list of references) has become the norm, replacing footnotes. A version for students is the *MLA Handbook for Writers of Research Papers* (MLA, 2nd edition, 1984, 221 pp.).

Comparable works for other disciplines are the *Publication Manual of the American Psychological Association* (American Psychological Association, 3rd edition, 1983, 208 pp.) and the *CBE Style Manual* (by the Committee on Form and Style of the Council of Biology Editors, American Institute of Biological Sciences, 3rd edition, 1972, 297 pp.). Most major newspapers have house styles, some of which are generally available and influential. *The New York Times Style Book for Writers and Editors* (ed. Lewis Jordan, McGraw-Hill, 1962, 124 pp.) and *The Washington Post Deskbook on Style* (ed. Thomas W. Lippman, McGraw-Hill, 2nd edition, 1989, 249 pp.) are typical. Similar are works of news services, such as *The UPI Stylebook* (ed. Bobby Ray Miller, United Press International, 1977, 200 pp.) and *The Associated Press Stylebook and Libel Manual* (ed. Christopher W. French, Addison-Wesley, 1987, 341 pp.). These works are primarily alphabetical lists of problems with recommendations (comparable to *ODWE*, above), but may include general information on matters of special concern in reportage. A guide for US government publications, the *United States Government Printing Office Style Manual* (US GPO, 1984, 479 pp.), began in 1894 and is now in its 28th version. In addition to matters of general style, it gives attention to legal records, the *Congressional Record*, and other specialized government publications. It also includes information on the printed

form of major foreign languages. A small supplement is devoted to *Word Division* (US GPO, 1987, 142 pp.).

See AUSTRALIAN ENGLISH, BBC ENGLISH, CANADIAN STYLE GUIDES, DICTIONARY OF MODERN ENGLISH USAGE, USAGE GUIDANCE AND CRITICISM.

**HUMOUR** BrE, **humor** AmE. Originally a mental disposition or temperament, fossilized in such forms as *good-humoured* and *ill-humoured*, humour is currently realized in the enjoyment of anecdotes, jokes, puns, repartee, riddles, wisecracks, and witticisms. Not all humour is verbal, and by no means everything that is humorous is also witty, though humour and wit are customarily neighbours, humour relating to situations and wit to the sayings the situations evoke. Some expressions of humour appear to be primordial and universal, transcending languages, independent of cultures, exacting sympathy with elementary human fears, aspirations, placations, aversions. This wordless humour is often presented graphically, as in cartoons, but, as language becomes its mediator, humour becomes increasingly culture-dependent. The JOKE usually presupposes a social bond, joker and audience drawing freely on a stock of common knowledge involving a shared history. Within this general societal humour there exist institutional types, associated with certain professions (the law, the Church) or social subgroups (children, the old, the family).

What is called a *sense of humour*, as if it were a skill like ability in mathematics or music, is a complex effect of people's experience as members of a culture, a nation, and various kinds of community. It might more appropriately be called a 'sense *for* humour': an ability to judge the acceptability of humour in certain situations, and a willingness to regard the capacity to laugh and to evoke laughter as legitimate behaviour. In social terms, there are times when people are free to make jokes, times when they need to make jokes, and times when joking is inhibited or disallowed.

The relationship between humour and society is obvious enough to prompt a common assumption, that particular societies, or nations, have symptomatic styles and preferences in humour. The assumption is challenged, however, by the fact that many jokes traverse the world and travel through time, as general comments on human nature and human thought, only modified in their presentation by local details of custom and setting. An ancient Roman joke tells how a man is accidentally knocked down in the street by a porter carrying a trunk. 'Look out!' says the porter. 'Why?' asks the victim, 'Is there another trunk coming?' This joke is an archetype with many subsequent realizations: for instance, in the slapstick film routines of workmen carrying planks that strike the same victim twice (one end at a time). See IRONY, NONSENSE, PATTER, PLAYING WITH WORDS, PUN, SATIRE.

**HYBRID**, also **hybrid word**. A WORD whose elements come from more than one language: *television* (from Greek *tele-*, Latin *vision*), *jollification* (from English *jolly*, Latin *-ification*). Attitudes to hybrids have been influenced by views on propriety and aesthetics. Traditionally, they have been considered barbarisms; purists have assumed that just as Latin, Greek, French, and English are distinct languages, so elements from these languages within English should be distinct. Hybridization has grown steadily in the 20c, with such words as *genocide, hydrofoil, hypermarket, megastar, microwave, photo-journalism, Rototiller, Strip-a-gram, volcanology*. See AFRICAN ENGLISH, ANGLO-HYBRID, BARBARISM, COMBINING FORM, INDIAN ENGLISH, THEMATIC VOWEL.

**HYPERBOLE**. [Stress: 'high-PER-bo-ly']. A term in RHETORIC for exaggeration or overstatement, usually deliberate and not meant to be taken (too) literally: 'Old Celtic myths have been springing up around these hills and lakes since the very start of time' (Tom Davies, 'Home & Garden', *Times Saturday Review*, 18 Aug. 1990). Everyday idioms are often hyperbolic: *a flood of tears, loads of room, tons of money, waiting for ages, as old as the hills, having the time of one's life*. Their purpose is effect and emphasis, but frequency of use diminishes their impact.

**HYPERCORRECTION**. Over-correction resulting in usages that may be regarded as amusing, deplorable, and/or tokens of the insecurity that prompted it. In NEW YORK City, highly stigmatized pronunciations (represented in print as, for example, *Toity-Toid Street* for Thirty-Third Street) are popularly associated with Brooklyn (although they are widespread throughout the work-

ing class). Speakers who want to dissociate themselves from this accent often 'correct' all forms which contain *oi*, so that *toilet* becomes 'terlet' and *boil* becomes 'berl'. Such hypercorrections have often themselves become STEREOTYPES and SHIBBOLETHS.

**HYPERTEXT**. A term in COMPUTING for text made up of short units (typically a paragraph, or 24-line screen) between which the reader may jump using links assigned in advance: see WORLDWIDE WEB. Unlike a book, in which the pages are in sequence, hypertext allows any of a number of pages to follow the one being read, in any order one wishes. A hypertext system, such as *Apple Hypercard*, contains a great many *frames*, each of which normally contains a single screenful of information. In each frame are several *buttons* or *arrows* which the reader can activate, and which call up another frame, on the same principle as a cross-reference in text on paper. Hypertext derives from an idea put forward in 1945 by the US computer designer Vannevar Bush, and the term was coined by the US entrepreneur Ted Nelson. Educational and other systems which include pictures and sound, are known as *hypermedia*.

## ■ HYPHEN ──────── ■

The PUNCTUATION mark (-), which has two main functions in present-day English: as a *link hyphen* (or *hard hyphen* in printing terminology), joining whole words or elements of words into longer words and compounds (*house-plant, Anglo-French*); as a *break hyphen* (or *soft hyphen*), marking the division of a word at the end of a line, especially in print (*divi-sion, liter-ature*).

**The link hyphen**. The use of the hyphen to mark COMPOUND WORDS has existed in English since the 16c, and from an earlier date in various forms in words such as *to-day* and *with-out*. It has always been variable and unpredictable. In recent use, it appears to be diminishing in some circumstances: for example, when the elements of a compound are monosyllabic (*birdsong, eardrum, playgroup; lambswool*, formerly *lamb's wool*), in longer formations where the elements are regarded as closely associated (*business-woman, nationwide*); where the two elements are regarded as having equal semantic weight, with the first acting as a modifier, forming a spaced pair (*road sign, snow goose*); and in prefixed forms such as *coordinate* and *reuse*. The absence of the hyphen in such cases is well established in AmE, and is becoming more common in BrE. The hyphen continues in BrE and AmE in both routine and occasional couplings when the elements seem to retain a stronger individual identity, and in ad-hoc formations: *boiler-room, filling-station*. In the second of these, *filling* is a noun ('a station for filling') and not a participle ('a station that fills'), which the absence of a hyphen might imply. Usage, however, is rarely consistent or completely logical in this regard. A hyphen is often retained to avoid awkward collisions of letters, as in *breast-stroke, co-worker*, and *radio-isotope*, but usage varies even in these cases, often in keeping the elements of compounds separate (*breast stroke, radio isotope*), and occasionally merging them (*breaststroke, radioisotope*).

The link hyphen also has a role in punctuation: (1) To establish such syntactic links as *truck-driver, labour-saving*, and *brown-eyed*. In the phrases *hard-covered books* and *French-speaking visitors*, the reference is to 'books with hard covers' and 'visitors who speak French'; here, hyphenation prevents misunderstanding and parallels the stress patterns of speech: *hárd-covered bóoks* and *Frénch-speaking péople* as opposed to *hard cóvered bóoks* and *French spéaking péople*. (2) To form expression with a phrasal base, such as *drink-affected* (affected by drink), *weed-infested* (infested with weeds), and *panic-stricken* (stricken by panic). (3) To avoid ambiguity in *twenty-odd people* (compare *twenty odd people*). (4) To connect the elements of associated words used attributively as in *a well-known woman* and *Christmas-tree lights*, but not predicatively as in *the woman is well known* and *the lights on the Christmas tree*. (5) Connecting nouns in apposition that form a single concept, such as *city-state* (a city that is also a state) and *player-manager* (a manager who is also a player), and in units such as *passenger-mile* (a mile travelled by one passenger: a statistical usage). (6) Connecting elements to form words in cases such as *re-enact* (where the collision of the first and second *e* might be awkward), *re-form* (meaning 'to form again' as opposed to *reform*), and some prefixed words such as those in *anti-, non-, over-,* and *past-*. Usage varies in this regard, especially as between BrE and AmE. In AmE, solid forms such as *reenact* and *nonstandard*

are common. In general terms, a great deal depends on how established and recognizable a formation is: when the second element begins with a capital letter, a hyphen is usual, as in *anti-Darwinian*. There are no hard-and-fast rules.

**The break hyphen.** The hyphen is used to divide a word at the end of a line, especially in print when words are spaced out to fill lines with justified margins. In handwritten texts, typed or word-processed material, and unjustified print, word-breaks can usually be avoided. In print, it has traditionally been a matter of pride with printers and publishers to ensure a careful division of words when line-breaks occur, taking account of the appearance and structure of the word. There are two basic approaches, *phonetic* (in terms of syllable structure) and *morphological* (in terms of word structure). Broadly, AmE favours a phonetic approach (preferring *trium-phant* to *triumph-ant*), while BrE has usually given greater weight to a morphological approach, although preferences are widely varied (*veg-etable, vege-table, ve-getable*). Newspapers in all English-speaking countries tend to produce word divisions that reflect neither criterion (such as *bat-hroom, se-arched, da-ily*), usually because the line-breaks in their computer typesetting programs are based on fairly crude principles such as division between two consonants. The traditional aim of word division at line-breaks is to distract the reader as little as possible. See DIAERESIS, OBLIQUE, PHRASE WORD, SENTENCE WORD, SYLLABICATION.

**HYPONYM**, also **subordinate term**. A WORD, PHRASE, or LEXEME of narrower or more specific meaning that comes 'under' another of wider or more general meaning: for example, *rose* under *flower* ('a rose is a kind of flower', 'flowers include roses and tulips'). In this relationship, the word *flower* is a *hyperonym, generic term*, or *superordinate term*. Many hyponyms belong in groups, such as *carpet, chair, desk, table, rug, stool*, all of which are *co-hyponyms* of the hyperonym *furniture* ('a carpet is an item of furniture'). Hyponymic relations are often imprecise, unstable, and multidimensional, depending on both context and how relationships are analysed. The same word may be a hyponym of several superordinates: *axe* as 'kind of tool' and 'kind of weapon'; *weapon* also a hyponym of *tool* ('a weapon is a kind of tool'). *Battle-axe* is 'a kind of axe' and 'a kind of weapon', but is unlikely to appear under *axe* in the SENSE of 'a kind of tool'.

*Rug* is in some contexts a synonym of *carpet* ('The cat sat on the rug/carpet'), in others a hyponym of *carpet* ('a rug is a kind of carpet'). See -ONYM, SEMANTICS.

# I

# I, i

[Called 'eye']. The 9th LETTER of the Roman ALPHABET as used for English. It originated in the Phoenician symbol *yod* (representing the sound of *y* in *yes*) which was adapted in GREEK to a vertical line for the vowel called *iota*. This was adopted by the Romans as *I* with both long and short LATIN vowel values, and also for the consonant value of *y*. In medieval times, a superscript dot was added to distinguish minuscule *i* in manuscript from adjacent vertical strokes in such letters as *u*, *m*, *n*. The variant form *j* emerged at this time and subsequently became a separate letter.

**Sound values**. It is difficult to fix a precise primary value for *i* in English. There is free variation between different values of *i* in the first syllable of words such as *digest*, *finance*, *minority*, *tribunal*. Elsewhere, there is a regular shift between related words: *child/children*, *five/fifth*, *crime/criminal*, *finish/final(ity)*, *social/society*, *admire/admirable*. Variation in sound is overlaid by two uncertainties in SPELLING: except word-initially, both *i* and *y* can represent the same sound, even as alternatives: *gipsy/gypsy*, *siphon/syphon*, *laniard/lanyard*, *drier/dryer*. Many spellings are available for the one sound in the final syllables of *souvenir*, *Kashmir* (contrast *cashmere*), *cavalier*, *weir*, *musketeer*, *sincere*, *appear*. The result is a varied distribution of values, as follows:

**Short I**. (1) In most monosyllabic words before pronounced word-final consonants: *ill*, *in*, *is*; *bid*, *big*, *bit*; *which*, *sing*, *dish*, *with*; *fifth*, *milk*, *kiln*, *film*, *filth*, *wind* (noun), *link*, *hint*, *plinth*, *lisp*, *list*. However, long *i* occurs in this position in *pint*, *ninth* and *child*, *mild*, *wild* (but not *build*, *gild*, *guild*) and in *bind*, *find*, *kind*, *wind* (verb), etc. Short *i* occurs in *give*, *to live*, but long *i* in *dive*, *five*, *alive*. Similarly, short *i* occurs in *river*, *liver*, but long *i* in *diver*, *fiver*. (2) In most polysyllables before a doubled consonant (*bitter*, *bitty*, *cirrus*, *irrigate*, *immigrant*) and commonly before single consonants (*city*, *finish*, *spirit*, *river*, *consider*, *imitate*, *iridescent*, *limit*, *litigation*, *magnificent*, *ridiculous*). (3) Occasionally before a consonant and word-final *e* (*give*,

*live*, *active*, *heroine*, *imagine*, *definite*), although *i* is normally long in this environment. (4) The sound of short *i* is often spelt with *y*, especially to represent the Greek letter upsilon, as in *myth*, *symbol*. Other vowel letters may also have this value: *e* in *pretty* and Greek-derived words such as *acme*, *catastrophe*; *o* in the plural *women*; *u* in *busy*, *business*. Certain unstressed vowels vary in pronunciation between short *i* and other values, especially schwa: *a* as in *furnace*, *cottage*, *e* as in *began*, *despair*, *hated*, *college*, *u* as in *lettuce*, *minute* (noun). (5) In RP, a modified short *i* occurs before single *r*, when *ir* is not directly followed by another vowel: *sir*, *stir*, *bird*, *girl*, *squirm*, *first*, *birth*, *circle*, *virtue*. The same modification occurs with the short values of *e*, *u*, *y*, producing the homophones *birth/berth*, *fir/fur*. (6) The letter *i* does not occur word-finally in traditional English spelling, its sound being represented by *y*, but such a short *i* or a lengthened variant (depending partly on accent) is found in some recent formations and loans: *taxi*, *safari*, *spaghetti*. A length distinction between this value and short *i* may be heard in *taxiing*, a distinction some speakers also make between the two vowels of *city*.

**Long I**. (1) Monosyllables and disyllables before one or sometimes two consonants preceding word-final *e*: *ice*, *tribe*, *wife*, *like*, *pile*, *time*, *fine*, *ripe*, *mire*, *kite*, *strive*, *size*; *idle*, *rifle*, *isle*, *title*, *mitre*. (2) In disyllabic verbs ending in a stressed Latin root, whose corresponding nouns often have short *i*: *ascribe/ascription*, *collide/collision*, *decide/decision*, *invite/invitation*, *provide/provision*, *reside/residence*. (3) In monosyllables before: *-gh* (*high*, *sigh*, *fight*, *plight*, *height*, *sleight*), but not otherwise after *e*: (*weigh*, *sleigh*, *eight*, *freight*; *-ld* (*child*, *mild*, *wild*, but not *build*, *g(u)ild*); *-nd* (*bind*, *blind*, *find*, *grind*, *hind*, *kind*, *rind*, *wind* (verb)); and in a single case each *-nt* (*pint*), *-nth* (*ninth*), and *-st* (*Christ*). Note also *whilst*. In monosyllabic and disyllabic roots, a following silent consonant sometimes signals the long value: *-g* (*align*, *benign*, *consign*), *-b* (*climb*), *-c* (*indict*), *-s* (*island*, *viscount*). (4) In many polysyllables with initial stressed syllables: *library*, *iron*, *island*, *item*, *final*, *libel*, *license*, *private*, *ivy*, *tidy* (but contrast *privy*, *city*). (5) The long value is not always stable: sometimes it remains in derivatives while losing stress (*final/finality, irony/ironic, library/librarian, virus/virology*), elsewhere becoming short while stress is retained (*arthritis/arthritic, bronchitis/bronchitic,* BrE *private/privacy*). (6) In initial stressed syllables directly followed by another vowel: *client, dial, diamond, diet, friar, ion, science, triangle, triumph.* The long *i* is kept when the stress shifts in derivatives: *science/scientific, triangle/triangular, triumph/triumphant.* (7) In some unstressed suffixes of Latin origin, such as *-ide* (*cyanide, sodium chloride*) and *-ite* (*Israelite, finite,* but optionally short in *plebiscite*). In other suffixes, usage varies. Long *i* occurs in *-ile* in BrE but generally not in AmE, which has a schwa or a syllabic consonant: *fertile, hostile, missile, volatile.* Long *i* occurs in such animal-related adjectives as *aquiline, bovine, equine,* but short *i* commonly in such general adjectives as *feminine, genuine, masculine* (although long *i* can also occur, especially in ScoE). Latin endings in *i* usually have long value (*alibi, fungi, termini*) as do Greek letter names (*pi, phi, psi, chi/khi*). (8) A unique spelling is *choir,* changed from *quire* to reflect its derivation from *chorus.*

**Continental I**. This is the 'ee' value of MIDDLE ENGLISH *i* before the Great Vowel Shift. It is found in recent loans from the ROMANCE LANGUAGES (*pizza, police, fatigue, routine, souvenir, mosquito*) and elsewhere (*bikini, kiwi, ski*). JAPANESE Romaji spellings also accord *i* this value: *Hirohito, Mitsubishi.* In final position in FRENCH loans, the *i* may be followed by a silent letter: *debris, esprit.* The spelling of this vowel sound in earlier French loans has been Anglicized as *ea* and *ee*: *league, esteem, canteen.* This value also occurs in native English words and older loans with the medial digraph *ie*: *field, fiend, frieze, grief, mien, piece, priest, shriek, siege.* A following *r* modifies this value in RP, but otherwise *bier, pierce, cashier* belong in this category. Occasionally the *ee* value of the *ie* may be shortened in speech to short *i*: *mischief.* The *ie* in *sieve* always has short value, and the *e* value in *friend* is exceptional.

**Unstressed I**. In unstressed position, *i* is commonly reduced to schwa, though in some accents, notably RP, tending towards its short value: *sordid, plaintiff, porridge, vestige, nostril, denim, raisin, tapir, premiss, limit, satirist, admiral, admiration.*

**Silent I**. (1) In the second written syllable of *business* and, for some people, in *medicine.* (2) Before another vowel in the unstressed syllables of *cushion, fashion, parishioner,* and commonly in *parliament.*

**Variations**. (1) The letters *i, y* were interchangeable in MIDDLE ENGLISH and remain so in several pairs of alternatives: short value (*gipsy/gypsy, lichgate/lychgate, pigmy/pygmy, sillabub/syllabub, silvan/sylvan*), long value (*cider/cyder, cipher/cypher, dike/dyke, siphon/syphon*); contrasting *ie* and *y* (*bogie/bog(e)y, cadie/caddy, pixie/pixy*). BrE *tyre* contrasts with AmE *tire.* However, these alternatives are distinct from such homophones as *calix/calyx, chili/chilly, die/dye.* (2) There is standard variation between *y* and *i* when a suffix is added to a word that ends in *y*: *happy, happier, happiest, happily, happiness; pity, pitying, pities, pitied, pitiable, pitiful.* However, *busy* keeps *y* in *busyness,* to distinguish it from *business.* Sometimes there are alternative forms (*drier/dryer*), or there is no *i* form (*slyness* only), or no *y* form (*gaily, daily*). The verbs *lay, pay, say* change *y* to *i* in their past tense only: *laid, paid, said.* The verbs *try, deny,* adopt *i* in *trial, denial.* (3) The digraph *ie* has the value of long *i* in open monosyllables: *die, lie, tie.* Nouns and verbs whose base form ends in *y* with the value of long *i* inflect with *ie* when followed by *s* and *d*: *try/tries, simplify/simplified.* (4) *I* replaces *e* when suffixes are added to base words ending in *-ce*: *face/facial, finance/financial, space/spacious* (but note *spatial*). For alternative spellings such as *despatch/dispatch, enquire/inquire* see under E. (5) Some Latin singulars ending in *-us* substitute *-i* in the plural (*fungus/fungi, radius/radii, terminus/termini*). This is sometimes optional (*cactuses, cacti*) and may include controversial usages such as *syllabuses, syllabi* (there being no justification in Greek or Latin for the form *syllabi*). Some Latin singulars ending in *-is* may change to plural *-es*: *axis/axes, basis/bases, oasis/oases.*

**Other functions**. (1) A following *i* may soften (that is, palatalize) the letters *c* and *g*: *electric/electricity, rigour/rigid.* (2) When a vowel letter follows, *i* may soften a preceding consonant, but lose its own sound value: for example, *c* sounding like *sh* in *racial, electrician, conscience, suspicion, conscious.* Similar palatalization occurs with *d* (*soldier*), *s* (*vision*), *ss* (*mission*), *t* (*nation*). (3) In a similar position, *i* is silent after (soft) *g*: *contagion, contagious, region, religion.* (4) In the system of English personal pronouns, the capitalized letter *I*, spoken with a long value, represents the first person singular. To represent distinctive pronunciations, however, such as in Scots and Southern AmE, the form changes to *Ah*. See HARD AND SOFT, J.

**ICON. 1.** A picture or image, especially a saint painted on a wooden panel and venerated in Orthodox Christianity. If something is *iconic*, it represents something else in a conventionalized way, as with features on a map (roads, bridges, etc.) or onomatopoeic words (as for example the words *kersplat* and *kapow* in US comic books, standing for the impact of a fall and a blow). **2.** An archetypal image: 'It is hopeless to retreat from the problem of racism to [Margaret] Mitchell's personal and Scarlett's fictional struggles against the role of the "icon" the "Southern Lady", a figure utterly entangled with the practice of slavery' (Patricia Storace, *The New York Review of Books*, 19 Dec. 1991). **3.** A person regarded as embodying a certain quality, style, or attitude: 'When Spike Lee, America's hottest black film director, decided to make a film about Malcolm X, the country's most controversial black icon, Hollywood sensed a blockbuster' (John Cassidy, *The Sunday Times*, 11 Aug. 1991). **4.** A stylized symbol, especially in COMPUTING: a small image on a screen representing a function or an option, such as a paintbrush (representing and permitting a painting-like activity on screen) or a wastebasket (representing and permitting the erasure of materia). Commonly, a program is started, a file obtained, etc., by pointing an arrow-like cursor at one icon in a menu-like group, generally using a hand-held mouse to move the cursor and activate the icon. Compare EMOTICON.

**IDIOLECT**. In LINGUISTICS, the language special to an individual, sometimes describe as a 'personal DIALECT'. See LECT.

**IDIOM**, also (archaic) **idiotism. 1.** The SPEECH proper to, or typical of, a people or place; a DIALECT or local LANGUAGE: *classics in the Tuscan idiom*. **2.** An expression unique to a language, especially one whose sense is not predictable from the meanings and arrangement of its elements, such as *kick the bucket* a slang term meaning 'to die', which has nothing obviously to do with kicking or buckets. In linguistics, the term *idiomaticity*

refers to the nature of idioms and the degree to which a usage can be regarded as idiomatic. Some expressions are more holophrastic and unanalysable than others: for example, *to take steps* is literal and non-idiomatic in *The baby took her first steps*, is figurative, grammatically open, and semi-idiomatic in *They took some steps to put the matter right*, and is fully idiomatic and grammatically closed in *She took steps to see that was done*. These examples demonstrate a continuum of meaning and use that is true for many usages. No such continuum exists, however, between *He kicked the bucket out of the way* and *He kicked the bucket last night* (meaning 'He died last night'). Such idioms are particularly rigid: for example, they cannot usually be passivized (no *\*The bucket was kicked*) or otherwise adapted (no *\*bucket-kicking* as a synonym for *death*).

**Creative adaptations**. Although idioms are normally simply slotted into speech and WRITING, they are occasionally subject to creative wordplay. The phrase *on the other hand*, a convention in the presentation of contrasting information (*on the one hand, . . . on the other hand*), is radically adapted in the following statement, from an article about animals:

> A female needs an area which will provide enough food and denning sites for raising kittens, even in a year when food is in short supply. On the other paw, a male has a very much larger home range, which usually overlaps with those of several females ('Just like Lions', *BBC Wild Life*, Jan. 1989).

**Spliced idioms**. It is not unusual for even fluent speakers in the heat of conversation to blend or splice two idioms or COLLOCATIONS whose forms and meanings are similar. The following specimens were collected in the late 1980s: 'That seems an interesting step to go down' (splicing *step to take* and *road to go down*); 'He stuck his ground' (splicing *stuck to his guns* and *stood his ground*); 'Language plays a decisive factor here' (blending *is a decisive factor* and *plays a decisive role*).

See CATCH-PHRASE, CATCHWORD, CLICHÉ, FIXED PHRASE, HACKNEYED, HOLOPHRASE.

■ **ILLITERACY** ————————— ■

The inability to read or write, or the actual or perceived state of being uneducated or insufficiently educated. Social judgement is so powerfully built into the term ILLITERATE that scholars now generally use more neutral terms, such as *non-literate* (for societies and individuals for whom literacy is not a relevant issue) and *pre-literate* (for societies and conditions before LITERACY emerged or was encountered and adopted). Formerly, the term *illiterate* was used to describe someone without book learning or a liberal EDUCATION (especially in classical LATIN and GREEK), even though such a person could read in a vernacular language or handle accounts and correspondence. However, the word also carried the connotation of 'unpolished', 'ignorant', or 'inferior', as in 'the disadvantage of an illiterate education' (Edward Gibbon, *The Decline and Fall of the Roman Empire*, volume 2, 1781, p. 75).

**Attitudes**. As schooling moved away from the classical languages, the term came to mean inability to sign one's name (generally on a marriage or a census document) or to read a simple passage. The term *illiterate* has been widely used pejoratively for usage which, though literate, has not measured up to the standards or expectations of the person commenting. *Semi-literate* is similarly employed: 'an illiterate style', 'a semi-literate letter'. Because of the prestige of LITERACY and its influence on patterns of speech, some observers have attacked 'illiterate speech', and on occasion writers of guides to 'GOOD' ENGLISH have employed such phrases to persuade readers away from certain usages: 'The first principle of illiterate speech—emphasis by repetition—is evident not only in grammatical patterns but also in PHRASEOLOGY; the basement-level speaker frequently iterates an idea and then immediately reiterates the very same idea in slightly different words. He is not quite sure you will understand him until he has said a thing at least twice' (Norman Lewis, *Better English*, 1956).

**Statistics**. In recent years, the term has been used to describe the condition of people unable to cope with printed materials relevant to their needs (*functional illiteracy*) and people unacquainted with the canon and conventions of an educated populace (*cultural illiteracy*). Precise descriptions and accurate estimates of illiteracy of any kind in English-speaking countries are difficult to obtain.

**Changing levels**. In the 1950s, the inability to read or write was not in itself detrimental to achievement, but in an increasingly technological society illiteracy usually limits employment and advancement. David Crystal has pointed out that, in the developed countries, it is becoming more rather than less difficult for people to achieve an acceptable standard of literacy:

> A democratic society and a free press presuppose high general literacy levels. There are now more diverse and complex kinds of matter to read, and people are obliged to read more if they want to get on. People who had achieved a basic literacy are thus in real danger of being classed as illiterate, as they fail to cope with the modern everyday demands of such areas as the media, business, bureaucracy, and the law. As a result of literate society continually 'raising the ante', therefore, the illiteracy figures rise, and the gap between the more and the less developed countries becomes ever wider ('Literacy 2000', *English Today*, Oct. 1986).

The inability to read and write not only prevents people from functioning fully within their communities, but also exerts an influence on national priorities and the use of human and material resources.

**IMPERATIVE**. The MOOD of the VERB used to express commands ('*Go* away'), requests ('Please *sit* down'), warnings ('*Look* out!'), offers ('*Have* another piece'), and entreaties ('*Help* me'). Sentences with an imperative as their main verb require the person(s) addressed to carry out some action. Hence, the subject of an imperative sentence is typically the second-person pronoun *you*, which is however normally omitted, as in '*Go* away', but appears in the emphatic 'You *do* as you're told!' First- and third-person imperatives refer to the doer of the action or the requirement to perform the action less directly: '*Let's go* now'; '*Someone close* the window'.

■ **IMPERIALISM** ──────── ■

A term relating to empires and their institutions and trappings. *Imperialism* and *imperialist* can be used neutrally, to refer to any empire or imperial institution. In the 19c, they were often used positively, with regard especially to the achievements and interests of the European mercantile empires. Currently, the terms are generally perceived as negative, under the influence primarily of Marxist critics of empire, bourgeoisie, and capitalism, and have been used to refer not only to overt empires such as that of Britain, but also to countries seen as more covertly (but equally nefariously) imperial, such as the US.

**Imperial English**. The domination and exploitation that are inherent in any empire often come to be associated with the imperial language, as with Latin in the Roman and English in the British Empire. Because of the complex social and emotional relationships within an empire, there is often a love/hate relationship between subject peoples and the élite that rules them and therefore also between those peoples and the language of their servitude. This is especially so where some local people receive preference because of their usefulness and loyalty, are privileged by visits to the 'mother country', and provide their children with education in schools whose medium is the imperial language. As a result, even after the immediate pressures of empire have gone, postcolonial societies find that they can live neither with nor without the imperial language.

**Post-imperial English**. In India, the Philippines, and many other countries, decades after independence English continues to dominate politics, EDUCATION, technology, law, and business, evokes memories of colonialism, and imposes various strains on societies often divided on ethnic grounds as well as between a majority and an élite that has inherited many of the attributes and trappings of the erstwhile imperialists. Some Indians accuse Britain of ensuring that nearly 50 years after independence Indians must use English rather than an indigenous language to talk to other Indians. Philippine historians often accuse turn-of-the-century American military authorities of imposing English in order to keep Filipinos from communicating effectively in their own languages. Resentment against English-speaking political and economic élites easily translates into resentment against the language of post-imperial power. Intellectuals in postcolonial societies often see ex-imperial languages as preventing the intellectualization of VERNACULARS, much as NORMAN FRENCH

in England first stunted then altered English. In a replay of the struggle of English to become a language of scholarship in a LATIN-dominated world, national languages such as Malay and Filipino are deliberately being intellectualized by nationalist linguists and writers through expansions in words, styles, and domains (often drawing on the resources of English for this purpose, as English drew on Latin). In this struggle, the major field of combat is the school: for example, in the Philippines, the medium of instruction was predominantly English until 1974, when a Bilingual Education Policy (slightly revised in 1987) mandated the use of Filipino for some subjects, as well as local vernaculars at lower levels. By the late 1980s, leading universities were successfully expanding the number of subjects taught in Filipino.

**Competitors with English**. In some countries, English offers an escape route from ethnic conflicts: as a 'neutral' language in such countries as India, Nigeria, and the Philippines, it is said to be more widely acceptable than local alternatives. Nationalists argue, however, that there are often local languages that unify populations at least as well, and often in less psychologically damaging ways. An example is Filipino (Tagalog), despite resistance from northern Ilocanos and southern Cebuanos; it is now more widely spoken than English, Ilocano, or Cebuano. The success of the national varieties of Malay in Malaysia and Indonesia is also a case in point.

**Cultural hegemony**. It takes time for patterns of dominance to change, and it is not easy to assess the extent of the intellectual, social, and cultural hegemony exerted by a language like English. Some non-native users of English advocate linguistic *détente*: watchful collaboration with a language only lately weaned, if weaned at all, from imperialism. They see the benefits of such collaboration in terms of a great good that is emerging from great ill, as English becomes the world's primary language. Other post-colonial observers, however, recall that to sup with the Devil one needs a long spoon. The Kikuyu writer NGUGI WA THIONG'O has described the predicament as follows:

> The oppressed and the exploited of the earth maintain their defiance: liberty from theft. But the biggest weapon

wielded and actually daily unleashed by imperialism against the collective defiance is the cultural bomb. The effect of the cultural bomb is to annihilate a people's belief in their names, in their languages, in their environment, in their heritage of struggle, in their unity, in their capacities and ultimately in themselves. It makes them see their past as one wasteland of non-achievement and it makes them want to distance themselves from that wasteland. It makes them want to identify with that which is furthest removed from themselves; for instance, with other people's languages rather than their own (*Decolonising the Mind*, 1986).

See CELTIC LANGUAGES, CLASSICAL LANGUAGE, COMMONWEALTH, CREOLE, ENGLISH.

**INCLUSIVE LANGUAGE**, also **inclusive usage**. Semi-technical terms for a use of language that includes rather than excludes particular groups, such as women and minorities: for example, the use of *humankind* or *people* rather than *mankind* or *men* when the whole human race is being discussed; the use of *Britain* rather than *England* when the entire UK is intended. See GENERIC PRONOUN, SEXISM.

**INDEFINITE ARTICLE**. In English grammar, the term for *a* and *an* when used to introduce a noun phrase: *a cup of coffee* or *an angry reply*. *A* occurs before consonant sounds (*a garden, a human, a use*) and *an* before vowel sounds (*an orange, an hour, an uncle, an MP, an SOS*). *An* is sometimes used before certain words beginning with an *h*, such as *an hotel, an historian*, particularly if the *h* is not pronounced. Some, however, pronounce the *h*, giving rise to controversy and being regarded by some others as slightly pretentious or precious. See ARTICLE, H.

**INDENTING**, also **indentation**, **indention**. The practice of setting a line of text further from the left margin than other lines, especially to start a PARAGRAPH. A poem or other block of text, especially a quotation, may also be indented so as to make it stand out from the surrounding text. Indenting is common in dictionaries and indexes, where it usually reverses the practice for text, effectively indenting every line except that of the headword. The space left by indenting is an indent(at)ion.

## ■ INDIAN ENGLISH ■

Formerly also **Indo-English**. Short forms *IndE*, *IE*. The English language as used in the Republic of India, a South Asian nation and member of the COMMONWEALTH. The term is widely used but is a subject of controversy; some scholars argue that it labels an established variety with an incipient or actual standard, others that the kinds of English used in India are too varied, both socially and geographically, and often too deviant or too limited, to be lumped together as one variety. They also argue that no detailed description has been made of the supposed variety and that the term is therefore misleading and ought not to be used. However, the length of time that English has been in India, its importance, and its range, rather than militating against such a term, make the term essential for an adequate discussion of the place of the language in Indian life and its sociolinguistic context. An estimated 30m people (4% of the population) regularly use English, making India the third largest English-speaking country in the world. Beyond this number is a further, unquantifiably large range of people with greater or less knowledge of the language and competence in its use. English is the associate official language of India, the state language of Manipur (1.5m), Meghalaya (1.33m), Nagaland (0.8m), and Tripura (2m), and the official language of eight Union territories (at the time of writing): the Andaman and Nicobar Islands; Arunachal Pradesh; Chandigarh; Dadra and Nagar Haveli; Delhi; Lakshadwip; Mizoram; and Pondicherry. It is one of the languages of the *three language formula* proposed in the 1960s for educational purposes: state language, HINDI, and English. It is used in the legal system, pan-Indian and regional administration, the armed forces, national business, and the media. English and Hindi are the *link languages* in a complex multilingual society, in which English is both a *library language* and a *literary language*. The *National Academy of Letters/Sahitya Akademi* recognizes Indian English literature as a national LITERATURE.

**History**. The first speaker of English to visit India may have been an ambassador of ALFRED the Great. The ANGLO-SAXON CHRONICLE states that in AD 884, Alfred sent an envoy to India with gifts for the tomb of St Thomas. His name appears in one later record as Swithelm, in another as Sigellinus. After this, there was little if any contact until the 16c, when European commercial and colonial expansion began. In 1600, English traders established the East India Company, and in 1614 James VI wrote to the Emperor Jehangir, accrediting Sir Thomas Roe as ambassador to the Moghul court:

James, by the Grace of Almightie God, the Creator of Heauen and Earth, King of Great Britaine, France and Ireland . . . To the high and mightie Monarch the Great Mogor, King of the Orientall Indies, of Chandahar, of Chismer and Corazon . . . Greeting. We hauing notice of your great fauour toward Vs and Our Subiects, by Your Great *Firma* to all Your Captaines of Riuers and Offices of Your Customes, for the entertaynment of Our louing Subiects the English Nation with all kind respect, at what time soeuer they shall arriue at any of the Ports within Your Dominions, and that they may haue quiet Trade and Commerce without any kind of hinderance or molestation.

The use of English dates from the trading 'factories' started by the Company: Surat (1612), Madras (1639–40), Bombay (1674), Calcutta (1690). European traders at that time used a form of PORTUGUESE, current since Portugal had acquired Goa in 1510. Missionaries were important in the diffusion of English in the 18c: schools such as St Mary's Charity Schools were started in Madras (1715), Bombay (1719), and Calcutta (1720–31). By the 1830s, an influential group of Indians was impressed with Western thought and culture, and its scientific advances, and wished to encourage the learning of English as a means through which Indians could gain a knowledge of such things. In a long official controversy over the medium of education for Indians, the *Anglicists* supported the *transplant theory* and the *Orientalists* the *nativist theory*. Thomas B. Macaulay, a member of the Supreme Council of India, settled the question in favour of English in an official Minute (1835):

To sum up what I have said, I think it clear that we are not fettered by the Act of Parliament of 1813; that we are not fettered by any pledge expressed or implied; that we are free to employ our funds as we choose; that we ought to employ them in teaching what is best worth knowing; that English is better worth knowing than Sanscrit or Arabic; that the natives are desirous to be taught English, and are not desirous to be taught Sanscrit or Arabic; that neither as the languages of law, nor as the languages of religion, have the Sanscrit and Arabic any peculiar claim to our engagement; that it is possible to make natives of this country thoroughly good English scholars; and that to this end our efforts ought to be directed. . . . We must at present do our best to form a class who may be interpreters between us and the millions who we govern; a class of persons, Indian in blood and colour, but English in taste, in opinions, in morals, and in intellect. To that class we may leave it to refine the vernacular dialects of the country, to enrich those dialects with terms of science borrowed from the Western nomenclature, and to render them by degrees fit vehicles for conveying knowledge to the great mass of the population.

In 1857, the first three western-style universities were established at Bombay, Calcutta, and Madras. Allahabad and Punjab (the latter now in Lahore, Pakistan) were added by the end of the 19c. By 1928, English was accepted as the language of the élite, and after independence in 1947, its diffusion increased. However, because IndE is essentially a contact language, convergence with Indian languages and socio-cultural patterns have resulted in many processes of Indianization.

**Variation**. There are three major variables for IndE: proficiency in terms of acquisition; regional or mother tongue; and ethnic background. In IndE there is a cline from educated IndE (the acrolect) to pidginized varieties (BASILECTS) known by such names as *Boxwalla(h) English*, *Butler English*, *Bearer English* or *Kitchen English*, and *Babu English*. The regional and mother-tongue varieties are often defined with reference to the first language of the speaker (*Bengali English*, *Gujarati English*, *Tamil English*, etc.) or in terms of a larger language family (*Indo-Aryan English*, *Dravidian English*). In this sense, there are as many Indian Englishes as there are languages in India. There are, however, shared characteristics which identify IndE speakers across language specific varieties. One variety, *ANGLO-INDIAN English*, is distinctive, because it emerged among the offspring of British servicemen and lower-caste Indian women, and is sustained among other things by a nationwide system of long-established English-medium private schools known as *Anglo-Indian schools*. Generally, however, when IndE is discussed, the term refers to the variety at the upper end of the spectrum, which has national currency and intelligibility and increasingly provides a STANDARD for the media, education, and pan-Indian communication. In grammar and spelling, standard BrE continues to have influence.

**Pronunciation**. (1) IndE is rhotic, /r/ being pronounced in all positions. (2) It tends to be syllable-timed, weak vowels being pronounced as full vowels in such words as *photography* and *student*. Word stress is used primarily for emphasis and suffixes are stressed, as in *readiness*. Distinctive stress patterns occur in different areas: *available* is often stressed in the north on the antepenultimate, in the south on the first syllable. (3) The alveolar consonants /t, d/ are retroflex. (4) The fricatives /θ, ð/ are aspirated /t, d/, so that *three of those* sounds like 'tʰree of dʰose'; /f/ is often pronounced as aspirated /p/, as in 'pʰood' for *food*. (5) In such words as *old, low* the vowel is generally /o/. (6) Among northern (Indo-Aryan) speakers, consonant clusters such as /sk, sl, sp/ do not occur in initial position, but have an epenthetic vowel, as in 'iskool' for *school* in the Punjab and 'səkool' in Kashmir. (7) The distinction between /v/ and /w/ is generally neutralized to /w/: 'wine' for both *wine* and *vine*. (8) Among southern (Dravidian) speakers, non-low initial vowels are preceded by the glides /j/ (as in 'yell, yem, yen' for the names of the letters *l, m, n*) and /w/ (as in 'wold' for *old* and 'wopen' for *open*). (9) South Indians tend to geminate voiceless intervocalic obstruents, as in 'Americ-ca'. Because gemination is common in Dravidian languages, double consonants in written English are often geminated: 'sum-mer' for *summer* and 'sil-lee' for *silly*. (10) Distinct kinds of pronunciation serve as SHIBBOLETHS of different kinds of IndE: Bengalis using /b/ for /v/, making *bowel* and *vowel* HOMOPHONES; Gujaratis using /dʒ/ for /z/, so that *zed* and *zero* become 'jed' and 'jero'; speakers of Malayalam making *temple* and *tumble* near-homophones.

A large number of IndE speakers, sometimes referred to as speakers of *General Indian English* (*GIE*), have a 17-vowel system (11 monophthongs and 6 diphthongs): /i:/ as in *bead*, /i/ as in *this*, /e:/ as in *game*, /ɛ/ as in *send*, /æ/ as in *mat*, /ɑ:/ as in *charge*, /ɒ/ as in *shot*, /o:/ as in *no*, /ʊ/ as in *book*, /u:/ as in *tool*, and /ə/ as in *bus*; /ai/ as in *five*, /ɔi/ as in *boy*, /aʊ/ as in *cow*, /ɪə/ as in *here*, /eə/ as in *there*, and /ʊə/ as in *poor*.

**Grammar**. There is great variety in syntax, from native-speaker fluency (the acrolect) to a weak command of many constructions (the basilect). The following represents a widespread middle level (the MESOLECT): (1) Interrogative constructions without subject/auxiliary inversion: *What you would like to buy?* (2) Definite article often used as if the conventions have been reversed: *It is the nature's way*; *Office is closed today*. (3) *One* used rather than the indefinite article: *He gave me one book*. (4) Stative verbs given progressive forms: *Lila is having two books*; *You must be knowing my cousin-brother Mohan*. (5) Reduplication used for emphasis and to indicate a distributive meaning: *I bought some small small things*; *Why you don't give them one one piece of cake?* (6) *Yes* and *no* as question tags: *He is coming, yes?*; *She was helping you, no?* (7) *Isn't it?* as a generalized question tag: *They are coming tomorrow, isn't it?* (8) Reflexive pronouns and *only* used for emphasis: *It was God's order itself* It was God's own order, *They live like that only* That is how they live. (9) Present perfect rather than simple past: *I have bought the book yesterday*.

**Vocabulary: loans**. LOANWORDS and LOAN TRANSLATIONS from other languages have been common since the 17c, often moving into the language outside India: (1) Words from Portuguese (*almirah, ayah, caste, peon*) and from local languages through Portuguese (*bamboo, betel, coir, copra, curry, mango*). (2) Words from indigenous languages, such as HINDI and Bengali. Some are earlier and more Anglicized in their spelling: *anna, bungalow, cheetah, chintz, chit/chitty, dacoit, dak bungalow, jodhpurs, juggernaut, mulligatawny, pice, pukka, pundit, rupee, sahib, tussore*. Some are later and less orthographically Anglicized: *achcha* all right (used in agreement and often repeated: *Achcha achcha, I will go*), *basmati* a kind of rice, *chapatti* a flat, pancake-like piece of unleavened bread, *crore* a unit of 10m or 100 lakhs (*crores of rupees*), *goonda* a ruffian, petty criminal, *jawan* a soldier in the present-day Indian Army, *lakh* a unit of 100,000 (*lakhs of rupees*), *lathi* a lead-weighted stick carried by policemen, *masala* spices, *paisa* a coin, 100th of a rupee, *panchayat* a village council, *samo(o)sa* an envelope of fried dough filled with vegetables or meat, *Sri/Shri/Shree* Mr, *Srimati/Shrimati/Shreemati* Mrs. (3) Words from Arabic and Persian through north Indian languages, used especially during the British Raj: *dewan* chief minister of a princely state, *durbar* court of a prince or governor, *mogul* a Muslim prince (and in the general language an important person, as in *movie mogul*), *sepoy* a soldier in the British Indian Army, *shroff* a banker, money-changer, *vakeel/vakil* a lawyer, *zamindar* a landlord. (4) Words taken directly from SANSKRIT, usually with religious and philosophical associations, some well known, some restricted to such contexts as yoga: *ahimsa* non-violence, *ananda* spiritual bliss, *chakra* a mystical centre of energy in the body, *guru* a (spiritual) teacher (and in the general language a quasi-revered guide, as in *management guru*), *nirvana* release from the wheel of rebirth, *rajas* a state of passion, *samadhi* spiritual integration and enlightenment, *sattwa/sattva* a state of purity, *tamas* a state of heaviness and ignorance, *yoga* a system of self-development, *yogi* one who engages in yoga. (5) CALQUES from local languages: *dining-leaf* a banana leaf used to serve food, *cousin brother* a male cousin, *cousin sister* a female cousin, *co-brother-in-law* one who is also a brother-in-law.

**Vocabulary: hybrids, adaptations, and idioms**. The great variety of mixed and adapted usages exists both as part of English and as a consequence of widespread code-mixing between English and especially Hindi: (1) HYBRID usages, one component from English, one from a local language, often Hindi: *brahminhood* the condition of being a brahmin, *coconut paysam* a dish made of coconut, *goonda ordinance* an ordinance against goondas, *grameen bank* a village bank, *kaccha road* a dirt road, *lathi charge* (noun) a charge using lathis, *lathi-charge* (verb) to charge with lathis, *pan/paan shop* a shop that sells betel nut and lime for chewing, wrapped in a pepper leaf, *police-wala* a policeman, *swadeshi cloth* home-made cloth, *tiffin box* a lunch-box. (2) Local senses and developments of general English words: *batch-mate* a classmate or fellow student, *body-bath* an ordinary bath, *by-two coffee* (in

the south) a restaurant order by two customers asking for half a cup of coffee each, *communal* used with reference to Hindus and Muslims (as in *communal riots*), *condole* to offer condolences to someone, *England-returned* used of one who has been to England, for educational purposes, a been-to, *Eve-teasing* teasing or harassing young women, *Foreign-returned* used of someone who has been abroad for educational purposes, *four-twenty* a cheat or swindler (from the number of a section of the Indian Penal Code), *head-bath* washing one's hair, *interdine* to eat with a member of another religion or caste, *intermarriage* a marriage involving persons from different religions of castes, *issueless* childless, *military hotel* (in the south) a restaurant where non-vegetarian food is served, *out of station* not in (one's) town or place of work, *outstation* (*cheque*) a cheque issued by a non-local bank, *prepone* the opposite of postpone, *ration shop* a shop where rationed items are available, *undertrial* a person being tried in a court of law. (3) Words more or less archaic in BrE and AmE, but used in IndE, such as *dicky* (the boot/trunk of a car), *needful* ('Please do the needful, Sri Patel'), *stepney* a spare wheel or tyre, and *thrice* ('I was seeing him thrice last week'). (4) The many idiomatic expressions include: *to sit on someone's neck* to watch that person carefully, and *to stand on someone's head* to supervise that person carefully; *Do one thing, Sri Gupta* There is one thing you could do, Mr Gupta; *He was doing this thing that thing, wasting my time* He was doing all sorts of things, wasting my time.

**Usage**. It is not easy to separate the use of English in India from the general multilingual flux. In addition to CODE-MIXING AND CODE-SWITCHING, other languages are constantly drawn into English discourse and English into the discourse of other languages, especially Hindi. In the English-language press, hybrid headlines are common: *JNU karamcharis begin dharna* (*The Statesman*, New Delhi, 12 May 1981), *Marathwada band over pandal fire* (*The Indian Express*, New Delhi, 9 May 1981), and *55 Jhuggis gutted* (*The Hindustan Times*, New Delhi, 3 May 1981). Matrimonial advertisements in the English-language press are equally distinctive: 'Wanted well-settled bridegroom for a Kerala fair graduate Baradwaja gotram, Astasastram girl . . . subset no bar. Send horoscope and details'; 'Matrimonial proposals invited from educated, smart, well settled, Gujarati bachelors for good looking, decent, Gujarati Modh Ghanchi Bania girl (25), B.A., doing the M.A. and serving'.

See ANGLO-INDIAN, BORROWING, HINDI-URDU, HINDLISH, INDIANISM, SOUTH ASIAN ENGLISH.

**INDIANISM**. An especially linguistic usage or custom peculiar to or common in India and IndE: *isn't it?* as a generalized question tag (*You are liking it here, isn't it?*); repeating a word for emphasis (*It was a small small box; Put put; Take take*). See -ISM.

**INDICATIVE**. A term for the grammatical MOOD in which statements are expressed: the sentence *I saw her yesterday* is in the indicative (mood). The indicative is the most common mood in English, and is used for both statements (*She knew him*) and questions (*She knew him?*). However, these may imply meanings typically associated with the imperative (where both *I should like to borrow your pen* and *Can I borrow your pen?* are indirect requests) and the subjunctive (a wish in *God should bless you in all your works* or after expressions of request, necessity, and the like, as in *It is imperative that she answers our letter immediately*, where the SUBJUNCTIVE is an alternative). See DECLARATIVE.

**INDIRECT OBJECT**. With VERBS that can be followed by two objects, the indirect object typically comes immediately after the verb: *Audrey* in 'I've sent *Audrey* a present'; *his son* in 'He bought *his son* a ball'. It is typically animate and the recipient of the direct object. The same idea is often expressed by repositioning the recipient with a *to* or *for*: 'I've sent a present to *Audrey*'; 'He bought a ball *for his son*'. Grammarians differ about whether the noun in the prepositional phrases should be labelled indirect object. Occasionally, an indirect object is inanimate: 'Give the kitchen a coat of paint.' In such cases, usually idiomatic uses of common verbs, the same idea cannot usually be re-expressed with *to* or *for* (never *Give a coat of paint to the kitchen*). See DIRECT OBJECT, DOUBLE ACCUSATIVE.

■ **INDO-EUROPEAN LANGUAGES, The** ———— ■

The language family, or family of families, of which English is a member, along with other European languages such as FRENCH, GERMAN, RUSSIAN, and SPANISH, and Asian languages such as Bengali, Gujarati, HINDI, and Persian, as well as the classical languages GREEK, LATIN, Pali, and SANSKRIT. It constitutes the most extensively spoken group of languages in the world. The view that similarities among certain languages of Europe and Asia resulted from a common origin had attracted scholars for several centuries before the British scholar Sir William JONES suggested in 1786 that Sanskrit, Latin, and Greek shared features derived from 'some common source which, perhaps, no longer exists'. He guessed that the GERMANIC LANGUAGES and even the CELTIC LANGUAGES had the same source. Within a century, the implications of Jones's suggestion had been studied in great detail and his postulated 'common source' is now called *Proto-Indo-European (PIE)* or simply *Indo-European (IE)*.

**Proto-Indo-European**. PIE is considered to have vanished soon after 2000 BC without leaving written records. Many details, especially its sound pattern, remain the subject of debate, and new theories of the date and place of the original 'Indo-Europeans' and the nature of their diaspora continue to be proposed. Their assumed homeland is a place where words shared by IE languages would have had a use. The word for *fish* was common to them but not the word for *sea*, so the territory of the Indo-Europeans appears to have had bodies of water but not a coastline. They had horses and goats, and grain but not grapes. Such evidence seems to point to an area in the northern part of eastern Europe. The era of IE is usually dated from *c*.3000 BC until shortly after 2000 BC. Again, the evidence is chiefly archeological and linguistic, and the conclusions inferential: for example, horses and goats did not appear in the assumed homeland much before 3000 BC. The breakup of the community of original speakers of PIE can be dated from the earliest records in IE languages. Thus, elements of Mycenean Greek are preserved on tablets from 1600 to 1200 BC, so IE had given way to its successors by then, and probably a good deal earlier. Some recent theories push these dates earlier still, holding that archeological evidence for the gradual spread of farming from Greece across Europe and into Britain points to an IE origin in Anatolia (now eastern Turkey) as early as 6000 BC.

**Features of Proto-Indo-European**. Like all historical reconstructions, PIE is hypothetical, designed to explain the features of the IE languages which can be studied in written records or in their living spoken form. The forms of PIE words are known only indirectly from its reflection in the earliest written records in IE languages. So Sanskrit *ásmi*, Latin *sum*, Greek *eimí*, and Old English *eom* can best be explained by assuming a PIE form like *es-, with a suffix related to modern English *me*: *esme. The sum of such reconstructions is a language with many stop consonants, several similar to those of modern English, but also another set with a following aspirate: *bh, dh, gh, gwh*. IE had several varieties of the nasal *m* and *n*, the liquids *l* and *r*, and the glides *w, y*, and schwa. But it had only one unstopped consonant, *s*. The vowels were *a, e, i, o, u* in long and short forms. As reconstructed, PIE words take forms like *bhrāter, brother, *yeug- to yoke, *wed-wet, leading to English *water*, Latin *unda* (source of English *undulate*), Greek *húdōr* (source of English *hydrant*), and Russian *voda* (borrowed into English in its diminutive form *vodka*).

PIE verbs are thought to have followed an inflectional pattern similar to that of English *sing, sang, sung*, varying the vowel to indicate tense. Verbs also took an inflection to indicate person, number, and mood. All the major parts of speech were highly inflected, for three genders (masculine, feminine, and neuter), and for eight cases that defined the function of the word in the sentence much as the modern English *s* defines the difference between *The cat is John* and *The cat is John's*. Such inflections were chiefly suffixes, rarely prefixes, but both kinds of affix were used for word-formation. Compound words similar to modern English *Whitehouse* and *Longfellow* were common.

**Indo-European culture**. Language is a record of culture. Reconstructed IE records a polytheistic people with a northern farmer's awareness of annual cycles, names for the chief celestial bodies and phenomena, names too for the earth and its varieties, wet and wild. Trees, notably the birch and fruit trees, and the animals that lurked in them, such as wolf and beaver, occupied the IE landscape; fish swam in their inland water, while above them flew several kinds of birds from sparrows to eagles. In the clearings were domestic animals, and the Indo-Europeans knew lice at close range.

The family was a vital group, from father and mother to son and daughter, and their home was the village. A patriarchal society seems to be reflected in the prominence of names for male relatives. Weaving and pottery created products for home use, for barter, and for the socially important exchange of gifts that IE languages record in the words for *give* and *take*. It is probably as much this cohesive agricultural social structure as conquest that enabled the Indo-Europeans to spread out of their homeland into regions from Britain to India, although the ancient mythologies and stories of India, the Hittites, and Greece suggest a stratified society of priests, warriors, artisans, and farmers, in which warfare was common and honourable.

**The Indo-European language families**. PIE gave rise to several 'families', related by common descent from one or other early offshoot. These are often classified as *satem* or *centum* languages (according to the development of the IE word for *hundred* with a *k* sound as in Latin *centum* or an *s* sound as in Sanskrit *satem*). It was once thought that the *centum* group (including English and Latin) was western and the *satem* group (including Sanskrit) was eastern, but Tocharian, deciphered in this century, is the easternmost IE language, and it is a *centum* language. Three IE families are no longer represented among living languages: Venetic in Italy, Tocharian in Central Asia, and Anatolian in what is now eastern Turkey (once represented by Hittite). Not all members of the surviving families, moreover, are still living: Latin and Old English are dead languages. The ongoing IE language families are:

**The satem languages**. (1) Indo-Iranian, including modern Persian and such Indic languages as Bengali, Gujarati, and Hindi. (2) Thraco-Phrygian, perhaps represented by modern Armenian. (3) Illyrian, perhaps represented by modern Albanian. (4) Balto-Slavonic, including modern Bulgarian, Lithuanian, Polish, Russian, and Serbo-Croat.

**The centum languages**. (1) Celtic, including modern Breton, IRISH Gaelic, Scottish GAELIC, and WELSH. (2) Germanic, including Danish, DUTCH, English, GERMAN, and Swedish. (3) Hellenic, including modern Greek. (4) Italic, including Latin and its Romance descendants, such as French, Provençal, ITALIAN, Spanish, Portuguese,

Catalan, and Romanian. The Germanic family stems from an unrecorded offshoot of IE known as *Primitive Germanic*. The Germanic languages fall into three groups: (1) East Germanic, represented only by GOTHIC, which ceased to be spoken in the 16c. (2) North Germanic, represented by the SCANDINAVIAN LANGUAGES. (3) West Germanic, represented by modern German, YIDDISH, DUTCH, FRISIAN, AFRIKAANS, and English.

By no means all early IE languages left written records. The SLAVONIC LANGUAGES can be traced no further back than the 10c; the earliest records of Albanian are from the 15c. There is no record at all of Germanic before it subdivided into eastern, western, and northern groups; the earliest records, runic inscriptions from the 3c or 4c, are Scandinavian.

**A double heritage.** The contemporary English language has a native GRAMMAR and VOCABULARY that stem directly from its Germanic heritage, and a borrowed vocabulary from other, mainly IE, languages, notably Latin, its offshoots, and Greek. This double vocabulary provides alternatives like *brotherly* from Germanic and *fraternal* from Latin, with nuances of difference: see BISOCIATION. Literary style often exploits the duality: though Milton is considered a Latinate writer, the second line in his couplet 'But O, as to embrace me she inclined, / I waked, she fled, and day brought back my night' is composed only of Germanic words, contrasting with the borrowed 'embrace' and 'inclined' in the previous line.

**The Indo-European diaspora.** The terms *Indo-European* and the older *Indo-Germanic* and *Indo-Celtic* aptly described (at the time they were coined) the spread of the language families from India in the east to Britain and Iceland in the west. Exploration, migration, and colonialism have, however, taken the diaspora further afield: the Western IE languages English, Spanish, French, and Portuguese are now major languages not just of Europe but of the Americas, Africa, and even Asia, where English is the associate official language of India, and English and Spanish are used in the Philippines. Smaller populations speaking IE languages are everywhere, and IE languages such as French and English often serve as languages of accommodation between speakers of other languages. Because of such developments, the term *Indo-European* is still historically, philologically, and taxonomically sound, but it has lost its geographical rationale.

See ARYAN, CELTIC LANGUAGES, DERIVATION, ETYMOLOGY, GREAT VOWEL SHIFT, GRIMM'S LAW, HISTORY OF ENGLISH, INDO-EUROPEAN ROOTS, INDO-GERMANIC, LANGUAGE, LANGUAGE FAMILY, PHILOLOGY, ROMANCE LANGUAGES, ROOT, ROOT-CREATION, ROOT-WORD.

**INDO-EUROPEAN ROOTS**. The hypothetical forms and meanings of Indo-European (IE) words reconstructed by comparative philologists through comparison of living languages, the surviving records of their older forms, and dead languages. IE ROOTS are usually printed with an asterisk (*) to show that they are unrecorded; many are also printed with a following hyphen (-) to indicate that an inflectional or derivational suffix follows. The form and meaning listed with a hypothetical root are those that plausibly explain the recorded forms and meanings; they are not primarily assertions about the details of the IE original, but statements about the relationship of extant words in IE languages that descended from it.

An IE root for *to fasten* appears to have had the forms *pag- or *pak-. It is the origin of LATIN, *pax* and hence of English *pacify*, *pacific*, and by way of FRENCH *paix*, of *peace* and *appease*. The sense development from *pak* appears to arise from the figurative specialization 'fastening together (by means of treaty)'. From the same IE root came Latin *palus* (stake fastened in the ground), whence English *pole*, as well as *pale*, *impale*, and *palisade* through French, and *pawl* through DUTCH. Three stakes fastened in the ground made an instrument of torture probably called *tripalium in Latin, from which comes French *travailler* (to work hard) and modern English *travail* and (from MIDDLE ENGLISH times when a trip was no pleasure) *travel*. One form of the root *pag-was the nasalized *pang-, which gave rise not only to the Latin source of MODERN ENGLISH *impinge* and *impact* but also to OLD ENGLISH *fang* (that which is fastened upon: plunder). In MIDDLE ENGLISH, the meaning of *fang* was specialized to the plunder of an animal, its prey; in Modern English it has become the tooth by which an animal fastens onto its prey.

Latin also had the descendant of *pagin *pagus* (staked-out boundary); a dweller within such a boundary was a *paganus*, a villager or rustic. The figurative sense gives us *pagan* directly from the Latin; the literal sense remains in *peasant*, from the same word by way of French. From *pagus* Latin also had *pagina* (little fastening), a frame onto which vines were fastened, and from those vines comes *propagate* by generalization, and *propaganda* (those things which are to be propagated) by metaphor; hence also a *page*, in which the columns of written text are like vines on a trellis. These examples illustrate some of the known outcomes of the IE root *\*pag-* or *\*pak-* in modern English. The reconstruction of the root takes into account not only these forms and meanings but such others as Greek *pēgnumi* (to fasten or congeal: compare *pectin*). The examples trace the outcomes from their source; the reconstruction traces the source back from its outcomes. See ETYMOLOGY.

**INFINITIVE**. The NON-FINITE VERB that has the uninflected form of the verb: *be, say, dig, make*. The term may be used alone (the *BARE INFINITIVE: I made him tell the truth*) or preceded by *to* (the *to-infinitive: I asked him to tell the truth*). The bare infinitive is commonly used after a modal auxiliary verb (*be* after the modal *may* in *We may be late*) and after the auxiliary *do* (*I did answer your letter, They don't know the difference*). It is also found in the complementation of a small number of main verbs such as *have, let, make, see* and *hear* (*I had Tom paint the fence; The soldiers let us pass; They heard us leave*). In some instances, either type of infinitive may be used: *Steven helped Susan* (*to*) *teach the children good manners; What Sidney did was* (*to*) *help Justin with his homework*. The *to*-infinitive has a wider distribution as the verb in an infinitive construction: (1) It may be subject (*To meet you was a great pleasure*), though a variant with postponed subject is more usual (*It was a great pleasure to meet you*). (2) It may be the object in various types of verb complementation: *I hope to see Judith and Percy soon; I asked John and Joyce to come to my party; Jeffrey and Rosalind want me to be there*. (3) It may be introduced by a *wh*-word: *Anton and Stella asked me what to advise their elder son*. (4) It may function in various semantic classes of adverbial: *To set the alarm, press four digits; He grew up to be a fine man; To be frank, the meeting was boring*. See SPLIT INFINITIVE, USAGE.

**INFLECTED**. A term in LINGUISTICS for a

language in which a word takes various forms, most commonly by alteration of an ending, to show its grammatical role: Greek *ho lúkos* the wolf (nominative CASE and subject of the sentence), *ton lúkon* the wolf (accusative case and object of the sentence). Languages vary in their degree of inflection. The INDO-EUROPEAN LANGUAGES were originally highly inflected, as shown by the forms of nouns, verbs, and adjectives in GREEK and LATIN. See LINGUISTIC TYPOLOGY.

**INFLECTION**, also especially BrE **inflexion**. A grammatical form of a word. Some languages make more use of inflections than others: LATIN is highly INFLECTED for nouns, adjectives, pronouns, and verbs, whereas FRENCH is highly inflected for verbs but less so for other parts of speech. Generally, verbs inflect for *MOOD, TENSE, PERSON, NUMBER*, while nouns and adjectives inflect for *NUMBER AND GENDER*. Such inflections may involve affixes, sound and spelling changes (including stress shifts), SUPPLETION, or a mixture of these. In English, there are relatively few inflections. Verbs inflect through suffixation (*look/looks/looking/looked*), but some irregular verbs have past forms that depart from the norm (*see/sees/seeing/saw/seen; swim/swims/swimming/swam/swum; put/puts/putting/put*). The verb *be* has eight forms: *am, are, be, been, being, is, was, were*. Nouns inflect for plurality and possession (*worker/workers/worker's/workers'*) and some adjectives inflect for their comparatives and superlatives (*big/bigger/biggest*). Seven pronouns have distinct object forms: *me, us, her, him, them, thee, whom*. See ACCIDENCE, CASE, ENDING, STRONG VERB, WEAK VERB.

**INFORMAL**. A term in LINGUISTICS for a situation or a use of language that is common, non-official, familiar, casual, and often colloquial, and contrasts in these senses with *formal*. Whereas *Would you be so good as to help me?* is highly FORMAL, *Lend us a hand, would you?* is highly informal.

**INGLIS** [Pronounced /ˈɪŋlɪz/ and /ˈɪŋlz/]. The word for *English* in northern MIDDLE ENGLISH and Older SCOTS, used from the 14c by writers of Older Scots as the name of their language, which they saw as the same as the language of England. In the late 15c, such writers began using the national name *Scottis* (pronounced /ˈskotis/ and /skots/) for the language of Lowland Scotland and both terms continued in use as more or less free alternatives, *Inglis* predominating. Sometimes, however, 16c Scottish writers used *Inglis* for the language of England alone:

> Lyke as in Latyn beyn Grew termys sum,
> So me behufyt quhilum, or than be dum,
> Sum bastard Latyn, Franch or Inglys oys,
> Quhar scant was Scottys.
>
> (Gavin Douglas, Prologue to Book I,
> *Æneid*, 1513)

> [Just as in Latin there are some Greek terms,
> So it behoved me at times, rather than be dumb,
> Some bastard Latin, French or English to use,
> Where Scots was scant].

The term *Scottis* was opposed to *Sotheroun* or *Suddroun* (Southern: the English of England), a less ambiguous term than *Inglis*. Only from the early 18c was the present-day terminology consistently applied, *Scots* for the VERNACULAR of the Scottish Lowlands and *English* for the language of England and the standard variety being imported into Scotland.

**INITIAL**, also **initial letter**, **point**. **1.** The first LETTER of a WORD, usually capitalized in a proper NAME: the *L* of *London*, the *G, B, S* of *George Bernard Shaw*. The practice of using initials or POINTS in handwriting and print has encouraged the growth of such ABBREVIATIONS as symbols, formulas, INITIALISMS, and ACRONYMS: for example, *a* stands, among others, for *acre* and *are* (units of land measurement); *e.g.* stands for LATIN *exempli gratia* for the sake of an example; *BBC* for *British Broadcasting Corporation*; *NATO* for *North Atlantic Treaty Organization*. **2.** The large ornamental letter at the start of a page or chapter, especially in an illuminated manuscript.

**INITIALESE**. An informal, sometimes pejorative term for a style that uses INITIALS to economize in space, effort, and expense. It assumes familiarity on the part of readers or listeners and is common in classified advertisements, in which time names and stock phrases are reduced to letters with or without points: *tel* telephone; *Mon, Sept.*; *ono/o.n.o.* or nearest offer. See -ESE.

**INITIALISM**, also **initial word**. An ABBREVIATION that consists of the INITIAL letters of a series of words, pronounced in sequence: *BBC* for *British Broadcasting Corporation*, pronounced 'bee-bee-cee'. A letter group such as *NATO*, pronounced as a word ('nay-toe') is commonly referred to as an ACRONYM. Both initialisms and acronyms have word-like qualities and take affixes (*pro-BBC*, *non-NATO*, *ex-IBMer*); they are sometimes referred to jointly as *letter words* or *letter names*, and the acronym is regarded by some lexicologists as a kind of initialism. The pronunciation of initialisms is usually straightforward, but writing sometimes poses problems: formerly, points were the norm (*B.B.C.*), but currently an unpointed style prevails in data processing and in the Armed Services and increasingly in commerce, advertising, and publishers' house styles. Although most names are upper case, there are such exceptions as the *Initial Teaching Alphabet* (or *initial teaching alphabet*), officially abbreviated as *i.t.a.* and *ita*. See LETTER WORD.

**INITIAL TEACHING ALPHABET**, short forms *i.t.a.*, *ita*, *I.T.A.*, *ITA*. A controversial adaptation of the Roman ALPHABET (sometimes called *an augmented Roman alphabet*) intended as an aid for children and adults learning to read and write English. It was devised in England in 1959 by Sir James PITMAN, based on the *phonotypy* of his grandfather, Sir Isaac Pitman, and on the *Nue Spelling* of the SIMPLIFIED SPELLING SOCIETY. It has 44 lower-case letters, each with one sound value: see extract. The additional letters are adaptations of forms already occurring in traditional orthography (t.o.), such as the digraphs *au*, *ng*, *th*. When the function of a capital is needed, an i.t.a. letter is written or printed larger. When learners become proficient in reading i.t.a. they are expected to transfer easily to t.o. Teachers who use it see this transfer as a progression and not a process of relearning. The alphabet was adopted on an experimental basis by some schools in the UK in 1960 and the US in 1963, and Pitman set up i.t.a. foundations in both countries to administer its use. The British foundation closed from lack of funds, its work taken up in 1978 by the *Initial Teaching Alphabet Federation*, a group of experienced and enthusiastic teachers.

The alphabet was tested for the U. of London by the researcher John Downing, whose report was favourable. His publications on the subject include *The Initial Teaching Alphabet* (Cassell, 1964), *The i.t.a. reading experiment* (Evans, 1964), *Evaluating the Initial Teaching Alphabet* (Cassell, 1967), *Reading and Reasoning* (Chambers, 1979). In 1975, the Bullock Report noted: 'It would appear that the best way to learn to read in traditional orthography is to learn to read in the initial teaching alphabet.' However, despite such conclusions and much initial interest, the mother-tongue English-teaching profession has since the 1970s massively ignored the alphabet, despite an increasing awareness of literacy problems in the English-using world. It continues, however, to be used on a modest scale in Australia, Canada, Malta, Nigeria, South Africa, Spain, the UK, and the US. Its advocates argue that it gives learners confidence and satisfaction, largely because of its consistency. Its opponents among spelling reformers consider it an unsatisfactory compromise through which the irregularities of t.o. are not removed but postponed. Its mainstream opponents see it as alien and confusing in appearance, expensive in terms of printing reading materials, uncertain in the ease with which transfer to t.o. occurs, and inconvenient in relation to the parallel process of teaching people to write. See SPELLING REFORM.

ꟃe Iniꟓial teꟙiꟙ aifabet Is not an attempt at speliꟙ reform ov ꟃe lꟙliꟃ lagweʒ, but an Iniꟓial lerniꟙ medium tu assist In ꟃe ackwisiꟓon ov literasy skills. It can be usd wiꟓ Infants or adults and uꟃers hu hav previusly feld. It breks ꟃe lerniꟙ prosess dun Into steʒes, cupiꟙ wiꟓ ꟃe difficultis ov speliꟙ wen confidens has ben aꟙevd wiꟓ a consistent orꟃografy. It meks for fast rediꟙ wiꟓ ꟃds comprehenꟓon.

**INKHORN TERM**, also **inkhornism**, **inkpot term**. Archaic: an obscure and ostentatious WORD usually derived from Latin or Greek, so called because such words were used more in WRITING than in speech. Thomas Wilson observed in 1553: 'Among all other lessons this should first be learned, that wee never affect any straunge ynkehorne termes, but to speake as is commonly received ... Some seeke so far for outlandish English, that they forget altogether their mothers language (*Art of Rhetorique*).' Among his examples of inkhornisms are: *revoluting*; *ingent affabilitie*; *ingenious capacity*;

*magnifical dexteritie*; *dominicall superioritie*; *splendidious*. See ARCHAISM, AUREATE DICTION.

**INTENSIFIER**. In GRAMMAR, a WORD that has a heightening effect (*very* in *very large*) or a lowering effect (*slightly* in *slightly fat*) on the meaning of the word that it modifies. Words that can be modified in this way are said to be *gradable*. Intensifying adjectives modify nouns (*great* in *a great fool*). Intensifying adverbs mainly modify verbs (*greatly* in *greatly admire*), gradable adjectives (*extremely* in *extremely foolish*), and other adverbs (*somewhat* in *somewhat slowly*). Some intensifiers go with certain gradable words: *entirely* with *agree*, *deeply* with *worried*, *highly* with *intelligent*. See COLLOCATION, IDIOM.

**INTERFERENCE**. In LINGUISTICS and LANGUAGE TEACHING, the effect of one language on another, producing 'instances of deviation from the norms of either language' (Uriel Weinreich, *Languages in Contact*, 1953). Interference occurs naturally in the speech of bi- and multilingual people and the efforts of learners of foreign languages. It affects all levels of language: accent, pronunciation, syntax, morphology, vocabulary, and idiom. Although it is natural, especially when speakers are tired, tense, excited, or distracted, it is often disapproved of in unilingual societies as a display of inadequate skill on the part of a foreign learner. See INTERLANGUAGE, MISTAKE.

**INTERFIX**. An element used to unite words and bases: the THEMATIC VOWELS *-i-* in *agriculture*, *-o-* in *biography*, and *-a-* in *Strip-a-gram* are interfixed vowels; the middle words in *editor-in-chief*, *writer-cum-publisher*, *Rent-a-Car*, and *Sun 'n Sand* are interfixed words; *-ma-* and *-ummy-* in *thingamabob/thingummybob* are interfixed syllables. Such elements generally fit into the RHYTHM of the language as weak vowels and syllabic consonants. In late 20c English, thematic vowels proper sometimes overlap with such other interfixable elements as the indefinite article and the agentive suffix *-er*, as in: *megalith*, *aquaphobic*, *Linguaphone*, *Funarama*, *SelectaVision*, *Select-a-game*, *Post-a-Book*, *Porta-phone*, *Rent-a-car*, *Comutacar*. Such coinages are often stunt words created as commercial names. In pronunciation, the *a*-element in all of these items is a schwa, but in many cases the function of the *a* is unclear: in *SelectaVision* it could be thematic like the *-e-* in *television*, a reduction of *-or* in *selector*, an indefinite article (*Select a vision*), or a mix of these. The range of such usages is large: (1) Like *-a-* in *megalith*: *Beat-A-Bug, Cup-a-Soup, gorillagram, Prismaflex, Relax-a-Dial, Rent-a-tux*. (2) Like *-e-* in *telephone*: *cineplex, Procretech, telecom*. (3) Like *-i-* in *carnivore*: *agri-biz, Chemi-Garded, Digipulse, flexitime, Healthitone, Multivite, NutriTime, VisiCalc*. (4) Like *-o-* in *cardiogram*: *biotech, Dento-Med, Film-O-Sonic, Fotopost, Frig-O-Seal, FructoFin, Thermoshell, Tomorrowvision*. (5) Like *-u-* in *acupuncture*: *Accu-Vision, CompuSex, Execu-Travel, Dentu Cream*. (6) Like *-y-* in *bathyscaphe*: *polywater, Skinnyvision*. See BLEND, COMBINING FORM.

**INTERJECTION.** A PART OF SPEECH and a term often used in dictionaries for marginal items functioning alone and not as conventional elements of sentence structure. They are sometimes emotive and situational: *oops*, expressing surprise, often at something mildly embarrassing, *yuk/yuck*, usually with a grimace and expressing disgust, *ow, ouch*, expressing pain, *wow*, expressing admiration and wonder, sometimes mixed with surprise. They sometimes use sounds outside the normal range of a language: for example, the sounds represented as *ugh, whew, tut-tut/tsk-tsk*. The spelling of *ugh* has produced a variant of the original, pronounced 'ugg'. Such greetings as *Hello, Hi, Goodbye* and such exclamations as *Cheers, Hurray, Well* are also interjections.

**INTERLANGUAGE. 1.** A LANGUAGE created for international communication, such as *Esperanto*, or used as a LINGUA FRANCA in a particular region, such as Hausa and PIDGIN English in West Africa. **2.** In LINGUISTICS, a language intermediate between two or more other languages, generally used as a trade jargon, such as *HINDLISH* in India and *TAGLISH*/Mix-Mix in the Philippines. **3.** In language teaching and applied linguistics, the transitional system of a learner of a foreign language at any stage between beginner and advanced. See ARTIFICIAL LANGUAGE, CODE-MIXING AND CODE-SWITCHING, -GLISH AND -LISH, LANGUAGE LEARNING.

**INTERNATIONAL CORPUS OF ENGLISH, The.** Short form **ICE**. An international electronic CORPUS of STANDARD ENGLISH involving at its outset 23 territories

worldwide: 9 with English as a native language (Australia, Canada, the Irish Republic, Jamaica, New Zealand, Northern Ireland, the UK, the US, and Wales as a distinct entity: with their own corpora); 9 with English as a second language, with official status (Hong Kong, India, Kenya, Nigeria, the Philippines, Singapore, Tanzania, Zambia, and Zimbabwe: with their own corpora); and 5 with English as a foreign language (Belgium, Denmark, Germany, the Netherlands, and Sweden: no national corpora). The project derives from the SURVEY OF ENGLISH USAGE at University College London, whose director Sidney GREENBAUM proposed it in 1988. The collection of texts began in 1990, with the aim that each national corpus would contain 1m words and all would be compiled, computerized, and analysed in similar ways. In addition, there would be supplementary projects dealing with: translations into printed English; English in international spoken communication; and English in teaching material for learners of the language. The texts in the supplementary corpora would be drawn from varieties similar to those in the national corpora. The aim of ICE as a corpus of corpora has been to make comparative studies easier for national varieties of English, both as a native and a second language. The SEU component (known as ICE-GB) would also provide the means for investigating recent changes in the language through a comparison with the original Survey corpus. Greenbaum noted in 1991:

> Although the standard varieties of British and American English are the most firmly established, other English-speaking countries have begun to claim linguistic independence, looking to their own varieties for what is correct or appropriate. At this stage, research can have practical applications in language planning by preventing the national standards from drifting too far apart. In that way research can help to preserve the international character of at least written English.
>
> ('ICE: the International Corpus of English', *English Today*, 28, October).

Greenbaum edited a book on the project, *Comparing English Worldwide: The International Corpus of English*, and compiled *The Oxford English Grammar*, both published by Oxford University Press in 1996, the year in which he died. Bas Aarts was appointed director of the SEU in 1997 and, despite the founder's death and ongoing difficulties in funding, the ICE projects continue, focusing in particular on the computer tagging and PARSING of corpus texts.

**INTERNATIONAL ENGLISH**. The English language, usually in its standard form, either when used, taught, and studied as a LINGUA FRANCA throughout the world, or when taken as a whole and used in contrast with *American English*, *British English*, *South African English*, etc. Compare INTERNATIONAL STANDARD ENGLISH, WORLD ENGLISH.

**INTERNATIONAL LANGUAGE**, sometimes **international auxiliary language**. A language, natural or artificial, that is used for general communication among the nations of the world: 'In the four centuries since the time of Shakespeare, English has changed from a relatively unimportant European language with perhaps four million speakers into an international language used in every continent by approximately eight hundred million people' (Loreto Todd & Ian Hancock, *International English Usage*, 1986); 'The success of English in its function as an international auxiliary language has often been regarded as a measure of its adequacy for the job' (Manfred Görlach, 'Varietas Delectat', in Nixon & Honey, *An Historic Tongue*, 1988). Compare LINGUA FRANCA, WORLD LANGUAGE. See BASIC ENGLISH, BROKEN ENGLISH, WORLD ENGLISH.

**INTERNATIONAL PHONETIC AL-PHABET**, short form *IPA*. An ALPHABET developed by the *International Phonetic Association* to provide suitable symbols for the sounds of any language. The symbols are based on the Roman alphabet, with further symbols created by inverting or reversing Roman letters or taken from the Greek alphabet. The main characters are supplemented when necessary by diacritics. The first version of the alphabet was developed in the late 19c by A. E. Ellis, Paul Passy, Henry Sweet, and Daniel JONES from a concept proposed by Otto Jespersen. It has been revised from time to time, most recently in 1989 (see accompanying charts). The IPA is sufficiently rich to label the phonemes of any language and to handle the contrasts between them, but its wide range of exotic symbols and diacritics makes it difficult and expensive for printers and publishers to

work with. As a result, modifications are sometimes made for convenience and economy, for example in ELT learners' dictionaries. Phoneme symbols are used in phonemic transcription, either to provide a principled method of transliterating non-Roman alphabets (such as Russian, Arabic, Chinese), or to provide an alphabet for a previously unwritten language. The large number of diacritics makes it possible to mark minute shades of sound as required for a narrow phonetic transcription. The alphabet has not had the success that its designers hoped for, in such areas as the teaching of languages (especially English) and SPELLING REFORM. It is less used in North America than elsewhere, but is widely used as a pronunciation aid for EFL and ESL, especially by British publishers and increasingly in British dictionaries of English. See ENGLISH PRONOUNCING DICTIONARY, LANGUAGE TEACHING, LEARNER'S DICTIONARY, PHONETIC TRANSCRIPTION, SPEECH, RESPELLING, WRITING.

**INTERNATIONAL PHONETIC ASSO-CIATION**, short form *IPA*. An association that seeks to promote the science of PHONETICS and its practical applications. It was founded in 1886 in France under the English name *The Phonetic Teachers' Association*, by a group of language teachers who used phonetic theory and transcription in their work. The journal *Dhi Fonètik Tītcer* started in France in the same year, edited by Paul Passy and printed in English in a phonetic script; its name was changed in 1889 to *Le Maître phonétique*. At first, the Association was concerned mainly with phonetics applied to teaching English, but interest expanded with the membership to the phonetic study of all languages. It acquired its present name in 1897. Although the Association played an important part in the European movement for the reform of LANGUAGE TEACHING in the late 19c, it is now best known for its regularly revised alphabet. See JONES, SPEECH.

**INTERNATIONAL SCIENTIFIC VO-CABULARY**. As used by Philip Gove, editor, *Webster's Third New International Dictionary*, 1961. A term for the classically derived vocabulary of science common to such languages as English, French, and Spanish. In *Webster's Third*, the letters ISV mark words 'when their language of origin is not posi-

## THE INTERNATIONAL PHONETIC ALPHABET

CONSONANTS

| | Bilabial | Labiodental | Dental | Alveolar | Postalveolar | Retroflex | Palatal | Velar | Uvular | Pharyngeal | Glottal |
|---|---|---|---|---|---|---|---|---|---|---|---|
| Plosive | p b | | | t d | | ʈ ɖ | c ɟ | k g | q ɢ | | ʔ |
| Nasal | m | ɱ | | n | | ɳ | ɲ | ŋ | ɴ | | |
| Trill | ʙ | | | r | | | | | ʀ | | |
| Tap or Flap | | | | ɾ | | ɽ | | | | | |
| Fricative | ɸ β | f v | θ ð | s z | ʃ ʒ | ʂ ʐ | ç ʝ | x ɣ | χ ʁ | ħ ʕ | h ɦ |
| Lateral fricative | | | | ɬ ɮ | | | | | | | |
| Approximant | | ʋ | | ɹ | | ɻ | j | ɰ | | | |
| Lateral approximant | | | | l | | ɭ | ʎ | ʟ | | | |
| Ejective stop | p' | | | t' | | ʈ' | c' | k' | q' | | |
| Implosive | ɓ ɓ | | | ɗ ɗ | | | ʄ ʄ | ɠ ɠ | ʛ ɗ | | |

Where symbols appear in pairs, the one to the right represents a voiced consonant. Shaded areas denote articulations judged impossible.

VOWELS

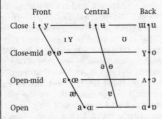

Where symbols appear in pairs, the one to the right represents a rounded vowel.

tively ascertainable but they are known to be current in at least one language other than English. . . . Some ISV words (like *haploid*) have been created by taking a word with a rather general and simple meaning from one of the languages of antiquity, usually Latin and Greek, and conferring upon it a very specific and complicated meaning for the purposes of modern scientific discourse.' Typically an ISV word is a compound or a derivative which 'gets only its raw materials, so to speak, from antiquity'. Compare CLASSICAL COMPOUND, COMBINING FORM.

**INTERNATIONAL STANDARD ENG-LISH**. Short form *ISE*. The STANDARD language used internationally. The term has two linked senses: (1) The sum-total of all STANDARD ENGLISH usage worldwide, but with particular reference to the norms of AmE and BrE, and possibly AusE, varieties which have established works of reference such as grammars, dictionaries, and style guides which broadly delimit national USAGE. (2) A more specific kind of standard usage that draws on such sources but increasingly has a transnational identity of its own, especially in print (as illustrated most particularly by the texts of 'quality' English-language newspapers worldwide) and the usage of such international organizations as the UNITED NATIONS. Compare INTERNATIONAL ENGLISH, STANDARD ENGLISH, TEIL, WORLD STANDARD ENGLISH.

**INTERNET, The.** Short form *the Net*. A worldwide range of computer networks made possible by a standard set of communication rules known as the *Internet protocol*, allowing for both data transmission and an electronic E-MAIL service. The latter passes messages from one electronic address to another (for which a computer requires a *modem*, a device that links it on demand to the general telephone system). The Internet derives from the ARPAnet used in the 1970s mainly by educational institutions. It has expanded to include millions of individuals and organizations who have various means of 'accessing' Internet 'gateways', as for example through such 'providers' as America Online (AOL), CompuServe, and Demon Internet. A key aspect of the Net is its *Domain Name System*, which specifies the location of computers sending and receiving transmissions. An *Internet address* consists of the user's account name followed by the symbol @ ('at'), a host organization's name, and one or more domains, as in *jsmith@au.edu*, where *au* stands for *American University* and *edu* is *education*. Because the system originated in the US, American addresses do not have a national domain, whereas addresses in other countries generally do: for example, *uk* for the United Kingdom, placed at the end. Because of the success and vast expansion of the Net in the later 1990s, congestion has arisen in the form of delays in 'downloading' (that is, receiving and storing) data. As a result, some organizations have created their own private *intranets*, which offer easier transmission and fewer breakdowns.

The Internet is inherently decentralized, there is no single controlling organization, it is not operated for profit, and has been described as 'anarchy by design'. This is because it grew out of the ARPAnet, an extensive military system created in 1969 by ARPA (the United States Defense Advanced Research Project Agency), which linked a number of US universities, research centres, etc., by means of an electronic 'nervous system' which had no headquarters. As a result, the ARPAnet could not be destroyed by an enemy strike at any one locality, and had in addition a capacity for rerouting information if any kind of disruption arose. For the same reason, no government or other organization can impose policy or watertight censorship on what transpires among users of the Internet, who have inherited a system created for very different reasons from those which make the Net useful for them. Most people now access the Net through commercial service providers, such as US-based America On-Line (AOL) and CompuServe and UK-based Demon Internet and Pipex. In 1981, only 213 computers were registered on the Internet, by 1989 there were *c*.80,000, by late 1990 over 300,000, in early 1992 over 700,000, by 1993 1–2m worldwide, and by 1996 probably more than 30m people in over 70 countries currently exchanging data, news, and comment. See COMPUTING, EMOTICON, NETIQUETTE, WORLD-WIDE WEB.

**INTERROGATIVE.** In GRAMMAR, the structure through which questions are asked, and a term used in the classification of sentence types, in contrast with *declarative*, *imperative*, etc. It is often used interchangeably with *QUESTION*, but some grammarians keep interrogative as a category of form and question as a category of meaning, while others do the reverse. The sentence *Can I borrow your pen?* is interrogative in form, but is a directive in meaning, requesting the listener to lend the pen.

**INTERVOCALIC.** A term in PHONETICS indicating that a consonant occurs between VOWELS: intervocalic /r/ in *merry* and /t/ in *butter*. See R, SPEECH.

**INTONATION.** The TONE pattern of SPEECH, produced by varying vocal pitch. Type and style of intonation are closely linked to patterns of RHYTHM and STRESS and cannot easily be described separately from them.

**INTRUSIVE *R*.** In some accents of English, including RECEIVED PRONUNCIATION, an /r/

pronounced between the vowels /ɔ, ɑː, ə/ and a following vowel when there is no *r* in the spelling, as in *Australia/r and New Zealand*, the *India/r Office*, *draw/r/ing room*. Homophonic effects sometimes occur, as in *law and order/lore and order*. Occasionally, comment on the intrusion is humorous; in Britain, *Laura Norder* is a friend of the police and an advocate of strong government. The /r/ is in phonological terms an inherent feature of the accent in question, but because it sometimes has an orthographic form (as in *czar of Russia*) and sometimes does not (as in *Shah of Persia*), it has been widely stigmatized in the latter case as a sound that should not be there and that makes no sense. The /r/ is accepted in the first of these phrases but often rejected as non-standard in the second. However, its use continues regardless of approval or disapproval, and generally goes unnoticed among those speakers who do it. See LINKING R, NEW YORK, RHOTIC AND NON-RHOTIC.

**INVERSION**, also **anastrophe**. **1.** Turning something round, as for example in English, when forming certain kinds of QUESTIONS from statements, such as *Are you coming?* from *You are coming*, by inverting the order of *you are*. **2.** In RHETORIC, speech in which the normal word order of statements is turned round, usually for emphasis or to mark priority and eminence: 'To the Most High and Mightie Prince, Iames by the grace of God King of Great Britaine, France and Ireland, Defender of the Faith, &c. the Translators of the Bible wish grace Mercie, and Peace through Iesus Christ our Lord' (dedication, the Authorized Version of the Bible, 1611). Journalistic uses of inversion that are often regarded as vices include inverting verb and subject in reporting clauses that come before quoted statements: for example, *Says Darren Beagle, chief programmer at Megabux Inc.*, '*This is the breakthrough we've all been waiting for.*' See CHIASMUS, QUESTION, WORD ORDER.

■ **IRISH** ─────────────────── ■

**1.** The adjective for Ireland, its people, languages, and traditions: *Irish* GAELIC, *the Irish language*, *the Irish Question*, *Irish whiskey*. Its nuances are varied, ranging from the sublime (*Irish patriot*) through such humorous and mischievous 'institutions' as the *Irish bull* and *Irish joke*, to facetious phrases like *an Irish hurricane* a flat calm with drizzling rain

*an Irish rise* a reduction in pay. Such expressions are sometimes deliberately used in Britain to express anti-Irish feeling. If something seems unusual, fey, or illogical, a common comment is: *That's a bit Irish.* **2.** Irish Gaelic: *In Connemara they speak Irish.*

**Irish and English**. The relationship between the English and Irish languages is at least eight centuries old. In that period, the fortunes of both have waxed and waned, and the contacts have been complicated by conquest, rebellion, religion, ethnicity, immigration, emigration, politics, and education. As English has advanced and Irish retreated, it has been said both that English 'murdered' Irish and that Irish 'committed suicide' in the face of English. It is certainly true that the main reasons for the replacement of Irish by English are social and political rather than linguistic. They include: (1) The large-scale settlements begun in the 16c by the Tudors and reinforced by the Stuarts and Cromwell in the 17c. (2) The penal laws of the 18c which reduced the native population to subsistence level and ensured that Irish was no longer the first language for those who hoped to improve their political or social position. (3) The introduction of National Schools in 1831, where English was the sole medium of instruction. (4) The years of famine in the mid-19c, which resulted in mass emigration and a belief that land and language were blighted.

**The heyday of Irish**. When in the 12c the Normans invaded Ireland, they found a secure language with strong and distinctive traditions. Speakers of Irish had Gaelicized not only the earlier people of the island and other Celtic settlers, but also later Pictish, Anglo-Saxon, and Norse settlers. The French, Flemish, Welsh, and English languages went to Ireland with the Normans and became in due course subject to pressure from Irish. Only within the eastern coastal region known as the Pale did English maintain a fragile grip. Medieval statutes show both the power of Irish and a wish to protect English against it: in 1285, a letter sponsored by the Bishop of Kildare and sent to the king suggested that Irish-speaking clerics should not be promoted because of their wish to maintain their language, and in 1366, the Statutes of Kilkenny (written in French) enjoined the English to use English names, customs, and language. However, Irish encroached even at the highest levels: in the 14c, the Earls of Ormond and Desmond spoke Irish and the latter, although Lord Chief Justice, wrote Irish poetry.

**The conquest of Ireland.** In the 16c, the English defeated the Gaelic order in Ireland; land was confiscated and plantation schemes brought in large numbers of English and later Scottish settlers. From 1600, English grew in strength and by 1800 was regularly used by up to 50% of the population. However, such was the growth in population that on the eve of the famines of 1846–8 there were probably more Irish-speakers in absolute terms than at any previous time. What began with Tudor pronouncements became more and more part of the social tissue of the island. As the 19c famines and mass emigrations proceeded, English consolidated its position. The Catholic Church became more reconciled to it and wary of Protestant proselytism through Irish, a process started by Elizabeth. Political leaders such as Daniel O'Connell were more concerned with emancipation than language and a school system was established, managed by the Catholic clergy, that excluded Irish from the curriculum. The steady decline of Irish was abetted by a general, pragmatic desire to acquire English. By the mid-19c, few Irish monolinguals were left and bilingualism had become a way-station on the road to English alone.

**The Gaelic League.** The founding of the Gaelic League in 1893 marked the start of the strongest wave of revivalist sentiment, which has endured in all its vicissitudes. Irish revivalism, an example of linguistic nationalism, arrived only when the language was already in grave peril. Its leaders were such Dublin intellectuals as Douglas Hyde and Eoin MacNeill, whose Irish was acquired rather than native. The movement largely failed to engage the support of the dwindling group of native speakers in the rural and impoverished *Gaeltacht*: an Irish-speaking area in the west that was idealized, romanticized, and kept at a safe remove. In addition, Irish was often linked with the strength of Catholicism, an association which permitted English to be depicted as the secular medium of a foreign culture, despite the fact that the Catholic Church promoted English even in Irish-speaking parishes.

**Irish since independence.** The Gaelic League had considerable success in fighting for Irish in schools and university but did not alter the language habits of the general population. When the Irish Free State was set up in 1921, Irish became a government responsibility. It was declared the national language, but accompanying the rhetoric was a serious and sometimes pessimistic concern for its fate. The government was often (and continues to be) accused of paying only lipservice to revival. It entrusted the task to the schools and it is therefore in education that the most important action has taken place over the last 70 years, such as compulsory Irish classes and making the gaining of an overall secondary school leaving certificate dependent on passing Irish (a rule no longer in effect). However, these efforts have not reversed the long decline: Ireland is now an overwhelmingly English-speaking country in which only 1–2% use Irish regularly and, even in the Gaeltacht, many parents bring up their children in English. Given the strong social currents of English in everyday life, it is hard to see what more the schools could have done than apply a thin wash of Irish across the land. See BORROWING, CELTIC LANGUAGES, HIBERNO-ENGLISH, SHELTA.

## ■ IRISH ENGLISH ■

Short form *IrE*. The English language as used in Ireland. Scholars currently employ three terms to describe this variety: ANGLO-IRISH, HIBERNO-ENGLISH, and *Irish English*. *Anglo-Irish* is the oldest and has long been associated with the English language in Ireland, English people in Ireland, and British politics in Ireland, as a result of which it can be ambiguous and Irish people often dislike its use as a generic term. *Hiberno-English* avoids this difficulty and identifies English in Ireland with the people of Ireland, not with outsiders. The term *Irish English*, although to some ears whimsical and paradoxical, is less academic and opaque, is not likely to be misinterpreted, and fits into the set *American English, British English, Indian English*, etc. It is used here as the generic term for all kinds of English in Ireland.

**The Germanic settlements.** It is not certain when, how, or in what forms English was first heard and used in Ireland. Trading links have existed between Ireland and

Britain for at least two millennia, but nothing is known about the contact languages used after the OLD ENGLISH dialects were established in Britain. Following the Viking invasions in the 9c, DANISH and NORSE settlements were established in the east and south of the island. In this way, Germanic dialects began to affect Irish Gaelic, especially in commerce, dress, and seafaring. In 1155, the English Pope, Adrian IV, granted Henry II of England permission to invade Ireland and bring about religious reforms. The subsequent invasion launched from

Wales, was a military success. The Treaty of Windsor suggests that, by 1175, half of Ireland was under Anglo-Norman control, and by 1250, almost three-quarters of the island had been divided into shires. The leaders of the invasion spoke French but the soldiers were Flemish, Welsh, and from southwest England. English was their LINGUA FRANCA and became established in all large settlements, especially in an area around DUBLIN known as the (English) Pale and in the Baronies of Forth and Bargy in Wexford.

## IRISH PLACE-NAMES

The place-names of Ireland reflect mixed linguistic origins over more than 2,000 years that include Irish Gaelic, Scandinavian, and Anglo-Scottish influences, and a range of hybrids and Anglicizations.

**Gaelic**. There are four broad types: (1) *Settlement names*. These include names based on the elements *baile* ('town') and *graig* ('village'): *Baile na Dtulach* ('town of the little hills'), Anglicized as *Ballynadolly* in County Antrim; *Graigin* ('little village'), Anglicized as *Graigeen* in County Limerick. (2) *Toponyms*. These include names based on *clár* and *magh* ('plain'), occurring both on their own, as in *Clare* (the name of a west-coast county) and *Moy* in County Tyrone, and in combination, as in *Magh Cosgrain* ('Cosgrain's plain'), now *Macosquin* in C. Derry; *coill* ('wood'), as in *Ceithre Choill* ('four woods'), now *Kerrykyle* in C. Limerick; *gleann* ('narrow valley'), as in *Gleann na Madaidhe* ('glen of the dogs') in C. Galway, now *Glennamaddy*; *inis* and *oileán* 'island', as in *Inis Fraoch*, now *Innisfree* in C. Donegal. (3) *Sites of battles*. These include: *Baile na Ruage* ('town of the rout'), now *Ballynarooga* in C. Limerick; *Drom Air* ('slaughter ridge'), now *Drumar* in C. Monaghan. (4) *Religious names*. These are both Christian and pagan, as in: *Domhnach mór* ('big church'), now *Donaghmore; Seanchill* ('old church'), now *Shankill* (in Belfast); *Sidh Dhruim* ('fairy ridge'), now *Sheetrim*; *Bóthar an Phúca* ('road of the Pooka', a supernatural being, cognate with Shakespeare's Puck), now *Boheraphuca*.

**Scandinavian**. Norse names, found mainly around the coast, include: those in *-ford* ('ford'), as in *Longford, Waterford*, and *Wexford*; *vig* ('bay'), Anglicized as in *Wicklow*; and *ey* ('island'), as in *Dalkey* ('thorn island'). *Leixlip* on the River Liffey derives from *Hlaxa Hlaup* ('salmon leap').

**Anglo-Scottish**. **1.** Some names, introduced under the Tudors and Stuarts, in the time of the Plantations (of settlers from both parts of Britain), are English, as with *Greencastle* in Antrim, *Jamestown* in Leitrim, and *Newcastle* in Tipperary, while others are Scottish, as in *Portmarnock* in Dublin, *Portstewart* in Derry, and *Stewartstown* in Tyrone. **2.** Some names are translations from Gaelic, as with *Blackrock* in Dublin, from *Carraig Dhubh* ('rock black'). **3.** Hybrid English and Gaelic forms occur, as in *Ardmore Point* in Wicklow, *Glenshane Pass* in Derry), *Maguiresbridge* in Fermanagh, and *the Mountains of Mourne* in Down. **4.** British-Irish blends occur, most notably in *Londonderry*, the name of a city in Northern Ireland. Protestant loyalists favour the London link, while Catholic nationalists insist on *Derry* alone.

**Gaelicization**. Like the Vikings, the Anglo-Normans were absorbed into the Celtic way of life, slowly relinquishing their language and customs. Laws, such as the Statutes of Kilkenny (1366), tried to ensure that they would continue to speak English and use English-style surnames, but such laws were increasingly ignored, so that by 1500 Irish Gaelic had virtually replaced English even in the towns. The Reformation in England in the 16c reinforced the solidarity between the settlers (who remained Catholic) and their co-religionists, the Irish, further weakening the role of English in the island. The English of the Anglo-Norman settlers and their descendants came to be called *Yola* (a variant of *old*) and the settlers themselves became known as the OLD ENGLISH.

**Language shift**. The main forms of present-day IrE can be traced to the second wave of settlers. From the middle of the 16c, large numbers of English and Scottish *planters* settled in Ireland, creating communities (*plantations*) that preserved a separate identity from the native population, from whom they were marked out by language, religion, and culture. By the beginning of the 17c, Irish was still the most widely used language, but within 250 years a massive shift had occurred. The 1900 census records 21,000 monoglot speakers of Irish in the country (5% of the population). Today, the figure is zero, but some 100,000 people speak Irish as one of their mother tongues, the younger bilinguals showing English influence in their Irish.

**Kinds of Irish English**. There are no dialect differences corresponding exactly with any county or other regional boundary in Ireland, but because of the different types of plantation, it is possible to distinguish three varieties of IrE: (1) *Anglo-Irish*, a middle- and working-class variety spoken over most of Ireland and deriving from the English of the 17c planters from England, modified by contacts with Irish, ULSTER SCOTS, and Hiberno-English. (2) *Ulster Scots*, a variety of Lowland Scots spoken mainly in Antrim, Donegal, and Down, influencing all forms of northern speech. (3) *Hiberno-English*, the mainly working-class variety used by communities whose ancestral language was Gaelic. Because of their long association, the three varieties tend to influence and shade into each other in various complex ways.

**Models of pronunciation**. In pronunciation, three main models are followed: (1) *Received Pronunciation*. Two small groups of people have RP accents: men educated in England, especially in the public (private) schools, and some individuals in the media. (2) *Received Irish Pronunciation*. A rhotic accent and the prestige pronunciation of Radio Telefís Eireann (Irish Radio and Television). It is closer to RP than other varieties of Irish speech and is favoured by middle-class speakers of Anglo-Irish. (3) *Received Ulster Pronunciation*. In Northern Ireland, many broadcasters speak standard English with a regional accent and are more influential as models than speakers of RP.

**Bilingual signs**. Since the Irish Republic is officially bilingual, English appears widely with Irish on public buildings and signs, and on official forms and documents, as in the following pairs on noticeboards at Dublin Airport: *Shops/Siopaí, Bar/Beár, Snacks/Sólaistí, Post Office/Oifig an Phoist, Telephones/Telefóin, Information/Fiasrúcháin*. Both languages appear on most road signs, the English below and capitalized, the Irish above in smaller traditional letters, as with: *Cill Fhionnúrach* over *Kilfenora*, *An Carn* over *Carran*, *Baile Uí Bheacháin* over *Ballyvaghan*, and *Lios Dúin Bhearna* over *Lisdoonvarna*. In many instances, the English names are Anglicizations of traditional Irish names, and the two correspond closely; in others they are quite different, as with *Baile átha Cliath* (pronounced 'bla-clee') over *Dublin*. See BELFAST, BRITISH ENGLISH, NEWFOUNDLAND ENGLISH, SCOUSE, ULSTER ENGLISH.

**IRISH GAELIC**. See CELTIC LANGUAGES, GAELIC, IRISH.

**IRISHISM** also, though rare, **Iricism**, **Hibernianism**, **Hibernicism**, **Irishry**. An Irish usage, custom, or peculiarity, and especially a form of language regarded as quintessentially Irish, including shibboleths and stereotypes such as the exclamations *begorrah* and *bejabers*, and such expressions as *a broth of a boy* and *the top of the morning to you*, well known in Britain, North America, and Australia, but used by Irish people only when consciously speaking 'stage Irish' for amusement or as a parody. Phonological, syntactic, and lexical Irishisms occur in: *Divil the bit of a shtick could I find for to bate the baisht with* I couldn't find a stick to beat the animal with; *Will you be* *after havin a cup of tea?—I will, to be sure; Wasn't it herself broke the delph into smithereens?* Rhetorical Irishisms are often plays on words (*He's teetotally obsnorious*), malapropisms (*That man's a confederate liar, so he is*), or Irish bulls (*Nuns run in that family*). See IRISH ENGLISH, -ISM.

**IRONY.** **1.** In RHETORIC, words with an implication opposite to their usual meaning. Ironic comment may be humorous or mildly sarcastic, as for example when, at a difficult moment, an act of kindness makes things worse, and someone says, 'Well, that's a *lot* better, isn't it?' Expressions *heavy with irony* are often used to drive a point home: 'I'm really looking forward to seeing him, *I don't think*'; 'You're pleased to see me? *Pull the other leg/one (it's got bells on)*.' In such usages, irony slides into *sarcasm*. **2.** In general usage, incongruity between what is expected and what happens, and an outcome that displays such incongruity. The sentence adverb *ironically* is often used to draw attention to it: 'Ironically, his kindness only made things worse.' In many instances, *ironically* serves virtually as a synonym of *paradoxically*. **3.** Wry awareness of life's incongruity and irrationality.

   Three kinds of irony have been recognized since antiquity: (1) *Socratic irony*, a mask of innocence and ignorance adopted to win an argument. Among the stock characters in early Greek comedy were two deceivers, the *eírōn*, a weak but wily underdog, who usually tricked the *alazōn*, a bombastic and stupid vagabond. In Plato's dialogues, Socrates often plays the *eírōn*, pretending ignorance and asking seemingly foolish questions so as to move a debate in the direction he wants. (2) *Dramatic or tragic irony*, a double vision of what is happening in a play or a real-life situation. In Greek tragedy, the characters were blind to fateful circumstances of which the audience was all too well aware, producing a privileged and often poignant appreciation of the plot. (3) *Linguistic irony*, a duality of meaning, now the classic form of irony. Building on the idea of dramatic irony, the Romans concluded that language often carries a double message, a second often mocking or sardonic meaning running contrary to the first.

   In modern times, two further conceptions have been added: (1) *Structural irony*, a quality that is built into texts, in which the observations of a naïve narrator point up the deeper implications of a situation. In the stories of the English humorist P. G. Wodehouse (1917 onward), Bertie Wooster reports verbatim the smooth, deflating comments of his butler Jeeves without any indication that he has understood or even noticed what Jeeves 'really' says. (2) *Romantic irony*, in which writers conspire with readers to share the double vision of what is happening in the plot of a novel, film, etc. By the 17c and 18c, a refined ironic style was established in European writing, as when Henry Fielding interrupted the action in his novels to address his readers directly and comment on events. When engaging in this game, writers combine creative egotism with a suave and knowing self-mockery. By the 19c, critics had become adept at detecting and dissecting irony in literature and in life. The Danish philosopher Kierkegaard raised irony to the cosmic level when he proposed in 1841 that it was a way of viewing all existence, and some writers and critics have since implied that God is the greatest ironist of all. The phrase *irony of fate* suggests that, like drama, life treats people as if wryly mocking them, delivering at a strategic moment the opposite to what is deserved or at first seemed likely. See FIGURATIVE LANGUAGE.

**IRREGULAR.** A term for linguistic forms that are exceptional in that they cannot be predicted by general RULES: *children* as the plural of *child*, because it is not formed, as most noun plurals are, by adding -*s*. See REGULAR.

**IRREGULAR VERB.** A VERB that does not follow the general rules for verb forms. Verbs in English are irregular if they do not have a normal -*ed* form like *talked, walked*. The -*ed* form has two functions: past and past participle. In some irregular verbs, these functions are served by different forms. Contrast *He talked for a long time* and *He has talked for a long time* with *He spoke for a long time* and *He has spoken for a long time*. There are other kinds of irregularity: *shut* serves as base form and -*ed* form. Since for all verbs (regular and irregular) the -*s* and -*ing* forms are constructed from the base by regular rules, it is only necessary to cite the base, past, and -*ed* forms to characterize irregular verbs. These three are termed the *principal parts* of the verb and are always given in the order: base, past, -*ed* participle.

## IRREGULAR VERBS IN ENGLISH

The table below gives the principal parts for most irregular verbs, including common alternatives and differences between BrE and AmE. Generally, the alternatives are possible in both varieties, but the form labelled BrE or AmE is found especially in that variety.

| Base | Past | -ed participle | Base | Past | -ed participle |
|------|------|----------------|------|------|----------------|
| awake | awoke, awaked | awoken, awaked | feed | fed | fed |
| beat | beat | beaten, beat | feel | felt | felt |
| become | became | become | fight | fought | fought |
| bend | bent | bent | find | found | found |
| bet | bet, betted (*BrE*) | bet, betted (*BrE*) | fit | fitted, fit (*AmE*) | fitted, fit (*AmE*) |
| | | | flee | fled | fled |
| bind | bound | bound | fly | flew | flown |
| bite | bit | bitten, bit | forget | forgot | forgotten, forgot (*AmE*) |
| bleed | bled | bled | | | |
| blow | blew | blown | forgive | forgave | forgiven |
| break | broke | broken | freeze | froze | frozen |
| bring | brought | brought | get | got | got, gotten (*AmE*) |
| build | built | built | | | |
| burn | burnt (*BrE*), burned | burnt (*BrE*), burned | give | gave | given |
| | | | go | went | gone |
| buy | bought | bought | grow | grew | grown |
| catch | caught | caught | hang | hung | hung, hanged |
| come | came | come | have | had | had |
| cost | cost | cost | hear | heard | heard |
| creep | crept | crept | hide | hid | hidden, hid |
| cut | cut | cut | hit | hit | hit |
| deal | dealt | dealt | hold | held | held |
| dig | dug | dug | hurt | hurt | hurt |
| do | did | done | keep | kept | kept |
| draw | drew | drawn | know | knew | known |
| dream | dreamt (*BrE*), dreamed | dreamt (*BrE*), dreamed | lead | led | led |
| | | | learn | learnt (*BrE*), learned | learnt (*BrE*), learned |
| drink | drank | drunk | | | |
| drive | drove | driven | leave | left | left |
| eat | ate | eaten | lend | lent | lent |

*Continued over*

Many irregular verbs exhibit changes in the middle vowel for one or both of the last two principal parts (*sing, sang, sung*) and have an *-en* inflection for the *-ed* participle (*speak, spoke, spoken*).

**Forms of BE**. The verb *be* is highly irregular, with eight forms: base *be*; present *am* (first-person singular), *is* (the *-s* form for third-person singular), *are* (second-person singular and all plurals); past *was* (first- and third-person singular) and *were* (second-person singular and all plurals);

*-ing* form *being*; *-ed* participle *been*. The *-s* forms of *have, do, say* are irregular (*has, does, says*), though the irregularity in pronunciation is obscured by the spelling of *does, says*.

**Modal verbs**. The modal auxiliaries have a defective paradigm since they only have the base forms and irregularly constructed past forms (*can, could; may, might*). *Must* is further exceptional in having only the base form.

All new verbs in English are regular, as

## IRREGULAR VERBS IN ENGLISH *continued*

| Base | Past | *-ed* participle | Base | Past | *-ed* participle |
|------|------|------------------|------|------|------------------|
| let | let | let | sit | sat | sat |
| lie | lay | lain | sleep | slept | slept |
| light | lit, lighted | lit, lighted | smell | smelt (*BrE*), smelled | smelt (*BrE*), smelled |
| lose | lost | lost | | | |
| make | made | made | speak | spoke | spoken |
| mean | meant | meant | spend | spent | spent |
| met | met | met | stand | stood | stood |
| mistake | mistook | mistaken | steal | stole | stolen |
| put | put | put | stick | stuck | stuck |
| read | read | read | strike | struck | struck |
| rid | rid, ridded | rid, ridded | swear | swore | sworn |
| ride | rode | ridden | swim | swam, swum (*AmE*) | swum |
| ring | rang, rung (*AmE*) | rung | | | |
| | | | take | took | taken |
| say | said | said | teach | taught | taught |
| see | saw | seen | tear | tore | torn |
| sell | sold | sold | tell | told | told |
| send | send | sent | think | thought | thought |
| set | set | set | throw | threw | thrown |
| shoot | shot | shot | understand | understood | understood |
| show | showed | shown | upset | upset | upset |
| shut | shut | shut | wake | woke, waked | woken, waken |
| sing | sang, sung (*AmE*) | sung | wear | wore | worn |
| | | | win | won | won |
| sink | sank, sunk (*AmE*) | sunk | write | wrote | written |

in *glitz, glitzed, glitzed.* Some irregular verbs also have regular forms: *sew, sewed, sewn* but also the regular *sew, sewed, sewed.* There are also some differences in irregular verbs between BrE and AmE: both *dived* and *dove* are found in AmE as pasts of *dive,* but only *dived* occurs in BrE. *Gotten* is used in AmE as an *-ed* participle in certain senses of the verb: *We've gotten more than we can use,* but not *We've got to do a lot better.* See STRONG VERB, T, WEAK VERB.

**ISLE OF MAN**. An island in the Irish Sea. The island was ruled by the Welsh during the 6–9c, then by the Norse until Magnus King of Norway ceded it and the Hebrides to Alexander II of Scotland in 1266. Granted to the Earls of Derby in 1406, it passed to the Dukes of Atholl in 1736, and was purchased from them by the British government partly in 1765, wholly in 1832. The island has its own parliament, the *Court of Tynwald,* comprising the governor, the Legislative Council, and the elected *House of Keys.* Acts of the British Parliament do not generally apply to the Isle of Man, which has a high degree of autonomy.

**Manx Gaelic** (also *Manx*). This Celtic language is closely related to Irish and Scottish GAELIC. It was probably introduced in the 4c by Irish settlers and may have replaced an earlier language similar in structure to Welsh. In the 10–13c, Manx was influenced by Norse, especially in its lexicon, but continued to be the main language of the island until the end of the 18c, when English began to assume a dominant role. Ned Maddrell, the last surviving speaker of Manx, died in 1974. The *Manx Society* has sought to sustain Manx as the second language of the island. The form now in use tends to be that of its classical literary period, the 18c, Anglicisms being replaced by coinages from Manx roots. It tends to be influenced in the spoken form by Irish Gaelic, since islanders can receive the Irish-language programmes of Radio Telefís Éireann.

**Manx English**. Welsh and Scandinavian influence gave way in the later Middle Ages to a distinctive Manx dialect of English that has close links, with varieties in Lancashire and shows substratum influence from Manx. Manx English is non-rhotic, has /æ/ in both *glass* and *gas*, distinguishes between *wh* and *w* as in *which witch*, tends to replace /ŋ/ by /n/ in *-ing* words, and often has a glottal plosive for /t/ (especially before syllabic *n* as in *beaten*, *touting*). Syntactic influence from Gaelic is found in the use of such preposition and pronoun constructions as *They returned with money at them* and *put a sight on her* (visit her). The Gaelic influence is stronger in vocabulary and includes words associated with farming (*collagh* a stallion), food (*braghtan* bread and butter), the home (*chiollagh* hearth), and folk traditions (*crosh caoirn* a cross made from twigs or rushes and placed over a door). See CELTIC LANGUAGES.

**-ISM**. A noun-forming SUFFIX, three of whose uses relate to language: (1) Forming words for concepts, activities, and conditions: *agrammatism, biculturalism, bilingualism, criticism, descriptivism, feminism, journalism, literary criticism, multiculturalism, obscurantism, plagiarism, prescriptivism, racism, sexism, symbolism*. (2) Forming linguistic and stylistic terms: *anachronism, aphorism, archaism, barbarism, classicism, colloquialism, dysphemism, euphemism initialism, malapropism, neologism, regionalism, solecism, syllogism, truism, verbalism, witticism*. (3) Forming words that identify usages as belonging to particular varieties of English: *Americanism, Anglicism, Australianism, Briticism, Canadianism, Gallicism, Indianism, Irishism, Latinism, New Zealandism, Scotticism*.

The suffix is widely used with considerable freedom and flexibility to label any regional or local usage, such as a *Newfoundlandism* or a *New Yorkism*, and for nonce purposes, as in: Simon Hoggart's 'Bushism of the week', in the *Observer* magazine during 1989, referring to the usage of US President George Bush. When asked to comment on the fall of the Berlin Wall, Bush is reported to have said: 'I wouldn't want to say this kind of development makes things to be moving too quickly at all . . . so I'm not going to hypothecate that it may—anything goes too fast' (17 Dec. 1989). Compare -ESE, -SPEAK. See POLITICALLY CORRECT.

**ISOGLOSS**. **1.** In DIALECT geography, an area within which a feature is used predominantly or exclusively. Such a feature (phonological, morphological, syntactic, semantic, lexical, or other) usually contrasts with some similar feature in adjoining areas. Thus, some native speakers of English pronounce /r/ after a vowel, as in *barn, hard, car*, while others do not: in the US this postvocalic /r/ is normally present in the Chicago area but absent in the Boston area. Such distinct areas are isoglosses. **2.** More commonly, the line on a dialect map which bounds the area of a certain usage. In England, an isogloss that stretches from the mouth of the Severn to Portsmouth separates the area of initial spoken /v/ from that of /f/, as in *vinger/finger, Vriday/Friday*, the *v*-forms being south-west of the line. No two isoglosses coincide exactly; there is always a transition area of partial overlapping. See DIALECTOLOGY.

# ■ ITALIAN ────────────── ■

A ROMANCE LANGUAGE, the official language of Italy and an official language of Switzerland, also spoken by Italian communities in Argentina, Australia, Britain, Canada, the US, Venezuela, and elsewhere. The term refers to both the STANDARD and literary language in contrast to the many DIALECTS and the entire complex of standard language and dialects, some of which are mutually unintelligible. In addition, some regional varieties, such as Friulian and Sardinian, are regarded as more or less distinct languages. Standard Italian is based on the medieval Tuscan dialect.

**Italian in English**. The influence of Italian on English is almost entirely lexical and has continued over many centuries. Since medieval times, Italian has had a strong influence on FRENCH, as a result of which many borrowings into English have had a distinctly Gallic aspect, as with *battalion* (16c: from *bataillon*, from *battaglione*), *caprice* (17c: from *caprice*, from *capriccio* the skip of a goat, a sudden sharp movement), *charlatan* (16c: from *charlatan*, from *ciarlatano*, from *ciarlare* to chatter), *frigate* (16c: from *frégate*, from *fregata*), *picturesque* (17c: from *pittoresque*, from *pittoresco*, with assimilation to *picture*), *tirade* (c.1800, from *tirade*, from *tirata* volley, from *tirare* to pull, fire a shot). Direct borrowings fall into four broad categories: (1) Terms from the centuries-old pan-

European tradition of using Italian to discuss and describe music: for example, *adagio, alto, andante, arpeggio, bel canto, cello, coloratura, con brio, concerto, contralto, crescendo, diminuendo, divertimento, fortissimo, libretto, mezzosoprano, pianoforte, pizzicato, scherzo, solo, sonata*. (2) Comparable literary, architectural, artistic, and cultural terms, such as *canto, conversazione, cupola, extravaganza, fresco, intaglio, novella, palazzo, stanza, tarantella*. (3) Internationalized culinary terms, such as *lasagne, minestrone, mozzarella, pasta, pizza, ravioli, spaghetti, tagliatelle, vermicelli*. (4) A variety of social words, including *alfresco, bimbo, bordello, bravo, condottiere, confetti, fiasco, ghetto, gigolo, graffiti, imbroglio, mafia, piazza, regatta*. Some loans have adapted spellings, as with *macaroni* (Italian *maccheroni*, earlier *maccaroni*), *seraglio* (Italian *serraglio*, ultimately from Persian). In addition, some words have moved to a greater or less extent from their original area of application into wider use, as with *crescendo, extravaganza, piano, solo*. Italian singular/plural inflections usually apply among terms restricted to musical, cultural, and culinary registers (*concerto/concerti, scherzo/scherzi*), but English inflections apply in general use (*concerto/concertos, scherzo/scherzos*).

**English in Italian**. The influence of English on Italian is essentially lexical and relatively recent. Noticeable in the 1930s, it has accelerated greatly since the 1960s, encouraged not only by the growing international use and prestige of English, but also by the adoption after the Second World War of English (to replace French) as the first foreign language in schools. Recent borrowings, often described as contributions to *Itangliano* (highly Anglicized Italian), include: *baby, boom, boy, budget, cartoon, catering, ceiling, club, control system, deadline, dee-jay, designer, egghead, fifty-fifty, flash, girl, happiness, identikit, killer, lady, leader, life-saver, market, partner, shop, shopping, show, spray, staff, standard, stop, style, target, trekking, trend*. The assimilation and use of many borrowings resemble the processes by which English is absorbed into French, including: (1) The adaptation of words to fit the gender and inflectional systems: *un bluff* a bluff, *bluffare* to bluff; *uno snob* a snob, *snobbare* to snob; *handicappati* the handicapped. Compounds may be reversed to conform to Italian norms, *a pocket radio* becoming *un radio-pocket*. (2) The restriction and adaptation of senses: *un flirt* an affair; *look* used only as a noun; *un mister* a sports coach. (3) The clipping of compounds: *un full* a full hand (of cards); *un night* a night club.

See CANADIAN ENGLISH, EARLY MODERN ENGLISH, EUROPEAN UNION, INDO-EUROPEAN LANGUAGES, LATIN, LINGUISTIC TYPOLOGY, MALTA, ROMANCE LANGUAGES.

**ITALIC**, also **italic script**, **italic type**, **italics**. A slightly slanted letter form based on a style of handwriting favoured by Italian humanists; introduced into European printing in 1501 by the Venetian printer Aldo Manuzio (Aldus Manutius). Originally a separate typeface, italic has long been combined with ROMAN as a marker for certain kinds of information in a text. In 16c English, it was often used for names and titles ('*Aristotle* wrote *De Caelo*'). Currently, it serves to highlight and emphasize titles, foreignisms, and words and phrases, and helps provide textual contrasts. Major quoted titles (books, plays, operas, films, musical compositions) are generally in italic (*The Wind in the Willows, Gone with the Wind*), but minor titles (poems in collections, articles in periodicals, or papers in scholarly works) are more commonly roman within quotation marks ('Ode to a Grecian Urn', 'Tense and aspect in Irish English'). The names in legal cases are also italicized: *Griffin* v. *Jones*. Italics are often used to mark exotic and unusual words in a text: 'Japanese columnists remind women readers of *gaman*, the tradition that they must endure their problems.' Similarly, words are italicized so as to draw the reader's attention to them: 'Ruskin called this attitude to nature *the pathetic fallacy*.' Italics highlight words which the writer wishes to emphasize, partially or fully: 'Hel-*lo*!'; 'He won't; not that he's afraid; oh, no! he *won't*.' In addition, phrases and sentences used as examples of usage in dictionaries are usually italicized to contrast with definitions in roman, and similar uses occur in textbooks. Sometimes entire texts are set in italic, sometimes sections of texts (such as introductions, summaries, and lead-ins), sometimes italic and roman alternate contrastively: paragraphs in italic with commentary in roman, or vice versa; a letter read in a novel or a character's thoughts in italics while the mainstream is in roman. See FOREIGNISM.

# J

## ■ J, j ──────────── ■

[Called 'jay', rhyming with *say*, to match the pronunciation of *K*. In ScoE, often rhymes with *high*, to match the pronunciation of *I*]. The 10th LETTER of the Roman ALPHABET as used for English. Around the 13c, it developed as a graphic variant of *i*, including use as the last element of a Roman numeral, *iij* three, *viij* eight. Its status was uncertain for centuries. Lists published as recently as the early 19c did not always have *i* and *j* as separate letters of the alphabet. In print, the distinction was being made fairly consistently in lower case by 1630, though not in the first editions of SHAKESPEARE. Introduced around 1600, upper-case *J* was not generally distinguished from *I* for another 200 years.

**Sound value and distribution**. (1) The STANDARD value of *j* in English is the voiced palato-alveolar affricate /dʒ/, whose voiceless equivalent is spelt *ch*: contrast *jeep/cheap*, *Jews/choose*. *J*, *dg*, and soft *g* compete to represent this sound, as in *judge* and *gem*. *J* is not normally used at the end of a word or a stressed syllable. In this position, *ge* and *dge* are the rule, as in *rage* and *dodge*. The only exceptions are a small number of loanwords, such as *hajj/hadj* (pilgrimage) from Arabic and *raj* (rule, government) from Hindi. (2) There is a strong tendency for *d* followed by an *i*-glide (in words like *grandeur*, *Indian*, *soldier*, *endure*) to move to the value of *j*, prompting such non-standard spellings as 'Injun' for *Indian* and 'sojer' for *soldier*. (3) *J* occurs most often word-initially before *a*, *o*, *u*, a position in which *g* normally has its hard value: *jab/gab*, *job/gob*, *jut/gut*. (4) *J* does not normally feature in words of Old English origin, the digraph *dg* representing the sound medially and finally (*cudgel*, *bridge*), but some *j*-words (*ajar*, *jowl*) may be of Germanic origin.

**Non-English influences**. (1) FRENCH has given English many words with initial *j*: *jail*, *jaundice*, *jaw*, *jay*, *jealous*, *jeopardy*, *jet*, *jewel*, *join*, *jolly*, *journal*, *journey*, *joy*, *juice*, *jury*, *just*. (2) French *g* has been changed to *j* in *jelly*, *Jeffrey*, *jest* and possibly in *jib*, *jig*. The form *judge* (French *juge*) is an orthographic

hybrid: initial French *j* and vernacular *dg* (marking a preceding short vowel). (3) Latin has contributed such words with initial *j* as *joke*, *jovial*, *jubilant*, *junior*, *juvenile*. (4) Other words with initial *j* tend to be exotic (*jackal*, *jaguar*, *jasmine*, *jerboa*, *ju-jitsu*, *jungle*), or recent, often AmE coinages (*jab*, *jam*, *jazz*, *jeep*, *jinx*, *jive*, and, with medial *j*, *hijack*). (5) Many proper names begin with *j*: *Jack*, *James*, *Jane*, *Janet*, *Jean*, *Jeffrey*, *Jim*, *Joan*, *John*, *Joseph*, *Julia*; as do the months *January*, *June*, *July*. (6) Medial *j* occurs commonly in Latinate roots after a prefix (*adjacent*, *conjunction*, *prejudice*, *reject*, *subjugate*) and such other Latinate words as *majesty*, *major*, *pejorative*. (7) Final *j* is rare, occurring only in such exotic forms as *raj* and *hajj/hadj*. (8) Since *j* differs in value in different languages, non-English values often occur in loans. The fricative of Modern French occurs in more recent loans (*bijou*) and in names (*Jean-Jacques*). GERMAN and some Slavonic languages pronounce *j* as a *y*-sound (*Jung*, *Janáček*). In SPANISH *j* represents the voiceless velar fricative /x/ (*Jerez*, *Juan*), which may be represented by *h* in English (*marihuana*) or fall silent. (9) Currently, *g/j* alternate in *gibe/jibe* and in the cognates *jelly/gelatine* and *jib/gibbet*, as well as in the personal names *Jeffrey/Geoffrey*, *Jillian/Gillian*. See G, I.

## JAMAICAN CREOLE, also **Jamaican English Creole**, **Jamaican Creole English**, **Jamaican**, **Patois**, **Patwa**, NATION LANGUAGE.

The general and technical term for the English-based CREOLE vernacular of Jamaica, a Caribbean country and member of the COMMONWEALTH. It has the most extensive and longest-standing literature and the widest media and artistic use of the varieties of CARIBBEAN ENGLISH CREOLE, and is the most fully studied. The wide appeal of Jamaican music, DUB poetry, and Rastafarian religion has spread the VERNACULAR throughout the Caribbean region as a widely heard (though frequently ill-understood) form of folk speech. Its influence is noteworthy in the UK, where it dominates other varieties of West Indian vernacular and has been a major factor in the evolution of BRITISH BLACK ENGLISH. In the US, Jamaican immigrant communities have also retained linguistic characteristics related to continued use of the language.

Jamaican Creole is relatively well researched, and within Jamaica, consensus has evolved on its artistic value and its distinctness from English, but despite this its use continues to be stigmatized and many literate Jamaicans do not value it. It is commonly viewed as an obstacle to education, an opinion actively countered by many who urge that the obstacle lies in failing to develop strategies for teaching English in the Creole environment. Because of the complex pattern of varieties between the English and Creole, Jamaica is often cited as a classic example of a *POST-CREOLE CONTINUUM*.

For those who have a command of both English and Creole, the one complements the other, English being more usual in formal public activity. Most of the population, however, use intermediate forms (mesolects). In radio and television, Jamaican is an established medium for advertisement, popular entertainment, and programmes with public participation. The news, however, is generally read in English. The use of Creole in newspapers is minimal, tending to be restricted to special columns. The *Dictionary of Jamaican English* (1967, 1980) has contributed to the stabilization of spelling in the press as well as to the readiness with which Creole is used by Jamaican writers. See BAJAN, CARIBBEAN ENGLISH.

**JAMAICAN ENGLISH**, short form *JamE*. The English language as used in Jamaica. The term is used primarily to refer to the formal speech of educated Jamaicans, but has also been used to refer to JAMAICAN CREOLE in authoritative scholarly works, such as the *Dictionary of Jamaican English* (1967, 1980). It is the preferred variety of STANDARD ENGLISH within Jamaica and functions as the formal language of the society. See CARIBBEAN ENGLISH.

**■ JAPAN** ─────────────── **■**

An island nation of East Asia. Language: Japanese (*Nippongo* or *Nihongo*). Japan has borrowed culturally and linguistically from CHINA (especially 6–9c), Western Europe (from the 16c), and the US (especially since 1945). The first contacts with European countries were with Portuguese merchants and Spanish Jesuit missionaries in the 16c; trade with The Netherlands and England was established in the early 17c. As a reaction against missionary activity, Japan discontinued contacts with all European nations except the Dutch until the 1850s, when US naval ships under Commander Matthew C. Perry forced a reopening to international commerce that led, after the Meiji Restoration of 1868, to rapid Westernization.

**The Japanese language**. Japanese shows some similarities to Korean and the Altaic languages. Although structurally and phonetically unrelated to Chinese, its writing uses borrowed Chinese characters, and a substantial portion of its vocabulary derives from their adapted Chinese readings (as with *Nihon*, above). Modern Japanese vocabulary contains native words (*wago*), words of classical Chinese origin (*kango*), and mainly Western loanwords (*GAIRAIGO*). Each type conforms to a pattern of open syllables, except syllabic /n/. Japanese is a syllable-timed language with a pitch accent. There are regional varieties, but STANDARD Japanese (based on the Tokyo dialect) is understood throughout the country.

Japanese writing uses Chinese characters (*kanji*) and two native syllabic scripts (the *kana*: hiragana and katakana) derived from them. *Hiragana* is a cursive script used for writing grammatical elements and some native words, and is the main medium for young children's books. *Katakana*, a more angular script, is used principally for onomatopoeic native words and transcriptions of foreign words and names, including BORROWINGS. Roman letters (*romaji*) are used for English and other European words in their original form, for loan material written as initials, for initials in foreign names, for Japanese words and names that may be read by non-Japanese (such as some company and product names), as a classifying device in some libraries, and for seating in some theatres and transport systems. Numbers are written in Chinese or Arabic symbols. Japanese scientific, technical, and official writing runs horizontally from left to right, whereas books, magazines, and newspapers generally run vertically, from top to bottom, and open from the right. Words in Roman script within vertical Japanese text are written on their side. Japanese English-language company names such as *National*,

*Sharp*, *Citizen*, *Brother* are written in romaji and/or in katakana; Japanese-language company names are sometimes written in Roman letters, and Roman abbreviations of names from either language are common: *JAL* (*Japanese Air Lines*), *NEC* (*Nippon Electric Company*), *NHK* (*Nihon Hōsō Kyōkai*). Western-style shops, cafés, apartment blocks, and office buildings often have foreign names, such as the *Sunshine City* commercial building in Tokyo.

**English in Japan**. English has played an important role in the modernization of Japan, especially through the reading and translation of Western works. Calls by some radicals after the Meiji Restoration for English to be adopted as the national language, in order to promote Japan's development, were unsuccessful. During the 1920–30s, the EFL specialists H. E. Palmer and A. S. HORNBY worked in Japan, the first as adviser to the Ministry of Education, with a special interest in oral methods and graded vocabulary lists, the second as one of the team which created *The Idiomatic and Syntactic English Dictionary*, first published in Tokyo (Kaitakusha, 1942), a work that evolved into the *Oxford Advanced Learner's Dictionary of Current English*. The majority of Japanese do not use English in everyday life, but recognize it as an important medium of international communication, especially for business and research. English as used by speakers of Japanese is characterized by the transfer of features from Japanese PHONOLOGY, GRAMMAR, VOCABULARY, and DISCOURSE conventions: for example, difficulty in distinguishing between and pronouncing /l/ and /r/ (the nearest Japanese sound being between the two); the use of *yes* to express simple agreement with a statement or question; 'go to shopping' for *go shopping*; 'silent' used to translate *shizuka* (which has a wider meaning of 'silent, quiet, or peaceful'); the transfer to English of loan expressions from other foreign languages, as in 'I have an arbeit' (from the loan *arubaito* a part-time job, from German *Arbeit* work). For most Japanese, however, the term *Japanese English* is used, not to refer to the English spoken by Japanese, but as a translation of *wasei eigo* ('Made-in-Japan English'), a term referring to local expressions drawn from English but used in uniquely Japanese ways, such as *imējiappu* ('image up') meaning 'improving one's image'.

**English in Japanese**. (1) *Loans*. English words are sometimes included in their original form within Japanese texts (for example, in advertisements and in some scientific writing), but are normally transcribed phonetically by katakana. This custom has assisted the entry into Japanese of loanwords (*gairaigo*) from English and other languages. There are over 1,000 such words in general use, and many thousands of scientific and technical borrowings: the *Kadogawa Gairaigo Jiten* (1969) defines some 25,000 such terms. For examples, see GAIRAIGO. (2) *Commerce and advertising*. Many modern Japanese products have English names written in their original form, often with katakana transcription, or only in katakana, and English words and phrases are often used in advertising to draw attention to the product, and give it an attractive, fashionable image.

**Decorative English**. English is ubiquitous as decoration on Western-style personal items such as clothes, fashion accessories, toiletries, and stationery. Goods for young people commonly feature popular characters such as Mickey Mouse, Alice in Wonderland, Snoopy, Beatrix Potter animals, and the local 'Kitty', often with related language, or bear English proverbs and inspirational mottos, such as *Let's sing a song with me!* Goods may be decorated with clippings or reproductions (not always accurate) from an English text, where the overall theme is appropriate but not the content, such as planting instructions accompanying a floral design. DECORATIVE ENGLISH is intended to be seen rather than read, the visual appeal of the foreign words taking precedence over their accuracy and appropriateness. The cosmopolitan form of the Roman script conveys a mood as much as a message, but the content may also embrace themes of youth, health, vitality, joy, and freedom (*for someone who seeks a long relationship with things nice*, on pocket tissues), or of romantic fantasy (*It's a romantic note book painted with a cute little cellophane-tape*, on a notebook; *This case packs my dream and eyeglasses*, on a spectacles case; *tenderness was completed a pastel*, on a pencil box). English composed by Japanese for Japanese is often a literal translation of Japanese thoughts and expressions, ranging from the clearly recognizable (*enjoy superb combination of almond and chocolate*, on a chocolate wrapping) to the obscure (*Soft in one*, hair conditioner; *ReSpice Enjoy fashion life. Nice to Heart and Just Impression* and *The New York City Theatre District is where you can and us, anyone*, on casual bags). The decorative use of scripts is a cultural tradition in Japan. Since the Second World War, the English language has become strongly associated with American culture, and its use as part of the design of Western-style goods perhaps serves to reinforce their role as symbols of modernity and sophistication.

**Japanese in English**. Borrowing from Japanese into English began in the 16c; since then, there has been a small but steady flow of words related to Japanese life and culture, such as *bonze* 16c, *sake*, *shogun* 17c, *mikado*, *shinto* 18c, *geisha*, *jinricksha* 19c, *aikido*, *bonsai*, *origami*, *pachinko* 20c. Areas of special interest include: (1) The arts: *bonsai*, *haiku*, *ikebana*, *kabuki*, *kakemono*, *koto*, *Noh*, *origami*, *sumi-e*, *ukiyo-e*. (2) The martial arts: *aikido*, *bushido*, *judo*, *jujitsu* (*jiujitsu*, *jujutsu*), *kendo*, *sumo*. (3) Cuisine: *miso*, *nori*, *sashimi*, *satsuma*, *soba*, *sushi*, *tempura*, *tofu*. (4) Commerce: *zaibatsu*, *yen*. (5) Religion: *koan*, *shinto*, *zazen*, *zen*. (6) People: *geisha*, *issei*, *mikado*, *ninja*, *nisei*, *samurai*, *sansei*, *shogun*, *yakuza*. (7) Furnishings, clothes, etc.: *fusuma*, *futon*, *kimono*, *obi*, *shoji*, *tatami*. (8) Entertainment: *enka*, *go*, *karaoke*, *nintendo*, *pachinko*. (9) Language: *hiragana*, *kanji*, *katakana*, *kunrei*. (10) Words taken from English, used in a special way in Japanese, and returned to English with their Japanese sense: *homestay* (from *hōmosutei*, from *home* and *stay*), *nighter* (from *naitā*, from *night* and *-er*), *salaryman* (from *sararīman*, from *salary* and *man*), and *wapuro* (abbreviating *word processor*). Such words have entered English in an adaptation of their Hepburn spellings, with long vowels not indicated by macrons: for example, *judo*, not *jūdō*. Early borrowings from Japanese, before systems of Romanization were established, particularly show modifications in spelling: for example, *soy* from *shōyu*, *tycoon* from *taikun*.

See ACRONYM, EAST ASIAN ENGLISH, KOREA, LINGUISTIC TYPOLOGY.

**JAPANESE PIDGIN ENGLISH**. An informal term applied, often pejoratively, to several varieties of English associated with JAPAN and the Japanese. They include: (1) A PIDGIN spoken from the early 20c by Japanese immigrants to Hawaii, and distinct from the other pidgins and creoles used in the islands. (2) Also *Bamboo English*. A pidgin used after World War II between some Japanese and the US occupation forces. American military involvement in other parts of East Asia later caused much of this pidgin to spread to other countries: for example, in Korea, the Philippines, Thailand, and during the Vietnam War, *mama-san* (Japanese: matron, especially one in charge of a geisha house, from *mama* mother, *san* honorific title) has been used to refer to any bar hostess, and *ichiban* (most, number one) means 'the best'. A humorous text in what was called *Korean Bamboo English* survives from the Korean War, apparently written by a US soldier. It blends elements of Japanese (and to a lesser extent Korean) with army slang, was published by Grant Webster in *American Speech* (1960), and begins:

> Taksan years ago, skoshi Cinderella-san lived in hootchie with sisters, . . . ketchee no fun, hava-no social life. Always washee-washee, scrubee-scrubee, make chop-chop. One day Cinderella-san sisters ketchee post cardo from Seoul. Post cardo speakee so: one prince-san have big blowout, taksan kimchi, taksan beeru . . . Cindy-san sisters taksan excited, make Cinderella-san police up clothes.

**JAPLISH**, also **Japalish**, **Janglish**. Informal terms, often wry, sometimes pejorative, for any mixture of Japanese and English. They may refer to Japanese spoken or written with an admixture of English or to English that shows Japanese influence: 'A great many Japanese speak English nowadays (or at least "Japlish", as the American colony calls it)' (*Harper's Magazine*, Jan. 1963); 'Japanese sometimes sounds like Japlish: *masukomi* for mass communications, *terebi* for television' (*Time*, 22 July 1966). A significant aspect of Japlish is the use of thousands of adapted English words in daily speech and writing: *dokutā sutoppu* ('doctor stop'), a physician's prohibition on certain activities, such as smoking; *Bajin Rodo* ('Virgin Road'), the title of a best-selling novel, referring to the aisle a bride walks down in church. See GAIRAIGO.

**JARGON**. An often pejorative general term for outlandish language of various kinds, such as speech perceived as gibberish or mumbo jumbo, SLANG, a PIDGIN language, or, most commonly, the specialized language of a trade, profession, or other group

(REGISTER). The term is often associated with law, medicine, and the sciences: *technical jargon*, *scientific jargon*. To non-members of professional, occupational, and other groups, their usage is filled with terms and syntax that are not typical of GENERAL ENGLISH and may therefore impede understanding among lay people, but to members of such a group, the usage is familiar and generally serves its purpose well. Because of ease and familiarity, however, they may use technical expressions and styles outside the group, either unthinkingly, because it seems best fitted for the topic in question, or on occasion to impress and even oppress.

**Jargon as verbal shorthand**. For those who understand it, jargon is a kind of SHORTHAND that makes long explanations unnecessary. When used by the members of a profession or group, it can be an efficient and effective language. For physicians, the surgical removal of a gall bladder is a *chole-cystectomy*. For lawyers, an *involuntary conversion* is loss or destruction of property through theft, accident, or condemnation. Studies of surgeons have found that the jargon used during surgery improves the communication of factual information with brevity and clarity. Comparably, computer science has evolved a jargon which communicates technical ideas among members of the group, including such expressions as *dynamic random access memory*, *read only memory*, *core dump*, and *cache buffer*.

**Jargon as group identification**. Ability to understand and use the jargon of a group is a badge of identification: one belongs, and those who cannot use the jargon of the group do not, even if they possess other skills necessary for membership. In a sense, the ability to use the jargon indicates that the user is conforming to the norms of the group, as well as accepting and understanding the basic ideas, principles, and practices of the group. In addition, using jargon can lend an air of authority and prestige to those who use it, especially if the jargon is associated with a profession that enjoys a high social position.

**The temptations of jargon**. While jargon has a legitimate function, it is probably more known for its ABUSE by people who use it to confuse, confound, needlessly complicate subject matter, and lend an air of importance and sophistication to their message and themselves. Jargon allows a speaker to make fairly simple ideas appear complicated, if not profound. It may sound more impressive to write that 'The argillaceous character of the formation is very prominent in some localities, although it is usually subsidiary to the arenaceous phase', rather than 'At some places the formation includes considerable clay, but generally it is made up chiefly of sand.' By and large, when people use jargon not to communicate but to impress, or use it to announce membership in a group, communication suffers.

See ACADEMIC USAGE, ARGOT, AUREATE DICTION, BAFFLEGAB, BUREAUCRATESE, CANT, CIRCUMLOCUTION, COMPUTERESE, CONFUSAGE, DOUBLESPEAK, DOUBLE TALK, EUPHEMISM, GOBBLEDYGOOK, INFLATED LANGUAGE, INKHORN TERM, JOURNALESE, LEGALESE, LEGAL USAGE, OFFICIALESE, PATOIS, PERIPHRASIS, PLAIN ENGLISH, PLEONASM, PRIVATE LANGUAGE, PSYCHOBABBLE, REDUNDANCY, SOCIOLOGESE, -SPEAK, TAUTOLOGY, TECHNOBABBLE, TRADE JARGON.

## ■ JESPERSEN, (Jens) Otto (Harry) ──────────── ■

[1860–1943]. Danish linguist and authority on LANGUAGE TEACHING and the GRAMMAR of English. Born at Randers, Jutland, he was educated at Frederiksborg School, Zealand, and at the U. of Copenhagen, where he began to study law but changed to languages, taking a degree in FRENCH, English, and LATIN in 1887. During a postgraduate year (1887–8), he went to England, where he attended Henry SWEET's lectures on PHONETICS at Oxford and met James MURRAY and other scholars. He obtained a D.Phil. in Copenhagen in 1891, and in 1893 was appointed Professor of English, a position which he held until his retirement in 1925.

While still an undergraduate, Jespersen made contact with some of the leaders of the Reform Movement of language teaching; he translated Felix Franke's book about the Movement's principles into Danish (1884) and wrote in Danish a grammar of English using the then revolutionary method of giving phonetic transcription (1885). In 1901, he published a book on language teaching, *Sprogundervisning* (revised edition, 1935), translated into English as *How to Teach a Foreign Language* (1904).

When Paul Passy in 1886 in Paris formed the organization that later became the INTERNATIONAL PHONETIC ASSOCIATION, he was joined by Jespersen, who participated in the creation of the IPA system of notation. Jespersen later supplied phonetic transcriptions of the entries in Brynildsen's *English and Dano-Norwegian Dictionary* (1902–7), which was the century's first pronouncing dictionary. His main contribution to phonetics is a compendium originally published in Danish but issued in German in 1904, *Lehrbuch der Phonetic*, with its companion volume *Phonetische Grundfragen*. A book on the phonetics of Danish came in 1906 and one on the phonetics of English in 1912; the latter, originally written in Danish, was issued in an English translation in 1950.

Jespersen's publications on LINGUISTICS and grammatical theory are numerous, including: *Language* (1922); *The Philosophy of Grammar* (1924); *Mankind, Nation and Individual* (1925); *Analytic Syntax* (1937). His system of analysis of English grammar is explained in *Essentials of English Grammar* (1933) and *A Modern Grammar on Historical Principles* (7 volumes, 1909–49). Jespersen's theory has in part been superseded, but the mass of material that he collected and systematized retains its value. Volume I contains original views on the history of English sounds, including his account of the GREAT VOWEL SHIFT (Jespersen's own term). His views on the general development of English are set out in *Growth and Structure of the English Language* (1905).

Language teaching to Jespersen was a means of bringing nations closer together. With the same object in mind he became actively involved in efforts to develop an international auxiliary language. In 1907, he helped create a reformed Esperanto called Ido, and in 1928 developed his own auxiliary language Novial, in which he sought to apply a principle concerning simplicity in grammar and vocabulary which echoed the words of the English philosopher Jeremy Bentham: 'That international language is best which in every point offers the greatest facility to the greatest number.' Neither Ido nor Novial had any success. See METANALYSIS, SOCIETY FOR PURE ENGLISH, USAGE GUIDANCE AND CRITICISM.

# ■ JEWISH ENGLISH ─────── ■

Short form *JE*. A collective term for several varieties of English spoken and written by Jews, marked by a range of lexical,

grammatical, and other linguistic and paralinguistic elements. At present, the most common variety is an English influenced by YIDDISH and HEBREW, used chiefly by Ashkenazim (Jews of Central and Eastern European origin or descent). This variety has introduced into colloquial AmE and BrE many neologisms, such as *maven*, *nebbish*, *nosh*, *shlep*. Other varieties include a Judezmo-influenced English used by Sephardim (Jews of SPANISH origin or descent), a 19c variety of AusE, and a formal variety that uses general English words, such as *academy* for Yiddish-origin *yeshiva*, *skullcap* for Yiddish-origin *yarmulka* or Hebrew-origin *kipa*, *ritual bath* or *ritualarium* for Yiddish- or Hebrew-origin *mikva*. The following characteristics describe mainly the American Ashkenazic variety of JE.

**Pronunciation**. (1) The following features are traceable to Yiddish influence: the substitution of /ŋg/ for /ŋ/ in present participles and other words, such as *singing* and *singer*; a raising of /ɔ/ in words like *off*, *cough*, *soft*; over-aspiration of /t/; confusion of /s/ and /z/ in pronouncing the PLURAL ending *-s* in some environments. Certain features of Eastern Ashkenazic NEW YORK City English of the immigrant generations (*c*.1880–1940) are still sometimes heard: pronunciation of such words as *circle*, *nervous*, *first* as if 'soikel', 'noivis', 'foist', and an intrusive /n/ in words like *carpenter* ('carpentner'), *painter* ('paintner'). (2) A widespread feature of Ashkenazic JE is replacement of Yiddish-origin word-final *-e* /e/, as in *pastrame*, *khale*, *shmate*, *tate*, *Sore* with *-i* /i/, as in *pastrami*, *khali* Sabbath loaf, *shmati* rag, *tati* daddy, *Sori* Sarah. (3) American Ashkenazic JE has numerous stylistic features, including those of pitch, amplitude, intonation, voice quality, and rate of speech, that reflect the influence of the Yiddish conversational style of the immigrant generations.

**Grammar**. (1) Yiddish and Hebrew LOANWORDS are integrated into English in four ways: by dropping infinitive endings (*davn* pray, from Yiddish *davnen*) then giving the verb English inflections (*davns*, *davned*, *davning*); by replacing Yiddish and Hebrew plural forms (*shtetlekh* small towns, *Shabatonim* Sabbath social gatherings) with English plurals (*shtetls*, *Shabatons*); by forming new derivatives with English affixes (*shleppy*, *shleppily*, *shleppiness*, *shleppish*, *shleppishly*); by extending the function of loans, for example, the Yiddish interjection *nebish* a pity, used (with the spelling *nebbish*) as an adjective meaning 'pitiful, unfortunate' (*a nebbish character*), and as a noun meaning 'unfortunate person, poor devil' (*What a nebbish he is!*). (2) Some verbs are used in a non-standard absolute way: *Enjoy, enjoy; Go figure; I'm entitled.* (3) The use of inversions for emphasis is common: *Shakespeare he is not; A roof over our heads we have.* (4) The use of Yiddish-origin constructions is frequent, and has spread into some forms of colloquial AmE: *I want you should do this; He is a boy is all* (that's all); *Don't be a crazy; Again with the complaints!* (complaining again); *Enough with the talk; Begin already!* (So begin!); *They don't know from nothing* (Don't know anything). (5) Similarly, Yiddish-origin idioms are often used, have spread into AmE at large, and are becoming increasingly widely used: *Get lost!; Eat your heart out; I need it like a hole in the head; I should live so long* (I would need to live a long time to see that); *You should be so lucky* (you are never going to be so lucky). (6) The use of rhetorical questions (usually CALQUES from Yiddish) is frequent and similarly spreading: *Who needs it?; What's with all the noise?; So what else is new?; What's to forgive?* (7) Several Yiddish morphological forms have become common formatives: the dismissive *shm-* in hundreds of REDUPLICATIONS: *Oedipus-shmoedipus, richshmich, value-shmalue*; the agent suffix *-nik: beatnik, kibbutznik, peacenik, realestatenik, spynik, noshnik, Freudnik*; the endearing diminutives *-ele* and *-l*, often appended to English given names (*Stevele, Rachele*), sometimes with a doubling of DIMINUTIVES (*Debbiinkele, Samchikele*), sometimes with common nouns (*roomele, roomkele, boyele, boychickl, storele, storkele*).

**Vocabulary**. (1) There are thousands of Yiddish and many Hebrew terms used in English that relate to Jewish life: *shadkhn* a matchmaker, *hesped* a eulogy, *kanehore* preserve us from the evil eye, *halevay* would that it be so. (2) There are many compounds of Yiddish and Hebrew loanwords with English words: *matse balls* round dumplings, *shana tova card* a Jewish New Year card, *sforim store* a Jewish bookstore. (3) Lexical items formed from general English words: *Jewish Star, Hebrew School*. (4) Semantic shifts in English words, often due to homophony with terms of Yiddish: *learn* to study torah (the law), from Yiddish *lernen*; *give* to take, from *gebn*, as in *Give a look*; *by*

with, from *bay*, as in *The money is by him.* (5) Informal ABBREVIATIONS for: vulgarisms of Yiddish origin (*TL* a sycophant, from Yiddish *tokhes leker* ass-licker); pejorative terms with English components (*JAP* Jewish American Princess); and Yiddish and Hebrew expressions (*B'H* meaning *with God's help, zal* an ACRONYM meaning *of blessed memory*).

**Social issues**. Speakers and writers of JE generally avoid terms with un-Jewish, especially Christian connotations, such as: *Christian name*, the preferred terms being *first name* or *given name*; *AD* and *BC*, preferring *CE* for *Common Era* and *BCE* for *Before the Common Era* (both JE coinages); idiomatic expressions alluding to Christian themes (*cross one's fingers, knock on wood/touch wood, the gospel truth, Christ! Jeez!*); terms with anti-Semitic denotations or connotations, such as *Hymietown* (New York City), *jew down* (to bargain sharply with), *Shylock*, and *Yid*.

See ARABIC, BIBLE, DIALECT (UNITED STATES) GERMANIC LANGUAGES, ISRAEL, PUN, SCHWA, SHIBBOLETH, SLAVONIC LANGUAGES, YIDDISHISM, YINGLISH.

**JIVE**, also **jive talk**. (1) The SLANG or JARGON associated in the earlier 20c with such African-American forms of music as jive (swing, jazz, etc.). (2) In the later 20c, an informal term for flattering, deceptive, exaggerated, meaningless talk, especially among black Americans (*Hey, don't give me that jive, man!*); DOUBLE TALK: 'Everything that we do must be aimed toward the total liberation, unification and empowerment of Afrika. Anything short of that is jive' (*Black World*, Oct. 1973). Compare BLARNEY, RAP.

■ **JOHNSON, Samuel** ────── ■

[1709–84]. English lexicographer, critic, poet, and moralist, who achieved through his *Dictionary of the English Language* (1755) and the model of his own writings preeminence in his lifetime as an authority on the language. Such comprehensive scholarly works as his edition of SHAKESPEARE (1765) and *The Lives of the English Poets* (1779–81) drew, like his DICTIONARY, on an encyclopedic knowledge of the authors of his age.

The Dictionary, commissioned by a group of London book-sellers, was in part a response to a widely felt need in the late 17c and early 18c for stability in the language and for canons of correctness in usage. As a language of scholarly communication, English was seen to lack the permanence and concision of LATIN, and the efforts of the French and Italian Academies in bringing about improvements in the vernacular were known and envied. Proposals, especially c.1660–1710, for establishing an English ACADEMY to 'fix' the language had come to nothing, and on publication of the Dictionary he was accorded the status of a one-man academy.

Work on the Dictionary took eight or nine years, and was carried out mainly in the large garret at Johnson's house in Gough Square, London. He is thought to have used an interleaved copy of Nathan Bailey's *Dictionarium Britannicum* as a foundation word list and had the help of some half a dozen amanuenses, who copied out the quotations which he had chosen. Johnson's perception of his task as a lexicographer changed while the Dictionary was in hand. When he published the *Plan of an English Dictionary* (1747), he saw himself as a verbal critic, condemning barbarous words and expressions, and guarding the purity of the language. But in the Preface (1755), he disclaimed that intention, saying that all the stubborn uncertainties of usage were not to be blamed on him, since his task was not to form, but merely to record the language.

**Johnson's influence**. The influence of his work on the development of the language has been widely assumed but cannot be proved and is difficult to assess. In particular, it is often held to have fixed English, spelling; printers' spelling had, however, been established largely in the modern form before 1700, and where Johnson differed from it in his dictionary entries (as in words such as *logick* and *errour*) his recommended form has often failed to survive. It is nonetheless likely that, through the countless abbreviated and miniature editions running well into the 19c, the Dictionary played a role in propagating a standard spelling among the less literate and in forming and restraining the writings of the educated. Earlier monolingual dictionaries were mainly concerned with 'hard' words: the bookish, Latinate, and technical vocabulary of Renaissance English. Except sometimes in providing etymologies, they were non-historical and paid little regard to literary usage. Johnson differed in seeking

to illustrate the meanings of words by literary quotation. He favoured the usage of the preceding century, Shakespeare, Milton, and Dryden alone accounting for a third of all quotations. The arrangement of his citations is chronological, and Johnson commonly surpasses his predecessors in the elegance of his definitions: *enchant* 'to subdue by charms or spells'; *graceful* 'beautiful with dignity'; *insinuative* 'stealing on the affections'. It can be said that Johnson provided a powerful but conservative model of language usage for at least a century after his time. See ENGLISH IN ENGLAND, JOHNSONESE, JOHNSONIAN, JOURNALISM, PHILOLOGY, PHRASAL VERB, PROSE, SPELLING REFORM.

**JOHNSONESE**. An often pejorative term for the elevated style of Samuel JOHNSON. His leanings towards a LATINATE vocabulary were remarked on in his own day (for example, by his biographer James Boswell). Thus, *repress the instantaneous motions of merriment* may be seen as a roundabout and obscure way of saying *stop laughing*. See -ESE.

**JOHNSONIAN**. A term applied to the style of Samuel JOHNSON or any style resembling it. His moralizing essays in *The Rambler* magazine (1750–2) best illustrate the style, not only in its long words, but in the antithetical balancing of phrases which often went with them: 'I could seldom escape to solitude, or steal a moment from the emulation of complaisance, and the vigilance of officiousness.'

**JOKE**. Something said or done to cause amusement. Making or 'cracking' a joke requires certain well-established devices, such as, in English, a ritual announcement often containing the word *one*: 'Have you heard this one?'; 'I heard a good one yesterday'; 'Do you know the one about the actress and the bishop at Stonehenge?' Any such statement or question is a formulaic summons to laughter. Technically, jokes are like chess: there is a limited number of moves, but the variations and combinations are infinite. Old jokes may enjoy an extended span of life through variations on the original formula: 'Who was that lady I saw you with last night?'—'That was no lady; that was my wife.' This tired old two-liner picks up a little energy if recast: 'Who was that lady I saw you with last night?'—'If it was last night, that was no lady.' Jokes can be refurbished to suit the latest fashion, appearing and reappearing indifferent generic settings, as *doctor jokes*, *elephant jokes*, *red-white-and-blue jokes*, *sick jokes*, *waiter jokes*, and even *anti-jokes*, in which the joke is the absence of a joke. See HUMO(U)R, POLITICALLY CORRECT, SCATOLOGY.

**JONES, Daniel** [1881–1967]. English phonetician, born in London and educated at Radley and University College Schools. He graduated in mathematics from King's College, Cambridge, in 1903, and received his MA in 1907, the year he was called to the Bar (Lincoln's Inn). However, he never practised law and, even during his legal training, spent time in Paris (part of 1905–6) studying PHONETICS under Paul Passy, whose niece he married in 1911. He gained an appointment in 1907 at U. College London, the year in which its Department of Phonetics was set up, and worked there for most of his life: as lecturer (1907–14), Reader (1914–21), Professor (1921–49), and Emeritus Professor (1949–67). He was the leading British phonetician during the first half of the 20c and had a profound effect on the study of pronunciation (for example, as a member of the *BBC Advisory Committee on Spoken English* from its formation in 1926) and was in part responsible for the selection of *RECEIVED PRONUNCIATION* or *RP* (which he named in the 1920s) as the norm for radio announcers. The works for which he is best known are *An ENGLISH PRONOUNCING DICTIONARY* (1917) and *An Outline of English Phonetics* (1918), both of which continue in revised editions. Jones spent most of his life working on PHONETIC TRANSCRIPTION. His views are summed up in *The PHONEME* (1950) and in his papers for the INTERNATIONAL PHONETIC ASSOCIATION (of which he was secretary, 1928–49, and President from 1950), especially *The Principles of the International Phonetic Association* (1949). See BBC ENGLISH, ENGLISH IN ENGLAND, LANGUAGE TEACHING, ORTHOEPY, PUBLIC SCHOOL PRONUNCIATION, SIMPLIFIED SPELLING SOCIETY, SPEECH, SPELLING REFORM.

**JONES, (Sir) William** [1746–94]. British philologist and jurist, born in London of Welsh parentage, and educated at Harrow and University College, Oxford. His *Grammar of the Persian Language* (1771) was considered definitive for many years. He studied law and was called to the Bar in 1774, becoming a judge of the high court in Calcutta in 1783. His philological pursuits, interest in Indian legal literature (rare among Europeans of his time), and his liberal political outlook, introduced him to Indian languages, including SANSKRIT. He founded the Asiatic Society in 1784, and in his presidential address of 1786 announced his view that 'the *Sanscrit* language . . . bear[s to GREEK and LATIN] a stronger affinity, both in the roots of verbs, and in the forms of grammar, than could possibly have been produced by accident; so strong indeed, that no philologer could examine them all three, without believing them to have sprung from some common source, which, perhaps, no longer exists. There is a similar reason, though not quite so forcible, for supposing that both the *Gothick* and the *Celtick* . . . had the same origin with the *Sanscrit*; and the old *Persian* might be added to the same family. . . .' By concentrating on systematic resemblances in the form of grammar, accepting that the common source no longer exists, and listing most of the chief language families that descended from that source, this statement embodies the founding principles of the historical study of the INDO-EUROPEAN LANGUAGES. See ETYMOLOGY, PHILOLOGY.

**JOURNALESE**. A general, usually non-technical term for the way in which journalists write (and speak), or are thought to write (and speak). It is used both neutrally (referring to newspaper STYLE at large) and more often pejoratively (implying that such a style is stereotyped, vulgar, and inclined to debase the language). The *Random House Dictionary* (1987) defines *journalese* as: '(1) a manner of writing or speaking characterized by CLICHÉS, occasional NEOLOGISM, archness, sensationalizing adjectives, unusual or faulty syntax, etc., used by some journalists, esp. certain columnists, and regarded as typical journalistic style; (2) writing or expression in this manner: *Get that journalese out of your copy! . . . That word's not English—it's journalese.*'

The characteristics of journalese arise from the nature of newspapers: ephemeral sheets of paper printed and published to strict deadlines, kept resolutely up-to-the-minute, and designed to attract and stimulate readers whose attention spans, for various reasons, are likely to be short. The profession and the public share a certain cynicism about how this is done:

> The late Nicholas Tomalin, one of the *Sunday Times*'s top reporters, named the three prime qualities for success some years ago. They were, he said, a ratlike cunning, a certain plausibility and a little literary ability. That's still true. I studied English and Drama at university. The drama techniques have probably been of far greater use (Liz Gill, 'Journalese: The Inside Story', *English Today* 11, July 1987).

**Technique**. Working to a deadline and rendering complex issues into reports of the right length and style produce their own structures, shortcuts, and standards of excellence. When a story is too long for the space available, it is cut, usually from the bottom up. Because of this and the need to get the main points quickly to the browsing reader, reporters pack these points into the first paragraphs. If there is a picture, then the story may be little more than a caption to that picture; when the story is unaccompanied, it stands or falls by its opening statement: the introduction or *intro*. The first sentence is often the most difficult to write. There is a technique known as the *dropped intro*, in which the key statement is delayed for several paragraphs and comes as a punch line, but the danger of delay is that many readers will not persevere far enough to enjoy it. More time can be spent on the intro than on any other part of the article.

**Stock expressions**. Stories also use *colour*: striking words or graphic details that attract interest, such as *White-haired granny Mrs X was yesterday found savagely beaten* . . . Such a style may be praised for its terseness or deplored because it is cliché-ridden and inelegant. It is, however, as deliberate in its own way and for its own purposes as Homer's use of phrases like *grey-eyed Athene* or *cloud-gathering Zeus*. It provides ways in which people can be recognized and pigeon-holed. The list of STOCK phrases includes: *bored housewife, devout Catholic, distinguished surgeon, grieving widow*. Comparably, especially in articles that strive for HUMOUR, words are used that relate to the characters or the occupations of the people concerned: when they face problems, teachers get *caned*, cooks are *browned off*, doctors might be *sickened*, butchers might be *beefing* about something, or *giving it the chop*.

**Clichés**. Many clichés and hackneyed expressions derive from or are favoured in newspaper writing, especially in relation to groups that can be stereotyped: *the ivory tower* (for the academic world: often concrete and plate glass), *the rat race* (competitive business), *the party faithful* (for loyal workers and voters for a political party), *mecca* (for any location attracting a particular group, other than for religious purposes, as in *fabulous, surfing mecca*).

Events and actions can be dressed with emotive and romantic words that add colour and are easily slotted into a report: such nouns as *burden, disaster, dream, fantasy, glamour, horror, nightmare, terror*; such adjectives as *amazing, bizarre, cataclysmic, devastating, heart-stopping, heart-warming, horrendous, moving, outrageous, scandalous, shattering, staggering*. Close to such stock words are EUPHEMISMS like *confirmed bachelor* (a homosexual man), *constant companion* (a lover), *fun-loving* (of a woman: sexually free-and-easy), *good-time girl, party girl* (a prostitute). Certain syntactic forms also occur so regularly as to be clichés: *amid mounting* (*Amid mounting calls for his resignation, X has decided to tough it out*), appositional *many* (*mothers, many with children in their arms*), *that was once* (*standing in the ruin that was once central Beirut*).

**Special uses of words**. Because they must be concise and make an immediate impact, journalists often use words in novel ways: (1) *CONVERSIONS*. Nouns are often put to use as verbs. Many of the first recorded instances of such changes have occurred in newspapers, especially in the US: *to interview, engineer, boom, boost, surge*. (2) *ATTRIBUTIVES*. The use of nouns to qualify other nouns: *death* as in *death car, death ride, death ship; top* as in *top politician, top referee, top team; rescue* as in *rescue worker, rescue party, rescue team*. (3) *REDUPLICATIONS*. Such coinages often rhyme, lodge easily in the memory, and sometimes become catch-phrases: *the jet set* (the leisured class which travels frequently); *the brain drain* (exodus of academics), *culture vulture* (someone who indiscriminately 'consumes' culture). (4) *ARCHAISMS*. Because they are short or perceived as popular, certain archaic words survive in newspaper usage: *agog, foe, hustings, scribe, slay*. (5) *NEOLOGISMS*. Journalists employ a variety of nonce and stunt forms, some of which are accepted in the language at large: *new-look, see-through, lookalike,* *lensman, weatherman, vocalist.* (6) *Kinds of* MODIFICATION. Word combination often leads to strings of adjectives and attributive nouns, a style that began in *Time* magazine in the 1920s, with the aim of providing impact and 'colour'. They may be relatively short (*London-born disc jockey Ray Golding . . .*) or long enough to become self-parodies, either pre-modifying a name (*silver-haired, paunchy lothario, Francesco Tebaldi . . .*) or post-modifying it (*Zsa Zsa Gabor, seventyish, eight-times-married, Hungarian-born celebrity . . .*).

**Immediacy of style**. (1) *Short* VERNACULAR *words*. Because of the need for conciseness and impact, journalists favour monosyllables and disyllables: *poll* for 'election'; *blast* for 'explosion'; *jobless* for 'unemployed'; *homeless* for 'destitute'. (2) *Emotive and inflated expressions*. The urge to promote excitement leads, especially in headlines, to such emotive and often inflated usage as: *fever* for 'excitement' (*World Cup fever grips Barcelona*); *rage* or *fury* for 'anger' (*Fury over Poll Tax*); *stricken* or *crippled* for 'disabled' (*stricken tanker adrift in Med*); *glory* for any sporting achievement (*glory day for Tottenham*); *storm* and *row* for 'controversy' (*storm over price-hikes*; *Cabinet row over inflation*). (3) *Quasi-illiterate usages*. For effect, some writers and publications, especially in Britain, favour eye dialect that suggests solidarity among philistines: *gonna, loadsamoney, showbiz, whodunnit, dontcha, wanna, wotalotigot*. (4) *Innuendo*. Especially in the tabloids, hints that are more or less explicitly muscular or sexual innuendo are often employed, especially as metaphors: *firm, harden, spurt, spill over, selling climax*. (5) *Allusive punning*. There appears to be a general increase in the use of a kind of punning allusion traditionally acceptable in US journalism but avoided in Britain: 'TV or Not TV' (*The Times*, 16 Oct. 1989); 'Know Your Rites', 'Heirs and Graces' (*The Listener*, 16 June 1988); 'Drapes of things to come', 'A test of skull on the Thames' (*The Times*, 26 July 1988).

# ■ JOURNALISM ─────────── ■

The enterprise of producing newspapers and magazines (including reporting, writing, editing, photographing, and managing) as well as the styles of writing used in such publications. The term came into use some two centuries after the practice had started. From the 18c, there were basically two styles: the elegant and ornate 'high'

style of Joseph Addison, Richard Steele, Samuel JOHNSON, and the other essayists, and the 'low' style of the so-called Grub Street hacks. Daniel DEFOE is often regarded as the first journalist, as distinct from the man of letters. With the rise of the popular press in the 19c, the more fashionable alternative terms were the *higher journalism* (Matthew Arnold's term) and the *gutter press*. To a large extent these modes are perpetuated in the division of modern British journalism into the *quality press* and the *tabloids*. By the mid-19c, the term was starting to fall into disrepute, to imply rather superficial social and political commentary and a style which was less than exemplary. In England in 1879, George Eliot commented rather scornfully on 'Journalistic guides to the popular mind', while *journalese*, recorded from 1882, was defined by the *OED c.*1900 as '"newspaper" or "penny-a-liner's" English'. The term *journalism* continues throughout the English-speaking world to retain a tinge of disapproval, and most of the epithets applied to the profession (such as *hacks, muck-rakers, rat packs, reptiles, scribblers*) are uncomplimentary.

It was, however, from the early 19c to the First World War that journalism enjoyed its greatest influence. Editors were raised to virtually legendary status, their editorials or 'leaders' being regarded as models of stylistic elegance and political authority, with an impact on current affairs which has never been surpassed. Especially under the editorship of Thomas Barnes, *The Times* became such a powerful voice in Britain (promoting the Reform Bill and condemning the Corn Laws) that by 1829 it had earned the sobriquet *The Thunderer*. Both Samuel Coleridge and Benjamin Disraeli served as leader-writers for the *Morning Post*, which also published poems by William Wordsworth, Thomas Hardy, and Rudyard Kipling. Although editors are not so strongly associated with newspapers in the US as in the UK, the names of Ambrose Bierce, A. J. Liebling, H. L. MENCKEN, Lincoln Steffens, and Tom Wolfe are especially notable in American journalism.

Newspapers will do whatever is necessary to catch and hold readers at the level at which they operate. 'Serious' or 'quality' newspapers cater to a minority with a higher level of education and interest. This minority is willing to read lengthy articles and expects a quasi-literary quality in what it reads. 'Popular' newspapers are aimed at the un-literary majority in any area. Many of their readers have no special interest in language and little time or inclination for detail. They also often have a great interest in social events and sport, and in the human side of the entertainment business. There is therefore a greater emphasis on 'gossip' and 'inside stories' than in the 'heavies' (the serious papers), although these also carry more muted versions of the same thing, often in the form of reviews. Adapting to their markets, newspapers differ in physical terms (with preferred formats such as *broadsheet* or *tabloid*; preferred headline styles; longer or shorter stories and features) and in the linguistic style that appeals to their target readerships.

The tradition of trenchant freelance political journalism founded by Defoe and continued by John Wilkes in the 18c was maintained in the 19c by William Cobbett and Charles DICKENS. In the 20c, the emphasis has moved from the editors who run newspapers to the entrepreneurs who own them, while new kinds of journalism have developed, contrasting *print journalists* with *radio journalists* and *television journalists*. See HEADLINE, JOURNALESE.

**JUTES**. According to the chronicler Bede (*c*.730), the name of a Germanic tribe which, with the Angles and Saxons, invaded Britain in the 5c and settled in Kent and part of the south coast, including the Isle of Wight. The Angles appear to have come from Schleswig and the Saxons from western Holstein and the north German coast from the Elbe westward. Since the Angles lived between the Saxons and the Jutes, the Jutes appear to have come from further north, probably the Jutland peninsula in Denmark, which may be named after them. See ANGLO-SAXON, KENTISH, OLD ENGLISH[1].

# K

[Called 'kay', rhyming with *say*]. The 11th LETTER of the Roman ALPHABET as used for English. It originated in the Phoenician consonant *kap*, which was adopted as *kappa* for GREEK. It reached the Romans via the Etruscans, but was little used in LATIN, in which *C* and *Q* were preferred as symbols for the voiceless velar stop /k/. The transliteration of Greek *K* into *C* was standard: *comma* not *komma*, *Socrates* not *Sokrates*. When *c* acquired a soft value before *e* and *i* in later Latin and the Romance languages, *k* was available to represent hard *c* in those positions, and was so adopted by most of the GERMANIC LANGUAGES. Old English, however, normally used *c* for /k/ (as in *cwic*, *cyning* for what later became *quick*, *king*), with *k* as an occasional variant. After 1066, under the influence of NORMAN-FRENCH spelling, both letters were widely used, but after a period of uncertainty (*could* being spelt both *coude*, *koude*) fairly distinct functions emerged for *c* and *k*, according to position and CONTEXT.

**Sound value and distribution**. In English, *k* normally represents a voiceless velar stop, whose voiced equivalent is *g*. It is typically used: (1) Before *e*, *i*: *kennel*, *keep*, *kit*, *kind*, *sketch*, *skirt*, *skin*. It occurs more rarely before other vowel letters (chiefly after *s*) in long-established English words: *skate*, *skull*, *sky* (contrast *scale*, *Scot*, *scud*). (2) After a long vowel (*take*, *break*, *meek*, *like*, *soak*, *broke*, *duke*) as well as after *oo* (*book*, *cook*). Further syllables may follow (*naked*, *token*). (3) In conjunction with preceding *c* after a short vowel, *ck* having the function of a doubled *c* or *k*: *sack*, *wreck*, *lick*, *mock*, *duck*; *bracken*, *reckon*, *wicked*, *rocket*, *bucket*. (4) After other consonants which follow a short vowel (whose value may be modified and lengthened before *l*, *r*, *w*): *walk*, *whelk*, *folk*, *milk*, *hulk*, *frank*, *pink*, *lark*, *jerk*, *ask*, *desk*, *hawk*; *sparkle*, *whisker*.

**Exotic and innovative usages**. (1) Recently coined or borrowed words use *k* without positional restrictions: names for exotic creatures, such as *kangaroo*, *koala*, have *k*, not *c*, before *a*, *o*, and *yak*, *trek* lack the usual *c* between short vowel and *k*. (2) *K* may be doubled between vowels in such words as *yakkity-yak* and *trekking*. (3) For visual effect, *c* and *q* are sometimes changed to *k*: as trade names (*Kleenex*, based on *clean*) and businesses (*Kwik-Fit*, based on *quick*). The change may take place for facetious, humorous, or sinister purposes: *Krazy Kats*, *Ku Klux Klan*. (4) Foreign names commonly occur with *k* in untypical positions: *Kaiser*, *Kremlin*, *Kuwait*.

**Digraphs**. (1) *Ck* is not a digraph in the sense of a combination creating a new pronunciation, but is common after short vowels in VERNACULAR words (*black*, not *\*blac* or *\*blak*), although the loanwords *bloc*, *chic*, and *dak*, *flak* occur. (2) *Kh* may constitute a digraph by representing a voiceless velar fricative /x/, rather as in ScoE *loch*, transliterating RUSSIAN *x* (*Kharkov*, *Khrushchev*) and similar sounds in other languages. However, in such words, the *h* is commonly ignored, and *kh* is pronounced as /k/: *khaki*, *khan*, *khedive*, *astrakhan*.

**Silent *K***. (1) In OLD ENGLISH and MIDDLE ENGLISH, initial *c* or *k* (like its voiced equivalent *g*) could be pronounced immediately before *n*. In this position, *k* has since fallen silent, but has been retained in writing in some twenty forms that include *knave*, *knee*, *knife*, *knot*, *knuckle*. This orthographic feature strikingly distinguishes several pairs of HOMOPHONES: *knave/nave*, *knight/night*, *know/no*. (2) In isolated cases, *ck* or *k* has been assimilated or elided before another consonant, as in *blackguard* ('blaggard') and *Cockburn* ('Coburn').

**Variations**. (1) *K* is inserted before vowels in inflected forms and derivatives of verbs ending in *c*: *bivouacked*, *picknicker*, *panicking* (but note *arced* not *\*arcked*, from *to arc*). (2) It occurs before *e* and *i* in place of a *c* in a related word or form: *cat/kitten*, *cow/kine*, *joke/jocular*, *urb/kerb*, *curfew/kerchief*. (3) It has been replaced in *ake*, which is now *ache*. (4) It has disappeared from *made*, which was formerly *maked*. (5) It no longer occurs in forms ending in *-ic*: *logic*, *music*, which were formerly *logick*, *musick*. (6) *Taken* has the poetic spelling *ta'en*, reflecting a common pronunciation in DIALECT in England and

Scotland. (7) The letter *x* has replaced *cks* in *coxcomb* and *ck* in *coxswain*, while *bucksome* was one of many earlier forms of *buxom*. In India, it sometimes replaces the Romanized SANSKRIT *ksh*, the names *Lakshman, Lakshmi* becoming *Laxman, Laxmi*. (8) For humorous, commercial purposes, such spellings as *socks* can become *sox*. (9) Alternations with *c* and *qu* in various combinations arise in loans from FRENCH: *block/bloc, manikin/mannequin, racket/racquet*. (10) BrE *barque, cheque, chequer, disc, kerb, mollusc, sceptic* are usually written *bark, check, checker, disk, curb, mollusk, skeptic* in AmE. However, some similar pairs of words are of distinct meaning and origin: *arc/ark, scull/skull*. See C, X.

**KAMTOK**. The English-based PIDGIN of CAMEROON, widely used for at least 100 years. When the Germans annexed the region in 1884, they found it so well established as a LINGUA FRANCA that they produced a phrase book in pidgin for their soldiers. Its speakers usually call it *pidgin* or *country talk* and linguists refer to it as *Cameroon(ian) Pidgin (English)*, but recently the media has begun to use *Kamtok*, to stress that it is local and useful, despite having no official status. It is the easternmost of a group of pidgins and CREOLES in West Africa that includes Gambian AKU (Talk), Sierra Leone KRIO, Ghanaian Pidgin, and Nigerian Pidgin, and is a mother tongue on plantations, in some urban settlements, and in families where the parents speak different languages. It is, however, rarely if ever the only mother tongue. Kamtok has various forms, reflecting the age, education, regional provenance, mother tongue, and linguistic proficiency of its users. Its literary use is complicated by three different sets of orthographic conventions: semi-phonetic (*Wi di waka kwik kwik*), English-based (*We dee walka quick quick*), and FRENCH-based (*Oui di waka quouik quouik*). It has been used by the media, in Bible and other religious translation, and in creative writing, uses that may lead to standardization. It has relatively high prestige, and is preferred informally among Africans of different ethnic groups, ranking just below French and English as a vehicle for mobility from rural villages into modern urban life. The former British West Cameroon has extensive influence from Nigerian Pidgin and STANDARD ENGLISH, while in the east there is more influence from French.

**Features**. (1) *Pronunciation*. Kamtok is non-RHOTIC and syllable-timed. It has seven vowels /i, e, ɛ, a, ɔ, o, u/ and four diphthongs /ei, ai, au, oi/. General English central vowels are replaced, SCHWA becoming /a/ as in /fada/ for *father*, /ɜ/ becoming /ɔ/ as in /tʃɔs/ for *church*, and /ʌ/ becoming /a/ or /o/ as in /graunat/ for *ground-nut* and /bɔt/ for *but*. Centring diphthongs are reinterpreted, so that *beer* is /bia/, *air* is /ea/ or /e/, *sure* is /ʃua/. Consonant clusters tend to be simplified, as in /tori/ for *story*, /maʃ/ for *smash*, or to be broken up by an instrusive vowel, as in /sipia/ for *spear* and /sikin/ for *skin*. (2) *Grammar*. Plurality is assumed from context, as in *tu pikin* two children, or indicated by the third-person plural pronoun *dem*, as in *ma pikin dem* my children. Time and aspect are either deduced from the context or indicated by a number of auxiliaries: *a bin go* I went; *i go go* he will go; *we wan go* we almost went; *wuna di go* you (plural) are going; *yu sabi chop* you habitually eat. Adjectives and verbs are structurally similar: *a big* I'm big, *a waka* I walk, *a go big* I'll be big, *a go waka* I'll walk, *som big man* a big man, *som waka man* a walker. Serial verbs are widely used: *I ron go rich di haus kam* He ran as far as the house and came back. Questions are marked by intonation alone (*I no go kam?* Will he/she not come?) or by a question initiator followed by a declarative form (*Usai i bin go?* Where did he/she go?). (3) *Vocabulary*. Most Kamtok words are from English, but many have been widened in meaning: *buk* a book, letter, anything written; *savi buk* ('know book') educated. There are many loan translations from local languages: *krai dai* ('cry die') a wake or funeral celebration; *tai han* ('tie hand') meanness. Non-English vocabulary relates to culture and kinship: *ngɔmbi* a ghost, spirit of the dead, *danshiki* a tunic-like shirt, *mbanya* co-wife in a polygamous family, *mbombo* someone with the same name as someone else, *njamanjama* green vegetables. See WEST AFRICAN PIDGIN ENGLISH.

**KELVINSIDE**. See MORNINGSIDE AND KELVINSIDE.

**KENSINGTON**, also **Kensingtonian**, **Kensington Hay**. An affected or overly refined ACCENT considered typical of the middle-class residents of the London borough of Kensington, especially formerly: 'Hilda had been deprived of her Five Towns

[Staffordshire] accent at Chetwynd's School, where the purest Kensingtonian was inculcated' (Arnold Bennett, *Hilda Lessways*, 1911). The phrase *Kensington Hay* satirizes both the affected pronunciation of 'high' as in *Kensington High Street*, and the aspirations of the speakers. Compare MORNINGSIDE AND KELVINSIDE.

**KENTISH**. A dialect of OLD ENGLISH, known in the 8c only from names in LATIN charters but in the 9c as a language used for the charters themselves. It may have descended from the speech of the JUTES, who are said to have settled in Kent in the 5c. See DIALECT (ENGLAND).

**KENYA**. A country of East Africa and member of the COMMONWEALTH. Languages: SWAHILI (official), English (second), indigenous languages. British control of Kenya was established by the Berlin Conference in 1885. The *British East African Protectorate* was established in 1895, opening the way to European settlers, especially in the area known as the *White Highlands*. In 1920, Kenya became a British colony. In 1944, African participation in politics was permitted. The Mau Mau rebellion lasted from 1952 to 1960 and Kenya gained its independence in 1963. English was the official language immediately after independence, but a constitutional amendment in 1969 instituted the use of Swahili in the National Assembly. In 1974, Swahili replaced English as the official language. At the time, President Jomo Kenyatta stated:

> The basis of any independent government is a national language, and we can no longer continue aping our former colonizers. . . . I do know that some people will start murmuring that the time is not right for this decision; to hell with such people! Those who feel they cannot do without English can as well pack up and go (public address, Nairobi, 1974).

English is, however, the language of higher education and of professional and social status, used by most senior administrators and military officers. The 1967 curriculum focuses on mathematics, science, and English, which is valued as the language of modernity and mobility, often used to express authority, even at the family level, if the parents know it. The mixing of English, Swahili, and the indigenous languages is common. The first newspaper in Kenya was the *African Standard* (established in 1902), now known as the *Standard*. Other English-language publications are the *Daily Nation* (established in 1960) and the *Weekly Review*. Both the Voice of Kenya radio and Kenyan TV broadcast in English as well as Swahili. Contemporary writers include NGUGI WA THIONG'O (b. 1938) and Mugo Gatheru (b. 1925). In terms of its linguistic features, Kenyan English is usually considered part of EAST AFRICAN ENGLISH, but the authenticity and homogeneity of both the regional and the national variety are currently controversial matters in Kenya.

The following points can, however, be made with some confidence: (1) In pronunciation, Kenyan English is non-rhotic. (2) The fricatives /θ, ð/ are generally replaced by the stops /t, d/: 'tree of dem' for *three of them*. (3) Affricates tend to become fricatives: 'inrisht' for *enriched*, 'hwis' for *which*, 'jos' for *judge*. (4) The consonants /b, v/ are often devoiced: 'laf' for *love* and 'rup' or 'rop' for *rub*. (5) The sounds /f, p/ may be hypercorrected to their voiced counterparts, *laughing* and *loving* becoming HOMOPHONES as 'lavin'. (6) Final -l is often deleted: 'andastandebu' for *understandable*, 'loko' for *local*, 'pipu' for *people*. (7) Usually uncountable nouns are often countable: *Thank you for your many advices*; *We eat a lot of breads*; *I held the child on my laps*; *A lady with big bums is attractive*. (8) The semantic range of some words has been extended: *dry* (of coffee) without milk or sugar, *medicine* chemicals, *hear* to feel (pain), to understand (language). (9) LOANWORDS and LOAN TRANSLATIONS from indigenous languages are common: *panga* a machete, *sufuria* a cooking pot, *sima* cornmeal paste, *clean heart* without guile.

**KEYWORD**, also **key word**. **1.** A WORD that serves as a crucial ('key') element in a usage, phrase, sentence, text, subject, concept, theory, or language: *Keywords: A Vocabulary of Culture and Society*, by Raymond Williams (Fontana/Croom Helm, 1976), a work in the form of a glossary of such words as *alienation, career, empirical, fiction, humanity, nationalist*, and *science*, described in the introduction as 'the record of an inquiry into a *vocabulary*: a shared body of words and meanings in our most general discussion, in English, of the practices and institutions which we group as *culture* and *society*'. **2.** A significant word for a person or group: 'Self-reliance and self-care were the keywords' (Mary Kenny, 'Paying the Price of Feminism', *Sunday Telegraph*, 6 Nov. 1988). **3.** A technical term for a term in a list through which it is possible to search an index, catalogue, filing system, or electronic database. **4.** Also CATCHWORD. A term in library science for a memorable or important word or term in the title, text, or abstract of an item being indexed and therefore used in the index entry. **5.** A term in cryptography for a word that is crucial in the enciphering or deciphering of a coded message.

**KINGMAN REPORT**. A British report on the teaching of English in England and Wales, presented in 1988 to the Secretary of State for Education by the Committee of Inquiry into Teaching of English Language under the chairmanship of Sir John Kingman. The Committee was asked to recommend a model to serve as a basis for training teachers in how the language works and to inform professional discussion, to consider how far the model should be made explicit to pupils, and to recommend what pupils should know about how English works. The model which it produced has four parts: the forms of the language; communication and comprehension; acquisition and development; historical and geographical variation. It has been criticized as a checklist of linguistic topics without an internal dynamic connecting the parts, or relating them to educational processes. Nonetheless, some of the Committee's arguments prepared the way for a greater emphasis on knowledge about language in the National Curriculum requirements for England and Wales (1989) than in previous curriculum discussion. See BULLOCK REPORT, COX REPORT, NEWBOLT REPORT, TEACHING ENGLISH.

**KING'S ENGLISH**. A traditional term in Britain that is earlier than, and more or less synonymous with, STANDARD ENGLISH: 'an old abusing of Gods patience and the Kings English' (Shakespeare, *The Merry Wives of Windsor*, 1.4; 1598). It is altered to *the Queen's English* when the monarch is a woman: 'Plea for the Queen's English' (title of a work by Henry Alford, 1869, in the reign of Victoria). Formerly invested with considerable respect, the term has in recent years been used less reverently: for example, in *The Queen's English: High Taw Tawk Prawpah-leah*

(London, Michael Joseph, 1985), the humorist Dorgan Rushton satirizes the ACCENT technically referred to as 'ADVANCED RP', mainly by means of eye dialect in which *shouting* is represented as 'shiteing', *family* as 'fear-mealy', and *taxi* as 'tex-yah'. See EYE DIALECT, LONDON, RECEIVED PRONUNCIATION.

**KING'S ENGLISH, The**. A usage manual published in 1906 by the brothers Henry W. FOWLER and Francis G. Fowler. It was aimed at writers who 'seldom look into a grammar or composition book'. *TKE* contain articles on VOCABULARY (concrete versus abstract words, MALAPROPISMS, LOANWORDS, SLANG, etc.), SYNTAX (relative pronouns, gerunds, *shall/will*, prepositions, etc.), what the Fowlers call 'Airs and Graces' (ARCHAISM, elegant variation, INVERSION, METAPHOR, etc.), PUNCTUATION, EUPHONY, QUOTATIONS and misquotations, MEANING, AMBIGUITY, and STYLE. Most sections are supported by illustrative examples drawn from unfabricated sources, in particular from unspecified 19c works by Meredith, Thackeray, George Eliot, and others, and from Victorian or Edwardian issues (exact dates not specified) of *The Times*, *The Daily Telegraph*, and *The Guernsey Evening Press* (the brothers lived on Guernsey, one of the CHANNEL ISLANDS). More than any earlier usage book, *TKE* introduced a new national pastime—the hunting and exhibiting of solecisms. See DICTIONARY OF MODERN ENGLISH USAGE. Compare AMERICAN LANGUAGE.

**KIRIBATI** [Pronounced /ˈkɪrɪbæs/]. A country of Oceania and member of the COMMONWEALTH. Languages: Kiribati (Gilbertese) and English (both official). Formerly known as the *Gilbert Islands*, and part of the British colony of the *Gilbert and Ellice Islands*, Kiribati gained its independence in 1979. See TUVALU.

**KOREA**. A country of East Asia, currently divided into *North Korea* and *South Korea*. The Korean language is agglutinative and usually regarded as a Uro-Altaic language. Ancient Korean was written in a script called *idu*, in which Chinese characters were used to represent Korean sounds as well as meanings (similar to the present-day Japanese *kanji*). In the 15c, an alphabet of 11 vowel and 17 consonant symbols (reduced later to 10 and 14) was devised and used for popular literature, while classical Chinese continued in use for official and scholarly purposes. Although banned during the last decade of the Japanese occupation, this system (known as *han-gul*) was revived and is used on its own or, to a lesser degree, in a mixed script with Chinese characters read as Korean words. English has had a considerable influence on the structure of the modern language. Over the last 40 years, English has generally been assigned as many school hours as Korean for students aged 12–18, and is in the main an analytical grammatical exercise that has affected the study and use of Korean, resulting in adjustments made to some Korean constructions so as to align them more closely with English: for example, greater use of the optional plural particle *-tul*. Although this is not a strict equivalent of the English plural inflection *-s*, many think that it is or should be. After the Korean War and partition, the need for English declined in North Korea but increased in the South, where it is the main foreign language. Almost all students have three years of it, and the 80% who attend high school have six years. There are many private English institutes, one for students preparing for college entrance examinations the other for people who want to speak the language. See EAST ASIAN ENGLISH, HAWAIIAN.

## KOREAN BAMBOO ENGLISH. See JAPANESE PIDGIN ENGLISH.

## KRIO, also **Creo**. An English CREOLE spoken in SIERRA LEONE, which developed when freed slaves were transported from Britain and Nova Scotia to Freetown in 1787 and 1792. The Krios were Christian, often literate, and valued as teachers and clerks along the entire West African coast. Sizeable settlements were established in GAMBIA, NIGERIA, CAMEROON, and smaller settlements in LIBERIA and GHANA, and Krio had an influence on all West African PIDGINS and creoles, with the possible exception of *Merico* in Liberia. Krio is spoken as a mother tongue by some 250,000 people in and around Freetown and by many more Sierra Leoneans as a second language. It has a dictionary (*A Krio-English Dictionary*, ed. C. N. Fyle & Eldred Jones), and is the only fully standardized West African creole. It has been used for translating SHAKESPEARE and parts of the BIBLE, and for plays, poems, and prose.

**Features**. (1) *Pronunciation*. Krio is non-rhotic, syllable-timed, and a tone language. It has seven monophthongs, /i, e, ɛ, a, ɔ, o, u/ and three diphthongs /ai, au, oi/. All vowels can be nasalized. Tone is significant, distinguishing grammatical as well as lexical meaning: for example, a customary low tone for auxiliaries becomes high for purposes of emphasis. (2) *Grammar*. There is little morphological variation, time and aspect being carried by pre-verbal auxiliaries, and plurality in the noun is either assumed or marked by *dɛm*: *I bin kil di arata dɛm kwik-kwik* He killed the rats quickly. Fluidity of word class is typical: Krio *plɛnti* can function as an adjective in *plɛnti pikin* plenty of children, as a verb *Pikin plɛnti* There are plenty of children, as a noun *plɛnti pwɛl* Many are spoilt, and as an adverb *I gɛt pikin plɛnti* He has children in plenty. **3.** *Vocabulary*. The majority of words derive from English: body parts such as *han* (hand, arm), *fut* (foot, leg), common verbs such as *bi*, *gɛt*, *go*, *kam*, *muf* (move), and auxiliaries *bin*, *de* (progressive), *kin*, *dɔn* (perfective), *nɔba* (negative perfective). English elements occur in many loan translations, such as *dei klin* (day clean: dawn), *drai ai* (dry eye: brave). There are also words from African languages: *akara* (bean-cake, from Yoruba), *bundu* (camwood, from Mende), *jakato* (garden egg, from Wolof), *kola* (kola nut, from Temne), *nono* (buttermilk, from Mandinka). See AKU, KAMTOK, WEST AFRICAN PIDGIN ENGLISH.

## KRIOL, also **Roper River Creole/Kriol**, **Roper Pidgin**. An English-based CREOLE spoken mainly in northern Australia, from western Queensland, across the Barkly Tablelands and Roper River Basin throughout much of the top half of the Northern Territory and into the Kimberleys of Western Australia. A CONTACT LANGUAGE between Aborigines and outside groups, it is now used in over 100 Aboriginal communities by more than 20,000 people, at least half of whom have it as their primary language. Kriol is a continuum of varieties, from *hebi Kriol* (heavy creole: the BASILECT) to *lait Kriol* (light creole: the ACROLECT). Speakers of *hebi Kriol* are mostly mother-tongue speakers of an Aboriginal language who use Kriol as a second language. Extreme *lait Kriol* includes virtually all the contrasts of mainstream English.

A word in Kriol may have several different pronunciations: *policeman* may be *balijiman* (basilect), *blijiman* (MESOLECT), *plisman* (acrolect). Most of the vocabulary is from English, in some cases with meanings altered to parallel the semantic range of equivalent words in Aboriginal languages: *kukwan* (from 'cooked one') means *ripe* as well as *cooked*. There are also some Aboriginal words: *munanga* a person of European descent. The grammar of Kriol shares some features with English-based PIDGINS and creoles in the Pacific: (1) The form of the transitive marker on verbs is *-im/-um*, as in *kilim* to hit, *kukum* to cook. Compare TOK PISIN *kilim, kukim*. (2) The use of *bin* as a completive auxiliary: *Ai bin rid det buk* I have read the book. Most of the limited Kriol morphology is associated with the verb and there are five prepositions which indicate grammatical relations: *blonga* (from 'belong'), as in *Aibin gibit im mani blonga daga* I gave him some money for food; *longa* (from 'long'), as in *Imbin bogi longa riba* He swam in the river. Other prepositions include *fo* for, *from* from, *garram* with, as in: *Olubat bin kaman from deya* They came from there; *Deibin hambagam mi fo daga* They pestered me for food; *Melabat kaan go garram yumob* We cannot go with you people. Kriol has a distinct orthography and a growing literature. In 1975, a school in Bamyili, where Kriol is a major language, was permitted to introduce it as the language of pre-school instruction. In 1979, permission was sought and obtained from the Northern Territory Department of Education for the introduction of a bilingual programme, despite opposition from those who did not consider Kriol a real language. See ABORIGINAL ENGLISH, AUSTRALIAN PIDGIN.

# L

## ■ L, l ■

[Called 'ell']. The 12th LETTER of the Roman ALPHABET as used for English. It originated in the Phoenician letter *lamed*, adopted into GREEK as *lambda* (Λ), which became the Roman letter L.

**Sound value.** (1) In English, the letter *l* represents a voiced alveolar lateral continuant, its articulation varying with accent and position: for example, in RP, a syllable-final velarization distinguishes the *l* in *pill* from that of syllable-initial *lip*. (2) A following *l* frequently gives a long value to the vowel letters *a, i, o*: *a* is like *aw* in *saw* (*all, fall, halt, talk, altercation, falsify*); *i* is like *y* as in *sky* (*child, mild, whilst*); *o* is like *owe* (*cold, poll, bolt, control*). However, pronunciation occasionally varies, as in such pairs as *holy/holiday, Polish/polish*.

**Double L.** (1) In MIDDLE ENGLISH, final *l* in monosyllables after a single vowel letter was often single (*al, ful, wel*) but except in recent coinages like *nil, pal* it is now doubled (*all, bull, cell, fill, gull, hall, mill, pull, will*). In long-established COMPOUNDS, however, such forms commonly have one *l*: *almost, also, although, until, welcome* BrE *wilful*. Contrast standard *all right* and non-standard but common *alright*. (2) Single *l* is usual when two vowel letters precede (*fail, haul, peel, coal, foul, tool*) or when *e* follows (*pale, while, pole, rule*). (3) Doubled *ll* usually signals a preceding short vowel: compare the related *vale/valley*. The chief exceptions are monosyllables such as *roll*, the anomalous adverb *wholly*, *tulle* (derived from a French place-name), and *camellia*. (4) On the other hand, single *l* occurs medially after both short and long vowels: compare *balance/ballot, bilious/billet, chalice/challenge, dolour/dollar, felon/fellow, gelatine/jelly, military/million, palate/pallet, talent/tallow, tranquillity/virility, valid/valley, vilify/villain*. (5) Discrepancies: *tonsillitis* with *ll* and *colitis, poliomyelitis, diverticulitis* with *l; fusilier* and *fusillade*; the pairs of alternates *colander/cullender, postilion/postillion, scalawag/scallywag; belletristic*, in which the *ll* derives from the three *l*s in the phrase *belles letters*. (6) The verb *to parallel* has the common inflected forms *paralleled, parallel-ing* and the less common and less accepted forms *parallelled, parallelling*. (7) An exotic *ll* occurs in SPANISH loans (*llama, guerrilla*), but is pronounced /l/, not as /j/ as in Spanish. (8) WELSH *ll*, as in the names *Llandudno, Llangollen, Llewellyn*, represents an alveolar lateral fricative, and is usually pronounced /l/ by non-Welsh-speakers.

**Doubling by affixation.** (1) Inherited from LATIN, when certain prefixes are assimilated: *ad-* (*allocation*), *con-* (*collocation*), and *in-* (*illustration, illegible*). (2) Inherited from Greek when the prefix *syn-* is assimilated: *syllable, syllogism*. (3) When *-less* attaches to a word ending in *l* (*soulless*) and when *-ly* is added to adjectives ending in *l*: *legally, coolly, beautifully*. Base words ending in *ll* add *y* (*fully*) and those ending in vowel plus *-le* normally add *-ly* (*palely, solely*); *wholly* from *whole* is anomalous. Base words ending in consonant plus *-le* replace the *e* with *y*: *able/ably, simple/simply*. The adverb *supply* (in a supple manner) can be written *supplely* to avoid confusion with to *supply*, but there is only one form *multiply* for both adverb and verb. Adjectives ending in *-ic*, with the exception of *public*, and *-ally*: *automatically, basically*.

**Syllabic L.** The letter *l* can function syllabically, as in *table*, whose second syllable is pronounced /əl/, but in *tabling* the *l* loses its syllabic status and is the first consonant in a second full syllable. Many words have a separate vowel letter where schwa occurs in speech before final *l*, and there is no difference in pronunciation in: *bridal/bridle, cubical/cubicle, gamble/gambol, idle/idol, mantel/mantle, metal/mettle* (cognates), *muscle/mussel* (cognates), *naval/navel*. Such endings can constitute a spelling problem, as with *principal* and *principle*. Such surnames as *Liddell, Revell, Waddell* have either syllable stressed, according to owners' preference, leaving strangers who have only seen the name uncertain how to pronounce it. Certain adjectives derived from nouns with syllabic *l* contain a *u* that relates to the Latin origin of the words concerned: *constable/constabular, muscle/muscular, scruple/scrupulous, table/tabular, triangle/triangular*.

**Epenthetic L**. The letter *l* is epenthetic in *chronicle, emerald, participle, principle, syllable*. In *fault, falcon, realm* the *l* at one stage disappeared, but was restored. See EPENTHESIS.

**L and R**. The sounds /l/ and /r/ are phonetically similar. The *l* in *belfry, marble, pilgrim* (cognate with *peregrine*), *plum* (cognate with *prune*), and *purple* evolved from *r*. *Glamour* derives from *grammar*, and the spelling *coronel* was replaced by French *colonel* in the 17c, although pronunciation still reflects the *r*. See *L*-SOUNDS, *R*-SOUNDS.

**Silent L**. (1) After *a*, before the consonant letters *f*/*v*, *k*, *m*: *calf*/*calve*, *half*/*halve*, *chalk, stalk, talk, walk, almond, alms, balm, calm, palm, psalm, salmon*. (2) After *o* before *k*, *m*: *folk, yolk, holm, Holmes* (contrast *film, helm*). (3) In *could, should, would*. (4) The vowel sound preceding *lk* (*chalk, folk*) is generally modified *a* or lengthened *o*, and in RP *a* is also lengthened before *lf, lm, lv* (*half, palm, calve*). Pronunciation may, however, be inconsistent, with *l* sometimes heard in *almond, calm, holm, palm*. (5) In some proper names, especially in England: always in *Alnwick* ('Annick'), *Lincoln* ('Linken'), generally in *Holborn* ('Hohben'). In most of the preceding words, *l* was once pronounced, but in *could* it was inserted unhistorically early in the 16c by ANALOGY with etymological *l* in *should, would*, which was already silent. *Samon* was respelt *salmon* by reference to Latin *salmo*. Conversely, an *l* has disappeared from *as, each, which, much* (compare *also*, Scots *ilk, whilk, muckle*, and German *als, welch*).

**British and American differences**. (1) Some disyllabic verbs ending in *l* and with second-syllable stress are usually written with *l* in BrE, *ll* in AmE: *appal*/*appall*, *distil*/*distill*, *enrol*/*enroll*, *enthral*/*enthrall*, *instil*/*instill*. Others have a single *l* in both varieties: *control, compel, dispel, impel, repel, annul*. Inflected and some derived forms have *ll* in both varieties: *appalled, controlling, distillation, enrolling, installation* (but *enrolment, instalment* chiefly in BrE). (2) Verbs ending in an unstressed vowel plus *l* (*to equal, travel, pencil*) normally double the *l* in inflected and derived forms in BrE (*travelled, travelling, traveller*), but not in AmE (*traveled, traveling, traveler*). BrE *callisthenics, chilli, councillor, counsellor, fulfil, jewellery, libellous, marvellous, skilful, tranquillity, wilful, woollen* correspond to AmE *calisthenics, chili, councilor, counselor,* *fulfill, jewelry, libelous, marvelous, skillful, tranquility, willful, woolen*.

**LABIAL**. A term in PHONETICS for a sound made with the lips or a lip, such as /p, f/. When both lips are used, the sound is *bilabial*: /p, b/. When the lower lip is raised towards the upper front teeth, the sound is *labio-dental*: /f, v/.

**LALLANS**. A name for the VERNACULAR speech of Lowland Scotland from the 18c to the present day, adopted after the Second World War by poets of the Scottish Renaissance movement in preference to *Synthetic Scots*, a term coined in the 1920s for eclectic literary SCOTS. Following Hugh MACDIARMID's aim of restoring dignity and copiousness to Scots, they composed much of their poetry in this form, which hostile critics ridiculed as *Plastic Scots*. The following excerpt from MacDiarmid's 'The Eemis Stane' (*Sangschaw*, 1925) demonstrates its eclecticism: the entire first line, and the archaic words *eemis* and *yowdendrift*, are lifted from John Jamieson's early 19c *Etymological Dictionary of the Scottish Language*:

> I' the how-dumb-deid o' the cauld hairst
>     nicht
> The warl' like an eemis stane
> Wags i' the lift;
> An' my eerie memories fa'
> Like a yowdendrift.
>
> [*how-dumb-deid* (Jamieson) 'the middle of
> the night, when silence reigns; Ayrshire';
> *cauld* (general) cold; *hairst* (general)
> autumn; *nicht* (general) night; *warl'*
> (general) world; *eemis* (Jamieson)
> insecurely balanced, toppling; *stane*
> (general) stone; *lift* (archaic) sky; *fa'*
> (general) fall; *yowdendrift* (Jamieson)
> 'snow driven by the wind']

Literary Lallans remains viable alongside other kinds of Scots verse and prose. It is the principal medium in *Lallans*, the journal of the Scots Language Society (1973– ). See DORIC, LOWLAND SCOTS.

**LAMINAL**. A term in PHONETICS for the blade of the tongue and sounds made with it. The sibilants /s, z, θ, ð/ are usually made with the tip and blade together, raised to the ALVEOLAR ridge.

■ **LANCASHIRE** ━━━━━━━━ ■

**1.** A north-western county of England. **2.**

The DIALECT of the county, part of NORTH-
ERN ENGLISH, and related to the CUMBRIAN
and GEORDIE dialects to the north, and the
YORKSHIRE dialect to the east, while also
having features of the MIDLAND dialect area.
Some scholars give the town of Rawtenstall
as the source of the alliterative 14c poem in
North Midland dialect, *Sir Gawain and the
Green Knight*. Although the Lancashire dialect is particularly associated with the cotton towns of the south-east, such as Burnley,
Bolton, and Rochdale, it has many varieties,
including the urban dialects of Manchester
and Liverpool.

**Pronunciation**. (1) Lancashire shares
many features of pronunciation with other
Midland and Northern regions of England,
accents ranging from the regional through
the RP-influenced to RP. (2) Regional pronunciation is non-rhotic, except for a small
and decreasing number of speakers in
Rochdale, Accrington, and Preston. (3)
Word-initial /h/ tends to be lost in frequently used words such as *house* and *hat*.
(4) The same vowel /a/ is used for words such
as *gas* and *grass*, *Sam* and *psalm*. (5) There is
usually no distinction between the vowels
in such words as *hoot* and *hut*, which are
homophones pronounced /hʊt/. Among
RP-influenced speakers, *book* is often pronounced /bʊk/, a usage that can be considered a SHIBBOLETH of Lancashire speech. (6)
The long /u/ vowel is sometimes diphthongized in such words as *moon*/muən/ and
*school* /skuəl/, especially to the north of
Burnley. (7) There is a tendency to use the
monophthongs /e, o, ɛ/ in words such as
*take, soap, square*, where RP has diphthongs.
(8) In the south, there is a tendency to round
the /a/ vowel when it precedes a nasal, particularly /m/ and /n/ in words such as
*ham*/hɒm/ and *hand*/hɒnd/. (9) Word-initial
/l/ as in *land* and *look* is often dark, and the
/l/ in -*ld* clusters is often lost, *old* and *cold*
being realized as 'owd' /aud/ and 'cowd'
/kaud/. (10) In words ending in /ŋ/ a final /g/
is sounded, as in 'long-g' /lɒŋg/ for *long*,
'sing-ging-g' for *singing*. (11) As in WELSH
ENGLISH, intervocalic consonants are sometimes lengthened in the south, making
*chapel* sound like 'chap-pel' and *biting* like
'bite-ting'. (12) In the west, especially
around Chorley and Southport, there has
been a tendency to add a parasitic nasal
after word-final plosives, as in *I've hurt my leg-
n* and *They were but lad-ns* They were only

boys. This feature is rare in the speech of
people under 60.

**Grammar**. (1) There are many working-
class structures such as multiple NEGATION
(*I haven't done nothing*), the use of *them* as a
demonstrative adjective (*I don't talk to them
people*), and the use of non-standard verb
forms (*I seen, he done*) . (2) In southern, rural
Lancashire, 'aw' and '(h)oo' continue to be
occasionally used for *I* and *she*: see verse
below. In the south-east, *thou* and *thee* have
been traditionally used, as in neighbouring
Yorkshire, as a marker of intimacy and solidarity. However, the standard pronouns *I*,
*she*, *you* are increasingly being used in all
sections of society. (3) There is a tendency
to drop the *to* in infinitive constructions, especially when the first verb ends in a *t*, as in
*What d'you want do?* (4) The definite article is
often reduced to /θ/ before both vowels and
consonants: see verse below. (5) The negative modal verb *maun't* (mustn't) is sometimes used in rural areas, but the positive
form *maun*, as used in Scots and in Northern
Ireland, is rare. (6) As in many northern
areas of Britain, such forms as *I've not seen it*
are more widely used than *I haven't seen it*.
(7) *Owt* (anything) and *nowt* (nothing) occur
frequently, as in *I didn't say owt* and *He gave us
nowt*. (8) *Right* and more recently *dead* and
*well* are used as colloquial intensifiers, as in
*We were right/dead lucky* and *They were well
merry* (quite drunk).

**Vocabulary**. Lancashire shares many
dialect words with other parts of northern
Britain, including *elder* an udder, *freet* super-
stition, *fuddle* a drinking bout, *mither* to
scold, and *oxter* an armpit. Items that do not
occur elsewhere include *alicker* vinegar,
*deggin'-can* watering can, *judy* a girl, *kay-
fished* left-handed, *maiden* a clothes-horse.
However, most of these words are no longer
widespread and are used only by old people,
comedians, and dialectologists.

**Literary Lancashire**. The first well-known
writer in dialect was John Collier (1708–86),
a schoolmaster who lived near Rochdale
and wrote under the pen name 'Tim
Bobbin'. The most famous is an admirer of
his, Edwin Waugh (pronounced 'Waff'), the
son of a shoe-maker who became a journeyman printer and later a fulltime writer
(1817–90). He wrote, among other things, of
the oppression of a work system that forced
a father to leave home to gain employment.

In the following lines, a woman 'reports' to her absent husband:

When aw put little Sally to bed,
Hoo cried, 'cose her feyther weren't theer,
So aw kiss'd th'little thing, an aw said
Thae'd bring her a ribbin fro' th'fair.
An' aw gav' her her doll, an' some rags,
An' a nice little white cotton-bo';
An aw kiss'd her again, but hoo said
'At hoo wanted to kiss *thee* an' o.
[*thae* thou/you, *bo*' ball, '*at* that, *o* all]

Like other writers of dialect, Lancashire poets have tended to be obsessed with standard spelling and inclined to use apostrophes freely to mark 'lost' letters, some of which were not sounded in STANDARD ENGLISH either (as in *kiss'd*, above). Organized interest in the dialect centres on the *Lancashire Dialect Society*, founded in 1951 largely through the efforts of the late G. L. Brook, Professor of English Language at the U. of Manchester. See CUMBRIA, DIALECT IN ENGLAND, MIDLANDS, SCOUSE.

# ■ LANGUAGE ────────── ■

**1.** A human system of COMMUNICATION which uses structured vocal sounds and can be embodied in other media such as writing, print, and physical signs. Most linguists currently regard the faculty of language as a defining characteristic of being human. **2.** A particular instance of this system, such as ARABIC, FRENCH, English, Kwakiutl, SANSKRIT, SWAHILI. **3.** Any more or less systematic and extensive means of communication, such as animal cries and movements, GESTURE, CODE (including in COMPUTING), and FIGURATIVE USAGE: *the language of dreams*; *machine language*. **4.** The usage of a special group, such as scientific and technical REGISTERS, JOURNALESE, SLANG. **5.** Usage that is socially suspect, often with a modifier, as in *bad/foul/strong language*, but sometimes alone, as in *Mind your language!*

**Students of language**. Language is the concern of LINGUISTICS, the systematic or scientific study of language, and those who practise it are (scientific) linguists. They do not, however, monopolize the study of language and languages, which takes various other forms. Many literary humanists, in particular, feel that objective analysis cannot replace the subjective insights of those steeped in LITERATURE; some deny or doubt the usefulness of linguistics.

**The nature and properties of language**. Language is a system in which basic units are assembled according to a complex set of rules. There is a major division between *natural language* (traditional human use of languages) and *artificial language* (devised languages like ESPERANTO; computer languages like BASIC). Human communication is multimodal, in that speech, gesture, writing, touch, etc., all interact. Language as such has the following properties:

**1.** *A vocal-auditory channel*. This channel is often referred to as *the phonic medium*, that is, sounds produced by the vocal organs, which are then received by the ear.

**2.** *Convertibility to other media*. Such media are writing and print (*the graphic medium*), sign language (a *visual medium*), and Braille (a *tactile medium*).

**3.** *Use of arbitrary symbols*. There is no link in most words between the form used and the meaning expressed.

**4.** *Duality or double articulation*. Language is made up of two layers: a layer of sounds, in which the units (phonemes) do not normally have meaning, but combine into another layer which does.

**5.** *Interdependence*. Language can be regarded as an integrated structure in which the role of every item is defined by that of all the other items in the same system.

**6.** *Open-endedness* (*productivity*, *creativity*). The number of utterances which can be produced is indefinitely large.

**7.** *Displacement*. Language is used to refer to events removed in time and place, and to situations which never existed, as in lying and telling imaginative stories.

**8.** *Continual change*. Language is always changing, and there is no evidence that overall progress or decay results from such change.

**9.** *Turn-taking*. Spoken language involves structured interchanges in which people take it in turns to talk.

In addition to these features, there has in recent years been a search for universal characteristics which are somewhat more abstract. The difficulty of finding such universals has led to renewed interest in assigning languages to different types.

**Language as a mental phenomenon**. Language appears to be behaviour that is controlled by maturation, in that it is 'programmed' to emerge at appropriate stages in an individual's development, as long as the nervous system and the environment are normal. Some language disorders are environmental; others may be inherited. Language ability is believed by most linguists to be genetically in-built, at least in its broad outlines, though the nature and extent of the innate contribution is controversial. The mental aspects of language are the concern of *PSYCHOLINGUISTICS*, which deals primarily with the acquisition, comprehension, and production of language. Some theoretical linguists also attempt to produce models of the human language faculty, though many of these are controversial. The link between language and thought is another contentious issue. Few linguists accept the claim that language determines thought, but many consider that language influences the way a person thinks.

**Language as a social phenomenon**. The social aspects of language are the concern primarily of *SOCIOLINGUISTICS* and *anthropological linguistics*. There have been various attempts to define the sociocultural notion of 'a language'. Political and geographical boundaries do not necessarily coincide with linguistic boundaries, nor do ethnic names: many Belgians, for example, speak FRENCH. Different varieties of the 'same' language may be mutually incomprehensible even within the same country: in England, a COCKNEY accent may not be understood by someone with a GEORDIE accent. Linguists usually therefore regard a language as being defined by those who speak it: the many varieties of English used around the world are all defined as English because this is the language the speakers agree that they are speaking. A variety, however, may be regarded by its speakers as a distinct language if there is a strong literary, religious, or other tradition, as in the case of SCOTS.

**Variation in a language**. Within a language, there are subdivisions traditionally known as *DIALECTS*, increasingly as *VARIETIES*, which are most commonly geographical but may also be social. A dialect is more than a simple difference of pronunciation. In the British Isles, many people speak the same dialect of English, but with different accents. Sometimes, one dialect becomes socially prestigious and is adopted as the norm; it is then usually referred to as the 'STANDARD' LANGUAGE. Social variation in language may be due to social class, ethnic origin, age, and/or sex, and within these, to the level of formality employed at any time. Sometimes this variation remains stable, but is often the forerunner of a change. LANGUAGE SHIFT usually appears as variation within a community, one variant increasing in frequency of use and in its distribution.

**Languages in contact**. The use of more than one language is common, particularly in frontier regions and in polyglot countries. Also common is the use of a restricted form of a language for a specialized purpose, such as AIRSPEAK, the restricted variety of English used worldwide for air traffic control. Occasionally, formal and informal varieties of the same language may differ to such an extent that they are used virtually as different languages, as until recently in modern Greece. Sometimes, contact between languages may give rise to a system so different from the original(s) that it can no longer be regarded as the same language. A *PIDGIN* is a limited language system, with rules of its own, used for communication between people with no common language. A *CREOLE* is a pidgin which has become the first language of a community. A *mixed language* is one in which elements from two or more languages have become so intertwined that it is unclear which is the 'basic' language.

**The world's languages**. There is no agreed figure for the number of languages spoken in the world today. Estimates cluster around 4,000–5,000, with a great deal of variation on either side. Some of the reasons for this uncertainty are: (1) From a linguistic point of view, some parts of the world remain unexplored, including areas where it is known that many languages are in use, such as New Guinea and Central Africa. The rate at which languages are dying, in the face of Western exploration, as in Amazonia, is an unknown factor. (2) Only after a great deal of linguistic enquiry does it become apparent whether a newly encountered community turns out to be speaking a new language or a dialect of an already 'discovered' language. (3) In some areas, it is not easy to decide on the status of what is spoken. Although normally those who can understand each other's spontaneous speech would be said to be speaking the same language, even if there were noticeable differences (as with AmE and BrE, or Cockney and WEST COUNTRY in England), in some places such relatively minor variants are considered important indicators of social, cultural, or political differences. In such cases, it proves necessary to talk of different languages, not different dialects. This has happened, for example, with Flemish and DUTCH, HINDI and URDU, and Swedish, Danish, and Norwegian. In these circumstances, a precise statement about the number of the world's languages is impossible to obtain. Similar differences are encountered when making estimates about the number of speakers of particular languages.

**Language and linguistics**. See ACROLECT, AGGLUTINATING, ANALYTIC, ARTIFICIAL LANGUAGE, BABY TALK, BASILECT, BILINGUALISM, CHILD LANGUAGE ACQUISITION, CLASSIFICATION OF LANGUAGES, COMPETENCE AND PERFORMANCE, CREOLE, DIALECT, DIGLOSSIA, FUSIONAL, GESTURE, INTERLANGUAGE, LANGUAGE ACQUISITION DEVICE, LANGUAGE CHANGE, LANGUAGE FAMILY, LANGUAGE LEARNING, LANGUAGE PLANNING, LANGUAGE SHIFT, LANGUAGE TEACHING, LEVEL OF LANGUAGE, LINGUISTICS, MESOLECT, MULTILINGUALISM, NATURAL LANGUAGE, PHILOLOGY, PIDGIN, PRIVATE LANGUAGE, PSYCHOLINGUISTICS, RESTRICTED LANGUAGE, SOCIOLECT, SOCIOLINGUISTICS, SPEECH, STRUCTURAL LINGUISTICS, TONGUE, TRANSLATION.

**Language groups**. See ARYAN, BANTU, CELTIC LANGUAGES, ENGLISH LANGUAGES, GERMANIC LANGUAGES, INDO-EUROPEAN LANGUAGES, PAPUA NEW GUINEA, ROMANCE LANGUAGES, SCANDINAVIAN LANGUAGES, SLAVONIC/SLAVIC LANGUAGES, SOUTH AFRICAN LANGUAGES.

**Individual languages**. See AFRIKAANS, ANGLO-NORMAN, ANGLO-SAXON, ARABIC, CELTIC, CHINA, CORNISH, CUMBRIC, DANISH, DUTCH, EARLY MODERN ENGLISH, ENGLISH, FILIPINO, FRENCH, FRISIAN, GAELIC, GERMAN, GOTHIC, GREEK, HAWAIIAN, HEBREW, HINDI, HINDIURDU, INGLIS, IRISH GAELIC, ITALIAN, JAPAN, KOREA, LATIN, LAW FRENCH, LOWLAND SCOTS, MALTA, MAORI, MIDDLE ENGLISH, MODERN ENGLISH, NORMAN FRENCH, NORN, NORSE, OLD ENGLISH, POLARI, PORTUGUESE, ROMANI, RUSSIAN, SABIR, SANSKRIT, SAXON, SCOTS, SCOTTISH GAELIC, SHELTA, SPANISH, SWAHILI, TAGALOG, URDU, WELSH, YIDDISH.

**LANGUAGE ACQUISITION DEVICE**, short form *LAD*. In LINGUISTICS, a genetic mechanism for the acquisition of language proposed by Noam CHOMSKY (*Aspects of the Theory of Syntax*, 1965). LAD was 'wired' with language universals and equipped with a mechanism which allowed children to make increasingly complex guesses about what they hear around them, aided by an in-built evaluation measure that enabled them to select the best GRAMMAR consistent with the evidence. It has, however, proved difficult to specify and test this theory, and Chomsky has abandoned it in favour of *parametric theory* (*Knowledge of Language*, 1986), which suggests that children are pre-programmed with some universals but only partially 'wired' with others. They have advance knowledge of certain basic language options, but have to discover by experience which occur in the language they are exposed to. In Chomskyan terminology, they know the parameters along which language can vary, but have to fix their values, perhaps by setting a 'switch' in one of two possible positions. According to this theory, languages are similar at deep, even though on the surface they appear different.

**LANGUAGE AWARENESS**. A term in LANGUAGE TEACHING and APPLIED LINGUISTICS for the development of greater awareness among schoolchildren of the nature and purpose of LANGUAGE. Promoters of language awareness seek to apply the findings of linguistic research to education at large. Courses in Modern Languages and in English that are based on language awareness encourage an appreciation of diversity among languages and varieties of languages, and of such matters as the mechanisms for speech, the nature of writing systems, and the historical development of language.

## ■ LANGUAGE CHANGE ─────── ■

The modification of forms of LANGUAGE over a period of time and/or physical distance. Such change may affect any parts of a LANGUAGE (PRONUNCIATION, ORTHOGRAPHY, GRAMMAR, VOCABULARY) and is taking place all the time. It may be abrupt (a change in spelling in a HOUSE STYLE) or gradual (a slight change in the pronunciation of a VOWEL). During the past nine centuries, English has undergone more dramatic changes than any other major European language. As a result, OLD ENGLISH or ANGLO-SAXON is not accessible to the modern English speaker in the way that Medieval Icelandic is to the modern Icelander. When people do notice change, their reactions are often negative (for example, the use of *disinterested* to mean *uninterested*), and conscious attempts are made to resist it. These are usually not successful in the long term. Deliberate attempts are sometimes made, however, by social pressure groups or by governments to change aspects of a language or its use.

**Sound change**. Changes in pronunciation were a primary interest of 19c comparative philologists who studied the historical relationships among groups of languages such as the Indo-European LANGUAGE FAMILY, which includes ENGLISH, FRENCH, GERMAN, GREEK, LATIN, and SANSKRIT. The establishment of regular correspondences among sets of sounds enabled them to reconstruct genetic relationships and the shifts responsible for the present differentiation of languages and DIALECTS: for example, a sound change which shifted /p/ to /f/ in some of the INDO-EUROPEAN LANGUAGES accounts for some major differences between the GERMANIC LANGUAGES and ROMANCE LANGUAGES. Compare the initial spoken consonant in Latin *pater* and Spanish *padre* with English *father* and German *Vater*. Many of these changes take a long time to complete and may never cover the entire range of a 'language'. Thus, one series of changes, the GREAT VOWEL SHIFT, is responsible for the present-day pronunciations of English *house*, *mouse*, but has never affected SCOTS, in which the pronunciations are *hoose*, *moose*, as was true of all English before the shift occurred.

**Grammatical change**. Major changes in SYNTAX and MORPHOLOGY have affected English over many centuries to the extent that speakers of MODERN ENGLISH are not able to understand Old English without training. The structure of Old English was more like Latin in that words had various inflectional endings to indicate their grammatical function. This situation has been much simplified: for example, the form of the definite article *the*, now invariant, once varied according to case, number, and gender, as in *se mona* (the moon: masculine, nominative, singular), *seo sunne* (the sun:

feminine, nominative, singular), and *þæt tungol* (the star: neuter, nominative, singular). Word order in Old English was more flexible because grammatical relations were made clear by the endings: *Se hund seah þone wifmann* (The dog saw the woman) could also be expressed as *þone wifmann seah se hund*, because the inflected forms of the definite article make it clear that 'woman' is the direct object in both cases. In Modern English, however, grammatical relations are indicated largely by word order, so that *The dog saw the woman* and *The woman saw the dog* (compare Old English *Se wifmann seah þone hund*) mean two different things. Modern English has also lost its system of classifying nouns into three grammatical genders, as still occurs in German.

**Lexical change**. Such change is caused by both internal and external factors. Internal change can mean the adaptation of both the meanings and forms of existing words and phrases through such factors as assimilation, elision, and reduction, as with the conversion of *Saint Audries* in *Saint Audries lace* into *tawdry* (cheap and ill-made, originally referring to the quality of the lace sold at St Audrey's Fair in Ely, England). External change includes the BORROWING OF WORDS, which may be occasional and minimal (as with LOANWORDS taken into English from Turkish) or frequent and massive (as with the flow into English of French, Latin, and Greek words). All such acquisition results in the introduction of new vocabulary and sometimes new word structures and patterns of WORD-FORMATION.

**Conclusion**. People often react negatively to change and regard it as due to ignorance, laziness, or sloppiness. This can be seen in the letters written to newspapers complaining that the contemporary uses of words like *disinterested*, *hopefully*, and *regime* are 'incorrect'. The spread of language change is basically a social phenomenon, as can be seen from recent sociolinguistic studies, which have shown that changes associated with prestige groups often have a greater chance of being adopted than others. Forms which from the point of view of one variety appear conservative may continue without comment in another, such as the use of *gotten* rather than *got* in *You've gotten more than you need*, which is conventional in Scots and in AmE, but is not now used in the English of England. Older forms may also survive in working-class NON-STANDARD speech (*hoose* in urban working-class Scots) and in informal styles (*workin* instead of *working* in many varieties), though sometimes older forms become restricted to formal or specialized contexts, as with the religious use of *brethren*. See ETYMOLOGY, PROGRESS AND DECAY IN LANGUAGE, SEMANTIC CHANGE.

**LANGUAGE FAMILY**. A group of languages which are assumed to have arisen from a single source: ENGLISH, FRENCH, GERMAN, GREEK, PERSIAN, RUSSIAN, SANSKRIT, and WELSH are all members of the INDO-EUROPEAN language family, and are considered to have descended from a common ancestor. Common ancestry is established by finding systematic correspondences between languages: English repeatedly has /f/ where Latin has /p/ in words with similar meaning, as in *father/pater*, *fish/piscis*, *flow/pluo* rain. It also often has /s/ where Greek has /h/, as in *six/héx*, *seven/heptá*, *serpent/hérpein* to creep. In addition, English and German compare adjectives in similar ways, as in *rich*, *richer*, *richest*: *reich*, *reicher*, *reichste*. These and other correspondences indicate that the languages are cognate (genetically related). Various related words can be compared in order to reconstruct sections of a hypothetical ancestor language. The process of comparison and reconstruction is traditionally known as *comparative PHILOLOGY*, more recently as *comparative historical linguistics*. This process formed the backbone of 19c language study, though in the 20c it has become one branch among many. A 'family tree' diagram (not unlike a genealogy) is commonly used to represent the relationships between the members of a linguistic family, in which an initial parent language 'gives birth' to a number of 'daughters', which in turn give birth to others. This can be useful, but is rarely an accurate representation of how languages develop, since it suggests clean cuts between 'generations' and between 'sister' languages, and implies that languages always become more divergent. In fact, languages generally change gradually, and there is often considerable intermixing among those which remain geographically adjacent. See LANGUAGE CHANGE, LINGUISTIC TYPOLOGY.

■ **LANGUAGE LEARNING** ───── ■

Short form *LL*. In principle, the learning of any language or of LANGUAGE itself; in practice, in LANGUAGE TEACHING and APPLIED LINGUISTICS, the term is usually limited to the learning of foreign languages. The psychological and neurological nature of such learning is not known, but some general statements can be made about its educational and social aspects. In broad terms, there are two kinds of foreign-language learning: *informal* ('picking a language up') and *formal* (taking an organized course).

**The market-place tradition**. Although not often discussed by applied linguists, the informal approach has been by far the commoner way of learning languages, especially among migrants, refugees, traders, sailors, soldiers, and the inhabitants of frontier settlements, garrison towns, and ports. This *market-place tradition* is primarily oral, usually haphazard, and part of a range of adhoc communicative strategies that include gesturing, drawing pictures, using interpreters, mixing elements from two or more tongues, and guesswork. The aim has seldom been to learn an approved or 'high' version of another language to the fullest possible extent, but rather to use language to get something else done ('to get by'). In the process, the boundaries between languages may not be well established. CODE-MIXING AND CODE-SWITCHING are common, especially where people know two or more language systems fairly well. One result of the widespread need to communicate at this level has been what are variously known as *CONTACT LANGUAGES*, *makeshift languages*, *TRADE JARGONS*, and *INTERLANGUAGES*, such as Bazar Malay, Lingua Franca, and Pidgin English. In course of time, under appropriate circumstances, some of these forms have evolved into new 'full' languages in their own right. In their early stages of stabilization and growth, such languages are known technically as *creoles*.

**The monastery tradition**. Because of its dominant position in most present-day societies, formal instruction in some kind of institution, in set periods of time, with one teacher and a class of learners in a room, has come to be seen as the 'proper' way to learn a language. Such formality, typical of present-day educational systems, is usually associated with certain assumptions about culture and utility: for example, it is traditionally applied more to prestige languages (such as FRENCH in Britain and English in France) than to minority or fringe languages (such as WELSH in Britain and Basque in France). In the Western world, the roots of formal learning of this type are classical, but the truly formative influence was the medieval training of religious novices in LATIN as an international language. This *monastery tradition* favours rote learning associated with repetition, the study of canonical texts, and grammatical analysis. Though rigorous and demanding, and greatly valued by many people, it sits apart from the world, favouring abstraction and standardization. It distances learning from immediate need, demanding discipline (often, especially formerly, by coercion: learning Latin *sub virga* or 'under the rod') and motivation (or at least submission) on the part of students.

**Attainment**. Formal language learning is incremental. It is absorbed (or not absorbed) in doses, and runs from zero to whatever ceiling is reached. Progress is usually marked by a reduction of dependence on the teacher and changes in the kind of help needed. Such changes are gradual and occur at different rates for different people and in different aspects of learning. There are no easily displayed tokens of attainment, but administrators, teachers, and students need indicators of attainment, and for this purpose three levels are generally assumed: *beginner, intermediate, advanced*.

**1. *Beginner***. In the classroom, learning is at first by courtesy of the teacher. At first, beginners understand little and produce nothing, then gradually they understand individual words, fixed formulas, and disconnected items in speech or text. There is often little creative scope, frustration is common, and regular praise and reassurance are essential. Translation is constant and often overt. Generally, learning to understand (*receptive ability*) is faster than learning to express (*productive ability*). Performance is usually poor at this stage and dominated by the mother tongue.

**2. *Intermediate***. When learners begin to produce their own phrases and sentences they can use their own creativity in making mental connections (sometimes correct, often wrong, constantly developing) between items already encountered and partly learned. They make guesses, set up provisional theories about what things

mean, or how they might be expressed, and modify them in the light of experience. Much of the learner's grasp of syntax is now established, though with gaps and shortcomings. Dependence on TRANSLATION (spoken or mental) is less compulsive. At this stage, many learners stop, their capacity fossilized. For more motivated students, however, it is the level at which the *performance skills* (speaking and writing) improve rapidly, given opportunity, stimulation, and time for assimilation.

**3. *Advanced***. Learners at the advanced stage use their own creativity and seek delicate discriminations of meaning, stylistic niceties, subtleties of culture and discourse, and greater acquaintance with the language. All going well, inner translation continues to decline and fluency, speed, and accuracy continue to develop. At this level, many learners achieve a close approximation to the skills of the native speaker of the target language.

**Conclusion**. The levels are not watertight. Individuals rise imperceptibly from one to the other, and may also slip back. Members of a class do not move forward uniformly, and the varying rates of fast, average, and slow learners may pose problems for teacher and students. Teachers, writers, and publishers often divide the levels into six: *absolute beginner, beginner-to-intermediate, lower intermediate, upper intermediate, early advanced, late advanced*, making it easier to structure courses and materials and conduct attainment tests. Although the market-place and the monastery continue to be well-separated styles of language learning, there is a growing tendency to open the classroom door and let the world in, or take students out into that world to immerse them for a time in 'real' usage, before returning to the classroom for a time of consolidation. See CHILD LANGUAGE ACQUISITION.

**LANGUAGE PLANNING**. The attempt to control the use, status, and structure of a language through a language policy developed by a government or other authority. Normally carried out by official agencies, such planning usually passes through several stages: a particular language or variety of a language is selected; codification is undertaken to stabilize it, for example by agreeing writing conventions for previously non-literate languages; the codified language is adjusted to enable it to perform new functions, for example by inventing or borrowing scientific vocabulary; and mechanisms are devised, such as teaching syllabuses and procedures for monitoring the media, to ensure that the language is used in conformity with the policy. This sequence is rarely appropriate for English, whose dominant role in the world gives it a unique position, but English is nonetheless officially planned into national education systems in various ways. In Britain, WELSH has been promoted through the National Curriculum in Wales as a subject to be compulsorily learnt within Wales, but is not compulsorily available to Welsh speakers or others outside Wales. In post-colonial nations the relationship of English to indigenous languages is often carefully defined: as the language of secondary and tertiary education in Tanzania while SWAHILI is the national language; as an official language recognized for legal purposes in India; as a library language in some subjects in some South American universities. Planning policy may be achieved through agencies at a number of levels in a state hierarchy. Governments may define their language policy throughout a country, ministries of education may define it within education, and institutions may contribute to planning through their own policies: for example, in the UK in the 1980s, local education authorities and individual schools attempted to define the roles of various especially migrant languages like Punjabi and Cantonese within particular regions or institutions. See ACADEMY, STANDARD.

**LANGUAGE SHIFT**. A term in LINGUISTICS for a massive shift in use from one language to another, as in Ireland from GAELIC to English (18–20c). In 1964, the US linguist Joshua A. Fishman introduced the dual notion *language maintenance and language shift* (*LMLS*) to discuss the situation of 'the minority language or small national language faced by pressures related to a much bigger national or international language'. To the latter, of which English is the pre-eminent example, he has given the name *language of wider communication* (*LWC*).

■ **LANGUAGE TEACHING** ────── ■

Short form *LT*. In principle, instruction in any LANGUAGE, under any conditions, for-

mal or informal; in practice, as the term is commonly used among language teachers and applied linguists, instruction in a second or foreign language within a system of education, such as the institutionalized teaching of FRENCH in Britain and English in France. More specifically, the teaching of a MOTHER TONGUE, home language, or national language may be referred to as *L1 teaching* (where L1 means *first language*) and the teaching of one or more other languages as *L2 teaching* (where L2 means *second language*).

**L1 and L2 teaching**. By and large, *L1 teaching* is that part of general education which deals with the transmission of a society's written culture and STANDARD speech (which may or may not involve training in an approved accent). It usually includes instruction in aspects of a particular literature, and it has traditionally included explicit instruction in GRAMMAR, SPELLING, PUNCTUATION, and COMPOSITION, matters that are currently controversial. *L2 teaching* for many centuries centred on acquiring a classical language, in Europe especially LATIN, sometimes GREEK or HEBREW, and elsewhere such languages as classical ARABIC, Mandarin Chinese (see CHINA), and SANSKRIT. In Britain, the teaching of a second vernacular (nonforeign) language has taken place, on a limited scale and mainly since the 19c, in Scotland and Wales, usually for those who have already had GAELIC or WELSH as their mother tongues, their general education proceeding in English as a second language which more often than not becomes their primary medium. Because there has been no significant other VERNACULAR in England since NORMAN FRENCH in the 14c, L2 teaching in that country has generally been concerned with 'foreign' languages. The most powerful L2 tradition in England, and elsewhere in the English-speaking world, has usually been the teaching of French.

**The literary method**. Throughout Western history, LITERACY and EDUCATION have run together. Only in the 20c has the technology of audio-recording allowed conversation to become an object of study. This change, along with a broad acceptance of democratic ideals in education as well as in politics, has made possible a vernacular rather than a classical education, or one that judiciously draws on both. For many centuries, language teaching in the European ('monastery') tradition of Christianity meant the teaching of the languages of religion, literature, and scholarship: Latin and to a limited extent Greek. In addition, in the Middle Ages in England, children of the aristocracy were taught Norman French, while English was a largely irrevelant vernacular. Although some attempt was made to teach spoken Latin (for example, in the English Abbot AELFRIC's *Colloquy*, a conversation reader, *c*. AD 1000), learning centred mostly on a close acquaintance with the most highly valued literary texts. With the Renaissance and the Reformation, and the return of classical Latin as a model, the language largely ceased to be used in speech; thenceforth, the aim was written mastery, learners imitating the style of 'the classics', and being led away from the 'debased' styles of less highly regarded texts. The 'golden' texts of Cicero, Horace, and Virgil were accepted, while the base metal of Apuleius, Geoffrey of Monmouth, Petrarch, and later Latin writers was ignored. The route to understanding lay through rote memorization of grammar and vocabulary and imitation that might or might not lead to creativity.

**The grammar–translation method**. Opposition to the literary tradition arose in and around Germany in the late 18c, with methods of teaching Latin and other languages that have in the 20c been given the name *the grammar–translation method/ approach*. Reformers sought to organize and simplify the traditional exposure to texts by using specimen sentences and emphasizing practice by translating in both directions. Through translation of specially constructed sentences that were keyed to lessons centred on particular grammatical points, learners could be exposed to the grammatical and stylistic range of the target language in an economical and systematic way. The reform was not, however, complete, and for the next 200 years the grammar–translation method and the less systematic literary method coexisted and often blended.

**The Reform Movement**. Dissatisfaction with the practice of teaching modern languages by such text-based methods came to a head in the *Reform Movement* of the 1880s–90s, among scholars and teachers in Germany, Scandinavia, France, and Britain

who were interested in the practical possibilities of a science of speech. It began with the publication in 1877 of Henry SWEET's *Handbook of PHONETICS*. With its analyses and specimens of different sound systems, this book opened up the prospect of teaching speech systematically and escaping from the ancient dependence on texts. In 1882, the German phonetician Wilhelm Viëtor expressed the growing impatience in the pamphlet *Der Sprachunterricht muss umkehren* (Language teaching must start afresh), initially published under a pseudonym. Paul Passy in France is credited with inventing the term *la méthode directe* (*the Direct Method*) to sum up the aims of the reformers; other names are the *Natural Method*, *New Method*, and *Phonetic Method*.

Writing in *Transactions of the Philological Society*, Sweet continued to publish analyses of the sound systems of various living languages, adding in 1884 the paper 'On the Practical Study of Language'. In the same year, Felix Franke in Germany published *Die praktische Spracherlernung* (The Practical Acquisition of Languages), in which while acknowledging his debt to Sweet he emphasized, in addition to the use of phonetic transcription, the psychological aspect of learning, the importance of creating the right associations, of avoiding translation as much as possible, and of entering into the spirit of the community concerned. Later in 1884, Franke's book was issued in a Danish translation by Otto JESPERSEN. In 1885, Sweet published what for the reformers came to stand as the model textbook of English for a foreign learner, *Elementarbuch des gesprochenen Englisch*, aimed initially at a German-speaking public, but subsequently issued in an English version, *A Primer of Spoken English* (1890).

**Phonetics**. Early in 1886, under the leadership of Paul Passy, a group of teachers in France formed the *Phonetic Teachers' Association* and started a journal in phonetic script entitled *Dhi Fonètik Tîtcer*. At Jespersen's suggestion, membership was made international; he joined in May, Viëtor in July, and Sweet in September. This body in due course developed into the *Association Phonétique Internationale* (in English the *INTERNATIONAL PHONETIC ASSOCIATION*, in German the *Weltlautschriftverein*), whose deliberations resulted in the IPA alphabet. In 1899, Sweet published *The Practical Study of Languages*. Two years later, Jespersen published his ideas in a book in Danish later issued in English as *How to Teach a Foreign Language* (1904). These complementary works by and large represent the Reform Movement, Sweet's concerned with principles, Jespersen's with classroom work. Their minor differences were typical of the movement as a whole.

**The direct method**. Reformers rejected the teaching of modern languages through grammatical paradigms, specimen sentences, and word lists. They wanted to base teaching directly on speech and to apply the results of phonetics in their courses so as to ensure sound pronunciation from the start. For the rest, they sought as close an approximation as possible to the way a child learns its first language. They adopted the principles of association, visualization, and learning through the senses, through pictures and through activity and play. They emphasized the learning of grammar by practice rather than precept, by making the responses to points of grammar automatic and unconscious. The mother tongue should be avoided as much as possible and translation reduced to a minimum. They held that learning a language in this way meant, in effect, the absorption of another culture. It was generally agreed that professional language teachers should receive phonetic training, and that at the school stage the teacher should preferably be of the same language background as the pupils. The aim of the teaching should be successful use of the target language, actively and passively, but should not include translation.

**The reformers' influence**. The movement has had a varied impact in different parts of the world. In Continental Europe, it is generally considered to have led, virtually within a generation, to a marked improvement in spoken English and other languages, especially in Scandinavia, Germany, and the Netherlands. The principles and practices of the movement continue to have a strong influence. In Britain, influence has been limited in the teaching of modern languages in schools but considerable in the teaching of English as a foreign and second language. Two EFL pioneers particularly influenced by the movement were Harold E. Palmer, author of *The Oral Method of Teaching Languages* (1921), and Daniel JONES, compiler of the *English Pronouncing Dictionary*

(1917). In the US, the movement had little success until the Second World War, although in 1914 Leonard BLOOMFIELD had noted in his *Introduction to the Study of Language*: 'It is only in the last twenty-five years and in the European countries that success in modern-language teaching has ever been attained', adding that 'most of our practice is half a century or so behind that of the European schools.' Bloomfield's interest is reflected in his *Outline Guide for the Practical Study of Foreign Languages* (1942), the text that inspired both the massive US wartime programme of language teaching and postwar theories of teaching and learning.

**The audio-lingual method**. In the US in the 1950s there developed a movement based on the precepts of structural linguistics and behaviourist psychology and known variously as the *audio-lingual method* (ALM), *audio-lingual teaching*, *audiolingualism*, *the structuralist approach*, and *structuralism*. The ALM dominated the teaching of English as a second language in North America for some 25 years, and materials prepared by Robert Lado and others at the U. of Michigan were widely used there and elsewhere. Its content derived from an analysis of the phonemes, morphemes, and sentence patterns of the target language, and it sought to automate classroom activity through *pattern practice* drills (exercises in the repetition of specific kinds of phrases and sentences, with systematic changes intended to extend the learner's skills), taught by techniques of *mimicry and memorization* known for short as *mim-mem*.

**The structural approach and the audio-visual method**. The American audio-lingual method differed considerably from two European approaches with similar names: (1) The British *structural approach* of Harold E. Palmer and Michael WEST in the 1920s–30s, which augmented the direct method with graded grammatical structures, word lists, and readers. (2) The French *méthode structuro-globale* (in English usually called the *audio-visual method*), which developed in the 1960s and used a combination of textbooks, tape recordings, filmstrips, slides, and classroom presentation. Although it appeared to be the ALM with illustrations, the French method was technological, not ideological.

**The situational approach**. Almost from the start of the Reform Movement, practitioners used conversation readers in their teaching, often with texts in phonetic script, such as E. T. True and Otto Jespersen, *Spoken English* (1891) and H. Palmer and F. G. Blandford, *Everyday Sentences in Spoken English* (1922). In the 1960s–70s, many textbooks took such a practical approach further, grouping their teaching units around situational themes such as *At the Hairdresser* and *The Post office*. The dialogues and narratives in the text derived from these settings, and teachers were expected to produce appropriate material to support action-based language use within the situation defined by the chosen topic. The strength of the topic was language appropriate to a situation, but its weakness, the difficulty of generalizing what is learned, led to its being used more in collaboration with other procedures than in its pure form.

**The notional–functional approach**. In the early 1970s there developed in Europe an approach to LT that focused on two kinds of semantic and performative criteria: *notions*, such as *time, place, quantity, emotional attitudes*, and *functions*, such as *describing, enquiring, apologizing, criticizing*. The introduction of such ideas has influenced subsequent syllabuses and coursebooks. However, courses whose content is entirely notional and functional are often difficult to teach and learn from, because some notions and functions presuppose a knowledge of grammar and vocabulary for which no provision may have been made. It is probable that no definitive list of notions or of functions exists or may even be possible, but the concept has proved useful.

**The communicative approach**. In the 1970s–80s there developed in both Europe and North America an approach to foreign- and second-language teaching that drew on the work of anthropologists, sociologists, and sociolinguists. In many ways a lineal descendant of the direct method, it has concentrated on language as social behaviour, seeing the primary goal of language teaching as the development of the learner's COMMUNICATIVE COMPETENCE. In addition to formal linguistic knowledge, learners are considered to need both rules of use to produce language appropriate to particular situations, and strategies for effective communication. Partly through the influence of the *Council of Europe Languages Projects*, the movement at first concentrated on

notional–functional syllabuses, which depended on analyses of semantic and functional categories of language use rather than on those of formal grammar. In the 1980s, however, the approach was more concerned with the quality of interaction between learner and teacher rather than the specification of syllabuses, and concentrated on classroom methodology rather than on content, which remained similar to that of situational and notional–functional course materials.

**The cognitive code approach**. This approach to language teaching, which developed especially in the US in the 1980s, advocates conscious (*cognitive*) awareness of the structure of the target language and argues that study of rules of pronunciation and grammar will give learners a practical command of that language. Some commentators see it as the *grammar-translation method* in a new form, others as essentially a rejection of behaviourism and the audiovisual method.

**A plethora of methods**. A wide range of approaches to L2 teaching are currently available, ranging from the *grammar-translation method* and the *communicative approach* (both 'mainstream', in the sense that they are used by large numbers of teachers) through the now less influential *audio-lingual method* or *structural method* with its behaviourist bias (favoured especially in North America in the 1950s–70s) to such radical 'fringe' approaches as Caleb Gattegno's *Silent Way* and Georgi Lozanov's *Suggestopedia*. The Silent Way seeks to give the learner maximum investment in the language-learning process, by reducing the spoken role of the teacher as much as possible. Highly formal charts for pronunciation and grammar, together with Cuisenaire rods for manipulation, provide the major teaching aids. Suggestopedia is based on the view that relaxation enables learners to exploit their capacities for language acquisition to the maximum degree. Emphasis is placed on comfortable surroundings, use of music and chanting, and trust in the authority of the teacher. Particularly used to assist memorization, the procedure relies on making LANGUAGE LEARNING different from the stressful effort to produce appropriate communication for predefined needs. Conferences for EFL and ESL teachers currently provide sessions on a sometimes overwhelming array of methods and blends of methods, and a plethora of books describes the main varieties in detail or in overviews. *Holistic methods* emphasize putting the learner into a frame of mind for learning or developing the education of 'the whole person', and diminishing the teacher's appearance as an authorityfigure. The *humanistic approach* similarly seeks to emphasize the shared interests and needs of teachers and students and provide a caring environment in which to learn. Many pragmatists, however, endorse no particular pedagogical or ideological position in their teaching, a style sometimes referred to as the *eclectic approach*. The on-going debate testifies to the variety and vitality of the profession.

**Public and community issues**. LT requires today, in every country, deliberate policy decisions by government on such issues as: which language should be encouraged; how many teachers should be employed; what training teachers should be given; how they should be valued in terms of pay and conditions; what average class size should be supported and at what rate of intensity; what teaching resources and materials should be supplied; what support should be given to research and development; what the degree of direct government intervention should be, in such matters as setting a syllabus, prescribing books, and inspecting the teaching; what standards of achievement are desirable and hence what examinations and qualifications should be promoted. Community attitudes (friendly or hostile) towards particular peoples and their languages also strongly affect teaching, as do popular assumptions about how successful members of the community will be in learning languages: for example, compare expectations about whether the average citizen will learn at least one foreign language in the Netherlands and in Britain.

**Teaching formats**. A further aspect of the public and community dimension of LT is the educational format in which it takes place: in a teacher-led class in a school or college; through distance learning by correspondence or radio or television (with or without an element of face-to-face tutoring); in one-to-one contact between a teacher and a learner; in solitary, self-study learning; in 'immersion teaching' (for ex-

ample, with immigrant children in Canada, where learners are immersed in an English-speaking or French-speaking life instead of experiencing the target language only in time-tabled class hours). Most of these formats are found in most countries; which one is being employed at a given time determines the different settings that will be necessary in the parameters of LT, in order to bring about effective LL. In addition, the ultimate aims of language teaching need to be clarified: whether it is part of general education, geared to instrumental needs such as the integration of immigrants into a particular society, or for such specific purposes as English for maritime communication (*SEASPEAK*) or air traffic control (*AIRSPEAK*).

**Conclusion**. Debates in L1 and L2 teaching in the 20c may be interpreted in terms of a tension between the *dual tradition* (the literary and grammar–translation methods) and the *reform movement* (the direct method and its various derivatives). The literary method has provided immediate contact with prestigious texts, serious subject matter, and a link with ancient traditions, while the various phases of grammar–translation have promised a less élitist approach, devising short-cuts to mastery of grammar or the social strategies necessary to become (more or less) part of the target-language community. Greater emphasis on writing or on speech has varied from time to time and place to place, but generally movements to renew or improve the effectiveness of teaching have consistently combined with movements to undercut the classical humanist traditions by appealing directly to usefulness. Reform movements have generally been equivocal about whether they are doing more efficiently the same things that previous traditions have done or whether they are subverting the previous traditions by changing the goals, substituting what any learner could do for what only a select few would wish to do. Each reform has therefore attracted adherents who imagined that they were undermining the values of previous education, together with those whose intention was to improve its effectiveness but not to question its goals.

See APPLIED LINGUISTICS, BERLITZ, PEDA-GOGICAL GRAMMAR, TEACHING ENGLISH, TEFL, TEIL, TESD, TESL, TESOL.

**LANGUE AND PAROLE**. Contrasting

terms in LINGUISTICS, proposed by Ferdinand de Saussure (*Cours de linguistique générale*, 1915) to distinguish between the language system of a group (*langue*) and instances of its use (*parole*) within language in general (*langage*). Compare COMPETENCE AND PERFORMANCE.

**LARYNX**. An anatomical term for the modified upper part of the trachea (windpipe) of air-breathing animals. It is commonly known as the *voice box* in humans because of its importance in the creation of the voice. It contains the VOCAL CORDS or folds and influences voice quality. The front cartilage of the larynx is the *Adam's apple*, prominent in adult males. See SPEECH.

**LATERAL**. A term in PHONETICS for a vocal sound in which air gets round central blockage by the tongue by escaping round the sides. The only English lateral is /l/ as in *large, hollow, barrel*; WELSH has /ɬ/ as in *Llanberis, Llangollen*. See L-SOUNDS.

## ■ LATIN ■

The classical and cultural language of Western Europe, a member of the INDO-EUROPEAN language family, and the precursor of the ROMANCE LANGUAGES. Particularly since the Renaissance, Latin has also been the scholarly and literary seed-corn for the VERNACULAR European languages. English has proved to be the most receptive among the GERMANIC LANGUAGES to direct as well as indirect Latin influence.

**Nature and influence**. Latin is a highly inflected language noted for conciseness of expression: for example, the one word *amābunt* translates the three English words *they will love*, while its passive form *amābuntur* translates *they will be loved*. For centuries, formal education in the British Isles has been closely associated with the teaching and learning of Latin. Especially in England, this training was provided in *grammar schools*, in which the term *grammar* was virtually synonymous with *Latin*. Such institutions in the 16c bear close comparison with 19–20c English-medium schools in such countries as India and Nigeria, and with contemporary grammar-based ways of teaching English in such countries as Japan and Korea. Both the terms and the style of the traditional grammatical study of English derive from Latin, and the formal analysis of English grammar widely taught until recent decades owes much to a Latin grammatical model derived in its turn from a GREEK model.

**Latin and English**. In the 4c, St Jerome's Vulgate Bible became the model for Christian writing in Latin. This model was further developed by St Augustine of Hippo (4–5c), a teacher of RHETORIC, in works like *Civitas Dei* (The City of God). His example was followed in England by such scholars as Aldhelm (7c), Bede (7–8c), Alcuin (8–9c), and AELFRIC (10–11c), while the translations from Latin into OLD ENGLISH by King ALFRED of Wessex (9c) laid the foundation of early English prose writing. The fluid interplay of languages in Britain during the Middle Ages is illustrated by three events in the 12c, all associated with the cycle of mythic and legendary material known as the *Matter of Britain*. First, the Oxford cleric Galfridus Monemutensis (Geoffrey of Monmouth), an Englishman with Welsh and Breton connections, wrote the Latin prose work *Historia regum Britanniae* (History of the kings of Britain, *c*.1135). He claimed that he translated this work from a very old book 'in the British tongue': that is, in a form of Celtic similar to Welsh. The History begins with the settlement in Britain of a great-grandson of the Trojan hero Aeneas, whose name was Brutus and who purportedly gave his name to the island. It ends with the legendary King Arthur, a Celtic hero adopted by the Anglo-Normans. The History was then translated into FRENCH, and further romanticized, as the *Roman de Brut* (1155) by Wace, an Anglo-Norman from Jersey in the CHANNEL ISLANDS. This work then served as the source for the *Brut*, an alliterative poem in the late 12c by the Worcestershire priest Layamon, in what is now called MIDDLE ENGLISH.

Latin continued to be the primary language of scholarship until the end of the 17c. Such scholars as William Camden wrote by preference in Latin, considering that to use English was to write in sand, and for major contributors to the canon of English literature, such as John Milton, Latin was an essential professional tool. In the late 17c, Sir Isaac Newton chosen Latin as the medium for *Philosophiae naturalis principia mathematica* (Mathematical principles of natural philosophy), better known as the *Principia* (1687), and this work was not translated into English until 1729. He chose Latin to ensure that the *Principia* would be widely read, but later wrote *Opticks* in English, its date of publication (1704) marking the point at which significant scholarly work began to appear in English first and, in due course, without any translation into Latin. Because of familiarity with the Classics, however, writers continued to evoke in English the images and phrases of ancient Rome, often only slightly adapted, and to allude fluently to topics that, until well into the 20c, their readership could generally grasp without editorial help. In addition, numerous Latin quotations and tags have enjoyed an extended life in English to the present day.

**Latin in English**. A large part of the lexicon of Latin has entered English in two major waves: mainly religious vocabulary from the time of Old English until the Reformation, and mainly scientific, scholarly, and legal vocabulary (slightly different in English and Scottish law), from the Middle Ages onwards. In the 17c, such makers of English dictionaries as John Bullokar deliberately converted Latin words into English, building on the already strong French component of the vocabulary so as to create a Latinate register of education and refinement. In it, words like *fraternity* and *feline* were set lexically and stylistically 'above' words like *brotherhood* and *cat*. These lexicographers' methods were straightforward: they turned the endings of Latin words into Anglo-French endings, a practice that has continued with minor modifications ever since: thus, *alacritas* became French-like *alacritie* (later *alacrity*), *catalogus* (Greek in origin) became *catalogue* (later *catalog* in AmE), *incantatio* became *incantation*, *onerosus* became *onerous*, *puerilis* became *puerile*, and *ruminare* (through its past participle *ruminatus*) became *ruminate*.

Many Latin-derived words in English occur in 'families'. For example, from the verb *cantare/cantatum* (to sing) come such words as *cant*, *canticle*, *cantor*, *descant*, *incantation*, *accent*, *incentive*, *precentor*, *recant* (with *enchant*, *enchantment* through French, and *cantata*, *canto* through Italian). From *monēre/monitum* (to warn) come *monitor*, *admonish*, *admonition*, *admonitory*, *premonition*. From *agere/actum* (to do, act) come *agent*, *agency*, *agile*, *agility*, *agitate*, *act*, *actor*, *action*, *enact*, *exact*, *inaction*, *inactivity*. From *currere/cursum* (to run) come *current*, *currency*, *cursive*, *cursor*, *cursory*, *concur*, *incur*, *excursion*, *occurrence*, *precursor*, *recurrent*. From *claudere/clausum* (to close, with the forms *-clud-/-clus-* after a prefix) come *clause*, *include*, *exclude*, *preclude*, *seclusive*, *conclusion*. From *dominus/domini* (master) and *dominare/dominatum* (to master) come *dominion*, *dominate*, *domination*, *dominie*, *domineering* (through French and Dutch), *domain* (through French). From *caput/capitis* (head) come *capital*, *capitalism*, *capitalize*, *decapitate*, *decapitation* (and through French *cattle*, *chapter*, *chattel*, *chief*). From *avidus/avidi* (greedy) come *avid*, *avidity*; from *rigidus/rigidi* (stiff) come *rigid*, *rigidity*, from *audax/audacis* (bold) come *audacious*, *audacity*; from *ferox/ferocis* (fierce) come *ferocious*, *ferocity*.

In addition, many words that in Latin actually perform grammatical functions have been turned into nouns in English: *caveat* (beware) as a synonym for a warning, *floruit* (he/she flourished) to mark the period when someone was in his or her prime (usually when precise birth and death dates are not known), *imprimatur* (let it be printed) for someone's approval of a published text, *quorum* (of whom) the minimum number of people necessary for a committee or similar meeting, *tandem* (at length) for a bicycle built for two. Similarly, many phrases and sentences of Latin are perpetuated as tags and mottoes: *ad astra per aspera* to the stars through hardships (the motto of the US state of Kansas), *per ardua ad astra* through difficulties to the stars (the motto of the Royal Air Force); *habeas corpus* you may have the body (a technical term in law); *ipse dixit* he said it himself (as a sometimes caustic comment); *non sequitur* it does not follow (a name for a certain kind of logical FALLACY). Further phrases have been abbreviated, and are part of the currency of everyday life, including writing: *AD* (for *anno Domini* in the year of the Lord, as part of calendar dating), *a.m.* (for *ante meridiem* before midday), *p.m.* (*post meridiem* after midday), *e.g.* (*exempli gratia* for the sake of example), *i.e.* (*id est* that is).

Currently, continuing a process of de-Latinization that has gathered momentum since the 18c (mainly because of the spread of LITERACY beyond the schools where Latin was a core subject), there is a tendency to translate such expressions into English (*time flies* rather than *tempus fugit*; *don't despair*, *don't give up* rather than *nil desperandum*), and to make Latin words more conventionally English: the plurals *cactuses* and *referendums* rather than *cacti* and *referenda*. In the train of such changes, and because the influence of Latin is still tenacious, there is often uncertainty and friction regarding usage: for example, in such vexed issues as the use of *data* and *media* as singular or plural nouns. See BORROWING, CLASSICAL ENDING, DERIVATION, HISTORY OF ENGLISH, LATINATE, LATINISM, LATIN TAG, NEO-LATIN.

**LATINATE**. Relating to, derived from, or in the style of LATIN. The term is used both for words in which the Latin form has been retained (such as *formula*, *latex*, *mausoleum*, *stimulus*) and for those in which adaptations have been made (such as *elucidate*, *legal*, *pungency*, *vociferous*). See AUREATE DICTION, INKHORN TERM.

**LATINISM**. A LATIN word or other element in another language: for example, in English the word *stimulus*, the phrase *non sequitur*, the sentence *Sic transit gloria mundi*, and the derivative *illegality* (from *illegalis*).

**LATIN TAG**. A LATIN phrase or other expression in English, such as *obiter dictum* ('a saying by the way') an incidental remark, *pro tem* (short for *pro tempore*) for the time being. Until the mid-20c, Latin TAGS were widely used, intentionally or otherwise, as a mark of EDUCATION, but in recent decades have grown less common (and often less understood) in educated circles, in which less common tags are often considered affected or unnecessary, even by those who know Latin. As a result, expressions like *Tempus fugit* are often loan-translated as 'Time flies'. Many tags are, however, firmly entrenched in everyday usage, whether in full or as abbreviations: in law (*de jure*, *habeas corpus*, *sub judice*), in medicine (*locum tenens*, *placebo*, *post mortem*), in logic (*argumentum ad hominem*, *non sequitur*, *reductio ad absurdum*), in administration (*ad hoc*, *quorum*, *sine die*), in religion (*Deo volente*, *Pax vobiscum*, *Requiescat in pace*), as sayings (*carpe diem*, *in vino veritas*), as set phrases (*mutatis mutandis*, *ne plus ultra*), as mottoes (*Nemo me impune lacessit*, *Semper fidelis*), and as academic footnotes and endnotes (*ibid.*, *op. cit.*, *passim*). Some have passed into the language at large: as phrases (*bona fides*, *magnum opus*, *modus operandi*, *per annum*, *prima facie*, *quid pro quo*, *sine qua non*, *terra firma*, *vade mecum*), and as

ABBREVIATIONS (*a.m.*, *c.*, *cf.*, *e.g.*, *i.e.*, *p.m.*, *R.I.P.*). See FOREIGNISM, NOTES AND REFERENCES.

**LAW FRENCH**. A fossilized form of NORMAN FRENCH used until the 18c in the courts of England. In 1362, French ceased to be a language of pleading, but its legal use was not officially abandoned until 1731. Many archaic French usages continue in the legal usage of England, such as: *amerce*, *implead*, *malfeasance*, *tort*. French word order is preserved in *attorney general*, *court martial*, *fee simple*, *malice aforethought*. The names of most legal roles in English are French in origin, such as: *attorney*, *bailiff*, *coroner*, *judge*, *jury*, *plaintiff*. The same is the case with the names of many crimes (such as: *arson*, *felony*, *libel*, *perjury*, *slander*, *trespass*) and of legal actions, processes, and institutions (such as *bail*, *bill*, *decree*, *evidence*, *fine*, *forfeit*, *gaol/jail*, *penalty*, *pillory*, *plea*, *prison*, *punishment*, *ransom*, *sentence*, *suit*, *summons*, *verdict*).

**LEARNER'S DICTIONARY**, also **English Learner's Dictionary**, **EFL dictionary**, **ELT dictionary**. A DICTIONARY intended for the use of foreign- and second-language learners and printed entirely in English. For foreign learners of most languages, bidirectional bilingual dictionaries (Italian–English, English–Italian, etc.) have been the norm, but since the 1960s the predominant type in TEFL and TESL has been a monolingual 'learner's dictionary', such as the *Oxford Advanced Learner's Dictionary of Current English* (1974 onward) and the *Longman Dictionary of Contemporary English* (1978 onward). See BASIC ENGLISH, ENGLISH PRONOUNCING DICTIONARY, GENERAL SERVICE LIST, HORNBY, JONES, TEFL, TESL.

**LECT**. A term in SOCIOLINGUISTICS for a speech variety; it is used relatively little on its own but often occurs in combination, as in *idiolect*. See ACROLECT, BASILECT, DIALECT, ENGLISH, GRAMMATICALITY, IDIOLECT, MESOLECT, PRIVATE LANGUAGE, SOCIOLECT.

**LEGALESE**. An informal, usually pejorative term for language that is typical of lawyers or that contains too much legal terminology. '"It is highly probable, and more likely than not in the light of [the TV series] 'L. A. Law's' nationwide popularity, that one or more jurors viewed this segment and was impressed by or even discussed same among themselves," he argued in his best legalese'

('Role Models for Attorneys?', *International Herald Tribune*, 11 May 1990). See -ESE, JARGON, LAW FRENCH, LEGAL USAGE, REGISTER.

**LEGAL USAGE**, also **legal English**. The REGISTER of the legal profession. The term covers the formulas and styles of both courts of law in all English-speaking countries and such documents as contracts and writs. In England, from the Norman Conquest in 1066 to the later 14c, the languages of law were FRENCH and LATIN, and both have left their mark on the English which succeeded them, especially in such terms as *lien* (French 'binding, tie': a legal claim on someone's property to secure the payment of debt) and *habeas corpus* (Latin 'you may have the body': a writ requiring that someone be brought before a judge or court, especially as a protection against that person's unlawful imprisonment). Legal usage in all English-speaking countries tends to be conservative, formal, syntactically complex, and often archaic, using expressions such as *aforesaid, hereinafter, thereto* that hardly occur in the language at large. Lawyers generally argue that the conventions and complexities of legal prose ensure that all possible contingencies are covered and ambiguities removed from documents on which legal decisions must rest. Critics reply that 'LEGALESE' makes lawyers necessary as interpreters as well as counsellors, may obscure the implications of contracts and other documents, and often worries people unnecessarily. The first excerpt below is part of a traditional contract, the second the same material recast in 'plain' language:

> GENERAL LIEN—The contractor shall have a general lien upon all goods in his possession for all monies due to him from the customer or for liabilities incurred by him and for monies paid on behalf of the customer, and if part of the goods shall have been delivered, removed or despatched or sold the general lien shall apply in respect of such goods as remain in the Contractor's possession.

> *Our right to hold the goods.* We have a right to hold some or all of the goods until you have paid all our charges and other payments due under this contract. These include charges, taxes or levies that we have paid to any other removal or storage business, carrier or official body.

In recent years, campaigners for PLAIN ENGLISH have sought simpler contracts and in some cases 'translations' of difficult usage, so that the public can grasp the meaning and intent of documents couched in legal terms. See LAW FRENCH.

**LENGTH MARK**. In PHONETICS, the mark (ː), used after a vowel to indicate that it is long, as when the RP pronunciation of *feast* is shown in IPA symbols as /fiːst/. For reasons of economy and simplicity, the colon (:) is often used instead: /fiːst/. Compare MACRON. See VOWEL QUANTITY.

**LESOTHO**. A country of southern Africa and member of the COMMONWEALTH. Languages: Sesotho and English (both official). The first BANTU-speaking peoples arrived in the area in the 16c. In 1854, the territory was incorporated by the Boers into the Orange Free State, but in 1869 became the British protectorate of *Basutoland*. The territory gained internal self-government in 1955 and independence as *Lesotho* in 1966.

■ **LETTER**[1] ───────────────── ■

An alphabetic symbol such as *A* or *a*, *B* or *b*. In WRITING based on the classical Roman ALPHABET, the separation of letters into *majuscules* (CAPITAL letters) and *minuscules* (small letters), the many variant alphabets (such as for English and Spanish), the typefaces available to them, and the distinctive joined letters of cursive handwriting have produced a wide range of letter forms.

**Naming letters**. In the GREEK alphabet, each letter has a name that is not directly related to its sound value (*alpha, beta, gamma*, etc.), but this practice is not common in ROMAN-derived ALPHABETS. The ways in which letters are referred to in English (*ay, bee, cee*, etc.) echo those of FRENCH, except that French *double-v* is English *double-u*, and the name of y may descend from the rounded OLD ENGLISH pronunciation of that VOWEL. Except for *h, w*, the names (*ay, bee, cee*, etc.) have a recognizable relationship with the sounds they commonly represent. The vowel letters are named by the long values in *mate, meet, might, moat, mute*, not the short values as in *pat, pet, pit, pot, putt/put*. Nine CONSONANTS in BrE and ten in AmE are named with a vowel after the sound value: with following *ee* in the case of *b, c, d, g, p, t, v* (and AmE *z*) and *ay* in the case of *j, k*. Six others are named with a preceding short *e: f, l, m, n, s, x*. The remainder (*h, q, r, w, y*, and BrE *zed*) have individual names.

**Letters as symbols**. When letters are used as symbols they may operate alone, in sets, or in combination with words: (1) Alone: capitals *A, B, C*, etc., to mark an educational or other grade, *X* to indicate a mystery; small letters such as *a, x*, and *y* as used in mathematical expressions. (2) In sets: *zzz* in cartoons and elsewhere, to represent sleep; the thousands of letter-based abbreviations, such as *BBC, NATO, e.g., i.e.*, UN/U.N. (3) In combination with a word, as an ABBREVIATION: BrE *L-plate*, where *L* means *Learner* (such plates being attached to the front and rear of motor vehicles); AmE *T-bill*, where *T* means *Treasury* (a reference to high-denomination promissory notes). (4) Combined with one or more words as part of a series: *B-movie* in the motion-picture industry; *C minor* in music. (5) Representing a shape: *X* in *Charing X* for the junction known as Charing Cross in London; *U-turn* a turn made through 180°. Some letters operate within established conventions, such as *A, B, C* and *X, Y, Z*, as the opening and closing letters of the Roman alphabet, often used to refer to sets of three things taken in order. *A to Z* means from the beginning to the end of something, such as a subject to be learned.

The uses of letter symbols are complex and varied, and include: economy of expression in generalizing and in labelling, mnemonic aid, the replacement and augmentation of numbers, and special effects. For example: through such formulas as *How do we get from Point A to Point B?* and *Flight X is now boarding at Gate Y*; *fonybas*, a mnemonic list of coordinating conjunctions (*for, or, nor, yet, but, as, so*), and *St Wapniacl*, once used to help US children memorize the departments of government in the order in which they were created (*State, Treasury, War, Attorney General, Post Office, Navy, Interior, Agriculture, Commerce, Labor*); alliterative sets of three (*the three Bs for Bach, Beethoven, Brahms*), the words sometimes adapted to fit the idea and the rhythm (*the three Rs for reading, 'riting, 'rithmetic*); *A, B, C* for 1, 2, 3, *B-51, F-18* (types of US aircraft) or *4A* (the top stream or track of the fourth year in a school).

**Special effects**. Although all letters are available for use as special symbols, *K* and *X* have been particularly popular for such purposes. The uses of *K* include: an abbreviation meaning one thousand (from *kilo*), 10K being 10,000 of a unit of currency; a token of alienness, as in *Amerika*, for the US conceived as dominated by Communists or Nazis; an eye-catching spelling for words in *q* and *c*, as with a company called *Kwik-Fit* and cartoon characters called *the Krazy Kids*. The uses of *X* include: a token for something unknown: *Mr X, Substance X, X-ray*; to represent *ex-*, as in *MX* for *missile experimental*, in *Xtra strong* and *X-ellent* (compare *D-grading* and *D-lightful*); for *Christ* in *Xmas*, representing the Greek letter *khi*; to signify censorship: *an X-rated movie*, not to be shown to minors; as the signature of an illiterate person; to mark a place on a map or where a signature should go on a paper (commonly called a cross and not necessarily identified as a letter); to represent a kiss, often in a series written in a letter.

**Letters in word use and word-formation**. Letter symbols are often attributive (*an A student, Type B behaviour*), and occur as abbreviations in compounds (*A-bomb, N-test* for *atomic bomb, nuclear test*). They may serve to emphasize significant words, whose full form may be taboo (*the F-word* for *fuck*), undesirable (*the big C* for cancer), or highly significant (*the big O* for the Olympics). Technical letter symbols in electrical engineering include *GeV* for *gigaelectron volt* and *TeV* for *teravolt*. Such symbols can include an AMPERSAND: *R & D* for *research and development*. However, it may not always be easy to distinguish letter symbols from initialisms: in Britain, *ABC* may refer to the socio-economic classes A, B, C taken together; in the 1983 general election in Canada, they meant *Anybody but Clark*; in Australia, they stand for the Australian Broadcasting Corporation; in Los Angeles, they have been used to mean *American-born Chinese*; in military terms, they mean *atomic, biological, chemical*.

See the entries for individual letters, A–Z, and ACRONYM, ACUTE ACCENT, AITCH, ASH, DIACRITIC, DIGRAPH, ENG, ESH, ETH, GRAVE ACCENT, INITIAL, INITIALISM, LETTER WORD, LITERAL, LONG *S*, ORTHOGRAPHY, SILENT LETTER, SPELLING, THORN, TRANSLITERATION, YOGH.

**LETTER**[2]. A piece of WRITING addressed and usually sent to someone. Personal and official letters date from remote antiquity, as for example between Hittite and

Egyptian rulers in the late second millennium BC. Until the invention of the telegraph, telephone, and E-MAIL, letters were the commonest means through which people living at a distance from each other could keep in touch, and the 19c growth of national and international postal systems created a boom in letter-writing. Writing and reading letters became a major aspect of literacy after Rowland Hill introduced the penny post in Britain in 1840.

**LETTER WORD**, also **letter name**. A WORD or NAME formed from the letters, usually the first letters, of several other words: *BBC* from British Broadcasting Corporation, *NATO* from North Atlantic Treaty Organization. It is a kind of ABBREVIATION, with two forms: the *INITIALISM* (*BBC* pronounced 'bee-bee-cee'); the *ACRONYM* (*NATO*, pronounced 'Nay-toe').

**LEVEL OF LANGUAGE**. A term in (structural) LINGUISTICS. In the second quarter of the 20c, language was modelled by some linguists as a series of layers arranged one on top of the other, with units of sound (*PHONOLOGY*) on the bottom layer, gathered into units of structure (*MORPHOLOGY*) above, which were then combined into larger grammatical units (*SYNTAX*) above them, and, according to some, into units of meaning (*SEMANTICS*) at the top. The two lowest levels each had a unit of its own, formed with the suffix *-EME*: *PHONEME* for phonology, *MORPHEME* for morphology. In some theories, this approach continued upwards with *lexeme* for an abstract lexical unit, and *tagmeme* sometimes used for syntax. The term has come into widespread, fairly loose usage to mean any one such layer: the phonological level, the syntactic level, etc. Originally, each level was studied independently of the others, at least in theory, and it was considered necessary to work from phonology upwards, finishing the study of one level before moving on to the next. A number of introductory textbooks of linguistics are organized in accordance with this model, which is still of value, although the strict separation of levels is no longer adhered to. In recent years, some linguists have tended to abandon the vertical 'layer cake' model in favour of a horizontal model with a *syntactic component* flanked by a *phonological component* on one side and a *semantic component* on the other. Syntax has this central role because it can be regarded as the component that links sound and meaning.

**LEXEME**, also **lexical item**, **lexical unit**. In LINGUISTICS, a unit in the LEXICON or VOCABULARY of a language. Its form is governed by sound and writing or print, its content by meaning and use. Thus, *penicillin* is the realization in print of a single English lexeme, while the nouns *crane* and *bank* represent at least two lexemes each: *crane* (a particular bird and a particular machine), *bank* (the shore of a river and a particular kind of financial institution). Most English dictionaries treat *crane n.* as a single headword with two senses (a case of POLYSEMY) and *bank n.* as two headwords, each with at least one sense: a case of HOMONYMY. Conventionally, a lexeme's inflections (such as *cranes*, *banks*) are considered variant forms, whereas such derivatives as *banker* are considered separate lexemes. In English as in other languages, lexemes may be single words (*crane*, *bank*), parts of words (*auto-*, *-logy*), groups of words (the compound *blackbird* and the idiom *kick the bucket*), or shortened forms (*flu* for *influenza*, *UK* for *United Kingdom*). See LEXICOLOGY, MORPHEME.

## ■ LEXICOGRAPHY ─────── ■

The procedure and profession of arranging and describing items of VOCABULARY in such works of reference as dictionaries, glossaries, thesauruses, synonym guides, usage guides, and concordances. Traditionally, lexicography has been of two kinds: *alphabetic lexicography*, the dominant form whose best-known product is the DICTIONARY properly so called, and *thematic lexicography*, which arranges words by themes or topics, usually accompanied by an index, of which such a 'classified' work of REFERENCE as *Roget's Thesaurus* is a leading example. By and large, however, lexicography is taken to be a process of describing words in an alphabetic list, and most lexicographers work on dictionaries of a relatively STANDARD kind. Equally traditionally, lexicography can be said to include the compilation not only of books about words (dictionaries, etc.), but also books about things (encyclopedias, etc.). Again, however, it is generally taken to centre on the making of wordbooks, which may be more encyclopedic (like many French and American works) or less encyclopedic (like many British works).

**Products**. The products of lexicography are varied. In terms of dictionaries proper, they range from the 20-volume *OXFORD ENGLISH DICTIONARY* and such large ('unabridged') one-volume US works as the *Webster's Third New International Dictionary* and the *Random House Dictionary of the English Language* through the desk, family, or collegiate dictionary (such as *Chambers English Dictionary* and *Webster's Ninth New Collegiate Dictionary*), to the concise or compact (*The Concise Oxford Dictionary*), the pocket (*The Pocket Oxford Dictionary*), and even smaller works (the *Collins Gem* series). Lexicographic work may be monolingual, bilingual or multilingual, and may be undertaken for general purposes or for (among others) small children, school and college students, or other special-interest groups. Whatever form they take, however, their compilation rests on the amassing and sifting of evidence about words and other expressions (for example citations from texts), and editorial guidelines as to what should be included, how it should be organized, and what special features (such as phonetics, etymologies, pictures, etc.) should be added.

**Sources and coverage**. All types of linguistic evidence are available to lexicographers, including introspection and discussion, the examination of pre-existing works of reference and other sources, and the formal use of survey questionnaires and citation corpora (both traditional, kept on cards, and electronic, stored in computer databases). Some classes of vocabulary item are normally excluded from most general dictionaries, but may appear in encyclopedic and specialist dictionaries, such as the binomial nomenclature of biology, and proverbs and quotations. After systematic exclusions are dealt with for the purposes of a general dictionary, what remains of the vocabulary is assessed for potential entries. Where large dictionaries seek to cover as much as possible, smaller dictionaries aimed at certain kinds of user have (often as the result of adhoc decision-taking) lists judged appropriate to their level. Specialist dictionaries have lists appropriate to their core topic (for example, *The Penguin Dictionary of Saints*, and Partridge's *Dictionary of Slang and Unconventional English*, etc.).

**Dictionary information**. Dictionaries generally give some or all of the following types of information in an order appropriate to the work in question: (1) Headword and any variants, sometimes with syllabication marked and HOMOGRAPH status indicated. (2) Pronunciation in a system of RESPELLING or phonetic symbols. (3) Grammatical information and usage labels (often in the form of ABBREVIATIONS or codes). (4) Number of senses as necessary. (5) Explanations proper. (6) Possible illustrative phrases or sentences. (7) COMPOUNDS, DERIVATIVES, PHRASAL VERBS, AND IDIOMS (if not listed separately). (8) ETYMOLOGY. (9) Points of USAGE. (10) Information about SYNONYMS and ANTONYMS.

**Conventions**. In presenting their information, most lexicographical works of reference (dictionaries, thesauruses, etc.) have two columns of densely organized information in small type. They use contrastive typefaces for distinct purposes, such as bold-face type for headwords, roman for definitions, italics for abbreviated codes and specimen words and phrases, and small capitals for cross-references. Square brackets may enclose special information, such as etymologies at the beginning or end of entries, while round brackets (parentheses) may add ancillary information in the body of the explanations. By and large, even when schools and colleges give students guidance on what to expect in a dictionary, the differences of format and emphasis from dictionary to dictionary are seldom discussed. As a consequence, for many people the complex layout of standard dictionaries may be intimidating. Thus, compounds may be main entries in one dictionary but sub-entries in another; abbreviations, word elements, biographical information, etc., may be in appendices at the back in one book, and interspersed through the main text in another.

**LEXICOLOGY**. An area of language study concerned with the nature, meaning, history, and use of words and word elements and often also with the critical description of LEXICOGRAPHY. Although formerly a branch of PHILOLOGY, lexicology is increasingly treated as a branch of LINGUISTICS, associated with such terms as *LEXEME*, *lexical field*, *lexical item*, *LEXICON*, *LEXIS*, on the premiss that they offer (or could offer, if tightly defined and widely adopted) a more precise and useful basis for the study of language than imprecise terms such as *WORD* and *VOCABULARY*.

**LEXICON**. **1.** A work of REFERENCE listing and explaining words: Henry G. Liddell & Robert Scott, *Greek–English Lexicon* (1843). A lexicon is usually a dictionary that deals either with a classical or scriptural language or a technical or facetious subject (Jonathon Green, *The Cynic's Lexicon: A Dictionary of Amoral Advice*, 1984). It may also, however, be a word list (Roland Hindmarsh, *The Cambridge English Lexicon*, 1980) or a thematic work of lexical reference (Tom McArthur, *The Longman Lexicon of Contemporary English*, 1981). **2.** A term in especially American LINGUISTICS for the VOCABULARY of a language or sub-language, consisting of its stock of LEXEMES.

**LEXIS**. A term in especially British LINGUISTICS for the VOCABULARY of a language or sub-language, consisting especially of its stock of LEXEMES. The term became popular because it is unambiguous, unlike *LEXICON*, and is GREEK in origin (fitting well with such other terms of Greek origin as *phonology* and *syntax*), in contrast with Latin-derived *vocabulary* (associated with Latinate *pronunciation* and Greco-Latin *grammar*).

**LIBERIA**. A country in West Africa. Languages: English (official), and over 20 Niger–Congo languages, including Kru and Mande. The region was mapped by the Portuguese in the 15c and later visited by the Dutch, British, and other Europeans looking for gold, spices, and slaves. The idea of a homeland for freed slaves was conceived by a group of US philanthropical societies, including the American Colonization Society, influenced by the British creation of Freetown in neighbouring Sierra Leone. Monrovia, named after President Monroe, was founded in 1822. The governors of Liberia were white Americans until Joseph Jenkins Roberts, a black born in Virginia, took over in 1841. He declared the *Free and Independent Republic of Liberia* in 1847. Freed slaves migrated from the US until the end of the Civil War in 1865, and black Americans have settled in small numbers ever since.

**Liberian English**. Liberia is the only black African country in which English is a native language and the only country in Africa owing its English more to the US than the UK. The variety originated first in contacts from the 17c between native speakers of BrE and AmE and such coastal peoples as the Kru (among whom English PIDGINS devel-

oped), and then in the settlement of repatriated blacks. Their descendants, known formally as *Americo-Liberians* and colloquially as *Mericos* and *Congos*, established and maintained the prestige of English and dominated Liberian society politically and economically, especially through the True Whig Party, until the 1980 coup, which was led by Samuel Doe, a non-Merico army sergeant. Sierra Leone Krio has had some impact on usage, and frequent travel to, and close political relations with, the US have given standard AmE and American BLACK ENGLISH continuing prestige and influence. English in Liberia can be described in terms of an ACROLECT (high-prestige form), several BASILECTS (low-prestige forms), and emerging MESOLECTS (intermediate forms). *Standard Liberian English* is acquired through, and is a mark of, a high level of education, is heard on radio and television, and is the speech of those locally referred to as *civilized*. At the other end of the continuum, the basilects include *Kru Pidgin English* (the oldest pidgin), *Settler English* (formerly *Merico*), the everyday usage of the Americo-Liberian settlers (closely related to Southern US English before the Civil War), and *Liberian Interior English*, used mainly by speakers of Mande in the non-coastal areas. *Soldier English* is a pidgin used since the early 20c by and with non-English-speakers in the army, and *Vernacular Liberian English* includes urban and rural mesolects that compromise between the standard and non-standard varieties.

**Features**. The close historical link with AmE gives Liberian English its distinctiveness in relation to other West African varieties. Phonologically, the varieties range from a rhotic standard associated with AmE to non-rhotic pronunciations influenced by Kru and Mande. Grammatically, the mesolects and basilects have the following features: (1) Non-standard auxiliaries: *He done come* He has come; *A was not know* I did not know; habitual *do* as in *I do see boy all de time* I see the boy all the time; progressive *de* as in *I de go* I am going. (2) Uninflected verbs: *You see da man?* Did you see the man?; *A know dem* I knew them; *Dey kesh grahapa* They caught grasshoppers. The distinction between Settler English and Kru Pidgin can be seen in Settler *Da pekin cryin*, Kru *Di pekin de krai* (The child is crying), Settler *I ain see him*, Kru *A neva siam*. Distinctively Liberian words include: *bugabug* termite, *dumboy* boiled, pounded cassava, *favour* to resemble (compare AmE), *fresh cold* a runny nose, head cold, *groundpea* peanut, groundnut, *jina* spirits, *kanki* measurement for rice (around two cups), *kwi* a foreigner, *outside child* a child acknowledged although born outside marriage, *sasse* cheeky, smart, sassy. Traditionally, the standard has been emphasized and the other varieties generally disparaged, but since the coup the compromise forms have begun to gain recognition in such public contexts as the media and informal greetings, as expressions of political and social solidarity. The mesolect in Monrovia is the centre of innovation, and is spreading throughout the country. Typically, the same kind of thing can be said at several different 'levels': acrolect *What you're saying, it's true, and I won't do it again*; mesolect *The thing you talking, that true, but I will not do it again*; basilect *The thing you telli me you no lie, but I can't do some again*. See WEST AFRICAN ENGLISH, WEST AFRICAN PIDGIN ENGLISH.

**LIGATURE. 1.** A term in PRINTING for two or more joined letters cast in the same piece of type: *æ* in *Cæsar*; *fl* in *florin*; *ffi* in *office*. Early typefaces had many ligatures, imitating connected letters in handwriting, but few are retained in contemporary English printed alphabets. Vowel ligatures such as *æ* are now commonly replaced by open *ae*, even when transcribing LATIN, Latinized GREEK, and OLD ENGLISH: *Caesar* not *Cæsar*; *Aelfric* not *Ælfric*. **2.** In PHONETICS, a mark like the slur in musical notation placed over or under a pair of symbols to show that they are spoken together: a͡ɪ, and a̯ɪ. Top ligature is favoured for letters with descenders, bottom ligature for letters with ascenders. Compare ASH, DIGRAPH.

**LINE BREAK, LINE-BREAK**. See HYPHEN, SYLLABICATION.

**LINGO**. An informal, slangy, usually dismissive term for: (1) A language that is perceived as strange and unintelligible: 'When men speak French, or any Out-landish Linguo' (J. Chubbe, *Miscellaneous Tracts*, 1770). (2) A hybrid PATOIS, often as used in an area where different language groups meet: *Border Lingo*, a name for the mix of English and Spanish in Texas, also known as *TEX-MEX*. (3) An unusual way of speaking that is hard to follow; SLANG or JARGON: 'I have often

warned you not to talk the court gibberish to me. I tell you, I don't understand the lingo' (Henry Fielding, *Tom Jones*, 1749). Compare -ESE, -SPEAK, TALK.

**LINGUA FRANCA**. [The plural is usually *lingua francas*, but sometimes Italian *lingue franche* and Latin *linguae francae*.] **1.** Originally, a name for the mixed language, based on ITALIAN and Occitan (Southern French), used for trading and military purposes in the Mediterranean in the Middle Ages. See SABIR. **2.** By extension, a semi-technical term for any additional (often compromise) language adopted by speakers of different languages, as a common medium of communication for any purposes and at any level. A lingua franca may be either a fully-fledged language (LATIN in the Roman Empire, Hausa at the present time in West Africa), or a PIDGIN or CREOLE (TOK PISIN in Papua New Guinea, KRIO in Sierra Leone). A language may become somewhat reduced if it is widespread as a lingua franca (SWAHILI in East Africa). FRENCH served widely in Europe as the lingua franca of diplomacy in the 18–19c, and English now serves as a lingua franca in many countries with linguistically diverse populations (such as India and Nigeria) and for many purposes (as with the restricted variety SEASPEAK, used by the world's merchant marine). See BUSINESS ENGLISH, LINGO, LINK LANGUAGE, POLARI.

**LINGUAL. 1.** Relating to the TONGUE, as with a *lingual protrusion lisp*, a lisp caused by the tongue coming forward too far. **2.** In PHONETICS, formed by (especially the tip of) the tongue, as with the consonants /d, t, n/; *a lingual sound*. **3.** Relating to LANGUAGES: *lingual skills*. The simple adjective is rare in this sense, but the combining form *-lingual* is common, as in *bi-*, *tri-*, and *quadrilingual* able to use two, three, and four languages respectively. There are two terms for 'able to use (only) one language': the commoner *monolingual* (a hybrid form using GREEK-derived *mono-* sole) and the etymologically more consistent *unilingual* (using LATIN-derived *un-* one). The latter is common in CanE, under the influence of FRENCH *unilingue*. Compare -GLOT. See BILINGUALISM, MULTILINGUALISM.

**LINGUISTIC ATLAS**, also **dialect atlas**. A book of maps which show the distribution of language features over a chosen area. The maps show, with conventional signs such as dots, circles, and triangles, the locations of features as used by native speakers, such as sounds, words, or syntactic features. Ideally, the speakers are directly interviewed in their home communities and their responses immediately noted, but the data are sometimes gathered by postal enquiry. Linguistic atlases have been made for Scotland by Angus McIntosh (1952, *An Introduction to a Survey of Scottish Dialects*) and J. Y. Mather and H. H. Speitel (1975, 1977, 1986, *The Linguistic Atlas of Scotland*, 3 volumes); for Wales by Alan R. Thomas (1973, *The Linguistic Geography of Wales*), and for England by Harold Orton, Stewart Sanderson, and John Widdowson (1978, *The Linguistic Atlas of England*). In North America, the overall project 'The Linguistic Atlas of the United States and Canada', for which fieldwork was begun in 1931, has been only partly achieved. Parts completed and published are: *The Linguistic Atlas of New England*, handbook and 3 volumes, by Hans Kurath (1939–43); *The Linguistic Atlas of the Upper Midwest*, 3 volumes, by Harold B. Allen (1973–6); *The Linguistic Atlas of the Gulf States*, 3 volumes, with others in preparation, by Lee Pederson (1986–9).

**LINGUISTIC GEOGRAPHY**, also **dialect geography** [1920s]. The study of regional dialect variation. See ISOGLOSS, LINGUISTIC ATLAS.

# ■ LINGUISTICS ——————— ■

The systematic study of LANGUAGE. Its aim is to look at language objectively, as a human phenomenon, in order to uncover general principles and provide reliable descriptions.

**History**. Although the formal study of language dates from at least the middle of the first millennium BC in India and ancient Greece, the era of scientific language study is commonly dated from the end of the 18c, when English was discovered to have the same ancestor as a number of European and Asian languages. This discovery initiated at least a century of intense interest in COMPARATIVE PHILOLOGY, which involved uncovering links between languages, writing comparative grammars of related languages, and reconstructing their common 'ancestors'. These activities stimulated a search for the mechanisms underlying LAN-

GUAGE CHANGE. In the 20c, a change of emphasis occurred, largely through the work of the Swiss linguist Ferdinand de Saussure, sometimes regarded as 'the father of modern linguistics'. He advocated separating DIACHRONIC (historical) from synchronic (contemporary or co-occurring) aspects of language study. He argued that language at any point in time is an interlocking structure, in which all items are interdependent, an insight which is now taken for granted in linguistics and forms the basis of 20c STRUCTURALISM. In the 1930s and 1940s, descriptive linguistics was developed largely in the US, as linguists sought to describe the fast-disappearing American-Indian languages, with Edward Sapir and Leonard BLOOMFIELD being regarded jointly as the 'fathers of American linguistics'. Midway through the 20c, Noam CHOMSKY triggered another change of direction, when he instigated work in *generative linguistics*, a concern for the principles in the minds of speakers which could *generate* language (account for their knowledge of language in an explicit way).

**Branches**. Linguistics comprises a large number of branches, several of them hybrids with other disciplines. Although *PHONETICS*, the scientific study of speech sounds, is usually regarded as an intrinsic part of linguistics, it is often taken to be a discipline in its own right, especially by phoneticians, who point to its 19c origins. Linguistics and phonetics together are therefore often referred to as *the linguistic sciences*. At its core, linguistics can be said to have three classic subdivisions: (1) *PHONOLOGY* the study of sound patterns; (2) *MORPHOLOGY and SYNTAX* the composition of words and sentences; (3) *SEMANTICS* the study of meaning. Some linguists consider that morphology and syntax can be subsumed under the traditional term *GRAMMAR*; others argue that phonology, morphology, syntax, and semantics all constitute the grammar of a language. Each can be studied synchronically or diachronically (or both together) and the order in which they have been dealt with within a grammar has fluctuated over the years. In the last quartercentury, some previously fringe areas have become increasingly important, notably: *PRAGMATICS* the study of language usage; *SOCIOLINGUISTICS* the study of the relationship between language and society;

*PSYCHOLINGUISTICS* language and the mind; *LINGUISTIC TYPOLOGY* the analysis of languages into types; *computational linguistics* the use of computers to simulate language processes; *stylistics* linguistic analysis applied to literature and style; *APPLIED LINGUISTICS* linguistics in relation to such practical activities as language teaching, LEXICOGRAPHY, and speech therapy. See CORPUS.

**LINGUISTIC SIGN**. A term in especially early 20c LINGUISTICS. Such a SIGN has two parts: a signifier (French *signifiant*), the form; something signified (*signifié*), what is referred to, the meaning. According to Ferdinand de Saussure, language was a system of signs, in which each formed part of an interdependent whole *où tout se tient* (where everything holds together). He stressed the arbitrary nature of the sign, evidently covering two notions of arbitrariness: (1) That there is mostly no connection between the two parts of the sign: there is no intrinsic link between the sound sequence *cow* and the animal it refers to. Apparent exceptions, as with onomatopoeic words (*bang, coo, quack*) are relatively few and vary from language to language. (2) That each language cuts up the world in different, arbitrary ways. This viewpoint is controversial, as linguists are divided as to whether there is an underlying reality which is managed differently by various languages, or whether the cutting up is as arbitrary as Saussure suggested. See SEMANTICS, SEMIOTICS.

## ■ LINGUISTIC TYPOLOGY ──── ■

Also **language typology**, **typology of language**. The classification of human languages into different types on the basis of shared properties which are not due to common origin or geographical contact. Linguistic typology therefore complements the long-established tradition of genetic classification, in which languages are assigned to a family on the basis of their presumed historical origin. The criteria used for dividing languages into types depend to some extent on the purpose of the classification, since a typology based on sound structure does not necessarily correlate with one based on word order. The most common classificatory criteria are morphological (word structure), syntactic (word order), and phonological (sound patterns).

**Morphology**. Investigation of the way in which different languages combine grammatical units (MORPHEMES) within WORDS is the longest-established aspect of typology. In the 19c, there was an attempt to assign languages to a number of basic morphological types, most commonly three, which divided languages according to the degree to which morphemes are fused together: (1) *Analytic or isolating languages*, in which each morpheme tends to form a separate word, as in Vietnamese *Com nâû ngoài trời ăn rất nhạt* (rice cook out sky eat very tasteless: 'Rice which is cooked in the open air is very tasteless'). (2) *Agglutinating languages*, in which several morphemes are juxtaposed within a word, as in Turkish *adamlardan* (*adam-lar-dan*, man-plural-from: 'from the men'). (3) *Fusional languages*, in which morphemes are fused together within a word, as in Latin *servorum* (of slaves), where the ending *-orum* is a fusion of *possession*, *plural*, and *masculine*. In practice, few languages are pure types, since many use all three processes, even though one favoured method tends to predominate. English has a tendency towards isolation (as in I *will now go out for a walk*), but both agglutination (as in *clever-ly* and *high-er*) and fusion (as in *gave*, in which *give* and *past* are fused) are also found.

Alternatively, languages may be classified morphologically according to the number of morphemes within a word: *analytic languages* (ideally, one morpheme per word, such as Vietnamese, with an estimated 1.06 morphemes per word) are opposed to *synthetic languages* (two or more morphemes per word, such as SANSKRIT with an estimated 2.59 morphemes per word). The most extreme form of synthesis is found in a *polysynthetic* language, such as Inuit (Eskimo), which has an estimated 3.72 morphemes per word. On this scale, English comes out as mildly analytic with 1.68 morphemes per word. *Inflected languages* are a variety of synthetic language in which a word takes various forms, most usually by the addition of suffixes, which show its role in the sentence. Many languages have some inflection (such as English *boys*, *the boy's mother*, *play/played*) but in a highly inflected language, such as LATIN, this process predominates. There are therefore two morphological scales, one which measures degree of fusion (*isolating—agglutinating—fusional*), the other degree of synthesis (*analytic—inflected—polysynthetic*). Since an isolating language is inevitably also an analytic language, English is at the low end of both scales.

**Syntax**. In the past quartercentury, basic word order has been the main criterion for classifying languages. In the early 1960s, it was observed that of the possible combinations of subject (S), verb (V), and object (O) within a sentence, only certain ones actually occur, and that these are not all equally likely. The commonest are those in which the subject comes first (SVO as in English, SOV as in Turkish), less common are those in which the verb comes first (VSO as in Welsh, VOS as in Malagasy), and least common are those in which the object comes first (OVS as in Hixkaryana, spoken in northern Brazil, OSV of which no sure example has yet been found). Many languages have mixed word orders, and not all languages have a firm order, so this classification has its flaws. However, English with its SVO structure, such as *The rabbit* (S) *gnawed* (V) *the carrot* (O), is a language with one of the two commonest word orders, even though some subsidiary orders are possible, such as *Up jumped the rabbit*.

The relative order of verb and object is often considered to be most important from the point of view of typology, since not all languages express overt subjects. The main interest in classifying languages in this way lies in the *implicational* relationships, in that certain other constructions are statistically likely to occur in each type. A VO language, such as English, is likely to have prepositions rather than postpositions (such as *up the tree* rather than *\*the tree up*), and auxiliaries before main verbs (such as *Bill may come* rather than *\*Bill come may*). It is also likely to have relative clauses (beginning with *who/which*, etc.) after the noun they refer to, such as *The burglar who stole the silver escaped* rather than *\*The who stole the silver burglar escaped*. The general principle behind these observations appears to be a preference for consistency in the position of the *head* (main word) in any construction with regard to its *modifiers* (items attached to it): so a VO language such as English is a '*head first*' *language* and an OV language such as Turkish is a '*head last*' *language*.

A controversial proposal by Noam CHOMSKY is that humans are genetically 'hardwired' with some universal features of language, but that these are supplemented with a number of options which have to be selected on the basis of exposure to a particular language: see LANGUAGE ACQUISITION DEVICE. The choice of one rather than another has complex ramifications throughout the language. Different language types are therefore the result of a number of fairly simple choices which are automatically available to humans. One proposal for such an option is between a *pro-drop language* (one which can optionally drop pronouns at the beginning of sentences, as in ITALIAN *Io sono Italiano/Sono Italiano* I am Italian/Am Italian) and one which does not usually do so, such as English. Pro-drop languages seem to behave somewhat differently over a range of constructions from languages which do not drop their pronouns.

**Phonology**. Phonological typology has received somewhat less attention, though some interesting work has been done on types of vowel system. In addition, a number of studies have proposed implicational hypotheses, such as if a language has fricative consonants, it will also have stop consonants. With regard to RHYTHM, some linguists divide languages into: (1) *Syllable-timed languages*, such as FRENCH and Japanese, in which the rhythm appears to be fairly even, with each syllable giving the impression of having about the same weight as any other. (2) *Stress-timed languages*, such as English and ARABIC, in which stressed syllables recur at intervals. In recent years, a somewhat 'weak' version of this view has gained ground. The absolute division has been replaced by a sliding scale, in which there are few pure types, though many which can be placed towards one or the other end of the scale. There is no doubt that English is on the stress-timed end of the scale. Another distinction is sometimes made between *tone* or *tonal languages*, such as Mandarin Chinese, and *intonation or non-tonal languages*, such as English. In a tone language, the pitch level of any syllable is of critical importance, since words are sometimes distinguished from one another purely by the tone, such as Mandarin *ma* with level tone (*mother*), with rising tone (*hemp*), with a dipping tone (*horse*), and a falling tone (*scold*). In a language such as English, however, sentence intonation plays a crucial role, as in *You saw him!* versus *You saw him?*, where difference in meaning is signalled by the intonation.

**Conclusion**. Linguistic typology is currently in a state of considerable flux and controversy. A wide range of criteria apart from those outlined above are currently under discussion, and it will be some years before reliable methods of classifying languages are firmly established. See LANGUAGE FAMILY.

**LINKING R**. In certain ACCENTS of English, including RECEIVED PRONUNCIATION, /r/ pronounced between a word or syllable ending in the vowels /ɔ, ɑː, ə/ and a following vowel: the *r* in *beer and a sandwich, car engine*. See INTRUSIVE *R*, NEW YORK, RHOTIC AND NON-RHOTIC.

**LINK LANGUAGE**. A semi-technical term for a language that allows communication between groups with no other common language: for example, HINDI in India, SWAHILI in East Africa. It may or may not be seen as neutral in relation to other languages used in a particular place. English serves as a link language in most of Africa and Asia: 'English is needed as a link language between the Indian states, and between the union government and the states' (Nayantara Sahgal, *South*, Aug. 1985). Compare LINGUA FRANCA.

**LIQUID**. A term in PHONETICS for a frictionless APPROXIMANT, especially an *r*- or *l*-sound. See CONSONANT, *L*-SOUNDS, *R*-SOUNDS.

# ■ LITERACY ─────────── ■

The ability to read and write in at least one language. This ability developed in West Asia in the third millennium BC, when the Sumerians developed a system of symbols to record spoken language. They were followed by the Syro-Palestinians who, between 2000 and 1000 BC, introduced a consonantal script using a small number of signs, the precursor of the alphabet. During the same period, increasingly complex commercial, administrative, and religious structures and growing urbanization led to the invention of WRITING systems in such other regions as Egypt, India, and China. In ancient cultures, literacy was rare and specialized, and therefore a token of considerable learning. In more recent centuries, however, the term has often been interpreted minimally: as at least the READING and writing of one's name, anyone unable

to do so being classed as *illiterate*. In the 20c, however, the ability to read and write has been delimited in many ways and *literacy* is often used interchangeably with *FUNCTIONAL LITERACY*: the production and understanding of simple oral or written statements reflecting the social, economic, and educational conditions of a particular region. Yet the threshold of literacy is indeterminate, making exact measurements difficult or culturally variable. In 1965, at a world congress of ministers of EDUCATION. UNESCO adopted the view that 'rather than an end in itself, literacy should be regarded as a way of preparing man for a social, civic and economic role that goes far beyond the limits of rudimentary literacy training consisting merely in the teaching of reading and writing' ('Literacy, Gateway to Fulfillment', special issue of *UNESCO Courier*, June 1980).

**Literacy in English**. The earliest written English was the concern of a small minority of men, first in the runic alphabet, whose letters were carved on objects for both practical and ornamental purposes, then in the Roman alphabet introduced in Britain by Christian missionaries at the end of the 6c. Education remained for many centuries a province largely of the Roman Catholic Church and the need for reading and writing was not greatly extended until the introduction of movable type and inexpensive paper in the late 15c. This helped standardize written versions of English, expand the uses of literacy, and give reading and writing greater circulation among the populace. Determining who is literate and for what purposes has always been difficult. The collection of statistics tends to be confounded by the under-representation of people marginalized from the economic and political centres of a culture: for example, in censuses, by incomplete records, and by variable standards of what should be measured. Data such as signatures or court and ecclesiastical testimony have been used to estimate the degree of literacy in particular locales at particular times, but tend to depend on self-reports and minimal evidence; they give no account of such skills as comprehension of printed matter. Moreover, reading and writing have had different constituencies and uses during different periods. Thus, in the 17c Protestant communities of early New England, where male literacy was well above 60% by

1700, it was considered important to help women acquire reading skills for religious purposes but not writing because its 'commercial uses lay beyond women's traditional sphere of activity' (Geraldine J. Clifford, 'Buch und Lesen: Historical Perspectives on Literacy and Schooling', *Review of Educational Research* 54, 1984).

**Ideology and literacy**. Deliberately taught rather than acquired like speech, literacy has traditionally been seen as a commodity delivered through political, educational, and religious bureaucracies. Reading, writing, and counting at sophisticated levels continued to be reserved first for the clergy and then for the sons of the aristocracy and of wealthy merchants; the term *literacy* in its 15–18c usages was regularly associated with a classical education and with priestly or civic élites. The literacy needs of most people, however, have tended to be functional: the production of reports, accounts, journals, and letters, and in recent times the completion of forms. Institutional arrangements for instruction in literacy according to the British and American models have, until the 20c, generally been aimed at achieving low to moderate levels of literacy for large numbers of people and higher levels for smaller privileged groups. Educational developments in 18c Scotland, linked with Presbyterianism, were typical: while the literacy rate for adult males jumped from 33% in 1675 to 90% in 1800, the increase was due to emphasis on reading, memorization, and recall of familiar material; neither writing nor the application of knowledge was demanded.

**Literacy, knowledge, and problem-solving**. The association of literacy with the acquisition of theoretical knowledge and the development of problem-solving abilities was by and large a product of the Industrial Revolution and, prior to the 20c, was generally confined to centres of education in cities. Country schools, whose pupils were needed to work the land and whose instructors were not always professionally certified, generally offered training in basic skills rather than fluency in written language. Both in town and country, however, children were drilled first on letter names and sounds, then on syllables and words. During the 19c, many reform-minded educators stressed the need for comprehension of reading materials, asserting that encountering words in context would lead students to a more rapid acquisition of meaning and a more appropriate use of emphasis and inflection. However, since lack of high-level literacy was regarded as neither degrading nor detrimental to economic or social advancement, 19c levels of literacy remained low while numbers of people described as literate grew.

During the 20c, attitudes to literacy have changed. School-based definitions of literacy and standards relating to year groups have been adopted in most English-speaking countries, as competency testing has replaced functional determinants. Paradoxically, because of heightened expectations and increased technological demands, many people who have exceeded traditional literacy criteria are now considered *semiliterate* or *functionally illiterate*. In addition, legislators, educators, and public activists throughout the English-speaking world have sought to broaden the social and personal dimensions of literacy through mandatory training in such things as *historical literacy* (awareness of the main outlines of history, especially as regards one's own country), *cultural literacy* (a knowledge of classical texts and great writers of one's own culture), *mathematical literacy* (also called *numeracy*), *symbolic literacy* (an appreciation of the value and use of symbols of various kinds), *media literacy* (familiarity with and a capacity to understand and to some extent evaluate the different media and what they provide), and *computer literacy* (familiarity with and ability to use a computer, without necessarily being able to write programs).

**Conclusion**. Literacy requirements, which often relate to and depend on such highly specific contexts as occupational need, continue to vary among social and economic groups, with low levels concentrated among the poor, the undereducated, and members of minority populations. Given the lack of contemporary agreement concerning its definitions and uses, literacy is best conceived as a continuum whose dissemination involves various kinds of behaviour at higher and lower levels, including reading, writing, speaking, listening, thinking, counting, coping with the demands of the state, of employment, and of social life. See ILLITERACY, SPELLING.

**LITERAL. 1.** A term traditionally opposed to *figurative* and *metaphorical*. Although it is generally unrelated to LETTERS, LITERACY, and LITERATURE, it suggests the influence of the letter as a measure of strictness and rightness: *the literal truth* is seen as being true in a basic and absolute way. If something is done *literally*, a person follows instructions 'to the letter', without flexibility or imagination. Paradoxically, however, the adverb *literally* is often used to mean *figuratively*: 'And with his eyes he literally scoured the corners of the cell' (Vladimir Nabokov, *Invitation to a Beheading*, 1960). See FIGURATIVE LANGUAGE. **2.** A term in proof-reading for a misprint such as the substitution of one letter for another, the omission or addition of a letter, or letters transposed (for example, *parodixical, responsiblity, asssumed, phenonemon, prniter*).

**LITERARY STANDARD**, also **Literary English**. A term used by Eric PARTRIDGE in the mid-20c for the English of literary prose:

> [It] lies beyond any matter of pronunciation, and is confined to written English,—and should it be used in speech, it is too bookish to be Received. Of Literary English—Literary Standard—it is necessary only to say that it is the more conventional, stylized, and dignified, more accurate and logical, sometimes the more beautiful form that Received Standard assumes, like evening dress, for important occasions (*Usage and Abusage*, 1947, revised 1957).

See LITERATURE, RECEIVED STANDARD AND MODIFIED STANDARD, STANDARD.

# ■ LITERATURE ─────── ■

**1.** Artistic creation through LANGUAGE and its products: *French literature, literature in English*. **2.** The texts of a group or subject: *scientific and technical literature, the latest literature on computers*.

**'Literary' literature**. It is impossible to define the primary sense of literature precisely or to set rigid limits on its use. Literary treatment of a subject requires creative use of the imagination: something is constructed which is related to 'real' experience, but is not of the same order. What has been created in language is known only through language, and the text does not give access to a reality other than itself. As a consequence, the texts that make up English literature are a part and a product of the English language and cannot be separated from it, even though there may be distinct university departments of English as 'language' and as 'literature'.

**Identifying a literary text**. Traditionally, literary texts have been easy to identify: an ode or a play is 'literary', but a menu or a telephone directory is not. There is, however, an indeterminate area of essays, biographies, memoirs, history, philosophy, travel books, and other texts which may or may not be deemed literary. Thomas Hobbes's *Leviathan* (1651) is commonly studied as a political text and John Bunyan's *Pilgrim's Progress* (1678–84) as a literary text, yet they share certain qualities, such as lively personifications; Bunyan creates Giant Despair and Little-faith, while Hobbes writes 'the Papacy is not other than the Ghost of the Deceased Roman Empire, sitting crowned upon the grave thereof'. As Edward Gibbon's *The History of the Decline and Fall of the Roman Empire* (1776–88) has grown less important as history, it has become more significant as literature. Many texts appear therefore to have literary aspects combined with other qualities and purposes, and ultimately individual or consensual choice must decide which has priority. Private and group judgement is also exercised in evaluative criticism. The word *literature* tends to be used with approval of works perceived as having artistic merit, the evaluation of which may depend on social and linguistic as well as aesthetic factors. If the criteria of quality become exacting, a *canon* may emerge, limited in its inclusions and exclusions, and the members of a society or group may be required (with varying degrees of pressure and success) to accept that canon and no other. Academic syllabuses for degrees in English have traditionally covered periods, focused on such well-established writers as Chaucer, Spenser, Shakespeare, Milton, and Wordsworth. Courses introduced more recently may include such topics as Women's Writing, with study of recent novelists like Doris Lessing and Margaret Atwood as well as Charlotte Brontë and Virginia Woolf, or Black American Literature, with James Baldwin and Richard Wright.

**Literature and language**. In the formative period of a written language, a successful literature may favour a particular dialect and contribute towards its becoming a national printed standard, in the case of English the East Midlands dialect from the 14c onwards. The prestige of literature can attract favour to an associated 'high style' that rejects aspects of common usage as vulgar. This favour prevailed for a time in some Continental European literatures, such as the *dolce stil* of 12c Italy and 17–18c classical French writing, but apart from the 18c cult of *poetic diction* has had little influence in the English-speaking world. Literature is an exceptional area of language use, which many people have regarded as the highest service to which language can be put and the surest touchstone of good usage. Its creation is dependent on the resources available to the author in any period, but those resources may be enriched and increased by a literary tradition in which quotations from and allusions to 'the classics' abound and many words have literary nuances. Writers have created such enduring neologisms as Spenser's *blatant*, Milton's *pandemonium*, and Shaw's *superman*.

**The language of literature.** In the 20c, much attention has been given to the language of literature and the question of whether there is in fact distinctively *literary language*. Many features thought of as literary appear in common usage. Metre and formal rhythm derive from everyday speech, words often rhyme without conscious contrivance, multiple meaning and word associations are part of daily communication, and tropes and figures of speech are used in ordinary discourse. However, literary language shows a greater concentration of such features, deliberately arranged and controlled. It may be said that communication is impossible without artifice, yet there is a difference between the colloquial simile that someone is 'as bold as brass' and T. S. Eliot's simile for the young man in *The Waste Land* (1922): 'One of the low on whom assurance sits / As a silk hat on a Bradford millionaire.' The difference lies not only in the originality and unexpected juxtaposition, but in the appropriateness of image to context, in the austere tone of the whole poem, in the evocation of a snobbish post-1918 attitude to men who had become rich through government contracts during the war.

**Language in literature.** Literary language may be drawn from any area or register of daily usage. Colloquialism and dialect are used in fictional and dramatic dialogue, as in this passage from *Sons and Lovers* (D. H. Lawrence, 1913):

'But how late you are!'
'Aren't I!' he cried, turning to his father.
'Well, dad!'
The two men shook hands.
'Well, my lad!'
Morel's eyes were wet.
'We thought tha'd niver be commin',' he said.
'Oh, I'd come!' exclaimed William.

In James Joyce's *Ulysses* (1922), Leopold Bloom reads an advertisement in a newspaper:

What is home without
Plumtree's Potted Meat?
Incomplete.
With it an abode of bliss.

and incorporates the jingle into his stream of consciousness. The pattern of metre and rhyme may transform into poetry a statement which has neither rare words nor unusual syntax:

The lad came to the door at night,
When lovers crown their vows,
And whistled soft and out of sight
In shadow of the boughs.
(A. E. Housman, 'The True Lover', 1896)

Prevailing literary fashion may make literary language seem artificial without impairing comprehension:

If aught of oaten stop or pastoral song
May hope, chaste Eve, to soothe thy
    modest ear,
Like thy own solemn springs,
Thy springs and dying gales.
(William Collins, 1721–59,
'Ode to Evening')

Experiment and the personal vision may challenge the reader to make a new response to language and to accept T. S. Eliot's dictum that 'genuine poetry can communicate before it is understood':

Now as I was young and easy under the
    apple boughs
About the lilting house and happy as the
    grass was green,
The night above the dingle starry,
Time let me hail and climb
Golden in the heydays of his eyes.
(Dylan Thomas, 1914–53, 'Fern Hill')

These extracts are from texts commonly accepted as part of literature, yet, out of context, they seem to present irreconcilable differences. Every literary work must be seen in its totality as a unique creation, often connected by similarities with other texts but dependent on none for its validity.

**LITOTES** [Stress: 'lie-TOE-teez']. In RHETORIC, a positive and often emphatic statement made by denying something negative, as when St Paul called himself 'a citizen *of no mean city*' (Acts 21: 39). Common phrases involving litotes include *in no small measure* and *by no means negligible*. See MEIOSIS.

**LIVERPOOL, LIVERPUDLIAN**. See SCOUSE.

**LOAN**. An item of language given, as if by a lender, from one language to another, used both on its own and in such combinations as *LOANWORD, LOAN TRANSLATION, LOAN BLEND*, and *loanshift*. The commonest loans are single words: *pizza* (from Italian to English), *babysitter* (from English to French, German, and other languages). Once adopted, loans usually show some adaptation: in sound, French *garage*, variously pronounced in English; in form, English *night* taken into Italian as a CLIPPING of *nightclub*; in grammar, English nouns borrowed into French and provided with a gender, *la babysitter* (feminine), *le golf* (masculine). Verbs adapt to the morphology of the borrowing language: in German, *babysitten* to babysit, past tense *babysittete*, past participle *gebabysittet*. See ASSIMILATION, BORROWING, CALQUE, CODE-MIXING AND CODE-SWITCHING, FOREIGNISM.

**LOAN BLEND**. A usage that combines a foreign LOAN with a native form: *Afrikanerdom*, combining *Afrikaner* (from Afrikaans) and the English suffix *-dom* as in *kingdom*. See BLEND.

**LOAN TRANSLATION**, also **calque**. A compound or complex LOAN in which, rather than borrow an expression directly, speakers analyse the parts and replace them with similar native forms: AmE *skyscraper* adopted into French as *gratte-ciel* (scrape-sky), into German as *Wolkenkratzer* (cloud-scrape).

**LOANWORD**, also **loan-word**, **loan word**. A WORD taken into one language from another: in English, *garage* from French, *leitmotif* from German. Such words are, on the ANALOGY of money, both 'loans' from Language A to B and 'borrowings' by B from A. Philologists use a three-word German system to discuss the process of lending and ASSIMILATION: *Gastwort, Fremdwort, Lehnwort*. A *Gastwort* (guest-word) is an unassimilated BORROWING that has kept its pronunciation, orthography, grammar, and meaning, but is not used widely: for example, *Gastwort* itself, with /v/ for the *W* of *Wort*, a capital letter because it is a noun, and the alien plural *Gastwörter*. Such words are usually limited to the terminology of specialists and italicized and glossed when used. A *Fremdwort* (foreign-word) has moved a stage further. It has been adapted into the native system, with a stable spelling and pronunciation (native or exotic), or a compromise has been made by translating all or part into a native equivalent: for example, *garage* and *Lehnwort* itself (which has for general purposes been converted to *loanword*). A *Lehnwort* proper is a word that has become indistinguishable from the rest of the lexicon and is open to normal rules of word use and word formation. It is seldom possible, however, to separate the stages of assimilation so neatly: Russian *sputnik* and *glasnost* entered English virtually overnight, with immediate derivatives like *anti-sputnik* and *pre-glasnost*. Assimilation into a language as widespread as English occurs on three levels: local, national, and international. For example, such a Mexican-Spanish word as *taco* may remain local in AmE, used only along the US–Mexican border, then become national, then international. Such a process often takes years, leaving many loans drifting uncertainly. See CALQUE, FOREIGNISM.

**LOCALISM**. An expression that belongs to a particular place or geographical variety of a language: for example, in Sierra Leone, *hot drink* means 'alcoholic beverage'; in ScoE, *loch* refers to a lake in Scotland, while *lake* is used for more general purposes. See -ISM, REGIONALISM.

■ **LOGIC** ──────────────── ■

In general usage, the process of reasoning and sound judgement, often taken to be the outcome of adequate education, an aspect of common sense, or both: *a logical decision*. In philosophy, the study and development of close reasoning, especially inference, traditionally the concern of logicians and mathematicians and currently important for computer programmers, computational linguists, and researchers into artificial intelligence. There are several kinds of logic, such as *formal logic* and *symbolic logic*, of philosophical systems that acknowledge its influence, such as *logical positivism*, and of techniques considered to incorporate logic, such as *logic arrays* and *logic circuits* in electronic technology.

**Classical logic**. The term *logiké* was coined by the Greek philosopher Alexander of Aphrodisias in the 3c, but systems of organized thinking had already developed well before this in Greece, India, and China. Western culture has inherited the Greek tradition mainly through Rome and the Arab world. In this tradition, logic is closely linked with grammar and rhetoric, and discussion of one often leads to discussion of the others. For the Greeks, both reasoning and language were encompassed in the word *lógos*, which they contrasted with *múthos*, a term that encompassed words, speech, stories, poems, fictions, and fables. Plato (5c BC) in *The Republic* represented Socrates as wishing to exclude poetry from the proper education of the young, and after some 2,500 years, this viewpoint still carries weight: logic, science, and reason are commonly set on one side and poetry, art, and myth on the other. To make his case, however, Plato used many devices from poetry and rhetoric: he so structured his dialogues that Socrates always won, often with the help of poetic analogies such as the Simile of the Cave. His pupil Aristotle laid the foundations of logic proper, as the study of inference from *propositions* arranged as formal *arguments*.

**Grammar and logic**. Because logic and GRAMMAR developed together they have overlapping terminologies: both use the term *sentence*, and deductive logic consists of a *logic of propositions* (also called *sentential logic*) and a *logic of predicates* (also called a *logic of noun expressions*). Logicians, grammarians, and rhetoricians are all interested in such matters as AMBIGUITY, FALLACY, paradox, syntax, and SEMANTICS, and in such modalities as necessity, possibility, and contingency; linguists who are concerned with grammar, computation, and artificial intelligence take as much interest in logic as in natural language. Logicians and mathematicians have created systems that contain both sets of abstract symbols and the rules necessary for their combination and manipulation in strings. Such symbols, rules, and strings are often idealizations of elements in, or thought to be in, natural language (but isolated from such everyday factors as dialect variation, personal idiosyncrasy, figurative usage, emotional connotation, colloquial idiom, social attitude, and semantic change). When such a system of symbols is adapted to practical ends, however, as in computer technology and artificial intelligence, *pure logic* becomes *applied logic*, operating within a real machine intended to do real work in real time.

Although many logicians, grammarians, and linguists have been interested in a universal calculus of language (something that would transcend natural language or allow the dispassionate description of all language), they have built their systems out of the natural languages that they know best: Greek for Aristotle and his disciples, Latin for medieval and Renaissance grammarians, and English for such present-day theorists as Noam Chomsky. Both prescriptive and descriptive grammarians of such Western languages as French and English have been influenced by logic and by the languages in which the principles of logic developed. Because it emerged in large part through the use and analysis of language, it has not been difficult to find quasi-logical patterns in language. Some analysts have been inclined to see logical orderliness either as inherent in language or as a reasonable goal of language planning, especially when a language is in the process of being standardized. Everyday language, however, has a persistent (even frustrating) tendency towards the illogical or non-logical, as for example in the use of double negatives (*I didn't do nothing*, which does not therefore mean 'I did something') and in idiomatic expressions (such as *it's raining cats and dogs*).

All analysts of language work towards orderliness, but some go further and engage in or recommend making certain aspects of language, such as the spelling of English, more 'regular' (that is, more rule-governed and therefore more logically consistent). They may also favour an artificial language such as Esperanto or Basic English that is (apparently) free from the illogic of natural language. Interest in such reforms has often gone hand in hand with particular conceptions of and assumptions about, progress, science, efficiency, education, literacy, and standards. Logic has therefore been used as a tool for both the description of natural language and its prescriptive improvement. In the development of the first grammars of English, the model was Latin and the analytical terms were Greek as used by the describers of Latin. Medieval and Renaissance models for vernacular prose as a vehicle of rational discourse were either Latin prose or vernacular prose written in the Latin style. Theories of sentences and parts of speech were those developed by classical grammarians and logicians, often the same people. The analysis of sentences into subjects and predicates, main and subordinate clauses, and the like, has paralleled the logician's view of propositions as the core of language and of binary division as a powerful conceptual tool.

**The limits of logic**. In the second half of the 20c, ancient practice has gained fresh impetus through the work of Noam Chomsky. Some features of his work are: (1) The definition of a language as a set of well-formed sentences, indefinite in number. (2) Abstract and diagrammatic analyses of sentences of standard written English. (3) The use of quasi-logical symbols such as S for sentence, NP for noun phrase, and VP for verb phrase, to sustain the analysis of such sentences. (4) Logical transformations performed on strings of symbols so as to produce further strings. (5) The creation of a generative grammar, that is, a set of explicit, formal rules that specify or generate all and only the sentences which constitute a language; in so doing, they are seen as demonstrating the nature of the implicit knowledge of that language possessed by an ideal native speaker-hearer. Such an approach has often been taken to be a break with the past, but is rooted in more than two millennia of logical and grammatical system-building. It remains a matter of debate whether natural language can be handled by linguistic theories that derive in the main from or are closely associated with aspects of formal logic. Natural language is a neural mechanism, apparently the result of genetic and social evolution.

While it is sometimes regular, logical, and precise, it is as often irregular, non-logical, and imprecise, and oftener still a mix of the two. It blends intellect with instinct, logic with inspiration, and the standard with the varied. Logic is closely associated with language and with its description and discussion in literate societies. As such, it is an essential tool, but one cannot deduce from this usefulness that it is the sole or even primary means by which natural language can be understood.

■ **LONDON** ─────────────── ■

A city on the River Thames in southern England, the ancient capital of England and the capital and seat of government of the United Kingdom of Great Britain and Northern Ireland. The city has experienced many languages: CELTIC, the LATIN of Roman Britain, OLD ENGLISH, NORMAN FRENCH, MIDDLE and MODERN ENGLISH, and the languages of immigrants, diplomats, merchants, and visitors. It is, in the late 20c, one of the world's great cosmopolitan and polyglot cities, identified in particular with four varieties of English: KING'S/Queen's ENGLISH, BBC ENGLISH, COCKNEY and more recently, ESTUARY ENGLISH. The primacy of London (in England, in the United Kingdom, and in the British Empire) has in the past given a certain status to the language used there. However, the city did not play a major part in Old English culture until the reign of Edward the Confessor (1042–66). Prior to that period, Winchester to the south-west was the seat of the Saxon kings and West Saxon was the literary dialect. Through the medieval period, London grew in importance, and the triumph of Middle English over Norman French in the 14c gave preference to the variety of the East Midland dialect that was becoming current in London. The poet Geoffrey CHAUCER, a Londoner of the time, generally used slightly older and more southern forms, with traces of Kentish.

**Capital and provinces**. The comparative stability of the Tudor period, with London as the seat of the royal court and major litigation, brought still greater regard for its superiority in language. In 1589, Puttenham advised the use of 'the vsual speach of the Court, and that of London and the shires lying about London with lx [sixty] myles, and not much aboue' (*The Arte of English Poesie*, 1589). The introduction of dialect speakers in drama, like Shakespeare's Welsh captain Fluellen and Scots captain Jamy in *Henry V*, and the use of 'stage southern' as affected by Edgar in *King Lear*, showed that Londoners were aware of their distinctive speech and amused by other varieties. The tendency is even more marked in later 17c comedy, in which country characters are differentiated by their speech: the restored Stuart court and the London location of groups like the new Royal Society made the city seem ever more significant than 'the provinces'. Discussions about the correct forms of English and the possibility of an ACADEMY to regulate the language were carried on mainly by London speakers.

Perhaps because London usage was taken for granted by so many of the influential, there is not an extensive record of its nature before the 19c. When dialogue was written for plays or novels, only speakers of other dialects were marked by deviant spelling, the established ORTHOGRAPHY being used for the rest. The hymnographer Isaac Watts, in his *Art of Reading and Writing English* (1721), dismisses the 'dialect or corrupt speech that obtains in the several counties of England' and lists words that are written differently from 'their common and frequent pronunciation in the City of London'. He adds that 'there are some other corruptions in the pronouncing of several words by many of the citizens themselves' and cites among others *yourn* for 'yours', *squeedge* for 'squeeze', *yerb* for 'herb'. However, Samuel Pegge notes, in *Anecdotes of the English Language* (1803), words whose pronunciation 'is a little deformed by the natives of London'; as well as Cockney features like the confusion of /v/ and /w/, he mentions some that 'savour rather of an affected refinement' like *daater* for 'daughter' and *saace* for 'sauce'.

**London English**. True Cockney is relatively limited, though some of its features are shared by Londoners who are not themselves Cockneys. Some vowel and diphthong sounds, notably the nasalization of the diphthong /aʊ/ as in *now* and the changing of /eɪ/ to /aɪ/ which makes *paper* sound like *piper*, are frequently heard, as is the dropping of initial *h* (*We're 'appy to 'elp you*). Characteristics of neighbouring counties are heard in London, particularly in the outer suburbs, which have penetrated into what were once rural areas of Surrey, Kent, and Essex. It would be an acute or very bold observer who could guarantee to analyse all the features of speech among a random selection of Londoners.

The speech of educated Londoners is not necessarily to be equated with RECEIVED PRONUNCIATION, but this is the model which has traditionally been followed by the upwardly mobile. In many instances, however, there appears in the later 20c to be a levelling-out in the speech patterns of younger, educated Londoners of many backgrounds, including RP, into a distinctive 'Estuary' accent and voice quality. Currently, however, the situation is complex, and London speech ranges from 'core' Cockney usage through a wide variety of intermediate forms to RP and forms of RP that some may regard as prestigious and others as affected or 'posh'.

See CAXTON, CHANCERY STANDARD, DIALECT (ENGLAND), DICKENS, EAST MIDLAND DIALECT, ENGLISH IN ENGLAND, HISTORY OF ENGLISH, JOHNSON, KENSINGTON, RHYMING SLANG, SHAKESPEARE, SHAW, STANDARD ENGLISH.

**LONDON-LUND CORPUS, THE**. A computerized CORPUS of texts in English associated with U. College London (UCL) and the U. of Lund in Sweden. In 1975, the Survey of Spoken English was established at Lund by Jan Svartvik with the aim of transferring to machine-readable form the section of texts derived from recorded speech by the SURVEY OF ENGLISH USAGE at UCL. This version of the SEU spoken texts reduces the amount of detailed information in the SEU transcriptions of the texts by omitting some of the original prosodic features and all paralinguistic features. The 87 spoken texts (all that had by then been processed at the SEU) became available in machine-readable form for distribution in the early 1980s. A selection of 34 texts of face-to-face conversations, totalling some 170,000 words, has been published in *A Corpus of English Conversation*, edited by Jan Svartvik and Randolph Quirk (Lund: Gleerup, 1980). The Lund Survey of Spoken English has since been engaged in developing a semi-automatic, interactive system of grammatical tagging that can be used primarily for research into the interrelationship of grammar and prosody.

**LONG *S***. Formerly, a variant of the lowercase LETTER *s* (roman form-ſ, italic ʃ) in initial and medial positions in words, such as ſin for sin, ſleep for sleep, ſhall for shall, himſelf for himself, graſs for grass, thouſand for thousand, conſcience for conscience poſſeſs for possess. After 1800, the greater convenience of s for all positions prevailed, and ſ fell into disuse in English. See ALPHABET, ESH.

**LONG WORD**. A polysyllabic WORD, especially of LATIN or GREEK origin, and often uncommon and difficult to spell or pronounce, such as *diuretic* or *phantasmagorical*. People often ask what the longest word in English might be, but the answer depends on what can be accepted as a word. Some chemical combinations have names of over 1,000 letters, but these are usually amalgams of combining elements rather than words as such. The longest word in the 1st edition of the *OED is floccinaucinihilipilification* (29 letters), 'the action or habit of estimating something as worthless', which the *Supplement* of 1982 topped with the lung disease *pneumonoultramicroscopicsilicovolcanoconiosis* (45 letters). See DERIVATION, HARD WORD.

**LOWER CASE**. In the present-day printed Roman ALPHABET, small LETTERS of varying size, known as *lower-case letters*, as distinguished from CAPITALS or *upper-case letters*. See CASE.

**LOWLAND SCOTS**, sometimes (especially formerly) **Lowland Scotch**. A common name for the Scottish dialects of Northern English that stresses both their location east and south of the Highland Line and their distinctness from the languages of the Highlands (*Gaelic* and *Highland English*). In the Middle Ages, Gaelic was known in Latin as *lingua Scotica* (the Scottish language) and some Gaels therefore claim that the Lowland tongue has usurped the name *SCOTS*. See DORIC, INGLIS, LALLANS.

**LOWTH, Robert** [1710–87]. English clergyman and grammarian, born in Winchester, educated at Winchester School and New College, Oxford. Appointed Bishop of London in 1777, Lowth was a philologist 'more inclined to melancholy than to mirth', who believed that Hebrew was spoken in paradise. His *Short Introduction to English Grammar* (1762) became a standard textbook, and his name has become synonymous with prescriptive GRAMMAR. Lowth's

reputation as a prescriptivist is not entirely deserved. Though he liberally illustrated his grammar rules with errors to be found in the English BIBLE and in STANDARD authors, his approach to correctness was not invariably rigid and, like most grammarians, he described English as well as prescribing its rules. While Lowth advised against ending sentences with prepositions, he acknowledged the construction as 'an idiom, which our language is strongly inclined to'. Lowth also distinguished between *shall* and *will* as the future auxiliary, yet he noted that the pattern is a new one that took hold in the language after 'the vulgar translation of the Bible'. Lowth was convinced that English is rule-governed, and he defended the regularity and simplicity of the language against a tradition which viewed it as too primitive to possess any grammar at all. His model was LATIN grammar, but he readily modified this to accommodate the idiosyncrasies of English. He also championed English language study in school, arguing that it facilitated the acquisition of the classics as well as the concept of universal grammar.

**L-SOUNDS**. There are various ways in which the LETTER l is expressed in English. In phonetic terms, /l/ is made by raising the tongue tip to make and maintain central contact with the ALVEOLAR ridge, allowing air to escape round the sides. Variations can be made by changing the shape of the tongue behind the apical closure. A *dark l* [ɫ] is made by pulling the body of the tongue backwards, and a *clear l* [l] by pushing it up and forward towards the hard palate. Dark l is characteristic of the speech of northern England (excluding Geordie) and southern Scotland; clear l is characteristic of southern Ireland and India. Both types are heard in Northern Ireland and northern Scotland, and widely in AmE. In the speech of southern England and in varieties that developed from it, such as AusE, /l/ tends to be clear before the vowel in a syllable, as in *lick* /lɪk/, and dark after it, as in *kill* /kɪɫ/. As the tongue takes up the position for /ɫ/, a transitional schwa-like sound may be heard: /kɪəɫ/. Dark l may be accompanied by lip rounding, which often begins on the transitional vowel, making it sound more like /ʊ/, as in /kɪʊɫ/. The transitional vowel indicates that a dark l follows immediately, and the /l/ is in effect redundant. In some varieties, such as that of south-east England (in particular Cockney) and AusE, dark *l* is frequently vocalized (turned into a vowel), because the tongue tip does not make a central closure with the alveolar ridge. This 'l' therefore sounds like a back vowel or /w/: /kɪʊ/, /kɪw/ for *kill*. In NZE, where the influence of ScoE is strong, /l/ can be dark in all environments, but the clear/dark distinction as in RP is widespread. If, instead of maintaining central contact, the tongue strikes the alveolar ridge momentarily, or is held close to it, the result to the ears of native speakers of English is a kind of /r/. Some languages, such as Chinese and Japanese, have a single phoneme, in which the tongue contact is optional. When speakers of these languages speak English, they appear to mix up /l/ and /r/, as in the shibboleths of Chinese English *velly solly* (very sorry) and Japanese English *I rub you* (I love you). Many personal-name diminutives in English have *l* rather than *r*, as with *Hal* for *Harry*, *Del* for *Derek*, and *Tel* for *Terry*. See CONSONANT, L, LATERAL, LIQUID, R-SOUNDS, SOMERSET, SPEECH.

**LYLY, John** [*c.*1554–1606]. English writer and Member of Parliament, born in Kent, and educated at Oxford and Cambridge. Known as 'the Euphuist', he was one of the first prose stylists to leave a lasting mark on the language. He wrote the two-part romance *Euphues, or the Anatomie of Wit* (1578) and *Euphues and his England* (1580), an early epistolary 'novel' with comments on religion, love, and style. His 'new English' favoured an ornate, classical style widely admired during the Renaissance and known to this day as *euphuism*.

# M

[Called 'em']. The 13th LETTER of the Roman ALPHABET as used for English. It originated in the Phoenician symbol *mem*, a zigzag line probably representing water (the word for which began with that letter: compare HEBREW *mayim* water). It was adapted by the Greeks as *mu* (M) and adopted with the same sound value by the Etruscans and the Romans.

**Sound value**. The sound represented by *m* is normally a voiced bilabial nasal, but before /f/ the closure may be labio-dental rather than bilabial (*comfort*), and before /b, p/ an *n* may be pronounced /m/: *none better* ('numbetter'), *input* ('imput'). Assimilation of this kind helped turn the late MIDDLE ENGLISH phrase *in kenebowe* ('in keen bow', that is, in a sharp curve) into present-day *akimbo*.

**Double *M***. (1) Final *m* is normally single in monosyllabic words: *am, aim, tame, rim, time, home, some, room, gum, fume, rhyme*. A suffix beginning with a vowel prompts *mm* after a short vowel (*jammed, brimming, drummer*), unless a silent consonant or final *e* in the base word intervenes (*thumbed, coming, damning*: contrast *damming*). (2) Medial *mm* normally signifies a preceding short vowel (contrast *comma/coma*), and also occurs in assimilations of Latin prefixes ending in *n*: *immaterial* (not \*inmaterial). Similarly, Greek *syn-* produces *mm* in *symmetry*. (3) *M*-doubling is inconsistent after short vowels, as shown by the pairs *camel/mammal, image/scrimmage, lemon/lemming*, prompting such common consequent misspellings as \*accomodate, \*ommit.

**Syllabic *M***. The letter *m* can function syllabically, as in *rhythm, chasm*.

**Silent *M***. The *m* is silent in initial Greek-derived *mn-* (*mnemonic, Mnemosyne*), but is pronounced after a prefix (*amnesia*). See B.

**MACAULAY, T(homas) B(abington)** [1800–59]. British essayist, critic, poet, and historian, born in Rothley Temple, Leicestershire, son of the Presbyterian philanthropist Zachary Macaulay, who hailed from the Hebrides, had been governor of Sierra Leone, and opposed slavery. His mother was a Quaker and the daughter of a Bristol book-seller. Macaulay was educated at a private school and Trinity College Cambridge. In 1830, he became Whig Member of Parliament for Calne in Wiltshire and helped pass the Reform Act of 1832. He became a member, then secretary, of the Board of Control that oversaw the work of the East India Company in India, and in 1834 went there to serve on the new Supreme Council of India. He played a part in the slow transfer of government from Company to Crown, and supported both freedom of the press and the equality of Indians and Europeans before the law. He set up a national system of education and in 1835 wrote the Minute that made English the subcontinent's future language of education: see INDIAN ENGLISH, CHURCHILL, PROSE.

**McDAVID, Raven I(oor), Jr** [1911–84]. American DIALECT geographer, born in Greenville, South Carolina, and educated at Furman U., completing a Ph.D. on Milton at Duke U. in 1935. McDavid came to an early appreciation of speech varieties and cultural STEREOTYPES when he found 'speech correctionists' from outside his native region eager to alter his locally standard dialect. In 1937, he attended a summer school at the U. of Michigan where Bernard Bloch, a fieldworker for the *Linguistic Atlas of New England*, taught linguistic geography and selected him as an informant for the course. The excitement of dialect study that summer shaped his subsequent career. During World War II, along with other linguists he prepared language materials to assist in the war effort; his tasks included studies of Burmese and pedagogical tools to assist Italians learning English. In 1945, McDavid turned full-time to fieldwork for the *Linguistic Atlas of the Middle and South Atlantic States* (*LAMSAS*) under the general direction of Hans Kurath. He conducted several hundred field interviews recorded in precise phonetic transcription, not only in the South Atlantic region, but later in the

Middle Atlantic and North Central States as well. McDavid joined the U. of Chicago in 1957 where he remained until retirement and beyond. When Kurath retired from active management of the *Linguistic Atlas* projects, McDavid became his successor. Editing *LAMSAS* and the *Linguistic Atlas of the North Central States* began under his direction and is continued today by his successors. With Kurath, he was co-author of the first comprehensive work drawing on *Atlas* files: *The Pronunciation of English in the Atlantic States* (1961). His abridgement and updating of MENCKEN'S *AMERICAN LANGUAGE* (1963) renewed the popularity of that book. His many essays were revised and collected in two volumes: *Dialects in Culture* (1979) and *Varieties of American English* (1980). See AMERICAN ENGLISH, GENERAL AMERICAN, SOUTHERN ENGLISH.

**MacDIARMID, Hugh**, pen name of *Christopher Murray Grieve* [1892–1978]. Scottish poet, critic, and polemicist, leader of the LALLANS movement. Born and educated in Langholm, a Border town whose dialect and traditions contributed to the striking individuality of his poetic style, Grieve was a founder (1928) of the National Party of Scotland (expelled 1933) and a member of the Communist Party (expelled 1938, rejoined 1956). Although passionately committed to Scottish cultural and political nationalism, he was at first unconvinced of the viability of SCOTS for 20c poetry. His discovery of the extent and expressiveness of Scots vocabulary, however, particularly as recorded in Jamieson's *Etymological Dictionary of the Scottish Language* (1808), prompted him to experiment with a Synthetic Scots, first for short lyrics, then for extended metaphysical poem-sequences (most importantly *A Drunk Man Looks at the Thistle*, 1926) showing a linguistic virtuosity and a spirit of philosophical exploration not attempted in Scots poetry since medieval times. His success in revitalizing poetry in the language has been marked.

**MACHINE-READABLE**. A term in COMPUTING meaning 'in a form that can be accepted by a machine, and particularly a computer'. Traditionally, this has meant that a TEXT is coded for electronic use, keyed into a computer, and stored on a laser disk or a magnetic tape, as for example when a paper DICTIONARY is converted to machine-readable form; currently, however, text on paper, either printed or typewritten, can be regarded as machine-readable if it can be processed ('scanned') on to a laser disk by an OCR (optical-character recognition) system (an optical scanner). In addition, because of developments in PRINTING and publishing, dictionaries and other works now generally are prepared directly on computer, so that machine-readable forms of books and other documents exist before any paper product is produced. With a machine-readable text, CONCORDANCES can be quickly produced, showing each occurrence of every word in context. The Oxford Text Archive serves as an international co-ordinating point for the effort to accumulate material in machine-readable form.

**MACRON**, also less formally **stroke**, **bar**. A traditional DIACRITIC in the form of a horizontal bar over a VOWEL letter (¯), to show that it is long (as in some renderings of LATIN and MAORI words). From its use in classical scansion to indicate a long syllable, it has come to indicate in English scansion that the syllable in which it occurs is stressed (contrasting with the *BREVE*). Similarly, the macron has been used over vowel symbols in the RESPELLING systems of English dictionaries and in teaching grammars to mark traditional 'long' vowels, which include diphthongs. See LENGTH MARK.

**MAIN CLAUSE**, also **principal clause**. A CLAUSE in a SENTENCE to which other clauses are subordinated, and which is not itself a subordinate clause. In a simple sentence, the main clause is the entire sentence. In a compound sentence, there is more than one main clause. Complex sentences contain a main clause and one or more subordinate clauses.

**MAJUSCULE AND MINUSCULE**. See CAPITAL, LETTER.

**MALAPROPISM** [Named after *Mrs Malaprop*, a character in Richard Sheridan's play *The Rivals* (1775), from the French *mal à propos* inappropriate]. An error in which a similar-sounding word is substituted for the intended one, a characteristic of the fictional Mrs Malaprop, who produced such errors as 'pineapple' for *pinnacle* ('He is the very pineapple of politeness!'), 'interceded' for *intercepted* ('I have interceded another letter from the fellow!'). See CONFUSIBLE, ELOCUTION, SLIP OF THE TONGUE.

**MALAWI**. A country of East Africa and member of the COMMONWEALTH. Languages: Chichewa, English (both official), and indigenous. The first European contact was in 1859, by the Scottish missionary David Livingstone. In 1878, the *African Lakes Company* was established; in 1883, Britain appointed a consul to the Kings and Chiefs of Central Africa; the territory became the British protectorate of *Nyasaland*, which became independent in 1964 as Malawi. English is the principal LINK LANGUAGE and the language of education from the fourth year of school, and is used in the media. See EAST AFRICAN ENGLISH.

**MALAYSIAN ENGLISH**. The English language in Malaysia, a country of South-East Asia, a member of the COMMONWEALTH and ASEAN. The name *Anglo-Malay* has been used to describe the variety that emerged during colonial times among expatriates and a local élite, serving as the vehicle through which such words as *compound/kampong*, *durian*, *orang utan*, and *sarong* have passed into GENERAL ENGLISH. Some English-medium schools were established in the 19c (in Penang in 1816, Singapore 1823, Malacca 1826, and Kuala Lumpur 1894), at the same time as Malay, Chinese, and Tamil schools were encouraged. Those members of the various ethnic groups who were educated in the English-medium schools came to use English increasingly in their occupations and their daily life; the 1957 census reported 400,000 people (some 6% of the population) as claiming to be literate in the language. When the British began to withdraw in the late 1950s, English had become the dominant language of the non-European élite, and with independence became with Malay the 'alternate official language'. However, the National Language Act of 1967 established Malay (renamed *Bahasa Malaysia* in 1963) as the sole official language, with some exceptions in such areas as medicine, banking, and business. Among Malaysians, the term *Malaysian English* tends to refer to a more or less controversial variety that centres on the colloquialisms of those educated at the English-medium schools. Its essence is distilled in the cartoons of K. H. Boon in the *Malaysian Post*: 'My-

self so thin don't eat, can die one, you know?'

English-medium education expanded after independence; there were close to 400,000 students in such schools when, in 1969, the Ministry of Education decided that all English-medium schools would become Malay-medium. By the early 1980s, the process through which Bahasa Malaysia has become the national language of education was virtually complete, but the shift prompted widespread concern that general proficiency in English would decline. To prevent this, English has been retained as the compulsory second language in primary and secondary schools. Some 20% of the present population (*c.*3.4m) understands English and some 25% of city dwellers use it for some purposes in everyday life. It is widely used in the media and as a reading language in higher education. There are seven English-language daily newspapers (combined circulation over 500,000) and three newspapers in Sabah published partly in English (circulation over 60,000). English is essentially an urban middle-class language, virtually all its users are bilingual, and CODE-SWITCHING is commonplace.

**Features**. (1) Malaysian English and SINGAPORE ENGLISH have much in common, with the main exception that English in Malaysia is more subject to influence from Malay. (2) Pronunciation is marked by: a strong tendency to syllable-timed rhythm, and a simplification of word-final consonant clusters, as in /lɪv/ for *lived*. (3) Syntactic characteristics include: the countable use of some usually uncountable nouns (*Pick up your chalks; A consideration for others is important*); innovations in phrasal verbs (such as *cope up* rather than *cope with*); the use of reflexive pronouns to form emphatic pronouns (*Myself sick* I am sick; *Himself funny* He is funny); and the multi-purpose particle *lah*, a token especially of informal intimacy (*Sorry, can't come lah*). (4) Local vocabulary includes: such borrowings from Malay as *bumiputera* (originally SANSKRIT, son of the soil) a Malay or other indigenous person, *dadah* illegal drugs, *rakyat* the people, citizens, *Majlis* (from ARABIC) Parliament, *makan* food; such special usages as *banana leaf restaurant* a South Indian restaurant where food is served on banana leaves, *chop* a rubber stamp or seal, *crocodile* a womanizer, *girlie barber shop* a hairdressing salon that doubles as a massage parlour or brothel, *sensitive issues* (as defined in the Constitution) issues that must not be raised in public, such as the status of the various languages used in Malaysia and the rights and privileges of the different communities; such colloquialisms as *bes* (from *best*) great, fantastic, *relac* (from *relax*) take it easy; and such hybrids as *bumiputera status* indigenous status, and *dadah addict* drug addict. See SOUTH-EAST ASIAN ENGLISH.

**MALDIVES, The**, also **the Maldive Islands**. A country of 19 atoll clusters in South Asia, and member of the Commonwealth. Languages: Divehi (official), also called Maldivian, related to Sinhala and with a script derived from ARABIC, and English, widely used in government and tourism. The Maldive sultanate was a British protectorate. See SOUTH ASIAN ENGLISH.

**MALTA**. A Mediterranean island nation and member of the COMMONWEALTH. Languages: Maltese/Malti, English (both official, English the medium of education), and Italian. Maltese, a variety of ARABIC with elements of several other Mediterranean languages, is the only Semitic language written in the Roman alphabet and used for official purposes in Europe. Malta was a Sicilian dependency from the late 11c and was controlled by the Knights of St John from 1530. It was a French colony from 1798 and a British colony from 1802, becoming self-governing in 1921, then an independent monarchy (with the Queen as head of state) in 1964, and a republic in 1974, the last British troops being withdrawn in 1979. The use of English is widespread, especially in the cities.

**MAORI**. The name of the indigenous people (*tangata whenua*) of New Zealand and their language. Maori is spoken by about one-third of the approximately 300,000 Maori population. With such other languages as HAWAIIAN, Samoan, and Tongan, it is a member of the Polynesian branch of the Malayo-Polynesian language family.

**Pronunciation**. The Maori pronunciation of *Maori* has a long *a* /ˈmaːɔri/, a usage which is fairly common in NEW ZEALAND ENGLISH alongside the traditional Anglicized /ˈmauri/. No single DIALECT has emerged as the basis for a STANDARD form of Maori.

Tribal variation in pronunciation is shown in such pairs as *inanga/inaka* (a kind of fish), *mingimingi/mikimiki* (an evergreen shrub), and the place-name *Waitangi/Waitaki*. In each of these cases, /ŋ/ is a North Island equivalent of a South Island /k/. In words conventionally spelt with *wh* (*whare, kowhai*), some tribes use a sound approximating to /f/, others a sound approximating to /hw/. Maori has the consonants /p, t, k, m, n, ŋ, f, h, r, w/ and the five vowels /i, ɛ, a, ɔ, u/, which can be either long or short. It also permits a maximum of one consonant sound before any vowel. Consequently, LOANWORDS from English may undergo considerable change: *sheep* to *hipi, Bible* to *paipera, London* to *Ranana*. The written consonant cluster *ng* is pronounced /ŋ/, as in *sing*, whether initial or medial. Maori *r* in many words corresponds to Hawaiian and Samoan *l*: *aroha*, Hawaiian *aloha* love; *whare*, Samoan *fale* house.

**Writing**. The language was unwritten before the arrival in the early 19c of British missionaries, who, in creating a written form for the language, did not always successfully equate its phonemes with the nearest equivalents in English. A major feature of their work was the decision that vowel length in Maori did not need to be reflected in spelling (although DIACRITICAL MARKS have since been optional). Some present-day scholars of Maori have adopted a system of doubling long vowels: *Maaori* instead of *Maori* or *Māori*; *kaakaa* instead of *kaka* or *kākā* (parrot); *kaakaapoo* instead of *kakapo* or *kākāpō*. However, since most printing of the language shows the older conventions, it seems likely that the missionaries' style will prevail.

**Influence on English**. All Maoris speak English, but few Pakehas (white New Zealanders) and a diminishing number of Maoris speak Maori with any fluency, although attempts are now being made to give greater prominence to Maori language and culture. From the beginning, European settlers adopted Maori names for physical features and tribal settlements, but such names came to be pronounced with varying degrees of adaptation. Thus, the place-name *Paekakariki*, pronounced /paɛˈkakariki/ by the Maoris, was Anglicized to /ˌpaɪkɒkəˈriːkiː/ and frequently reduced to the disyllabic /ˈpaɪkɒk/. The place-name *Whangarei* /ˈfaŋarei/ was Anglicized to

/'wʊŋə'rei/. Most of the Maori names for the distinctive flora (*kowhai, nikau, pohutukawa, rimu, totara*) and fauna (*kiwi, takahe, tuatara, weta*) were also adopted and varyingly adapted into NZE. The issue of how far English-speakers should attempt to adopt native Maori pronunciations of such words has, for many years, been a major point of linguistic discussion in New Zealand. Broadcasting now attempts, not always successfully, to use a Maori pronunciation at all times.

**Status**. In the later 19c and early 20c, the use of Maori was officially discouraged in schools. Many Maoris concurred with this policy, seeing English as the language which was likely to give their children the greater advantage in later life. In more recent times, there has been a resurgence in the use of Maori as a marker of ethnic and cultural identity. *Language nests* or *kohanga reo* have been established for pre-school children, and many Maori people aim at bilingualism. Although Maori has now been recognized as an official language in the courts, it is still too early to say what effect this growing recognition of Maori will have in the long term.

**MAORI ENGLISH**. A widely used term for a variety of NEW ZEALAND ENGLISH. Its features, however, remain poorly defined and to the extent that the variety is neither spoken by all Maoris nor exclusively by Maoris the label is misleading. It is spoken by Pakehas (whites) in areas where there are many Maoris or as a means of showing solidarity with them. MAORI English is primarily identifiable through voice quality and a greater tendency towards syllable timing than is normal in Pakeha English (the usage of white New Zealanders). Certain vowel qualities appear to differ from those in standard NZE, but reliable descriptions are not yet available. In a survey of Maori schoolchildren by Richard A. Benton in 1963–4, it was found that they sometimes made no distinction between /ð/ and /d/, /θ/ and /t/, /s/ and /z/, /k/ and /g/, that /t/ and /d/ were sometimes interchanged, and that /ŋ/ was replaced by /n/. The use of the high-rise terminal intonation pattern for statements was also commented on. It is not clear to what extent these are maturational 'problems' and, if not, to what extent they also beset Pakehas. The high-rise terminal is today widespread among Pakehas, including the middle class, and variation between /ŋ/ and /n/ is a notorious shibboleth throughout the English-speaking world.

Similar problems arise in interpreting data on the grammar of Maori English. The above study mentions constructions such as *I went down the henhouse, Me and Bill went there, He learned me to do it,* all common non-standard forms in English elsewhere. It also mentions constructions that may be more representative of Maori English: *I went by my Auntie's; Who's your name?; To me, the ball.* Recent research shows some grammatical differences between Maori and Pakeha speakers, such as the omission of *have* before some past participles and before *got to.* The use of the tag question *eh?* is stereotypical, but also occurs in other varieties of NZE and elsewhere. Typical vocabulary items include both Maori and non-Maori words: *kai* food, *fellers* /'fʌləz/ people, males (often in the vocative *you fellers*). There is another variety, mainly written and not usually called *Maori English,* in which far more Maori vocabulary is used. In it, the elements are neither italicized nor glossed: 'This indeed may be the nub from which this book gains perspective—that even after 145 years of Pakeha terms of reference, ka tu tonu the Maori. And so they should remain as yet to be consulted tangata whenua. Whether this book bears fruit will depend on a response to the kaupapa laid down on marae throughout Aotearoa at the feet of the manuhiri' (Philip Whaanga, *New Zealand Listener,* 5 Apr. 1986). The average Pakeha New Zealander will not understand enough Maori to know precisely what is being said here. It is not clear whether the variety reflects CODE-SWITCHING in Maori speech or is a literary style that may provide a model for spoken usage. In either case, it seems to be a new development and may mean that a more prestigious kind of Maori English will soon emerge. See DIALECT (NEW ZEALAND).

**MARITIME PIDGIN**, also **Nautical Jargon**. A trade JARGON widely used by sailors, many of whom were multilingual, on European vessels from the 17c. Some scholars argue that it was passed on to others with whom the sailors came into contact, providing the origin of the European-based PIDGINS and CREOLES. Evidence can be found in the fact that most pidgins and creoles have a nautical element, though that should not be surprising since many of these languages are spoken in maritime areas. Not much support can be found for the so-called *nautical jargon theory* of the origin of pidgins, but the role of sailors in spreading linguistic features across vast areas accounts for some lexical similarities among such widely separated pidgins as *Hawaii Pidgin English*, *Chinook Jargon*, and *Eskimo Jargon*: for example, *kanaka* [Hawaiian: person, man] in Chinook Jargon and the English and French-based Pacific pidgins, and *kaukau* [from Chinese Pidgin English *chowchow*] in Eskimo Jargon and Hawaii Pidgin English.

**MARITIME PROVINCES, The**, also **the Maritimes**. The Atlantic provinces of mainland Canada: New Brunswick, Nova Scotia (which includes Cape Breton Island), and Prince Edward Island. When Newfoundland is added, the collective term is *the Atlantic Provinces*. The regional accents of the Maritimes have features in common with Newfoundland and differ considerably from usage to the west; the urban accents of Fredericton, Halifax, and other centres of population are similar to inland urban CanE. The territory is roughly the region called *Acadian* by the French. It was also claimed by the English and settled by both in the 17c, changing hands several times until 1713, when it was ceded to Britain. A complex settlement history explains its variety of rural dialects, some of which were influenced by Acadian FRENCH, some by GERMAN (in Lunenburg County, Nova Scotia, settled in 1753), some by GAELIC (Cape Breton, settled 1802–28 by 25,000 Highlanders during the Clearances in Scotland), as well as various dialects of England. In 1783, the arrival of Loyalists after the American War of Independence almost tripled the English-speaking population.

The main differences between standard Canadian and the Maritimes appear to arise from the earlier settlement of the Maritimes (from 1713) than Ontario (from 1783), but it has also been suggested that they arise from the localities from which the Loyalists migrated. Most of the new arrivals in the Maritimes were from New England, while those moving into central Canada were primarily from further west and were the first settlers there. A well-known SHIBBOLETH of pronunciation is mentioned by a character in Margaret Atwood's *Lady Oracle* (1977): 'Being from the Maritimes, he said *ahnt* ... whereas I was from Ontario and said *ant*' (for *aunt*). Regional grammar includes the use of *some*, *right*, *real* as intensifiers: *It's some hot*; *It's right hot*; *It's real hot*. Regional vocabulary shares some terms with Newfoundland and some with New England, and includes: *banking* the storing of illegally trapped lobsters until the season opens; *bogan* a backwater; *make*, *make cod*, *make fish* to dry fish or cod; *malpeque* a famous oyster, from Malpeque Bay, Prince Edward Island; *tern* a three-masted schooner. See DIALECT (CANADA).

**MARKED AND UNMARKED TERMS** [Originating in the work of the Russian linguist Nikolay Trubetzkoy (1890–1938) in relation to pairs of phonemes]. Terms in LINGUISTICS which designate a contrasting pair, one possessing a special 'mark', the other neutral: in *play/played*, *play* is unmarked and neutral, and *played* has the mark *-ed*. Similarly, *host* is unmarked, but *hostess* is morphologically marked for femaleness. The mark is not necessarily visible or audible: in the pair *horse/mare*, *horse* is the more general, unmarked term, while *mare* is marked for femaleness. In the pair *cow/bull*, *cow* is unmarked, while *bull* is marked for maleness. The terms are sometimes extended to wider, typological characteristics of languages, and also to social situations, to distinguish between normal (unmarked) behaviour and a less common variant.

**MASCULINE**. A term relating to grammatical GENDER in nouns and related words, contrasting with *FEMININE* (as in FRENCH) and feminine and *neuter* (as in GERMAN and LATIN). Words denoting male people and animals in such languages are usually masculine, but grammatical gender is not about sex: in French *le courage du soldat*, the courage is as masculine as the soldier. In English, the term is confined to personal pronouns (*he/him/himself/his*) and some nouns (such as *drake* in contrast with *duck*).

**MASS NOUN**. See COUNTABLE AND UNCOUNTABLE.

**MAURITIUS**. An Indian Ocean country and member of the COMMONWEALTH. Languages: English (official), a FRENCH-based CREOLE called Morisiê, French, HINDI, URDU, and Hakka Chinese. A French colony from 1715 and a British colony from 1810, Mauritius gained independence in 1968. The Creole minority is descended from African slaves and French settlers, the Indo-Mauritian majority from indentured labourers brought to the islands by the British after the abolition of slavery in 1833. The mixture of influences is noticeable in place-names, such as the districts of *Rivière du Rempart*, *Pamplemousses*, *Flacq*, *Moka*, *Black River*, *Plaines Wilhems*, *Grand Port*, *Savanne*. Local newspapers print articles in English and French side by side.

**MEANING. 1.** The purport or message conveyed by WORDS, PHRASES, SENTENCES, SIGNS, SYMBOLS, and the like: *'Semantics' means 'the study of meaning'*; *A red traffic light means drivers have to stop and a green one means they can go.* **2.** Signification, sense, interpretation, as in *The Meaning of Meaning*, the title of a book on SEMANTICS by C. K. Ogden & I. A. Richards (1923); any instance of these, as in *What is the meaning of the word 'semantics'*? **3.** What a speaker or writer intends: *What do you mean?*; *They don't mean any harm.* See LANGUAGE, SEMIOTICS.

**MEDIA** [Coined in the 1920s, as a shortening of mass media]. A collective term for newspapers, broadcasting, and other vehicles of widespread communication and entertainment, often used attributively in such phrases as *Media Studies* and *media education*. In the later 20c, the usage has been increasingly detached from its singular form *medium*, and often therefore takes a singular verb (as in 'someone the media is interested in these days'). In this, the term resembles *data*, whose sense and intent are now collective rather than plural. The traditional information media are speech, writing, and print ('Cogitations [are] expressed by the Medium of Words', Francis Bacon, *Advancement of Learning*, volume 2, 1605), but since the later 19c systems of electrical and electronic communication have increasingly done more than simply convey information from person to person: they inform and entertain huge audiences, now often in their hundreds of millions worldwide. Although the televisual media have now in 'mass' terms superseded the print media, such electronic media as the INTERNET are vastly extending and adapting print and blending it with visual and vocal material.

Following the spread of television as a news medium, the Canadian communication theorist Marshall McLuhan expressed in the 1960s a radical view of society as shaped more by the style and nature than the content of the media (hence his comment 'the medium is the message'). It is currently widely agreed that the media are not neutral, impassive agencies that transmit news and views, but are themselves influential selectors, shapers, manufacturers, and even on occasion fabricators of news and views.

**MEIOSIS** [Stress: 'my-OH-sis']. In RHETORIC, a kind of understatement that dismisses or belittles, especially by using terms that make something seem less significant than it really is or ought to be: for example, calling a serious wound a *scratch*, or a journalist a *hack* or a *scribbler*. Compare LITOTES.

**MELANESIAN PIDGIN ENGLISH**, also **Melanesian Pidgin**. The name commonly given to three varieties of PIDGIN spoken in the Melanesian states of Papua New Guinea (*TOK PISIN*), Solomon Islands (*Pijin*), and Vanuatu (*BISLAMA*). Although there is a degree of mutual intelligibility among them, the term is used by linguists to recognize a common historical development and is not recognized by speakers of these languages. The development of Melanesian Pidgin English has been significantly different in the three countries. This is due to differences in the SUBSTRATE languages, the presence of European languages other than English, and differences in colonial policy. In Papua New Guinea, there was a period of German administration (1884–1914) before the British and Australians took over. The people of Vanuatu were in constant contact with the French government and planters during a century of colonial rule (1880–1980) and for a time there was a condominium rule by the British and French; contact with French has continued after independence in 1980. However, Solomon Islanders have not been in contact with any European language other than English.

**MELIORATION**, also **amelioration**. A process of SEMANTIC CHANGE in which there is an improvement or 'upward' shift in the meaning of a word: for example, *nice* has meant foolish, stupid (13–16c), lascivious, loose (14–16c), extravagant, elegant, rare, strange (15–16c), effeminate, shy, tender, slender, delicate, unimportant (16–17c), over-refined (17–18c), careful, precise, intricate, difficult, fastidious (16–19c), dainty, appetizing (18–19c), refined, cultured, discriminating (17–20c), and agreeable, pleasant (18–20c). See PEJORATION.

**MENCKEN, H(enry) L(ouis)** [1880–1956]. American journalist and social critic, born in Baltimore, Maryland, and educated at a local private school and the Baltimore Polytechnic. He is remembered chiefly for his monumental work *The AMERICAN LANGUAGE* (*AL*, 1919), which was instrumental in establishing the scholarly study of English in the US. A lifelong resident of Baltimore, Mencken began writing for the city's newspapers in 1899 and continued doing so for most of his career. He was an iconoclast, noted for cynically witty essays in literary, social, and political criticism. Among his favourite targets were religion, the cultural barrenness of the American South, the motives of politicians, and an English cultural tradition in America that he identified as puritanism.

Mencken was an autodidact whose interest in language led him to read widely and to collect citations of all aspects of AMERICAN ENGLISH. His goal was to make the study of language accessible to the general reader. The 1st edition of *AL* claimed that Americans spoke a separate language of their own making that they could take pride in, not an imperfect imitation of the language of England. The language that he described as *American* was full of regional variation, new words borrowed from immigrant groups, figurative usage from such institutions as railroading and baseball, jaunty slang, and raucous vulgarisms. Americans in the era following World War I found in *AL* verification of their cultural independence as the US became an international power.

Incorporating new information from both scholars and general readers, Mencken brought out revised and enlarged editions of *AL* in 1921 and 1923. In 1925, he was instrumental in founding the journal *American Speech*, which he hoped would be sold at corner news-stands. Though the journal never attained such popularity, Mencken's publications and his personal encouragement influenced a number of scholars to turn their attention to the study of the English language in America. The 4th edition of *AL* (1936), along with two supplements (1945, 1948), is an unrivalled compendium of information about English in the US and its historical development before the mid-century. In later editions, Mencken abandoned his earlier thesis that BrE and AmE were developing as separate languages in favour of the view that they were merging, but with American as the dominant partner. See AMERICANISM, AMERICAN LANGUAGE, EDUCATED ENGLISH, GENERAL AMERICAN.

**MESOLECT**. The variety of language in a POST-CREOLE CONTINUUM intermediate between *BASILECT* and *ACROLECT*, often retaining semantic and syntactic features not found in the acrolect and tending to vary from speaker to speaker, such as between standard Jamaican English and Jamaican Creole. See DIALECT, LECT.

**METANALYSIS**. A technical term for a change in the way the elements in a WORD, PHRASE or SENTENCE are interpreted and used, such as: Middle English *a naddre* reinterpreted as *an addre* (Modern *an adder*); Perso-Arabic *nāranj* becoming Old Provençal *auranja* then French and English *orange*, the /n/ being attracted to the article in both languages (but retained in Spanish *una naranja*).

**METAPHOR**. In RHETORIC, a figure with two senses, both originating with Aristotle in the 4c BC: (1) All FIGURES OF SPEECH that achieve their effect through association, comparison, and resemblance. Figures like *ANTITHESIS, HYPERBOLE, METONYMY, SIMILE* are all species of metaphor. Although this sense is not current, it lies behind the use of *metaphorical* and *figurative* as ANTONYMS of *literal*. (2) A figure of speech which concisely compares two things by saying that one is the other. A warrior compared to a lion becomes a lion: *Achilles was a lion in the fight*. In such usages, the perception of something held in common brings together words and images from different fields: warriors and lions share bravery and strength, and so the warrior is a lion among men and the lion is a warrior among beasts.

**Description**. When introducing students to the idea of metaphor, teachers have generally adopted the approach of the Roman rhetorician Quintilian (1c AD), using the simpler figure simile (*He fought like a lion*) as a way in to the more complex metaphor (*He* *was a lion in the fight*). A typical definition on this principle is: 'A metaphor is like a simile condensed. In a simile the comparison is explicitly stated with the help of some such word as *like* or *as*, whilst in a metaphor the comparison is implied by an identification of the two things compared' (Ronald Ridout & Clifford Witting, *The Facts of English*, 1964). Such descriptions have helped generations of students recognize metaphors, but do not comment on the creative process at work. Aristotle provided a formula for creating metaphors which pointed to something inherent in all kinds of comparison. He proposed a ratio (*análogon*) of the type *A is to B*, as *X is to Y*, exemplified as *Life is to old age, as day is to evening*. This ratio demonstrated that *life* and *day* can come together because of a third shared factor, *time*. He then switched the second terms to get *A is to Y*, as *X is to B*, producing: *Life is to evening, as day is to old age*. Such a cross-over creates such phrases as *the evening of life* and *day's old age* (*Poetics*, 31. 11). Here, terms from distinct contexts are first aligned, then spliced, demonstrating the close relationship between metaphor and ANALOGY. In 1936, the English critic I. A. Richards provided labels for the three aspects of metaphor implied by Aristotle: the original context or idea is the *tenor* of the metaphor, the borrowed idea is the *vehicle*, and the shared element the *ground*. In Aristotle's example, *life* is the tenor, *day* the vehicle, *time* the ground. Commentators, however, are not usually precise about where the metaphor proper resides: it is sometimes defined as the vehicle alone, sometimes as the combination of tenor and vehicle, and sometimes as tenor, vehicle, and ground together.

Metaphor is often used in naming and in extending the senses of words. Its capacity to name was exemplified in the US in 1966, when a group of black activists adopted the name *Black Panther*. At about the same time, people who disliked the police began calling them pigs. As a result, the sentence *Black Panthers hate pigs* could occur and be suitably interpreted in a context far removed from 'real' black panthers and pigs. In George ORWELL'S *Animal Farm* (1945), pigs stand for Communist Party members, dogs for the police, and humans for the Russian *ancien régime*. Because of the meanings given to *pig* and *man*, the story's close is particularly potent as a comment on the fate of revolutions:

Twelve voices were shouting in anger, and they were all alike. No question, now, what had happened to the faces of the pigs. The creatures outside looked from pig to man, and from man to pig, and from pig to man again; but already it was impossible to say which was which.

**Extended metaphors**. Orwell's tale is an ALLEGORY, based on the *master metaphor* 'farm is to state as animals are to citizens', and its plot runs parallel to real life. The result of its use throughout a text is an *extended metaphor*, a device which can operate at many levels of speech and writing. The same imagery may run through a text, as a writer develops an analogy between the topic of immediate interest and another topic considered relevant and informative:

The architect delivers a number of completely impersonal plan drawings and typewritten specifications. They must be so unequivocal that there will be no doubt about the construction. He composes the music which others will play. Furthermore, in order to understand architecture fully, it must be remembered that the people who play it are not sensitive musicians interpreting another's score. . . . On the contrary, they are a multitude of ordinary people (S. E. Rasmussen, *Experiencing Architecture*, 1959).

Here, the writer splices architecture and music, so that tenor and vehicle run together through the whole paragraph.

**Metaphoric networks**. In addition to this extension of a theme through a single discourse, networks of metaphor criss-cross language at large, especially in the form of IDIOMS and sayings. In PROVERBS, similar advice may be proffered through different images: *A stitch in time saves nine, Look before you leap, Don't count your chickens before they're hatched, Don't cross your bridges before you come to them*. Idioms all drawn from the same source may reflect a significant element in a society and culture: for example BrE cricketing expressions, used to talk about arguments, contests, and life itself. A politician might *go in to bat* in the House of Commons, intent on *knocking the Opposition for six*, only to be *clean-bowled*, *stumped*, or *caught out* by an opponent. If people do things *off their own bat*, they do them without help from anyone else, and if they live to be a hundred, they *knock up their century*, in which case they have had *a (jolly) good innings*. The master metaphor animating such usages can be compactly expressed as: *Life is a Game of Cricket*.

**The universality of metaphor**. Because metaphor is so pervasive in linguistic and cultural terms, it is often seen as central to thought and ordinary, non-literary language. In such speculation, the broader Aristotelian interpretation of metaphor is evoked. Language is seen as a system of SYMBOLS running parallel to reality, its purpose to blend form and meaning. All models of existence are associative make-believe: 'Existence is *like* X or Y', 'It is *as if* there were a Heavenly Father', or as T. R. Wright has put it: 'If narrative is the way we construct our sense of identity, metaphor is how we think, especially in areas in which we need to build our knowledge of the unknown by comparison with the known' (*Theology and Literature*, 1988). He adds that theology 'has always been irredeemably riddled with metaphor'. The Christian Gospels 'make Jesus repeatedly risk and often suffer the misunderstanding of the literal-minded', so that in Matthew (16: 6–7) the disciples say that they have no bread when Jesus warns them against accepting the leaven of the Pharisees, while in John (3: 4) Nicodemus wonders how a man can enter his mother's womb a second time so as to be 'born again'. Most religions and ideologies are imaginative in the shapes they lend reality, asserting the virtues of Image X over Picture Y or Model Z. Wright considers that it is not so important to replace one metaphor with another ('addressing God continually as Mother instead of Father, She rather than He') as to understand the processes involved in concretizing infinity and 'recognize the metaphorical status of all these terms'.

**Dead metaphors**. Whether such a status is recognized or not, metaphors and models tend to have a time of vigour, after which they may 'fade' and 'die'. Traditionally, those that have lost their force have been called *dead metaphors*; as such, they may still continue in service as CLICHÉS and *hackneyed expressions*. Many venerable metaphors have been literalized into everyday items of language: a clock has a *face* (unlike human or animal face), and on that face are *hands* (un-like biological hands); only in terms of clocks can hands be located on a face. Again, *decide* began as a metaphor, where Latin *decidere* meant *to cut through* something in order to achieve a conclusion or a solution. In their turn, *conclusion* and *solution* were once metaphorical (Latin *concludere* to shut up, and *solvere* to unfasten). The deadness of a metaphor and its status as a cliché are relative matters. Hearing for the first time that 'life is no bed of roses', someone might be quite swept away by its aptness and vigour. See FIGURATIVE LANGUAGE, MIXED METAPHOR, PERSONIFICATION.

**METATHESIS** [Stress: 'me-TA-the-sis']. The transposition of elements of language, usually two sounds and/or letters in a word: Old English *bridd* becoming Modern English *bird*, Middle English *Manisk* becoming Modern English *Manx*. Non-standard *aks* in *Don't aks me* metathesizes standard *ask*. Compare SLIP OF THE TONGUE, SPOONERISM.

**MÉTIS** [Through French from Latin *mixticius*, mixed, from *miscere/mixtum* to mix. Compare *miscegenate*], also **mixed-bloods**, and pejoratively **half-breeds**. Canadian names for individuals and communities of Amerindian and European descent (usually from European fur traders and Native women), especially those who settled in the 19c in the valleys of the Red, Assiniboine, and Saskatchewan rivers: French-speaking Roman Catholic Métis (also called *les bois brûlés*: burnt woods) and English-speaking Métis (also called *English half-breeds* or *Métis anglais*). The latter were usually descendants of Scots employed by the Hudson's Bay Company and if so were also called *Hudson Bay Scots* or *improved Scotsmen*. For some, the term *Métis* is properly restricted to the French group. The Métis have founded various political and cultural organizations, mainly to pursue land claims, often in alliance with status and non-status Indians. The Constitution Act of 1982 recognized them as an aboriginal people. PIDGIN languages spoken by the Métis were used in the fur trade, centred in the Red River Valley, now in the province of Manitoba. The best-known English-based DIALECT is *Bungee* (from Ojibwa *panki* a little), also known as the *Red River dialect*. Howard Adams has recalled: 'In all the twenty years I spent in my halfbreed home, a bed was known as a *paillasse* (*pa-jas*). Doughnuts made by Métis women were called "la bange" [French *beignet*]. . . . When I first went into mainstream society my Métis ways were ridiculed and my language of "Metchif patois", a combination of English, French, and Cree, was openly mocked' (*Prison of Grass: Canada from the Native Point of View*, 1975, p. 175). The writer Maria Campbell reported in an interview: 'We talk English, but we talk such a broken mixture of French, English, Gaelic and Cree, all mixed together' (to Doris Hills in 'You Have to Own Yourself', in *Prairie Fire*, 1988).

**METONYMY**. A FIGURE OF SPEECH which designates something by the NAME of something associated with it: *the Crown* substituting for monarchy, *the stage* for the theatre, *No. 10 Downing Street* for the British Prime Minister, *the White House* for the US President. A word used metonymically (*crown*, as above) is a *metonym*. Metonymy is closely related to and sometimes hard to distinguish from *METAPHOR*. It has sometimes been seen as a kind of *SYNECDOCHE* and sometimes as containing synecdoche. Both metaphor and metonymy express association, metaphor through comparison, metonymy through contiguity and possession. Many standard items of vocabulary are metonymic. A *red-letter day* is important, like the feast days marked in red in church calendars. The word *redcap* (a porter) originally referred to a piece of red flannel tied for visibility around the caps of baggage carriers at New York's Grand Central Station. On the level of SLANG, a *redneck* is a stereotypical member of the white rural working class in the Southern US, originally a reference to necks sunburned from working in the fields. See FIGURATIVE LANGUAGE.

■ **MIDDLE ENGLISH** ─────── ■

Short forms *ME*, *M.E.* From one point of view, the second stage of the single continuously developing ENGLISH language; from another, a distinct language that evolved from OLD ENGLISH (OE) and slowly turned into MODERN ENGLISH (ModE). ME began when the linguistic effects of the Norman Conquest were complete (*c.*1150) and came to an end at the start of the period that scholars generally call EARLY MODERN ENGLISH (*c.*1450). Three features of ME contrasted with OE: a greatly reduced system of grammatical inflections; greatly increased lexical borrowing from other languages, in particular FRENCH and LATIN; and a highly varied and volatile ORTHOGRAPHY. Surviving texts indicate that there was no uniform way of writing ME, and as a result texts are sometimes easy to read without much help, sometimes more difficult, and sometimes well-nigh impossible. The following sentence, from CHAUCER's late 14c translation of Boethius, *De Consolatione Philosophiae* (*On the Consolation of Philosophy*: opening, Book I, prose VI), is representative:

> First woltow suffre me to touche and assaye the estat of thy thought by a fewe demaundes, so that I may understonde what be the manere of thy curacioun?

Word for word in more or less modern usage, this sentence runs:

> First wilt thou suffer me to touch and try the state of thy thought by a few demands, so that I may understand what be the manner of thy curation?

In more relaxed modern usage still, it might be:

> First will you let my try the state of your thinking by asking a few questions, so that I can understand the way you cure people?

In the original sentence, many words have the same spelling (but generally not the same pronunciation) as ModE, and their meaning is often the same (*first, me, and, the, of, thy, thought, by, a, so, that, I, may, what, be*), some have a similar spelling (but not pronunciation) to present-day usage, and much the same meaning (*touche, estat, fewe, understonde, manere*), or similar spellings but rather different meanings and uses (*suffre, demaundes*), and some are variously alien at first encounter yet become less so after translation (*woltow, assaye, curacioun*). In terms of grammar, the most obvious difference between ME and strict standard ModE (as shown by means of this specimen sentence) is the loss of the second-person pronoun (*thou*, etc.) in everyday usage, though the form was present in Early ModE and continues to be widely and easily understood. Another is the loss of the subjunctive form as used in *so that I may understonde what be*. In terms of pronunciation, ME can very broadly be said to blend Germanic and Romance sound systems, words of Germanic origin being pronounced more or less with the values of Old English, words of Romance origin being pronounced more or less as in Norman French.

**Background**. As a spoken VERNACULAR, ME was continuous with OE, but as a written medium it did not have the erstwhile autonomy or prestige of OE prose and verse. Instead, it competed unequally with Latin and French through most of its history. Latin was the dominant literary and ecclesiastical language in Europe long before the Norman Conquest and well into the Renaissance, while NORMAN FRENCH became after the Conquest the primary language of the cultivated classes of England, sharing with Latin high prestige in literature and administration; the legal profession in particular was permeated by French and Latin. As a result, English, the language of a conquered people, made scant literary and official appearance in documents during the two centuries after the Conquest, and no dialect had precedence over any other. In the 14c, Chaucer's much-admired contemporary John Gower wrote his vast poem *Confessio Amantis* (*The Lover's Confession*) in English (yet with a Latin title), but also wrote long poems in Latin and French. Such multilingual expertise was normal among the writers and scholars of the day.

**Dialects**. The four great DIALECT boundaries of OE developed in ME as follows: (1) The vast Mercian dialect area divided into East Midland and West Midland. (2) Kentish became part of a wider South-Eastern dialect to the south of the River Thames. (3) West Saxon, latterly the most prestigious OE dialect, especially for literature, shrank westward to become the South-Western dialect, which entirely lacked the prominence of its OE ancestor. (4) Northumbrian divided into the Northern dialects of England and the Lowlands of Scotland. Scholars generally refer to ME north of the border as Middle SCOTS, which developed its own courtly use and literature. In addition to the growth of a separate national variety in Scotland, slowly spreading at the expense of GAELIC, ME was carried through invasion and settlement westward into Wales and Ireland. Although the city of London was close to the South-Eastern dialect, the distinctive usage of the capital towards the end of the ME period was primarily influenced from north of the Thames, by East Midland. It was the high form of this eclectic metropolitan variety that in due course became the primary source of modern standard English.

**Pronunciation and spelling**. (1) In the main, the sounds of ME were the same as those of OE, and for several lifetimes after the Norman Conquest the written language retained many of the characteristic features of OE orthography. In due course, however, script and style changed radically under the influence of NORMAN FRENCH, obscuring for later readers the continuity of the pronunciation system. Whereas OE spelling was relatively stable and regular, ME spelling varied greatly from place to place, person to person, and period to period, offering many variants for the same words: for example, OE *lēaf* (ModE *leaf*) became ME *lief, lieif, leif, lefe, leue, leeue, leaue*, etc. (2) The special OE letters ash (*æ*), wynn (*ƿ*), yogh (*ʒ*), and eth (*ð*) went out of use early in the ME period; thorn (*þ*) remained longer and appears sporadically in early 15c Chaucer manuscripts. (3) The distinctive short and long vowel pairs of OE gave way to a system in which the lax or tense state of the tongue (and not the duration of the sounds themselves) distinguished such sounds as the /ɛ/ of *vers* (verse) from the /e/ of *wep* (weep). (4) Some ME sound changes altered vowel values, resulting for example in the present-day vowel differences between singular *child, staff* (a large stick) and plural *children, staves*. (5) The OE pronunciation of the first consonant in the initial cluster *cn-* (as in *cnāwan* to know) continued for centuries, though the new spelling was *kn-*. It died out only in the later stages of ME, leaving its mark, however, in contemporary spelling, as in *know, knee, knight* (with their 'silent' fossil *k*). (6) Similarly, the voiceless velar or palatal fricative of OE (as in German *ach* and *ich*) continued in use for most of the period in England and continues to the present day in Scots. It has usually been represented in ModE by *gh*, leaving its silent fossils in such words as *dough, night, through, thought, thorough*. In Chaucer's line 'A knight ther was, and that a worthy man', *knight* (OE *cniht*) was pronounced /knɪxt/ or /knɪçt/. (7) Consonants coming between vowels were increasingly elided, with the result that many OE disyllables have been reduced to ModE monosyllables: for example, earlier OE *hlāfweard* ('loaf-ward') became later OE/early ME *hlāford* and *laford*, then 13c *louerd*, and 15c *lord*; OE *fuʒel* (bird) developed into 12c *vuhel*, 13c *fuwel*, 14c *fouxl* and *foul* (etc.), becoming 16c *fowle*, *foule* (etc.), and ModE *fowl*. (8) The voiced values /v/ and /z/ of the OE letters *f* and *s* became distinctive sounds in their own right, distinguished *fat* from *vat* and *seal* from *zeal*.

**Grammar**. (1) While the sound system of ME was relatively unchanged from OE, the inflectional system was greatly reduced, possibly because of close, long-term contacts between native OE speakers and first Danish- then French-speaking settlers. (2) The main classes of verb inflection survived, but the distinction in STRONG VERBS between the singular and the plural of the past was on its way out in Chaucer's day: for example, for the verb *bind* (from OE *bindan* to bind), he had the past singular *bond* (from OE *band*) and past plural *bounde* (from OE *bundon*), but *bond* was soon to vanish as ModE *bound* took over both the singular and plural. (3) The occasional surviving inflectional suffixes for the plural and the infinitive in Chaucer's day likewise soon disappeared, and the four-case OE inflections for the noun were reduced to two (common and possessive) as in ModE. (4) The OE function words (pronouns and articles, conjunctions, prepositions, and auxiliary verbs) remained in ME and largely survive to the present day.

**Vocabulary**. (1) By and large, the everyday vocabulary of OE has survived into ME and ModE, as in the following sets, with OE first, then typical ME, then ModE: *bricg*, *bregge*, bridge; *fæstnian*, *festen*, *fasten*; *īegland*, *eland*, *island*; *langung*, *longinge*, *longing*; *nīwe*, *newe*, *new*; *strang*, *stronge*, *strong*. (2) As a result of the Norman Conquest and the great social and political changes that came in its wake, many OE words fell entirely out of use, often being supplanted by words of French provenance: for example, *eftsīð* was replaced by *retorn*, *retorne*, *retourne*, etc. (return), *eorlscipe* ('earlship') by *nobilite*, *nobylyte*, etc. (nobility), and *lārcwide* by *conseil*, *counseil*, etc. (counsel). (3) In the centuries immediately after the Conquest, English took on the basic forms and patterns of its present-day dual Germanic and Romance vocabulary: for example, native-based *freedom* as against French-based *liberty*; *hearty* versus *cordial*; *kingly* and *royal* (and also *regal*, directly from Latin); *knight* and *chevalier*, *knighthood* and *chivalry*; *lawful* and *legal*, *unlawful* and *illegal*, *unlawfulness* and *illegality*; *pig* and *pork*, *sheep*

and *mutton*, *calf* and *veal*, *cow* and *beef*. See BISOCIATION, NORMAN FRENCH.

**Intelligibility**. ME words generally bear a fair resemblance to their present-day descendants, with the result that reading ME without help, though by no means always easy, is far simpler than reading OE: the OE sentence *Gemiltsa mīnum suna* (*c*.1000) is entirely foreign to speakers of ModE, but the ME equivalent *Haue mercy on my sone* (though only about 385 years more recent and with a distinctive pronunciation) shows its antiquity in only two small oddities of spelling. The grammatical functions signified by the suffixes on all three OE words in this sentence are gone; the grammatical function of *my sone* is indicated not by a case ending as in OE but by the preposition *on* (absent in OE); and the function of *haue* is indicated by word order. The OE word *gemiltsa* has vanished, replaced by a phrase composed of OE *haue* in its ME form, and ME *mercy*, borrowed from French. See ANGLO-IRISH, CAXTON, CHANCERY STANDARD, ENGLISH LITERATURE, GREAT VOWEL SHIFT, HISTORY OF ENGLISH, LAW FRENCH, PROSE.

**MIDLAND. 1.** For the UK, see MIDLANDS. **2.** For the US, see DIALECT (AMERICA).

**MIDLANDS, The**. A region of England often associated with DIALECT and contrasted with *the North* and *the South*. It is generally held that there were five main dialect areas in medieval England: *Northern*, *East Midland*, *West Midland*, *Southern*, and *Kentish*. The Midland group are described as having clearly defined boundaries. They were found north of the Thames and Severn and south of a line from the mouth of the Humber to the west coast, south of Heysham, and the line of the Pennines divided the East Midland and West Midland areas. Some dialectologists consider that such boundaries continue to be significant in contemporary language research, others that the post-industrial urban dialects of the cities of BIRMINGHAM, Wolverhampton, Leicester, and Peterborough now exert greater influence than those of the rural areas. Apart from speakers of RP, most people in the English Midlands share features of pronunciation with speakers from the North rather than the South. They often use /ʊ/ not /ʌ/ in words such as *but*, *come*, *fun*, *some* (*put* and *putt* being homophones), and use

## EXCERPTS FROM TWO MIDDLE ENGLISH TEXTS

Below are two brief textual specimens. The first is from the 13–14c: the opening
lines of an anonymous lyric poem. The second belongs to the late 14c, and is also
anonymous: the work of a West Midlands poet that continues the alliterative
verse patterns of OE.

### 1. *Verse: Alison*

> Bytuene Mersh and Averil,
> When spray biginneth to springe,
> The lutel foul hath hire wyl
> On hyre lud to synge.
> Ich libbe in love-longinge
> For semlokest of alle thinge—
> He may me blisse bringe;
> Icham in hire baundoun.

TRANSLATION

> Between March and April,
> When the twigs begin to leaf,
> The little bird is free
> To sing her song.
> I live in love-longing
> For the seemliest of all things—
> She may bring me bliss;
> I am in her power.

(From *The Norton Anthology of Poetry*, coordinating editor Arthur M. Eastman, New
York 1970, p. 5)

### 2. *Verse: Sir Gawain and the Green Knight* (opening lines)

> Sithen the sege and the assaut was sesed at Troye,
> The borgh brittened and brent to brondes and askes,
> The tulk that the trammes of tresoun there wrought
> Was tried for his tricherie, the trewest on erthe.
> Hit was Ennias the athel and his highe kynde,
> The sithen depreced provinces, and patrounes bicome
> Welneghe of al the wele in the west iles.

TRANSLATION

> After the siege and the assault were ceased at Troy.
> The city crumbled and burned to brands and ashes,
> The man who the plots of treason there wrought
> Was tried for his treachery, the truest on earth.
> It was Aeneas the noble and his high race,
> Who after subjugated provinces, and lords became
> Wellnigh of all the wealth in the western isles.

(Adapted from the version in *The Norton Anthology of English Literature*, general
editor M. H. Abrams, 5th edition, vol. 1, New York, 1986, pp. 232–3)

/a/ for the RP sounds /æ/ and /ɑ/, so that the vowel sound is the same in *bat* and *bath*, *lass* and *last*, *pat* and *path*. The speech of the Midlands is not, however, homogeneous. People in the West are more likely to use /ŋg/ for /ŋ/ in words such as *singing* /sɪŋgɪŋ/ and *tongue* /tʊŋg/, to use /ɒn/, not /an/, in words such as *man* and *pan*, and to be to some degree rhotic in words such as *far* and *farm*. People in the northeast of the region are generally likely to use /z/ in *us*, to substitute /r/ for /t/ in *got a* ('gorra'), and to use an alveolar tap for /r/ instead of the more widely used post-alveolar approximant of RP. See DIALECT (ENGLAND), EAST ANGLIA, EAST MIDLAND DIALECT.

**MINCED OATH**. A semi-technical term for a SWEARWORD modified so as to be used without giving offence: *God* modified to *Gosh*, *shit* to *shoot*. Two forms of modification are common: (1) Creating a nonsense equivalent: (*by*) *God* becoming (*by*) *Golly/Gosh/Gum*; *Jesus* becoming monosyllabic *Gee* or disyllabic *Jeepers*, and *Jesus Christ* becoming *Jeepers Creepers*; *hell* becoming *heck*. (2) Substituting an everyday expression of similar sound and length, sometimes with an associated meaning, sometimes with no association whatever: *bloody* becoming *ruddy*; *damn* (*it*) becoming *darn* (*it*); *fuck* becoming *flip*. See EUPHEMISM, SWEARING, TABOO.

**MINIMAL PAIR**. In PHONETICS, a pair of words that differ in one PHONEME such as *pin* and *bin* /pɪn, bɪn/ or *rich* and *wretch* /rɪtʃ, rɛtʃ/. *Sick* and *sink* are a minimal pair, the latter having an extra phoneme; *slink* and *shrink* are not minimal, as they differ in two phonemes. Minimal pairs are used in order to ascertain the phonemes of a LANGUAGE or DIALECT. Some differences are however phonetic rather than phonemic: for example, the differences in the vowels of *feed* and *feel* can be ascribed to the influence of the following consonants, and so the vowels are allophones of the same phoneme and not independent phonemes. The contrasting vowels of *bead* and *bid*, on the other hand, are in the same environment (in this instance, preceded by /b/ and followed by /d/), and must therefore belong to different phonemes. Pairs that are different in one dialect may be identical in another: for example, *cod* and *cawed* contrast in RP, but are identical in some Irish dialects. See OPPOSITION.

**MISKITO COAST CREOLE**, also **Miskito Coast Creole English**, **Nicaraguan English**. The language of the Creoles of the Miskito Coast (the Caribbean coast of Nicaragua and Honduras, named after Carib Indians known as Miskitos). Its focus is Bluefields, Pearl Lagoon, and Corn Island in Nicaragua and it is a second language of many Amerindian and SPANISH speakers. It dates from the mid-17c and is similar to other varieties of CREOLE, but its vocabulary has been influenced by Spanish and Chibcha. See CARIBBEAN ENGLISH CREOLE.

**MISPRONUNCIATION**. Wrong PRONUNCIATION, usually of a specific sound: for example, when a foreign learner of English says 'chilled' for *child* (on the analogy of *build* and *gild*); or, in the accentual pattern of a word, stressing *cement* on the first syllable and eliding the *t*, so that it sounds like *seaman* or *semen*. Within one language, what is correct in one variety may be incorrect in another: in most accents of English, the word *loch* (as in the name *Loch Lomond*) is a homophone of *lock*, but in ScoE it ends with the velar fricative /x/, as in German *ach*; most Scots regard the pronunciation 'lock' as incorrect, and many find it irritating. Among native speakers of English, the mispronunciation of a word or name usually arises from unfamiliarity, either because an item is exotic (as with 'makizmo' for *machismo*) or because it derives from Latin or Greek (as with 'fthizzis' for *phthisis*, usually pronounced 'thigh-sis' or 'tie-sis'). Many English words of classical origin have two or more possible pronunciations. Sometimes both or all the variants are accepted, as with 'hibbiskus' and 'highbiskus' for *hibiscus*, and with 'HEDGE-emony', 'he DGEMony', and 'heGGEMony' for *hegemony*. Sometimes one or the other is widely regarded as an error, as with *lamentable*, when stressed on the second syllable.

**MISRELATED PARTICIPLE**. See PARTICIPLE.

**MISTAKE**. A misapprehension of meaning or a fault in execution. Mistakes can be divided into two types: *competence mistakes* (sometimes technically called *errors*), that arise from ignorance of or ineptness in using a language (as when an EFL learner says 'He no comes today' or a native user spells *receive* 'recieve'); *performance mistakes* (technically *mistakes*), where one knows what to say or write but through tiredness, emotion, nervousness, or some other pressure makes a SLIP OF THE TONGUE, leaves out a word, or mistypes a letter. People are particularly frustrated if a slip in performance is seen as a gap in their competence.

Native speakers, however, tend to get away with more slips than foreigners; in CONVERSATION, they can stop, start, change grammatical direction, mispronounce and then correct themselves, and so forth, without much or any censure, but a foreign user's shortcomings are on display all the time. Advanced users of a second language often appear to set themselves higher standards for that language than for their own, partly because they are more conscious of the mistakes they make in it. In educational circles, conservative teachers tend to treat mistakes as disease-like symptoms that need isolation through red ink. Radical teachers tend to overlook mistakes in the interests of good relations, students' confidence, and their ability to communicate and create. Neither extreme appears to be efficient in teaching the mother tongue or another language: the first intimidates and depresses, while the second may invite chaos. See ACCEPTABILITY, BAD ENGLISH, BARBARISM, CATACHRESIS, CORRECT, DEVIANT, FREUDIAN SLIP, GRAMMATICALITY, LITERAL, MALAPROPISM, MISPRONUNCIATION, PLEONASM, SOLECISM, SPOONERISM, TAUTOLOGY.

**MIXED METAPHOR**. A feature of STYLE in which unrelated and sometimes discordant METAPHORS occur together: 'The butter mountain has been in the pipeline for some time' (President of Farmers' Union, BBC1 news, 1987).

**MODALITY**. In syntactic and semantic analysis, a term chiefly used to refer to the way in which the meaning of a sentence or clause may be modified through the use of a MODAL VERB, such as *may*, *can*, *will*, *must*. In a wider sense, the term is used to cover linguistic expression of these concepts other than through the modal auxiliaries: 'It will *possibly* rain later this evening'; '*I am sure* that the plane has landed by now'; '*You have my permission* to smoke now'; '*I am obliged to* go.' Adverbs such as *possibly*, *perhaps*, *probably*, *certainly*

have been called *modal adverbs*, and such adjectives as *possible* have been called *modal adjectives*. The term is also extended to include the subjunctive mood and the past verb forms used to express hypothetical meaning (that is, that the situation is unlikely to occur or has not occurred): 'I wish I *knew* her'; 'If I *saw* him, I *would recognize* him'; 'If you *had said* that, I *would* not *have minded*.' In case grammar, *modality* refers to one of the two underlying constituents of sentence structure (the other being *proposition*). The modality includes those features that relate to the sentence as a whole, such as tense and negation.

■ **MODAL VERB** ─────────── ■

Also **modal auxiliary, modal**. A VERB, normally an AUXILIARY VERB such as English *must* and *should*, used to express MODALITY. In English, such verbs have largely replaced the subjunctive mood, and three kinds of modality can be distinguished for them: (1) *Epistemic modality*, which expresses a judgement about the truth of a proposition (whether it is possible, probable, or necessarily true): *John may be in his office*. (2) *Deontic modality*, which involves the giving of directives (in terms of such notions as permission and obligation): You *must leave immediately*. (3) *Dynamic modality*, which ascribes such properties as ability and volition to the subject of the sentence: *I can come*. Often the same modal verb is used for more than one kind of modality: *may* for possibility (*It may rain tomorrow*) and permission (You *may smoke now*); *must* for necessity (*The plane must have landed by now*) an obligation (*I must go*).

**Central and marginal modals**. The central modal verbs are *can*, *could*, *may*, *might*, *must*, *shall*, *should*, *will*, *would*. The marginal modal verbs, sometimes called *semi-modal verbs*, are *dare*, *need*, *ought to*, *used to*. All share the following characteristics: (1) They are auxiliary verbs. (2) They have no third-person -*s* form: *She may go*, *They may go* (contrast *She goes*, *They go*). (3) They have no non-finite forms (no infinitive, -*ing* participle, or -*ed* participle), and therefore in standard English can appear only in initial position in the verb phrase, and cannot occur with each other (although 'double modal' forms such as *might could go* occur in some non-standard varieties, such as Southern US English). (4) All except *ought* and *used* are followed by the bare infinitive without *to*. (5) They have idiosyncratic semantic and formal features, affecting particularly their use in the past tense and in negation.

**Kinds of modals**. (1) Epistemic modals: *may* (*He may be at home*), *might* (*It might get too hot*), *must* (*It must be your sister on the phone*), *ought to* (*They ought to have heard by now*), *should* (*The show should be over soon*), *will* (*That will be the doctor*), *would* (*Who would have guessed he was so young?*). (2) Deontic modals: *can* (*You can leave now*), *could* (*Could I go now please?*), *may* (*You may smoke*), *might* (*Might we have another one?*), *must* (*You must be patient*), *need* (*You needn't say anything*), *ought to* (*I ought to write more often*), *shall* (*You shall have my resignation letter tomorrow*: a promise or a threat), *should* (*You should write more legibly*). (3) Dynamic modals: *can* (*Neil can drive a car*), *could* (*He couldn't drive at that time*), *dare* (*I daren't tell/don't dare tell my parents*), *shall* (*We shall allow no obstacle to impede our programme*), *will* (*I will stay as long as I wish*).

**Future expressions**. *Shall* (with first-person subjects only, particularly in Southern England) and *will* (often contracted to *'ll*) express future time and are often said to comprise the future tense: *I shall be back next week*; *He will be here soon*. Other ways of expressing the future include the semi-auxiliaries (see below) *be going to* (*It's going to rain*) and *be to* (*She is to be married tomorrow*), the present continuous (*I'm leaving for New York next week*), and the simple present (*The plane leaves at noon*).

**Marginal modals and semi-auxiliaries**. *Dare*, *need*, *ought to*, and *used to* share most of the characteristics of modal verbs but are marginal for various reasons. Unlike the central modals, *ought* and *used* are followed by *to* and despite prescriptive objections often combine with *do* in negative and interrogative constructions, like a full verb: especially in England, *They didn't ought to say that* alongside the more traditionally acceptable *They oughtn't to say that*; *Did he used to play the violin?*, alongside the rare *Used he to play the violin? Used to* also differs semantically from central modals, since it conveys aspect (habitual situation) and not modality. In negative and interrogative contexts, *dare* and *need* may be either modals (*I daren't object*; *Need I say more?*) or full verbs with preceding *do* and following *to*-infinitive (*I don't dare to object* or the blend without the *to*, *I don't dare objects*; *Do I need to say more?*).

Elsewhere, they are full verbs: *I dare/dared to object*; *I need/needed to say more*. There are a number of semi-auxiliaries that express modal or aspectual meanings, such as *be able to*, *be about to*, *be bound to*, *be going to*, *have to*, *have got to*. They can be used as non-finite forms and are therefore convenient substitutes for modals in non-finite positions: for example, the use of *You may be able to see me tomorrow* instead of the impossible *\*You may can see me tomorrow*.

**Negation**. When a verb phrase containing a modal is negated, the negation applies in some instances to the modal and in other instances to the proposition: for example, the modal is negated in *You may not leave* (You are not allowed to leave), whereas the proposition is negated in *I may not be on time* (It is possible that I won't be on time). The difference may affect the choice of the auxiliary: for example, epistemic *must* (*It must be your sister on the phone*) usually forms its negative equivalent through *may not* for negating the proposition (*It may not be your sister on the phone*: It is possible that it is not your sister on the phone) and *can't* for modal negation (*It can't be your sister on the phone*: It is not possible that it is your sister on the phone).

**Past tense**. *Can*, *may*, *shall*, *will* have the past-tense forms *could*, *might*, *should*, *would*. These forms are chiefly used to express tentativeness or conditionality rather than past time, so that there is no time difference between *I may see you later* and *I might see you later*, or between *Can you pass the salt?* and *Could you pass the salt?* The past forms, however, are used for past time in indirect speech (*I may see you later* is reported as *She said that she might see me later*). There are no past forms for *must*, *dare*, *need*, *ought to*. The epistemic modals indicate the *past* time of the proposition by using *have*: *Andrew may/might have been in his office*; *You must have seen them*; *They will/would have landed by now*. The deontic modals *ought to have* and *should have* express past obligation, usually with the implication that it was not fulfilled: *You ought to have phoned* (but you didn't); *They should have come in*. Dynamic *could* (was able to) and *would* (was willing to) are used for past time in negative contexts (*He couldn't type*; *They wouldn't help us*).

*Would* is commonly used in the main clause of a sentence expressing a hypothetical condition: *If I were you, I would buy it*; *If you had seen them, you would have been shocked*.

Sometimes, in BrE, *should* is used with a first-person subject in place of *would*: *If I had seen them, I should have reported it.* *Would* and *should* appear in other hypothetical contexts: *I was at the demonstration, but it would take too long to tell you what happened.* *Should* may also appear after evaluative expressions (*It's odd that he should say that*; also *It's odd that he says that*) and expressions of necessity, intention, and the like (*We insisted that he should stay*). See DIALECT (AMERICA), SCOTS.

**MODERN ENGLISH**, short form *ModE*, *MnE*. Also sometimes **New English**. **1.** The third stage in the history and development of the ENGLISH language, *c.*1450 to the present day, often divided into *EARLY MODERN ENGLISH* (*c.*1450–1700) and (*Late/Later*) *Modern English* (*c.*1700 to the present day.) **2.** Late Modern English treated as a fourth stage in the history and development of the language. See HISTORY OF ENGLISH.

***MODERN ENGLISH USAGE***. See DICTIONARY OF MODERN ENGLISH USAGE.

**MODIFICATION**. A term for the dependence of one grammatical unit on another, the less dependent unit being delimited or made more specific by the more dependent unit: the adjective *good* modifying the noun *weather* in the phrase *good weather*; the noun *diamond* modifying the noun *mines* in *diamond mines*; the adverb *strikingly* modifying the adjective *handsome* in *strikingly handsome*. A distinction is made between *premodification* (modifying by preceding) and *post-modification* (modifying by following). In *diamond mines in South Africa*, *diamond* is a premodifier and *in South Africa* is a postmodifier. The example illustrates a phrase (here a prepositional phrase) used as a modifier (here a post-modifier of a noun). Clauses may also be modifiers in phrases, usually post-modifiers of nouns, such as the relative clause in 'the bag *that you are carrying*'. The dependence of a subordinate clause on its superordinate clause is generally not described in terms of modification: the subordinate clause in 'I know *that you are there*' is not said to be a modifier. Some grammarians, however, use the term *sentence modifier* for adverbials (including adverbial clauses) that express a comment on the sentence or clause: *fortunately* in

'*Fortunately*, no one was hurt'; *in all probability* in '*In all probability*, it is closed by now'; the *since-clause* in '*Since you're here*, you may as well make yourself useful.' Although the distinction is obvious between such examples and clear instances of adverbials functioning as modifiers of verbs (such as 'The band is playing *too loudly*'), there is no agreement on how to draw the line between sentence modifiers and verb modifiers or on how many relational categories to establish for adverbials. See JOURNALESE.

**MONOPHTHONG**. In PHONETICS, a VOWEL whose quality is relatively constant, in contrast to a DIPHTHONG or *triphthong*. Some varieties of English have more monophthongs, some have fewer: in RP there are 12 (as in *see*, *sit*, *set*, *hat*, *arm*, *got*, *saw*, *pull*, *pool*, *cup*, *fur*, and the first syllable of *ago*); in ScoE there are 11, rather differently distributed (as in *say*, *see*, *sit*, *set*, *hat/arm*, *got/saw*, *so*, *pull/pool*, *cup/fur*, and the first syllables of *never*, *ago*).

**MONOSYLLABLE**, formerly also **monosyllabon**. A WORD of one SYLLABLE. 'Native' English is often said to be inherently monosyllabic ('Words monosillable which be for the more part our natural Saxon English,' George Puttenham, *The Arte of English Poesie*, 1589), as opposed to polysyllabic Latinisms and other borrowings. Certainly, many common monosyllables are Germanic in origin (such as *am*, *be*, *can*, *dog*, *eye*, *fox*, *gun*, *hot*, *it*, *jump*, *key*, *leap*, *mum*, *nut*, *odd*, *pot*, *queen*, *run*, *say*, *two*, *up*, *vat*, *who*, *you*), but the same Germanic source also provides such POLYSYLLABLES as *cold-bloodedly* and *longwindedness*. The many monosyllables from non-Germanic sources include *act* and *flex* from Latin, *bloc* and *joy* from French, *crag* and *loch* from Gaelic, *gong* and *kris* from Malay, *steppe* and *tsar* from Russian, and *gene* and *zone* from Greek. A tendency to clip words does, however, provide some support for the idea of Anglo-Saxon *monosyllabism* (addiction to monosyllables or the quality of being monosyllabic), as with *cred* from the Latinate word *credibility*, *mob* from the Latin phrase *mobile vulgus*, and *zoo* from the hybrid Greco-Latin and vernacular *zoological gardens*. A person who is monosyllabic in style tends to be curt and keep to short words, especially simply *yes* and *no*. See CLIPPING.

**MONOTRANSITIVE**. See TRANSITIVE AND INTRANSITIVE.

**MONTSERRAT**. A British dependency in the Leeward Islands. Languages: English, CREOLE. Columbus named the island when he visited it in 1493, its terrain reminding him of Montserrat in Catalonia (from Latin *Mons Serratus* Saw-Toothed Mountain). In 1632, the island was colonized by English and Irish settlers from St Christopher, followed by more Irish from Virginia. Slaves from Africa began arriving in 1664. Although the French took the island for brief periods in 1664, 1667, and 1782, it remained British, but did not become a colony until 1871. In 1958, it became a member of the Federation of the West Indies, and did not seek independence on the dissolution of the Federation in 1962. The island's active volcanoes are known as *soufrières* (French: sulphurous ones).

**MOOD**. In traditional GRAMMAR, a term for a form of the verb that affects the general meaning of the sentence and for the sentence or clause type in which it occurs. Three moods are customarily recognized for English: the *INDICATIVE* (*God helps us*); the *IMPERATIVE* (*Help us*); and the *SUBJUNCTIVE* (*God help us*).

**MORNINGSIDE AND KELVINSIDE**. Accents of English in Scotland, named after middle-class districts of EDINBURGH and GLASGOW; in effect one accent, generally regarded as an affected, hypercorrect imitation of RP. In popular and literary caricatures since the 1940s, it is identified with two shibboleths in particular: a raised realization of the short, front vowel /a/, frequently represented as *e*, as in 'ectually' for *actually*; a single, narrowed realization of the SCOTTISH ENGLISH diphthongs in *five*, *time* ('faive', 'taime'). The features come together in 'Eh'm quate well aware of the fect' (Mrs M'Cotton, in Helen W. Pryde's *McFlannels United*, 1949). The names are also used by speakers of the vernacular for any 'anglified' variety of ScoE, especially the near-RP speech of lawyers, architects, and other professional people. Compare KENSINGTON. See AFFECTATION, ANGLIFY.

**MORPHEME**. In LINGUISTICS, a minimal unit of form and meaning. There are many variations in how the term is used and understood, arising in the main from a distinction between language as arrangement and language as process: (1) As proposed by the US structural linguist Leonard BLOOMFIELD (*Language*, 1933), the morpheme is the unit of MORPHOLOGY and therefore grammatical. In this approach, language analysed as a static arrangement of data consists of minimal units of form and meaning, each of which can be physically identified. The sentence *The cats were sitting unhappily in the rain* is analysable into the morphemic string *the + cat + s + were + sit(t) + ing + un + happy + ly + in + the + rain*. The 8-word sentence consists of 12 morphemes, all of equal status. (2) As proposed by the French linguist Joseph Vendryes (*Le Langage*, 1921), the morpheme is one of two units, one grammatical, one semantic, and each in its own sense minimal. Language in this approach is the outcome of processes which may or may not all have observable forms, but which can be analysed as units of grammatical meaning (*morphemes*) and units of lexical meaning (for Vendryes *semantemes*, but now known, more or less, as *LEXEMES*). Here, morphemes are the glue that holds lexemes together, and the specimen sentence can be analysed as: *the + CAT + s + (BE + past/plural) + SIT(T) + ing + un + HAPPY + ly + in + the + RAIN* (in which the lower-case items are morphemes, the upper-case lexemes). The 8-word sentence in this analysis contains 8 morphemes and 5 lexemes.

There have been many variations on these themes. The US linguist Dwight Bolinger (*Aspects of Language*, 1968) divided Bloomfield's morpheme into a *system morpheme* (the glue) and a *source morpheme* (the lexical content), while the French linguist André Martinet (*Éléments de linguistique générale*, 1970) subsumed Vendryes's morpheme and lexeme under a unifying unit the *moneme*. In this approach, the specimen sentence has 13 monemes divided into 8 morphemes and 5 lexemes. Currently, whatever the terms used, linguists tend to agree on three points: (1) Grammatical and lexical units need to be distinguished: for example, the two elements *cat* and *s* in the word *cats* are different aspects or levels of language. (2) Not all the features in a stretch of language are physically realized: for example, *cats* may exhibit a marker of plurality, but *sheep* does not. (3) One unit of form may serve more than one end: for example, *were* in the specimen sentence above combines BE and *past*. The traditional structuralist approach assumes that all the morphemes of a language can in principle be listed in a *morpheme inventory*, like a PHONEME inventory, but because of the complexities involved, few such lists have been attempted and none exists for English.

In later STRUCTURAL LINGUISTICS, the *morpheme* has been defined as the abstraction behind a *morph* (a form that has semantic distinctiveness). It may subsume two or more *allomorphs*, morphs that have common semantic identity but differ in their pronunciation according to well-defined rules: for example, the prefixes *in-*, *im-*, *il-* are allomorphs of the same morpheme (in this case a negative prefix) in the words *insincere*, *impolite*, *illogical*, the choice of prefix being determined by the initial sound of the stem that follows the prefix. When it deals with morphs and morphemes, morphology is known as *morphemics*. See -EME, LEVEL OF LANGUAGE.

**MORPHOLOGY**. In LINGUISTICS, the study of the structure of words, as opposed to SYNTAX, the study of the arrangement of words in the higher units of phrases, clauses, and sentences. The two major branches are *inflectional morphology* (the study of inflections) and *lexical morphology* (the study of WORD-FORMATION). See ACCIDENCE, INFLECTION, LINGUISTIC TYPOLOGY, MORPHEME.

**MOTHERESE**. A term used in the study of CHILD LANGUAGE ACQUISITION for the way mothers talk to their young children. Its features include simplified grammar, exaggerated speech melody, diminutive forms of words such as *doggie*, and a highly repetitive style. There is also a tendency to expand or comment on what the child has just said: when a child says *Castle down*, and the mother replies, *Yes, the castle's fallen down*. Although originally mothers were the focus of research study, similar conversational patterns have been observed in fathers' speech (sometimes referred to as *fatherese*) and in the speech of others who look after young children, such as grandparents and nannies (users of *caretaker speech*). These patterns, however, are not identical: for example, research indicates that fathers tend to be more intense and demanding in talking to young children, using more direct questions and a wider range of vocabulary. See BABY TALK, -ESE.

**MOTHER TONGUE**. A general term for the language of the childhood home, learned 'at one's mother's knee', often used synonymously with *NATIVE LANGUAGE*. Although the implication is usually clear, there is no necessary connection between a child's use of language and the language of its mother: some children learn the language of a nurse or ayah first; a mother may talk to her child in a language not originally her own; the mother may be dead. The term is often used to mean a national language, such as French whether or not it is the first or preferred language of all members of the nation, as with Basques and Bretons in France. Compare FIRST LANGUAGE/SECOND LANGUAGE.

**MULCASTER, Richard** [1530?–1611]. English scholar, schoolmaster, author, and liberal educational theorist; the poet Spenser's headmaster at the Merchant Taylors' School in London and perhaps SHAKESPEARE's model for the pedant Holofernes in *Love's Labour's Lost*. Mulcaster's *The First Part of the Elementarie* (1582) was the period's most significant pronouncement on English. It took an innovative stand in the movement on reforming SPELLING, issued the first call for a comprehensive DICTIONARY of English, defended the right of BORROWING words from other languages, and exhibited unlimited pride in English. He said that it is the learning in a language and not any inherent virtue that makes it esteemed, and English can be as learned and expressive as any: 'I loue Rome, but London better, I fauor Italie, but England more, I honor the Latin, but I worship the English.' See EARLY MODERN ENGLISH.

**MULTICULTURALISM**. **1.** Also *cultural pluralism*. Sociological terms for the co-occurrence of many cultures (including hybrid forms) in one area, as in the cities of Auckland, Bombay, London, New York, Singapore, Sydney, and Toronto. **2.** A sociopolitical policy of encouraging the coexistence and growth of several cultures in one place. The term *multicultural* is sometimes used as a synonym of *multiracial*: 'Although Britain has a multi-cultural society, where are the black faces among the television announcers, newscasters and sports commentators?' (*Daily Telegraph*, 20 July 1973). In recent years, the terms *multicultural*, *multiculturalism*, *multiculturalist*, etc., have been used, both positively and negatively, to identify and discuss a movement that confronts certain perceived biases in Western and especially US society, particularly in education and on college campuses: 'It is in its most intense and extreme form ... that multiculturalism is on its way to being a major educational, social and eventually political problem. This version is propagated on our college campuses by a coalition of nationalist-racist blacks, radical feminists, "gays" and lesbians, and a handful of aspiring demagogues who claim to represent various ethnic minorities' (Irving Kristol, 'The Tragedy of Multiculturalism', *Wall Street Journal*, 31 July 1991). See, AUSTRALIAN ENGLISH, POLITICALLY CORRECT, SEXISM.

**MULTILINGUALISM**. The ability to use three or more languages, either separately or in various degrees of CODE-MIXING. There is no general agreement as to the degree of competence in each language necessary before someone can be considered multilingual; according to some, a native-like fluency is necessary in at least three languages; according to others, different languages are used for different purposes, competence in each varying according to such factors as REGISTER, occupation, and education. Where an individual has been exposed to several languages, as for example in India, Nigeria, or Singapore, one language may be used in the home, another professionally, another passively for listening or reading, another spoken but not written or read, and so forth. See BILINGUALISM, LANGUAGE PLANNING, LINGUAL, MULTICULTURALISM.

**MULTIPLE MEANING**. See MEANING, POLYSEMY, SEMANTIC CHANGE, SEMANTICS.

**MULTIPLE NEGATION**. See DOUBLE NEGATIVE, NEGATION.

**MUMMERSET** [A blend of *mummer*, one who mutters and murmurs, or takes part in a mime, and *SOMERSET*], also **Mummersetshire**. An imaginary rustic county of England and its dialect: 'Nowadays you can't be sure if they *are* eggs, even when somebody on television says they are in B.B.C. Mummerset' (C. Mackenzie, *Paper Lives*, 1966). This form of stage WEST COUNTRY is drawled and emphasizes retroflex /r/ ('Arrr, that'll be roit, zurr'). It replaces /s/ with /z/, /f/ with /v/ ('We ain't zeen 'im zince last Vroiday'), and uses special forms of *be* ('We be happy yere, bain't we?'). Comedians sometimes add pseudo-dialect words to the brew. See BURR.

**MURRAY, Sir J(ames) A(ugustus) H(enry)** [1837–1915]. Scottish lexicographer and philologist. Born in Denholm, Roxburghshire, he had no formal education after the age of 14, acquiring his erudition by private study. He moved from Hawick to London in 1864 in the hope that milder southern winters might help his first wife's health, but she died shortly afterwards. From 1870 to 1885, he was English master at Mill Hill School in north-east London. He joined the circle of professional and amateur scholars who were establishing the scientific study of PHONETICS, Early English, and DIALECTOLOGY. From 1868, he was active in the Philological Society, and, urged on by F. J. Furnivall, produced several editions of SCOTS texts for the Early English Text Society. In 1873, he brought out *The Dialect of the Southern Counties of Scotland*, on which all subsequent work on the history and description of Scots has depended. His entry on the English Language in the 9th edition of the *Encyclopaedia Britannica* (1878) has long been regarded as a classic.

In 1876, Murray was invited by the publisher Macmillan to produce a major new dictionary of English. Although this proposal came to nothing, it reawakened the interest of Furnivall and others in the Philological Society's own lapsed project for a new historical dictionary. The upshot was its relaunching by Murray in 1879 at Mill Hill. With the help of hundreds of new volunteer excerptors, he augmented the collection of quotations (already over 2m on slips) assembled by Coleridge and Furnivall. At the same time, following the principles set out in R. C. Trench's paper of 1857, he laid down plan and methodology, after which, in the face of financial and other difficulties, he began to produce copy for *A New English Dictionary on Historical Principles* (later renamed *The OXFORD ENGLISH DICTIONARY*) at the remarkable rate of over 200 dictionary pages per year. In 1885, he gave up his part-time post at Mill Hill School and moved to Oxford to devote himself exclusively to the dictionary. He edited some 7,207 of its 15,487 pages, the remainder being divided among Henry Bradley, William Craigie, and Charles Onions. Because of the influence on later historical dictionaries of the methods he devised and of the editorial standard he set, and his own prodigious achievement as a dictionary compiler, Murray is widely regarded as the greatest ever lexicographer.

# N

## N, n

[Called 'en']. The 14th LETTER of the Roman ALPHABET as used for English. It originated as the Phoenician symbol *nun*, adopted by the Greeks as *nu* (N), a form which the Romans adopted in their turn.

**Sound value**. In English, the letter *n* represents a voiced alveolar nasal. Before a vowel, the sound–symbol correspondence is regular (*name, many*), but in loans from French a preceding medial *g* indicates a *y*-sound after the *n* (*cognac*: 'conyack'). In FRENCH loans *n* may nasalize a preceding vowel, but have no clear sound of its own (*restaurant, lingerie*). Articulation may be affected by a following consonant: *b, p* may give the value of *m*, as in *inbred* ('imbred') and *input* ('imput'), and following hard *c, k, g, q, x* may produce a velar nasal 'ng': *zinc, increase, ink, sing, anger, concrete, congress, conquer, anxious*.

**Double *N***. (1) In monosyllables following an initial consonant and vowel, *n* is normally single (*ban, can, fan, man, ran, tan, ten, tin, ton, tun*), with doubling before inflections beginning with a vowel (*bans, banned, banning*). *Nn* follows the initial short vowel in *inn, Ann*, but not in grammatical words (*an, in, on*). (2) In disyllables, after a short vowel, especially before *-er, -a, -y*: *manner, tenner, dinner, gunner*; *manna, henna*; *canny, tinny*. The pairs *dinner/diner, tinny/tiny* show the force of the doubling. However, many other words do not observe this pattern: *any, canon* (beside *cannon*), *enemy, honour, linen, money, tenor*. A single *n* is usual before *-ish* (*banish, replenish, finish* (compared *Finnish*), *astonish, punish, Spanish*) and *-ion* (*companion, minion, pinion, onion, bunion*). Many such words derive from French, but do not follow modern French use of *nn/n*: *dîner, ennemi, étonner, honneur, manière, monnaie*. (3) With the Germanic prefix *un-* before *n* (*unnecessary, unnerved*) and Latin prefixes ending in or assimilated to *n* (*annul, connect, innate, innocent*). (4) When the Germanic suffix *-ness* is added to words ending in *n*: *barrenness, openness* (but usually with a geminated or 'double' pronunciation). (5) In the comparative of adjectives ending in *n* following a short vowel if stressed (*thinner, thinnest*), but not if unstressed (*commoner, commonest*).

**Syllabic *N***. The letter *n* may have syllabic value after alveolar consonants, as in the negative contractions *hadn't, isn't, mightn't* and the name *Haydn*. In similar environments, syllabic *n* can alternate with /n/ preceded by schwa. The SCHWA may, however, be spelt with a range of vowel letters: *beaten, raisin, fashion, cotton*. These variations can cause uncertainty: for example, in the endings *-ant, -ent*: *resistant, consistent*. See A.

**Epenthetic *N***. Sometimes, an epenthetic *n* has been inserted in a word: *messenger, passenger*, from *message, passage* (compare French *messager, passager*). See EPENTHESIS.

**Transfer**. (1) Some nouns have lost an initial *n* that has been transferred to the indefinite article: *an adder* from *a nadder, an apron* from *a naperon, an umpire* from *a noumpere*. (2) Conversely, the *n* of *an* has sometimes been transferred to a following noun: *a newt* from *an ewt, a nickname* from *an ekename, the nonce* from *then anes*. See METANALYSIS.

**Silence**. (1) Word-final *n* is silent after *m* (*damn, hymn, autumn, column*), including inflected forms (*condemned, condemning*), but is pronounced in derived forms where a vowel follows (*autumnal, condemnation, hymnal, solemnity*). (2) *N* is sometimes preceded by a silent *g, k, p*: *gnat, feign, foreign; knit, know; pneumatic, pneumonia*. See G, K, P.

**Other patterns**. Many words in older English which ended in *n* (often an inflection) have lost the *n* with the inflection. Nevertheless, there are some pairs of words in which one member is without and another has kept the final *n*: *a/an, drunk/drunken, maid/maiden, my/mine, oft/often, ope/open*. One of the terms often has an archaic or poetic flavour: *maiden, oft, ope*. The inflectional function survives in the *olden of olden days/times*.

## NAME

[From Old English *nama*, cognate with Latin *nomen* and Greek *ónoma/ónuma*]. A general, non-technical term for a WORD or PHRASE that designates a person (*woman*, *Helen*), an animal (*cat*, *Felix the Cat*), a place (*Helensburgh*, first a town in Scotland, then by commemorative extension a town in Australia), or a thing (the mineral *stone*, the subject or activity *electrical engineering*, the novel and motion picture *The Hound of the Baskervilles*). The same name may serve to designate more than one distinct though linked referent: for example, *Saint Helena* denotes both a saint and the island 'named' in her honour.

**Common and proper names**. Traditionally, names fall into two categories: (1) The *common name*, which designates a member of a class, such as *cat*, *tomcat*, *stone*, *rhinestone*, *verse*, *blank verse*. Generally, common names are written without initial capital letters. (2) The *proper name*, which designates a specific entity: *Helen*, *Troy*, *Helen of Troy*; *Henry*, *Henry Smith*, *Henry VI* (both a person and a play). Generally, proper names are written with initial capital letters for each of their constituents, especially if they are nouns or adjectives: *Prince Hal*, *Blind Harry*. Occasionally, however, the capitals are dropped for effect, as in the name of the American poet *e. e. cummings* (1894–1962), and the names of some periodicals (such as the Australian literary magazine *overland*). Many common names take the form of generic phrases that open with an embedded proper name, and therefore contain a capital letter, as in *Cheddar cheese*, *Siamese cat*, *Trojan horse*, *Wellington boot*. See NOUN.

**The study and classification of names**. The descriptive and historical study of proper names is *onomastics*, and the study of common names (particularly as they form lexical systems or terminologies and vary from one group of speakers to another) is *onomasiology*. Proper names are distinguished, according to referent, as: personal names (*William Smith*, *Heather Gibson*); PLACE-NAMES (*Alice Springs*, *Chicago*); names of events (*Armageddon*, *the Boer War*); names of institutions (*the British Museum*, *the Library of Congress*); names of vehicles (*Ford*, *Pontiac*; *The Orient Express*, *the Queen Elizabeth II*); and works of art such as books and plays (*Pickwick Papers*, *Othello*), paintings (*the Mona Lisa*, *the Laughing Cavalier*), and musical compositions (*Eine kleine Nachtmusik*, *Finlandia*). Name study is logically a branch of linguistics, with an affinity to such other subjects as anthropology and topography, but in practice it is an independent discipline that combines the interests of philologists, linguists, historians, geographers, encyclopaedists, sociologists, psychologists, genealogists, literary critics, and others. See FORM OF ADDRESS.

**Associated meaning**. The associations evoked by proper names may be either public (as with *Chernobyl*, a Ukrainian city associated throughout the world with a nuclear accident in 1986) or private (for example, someone associating the name *Rex* with pain and fear, because once bitten by a dog with that name). Public associations with some place-names are so strong that the names may come to be used in a sense that was originally no more than an association: for example, *Fleet Street*, a street in London, was until the late 1980s the location of many British newspaper offices, and came to mean, by metonymy, the British national press. It continues to be so used even though all London newspapers are now located elsewhere. Personal names often have both public and private associations that derive from particular individuals with those names: for example, *Mary* used to be, in the words of a popular song, 'a grand old name', the epitome of feminine virtue. Recently, however, it has been declining in popularity over much of the English-speaking world, and is now widely regarded as old-fashioned and pietistic. It may continue, however, to be used in certain families, for the sake of tradition, and may evoke the memory of a particular Mary whenever mentioned. See ACRONYM, BBC PRONUNCIATION UNIT, CLIPPING, EPITHET, EPONYM, ETHNIC NAME, FORM OF ADDRESS, LETTER WORD, ONOMATOPOEIA, -ONYM, PLACE-NAME, PROPER NOUN, TRADEMARK, WORD.

**NAMIBIA**. A country of southern Africa and member of the Commonwealth. Languages: English (official), Afrikaans, Damara, German, Herero, Kavango, Ovambo, Nama, etc. Because of the Namib Desert, British and Dutch missionaries did not penetrate the region until the late 18c. The Germans colonized it as *German West Africa* in 1892–3, but lost it during the First World War to South Africa, which governed it from 1920 as *South West Africa*, under a League of Nations mandate. The United Nations sought to make it a trusteeship after 1946, but South Africa refused to co-operate. In 1966, the UN mandate was withdrawn. In 1968, the territory's name became Namibia. South Africa governed the territory without international recognition until independence in 1990. English, Afrikaans, and German were all official until independence, when English was declared the sole official language.

**NASAL.** A term used generally and in PHONETICS for a SPEECH quality influenced by air passing through the nose. When a nasal consonant is produced, the velum is lowered to allow air to pass out through nose as well as mouth: /m, n, ŋ/ as in *am, an, sing*. These consonants are generally referred to as *nasal consonants* or *nasals*. *Nasalization* is the production of resonance in the nose to accompany a speech sound, as in French *bon* but not *bonne*. English vowels may be partially nasalized when followed by a nasal consonant. Some ACCENTS of English are more nasal than others; some people's voices are said to sound nasal or are described as having a *nasal accent* or a (*nasal*) TWANG. Nasality is a feature of most varieties of AmE and CanE and some kinds of LONDON English. It is the consequence of a setting of the VELUM which causes a degree of nasal resonance greater than the user of such a term as *twang* would consider normal. Reduced nasal resonance is also described as *adenoidal*. There is no fixed norm. See ENG, NEW ENGLAND, SCOUSE.

**NATIONAL CURRICULUM.** See COX REPORT, KINGMAN REPORT.

**NATIONAL LANGUAGE.** A language officially designated the language of a nation or country, usually for cultural and/or ethnic reasons. Such a language may or may not be the *OFFICIAL LANGUAGE* of the country in question (that is, used in its government and administration): for example, in Botswana, the national language is Setswana, but the official language is English. Compare NATIVE LANGUAGE.

**NATION LANGUAGE.** A term coined by the poet and scholar Edward Brathwaite to present Caribbean CREOLE in a positive light, especially in its artistic and literary use (*History of the Voice: The Development of Nation Language in Anglophone Caribbean Poetry*, London: New Beacon, 1984). His concern has been to break away from the traditions of speakers of English in the Caribbean and elsewhere. He acknowledges the English lexical sources of Creole, but affirms the Africanness of its rhythms, experiential content, and personality, as well as its cultural links with West Africa. He opposes the term to DIALECT, whose pejorative connotations he sees as inappropriate and limiting. See CARIBBEAN ENGLISH.

**NATIVE LANGUAGE.** A general term often used synonymously with *MOTHER TONGUE*. It dates from the Middle Ages, when it was widely believed that language is physically inherited, one's birth determining both language and nationality. Because of this association with birth and birthright and the confusion associated with the word *native*, some linguists consider that the term should, like *NATIVE SPEAKER*, be avoided or used with caution in scholarly work. See FIRST LANGUAGE, SECOND LANGUAGE.

**NATIVE SPEAKER.** A person who has spoken a certain language since early childhood: *A native speaker of French*. Native speakers are often appealed to, including by linguists, over questions of CORRECT usage, because traditionally the language in which they are fluent has been regarded as their exclusive property. Some linguists, however, have in recent years argued that no one is 'born' into a language (as the ETYMOLOGY of the usage suggests) but acquires it from an environment that may in fact change in childhood, adolescence, or later, causing an individual to develop a second language into a medium as personal as the first (sometimes losing skills in the earlier 'mother tongue'). Whether such a *non-native speaker* is able to acquire the same command of the language as a native speaker is a much-debated question to which there is no simple answer. *Native* and *non-native* are not clear-cut homogeneous categories; each group comprises wide variations depending on such individual factors as regional or national origin, age of learning (for non-natives), degree of formal training, aspirations, and sense of identity.

**NATIVE USER.** A term increasingly used in LANGUAGE TEACHING and APPLIED LINGUISTICS in preference to *NATIVE SPEAKER*, to emphasize that language includes writing and print as well as speech. See FOREIGN USER.

**NATIVIZATION**, also **nativisation**. **1.** The process by which a transplanted language become native to a people or place, either in addition to or in place of any language or languages already in use, as with English in Ireland and both English and French in West Africa. The process is often given a specific name, such as *Africanization* or *Indianization* (in the case of English), and takes place at every level of language, local users of that language developing, among other things, distinctive accents, grammatical usages, and items of vocabulary, such developments generally linked with their other or former languages. **2.** The process by which a PIDGIN language becomes a creole, as with TOK PISIN in Papua New Guinea. **3.** The process by which a foreign word becomes 'native' to a language, as in the various pronunciations of French *garage* in English. Compare ENGLISHIZE.

**NATURAL LANGUAGE**. A term in linguistics for language as it naturally occurs in humans. Compare ARTIFICIAL LANGUAGE.

**NAURU**. A country of Oceania, an island of 21 square miles, and member of the COMMONWEALTH. Languages: Nauruan (official), English. A German colony since the late 19c, Nauru became a League of Nations mandate in 1920 and later a UN trust territory administered by Australia, gaining internal self-government in 1966 and independence in 1968.

**NDJUKA**. An English-based CREOLE of SURINAM spoken since the 18c by the Eastern Bush Negroes (the Aucan or Ndjuka and the Boni or Aluku). The language developed among runaways from plantation slavery. It is closely related to *SRANAN* and to a limited degree mutually intelligible with it. Ndjuka is unusual among creoles in having its own syllabic writing developed by its speakers, a system with strong similarities to indigenous scripts of West Africa.

**NEAR-RP**. A term in PHONETICS and SOCIOLINGUISTICS for an ACCENT of English considered close to but not identical with RECEIVED PRONUNCIATION, even though speakers of such an accent and others hearing them may regard it as the same. See MORNINGSIDE AND KELVINSIDE, NEW ZEALAND ENGLISH.

■ **NEGATION** ─────────── ■

A grammatical term for the process that results in changing a positive (affirmative) sentence or clause into a negative one: from *They came* to *They did not come*. This is sometimes known as a contrast in *polarity*. In English, a sentence is typically negated through the verb, by the insertion of *not* or its contraction *n't* after the first or only verb: *It is raining* becoming *It is not/isn't raining*. If an auxiliary verb is present, as with *is* in the above sentence, *not* follows it or *n't* is attached to it as an enclitic (*must not*, *mustn't*). If no auxiliary is present, then the relevant form of the auxiliary *do* (*do*, *does*, or *did*, according to tense and person) is inserted to effect the negation: *I know him* becoming *I do not/don't know him*.

**Special cases**. (1) The verb *be* is used in the same way when no auxiliary is present: *Justin was ill* becoming *Justin was not/wasn't ill*. (2) The verb *have* allows both alternatives, but in a variety of forms. The negation of *Benjamin has his own bedroom* can be *B. has not his own b.* (traditional BrE), *B. hasn't his own b.* (its informal variant), *B. has not got his own b.* (a current emphatic, especially BrE usage), *B. hasn't got his own b.* (its common, informal equivalent), *B. does not have his own b.* (a widely used formal, especially AmE usage), *B. doesn't have his own b.* (its common, informal equivalent). (3) See MODAL VERB.

**Contracted forms**. The contraction *n't* is typically informal, especially in speech, except when the negation is emphasized, as in a denial of something said before, in which case the full *not* is used and stressed. With many auxiliaries, there is often also a possibility of auxiliary contraction in informal English: *It isn't fair It's not fair* (more common); *He won't object* (more common) or *He'll not object*; *They haven't finished* (more common) or *They've not finished*.

**Tag questions**. When tag questions are used to invite confirmation, positive sentences are normally followed by negative tag questions (*David is abroad, isn't he?*) and negative sentences by positive tag questions (*David isn't abroad, is he?*). Positive sentences are sometimes followed by positive tag questions (*So David is abroad, is he?*), indicating an inference or recollection from what has been said. Occasionally, they suggest suspicion or a challenge: *So that's what Doris wants, is it?*

**Expressions used with negation**. Some expressions are found exclusively or typically in negative sentences: the *not . . . any* relationship in *Doris hasn't produced any plays*, contrasted with *Doris has produced some plays*; the *not . . . either* relationship in *David doesn't smoke a pipe, either* (in response to such statements as *John doesn't smoke a pipe*), contrasted with *David smokes a pipe, too* (in response to *John smokes a pipe*).

**Negation other than through the verb**. *No*, *not*, and other negative words may be introduced in order to negate a sentence: *Jeremy has no difficulties with this* (compare *Jeremy hasn't any difficulties with this*), *Ray said not a word to anybody* (compare *Ray didn't say a word to anybody*); *Maurice will never make a fuss, will he?* (compare *Maurice won't make a fuss, will he?*); *Nothing surprises them, does it?* (compare *There isn't anything that surprises them, is there?*); *Mervyn hardly ever makes a mistake, does he?* (compare *Mervyn doesn't ever make mistakes, does he?*).

**Implied contrasts**. The negative particle or word extends its scope over the whole or part of the sentence. The extent is manifested when expressions associated with negatives are present, as in the difference between *I didn't read some of the papers* (that is, I read others) and *I didn't read any of the papers* (that is, I read none). The *focus* of the negation (marked intonationally in speech) is the part of the sentence which presents a negative contrast: *Ted doesn't teach history* may imply that someone else does or that Ted teaches something else.

**Double negation**. Prefixes such as *un-* and *in-* make the word negative but not the sentence in which it is used: *unhappy* in *They are unhappy about their new house*; *insensitively* in *They spoke rather insensitively to him when he lost his job*. Such words may be combined with another negative to cancel out, to a large extent, the force of the negative prefix: *Jeremy was not unhappy*, meaning that he was fairly happy. See LITOTES. This type of double negation, which results in a positive meaning, is different from the kinds of *multiple negation* found in both general non-standard English (*I didn't see nothing*: I didn't see anything) and in some DIALECTS (Glasgow *Ah'm no comin neer Ah'm no*: I am not coming neither I am not). Such usages are widely stigmatized and equally widely used. See DOUBLE NEGATIVE.

**NEO-LATIN**, also **New Latin**. A variety of LATIN current during and after the Renaissance, especially in academic and scientific discourse. One of its features is a stratum of GREEK associated with scholarly and highly technical usage. See BISOCIATION, CLASSICAL LANGUAGE.

**NEOLOGISM**, A new WORD or sense of a word and the coining or use of new words and senses. Most neologisms in English belong in the following categories: (1) Compounding: *couch potato*, someone constantly slumped on a couch watching television: *video-conferencing*, a number of people taking part in a conference or conferences by means of video equipment rather than all meeting in one place. (2) DERIVATION: *yuppie*, formed from *yup*, the initial letters of the phrase 'young urban professional' by adding the suffix *-ie*; *yuppiedom*, the condition of being a yuppie, formed from *yuppie* by adding the further suffix *-dom*. (3) Shifting meaning: *spin*, a journalist's term for a special bias or slant given to a piece of writing. (4) Extension in grammatical function: the nouns *quest* and *host* used as verbs. (5) ABBREVIATION: in Stock Exchange usage, *arb* from *arbitrager* or *arbitrageur*, one who sells securities or commodities simultaneously in different markets to benefit from unequal prices; the computer acronym *GIGO*, meaning *garbage in, garbage out*. (6) BACK-FORMATION: *disinform* formed from *disinformation* (and not the reverse). (7) Blending: *harmolodic* mixing *harmony* and *melodic*. (8) BORROWING: loanwords such as *glasnost* from Russian; CALQUES or LOAN TRANSLATIONS such as *found object* from French *objet trouvé*. (9) Very rarely, ROOT-CREATION, or COINAGE from sounds with no previous known meaning whatever: *googol, Kodak* (both apparently formed *ex nihilo*). See BARBARISM, BLEND, COMPOUND, JOURNALESE, NONCE WORD, SEMANTIC CHANGE, TIMESPEAK, WORD-FORMATION. See panel.

**NEPAL**. A country in South Asia. Languages: Nepali/Gurkhali (official), the mother tongue of 58% of the people; other languages such as Bhojpuri and Gurung; English, the primary foreign language, but more prevalent than this status suggests. Although influenced by Britain and providing Gurkha soldiers for both the British and Indian armies, Nepal was never part of the

## DECADES OF NEOLOGIZING

New words are often the subject of scorn because they are new, because they are perceived as unaesthetically or improperly formed, or because they are considered to be unnecessary. They are, however, a normal part of language change; with frequent use and the passage of time they become unremarked items in everyday use, as can be seen from many of the items in the following representative decade-by-decade lists of neologisms:

**1940s**. acronym, airlift, apartheid, atomic age, automation, baby-sit, bikini, blockbuster, call girl, circuitry, cold war, crash landing, debrief, declassify, doublethink, flying saucer, freeze-dry, genocide, gobbledygook, gremlin, guided missile, hydrogen bomb, nerve gas, petrochemical, quisling, radar, snorkel, spaceship, starlet, tape recorder, task force, vegan, VIP, xerography, zero in.

**1950s**. A-OK, automate, beatnik, brainwashing, common market, cosmonaut, countdown, desegregation, discotheque, do-it-yourself, egghead, hard sell, H-bomb, hotline, Kremlinology, LSD McCarthyism, moonlighting, moonshot, Ms, name-dropping, nuke, overkill, panelist, paramedic, parenting, sci-fi, scuba, senior citizen, sex kitten, shopping mall, soft sell, space medicine, sputnik.

**1960s**. affirmative action, biodegradable, bionics, brain drain, cable television, counter-productive, cryonics, cybernation, disco, Eurocrat, Eurodollar, fastfood, genetic engineering, jet lag, microelectronics, microwave oven, pleabargaining, pop art, postcode/postal code (BrE), quasar, reverse discrimination, sitcom, space shuttle, theme park, tokenism, underachiever, uptight, ZIP Code (AmE).

**1970s**. boat people, bottom line, condo, corn row, downsize, ecocatastrophe, ecofreak, empty nester, flextime, gas guzzler, gasohol, hit list, junk food, Legionnaire's Disease, Mediagate, miniseries, nouvelle cuisine, petrodollars, shuttle diplomacy, supply-side economics, Watergate, Watergatology.

**1980s**. cash point, channelling, couch potato, Filofax, glasnost, golden handcuffs, golden handshake, golden parachute, gridlock, home shopping, kiss-and-tell book, necklacing, New Agers, perestroika, personal organizer, power breakfast, silent majority, telemarketing, wholefoodie, whoopie, yuppie, yuppiedom.

**1990s**. New words which may become established include: Britpop, carjacking, charm offensive, ethnic cleansing, European Union, home page, intranet (source: *The Oxford Dictionary of New Words*, 1997).

British Empire. English in Nepal is unique in that it was introduced neither by colonization nor by missionaries. Until 1950, Nepal was a closed society ruled by hereditary prime ministers, but a tradition of English instruction came primarily from India, in whose universities most Nepalese teachers were educated. Since the 1960s, Nepal has had an open-door policy and English has become a major language of travel, tourism, and regional communication. In 1951, as part of a process of democratization, use of English in the media received some support. In 1985, there were 417 Nepali- and 32 English-language periodicals. English is widely used in advertising and there is a small body of creative writing. Radio and television have contributed to the diffusion of English and are used for teaching it. CODE-MIXING AND CODE-SWITCHING with English are as common as in other parts of South Asia; Nepalese English has much in common with that of northern India. See SOUTH ASIAN ENGLISH.

**NETIQUETTE** [A blend of *net* and *etiquette*]. Guidelines relating to behaviour when posting messages to an electronic newsgroup, especially on the INTERNET: 'a set of rules that reflect longstanding experience about getting along harmoniously in the electronic environment (electronic mail and computer newsgroups)' (Philip E. Margolis, *Random House Personal Computer Dictionary*, 2nd ed., 1996). These include: (1) keep your message short; (2) provide a clear, concise, and relevant subject heading for your message; (3) do not use all capital/upper-case letters all the time; it is considered to be shouting; (4) do not criticize the person, criticize the idea; (5) do not criticize people's spelling and grammar.

**NETWORK STANDARD**. A variety of PRONUNCIATION supposedly favoured by radio and television announcers on US national network broadcasts, in effect a pronunciation without any features easily recognizable as characteristic of any region or social group. Thus, most Americans are rhotic (that is, they pronounce *r* where it is spelled); its non-pronunciation (except before vowels) is characteristic of eastern New England, New York City, and the South. Consequently, network STANDARD is rhotic. Similarly, it neither diphthongizes the vowel of *caught*, as in the South, nor pronounces it long and tense, as in parts of the Northeast. On the other hand, in some regions of the US *caught* and *cot* are distinct in pronunciation (typically with a rounded vowel in the first and an unrounded vowel in the second); in other regions, they are HOMOPHONES. However, the different treatments of these words are not perceived as regional features by Americans; consequently, both options are appropriate for network standard. Because many national TV announcers have tried to avoid regionally identifying language, their homogenized speech has been given the name *Network standard*. The word *standard* is, however, misleading because it suggests a more formally recognized variety than exists. *Network standard* is the closest American analogue to British RECEIVED PRONUNCIATION, but it is a distant one. It is best defined negatively as an AmE variety that has no regional features, does not mark class, is not

learned collectively in childhood, and has never been institutionalized or set up as a pronunciation model. See DIALECT (AMERICA), GENERAL AMERICAN.

**NEUTER**. A term referring to grammatical GENDER in nouns and related words, contrasting with *masculine* and *feminine* in languages that have three genders such as GERMAN and LATIN. Although there is some connection between natural and grammatical gender in such languages, a word which is grammatically neuter may be semantically quite different: in German *das Kind* (the child); *das Mädchen* (the girl). The personal pronoun *it* is sometimes said to be neuter in gender, but more accurately it is non-personal since it may be used to refer to animals and babies.

**NEUTRAL VOWEL**. See SCHWA.

**NEWBOLT REPORT**. A report on the teaching of English in England and Wales, presented to the Board of Education in 1921 by a committee chaired by Sir Henry Newbolt. Entitled *The Teaching of English in England*, the report argued that English was unduly neglected as a subject in many schools, and insisted that it should be built into the total educational experience. Cautiously rather than enthusiastically progressive, it covered the whole range of education, from elementary schools to universities, and argued that the understanding of literature should have a central role and that emphasis should be placed on teaching pupils how to form well-constructed arguments. See BULLOCK REPORT, KINGMAN REPORT.

**NEW ENGLAND**. The name of the six north-easternmost states of the US (Maine, Vermont, New Hampshire, Massachusetts, Connecticut, and Rhode Island); the site of the second oldest permanent English settlement on the North American mainland. The New England colonies were populated by Puritans mainly from EAST ANGLIA, who came to the New World primarily for religious reasons. Because of their predominantly common origin and cultural unity, the New England settlers formed a more homogeneous community than did colonists elsewhere.

**The Puritan inheritance**. The character of the colonists was early famed for its seriousness, emphasis on the work ethic, and a social consciousness that sprang from the scriptural injunction to charity; this was, however, often expressed as a tendency to enforce their view of what is good on those who did not share it. The conflict between Puritanism and pleasure can be seen in much of American social life to the present day. New England has served as the schoolhouse and conscience of the US. One of its most famous sons, Noah WEBSTER, was a force in shaping the DICTIONARY and schoolbook tradition of the country; his name has entered the lore of the nation as a synonym for dictionaries.

**Linguistic features**. The terms applied popularly to present-day New England speech are often the same as those used in the 17c to characterize the language of the English Puritans: a NASAL TWANG, high-pitched, harsh, and unmusical. In fact, however, New England is divided between two rather different DIALECTS: *Eastern New England*, with Boston as its hub, and *Western New England*, which blends into upper New York State as the wellspring of the *Inland Northern* dialect that sweeps across the northern tier of states to the Pacific. One of the defining characteristics of these two dialects is their treatment of *r* when not followed by a vowel. Eastern New England is non-rhotic, articulating it much as British RP does, with a gliding vowel. Western New England, on the other hand, is RHOTIC, as is most of the US. See DIALECT (AMERICA).

**NEW ENGLISH**. A term in LINGUISTICS for a recently emerging and increasingly autonomous variety of English, especially in a non-Western setting such as India, Nigeria, or Singapore. Two works of the 1980s have had virtually the same title: *New Englishes*, ed. John Pride (US: Newbury House, 1982), and *The New Englishes*, by John Platt, Heidi Weber, and Ho Mian Lian (UK: Routledge & Kegan Paul, 1984). The term is sometimes used generically: 'The first documented evidence of the New English of Sierra Leone (NESL)' (Joe Pemagbi, 'Still a Deficient Language?', *English Today* 17, Jan. 1989). See ENGLISHES.

**NEWFOUNDLAND ENGLISH**. The English language as used in the Canadian island and province of Newfoundland for almost 500 years, and the oldest variety in the Americas, dating from the early 16c. It derives primarily from the speech of early settlers from the English WEST COUNTRY and later Ireland, and is the outcome of long, stable settlement and relative remoteness. Many Newfoundland *townies* have features of pronunciation, grammar, and vocabulary that are distinct from the rest of Canada, and the varied DIALECTS of the *baymen* are possibly the most distinctive in the country. Because of such factors the English of Newfoundland is something more than a dialect of CANADIAN ENGLISH, and can be described as a variety with a standard and dialects of its own. Harold Paddock, in *Languages in Newfoundland and Labrador* (1982), delineates five main dialect areas on the island. In a survey by Sandra Clarke (reported in Paddock), the residents of St John's ranked six local ACCENTS in terms of prestige: first, BrE Received Pronunciation, then upper-class St John's Irish, Canadian Standard English, non-standard St John's 'Anglo-Irish', and a non-standard regional dialect of the southern shore.

**Pronunciation**. (1) Newfoundland speech is mainly RHOTIC. (2) There is English West Country influence in initial /v/ for /f/ and /z/ for /s/: 'a vine zummer' for *a fine summer*. (3) There is Irish influence in /t, d/ for /θ, ð/: 'tree of dem' for *three of them*. (4) Initial /h/ is unstable, sometimes added before the vowels of stressed syllables ('helbow' for *elbow*), sometimes dropped ('eel' for *heel*). (5) Final consonant clusters are often simplified: 'a soun in the loff' for *a sound in the loft*. (6) Certain vowel distinctions are commonly not made: *boy* is a HOMOPHONE of *buy*, *speak* rhymes with *break* and *port* with *part*.

**Grammar**. Dialect usage includes: (1) The use of *is* or *'m* for present forms of *be*: *I is*, *you is*, *he is*, *we is*, *they is*; *I'm*, *you'm*, *we'm*, *they'm*. (2) The negative forms *baint'e* are you not, *I idden* I am not, *you idden* you are not, *he idden* he is not, *tidden* it is not (reflecting West Country influence). (3) Distinctive forms of *do*, *have*, *be*: *They doos their work*; *I haves a lot of colds*; *It bees cold here in winter*; *Do Mary work here?*; *Have she finished?*; *'Tis cold here now*. (4) In some areas, an *-s* in all simple present-tense verb forms (*I goes*, *he goes*, *we goes*, etc.), distinguishing the full-verb use from the auxiliary use of *do*, *have*, and *be*. (5) Weak rather than strong forms in some irregular verbs: 'knowed' for *knew*, 'throwed' for *threw*. (6) Four variants for the perfect: *I've done*, *I've a-done*, *I bin done*, *I'm after doin*. (7) *He/she* as substitutes for inanimate countable nouns: *We'd have what we'd call a flake-beam, a stick, say, he'd be thirty feet long.* (8) In some areas, the form *un* or *ən* as a masculine pronoun and for *it*: *Tom kicked un* (the shovel). If, however, the shovel rather than the rake is stressed, *he* is used: *Tom kicked he.* (9) Some expressions of HIBERNO-ENGLISH origin: *It's angry you will be; It's myself that wants it.*

**Vocabulary**. (1) Expressions that are archaic or obsolete elsewhere: *angishore* a weak, miserable person (from Irish Gaelic *ain dei seoir*), sometimes transformed to *hangashore*; *bavin* brushwood used for kindling; *brewis* (from SCOTS, pronounced 'brooze') stew (applied to a mix of soaked ship's biscuits, salt codfish, and pork fat). (2) Words for natural phenomena, occupations, activities, etc., such as terms for seals at various stages of development: *bedlamer, dotard, gun seal, jar, nog-head, ragged-jacket, turner, white coat.* (3) A local word familiar elsewhere in Canada is *screech*, a potent dark rum (from Scots *screech* whisky). (4) A *livyer* (live here) is a permanent inhabitant, while a *comefrom-away* (sometimes shortened to *CFA*) is an outsider or mainlander. See DIALECT (CANADA), IRISH ENGLISH, MARITIME PROVINCES.

**NEW ORLEANS**. A city in Louisiana whose distinctive variety of AMERICAN ENGLISH is the result not only of the influence of its founders from Spain and France (who governed the region before the 19c) but also waves of migrants from Ireland, Germany, Italy, and most recently Vietnam. West African influence through pan-Caribbean creole is also apparent. The term *CREOLE*, as defined by local whites, applies to white descendants of early French or Spanish settlers. As defined by blacks, it applies to persons of Afro-French parentage. Both express 'authentic' local identity. Some of the dialect's characteristics come directly from FRENCH, either locally or from present and former French-speaking regions of the state, such as the obsolescent *banquette* for (AmE) sidewalk, (BrE) pavement, and the phrases *make the groceries* to shop for groceries, *make menage* to clean (the) house, and *save the dishes* to put the dishes away. The city has locally well-understood STEREOTYPES based on race, class, and neighbourhood, though linguistic features criss-cross these in complex ways. Typical grammatical features include a widespread tendency to use *had* +

past participle for the simple past (as in *Yesterday I had run into him*) and the tags *no* (as in *I don't like that, no!*) and the more widely current Coastal Southern *hear* (as in *I'm having another piece of pie, hear?*).

**Yat**. The most distinctive local variety is *Yat*, called by one observer 'the COCKNEY of New Orleans'. The name is said to derive from the greeting *Wha y'at?* 'What are you at?' Associated with such working-class districts as the Irish Channel and old Ninth Ward, it is also heard in other parts of the city and recently in some suburban *parishes* (government units in Louisiana that correspond to *counties* in much of the rest of the US). Outsiders confuse Yat with *BROOKLYNESE*; its stereotypic features include such quasi-phonetic spellings as *berlin* boiling, *dat* that, *earl* oil, *mudder* mother, and *taught* thought.

**Cuisine**. The city has a varied cuisine with characteristic vocabulary, much of it from Louisiana French: *beignet* (pronounced 'bane yea') a square doughnut dusted with powdered sugar, *debris* pan gravy, *etouffee* stewed, *file* (pronounced 'fee-lay') thickener for soups and stews derived from young sassafras leaves, *jambalaya* a dish prepared with rice, seasoning, and meat or seafood, *praline* (pronounced 'prah-leen') a confection made with pecans and brown sugar. Other terms are from English: *cajun* popcorn deep-fried crawfish/crayfish tails, *dirty rice* a spicy rice dish with chicken giblets, *king cake* a ring-shaped coffee cake traditionally served from Epiphany to Shrove Tuesday, *po' boy* a sandwich of the type known elsewhere in AmE as a *grinder, hoagie*, or *submarine*. See CAJUN.

**NEWSPEAK**. A simplified ARTIFICIAL LANGUAGE based on English in George ORWELL'S novel *Nineteen Eighty-Four* (1949). Almost any Newspeak word could serve as any part of speech; hence the verb *think* did duty for the noun *thought*, and Newspeak replaced *Newspeech*. Affixes were common: *ungood, goodwise*. The regular *stealed* and *mans* replaced irregular forms like *stole* or *men*. Compounds were frequent: *doublethink, oldthink, Oldspeak* (standard English). Other words were telescoped: *Ficdep* Fiction Department, *Ingsoc* English Socialism, *Minitrue* Ministry of Truth. Newspeak was intended not only to express but to form politically acceptable habits of thought, 'at least so far as thought is dependent on words'. It therefore excluded ambiguities and shades of meaning, along with words for unacceptable concepts like *honour* and *democracy*. Its ideological slant rendered it unable to express or translate such statements as the Oldspeak 'all men are created equal', because the concept of political equality was *crimethink*. *Newspeak* has become a term in the language at large for misleading (especially political) jargon, and is the source for a large number of words modelled on it, such as *nukespeak* and *teenspeak*. See BASIC ENGLISH, -SPEAK.

■ **NEW YORK** ─────── ■

A city and port at the mouth of the Hudson River, in the state of the same name: a major city of the US and of the English-speaking world, and the centre of one of the largest US urban areas. It occupies Manhattan and Staten Island, the western end of Long Island, and part of the adjacent mainland, and its conurbation extends into the states of New Jersey and Connecticut. It typifies the American concept of the melting-pot, having received through Ellis Island many waves of immigrants, especially from Europe and Latin America. Many languages are spoken in the city, which is the centre of a sub-dialect within the general Northern DIALECT area of AMERICAN ENGLISH.

**Pronunciation**. (1) New York pronunciation has a long, tense, very round vowel in words like *caught*, and a long, tense, relatively high vowel in words such as *cab*. (2) Like eastern New England and the American South, it is a non-RHOTIC (non-*r*-pronouncing) variety and, also like eastern New England and some accents of England (including RP), it has the LINKING *r* and IN-TRUSIVE *r*. When a word ending in *r* (which would normally not be pronounced) is followed closely by a word beginning with a vowel, the linking *r* is sounded: *gopher* is pronounced 'gopha', but in *The gopher is lost* the *r* is pronounced. By ANALOGY, an intrusive *r* occurs where it is not etymologically or orthographically justified: *sofa* rhymes with *gopher*, but in *The sofa/r is lost* an *r*-sound often intrudes. In contrast, the Southern US shares neither the linking nor intrusive *r*-sounds with the other non-rhotic varieties, indeed often losing an *r*-sound even between vowels, as in *ve'y* for *very* and *Ca'olina* for *Carolina*. Non-rhotic pronunciation differs widely in its prestige, depending on

where it occurs. In the American South, *r*-lessness is a universal feature of many areas at all social levels. In New York City, on the other hand, it correlates strongly with class differences and has low prestige. In his investigations, William Labov found that *r*-pronouncing was more common among the employees of up-market department stores and shops than among those of businesses with merchandise of lower quality and prices. He also found more *r*-pronouncing in 'careful', self-conscious speech than in spontaneous dialogue. There is also an upper-class, old-family New York English, but it has been little studied and its features are not widely known.

**Low prestige**. New York English has low prestige even among its own speakers. Their reaction, which has been dubbed 'linguistic self-hatred', is not typical of many other areas, where the local speech-ways are usually regarded as indicating that the speaker is honest, friendly, sympathetic, intelligent, and reliable. New Yorkers' discomfort with their speech patterns may reflect the low regard the rest of the nation has for those patterns. It is, however, odd that the major city of the nation (its cultural and financial centre) should be low in linguistic prestige. In fact, the STEREOTYPE of New York English is the language of a lower socioeconomic group, as though LONDON English were to identify with COCKNEY usage, without the affectionate respect often accorded to it. See BROOKLYNESE, DIALECT (AMERICA), JEWISH ENGLISH.

■ **NEW ZEALAND ENGLISH** ─── ■

Short form *NZE*. The English language as used in New Zealand, a country of the Southern Pacific and a member of the COMMONWEALTH. English has been used in New Zealand for over 200 years, from the first visit of Captain James Cook and his English-speaking crew in 1769. He recorded in his diary some MAORI words, such as *pah* (a fortified village) and on a later visit *pounamu* (greenstone or nephrite), that later became part of the vocabulary of all New Zealanders. However, a more realistic starting-point is 1840, when the Maori, inhabitants of the islands since the 9c, ceded *kawanatanga* (governorship, interpreted by the British as sovereignty) to the British Crown in the Treaty of Waitangi. From that time, settlers from the British Isles began to arrive in increasing numbers, bringing their regional modes of speech with them.

**Australian and New Zealand English.** Parallels are often drawn between AusE and NZE. Although the two varieties are by no means identical, they are often indistinguishable to outsiders. Some phoneticians consider that there is a social and historical continuum in which three varieties of pronunciation can be identified: *Cultivated New Zealand, General New Zealand,* and *Broad New Zealand.* If this is so, NZE is similar to AusE, in which these categories are generally established, but other phoneticians regard the matter as unproved. Many speakers of NZE share with many speakers of AUSTRALIAN ENGLISH and CANADIAN ENGLISH the habit of using an upward inflection of the voice in declarative sentences, often considered by non-New Zealanders to produce a tentative effect, as if inviting confirmation of a statement. This intonational pattern, however, serves to check that someone is still following what one is saying. See AUSTRALASIAN ENGLISH.

**Pronunciation.** NZE is non-rhotic, with the exception of the *Southland* BURR, the use by some speakers in Southland and Otago, South Island, of an /r/ in words like *afford* and *heart*. It is believed to derive from ScoE, since Otago was a predominantly Scottish settlement. It has been said that the norm of educated NZE is the RECEIVED PRONUNCIATION of the BBC World Service. There are, however, relatively few RP-speakers in New Zealand, a larger proportion speaking what is now called *NEAR-RP*. Its consonants do not differ significantly from those in RP except that a *wh/w* distinction is often maintained in words like *which/witch*. In words like *wharf*, where no near-HOMONYM *\*warf* exists, aspiration is less detectable.

Features of General New Zealand include: (1) Such words as *ham, pen* perceived by outsiders as 'hem', 'pin'. (2) Centralization of short *i* to SCHWA: *ships* pronounced /ʃəps/ in contrast with General Australian /ʃips/. These usages are sometimes stigmatized in print as 'shups' and 'sheeps' respectively. (3) The maintenance of RP 'ah' in *castle* /kɒːsl/, *dance* /dɒːns/ by contrast with General Australian /kæsl, dæns/. (4) Schwa used in most unstressed syllables, including /ə'fekt/ for both *affect* and *effect*, and /'rʌbəʃ/ for *rubbish*. (5) A tendency to pronounce *grown, mown, thrown* as disyllabic with a schwa:

'growen', 'mowen', 'throwen'. (6) A distinctive pronunciation for certain words: *geyser* rhyming with 'riser', *oral* with 'sorrel'; the first syllable of *vitamin* like 'high', as in AmE and ScoE; the *Zea* of *Zealand* pronounced with the vowel of *kit*. Occasional pronunciations such as *basic* /'bæsɪk/ and *menu* /'miːnjuː/ are also heard. (7) A tendency to diphthongize some long vowels, opening with a schwa, as in *boot* /bəuːt/ and *bean/been* /bəiːn/. (8) Lengthening of final *-y* in such words as *city, happy*: /'səti:/, /'hæpi:/. (9) Full pronunciation of *-day* in *Monday, Tuesday,* etc. (10) A policy of the Broadcasting Corporation that words and place-names of Maori origin be pronounced by announcers as in Maori, rather than in Anglicized forms. *kowhai* not /'kəu(w)aɪ/ but /'ɔːfai/.

**Grammar.** (1) Standard NZE is to all intents and purposes the same as standard BrE. However, the plural forms *rooves* and *wharves* are preferred to *roofs* and *wharfs*, and in spelling New Zealanders like Australians use *-ise* as in *centralise*, not *-ize*. Although *-ise* is common in BrE, *-ize* is widely used. (2) Nouns of Maori origin often appear in NZE, as in Maori itself, without a plural marker: *iwi* a tribe, as in *A Maori nation exists comprising various iwi* (not *iwis*); *marae* a courtyard of a meeting house, as in *Marae have always been open to all* (not *maraes*). The word *Maori* itself is now commonly spoken and written in plural contexts without a final *-s*: *the powerlessness which frustrates so many Maori*. Such usage is, however, currently controversial. (3) In recent works of literature, Maori speakers of non-standard English have begun to be portrayed, drawing attention to syntactic aspects of Maori English: *Here's your basket nearly finish* (Patricia Grace, 1986); *You big, brave fellow, eh?* (Bruce Mason, 1963).

**Vocabulary.** In the absence of a comprehensive dictionary of NEZ on historical principles, the number of distinctive words cannot be estimated with any certainty, but the total is likely to be less than a third of the 10,000 claimed for AusE. This vocabulary falls into five classes: LOANWORDS from Polynesian languages, words showing extension of or departure from the meanings of general English words, the elevation of regional BrE words into standard currency, loanwords from AusE, and distinct regional word forms. In more detail, these are:

*Loanwords from Maori.* In addition to names of flora and fauna, there is an in-

## NEW ZEALAND PLACE-NAMES

The place-names of New Zealand reflect mixed linguistic origins over some 200 years. According to the New Zealand Geographic Board, the body charged by Act of Parliament with registering place-names, 58% of officially recognized names (including those of rivers and mountains) are of Maori origin and 42% of European origin. The numerical breakdown between the two islands reflects the patterns of Maori and European settlement: in the North Island, 79% Maori and 21% European; in the South Island, 33% Maori and 67% European.

**1. *Maori names*.** These are of two kinds: those which conform to the sound and spelling pattern of the Maori language, such as *Awakino* (valley + ugly: 'ugly valley'), *Maunganui* (mountain + big: 'big mountain'), *Waikaremoana* ('great lake of rippling water'), and *Waitangi* ('weeping water, waterfall'); and those which have changed with time or been altered by Europeans, as in *Amuri* from Maori *Haumuri* ('east wind'), and *Pitone* from Maori *Pito-one* ('end of the beach'). The longest officially recognized place-name is *Taumatawhakatangihangakouauotamatepokaiwhenuakitanatahu*, the name of a hill in southern Hawkes Bay, North Island. It means 'The hill on which Tamatea, circumnavigator of the land, played his kouau (flute) to his loved one'.

**2. *European names*.** Most place-names of European origin are English: (1) Transfers of names for places that settlers were associated with in the British Isles, such as *Christchurch, the Canterbury Plains*, and *Dunedin* (an alternative name for Edinburgh); (2) Names commemorating people, as with *Clive, Greytown, Nelson*, and *Onslow*; (3) Names reflecting new experiences, as with *Bay of Plenty, Cape Foulwind*, and *Poverty Bay*. There has been a scattering of other European influences, such as French *Aiguilles Rouges* ('red needles'), Danish *Dannevirke*, Austrian *Franz Joseph* (named for an emperor), and the Dutch second element in the hybrid name *New Zealand* ('sea land').

---

creasing number of Maori loanwords for abstract concepts and tribal arrangements and customs: *aue* an interjection expressing astonishment, distress, etc., *haere mai* a term of greeting, *iwi* a people, tribe, *mana* power, prestige, authority, *manuwhiri* a visitor, guest, *mauri* the life principle, *rahui* a sign warning against trespass, *tupuna* an ancestor. There are also some verbs, such as *hikoi* to march, *hongi* to press noses. Some Maori words have been Anglicized to such an extent that they no longer look like Maori words: *biddy-bid* a plant with prickly burrs (Maori *piripiri*), *cockabully* a small fish (Maori *kōkopu*), *kit* a flax basket (Maori *kete*).

***Loanwords from Samoan***. Samoan loanwords are not widely used by non-Samoan New Zealanders. They include: *aiga* an extended family, *fale* a house, *palagi* a non-Samoan, *talofa* a ceremonial greeting, and the returned loanword *afakasi* a half-caste.

***Extensions and alterations***. Adaptations of general English words include: *bach* a holiday house at beach (a clipping of *bachelor*), *creek* (also AusE) a stream, *crook* (also AusE) ill, *go crook at* (also AusE) to be angry with, *farewell* as in *to farewell someone* (also AusE) to honour that person at a ceremonial occasion, *section* a building plot, *tramp* to walk for long distances in rough country, hence *tramper* one who does this.

***Standardization of British English dialect words***. BrE dialect words promoted to standard, all also AusE, include: *barrack* to shout or jeer (at players in a game, etc.), *bowyang* a band or strip round a trouser-leg below the knee, to prevent trousers from dragging on the ground, *burl* a try or attempt, as in *give it a burl*, *chook* a chicken, fowl, *dunny* a lavatory, *larrikin* a hooligan, *lolly* a sweet of any kind, especially boiled, *Rafferty's rules* no rules at all, *smooge* a display of amorous affection, *wowser* a killjoy or spoilsport.

**Loanwords from Australian English**. Words acquired from AusE include, from the preceding section, *larrikin*, *Rafferty's rules*, and: *backblocks* land in the remote interior, *battler* someone who struggles against the odds, *dill* a fool, simpleton, *ocker* a boor, *offsider* a companion, deputy, partner, *shanghai* a catapult. However, many AusE words are not used in NZE, especially words of Aboriginal origin and words associated with the swagmen (old-time itinerant workers). Similarly, many NZE words are unknown in Australia, especially words of Maori origin like the common fish names *hapuku*, *kahawai*, *tarakihi*, *toheroa*.

**Distinct word forms**. Regional coinages include compounds, fixed phrases, and diminutives: (adjective + noun) *chilly bin* a portable insulated container for keeping food and drink cool, *silver beet* seakale beet; (noun + noun) *Canterbury lamb* from the name of a province, *kiwifruit* the Chinese gooseberry; (diminutive suffix *-ie*) *boatie* a boating enthusiast, *postie* a person delivering post (shared with ScoE and CanE), *truckie* a truck-driver (also AusE), *wharfie* a waterside worker, stevedore (also AusE); (diminutive suffix *-o*, *-oh*): *bottle-oh* a dealer in used bottles, *compo* compensation, especially for an injury.

**English and Maori**. The most significant social issue relating to language is the relationship between the European majority and the Polynesian minority. This includes issues such as the status of Maori as an official language on a par with English in the courts and the pronunciation of Maori words, including place-names, in English. See *l*-SOUNDS, MAORI ENGLISH.

**NEW ZEALANDISM**. A word, phrase, idiom, or other usage peculiar to, or particularly common in, New Zealand. Such expressions are drawn from the MAORI language (*Pakeha* a white New Zealander) or are adaptations of GENERAL ENGLISH (*grass fence* a strip of long grass along an electric fence, a barrier to sheep even when the current is off). See NEW ZEALAND ENGLISH.

**NGUGI WA THIONG'O**, also written **Ngũgĩ**; formerly *James Ngugi* [b. 1938]. Kenyan (Kikuyu) teacher, critic, dramatist, and novelist, born in Limuru, and educated in Kenyan schools and at Makerere U., Uganda, and Leeds U., England. His first works were in English, set against a background of social and political upheaval as Kenya moved towards independence from Britain in the 1950s and early 1960s. Ngugi's style has been described as biblical in its purity, and expresses an African Marxist viewpoint. His writings in English include the novels *Weep Not Child* (1964), *The River Between* (1965), *A Grain of Wheat* (1967), and *Petals of Blood* (1977), and the plays *The Black Hermit* (1968), *This Time Tomorrow, The Rebels, The Wound in the Heart* (all 1970), and *The Trial of Dedan Kimathi* (1976, with Micere Mugo). When he completed *Petals of Blood*, he gave up English as the medium for his fiction, but continued to use it to translate his works and for non-fictional purposes. He argued that to provoke and cultivate the social and political reforms needed in Kenya requires novels and plays in the local languages. For this, his medium is Kikuyu (or Gĩkũyũ, as he writes the name). With Ngugi wa Mirii, he produced the play *Ngaahika Ndeenda* (1980), translated as *I Will Marry When I Want* (1982). It was immediately banned. In *Detained: A Writer's Prison Diary* (1981), he describes his one-year detention without trial in 1978. His Kikuyu novels are *Caitaani Mutharabaini* (1980), translated as *Devil on a Cross*, and *Matigari Ma Njiruungi* (1986), translated as *Matigari*. In these, Ngugi draws on oral traditions and tribal values to attack neo-colonialism, and their apparently plain language is laden with aphorisms, symbols, and slogans. His works are widely read in Kenya by people far from the modern metropolitan centres. Ngugi discusses the language issue in *Decolonising the Mind: The Politics of Language in African Literature* (1986), a work dedicated to 'all those who write in African languages, and to all those who over the years have maintained the dignity of the literature, culture, philosophy, and other treasures carried by African languages'. He adds in the preface: 'If in these essays I criticise the Afro-European (or Eurafrican) choice of our linguistic praxis, it is not to take away from the talent and the genius of those who have written in ENGLISH, FRENCH, or PORTUGUESE. On the contrary I am lamenting a neo-colonial situation which has meant the European bourgeoisie once again stealing our talents and geniuses as they have stolen our economies.' In the same work, he says:

'This book . . . is my farewell to English as a vehicle for any of my writings. From now on it is Gĩkũyũ and Kiswahili all the way.'

# ■ NIGERIA ──────────────── ■

A country of West Africa and the most populous country in Africa. Languages: English and the main languages of each state (official); the most widely spoken of the estimated 400 indigenous languages are Hausa (27%), Igbo (11%), Yoruba (18%); Nigerian Pidgin English is a widely used LINGUA FRANCA. English is the language of education after the first three years of primary school.

**History**. The Portuguese established the first trading posts along the Guinea coast in the 15c and various European nations traded in the area for gold, ivory, and slaves. British contacts with Nigeria go back at least to the 16c and varieties of English were well established in coastal areas in the 18c. British missionaries began to teach English in Nigeria during the first half of the 19c, but relations between Britain and parts of Nigeria were not formalized until 1861 when the settlement of Lagos was declared a colony. The Berlin Conference of 1885 recognized Britain's claim to the *Oil Rivers Protectorate* created in 1882 in the Niger delta area. This was enlarged and renamed the *Niger Coast Protectorate* in 1893. The *Protectorate of Southern Nigeria* and the *Protectorate of Northern Nigeria* were created in 1900 from territories controlled by the Royal Niger Company. These were amalgamated into the *Colony and Protectorate of Nigeria* in 1914. Nigeria became independent in 1960, a republic within the Commonwealth in 1961, and a federal republic in 1963.

**Nigerian English**. A wide spectrum of English is used in Nigeria, including standard English whose spoken forms are influenced by various mother tongues, more general English whose structures are influenced by the mother tongues, the Indian English of many traders and teachers, and Nigerian Pidgin English, which is part of the continuum of WEST AFRICAN PIDGIN ENGLISH is used throughout the country as a lingua franca. It is sometimes acquired as a mother tongue in such urban areas as Calabar and Port Harcourt, but almost always in conjunction with one or more local languages. It has many forms that reflect mother-tongue and English influence and,

although a number of PIDGIN dictionaries have been written and cyclostyled, it has not yet been standardized. It has been used in prose by many writers, including Chinua Achebe, and as a vehicle for poetry by Frank Aig-Imoukhuede and for drama by Ola Rotimi.

**Pronunciation**. (1) All varieties of Nigerian English are non-rhotic. RP is no longer the norm for the media, but continues to have prestige and to influence pronunciation. (2) There is a tendency towards syllable-timing that becomes more pronounced as one moves from standard English to Pidgin. Polysyllables tend to have all syllables equally stressed. (3) The central vowels /ə/ and /ɪ/ in RP tend to be replaced by /a/, /ɔ/, or /ɛ/, so that *but* can rhyme with *got* or in hypercorrect forms with *get*, and all three can occur in *church*. (4) There are fewer vowel contrasts in Nigerian English: often no distinction between *cheap* and *chip*, *caught*, *court*, and *cot*, *pool* and *pull*. (5) The diphthongs in RP *day* and *dough* tend to become the single vowels /e/ and /o/; those in *hear* and *hair* tend to have the SCHWA replaced by /a/. (6) There are differences in the pronunciation of consonants in different parts of the country. The initial consonants in *thin* and *then* tend to be replaced by /t, d/ in Igbo and Yoruba-influenced English, and by /s, z/ in Hausa-influenced English. Igbo and Yoruba speakers tend to replace the final consonant /ʒ/ as in *rouge* by *sh* ('roosh'), while Hausa speakers often use /dʒ/ ('roodge').

**Grammar**. Educated Nigerians use standard forms especially in the written medium, but the following features are widely described as occurring in general Nigerian English: (1) Uncountable nouns are often treated as countable: *I had only fruits to eat*; *I am grateful for your many advices.* (2) Definite articles are sometimes used as if the rules of standard English have been reversed: *Lorry was overcrowded*; *What do you think of the Structuralism?* (3) The use of prepositions can differ from BrE and AmE norms: *He came to my office by four o'clock* (that is, at four o'clock); *She is the best teacher for our school* (in our school). (4) PHRASAL VERBS are sometimes used differently (as in *He couldn't cope up with any more money worries*) or drop their particles (*Pick me at the corner*: not *pick me up*). (5) The MODAL VERBS *could* and *would* are often used instead of *can* and *will*: *He has* assured me that he could come tomorrow; They say that he would be attending our next meeting. Will is also sometimes used for would: I will first of all like to thank you. (6) Themselves is often used with like/love for each other: The husband and wife loved themselves dearly; Why do they like themselves so much?

**Vocabulary**. There are three groups of distinctive words in Nigerian English: (1) BORROWINGS from local languages and Pidgin: danshiki (Hausa) male gown, oga (Yoruba) master, boss, obanje (Igbo) spirit child, dash (Pidgin) to give, a gift. (2) LOANTRANSLATIONS from local languages: have long legs to exert influence, throw water to offer a bribe. (3) Items given local meanings or coined for local purposes: come, as in I'm coming I'll be with you soon, You've come! Welcome; decampee a person who moves to another political party; hear to understand, as in I hear French; senior elder, as in senior sister elder sister. See WEST AFRICAN ENGLISH.

**NOMINAL**. **1.** Relating to nouns: a nominal group. **2.** A NOUN or PRONOUN: He and bridge are the nominals in the sentence He crossed the bridge. **3.** An ADJECTIVE functioning as a noun: the poor (poor people); the accused (the accused person). The terms nominal group and nominal clause mean the same as noun phrase and noun clause. A nominal clause is a finite or non-finite clause that resembles a noun phrase in the range of its functions; for example, as the subjects of sentences, That he can't lift his arm in That he can't lift his arm worries me, and Smoking cigarettes in Smoking cigarettes can cause cancer. Compare SUBSTANTIVE.

**NOMINALIZATION**. **1.** The process or result of forming a NOUN from a word class: writing/writings and shaving/shavings derived from write and shave by adding -ing; sanity derived from sane by the addition of the noun-forming suffix -ity; nominalization derived from nominalize by adding -ation. **2.** The process or result of deriving a noun phrase by a transformation from a finite clause: their rejecting my complaint or their rejection of my complaint from They rejected my complaint.

**NONCE WORD**, also **nonce-word** [From MIDDLE ENGLISH for the nanes, metanalysis of *for then anes for the one (thing), present-day for the nonce for the time being, for the work in hand. In medieval poetry, variants of

the word nonce were used to complete lines, often plural and rhyming with bones or stones: 'Eneas hymself doun layd for the nanis, / And gave schort rest vnto his wery banis' (Gavin Douglas, Æneis, 1513).] The term nonce-word was adopted in the preparation of the OED (1884) 'to describe a word which is apparently used only for the nonce' (= on one occasion). From this usage have come by analogy such further forms as nonce combination, nonce form, nonce meaning, nonce usage (all often hyphenated). Because of the special functions, ephemerality, and even eccentricity of such usages, it is not easy to exemplify them. Recent occurrences, however, have included the verb to perestroik, formed from the Russian loanword perestroika, as if it were 'perestroiker' (one who perestroiks), and the noun Excaliburger, for a hamburger sold at Tintagel in Cornwall, a site associated with the legendary King Arthur, whose sword was called Excalibur. Nonce forms sometimes become regular, widely used words, as with mob in the early 18c, clipped from Latin mobile vulgus (the fickle crowd). See BLEND, BUZZ WORD, NEOLOGISM, ROOT-CREATION, STUNT WORD.

**NON-FINITE VERB**, also **nonfinite verb**. A form of the VERB that does not display a distinction in tense, in contrast with FINITE VERB (where there is a distinction between present tense and past tense: hopes, hoped). A non-finite verb is either an INFINITIVE or a participle. There are two infinitives: the to-infinitive ('Estelle wants to dance with Matthew'); the bare infinitive ('Philip will come with Matthew'). There are two participles: the -ing participle or the present participle ('James is playing cards') and the -ed participle or (according to its function) the past participle or passive participle ('James has visited me recently'; 'Jane was helped by Jeremy').

## ■ NONSENSE ──────────── ■

Words or language with little or no meaning and perhaps an absurd or trivial quality. The form non-sense is occasionally used as a neutral antonym of sense. The term is often attributive: a nonsense book, nonsense verse.

A nonsense syllable is formed by putting a vowel between consonants to produce a non-word, as in the sequence dib, gib, kib, mib, pib, zib, from which the forms bib, fib, lib, nib are excluded because they 'make sense' (that is, form known words or abbreviations). Nonsense syllables have often been used by psychologists in experiments that test memory and learning. The use of *nonsense words* is venerable: sometimes, like children's rhymes and folk expressions, they serve to fill out a phrase or a character (as with the giant who says *fee-fi-fo-fum, I smell the blood of an Englishman*); sometimes they garble words that once made altogether too much sense, like the references to plague behind *Ring-a-ring-a-roses, a pocket full of posies, hush-a, hush-a, all fall down*. Often, however, nonsense appears to be spontaneous and a matter of whimsy: for example, in 1862 the painter and poet Edward Lear wrote the following to his friend Evelyn Baring:

> Thrippsy pillivinx,
>     Inky tinky pobblebockle
> abblesquabs?—Flosky! Beebul trimble
> flosky!—Okul scratchabibblebongibo,
> viddle squibble tog-a-tog, ferrymoyassity
> amsky flamsky ramsky damsky
> crocklefether squiggs,
>             Flinkywisty pomm,
>             Slushypipp

The French linguist Jean-Jacques Lecercle draws attention to this letter in *The Violence of Language* (1990), saying first that it appears to be an incomprehensible hoax: 'The only surprise is that a man of 50 should still indulge in such childish games.' He notes, however, that the text is not entirely chaotic: it is English nonsense (not French), is laid out as a letter, suitably opens and closes, and is properly punctuated and (apparently) spelt. The words are clear-cut, some look credible, and here and there a bit of 'sense' creeps in (except that it may not be safe to assume that *ink*, *scratch*, and *tog*, or *-le* and *-y* are doing their usual jobs). Questions, exclamations, and statements also present themselves clearly, and so it is 'only' at the level of meaning that the system breaks down. Lecercle adds:

> But perhaps I am looking for the wrong meaning. If I forget denotation and look for connotation, in other words if I go from semantics to pragmatics, the text as a whole acquires meaning. . . . We all have to write official letters, full of the expression of high-flown but empty feeling, of conventional phrases and clichés. . . . Hollowness, sometimes even hypocrisy, are the order of the day. Would not a semantically empty text, keeping only the pragmatic skeleton of a conventional letter, aptly embody the

artificiality of such letters? Lear's meaning, if my hypothesis is correct, is satirical.

Lecercle draws this meaning almost painfully from Lear's text, his conclusion pointing to a distinctive feature of nonsense: that people often work on it, like a Delphic prophecy, to eliminate as much of the *non-* as they can.

In recent years, especially in JAPAN, a kind of pseudo-English has begun to appear regularly on the packaging of goods, on T-shirts, and the like: *Joyful, let's dash in a sky* and *When I jumped far beyond your imagination, I found myself a gust of wind*. Such surreal snippets may now have become trendy in the English-speaking world. In 'English know-how, no problem' (an article in *The Independent on Sunday*, 9 Sept. 1990), the American writer Bill Bryson discusses such a 'message' on a British-made jacket seen in London: *Rodeo— 100 per cent Boys for Atomic Atlas*. 'What', he asks, 'do these strange messages mean? In the literal sense, nothing of course. But in a more metaphoric way they do rather underscore the huge, almost compulsive, appeal of English in the world. It is an odd fact that almost everywhere on the planet products are deemed more appealing, and sentiments more powerful, if they are expressed in English, even if they make next to no sense.' See DECORATIVE ENGLISH.

**Nonsense verse**. The humour of nonsense verse is usually emphasized by rare words, neologisms, and unexpected juxtapositions. Often intended for children, such verse also appeals to an adult sense of the ridiculous or whimsical. In English, Edward Lear and Lewis CARROLL are its best-known exponents. Carroll's poem 'The Hunting of the Snark' developed from a single line ('For the Snark *was* a Boojum, you see') that occurred to him while out walking one day in 1874. Whenever asked if the poem had allegorical, satirical, or other significance, he would answer, 'I don't know.' In the poem, Carroll is imprecise about the nature of Snarks, but makes it clear that Boojums are a kind of Snark, and a dangerous kind at that. The poem ends with the line out of which it first grew:

> 'It's a Snark!' was the sound that first
>     came to their ears.
> And seemed almost too good to be true.
> Then followed a torrent of laughter and
>     cheers:

Then the ominous words 'It's a Boo—'
Then silence. Some fancied they heard in
  the air
A weary and wandering sigh
That sounded like '—jum!' but the others
  declare
It was only a breeze that went by.

They hunted till darkness came on, but
  they found
Not a button, or feather, or mark,
By which they could tell that they stood
  on the ground
Where the Baker had met with the
  Snark.

In the midst of the word he was going to
  say,
In the midst of his laughter and glee,
He had softly and suddenly vanished
  away—
For the Snark *was* a Boojum, you see.

Successful nonsense verse must respect the
structure and syntax of a language; comic
NEOLOGISMS need to be rooted in the familiar. In the opening lines of Carroll's
'Jabberwocky':

  'Twas brillig, and the slithy toves
  Did gyre and gimble in the wabe.

the reader can deduce that *toves* and *wabe*
must be nouns, *slithy* an adjective and *gyre*
and *gimble* verbs.

See ACCEPTABILITY, BABY TALK, CUMBRIC,
DECORATIVE    ENGLISH,    GRAMMATICALITY,
MINCED OATH.

## NON-SEXIST LANGUAGE/USAGE. See
SEXISM.

## NON-STANDARD, NONSTANDARD. A
term for usages and varieties that are not
part of a STANDARD language: such socially
marked usages as *He ain't comin', I seen him;*
such regionally marked usages as *Ah dinnae
ken* (Scots: I don't know); such regional varieties of English as Geordie in England and
Brooklynese in the US. The term has three
uses: as a neutral alternative to *sub-standard;*
as one in a set of three (*standard, non-
standard, sub-standard*); as a EUPHEMISM for
*sub-standard.* It is not always easy to establish
which use is dominant in particular texts
and contexts.

## NORM. A STANDARD, model, or average,
often used of social behaviour and consensus in the use of a language: *deviations from*

*the norm; linguistic norms.* See DEVIANT, NOR-
MATIVE, REFERENCE NORM, REGULAR, RULE.

## NORMAN FRENCH. The variety of Old
Northern FRENCH adopted in the 10c by
the *Normans,* Norse settlers who gave their
name to Normandy. It extended to England
after the Norman Conquest in 1066. In its
British context, it is often referred to as
*ANGLO-NORMAN.* Although native only to the
aristocracy and their immediate retainers,
Norman French was until the 13c dominant
in England and important in Wales, Scotland, and Ireland. It influenced English and
was in turn influenced by it, as well as by
Central (Parisian) French, which as the
language of the French court was considered more refined. In Chaucer's *Canterbury
Tales* (14c), the Prioress is singled out as a
speaker of English French: 'And Frensh she
spak ful faire and fetisly, / After the scole of
Stratford atte Bowe, / For Frensh of Paris was
to hir unknowe.' By the end of the Hundred
Years War (mid-15c), French was no longer a
living tongue in England, although elements of it were preserved for centuries afterwards, as in *Law French.* Its last British
remnant is in the Channel Islands.

Among the many Old French words in
English, the oldest have a Norman French
aspect (sometimes with doublets from Central French, shown in parentheses): (1) Hard
*c* as opposed to *ch* as in *chair: caitiff, capon,
car* (*chariot*), *carrion, carry, castle, catch* (*chase*),
*cater, cattle* (*chattels*), *cauldron, decay, escape,
pocket* (*pouch*). The Modern French equivalent is the *sh*-sound in *chateau.* (2) Hard *g* as
opposed to *j* as in *James: gammon, garden,
garter. Gaol* has a Norman French spelling
but a Central French pronunciation,
whence the alternative *jail.* The Modern
French equivalent is the *zh*-sound in *jardin.*
(3) A *w* as opposed to a *g(u): ewer, reward* (*regard*), *wage* (*gage*), *wait, wallop* (*gallop*), *ward*
(*guard*), *warden* (*guardian*), *warranty* (*guarantee*), *warren, waste, wicket, wile* (*guile*), *wise*
(*guise*). The Modern French equivalent is the
*g(u)* in *garde, guichet.* (4) The *ch* in *chair, cherry,
chisel, patch* (*piece*), etc. The Modern French
equivalent is the *s*-sound in *cerise.* (5) The *sh*
in *ashet* (ScoE), *brush, cushion, fashion, leash,
mushroom, parish, push, usher,* etc. The Modern French equivalent is the *s*-sound in
*façon, pousser. Sh* is notable in English verbs
formed on Norman French verbs in *-ir: abolish, finish, perish, polish.* (6) The *qu* in *conquest*
(but not *conqueror*), *enquire, quality, quarter,*

*question, quit*, etc. The Modern French equivalent is the *k*-sound in *quitter*. (7) An *ai*, *ei*, or *ey* spelling (and an *ee* or *ay* pronunciation): *convey* (*convoy*), *deceive*, *faith*, *heir*, *leisure*, *prey*, *receive*, *veil*. The Modern French equivalent is the *wa*-sound in *loisir*.

**NORMATIVE**. A term in LINGUISTICS and EDUCATION for belonging to or serving to establish and maintain a norm, as in *normative grammar*. If a language, variety of a language, or culture depends for its norms on another community, it is *exonormative*; if it does not, it is *endonormative*. Most colonies and many post-colonial societies have exonormative rules: until recently AusE was exonormative in terms of BrE, but has in recent years become increasingly endonormative.

**NORN**. A variety of NORSE once spoken in and around the Northern Isles of Scotland, and known as *Orkney Norn* and *Shetland Norn*. Orkney and Shetland were settled in the 9c by Norse-speaking farmers, mainly from south-western Norway, who imposed their language on the local Pictish people. At about the same time there were settlements by Scandinavians in Caithness and in the West Highlands and Islands. But nowhere else in the British Isles did links with Scandinavia endure so long and leave such striking imprints on dialects, place-names, culture, and folk memory. There was Scots influence in the family of the earls of Orkney from the 12c, but after the accession of the Lowland Scottish Sinclairs to the Earldom in 1379, and the pledging of Orkney and Shetland in 1468/9 by the King of Norway and Denmark to the King of Scots, the islands became dominated by SCOTS-speaking rulers, administrators, and clerics. From the 16c or earlier, Scots appears to have been the 'high' and Norn the 'low' language.

It has been conjectured that Norn was superseded by Scots in Caithness in the 15c and by GAELIC in the West Highlands and Islands in the 16c, but it appears to have endured to the later 18c in Orkney and perhaps into the 19c in Shetland. Garbled fragments (rhymes, proverbs, riddles, and snatches of songs) persisted in Orkney and especially Shetland folklore to the 20c (as late as 1958 on the island of Foula). The scanty earlier records reveal a language related to Faroese, but with a decaying inflec-

tional system, as in this passage from the Lord's Prayer, as recorded by James Wallace in *Account of the Islands of Orkney* (1700): *Ga vus da on da dalight brow vora, firgive vus sinna vora, sin vee firgive sindara mutha vs* (Give us each day our daily bread, Forgive us our sins, as we forgive sins against us). The equivalent Old Norse was: *Gef oss dag um dag dagligt brauð vort, fyrirgef oss syndir va\*p1rar, sem vér fyrirgef syndir i móti oss*. Local documents in Older Scots (from 1433) contain many administrative and legal terms of Norn origin, and court records (from the early 17c) introduce many originally Norn words, including: *galt* boar, *grind* gate, *heavie* straw basket, *row* to 'roo' or pluck (sheep), *spick* fat, blubber, *voe* inlet, *voir* springtime. See ORKNEY AND SHETLAND DIALECTS, SCANDINAVIAN LANGUAGES.

■ **NORSE** ─────────────────── ■

Also *Old Norse*, *Scandinavian*, and (with particular reference to its use in England) DANISH. The SCANDINAVIAN LANGUAGES in an early, relatively homogeneous form. OLD ENGLISH and Old Norse were related and to some extent mutually intelligible. Despite differences in grammar, communication appears to have been widespread, especially in the early Middle Ages when Danes settled in much of England and the country was ruled by Danish kings (1016–42). The numerous PLACE-NAMES in -*by*, -*thorp*, -*thwaite*, -*toft* testify to the density of the settlement known as the DANELAW. Many words were identical or similar in the two languages, such as *folk*, *hus*, *sorg* (sorrow), which were both English and Norse, and such correspondences as Old English *fæder*, *gærs/græs*, *wif*, Old Norse *faðir*, *gras*, *vif* (father, grass, wife). Norse came to exercise a marked influence on English, especially when the Norman Conquest in the 11c broke the continuity of the Old English standard based on the West Saxon dialect. Norse influence has taken two forms: influence on English at large and influence on NORTHERN ENGLISH and SCOTS.

**Influence on English at large**. Much of the everyday vocabulary of English is of Norse origin: *call*, *cast*, *fellow*, *gape*, *happy*, *hit*, *husband*, *ill*, *leg*, *loose*, *low*, *sister*, *skill*, *skirt*, *sky*, *take*, *weak*, *window*, *wrong*. Occasionally, both the English and the Norse form of the same word have survived as DOUBLETS: *shirt* (English), *skirt* (Norse). Norse borrowings include such legal and administrative terms as *hustings*, *law*, *bylaw*, *outlaw*, and *riding* (as in the North Riding of Yorkshire and as used in CanE for a parliamentary constituency), but the overwhelming majority of Norse words in English are general, everyday expressions, such as must have arisen from close social contact between the two peoples, an impression reinforced by the Norse origin of a number of English grammatical words: *they/their/them*, *though*, *both*. It is also possible that some syntactic structures common to MODERN ENGLISH and Scandinavian but unknown in other GERMANIC LANGUAGES (such as *the house we live in*) had their origin in the Danelaw.

**Influence on Northern English and Scots**. A large number of Norse words which have not spread into English at large survive in the usage of northern England and Scotland: *gate* a street, *ken* to know (used in general English only in the phrase *beyond our ken*), *lake* to play, *neb* beak. Sometimes the Norse form is regional while a corresponding English form is standard: *garth/yard*, *kirn/churn*, *kist/chest*, *skell/shell*. In other cases of north–south doublets, both forms now belong to general English: *kirk/church*, *skirl/shrill*, *screech/shriek*. See SCOTS.

**Conclusion**. The extensive Norse settlements in the British Isles during the Viking age, followed by a long period of coexistence, have had a profound influence on English. Because of close kinship, Scandinavian influence is less immediately obvious than other foreign influences, yet it has altered basic vocabulary and grammar, and has permeated DIALECT usage even more than the STANDARD LANGUAGE. In its origin and earliest form, English is classed with the West Germanic languages, a group which comprised the ancestors of Dutch, Frisian, and German, but a detailed comparison of the languages in their present form might place English nearer to the North Germanic group. See IRISH ENGLISH, NORN.

**NORTHERN ENGLISH**. An occasional term for: (1) The Northumbrian DIALECT of OLD ENGLISH and its successor dialects in the North of England and in Scotland. (2) English as used in the North of England, sometimes extended to include SCOTS and SCOTTISH ENGLISH. See CUMBRIA, DIALECT IN ENGLAND, GEORDIE, LANCASHIRE, L-SOUNDS, NORSE, NORTHUMBRIA, SCOUSE, YORKSHIRE.

**NORTHERN IRISH ENGLISH**. English used in Northern Ireland, of which there are four varieties: (1) ULSTER SCOTS, also known as *Scotch-Irish*, brought to the area in the 17c by Lowland Scots. It is the most northerly variety, found in Antrim, Down, Derry/Londonderry, and in eastern and central Donegal in the Irish Republic. (2) ANGLO-IRISH or ULSTER ENGLISH, introduced by 17c settlers from England. It stretches northward from Bundoran in the west to Dundalk in the east, has much in common with southern Anglo-Irish, and has been influenced by Ulster Scots. (3) HIBERNO-ENGLISH, influenced by GAELIC. It is most widely found in rural Armagh, Donegal, Fermanagh, and Tyrone. There is a further pocket in the Glens of Antrim, where Irish Gaelic was reinforced by Scottish Gaelic and survived into the 1940s. (4) The distinctive speech of BELFAST. See IRISH ENGLISH, L-SOUNDS.

**NORTHUMBERLAND BURR**. See BURR, R-SOUNDS.

**NORTHUMBRIA**. A kingdom of the Angles before the unification of England, from the Humber to the Forth. In the 7c, its leadership was recognized by the other kingdoms and its monasteries were in the forefront of European religious life. The Venerable Bede was a monk at Jarrow and the Lindisfarne Gospels demonstrate great skill in the illuminating of manuscripts. In the 9c the kingdom was overwhelmed by Danes and in the 10c the Scots (speakers of GAELIC) extended their border from the Forth to the Tweed, acquiring a province of speakers of Northumbrian English. In 944, when the last Danish king was expelled from York, Northumbria became an earldom of England. The Northumbrian dialect was ancestral to NORTHERN ENGLISH and SCOTS and is preserved in glosses on the Lindisfarne and other gospels, in manuscripts of Caedmon's *Hymn* and Bede's *Death Song* (8–9c), and in runic inscriptions (8–10c). See GEORDIE, RUNE.

**NOTATION**. A process or system of representing something audible or abstract by means of graphic symbols, such as *musical notation*, *phonetic notation*, or *mathematical notation*. See ETYMON, PHONETIC TRANSCRIPTION, TRANSLITERATION.

# ■ NOTES AND REFERENCES —— ■

Additions to works of scholarship and science such as supplementary points of information and details of the sources to which writers have referred. There is no sharp distinction between the two categories: notes can consist of or contain references, and references may be annotated. Notes, however, are often more substantial than references (for example, in monographs), and tend to be either *footnotes* (at the bottom of a page) or *endnotes* (at the end of a chapter or entire work). *Sidenotes*, set in a margin, also sometimes occur. Scholarly notes are usually signalled by superscript numbers at appropriate points in a text, but such symbols as asterisks and obelisks may be used instead for footnotes. References, on the other hand, tend to be listed in appendices whose titles and locations are usually given on the contents page of the work in question. The advantage of footnotes to the reader is ease of reference; the disadvantage to both reader and typesetter is that long notes are likely to run over to the lower part of the next page. The advantage of endnotes, especially for the printer and publisher, is that they are all arranged sequentially in one place, regardless of the length of individual notes. The disadvantage for the reader is that they are at a distance from the various parts of the text to which they relate, but this disadvantage may be lessened if the notes are so organized as to provide a linked set of supporting comments on the text. For texts which authors and publishers wish to keep free of superscript symbols, endnotes are keyed to such points of reference as page numbers or repeat identifying phrases from the text. All such addenda are generally kept as brief as possible, but endnotes can sometimes be in effect supplementary essays. Endnotes, bibliographies, lists of works referred to, and the like, are usually set in a smaller typesize than the main text. Footnotes, the compactness of which is especially desirable, may be set even smaller, several sizes down from the text type. Generally, the bulk of any set of notes and references is taken up by citations of the authors, titles, dates, etc., of publications. These may be presented in either of two ways: in note form, often in a *reference list*, such as 'See K. Wales, *A Dictionary of Stylistics*, 1989'; or in bibliographical form, such as 'Wales, K. 1989. *A Dictionary of Stylistics*. Harlow:

Longman'. See ACADEMIC USAGE, ASTERISK, BIBLIOGRAPHY, WRITING.

# ■ NOUN ———————————— ■

A PART OF SPEECH or WORD CLASS typically used in a variety of sentence functions such as subject and object, generally in combination with the definite or indefinite article and modifiers and traditionally regarded as 'naming' or identifying persons and things.

**Form**. In English, many especially monosyllabic nouns cannot formally be identified as such (*woman, girl, dog, cat, king, war*), whereas in some languages, such as LATIN, they have distinctive endings (*femina, puella; canis, faelis; bellum*). Many polysyllabic nouns, however, are identifiable by suffixes used to derive nouns from other nouns or from verbs and adjectives: -*ing* (*farming, swimming*); -*er* (*dancer, writer*); -*ation* (*association, organization*); -*ity* (*morality, reality*); -*ness* (*darkness, kindness*); -*ism* (*humanism, racism*), -*ist* (*rationalist, socialist*).

**Function**. In a noun phrase, a noun functions as the main or only word which can be subject ('The *crew* boarded the vessel'), direct object ('They will clean up the *waste*'), indirect object ('I told the committee my *views*'), subject complement ('One fascinating discovery was a *musket*'), object complement ('Everybody thought her the best *candidate*'), adverbial ('We saw them last *night*'), complement of a preposition ('We did it for *Tony*'); modifier of another noun ('*income* tax').

**Subclasses**. There are a number of grammatical and semantic subclasses of nouns: common or proper (*Jane, Jeremy*); animate (*child*) or inanimate (*pencil*); abstract (*opinion*) or concrete (*glass*), countable (*student*) or uncountable (*information*). In the sentence Pick up the book, the noun *book* is common, inanimate, concrete, and countable. In the sentence Barbara came too, the noun *Barbara* is proper, animate, concrete, and in this instance uncountable. A noun may have one feature in one context and the opposite feature in another: *glass* is countable in Have another glass of orange juice, uncountable in That dish is made of cut glass.

**Number**. Countable nouns make a distinction between singular and plural in number. The distinction is generally indicated by a difference between singular and plural

## LATIN ABBREVIATIONS, ETC., FOR NOTES AND REFERENCES

To save space, but also as a legacy from the days when Latin was the language of pan-European scholarship, authors and editors have tended to use, in texts and notes, Latin terms of reference, usually in abbreviated form and often printed in italic. The most common traditional usages are:

*c.*, *ca.* Short for *circa* 'around': indicating an approximate date or figure, as in 'Chaucer was born *c*.1340' and '*c*.3 m' (for 'around three million').

*cf.* Short for *confer* 'compare': inviting the reader to compare an entry, topic, or work with one or more others, as in '*cf.* Havelock, *Preface to Plato*', '*cf.* analogy, metaphor, simile'.

*e.g.* Short for *exempli gratia* 'for the sake of example': preceding an example of the point being discussed.

*et al.* Short for *et alii* (masculine), *et aliae* (feminine), *et alia* (neuter), 'and others': coming after the first of a list of names whose other elements the writer does not wish to provide or repeat: 'R. Quirk *et al.*, *A Comprehensive Grammar of the English Language*.'

*etc.* Short for *et cetera* 'and so on': used widely, both formally and casually, for more of the same: 'books, magazines, newspapers, etc.'

*fl.* Short for *floruit* 'flourished': indicating the period in which someone lived, usually because actual life dates are not known: 'Gautama the Buddha, *fl.* 6th century BC'.

*ibid.* Short for *ibidem* 'in the same place': referring the reader to a publication mentioned in an immediately preceding note: *Ibid.* p. 330.

*id.*, *ead.* Short for *idem* 'the same man', *eadem* 'the same woman': used after the first reference in notes that have more than one reference to works by the same author, to save repeating the author's name.

*i.e.* Short for *id est* 'that is': used in running text to gloss or clarify a statement just made: '. . . the work of an *ovate* i.e. a minor druid'.

*loc. cit.*, *l.c.* Short for *loco citato* 'in the place cited': used in notes to indicate a passage already cited: 'Urdang, *loc. cit.*'

*NB* or *N.B.* Short for *nota bene* 'note well': used to call attention to something the writer considers important: '*NB* difficulties in dating such texts'.

*op. cit.* Short for *opere citato* 'in the work cited': used in notes to indicate reference to a publication already cited: 'Urdang, *op. cit.*, p. 18'.

*passim* 'here and there': used to inform the reader that the topic under discussion is treated in various parts of a cited publication: 'Chap. 5, *passim*' (that is, throughout Chapter 5), 'Chap. 5 *et passim*' (throughout Chapter 5 and elsewhere).

*q.v.* Short for *quod vide* 'which see': once a common device to indicate in passing that something is treated fully elsewhere, in its proper place: 'In 1792, the Jacobins under Georges Danton (*q.v.*) seized power' (that is, see the entry *Danton*). Plural *qq.v.*

*sic* 'thus': used parenthetically by writers and editors, especially in square brackets, to distance themselves from a dubious or erroneous usage, but also sometimes to draw attention to it, perhaps highlighting it in order to mock it: '. . . but they did not recieve [*sic*] the letter'.

*viz.* Short for *videlicet* 'it is permitted to see' (understood as 'namely', 'to wit'): a reference in apposition that specifies examples or identifies a person or thing, as in 'The Magi, *viz.* Melchior, Caspar, and Balthazar'.

forms (*cat/cats*, *sample/samples*, *phenomenon/phenomena*).

**Gender**. English does not have GENDER classes of nouns as in Latin and GERMAN, but some nouns have male and female reference: *father, boy; mother, girl*. There are some pairs of nouns one of which has a suffix marking a male/female contrast: *host/hostess, hero/heroine, usher/usherette; widow/widower*. The gender reference of human nouns becomes manifest when *he* or *she* relates to the noun: *My neighbour said she/he wanted to speak to you*. Non-human animate nouns (and nouns relating to young children, depending on the circumstances) allow male, female, or non-sexual reference: *Don't touch the dog; he/she/it has fleas*.

**Case**. Old English had, like Latin, a complex CASE system for its nouns. Modern English, however, only makes two case distinctions: common case (*Tom*) and genitive case (*Tom's*). For regular plurals, the distinction is found only in punctuation, but not in pronunciation: *students/students'* (contrast *men* and *men's*).

See ABSTRACT AND CONCRETE, ANIMATE NOUN, COMMON NOUN, COUNTABLE AND UNCOUNTABLE, NAME, NUMBER, OLD ENGLISH, PROPER NOUN, SUBSTANTIVE.

**NOUN CLAUSE**. See RELATIVE CLAUSE.

**NOUN-INCORPORATION**. A term in WORD-FORMATION for the creation of a compound in which a noun is incorporated into a verb as its first element: *baby-sit, house-hunt, sleep-walk*. Such forms go back at least to the Middle Ages, as with *backbite* (*c*.1300) to bite someone on or behind the back. They are often nonce or stunt usages, sometimes with a touch of humour: *backseat-drive, ballroom-dance*. They generally have two sources: (1) BACK-FORMATION: *eavesdrop* from *eavesdropper*; *kidnap* from *kidnapper*; *mass-produce* from *mass production*; *window-shop* from *window-shopping*. (2) The conversion of a noun-noun compound to use as a verb: *fingerprint*, as in *fingerprinting suspects*; *scent-mark*, as in: 'How often a cat scent-marks varies according to how old it is' (*BBC WildLife*, Jan. 1989).

**NUCLEUS**. **1**. In PHONETICS, the central, most prominent part of a SYLLABLE, consisting of a vowel or vowel-like consonant, such as the [a] sound in *bat* or the [l] sound in *battled*. **2**. In phonetics, the syllable that carries the tone change; the tonic syllable.

## ■ NUMBER[1] ────────── ■

A concept associated with quantity, size, measurement, etc., and represented by a word such as *three*, a symbol such as 3, a group of words such as *eighty-three point five*, or a group of symbols such as *83.5*. Every number, regardless of the language in which it is expressed, occupies a unique position in a series, such as 3 in the series *1, 2, 3, 4, 5, . . .* , enabling it to be used in such arithmetical processes as addition, subtraction, multiplication, and division. There are two basic kinds of number in such languages as English and French: *cardinal numbers* (the term deriving ultimately from Latin *cardo/cardinis* a hinge: that is, something on which other things turn or depend), denoting quantity and not order (as in *1, 2, 3, 4*); and *ordinal numbers* (the term deriving ultimately from Latin *ordo/ordinis* order), denoting relative position in a sequence (as in *1st, 2nd, 3rd, 4th*). Grammatically, the number system of a language contrasts with its system of quantifiers: for example, *one house* with *a house*, and *two/three/forty people*, etc., with *some people*, *several people*, and *many people*, etc.

**Numbers as words**. A spoken number is a WORD or phrase in a language, but a written number may be realized as either a word or phrase or a symbol or groups of symbols, usually a *figure* such as *1, 2, 12, 21*. Written words are generally used for low numbers, from *one* to *ten* or *twelve* (as in the phrases *three blind mice, the seven wonders of the world*, and *the twelve signs of the Zodiac*). They are also often used for numbers up to *100* (with hyphenation for compound forms such as *twenty-one* and *eighty-three*) and for large round figures as in *a thousand years* and *four million visitors a year*. Words may or may not be used to express percentages, which may be given as *ten per cent, 10 per cent*, or *10%* depending on house style or personal preference. Most house styles and editors aim for consistency in whichever forms they have chosen.

**Numbers as symbols**. Arabic figures are commonly used for numbers above *ten* or *twelve* (as in *The ship sank with the loss of 18 lives*), before abbreviations (as in *8 pm* for *eight o'clock in the evening, 7K* for *seven thou-*

sand, and *3m* for *three million*), and for dates, addresses, and exact sums of money. Large numbers such as *118,985* are usually given as figures; when spoken, there is one significant difference between British and American usage: BrE always has *and* after *hundred*, as in *one hundred and eighteen thousand, nine hundred and eighty-five*, while AmE generally does not, as in *one hundred eighteen thousand, nine hundred eighty-five*. In large numbers, commas are generally used after the figures representing millions and thousands (*1,345,905*), but spaces are also, perhaps increasingly, used for this purpose (*1 345 905*); commas or spaces may or may not be used for thousands alone (*2,345* and *2 345*), for which solid numbers are also common (*2345*). Telephone numbers are generally written with spaces between regional and local numbers (*01223 245999*), and reference numbers are generally solid (*N707096*). Plural *s* after a set of numbers is often preceded by an apostrophe, as in *3's and 4's* or *the 1980's*, but many house styles and individuals now favour *3s and 4s* and *the 1980s*.

**Numbers in -illion**. Formerly, BrE and AmE differed greatly in their use of numbers representing multiples of *million*: for example, in Britain, France, and Germany, *billion* was 'one million million', or $10^{12}$ (10 to the power 12), while in the US and Canada it was 'one thousand million' or $10^9$. The North American equivalent to the British *billion* was the *trillion*. In the last decades of the 20c, however, the North American use has become universal, providing the set *million, billion, trillion, quadrillion, quintillion, sextillion, septillion, octillion, nonillion, decillion*. The *-illion* pattern has prompted some word-play, especially in AmE, that makes use of various initial consonants and syllables: 'The savings-and-loan industry bailout, which as of yesterday afternoon was expected to cost taxpayers $752.6 trillion skillion, is now expected to cost $964.3 hillion jillion bazillion' (Dave Barry, 'Give or Take a Whomptillion', *International Herald Tribune*, 13 June 1990). The widely-used *zillion*, with its end-of-

alphabet prefix, usually suggests the ultimate in facetious scale, but Barry's *ba-* adds even more force. See LETTER[1], QUANTIFIER.

**NUMBER**[2]. A grammatical category used in describing parts of speech that show contrasts of *PLURAL, SINGULAR, dual*, etc. In English, the number system is basically a two-term contrast of singular and plural, shown in nouns and some pronouns and determiners, and to some extent in verbs. Even dual words, such as *both, either, neither*, take singular or plural verb CONCORD: *both* taking the plural; *either, neither* usually taking the singular. English nouns, as far as number is concerned, can be divided into: singular only, plural only, and words that can be both. Singular-only nouns are: (1) Uncountable nouns which can occur with such uncountable-specific words as *much, little: much money, little sugar*, etc. (2) Most proper nouns: *Edinburgh, the Thames* (in which other restrictions apply). Plural only nouns are: (1) Countable: *people* in *six people*, but not in *the European peoples*. (2) Usually uncountable: *not enough clothes* (not *\*six clothes*); *many thanks* (not *\*five thanks*); *trousers* (*a pair of trousers* and not usually *three trousers*). The vast majority of countable nouns can be both singular and plural (*book/books, fox/foxes, mouse/mice*), but a few have no distinct plural form (as with *one sheep/three sheep*). Many nouns, however, have both countable and uncountable uses, in which case they may have a plural in some uses (*What an excellent wine/What excellent wines!*) but not in others (*I never drink wine*). Pronouns having distinct singular and plural forms include *personal, reflexive*, and *possessive*. Number contrast is neutralized with *you*, but the second-person reflexive forms distinguish *yourself* and *yourselves*. Demonstrative pronouns also have separate forms, singular *this, that* being used both with singular countable nouns (*this restaurant*) and with uncountable nouns (*this food*). Number contrast in verbs, except in the verb *be*, is confined to the distinct third-person singular tense form (*look/looks*). See PRONOUN, QUANTIFIER.

# O

## ■ O, o ───────────────── ■

[Called 'oh']. The 15th LETTER of the Roman ALPHABET as used for English. It originated as the Phoenician consonant symbol *'ain*, representing a pharyngeal plosive (or 'glottal catch'). It had a roughly circular form and meant 'eye'. The Greeks adopted it as a vowel symbol, at first for both long and short values. Later, a letter *omega* (Ω) (that is *O-mega*, 'big O') was created for the long value, with O, known as *omicron* (that is, *O-micron*, 'little o'), kept for the short value. LATIN took over only omicron, for both long and short values.

**Sound values.** In English, as well as long, short, and DIGRAPH values, *o* has some irregular values, often overlapping with values of *u*. In some words, the letter *o* has a different value in different accents. Native speakers differ as to whether *log* and *dog* rhyme, whether *bother* has the vowel of *father*, whether *horse* and *hoarse* are HOMO-PHONES, and whether *your* is pronounced like *yore* or as *ewer*. The sound values are listed in the following paragraphs as *short O, word-final long O, pre-consonantal long O, O with the value of U, O and the inflections of DO*, and *O with doubled consonants*.

**Short O.** (1) In monosyllables before consonants, but not before *h, r, v, w, y*: *mob, lock, botch, odd, soft, log, dodge, doll, on, top, Oz*. The biblical name *Job*, however, has long *o*. (2) In polysyllables such as *pocket, soccer, biography, geometry*. (3) Before consonant plus *e* in *gone, shone*, in one pronunciation of *scone* (contrast *tone*), and before *ugh*, representing /f/, in *cough, trough*. (4) In RP and related accents, a lengthened variant of short *o* occurs before word-final *r* (or, *nor*), medially as in *corn, adornment*, and before final silent *e* as in *ignore*. The same value occurs as *oa* uniquely in *broad*, as *ou* in *ought, thought*, etc., and is sometimes heard (as it commonly was in old-fashioned RP) instead of short *o* in *off, often, lost*, sometimes facetiously or mockingly rendered as *aw* in 'crawss' (*cross*), 'Gawd' (*God*), the poet John Keats, a Londoner, rhymed *crosses* and *horses*. This value is also spelt *au, aw*, as seen in the sets *sauce/source, fraught/fought/fort*. (5) In other accents, this distinction does not occur: in most Scottish accents, for example, the same vowel is heard in *cot, caught, ought*, and *sauce* does not rhyme with *source*. (6) In RP and related accents, the vowel sound in *word, work, world, whorl* is the same as that in *were*, and the set *whirled, whorled, world* is homophonous.

**Word-final long O.** (1) Standard long *o* occurs word-finally spelt simply as *-o* in the monosyllables *fro, go, so*, and in polysyllabic loans (*hero, piano, potato, radio, tomato, zero*), but in *lasso* final *o* usually has the value of long *u*. There is often uncertainty whether such loans form their plurals with *-s* (*armadillos*) or *-es* (*potatoes*) or optionally either (*lassos, lassoes*). Those ending in vowel plus *o* add *s*: *cameos, radios, duos*. Syllable-final long *o* is found in *coaxial, cloaca, oasis* (compare *coax, cloak, oats*), *poet, coerce, coeval*, etc. (2) The same sound occurs word-finally as *-oe* in the monosyllables *doe, foe, floe, hoe, sloe, throe, woe* and in some polysyllables (*aloe, felloe, oboe*), but *shoe, canoe* give *-oe* the value of long *u*. (3) Long *o* occurs as *-oh* in *oh, doh, soh*, as *-ough* in *dough, though* (but not other *-ough* words), and as *-ow* as in some 14 words: *how, blow, crow, know, low, mow, row, show, slow, snow, sow, stow, tow, throw*. Of these, the forms *bow, row, sow* have different meanings (that is, are different words) when they rhyme with *how*. (4) The long *-o* value of the *-ow* ending occurs in disyllables of mainly vernacular origin, after *d* (*meadow, shadow, widow*), after *ll* (*gallows, swallow; bellow, yellow; billow, willow; follow, hollow*), after *nn* (*minnow, winnow*), and after *rr* (*arrow, barrow; borrow, sorrow; burrow, furrow*); and also in *window* (from a Scandinavian compound of *wind* + *eye*) and *bungalow* (from Hindi). (5) The diphthong value of final *-ow* (*now, vow*) is rare in polysyllables: *allow, endow*. (6) Some FRENCH loans have a final silent consonant after long *o*: *apropos, depot*. (7) Final long *o* may become *i* in the plural of ITALIAN loans: *libretto/libretti, virtuoso/virtuosi*.

**Pre-consonantal long O.** (1) Simple *o* before *ld* (*bold, cold*), *lst* (*bolster, holster*), *lt* (*bolt, molten*), *ll* (*stroll, troll*), *lk* (*folk, yolk*). Sometimes also before final *st*, *th* (*ghost*, *most*, *past*; *both*, *sloth*, but contrast short *o* in *lost*, *cloth*, etc.). The anomalous long *o* in *only* contrasts with the related forms *one*, *alone*, *lonely*, which all have following *e*; however, a parallel may be seen in *nobly*. (2) Before a single consonant, with a following *a* or a magic *e* after the consonant: *soap*, *choke*. (3) Digraphs *ou* and *ow* often before *l* or *n* (*boulder*, *poultry*, *shoulder*, *smoulder*; *bowl*, *own*, *sown*), but contrast the diphthong value in *howl*, *down* and the more usual vowel spellings in *foal*, *sole*, *loan*, *tone*. Before *r* in RP, this value becomes that of *or* in *course*, *court*, *source*. (4) Uniquely as *oo* in *brooch* (contrast *broach*).

**O with the value of U**. (1) The letter *o* often has one of the values of *u*, phonetically central and short as in *but*, close and short as in *put*, or close and long as in *truth*. (2) The short *u*-value is common in monosyllables, especially before *n* (*son*, *front*, *monk*, *month*, *sponge*, *ton*, *tongue*, *won*), and in some words with silent *e* (*some*, *come*, *done*, *none*, *love*, *dove*). *One*, *once* contain the further anomaly of an unspelt initial /w/. The short *u*-value is heard before nasals, *l*, *r*, *th*, *v*, and *z* in such polysyllabic words as *above*, *accomplish*, *among*, BrE *borough*, *brother*, *colour*, *comfort*, *conjure*, *cover*, *dozen*, *dromedary*, *frontier*, *govern*, *Monday*, *money*, *mongrel*, *monkey*, *mother*, *nothing*, *onion*, *other*, *shovel*, *slovenly*, *smother*, *somersault*, *stomach*, *wonder*. Pronunciation varies, however: *Coventry*, *constable* occur in BrE with both short *o* and *u* values. This use of *o* for short *u* has been explained as a graphic device in MIDDLE ENGLISH to reduce the confusing succession of vertical strokes (minims) that would otherwise arise in manuscript in a word such as *money*. (3) Longer (close) values of *u*, as in *put* or *truth*, occur: with simple *o*, in *do*, *to*, *two*, *who*, *lasso*; with *o* before a consonant plus *e*, in *lose*, *whose*, *move*, *prove* (contrast *choose*, *booze*, *use*, *hose*, *drove*); with *oe* in *shoe*, *canoe*; in such special cases as *bosom*, *Domesday*, *tomb*, *whom*, *wolf*, *woman* (but *o* with the value of short *i* in the plural *women*), *womb*.

**O and the inflections of DO**. The forms of *do* are highly anomalous: the long-*u* value of *o* in *do*, the short-*u* value in *does* (contrast plural of *doe*), and the long-*o* value of *don't*, matching *won't*.

**O with doubled consonants**. When followed by doubled consonants, *o* often has a short value, but before double *l*, whether

final or medial, both values occur: *doll*, *loll*, but *poll*, *roll*; *dolly*, *follow*, but *swollen*, *wholly*. Doubled *l* in *holly* distinguishes its short *o* from the long *o* in *holy*. Many words are pronounced with a short *o* preceding a single consonant, despite parallels with doubled consonants (*body*/*shoddy*, *proper*/*copper*) or with long vowels (*honey*/*phoney*, *hover*/*rover*). Other examples of single consonants after short *o* include *colour*, *holiday*, *honour*, *honest*, *money*. On the other hand, doubled *r* distinguishes short *o* in *sorry*, *lorry* from longer *o* in *story*, *gory*, though not in *historical*.

**Digraphs**. *O* is the first element in the following digraphs:

**OA**. The digraph *oa* has the values of: (1) Long *o* as in *no* (*soap*, *cloak*). (2) The open *aw*-sound before *r* in RP and related accents (*coarse*, *hoarse*).

**OE**. The digraph *oe* has the value of long *o* as in *no* (*woe*, *woeful*), or of *ee* in such Greek-derived forms as BrE *amoeba*, *foetus*, or of the first *o* in *colonel* in such German names as *Goethe* and *Goebbels*.

**OI and OY**. (1) The digraphs *oi* and (usually as a word- or syllable-final variant) *oy* are diphthongs: short *o* preceding short *i*, as in *boil*, *boy*. They are common in monosyllables and incorporate a glide before a vowel at a syllable boundary: *join*, *noise*, *voice*, *oyster*, *royal*, *voyage*, *buoyant*. (2) Rare final *oi* occurs in *borzoi* (from Russian) and *envoi* (Anglicized from French). (3) Special occurrences include: *porpoise*, *tortoise* with *oi* often reduced to schwa; a unique use in *choir* (rhyming with *friar* and *wire* and respelt from *quire*); in recent French loans, the value of /wa/ (*boudoir*, *reservoir*). (4) The *oi* combination is not always a digraph: compare *coin*/*coincide*.

**OO**. (1) The digraph *oo* is generally considered to have the value of long *u* as in *rule* (*booty*, *choose*), but with variation depending on accent. Exceptionally, it has the value of short *u* in *blood*, *flood*. (2) In RP and related accents, *oo* in some words is long *u* as in *truth* (*food*, *soon*), but elsewhere has the shorter *u* of *put* (*good*, *hood*) especially before *k* (*book*, *cook*, *look*). In *room*, both values occur in free variation. Similar variations occur before *r*: *door*, *floor*, *moor*, *poor*. (3) The form *too* developed in the 16c as a stressed variant of *to*; GERMAN has *zu* for both senses. (4) Occasionally, *oo* corresponds to French *ou* (contrast cognate *troop*/*troupe*), and *-oon* to French *-on* (*balloon*/*ballon*). (5) A few *oo* words are exotic: *bamboo* (probably Malay), *typhoon* (Chinese), *taboo* (Tongan). The digraph formerly occurred in *Hindoo*, now *Hindu*, and the alternative *tabu* exists for *taboo*. (6) *Zoo* is a clipping of *zoological garden*, but uniquely in *zoology* the second *o* functions simultaneously as part of the *oo* digraph and as a normal short *o*. (7) *Oo* becomes *ee* in the plural of *foot*, *goose*, *tooth*: *feet*, *geese*, *teeth*.

***OU and OW***. (1) The digraphs *ou* and (usually its word-final variant) *ow* can represent a diphthong, as in *cow*, *cloud*, *flour*, *flower*. Word-final *ou* occurs exceptionally in archaic *thou*, but *ow* is sometimes used medially. It is contrastive in *foul/fowl*, and is an alternative spelling in *to lour/lower* and formerly in *flour/flower*. (2) *Ou* has other values, as in *soul* (rhyming with *pole*), *sought* (with *bought*), *source* (with *course*), *soup* (with *loop*), *scourge* (with *urge*), and *touch* (with *hutch* and *much*). See **U**. (3) Final *-ow* as long *o* in *know* occurs in some 50 words as compared to some 15 with final *-ow* as in *bow*, *brow*, *cow*, *dhow*, *how*, *now*, AmE *plow*, *prow*, *row*, *sow*, *vow*, *wow*, *allow*, *endow*. (4) On its own, the form *wound* is ambiguous: the past tense of *to wind* has the standard diphthong value, but the noun has the value of *ou* in *soup*. (5) Exceptionally, *ow* has the value of short *o* in *knowledge*, *acknowledge*. (6) *Ou* becomes plural *i* in the plurals of such pairs as *louse/lice*, *mouse/mice*.

***-OUGH***. (1) Some *-ough* spellings have the standard value of *ou* (*bough*, *drought*, BrE *plough*). Variants are AmE *plow* and archaic *enow*, which was an alternative pronunciation of *enough*. (2) Other *-ough* spellings give *o* different values: short *o* in *cough*, *trough*; in RP, the *aw* sound in *ought*, *bought*; long *o* in *though*; schwa in *thorough*, *borough* in BrE, sometimes long *o* in AmE; and silent *o* in *tough*, *rough*, *through*.

***O and schwa***. (1) Unstressed *o* may be more or less reduced to the value of SCHWA, or elided altogether. In pronunciations of the word *police*, the full range can be heard, from long *o*, through short *o* and schwa, to zero value with initial consonants as in *please*. (2) There is also often variation between AmE, in which the *o* in *omit*, *co-caine*, *testimony*, *territory*, *phenomenon* (second *o*) may have one of its full values, and BrE where it is normally reduced. (3) Most typically, *o* (like other vowel letters) has the value of schwa after the main stress in polysyllables, especially in words ending in *l*

(*petrol*, *symbol*), *m* (*fathom*, *bottom*), *n* (*cotton*; *cushion*, *fashion*; *ration*, and *-ation* words generally), *r* (*error*, *doctor*). (4) Homophones sometimes occur as a result of such reduction: *baron/barren*, *gambol/gamble*, *petrol/petrel*, *lesson/lessen*, *minor/miner*.

***O and stress shift***. In polysyllabic derivatives, the value of *o* may shift between long, short, and schwa (in unstressed position), as the spoken structure of the word changes: (1) *Atom* has schwa for its *o*, but in *atomic* has the short-*o* value. (2) *Colony* has the short-*o* value for its first *o*, schwa for its second, but *colonial* has schwa for its first *o* and the long-*o* value for its second. Such effects occur before suffixes like *-(i)al*, *-ic(al)*, *-y*, *-ety*, as in *colony/colonial*; *atom/atomic*; *economy/economic(al)*; *symbol/symbolic*; *tone/tonic*; *geology/geological*; *photograph/photographer/photographic*; *proper/propriety*; *social/society*. See **SUFFIX**.

**Agentive *-or/-er***. The suffix *-or* is mostly used with Latin roots (*doctor*, *professor*), especially after verbs ending in *-ate* (*dictator*, *perpetrator*). It is normally pronounced with schwa, although occasionally the full value of *-or* is heard: *actor*, *vendor*. However, *-or* varies with *-er* in a number of patterns. BrE legal spelling may use *-or* where lay writing has *-er*: *grantor/granter*. A technical device may be distinguished by *-or* from a human agent with *-er*: *adaptor/adapter*, *conveyor/conveyer*. In other cases, *-or* and *-er* are in free variation: *advisor/adviser*, *impostor/imposter*, *investor/invester*. *Caster/castor* sometimes differ in meaning, and *censor/censer* always do.

**Silent O**. (1) In *jeopardy*, *Leonard*, *leopard*, *people*, but the *o* in *yeoman* has long value and the *e* is silent. (2) The second *o* in *colonel*.

**American and British differences**. (1) The once widespread unstressed ending *-our* (as in *emperour*) has since the early 19c been increasingly rewritten *-or*: universally in *emperor*, *governor*, *horror*, *terror*, and in AmE in such forms as *ardor*, *behavior*, *candor*, *dolor*, *endeavor*, *favor*, *harbor*, *labor*, *odor*, *parlor*, *rigor*, *savior*, *vapor*. *Glamour* and *saviour* are, however, still widely written with *-our* in AmE. AmE has *o* in all derivatives, while BrE has *o* alone in many (*honorary*, *vaporise*, *vigorous*), but not all (*behaviourism*, *favourite*, *honourable*, *colourist*). In many rarer forms, such as *torpor* and *stupor*, *-or* is universal. (2) AmE writes BrE *amoeba*, *foetus*, *oesophagus*, *moustache* without the *o* and *manoeuvre* as *maneuver* (but note the common spellings *onomatopoeia*, *subpoena*). (3) Contrast AmE *mold*, *molt*, *smolder*, BrE *mould*, *moult*, *smoulder*. (4) AmE has *plow* for BrE *plough*.

**OBJECT**. A major functional element in the structure of CLAUSES, present in any sentence with a transitive verb. With verbs that can have two objects, the *indirect object* generally refers to the recipient of what is denoted by the *direct object*. In *I sent my bank a letter* (Subject/Verb/Object/Object), *my bank* is the indirect object, *a letter* the direct object. In the equivalent *I sent a letter to my bank*, some grammarians regard *to my bank* as also an indirect object. Pronouns in any object position must take their object forms, as with *I* and *they* in *Please send me them*. Despite the closer position of the indirect object to the verb in *I sent my bank a letter*, with most verbs it is the indirect object that is more easily omitted: *I sent a letter*, not *\*I sent my bank*. Exceptions include *pay* (*You can pay me*), *teach* (*She teaches the top class*), and *tell* (*You can tell me, if you wish*), where such direct objects as *the money*, *French*, and *the news* are omitted. In such constructions, some grammarians see the retained object as the direct object, while others see it as the indirect object.

**OBLIQUE**, also **diagonal**, **oblique dash**, **oblique stroke**, **slash**, **solidus**, **virgule**. The PUNCTUATION MARK (/), a forward-sloping line used in writing and printing. The device has six main uses: (1) To indicate vulgar fractions (*23/24* for *twenty-three twenty fourths*) and ratios (*miles/hour* for *miles per hour*). (2) As part of certain abbreviations and related symbols, such as *c/o* care of, *i/c* in charge, and the percentage sign %. (3) To mark the ends of lines of poetry when set in a prose text (as in *Tyger Tyger, burning bright / In the forests of the night*). (4) To unite alternatives as in *and/or*, *colour/color*, *his/her*, and *s/he* (for 'she or he'). (5) To indicate routes, as in *London/New York/San Francisco*. (6) In PHONETICS, to mark off phonemic transcription, as in /wik/, denoting the pronunciation of the words *week* and *weak*. The reverse oblique (\), is known as a *back-slash*.

**OFFICIAL ENGLISH**, also **Official English Movement**. Collective names for campaigning groups whose aim is an amendment of the US Constitution, making English the official language of the republic. The organization *US English* belongs within this grouping. See ENGLISH LANGUAGE AMENDMENT, ENGLISH-ONLY MOVEMENT.

**OFFICIALESE**. A style common in statements and texts issued by the representatives of governments and large institutions, especially civil servants. The term is usually pejorative and the style is particularly criticized for obscure, polysyllabic, pompous, and/or pedantic usage. See BUREAUCRATESE, JARGON.

**OFFICIAL LANGUAGE**. A LANGUAGE used for official purposes, especially as the medium of a national government. English is not the statutory or *de jure* official language of either the UK or the US, but is the *de facto* official language. It is, however, the sole statutory official language of Namibia; with FRENCH, it is one of the two statutory official languages of Canada; with Mandarin Chinese, Malay, and Tamil, it is one of the four statutory official languages of Singapore; and with Chinese, French, RUSSIAN, and SPANISH is one of the five official languages of the UNITED NATIONS. See NATIONAL LANGUAGE.

## ■ OLD ENGLISH[1] ─────── ■

Also **Anglo-Saxon**. Short forms *AS*, *A.S.* From one point of view, the earliest stage of the single continuously developing ENGLISH language; from another, the language from which two other more or less distinct languages successively evolved, first MIDDLE ENGLISH (ME), then Modern English (ModE); from a third point of view, the common ancestor of English and SCOTS, the two national GERMANIC LANGUAGES of Britain. OE was spoken and written in various forms for some eight centuries (5–12c). Although its texts are as unintelligible to present-day English speakers as LATIN to speakers of FRENCH, after even modest exposure they can begin to make progress, as with the following (from the OE version of Bede's *Ecclesiastical History of the English People*):

> Breten is gārsecges īegland, þæt wæs gēo geāra Albion hāten.

Translated word for word and with the same word order, this sentence runs:

> Britain is sea's island, that was ago years Albion called.

Translated more freely, it is:

Britain is an island of the sea that was formerly called Albion.

In the original sentence, word order in the main clause is the same as in ModE, but in the subordinate clause differs markedly from it (with echoes of German). Some words are the same as or very like ModE words (*is*, *Albion*; *Breten*, *wæs*), some are further removed but easily identifiable after translation (*ī egland* island, *geāra* years), and some are alien (*gārsecges* of the sea, *gēo* formerly, *hāten* called).

**Background**. Old English consisted of several West Germanic DIALECTS taken to Britain from the north-western European mainland in the middle centuries of the first millennium AD. Germanic settlement was very limited during the late Roman period, but expanded greatly after the departure of the Romans in the early 5c. The language was never fully homogenized as a literary and administrative medium, but nonetheless made greater progress in this direction (despite the primacy of LATIN) than most other European vernaculars. Writing in Latin in the 8c, the Northumbrian historian Bede identified the settlers of three hundred years earlier as three peoples, the Jutes, Angles, and Saxons; the ANGLO-SAXON CHRONICLE, written entirely in OE from the 9c to the 12c, described by year, from the settlers' point of view, the progress of various leaders and groups as they overcame the resistance of the Romano-Celtic Britons from the 5c to the 7c.

By the 8c, OE-speakers held territories roughly equivalent in size and distribution to the later kingdom of England. Four major varieties of the language can be distinguished in surviving documents: *Kentish*, associated with the JUTES, who probably migrated from what is now Denmark; *West Saxon*, in the southern region called Wessex, ultimately the most powerful of the SAXON kingdoms, whose founders originated in northern Germany; *Mercian*, the Anglian dialect spoken in Mercia, a kingdom stretching from the Thames to the Humber; and *Northumbrian*, the northernmost of the Anglian dialects, spoken from the Humber to the Forth. The Angles (in OE *Engle*) appear to have originated in Angeln, now in Schleswig, and gave their name to the language, *Englisc*, but it was the Saxons of Wessex who brought their dialect closest to

a standard literary medium: see ALFRED. The last document in OE, an annal of the *Anglo-Saxon Chronicle* dated 1154, shows features of early Middle English, which was strongly influenced by the impact on OE of DANISH during the 9–11c and NORMAN FRENCH from the 11c onward. The following sections, however, discuss OE without reference to such influences.

**Pronunciation and spelling**. OE had speech patterns similar to those of its fellow North Sea Germanic languages Old FRISIAN and Old DUTCH. It was written first in runic letters then in an adaptation of the Roman ALPHABET that incorporated several such letters to represent distinctive OE sounds (see below).

*Stress*. In polysyllables, OE stress typically falls on the first syllable, as in ModE: *mórgen* morning, *séttan* to set. When the first syllable is a prefix, however, nouns and adjectives stress the prefix (*ándswaru* answer, *ándward* current, present), but verbs do not (*forgí efan* to forgive, *tōbérstan* to burst). Two prefixes are never stressed, whatever the part of speech: *be-* (*beswíllan* to soak), and *ge-* (*gefrémed* done, from *fremman* to do; *gepólian* to tolerate, from *pólian* to endure; *gerégnad* ornamented).

*Vowels*. The monophthongs of OE consist of seven pairs of short and long vowels: (1) Short, *a*, phonetically /a/, as in *nama* name; long *ā* /ɑː/, as in *stān* stone. (2) Short *æ* /æ/, as in *glæd* glad; long *ǣ* /æː/, as in *dǣd* deed. (3) Short *e* /ɛ/, as in *etan* eat; long *ē* /eː/, as in *hē* he. (4) Short *i* /ɪ/, as in *cwic* alive; long *ī* /iː/, as in *wīn* wine. (5) Short *o* /ɔ/, as in *god* god; long *ō* /oː/, as in *gōd* good. (6) Short *u* /ʊ/, as in *sunu* son; long *ū* /uː/, as in *nū* now. (7) Short *y* /y/, as in *cyning* king; long *y* /yː/, as in *ȳtmǣst* utmost: compare French *tu* and *ruse*. The diphthongs of OE consist of three pairs of short and long vowels in which the stress falls on the initial vowel: (1) Short *ea* /æa/, as in *eald* old; long *ēa* /æːa/, as in *ēast* east. (2) Short *eo* /ɛo/, as in *eorl* earl; long *ēo* /eːo/, as in *dēop* deep. (3) Short *ie* /ɪɛ/, as in *ieldu* age; long *īe* /iːɛ/, as in *hīeran* to hear.

*Consonants*. The consonants of OE are mostly the same as those of ModE. Differences include: (1) The pronunciation of all consonants in all written positions, notably /r/ and initial /g/ as in *gnagan* to gnaw, initial /k/ as in *cnēo* knee, initial /h/ as in *hlāf* bread, and initial /w/ as in *wrītan* to write. (2) Double letters represent geminated sounds

## EXCERPTS FROM TWO OLD ENGLISH TEXTS

The literary and other texts of OE are among the oldest specimens of vernacular writing in Europe. Below are two brief specimens, with modern translations. The verse was committed to writing *c.* AD 1000 but was composed much earlier; its layout shows the typical OE metrical unit, the half-line. The prose represents the style of 10c Saxon annalists.

### 1. *Verse: Beowulf, lines 710–13*

> þa cōm of mōre      under misthleoþum
> Grendel gongan;      Godes yrre bær;
> mynte se mānscaþa      manna cynnes
> sumne besyrwan      in sele þām hēan.
> Wōd under wolcnum      to þæs þe hē wīnreced,
> goldsele gumena      gearwost wisse
> fættum fāhne.

A CLOSE TRANSLATION

> Then came out of the moorlands      beneath the mist-slopes
> Grendel stalking;      he bore God's ire;
> The evil one meant      of human kind
> Someone to snare      in the high hall.
> He went on under the clouds      till their wine-hall,
> The gold-hall of men      he could clearly make out plated in gold.

A FREE TRANSLATION

Down off the moorlands' misting fells came Grendel stalking; God's brand was on him. The spoiler meant to snatch away from the high hall some of the human race. He came on under the clouds, clearly saw at last the gold-hall of men, the mead-drinking place nailed with gold plates.

(Michael Alexander, Beowulf, Penguin Classics, 1973)

### 2. *Prose: The Anglo-Saxon Chronicle (years 981, 982)*

981. Hēr on þìs gēare wæs Sancte Patroces stōw forhergod, and þȳ ilcan gēare wæs micel hearm gedōn gehwǣ be þām scǣriman ægþer ge on Defenum ge on Wēalum.

982. Hēr on þȳs gēare cōmon ūpp on Dorsætum iii scypu wīcinga and hergodon on Portlande. þȳ ilcan gēare forbarn Lundenbyrig. And on þām ylcan gēare forþfērdon twēgen ealdormenn, Æþelmær on Hamtūnscīre and Eadwine on Sūþseaxum.

A CLOSE MODERN RENDERING

981. [Here in this year] St. Petroc's, Padstow, was ravaged, and in the same year much harm done everywhere along the sea-coasts, in both Devon and Cornwall.

982. [Here in this year] Three ships of vikings came up into Dorset, and ravaged in Portland the same year. Also that year, London was burnt, and [in that same year] two ealdormen passed away, Aethelmaer in Hampshire and Eadwine in Sussex.

(Ann Savage, The Anglo-Saxon Chronicles, Phoebe Phillips, 1982) (as in Italian): for example, OE *biden* and *biddan* differ phonetically in the same way as ModE 'bidden' and 'bid Den'. (3) Two consonants are absent from present-day mainstream English. The sound represented by non-initial *h*, as in *niht* night, is a voiceless palatal fricative (compare GERMAN *ich*) or a voiceless velar fricative (compare German *ach*, ScoE *loch*, Scots *nicht*). The sound represented by *g* after or between back vowels is a voiced velar fricative (compare one pronunciation of German *sagen* to say). Initial *h* has the same pronunciation as in present-day general English; *g* in other positions is as shown below in point 7. (4) There are several distinctive letters: ASH (æ), ETH (ð), THORN (þ), WYNN (ƿ), YOGH (ȝ). For details, see the entries for each. (5) The letters *f* and *s* each have voiceless and voiced values, the letters *v* and *z* not normally being used. Such words as OE *fæt* (fat) and *fæt* (vat) are therefore pronounced as homophones with either /f/ or /v/, according to dialect: compare present-day WEST COUNTRY speech in England. Similarly, thorn may represent either a voiceless /θ/ or a voiced /ð/: compare the current use of the digraph *th* in *three* and *these*. (6) The letter *c* is used as follows: before the 'hard' vowels *a*, *o*, *u*, *y* and all consonants, it has the value /k/, as in *cald* cold, *clipian* to summon, *cwic* alive, *cyning* king: before the 'soft' vowels *e*, *i*, it generally has the value /tʃ/, as in *ceaster* ('chester') town, *cirice* church. (7) Similarly, *g* is pronounced /g/ before *a*, *æ*, *o*, *u* and before consonants, as in *gāst* spirit, *god* god, *grim* fierce, and /j/ (as in ModE *yet*) before *e* and *i*, as in *gēac* cuckoo, *gif* if. (8) The letter combinations *sc* and *cg* are pronounced like *sh* and *dge* in present day *shed* and *sedge* respectively: *scip* ship, *bricg* bridge.

**Grammar**. Textbooks of OE grammar distinguish eight parts of speech: nouns, adjectives, pronouns, verbs, adverbs, prepositions, conjunctions, and interjections. Unlike ModE, OE is highly inflected; the major aspects of its morphology are traditionally set out in paradigms, much as in textbooks of Latin, with declensions for nouns, adjectives, and pronouns, and conjugations for verbs. Its morphology and syntax are too extensive and complex to cover here; the following sections present only highlights.

**Declensions**. To discuss nouns, pronouns, and adjectives, grammarians of OE use the three categories number, gender, and CASE, with three subcategories for number (singular, sometimes dual, and plural), three for gender (masculine, feminine, and neuter), and four or five for case (nominative, accusative, genitive, and dative, the last serving an instrumental function for nouns, while there is a distinct instrumental case in certain parts of the declensions of adjectives and pronouns).

The paradigm given in Table 1 shows the declension of nouns ending in *-an* (generally referred to as 'weak' nouns). In this case, the noun (*nama* name) is masculine. Table 2 shows the declension of a 'strong' noun (*stān* stone) in effect, any form other than with *-an* endings. Here, for convenience of comparison, the noun is also masculine.

Table 3 gives the declension for the singular only of the definite article (a subclass of pronoun also translated as *that*). In ModE, the definite article is invariable (only *the*), while the demonstrative pronoun has two forms (*that/those*); in OE, however, the forms varied through three genders, two numbers, and five cases. The plural forms are simpler: nominative and accusative *þā* for all genders; genitive *þāra*; and dative *þǣm*.

Table 1. *Declension of masculine weak noun* nama

|      | Singular | Plural |
|------|----------|--------|
| Nom. | *nama* (name: subject) | *naman* (names: subject) |
| Acc. | *naman* (name: object) | *naman* (names: object) |
| Gen. | *naman* (of a name, name's) | *namena* (of names, names') |
| Dat. | *naman* (to/for/with a name) | *namum* (to/for/with names) |

Table 2. *Declension of masculine strong noun* stān

|      | Singular | Plural |
|------|----------|--------|
| Nom. | *stān* | *stānas* |
| Acc. | *stān* | *stānas* |
| Gen. | *stānes* | *stāna* |
| Dat. | *stāne* | *stānum* |

Table 3. *Declension of definite article* sē (*singular only*)

|       | Masculine | Feminine | Neuter |
|-------|-----------|----------|--------|
| Nom.  | *sē*   | *sēo*  | *þæt* |
| Acc.  | *þone* | *þā*   | *þæt* |
| Gen.  | *þæs*  | *þǣre* | *þæs* |
| Dat.  | *þæm*  | *þǣre* | *þæm* |
| Inst. | *þȳ*   | *þǣre* | *þȳ*  |

The OE for 'the/that name' as subject of a sentence is *sē nama*, as object is *þone naman*; 'the/those stones', as both subject and object, is *þā stānas*.

**Conjugations**. The tenses of the verb in OE are comparable to those of ModE, which contains remnants of the major distinction in OE verbs: between 'strong' and 'weak' forms. The main difference lies in the formation of the preterite (the simple past tense). The preterite of STRONG VERBS is formed by changing the vowel of the root according to a series known as 'vowel gradation' (in ModE, for example, the change from *swim* to *swam*). The preterite of weak verbs is formed by adding a suffix containing *d* (as in ModE *walk* to *walked*). There are seven conjugations or classes of strong verbs and three of weak verbs. In Tables 4 and 5, the present and preterite paradigms of the indicative mood of the strong verb *þindan* (to bind) and of the weak verb *hīeran* (to hear) are set out for comparison.

**Basic word order**. (1) In phrases, adjectives and genitives generally precede nouns: *micel flōd* a great flood: *Westseaxna cyning* king of the West Saxons. Two coordinate adjectives are usually separated, one preceding and the other following the noun, after *and*: *gōda þēow and getrēowa* (good servant and faithful), good, faithful servant.

Table 4. *Conjugation of strong verb* bindan, *indicative mood*

| Person | Singular | Plural |
|---|---|---|
| | Present | |
| 1st | binde | bindaþ |
| 2nd | bindest/bintst | bindaþ |
| 3rd | bindeþ/bint | bindaþ |
| | Preterite (with vowel change) | |
| 1st | band | bundon |
| 2nd | bunde | bundon |
| 3rd | band | bundon |

Table 5. *Conjugation of weak verb* hīeran, *indicative mood*

| Person | Singular | Plural |
|---|---|---|
| | Present | |
| 1st | hīere | hīeraþ |
| 2nd | hīerst | hīeraþ |
| 3rd | hīerþ | hīeraþ |
| | Preterite (with d-element) | |
| 1st | hīerde | hīerdon |
| 2nd | hīerdest | hīerdon |
| 3rd | hīerde | hīerdon |

Compare the fossilized ModE idiom 'twelve good men and true'. A title follows a proper name, the opposite of ModE: *Æþelred cyning* King Ethelred. (2) In sentences, inflection for case allows a certain freedom of word order, more or less as in Latin. There are, however, three common orderings in OE prose and verse: SV (Subject–Verb) and SVO (Subject–Verb–Object), as in *hēo beswāc hine* She betrayed him; S . . . V, especially in subordinate clauses, as in the clause which appeared above, *þæt wæs gēo geāra Albion hāten* (that was formerly called Albion); VS, which is used for both questions (*Hwǣr eart þū nū?* Where art thou now?) and statements, whether positive or negative (*Ne cōm se here* Not came the army: The army did not come).

**Vocabulary**. (1) The core OE wordstock was shared with the other West Germanic languages and like theirs was subject to the sound changes of GRIMM'S LAW and Verner's Law. (2) Borrowing from non-Germanic languages was relatively rare, but there were significant LOANWORDS from LATIN and GREEK. Some Latin words were acquired before the Anglo-Saxons settled in Britain, such as *strǣt* street (from *strata via* paved way) and *w(e)all* wall (from *vallum* rampart); others were borrowed afterwards, such as *fēfor* fever (from *febris*) and *mægister* master (from *magister*). Greek loans usually came through Latin, as with *biscop* (from *episcopus* from *epískopos*) and *scōl(u)* school (from *schola* from *skholḗ*). (3) Because of inflection, the structure of OE nouns, adjectives, and verbs differs greatly from that of ModE; for example, whereas ModE has one form *drink* for both noun and verb, OE has two, the noun *drinc* and the verb *drincan*. (4) Compound words were common, including as personal names: *Ælfred* Elf Council (original form of *Alfred*), *Ætheldreda* Noble Strength (original form of *Audrey*), *bretwalda* ruler of Britain (a title for the foremost king of his time), *ealdormann* nobleman (ancestral form of *alderman*), *eallwealda* or *ælwalda* ruler of all, *Edwin* Prosperous Friend, *hēahgerēfa* high reeve (an official), *sǣweall* sea wall, *stormsǣ* stormy sea, *sweordbora* sword-bearer, *synnfull* sinful. (5) DERIVATION was also common: for example, with the prefix *be-* around, as in *berīdan* to ride around; with *for-* as an intensifier, as in *forlorenness* utter lostness, perdition; with *on-* un-, as in *onlūcan* to unlock; the suffix *-end* for an agent, as in *hǣlend* healer, saviour, *wīgend* warrior; *-ing* son of, as in *Ælfred*

*Æþelwulfing* Alfred son of Ethelwulf, *hōring* son of a whore, fornicator; and *-ig*, as in *cræftig* strong (the ancestral form of *crafty*), *hālig* holy. (6) A range of compounds and derivatives was created as loan translations of Latin terms, such as *tōcyme* (to-come) to match *adventus* (advent), *gōdspel* (good news: the ancestral form of gospel) to match *evangelium*, and *þrīnnys* (threeness) to match *trinitas* (trinity). See AELFRIC, BARNES, BEOWULF, CELTIC LANGUAGES, DANELAW, DORSET, HISTORY OF ENGLISH, NORSE, NORTHERN ENGLISH, NORTHUMBRIA, PLAIN ENGLISH, PURE, RUNE, SAXONISM, SCANDINAVIAN LANGUAGES, Y.

**OLD ENGLISH**[2]. The first English settlers in Ireland, dating from the late 12c, and their language; in Irish GAELIC, they were known as *Na SeanGhaill* (The Old Foreigners). The term *Old English* was applied to them by later settlers, from the 16c onward: 'Howbeit to this day, the dregs of the old auncient Chaucer English are kept as well there [in Wexford]' (Holinshed's Chronicle, 1586); 'Their advice was always prefaced by profuse professions of the traditional loyalty of the Old English community to the Crown' (R. F. Foster, *Oxford Illustrated History of Ireland*, 1989, p. 117). See HISTORY OF ENGLISH, IRISH ENGLISH.

**ONOMATOPOEIA**. [Through LATIN from GREEK *onomatopoiía* making a name. Derived adjectives: both *onomatopoeic* and *onomatopoetic*]. A FIGURE OF SPEECH in which: (1) Words are formed from natural sounds: *ping*, *rat-a-tat-tat*. (2) Words are used and sometimes adapted, including visually, to suggest a sound: *snow crackling and crunching underfoot*, *R-r-i-i- p-p!* (of cloth tearing). In onomatopoeic usage, sound and sense echo and reinforce each other, often using ALLITERATION and ASSONANCE; hence the alternative but more inclusive term ECHOISM. Onomatopoeia is common: (1) In children's stories: *Only a bee tree goes, 'Buzz! Buzz!'* (2) In comic books and cartoons: *WHAM! KABOOM!* (3) In the language of advertising: *All 3 Kodak disc cameras go bzzt, bzzt, flash, flash. One goes tick, tock, beep, beep. And anyone who gets one for the holidays will go ooooohh!* (4) When writers want to build up a phonaesthetic effect: 'The childhood dreams of . . . the grinning Fe-Fi-Fo-Fum giant swinging his axe . . . the slush-slurp of the Creature emerging from the Black Lagoon' (James Herbert, *Shrine*, 1983). See PHONAESTHESIA.

**-ONYM**. [Through LATIN from GREEK *ónuma/ónoma* name]. A word base or combining form that stands either for a WORD (as in *SYNONYM*) or a NAME (as in *pseudonym*). Words containing *-onym* have two kinds of adjective: with *-ous*, as in *synonymous* (having the nature or quality of a synonym: *synonymous words*) or with *-ic*, as in *synonymic* (concerning synonyms: *synonymic relationships*). The form *-onymy* indicates type, as with *synonymy* (the type of sense relation in which words have the same or similar meaning) and *eponymy* (the category of word-formation that concerns words derived from people's names). Because *-onym* begins with *o* (the commonest Greek THEMATIC VOWEL, as in *biography*), the base form is sometimes taken to be *-nym*, an assumption reinforced by the initial *n* of the equivalent terms *nomen* in Latin and *name* in English. As a result, some recent technical terms have been formed on *-nym*: for example, *characternym* and *paranym*. See ACRONYM, ANTONYM, EPONYM, HETERONYM, HOMONYM, HYPONYM, RETRONYM.

**OPPOSITION. 1.** In LINGUISTICS, a functional contrast between partially similar elements in a language system: for example, between the meanings and uses of the negative prefixes *un-* and *non-* in *unprofessional* and *nonprofessional*, where *un-* is judgemental and *non-* is neutral. **2.** In PHONETICS, the nature of the contrast between a pair of PHONEMES: for example, /t/ is a voiceless alveolar stop and /d/ is a voiced alveolar stop. The two consonants agree in place and manner of articulation, but fall into the opposition of voicing. See MINIMAL PAIR.

■ **ORKNEY AND SHETLAND DIALECTS** ──────────── ■

The DIALECTS of the Northern Isles of Scotland: conservative varieties of SCOTS heavily influenced by the NORN which they superseded. The most similar mainland varieties are the most conservative of the Central Scots dialects: west Angus and east Perthshire.

**Pronunciation.** (1) Retention of the old front rounded vowel /ø/, written *ui*, *u-e*, or *ö*, as in *guid/gude/göd* and *scuil/scule/scöl*. (2) The preservation of the initial consonant clusters *kn-*, *gn-*, and *wr-*, as in *knee* /kniː/, *gnaw* /gnaː/, and *wrong* /wraŋ/. (3) Due to the Norn substratum: the stopping of the voiced and voiceless dental fricatives (*this* and *blithe* pronounced 'dis' and 'blide'; *three* and *earth* pronounced 'tree' and 'eart'; unvoiced realizations of /dʒ/ ('chust' for *just*). (4) Shetland tends to simplify /tʃ/ to /ʃ/: 'sheese' for *cheese*. (5) Shetland, like Icelandic, merges /hw/ and /kw/, in most localities as /kw/ (*white* pronounced 'quite'), but in south Mainland as /hw/ (*quite* pronounced 'white'), or with the sounds interchanged ('kweel' for *wheel*, 'hween' for *queen*).

**Grammar**. (1) Familiar *thou/the/thy* alongside respectful *ye/you/your*. (2) Probably of Norn origin is the use of gender-marked personal pronouns, especially *he*, for weather, time, and other natural phenomena: *He was blaain a gale* It was blowing a gale. (3) Commonly, perfective *be* rather than *have*: *I'm walked a piece the day* I've walked a long way today. (4) Limited use of simple inversion to form questions, as an alternative to the use of an auxiliary: *Whit tinks du?/Whit does du tink?* What do you think? and—a further example of (3) *Is du heard aboot yun afore?* Have you heard about that before? (5) Characteristic reflexive usages, especially in the imperative: *Heest dee!* Hurry up!; *Dip dee a meenit!* Sit down for a minute!; *A'll geng an rest me whin a'm pitten da bairns ta da scöl* I'll go and have a rest when I've put the children to school.

**Vocabulary**. (1) The vocabularies of the Northern Isles are distinct from those of other Scots dialects, mainly in their massive borrowing from Norn, of which over a thousand items survive. Typical examples of those in everyday use are: *benkle* dent, crumple; *frush* splutter, froth; *gaan* gawp; *glaep* gulp down, swallow greedily; *oag* crawl; *peedie* (Orkney)/*peerie* (Shetland) little; *roog* heap, pile; *skoit* peep, take a look; *smucks* carpet slippers; *spret* rip open, burst; *tirn* angry; *trivvel* grope, feel one's way. (2) Some words are structurally unusual for Scots, such as *andoo* to row a boat slowly against the tide, *brigdie/brigda* a basking shark, *fluckra* snow in large flakes, *glimro* phosphorescence (Orkney), *hyadens* animal carcasses (Shetland). (3) Some words fossilize Old Norse inflectional endings: the strong masculine *-r* in *ilder* fire (in the now-obsolete Shetland sea-language), *shalder* an oyster-catcher; the weak masculine *-i* in *arvie* chickweed, *galtie* a pig, boar, *hegrie* a heron; the weak feminine *-a* in *arvo* chickweed, *shaela* hoar-frost (Shetland); the vocative in the

former Birsay terms of address *gullie* to a man, *gullo* to a woman; and the gender distinctions in the Shetland sea-terms *russie* a stallion, *russa* a mare. (4) Some nouns contain the Old Norse suffixed definite article (*i*)*nn*: *croopan* trunk of the body, *fyandin* the devil (Shetland), *knorin* boat (Shetland), and the Shetland sea-terms *birten* fire, *hestin* horse, *monen* moon, and *sulin* sun. (5) Unique to Shetland, though now mostly archaic, are words borrowed from Dutch fishermen, who have visited Shetland since the 17c: *blöv* to die, *forstaa* to understand, *kracht* energy, *maat* a friend, *stör* a penny. See DIALECT (SCOTLAND).

**ORTHOEPY** [From Greek *orthoépeia* right speech, correct diction]. A term used mainly in the 17–18c for the part of GRAMMAR that deals with 'correct' PRONUNCIATION and its relation to 'correct' writing (*ORTHOGRAPHY*). The principles of orthoepy influenced a number of pronouncing (*orthoepic*) dictionaries of the time, such as William Kenrick's *A new Dictionary of the English Language: containing not only the explanation of words . . . but likewise their orthoepia or pronunciation in speech* (1773). Orthoepy, although primarily associated with ELOCUTION, is ancestral to PHONETICS and its application to language teaching, as in Daniel JONES's *English Pronouncing Dictionary* (1917).

**ORTHOGRAPHY** [Through FRENCH and LATIN from GREEK *orthographía* correct writing]. **1.** A term for CORRECT or accepted WRITING and SPELLING and for a normative set of conventions for writing and especially spelling. In the 15–16c, there was considerable variety and uncertainty in the writing and printing of English. Advocates of standardized spelling emphasized the importance of regularization by referring to it as *trewe ortografye*, *trew orthographie*, etc. **2.** The study of letters and how they are used to express sounds and form words, especially as a traditional aspect of GRAMMAR; the spelling system of a language, whether considered 'true' and 'correct' or not. In linguistics, however, the name for the study of the writing system of a language and for the system itself is more commonly *graphology*, a level of language parallel to *phonology*. The earlier, prescriptive sense of the term continues to be used, but the later, more neutral sense is common among scholars of language. The orthography of English has standardized on two systems, British and American. While far from uniform in either system, it allows for much less variation than is possible, for example, in the orthography of Scots. See ABBREVIATION, ACRONYM, COMPOUND WORD, ORTHOEPY, SENTENCE, SHAKESPEARE, SPELLING REFORM, TECHNO-SPEAK, TRADITIONAL ORTHOGRAPHY.

■ **ORWELL, George** ──────── ■

[1903–50]. Pen name of *Eric Arthur Blair*, English novelist, journalist, and political thinker. The adoption in 1933 of the pen name, taken from the River Orwell in East Anglia, marked his transformation from a member of the establishment of the British Empire into a social, political, and literary radical. He was born in Montihari, Bengal, India, the son of a British civil servant, and educated at Eton (where Aldous Huxley was one of his masters). From there he went in 1922 to serve in the Indian Imperial Police in Burma, but resigned because he disliked imperialism 'and every form of man's dominion over man'. In England in 1927, he became a reviewer and columnist, living for a time in the poverty described in the 'documentary novel' *Down and Out in Paris and London* (1933). Six more works appeared before the Second World War: the novels *Burmese Days* (1934), *A Clergyman's Daughter* (1935), *Keep the Aspidistra Flying* (1936), *Coming Up for Air* (1939), and the non-fiction *The Road to Wigan Pier* (1937), *Homage to Catalonia* (1938). They range from reflections on his life in Burma and on class differences and unemployment in England to his experiences in the Spanish Civil War, in which he was wounded in the throat while fighting for the Republicans against Fascism. Orwell at first saw himself as an anarchist, then a socialist, but later sought to avoid political labels. He was opposed to totalitarianism in any guise. He died of tuberculosis, a disease from which he had suffered for many years. He is best known for his two post-war anti-totalitarian satirical novels, *Animal Farm* (1945) and *Nineteen Eighty-Four* (1949), the latter introducing the concept of *NEWSPEAK*. From the same period comes the essay 'Politics and the English Language' (first published in *Horizon*, 1946), still frequently included in anthologies and widely admired for its advice on prose style.

**Attitude to English**. Like others of his time, background, and social position,

Orwell was a polyglot: LATIN and GREEK; FRENCH; Hindustani and Burmese; SPANISH. He did not, however, accept contemporary standards for English; he often derided the variety of BrE common among his fellow Etonians, along with the variety employed on the BBC, seeing them as dangerous establishment tools. In its place, he advocated an artificial amalgam of lower-class varieties, including the *dropped aitch*, to be taught in schools. Orwell was not averse to the official promulgation of an invented variety of English. The Newspeak of *Nineteen Eighty-Four* is not, therefore, evil simply because it is artificial, but because its goals are untruth and mind control, and because its means to this end are the suppression of words for forbidden concepts (like *honour*, *justice*) and the ready conversion of parts of speech (like the verb *speak* as a noun, instead of *speech*). Orwell was in most ways a language conservative while he was a social individualist and a political adherent of 'democratic socialism', as he called it. His books sometimes champion those who speak non-standard English, but his essays severely oppose linguistic change and by implication condemn the diversity that change brings.

**Rules for writing English**. In 'Politics and the English Language', Orwell wrote that 'one can often be in doubt about the effect of a word or a phrase, and one needs rules that one can rely on when instinct fails. I think the following rules will cover most cases: (1) Never use a METAPHOR, SIMILE or other FIGURE OF SPEECH which you are used to seeing in print. (2) Never use a LONG WORD where a short one will do. (3) If it is possible to cut a word out, always cut it out. (4) Never use the PASSIVE when you can use the ACTIVE. (5) Never use a foreign phrase, a scientific word or a JARGON word if you can think of an everyday English equivalent. (6) Break any of these rules sooner than say anything outright barbarous.' The double implication (that half a dozen rules would 'cover most cases', and that all writers worthy of the name would agree about what was 'outright barbarous') reveals Orwell's conservative stand on the complexities of language variety. See SATIRE, USAGE GUIDANCE AND CRITICISM.

**OTTAWA VALLEY**. A distinctive DIALECT region of Canada that extends along the Ottawa River from north-west of Montreal through the city of Ottawa and north to Algonquin Park. While the speech of the major towns is standard spoken CanE, that of the rural districts is strongly influenced by IrE, both from Ulster and the South, with small pockets of Lowland and Highland ScoE, and GAELIC, GERMAN, and Polish influence. The stereotypical feature of the accent is the local place-name *Carp* as /kærp/. Syntax includes *for to* as an infinitive complement: *Mary wants for to leave*. Vocabulary includes *(cow) byre* a cow-shed, *cow barn*, *moolie* a cow without horns, *snye* a channel (from French *chenail*), and *weight-debuckety* or *weighdee* a teeter-totter, see-saw. See DIALECT (CANADA).

**OXFORD ACCENT**. A form of RECEIVED PRONUNCIATION regarded as typical of faculty and students at the U. of Oxford, as opposed to the townspeople of Oxford. It was widely regarded, especially before the Second World War, as affected: 'It might be said perhaps that the "Oxford Accent" conveys an impression of a precise and rather foppish elegance, and of deliberate artificiality' (*Society for Pure English Tract 39*, 1934). See AFFECTATION.

**OXFORD ENGLISH**. **1.** English spoken with an *OXFORD ACCENT*, widely considered, especially in the earlier 20c, to be 'the best' BrE usage, but also regarded by many as affected and pretentious. **2.** A term used by Oxford University Press in recent years virtually as a trade name in the promotion of English-language reference books and ELT course materials. It occurs in the title of *Oxford English: A Guide to the Language*, ed. I. C. B. Dear (1983). This work is presented as 'a guide to correct written and spoken English and an accessible introduction to the language in all its aspects'. See BBC ENGLISH[1], CAMBRIDGE ENGLISH, RECEIVED PRONUNCIATION.

# ■ *OXFORD ENGLISH DICTIONARY* ────────────── ■

Short form *OED*. The foremost DICTIONARY of the English language, initiated by the Philological Society as *The New English Dictionary on Historical Principles* (*NED*) and published by Oxford University Press, 1st edition 1928 (12 volumes, with later Supplements), 2nd edition 1989 (20 volumes). Shortly after its founding in 1842, the Philological Society appointed an 'unregistered words committee' to collect English words not listed in existing dictionaries, and its members, Herbert Coleridge, Frederick Furnivall, and Richard Chenevix Trench, came to the conclusion that a large new work was required. In 1857, Trench read two papers to the Society, jointly entitled 'On Some Deficiencies in our English Dictionaries'. They covered the need to find better ways to manage obsolete words, describe derivational families, provide accurate and dated citations, list important senses of words, distinguish synonyms, cover literary sources, and eliminate redundant material.

For Trench and his associates, a dictionary was a factual inventory rather than a tool for selecting only the 'good' words of a language (however decided); a lexicographer was therefore a historian rather than a moralist, judge, or teacher. An adequate dictionary of the language would record all possible words, much as the botanist Linnaeus had sought to record all possible plants. As a result of his recommendations, the Society passed resolutions in 1858 calling for a new dictionary 'on historical principles'. It would follow the lead established in Germany by the classicist Franz Passow and the philologists Jakob and Wilhelm Grimm. In 1812, Passow had recommended, for the compilation of a Greek lexicon, that definitions should be supported by textual citations organized chronologically, and in 1838 the brothers Grimm had begun the *Deutsches Wörterbuch*, aiming to cover all the words of German 'from Luther to Goethe'. The Society resolved in its turn to cover all the words of English from AD 1000 onward, their definitions emerging from citations garnered by volunteers in many countries reading thousands of texts.

**Preparation**. Coleridge, as first editor, supervised the work of two committees, one dealing with literary sources, the other with etymology, and looked after the submission of citations, a process facilitated by the recent development of a good international postal system. On his premature death in 1861 at 31, the editorship passed to Furnivall, who realized that an efficient system of excerpting was needed. This meant that for the earlier centuries printed texts had to be prepared of manuscripts not hitherto easily available; he therefore founded in 1864 the *Early English Text Society* and in 1865 the *Chaucer Society*, preparing editions of texts of general benefit as well as immediate value to the project. None of this work, however, led to compilation; it was entirely preparatory and lasted for 21 years. There were in the end some 800 voluntary readers. Their enthusiasm was enormous, but in a process which depended on paper and pen alone a major drawback was the often arbitrary choices made by the relatively untrained volunteers regarding what to read and select, what to discard, and how much detail to provide.

**Compilation**. The first editor properly so called was the schoolmaster James A. H. MURRAY. When appointed in 1879, he took over from Furnivall nearly two tons of material, mainly slips of paper. The Society and Murray entered into an agreement with the Delegates of the Clarendon Press, Oxford U., that the Press would publish the Society's *New English Dictionary on Historical Principles*, often also known as 'the Society's Dictionary' and 'Murray's Dictionary'. It was agreed that the work would take ten years to complete, be published at intervals in fascicles, and in its final form would consist of four volumes of some 6,400 pages. Its aim was 'to present in alphabetical series the words that have formed the English vocabulary from the time of the earliest records (*c.*AD 740) down to the present day, with all the relevant facts concerning their form, sense-history, pronunciation, and etymology', but excluding words and meanings that did not survive the Norman Conquest in the 11c; it would include 'not only the standard language of literature and conversation, whether current at the moment, or obsolete, or archaic, but also the main technical vocabulary, and a large measure of dialectal use and slang' (preface, 2nd edition).

**The editors**. The Dictionary had four cooperating editors between 1879 and 1928, each working with a staff of about six assistants. The first fascicle of 352 pages (*a–ant*) was published in 1884. In the same year, Henry Bradley joined Murray as one of his assistants, and the project moved from Mill Hill School, where Murray had been a master since 1870, to Oxford. There the work continued in two separate locations. Murray and his assistants worked in the famous *Scriptorium* (a garden shed fitted with pigeon-hole shelving in his home at 78 Banbury Road); the teams of Henry Bradley,

William Craigie, and C. T. Onions, at the Old Ashmolean building in Broad Street.

**The First Edition**. Although the project continued to belong officially to the Philological Society, its presence in Oxford and the expense of sustaining it tended to make it more and more an Oxford undertaking. In 1895, this was reflected by the appearance for the first time, above the title on the cover of the fascicle *deceit–deject*, the words *The Oxford English Dictionary*. When, after 71 years of preparation, the complete work appeared in 1928, it was *The Oxford English Dictionary*, consisting of 12 volumes of 15,487 pages covering 414,825 words backed by 5m quotations, of which some 2m were actually printed in the dictionary text.

**The Supplements**. In 1933, Craigie and Onions issued a *Supplement* of 867 pages, intended to include details of all words and meanings that had come into the language while the *OED* was in preparation, but it fell well short of that target. In 1933, the team was dispersed and the enterprise brought to a close for a quarter of a century. A new *Supplement* was set in hand in 1957, under the editorship of Robert W. Burchfield. This work followed the pattern of the original in taking approximately four times as long to compile as the initial forecasts suggested, and ending up as four volumes instead of the one proposed volume of 1,275 pages. *The Oxford English Dictionary Supplement* (*OEDS*) reached out to the vocabulary of all parts of the English-speaking world, approximate parity of treatment being given to the major forms of English in the United Kingdom, North America, Australia, New Zealand, and elsewhere. Volume A–G was published in 1972, H–N in 1976, O–Scz in 1982, and Se–Z in 1986. The independent existence of the *OEDS* was brought to a close by plans in the early 1980s for an electronic merging of the 12 volumes of the *OED* and the four volumes of the *OEDS*.

**The Second Edition**. Preparation for this began in 1983 and editorial work started the following year under the administrative direction of Timothy J. Benbow, and with John A. Simpson and Edmund S. C. Weiner as co-editors. An electronic system for integrating the original text and the supplements was created with help in the form of equipment and expertise from IBM (UK) Ltd. The U. of Waterloo in Ontario, Canada, helped develop the software for parsing the text, with a grant from the government of Canada. The project also received a grant from the UK Department of Trade and Industry. More than 120 keyboarders of International Computaprint Corporation in Tampa, Florida, and Fort Washington, Pennsylvania, USA, started keying in over 350m characters, their work checked by 55 proofreaders in England. There were four major changes to the text: Murray's system for indicating pronunciation was replaced by the INTERNATIONAL PHONETIC ALPHABET; all foreign alphabets except Greek were transliterated; the initial capital letter given for each headword was replaced by a system that reflected the normal facts of the language in respect to capitalization (for example, *American/amity*, *Lady day/lady-bird*); and important changes were made to the typographical layout. The two sets of information were merged in 1987, and some 5,000 additional modern words and meanings were inserted. This edition was published in 1989 in 20 volumes. It has 21,728 pages and contains some 290,500 main entries, within which there are a further 157,000 combinations and derivatives in bold type (all defined), and a further 169,000 phrases and undefined combinations in bold italic type, totalling 616,500

word forms. There are some 2.4m illustrative quotations, some 6m words of text, and over 350m characters. The electronic base takes up 540 megabytes of storage.

**The electronic *OED*.** The text of the First Edition was made available on CD-ROM in 1988, and a CD-ROM version of the Second Edition appeared in 1992. Its electronic text, which has the capacity of indefinite adaptation and extension, is structured in such a way that it can yield any desired combinatorial information, such as all entered words of Arabic origin, all words or meanings first recorded in the year 1819, or all the illustrative quotations cited in the *Dictionary* from the works of a given author.

**OXYMORON**. [From Greek *oxúmōros* sharp and dull. Stress: 'awk-si-Mo-ron']. A term in RHETORIC for bringing opposites together in a compact paradoxical word or phrase: *bitter-sweet*; *a cheerful pessimist*. The term is often used for social comment, humorously or cynically (such as in reference to *military intelligence*, conceived as a contradiction in terms) and dramatically, as in 'It has become an oxymoron to speak of the Lebanese nation' (Jim Hoagland, *The Washington Post*, Apr. 1989).

# P

■ **P, p** ─────────────────────────── ■

[Called 'pee']. The 16th LETTER of the Roman
ALPHABET as used for English. It originated
in the Phoenician symbol *pe*, which was
adopted by the Greeks as *pi* (*Π*), an earlier
form of which the Romans adopted as P.

**Sound values**. In English, the letter *p* is
normally pronounced as a voiceless bilabial
plosive, as in *pip*. Phonetic variations in
English include a less aspirated value after
initial *s*, as in *spot*, and an unreleased plosive before other consonants, as in *slipped*
(as opposed to the gently released *p* in *slip-
per*). In final position, spoken /p/ may or may
not be released: *slip*, *snap*.

**Double P**. (1) Final *p* is normally single
(*tap*, *step*, *tip*, *stop*, *cup*, *kidnap*, *worship*), the
form *steppe* probably reflecting FRENCH or
GERMAN spelling, as the original RUSSIAN
has only single *p*. Monosyllables double the
final *p* after a single short vowel before a
suffix beginning with a vowel (*stopping*,
*stopper*, *stopped*). Few polysyllables end in *p*;
if they do, the *p* is generally not doubled before suffixes: *galloped*, *gossiping*, *syrupy*. However, BrE treats *kidnap*, *worship* as though
based on monosyllables (*kidnapped*, *worship-
ping*), though AmE often follows the polysyllabic pattern (*kidnaped*, *worshiping*). (2)
The doubling of medial *p* after stressed simple short vowels is inconsistent, as in the
pairs *apple/chapel*, *pepper/leper*, *copper/proper*.
In *coppice* there is doubling, whereas related
*copse* has a single *p*. (3) When *p* is preceded
by some Latin prefixes, it is doubled because
of the assimilation of a consonant, as in *apparent* (ad-parent), *oppose* (ob-pose), *suppress*
(sub-press).

**Epenthetic P**. (1) The nasal equivalent of
*p* is *m*. The phonetic closeness of the sounds
represented by these letters has prompted
an epenthetic *p* after *m* in *empty* (earlier
*emti*), and in the variants *sempstress/
seamstress*, *Thompson/Thomson*, and *Hamp-
stead/Hamstead* (part of London and part
of Birmingham, respectively). (2) Phonetically, there may be the same epenthetic
*p*-quality in *dreamt* ('drempt') as in *empty*. (3)
The *p* in related forms such as *redeem/*

*redemption*, *consume/consumption* has been
carried over from Latin etyma. See EPENTHE-
SIS, ETYMON.

**PH**. (1) The DIGRAPH *ph* with the value /f/
originated as the Latin transcription of
Greek *phi* (*Φ*), which originally had the
value of a heavily aspirated /p/ (comparable
to the sound in *uphold*). *Ph* pronounced /f/ occurs almost only in roots of GREEK origin
(*pharmacy*, *philosophy*, *photograph*), but has
been adopted by analogy in occasional
words of non-Greek derivation, such as
*nephew* (compare French *neveu*, German
*Neffe*), BrE *sulphur* (compare LATIN and AmE
*sulfur*). The *ph* in the name *Stephen* is pronounced /v/ and is alternatively *v* as in
*Steven*. (2) *Ph* before *th* is often pronounced
/p/, for example 'diptheria' for *diphtheria*,
'dipthong' for *diphthong*, 'opthalmic' for
*ophthalmic*, and this leads to spellings without *h*. See F.

**Silent P**. (1) Initially, in words of Greek derivation before *n* (*pneumonia*), *s* (*psalm*), *t*
(*pterodactyl*), producing combinations that,
if pronounced, would be alien to English
phonology. Middle English sometimes omitted *p* in *salme*, *salter*, but in Modern English
it is seen in *psalm*, *psalter*, *pseudo-*, *psittacosis*,
*psoriasis*, *psyche*, *Ptolemy*, *ptomaine*, etc. Of
GAELIC origin, *ptarmigan* probably acquired
its *p* by analogy with Greek derivations. (2)
Occasionally, as when preceding a syllable
beginning with its voiced equivalent *b*, the
sound of *p* is assimilated, so effectively becoming silent, as in *cupboard* ('cubberd'),
*raspberry* ('razb(e)ry'). (3) The *p* of *receipt* is
an etymologically motivated insertion and
was formerly often also inserted in *conceit*
and *deceit*, but Samuel JOHNSON kept it only
in *receipt* on grounds of common usage. (4)
Silent *p* occurs in *sapphire*, whose first *p* was
introduced as MIDDLE ENGLISH *safir* on etymological grounds. It also occurs in such
French loans as *corps* and *coup*. (5) Whether
*p* is pronounced after *m* in, for example,
*empty*, *exempt*, *tempt*, *prompt*, *consumption* (as
well as in *dreamt*) is unclear; at all events,
the preceding bilabial *m* prepares the lips
for *p* and is released as for /p/ with the
following consonant.

# ■ PAKISTANI ENGLISH ───── ■

Short forms *PakE*, *PE*. The English language as used in Pakistan, a variety of SOUTH ASIAN ENGLISH close to that of northern India. English has had co-official status with URDU since independence in 1947, but the constitution of 1959 and the amendments of 1968, 1972, and 1985 recognize URDU as pre-eminent and restrict the use of English, the aim being its eventual replacement. Both are minority languages. In 1981, the president appointed a study whose report recommended that 'Urdu should continue to be the only medium of instruction at the school level, with no exception' (1982), but that English and ARABIC be introduced as additional languages from class six (sixth grade: age 11); a federal agency should ensure that the policy is implemented. English is an important medium in a number of leading educational institutions. It is the main language of technology, international business, and communication among a national élite, and a major element in the media. The constitution and the laws of the land are codified in English, and the *Pakistan Academy of Letters* recognizes works in English for its literature award. It also has a considerable influence on the vernacular languages; S. Hands notes that in personal interaction, 'the use of an English word is believed to add a note of refinement and elegance to conversation in the "lower" languages' (*Pakistan: A Country Study*, 4th edition, The American University, Washington, DC, 1983).

**Pronunciation and grammar**. (1) PakE is RHOTIC, tends to be syllable-timed, and shares many features with northern INDIAN ENGLISH. (2) Some pronunciation features are typical of speakers of regional languages: for example, speakers of Punjabi have difficulty with such initial consonant clusters as /sk, sp/ (saying 'səport' and 'səkool' for *sport* and *school*); Urdu speakers also have difficulty with initial consonant clusters (saying 'isport' and 'iskool' for *sport* and *school*); Pashto speakers have no such difficulty, but use /p/ for /f/ ('pood' for *food*). (3) Distinctive grammatical features relate to uses of the verb, article, relative clause, preposition, and adjective and verb complementation, all shared with IndE. Features of the indigenous languages influence use of English and CODE-MIXING AND CODE-SWITCH-

ING are common, including among the highly educated.

**Vocabulary**. (1) BORROWINGS from Urdu and the regional languages: *atta* flour, *tehsil* district, *ziarat* religious place. (2) LOAN TRANSLATIONS from these languages: *cousin-brother*. (3) Terms shared with Indian English: *crore* ten million, *lakh* one hundred thousand, *-wallah* a word element denoting 'one who does something as an occupation', as with *policewallah*. (4) Hybrids of English and local languages: *biradarism* favouring one's clan or family, *gheraoed* surrounded by protesters in an office or similar place and unable to leave, *goondaism* hooliganism, thuggish behaviour. (5) English words, especially compounds, adapted for local use: *age-barred* over the age for (particular work), *load-shedding* intermittently shutting off a supply of electricity.

**Media and literature**. Pakistan has a strong English-language press. Most major cities have daily and weekly newspapers; in all, there are 20 dailies, 35 weeklies, 33 fortnightlies, 152 monthlies, and 111 quarterlies. They include *The Muslim*, *Daily News*, *Dawn*, *Morning News*, *Star*, *Pakistan Times*, and *Khyber Mail*. Pakistani literature in English is developing in various genres and several writers have acquired national and international recognition, such as Ahmad Ali, Bapsi Sidhwa, Zulfikar Ghose, A. Hashmi, and Hanif Kureishi. The educated variety used by Pakistan radio and television serves as the model for teaching and learning English throughout the country.

**PALATE**. An anatomical term for the roof of the mouth, behind the ALVEOLAR ridge, often described as having two parts: the *hard palate* (the roof of the mouth proper) and the *soft palate* (the VELUM). The adjective *palatal* is used to describe sounds made by raising the front of the tongue towards the hard palate. See CONSONANT, SPEECH.

**PALINDROME**. **1.** A WORD, PHRASE, or longer expression that reads the same backwards as it does forwards: for example, the words *level* and *noon*, and the phrases *Madam, I'm Adam* and *Able was I ere I saw Elba*. **2.** Also REVERSAL, *semordnilap* (a backward palindrome). A word that spells another word when reversed: for example, *doom*, *evil*, *warts*, and the trade names *Serutan*, *Trebor*.

**PANAMA**. Languages: Spanish (official), English (a common second language because of US influence), and Chibcha. The region was under Spanish control from 1538 to 1821, was part of Colombia until 1903, and with US backing has been distinct ever since. See CARIBBEAN ENGLISH CREOLE.

**PAPUA NEW GUINEA**, also **Papua Niugini**. A state in the south-west Pacific, occupying the eastern half of the island of New Guinea and some 600 islands, the largest of which are New Britain, New Ireland, and Bougainville. Prior to independence in 1975, the southern half (Papua) was an Australian colony and the northern part (New Guinea) was administered by Australia under a mandate from the United Nations given after the First World War, when it ceased to be a German colony. The island of New Guinea was peopled by different waves of migrants, whose history is largely unknown. The terrain is rugged. Travel by air is more important than by road. Port Moresby, the capital, is not connected by road to any other urban area. The coastal population is thinly clustered in villages, but over one-third of the total population live in highland valleys. While settlement by Europeans has extended over a century, contact with many internal regions is fairly recent. Most of these communities were not known before 1930. Even in the 1950s, Australian administrative patrols were still establishing contact with people in remoter areas. These conditions have fostered cultural and linguistic diversity; there are some 700–750 languages belonging to two families, Papuan and Austronesian, as well as an indigenous PIDGIN, Hiri Motu, and an English-based pidgin, TOK PISIN. Both serve as LINGUA FRANCAS and share official status with English. See MELANESIAN PIDGIN ENGLISH.

**PARADIGM** [From Greek *parádeigma*, a pattern, an example, a basis for comparison. Stress: 'PA-ra-dime']. In GRAMMAR, a set of all the (especially inflected) forms of a word (*write, writes, wrote, writing, written*), especially when used as a model for all other words of the same type. Paradigms serve as models for word forms in LATIN and GREEK (in which key words represent the patterns of numbered groups of nouns, adjectives, verbs, etc.) and to a lesser extent for such other languages as French and Spanish (principally for verbs). Their use is limited in English, because it is not a highly inflected language. See CONJUGATION, SUFFIX.

**PARADIGMATIC AND SYNTAGMATIC**. Contrasting terms in (structural) LINGUISTICS. Every item of language has a *paradigmatic relationship* with every other item which can be substituted for it (such as *cat* with *dog*), and a *syntagmatic relationship* with items which occur within the same construction (for example, in *The cat sat on the mat, cat* with *the* and *sat on the mat*). The relationships are like axes, as shown in the accompanying diagram.

|  | *syntagmatic* |  |  |  |
|---|---|---|---|---|
|  | The cat | sat | on | the mat. |
| *paradigmatic* | His dog | slept | under | that table. |
|  | Our parrot | perched in | its cage. |

Paradigmatic contrasts at the level of sounds allow one to identify the phonemes (minimal distinctive sound units) of a language: for example, *bat, fat, mat* contrast with one another on the basis of a single sound, as do *bat, bet, bit*, and *bat, bap, ban*. Stylistically, rhyme is due to the paradigmatic substitution of sounds at the beginning of syllables or words, as in: 'Tyger! Tyger! burning *bright* | In the forests of the *night*.'

On the lexical level, paradigmatic contrasts indicate which words are likely to belong to the same word class (part of speech): *cat, dog, parrot* in the diagram are all nouns, *sat, slept, perched* are all verbs. Syntagmatic relations between words enable one to build up a picture of co-occurrence restrictions within SYNTAX, for example, the verbs *hit, kick* have to be followed by a noun (*Paul hit the wall*, not *\*Paul hit*), but *sleep, doze* do not normally do so (*Peter slept*, not *\*Peter slept the bed*). On the semantic level, paradigmatic substitutions allow items from a semantic set to be grouped together, for example *Angela came on Tuesday* (Wednesday, Thursday, etc.), while syntagmatic associations indicate compatible combinations: *rotten apple, the duck quacked*, rather than *\*curdled apple, \*the duck squeaked*.

**PARADOX**. A term in RHETORIC for a situation or statement that is or seems self-contradictory and even absurd, but may contain an insight into life, such as *The child is father of the man*. Rationally, a child cannot be a father, but one can propose in this figurative way that the nature of one's early life affects later ideas and attitudes. A series of paradoxical statements that involve AN-TITHESIS, climax, metaphor, and repetition, opens Charles DICKENS'S *A Tale of Two Cities* (1859):

It was the best of times, it was the worst of times, it was the age of wisdom, it was the age of foolishness, it was the epoch of belief, it was the epoch of incredulity, it was the season of Light, it was the season of Darkness, it was the spring of hope, it was the winter of despair, we had everything before us, we had nothing before us, we were all going direct to Heaven, we were all going direct the other way.

Some writers, such as Oscar Wilde, have made an art of the paradoxical and epigrammatic: 'Nowadays people know the price of everything, and the value of nothing' (*The Picture of Dorian Gray*, 1891). Compare IRONY.

**PARAGRAPH**. Currently, a piece of WRITING or print of variable length and having a variety of internal structures, arranged as a single block of TEXT. It can contain only one SENTENCE, but generally consists of two or more sentences presenting an argument or description. The beginning of a paragraph is usually *indented* in print, unless preceded by an interlinear space, but not always in handwriting or word processing, nor in display material. Sometimes, both INDENTING and extra line space are used to make each paragraph stand out strongly.

The layout of texts in European languages has changed considerably since the Middle Ages, when the paragraph was not a consistently organized unit of PROSE, and prose was not a highly developed form of writing. The development of PRINTING in the 15c encouraged the use of paragraphs as blocks of lines that could be manipulated easily by the printer and helped break up the appearance of page after page of print. However, balance in the presentation of lines of print, whole pages, and the effect of the message has been a minor consideration in teaching COMPOSITION and in the development of print. Nonetheless, the general view has arisen that just as a chapter (with or without a heading) is a section in the progression of an argument or a story, so within the chapter a paragraph (with or without a subheading) is part of the same orderly progression.

By and large, until the 19c, paragraphs tended to be long and to consist of PERIODIC SENTENCES, one period sometimes taking up a paragraph running over one or more pages. In manuals of instruction, however, especially where sections have been logically ordered (and numbered), paragraphs have tended to be shorter. The scripts of PROSE plays have always had marked-off sections opening with characters' names (on a par with verse drama). In novels and other works of fiction, along with the increasing use of separated-off DIALOGUE (similar to the style of scripts), 19c writers reduced the lengths of their paragraphs, a process that has continued in the 20c, particularly in journalism, advertisements, and publicity materials, where paragraphs are often short and built out of sentence fragments. Writers of fiction often use the same effect to present swift action, changes in thinking, and the like.

Traditionally, teachers of COMPOSITION have taught students to begin a new paragraph when beginning a new topic or subtopic in an essay or other piece of prose. The aim has been to produce logically ordered sentences, the first of which is a *topic* or *key sentence* that sets the scene. This ideal continues to be widely valued, but is not the only basis, or even a principal basis, on which paragraphs are constructed by professional writers. In the process of drafting their material, they may combine and recombine paragraphs. Two influences are: relationships with material in preceding and following paragraphs, and the 'eye appeal' of different lengths of paragraph arranged in relation to the size of page and typeface used. Paragraph construction is therefore as much a matter of layout and visual balance as of content and logical relationship between preceding or subsequent paragraphs. For purposes of highlighting or emphasis, longer paragraphs may be divided up, sometimes turning a proposed topic sentence into a *topic paragraph*. Paragraphs in academic works, works of reference, religious scriptures, specialist journals, consumer magazines, quality newspapers, and tabloid newspapers all follow different rules of thumb in their construction. See PUNCTUATION.

**PARALLELISM**. In RHETORIC, a device in

which a formula or structural pattern is repeated, as in the LATIN sequence *veni, vidi, vici* and its English translation *I came, I saw, I conquered*. It occurs in sayings and proverbs (such as *Now you see them, now you don't* and *Out of sight, out of mind*), and in verse and poetic prose ('My mother groaned, my father wept— / Into the dangerous world I leapt' (William Blake, *Songs of Experience*)). See ANTITHESIS, REPETITION.

**PARAPHRASE**. **1.** The (more or less) free rewording of an expression or text, as an explanation, clarification, or TRANSLATION: 'Paraphrase, or translation with latitude, where the author is kept in view . . . , but his words are not so strictly followed as his sense' (John Dryden, preface to his translation of Ovid, 1680). **2.** An act or result of rewording, such as a simplified version of a legal document: a plain-English paraphrase of *The contractor shall have a general lien upon all goods in his possession for all monies due to him from the customer* is *We have a right to hold some or all of the goods until you have paid all our charges*. **3.** To make a paraphrase; to translate or define loosely: the COMPOUND WARD *teapot* can be paraphrased or explained by the phrase *a pot for tea* but not by *a pot of tea*.

**PARATAXIS** [Stress: 'pa-ra-TA-xis']. **1.** Placing together phrases, clauses, and sentences, often without conjunctions, often with *and, but, so*, and with minimal or no use of subordination. A paratactic style is common in orature (oral literature) and in fast-moving prose, especially if intended for young listeners or readers:

> Not always was the Kangaroo as now we do behold him, but a different Animal with four short legs. . . . He was grey and he was woolly, and his pride was inordinate: he danced on a sandbank in the Middle of Australia, and he went to the Big God Nqong. He went to Nqong at ten before dinner-time, saying: 'Make me different from all other animals; make me popular and wonderfully run after by five this afternoon.'

(Rudyard Kipling, 'The Sing-Song of Old Man Kangaroo', *Just So Stories*, 1902). **2.** Punctuating two or more sentences as if they were one, as in *I came, I saw, I conquered* (translating Latin *Veni, vidi, vici*) and *Come on, let's get going!* See COMMA, COORDINATION.

**PARENTHESIS** [Stress: 'pa-REN-the-sis'.

Plural *parentheses* ('-seez')]. **1.** In GRAMMAR, a qualifying, explanatory, or appositional word, phrase, clause, or sentence that interrupts a construction without otherwise affecting it. A written or printed parenthesis may be marked by pairs of COMMAS, DASHES, or round BRACKETS/parentheses: *Our new manager (he has just this minute arrived) would like to meet you*. A spoken parenthesis has the same intonation as an aside. **2.** In the plural, a name for round brackets: the general term in AmE, but a less common, more technical term in BrE (short form *parens*). See ACADEMIC USAGE, ASIDE.

**PARONOMASIA**. See PUN.

**PARSING** [From the verb *parse*, from Latin *pars/partis* a part, abstracted from the phrase *pars orationis* part of speech]. **1.** Analysing a SENTENCE into its constituents, identifying in greater or less detail the syntactic relations and parts of speech. **2.** Describing a WORD in a sentence, identifying its part of speech, inflectional form, and syntactic function.

**Traditional parsing**. Parsing was formerly central to the teaching of GRAMMAR throughout the English-speaking world, and widely regarded as basic to the use and understanding of written language. When many people talk about formal grammar in schools, they are referring to the teaching of *parsing* and *CLAUSE ANALYSIS*, which virtually ceased in primary and secondary education in the English-speaking world in the 1960s, and in tertiary education has been superseded by linguistic analysis. The argument against traditional parsing is threefold: that it promotes old-fashioned descriptions of language based on LATIN grammatical categories; that students do not benefit from it; and that it is a source of frustration and boredom for both students and teachers. The argument in favour of parsing is fourfold: that it makes explicit the structure of speech and writing, exercises the mind in a disciplined way, enables people to talk about language usage, and helps in the learning and discussion of foreign languages. A compromise position holds that the formal discussion of SYNTAX and function can be beneficial, but should take second place to fluent expression and the achievement of confidence rather than dominate the weekly routine.

**Computational parsing**. When a computer parses, it analyses a string of characters in order to associate groups in the string with the syntactic units of a grammar. Computers do this mostly for programming languages but also sometimes for English. Programming languages are defined by simple but precise grammars, and the translation of these languages into machine language requires knowing which rules apply to each statement. Typical grammars for computer languages take a few dozen rules and parse input at the rate of several seconds per statement. The grammars for such languages are designed to be unambiguous: only one 'parse' is possible for each statement. Computer scientists have often thought of applying similar techniques to natural language, but a language like English requires hundreds or thousands of rules, does not conform to the neat mathematical models that allow the rapid parsing of computer languages, often contains ambiguities, and has not yet been described in sufficient detail to be successfully parsed by a machine.

■ PARTICIPLE ──────────────── ■

In grammatical description, the term for two non-finite VERB forms, the *-ing* participle (known traditionally as the *present participle*) and the *-ed* participle (known traditionally as the *past participle* or *passive participle*).

**The *-ing* (present) participle**. This verb form ends with the inflection *-ing* and is used in combination with a form of the auxiliary *be* for the progressive continuous, as in: *am driving, was playing, will be going, has been talking*. It is also used as the verb in an *-ing* participle clause, as in: *Marvin and Jane liked playing with their grandchildren; Despite his protestations, Stanley was not averse to having a birthday party; John and Linda were happy to see Daniel behaving himself during the meal; After giving her lecture, Venetia had lunch with me at the College; The young man driving me to the shopping centre was Jeremy.*

**The *-ed* (past) participle**. This verb form ends with the inflection spelled *-ed, -d,* or *-t* for all regular verbs and many irregular verbs, but many irregular verbs form it with an *-en* or *-n* inflection (as in *stolen, known*) or with a change in the middle vowel (as in *sung*, in which case it is often identical with

the simple past form, as with *sat*), or a combination of the two methods (as with *written*). The *-ed* participle combines with a form of the auxiliary *have* for the perfect: *has cared, had said, may have walked*. It combines with a form of the auxiliary *be* for the passive: *is paid, was told, are being auctioned, could have been seen*. It is also used as the verb in an *-ed* participle clause: *I had my study redecorated; Asked for his opinion, Ian was non-committal; Among the objects recovered from the ship was a chair stamped with the captain's initials.*

**Attributive uses**. Both participles may be used in the attributive position like an adjective, but only if the participle indicates some sort of permanent characteristic: *running water, the missing link, a broken heart, lost property*. The phrase *The Laughing Cavalier* is possible as the name of a picture (the man is laughing for all time), but *\*Who is that laughing man?* would be odd in most contexts. The *-ed* participle usually has a passive meaning (*listed buildings, burnt almonds, written instructions*), but may be used actively with some intransitive verbs (*an escaped prisoner*). Some participles that are not permanent enough to be used attributively alone are acceptable when modified (*their long-awaited visit*).

**Participles and word-formation**. There is a range of usage between participles which remain fully verbal (*running* in *swiftly running water*) and those that in some contexts are completely adjectival (*interesting* in *a very interesting idea; disappointed* in *a very disappointed man*). There are also some participle-like formations for which there are no corresponding verbs: *an unexplained discrepancy, an unconvincing narrative*, for which there are no conventional verbs *\*to unexplain* and *\*to unconvince; a bearded man, a forested hillside, a blue-eyed cat, a one-armed bandit*, common constructions which are aspects of word-formation rather than grammar.

**Participial clauses**. Traditionally known as *participial phrases*, such clauses function in various ways: (1) They can follow noun phrases (like abbreviated relative clauses): 'The train (which is) *now standing at Platform 5 is . . .*', 'The food (that was) *served on the plane was . . .*'. (2) They can function rather like finite subordinate clauses, with or without a conjunction, and with various meanings, often of time ('While *running for the* *train*, he lost his wallet'), reason ('*Jostled by the crowd*, he did not really see what happened'), or result ('The train started suddenly, *throwing an elderly passenger to the floor*'). (3) They can follow an object + verb of the senses: 'We could all hear him *singing in the bath*'; 'He didn't see the soap *lying on the floor*.' Occasionally this multiplicity of functions may lead to ambiguity: 'I witnessed a sergeant push his way past supporters *drinking openly in the aisle*' (letter in the *Daily Telegraph*, 27 May 1988).

**The dangling participle**. When a participial clause contains its own subject, it is called an *ABSOLUTE CLAUSE*, as in '*Weather permitting*, we'll go sailing this weekend'. When, as is more usual, such a clause does not contain a subject, it normally refers grammatically to the subject of the main clause: in 'I made my way, *depressed*, to the ticket office', it is clear who was depressed, and in 'The woman on the chair beside me was tipped on to my lap, *complaining all the time*' it is clear who was complaining (both from Colin Thubron, *Behind the Wall*, 1987). Failure to maintain such a clear relationship leads to the so-called *dangling, hanging, misrelated*, or *unattached participle*, as in: 'Her party was the first to discover that there were no sleepers left. The entire section had been booked. *Faced with a forty-four hour journey*, this was not good news' (Patrick Marnham, *So Far from God*, 1985).

With participles that attach themselves to the wrong noun, the effect may be momentarily confusing even if the writer's meaning is clear: '[Sir Mortimer Wheeler's] celebrity on television was so great that, *boarding an empty bus late one rainy night when in a white tie with rows of medals*, a conductress arranged with the driver to take him to the door of Wheeler's small house off Haymarket' (Anthony Powell, *To Keep the Ball Rolling*, 1982). Here, the meaning may be fairly obvious, but on first reading it is the conductress who boards the bus. In the following example, it is the lines that apparently provided the clues '*By taking a great many such observations and analysing them statistically*, the lines gave crucial clues about the intervening space between us and quasars, and therefore of the early universe's history' (in 'Bonfire of the Cosmos', *Observer*, 16 Apr. 1989). Sometimes, the pictures presented are simply absurd: '*After travelling by road all day . . .* , the 123-room Sahara Palace is an air-conditioned all-mod-cons watering hole'

(*Daily Telegraph*, 22 Sept. 1984); 'There, *coasting comfortably down the attractive green coastline*, the town of Malacca with its prominent hill was very evident' (Tim Severin, *The Sindbad Voyage*, 1982).

**Participial prepositions and conjunctions**. Apparent exceptions to the rule that participles should be properly attached are a number of participle forms that now function as prepositions, such as *following* in 'There was tremendous clearing up to do *following the storm*', and *including* in 'We all enjoyed ourselves, *including the dog*'; and participle forms that are now conjunctions, such as *providing* (*that*) and *provided* (*that*) in 'Everything will be all right, *providing/provided* you don't panic', and *given* in '*Given the difficulties*, I'd say it was a success.'

**PARTICLE**. A WORD that does not change its form through INFLECTION and does not fit easily into the established system of PARTS OF SPEECH. Among individual words commonly so classed are the negative particle *not* (and its contraction *n't*), the infinitival particle *to* (*to go*; *to run*), the imperative particles *do*, *don't* (*Do tell me*; *Don't tell me*) and *let*, *let's* (*Let me see now*; *Let's go*). There is also a set of adverbial and prepositional particles that combine with verbs to form PHRASAL VERBS (*out* in *look out*; *up* in *turn up*) and PREPOSITIONAL VERBS (*at* in *get at*; *for* in *care for*). The term *pragmatic particle* is sometimes used for words that play a role in maintaining discourse and are also known as *fillers* and *discourse markers*: *oh, ah, well, yes, no, actually, anyway*. See ADVERBIAL PARTICLE, PREPOSITION.

**PART OF SPEECH**. A GRAMMATICAL CATEGORY or class of words. Traditional grammars of English generally list eight parts of speech: *NOUN, PRONOUN, VERB, ADJECTIVE, ADVERB, PREPOSITION, CONJUNCTION, INTERJECTION*. The parts of speech are traditionally defined by a mixture of formal and notional criteria. This mixture has posed problems for 20c grammarians, and since the development of structural LINGUISTICS, many have come to prefer the term *WORD CLASS*, for which the criteria are rigorously restricted to form alone. Some contemporary linguists and grammarians prefer to avoid the traditional term; others use it by and large in the same sense as word class, and treat the two as interchangeable. The contemporary categories, based on formal criteria and however named, are more numerous than the traditional parts of speech and can be subcategorized. In English, for example, grammarians recognize a class of DETERMINERS that introduce noun phrases, and subclasses of determiners include: the definite article *the* (*the weather*); the indefinite article *a/an* (*a pipe*); the DEMONSTRATIVES (*that painting*); the possessives (*our family*); and the indefinite pronouns (*some money*). Similarly, verbs may be distinguished as full verb and AUXILIARY VERB, and within the auxiliary class there is the class of modal auxiliary or MODAL VERB (*can, may, will,* etc). See ADVERBIAL, ARTICLE, PARTICIPLE, PARTICLE.

## PARTRIDGE, Eric (Honeywood)

[1894–1979]. New Zealand-born lexicorgrapher, and writer on USAGE and other subjects, born in Waimata Valley, North Island, and educated in Australia. His studies at the U. of Queensland were interrupted by four years as a private in the Australian infantry during the First World War, in which he saw action at Gallipoli and the Somme. In the Second World War, though over military age, he again volunteered. After a spell as an army education officer he was invalided out, only to join the Royal Air Force, in which, after serving as a storeman, he became clerk to 'Writer Command', a group of writers including H. E. Bates, John Pudney, and W. Vernon Noble. The group was commissioned to publicize the Service. His military experiences, and encounters with all sorts and conditions of men, reinforced a lifelong interest in the underside of the language.

After graduating, he became a Queensland Travelling Fellow at Oxford. Having gained an MA and B.Litt. simultaneously there, he taught at the universities of Manchester and London, but boredom and dislike of lecturing made him found his own publishing firm, Scholartis, in 1927. Partridge's most important publications were (with John Brophy) the discursive glossary *Songs and Slang of the British Soldier in the Great War* (1930) and his annotated version of *A Classical Dictionary of the Vulgar Tongue*, by Francis Grose (1931). Cecil Franklin, chairman of the London publishers Routledge & Kegan Paul, saw the potential of these works, and, when Scholartis closed because of the Depression in 1931, commissioned Partridge to produce a comprehensive dictionary of SLANG.

Published in 1937, *A Dictionary of Slang and Unconventional English* was a worldwide success. It was followed by: *Usage and Abusage: A Guide to Good English* (1942); *Shakespeare's Bawdy* (1947); *A Dictionary of the Underworld* (1950); *Origins: An Etymological Dictionary of English* (1958); *A Dictionary of Catch Phrases* (1977); and over 20 other books of essays on language, some prescriptive, some descriptive. Partridge's influence has been twofold: generating curiosity about the language among its speakers in all walks of life; working for the adequate lexicographical coverage of COLLOQUIAL and TABOO usage, a procedure now, partly as a result of his influence, standard for major dictionaries.

## PASSIVE (VOICE).

A grammatical term that contrasts with *active* (*VOICE*): where the sentence *Helen met the visitors* is in the active voice, the sentence *The visitors were met by Helen* is in the passive voice. The American grammarian Dennis Baron (in 'Going out of style?', *English Today* 17, Jan. 1989) has argued that since the 1940s, especially in the US, writers of guides to good writing have increasingly urged their readers to avoid or minimize passive constructions: the passive voice has not only become associated with general wordiness and confusion but also, especially in its 'agentless' form, with evasiveness and deception, as in *The bombs were dropped on innocent civilians* (by whom?). In 1946, George ORWELL, in his essay 'Politics and the English Language' (*Horizon*, vol. 13), proposed the principle 'Never use the passive where you can use the active.' However, as has often been pointed out, Orwell (like other commentators opposed to the passive) has none the less used it freely.

Baron notes that critics who downgrade the passive apply to its use such adjectives as 'lazy', 'hazy', 'vague', 'distant', 'watery', and 'wordy'. He also draws attention to William Zinsser's observation: 'The difference between an active-verb style and a passive-verb style—in pace, clarity and vigor—is the difference between life and death for a writer' (in *On Writing Well*, Harper & Row, 1980). Opposition to the passive has been strong in recent years in two areas: among many campaigners for plain English and in *style checkers*, word-processing aids to the editing of especially business documents. *Webster's Dictionary of English Usage* (1989), however, lists three situations in which the passive has generally been regarded as useful: (1) When the receiver of the action is more important than the doer, as in *The child was struck by the car*. (2) When the doer is unknown (*The store was robbed last night*), unimportant (*Plows should not be kept in the garage*), or too obvious to be worth mentioning (*Kennedy was elected president*). (3) In scientific writing, because it helps establish a tone of detachment and impersonality. The dictionary's entry on *passive* concludes: 'The point, finally, is that sentences cast in the passive have their uses and are an important tool for the writer. Everyone agrees you should not lean too heavily on passive sentences and that you should especially avoid awkwardly constructed passives. The few statistical studies we have seen or heard of indicate that you are likely to use the active voice most of the time anyway' (p. 721). See ACADEMIC USAGE, PASSIVIZATION, TENSE, VERB.

**PASSIVIZATION**. **1.** Turning an active sentence or clause into a corresponding PASSIVE sentence or clause: *Jane opened the door* becoming *The door was opened by Jane*. **2.** The corresponding transformational rule formulated at the earliest period of GENERATIVE GRAMMAR, intended to reflect the relationship of the two sentences and to derive the passive sentence from its basic active sentence. In effect, the rule moved the active object to subject position, moved the active subject into a *by*-phrase (which can be optionally deleted), and added the auxiliary verb *be* and (on the following main verb) the passive participle inflection (*-ed* in regular verbs). Passivization applies when the active sentence contains an object. If the sentence contains two objects (an indirect object followed by a direct object) each object may become the passive subject: the active sentence *Natalie showed Derek* [IO] *the photographs* [DO] becoming either *Derek was shown the photographs* (*by Natalie*) or *The photographs were shown to Derek* (*by Natalie*). Prepositional verbs, such as *look at* and *approve of*, often occur in the passive. The noun phrase following the preposition is the prepositional object and can often be made passive subject, the preposition being left 'stranded' at the end: *All the professors approved of the Provost's action* becoming *The Provost's action was approved of* (*by all the professors*).

**PAST**. A term for a TENSE of the VERB concerned with events, actions, and states that no longer occur. The *simple past* (or *PRETERITE*) is regularly formed with *-ed* (*walked*). The complex past forms are: the *past continuous* (or *past progressive*) which combines a past form of auxiliary *be* with the *-ing* participle (*was walking*); the *past perfect* (or *pluperfect*), which combines auxiliary *had* with the *-ed* participle (*had walked*); the *past perfect continuous*, which combines these two (*had been walking*). Compare FUTURE, PRESENT.

**PAST PARTICIPLE**. See PARTICIPLE.

**PAST PERFECT**. See PERFECT, PLUPERFECT.

**PATOIS** [Pronunciation: 'patwa']. **1.** A non-technical term for a DIALECT, especially if it has low status in relation to a STANDARD, literary language: *peasants speaking a local patois*. Although it is strongly associated with French, the term has been used for such a variety of any language, often to suggest low, mixed usage: ' "Alas" cried she, in a *patois* dialect, between French and Spanish' (Charlotte Smith, *Ethelinde*, 1789); 'To ascertain that she had nothing *patois* in her dialect' (Hannah More, *Female Education*, 1799). **2.** The SLANG or JARGON of a particular group: *a criminal patois*. **3.** Also sometimes *Patwa*. A common name for a Caribbean CREOLE, especially Jamaican Creole (usually without the definite article): 'She said something in patois and went on washing up' (Jean Rhys, *Voyage in the Dark*, 1934). The meaning varies according to location. In Dominica, St Lucia, Grenada, and Trinidad, it refers to the French-based Creole of the Lesser Antilles. In Guyana, the term is not popular, *Creolese* being preferred. In those countries where French-based Creole is the major VERNACULAR (St Lucia and Dominica), there is a growing feeling that the term is pejorative and *Creole* or *Kweyol* is often used instead. Compare ARGOT, BRITISH BLACK ENGLISH, CANT, LINGO.

**PATTER** [From Latin *Paternoster* Our Father (the name of a common Christian prayer), used as a verb meaning 'to gabble, recite quickly', then as a noun for any gabbling ritual or routine]. **1.** Rapid, fluent speech that may or may not make sense or be sincerely intended, like someone going meaninglessly through a ritual learned by heart. **2.** The stylized LINGO of salesmen, hucksters, sideshow barkers, conjurors, and comedians: 'Nothing up my sleeve, ladies and gentlemen, nothing down my trousers, and we take the bunny rabbit like so, you see—everybody see?—and—hey presto! No more bunny rabbit!' **3.** Stylized DIALOGUE, such as the rehearsed routines of stand-up comics, one of whom is the straight man, the other the funny man. **4.** Especially in GLASGOW in Scotland, words used with skill: *Ah like yur patter, Jimmy—yur patter runs like watter.* Someone fluent and garrulous, whether sincere or otherwise, is a *patter merchant.* From this usage, the term has been extended to Glasgow dialect, often called *the patter.* See BLARNEY, NONSENSE, RAP.

**PEDAGOGICAL GRAMMAR**, short form *ped grammar.* A term in LANGUAGE TEACHING and applied linguistics for a book or set of books designed to help learners of a foreign or second language, or for a way of presenting GRAMMAR that is intended to help students.

**PEJORATION**. A term in LINGUISTICS for the process of SEMANTIC CHANGE in which there is a depreciation or 'downward' shift in the meaning of a word, phrase, or lexeme: for example, Old English *cnafa* (boy: compare German *Knabe*) became Modern English *knave* someone dishonest; Latin *villanus* (a farm servant) became Middle English *vilain/vilein* (a serf with some rights of independence), then Modern English *villain* (a scoundrel, criminal). See MELIORATION.

**PEJORATIVE** [Stress: 'pe-JAW-ra-tiv']. **1.** A term in PHILOLOGY and SEMANTICS that refers to a complex word whose meaning is 'lower' than that of its base: *princeling*, a minor or very young prince. **2.** A term in LINGUISTICS and lexicography that refers to an expression, tone, or style that serves to devalue, disparage, or dismiss the subject being talked or written about: *illiterate* is pejorative when used to describe people who can read and write, but not to a level acceptable to the speaker (*What an illiterate scrawl!*); *Dago*, a pejorative nickname that distances and devalues people from or in Iberia and Latin America. Compare DEROGATORY.

**PERFECT**. A term for an aspect of the VERB concerned with completion. In the Slavonic languages, the *perfective* and *imperfective* are signalled by inflections on the verb, the perfective denoting the completion of the activity and the imperfective its non-completion. In English, the perfect (also sometimes termed the perfective) contrasts with the non-perfect, and is formed by a combination of the auxiliary *have* and an *-ed* participle: *present perfect* (*has/have discovered*); *past perfect or pluperfect* (*had discovered*); *present continuous progressive perfect* (*has/have been discovering*); *past continuous progressive perfect* (*had been discovering*); *future perfect* (*will have discovered*); *future continuous progressive perfect* (*will have been discovering*). In general, the perfect indicates a previous indefinite period with which the action of the verb takes place. For the present perfect, that period begins in the past and extends to the present: *I have lived in London since I was born* (until the present time); *She has broken her arm* (and the effect is still noticeable); *I haven't seen the film* (but may still do so). The past perfect indicates an action previous to another action within a past period: *Tom had not seen his parents since they were divorced.* The past perfect can also denote a past action (past before the past) without any aspectual force, in which case it is often replaced by the simple past: *After he (had) consulted his solicitor, Colin refused to sign the contract.* The future perfect refers to an event before a future event: *Pat will have finished her essay by the time we arrive.* See TENSE.

**PERFORMATIVE VERB**. A term used in philosophy and linguistics for a type of VERB (*apologize, forbid, inform, promise, request, thank*) that can explicitly convey the kind of speech act being performed. In saying *I apologize for my behaviour*, someone is making an apology, which could also be done in part at least without such a verb: *My behaviour was utterly deplorable.* Generally, the performative verb in such sentences is in the simple present active and the subject is I, but the verb may be in the simple present passive and the subject need not be I: *Smoking is forbidden; The committee thanks you for your services.* A test for whether a verb is being used performatively is the possible insertion of *hereby: I hereby apologize; The committee hereby thanks you.* In *hedged performatives*, the verb is present but the speech act is performed indirectly: in saying *I must apologize for my behaviour*, the speaker is expressing an obligation to make an apology, but implies that the acknowledgement of that obligation is the same as an apology. In contrast, *I apologized* is a report, and *Must I apologize?* is a request for advice.

**PERIOD**. In the classical study of language, dominant in English during the 16–19c, the term for a SENTENCE regarded as 'complete' because it is composed of a balanced group of main and dependent clauses. If a period (also known as a *PERIODIC SENTENCE* or a *POINT*) was well formed, it was called *well-rounded* or *well-turned*; 'If you will not take this as an excuse, accept it at least as a well-turned period, which is always my principal concern' (Thomas Gray, letter to N. Nicholls, 1764). The term also applied, especially in the 16c, to a pause at the end of a spoken sentence. By the early 17c, it was being used, alongside *full stop* and *full point*, for the PUNCTUATION MARK (.), which served to signal the closing pause. In elocution, this mark is associated with the silent counting of time: 'A Comma stops the Voice while we may privately tell one, a Semicolon two; a Colon three; and a Period four' ( John Mason, *An Essay on elocution*, 1748). The theory and practice of pauses associated with punctuation marks has lost most of its force in the 20c, but some teachers continue to use aspects of it, and when reading aloud many people pause for breath or effect at the end of sentences. Currently, *period* is the most widely used and understood term for the point at the end of a sentence: it is the dominant term in North America, but in the UK takes second place to *full stop*. Especially in colloquial AmE, the word *period* is often used as an interjection to indicate that someone has made a decision and has nothing more to say on the matter: 'I forbid them to go, period.' See DOT, ELLIPSIS.

**PERIODIC SENTENCE**, also PERIOD, POINT. In traditional GRAMMAR, RHETORIC, and COMPOSITION, a complete SENTENCE, usually characterized by an intricate relationship among its clauses. It is the classical 'rounded sentence', avowedly expressing a complete thought, adopted by writers in the European vernaculars from the prose stylists of Greece and Rome. The subordinate forms in a period are often nested one within the other, like Chinese boxes; in its most complex forms it can be cumbrous and hard to follow. Intricate periods were much used and admired until the late 19c.

The following is a typical Augustan period, in which the first *who* is separated from its verb *had* by 51 other words:

> This discovery was now luckily owing to the presence of Joseph at the opening of the saddlebags; *who*, having heard his friend say he carried with him nine volumes of sermons, and not being of that sect of philosophers who can reduce all the matter of the world into a nutshell, seeing there was no room for them in the bags, where the parson had said they were deposited, *had* the curiosity to cry out, 'Bless me, sir, where are your sermons?' (Henry Fielding, *Joseph Andrews*, 1742, italics added).

The period is unusual in present-day English, although it may occur in the language of the law and similar registers. When it occurs, it is usually designed to hold the reader in suspense as to the point being made. In the following, the serial descriptions ('Never to feel . . . ; never to be able to . . . ; to be aware of . . .') are concluded by an assertion ('whether or not . . .') in which the subject and negated verb are postponed to the very end:

> Never to feel wholly what you wish to feel—and to wish it all the more intensely for that very reason; never to be able to believe in the veracity of whatever feelings you do have—and to make threatening gestures towards anyone who has his own doubts about them; to be aware of a sickening gap between assertion and inner state every time you open your mouth—not least when you open your mouth precisely to deny that there is such a gap . . . whether or not it is a crime to feel the 'throes' and 'pangs' of that kind of insincerity I do not know (Dan Jacobson, *Adult Pleasures*, 1988).

**PERIPHRASIS** [From Greek *periphrasis* talking around. Stress: 'pe-RI-fra-sis']. In RHETORIC, the use of more rather than fewer words, especially to talk about something in an indirect and circuitous way. The adjective *periphrastic* is used both directly in relation to this sense of periphrasis and to refer to the use of *more*/*most* for the comparative and superlative DEGREES of adjectives and adverbs, which is less compact than the use of *-er*, *-est*. See CIRCUMLOCUTION, TAUTOLOGY.

**PERSON**. A grammatical and semantic

category applying to PRONOUNS and VERBS and used in describing the roles of people and things.

**Pronouns**. In STANDARD ENGLISH, the first-person pronouns are the speakers(s) or writer(s) together with any others included in the plural (*I*, *me*, *we*, *us*). The second-person pronouns are the addressee(s) and possibly others in the plural (*you* and archaic singular *thou/thee*). The third person pronouns are others being referred to (*she*, *her*, *he*, *him*, *it*, *one*, *they*, *them*). MELANESIAN PIDGIN ENGLISH makes a further distinction by having two words to correspond to *we*, one including speaker, listener, and possibly others (*yumi*: you-me) and one excluding the listener (*mipela*, me-fellow: 'me and someone else'). There can also be different words for *you*, implying greater or lesser degrees of intimacy or formality, as with French *tu/vous*, comparable to the archaic and dialectal English distinction *thou/you*. The distinctions of person are shown not only in PERSONAL PRONOUNS but also in reflexive pronouns (*myself*) and possessive pronouns (*my*, *mine*).

There is no necessary correspondence between the grammatical and semantic category of person. In SPANISH, the formal pronouns *usted/ustedes* (*you*, singular/plural) semantically address people but are grammatically third-person pronouns. *Usted* derives from an original *vuestra merced* (your grace), and parallels the highly formal convention in English in *Does Madam wish to look at some other hats?* (addressed to a customer). Comparable usages in present-day English are the royal and editorial *we* and the generalized *you*. This use of *we* is semantically singular while grammatically plural, as in Queen Victoria's remark, 'We are not amused.' The generalized *you*, as in *You never can tell, can you?*, is second person grammatically but semantically includes others. Usage is sometimes ambiguous between the addressed and generalized *you*, prompting the question *Do you mean me or everybody?* Generic or inclusive *he* is a long-established usage in which the third-person masculine represents both man and woman (*Ask anybody and he'll give you the same answer*). Those who defend its use argue that sexist bias is not present in it or intended by it, and that the meaning is clear. Those who object to it argue that it misrepresents half the human race and reinforces male bias and social dominance. See GENERIC PRONOUN. In collo-

quial usage, *they* is often used instead (*Ask anybody and they'll give you the same answer*).

**Verbs**. In highly inflected languages like Latin, person is indicated in the verb itself: *amo* I love, *amas* thou lovest, *amat* he/she/it loves, *amamus* we love, *amatis* you (plural) love, *amant* they love. As a result, pronouns are used for other purposes, such as emphasis. In English, however, only the third-person singular of the present tense normally has a distinct form: *he loves*, *she likes*, *it does*. See VOICE.

**PERSONAL PRONOUN**. A PRONOUN that refers mainly but not exclusively to a person or people, and that in many languages makes distinctions of PERSON (often first, second, and third person), NUMBER, GENDER, and CASE. In English, most such pronouns distinguish subject and object case (*I/me*, *he/him*, *she/her*, *we/us*, *they/them*, and archaic *thou/thee*) and are the only words that do so (except for *who/whom* and *whoever/whomever*). Two pronouns, *you* and *it*, are without case distinction. In addition to its references to things, *it* can refer to information: *They're cheaper this week: I read it in the paper. It* also has some purely grammatical functions, as in *It's raining* and *I hate it when people shout*, in which it is known as *existential it*. The term personal pronoun is sometimes extended to cover *possessive pronoun*. See DUMMY, PERSON.

**PERSONIFICATION**. In RHETORIC, discourse in which animals, plants, elements of nature, and abstract ideas are given human attributes: 'bask in Heaven's blue smile' (Shelley). It has been regarded as both a figure in its own right and as an aspect of METAPHOR in which non-human is identified with human: 'Life can play some nasty tricks'. It is common in VERSE: 'Slowly, silently, now the moon / Walks the night in her silver shoon' (Walter de la Mare, 'Silver', 1913). The representation of the moon as female is similar to the application of *she* to ships, cats, countries, and certain abstractions: 'He seems to want to destroy poetry as poetry, to exclude her as a vehicle of communication' (Eric A. Havelock, *Preface to Plato*, 1963).

**PHARYNX**. An anatomical term for the cavity of the upper throat through which air passes from the LARYNX to the mouth and nose. Sounds made in the pharynx are *pharyngeal*, such as the open back vowel of *palm* in RP and certain fricative consonants in ARABIC. See GUTTURAL.

**PHATIC COMMUNION**. [From Greek *phátos* spoken: coined by the Polish anthropologist Bronisław Malinowski, 1923]. LANGUAGE used more for the purpose of establishing an atmosphere or maintaining social contact than for exchanging information or ideas: in speech, informal comments on the weather (*Nice day again, isn't it?*) or an enquiry about health at the beginning of a CONVERSATION or when passing someone in the street (*How's it going? Leg better?*); in writing, the conventions for opening or closing a letter (*All the best, Yours faithfully*).

■ **PHILIPPINE ENGLISH** ──── ■

Also **Filipino English**. The English language as used in the Philippines, a state of South-East Asia consisting of more than 7,000 islands. The 1980 census counted the number of Filipinos with some competence in English as around 65%: some 35m people. Ability ranges from a smattering of words and phrases through passive comprehension to near-native mastery.

**Background**. Filipino experience of Western colonialism and its linguistic effects has been unique, in that there have been two colonizers in succession: Spain from the 16c and the US from 1898, when English arrived in the islands. It spread rapidly, to the detriment of SPANISH, because it was the new language of government, preferment, and education. Incentives to learn English, included recruitment into the civil service and study in the US. In 1935, US-educated *pensionados* (scholars) became leaders of the Senate and the House of Representatives as well as members of the cabinet. English was used universally in the elementary-school system set up by the colonial government, which brought in American teachers. Education was the last government department to be indigenized, with US superintendents still functioning under the Commonwealth government before the outbreak of World War II. In the Philippines there are some 85 mutually unintelligible though genetically related languages of the Malayo-Polynesian family, such as TAGALOG, Cebuano, Ilocano, Hiligaynon, Waray, and Bicol. These languages of the home serve as SUBSTRATES whose features have variously influenced the development of Philippine English.

**Pronunciation**. (1) Philippine English is RHOTIC, but the local /r/ is an alveolar flap, not an AmE retroflex. (2) It is syllable-timed, following the rhythm of the local languages; full value is therefore given to unstressed syllables and SCHWA is usually realized as a full vowel. (3) Certain polysyllables have distinctive stress patterns, as with *elígible, estáblish, cerémony*. (4) Intonation is widely characterized as 'singsong'. (5) Educated Filipinos aim at an AmE accent, but have varying success with the vowel contrasts in *sheep/ship, full/fool, boat/bought*. (6) Few Filipinos have the /æ/ in AmE *mask*; instead, they use /ɑ/ as in AmE *father*. (7) The distinction between /s, z/ and /ʃ, ʒ/ is not made: *azure* is 'ayshure', *pleasure* 'pleshure', *seize* 'sees', *cars* 'karss'. (8) Interdental /θ, ð/ are often rendered as /t, d/, so that *three of these* is spoken as 'tree of dese'.

**Grammar**. The following features occur at all social levels: (1) Loss of the singular inflection of verbs: *The family home rest on the bluff of a hill*; *One of the boys give a report to the teacher every morning*. (2) Use of present perfect for simple past (*I have seen her yesterday* I saw her yesterday) and past perfect for present perfect (*He had already gone home* He has already gone home). (3) Use of the continuous tenses for habitual aspect: *He is going to school regularly* He goes to school regularly. (4) Use of the present forms of auxiliary verbs in subordinate noun clauses rather than past forms, and vice versa: *He said he has already seen you* He said he had already seen you; *She hoped that she can visit you tomorrow* She hoped that she could visit you tomorrow; *He says that he could visit you tomorrow* He says that he can visit you tomorrow. (5) An apparent reversal of the norms for the use of the definite article: *He is studying at the Manuel Quezon University*; *I am going to visit United States*. (6) Verbs that are generally transitive used intransitively: *Did you enjoy?*; *I cannot afford*; *I don't like*.

**Vocabulary and idioms**. (1) Loans from Spanish: *asalto* a surprise party, *bienvenida* a welcome party, *despedida* a farewell party, *Don/Doña* title for a prominent man/woman, *estafa* a fraud, scandal, *merienda* mid-afternoon tea, *plantilla* faculty assignments and deployment in an academic department, *querida* a mistress, *viand* (from *vianda* provisions for a journey) a dish served to accompany rice in a Filipino meal. (2) LOAN-WORDS from Tagalog: *boondock* (from *bundok*) mountain (compare the AmE extension: *the boondocks*), *carabao* (from *kalabaw*) a water buffalo, *kundiman* a love song, *sampaloc* (from *sampalok*) the fruit of the tamarind, *tao* man (as in *the common tao*). (3) LOAN TRANSLATIONS from local usages: *open the light/radio* turn on the light/radio (also found in IndE), *since before yet* for a long time, *joke only* I'm teasing you, *you don't only know* you just don't realize, *he is playing and playing* he keeps on playing, *making foolishness* (of children) misbehaving, *I am ashamed to you* I am embarrassed because I have been asking you so many favours. (4) Local NEOLOGISMS: *agrupation* (from Spanish *agrupación*) a group, *captain-ball* team captain in basketball, *carnap* to steal (kidnap) a car, *cope up to* keep up and cope with (something), *hold-upper* someone who engages in armed hold-ups, *jeepney* (blending *jeep* and *jitney*, AmE a small bus) a jeep converted into a passenger vehicle.

**Written models**. Because of the influence of reading and writing and the academic context in which English is learned, local speech tends to be based on written models. Filipinos generally speak the way they write, in a formal style based on Victorian prose models. Because of this, spelling pronunciations are common, such as 'lee-o-pard' for *leopard*, 'subtill' for *subtle*, and 'wor-sester-shire sauce' for *Worcestershire sauce*. Style is not differentiated and the formal style in general use has been called the *classroom compositional style*. When style differentiation is attempted there may be effects that are comical from the point of view of a native speaker of English: 'The commissioners are all horse owners, who at the same time will appoint the racing stewards who will adjudicate disputes involving horses. Neat no?' (from a newspaper column).

**Code-switching**. A register has developed for rapport and intimacy that depends on CODE-MIXING AND CODE-SWITCHING between Filipino and English. It is largely confined to Metro Manila and other urban centres and used extensively in motion pictures and on television and radio as well as in certain types of informal writing in daily newspapers and weekly magazines. Examples:

(1) '*Peks man*,' she swears, '*Wala pang nangya-yari sa amin ni Marlon*. We want to surprise each other on our honeymoon.' ['Cross my heart,' she swears. 'Nothing yet has happened between Marlon and me . . . '] (from a movie gossip column).

(2) Donna reveals that since she turned producer in 1986, her dream was to produce a movie for children: '*Kaya, nang mabasa ko ang Tuklaw sa Aliwan Komiks, sabi ko*, this is it. And I had the festival in mind when finally I decided to produce it. *Pambata talaga kasi ang Pasko*,' Donna says. ['That is why when I read the story "Snake-Bite" in the Aliwan Comic Book, I told myself, this is it. . . . Because Christmas is really for children'] (from a movie gossip column).

**Social issues**. Philippine English is currently competing in certain domains with the rapidly spreading and developing Filipino, which is in a process of register-building sometimes called *intellectualization*. Filipino is not fully developed for academic discourse, especially in the sciences, and there is an ongoing debate on the use of Filipino instead of English for school work and official purposes. There is also conflict between the learning of Filipino for symbolic purposes and the learning of English for utilitarian, largely economic, purposes. The two official languages are propagated through a bilingual education scheme begun in 1974: mathematics and science continue to be taught in English although it is envisaged that when possible the teaching of these subjects at certain grade levels shall be in Filipino. The print media are dominated by English, but television, radio, and local movies are dominated by Filipino.

English in the Philippines shares patterns of development and constriction with English in Malaysia. From a situation similar to that of Singapore, where a premium is placed on learning English and using it extensively, the Philippines has now moved on to a stage at which English is used only in such domains as academic discourse and international relations. Philippine English has developed a vigorous literature. It is in the process of standardization, with a variety no longer marked by regional accents associated with regional languages, but a converging variety that originates in Manila. This form is propagated largely through the school system, the mass media, and tourism. Because of code-switching, it seems unlikely that a colloquial variety of English alone will develop. The future is open, without clear trends. On the one hand, code-switching may end up in code-mixing, resulting in a local creole. On the other hand, the need for international relations, the dominance of the print media, and the continued use of English in education may exercise a standardizing role, making it possible for the Philippine variety to be mutually intelligible with other varieties of English. It is also possible that the present system of bilingual education will be converted into a purely monolingual Filipino scheme in which English is taught as a foreign language and becomes available only to an élite. See FILIPINISM, SOUTH-EAST ASIAN ENGLISH, TAGLISH.

■ **PHILOLOGY** ─────── ■

[From Greek *philología* love of language]. The traditional study of LANGUAGE, which reached its peak as *comparative philology* in the later 19c. Overshadowed in the 20c by its offspring LINGUISTICS, it continues in a more muted fashion, sharing much with the subdiscipline *historical linguistics*, and focusing particularly on the evolution of languages, especially in terms of their groupings ('families') and their elements. Languages appear to change in the direction of greater diversity: one language tends to be superseded by several; a written 'dead' language preserves evidence of the earlier forms from which 'living' languages developed. Thus, Latin *planctus* gave way to French *plainte* and Italian *pianto*; LATIN *planus* to FRENCH *plain* and ITALIAN *piano*. The descendants of the Latin words have diverged to the point that, though Italian is related to French, they are now foreign to each other, as is their common 'parent' to both. The changes, moreover, are regular: Italian reduces the Latin *-us* ending to *-o*, French reduces it to *-e* or deletes it entirely; Latin *a* becomes French *ai* and remains unchanged in Italian; and Latin *pl* becomes Italian *pi* and remains unchanged in French.

Not so regular is the change of MEANING: Italian *piano* has at least one meaning ('soft' as opposed to 'loud') not in the related Latin or French. In the combination *piano e forte* (soft and loud), *piano* in due course became the name for a keyboard instrument, the *pianoforte*, more capable of dynamic variation than came before it. By abbreviation, this new instrument is now usually called a *piano* in

English and various other languages. The special meaning of the Italian phrase results from its cultural context and the distinctive feature of the instrument it names. The English word still names the same instrument, but the clipping discards 'and loud' from the original Italian phrase and hence becomes an arbitrary label and no longer a description. Over the centuries, philologists have learned to trace and tease out such facts and processes as these, and over the last century philology has concerned itself with all such changes and with the linguistic relationships they result in.

Written documents provide the information needed for this study, but, by mapping such relationships, philologists can also reconstruct further relationships among stages of earlier languages that left no written records. Thus, philologists give the name *Germanic* to the language that is the source of English as Latin is the source of French; but Germanic, unlike Latin, vanished without leaving written testimony. Present-day understanding of the family of INDO-EUROPEAN LANGUAGES therefore results from studies that systematically combine textual analysis and hypothetical reconstruction.

**History**. The ancient Greeks wrote about their own language, having little interest in comparing Greek with what they considered lesser (barbarian) languages. Roman writers, impressed by such thinking, undertook some comparisons of their Latin with Greek, for though not mutually intelligible, the two have many similarities of VOCABULARY (Latin and Doric Greek both have *māter* for mother) and of GRAMMAR (both have three grammatical GENDERS and similar declensional systems). From such hints, some Roman writers concluded that Latin had descended from Greek, a view abandoned only with the development of comparative philology around 1800, which demonstrated that Greek and Latin descended collaterally from a putative common ancestor, Indo-European (IE).

In the Middle Ages, Latin ceased to be an everyday spoken language, and the VERNACULARS descended from it, such as French and Italian, grew in prestige. Writers like Dante gave some consideration to the relationship among vernaculars and their kinship with Latin, that is, to comparative and historical concerns. Such consideration, aided from the Renaissance onwards by the publication of many early manuscript texts as printed books, yielded further knowledge of individual language families such as the CELTIC and GERMANIC. But speculation concentrated on vocabulary and took no account of systematic relationships, and hence failed to discern larger 'genetic' connections. On the rare occasions where a common parent language was postulated, the language was (for cultural and even doctrinal reasons) usually HEBREW. As late as 1807, the writer Alexander Pirie could maintain that 'The originality of the Hebrew language being incontrovertible, nothing can be more natural than that all other languages should in some respects be derivatives.' Such arguments distracted from the successful study of IE, with which Hebrew has no genetic connection.

European IMPERIALISM put 18c scholars in touch with such Asian languages as SANSKRIT, and in 1786 Sir William JONES announced his belief that the grammar of Sanskrit revealed its close affinity with Greek and Latin, suggesting the derivation of all three from 'some common source ... which no longer exists'. Jones's belief, which served to unite previously fragmented studies of individual language families, underwent elaboration in the 19c, especially by F. von Schlegel, Franz Bopp, Rasmus Rask, and Jacob Grimm early in the century and later by A. F. Pott, K. Verner, Ferdinand de Saussure, K. Brugmann, and B. Delbrück.

These scholars concentrated on refining knowledge of the relationship of later languages (such as French and Italian) with their earlier written forms (such as Latin), the relationship of these earlier written forms (such as Latin and Sanskrit) with each other, and the relationship of them all with the unrecorded 'common source', whether the lost Germanic original of the Scandinavian, GOTHIC, GERMAN, and English languages, or the lost Indo-European original of Germanic, Latin, Greek, and Sanskrit. These relationships are usually set out in a form devised by A. Schleicher, resembling a genetic 'family tree' owing much to biological classification and Darwinism. The materials for establishing such a schematic form are the usual objects of language study: VOCABULARY, GRAMMAR (especially MORPHOLOGY), and sounds with their orthographic equivalents, as in the French and

Italian words derived from Latin (above). However, vocabulary is at once the most tempting and the most treacherous evidence for the study, because, unlike sounds or grammatical forms, WORDS readily migrate from one language to another. Currently, linguists generally prefer the synchronic study of spoken language to the diachronic comparison of words in texts, and have tended to regard philology as pre-scientific. Others have sought to bring elements of old and new together in panchronic studies that give equal importance to past and present. However regarded, philology (in association with traditional grammar and ETYMOLOGY) has built a formidable edifice which few scholars ignore when writing about or teaching the history of languages. See LANGUAGE FAMILY, MURRAY, SEMANTIC CHANGE, SEMANTICS, SWEET.

**PHONAESTHESIA** BrE, **phonesthesia** AmE, also **phonetic symbolism**, **sound symbolism**. Vocal sound that suggests meaning, as in onomatopoeic or echoic words like *cock-a-doodle-doo, cuckoo*. The term is often used to refer to the occurrence of the same consonant cluster in a series of words with similar meanings: *sl-* in *sleaze, slide, slime, slip, slope, sludge, slump, slurp, slurry*, suggesting downward movement and a rushing, sucking sound; *-sh* in *bash, dash, crash, flash, gush, hush, rush, splash, whoosh*, suggesting swift or strong movement. These clusters are sometimes referred to as *phon(a)esthemes*, two of which may occur in one word: *sl* and *sh* in *slash, slosh, slush*. Such phonetic and aesthetic elements, often used to effect in verse and rhetoric, are semantically imprecise, and do not necessarily apply to all the words of a certain type: *sleep* and *sleeve, dish* and *sash* do not normally have the same nuances as *slime* and *splash*. Compare ALLITERATION, ASSONANCE, ECHOISM, ONOMATOPOEIA, ROOT-CREATION.

**PHONE**, Also **speech sound**. In PHONETICS, an elementary spoken sound, the smallest segment of speech recognized by a listener as a complete vowel or consonant. Because all speakers sound slightly different, and any one speaker produces vowels and consonants differently on different occasions, the number of phones in a language is indefinitely large. They are grouped into a small number of PHONEMES or units of distinctive sound.

**PHONEME**. In PHONETICS and LINGUISTICS, the basic theoretical unit of distinctive sound in the description of SPEECH, out of which syllables are formed, such as the three units /b, ɪ, t/ (consonant, vowel, consonant) in /bɪt/ (*bit*). The *OED* (1989) defines the phoneme as 'A phonological unit of language that cannot be analysed into smaller linear units and that in any particular language is realized in non-contrastive variants'. The *Longman Dictionary of Applied Linguistics* (1985) defines the phoneme as 'the smallest unit of sound in a language which can distinguish two words', giving the examples *pan* and *ban*, that differ only in the contrast of the phonemic consonants /p/ and /b/, and *ban* and *bin*, that differ only in the phonemic vowels /æ/ and /ɪ/. The number of phonemes varies from language to language, and from variety to variety within a language. Any such number, as for example the 24 consonants and 20 vowels of RP, are known as a *phoneme inventory*. A PHONE is a realization in sound of a phoneme, and an *allophone* is one such realization among others: for example, English /n/ is normally alveolar, but is dental before the dental fricative /θ/ in *tenth* [tɛnθ]. There are no *minimal pairs* contrasting dental and alveolar [n], and so the difference is not phonemic: because of this, the two forms are said to be allophones of the same phoneme /n/. When allophones occur in different environments, only one over occurring in one environment, they are said to be in *complementary distribution*. The term *allophone* is also used to include the *free variant*, a sound that can be substituted for another without bringing about a change of meaning. Examples include the various r-sounds of English and the use of the GLOTTAL STOP as a variant of [t] in a word like *water*. See BLOOMFIELD, -EME, MINIMAL PAIR.

**PHONEMIC TRANSCRIPTION**. See PHONETIC TRANSCRIPTION.

**PHONETIC**. **1.** Relating to speech sounds and their production: *phonetic elements, phonetic change.* **2.** Corresponding to or representing pronunciation in written or printed form: *phonetic as opposed to ideographic writing, a phonetic alphabet, a phonetic transcription, phonetic spelling.* **3.** Relating to PHONETICS; *phonetic training.* See PHONIC.

**PHONETICS**. The science or study of the sounds of SPEECH. There are three kinds: (1)

*Articulatory phonetics*, the oldest branch of the subject, which investigates the ways in which sounds are made. Here, the phonetician is trained to recognize, produce, and analyse speech sounds. During the 20c, phonetics has developed as a laboratory subject, in which instruments are used to study the production of speech in the vocal tract: for example, by monitoring the positions and movement of organs, or breath flow and air pressure. Electropalatography uses an artificial PALATE to record, display, and store data on articulatory movements inside the mouth. (2) *Acoustic phonetics* is concerned with the study of speech as heard: that is, its *waveform.* For the study of vowels and consonants, the waveform is presented as a spectrogram, on which sounds appear as recognizable visual patterns. For the study of INTONATION, the PITCH, or more precisely the *fundamental frequency*, usually called *Fo* ('ef nought'), is extracted and displayed. A *speech workstation* is a machine, usually based on a computer, that analyses and displays speech, and allows the user to replay, edit, or annotate the waveform. (3) *Experimental phonetics* usually involves the manipulation of the waveform and makes psycho-acoustic tests to identify which aspects of sounds are essential for understanding, and for the recognition of linguistic categories. Major applications of phonetics have been made in such areas as LANGUAGE TEACHING, speech therapy, and automatic speech synthesis and recognition. See ACCENT, CONSONANT, INTERNATIONAL PHONETIC ALPHABET, INTERNATIONAL PHONETIC ASSOCIATION, PHONEME, PHONETIC TRANSCRIPTION, PHONOLOGY, PRONUNCIATION, RHYTHM, STRESS, SWEET, VOICE, VOWEL.

**PHONETIC TRANSCRIPTION**. A written or printed representation of SPEECH using a phonetic alphabet. Whereas, in standard orthography, the same letters can be used to represent different sounds (the *y* in *sky* and *syrup*), and different combinations of letters can be used to represent the same sound (the *ee* of *meet* and the *ea* of *meat*), a phonetic symbol always represents the same sound, and a sound is always represented by the same symbol. Speech can be transcribed phonetically at different levels of detail and accuracy. In general terms, there are two kinds of transcription: (1) *Phonetic transcription* proper, which draws on the total resources of a phonetic alphabet to mark minute distinctions in sound and places symbols in square brackets, [t]. Such transcriptions are used especially to represent the usage of individual speakers, and are informally known as *narrow transcriptions*. (2) *Phonemic transcription*, which provides a symbol for each PHONEME in a text and places the symbols between obliques, as in /t/. Such transcriptions are used to represent an idealized description of the system of a speech community. It is the kind used in pronouncing dictionaries, and is referred to informally as *broad transcription*.

Contemporary phoneticians generally take their symbols from the INTERNATIONAL PHONETIC ALPHABET, but other symbols are also in use, especially in North America. All such symbols are mnemonic labels that ignore phonetic detail, as when the initial consonants of *tea*, *two*, and *train* are phonemically written /t/, even though they are all phonetically slightly different. In many cases, DIACRITICS are added to phonemic symbols to give further detail: for example, a superscript *h* added to /t/ to indicate aspiration, /tʰ/. A third kind of transcription is *prosodic transcription*, for which there is no generally agreed system of symbols. Its purpose is the representation of rhythm, stress, and intonation, and it has elements in common with musical notation. Generally, a text representing speech is divided into its actual or probable tone groups, the boundaries between groups being marked with a bar (/), usually doubled to mark the end of a major tone group (//), the rough equivalent to a sentence. Next, the accented syllables are identified, then the pitch contours associated with these syllables are marked in.

**PHONIC. 1.** Relating to vocal sound: *phonic substance*, *phonic vibrations*. **2.** In PHONETICS, a term used in contrast with *PHONETIC* to mean 'relating to speech sounds': *the phonic medium*, *the phonic method of teaching reading*, *a phonic reader* (a book). **3.** In physiology, relating to a nerve centre that excites the organs of speech and to vibration of the vocal folds or cords.

**PHONICS. 1.** An obsolete term for the science of *PHONETICS*. **2.** A method of teaching READING and SPELLING based on the phonetic interpretation, element by element, of spelling, often contrasted with the *look-and-say* method.

**PHONOLOGY**. The study of sound patterns in languages, sometimes regarded as part of PHONETICS, sometimes as a separate study included in LINGUISTICS. Phonologists study both PHONEMES (vowels and consonants) and *prosody* (STRESS, RHYTHM, and INTONATION) as subsystems of spoken language. Phonological patterns relate the sounds of speech to the grammar of the language; a common 20c model has three levels or components: phonology, SYNTAX, and SEMANTICS. Patterns that can be measured on laboratory instruments are generally regarded as part of phonetics, whereas phonological patterns tend to be more abstract and idealized. Until the 1960s, phonology was largely concerned with *phonemics*, the study of phonemes and phonemic systems, and often considered synonymous with it, especially in the US. Since then, however, attention has concentrated on the formulation of rules to account for sound patterns, its scope widening to include prosodic phenomena and patterns of connected texts. See LEVEL OF LANGUAGE, LINGUISTIC TYPOLOGY.

■ **PHRASAL VERB** ─────── ■

[First used in print by Logan Pearsall Smith, in *Words and Idioms* (1925), in which he states that the OED Editor Henry Bradley suggested the term to him], also **verb phrase**, **compound verb**, **verb–adverb combination**, **verb–particle construction (VPC)**, AmE **two-part word/verb and three-part word/verb** (depending on number of particles: see below).

A type of VERB in English that operates more like a phrase than a WORD, such as *go up* (as in *The balloon went up*), *put off* (as in *Don't put it off any longer*), and *take down* (as in *That'll take him down a peg or two*). Such composites derive primarily from verbs of movement and action (*go*, *put*, *take*) and ADVERBIAL PARTICLES of direction and location (*up*, *off*, *down*). The base verbs are mainly monosyllabic and may underlie a range of phrasal verbs: for example, *get* underlying *get up*, *get down*, *get in*, *get out*, *get on*, *get off*, *get away*, *get back*. The combinations are used both literally and figuratively, and are often idioms or elements in idioms: *to get away with murder*, *to get on like a house on fire*, *to get back at someone*, *to get up to mischief*.

**History**. Although the phrasal verb has

been present in English for many centuries, it has only recently been described in detail. Citations in the *OED* date from Middle English: for example, *turne aboute* 1300; *gon doun* 1388. They are common in Shakespeare: 'So long, that ninteen Zodiacks haue gone round' (*Measure for Measure*, 1603). Such verbs have often been used to translate Latin verbs (*to putte downe . . . calare, deponere*: *Catholicon Anglicum*, 1483) and to define verbs of Latin origin in English (*abrogate . . . take away*: Cawdrey, *Table Alphabeticall*, 1604). The 18c lexicographer Samuel JOHNSON was among the first to consider such formations seriously:

> There is another kind of composition more frequent in our language than perhaps in any other, from which arises to foreigners the greatest difficulty. We modify the signification of many words by a particle subjoined; as to *come off*, to escape by a fetch; to *fall on*, to attack; to *fall off*, to apostatize; to *break off*, to stop abruptly . . . These I have noted with great care (Preface, *Dictionary of the English Language*, 1755).

**Grammar**. Grammarians have adopted two main position with regard to the nature and use of phrasal verbs: (1) That the literal use of a form like *go up* is not a phrasal verb as such, but a verb operating with a particle: *The balloon went up into the air*. The term *phrasal verb* should properly be reserved for figurative and idiomatic uses: *The balloon went up* (= The crisis finally happened). Here, it is the holistic and semantic aspect of *go up* which is considered to identify the type, not syntax or morphology. (2) That the term covers both the literal and figurative/idiomatic uses and therefore includes syntax, morphology, and semantics: that is, both senses of *go up*, as above. This is the position adopted in the following review, which begins with a consideration of the grammatical aspects of phrasal verbs under three headings: transitivity and word order; particles functioning as adverbs and/or prepositions; and the position of adverbs.

***Transitivity and word order***. Phrasal verbs may be intransitive ('When they *went away*, she *got up* and *went out*') or transitive ('She *put* the book *down*, then *picked* it *up* again'). If the verb is transitive, the object can go before or after the particle without affecting meaning: *She put the book down*,

*She put down the book*. If, however, the object is a pronoun, it comes between verb and particle: *She put it down*, not *\*She put down it*. However, young children and occasionally adults for emphasis have been known to place the pronoun last: *Put down IT!*

***Adverbial and prepositional particles***. A sentence containing a verb followed by a prepositional phrase can usually (but not always) be shortened so as to turn preposition into adverb: *He carried the box up the stairs* becoming *He carried the box up* (stairs understood). If a further prepositional phrase is added, two particles (the first adverbial, the second prepositional) may occur in sequence: *He carried the box up to his room*. The syntactic relationships in such sentences can be shown by bracketing: (*He carried the chair up*) (*to his room*). Usage may appear inconsistent with regard to compound forms: *into*; *out of*; BrE *on to*, AmE *onto*; *off of*, nonstandard in BrE, often standard in AmE. However, in terms of phrasal verbs, such usage is straightforward: the sentences *She took the books into the room*, *She took the books out of the room*, *She lifted the books on to/onto the table*, and *She lifted the books off (of) the table* all reduce to *She took the books in/out* and *She lifted the books on/off*. The particle *out* is followed in England by *of* in such sentences as *They looked out of the window*, but in AmE, CanE, ScoE the form is generally *They looked out the window*.

***The position of adverbs***. Adverbs often appear alongside the particles of phrasal verbs. With intransitive usages, the adverb can take any of the positions in: *He happily ran away*, *He ran happily away*, *He ran away happily*, the last probably commonest. With transitive usages, the adverb goes either before the verb or after the object or particle, whichever is last: *She eagerly picked the letter up*, *She picked up the letter eagerly*, *She picked the letter up eagerly*, *She picked it up eagerly*, no usage predominating, but in most contexts there are no such forms as *\*She picked the letter/it eagerly up*. (Notes such relatively rare possibilities as *He pushed the letters clumsily through*).

**Adverbial particles**. The particles commonly used are: *aback, about, ahead, along, apart, aside, around, away, back, beyond, down, forth, in, off, on, out, over, past, round, through, up*. The commonest are *down, in, off, on, out, up*. BrE favours *about* (*running about*), AmE (*a*)*round* (*running around*). A verb–particle combination may have: any of the meanings of the verb plus any of the meanings of the particle, and any meanings that emerge jointly in particular contexts, including a distinct figurative and often holistic meaning. For example: (1) The phrasal verb *get up* may be intransitive (*They got up*) or transitive (*Get them up*), may mean 'move from lower to higher' (*He got the child up on to the wall*), 'move from far to near' (*One of the other runners got up to him and passed him*), 'gather, accumulate' (*The engine got up steam*), 'organize, make' (*He can get up the plot of a new film in no time at all*), and something like 'put on special clothes' (*They got themselves up as pirates*). (2) The particle *up* can mean upward direction (*The smoke rose up*), approaching direction (*He swam up to the boat*), completion in the sense that nothing is left (*They used up all the oil*), completion in the sense that something is done as fully as possible (*They tidied the room up*), and emphasis (*Hurry up!*). It may also have several nuances, as with *Drink up!*, both completive and emphatic.

**The use of phrasal verbs**. Such verbs are often informal, emotive, and slangy, and may contrast with Latinate verbs, as in *They used up/consumed all the fuel*; *They gathered together/assembled/congregated in the hall*; *The soldiers moved forward/advanced*. *Putting off* a meeting parallels *postponing* it; *driving back* enemy forces *repels* them; *putting out* a fire *extinguishes* it; *bringing back* the death penalty *restores* it. However, such pairing often depends on context and collocation. In some cases, one phrasal verb may match several Latinate verbs: *bring back* = *restore* (the death penalty), *return* (money to someone), *retrieve* (a shot bird or animal from where it has fallen). In other cases, one Latinate verb may match several phrasal verbs: *demolish* matching *knock down*, *tear down*, *blow up* as variants in destructive style. It is sometimes possible to match the elements of phrasal verbs and Latinate verbs: *climb up* with *a/scend*, *climb down* with *de/scend*. See BISOCIATION.

**Literal and figurative usages**. The verb *bring in* is used literally in *The milkman brought in the milk*, figuratively in *The prime minister brought in a new policy*. Only in the second sense can *bring in* be matched with *introduce* (itself originally metaphorical in Latin): not *\*The milkman introduced the milk*, unless a joke is intended. Jokes and cartoons are often based on a deliberate confusion of phrasal-verb meanings: as when someone

says, '*Put* the kettle *on*' (taken to mean heat some water in a kettle for tea), then notes with appreciation, '*Mmm*, it suits you' (crossing over to *putting on* clothes and leaving the listener to imagine someone wearing a kettle). An artist might build a cartoon round the literal/figurative contrast in *Where did you pick up that idea?*, with someone searching through garbage for inspiration, and the headline *OIL WILL RUN OUT SOON* might be supported by a picture of barrels with legs leaving a room.

**Derived phrasal verbs**. In addition to the traditional combination of verb of movement plus directional particle, phrasal verbs are commonly created from adjectives, nouns, and Latinate verbs: (1) *From adjectives*. Basically, with *-en* verbs: *brighten/ brighten up*, *flatten down/out*, *freshen up*, *harden off*, *loosen off/up*, *slacken off/up*, *smarten up*, *soften up*, *tighten up*, *toughen up*. Where verbs in *-en* cannot be formed (that is, from adjectives ending in *n*, *ng*, *m*, *l*, *r*, *th*, or a spoken vowel), the particle is added directly: *calm down* to become/make calm, *cool off* become/make cool, *even out* to become/make even, *tidy up* to make tidy. (2) *From nouns*. By telescoping an expression containing a phrasal verb and a special noun: *hammer out* encapsulating *beat out with a hammer*; *channel off* telescoping *carry or run off by means of a channel*; *brick up* meaning *close up with bricks*. many phrasal verbs emerge in this way: *bed down*, *board up*, *book out*, *button up*, *dish out*, *fog up*, *gang up*, *hose down*, *iron out*, *jack up*, *mist up*, *saddle up*, *sponge down*, *wall in*. (3) *From Latinate verbs*. Particles are added, usually as completives and intensives, to two- and three-syllable verbs of Latin origin: *contract out*, *divide off/up*, *level off*, *measure off/out*, *select out*, *separate off/out*. Such usages are sometimes described as barbarous and pleonastic, but such criticism does not affect their widespread use.

**Nouns from phrasal verbs**. Two kinds of noun are formed from such verbs: (1) *The major pattern*. In speech, the level stress of *bréak dówn* changes to the compound stress of *BRÉAKdown*. In writing and print, nouns like this are either solid (*breakdown*) or hyphenated (*round-up*). The solid form is common when a usage is well established and is favoured in AmE. Hyphenation is common for newer usages and is favoured in BrE, in which a solid form may seem confusing or odd, especially when vowels come together: *cave-in* as *cavein*, *make up* as *makeup*. Typical nouns are: *blackout*, *breakout*, *break-up*, *build-up*, *getaway*, *get-together*, *hold-up*, *mix-up*, *sit-in*, *take-off*, *white-out*. (2) *The minor pattern*. By a process of inversion: when a disease *breaks out*, there is an *outbreak* of that disease. Again, compound stress occurs: *OUTbreak*. In writing and print, the presentation is usually solid. Typical nouns are: *input*, *onrush*, *outflow*, *output*, *overflow*, *overspill*, *throughput*, *upkeep*, *upsurge*, *uptake*. The contrasting patterns sometimes prompt different forms with different meanings: a *breakout* usually of people, an *outbreak* usually of disease and trouble; a *layout* in design and decoration, an *outlay* of money and goods; a *lookout* posted to observe, an *outlook* usually relating to weather, attitude, and prospects. Most phrasal nouns relate to situations. The few which relate to things and people tend to be dialectal, idiomatic, and slangy: BrE *layabout* someone who lays/lies idly about; AmE *dropout* someone who drops out of society or education; *write-off* a car so badly damaged that it is written off the books of an insurance company; *blow-up* a photograph blown up like a balloon. As with the verb forms, phrasal nouns can run parallel with Latinate nouns that tend to be elevated, technical, and formal where the phrasal nouns are colloquial, informal, and slangy: *break-up/disintegration*, *checkup/examination*, *letdown/disappointment*, *let-up/relaxation*, *sellout/betrayal*, *shake-up/reorganization*.

**Compounds and attributives**. Phrasal nouns can occur in compound and attributive formations: (1) With the phrasal noun first: *blackout regulations*, *breakdown service*, *check-up period*, *getaway car*, *input time*, *overflow pipe*, *round-up time*. (2) With the phrasal noun second: *aeroplane take-off/airplane takeoff*, *traffic holdup*, *cholera outbreak*, *enemy build-up*, *population overspill*, *student sit-in*. (3) With the phrasal noun between other nouns: *cattle round-up time*, *truck break-down service*, *population overspill problem*.

**Phrasal-verb idioms**. Idiomatic usages are usually colloquial and informal, more or less obvious figurative extensions of ordinary uses. Expressions used to gloss them are often more formal, less direct, and less emotive, as with: *bring down* or defeat (a government), *bring in* or introduce (a new law), *bring off* or clinch (a deal), *bring on* or encourage and train (a student), *bring out* or

publish (a book), *bring up* or raise (a child); be *carried away* or overwhelmed (by one's emotions), *carry off* or win (a prize), *carry on* or continue (one's work), *carry out* or perform (one's duty), *carry through* or sustain (a project, to the end); a machine *coming apart* or disintegrating, a deal *coming off* or succeeding, work *coming on* or improving, soldiers *coming through* or surviving, something *coming up* or happening; *cutting back* or economizing (on expenses), *cutting down* or reducing (one's expenses), *cutting in on* or interrupting (a conversation), *cutting* people *off* or isolating them, *cutting* something *out* or excising or eliminating it; *getting down* or alighting (from a train), *getting* all the information *in* or collecting it, *getting on* or succeeding (in life), *getting off* or disembarking, or being allowed to go free, after an offence, *getting out of* or escaping from (a prison), and *getting out* or producing and publishing (a magazine), *getting up* or increasing (pressure), and *getting up* or rising from one's bed in the morning. Similar lists can be made for such other everyday verbs as *be, do, go, keep, make, pass, pull, put, run, set, take, turn*.

**Phrasal verbs and prepositions**. There is a continuum between the phrasal verb as described above and verbs followed by phrases in which the preposition may or may not be part of the phrase. A phrasal verb can be formed elliptically from a verb plus prepositional phrase (like *He took the box up* from *He took the box up the stairs*). A transitive usage may not be separable (like *pick up the book/pick the book up*), but may have distinct meanings depending on where the particle is placed (*get round someone*, *get someone round*). Particles may not be clearly either adverbial or prepositional, as with *off* in BrE *get off the bus* (compare widespread AmE *get off of the bus*). Some prepositions may be attached to verbs preceding them, usually for figurative reasons: where the sentence *He came across the street* is analysable as (*He came*) (*across the street*), the sentence *He came across an old friend* makes more sense as a phrasal form: (*He came across*) (*an old friend*), *come across* glossed as *meet by chance*. Some grammarians and lexicologists call a usage like *come across* a *prepositional verb*, because the particle is not adverbial but prepositional. Such a terminology, if extended, should turn phrasal verbs proper into 'adverbial verbs', but has not yet done so. Other commentators call the usage a *fused* or *non-separable phrasal verb*, because the preposition has been 'stolen' from its own phrase and fused with the preceding verb in an idiom. Others still consider some particles so equivocal that they are neither adverbs as such nor prepositions as such, but 'adpreps'. Usages include: *act for* represent, *bargain for* expect, *call for* demand, *come by* obtain, *get at* imply, *go for* attack. The issue is further complicated by occasions when the fusion occurs between a phrasal verb proper and a following preposition, as with *look down on* hold in contempt, *check up on* investigate, *go along with* accept, *face up to* confront, *look back on* recall, *look forward to* have good expectations of, *look up to* admire, *meet up with* encounter.

**Stress**. In normal speech, if no special emphasis is employed, the adverbial particle in a phrasal verb proper is stressed: *to píck úp a bóok/píck a bóok úp*. The preposition in a two-part fused (prepositional) verb is not usually so stressed: *They dídn't bárgain for thát*. In a three-part fusion, the stresses combine the patterns: *to lóok UP to sómeone, lóok DOWN on sómeone*.

**Productivity**. Phrasal verbs have always been common, but have increased in number since the mid-19c and even more so since the mid-20c, especially in AmE. As a result, a number of dictionaries of phrasal verbs have been published since 1974 and increasingly dictionaries for both native and foreign users have given phrasal verbs main-entry or high secondary status. They are increasingly the subject of special attention in courses for foreign learners of English, and it was in this area that the category came of age as a distinct aspect of grammar, word-formation, and usage. See PREPOSITIONAL VERB, SLANG, WORD-FORMATION.

**PHRASE**. **1.** In general usage, any small group of WORDS within a SENTENCE or a CLAUSE, such as 'in general usage', 'small groups', and 'a clause'. Such a group is usually recognized as having a syntactic structure: groups like *usage any* and *or a* would not normally qualify as phrases. **2.** In grammatical theory, a unit that does not have the structure of a sentence or clause, and cannot therefore be analysed in English in terms of subject, verb, and object. There are five types of phrase, named after their main word: *noun phrase* (*a very bright light*); *verb phrase* (*may be eating*); *adjective phrase*

(*extraordinarily happy*); *adverb phrase* or *adverbial phrase* (*quite casually*); *prepositional phrase* (*in our city*). In traditional analyses, a phrase must consist of more than one word, as in the everyday use of the term, but in contemporary GRAMMARS one, two, or more words that function in the same way are all phrases. A noun phrase is therefore the subject of all three sentences 'The work is in progress', 'Work is in progress', 'It is in progress'.

A phrase may have another phrase embedded in it: the prepositional phrase *for your information* contains the noun phrase *your information*; the noun phrase *a somewhat easy question* contains the adjective phrase *somewhat easy*. A phrase may also have a clause embedded in it: the noun phrase *the play that I saw last night* contains the relative clause *that I saw last night*. In most traditional grammars, constructions that do not have a finite verb are considered phrases, so that the infinitive construction 'To miss the party would be a pity' and the participle construction in 'His hobby is *painting landscapes*' are phrases. In many contemporary grammars, these are regarded as clauses. In generative grammar, the term is treated even more widely: in 'I *know that they are waiting*' the verb phrase consists of everything but the subject I, since it is taken to include the complementation of the verb, in this instances a *that*-clause. See FIXED PHRASE.

**PHRASEOLOGY**. [Stress: 'fray-ze-OL-o-jy']. A way of expressing oneself; the way in which WORDS and PHRASES are used, especially by particular individuals or groups: *confused phraseology, legal phraseology*.

**PHRASE WORD**. An occasional term in WORD-FORMATION for a WORD formed from a PHRASE. There are at least six types: (1) Attributive phrase words, as italicized in 'a *state-of-the-art* description' (more below). (2) Nouns followed by prepositions and other nouns, on the model of certain French COMPOUND WORDS, as in *man-at-arms* and *tug-of-war* (more below). (3) Phrases turned into lexical bases by the addition of suffixes, as in *never-say-die-ism* and *state-of-the-artistry*. (4) Stunt formations of various kinds, such as *whodun(n)it*, the informal name for a murder mystery, and its derivative *whodunitry*, the activity of producing such books. (5) Such vague words as *whatchamacallit* and BrE *thingummyjig*, AmE *thingamajig*. (6) PHRASAL VERBS and their noun derivatives: *get together* ('They *got together* and discussed the matter'); *a get-together* ('I enjoy these family *get-togethers*').

**Attributive phrase words**. There are as many attributive phrase words as there are types of phrase. They are often based on idioms, proverbs, and common expressions (*run of the mill* in 'a *run-of-the-mill* TV show'), or cover a concept or situation ('the *arms-to-Iran-for-hostages-plus-money-for-the-"contras"* scandal'). Their orthography is diverse. They may be linked by hyphens, (which is probably the general rule), enclosed in quotation marks, capitalized, a mix of these, or left as straight phrases. In writing, an attempt is usually made to highlight such phrase words visually. In speech, they may be spoken quickly and deliberately as a unit. The lists which follow (taken from 1980s citations without major changes in their printed forms) cover the main types:

*Noun-based*. An able-baker-charlie-dog sequence; a Hound of the Baskervilles image; a 'Power of the Human Mind' theory.

*Verb-based*. **1.** *Infinitive*: a made-to-measure suit; ready-to-wear clothes; right-to-die legislation. **2.** *Participial*: the 'standing up for America' syndrome; the having-your-cake-and-eating-it-too category; dyed-to-match co-ordinates. **3.** *Modal*: a must-win context; more a will-try than a can-do situation.

*Adjective-based*. A 'best-buy' computer system; 'good news, bad news' jokes; a 'good news' newspaper; stiff-upper-lip Brits; a larger-than-life picture; a holier-than-thou approach.

*Number-based*. A seven-days-a-week service; a three-week vacation; a 40-pound weight; a three-year-old boy; a 1989 Audi Quattro.

*Preposition-based*. (1) *Preposition first*: behind-the-scenes information peddling; over-the-counter medication; round-the-clock surveillance. (2) *Preposition midway*: a back to the land movement; the signal-to-noise ratio; a rags-to-riches story; an Aid-to-El Salvador group; hole-in-the-corner affairs; a balance-of-payments problem; an end-of-May opening date; a made-for-TV movie; a once-upon-a-time story.

*Coordination-based*. An 'accuse and demand' approach; a down-and-out alcoholic; hit-and-run drivers; an open-and-shut case; a rock-and-roll eccentric; a 'them' and 'us' mentality; a tough-but-vulnerable look.

*Wh-words-based*. You-know-who; a 'what-if' question; a what-went-wrong puzzle; how-to-massage books; that how-do-I-get-out-of-here feeling.

*Negation-based*. A no-man's-land; a no-win situation; a won't-go-away loneliness; a nobody-cares feeling.

**Phrase words on the French model**. One variety of French *mot composé* (compound word) is phrasal in form and joins nouns by means of a preposition: *pomme de terre* potato, *arc-en-ciel* rainbow, English acquired this pattern through Norman French: *editor-in-chief* (compare French *rédacteur-en-chef*). Common usages: *brothers-in-arms*, *cost of living*, *jack-in-the-box*, *man-at-arms*, *man-of-war*, *poet-in-residence*, *president-for-life*. Stunt variations include: *computer-on-a-chip*, *cynic-in-residence*, *hamburgers-on-the-hoof* (beef cattle), *trainee-in-terror*. See STUNT WORD.

# ■ PIDGIN

A term used in both a general and a technical sense for a CONTACT LANGUAGE which draws on elements from two or more languages: *pidgin Portuguese*; *a Spanish pidgin*.

**The general sense**. As generally understood, a pidgin is a hybrid 'makeshift language' used by and among traders, on plantations (especially with and among slaves of various backgrounds), and between Europeans and the indigenous peoples of Asia, Africa, and the Americas, especially during the heyday of European expansion (17–20c). Because the word has often been used and discussed pejoratively, it carries such connotations as 'childish', 'corrupt', 'lazy', 'inferior', 'oversimplified', and 'simple-minded'. Etymologically, there appears to have been only one pidgin: *Pidgin English*, also known as *Business English*, *Pidgin-English*, *pidgin-English*, *Pigeon English*, *Pigeon-English*, *bigeon*, *pidgeon*, *pidjin*, *pidjun*. This was a TRADE JARGON used from the 17c onward between the British and Chinese in such ports as Canton. In 1826, B. Hall wrote: 'I afterwards learned that "pigeon", in the strange jargon spoken at Canton by way of English, means business'; in 1845, J. R. Peters noted: 'Pidgeon, is the common Chinese pronunciation of business' (*OED*). It should be noted, however, that *Chinese (Coastal) Pidgin English* or *China Coast Pidgin* is now a technical term referring to a contact language used between speakers of English and Chinese from the first half of the 18c until the early 1970s.

**The technical sense.** Sociolinguists in particular use the term to describe a phenomenon whose study has greatly increased since the Second World War. For them, a pidgin is a marginal language which arises to fulfil certain restricted communicative functions among groups with no common language. In sociolinguistic terms, there have been many pidgins and the process known as *pidginization* is seen as liable to occur anywhere under appropriate conditions. This process of simplification and hybridization involves reduction of linguistic resources and restriction of use to such limited functions as trade. The term is sometimes extended to refer to the early stages of any instance of second-language acquisition when learners acquire a minimal form of the target language often influenced by their own primary language. There is, however, some disagreement among scholars over the number of languages in sufficient contact to produce a pidgin. Some investigators claim that any two languages in contact may result in a degree of linguistic improvisation and compromise, and so lead to pidginization. Such a viewpoint includes in the category of pidgin FOREIGNER TALK and other classes of makeshift and often transitory communication. Other investigators argue that only in cases where more than two languages are in contact do true pidgins spring up. In situations where speakers of more than two languages must converse in a medium native to none of them, the kinds of restructuring are more radical than in other cases and likely to be more durable.

The names given to pidgin languages by linguists refer to their location and their principal *lexifier* or *base language*: that is, the language from which they draw most of their vocabulary. *Papuan Pidgin English* therefore refers to the pidgin that is spoken in what was formerly the Territory of Papua, and that draws most of its vocabulary from English and is therefore an English-based pidgin; HAWAII PIDGIN ENGLISH is the pidgin English spoken in Hawaii. In addition and often prior to such academic names, pidgins may or may not be identified as such and often have specific names, retained by scholars when discussing them, such as *Bazaar Hindustani/Hindi, Korean Bamboo English, français petit-nègre*. Even after a pidgin develops into a CREOLE, the name may continue to be used, such as *Roper Pidgin*, also known as *Roper River Creole*. A language may also have both pidgin and creole varieties, as with TOK PISIN in PAPUA NEW GUINEA.

**Features.** A pidgin is characterized by a small vocabulary (a few hundred or thousand words) drawn largely from the superstrate language (that is, the language of the socially dominant group), together with a reduction of many grammatical features, such as inflectional morphology, as in Tok Pisin *mi kam* can mean 'I come', 'I am coming', 'I came', and *wanpela haus* means 'house' while *tupela haus* means 'two houses'. One source of grammar is the socially subordinate substrate language(s). Often though not always, where pidgins develop, one group is socially superior and its full language is more or less inaccessible to the other group(s), so that there is little motivation or opportunity to improve performance. Where the needs of communication are minimal and confined to a few basic domains such as work and trade, a casual and deficient version of language can be enough, as has been the case with *Kisettla* (settlers' language), the pidgin Swahili used between the British and Africans in Kenya. Many pidgin languages arose in the context of contact between European colonizers who enslaved or employed a colonized or transported population on plantations, in ports, in their homes, etc.

A notable feature of pidgins is lack of grammatical complexity; for this reason, they are often referred to at best as simple or simplified languages, at worst as bastardized or broken forms of another language. In popular accounts, simplicity is attributed to lack of grammar, but linguists agree that pidgins have a distinctive grammatical structure. The grammar of a pidgin language is constructed according to a principle which dictates that there should be a close relation between form and meaning. There is a tendency for each MORPHEME (or word element) to occur only once in an utterance, and for it to have only one form. Non-pidgin languages generally have built-in redundancy and require the expression of the same meaning in several places in an utterance: for example, in the English sentences *One man comes* and *Six men come* singular and plural are marked in both noun and modifier, and concord is shown in both noun and verb. However, the equivalents in Tok Pisin (Papua New Guinea Pidgin English) show no variation in the verb form or the noun: *Wanpela man i kam* and *Sikspela man i kam*.

Because they lack redundancy, pidgins depend heavily on context for their interpretation. Most pidgins have little or no inflectional morphology. Where English marks possession by adding *'s* (as in *John's house*), Tok Pisin has *haus bilong John*. Here, *bilong* has been taken from English, but has shifted its function from verb to preposition, and can be paraphrased as 'belonging to'. Pidgin languages tend to have only a small number of prepositions and they use them to mark a variety of grammatical relations which in other languages would be expressed by a much greater number of prepositions. Pidgins are highly regular and have fewer exceptions than many other languages, which makes them easier to learn. Another property is multifunctionality: the same word can function in many ways. In English, the word *ill* functions as an adjective (in *He is ill, an ill wind*). The corresponding noun is *illness*, derived by a regular process of word-formation. In Tok Pisin, however, the word *sik* can function as both noun and adjective: *Mi sik* I am ill; *Em i gat sik malaria* He has malaria. Pidgins may compensate for lack of vocabulary by circumlocution: in Tok Pisin, *Singsing taim maus i pas* to sing with the mouth closed (= to hum). Where English has *branch*, Tok Pisin, has *han bilong diwai* hand of a tree.

In analysing the syntactic elements of pidgins, it is often impossible to separate the influence of substrate from superstrate language: as in the case of Tok Pisin, the influence of local languages from that of English. In Tok Pisin, the particle *i* is a so-called *predicate marker*, occurring in such sentences as *Ol man i kisim bigpela supia* (The men—predicate marker—got big spears). It is plausible to derive this marker from the use of resumptive pronouns in nonstandard English, such as *he* as in *John, he got a new car*, as well as from similar syntactic patterns in Austronesian languages. Such a use of pronouns as predicate markers is widespread across pidgins, occurring in some of the French-based Indian Ocean creoles as well as in Chinook Jargon.

**Classification**. Pidgins can be classified into four types according to their develop-ment: JARGON, stable pidgin, extended or expanded pidgin, and creole, each characterized by a gradual increase in complexity. (1) *Jargon*. In this stage, there is great individual variation, a very simple sound system, one- or two-word utterances, and a very small lexicon. Jargons are used for communicating in limited situations: trade jargons generally, and *Chinook Jargon*, a trade language spoken along the north-west Pacific coast of North America from the 18c. (2) *Stable pidgin*. This is more regular and more complex and there are social norms regarding its use, was with *Russenorsk*, a trade pidgin used in northern Norway by Russian merchants and Norwegian fishermen over some 130 years (1785–1917). Because the language was used for seasonal trade, it did not expand much structuarally and had a core vocabulary of *c*.150–200 words. (3) *Extended* or *expanded pidgin*. Other pidgins, such as *Tok Pisin*, not only stabilized but expanded to become more grammatically complex, and to serve as well-established lingua francas, sometimes with official or other status. (4) *Creole*. At this stage, the pidgin is creolized: that is, it is acquired as a first language by children, particularly in urban areas. This is the stage of, for example, Tik Pisin in Papua New Guinea and KRIOL (also known as Roper River Creole) in the Northern Territories of Australia. It is generally impossible to identify structural features which distinguish expanded pidgins from emerging creoles, since both exhibit increased structural complexity and share many features. The difference lies more in social use than in form.

**Theories of origin**. Various theories have been proposed to account for the origin of pidgin languages, and fall into three broad types: *monogenetic, polygenetic,* and *universalist*.

**Monogenesis**. This theory asserts a common origin for all European-based pidgins. Some monogenetic theorists claim that they all descend from a nautical jargon used for communication among sailors from different backgrounds. Others have argued that they descend from a 15c Portuguese pidgin which could in its turn have been a relic of *Sabir*, the LINGUA FRANCA of the Crusaders and a Mediterranean trading language. It is claimed that this language was relexified (that is, renewed with vocabulary from different sources) as it came into contact with such other European languages as English and Dutch. Both the nautical-jargon and Sabir theories take as supporting evidence the fact that many pidgins share common words like *save* (to know; compare English *savvy*) and *píkinini* (child: compare English *piccaninny*). Both words are of Spanish/Portuguese origin, from *saber/sabir* (to know) and *pequeño* (small), and are widely used in English-based pidgins and creoles in the Caribbean and Pacific. Such pidgins could either have been directly inherited locally or transmitted from one location to another by sailors, who undoubtedly account for some of the lexical sharing across unrelated pidgins, although their role in the formation of stable pidgins was probably not great. However, it is difficult to account for the many differences among pidgins by appealing entirely to relexification, and neither approach explains the origin of the many non-European-based pidgin languages.

*Polygenesis*. This theory stresses distinctness and appeals to the influence of substrate languages, such as the influence of African languages in the formation of the Atlantic pidgins. According to one view, pidgins arise out of the imperfect learning of a model language by slaves or as a result of deliberate simplification, for example by Europeans in a master/slave relationship. There is evidence that the Portuguese taught a simplified version of their language to those they traded with along the west coast of Africa.

*Universalism*. This view argues for the universal nature of the social and psychological factors which occur in language contact. The *baby-talk theory* is based on the idea that certain systems of communication emerge in response to particular social and historical circumstances. There is evidence for this hypothesis in the fact that BABY TALK, foreigner talk, and pidgins show certain similarities of structure. Baby talk expressions such as *Daddy go bye-bye* are similar to the reduced versions of language used to address foreigners.

There is no doubt that the native languages of colonized, enslaved, and transplanted populations provided important input to pidgins, but there are also many features which can be explained only by reference to the superstrate languages of the colonizers, enslaves, and transplanters. At present, therefore, no single theory

can adequately explain the origin of pidgin language.

See ABORIGINAL ENGLISH, ACROLECT, AFRICAN ENGLISH, AKU, AUSTRALIAN PIDGIN, BASIC ENGLISH, BASILECT, BEACH LA MAR, BEARER ENGLISH, BROKEN, CARIBBEAN ENGLISH CREOLE, CHINA, FIJI, FRACTURED ENGLISH, FRENCH, INTERLANGUAGE, JAMAICAN CREOLE, JAPANESE PIDGIN ENGLISH, KAMTOK, KRIO, LECT, LINGO, MARITIME PIDGIN, MELANESIAN PIDGIN ENGLISH, MESOLECT, SABIR, SOLOMON ISLANDS PIDGIN ENGLISH, TALK, WEST AFRICAN PIDGIN ENGLISH.

**PITCH**. A term used generally and in PHONETICS for the level of the VOICE. Pitch depends on the frequency with which the vocal cords (or folds) vibrate to produce *voice*: the more rapidly, the higher the pitch perceived. When voices quaver, there is a fluctuation of pitch, especially in a *falsetto* (an especially male voice which is unnaturally high), the vocal cords having been greatly contracted. When a voice has a very low pitch, it is said to *creak*. *Creaky voice*, common among male RP-speakers, tends to occur at the end of a statement, as the voice falls low. *Pitch range* refers to the difference between high and low pitch. The greater the range, the greater the impression given of emotion. See ACCENT, TONE.

**PITMAN, (Sir) Isaac** [1813–97]. English educational reformer, businessman, and inventor of the Pitman shorthand system. Born in Trowbridge, Wiltshire, the son of a hand weaver, he left school at 13 and served for a time as a clerk in a textile mill. He then trained as a teacher in 1831, taught as headmaster in various schools, and finally had a school of his own. Intrigued by John Walker's pronouncing dictionary and Samuel Taylor's shorthand, he developed a system of his own based on the representation of sound, described first in *Stenographic Sound Hand* (1837), then in *Phonography* (1840). The latter was also called 'the Penny Plate' (because it was sent out by the new penny post) and was the world's first correspondence course. It was initially offered free of charge, a mark of Pitman's concern for 'educating anyone of any class from anywhere who could read and had the desire to learn' (Frances Moss, *Pitman: 150 Years of Innovation in Business Education*, 1987).

The system classifies speech sounds into groups, consonants being shown as strokes and generally paired (for example, a lightly written stroke for *f* and a heavier variant for *v*), vowels as dots and dashes, and abbreviations of consonant clusters (*str*), syllables (*der*), and affixes (*tion*) as circles, loops, and hooks. The system was refined through many editions, changes often causing confusion among users. The 10th edition of *Phonography* (1857) established the vowels as they have continued to be used, and the *New Era edition* (1922) contained extra devices for high-speed reporting at up to 250 words per minute. The Pitman system benefited from the spread of British imperial administration in the later 19c.

In 1843, Pitman set up his *Phonetic Institute* in Bath as a publishing house and marketing operation. His success in recording verbatim an anti-Corn Law speech by William Cobden gained converts to his system and in due course his shorthand was used for preparing Hansard, the official record of Parliament. He founded *The Phonotypic Journal* in 1840, which was for a time *The Phonetic Journal*, became *Pitman's Shorthand Weekly* in 1892, and *Office Training* in the 1930s. In 1870, *Pitman's Metropolitan College* opened, perhaps the first school of business education in the world, with a syllabus covering office routine, accounting and law, and shorthand and typing. In addition to being used throughout the world for English, Pitman's system of shorthand has been adapted for such languages as Arabic, Dutch, French, German, Hebrew, Hindi, Japanese, Latin, Persian, Spanish, Welsh, and Tamil. His system of phonetic English spelling had little impact, however, although it served as the basis of the *Initial Teaching Alphabet*, devised by his grandson James Pitman in 1959.

**PITMAN, (Sir) (Isaac) James** [1901–85]. English publisher and educational reformer, grandson of Isaac Pitman. He was born in London, and educated at Eton and Oxford, where he studied modern history. He played rugby for Oxford and for England, and was a noted boxer, runner, and skier. He joined his father Ernest and his uncle Alfred in the family business and was for a time headmaster of one of the Pitman's Colleges (in Maida Vale in the 1920s). He became chairman and managing director of Sir Isaac Pitman & Sons (*c.*1932), was Chairman of the Joint Examining Board (1935–50), a director of the Bank of England

(1941–5), first Director of Organization and Method in the Civil Service (1943–5), President of the Society of Commercial Teachers (1951–5), and Conservative Member of Parliament for Bath (1945–64). In 1959, he published *The Ehrhardt Augmented (40-sound 42-character) Lower-Case Roman Alphabet* (in which *Ehrhardt* is the name of a typeface), which described a system that later became known as the INITIAL TEACHING ALPHABET, designed to help children learn to read more easily and successfully. Based on original work by his grandfather, it became a lifelong passion to whose promotion in the UK and elsewhere he contributed large sums of his own money, lobbying education ministers, school inspectors, and chief education officers, and attending conferences of teachers. His *Initial Teaching Alphabet Foundation* benefited from a large donation in the US, but disagreements led to litigation, and the movement lost momentum: 'Most teachers continued to prefer books in ordinary type. They never wholly believed claims that there were no difficulties in transferring from i.t.a. to traditional orthography' (Archibald Clark-Kennedy, obituary, *The Times*, 3 Sept. 1985). By the 1980s, the system had disappeared from most of the schools that had taken it up.

**PLACE-NAME**, also **placename**, **place name**. Technically **toponym**. The proper name of a locality, either natural (as of bodies of water, mountains, plains, and valleys) or social (as of cities, counties, provinces, nations, and states). In an island like Britain, settled by successive waves of peoples, the place-names embody its history. Celtic, Roman, Anglo-Saxon, Scandinavian, and Norman names vie with one another today as their name-givers did in past centuries. The elements that make up place-names reflect a polyglot heritage: -*coombe* from Celtic *\*kumbos* (Welsh *cwm*) for a hollow or small valley, as in *Cwmbrân* and *Cwm Rhondda* in Wales, *Coombe* and *High Wycombe* in southern England, and *Cumloden* and *Cumwhitton* in northern England. The variants -*chester* appear in *Chester* and *Manchester*, -*caster* in *Lancaster*, and -*cester* in *Cirencester* and *Gloucester*, and come from Latin *castra* (a military camp). Forms of the Old England *burh* (dative case *byrig*), a fortified settlement, appear in England as -*bury* in *Canterbury*, -*borough* in *Scarborough*, and -*brough* in *Middlesbrough*, and in Scotland as -*burgh*, in *Edinburgh* (with mainland European cognates in *Hamburg* in Germany and *Skanderborg* in Denmark). The Scandinavian -*by* (a farm or village) can be found throughout northern and eastern England, in such names as *Derby*, *Grimsby*, *Romanby*, *Walesby*, and *Whitby*.

In more recently settled English-speaking countries, names are often commemorative of places in the motherland, as with the city of *Boston* in Massachusetts in the US (after the town in Lincolnshire in England) and the town of *Hamilton* in Ontario, Canada (after the town near Glasgow in Scotland). They may also commemorate well-known people in the motherland or the new settlement: for example, the settlements and features called or incorporating the name of Queen Victoria in Cameroon (now Limbe), southern Africa, Canada, and Australia. Sometimes the names are simply descriptive, wherever they are found: *the Black Isle* a peninsula in Scotland, *North Island* in New Zealand, and *the Rocky Mountains* in the US and Canada.

Some place-names have two or more elements: a generic for the kind of place and a specific for a particular locale. The generic usually comes last, as in *Atlantic Ocean*, *British Isles*, *Malvern Hills*, *Madison Avenue*, *New York City*; sometimes, however, it comes first, as in *Cape St Vincent*, *Mount Everest*, *Lake Huron*; and sometimes the elements are joined by *of*, as in *Bay of Fundy*, *Cape of Good Hope*, *Gulf of Carpentaria*. Some names which might be expected to have a generic lack one: for example, *the Matterhorn*, *the Himalayas*. In a few instances, British and American practice differs: *River Thames* as against *Mississippi River*; *County of Warwick* and *Warwickshire* as against *Clinton County*, with *county* used attributively in Ireland, as in *County Clare* and *County Tyrone* (and in the one instance of *County Durham* in England). See place-name panels for AMERICAN, AUSTRALIAN, CANADIAN, ENGLISH, IRISH, NEW ZEALAND, SCOTTISH, SOUTH AFRICAN, WELSH.

**PLAGIARISM** [From Latin *plagiarius* a kidnapper, literary thief]. The appropriation of someone's artistic, musical, or literary work for personal ends. Because most artists are affected by other artists, it is not always easy to decide where legitimate influence ends and plagiarism begins. The term is usually reserved, however, for the flagrant lifting of material in an unchanged or only slightly changed form and its dissemination as the plagiarist's own work. In oral and scribal societies, most performers 'plagiarized', in the sense that they borrowed material but failed to identify their sources. It is unlikely, however, that this interaction was considered reprehensible. In addition, insofar as educational institutions invite students to model themselves on others, a degree of plagiarism and pastiche are built into the acquiring of creative skills. The concept of plagiarism as a serious legal offence became clear-cut with the growth of printing and the establishment of authors and publishers as people and institutions with property rights. See DERIVATIVE QUOTATION.

**PLAIN**. A term for direct and unambiguous language: 'Speketh so pleyn at this tyme, I yow preye, / That we may understonde what ye seye' (Chaucer, the Host speaking to the Clerk of Oxford in *The Canterbury Tales*); *The Complete Plain Words* (title of a British usage manual by Sir Ernest Gowers, 1954). *Plain* has been used since the late Middle Ages to contrast with *ornate*, *academic*, *technical*, *Latinate*, etc., and phrases such as *plain English*, *plain language*, *plain style* have been used to contrast with such expressions as *double Dutch*, *gobbledygook*, *jargon*, and *mumbo jumbo*. The contrast of *plain style* with other styles of language originates in ancient Greece and Rome, when RHETORIC recognized three styles: the grand or high style, the middle style, and the plain or low style, each appropriate to certain audiences, occasions, and purposes. The grand declamatory style was suited to high themes, people, and occasions (with the risk of becoming grandiose), the moderate middle style was suited to instruction and education (with the risk of becoming bland or pedantic), and the simple style was suited to ordinary life and public speaking (with the risk of becoming coarse, colourless, or patronizing). During the Renaissance and Reformation (15–16c), styles tended to polarize between the classical, academic, and ornate on the one side and the popular, vernacular, and plain on the other, a division that mirrored religious disputes. Protestants, especially of the 'Low Church' in England, favoured *Puritan plain style* and Quaker *plain language* in their worship, speech, and writing. Both forms influenced the development of prose writing in the British Isles, North America, and elsewhere. See ANGLO-SAXON, COMPLETE PLAIN WORDS, SAXONISM.

# ■ PLAIN ENGLISH ──────── ■

**1.** English that is straightforward and easy to understand: 'Which ye shalle here in pleyne Englische' (*Chaucer's Dreme*, 1500). **2.** Blunt, no-nonsense language: 'If we double the thickness, the outside will be but one twenty-fifth as useful, or in plain English, nearly useless' (US government report, 1868). **3.** Strong or foul language: 'With Princess Anne, who was apt to express herself in plain English when she found herself upside down in a water jump surrounded by clicking Nikons, there were some explosions' (Profile, *Observer*, 3 Sept. 1989). **4.** In the later 20c, a term closely associated with an at-first diffuse but increasingly focused international movement against overly complex and misleading, especially bureaucratic, usage: 'Award winners for plain English included the Association of British Insurers for the booklet "About insurance—some key facts" ' (*Plain English Campaign Magazine* 26, June 1989).

**Historical background**. In the 17–18c, the British middle and upper classes generally fovoured an ornate style of language, but towards the end of the 18c, as the Romantic movement and the Industrial Revolution gained momentum, this 'Augustan' style was modified. Even so, however, English prose generally continued to be highly Latinate and often difficult and intimidating for people who had received little more than a basic education. For this and other reasons, purists and revivalists such as the dialectologist William Barnes advocated the use of a more native or Germanic English, arguing for suck words as *fore-elders* instead of *ancestors* and *birdstow* rather than *aviary*. This approach did not, however, necessarily make usage clearer, because many Saxonisms were as difficult to learn and use as their classical equivalents. A late form of purism or nativism found expression in the 1920s in C. K. Ogden's BASIC ENGLISH, which was intended to embody the virtues of plain usage; its vocabulary of 850 words is largely Germanic. In the later 20c, however, advocates of a plainer English have not proposed the native rather than the Latinate, but rather avoiding any usage, whatever its source or inspiration, that confuses or misleads readers or listeners; the demonology of the plain English movements includes such opponents as *bafflegab*, *gobbledygook*, *doublespeak*, and *psychobabble*.

**Plain English movements**. In recent decades there have been significant campaigns promoting plain English in the UK, the US, Australia, Canada, and elsewhere. The terms *plain English movements* and *plain language movements* cover all drives towards the use of simpler language, especially in official, legal, and commercial writing (as in forms, contracts, business letters, and descriptions of products) and medical usage (including labels on medicinal products). In the UK, campaigning tends to be from the bottom up, a grass-roots activism with some official support; in the US, it has tended to be from the top down, especially government-initiated moves with popular approval.

The name *Plain English Campaign* or *PEC* (without the definite article) stands for a pressure group in the UK that campaigns for plain English while also offering commercial and other services that help sustain its momentum and funds. These services provide a means through which government, business, and individuals can obtain help in writing and checking plain-English texts (including forms and leaflets for public use) and document design that makes the transmission of information easier. Another UK organization in the *Plain Language Commission*. In the US, the Doublespeak Committee of the NCTE (National Council of Teachers of English) offers annual *Doublespeak Awards*, ironic tributes focusing on unsatisfactory and evasive language, especially as used by government (first awards, 1974). In the UK, PEC and the National Consumer Council present annual awards both to encourage organizations that have met their standards in the use of plain English and to draw critical attention to some that have not, by means of *Golden Bull Awards* for particularly unsatisfactory texts (first awards, 1982). PEC has also launched a scheme through which organizations can seek an endorsement of the language and design used in their documents. This takes the form of the *Crystal Mark*, a logo-like symbol displayed on leaflets, products, and the like.

**PLAIN LANGUAGE**. **1.** Usage without social pretensions, overly complex structures, and such actual or supposed frills as poetic flourishes, foreignisms, and technical jargon. **2.** Plain English: *Drafting Documents in Plain Language* (title of book published by the US Practising Law Institute, 1980). **3.** The usage of the Protestant denomination known as the Quakers or Society of Friends (founded in the 17c), which favoured the use of *thou* and *thee* long after it ceased to be part of mainstream English.

**PLATITUDE**. A commonplace statement or remark, especially if presented as though newly minted or uttered with an air of solemnity, as in 'I've said it before and no doubt I'll say it again: *There is no smoke without fire*.' Compare CLICHÉ, PROVERB.

**PLAYING WITH WORDS**, also **wordplay**. Any adaptation or use of words to achieve a humorous, ironic, satirical, dramatic, critical, or other effect. Whereas a play *on* words is a PUN, playing *with* words is verbal wit or dexterity at large and includes puns. One may play with the sound, spelling, form, grammar, and many other aspects of words: (1) *Sound*. 'Oh why can they not be made to see that all they have found is another man? A fellow man. A yellow man. A Jell-O man. A hollow man . . .' (Colleen McCullough, *A Creed for the Third Millennium*, 1985), alluding to T. S. Eliot's religious poem 'The Hollow Men' (1925). (2) *Spelling*. In 1653, Isaak Walton published *The Compleat Angler*, 'compleat' being his normal spelling for 'complete'. In 1987, Valerie Grove published *The Compleat Woman*, echoing Walton. In a review, Carol Rumens noted: 'Depicted on the back-jacket with her brood of four, Valerie Grove is clearly on her way to becoming compleat in her own right' (*Observer*, 18 Oct. 1987). (3) *Form*. Writing for the *New York Times* in 1988, William Safire referred to advertising usage as 'the work of the copywrongers . . . copywriters who make mistakes in grammar on purpose'. (4) *Grammar*. The British reference book *Who's Who* (founded 1849) contains biographies of 'people of influence and interest in all fields'. Its sister publication, *Who Was Who*, records the deceased. In 1987, a publisher brought out *Who's Had Who*, discussing known and alleged sexual relations among the famous. (5) *All of language*. In *Ulysses* (1922), Joyce employs such expressions as *Lawn Tennyson, gentleman poet*, and *a base barreltone voice*. In *Finnegans Wake* (1939) he has the *hanging garments of Marylebone* and *all moanday, tearsday, wailsday, thumpsday, fightday, shatterday*. See BLEND, HUMOUR, NONCE WORD, NONSENSE, TECHNOSPEAK, TIMESPEAK.

**PLAY ON WORDS**. See PLAYING WITH WORDS, PUN.

**PLEONASM**. A traditional term for the use of more words than necessary, either for effect or more usually as a fault of style, and any instance of that use, as in: *They both got one each* rather than *They both got one* or *They got one each*; *That's a more superior product* (*superior* already denotes 'more'); *It's a really new innovation* (an *innovation* is already *new*). Some common pleonasms attract little comment, such as *free gift* (gifts are by definition free). Many famous writers have been pleonastic, including Shakespeare's double superlative 'The most unkindest cut of all' (*Julius Caesar*). See CIRCUMLOCUTION, PERIPHRASIS, REDUNDANCY, TAUTOLOGY.

**PLOSIVE**. In PHONETICS, a stop CONSONANT that is released quickly, with a brief explosive sound known as a *release burst*. English voiceless plosives, such as /p, t, k/, are often followed by aspiration, particularly in IrE. The process is known as *plosion*. See ARTICULATION.

**PLUPERFECT**. A traditional term for the past PERFECT tense: *had come* in *Aren't they here? I thought they had come.*

■ **PLURAL** ─────────── ■

A term contrasting with SINGULAR (and *dual*) in the NUMBER system of a language. In English, it refers to 'more than one' (*one and a half hours*) as well as 'two or more' (*five hours*). Where there is a contrast with dual words such as *both* and *neither*, plurals refer to a minimum of three: *all her brothers*, *any of her brothers*, and *none of her brothers* entail that she has at least three. The word *every*, though it takes singular concord, also implies three or more. Although the principles for forming plurals in English are relatively simple, the history of the language has led to some complications.

**Pronunciation**. (1) The majority of countable nouns make their plurals by adding -*s* to the singular, except words ending in a sibilant, which add -*es* unless there is already an *e* in the spelling: *buses, ditches, wishes, bases, garages, judges*. The spelling -*es* is generally pronounced like *iz*, but the -*s* ending is pronounced in two different ways: usually an *s*-sound after a voiceless sound (*taps, cats, locks*), but a *z*-sound if the preceding sound is voiced (*tabs*, *cads*, *logs*, *boys*, *lines*). (2) Nouns ending in a consonant plus *y* usually change the *y* to *i*, and add -*es* (*mysteries*, *parties*), but proper nouns may retain the letter *y* (*the Henrys*; *the two Germanys*: but compare *the two Maries*, *the Ptolemies*) as do compounds with -*by* (*lay-bys*, *stand-bys*). (3) Some nouns ending in -*o* and generally of foreign origin simply add *s* (*photos*, *radios*), but others have -*es* (*heroes*, *zeroes*), and some have either (*mosquitos/mosquitoes*). (4) Nouns written with a final *f* or *fe* take regular or weak plurals (*cliffs*), irregular or strong plurals (*halves*, *knives*), or either (*dwarfs/dwarves*, *hoofs/hooves*, *scarfs/scarves*).

**Compounds**. Most compound nouns form their plurals in the usual way (*boyfriends*, *crime reporters*, *sit-ins*), but some pluralize both elements (*women pilots*). In traditional and rather formal usage, some pluralize the first element (*runners-up*, *courts martial*, *brothers-in-law*), but often they have a more colloquial alternative (*runner-ups*, *court martials*, *brothers-in-laws*).

**Place-names**. Most place names ending in -*s* are singular: *Athens*, *Paris*, *Naples*, *the Thames*, *Wales*. Even names of countries which appear plural normally take singular concord (*The Netherlands/the United States is . . .*), although plural concord is possible if the meaning is, for example, a national or other comparable sports team (*The Netherlands are playing well*). However, mountain ranges and groups of islands are normally plural only: *the Himalayas/the Hebrides are . . .*

**Plural-only usages**. (1) Some plural nouns in -*s* have no singular form: *clothes*, *remains*, *thanks*. (2) Other plural-only words may appear to have singular forms, but these are either part of a singular/plural countable pair with a different meaning (plural only for *arms* meaning weapons, *arm/arms* for the parts of the body) or the singular form is an uncountable noun with a different meaning (£*500,000 damages* compared with *storm damage*). (3) Some words referring to tools and clothes with two parts are plural only (*scissors*, *tights*). The normal way of counting them is *a pair of scissors*, *two pairs of trousers*, etc.

**Words ending in -s**. (1) Although some singular words ending in -*s* add -*es* for plural (*buses*, *businesses*), other have the same form in both singular and plural: (BrE) *an innings*, *two innings* (compare AmE *an inning*), and

*means* in *every means in my power*, *by all means*, *by no means*. (2) Some uncountable nouns end in -*s*, the best-known of which is *news*. Others include names of games (*billiards*, *bowls*) and words for subjects and sciences with an -*ics* ending (*mathematics*, *physics*, *politics*). (3) Some -*ics* words are singular or plural according to sense (*Economics is an arid subject*; *What are the economics of buying a house in Spain?*), while others give rise to uncertainty: *Metaphysics is/are too difficult for me*. In some cases, a singular may have been back-formed from the -*ics* form: *a statistic*, from *statistics*. (4) Diseases can give rise to doubt: *Measles is/are nasty*; *I had it/them as a child*. The feeling that an -*s* ending means a plural is strong, and even such countable nouns as *crossroaads*, *headquarters*, *golf links* may by followed by a plural verb when the reference is to a single place: *The headquarters is/are in London*.

**Other plural forms**. (1) From Old English: *child/children*, *ox/oxen*, *man/men*, *woman/women*, *foot/feet*, *tooth/teeth*, *goose/geese*, *louse/lice*, *mouse/mice*, *penny/pence*. (2) 'zero' plurals (mainly with the names of animals) where singular and plural are the same: *one sheep/twenty sheep*; *a deer/some deer*; *a salmon/several salmon*. In the usage of hunters, the names of animals, birds, and fish are often singular in form: *went shooting lion*; *shot three buffalo*. The word *fish* has two plurals, one unchanged (*hundreds of dead fish*) and with a collective implication, the other regular (*lots of little fishes*) and implying individuals together. Zero plurals are common with measurements: *She only weighs 98 pound(s)*, *though she is 5 foot/feet 5 inches*; *I'll take three dozen*. (3) Some plural-only words such as *cattle*, *clergy*, *people* (a plural of *person*, alongside *persons*), and *police*. (4) Some foreign plurals, such as *formulae*, *kibbutzim*, *mujahedin*, *phenomena*, and *radii*. The plural of French words ending in -*eau* may be written with an -*x* or an English -*s*: *chateaux*, *bureaus*. *Graffiti* is an Italian plural, but the singular *graffito* is rarely used in English.

**Classical plurals**. Latin plurals in English are: -*i* for words ending in the masculine inflection -*us* (*stimulus/stimuli*); -*ae* for singular words ending in feminine -*a* (*larva/larvae*); -*a* for words ending in neuter -*um* (*bacterium/bacteria*); -*ces* for words ending in -*x* (*appendix/appendices*). Greek plurals in English are: -*a* for words ending in neuter -*on* (*criterion/criteria*); and -*es* for words ending in *-is* (*analysis/analyses*). The situation with words of Latin and Greek origin which have kept their inflected nominative endings (*formula, memorandum, radius*) is complex and falls into three types: (1) With fully Anglicized plurals: *bonuses, rhinoceroses*. (2) Generally with classical plurals: *synthesis/ syntheses, radius/radii, stimulus/stimuli*. (3) With two plurals, the classical for formal contexts and specialized meanings, the vernacular for informal and general use: *appendix* with *appendices* and *appendixes*; *cactus* with *cacti* and *cactuses*; *formula* with *formulae* and *formulas*; *referendum* with *referenda* and *referendums*. There is widespread uncertainty about words ending in *-a*, which may represent a Latin singular or plural or a Greek plural. In terms of their origin, Latin *agenda, data, media, strata* and Greek *criteria, phenomena* are plurals, but have to some extent been reclassified in English. In this matter, however, acceptability varies. *Data* is often an uncountable noun (*There isn't much data*), but use of *criteria, media* (press and television), *phenomena, strata* (level of society) as singular nouns is often stigmatized. See CLASSICAL ENDING, ENDING, S.

**POETIC DICTION**. A term for a poetic STYLE prevalent in the 18c and marked by some or all of the following features: fanciful epithets, such as *the finny tribe* for 'fish' and *feathered songsters* for 'birds'; stock adjectives and participles, as in *balmy breezes, purling brooks, honied flowers*; artificial and ornate usage, such as 'Hail, sister springs, / Parents of silverfooted rills' (Crashaw); classical references, such as 'Of Cerberus and blackest midnight born, in Stygian caves forlorn' (Milton); complex figures of speech, as in 'My love was begotten by Despair / Upon Impossibility' (Marvell); archaism, as in 'and thither came the twain' (Tennyson); sentimentality, such as 'Absent from thee, I languish still' (Wilmot); unusual word order, such as 'This noble youth to madness loved a dame / Of high degree' (Dryden). The view that because poetry and prose have distinct conventions they should also have distinct styles and usages was favoured well into the 18c. In 1742, Thomas Gray wrote that 'the language of the age is never the language of poetry', a view challenged by Wordsworth (Preface, *Lyrical Ballads*, 1798), who argued against 'what is usually called poetic diction'. He considered that there should be no significant difference between the language

of poetry and that of everyday life. However, despite an increasing 19–20c tendency to use similar styles and usages in poetry and prose, poetic usage continues to be widely regarded as more rarefied or 'flowery' than most kinds of prose.

■ **POETRY** ──────────────────────── ■

Literary composition in verse form. It is often the case that to discuss a piece of work as poetry implies evaluating its quality, while to discuss it as verse relates to technique used in creating it. The terms, however, are blurred: the phrase *bad poetry* may refer to technique and the phrase *superb verse* may imply poetic excellence. In general, however, verse is the basis that supports a structure of sufficient quality to be called a poem.

**The poetic medium**. Poetry need not be written: early poetry was oral, transmitted and preserved through the mnemonic and performative skills of bards with no awareness of script or print. The written code accommodates poetry and adds the aesthetic effect of lines grouped on a page, or even of poems shaped in a visual pattern, like George Herbert's 'Easter Wings'. Other phonic features are added to the basic metrical pattern of verse, with or without rhyme. Thus, the sound of words may be directly onomatopoeic or may give a less overt effect of sound symbolism. Both are heard in Tennyson's 'Come Down, O Maid' (1847):

> The moan of doves in immemorial elms
> And murmuring of innumerable bees.

Slow or rapid movement can be suggested by a deliberate pattern of sounds and syllables as in Alexander Pope's *Essay on Criticism* (1711):

> When Ajax strives some rock's vast
>    weight to throw,
> The line too labours, and the words
>    move slow;
> Not so, when swift Camilla scours the
>    plain,
> Files o'er th'unbending corn, and skims
>    along the main.

Alliteration is not a part of most modern verse structure, but has a tradition dating back to Old English. Many poets have made it a feature for rhetoric or emphasis. Imagery in poetry conveys ideas obliquely, drawing from almost any area of human experience to create a response more effective than direct exposition. SHAKESPEARE makes frequent references to disease and corruption in *Hamlet* to suggest evil in the state of Denmark. In 'Dover Beach', Matthew Arnold likens his uncertainty and loss of faith to an ebbing tide. Images are often presented through figures of speech like simile and metaphor. These are also found in PROSE and to a lesser extent in everyday discourse. They are especially distinctive of poetry, however, because of their frequency and the stronger focus of attention given by verse forms.

**The poetic message**. The appeal of poetry is semantic as well as phonic. The poet has something to convey in language, which may range from the half-concealed situation in many of Shakespeare's sonnets, through Wordsworth's specific description and reflection of experience in 'The Daffodils', to the overt message of the 'Song of the Shirt' by Thomas Hood. In general, the poem gains by not being too explicit in its personal statement. The meanings and associations of a word may not be in harmony with its sound: although *paraffin* contains a pleasing phonemic sequence, it would not usually be regarded as a 'poetic' word; *equilibrium* refers to a good state of being but has not a traditional poetic sound. Polysemy, abundant in English, enriches poetic language, as when T. S. Eliot uses the theological and linguistic meanings of *word* to write of Christ in his nativity as:

The word within a word, unable to speak a word.

('Gerontion', 1920)

The pun is not currently in fashion for serious writing, but could once be used with telling effect:

Therefore I lie with her, and she with me,
And in our faults by lies we flattered be.
(Shakespeare, Sonnet 138)

**The language of poetry**. Concentration of special linguistic effects in a regular pattern tends to produce artificial diction. Rigid conventions about poetic usage have been less powerful in English than in some languages, but there have been times when poets have moved away from the familiar and everyday: particularly so in the 18c, with circumlocutions like *the finny tribe* for *fish* and *the bleating kind* for *sheep*. New generations of poets often demand a return to 'or-

dinary' language, as Wordsworth led the Romantic reaction against 18c POETIC DICTION with a call for 'a selection of the real language of men in a state of vivid sensation'. In the 1930s, the 'New Country' poets, such as W. H. Auden, Stephen Spender, and Cecil Day Lewis, wanted to write language that was accessible to ordinary people.

In the 20c, language has been accepted in poetry that would once have been considered too colloquial, commonplace, or even obscene, but this too can become mannered and removed from common usage. Poetry will always be to some extent artificial; selection and compression within the chosen form, even of free verse, distances the poem from daily usage. True poetry, however, is never entirely severed from the speaking voice; a certain latitude, however, sometimes called *poetic licence*, allows the poet to take liberties with language. In the classical set of genres, poetry was epic or lyric according to the degree in which the poet's direct voice was heard. Later theory has absorbed both genres under the general heading of poetry and added forms for specific purposes, such as elegy and pastoral. The frontier between poetry and prose is not always closely guarded or easy to delineate. If prose has a markedly high proportion of rhythm and other features associated with poetry, it is *poetic prose* or even *prose poetry*. An extended SIMILE with imagery and careful choice of words can give poetic quality to a passage in a novel, as:

Her words faded. So a rocket fades. Its sparks, having grazed their way into the night, surrender to it, dark descends, pours over the outlines of houses and towers; bleak hill-sides soften and fall in.
(Virginia Woolf, *Mrs Dalloway*, 1925)

Some of the highest literary uses of English have been in poetry. Poets have wanted not only to create beauty but also to express themselves memorably; the attitudes, fashions, and beliefs of many periods are made permanent in poetry. It appeals to the senses as well as the intellect. Of the two, sensory attraction is the more important; without emotive beauty, versified philosophy has little to recommend it. Although a relatively objective metalanguage can be devised to describe and discuss poetry, individual response to it is necessarily subjective. See ALLITERATION, ASSONANCE, BIBLE, BURNS, ENGLISH LITERATURE, LITERATURE, NONSENSE, RHYTHM, STRESS.

**POINT**. **1.** The sign (.), in WRITING made with the point of a pen or pencil, known as a *period*, *full stop*, or *full point* when used to close a sentence that expresses a statement, including elliptical sentences and SENTENCE fragments, as in: *They did not want to refuse. They didn't want to. On the contrary.* The point marks the close of, or elements in, many AB-BREVIATIONS (*Thurs., Cen., a.m., B.B.C.*) and follows INITIAL letters, as with the *M* in *William M. Thackeray*. It is, however, increasingly omitted in INITIALISMS (*BBC, GMT*), almost always omitted in ACRONYMS (*Nato, yuppie*), and, especially in BrE, generally omitted in abbreviations such as *Mr* and *Dr*. A set of *ELLIPSIS POINTS* is used to mark gaps in writing, especially words omitted from a quotation, as in: 'All the business of war, and indeed all the business of life, is to endeavour to find out what you don't know' reduced to 'All the business of war . . . is to . . . find out what you don't know' (quoting the Duke of Wellington, *Croker Papers*, 1885). When such points are used to mark a pause, they are called *suspension points*, as in *Tell him, uh . . . to wait a moment*. **2.** Also *decimal point*. The sign (.) or (·) used in decimal numbers, as in 2.22 or 2·22. Compare the *decimal comma* in Continental European practice, as in 2,22. **3.** A periodic sentence. **4.** In phonetics and orthography, a diacritic mark with various values: for example, in the modern transcription of Old English, sometimes placed above the letter *c* to indicate that it is pronounced 'ch' as in *church*, in such words as *ċild* (child) and *ċiriċe* (church). See DIACRITIC, DOT, PUNCTUATION.

**POLARI**, also **Palarie, Parlyaree, Parlary**, etc. [From Italian *parlare* to talk]. A once-extensive ARGOT or CANT in Britain and elsewhere, among sailors, itinerants, people in show business, and some homosexual groups. It survives as a vocabulary of around 100 words, some of which have entered general BrE slang: *mank(e)y* rotten, worthless, dirty (from Italian *mancare* to be lacking), *ponce* an effeminate man, pimp (from Spanish *pu(n)to* a male prostitute, or French *pront* prostitute, *scarper* to run away (probably from Italian *scappare* to escape, perhaps influenced by Cockney rhyming slang *Scapa Flow* go). A composite of different Romance sources, it was first taken to England by sailors, may derive ultimately from LINGUA FRANCA. A sample of present-day argot runs: 'As feely homies, we would zhoosh our riahs, powder our eeks, climb into our bona new drag, don our batts and troll off to some bona bijou bar' (Ian Hancock, 'Shelta and Polari', in P. Trudgill (ed.), *Language in the British Isles*, 1984) [*feely homies* young men, *zhoosh our riahs* fix our hair, *eeks* faces, *bona* nice, *drag* clothes, *batts* shoes, *troll* wander, *bijou* small]. See LINGO.

**POLITICALLY CORRECT**, short forms *PC, P.C.* 'Marked by or adhering to a typically progressive orthodoxy on issues involving esp. race, gender, sexual affinity or ecology' (*Random House Webster's College Dictionary*, 1991). The phrase is applied, especially pejoratively by conservative academics and journalists in the US, to the views and attitudes of those who publicly object to: (1) The use of terms that they consider overtly or covertly *sexist* (especially as used by men against women), *racist* (especially as used by whites against black), *ableist* (used against the physically or mentally impaired), *ageist* (used against any specific age group), *heightist* (especially as used against short people), etc. (2) Stereotyping, such as the assumption that women are generally less intelligent than men and blacks less intelligent than whites. (3) 'Inappropriately directed laughter', such as jokes at the expense of women, the disabled, homosexuals, and ethnic minorities. The abbreviation *PC* is also used as a term for people perceived as 'politically correct': ' "Community" is a rallying cry among PCs. They tend to use it. . . . as an all-purpose buzz word' (Mike Bygrave, 'Mind your Language', *Guardian Weekly*, 26 May 1991). Both the full and abbreviated terms often imply an aggressive intolerance of views and facts that conflict with their 'progressive orthodoxy'. The Random House dictionary quoted above was accused by the reviewer Anne Hopkins ('Defining Womyn (and Others)', *Time*, 24 June 1991) of failing to 'protect English from the mindless assaults of the trendy' because its editors listed such usages as *chairpersonship, herstory, humankind*, and *womyn* alongside *chairmanship, history, mankind*, and *women*, thereby giving them, in the opinion of the reviewer, a respectability that they did not merit. Compare MULTICULTURALISM. See GENDER BIAS, SEXISM, STEREOTYPE.

**POLYSEMY** [Stress: 'po-ly-semy'], also **multiple meaning**. A term in LINGUISTICS for words or other items of language with two or more SENSES, such as *walk* in *The child started to walk* and *They live at 23 Cheyne Walk*. Such senses may be more or less distant from one another: *walk* (action), *walk* (street) are relatively close, but *crane* (bird), *crane* (machine) are much farther apart. It is generally agreed, however, that in each case only one word is being discussed, not two that happen to have the same form (to which the name HOMONYMY is given). There is an extensive grey area between the concepts of *polysemy* and *homonymy*. A word like *walk* is polysemous (*went walking, went for a walk, walk the dog, Cheyne Walk*), while a word like *bank* is homonymous between at least *bank* for money and *bank* of a river. Dictionaries usually put polysemous words with all their senses in one article and homonymous words in two or more articles, dividing each into senses and subsenses as appropriate. In doing this, lexicographers generally take the view that homonymy relates to different words whose forms have converged while polysemy relates to one word whose meanings have diverged or radiated. See JANUS WORD, RADIATION, SEMANTIC CHANGE.

**PORTUGUESE**. A Romance language of Western Europe, closely related to SPANISH and the earliest of the major colonial languages originating in Europe. It is spoken by 135m people worldwide: in Europe, as the national language of Portugal (including the Azores and Madeira, islands in the Atlantic); in the Americas, as the official language of Brazil; in Africa, as the official language of Angola, Cape Verde, Guinea-Bissau, Mozambique, and Saõ Tomé and Príncipe; in Asia, as the official language of the Portuguese colony of Macao, near Hong Kong, and in ex-colonial territories such as Goa in India and East Timor in the Indian Ocean. It is also spoken by immigrant communities in Canada, France, the US, and elsewhere, and has given rise to or influenced PIDGINS and CREOLES in many parts of the world. Like Spanish, it was influenced by ARABIC during the centuries of Muslim dominance in the Iberian peninsula. Although Portugal is the oldest ally of England (since the 14c), the impact of Portuguese on English has been slight. LOANWORDS (some of them undergoing adaptation) include *albino, auto-da-fe, ayah, caste, madeira, marmalade, molasses, palaver,* and *port* (wine). Many such words have reached English indirectly, as with *ayah* and *caste*, which are the outcome of Portuguese influence on English in India. See BORROWING, INDIAN ENGLISH, ROMANCE LANGUAGES.

**POSITIVE**. **1.** Also *affirmative*. Terms for a sentence, clause, verb, or other expression that is not *negative*: *They are coming* as opposed to *They are not coming*. **2.** A base form, as with the positive as opposed to the COMPARATIVE or SUPERLATIVE DEGREES of an ADJECTIVE (*new* as opposed to *newer* and *newest*) or ADVERB. See NEGATION.

**POSSESSION**. The grammatical concept of one person or thing belonging to another, shown in English in four ways: (1) By verbs such as *have, own, belong to*. (2) By possessive pronouns that function as determiners: *my house*. (3) By the genitive or possessive case of nouns marked in writing by the possessive APOSTROPHE: *John's book; the Smiths' farm*. (4) By the *of*-construction: *the end of the road*. These cover a wide range of meaning from practical ownership (*my clothes; I have a dog*) through kinds of association (*their parents; our country; Shakespeare's birthplace*), to more general and often figurative and idiomatic relationships (*have an appointment; a day's journey; a lover's quarrel; the story of his life*). The genitive is also used to introduce the subject of a gerund, as in *It's funny your saying that*. In some instances, a genitive and an *of*-construction are both possible, though not interchangeable in all contexts. The genitive construction is likeliest when the possessor is personal or at any rate animate, or is in some way perceived as having personal aspects: *Dr Johnson's house; a dog's breakfast; God's love; Scotland's national poet; the world's pressing needs*. The *of*-construction is preferred with things not considered capable of possessing anything: *the lid of a box* rather than *a box's lid*. See GENITIVE CASE, GERUND, SAXON GENITIVE.

**POSSESSIVE PRONOUN**. A PRONOUN which expresses possession. Strictly applied, the term covers eight items used independently, as in *The house is ours*: *mine, thine* (archaic), *yours, his, hers, its, ours*, and *theirs*. More loosely, it includes eight items used attributively, as in *This is our house*: *my, thy* (archaic), *your, his, her, its, our*, and *their* (a set also labelled *possessive determiners* and *possessive adjectives*). The distinction between the two groups is the same as with any pronouns and DETERMINERS. Possessive determiners never take apostrophes: *its* is the determiner, while *it's* is short for *it is* or *it has*.

**POST-CREOLE CONTINUUM** A chain of language varieties which arises linking a CREOLE (also known as the *BASILECT*) to its SUPERSTRATE language (also known as the *ACROLECT*) via intermediate varieties referred to collectively as the MESOLECT: for example, the Jamaican post-creole continuum, ranging from Jamaican creole proper to a Jamaican standard English based on standard BrE. The following are Guyanese English Creole forms for standard English *I gave him*: Basilect *Mi gii am*; Mesolect *A giv im*; Acrolect *A geev him*. The differences between coexistent varieties in such a continuum are generally greater than might be expected in a community with 'normal' processes of dialect formation, particularly in terms of the amount and degree of syntactic and semantic variation. A post-creole continuum may develop when, after a period of relatively independent linguistic development, a post-pidgin or post-creole variety comes under a period of renewed influence from the superstrate (the *relexifier language*, or principal source of vocabulary). This is generally described as *decreolization*.

**POSTVOCALIC**. A term in PHONETICS referring to consonants that occur after a VOWEL: post-vocalic *r* in *work*. See R-SOUNDS.

**PRAGMATICS**. A branch of LINGUISTICS which originally examined the problem of how listeners uncover speakers' intentions. It is sometimes defined as the study of 'speaker meaning', as opposed to linguistic meaning: the utterance *I'm thirsty* might need to be interpreted as *Go and buy me a drink* and should not necessarily be taken at face value as a simple statement. The term is usually attributed to the British philosopher Charles Morris (1938–71), who distinguished between *SYNTAX* (the relations of sings to one another), *SEMANTICS* (the relations of signs to objects), and *pragmatics* (the relations of signs to interpretations). Recently, pragmatics has expanded into a wide and somewhat vague topic which includes anything relating to the way in which people communicate that cannot be captured by conventional linguistic analysis. Within pragmatics, *discourse analysis* (the study of language in discourse) has become a major focus of attention.

**PRÉCIS**, also **precis** [From French 'cut short'. Pronunciation: 'PRAY-see']. Plural identical in spelling, but pronounced '-seez']. **1.** A concise summary or abstract: *to make a précis of a report*. The term *précis-writing* has been commonly used in schools, especially in Britain, to refer to the teaching and practice of writing summaries. **2.** To summarize: *to précis a report*. See ABRIDGEMENT.

**PREDICATE**. A traditional grammatical term for a major constituent of the SENTENCE, part of a binary analysis that divides the sentence into subject and predicate. In the sentence *Pat has joined our club*, *Pat* is the subject and *has joined our club* is the predicate. In both grammar and logic, the predicate serves to make an assertion or denial about the subject of the sentence. In some analyses, the predicate does not include optional constituents, so that *today* is not part of the predicate in *Pat has joined our club today*.

**PREDICATIVE ADJECTIVE**, also **predicate adjective**. An ADJECTIVE that occurs in the PREDICATE: *silent* in *Eliot remained silent*; *uncomfortable* in *Naomi made her brother uncomfortable*. The relationship of the adjective is with the subject, following a linking verb (for example *remain*: compare *Eliot was silent*), or with the direct object that the adjective follows (compare *Her brother became uncomfortable*). Some adjectives can only be used predicatively: *asleep* (*The children were all asleep*, but not *\*the asleep children*); *aware* (*They were not aware of the danger*, but not usually *\*an aware person*). Increasingly commonly, the term *predicative adjective* is used to refer only to such adjectives, in contrast to *attributive adjective* (an adjective used before a noun). Some adjectives can only be used attributively: for example, *undue*, as in *undue pressure* (not *\*the pressure is undue*). See ATTRIBUTIVE, COMPLEMENT.

■ **PREFIX** ─────────────── ■

**1.** A term in WORD-FORMATION for an AFFIX added at the beginning of a word or base to form a new word: *re-* added to *write* to form *re-write/rewrite*. **2.** A general term for a word, letter, number, or other item placed before something else: the letter *A* in the sequence *A133*; the COMBINING FORM *auto-* prefixed to *biography* to form *autobiography*.

**Productivity**. A prefix is *productive* when it contributes to the meaning of a word (the *un-* in *unhappy* having the meaning 'not') and can be added freely to other, comparable words (*unable*, *unkind*). It is *non-productive* when it occurs in a word but does not contribute to its meaning: *con-* in *condition*. The meaning of the word *condition* is unrelated to the union of *con-* and *-dition* and there is no independent base word *\*dition*. A prefix is *vestigial* when only a trace of it can be detected by scholars: the *s* of *spend*, which was once *expend*. The same prefix may be productive in some words (*dis-* in *disconnect*, *dislocate*), non-productive in others (*dis-* in *disaster*, *distribute*), and vestigial in others still (*sport*, once *disport*). There are 'twilight' states: *re-* when productive means 'again' (*redo*, *reconnect*) and when non-productive (as in *remiss*) has no meaning, but in *rejuvenate*, *repair* the meaning 'again' is present even though the bases to which *re-* attaches (*\*juvenate*, *\*pair*) are not independent words.

**Provenance**. The prefixes of English derive from: (1) OLD ENGLISH: *a-* in *asleep*, *be-* in *bespatter*, *un-* in *unready*. (2) FRENCH: *dis-* in *disappear*, *mis-* in *misgovern*. (3) LATIN: *ante-* in *anteroom*, *in-* in *inactive*, *pre-* in *preconceive*. (4) GREEK: *a-* in *amoral*, *anti-* in *anti-war*, *meta-* in *metaphysical*. Prefixes with different backgrounds can, however, fall into relational sets: vernacular *over-*, as in *over-sensitive* more sensitive than necessary or desirable; Latin *super-*, as in *supersensitive* very sensitive (especially of instruments, film, etc.); Greek *hyper-*, as in *hypersensitive* excessively sensitive (especially to allergens). The negative prefixes of English form a range of usages that are sometimes irregularly paired (*ungrateful/ingratitude*, *unlikeable/dislike*, *unstable/instability*), are sometimes a source of confusion (*disinterested/uninterested*), and are sometimes delicately contrastive (*unmoral*, *immoral*, *amoral*, *non-moral*).

**Pairing**. In English, SUFFIXES often occur in chains (such as the *-istically* in *characteristically*), but prefixes do not. They usually occur singly (*un-* in *unhappy*, *re-* in *re-write*), but sometimes occur in pairs: *un-*, *re-*, in *unremarried* not married again; *anti-*, *dis-*, in *antidisestablishment*. In these examples, both prefixes are productive (that is, *married* and

*establishment* are independent base words), but pairing is commonly the addition of a productive to a non-productive prefix: productive *in-* to non-productive *re-* in *irredeemable* (no *\*deemable*); *in-* added to *con-* in *inconclusive* (no *\*clusive*). Sometimes, the same prefix may be added twice, usually with a hyphen: *meta-metalanguage*, *re-reconstructed*, *co-conspirator* (the productive *co-* beside the non-productive *con-*). Very occasionally, a three-prefix chain occurs: *non-reproductive*, in which *non-* is fully productive, *re-* is partly productive (*reproduction* being more than an extension of *production*), and *pro-* is non-productive (no *\*ductive*).

■ **PREPOSITION** ─────────────────── ■

One of the traditional PARTS OF SPEECH into which words are classified. It is a closed class, in that few new prepositions ever enter a language.

**Kinds of preposition**. (1) *Simple preposition*. Traditionally, the preposition proper: one- or two-syllable words, such as *at*, *from*, *through*, *without*. Many such words, however, also have adverbial roles: *up* is prepositional in *They took the boxes up the stairs*, adverbial in *They picked the boxes up/They picked up the boxes*. (2) *Compound preposition*. Two prepositions used together as one: *in* and *to* as *into*. Such forms are primarily conventions of writing and print and may vary according to the kind of English: BrE generally has *on to* and AmE *onto*. Forms like *into*, *on to/onto*, and *out of* are all compounds in speech, because of their rhythm and stress: the first preposition is stressed (*INto*), and the second is usually reduced. This point is reflected in the non-standard spelling of *out of* (*Will ya get outa here?*), where *a* stands for *of* reduced to schwa. (3) *Complex preposition*. A two- or three-word phrase that functions in the same way as a simple preposition: *according to*, as in *According to John, they are coming tomorrow*; *as well as*, as in *We're going as well as John*; *except for*, as in *They did everything, except for some work we'll finish tomorrow*; *in favour of*, as in *They voted in favour of the local candidate*.

**Prepositions and complements**. Unlike such major word classes as verbs and nouns, which have a more independent status, prepositions do not stand alone but need a *complement*. Typically, this is a noun or pronoun (*dawn* in *at dawn*, *you* in *after you*) but can be other parts of speech (*then* in *by* *then, short* in *in short*). Prepositions can also be followed by an *-ing* clause (after *of* in *A man has no reason to be ashamed of having an ape for his grandfather*) or by a *wh*-clause (*For what we are about to receive . . .*). They are not normally followed by *that*-clauses, although apparent exceptions are clauses introduced by complex conjunctions: *in that*, as in *The box was difficult to find, in that nobody knew where to look*; *except that*, as in *I wouldn't have gone, except that I'd promised*. Prepositions are not followed by *to*-infinitives, and there is a distinction between preposition *to* (as in *We look forward to seeing you/to your visit*, not *We look forward to see you*) and the *to* particle plus an infinitive (*We hope to see you soon*, not *We hope to seeing you soon*).

**Semantics**. In terms of meaning, prepositions range through various relationships: (1) Space and time, many being used for both: *at* in *They met at Heathrow Airport at six o'clock*. (2) Cause and purpose: *for* in *She did it for reasons of her own*. (3) Agent and instrument: *by* in *work done by an assistant; with* in *opened with a knife*. (4) The versatile *of*: possessive (*a friend of mine, the lid of the box*); assigning origin (*of royal descent*); indicating creation (*the works of Shakespeare*); referring to depiction (*a picture of Loch Fyne in winter*); indicating a subject of conversation (*telling them of his travels*); stating source and manufacture (*made of cotton*). (5) There are also many figurative meanings, such as the zeugma of *He left in a rage and a taxi*. (6) Normally, when the same preposition governs two consecutive phrases and has the same signification in both, it does not need to be repeated (*She works in London and Glasgow*), but on occasion, repetition is essential for the sake of clarity: *They lived in hope in Edinburgh* (because the significations are different: not *They lived in hope and Edinburgh*).

**Usage: the ends of sentences**. Because, in etymological terms, *preposition* means 'placing before', and Greek and Latin prepositions precede their complement, the classical prescriptive rule emerged for standard English that sentences should not end with a preposition. However, although English prepositions often do precede their complement, there are structures in which this is impossible (*What did you say that for?; What are you getting at?*) and some which have no grammatical complement (*The bed hadn't been slept in; It hardly bears thinking about; He's nothing to look at*). Traditionally, such usages

have been described as more or less ungrammatical, often with the result that alternatives have been preferred or recommended (*Why did you say that?* instead of *What did you say that for?*). The resultant insecurity sometimes produces stilted inversions like *To whom do you think you are talking?* for *Who do you think you're talking to?* One such manoeuvre in a government report is said to have led Winston Churchill to make his famous marginal comment: *This is the sort of bloody nonsense up with which I will not put* ('bloody nonsense' often being changed to 'English' in quotations). With relative clauses, there are usually two positions for a preposition, the end position being less formal: *This is the house in which she lived* as against *This is the house (that) she lived in*. In using such constructions, both native and non-native speakers of English sometimes either forget the preposition (*He is the person you have to give it*, forgetting *to*) or repeat it (*He is the person to whom you have to give it to*).

**Usage: prepositions and other parts of speech**. Prepositions overlap with other parts of speech, especially ADVERBS and conjunctions. The grammatical classification of an item therefore often depends on use in context: in the sentence *Jack and Jill went up the hill*, *up* is a preposition, but in *They climbed up (and up)*, it is an adverb. Such adverbs are sometimes called *prepositional adverbs*, sometimes *adverbial particles*. In other instances, there are related prepositional and adverbial forms. In standard English in England, *out* is adverbial only (*I opened the window and looked out*), the related prepositional form being *out of* (*I looked out of the window*). However, in AmE and ScoE, *out* is both adverbial and prepositional (*I looked out the window*). *Near* (*to*) and *close* (*to*) function like prepositions, but are like adjectives and adverbs in having comparative and superlative forms, and can be modified by an intensifier: *He sat nearer (to) the fire/very near the fire*. Other prepositions overlap with conjunctions. The distinction is again one of usage and function: *We waited until she arrived* (conjunction plus clause), *We waited until her arrival* (preposition plus noun phrase). Some words are conjunctions, prepositions, and adverbs: *since* in *We haven't heard from him since he left* (conjunction): *We haven't heard since January* (preposition); *We haven't heard since* (adverb). At times, the distinction between preposition and conjunction is not easy to make and may lead to controversy, as with *as* and *than*. Depending on whether they are seen as conjunctions (needing subject pronouns) or prepositions (able to take object pronouns), in such comparisons as *I'm not as rich as she/her* and *He's taller than I/me* the first option may be viewed as correct (but stilted), the second as usual (but sometimes stigmatized).

**Usage: like**. Some people, regarding *like* as a preposition (*Do it like this*), object strongly to its use as a conjunction, as in *Do it like I told you*, rather than *Do it the way I told you*; *Like he said, it's good for you*, rather than *As he said, . . .* ; *It's like he wanted to get away*, as opposed to *It's as if/though he wanted to get away*. These uses are, however, widespread. There are also some prepositions that introduce non-finite clauses but are never conjunctions, as with *on* in *On seeing us, he rushed away without saying a word*.

**Marginal prepositions**. These are words that have some of the characteristics of prepositions but also strong affinities with other word classes. They include some *-ing* and *-ed* forms which also have verbal use: *considering* (as in *Considering all the trouble he has caused, he should . . .*), *following*, *regarding*, *given*, *granted*. There are also such hard-to-classify words as *bar* (as in *all of them bar one*), *worth* (as in *It's worth much more*), and *minus* and *plus* (as in *minus four, plus ten*). *But* and *except* as prepositions can be followed not only by noun phrases (*There's nobody here but/except me*) but also by a bare infinitive (*They do nothing but complain*).

**The prepositional phrase**. This is a preposition and its complement together: *in the house*; *near the end*. Such a unit functions in different ways in a sentence: it can follow a noun in a noun phrase ('the man *in the white suit*'); it can follow particular verbs and adjectives ('Come and look *at my etchings*', 'Are you fond *of animals*?'); and it can function as an adverbial ('Put that thing *on the floor*'). This versatility sometimes leads to absurdity, when a prepositional phrase meant to have one function is misplaced and can be understood in another: *Staff are requested not to eat anything outside the canteen except for the duty telephone operator*. See next entries, and PHRASAL VERB.

**PREPOSITIONAL VERB**. In one school of grammatical theory, the term for an often idiomatic combination of VERB and PREPOSITION: *approve of* in *They fully approved*

*of his actions*; *get at* in *I really don't know what you are getting at*. Sometimes, such a verb is synonymous with a single verb: *come across* with *find* in *They came across the manuscript by accident*. The phrase that follows the preposition (*the children* in *Look after the children*) is a *prepositional object*. According to this view, some such verbs have two objects, one of them coming between the verb and the preposition: *blame on* in *Blame the noise on the children*. Other grammarians, however, argue that here the *on* is part of a traditional prepositional phrase. A *phrasal-prepositional verb* is a combination of a verb and two PARTICLES, the first an adverb, the second a preposition: *put up with*, meaning 'tolerate', as in *I can't put up with this noise any longer*. See PHRASAL VERB.

**PRESCRIPTIVE**. See DESCRIPTIVE AND PRESCRIPTIVE GRAMMAR.

**PRESENT**. A term for the TENSE of the VERB concerned primarily with events, actions, and states that apply at the time of speaking or writing (*The work goes on*), but also used to express FUTURE time (*We go to France tomorrow*), universal truths (in the simple present only: *Water is wet*), and PAST time in certain narratives, often of an informal or colloquial nature ('The narrative present': *He crosses the street and shoots them*). There are several types of present tense. The *simple present tense* has the form of the verb without inflections (*mention*) or with the third-person singular *-s* (*Everybody mentions his name*). The complex present tenses are: the *present continuous* or *present progressive*, which combines a present form of auxiliary *be* with the *-ing* participle (*is mentioning*); the *present perfect*, which combines a present form of auxiliary *have* with the *-ed* participle (*has mentioned*); the *present perfect continuous*, which combines these two (*has been mentioning*).

**PRETERITE**, also AmE **preterit**. A traditional term for the simple PAST tense of the verb (such as *climbed* in *They climbed the hill yesterday*) and for a verb in this tense.

■ **PRINT AND PRINTING** ────── ■

The process, business, art, and outcome of producing standardized LETTERS and TEXTS, often accompanied by diagrams, pictures, and other addenda, by applying ink to paper and other surfaces so as to produce many copies of the same piece of work. Printing is often treated as an aspect or offshoot of WRITING, but differs from it in at least four ways: (1) Writing varies from person to person, but print retains invariant shapes regardless of who uses it. (2) Writing follows relatively informal rules of positioning and sequencing on paper, but printing keeps rigidly to such conventions as margin sizes, line spaces, number of lines per page, and type chosen for a project. (3) Whereas writing is slow and produces approximate copies only through handcopying or the use of carbon paper or photocopying, printing is rapid and produces identical copies in sequence until the process stops or ink and paper run out. (4) The legibility of handwriting varies, but the legibility of print is consistent.

**Origins**. The art of making inked reproductions from woodblocks and movable signs was developed in the 6–8c by the Chinese and Koreans. It is uncertain how the practice was disseminated from East to West. The Islamic world was not interested in printing, but reports that reached Europe of such an invention appear to have prompted speculation and experiment. The Western invention of printing from movable type is generally ascribed to Johann Gutenberg, a goldsmith from Mainz in Germany. Although scholars dispute the details of the early production of his press, the first dated item is a copy of a 42-line Bible, which a scribe finished *rubricating* (entering CAPITALS and other matter) on 24 August 1456. There had been printing from woodblocks before Gutenberg. His genius was to perfect a number of separate but available technologies for printing from type. He appears to have devised a successful mould for casting regularly sized and spaced metal type, a heavy ink that would adhere to this type, and a variation of a press that would give an impression on paper. His 42-line Bible and other productions, far from being rudimentary initial experiments, are technically superior works of layout and typography.

**Development**. By the early 16c, printing and systems for distributing printed materials had spread throughout the main cities of Europe and stabilized. The English merchant William CAXTON learned the art in Cologne and practised it in Bruges before

setting up the first printing press in England, in Westminster in 1476. The first printing in India (by Portuguese Jesuits in Goa) was in 1556; in the North American colonies of England it was in Boston in 1638; in French Canada in Quebec City in 1752; in Australia, 1796; in New Zealand, 1835. At first, printed materials imitated manuscripts in subject matter, design, and distribution, but printing gradually established its own conventions. By the 1520s, large numbers of relatively cheap, fairly rapidly distributed books had become available to an expanded reading public. The technology remained stable until the end of the 18c, though markets for printed matter grew, especially for journals and newspapers. Because of the quantities involved and the capital-intensive nature of the business, the early printing and publishing of books tended to be centralized. In Britain, in the early centuries of printing, the government encouraged centralization in London and the universities of Oxford and Cambridge, because printing and publishing could easily be controlled and censored from there. In the 19c, however, a great expansion took place because of the spread of education, large and small printers set up shop in many places, and publishers (becoming from the 18c steadily more distinct from printers) became established outside the major centres in England, Scotland, and Ireland. The technology also changed with new kinds of presses and, by the end of the century, with new systems for typesetting. In the 20c, there has been a pronounced shift towards general LITERACY and a vast provision of printed materials throughout the world and in particular throughout the English-speaking world.

**Nature and impact**. A printed book not only involves a different technology from a manuscript, but results in a different product. Whereas manuscripts were copied in very small quantities, early books were printed in editions that averaged 250 to 1,250 copies. In the late 20c, however, an academic book might have 1,500 copies and a best-selling popular paperback a first print-run of 250,000. This economy of scale means that material can be rapidly disseminated. In the early centuries of printing, pamphlets and other more ephemeral material, often religious or political, could present issues of immediate importance. Many debates in the Reformation took place in print and in England little pamphlet wars, such as the late 16c Marprelate Controversy (in which anonymous tracts, printed on a secret press, irreverently attacked bishops and defended Puritanism), set the stage for sustained radical writing during the following century. The quantity of books available helped increase the numbers of the reading public, which in turn increased the number of books and the importance of literacy as a social tool. Although writing and reading have been associated with a minority educated class, printers from Caxton onwards, and especially from the 19c onwards, have often tried to extend readership by publishing popular and entertaining works. Currently, most books in English are aimed at specific audiences, but some would-be best-sellers are directed at an undifferentiated mass of millions of potential readers. For newspapers and magazines, the size of the audience is greater still. Increasingly sophisticated textbooks, books of self-instruction, and works of reference have also been a consequence of printing. Although rudimentary in the early centuries, they have become so refined that a surgeon can perform complex procedures based on text alone.

**Printing and culture**. Some scholars, following Harold Innis and Marshall McLuhan, suggest that print has created its own mental world, that it has been an agent of cultural change at a profound level. Although the attractiveness of such a theory may arise as much from a need to define literacy during a period of flux (the advent of cinematic and electronic media), the notion of a 'culture' associated with print bears cautious examination, especially in the way the press disseminates written language and at the same time changes it. Because of the nature of their work, printers affect the shape and style of printed matter. Traditional SPELLING and PUNCTUATION have been standardized by print and syntax and style influenced by it. The history of dictionaries and encyclopedias is closely bound up with the history of printing; a profound reliance on alphabetic order, though generated in the late Middle Ages, is basic to the culture of print: see DICTIONARY. The most pervasive text in English was once the BIBLE, but is now the telephone book. Although spoken English has retained its diversity, printed English shows less variation. Notions of correctness, for centuries part of the study of Latin manuscripts, have been passed on in the vernacular legacy of print; such notions spill over from print into speech, so that 'correct' speech follows bookish patterns.

See AMPERSAND, DIAERESIS, ITALIC, LIGATURE, LOWER CASE, ORTHOEPY, ORTHOGRAPHY, POINT, TRANSLITERATION.

**PRIVATE LANGUAGE**. LANGUAGE used for private or in-group purposes; a particular language or variety of a language used for such purposes, such as adolescent SLANG, criminal ARGOT, and technical JARGON. A private language that is intended to be opaque to all or most outsiders is known technically as a *cryptolect* ('hidden dialect'). Such languages are difficult to study because they often change rapidly and investigators have difficulty gaining admission to the groups that use them. The *travellers* or *travelling people* of Europe and North America, a group that includes but is not limited to *Gypsies* or *Romanies*, use various cants and forms of ROMANI as a *language of the roads*, to mark their ethnic identity and exclude outsiders. The linguist Ian Hancock, of Romany descent, has reported on these cryptolects: for example, in 'Romani and Angloromani' (in P. Trudgill (ed.), *Language in the British Isles*, 1984).

In California, a more localized private language called *Boontling* (also *Boonville Lingo*) has been used since the 1880s around Boonville in the upper Anderson Valley of Mendocino County. Used as the secret language of sheep-shearing crews and baseball teams, and to keep adult discussions secret from children, Boontling was most effective in separating locals from outsiders, who could not easily fathom its altered pronunciations, abbreviations, and personal associations. Among its evasive usages were: *burlap* (sometimes shortened to *burl*) to have sexual intercourse, *dreef* coitus interruptus, *keeboarp* premature ejaculation, *moldunes* breasts, *nonch harpins* objectionable talk, especially about sexual matters.

Perhaps the most common form of private usage in English occurs in families. Parents often coin private usages, such as nicknames and child-orientated EUPHEMISMS for bodily parts and functions, and adopt expressions used by their children when they were learning to speak. Twins are also sometimes credited with developing a private language that only they can understand. Family usages are often sustained for years without outsiders knowing much or anything about them. Perhaps the most opaque and isolated form of private language is that of schizophrenics. Although private language is widespread, no definitive study of the subject as a whole currently exists. See BACK SLANG, CANT, DOUBLE TALK, POLARI, RHYMING SLANG.

# ■ PROGRESS AND DECAY IN LANGUAGE ─────── ■

Two kinds of assumption are commonly made about languages: that they move from worse to better states (progress, amelioration); that they move from better to worse states (decay, deterioration). The Stoics of ancient Greece took the view that languages decay, whereas some social Darwinians in the 19–20c have held that languages improve as they evolve. A mixed viewpoint is also intermittently found: that some aspects of a LANGUAGE are deteriorating while others are improving. However, language change is an inevitable process and is the result of many factors, both linguistic and social. The interpretation of such change in terms of the improvement or deterioration of a language appears to be more a matter of social standpoint than linguistic observation.

**Life cycles in language**. In the 19c, it was widely believed in Western society that languages have a life cycle like animals and plants, in which they progress to a mature stage, then gradually decay. An inflected language such as classical Latin was a favoured example of a mature language, and English was thought by some to be in a state of disintegration because it was gradually losing its word endings ('English has no grammar'). This view, once held by scholars and lay people alike, is currently regarded as mistaken by most linguists. A later view, endorsed by Otto Jespersen, held that a fairly analytic language such as English represented the best and most evolved type of structure. This view is also now regarded as unfounded by most linguists.

**States of language**. There appears to be no reason for supposing that any one language is inherently superior to any other, either socially or structurally. PIDGINS and CREOLES, which are languages in the process of development, are linguistically 'impoverished' in that they do not initially have the range of vocabulary and constructions found in 'full' languages. Some languages are widespread for political or social reasons, rather than because of any intrinsic superiority. Over the centuries, very different kinds of languages have held dominant cultural positions and had high prestige. See CLASSICAL LANGUAGE. Conversely, languages which decline and die out do so when they become subject to powerful social pressures, as with GAELIC, which has declined in Scotland because English has for many years been the dominant language of the United Kingdom.

**The decline of English?** The view that English is 'going to the dogs' is widely held, especially by older people with conservative views. It is frequently expressed in newspapers, both in letters to the editor and feature articles, which often assert that change arises from lack of care and proper education ('slovenly language', 'sloppy speech', 'illiteracy in the classroom'). The changes referred to, however, appear to be continuous and inevitable. Sometimes, changes occur which happen repeatedly in the languages of the world, such as loss of the final consonant in a word. At other times, the need to maintain patterns may cause large-scale restructuring: vowel changes in English obscured the connection between many singular and plural words, such as *cow/kine* and *brother/brethren*, so new plurals (*cows, brothers*) replaced the old ones. These either fell out of general use (*kine*) or acquired a specialized sense (*brethren*), though two of the old -*en* plurals remain in general use (*children, oxen*). At other times, changes take place under the influence of other languages, or other varieties of English: at an early stage, English borrowed numerous Latin words, and currently BrE is heavily influenced by AmE. In such changes, however, there is nothing either progressive or decadent. They simply occur.

**Features of change**. A social group with overt or covert prestige usually initiates a change, sometimes consciously, sometimes unconsciously, though it can only bring about an innovation that was liable to occur in any case. There are usually several directions in which a language can move at any one time, and social factors can push it towards one rather than another. Currently,

BrE and AmE are adopting different paths over intervocalic /t/, which is inherently unstable. In a word such as *bitter*, the /t/ is increasingly being replaced by a glottal stop in BrE, but by /d/ in AmE, where the words *bitter* and *bidder* can be indistinguishable. Some people are indifferent to such changes. Others regard them as reprehensible and a symptom of a wider malaise in society, even though the · changes are independent of social conditions. Disapproval of a change may therefore be more indicative of the disposition of the commentator than the state of the language. Such disapproval may, however, influence individuals in their response to changes, if they are aware of them. Occasionally, social pressure may postpone or reverse a change: for example, initial /h/ is an unstable element in some varieties of BrE, but is preserved by a popular belief that it is 'wrong to drop aitches'. See AESTHETICS, LANGUAGE CHANGE, SEMANTIC CHANGE.

**PROGRESSIVE**, also **continuous**. Terms for a VERB form that basically denotes duration. In English, the contrast is between progressive (*She is repairing computers*) and non-progressive (*She repairs computers*). The progressive is constructed in English by a combination of a form of the verb *be* and the *-ing* form of the following verb: *was talking, may be calling, has been seeing, is being investigated*. The English progressive is generally considered to be an *ASPECT* (the way in which the temporal situation is viewed by the speaker), as contrasted with a *TENSE* (the location of the situation in time). However, the marking of aspect is always combined with the marking of tense: *is reading* is present progressive; *was reading* is past progressive.

**PROLEPSIS. 1.** A term in RHETORIC for treating a future event as if it has already happened: *I'm dead—Get away before they kill you too!* **2.** A debating device in which one raises an objection to one's own case before an opponent can do so: *I am well aware that the cost of the project is high, but consider the consequences of not going ahead.* **3.** In traditional GRAMMAR, a structure anticipating another that comes later: *that old man in 'That old man*, I just saw *him* again.'

■ **PRONOUN** ─────── ■

A traditional PART OF SPEECH that is typically used as a substitute for a noun or noun phrase. In contemporary grammatical theory, pronouns are sometimes viewed as a subclass of nouns. They constitute a closed class, in that few new pronouns ever enter a language.

**Subclasses**. There are eight subclasses: PERSONAL PRONOUNS (*I, we, they*, etc.); possessive pronouns (*my/mine, our/ours, their/theirs*, etc.); REFLEXIVE PRONOUNS (*myself, ourselves, themselves*, etc.); DEMONSTRATIVE PRONOUNS (*this, that, these, those*); RECIPROCAL PRONOUNS (*each other, one another*); interrogative pronouns (*who, what*, etc.); relative pronouns (*who, that*, etc.); indefinite pronouns (*any, somebody, none*, etc.). Some forms belong to more than one subclass: *who* is an interrogative pronoun in *Who is that?* and a relative pronoun in *the child who did that* . . . Some may belong to other parts of speech: *any* is a pronoun in *Do you want any?* and a determiner (like the definite article, introducing a noun phrase) in *Do you want any money?* The possessive pronouns have two sets of forms: one strictly speaking a determiner (*my* in *You have my book*), the other a pronoun (*mine* in *That book is mine*).

**Form**. Some of the sets of pronouns have distinctions in PERSON, NUMBER, CASE, or GENDER. Personal pronouns have distinctions in: person (*I, you, she*); number (*I, we*); gender (in the third-person singular only: *he, she, it*); case (subjective *I*, objective *me*). Possessives may be viewed as genitives of personal pronouns and make similar distinctions, as do reflexives (which do not have case). Demonstratives have distinctions in number (*this, that* versus *these, those*) and in physical or metaphorical distance (*this, these* are nearer to speaker than *that, those*). The reciprocals have genitives (*each other's, one another's*), as do the indefinites ending in *-body* and *-one* (such as *somebody's, anyone's*). Finally, the interrogatives and relatives have distinctions in gender (personal *who* and normally non-personal *what* for interrogatives, personal *who* and non-personal *which* for relatives), and in case (subjective *who*, objective *whom*, genitive *whose*).

**Function**. In contemporary grammar, the pronoun by itself usually constitutes a noun phrase, though with certain restrictions some pronouns may be modified: *something colourful; those who know; what else*. As the main or only word in the noun phrase, it has the same set of syntactic functions as a noun. Many of the pronouns have important discourse functions. They contribute to cohesion in discourse by referring back to a previous unit in anaphora (*he* in *While Matthew was in Jerusalem, he joined a peculiar cult*) or forward to a subsequent unit in cataphora (*Although she is studying hard, Deborah finds time to help me*). Some of the pronouns are used in deixis to refer directly to persons or things in the situation of the discourse: *I* for the speaker or writer and *you* for the person or persons addressed, and *it* in *Pick it up* (where the thing referred to by *it* is not previously named). See GENERIC PRONOUN, RASTA TALK.

**PRONUNCIATION. 1.** The act or result of producing the sounds of SPEECH, including ARTICULATION, INTONATION, and RHYTHM. **2.** The sound system of a language: *German pronunciation*. **3.** An accepted standard of sound and rhythm for elements of spoken language: *the proper pronunciation of 'controversy'; the mispronunciation of vowels*. **4.** The phonetic representation of a sound, word, etc.: see TRANSCRIPTION. Because of the vagaries of the spelling system of English, most larger dictionaries have since the 18c provided guidance on the pronunciation of words, usually immediately after the headword of an entry, and either in a system of *respelling* or, since the end of the 19c, in phonetic symbols. EFL learner's dictionaries published in the UK currently use the INTERNATIONAL PHONETIC ALPHABET to represent the phonemes of RECEIVED PRONUNCIATION (RP), an ACCENT of England that has served as a *pronunciation model* (the target at which the learner aims) since the early 20c. Some learners' dictionaries provide AmE equivalents. Works that concentrate on pronunciation alone include Daniel JONES, *An* ENGLISH PRONOUNCING DICTIONARY (*EPD*, 14th edition, revised by A. C. Gimson, 1977), and J. C. Wells, *The Longman Pronunciation Dictionary* (1990). In dictionaries for native speakers, respelling systems are generally preferred in the US, while in the UK publishers are currently divided, some favouring respelling, others (such as Oxford University Press) moving over to IPA symbols. See BBC ENGLISH[1], BBC PRONUNCIATION UNIT, ELOCUTION, MISPRONUNCIATION, ORTHOEPY, PHONETICS, PUBLIC SCHOOL PRONUNCIATION, SPELLING PRONUNCIATION.

**PROPER.** A general term for what is right, suitable, or appropriate (*the proper technical*

term; *proper conduct*), often implying a wish or need to 'do the right thing' socially (*They were always very proper in everything they did*). The term has sometimes been attached to groups and places: 'She was only a mild rebel: there was still too much of the Proper Bostonian in her' (J. Cleary, *High Road to China*, 1977). Traditionally, a *proper accent* has been the accent considered most suitable for polite, dignified, educated usage, among ladies and gentlemen: in England, RECEIVED PRONUNCIATION. Such non-standard expressions as *He don't talk proper* have long been widespread, marking the social and linguistic gap between speakers of vernacular and standard English: 'Perhaps she'll 'ave another go at teachin' me to speak proper, pore soul' (Margery Allingham, *The Tiger in the Smoke*, 1952); ironically, 'How to talk proper in Liverpool' (subtitle of *Lern Yerself Scouse*, 1966, by Frank Shaw, Fritz Spiegl, & Stan Kelly). The term *proper English* is often used to mean STANDARD ENGLISH: 'Debates about the state and status of the English language are rarely debates about language alone. Closely linked to the question, what is proper English? is another, more significant social question: who are the proper English?' (publisher's statement opening Tony Crowley's *Proper English: Readings in Language, History and Cultural Identity*, Routledge, 1991). See AESTHETICS, CORRECT, GENTEELISM, GOOD ENGLISH.

**PROPER NOUN.** A category of NOUN, distinguished on grammatical and semantic grounds from COMMON NOUN, and written with a CAPITAL letter. Proper nouns are primarily NAMES of persons (*John, Churchill*), places (*India, Edinburgh*), and various periods of time (*Sunday, August*). Their reference is said to be unique in context and definite; sometimes *the* is used with the noun (*The Hague*), but most names are definite without requiring the definite article. Grammatically, indefinite *a/an* and most other determiners are not used with proper nouns, nor is there normally a singular/plural contrast: (*Mount*) *Kilimanjaro, the Seychelles*, but not *\*a Kilimanjaro, \*a Seychelle*. There is, however, no clear demarcation between proper and common nouns, regardless of the initial capital. People can speak of *Churchills*, who could be members of the Churchill family, people with that surname, or people figuratively compared to Winston Churchill. There might be *a different Churchill* (not

Winston), *a Sunday in June, that memorable August, the Edinburgh of her childhood*, and so on. Here, for specific purposes, proper nouns have effectively been converted into common nouns. Common nouns can also on occasion behave like proper nouns, as in: *I do not fear you, Death.* Nationality nouns (*Americans, a New Zealander, the Japanese*) lie on the borderline between proper and common nouns. Some grammarians distinguish the *proper noun* (a single noun like *London; the* and a single noun: *the Pennines*) from the *proper name*, a wider category which includes these and also such word groups as *the United States (of America), the Houses of Parliament, the Royal Navy, A Tale of Two Cities, The Concise Oxford Dictionary.*

**PROSCRIPTIVE**. A grammatical or other rule is proscriptive if it forbids the use of a particular feature of language on the grounds that it is incorrect or undesirable: proscribing the use of the verb *infer* in such a sentence as *What are you inferring?* and prescribing instead the verb *imply*. See DESCRIPTIVE AND PRESCRIPTIVE GRAMMAR.

■ **PROSE** ────────────── ■

[From Latin *prosus* direct or straightforward. *Prosa oratio* was the Latin equivalent of Greek *pezós lógos* speech that goes on foot, as opposed to *émmetros lógos* ('measured speech') or verse, whose high prestige was reflected in the image of riding on horseback.] A form of written DISCOURSE based on the sentence and without the stylized patterning of VERSE. A negative perception of prose, which has persisted from classical times virtually to the present day, sees it as a medium that lacks strong features and creative vigour: whence the use of *prosaic* to mean 'dull, commonplace, unimaginative'. This ancient perception has, however, diminished greatly in the 20c, in the course of which prose has become the dominant form of printed discourse and verse has become largely peripheral.

The term covers two kinds of procedure: employing physical features such as the non-metrical line, the PARAGRAPH, and SENTENCE-based PUNCTUATION, and styles of discourse that serve narrative, expository, descriptive, persuasive, dramatic, and other ends. Prose writing is so similar in many ways to carefully organized SPEECH, and the two have been linked for so long in

the world of education, that prose is often thought of as simply speech transferred to paper. Everyday speech, however, is much less tightly structured than most types of prose, and its dynamics are quite distinct from those of formal writing. Colloquial English, for example, is not arranged according to the classical theory of the well-formed sentence ('a sentence is a complete thought'), long a key criterion for producing and evaluating prose. Such a criterion has been used by elocutionists and others in attempts to 'improve' speech, but without great success: spoken usage that is too 'prosy' sounds artificial and perhaps pretentious. In the classical world, the study and use of prose were linked with RHETORIC, GRAMMAR, and LOGIC, but whereas the rhetorical tradition was oral in origin, the beginnings of grammar and logic lay in the use and study of writing. Lacking the mnemonic quality and often the histrionic roles of verse, prose has depended largely on writing (not oral delivery) for its transmission, and has come only within the last 300 years to serve as a regular vehicle for 'high' literary genres such as drama and the epic (the latter essentially in the form of the novel).

**Kinds of prose**. Because of its wide present-day use, prose ranges across many activities, including: the writing of technical instructions; the presentation of information in newspapers and other periodicals; legal, business, and other reports; personal letters; and the writing of fiction and drama. *Literary prose*, considered by many to be its highest form, shares with verse (despite the classical view) an intensification and stylization of rhythm and a greater than usual attention to rhetorical features and aesthetic factors such as euphony and assonance. Its status as prose is sustained, however, by the absence of recurring metrical patterns, however 'poetic' in form and content such texts may be. Many writers of literary prose have followed Aristotle's dictum that it 'must neither possess metre nor be without rhythm' (*Rhetoric*, 3. 8), and at times it can have a quality close to *free verse* or *blank verse*. Just as the line of demarcation is not always easy to find between prose and verse, so there is no easy demarcation between one kind of prose and another. Prose discourses occupy a spectrum in which the extremes are easily identified: 'poetic' prose on one side, 'technical' or 'functional' prose on the other, with the middle ground often uncertain.

**Prose and style**. Although STYLE is sometimes thought to reside only in 'good' literary writing (however judged), it is a factor in all writing; every specimen of prose from instructions on how to put together a piece of furniture to James Joyce's *Ulysses* has features that can be described, analysed, and evaluated by stylistic and aesthetic criteria. The evolution of Western prose has produced a variety of styles, often characteristic of a particular period, writer, or function. The traditional division of styles has been into *high*, *middle*, and *low*, according to the rhetorical principle of *decorum* (that the manner of writing should be adapted to subject and recipient). This socially ranked system, however, has not proved useful in contemporary analysis because it lacks objectivity (though it partly incorporates the present-day linguistic category of REGISTER). Like other Western European VERNACULARS, English developed in the shadow of LATIN, and its models for prose were therefore Latinate, at first through translation, imitation, and experiment, later as a consequence of its hybrid inheritance. Because of the classical legacy (and despite specific differences), the prose styles of English have much in common with those of FRENCH, ITALIAN, SPANISH, GERMAN, and other languages also influenced by Latin models. It is possible therefore to talk of a broad European prose tradition of which English is part.

**Old and Middle English prose**. OLD ENGLISH prose writing was largely a matter of translation from Latin, as in the works of ALFRED the Great (9c), but original vernacular prose was produced by such writers as AELFRIC (10–11c) and the clerics who compiled the ANGLO-SAXON CHRONICLE. By and large, the style is straightforward and unadorned. In the centuries immediately after the Norman Conquest (1066), the development of MIDDLE ENGLISH prose waited on the decline of French as the language of aristocracy and government and of Latin as the dominant language of religion and learning. There was therefore little demand for vernacular prose in the Middle Ages and as a result it was generally poorly structured in comparison with Latin. However, the vernacular sermon added persuasive rhetorical strength to some English prose

texts, notably in the writings of John WYCLIFFE, Geoffrey CHAUCER, and William CAXTON.

The following excerpts are typically from translations, or associated with them: the Old English version of the Venerable Bede's *Historia Ecclesiastica Gentis Anglorum* (*Ecclesiastical History of the English People*, early 8c); Chaucer's rendering in the 14c of Boethius, *De Consolatione Philosophiae* (*On the Consolation of Philosophy*: 6c); and Caxton's prologue to the *Eneydos*, his version of a French version of Virgil's *Aeneid* (1490), which moved towards EARLY MODERN ENGLISH. The slashes (virgules) in Caxton's text were an experiment in punctuation, and are roughly equivalent to commas.

*Old English*. Breten is gārsecges īegland, þæt wæs gēo geāra Albion hāten: is gesett betwix norþdǣle and westdǣle, Germānie and Gallie and Hispānie, þǣm mǣstum dǣlum Eurōpe, micle fæce ongeān. þæt is norþ eahta hund mīla lang,and twā hund mīla brād. Hit hæfþ fram sūþdǣleþā mægþe ongeān þe man hætt Gallia Belgica. Hit is welig, þis īegland, on wæstmum and on trēowum missenlicra cynna, and hit is gescrēpe on lǣswe scēapa and nēata, and on sumum stōwum wīngeardas grōaþ.

[*A close translation*: Britain is a sea island, that was in former years called Albion: it is set between the north-parts and west-parts [that is, to the north and west] of Germany, Gaul, and Spain, the greatest parts of Europe, by much space opposite [that is, at a considerable distance]. It is north eight hundred miles long, and two hundred miles broad. It has on south-part the nation opposite that one calls Belgian Gaul. It is rich, this island, in fruit and trees of various kinds, and it is suitable for pastures of sheep and cattle, and in some places vineyards grow.]

*Chaucer*. The poete of Trace, *Orpheus*, that whylom hadde right great sorwe for the deeth of his wyf, after that he hadde maked, by his weeply songes, the wodes, moevable, to rennen; and hadde maked the riveres to stonden stille; and hadde maked the hertes and the hindes to joignen, dredeles, hir sydes to cruel lyouns, *for to herknen his songe*; and hadde maked that the hare was nat agast of the

hounde, which that was plesed by his
songe: so, whan the moste ardaunt love
of his wif brende the entrailes of his
brest, ne the songes that hadden
overcomen alle thinges ne mighten nat
asswagen hir lord *Orpheus*, he pleynede
him of the hevene goddes that weren
cruel to him; he wente him to the
houses of helle. And there he temprede
hise blaundisshinge songes by
resowninge strenges, and spak and song
in wepinge al that ever he hadde
received and laved out of the noble
welles of his moder *Calliope* the goddesse;
and he song with as mochel as he
mighte of wepinge, and with as moche
as love, that doublede his sorwe, mighte
yeve him and techen him; and he
commoevede the helle, and requerede
and bisoughte by swete preyere the
lordes of sowles in helle, of relesinge;
*that is to seyn, to yilden him his wyf.*

**Caxton**. How wel that many honderd
yerys passed was the sayd booke of
eneydos wyth other werkes made and
lerned dayly in scolis specyally in ytalye
& other places / whiche historye the sayd
vyrgyle made in metre / And whan I had
aduised me in this sayd boke. I delybered
and concluded to translate it in to
englysshe And forthwyth toke a penne &
ynke and wrote a leef or tweyne / whyche
I ouersawe agayn to correcte it / And
whan I sawe the fayr & straunge termes
therin / I doubted that it sholde not
please some gentylmen whiche late
blamed me sayeng y$^t$ in my translacyons
I had ouer curyous termes whiche coude
not be vnderstande of comyn peple / and
desired me to vse olde and homely
termes in my translacyons, and fayn
wolde I satysfye euery man / and so to
doo toke an olde boke and redde therin /
and certaynly the englysshe was so rude
and brood that I coude not wele
vnderstande it. And also my lorde abbot
of westmynster ded do shewe to me late
certayn euydences wryton in olde
englysshe for to reduce it in to our
englysshe now vsid / And certaynly it
was wreton in suche wyse that it was
more lyke to dutche than englysshe I
coude not reduce ne brynge it to be
vnderstonden /

**Elizabethan and Jacobean prose**. In the
16c and 17c, more and more writers chose

to develop English prose rather than continue with Latin. Although their prose still
followed Latin models, it necessarily accom-
modated itself increasingly to such vernacular usages as the compound noun and the
phrasal verb, as well as less formal syntactic
constructions. Elizabethan prose often
seems self-conscious in attempting to imitate Latin, with the Roman lawyer and
orator Cicero as the supreme model. Style
was based on the periodic sentence, formal
and ordered in structure, building to its climax before the full meaning is revealed.
This apparent neo-classical artificiality
tightened up the loose, rambling style of
Middle English and took on a powerfully
disciplined form in the preface to the
Authorized Version of the BIBLE:

> But how shall men meditate in that,
> which they cannot vnderstand? How
> shall they vnderstand that which is kept
> close in an vnknowen tongue? as it is
> written, *Except I know the power of the voyce,
> I shall be to him that speaketh, a Barbarian
> and he that speaketh, shalbe* [sic] *a Barbarian
> to me*. The Apostle excepteth no tongue;
> not Hebrewe the ancientest, not Greeke
> the most copious, not Latine the finest.
> Nature taught a naturall man to
> confesse, that all of vs in those tongues
> which wee doe not vnderstand, are
> plainely deafe; wee may turne the deafe
> eare vnto them. . . . Translation it is that
> openeth the window, to let in the light;
> that breaketh the shell, that we may
> eat the kernel; that putteth aside the
> curtaine, that we may looke into the
> most Holy place; that remooueth the
> couer of the well, that wee may come by
> the water, euen as *Iacob* rolled away the
> stone from the mouth of the well, by
> which meanes the flockes of *Laban* were
> watered. Indeede without translation
> into the vulgar tongue, the vnlearned
> are but like children at *Iacobs* well
> (which was deepe) without a bucket or
> something to draw with: or as that
> person mentioned by *Esay*, to whom
> when a sealed booke was deliuered, with
> this motion, *Read this, I pray thee*, hee was
> faine to make this answere, *I cannot, for it
> is sealed*.

A highly artificial but influential style was
that of John LYLY, named *euphuism* from the
hero of his prose romances. It was characterized by long periodic sentences, with
abundant tropes and figures of RHETORIC,

classical ALLUSIONS, and improbable analogies from the natural world. SHAKESPEARE parodied it in *Love's Labour's Lost* (*c*.1595) and elsewhere. A more restrained style, formal but somewhat less mannered, was achieved by Sir Philip Sidney in his *Arcadia* (1581) and *Defence of Poetry* (1579–80). The excitement of English as an emerging literary language in its own right brought exuberance to contemporary writing. Francis Bacon (1561–1626) criticized the tendency of the periodic style to mask sense with rhetoric. His own style was sometimes rhetorical, but produced greater simplicity, combined with balance and antithesis, in his *Essays* (1597–1625).

**Restoration and Enlightenment prose**. The Restoration period saw the emergence of a distinctly native prose style, whose seeds were sown in the polemical writings of the Civil War. The new prose was simpler and less ornate, further from Latin syntax, more familiar in tone, though still polished and urbane. The beginnings of JOURNALISM strengthened the closer relationship between writer and reader; the political prose of Hobbes and the critical prose of Dryden are typical. Prose was increasingly used for instruction as well as for persuasion and entertainment. The members of the ROYAL SOCIETY (founded in 1662) were expected to prefer 'the language of artizans, countrymen, and merchants, before that of wits and scholars'. The polite, familiar style was further developed in the early 18c by Addison, Defoe, Steele, and Swift. The following is from Daniel DEFOE'S *An Essay upon Projects* (1697), relating to the establishing of an English equivalent of the Académie française (see ACADEMY):

I had the Honour once to be a Member of a small Society, who seem'd to offer at this Noble Design in England. But the Greatness of the Work, and the Modesty of the Gentlemen concern'd, prevail'd with them to desist an Enterprize which appear'd too great for Private Hands to undertake. We want indeed a *Richlieu* to commence such a Work: For I am persuaded, were there such a *Genius* in our Kingdom to lead the way, there wou'd not want Capacities who cou'd carry on the Work to a Glory equal to all that has gone before them. The *English* Tongue is a Subject not at all less worthy the Labour of such a Society than the

*French*, and capable of a much greater Perfection. The Learned among the *French* will own, That the Comprehensiveness of Expression is a Glory in which the *English* Tongue not only Equals but Excels its Neighbours.

With the rise of the essay and the novel in the 18c, prose took the assured and accepted place in literature that it already held in legal, commercial, and other uses. Critical responses, both casual and professional, which had previously been mainly confined to poetry, came to be applied to literary prose as well. In addition, a good prose style was considered a desirable accomplishment for the cultivated, and attention to models of 'good writing' in essays, letters, etc., became more and more a required part of education. However, in the late 18c there was a return to the periodic Latinate style. JOHNSON wrote with involved syntax and the frequent use of classical words, and Burke (1729–97) in political prose and Gibbon (1737–94) in historical prose followed a similar style. At the same time, a comparable prose was developing in North America, and is enshrined in the Declaration of Independence of 4 July 1776 (signed by John Hancock on behalf of Congress), which opens with the following statement:

When in the Course of human Events, it becomes necessary for one People to dissolve the Political Bands which have connected them with another, and to assume among the Powers of the Earth, the separate and equal Station to which the Laws of Nature and of Nature's God entitle them, a decent Respect to the Opinions of Mankind requires that they should declare the causes which impel them to the Separation. We hold these Truths to be self-evident, that all Men are created equal, that they are endowed by their Creator with certain unalienable Rights, that among these are Life, Liberty, and the Pursuit of Happiness—That, to secure these Rights, Governments are instituted among Men, deriving their just Powers from the Consent of the Governed, that whenever any Form of Government becomes destructive of those Ends, it is the Right of the People to alter or to abolish it, and to institute new Government (*A Declaration by the Representatives of the*

*United States of America, in General Congress Assembled*, 4 July 1776).

**Prose in the nineteenth century**. This century brought as much variety and abundance in prose style as in other things. The reading public expanded on an unprecedented scale, the popularity of the novel in particular giving impetus to prose writing for entertainment and the growth of JOURNALISM making it a major vehicle of news and opinion. Although there are marked differences between the leading novelists of the period, they shared a desire to write accessibly and to keep the interest of the reader, who is addressed directly, as a friend. Narrative style became more assured in the hands of Austen. DICKENS, Thackeray, Eliot, Hardy, and many other both 'literary' and 'popular' writers. A more didactic type of prose, designed to inform and convince, was practised by Arnold, Carlyle, Macaulay, and others. The following is from Macaulay's essay on Bacon, in the *Edinburgh Review* (1837):

> We have often heard men who wish, as almost all men of sense wish, that women should be highly educated, speak with rapture of the English ladies of the sixteenth century, and lament that they can find no modern damsel resembling those fair pupils of Ascham and Aylmer who compared, over their embroidery, the styles of Isocrates and Lysias, and who, while the horns were sounding and the dogs in full cry, sat in the lonely oriel, with eyes riveted to that immortal page which tells how meekly and bravely the first great martyr of intellectual liberty took the cup from his weeping gaoler. But surely these complaints have very little foundation. We would by no means disparage the ladies of the sixteenth century or their pursuits. But we conceive that those who extol them at the expense of the women of our time forget one very obvious and very important circumstance. In the time of Henry the Eighth and Edward the Sixth, a person who did not read Greek and Latin could read nothing, or next to nothing. The Italian was the only modern language which possessed anything that could be called a literature. All the valuable books then extant in all the vernacular dialects of Europe would hardly have filled a single shelf.

Prose writing in English took firm root during this century in many parts of the world, particularly in the US but also in Australia, Canada, India, and New Zealand.

**Prose in the twentieth century**. More prose-writing in English has probably been published in this century than in all past centuries combined. Because, however, the quantities involved are so vast and the objectives and styles have been so varied, it is virtually impossible to make more than a few provisional general statements about 20c prose. It can, for example, be argued that there has been in literary and journalistic writing a move away from (often in tandem with a distaste for) the elevated literary and classical style, towards the more direct, immediate, and colloquial. By and large, although every kind of prose can be found in English in the late 20c, there is a general tendency towards factual and referential writing, favouring shorter sentences and a vocabulary as simple as the subject allows. See CHURCHILL, COMPOSITION, CONVERSATION, DIALOGUE, LITERATURE, ORWELL, PERIODIC SENTENCE, STYLE, TEXT, WRITING.

**PROVERB**. A short traditional saying of a didactic or advisory nature, in which a generalization is given specific, often metaphorical, expression: *A stitch in time saves nine*, meaning that action taken now will prevent a small problem becoming larger. Proverbs are found in many languages and cultures. A common idea may be given different local references: English *carrying coals to Newcastle* equivalent to Greek *sending owls to Athens*. Proverbial sayings were popular in the Middle Ages and treated as accepted wisdom. In the 16c and 17c, they were often used in literature, to support arguments and give emphasis to the author's views.

Proverbs are often of linguistic interest and may show lexical change. The saying 'Do not spoil the *hog* for a halfpenny-worth of tar' is recorded in 1600, but changed to *sheep* in 1651 and *ship* in 1823. The mnemonic needs of oral transmission may appear in: rhyme 'Birds of a feather flock together'; ASSONANCE 'A stitch in time saves nine'; ALLITERATION 'Look before you leap'. Two proverbs may seem contradictory when in fact they contain truths applicable to different situations: *Too many cooks spoil the broth* as against *Many hands make light work*. Proverbs in present-day usage may often be regarded as clichés, but their persistence indicates their sociolinguistic importance. Commonly, when they occur in informal conversation, only the opening phrase is used: *Well, a stitch in time, you know*; *Don't count your chickens* (before they are hatched). See METAPHOR, QUOTATION.

**PROVINCIALISM**. A usually pejorative term for a lack of social and linguistic sophistication regarded as typical of provinces and provincials, and for a WORD or other usage that is not accepted in the capital or the main cultural centre(s) of a nation. See -ISM, STYLE.

**PSYCHOBABBLE**. [From the title *Psychobabble: Fast Talk and Quick Cure in the Era of Feeling*, 1977, a book by the US journalist Richard D. Rosen: compare TECHNOBABBLE]. A form of JARGON in which terms from psychology, psychiatry, psychotherapy, and related fields are used to impress the listener, give an appearance of scientific objectivity to mundane ideas, or inflate what someone has to say. According to Rosen, it is 'a set of repetitive verbal formalities that kills off the very spontaneity, candour and understanding it pretends to promote'. A person engaged in psychobabble might seek 'ego reinforcement through consciousness raising by going where the energies are in my extrinsic peer group orientation'.

# ■ PSYCHOLINGUISTICS ─── ■

The branch of knowledge which studies the mental aspects of language, combining LINGUISTICS and psychology. It overlaps with a wider, more general field known as the *psychology of language*, which includes the relationship of language to thought, and with an even wider one, the *psychology of communication*. Psycholinguistics, as the study of language and the mind, is usually distinguished from *neurolinguistics*, the study of language and the brain.

Many people date psycholinguistics proper from the mid-1960s, when an upsurge of interest followed on from the work of Noam CHOMSKY, who argued that language was likely to be genetically programmed. Chomsky's ideas triggered an avalanche of work by both linguists and psychologists on CHILD LANGUAGE ACQUISITION, and also an interest in finding out whether his theory of transformational-generative

grammar had 'psychological reality', in the sense of reflecting the way people store or process language. Much of this early work turned out to be somewhat naïve and had disappointing results. Because Chomsky repeatedly revised his theories, a number of psychologists decided that linguistic theory was too changeable to provide a secure basis for their work. The field has therefore become somewhat splintered, even though it continues to expand. Considerable progress has been made in major areas like CHILD LANGUAGE ACQUISITION, speech comprehension, and speech production.

**Child language acquisition**. Children all over the world show similarities in the way they acquire language, whose development appears to be maturationally controlled (pre-programmed to emerge at a particular point in development, providing that the environment is normal and the child unimpaired). Moreover, at each stage, child language is not just a substandard form of adult language, but an independent system with rules of its own. The nature of the genetic input is still under discussion, as is the question of how children abandon immature rules, such as *What kitty can eat?* for *What can kitty eat?*, since they are apparently impervious to direct corrections. See LANGUAGE ACQUISITION DEVICE.

**Speech comprehension**. Understanding speech is now known to be an active rather than a passive process, in which hearers reconstruct the intended message, based on outline clues and their own expectations. This can be demonstrated by presenting them with a confusing sentence such as *Anyone who shoots ducks out of the line of fire* (Any person who uses a gun gets down quickly out of the line of fire). This is a so-called *garden path sentence*, in which hearers are 'led up the garden path' (misled) as they try to impose their expectations of a subject–verb–object pattern on a sentence which requires a different interpretation. Further evidence of the active nature of comprehension comes from experiments with homonyms, such as *It's a rose/They all rose*, when all meanings of a linguistic form turn out to be briefly considered before the unwanted ones are suppressed.

**Speech production**. Producing speech is a complex procedure, in which future stretches of speech are prepared while others are being uttered, as shown by slips of the tongue such as *The curse has walked for you* (The course has worked for you). At the same time, more than one candidate is possibly being considered for each word slot: in an error such as *I looked in the calendar* (catalogue), the speaker has possibly activated several three-syllable words beginning with *ca-*, narrowed it down to those involving lists, then accidentally suppressed the wrong one. See MALAPROPISM, SLIP OF THE TONGUE. An important issue is to discover not only how the mind activates a required word or construction, but also how it suppresses the numerous alternatives which are subconsciously considered.

**PUBLIC SCHOOL ENGLISH**. The English language as used in the public (in fact private) boarding- and day-schools of Britain, and especially England, the foremost of which are Eton, Winchester, Westminster, Harrow, Rugby, Charterhouse, and Shrewsbury ('the Seven Public Schools'). The variety is distinguished primarily by the so-called *public school accent* (known technically as RECEIVED PRONUNCIATION) and to some extent by *public school slang*, which tends to vary from school to school. See PUBLIC SCHOOL PRONUNCIATION, RECEIVED STANDARD AND MODIFIED STANDARD.

**PUBLIC SCHOOL PRONUNCIATION**, short form *PSP*. The name chosen by Daniel JONES for the model of English in his ENGLISH PRONOUNCING DICTIONARY (1917). In the edition of 1926 he changed it to RECEIVED PRONUNCIATION (*RP*). See PUBLIC SCHOOL ENGLISH.

**PUERTO RICO**, formerly *Porto Rico*, a name still often used in the US. The easternmost island of the Greater Antilles. Languages: SPANISH and English (official). Originally inhabited by Carib and Arawak Indians, the island was visited by Columbus in 1493 and was a Spanish colony until ceded to the US in 1898. In 1952, Puerto Rico became a semi-autonomous Commonwealth in association with the US; discussion as to whether the island should seek to become a state of the Union, become an independent nation, or maintain the status quo tends to dominate local politics. The English of Puerto Ricans at home and in the US ranges from that of the learner to the native speaker; like *CHICANO ENGLISH*, it presents difficulties in distinguishing the

usage of individuals from that of groups. The American linguist Rose Nash has characterized Puerto Rican usage as ranging through four types: English comparable to standard usage in the US and other anglophone Caribbean communities; SPANGLISH, which adds Spanish to English, as in lexical CODE-SWITCHING ('He has that special *manera de ser*') and adaptations from Spanish ('Please *prove* the light', from *probar* to test; 'I *assisted to* the *reunion*', from *asistir* to attend, *reunión* meeting); *Englañol*, which adds English to Spanish, as in lexical code-switching ('Se solicitan dos *clerk typists*'), and is common among bilingual adults; Spanish comparable to standard usage elsewhere in Latin America. See AMERICAN ENGLISH, CARIBBEAN ENGLISH.

**PUN**, also **paronomasia** [Stress: 'pa-ro-no-MAY-si-a']. **1.** The conflating of HOMONYMS and near-homonyms to produce a humorous effect: (in speech and writing) *Is life worth living?—It depends on the liver*; (in speech alone) *At his funeral, four of his drinking companions carried the bier/beer*. **2.** A comparable play on words and phrases with similar sounds, sometimes requiring the (often forced) adaptation of one word or phrase to fit the other: *My wife's gone to the West Indies.—Jamaica?* (Did you make her?)—*No, it was her own idea*. In the 16–17c, puns were common among dramatists and writers. In SHAKESPEARE's *Romeo and Juliet*, when Mercutio is dying, he says, 'Ask for me tomorrow and you shall find me a grave man.' In *Macbeth*, when Lady Macbeth plans to incriminate King Duncan's attendants in his murder, she says: 'If he do bleed, I'll gild the faces of the grooms withal, for it must seem their guilt (gilt).' On this liberal approach to puns, Ernest Gowers has observed (in his 1965 edition of Henry Fowler's *Modern English Usage*): 'Now that we regard puns merely as exercises in jocularity, and a pretty debased form even of that, we are apt to be jarred by the readiness of Shakespeare's characters to make them at what seem to us most unsuitable moments.'

The pun lost status in English, despite (or perhaps because of) a wealth of homonyms. In the 18c, Joseph Addison considered puns false wit, and increasingly since then critics have taken the same view. Currently, puns are widely considered so low a form of wit that they prompt a ritual groan, but despite this apparent disapproval the pun continues to thrive. They are, for example, common as a means of attracting attention in journalism and commerce: (1) In newspaper headlines: *Honoring a Pole Apart* (*Time*, Oct, 1980), on Nobel Prize winner Czesław Misłosz; *Rejoycing with the Ulysses set* (*International Herald Tribune*, 22 June 1984), on James Joyce's novel *Ulysses*; *Regimental ties* (*Observer*, 6 Oct. 1985), a title for reviews of military books. (2) In the names of businesses: *Lettuce Entertain You* (a restaurant); *Curl Up and Dye* (a hair stylist); *Molly's Blooms* (a Dublin florist, playing on the name of the Joycean character Molly Bloom). Part of the problem of the pun, however, is straining for effect, working with near-puns rather than with puns properly so called: as the woman said when she received greenery instead of flowers, 'with fronds like these, who needs anemones?' See DOUBLE MEANING, HUMOUR, JOURNALESE, PLAYING WITH WORDS.

## ■ PUNCTUATION ──────── ■

The practice in WRITING and PRINT of using a set of marks to regulate texts and clarify their meanings, principally by separating or linking words, phrases, and clauses, and by indicating parentheses and asides. Until the 18c, punctuation was closely related to spoken delivery, including pauses to take breath, but in more recent times has been based mainly on grammatical structure. There are two extremes in its use: *heavy punctuation* and *light punctuation*. In the 18–19c, people tended to punctuate heavily, especially in their use of commas. Currently, punctuation is more sparing, but individuals and house styles vary in what they consider necessary; the same writer may punctuate more heavily or lightly for some purposes than for others.

**Origins**. In antiquity and the early Middle Ages, points were used, either singly or in combination, to separate sentences, or in some cases (such as Roman inscriptions) to separate words. Key figures in the development of punctuation up to 1600 are St Jerome in the 5c AD (in Latin translations of the Bible), Alcuin in the 8c (Anglo-Saxon tutor at the court of the Emperor Charlemagne, responsible for a new spelling and punctuation system for biblical and liturgical manuscripts), two Venetian printers (grandfather and grandson) both named Aldus Manutius in the 15c–16c (who developed a system using marks equivalent to

the present-day PERIOD, COLON, SEMICOLON, and COMMA), and the Elizabethan critic George Puttenham (whose *Arte of English Poesie*, 1589, included advice on punctuation as a means of marking a text for sense and metre). The declamatory basis for punctuation was, however, replaced in the 17c by the syntactic approach of the playwright and grammarian Ben Jonson (incorporated posthumously in his *English Grammar* of 1640). Before the 17c, and especially in the work of William CAXTON and other early printers, punctuation was haphazard and erratic, with little attention paid to syntax.

**Older terms and marks**. Most of the principal terms and marks now in use in English date from the 15–16c, and some of the names are first attested in the writing of Puttenham or his contemporaries. Most are of Greek origin, and referred originally not to marks but to the sections of text that they marked off. For example, the terms *colon* and *comma* originally denoted the parts of a line or SENTENCE in verse, not prose: a *kôlon* was at first a part of a strophe (a section of a poem), and only later came to refer, by analogy, to a clause in a sentence; a *kómma* (from *kóptein* to cut) was a 'piece cut off' (a short clause). The term APOSTROPHE (from *apó* away, *stréphein* to turn) denoted a mark of 'turning away' (elision), and the term HYPHEN (from *huphén* in one) was used by the grammarians of Alexandria to denote a symbol that links elements meant to be read as one word. The use of the hyphen to divide words at the ends of lines of text dates from the 14c, and evolved from a marginal tick or check mark used to show that the final word of a line was not complete. Eventually, the terms for sections of text were transferred to the signs that mark the sections off one from another; no one now calls a phrase a *comma* or a clause a *colon*, nor do the marks now precisely relate to such segments of text. Generally, however, the historical connection continues.

**More recent terms and marks**. Other terms are more recent and have superseded older equivalents. The Greek-derived PERIOD came to refer to a punctuation mark around 1600, another example of a term that originally referred to sentence structure (in this case, a complete sentence). The terms STOP and *full stop*, for the same mark, date from about the same time: both occur in Shakespeare with reference to the ending of a speech or discourse: for example, in *The Merchant of Venice* (3. 1. 17), 'come, the full stop'. Earlier terms were POINT (found in Chaucer and still in use, especially in the terminology of printing) and the Latin *punctus*. *Full point* has also long been in use. Currently, *period* is the common usage in AmE and *full stop* in BrE. The term QUESTION MARK has been used for less than a century: the earlier term was *mark/point of interrogation* (late 16c). It is a descendant of the *punctus interrogativus*, one of the marks found in 10–13c liturgical manuscripts, where it indicated inflection of the voice. The terms *mark/note of exclamation* and SEMICOLON both date from the 17c. The term DASH, which originally meant 'a blow', reached its present meaning in punctuation via the sense 'hasty stroke of the pen', often the case in writing. *Bracket* is not attested in this context until the 18c; the earlier term *parenthesis* (which continues in use, usually in the plural) generally refers also to the part of the sentence that the punctuation delimits, but in AmE is also used for what are in BrE called *round brackets*. The symbols now in use have evolved from many centuries of practice. The points derive from classical practice, the *comma* was a development of the late medieval *virgule* or *stroke* (/), also used as a separator, and the *semicolon* came into use in the Byzantine era; in Greek, it was and is used to mark a question.

**Uses: linking and separating**. Currently, punctuation serves to clarify the meaning of written language by marking strings of words into associated groups. It is based mainly on grammatical structure and has both a *linking function* and a *separating function*: linking in the listing use of commas as in *They bought a newspaper, two magazines, and a cassette*; separating in the short sentences *We didn't know. But they knew from the start*.

*Points and commas*. The marks most commonly used are the point/period/full stop and the comma. These generally signal or establish boundaries, the period marking out sentences and the comma marking out associated words within sentences. The single comma may cause difficulty because it is a flexible and often optional mark and has applications that need to be weighed carefully in a specific piece of writing. Usage varies as to its inclusion in statements such as *a large, untidy house* and *a little*

*black dog*: it is generally included when the notions underlying the words are of different kinds, as with *large* and *untidy* (whereas *little* and *black* go together in describing the type of dog in question). As a rule of thumb, if *and* can be inserted idiomatically between the adjectives, a comma tends to be used (*a large and untidy house*, therefore *a large, untidy house*); but if *and* cannot be so inserted, a comma is not used (*\*a little and black dog*, therefore *a little black dog*). Paired commas are more straightforward; they mark parenthesis in ways similar to dashes and brackets, although with less effect. Note the increased emphasis on the words 'and helpful' in the following:

(1) People in the north are more friendly and helpful than those in the south.

(2) People in the north are more friendly, and helpful, than those in the south.

(3) People in the north are more friendly (and helpful) than those in the south.

(4) People in the north are more friendly—and helpful—than those in the south.

Brackets often replace pairs of commas when the words marked off are added comment, especially explanation: *He is (as he always was) a rebel*. The following extract shows commas, brackets, and dashes used in one fairly long sentence:

The why and wherefore of the scorpion— how it had got on board and came to select his room rather than the pantry (which was a dark place and more what a scorpion would be partial to), and how on earth it managed to drown itself in the ink-well of his writing-desk—had exercised him infinitely.

(Joseph Conrad, *The Secret Sharer*)

*Colons, semicolons, and dashes*. The colon and especially the semicolon are often avoided in writing by hand because of uncertainty as to their precise uses, a view that they are rather formal and old-fashioned, and best left to certain kinds of printed text. In less formal writing, the dash is often a catch-all mark to take the place of both colon and semicolon, obviating the need to distinguish them or think about more subtle kinds of punctuation. They can be effective when used sparingly, in linking thoughts that go more closely together than separate sentences would allow and, in the case of the colon, in leading from one idea to its consequence or logical continuation, especially in the use of the colon at the end of a sentence, leading to a quotation or a list. The following sentences show how a semicolon can link two parallel statements, whereas a colon serves better when the intention is to lead from one thought to the next:

*semicolon*   There was no truth in the accusation; it was totally false.
*colon*   There was no truth in the accusation: they rejected it utterly.

Division into separate sentences, though grammatically satisfactory, implies a separateness (which the voice conveys with a longer pause) that is not always appropriate:

*point*   There was no truth in the accusation. They rejected it utterly.

Compare the following, in which the second sentence is quite distinct:

There was no truth in the accusation.
The other problem was why they had not been warned.

In the following extract, the semicolons provide continuity of thought in the first sentence, with distinctness in the short sentences that follow:

Her husband . . . was intent on listening to a Beethoven symphony on the gramophone and frowned across the room at Maggie to keep her voice down; he made an irritable gesture with his hand to accompany the frown; he was not in the least disenthralled with Maggie; he only wanted to savour the mighty bang-crash and terror of sound which would soon be followed by the sweet 'never mind', so adorable to his ears, of the finale. He was a sentimental man. Maggie and Mary lowered their voices.

(Muriel Spark, *The Takeover*)

Some writers, such as Henry James, are sometimes accused of overusing the semicolon, producing sentences that continue for half a page or more. In the following sentence, however, the colon and commas are effectively used:

The sense of the past revived for him nevertheless as it had not yet done: it made that other time somehow meet the future close, interlocking with it, before his watching eye, as in a long

embrace of arms and lips, and so handling and hustling the present that this poor quantity scarce retained substance enough, scarce remained sufficiently *there*, to be wounded or shocked.

(Henry James, *The Golden Bowl*)

Without careful use of separating punctuation marks, the following, from the same source, would be almost unintelligible:

What had happened, in short, was that Charlotte and he had by a single turn of the wrist of fate—'led up' to indeed, no doubt, by steps and stages that conscious computation had missed—been placed face to face in a freedom that partook, extraordinarily, of ideal perfection, since the magic web had spun itself without their toil, almost without their touch.

***Avoiding ambiguity***. Punctuation also plays an important role in the avoidance of ambiguity or misunderstanding, especially by means of the comma (which separates) and the hyphen (which links), as in *They did not go, because they were lazy* as opposed to *They did not go because they were lazy*, in *twenty-odd people* as opposed to *twenty odd people*, and in sentences like *From then, on meeting a friend he would smile* as opposed to *From then on, meeting a friend was a great pleasure for him*. A carefully entered hierarchy of punctuation adds clarity to a long or complex sentence, as in the following:

I came out of the house, which lay back from the road, and saw them at the end of the path; but instead of continuing towards them, I hid until they had gone.

A period/full stop would also be possible here in the place of the semicolon, but it would break the continuity.

***Hyphen and apostrophe: recent developments***. In everyday use and in ephemeral writing such as newsprint, punctuation is generally less precisely used than in more formal and permanent forms of writing and printing. The use of some marks is declining, especially the hyphen and the apostrophe. The hyphen is currently less common in forming compound words (such as *newspaper*, *worldwide*) and in separating vowels that may have the values of digraphs when placed together (as in *coordinate*, *makeup*). Arguably, the possessive apostrophe is needed only to distinguish number, as in *the girl's books* and *the girls' books*. In other cases, it could be (and increasingly is) dispensed with without any loss of clarity in such phrases as *Johns books* and *their mothers voice*; these are as comprehensible today as they were before the mark was introduced. It is also disappearing in names, such as *Smiths books* and *Lloyds Bank*.

See ASTERISK, DIACRITIC, EXCLAMATION MARK, QUOTATION MARKS, RELATIVE CLAUSE.

**PUNCTUATION MARK**. Any one of a set of conventional marks or characters used in organizing written and printed language, such as a *comma* (,) or an *exclamation mark/point* (!). See PUNCTUATION.

**PURISM**. Scrupulous observance of, or insistence on, purity or correctness in LANGUAGE and STYLE, an attitude often considered by others as excessive. Purists may have specific plans for reforming languages in such areas as spelling, vocabulary, and grammar. One of the earliest English treatises on logic, Ralph Lever's *The Arte of Reason, Rightly Termed Witcraft* (1573), rejected Latinate terms in favour of a native technical vocabulary: in addition to *witcraft*, he coined among other terms *foreset* subject, *backset* predicate, and *gainset* opposite. In the 19c, the philologist William Barnes wrote an English grammar, the *Outline of English Speech-Craft* (1878), using invented vocabulary such as *thought-wording* proposition, *speech-thing* subject, and *timetaking* predicate. Some words did catch on: the rhetorician John Earle (1890) credited the 19c movement with popularizing *openmindedness*, *seamy*, *shaky*, and *unknowable*.

In present-day terms, purists are reformers who seek to root out presumed errors in grammar and usage and offer what they feel to be more correct alternatives. They usually object to the state of the language and/or the direction in which it appears to be going, suspect and disapprove of new words or of old words with new meanings, insist on the literal meaning of words, and insist on logic in usage. In addition, they tend to see themselves individually as acting on behalf of an unclear ultimate authority. There are few self-confessed purists among the critics of the English language today; *purism* is generally a negative term, and by and large *purists* are regarded as hypercorrective extremists. It is not unusual, however, to find grammar and usage critics denying that they are purists while engaging in all the traditional forms of purism. See PLAIN, PURE.

**PURPLE PASSAGE**, also **purple patch**, **purple prose**. A piece of writing marked by a florid, fanciful style:

> There are few of us who have not sometimes wakened before dawn, either after one of those dreamless nights that make us almost enamoured of death, or one of those nights of horror and misshapen joy, when through the chambers of the brain sweep phantoms more terrible than reality itself, and instinct with that vivid life that lurks in all grotesques, and that lends to Gothic art its enduring vitality, this art being, one might fancy, especially the art of those whose minds have been troubled with the malady of reverie.
>
> (from Oscar Wilde, *The Picture of Dorian Gray*, 1890, ch. 11)

See POETIC DICTION.

# Q

[Called 'kew', rhyming with '*few*']. The 17th LETTER of the modern Roman ALPHABET as used for English. It originated as the Phoenician symbol *qop*, which had the value of a voiceless uvular plosive: a *k*-like sound made well back in the mouth. It was initially adopted by the Greeks as *koppa*, to represent /k/ before a back vowel; but classical GREEK preferred the letter *kappa*, the ancestor of *K*, and *koppa* fell into disuse. The Etruscans used three Greek letters, *gamma*, *kappa*, and *koppa*, for variants on /k/. *Koppa* was used specifically before /u/, a practice followed by LATIN, which gave the letter its characteristic curved tail as Q. This letter was little used in OLD ENGLISH, which used the digraph *cw* in words now spelt with *qu*: *cwen/queen*, *cwic/quick*. FRENCH inherited the digraph *qu* from Latin, and after the Norman Conquest it was increasingly used in written English by French-influenced scribes, so that by 1300 *cw* had been supplanted. For a time, *qu* spread further especially in Northern English, to words now spelt with *wh*. This pattern persisted longest in Scots, in which, for example, *what* was written *quhat* until the 18c, and *quh* survives in such surnames as *Colquhoun* ('Cahoon'), *Farquhar* ('Farker'), and *Urquhart* ('Urkart').

**Sound value and occurrence**. (1) In English, *q* has the same value as *k* or hard *c*, and is generally followed by *u*, with the joint pronunciation /kw/: *quaint, quibble*. (2) Loss of /w/ in French led to spelling changes that obscure the common ancestry of such English/French pairs as *quash/casser, quire/cahier*. On the other hand, English has developed *qu* in words that in French had, and still have, *cu*: *esquire/écuyer, squirrel/écureuil*. (3) In English, *qu* typically occurs word-initially before *a, e, i, o* (*quack, quash, quail, quest, queer, quit, quite, quote*) and after *s* (*squat, squeal, squirrel*). (4) Medial *qu* also occurs: *adequate, banquet, equal, frequent, liquid, request*. (5) When the Latin prefix *ad-* precedes *qu*, it is assimilated as *ac*: *acquaint, acquire, acquit*. However, initial *a* sometimes also precedes *qu* without *c* (*aquatic, aquiline*) with no distinction in pronunciation.

**Exotic Q, QU**. (1) Though rarely so used, *q* without *u* has the same value as *k* and as *c* before *a, o, u*. It is used as a TRANSLITERATION of the HEBREW letter *quph* and ARABIC *qaf* (cognate with Phoenician *qop*), both uvular plosives given the value /k/ in everyday English: *Iraq, qaf, Qatar, Qur'ān* (Koran). (2) In the Pinyin script for Chinese, *q* represents the *ch* sound in *cheese*, as in *Qian-long, Qin-huang-dao*: see CHINA. (3) Words that have entered English in recent centuries from Romance languages have mostly kept the value of *qu* as /k/: word-finally with *e* (*arabesque, grotesque, mosque, opaque, picturesque, unique*), medially (*bouquet, coquette, mosquito*), and occasionally initially (*quiche*, but not *queue*), especially in names (*Quezon City* in the Philippines). The recent French LOAN *questionnaire* is sometimes pronounced with /k/, but usually with /kw/ by ANALOGY with the earlier loan *question*. *Quay* is an 18c respelling of *kay* or *key*, by analogy with French *quai*. There is an alternation between /kw/ in *conquest* (compare *quest, request*) and *liquid*, and /k/ in *conquer/conqueror* and *liquor*. (4) In the ACRONYMS *Qantas* (Queensland and Northern Territory Aerial Services) and *QARANC* (Queen Alexandra's Royal Army Nursing Corps) the *q* is pronounced as /kw/, as if followed by a u: 'Kwontas', 'Kwarank'. (5) Forms with medial *cqu* pronounced /k/, include: *lacquer, lacquey* (now *lackey*), and *racquet* (also *racket*). (6) AmE generally has *bark, check, licorice* where BrE keeps the *q* in *barque, cheque, liquorice*.

**QUALIFY**. A traditional term used to indicate that one grammatical unit depends on another: in the phrase *brave attempts*, the adjective *brave* is said to qualify the noun *attempts*; that is, the adjective indicates the 'quality' or nature of the noun. Contemporary GRAMMARS generally use the term *modify*. See MODIFICATION.

**QUANTIFIER**. A category of DETERMINER or PRONOUN used to express quantity. Most quantifiers have a limited distribution that depends on the countability of the nouns they relate to. *Many, a few, few,* and *several* relate only to plural countable nouns (*many* newspapers, *a few drinks, few people, several men*), in contrast to *much, a little, and little,* which relate to uncountable nouns (*much confusion, a little information, little news*). *Enough* can relate to both types of noun (*enough newspapers, enough information*), as can *some* and *any* (*some help, any houses*). However, *some* and *any* can also be used with singular countable nouns with non-quantitative functions: *Some chicken!* means 'What a poor chicken!' or 'What a wonderful chicken!', depending on tone and emphasis; *Any fool knows that* means 'There is nothing special about knowing that'. Distinctions in the use of certain quantifiers are contrastive and subtle: *few newspapers* (not many newspapers), *a few newspapers* (some newspapers); *little* help (virtually no help at all), *a little* help (some help but not much). It is useful to treat *a few* and *a little* as distinct quantifiers and not simply as the indefinite article followed by *few* and *little.* Neither is used with a singular countable noun (*a few raisins, a little rice,* but not \**a raisins,* \**a rice,* \**a few raisin,* \**a little raisin*). In addition, both *little* and *a little* have to be distinguished from the ordinary adjective *little* (small). Ambiguity is possible with nouns that can be both countable and uncountable: out of obvious context, *a little chicken* could mean either a small bird or a small quantity of the meat of a chicken.

*Few* and *little* have negative force, as is shown by the fact that, like negatives, they take positive question tags: *Few of us really think that, do we?* Contrast: *A few people believe that, don't they? Few* and *little* have comparative and superlative forms (*fewer, fewest; less, least*), while *much* and *many* share *more* and *most.* Traditionally, *fewer* and *fewest* have been described as modifying only countable nouns (*fewer houses, the fewest men possible*) and *less* and *least* as modifying only uncountable nouns (*less wine, the least fuel possible*), and many people regard this as the only acceptable USAGE in STANDARD ENGLISH. However, widely throughout the English-speaking world *less* and *least* are used with countable nouns (*less people, the least working hours*), regardless of criticism and in many instances without the least awareness of the basis for the criticism. *Much* tends to be non-assertive in informal English; it prefers negative or interrogative contexts: *We don't have much money, How much money do you need?* In affirmative statements, a quantitative phrase such as *a lot (of)* and *a great deal (of)* is often preferred: *That explains*

a lot (*of what I've heard*) or *That explains a great deal* rather than *That explains much.* Quantifiers can be pre-modified by *very, so, too, as,* as in *very few people, so little help, too many cooks,* and *as much work as possible.* Some words and phrases used as quantifiers can also be used as intensifiers, as in: *much less; many more; a little better; a lot older; a lot too old; a bit too much.* Some of these words are also used for duration and frequency: *We waited a little; They eat a lot.* This can lead to ambiguity; in *She eats a lot* and *He doesn't read much,* if the items are quantifying pronouns, the meaning is *a lot of food* and *a lot of books,* but if they are adverbs of frequency, the meaning is *She's constantly eating* and *He doesn't often read.* Compare NUMBER[1].

**QUANTITY**. In prosody and PHONETICS, a distinction between sounds and syllables based partly on DURATION (length). The concept has traditionally been important in discussing LATIN vowels, whose values are either long or short; it is less important in English. The first syllables of such words as *thimble, bauble, table* tend to have greater duration than short syllables ending in a short vowel (the first syllables of *bubble, nibble*), on account of the durations of the vowels and consonants that they contain. Syllable duration is also conditioned by context, syllables being shortened when unstressed and lengthened in word-final position. All is relative: there are no fixed durations corresponding to 'long' and 'short' respectively. Longer syllables are more able to carry a pitch change or tone, and may for this reason be more likely to attract stress: the long second syllable of *arena* is stressed but the short second syllable of *cinema* is not. Partly because the concept of length is ill defined, and partly because other patterns are involved, some phoneticians consider it preferable to follow the example of the ancient Hindu grammarians and define quantity in terms of *weight* ('heavy' and 'light' syllables) rather than length. See RHYTHM, VOWEL QUANTITY.

# ■ QUEBEC ───────── ■

Also **Québec**. The name of both the largest province of Canada (home of the largest FRENCH-speaking community in North America) and of its capital city (founded by Samuel Champlain in 1608). Out of a population of *c*.6m, 82% speak French, 16%

English. ITALIAN and GREEK are prominent immigrant languages, and Cree and Mohawk are prominent indigenous languages. The first Europeans to settle in the region were the French in the 17c, and their colony was known as *Nouvelle France* (New France) until well into the 18c. In its heyday, the French empire in North America stretched from the valley of the St Lawrence down the Ohio and Mississippi rivers to the Gulf of Mexico, limiting British expansion west. In the late 20c, however, Quebec is the only politically significant French-speaking community in North America.

**Quebec French**. The French of Quebec descends from the speech of 17c Normandy and Picardy. Distinctive and varied, it has a broad form known as *joual* (pronounced 'zhwal': a variant of *cheval* horse). The traditional standard of education and the media has been that of Paris, often referred to as *le français international*. Local French of all varieties and most social levels has been stigmatized both in France and in Quebec as a patois marred by its accents, its ARCHAISMS, and its ANGLICISMS.

**Quebec English**. British Empire Loyalists from the US, after the end of the War of Independence in 1783, were the first significant English-speaking settlers in Quebec. They founded the Eastern Townships southeast of Montreal. By 1831, ANGLOPHONES of British descent were in the majority in Montreal itself, but an influx of rural francophones, who filled the ranks of the urban working class, had by 1867 reversed that trend. By 1981, 66% of the city's population was French-speaking. Such facts explain why English is used in Montreal (and more generally in Quebec) is not as homogeneous as other Canadian regional Englishes. Rather it exists as a continuum, from long-established unilingual anglophones broadly similar to anglophones in Ontario through bilinguals of various kinds to francophones using English as a second language. Until 1970, Montreal was the economic capital of Canada, but many controlling anglophone companies relocated, especially in Toronto, as a result of mounting separatist pressures in the 1970s and early 1980s among the French majority and under the government of the secessionist Parti Québécois (1976–85).

Much has been written in French on the effects of English on French in Quebec. In such works, the dominating role of English in North America has generally been considered pernicious, and francophones have often been urged to *éviter les anglicismes* (avoid Anglicisms) and not *commettre un anglicisme* (commit an Anglicism) in their French. The French of Quebec and Canada as a whole, however, continues to be heavily influenced by both CANADIAN ENGLISH and AmE, as for example the widespread use of *bienvenu(e)*, the equivalent of *You're welcome* (in response to *merci* thank you), rather than the *de rien* (It's nothing) of France. There has been little comparable concern in Quebec about the effects of French on English and there have been few studies of Quebec English. However, the research that has been done indicates that in Montreal, for socio-economic reasons, English was until *c*.1975 regarded in both communities as the language of prestige. In the last 15 years, however, under the impact of pro-French legislation, French has gained greatly in prestige. In addition, English in Montreal tends to favour the norms of AmE more than English in Ontario, and Montrealers are less likely to employ Canadian Raising in their speech.

The most marked feature of local English is the influence of French. Many expressions have simply moved into English, such as: *autoroute* highway, *caisse populaire* credit union, *depanneur* convenience store, corner shop, and *subvention* subsidy. Anglophones who speak French constantly use such loan expressions as: *give a conference* give a lecture (from *donner une conférence*), *sc(h)olarity* schooling (from *scolarité*), and *syndicate* a trade union (from *syndicat*). The Gallicisms of francophones when speaking English range from such easily grasped expressions as *collectivity* (for *community*) and *annex* (for the *appendix* to a document) to a commonplace misuse of *faux amis*, such as *deceive* in *I was deceived when she didn't come* (from *décevoir* to disappoint), *reunion* in *We have a reunion at 5 o'clock* (from *réunion* a meeting), and *souvenir* in *We have a good souvenir of our trip to Louisiana* (from *souvenir* a memory). See CAJUN, CANADIAN LANGUAGES, DIALECT IN CANADA, MÉTIS.

**QUEEN'S ENGLISH**. See KING'S ENGLISH.

# ■ QUESTION ─────── ■

In general usage, a form of language that invites a reply, marked in spoken English with specific patterns of intonation and in written and printed English by a closing QUESTION MARK (?). In GRAMMAR, a term in the classification of sentences, referring to types distinguished by form and function from such other sentence types as *statement* and *command*. If the term is used functionally, sentences said with a rising intonation (*You don't believe me?*) can be included, while rhetorical questions (*How could I possibly forget!*) and exclamations in INTERROGATIVE form (*Isn't he lucky!*) are not. In formal terms, questions are of three main types:

**Yes–no questions**. Questions to which the answer could be a *Yes* or *No*, with or without further detail, as with *Did you telephone Robert?* Formally, they begin with a verb: *be, have*, or *do*, or a modal verb, followed by the subject: *Are you all right?*; *Do you understand?*; *Have you enough money?/Do you have enough money?*; *Will you telephone Robert?*; *Can I help you?* Their usual intonation pattern is a rising TONE on and after the tonic syllable, but, when rhetorical or emphatic, they are said with a falling tone.

**Wh-questions**. Questions beginning with an interrogative word. With the exception of *how*, these all begin with the letters *wh-*: *who(ever), whom, whose, what(ever), which, when, where(ver), why(ever)*: *Why did he leave and where has he gone?* Such questions are sometimes called *information questions* because they are seeking new information. They contrast with *yes–no* questions, but like them usually involve inversion of subject and verb. Their usual intonation pattern is a falling tone on and after the tonic syllable, but when rhetorical or emphatic are said with a rising tone.

**Alternative questions**. These offer a choice of answer: *Are you expecting Robert or his brother?*; *Shall I telephone or write?*; *Who are you expecting—Robert or his brother?* If the question begins with a verb, the usual intonation pattern is a rising tone on each of the alternatives before the last and then a falling tone on the last alternative. If the question begins with an interrogative word, the usual pattern is a fall on the first part, followed by the same pattern in the second part as for a question beginning with a verb.

**Inversion**. All three types generally involve INVERSION of the subject and an auxiliary or modal verb. This inversion applies also to questions containing *be* as the sole verb (*Are you ready?*) and in BrE sometimes to *have*

(*Have you any wool?* as opposed to *Do you have any wool?* and *Have you got any wool?*). All other verbs use *do* if there is no auxiliary or modal: *Where does she live?*; *What did you do?* The only exception to this inversion rule is when *who, what*, or *which* is part of the subject. Contrast: *Who told you that?* (where *who* is subject) and *Who(m) did you tell?*

**QUESTION MARK**, also especially AmE **interrogation mark, interrogation point**. The PUNCTUATION mark (?). Its primary use is to show that a preceding word, phrase, or sentence is a direct QUESTION: *Do you want more to eat?* It is not used in indirect speech, because a reported question is part of a statement: *I asked you whether you wanted more to eat.* The question mark is sometimes repeated in informal usage or followed by an exclamation mark/point in order to indicate a specially strong question (*What did you say??*; *What did you say?!*). It is also used, often in brackets, to express doubt or uncertainty about a word or phrase that immediately follows or precedes it: *Julius Caesar, born* (?) *100 BC*; *They were then seen leaving the house (in tears?) and walking away.*

**QUESTION TAG**. A short QUESTION tagged on to the end of a statement (DECLARATIVE sentence). Some languages have an invariable question tag that can be added to almost any statement: FRENCH *n'est-ce pas?* (isn't it?); SPANISH *verdad?* (truly?). In IndE and some other varieties, *isn't it?* is used in this way (*You are going tomorrow, isn't it?*), while *yes* and *no* are used for confirmation (*You are coming, yes?*; *She is going there, no?*). In many kinds of English, an enclitic tag is used for confirmation and other purposes: *eh?* is a SHIBBOLETH of CanE and common in BrE (*You like that kind of thing, eh?*), and in some varieties of ScoE *eh no?* is common (*You're comin as well, eh no?—aren't you?*). Many AmE speakers use *huh?* or *uh?* (*You coming, huh?*). Other common informal tags are *right?* and *OK?* (*He'll be there, right? I'll see you soon, OK?*).

STANDARD ENGLISH throughout the world requires the question tag to correspond to the subject and verb of the preceding sentence. Such tags consist of a single-word verb (*be* or *have* as main verbs, an auxiliary, or a modal) plus a subject pronoun, as in *It's a nice day today, isn't it?*, *You have enough books, haven't you* (especially BrE) and *You have enough books, don't you?* (especially AmE), *She went home last night, didn't she?*, and *You could help if you wanted, couldn't you?* Question tags are normally negative after a positive statement, and vice versa. When spoken on the rising tone of *yes–no* questions, they may genuinely be asking for information or be expressing surprise or uncertainty: *You're not going to tell them, are you?* However, tags are more usually spoken on the falling intonation of statements, to invite or expect agreement with the preceding statement: *Lovely day we're having, aren't we?*; *It's been a mild winter, hasn't it?* Question tags can also be used with imperatives: *Wait a minute, will you?*; *Send us a postcard, won't you?*; *Let's go together, shall we?* Another possibility is for the tag to agree with a subordinate clause: *I don't think they'll come now, will they?*; *That's a nice mess you've got us into, haven't you?* Occasionally, a positive statement is followed by a positive tag, with a rising intonation. This may simply signify an inference or even a request for clarification (*He'll be 21 next year, will he?*), but the structure often suggests sarcasm or suspicion: *So he's innocent, is he?*; *It fell off the back of a truck, did it?* (implication: I doubt that very much). See TAG QUESTION.

■ **QUIRK, (Charles) Randolph** ─────────── ■

British linguist. Born in the Isle of Man in 1920, he studied at U. College London, and was awarded the degrees BA, MA, Ph.D., D.Litt. from the U. of London. He was a lecturer in English at UCL (1947–52), Reader in English Language and Literature at the U. of Durham (1954–8), Professor of English Language at Durham (1958–60) and at UCL (1960–8), and Quain Professor of English Language and Literature at UCL (1968–81). He chaired a governmental Committee of Inquiry which reformed the training of speech therapists in the UK (HMSO, 1972), served as Vice-Chancellor of the U. of London (1981–5), as President of the British Academy (1985–9), was awarded the CBE in 1976, was knighted in 1985, and raised to the peerage as Lord Quirk of Bloomsbury in 1994. His scholarly activities cover a wide range of studies in the English language and related subjects. They include: the PHONOLOGY, MORPHOLOGY, VOCABULARY, and SYNTAX of OLD ENGLISH; editions of Old Icelandic texts; the language of DICKENS and SHAKESPEARE; the teaching of the English language; lexical studies of English in vari-

ous periods; English as an international language; research and publications on modern English syntax.

He founded the *SURVEY OF ENGLISH USAGE* in 1959, continuing as its Director until 1981. At this research unit, he supervised the compilation and analysis of a corpus of spoken and written samples of the language used by adult educated native speakers of BrE. In association with researchers at the Survey, he developed techniques for eliciting usage and attitudes to usage. The analyses derived from the data in the Survey corpus and in elicitation experiments have resulted in numerous publications by Quirk himself and by scholars from all over the world, in particular the two major reference grammars on which he collaborated: *A Grammar of Contemporary English* (1972) and *A Comprehensive Grammar of the English Language* (1985). His approach to research has been theoretically eclectic and focused on the functions of language. He assigns priority to the meticulous examination of language data and to total accountability of the data. The pursuit of these priorities has induced him to assert the prominence of ANALOGY and gradience in the functioning of the language system; language categories are viewed as overlapping rather than discrete, and peripheral subcategories or individual items are shown to share to varying extents the features of the central members of a category. In his view, the description of English must take account of the stylistic variation occasioned by the relationship between participants in a DISCOURSE, the medium, the educational and social standing of the participants, and the subject matter of the discourse. He envisages the English language as having a common core shared by regional and stylistic varieties.

■ **QUOTATION** ─────────── ■

The act or practice of repeating a phrase, sentence, or passage from a book, speech, or other source, an occasion of doing this, and the words used: *a speech full of quotations*. The informal noun *quote* is also widely used, especially by journalists: *Can I have a quote on that? That's the quote of the week.* In classical and medieval times, reciting and quoting were closely related; because books were rare and not always at hand when needed, it was necessary to memorize and be able to repeat large parts of important texts, especially scripture. Unlettered people, the vast majority, could only learn them if the literate could quote them *verbatim* (Latin: word for word). Preachers and orators would use and identify specific quotations for insertion in their sermons and speeches, to add weight and substance to what they said. When necessary, especially in matters of religion and law, texts would be produced, places of reference marked, and relevant sections read aloud or pointed out. Because of this, *quotation* also referred to the provision of references to parts of texts, to the listing of such references, and to copying out quotable excerpts by hand.

**Quotation, plagiarism, allusion**. The concept of quotation depends on identifying (briefly or in detail) the source to which reference is made and from which words have been taken. It also usually requires justification, explicitly stated or implicitly accepted: one quotes in order to substantiate a claim, bolster an argument, illustrate a point, demonstrate a truth, catch out an opponent, amuse an audience, or impress one's listeners or readers. A spoken quotation may be presented in a variety of ways: for example, with a lead-in that relates quotation to topic, followed by something on the person to be quoted, then the quoted matter itself, as in: 'Talking about the Canadian predicament, the former prime minister Mackenzie King put it this way: "If some countries have too much history, we have too much geography."' Another possibility is: 'The humorist Stephen Leacock described the matter as follows in 1994: "In Canada, we have enough to do keeping up with two spoken languages without trying to invent slang, so we just go right ahead and use English for literature, Scotch for sermons, and American for conversations."' The written forms used here to frame these quotations show how they are conventionally integrated into running text. Quotations in isolation, however, are usually set apart in paragraphs of their own, with plenty of white space, have the quoted matter first, then the name of the originator, often followed by such information as source and date, all of which may be presented in a variety of formats. For example:

*Without quotation marks and with a dash, etc.*

America is God's Crucible, the great Melting-Pot where all the races of Europe are melting and re-forming!—Israel Zangwill, *The Melting Pot*, 1908.

*Without quotation marks and with parentheses, etc.*

The most important thing to know about Americans—the attitude which *truly* distinguishes them from the British and explains much superficially odd behaviour—is that *Americans believe that death is optional* ( Jane Walmsley, 'A Native's Guide to Ameri-think', *Company*, Mar. 1984).

*With quotation marks (British style), and both a dash and parentheses, etc.*

'The Irish are a fair people—they never speak well of one another'—Samuel JOHNSON, quoted in James Boswell, *Life of Johnson* (1775, vol. 2, p. 307).

*With quotation marks (American style), and both a dash and parentheses, etc.*

"And while we don't exactly hate New Zealanders, we're not exactly fond of each other. While they regard us as vulgar yobboes, almost Yank-like, we think of them as secondhand, recycled Poms."—Phillip Adams, *The Age* (Melbourne: 18 June 1977).

If sources are not identified by such means as these, and the borrowed materials is substantial and presented explicitly or implicitly as a writer's own, the person who does so may have engaged in PLAGIARISM, the theft of someone else's words. If, however, the unassigned quotation is brief, appropriate to a situation, and belongs by more or less general agreement to a shared cultural tradition, it is neither quotation nor plagiarism, but ALLUSION: the oblique and entirely legitimate reference to a source, part of whose effect is the pleasure (or frustration) listeners or readers feel as they identify (or fail to identify) the source in question. In addition, many expressions that belong entirely in the public domain, such as proverbs and idioms, may have a quotation-like flavour, or be quotations so often quoted that they have become detached from their sources. This is generally the case, for example, with *The pen is mightier than the sword*, a statement as proverbial as *A stitch in time saves nine*. It may be thought to have a Biblical or Shakespearian feel to it, but comes from the work of the 19c English politician, novelist, and poet Edward Bulwer-Lytton:

Beneath the rule of men entirely great
The pen is mightier than the sword.
(*Richelieu, or the Conspiracy*, a play in blank
verse, 1838, 2.2)

**Misquotation and non-quotation**. Until
the 20c, quotation was largely from written
and printed sources; in recent decades,
however, quotations have increasingly been
taken from live performance, especially
speeches and interviews, the taking of excerpts being done in shorthand or, more recently still, with the help of tape recorders.
As a result, 'quotees' are increasingly aware
of the risks of being *misquoted* or may take
refuge from the consequences of what they
have said by claiming that they were misquoted. People in the public eye may seek to
establish ground rules for interviews and
statements to the media: these range from
the more informal *Don't quote me (on this)* to
the more formal *This is off the record* and perhaps the requirement that a statement be
*unattributed*, except perhaps to 'a usually
reliable source'. Such requirements may or
may not be respected; they may or may not
even be meant to be respected, but intended
instead to serve as an indirect way of gaining publicity.

**The 'quotation industry'**. Out of the tradition of quoting chapter and verse from
the BIBLE, of quoting lines from great writers and orators, and of quoting the remarks
of the famous, there has grown a minor
industry that marshals and highlights the
comments, aphorisms, quips, *bons mots*, and
verbal *faux pas* of the celebrated, notorious,
or fashionable. It includes: (1) The compiling and publishing of anthologies of observations by famous people, works promoted
and purchased as a means through which
public speaking may be enlivened ('quotes
for all occasions') or readers can enjoy instances of language used to good effect. (2)
Brief, topical features in newspapers and
other periodicals with such names as *Quotes
of the Week* or *They Said It*, listing significant,
thought-provoking, egregious, or fatuous
observations or remarks made by people
currently in the limelight. The existence of
such items not only requires journalists to
find material to fill them but may prompt
public or would-be public figures to formulate snappy one-liners that might be
listed and attributed. See DIALOGUE, DIRECT
AND INDIRECT SPEECH, ELLIPSIS, PROSE,
PUNCTUATION.

# ■ QUOTATION MARKS ──────── ■

Also less formally **quote marks**, **quotes**;
in BrE also called **inverted commas** and
informally **speech marks**. PUNCTUATION
marks used to open and close quoted matter
and direct SPEECH either *single* (' ') or *double
quotation marks* (" "). Double marks are traditionally associated with American PRINTING
practice (as in the Chicago style) and single
marks with British practice (as in the
Oxford and Cambridge styles), but there is
much variation in practice; double marks
are more often found in British texts before
the 1950s, and are usual in handwriting.
Quotation marks are a relatively recent invention and were not common before the
19c. Traditional texts of the Bible do not use
them and do not suffer from the omission.
Quotation marks can be untidy, especially
in combination with other punctuation
marks and when marks occur within
marks. Some writers have therefore avoided
them, notably James Joyce, who used dashes
to introduce direct speech. Single quotation
marks are tidier, less obtrusive, and less
space-consuming than double marks, and
for this reason are increasingly preferred in
Britain and elsewhere in printing styles,
especially in newspapers. The uses of
quotation marks for direct speech, quoted
material, and other purposes are discussed
separately below; there is considerable overlap among the various categories.

**Direct speech**. Quotation marks indicate
direct speech (that is, the words of a speaker
quoted, more or less exactly) in such forms
as BrE *He said, 'Come with me'* and AmE *He
said, "Come with me"*, and BrE *'Come with me,' he
said* and AmE *"Come with me," he said*. The
marks are normally placed outside other
punctuation in sentences of direct speech,
such as a final period or full stop, or a
comma when the direct speech is
interrupted:

> BrE   'Go away,' she said, 'and don't
>        come back.'
> AmE   "Go away," she said, "and don't
>        come back."

In BrE, they are often placed inside other
punctuation marks when they refer to a
part of the sentence that is contained
within the other marks, as in *When you said
'Go away', I was shocked*. In AmE, however,
the quotation marks are normally placed
outside other punctuation in all circumstances, as in *When you said "Go away," I was*

*shocked*. Quotation marks are not used in indirect (reported) speech, except occasionally when the enclosed words are regarded as equivalent to a quotation, as in:

BrE He then declared that 'I was incompetent'.

AmE He then declared that "I was incompetent."

In BrE, the quotation marks are placed within other punctuation because the words referred to are a quotation within the structure of the whole sentence.

Opening marks are given when direct speech is resumed after an interruption such as a reporting clause, as in the examples above. Normally, a COMMA or other punctuation mark separates the ending or resumption of direct speech from its interruption:

BrE 'Certainly not,' he exclaimed. 'I would sooner die.'

AmE "Certainly not," he exclaimed. "I would sooner die."

Different practices have been advocated from time to time, but the practice described here now prevails. In extended DIALOGUE, the words of each speaker are normally given on a new line when the speaker changes. Speakers are often not named after their first appearance in a run of speech, except to describe some special feature or manner of speaking (as in *he exclaimed* or *she said proudly*). The following is from BrE:

'Where is Joseph?'
'I don't know.'
'Why isn't he here?'
'I don't know.'
'You drove out with him last night.'
'Yes.'
'You returned alone.'
'Yes.'
'You had a rendezvous with the rebels.'
'You're talking nonsense. Nonsense.'
'I could shoot you very easily. It would be a pleasure for me. You would have been resisting arrest.'
'I don't doubt it. You must have had plenty of practice.'
(Graham Greene, *The Comedians*, 1960)

The following is from AmE:

"He's a dear old friend," she said to Spizer. "We've known each other since we were kids."

"Childhood sweethearts?" Spizer said generously.
"No, just dear friends."
"I did have a dinner date with Marty," Martha said. "If you had only called."
"Not a word more," Spizer said. "I'm taking both of you to dinner. How many real friends do we have in this world? And you don't know," he said to Stephan, "how lucky you are."
(Howard Fast, *The Immigrants*, 1977)

**Headings and titles**. Quotation marks are also generally used to designate cited headings and titles, which are in effect equivalent to quotations. Printing practice varies in this regard, italics being widely used to denote titles of books, journals, and newspapers, and quotation marks to denote titles of individual articles or sections within larger works, as in: See Chapter 3, 'The Middle Ages', and J. Smith, 'Some Observations on Magic and Ritual in the Middle Ages,' in *Journal of the Historical Society* 3 (1967), 6–16. In many scientific works, however, titles of papers are printed without quotation marks.

**Highlighting**. Quotation marks may also serve to alert the reader to a special or unusual word or use of a word, such as a foreign expression (as in *You need a lot of 'savoir faire'*), or to indicate a word or use that is not the writer's own (as in *Several 'groupies' followed the band on their tour*). The latter usage is often formally referred to as *scare quotes*, because the marks frequently serve as a warning to the reader that there is something unusual or dubious (in the opinion of the writer) about the quoted word or phrase. In CONVERSATION, speakers may indicate their use of such scare quotes by making finger movements that suggest quotation marks: see QUOTE UNQUOTE. This use is close to quotation, the implication being something like *Several groupies, as they are often called, followed the band on their tour*.

**Special conventions**. **1.** When quoted material or direct speech extends continuously over several paragraphs, new paragraphs begin with opening quotation marks, and closing marks are given only at the end of the last paragraph. **2.** When quoted material occurs within other quoted material, BrE and AmE adopt opposite conventions. The normal practice in BrE is to use single quotation marks in the first (enclosing) instance and double marks in the second (enclosed) instance: *He asked, 'Have you seen "The Laughing Cavalier"?'* In AmE, double marks are commonly used in the first instance and single in the second instance: *He asked, "Have you seen 'The Laughing Cavalier'?"* In both cases, the question mark comes after the marks that relate to the quoted names, and before the mark or marks that close the sentence of speech. See DASH, DIRECT AND INDIRECT SPEECH.

**QUOTE UNQUOTE**. As a convention of dictation, a speaker may warn that a QUOTATION is coming by saying *quote* and indicate that it has been completed by saying *unquote*. The usage has been carried over into conversation and public speaking: 'He expressed the personal opinion that the picture was quote great for America unquote' (Peter Ustinov, *Loser*, 1961). Here, the words are kept apart, but in a further development they come together as a phrase, *quote unquote*, used to indicate that what has just been said would be in QUOTATION MARKS if written: 'If you're a liberal, quote unquote, they're suspicious of you' (*The Random House Dictionary*, 1987). The practice, in either form, distances speakers from words that they wish to emphasize are not their own.

# R

[Called 'ar']. The 18th LETTER of the Roman ALPHABET as used for English. It originated in Phoenician and was adopted and adapted by the Greeks as *rho* (P). When the Romans adopted it, they adapted it further to distinguish *R* from *P*.

**Sound values**. In English, the letter *r* is pronounced in different ways in different accents, but normally has only one sound value in the speech of any individual. As well as occurring before and after vowels (*rear*, *roar*), *r* is also heard after initial consonants as in *brown*, *crown*, *frown*, *ground*, *proud*, *shroud*, *trout*, *thrown*, and after *s* + consonant as in *spray*, *stray*, *scream*. After a vowel, *r* may precede other consonants as in *barb*, *bard*, *dwarf*, *morgue*, *arc*, *ark*, *arch*, *barque*, *hurl*, *harm*, *barn*, *farce*, *hears*, *furs*, *burst*, *harsh*, *hurt*, *earth*, *serve*, *Xerxes*, *furze*. Final *r* cannot immediately follow a consonant in English as it does in Welsh (for example, *theatr*), but to form a syllable requires a vowel letter either after it (*acre*, BrE *theatre*) or before it (*later*, AmE *theater*).

**Rhotic and non-rhotic**. A major variation with implications for spelling concerns not how, but when, *r* is pronounced. The accents of English fall into two groups: *RHOTIC* or *r*-sounding ACCENTS (in which *r* is pronounced in all positions in *red*, *credit*, and *worker*) and *non-rhotic* or *r*-less accents in which *r* is pronounced only before a vowel (that is, in *rice* and *price*, but not in either position in *worker*). The presence or absence of /r/ in the pronunciation of words like *worker* has an effect on the pronunciation of preceding vowels. Rhotic speakers generally distinguish certain words which are homophones for non-rhotic speakers, such as *farther/father*, *iron/ion*, *tuner/tuna*. They do not, however, always distinguish words in the same way: for example, Scots and non-Southern Americans distinguish *sauce/source* (HOMOPHONES in RP) with different vowel sounds and different realizations of /r/. In some non-rhotic accents, final *r* is pronounced when the following word begins with a vowel (LINKING *R*) and an unwritten /r/ (INTRUSIVE *R*) is commonly pronounced in contexts like *Africa/r and Asia*, *law/r and order*, and *draw/r/ing*. See *R*-SOUNDS.

**Rhotacizing and de-rhotacizing**. Non-rhotic speakers often cannot tell from pronunciation when to put *r* in a word and when to leave it out, and are prone to misspellings such as *rhotacizing* (inserting an *r*) in *\*surport* for *support*, and *de-rhotacizing* (removing an *r*) in *\*suprise* for *surprise*. Some written forms reflect this ambivalence. *Marm* as a clipped form of *madam* reflects non-rhotic pronunciation and rhymes with *charm*, whereas the *r*-less spelling *ma'am* accords with both types of accent and can rhyme with either *calm* or *jam* (however pronounced). Paradoxically, the AmE vulgarism *He bust his ass* doubly de-rhotacizes *He burst his arse*, but is common in rhotic AmE speech. Poets on both sides of the Atlantic have sometimes exploited the non-rhotic pronunciation for the sake of rhyme, as in *crosses/horses* (Keats) and *quarter/water* (Longfellow). The insertion of a vowel after *r* in *alarum*, *chirrup*, *sirrah* (for *alarm*, *chirp*, *sir*) preserves (and emphasizes) the *r*-sound in non-rhotic speech.

**Double R**. (1) In word-final position, in some monosyllables when preceded by a single vowel: *err*, *purr*, *whirr* (also *whir*) (but contrast *blur*, *cur*, *her*, *slur*, *spur*, *stir* and note *bur/burr*). (2) Medially, in disyllables ending in -*y* (*carry*, *berry*, *lorry*, *hurry*) and -*ow* (*narrow*, *borrow*, *furrow*). (3) Some medial doubling derives from Latin: *error*, *horror*, *terror* and the root *terra* (Earth, land), as in *terrestrial*, *Mediterranean*. Double *r* can also be a consequence of the assimilation of certain LATIN prefixes to roots beginning with *r*: *ad-* in *arrive*, *con-* in *correct*, *in-* in *irremediate* and *ir-rigate*, *sub-* in *surreptitious*. (4) When suffixes beginning with a vowel are attached to stressed syllables ending in *r*: *blurred*, *averred* (contrast *severed*), *deferring* (contrast *suffering*), *referral*, *referrable* (optionally also *referable*, often with stress on the initial syllable: compare *reference*). (5) The discrepancy of *rr* in *embarrass*, but *r* in *harass* reflects French *embarrasser*, *harasser*. The *OED* attests variation in both words in English. (6) In some words, although doubling is obligatory in the source language, it is optional in English borrowings: English *garrotte/garotte*, *guerrilla/guerilla*, Spanish *garrote*, *guerrilla*.

**Syllabic R**. Difficulties in spelling arise from complex, unpredictable relationships between *r* and preceding unstressed vowel sounds and letters. Like the phonetically similar consonants *l*, *m*, *n*, the letter *r* functions in rhotic accents simultaneously as a spoken vowel and as a consonant (though less obviously in non-rhotic speech). The *r* is then syllabic, as in *acre*. In non-rhotic accents, the *r*-sound has disappeared in these contexts, leaving schwa, with the result that pairs like *beater/beta*, *pucker/pukka*, *rotor/rota*, *peninsular/peninsula* are homophones in RP and similar accents. This syllabic *r* or the schwa which has replaced it may combine with a preceding long vowel or diphthong to form a single syllable, with the result that such words as *lair*, *layer* are homophones and rhyme with *mayor/mare* and *prayer*.

In *acre* (with 'magic' *e*), and BrE *centre*, AmE *center*, the schwa in non-rhotic pronunciation is represented by the *r* (the final *e* being silent). The effect is striking in inflected forms such as BrE *centred* (compare *entered*). Syllabic *r* creates uncertainty in spelling, because the schwa sound may be spelt with any vowel letter or several digraphs: *lumbar*, *cancer*, *nadir*, *rector*, *murmur*, *martyr*, *neighbour*. Pronunciation (especially in RP and related accents) is no guide; when in doubt, the less confident writer often settles on an -*er* form: *\*burgler* for *burglar*, *\*docter* for *doctor*.

The problem of spelling syllabic *r* (or final schwa) is compounded by numerous pairs of homophones: *altar/alter*, *auger/augur*, *calendar/calender*, *caster/castor*, *censer/censor*, *dolar/dolour*, *filter/philtre*, *fisher/fissure*, *friar/frier*, *hangar/hanger*, *lumbar/lumber*, *manner/manor*, *meddler/medlar*, *meter/metre*, *miner/minor*, *prier/prior*, *raiser/razor*, *rigger/rigour*, *roomer/rumour*, *sailer/sailor*, *sucker/succour*, *taper/tapir*, *tenner/tenor*. Homophone pairs in which the schwa + *r* sequence is medial pose similar problems: *humerus/humorous*, *literal/littoral*, *savory/savoury*, *stationary/stationery*, *summary/summery*. Further problems for learners and weak spellers arise with words which have similar phonological but different orthographic patterns: *ministry/monastery*, *mystery/history*, *disparate/desperate*, *deliberate/elaborate*, *disastrous/boisterous*, *leprous/obstreperous*, *wintry/summery*.

**Simple vowels before *R***. (1) The values of vowel letters before *r* are often modified. In monosyllables, if *a* and *o* precede *r*, they are lengthened: *star*, *hard*, *harm*, *barn*, *harsh*, *cart*, *carve*; *ford*, *torn*. However, *e*, *i*, *u*, *y* typically merge their values in RP to a lengthened schwa: *her*, *sir*, *cur*, *herd*, *turf*, *urge*, *irk*, *bird*, *curd*, *fern*, *turn*, *hurt*, *serve*, *myrrh*. The vowel digraphs *ea* and *ou* when followed by *r* may also have this value: *earn*, *journey*. These alternatives generate pairs of homophones: *berth/birth*, BrE *curb/kerb*, *earn/urn*, *fir/fur*, *heard/herd*, *pearl/purl*, *serf/surf*, *serge/surge*, *tern/turn*. Such long pronunciations also occur in the stressed final syllables of disyllables: *impart*, *suborn*, *concern*, *confer*, *concur*. However, when a *w*-sound precedes these vowel + *r* patterns, the values of *a* and *o* are commonly altered to those of *o* and *u* respectively, as in *dwarf* (compare *orphan*), *word* (compare *curd*), but not after silent *w* (*whore*, *sword*). (2) Especially in the accents of England, if an unstressed vowel between two *r*s is elided, single *r* may be heard as in *February* ('Febry', 'Febuary'), *library* ('libry'), *literary* ('litry'), *temporary* ('tempry').

**Long vowels before *R***. The greatest complexity arises after long vowels or diphthongs, as a result both of the rhotic/non-rhotic split and of the effect of *r* on preceding vowels. When final silent *e* follows *r*, preceding vowels are typically long, but often modified: compare *hare/hate*, *here/eve*, *hire/hive*, *more/mope*, *lure/lute*. Different spellings for these vowels produce inconsistency in many common words: (1) *Pare* compared with *pair*, *pear* and contrasted with *bar* and anomalous *are*. (2) *Here* compared with *hear* and contrasted with *were*, *there*, *where* and the two pronunciations of *tear*. (3) *Fire* contrasted with *fiery*, *wiry*. (4) *Pure* compared with the varying value of -*ure* in *sure*. (5) *Sore*, *morning* are homophones of *soar*, *mourning* only in some accents. (6) The -*our* sequence is confused. The forms -*our* and -*ower*, as in *flour/flower*, may represent the standard value, but *course*, *court*, *four* have the vowel of *or* in RP; there is uncertainty about rarer words such as *dour*, *gourd*; and the common word *your* may be a homophone of *yore* or of *ewer*. In many non-rhotic accents, *sore/soar/saw* (but not *sour*, *sower*) are homophones. Similar variety prevails with the vowels in *moor/more/maw*. The oldest forms of RP, and many other accents, distinguish all three; others merge the first or last two; while recent RP and related accents merge all three.

**Intervocalic R**. In polysyllables, r between vowels may follow a short or long vowel: (1) Short *a, e, i, o, y* (not *u*) before *r* in stressed syllables: *arid, character, parachute, erudite, miracle, spirit, coracle, origin, courier, syrup, pyramid*. (2) Long vowels in stressed syllables: *area, parent, vary, hero, period, pirate, virus, story, floral, during fury, spurious*. (3) The vowel before *rr* in the stressed syllables of polysyllables normally has the standard short value: *carry, barrier, error, ferry, mirror, stirrup, sorrow, hurry*. However, values differ between *warring/warrior*, the noun *furrier* and the comparative of the adjective *furry*, and between the verb *to tarry* and the adjective *tarry* from *tar*.

**Distinctive combinations**. (1) Initial *r* follows silent *w* in some words of OLD ENGLISH origin: *wrap, wraith, wreck, wriggle, write, wrong, wrought, wrung*. (2) The digraph *rh* occurs word-initially in GREEK-derived words, representing classical Greek *r* with rough breathing ('hr'): *rhapsody, rhetoric, rhinoceros, rhododendron, rhubarb, rhythm*. In word-medial and word-final positions, the combination is *rrh*, following the classical Greek practice: *antirrhinum, catarrhine, diarrhoea/diarrhea, haemorrhage/hemorrhage, platyrrhine; catarrh, myrrh*. (3) *Rh* also occurs initially in WELSH names: *Rhoddri* (man's first name), *Rhondda* (place-name). (4) The combination *shr* and *sr* occur in IndE in SANSKRIT loanwords such as the titles *Sri/Shri/Shree* and *Srimati/Shrimati/Shreemati*, as in *Sri* and *Srimati Gupta* (Mr and Mrs Gupta). (5) Initial *vr* occurs in *vroom* (the noise of a powerful engine revving).

**Historical points**. (1) There has been occasional variation between *r* and other alveolar consonants: *glamour* derives from *grammar*; *colonel* was formerly *coronel* (see L); the *rr* in *porridge* and single *r* in *porage* were originally the *tt* in *pottage*: compare SCOUSE. (2) The *r*-sound has disappeared in *speak* (compare GERMAN *sprechen*), in *palsy* (ultimately from Greek-derived *paralysis*), and in the colloquial forms *bust* for *burst, cussed* for *cursed*. (3) Sometimes, an *r*-sound has switched position with a following vowel, as in *burn/brand* and *work/wrought* (dating from Old English), *brid* (in MIDDLE ENGLISH) now *bird*; *r* occurring before the vowel in *three* but after it in *third, thirty*: see METATHESIS.

**American and British differences**. Variation in the use of *r* occurs between most BrE forms ending in consonant + *re* and their AmE equivalents, which are written consonant + *er*: BrE *calibre*/AmE *caliber, centre/center, fibre/fiber, goitre/goiter, litre/liter, manoeuvre/maneuver, meagre/meager, metre/meter, ochre/ocher, reconnoitre/reconnoiter, sabre/saber, saltpetre/saltpeter, sceptre/scepter, sombre/somber, spectre/specter, theatre/theater*. However, no such difference arises after a long vowel + *c* or *g*: both varieties have the same spellings for *acre, lucre, mediocre*, and *ogre*. See BURR, RHOTACISM.

**RADIATION**. In LINGUISTICS, a process of SEMANTIC CHANGE in which there is a multiplication in the senses of a word, phrase, or lexeme, whether within one language or across a number of languages. For example, in classical Greek, *pápuros* originally referred to a reed common in Egypt, used among other things for making into a writing surface. The word then came to refer to the writing material produced, and this is the dominant sense of the Latinate English word *papyrus*. In addition, *pápuros* has been adapted into other languages (into English as *paper*) without the original sense 'reed' and referring to writing material made from any source, whether reeds, cotton, linen, or wood pulp. In addition, the meaning of *paper* has radiated to include a written document or documents (from the 14c), a newspaper, a written or printed essay, a bill of exchange, and money (from the 17c), and a set of questions in an examination (from the 19c). See POLYSEMY.

**RAP**. An informal term associated with inner-city neighbourhoods and popular radio and television, especially among blacks in the US: (1) To talk rapidly, rhythmically, vividly, and boastfully, so as to compete for prestige among one's peers and impress one's listeners. The verse of the American boxer Muhammad Ali (formerly Cassius Clay) is an early form of rapping: 'Only last week / Ah murdered a rock / Injured a stone / Hospitalized a brick / Ah'm so mean / Ah made medicine sick'. (2) The ritualized repartee (especially young male) blacks, associated with the *hip* or *cool* street talk also known as *sounding, capping*, and *playing the dozens*, which includes assertions, taunts, and insults. Currently, rapping is closely associated with *hip hop*, a flamboyant youth style originating in the streets of the South Bronx in New York City in the early 1970s and including graffiti art, break-dancing, and Afrocentric ways of dressing. (3) To perform a rhyming, usually improvised monologue against a back-ground of music with a strong beat: in a street, the music is usually from a portable radio/cassette-player (a *ghetto-blaster* or *boom box*); in a broadcasting studio, it is from a background of recorded music or is reduced to a heavy bass beat produced by a drum machine or synthesizer. (4) A song or poem performed in this way, the performer being a *rapper* and the overall effect being *rap music*. On television, the background may be a series of fragments of music or video scenes. Jon Pareles observes:

> To say that rap reflects television doesn't discount its deep roots in black culture; the networks didn't invent rap, ghetto disk jockeys did. Rap comes out of the story telling and braggadocio of the blues, the cadences of gospel preachers and comedians, the percussive improvisations of jazz drummers and tap dancers. It also looks to Jamaican 'toasting' (improvising rhymes over records), to troubadour traditions of social comment and historical remembrance, and to a game called 'the dozens,' a ritual exchange of cleverly phrased insults. ('The Etymology of Rap Music', *The New York Times*, Jan. 1990).

Pareles considers that rap's chopped-up style reflects the impact of television, in which programmes are accompanied and interrupted by commercials, previews, snippets of news, and the like, as well as by using a remote control to 'zap' from channel to channel. See AFRICAN-AMERICAN VERNACULAR ENGLISH, BLARNEY, DUB, JIVE, PATTER, REGGAE.

**RASTA TALK**, also **Rasta**, **Dread Talk**, **Iyaric**, **I-lect**, **the language/speech of Rasta(fari)**. The usage of the Rastafarian community in the Caribbean, UK, US, and elsewhere, derived from JAMAICAN CREOLE, with elements from the Old Testament of the BIBLE and the black consciousness movement. *Rastafarianism* (also *Rastafari*, *Rastafaria*; informal *Rasta*, *Ras*) originated among the poor in Jamaica in the 1930s. Haile Selassie is regarded as the incarnation of God (*Jah*), through whom, despite his death in 1975, the faithful of the black diaspora will be taken out of *Babylon* (the oppressive white power system) to the promised land of Ethiopia. Since the 1960s, young middle-class people have also been included among their number.

Rastas reject both STANDARD ENGLISH and CREOLE; their alternative usage emerged in the 1940s as an argot among alienated young men, became a part of Jamaican youth culture, and has been significant in the growth and spread of *DUB* poetry and *REGGAE* music. A major syntactic difference from Creole is the use of the stressed English pronoun *I* (often repeated for emphasis and solidarity as *I and I*) to replace Creole *mi*, which is used for both subject and object. *Mi* is seen as a mark of black subservience that makes people objects rather than subjects. The form *I and I* may also stand for *we* and for the movement itself:

> I and I have fi check hard . . . It change I . . . now I and I [eat] jus' patty, hardo bread, from Yard (*New York Magazine*, 4 Nov. 1973). [I was greatly affected . . . It changed me . . . Now I only eat patties, hard-dough bread, from Jamaica (a reference to Rasta vegetarianism).]

> At the same time I fully know why leaders of societies have taken such a low view of I n I reality. They hold Rasta as dangerous to their societies (Jah Bones, 'Rastafari: A Cultural Awakening', appendix to E. E. Cashmore, *The Rastafarians*, Minority Rights Group Report 64, 1984).

Because of its significance as a mark of self-respect and solidarity, *I* often replaces syllables in mainstream words: *I-lect* Rasta dialect, *Iyaric* (by analogy with *Amharic*) Rasta language, *I-cient* ancient, *I-man* amen, *I-nointed* anointed, *I-quality* equality, *I-sanna* hosanna, *I-thiopia* Ethiopia. Other items of vocabulary are: *control* to keep, take, look after, *dreadlocks* hair worn long in rope-like coils (to signify membership of the group), *dub* a piece of reggae music, rhythmic beat, *queen* a girlfriend, *Rastaman* a male, adult Rastafarian, *reason hard* to argue, *sufferer* a ghetto-dweller, *trod* to walk away, leave, *weed of wisdom* and *chalice* (by analogy with Holy Communion) marijuana, ganja (regarded as a sacred herb). Rasta word-play includes the etymology *Jah mek ya* (God made here) for *Jamaica*, and the adaptations *blindjaret* for *cigarette* (pronounced 'see-garet') and *higher-stand* in preference to *understand*.

# ■ READING ─────────── ■

The process of extracting meaning from written or printed language: one of the four language skills (listening, speaking, reading, WRITING) and one of the two key aspects of LITERACY (reading and writing). The activity is of two kinds: *reading aloud*, so that others can hear (and benefit from) what is being read, and *silent reading*.

**Reading aloud.** People who are learning to read often read aloud, in order to relate what they see to the spoken language. Depending on the skill and confidence of the novice reader, this may be accompanied by tracing the line of text word by word with the index finger. In scribal societies, reading aloud appears to have been the norm, even for private, personal purposes. The shift to mature silent reading may have been encouraged by the advent of print, the spread of literacy, an awareness that reading aloud disturbs others within earshot, a view among teachers that saying (or muttering) what is being read indicates a low level of skill, and perhaps also appreciation of a silence that makes the message more personal. Reading aloud in public is an ancient practice that lies at the roots of publishing ('making public'), and in many parts of the world continues to be an important means of disseminating information and educating the young. It includes *dictation* that is read out to be written down by students and *lecturing* from a prepared text at a pace that allows note-taking: compare French *lecture* (reading). Reading aloud well involves control of breath, voice, and body, a capacity to look up from a text and back without losing one's place, and, depending on subject and occasion, an element of drama and display. In public presentations, such reading has traditionally been from a document held in the hand or placed on a *lectern* (a special sloping surface that holds whatever is being read). On television, however, there is increasing use of an electronic prompting device (a *teleprompter* or trade name, an *Autocue*) placed between reader and audience. This enlarges the elements of a script line by line, so that someone may see it easily and use it without appearing (too obviously) to be reading.

**Silent reading.** Private reading is so basic a skill in present-day society that its nature is little discussed and its existence largely taken for granted. It differs from other forms of scanning one's surroundings by being focused, sustained, relatively disciplined, and accompanied by thinking about the meaning of what one sees. The concept of reading is often extended to other kinds of disciplined, reflective activity, such as 'reading' someone's face for a message, 'reading' a landscape for information, or asking *Do you read me?* (Have you understood me?) after sending a radio message. One can also 'read' semaphore signals at a distance, braille by touch, and Morse code by listening. The eye movements that occur in conventional reading consist of jerks and stops. Each jerk entails a change in focus, and is technically known as a *saccade* (from French: the jerk on the reins of a rider controlling a horse); each stop is a *fixation*, a moment of stability in which signals are transmitted from retina to brain. On average, readers make three or four fixations a second, and each may register several letters or several words, depending on such factors as distance from text, size and kind of lettering, and familiarity with language, orthography, and subject matter.

Readers use both visual and phonetic skills, combining a capacity to decipher writing and print letter by letter with an indirect awareness of the heard equivalents of what is graphically displayed. This cross-association of graphic and phonic symbols appears to be natural: readers may at any time audibly or inaudibly say a syllable or word so as to help grasp its nature, function, and meaning: in doing this, they may be returning to the historically and individually 'early' stage of moving the lips while interpreting the signs of the text. In this process, they are not usually put off by homophones, such as *right* and *write* or *dun* and *done*, which suggests that visual interpretation can function independently of phonetic backup. They may, however, be put off by homographs and polysemous words, such as the various uses of *bank* and *crane*. The fact that some people read so fast (over 500 words per minute) that they exceed the capacity of their phonetic backup to check what they are seeing is evidence for an element in reading that is not in any way tied to physical sound or 'sounds' in the mind.

**Learning to read.** There has long been controversy among teachers of reading over the primary means by which children learn (or should learn) to read. Attitudes and policies tend to vary between a *whole-language*, *whole-word*, *global*, *holistic*, or *look-and-say* approach on the one hand (in which words are minimal units to be learned as gestalts) and a *symbol-to-sound*, *code-based*, *atomistic*, or *phonic* approach (in which reading is like cracking a code that consists of correspondences between speech sounds and graphic symbols, with letters or *graphemes* as the prime units). Some teachers favour one approach over the other, while many favour a compromise that allows a judicious use of elements from both approaches. Some also make a distinction between a 'whole language' approach in which children work from so-called 'real books' (as opposed to specially prepared readers) and the older 'look and say' method that is closely associated with readers, reading schemes, flash cards, and other aids. There is some evidence that concentrating on the atoms of reading in the early stages leads to a higher rate of word recognition later, followed by an expansion of global comprehension through the quality and interest of what is being read. It is also likely that strategies may differ depending on the writing system used: for example, learning to read the blend of logographic and syllabic signs used for Japanese may require a different approach from learning the set of signs used for such 'alphabetic' languages as Spanish, Italian, German and English.

**Six stages?** The American researcher Jeanne S. Chall (*Stages of Reading Development*, New York, 1983, and with Steven A. Stahl, 'Reading', *International Encyclopedia of Communications*, New York, 1989) has proposed that reading in English proceeds through six (relatively idealized) stages, more or less as follows (with ages specific to educational experience in the US):

***Stage 0: Pre-reading and pseudo-reading***. Before they reach the age of 6, children are likely to 'pretend' to read, retelling a story when looking at the pages of a book that has already been read to them, increasingly naming letters, recognizing some signs, printing their own names, and playing with the general paraphernalia of literacy. This process develops naturally as a response to being read to by adults or older children who take a close and warm interest in that response. Most children at this stage can understand simple picture books and the stories read to

them, but have a hazy perception of what reading really is.

***Stage 1: Initial reading and decoding***. Between 6 and 7, children may learn the relations between sounds and letters and between spoken and printed words, read simple texts containing short, high-frequency words that are spelt more or less regularly, and 'sound out' monosyllables. If they receive instruction in *phonics*, they are often read to from a level just above their own ability to read. Generally, their level of reading at this stage is well below their capacity to manage speech. Although it is not easy to quantify words known and used, Chall estimates that they can understand some 4,000 spoken words and some 600 written or printed words. A reading specimen of this stage is:

'May I go?' said Fay. 'May I please go with you?' (from *American Book Primer*).

***Stage 2: Confirmation and fluency***. Between 7 and 8, children may consolidate their skills, increasing their range of reading, their fluency, their general vocabulary, and their ability to decode the elements of words. Again, help may often include being read to at a level above their own ability. At the end of this stage, they can understand an estimated 9,000 spoken words and 3,000 written or printed words. A reading specimen of this stage is:

Spring was coming to Tait Primary School. On the new highway big trucks went by the school all day (from Ginn 720, Grade 2).

***Stage 3: Reading for learning***. Between 9 and 14, reading is no longer an end in itself but becomes a means by which further knowledge and experience can be gained. Use extends beyond the immediate subjects of school and includes textbooks, reference books, and periodicals (from comic books to newspapers and encyclopaedias). Reading becomes part of a general experience of language that is likely to include explicit discussion of language skills, especially writing and spelling. At the beginning of this stage, listening comprehension of the same material is more effective than reading comprehension, but by the end the two are roughly equal. For some young people, reading may have edged ahead. Two reading specimens of this stage are:

She smoothed her hair behind her ear as she lowered her hand. I could see she was eyeing *beauty* and trying to figure out a way to write about being beautiful without sounding even more conceited than she already was (from Ginn 720, Grade 5).

Early in the history of the world, men found that they could not communicate well by using only sign language. In some way that cannot be traced with any certainty, they devised spoken language (from Book F, *New Practice Reader*, Graves *et al.*, 1962).

***Stage 4: Multiplicity and complexity***. From 14 to 17, if all has gone well, students are reading fairly widely from a range of increasingly complex materials, both narrative and expository, and varied in viewpoint. Such materials are both technical and non-technical, literary and non-literary, and may involve a parallel study of words and their elements. For poorer performers, listening and reading comprehension are about the same, but for stronger performers reading comprehension is better than listening comprehension, especially in technical subjects. A specimen for this stage is:

No matter what phenomena he is interested in, the scientist employs two main tools—theory and empirical research. Theory employs reason, language, and logic to suggest possible, and predict probable, relationships among various data gathered from the concrete world of experience (from A. B. Kathryn, 'College Reading Skills', in John & Mavis Biesanz (eds.), *Modern Society*, 1971).

***Stage 5: Construction and reconstruction***. Beyond 18, young adults should have developed the capacity to read for their own purposes, using their skill to integrate their own knowledge with that of others and to assimilate their experience of the world more effectively. In stronger performers, it is rapid and efficient, and serves as a basis for a lifetime of reading for personal and occupational purposes. Interested readers go beyond their immediate needs and in the writing of essays, reports, summaries, and other materials continue to integrate the four skills. A reading specimen for this stage is:

One of the objections to the hypothesis that a satisfying after-effect of a mental connection works back upon it to

strengthen it is that nobody has shown how this action does or could occur. It is the purpose of this article to show how a mechanism which is as possible psychologically as any of the mechanisms proposed to account for facilitation, inhibition, fatigue, strengthening by repetition, or other forms of modification could enable such an after-effect to cause such a strengthening (from Edward L. Thorndike, 'Connectionism', *Psychological Review* 40, 1933).

**Conclusion**. The above stages resemble the developmental phases of the child's mind as proposed by the Swiss researcher Jean Piaget. They are both a generalization from objective study and an idealized assumption about an average child who progresses fairly smoothly through such stages in an English-speaking society that has an adequate educational system, without any significant social or personal problems. The order may be universal, but the age ranges will vary between individuals, cultures, and countries. Unfortunately, not all climb smoothly from the bottom to the top of this ladder and not all societies provide an adequate educational service. In addition, many competent readers might have serious difficulty with the specimen that Chall provides for Stage 5, many adequate readers with the specimen at Stage 4, and so on down the line to the large percentage of people whom English-speaking societies now recognize as *functionally illiterate*: that is, those who, for whatever reason, never managed to get successfully through Stage 1 or 2. Recent definitions of literacy have classed as illiterate all those who read less efficiently than they would like, including many who have moved well beyond Stage 2. See CHILD LANGUAGE ACQUISITION, DYSLEXIA, EDUCATION, ILLITERACY, PROSE, SPELLING.

**REBUS**. A device that uses letters, numbers, or pictures to represent WORDS: for example, *MT* used to mean *empty*; *B4* to mean *before*. The rebus is usually a puzzle that demands some lateral thinking to decipher it, as in *MIN* (half a minute) and *CCCCCCC* (the Seven Seas). The idea is as old as Egyptian hieroglyphics and came into English in the Middle Ages in heraldic devices and pictorial representations of names.

**RECEIVED**. When used of language, *received* usually refers to what is accepted and approved in educated, especially middle-class society: 'The tip of the tongue for received English is not so advanced towards the teeth or gums, as for the continental sound' (A. J. Ellis, *On Early English Pronunciation*, vol. 4, 1874).

# ■ RECEIVED PRONUNCIATION ————— ■

**1.** PRONUNCIATION regarded as correct or proper, especially by arbiters of usage: 'the theoretically received pronunciation of literary English' (A. J. Ellis, *On Early English Pronunciation*, vol. 1, 1869); 'Edinburgh and Dublin have their received pronunciations' (Simeon Potter, *Changing English*, 1969). **2.** [1920s: with initial capitals]. Short form *RP*. A term in PHONETICS, applied LINGUISTICS, and LANGUAGE TEACHING for the ACCENT generally associated with educated BRITISH ENGLISH and used as the pronunciation model for teaching it to foreign learners. This accent has been referred to technically as: *Received Standard English* (or *Received Standard*) and *Public School English* by Henry Cecil Wyld; *Public School Pronunciation* (*PSP*) by Daniel JONES, prior to using the term itself; *General British* in the *Oxford Advanced Learner's Dictionary* (3rd edition, 1974: in contrast to *General American*); *standard southern pronunciation*; and *standard (spoken) British English*. Since its initial description by Jones in the *ENGLISH PRONOUNCING DICTIONARY* (*EPD*) in 1917, it has probably become the most described and discussed accent on earth.

**Attitudes to RP**. The terms *Received Pronunciation* and *RP* are not widely known outside the immediate circle of English-language professionals, but the form that they refer to is widely known as the spoken embodiment of a variety or varieties known as *the KING'S ENGLISH*, *the Queen's English*, *BBC ENGLISH*, *OXFORD ENGLISH*, and *PUBLIC SCHOOL ENGLISH*. It is often informally referred to by the British middle class as a *BBC accent* or a *public school accent* and by the working class as *talking proper* or *talking posh*. In England, it is also often referred to simply as *Standard English*. Its 'advanced' (that is, distinctive upper-class and royal) form is sometimes called *la-di-dah* (as in talking la-di-dah) or *a cut-glass accent*, especially if used by people judged as not really 'from the top drawer'. RP has been described by many of its users

and admirers in the UK and elsewhere as the best pronunciation for BrE, for the countries influenced by BrE, or for all users of English everywhere. Americans do not normally subscribe to this view, but many of them admire RP as the representative accent of educated BrE while some associate it with the theatre and, in men, with effeminacy.

Many British people dislike Received Pronunciation, usually arguing that it is a mark of privilege and (especially among the Scots, Northern Irish, and Welsh) of social domination by the (especially southern) English. It has, however, a considerable gravitational pull throughout the UK, with the result that many middle- and lower middle-class people, especially in England, speak with accents more or less adapted towards it. These accents are therefore known among phoneticians as *modified regional accents* and *modified RP*. Comparable accents in Australia, Ireland, New Zealand, Scotland, South Africa, and elsewhere are often referred to as *NEAR-RP*. It has always been a minority accent, unlikely ever to have been spoken by more than 3–4% of the British population. British phoneticians and linguists have often described it as a 'regionless' accent in the UK and especially in England, in that it is not possible to tell which part of the country an RP speaker comes from; it is never, however, described as a 'classless' accent, because it identifies the speaker as a member of the middle and upper classes. Because it is class-related, it is socially and politically controversial and can lead to embarrassment when discussed.

**General background**. RP is often taken to have existed for a relatively long time, evolving from a prestigious accent well established in England by the 17c, when comparisons began to be made between the speech of the court and the nobility in LONDON and that of their peers from the provinces. John Aubrey (*Brief Lives*, mid-17c) provides a hearsay report that Sir Walter Raleigh had a Devon accent; Samuel JOHNSON in the 18c is on record as speaking with a Staffordshire accent. Although there was an increasingly homogeneous and fashionable style of speech in the capital in the 18–19c, little is known about it. It probably served in part at least as a model for the middle classes and may have been common at such ancient public schools as Eton, Harrow, Rugby, and Winchester, but there is no evidence that a uniform accent was used or promoted in these schools until the later 19c. However, by the beginning of the 20c, it was well established, and in 1917, at the height of the First World War, Jones defined his model for English as that 'most usually heard in everyday speech in the families of Southern English persons whose menfolk have been educated at the great public boarding-schools', and called it *Public School Pronunciation* (*PSP*).

The heyday of Empire, approximately 1890–1940, was also the high point of RP, which has been described by such terms as 'patrician' and 'proconsular'. Its possession was a criterion for the selection of young men as potential officers during the First World War and it has been the accent favoured for recruits to the Foreign Office and other services representing the British nation (largely drawn from the public schools, with a slight enlargement of the catchment area in recent years). Newcomers to the British establishment have tended to ensure that their children acquire RP by sending them to the 'right' schools or, especially in the past in the case of girls, to elocution teachers. In these schools the accent has never been overtly taught, but appears to have been indirectly encouraged and often promoted through peer pressure that has included mockery of any other form of SPEECH. It has been the voice of national announcers and presenters on the BBC since its founding in the 1920s, but in the 1970s–80s there has been a move towards modified regional accents among announcers and presenters, and towards distinct (but generally modified) regional accents among presenters on popular radio channels and meteorologists and sports commentators on television.

**Generalities and characteristics**. (1) The description of RP in A. C. Gimson, *An Introduction to the Pronunciation of English* (Edward Arnold, 3rd edition, 1980), is widely regarded as standard. Its 4th edition (1990) has been revised by Susan Ramsaran. (2) RP is often used as a reference norm for the description of other varieties of English. An idealized representation has been available for this and other purposes for at least 20 years, with minor differences in the house styles of such publishers as Oxford University Press and Longman. A comparison between RP and 'GenAm' (General American) is a key element of John C. Wells's *Longman*

*Pronunciation Dictionary* (1990). (3) RP differs little from other accents of English in the pronunciation of consonants, which are 24 in number. It is a non-rhotic accent that includes the linking/intrusive /r/ (widely noted in such phrases as *law/r and order*), which is not however taught as part of the EFL/ESL pronunciation model. (4) Wells (above) lists the following 22 basic values of RP vowels: /ɪ/ as in *kit, bid, hymn, intend, basic*; /e/ as in *dress, bed*; /æ/ as in *trap, bad*; /ɒ/ as in *lot, odd, wash*; /ʌ/ as in *strut, bud, love*; /ʊ/ as in *foot, good, put*; /iː/ as in *fleece, sea, machine*; /eɪ/ as in *face, day, steak*; /aɪ/ as in *price, high, try*; /ɔɪ/ as in *choice, boy*; /uː/ as in *goose, two, blue*; /əʊ/ as in *goat, show, no*; /aʊ/ as in *mouth, now*; /ɪə/ as in *near, here, serious*; /eə/ as in *square, fair, various*; /ɑː/ as in *start, father*; /ɔː/ as in *thought, law, north, war*; /ʊə/ as in *cure, poor, jury*; /ɜː/ as in *nurse, stir*; /i/ as in *happy, radiation, glorious*; /ə/ as in the first vowel of *about* and the last of *comma*; /u/ in *influence, situation, annual*.

**Current situation**. Although RP continues to be socially pre-eminent in Britain, and especially England, it has in recent years become less monolithic both phonetically and socially. Phoneticians recognize several varieties and also a generation gap. In the introduction to the 14th edition of the *EPD* (1977), Gimson noted of RP that its 'regional base remains valid and it continues to have wide intelligibility throughout Britain . . . [but there] has been a certain dilution of the original concept of RP, a number of local variants formerly excluded by the definition having now to be admitted as of common and acceptable usage. Such an extended scope of usage is difficult to define.' He retained the name, however, because of its 'currency in books on present-day English'. Even so, the observations of the phonetician David Abercrombie in 1951 still largely apply:

This R.P. stands in strong contrast to all the other ways of pronouncing Standard English put together. In fact, English people are divided, by the way they talk, into three groups; first, R.P. speakers of Standard English—those [regarded as being] without an accent; second, non-R.P. speakers of Standard English—those with an accent; and third, dialect speakers. I believe this to be a situation which is not paralleled in any other country anywhere ('R.P. and Local

Accent', in *Studies in Linguistics and Phonetics*, 1965).

In the 15th edition of the *EPD* (1997), Peter Roach and James Hartman have replaced 'the archaic name *Received Pronunciation*' with *BBC English*, to contrast with *Network English* for AmE. The system remains, however, essentially the same.

**RP and EFL**. Because most British teachers of English have spoken with RP or modified-RP accents, overseas learners have until recently tended to assume that it is the majority accent of BrE. It retains its position as the preferred target for COMMONWEALTH ESL learners, although in countries such as India and Singapore local pronunciations with a degree of prestige have emerged and may in due course replace it or operate alongside it. In EFL, it competes more and more with equivalent forms of AmE, but is strongly buttressed by the investment in RP made by British ELT publishers, especially in learners' dictionaries. It is generally selected as a matter of course as the reference norm for discussing spoken BrE (and often other varieties of English), as well as for such activities as automatic speech synthesis, but since most British people do not speak or even know RP as a coherent system, general statements about BrE keyed to Received Pronunciation can often be misleading and confusing.

See ADVANCED, AMERICAN ENGLISH AND BRITISH ENGLISH, AUSTRALIAN ENGLISH, CLIPPED, ENGLISH IN ENGLAND, R, INTRUSIVE *R*, LINKING *R*, KENSINGTON, *L*-SOUNDS, NEW ZEALAND ENGLISH, OXFORD ACCENT, RHOTIC AND NON-RHOTIC, *R*-SOUNDS, SCOTTISH ENGLISH, SOUTH AFRICAN ENGLISH, TEFL.

## RECEIVED STANDARD AND MODIFIED STANDARD

**RECEIVED STANDARD AND MODIFIED STANDARD**. Contrastive terms proposed by Henry Cecil Wyld at the beginning of the 20c for two kinds of PRONUNCIATION in Great Britain:

> It is proposed to use the term *Received Standard* for that form which all would probably agree in considering the best, that form which has the widest currency and is heard with practically no variation among speakers of the better class all over the country. This type might be called Public School English. It is proposed to call the vulgar English of the Towns, and the English of the Villager who has abandoned his native

Regional Dialect *Modified Standard*. That is, it is Standard English, modified, altered, differentiated, by various influences, regional and social. Modified Standard differs from class to class, and from locality to locality; it has no uniformity, and no single form of it is heard outside a particular class or a particular area. (*A Short History of English*, 1914)

See PUBLIC SCHOOL ENGLISH, RECEIVED PRONUNCIATION.

## RECEIVED STANDARD ENGLISH

**RECEIVED STANDARD ENGLISH** [Introduced by Henry Cecil Wyld]. An occasional technical term for the ACCENT of English generally referred to by phoneticians and EFL/ESL teachers as *RECEIVED PRONUNCIATION*. Compare RECEIVED STANDARD AND MODIFIED STANDARD, STANDARD ENGLISH.

## RECIPROCAL PRONOUN

**RECIPROCAL PRONOUN**. A term sometimes used for the compound PRONOUNS *each other* and *one another*, which express a two-way interaction: *Romeo and Juliet loved each other/one another* (Romeo loved Juliet and Juliet loved Romeo). In meaning, reciprocal pronouns contrast with reflexive pronouns: *The Montagues and the Capulets loved themselves* (The Montagues loved the Montagues, and the Capulets loved the Capulets). Reciprocal pronouns are, however, like reflexives in not normally being used as subjects: not \**They wondered where each other/one another was*.

## REDUNDANCY

**REDUNDANCY. 1.** In general usage, more of anything than is (strictly) needed, usually resulting from REPETITION or duplication; PLEONASM or TAUTOLOGY. In the sentence *They also visited us last week too*, either *also* or *too* is redundant, because both words express the same idea. **2.** Technically, both the repetition of information (or the inclusion of extra information so as to reduce errors in understanding messages) and part of a message which can be eliminated without loss of essential information. Languages differ in the degree and kinds of redundancy they make use of: LATIN syntax has a much higher level of redundancy than English syntax. In the sentence *Milites novi hodie venerunt*, as compared with its translation *The new soldiers came today*, plurality is marked three times in Latin (*-es* in *milites*, *-i* in *novi*, *-erunt* in *venerunt*) but only once in English (*-s* in *soldiers*). FRENCH often has greater redundancy in writing than in speech: in *Les nouveaux soldats sont venus aujourd'hui*, the plural is carried in speech by *les*, *sont* and in writing by *les*, *-x*, *-s*, *sont*.

**Redundancy and information**. Redundancy can be described as the difference between the possible and actual information in a message. This difference may be repetition or other encodings beyond the minimal possible length. A message entirely without redundancy may contain the maximum amount of information, but cannot be corrected if it is corrupted in some way, because there is no 'spare' material to check with. In the Latin sentence above, three items would have to be lost before the plural message is lost. In the English equivalent, the loss of one *-s* would change the message drastically. To avoid misunderstandings, people generally repeat themselves more when speaking than writing. This corresponds to the greater possibility of error in listening than reading.

**REDUPLICATION**. The act or result of doubling a sound, word, or word element, usually for grammatical or lexical purposes. In classical Greek, grammatical reduplication serves to form the perfect of the verb, by means of a prefixed syllable that repeats the initial consonant: *lúo* I loosen, *léluka* I have loosened. A mix of grammatical and lexical reduplication occurs in various languages: for example pluralizing in Malay *contoh* example, *contoh-contoh* examples, *raja* king, *rajaraja* kings. A word in which this process occurs is a *reduplication* or (more commonly) a *reduplicative*. In English, lexical reduplication is found: (1) In occasional borrowings, such as *beriberi*, a disease caused by deficiency of vitamin $B_1$, (from Sinhala, an emphatic doubling of *beri* weakness). (2) In echoic or otherwise phonetically suggestive words, such as *tut-tut/tsk-tsk*. In most cases, some elements contrast while others are repeated, as with *mishmash* and *hanky-panky*. Such words are often informal and whimsical, with contrasts that affect vowels (*mish-mash*, *pingpong*, *pitter-patter*, *tick-tock*, *tittle-tattle*) or consonants (*mumbo-jumbo*, *niminy-piminy*), the latter often involving an opening *h*-sound (*hanky-panky*, *harum-scarum*, *helter-skelter*, *hocus-pocus*, *holus-bolus*, *hugger-mugger*). Less precisely reduplicative resemblances occur in such words as *hunky-dory* and associations can be made between actions in such words as *walkie-talkie*. (3) In such occasional emphatic repetitions as *no-no* in the slang expression *It's a no-no* (It's something definitely not to be done). (4) In pidgin and creole usages, such as Tok Pisin *lukluk* to stare (from *look*) and *singsing* a festival (from *sing*), Kamtok and Krio *bɛnbɛn* crooked (from *bend*), and Kamtok and Nigerian Pidgin *katakata* confused (from *scatter*). See ALLITERATION, ASSONANCE, ECHOISM, JEWISH ENGLISH, JOURNALESE, SCOTS, SINGSONG.

**REFERENCE**. **1.** Referring to or mentioning someone or something, either directly or indirectly, and often in the form of an AL-LUSION or a QUOTATION. **2.** Also *objective reference*. In logic and linguistics, the activity or condition through which one term or concept is related to another or to objects in the world. **3.** In sociology and psychology, the process by which, or the extent to which, people relate to elements in society as norms and standards for comparing such things as status and values. **4.** An indication or direction in a text or other source of information to all or part of one or more other text, etc., where further, related information may be found. **5.** The text or other source to which one is directed or referred. The term is often attributive in senses 4 and 5, as in *reference book*, *reference library*, *reference materials*. It may also be part of an *of*-phrase, as in *frame of reference*, *point of reference*, *work of reference*. **6.** To provide a book or other source of information with references (*books that are all thoroughly referenced*) or to arrange (data, notes, etc.) for easy reference (*all the background material is referenced in an appendix*).

Reference materials have in the past depended mainly on surfaces that serve as receptacles of pictures and language symbols, from paintings on cliff faces, in caves, and on walls, through clay tablets and manuscripts of various kinds, to printed books and other products. Especially in the 20c, however, they have been extended to include audio- and video-recordings and electronically stored information on tape and disk. Distinct genres of reference book, such as the *atlas* for maps, the *DICTIONARY* for words, the *directory* for a variety of general or specific information (such as names, addresses, and telephone numbers), the *encyclopedia* for facts and opinions, the *gazetteer* for geographical information, have emerged over many centuries, gaining their present-day forms especially in the expansion of book publishing in the 18–20c.

ALPHABETICAL ORDER, BIBLIOGRAPHY, CONNOTATION AND DENOTATION, DEIXIS, DICTIONARY OF MODERN ENGLISH USAGE, LEXICOGRAPHY, LEXICOLOGY, LINGUISTIC ATLAS, NOTES AND REFERENCES, OXFORD ENGLISH DICTIONARY, POLYSEMY, QUOTATION, ROGET'S THESAURUS, SEMANTICS, SENSE.

**REFERENT**. **1.** The object or event to which a term or a symbol refers. The term *table* has many referents, the majority of which have a flat top and four legs. **2.** In logic, the first term in a proposition to which succeeding terms relate. See REFERENCE, SEMANTICS, SEMIOTICS, SENSE.

**REFINED**. **1.** Purified, freed from impurities: *refined iron*. **2.** Cultured, civilized, wellbred; not vulgar or coarse: *refined courtiers, a refined education*. **3.** (Of language) cultivated, polished, elegant: *a refined accent*. See AESTHETICS, PURE, STANDARD.

**REFLEXIVE PRONOUN**. A PRONOUN that ends in *-self* or *-selves*. Such pronouns are used when the direct and sometimes the indirect object of a verb 'reflects' or refers back to the subject: *I blame myself for what happened*; *They have allowed themselves another week*. Occasionally some other part of the sentence may also reflect the subject: *She pulled the box towards herself*. In standard English, a reflexive pronoun cannot usually serve as the subject of a sentence (no *\*Myself did it*), but especially in Scotland and Ireland, under the influence of Gaelic, there is a mock-prestigious use of the third-person singular (*Is himself at home?*, *It was herself answered the phone*), deriving from usages that formerly referred to kings and chiefs: *Himself has eaten, the rest of the world may eat*.

**REGGAE** [Probably from JAMAICAN CREOLE *rege(-rege)* rags, ragged clothes, perhaps with echoes of AmE *ragtime*]. Music with a heavy four-beat rhythm, with accents on one and three rather than two and four as in rock music. Reggae began in Kingston, Jamaica, and has cultural, social, and political implications in the Caribbean, UK, US, and elsewhere. The lyrics propose solutions to black problems ranging from social revolution to redemptionist prophecy, and are often a vehicle for Rastafarianism, as in:

Babylon system is the vampire
Sucking the children day by day.
(Bob Marley, 'Babylon System', 1979)

I hear the words of the Rasta man say
Babylon your throne gone down, gone down.
(Bob Marley and the Wailers, 'Rasta Man Chint')

Lyrics are sung in Jamaican Creole, Jamaican English, or a mixture of both, 'often expressing rejection of established "whiteman" culture' (F. G. Cassidy & Robert Le Page, *Dictionary of Jamaican English*, 1980). See DUB, RAP, RASTA TALK.

**REGIONALISM**. A term in LINGUISTICS for a WORD or other usage belonging to a region, either of the world or a country. An *Americanism* is a regionalism of English in world terms, while a *Kentuckyism* or *New Yorkism* is a regionalism in US terms. See ISM. Compare LOCALISM.

**REGISTER**. In SOCIOLINGUISTICS and STYLISTICS, a VARIETY of language defined according to social use, such as scientific, formal, religious, and journalistic. The term has, however, been used variously in different theoretical approaches, some giving it a broad definition (moving in the direction of *variety* in its most general sense), others narrowing it to certain aspects of language in social use (such as occupational varieties only). The term was first given broad currency by the British linguist Michael HALLIDAY, who drew a contrast between varieties of language defined according to the characteristics of the user (*dialects*) and those defined according to the characteristics of the situation (*registers*). Registers were then subclassified into three domains: *field of discourse*, referring to the subject matter of the variety, such as science or advertising; *mode of discourse*, referring to the choice between speech and writing, and the choice of format; and *manner of discourse*, referring to the social relations between the participants, as shown by variations in formality. See CONTEXT, JARGON, RESTRICTED LANGUAGE. For some specific registers, see ACADEMIC USAGE, BIBLICAL ENGLISH, COMPUTER USAGE, JOURNALESE, LEGAL USAGE, TECHNOSPEAK.

**REGULAR**. A term in general use and in LINGUISTICS for items and aspects of language that conform to general RULES. A *regular verb* in English has four forms, and the construction of three of those forms is predictable from the first (uninflected) form: *play, plays, playing, played*. On the other hand *speak* is an IRREGULAR verb. It has five forms, the last two of which are unpredictable: *speak, speaks, speaking, spoke, spoken*. See ANALOGY.

# ■ RELATIVE CLAUSE ─────── ■

In grammatical description, the term for a CLAUSE introduced by a relative word or a phrase containing a relative word. There are three types of relative clause: the *adnominal relative clause*; the *sentential relative clause*; the *nominal relative clause*.

**The adnominal relative clause** (also *relative clause, noun clause*). This clause modifies a noun as in: *(the book) that I have just read*. It may be introduced by a RELATIVE PRONOUN such as *who, which, that*, or by a phrase containing a relative pronoun, such as *for which, to whom, in the presence of whom*, or by a relative adverb, such as *where, when*: *(the hotel) where he stayed*. Under certain circumstances, the relative pronoun may be omitted: *(the music) she composed*; *(the safe) I put the money in*. Adnominal relative clauses of the type *(She told me the reason) that they gave* are to be distinguished from the superficially similar appositive clause that also modifies a noun: *(She told me the reason) that they left*. The appositive clause is introduced by the conjunction *that*, which may sometimes be omitted: *(the reason) they left*. The difference between the two types of clause is that the appositive clause is complete in itself (*they left*, not *they left the reason*), whereas the relative clause requires the relative item to be present or to be understood, since it functions in the clause (*they gave that*, meaning *they gave the reason*). The relationship between a noun and its appositive clause differs from that between a noun and its relative clause in that it may be expressed by inserting the verb *be* between the two: *The reason is that they left*. Furthermore, the nouns that are modified by an appositive clause are restricted to a small set of general abstract nouns such as *fact, idea, news, report*.

**Restrictive and non-restrictive clauses**. The two major types of adnominal relative clauses are *restrictive relative clauses* and *non-restrictive relative clauses*. A *restrictive relative clause* (also *defining relative clause*) is a relative clause with the semantic function of defining more closely what the noun modified by the clause is referring to. In the sentence *My uncle who lives in Brazil is coming to see us*, the relative clause *who lives in Brazil* restricts the reference of *my uncle*. The restrictive modification would distinguish this uncle from any others who might have been included. A *non-restrictive relative clause* (also *non-defining relative clause*) adds information not needed for identifying what a modified noun is referring to. The sentence *My uncle, who lives in Brazil, is coming to see us* contains the non-restrictive relative clause *who lives in Brazil*. This clause provides information about the uncle, but his identity is presumed to be known and not to need further specification. Non-restrictive relative clauses are usually separated from the noun phrases they modify by parenthetical punctuation (usually COMMAS, but sometimes dashes or brackets). In speech, there may be a pause that serves the same function as the parenthesis.

**The sentential relative clause**. This clause does not modify a noun. It may refer back to part of a sentence (*She exercises for an hour a day, which would bore me*: that is, the exercising would bore the speaker), to a whole sentence (*He kept on bragging about his success, which annoyed all of us*: that is, the continual bragging about his success annoyed everybody), or occasionally to more than one sentence (*I didn't enjoy the work. The weather was atrocious. I felt thoroughly homesick. And the locals were unpleasant. Which is why I have never been back there again*). *Which* is the most common relative word to introduce a sentential relative clause, sometimes within a phrase (*in which case, as a result of which*), but other relative expressions with this type of clause include *whereon, whereupon, from when, by when*.

**Nominal relative clauses**. In the adnominal and sentential relative clauses, the relative word has as *antecedent*, a word or longer unit to which the relative word refers back: in *the game which they were playing*, the antecedent of *which is the game*, since in its clause *which* substitutes for *the game* (they were playing the game). The relative word in the nominal relative clause has no antecedent, since the antecedent is fused with the relative: *I found what* (that which; the thing that) *you were looking for; He says whatever* (anything that) *he likes*. Because they are free of antecedents, such clauses are sometimes called *independent* or *free* relative clauses. See ADJECTIVE CLAUSE.

**RELATIVE PRONOUN**. A PRONOUN that alone or as part of a phrase introduces a RELATIVE CLAUSE: *who* in *the man who came to dinner*; *on whom* in *the woman on whom I rely*. The relative pronoun refers to an antecedent (*the man/who, the woman/on whom*), and functions within the relative clause: as subject in *who came to dinner*; as complement of a preposition in *on whom*. There is a gender contrast between the personal set of *who* pronouns and the non-personal *which* pronoun, and there are case distinctions in the *who* set: subjective *who(ever)*, objective *whom(ever)*, genitive *whose*. However, except in a formal context, *who(ever)* replaces *whom(ever)*. *That* can be used as a relative pronoun in place of *who, whom*, or *which*, except as complement of a preposition: *the woman who/that I rely on*, but only *the woman on whom I rely*. *That* can be omitted when functioning as object (*a man that I know; a man I know*), but not as subject (*a man that knows me*). The omitted pronoun is sometimes referred to as *zero relative*.

**REPETITION**. Doing, saying, or writing the same thing more than once. The recurrence of processes, structures, elements, and motifs is fundamental to communication in general and language in particular. Such repetition occurs at all levels, starting with rhythm. The distinctive RHYTHM of English derives from recurring syllabic stresses: *If whát/ you sáy/ is trúe/ I'd bétt/er gó*. Poetry intensifies such rhythms, iambic pentameter in particular formalizing the stress-timed rhythm of English: 'While thús/ I stóod,/ intént/ to sée/ and héar,/ One cáme,/ methóught,/ and whís/per'd ín/ my éar' (Pope, 1715). In addition, the repetition of shared sounds creates rhyme. These lines of Pope's have the rhyme pattern *aabb*: *hear/ear, raise/praise*. The use of poetic and rhetorical devices such as ALLITERATION and ASSONANCE produces repetition of sounds and letters and other effects, as in the jingle-like:

> Nature, it seems, is the popular name
> for milliards and milliards and milliards
> of particles playing their infinite game
> of billiards and billiards and billiards
>                              (Piet Hein, *Grooks*, 1966)

Similarly, syntactic and rhetorical repetition can produce emphatic or climactic effects:

> Lord Wilson's memoirs are not as dull as Lord Stockton's, nor as sad as Lord Avon's, nor as queer as Lord Bradwell's, but Lord! they are as worthless as any of them (*Independent*, 21 Oct. 1986).

See ANADIPLOSIS, ANAPHORA, PARALLELISM, REDUPLICATION, TAUTOLOGY.

**REPORTED SPEECH**. See DIRECT AND INDIRECT SPEECH.

**RESPELLING**, also **re-spelling**. A lexicographical technique or system in which the PRONUNCIATION of English words is shown by means of a fixed set of letters and diacritics in which each letter unit has only one value: for example, *o* with the value in *hope* (usually regardless of accent variations). Most present-day respelling systems include the schwa or weak vowel [ə]. A dictionary that uses such a system not only describes it in detail in the introduction but also usually displays a set of key word-values at the bottom of each page, for easy consultation. In Britain, the key words of the *Chambers English Dictionary* (1988) are: '*fāte; fär; hûr; mīne; mōte; för; mūte; mōon; fŏŏt; dhen* (then); *el'əmənt* (element).' In the US, the key words (etc.) of *The Random House Dictionary* (1987), with the key letters in roman, are: '*act, cāpe, dâre, pärt; set, ēqual; if, īce; ox, ōver, ôrder; oil, bŏŏk, bōōt, out; up, ûrge; child, sing; shoe; thin, that*; zh as in *treasure*. ə = *a* as in *alone, e* as in *system, i* as in *easily, o* as in *gallop, u* as in *circus*; *ᵊ* as in *fire* (fī*ᵊ*r), *hour* (ou*ᵊ*r). l and n can serve as syllabic consonants, as in *cradle* (krād'l), and *button* (but'n).' The only current alternative to respelling is phonetic symbols, such as those of the International Phonetic Alphabet. IPA symbols representing the RP accent are standard in British learners' dictionaries and have become more common in recent years in British mother-tongue dictionaries: compare recent editions of *The Concise Oxford Dictionary*: the 7th in 1982 has respelling; the 8th in 1990 uses IPA. Respelling remains standard in the US.

**RESTRICTED LANGUAGE**. A reduced form of a LANGUAGE: 'Some REGISTERS are extremely restricted in purpose. They thus employ only a limited number of formal items and patterns [and] are known as *restricted languages'* (M. A. K. Halliday *et al.*, *The Linguistic Sciences and Language Teaching*, 1964). Such a system is often artificial and highly specialized, created and used with a particular end in mind: for example, BASIC ENGLISH, limited in its syntax and lexis, but meant to be used as an international medium; SEASPEAK, a form of English limited to specific procedures and terms, serving to facilitate the safe movement of shipping; *headlinese*, a register reduced in syntax and lexis, used to draw attention to news and other reports, and to indicate their content. See AIRSPEAK, ARTIFICIAL LANGUAGE, CONTACT LANGUAGE, ELABORATED AND RESTRICTED CODE, HEADLINE, JARGON, PIDGIN.

**RETROFLEX**. Sometimes *retroflexed*. A term in PHONETICS for sounds, especially /r/, made with the tip of the tongue curled back and raised towards the palate. These R-SOUNDS occur in such rhotic varieties of English as AmE (non-Southern), CanE, IndE, IrE, and the accents of south-west England, in which postvocalic /r/ coalesces with a following alveolar consonant in words like *worse* and *hard*. The process is known as *retroflexion*. In the languages of the Indian subcontinent, retroflex consonants such as /t/ and /d/ are common and occur in South Asian English.

**RETRONYM**. A semi-technical term for a phrase coined because an expression once used alone needs contrastive qualification: *acoustic guitar* because of *electric guitar*, *analog watch* because of *digital watch*, *manual typewriter* because of *electric/electronic typewriter*, *mono sound equipment* because of *stereo sound equipment*.

**REVERSAL**, also **retronym**. Semi-technical terms for a word that spells another word backwards: *doom*, *straw*. Deliberate reversals form a new word: the trade name *Trebor*; the BrE slang *yob* ('a backward boy': a lout). Such reversals are sometimes used for effect in utopian and satirical writing, such as Samuel Butler's novel *Erewhon* (1872), set in a land where Victorian ideas and values are reversed. Erewhonians have such names as *Yram* and *Nosnibor*.

■ **RHETORIC** ────── ■

**1.** The study and practice of effective COMMUNICATION. **2.** The art of persuasion. **3.**

An insincere eloquence intended to win points and get people what they want. All three senses have run side by side for more than 2,000 years. In the late 20c, rhetoric has an explicit and an implicit aspect. Explicitly, many 20c language professionals refer to rhetoric as archaic and irrelevant, while for some philosophers of communication and for many teachers of writing it is a significant and lively issue. In the latter circles, there is discussion of a 'new rhetoric' that blends the best of the old with current insights into the nature of communication. It is, however, an ironic measure of the centuries-old strength of rhetoric that many of its principles, concepts, and devices are taken as given by educated users of languages like English, French, and German. Terms like *ANALOGY*, *ANTITHESIS*, *dialectic*, and *METAPHOR* had their beginning among the rhetoricians of ancient Greece, as did many of the techniques of court-room argument, public speaking, advertising, marketing, and publicity.

**Origins**. In ancient societies with no awareness of writing, the ability to speak informatively, cohesively, and memorably was essential and admired. In such societies, chiefs, bards, and seers used a variety of techniques to gain attention and ensure retention of information (in their own as well as their listeners' minds). Linguistic techniques included: RHYTHM; REPETITION; formulaic lists and descriptions; kinds of EMPHASIS; balance and antithesis; ELLIPSIS; and words and devices to evoke mental images. In the course of time, such techniques were organized into bodies of received knowledge. In some societies, they were largely a part of religious ritual, as in India; in others, such as Greece, they were part of the craft of speaking which in the 5c BC became the foundation of education in city states like Athens and Sparta.

**Greek rhetoric.** The story is told of exiles who returned to Syracuse, a Greek colony in Sicily, after the overthrow of a tyrant. Because they needed to organize their claims to appropriate land, they hired teachers to help them argue their cases, and, as a result, the craft of rhetoric emerged through pleading in the Syracusan court. Itinerant teachers known as *sophists* (wise ones) then taught this forensic art alongside logic, a subject which was associated with the new craft of writing. Rhetoric's foremost exponents and analysts were Gorgias, Isocrates, Plato (all 5–4c BC), and Aristotle (4c BC). Of their rhetorical works, however, only Plato's *Phaedrus* and Aristotle's *Rhetoric* have survived. As writing became commoner, elements of the oral craft were transferred to prose composition and efforts were made to harmonize the rules of speech and writing with those of logic. The devices of rhetoric, however, did not lose their links with poetry or their practical ties with the law. As a result, rhetoric came to be viewed in two ways: as the high moral and philosophical art of speech and writing, and as a low art of winning arguments and impressing the gullible.

**The five canons**. Many manuals were compiled on the subject, such as the Latin treatise *Rhetorica ad Herennium* ('Oratory for Herennius': anonymous, 1c BC). These works usually listed five *canons* or *offices* of rhetoric, concerned with gathering, arranging, and presenting one's material:

**1. Greek *heúresis*, Latin *inventio***. Finding or researching one's material. The speaker or writer assesses an issue and assembles the necessary material.

**2. Greek *táxis*, Latin *dispositio***. Arranging or organizing one's material. Here, the orator puts the parts of the discourse in order, starting with the *exordium* or formal opening, then proceeding with the *narration*, including the division into various points of view, with proofs and refutations, and closing with the *conclusion*.

**3. Greek *léxis*, Latin *elocutio* or *educatio***. The fitting of language to audience and context, through any of three styles: the high-and-grand, the medium, and the low-and-plain. Included in this 'style' section are the traditional rhetorical devices and figures of speech.

**4. Greek *hupókrisis*, Latin *pronuntiatio* or *actio***. Performance, including the arsenal of techniques to be used in proclaiming, narrating, or in effect acting. This aspect was concerned with live audiences but also covered work on papyrus and parchment.

**5. Greek *mnémè*, Latin *memoria***. Training of the mind, to ensure accurate recall and performance in public assembly or court of law.

In all such discourse, the speaker could appeal to *páthos* (the emotions, the heart),

to *lógos* (reason; the head), and/or to *êthos* (character; morality).

**Roman rhetoric**. Republican Rome shared the Greek interest in debate and legal argument, and therefore considered rhetoric essential to public life. Classics like Aristotle's *Rhetoric* were augmented by the lawyer Cicero (2–1c BC), who produced among other works the *De inventione* (On Making your Case) and the *De oratore* (On Being a Public Speaker), and by Quintilian (1c AD), author of the *Institutio oratoria* or *Institutiones oratoriae* (Foundations of Oratory). The systematization of rhetoric served the Empire well, helping to develop Latin as a language of literacy throughout the dominions. Imperial Rome, however, generally discouraged free and democratic debate, with the result that style and effect became more important than integrity.

**Medieval and Renaissance rhetoric**. Aristotle and Cicero had a profound influence on education in medieval Christendom. Through the works of Martianus Capella (5c), Cassiodorus (5–6c), and St Isidore of Seville (6–7c), their principles became part of Scholasticism, leading to the *trivium* (the three ways) of grammar, rhetoric, and logic-cum-dialectic, studied by aspirants to Latin learning and clerical orders. The trivium was the foundation for the *quadrivium* (the four ways) of arithmetic, geometry, astronomy, and music-cum-harmony. Together, these made up 'the seven liberal arts', the core programme of theocratic and general education. Cicero had been the first to use the phrase *artes liberales* (liberal arts), the model not only for medieval and Renaissance scholarly debate but for contemporary liberal arts colleges and degrees and the education they seek to provide. When the complete text of Quintilian was rediscovered in a Swiss monastery in 1416, it helped animate the revival of classical learning known as the Renaissance. Scholars like Peter Ramus (16c), however, saw rhetoric less as a way of developing speech than as a means of teaching writing, whose importance was much greater than in classical times, both to the Church and the new nation-states. The five ancient canons were reorganized, assigning *invention* and *disposition* to dialectic and largely ignoring *memory* (although learning by heart remained a prime element in education). Renaissance rhetoric served the growth of literacy in the vernaculars as well as Latin, focusing on composition, style, and the figures of speech.

**Rhetoric and English**. During and after the Renaissance, rhetoric dominated education in the humanities in England, Scotland, and France, remaining little changed until the later 19c. During this period, the ancient tension between 'good' and 'bad' rhetoric continued, as the following extracts indicate. The first, from *The Schoolmaster* (Roger Ascham, 1563), praises Cicero and everything Latinate; the second, from *Hudibras* (Samuel Butler, 1663) mocks the ornate and empty:

Ascham. There is a way, touched in the first book of Cicero *De oratore*, which, wisely brought into schools, truly taught, and constantly used, would not only take wholly away this butcherly fear in making of Latins but would also, with ease and pleasure and in short time, as I know by good experience, work a true choice and placing of words, a right ordering of sentences, an easy understanding of the tongue, a readiness to speak, a facility to write, a true judgment both of his own and other men's doings, what tongue soever he doth use.

Butler. For rhetoric, he could not ope His mouth but out there flew a trope; And when he happened to break off In the middle of his speech, or cough, He had hard words ready to show why, And tell what rules he did it by.

The fragmentation of rhetoric that began in the Renaissance created whole new subjects in succeeding centuries. The third and fourth canons (*elocution* and *pronunciation*) became in the 18c courses in 'proper' speech, taught by actors like Thomas Sheridan and John Walker, both of whom published pronouncing dictionaries of English.

During the 17–19c, the methods of Cicero and Quintilian were standard in British and American universities. Yet, while students learned the classical languages and their rhetoric, their teachers were often in the forefront of change to English. The Scottish scholar Adam Smith chose English rather than Latin when giving his lectures; his friend Hugh Blair was appointed to the first chair of Rhetoric and Belles Lettres at the U. of Edinburgh in 1762, the precursor of all chairs of English language and literature

around the world. In 1806, the first Boylston Professor of Rhetoric and Oratory at Harvard, Massachusetts, was John Quincy Adams (later sixth US president). He was charged to instruct students in accordance with the models and exercises of Quintilian, but when Francis J. Child occupied the same chair in 1851, it was as Professor of English. In 18c society at large, issues of judgement and taste became more important than aesthetics and rhetoric, and among Romantics in the 18c and 19c freedom and feeling were more intriguing than discipline and refinement. As the 19c progressed, the ancient theorists became of less and less interest, except to classical scholars, and rhetoric became for many either the (empty) forms of public speaking or the study of writing and composition in schools. Some of the ancient aims and practices were, however, sustained in the debating societies of British universities and the departments of speech and public address in US colleges.

**Conclusion**. The ancient rhetoricians assumed that truth was absolute and separable from a text. Many 20c critics and scholars, however, see truth as relative and texts as self-contained objects whose 'truth' is re-made by every reader. The ancients regarded discourse as dynamic, embodying an intention and a design fitted to an audience, much as politicians and lawyers still see it. Many present-day literary critics, however, see discourses and especially texts as complete in themselves and distinct from their creators, the intention and ideas of the creator having reduced importance or no importance at all if they are not directly shown in the text. The dynamic therefore lies not with the writer but with the reader, in the re-creation of meaning. The emphasis has accordingly been on structure, coherence, and interpretation rather than on creation and the techniques of dissimulation that may accompany it, except insofar as these can be deconstructed to reveal a variety of possible interpretations. Even so, classical rhetoric survives. It has given shape to much of the Western world's inheritance of oracy and literacy. Everyone who speaks and writes a Western language or any language influenced by the forensic and literary traditions of the West is willy-nilly affected by it. Anyone who speaks in public or writes for professional purposes engages in the processes first listed in the five canons. In journalism and publishing, on radio and television, in the theatre and cinema, the old names may or may not be known, but the tools continue to be used.

See DISCOURSE, ELOCUTION, FIGURATIVE LANGUAGE, GRAMMAR, IRONY, PLAYING WITH WORDS, RHETORICAL QUESTION, STYLE.

**RHETORICAL QUESTION**. A QUESTION that expects no answer. The answer may be self-evident (*If she doesn't like me why should I care what she thinks?*) or immediately provided by the questioner (*What should be done? Well, first we should . . .*). The question is often asked for dramatic effect. Rhetorical questions are sometimes announced with such a phrase as *I ask you* (when nothing is in fact being asked): 'Garn! *I ask you*, what kind of a word is that? / It's Ow and Garn that keep her in her place, / Not her wretched clothes and dirty face' (Alan Jay Lerner, *My Fair Lady*, 1956).

**RHOTIC AND NON-RHOTIC**. Terms coined by the British phonetician John Wells for two kinds of spoken English, a fundamental contrastive feature in the language. In one set of accents of English, *r* is pronounced wherever it is orthographically present: *red, barrel, beer, beard, worker*. Such a variety is variously known as *rhotic, r-pronouncing*, or *r-ful(l)*. In another set of accents, *r* is pronounced in syllable-initial position (*red*) and intervocalically (*barrel*), but not postvocalically (*beer, beard, worker*). In such positions it is vocalized (turned into a vowel) and not pronounced unless another vowel follows. Such a variety is variously known as *non-rhotic, non-r-pronouncing*, or *r-less*. The mainly rhotic and non-rhotic communities in the English-speaking world are: (1) *Rhotic*. Canada; India; Ireland; southwestern England; Scotland; the northern and western states of the US apart from the Boston area and New York City; Barbados. (2) *Nonrhotic*. Black Africa; Australia; the Caribbean, except for Barbados; England apart, in the main, from the south-west; New Zealand; South Africa; the southern states, the Boston area of New England, and New York City vernacular speech; and Black English Vernacular in the US; Wales. Foreign learners from such backgrounds as the Romance languages and Arabic and those who have Network American as their pronunciation model tend to be rhotic. Foreign learners in Black Africa, and from

China and Japan, as well as those who have RP (BBC English) as their model tend to be nonrhotic. See R, R-SOUNDS.

**RHYME**, also **rime**. A general and literary term for the effect produced by using words that end with the same or similar sounds: in the last stressed vowel (*fire/lyre/ desire/aspire*) and in following vowels and consonants (*inspiring/retiring*; *admiringly/conspiringly*). Rhyme has been a major feature of English VERSE since the early medieval period and is widely regarded as essential to it, although a great deal of verse is unrhymed. See POETRY.

**RHYMING SLANG**. A form of SLANG that may have originated in the 18c, probably among the London Cockneys, as part of creative word-play and thieves' cant. It is unlikely, however, that there was ever a systematic code of rhymes used to create a PRIVATE LANGUAGE. Rhyming slang was part of the general patter of traders and others, used as much for amusement as for secret communication. It was never a major feature of COCKNEY usage, and became more widely known through its use on radio and television. There are two stages in its formation and use:

**1. *Creating two-term phrases***. The effect depends on the creation of a binary expression that rhymes with a single everyday word: *apples and pears* with *stairs, ball of chalk* with *walk, bowl of water* with *daughter, Bristol City* with *titty, butcher's hook* with *look, trouble and strife* with *wife*. The rhyme need not be perfect and is sometimes based on an existing slang usage: *Lakes of Killarney/barmy, cobbler's awls/balls*, where *barmy* means 'mad' and *balls* stands for 'testicles' and by extension 'nonsense'.

**2. *Dropping the second term***. The second element in the pair may then be dropped: *Bristol Cities* becomes *Bristols*, as in *Get a load of those Bristols* (Just look at those breasts), *butcher's hook* becomes *butcher's*, as in *Take a butcher's at him* (Take a look at him), and *cobbler's awls* becomes *cobbler's*, as in *What a load of old cobblers* (What crap).

Rhyming slang may never have been limited to London and is found in other parts of the British Isles, in Australia, and in the US. It is, however, most commonly associated with London, at least as regards its origins, and much of its spread has been due to the broadcasting and other dissemination of Cockney and pseudo-Cockney usages.

# ■ RHYTHM ■

**1.** The flow and beat of such things as sound, melody, SPEECH, and art. **2.** In music, the arrangement of beats and lengths of notes, shown in notation as *bars* or groups of beats, the first beat of each bar carrying the stress. **3.** In poetics, the arrangement of words into a more or less regular sequence of long and short syllables (as in the quantitative metre of LATIN) or stressed and unstressed syllables (as in the accentual metre of English), and any arrangement of this kind. **4.** In PHONETICS, the sense of movement in speech, consisting of the *STRESS*, *quantity*, and *timing* of syllables. The rhythm of a language is one of its fundamental features, acquired early by a child and hard for an adult to change. Its basis is pulses of air in the lungs: technically, in the pulmonic airstream mechanism. Such a pulse or beat is produced by the intercostal respiratory muscles and is known as the *breath pulse*, *syllable pulse*, or *chest pulse*. This pulse serves as the basis for the syllable and a flow of such pulses creates the series of beats in the flow of syllables. Occasionally, a pulse can occur but be silent, as when someone says ʼ*kyou* for *thank you*; this is technically referred to as *silent stress*. When a chest pulse has greater force, it produces a *stress pulse* whose outcome is usually a stressed SYLLABLE. Ordinary chest pulses occur at a rate of about five per second, stress pulses less frequently. David Abercrombie notes: 'These two processes—the syllable process and the stress process—together make up the pulmonic mechanism, and they are the basis on which the whole of the rest of speech is built' (*Elements of General Phonetics*, 1967, p. 36).

**Stress-timed and syllable-timed languages**. The two processes are coordinated in different ways in different languages, and the way in which they are combined produces a language's rhythm, which is fundamentally a matter of timing the pulses. In order to account for differences in timing among languages, a distinction is often drawn between *stress-timing* and *syllable-timing*, according to whether the foot or the syllable is taken as the unit of time. Broadly speaking, the languages of the world divide into *stress-timed languages* such as English, Modern GREEK, and RUSSIAN, and *syllable-timed languages* such as FRENCH and Japanese; many languages, such as Arabic and Hindi, do not fit either category, and it is doubtful whether any language fits either category perfectly. In any language, timing is not uniform throughout speech: it is affected by TONE group boundaries, and slows down in final position. Nevertheless, the distinction is a useful pedagogical device: English learners of French can aim at syllable-timing, and French learners of English can aim at stress-timing. In some styles of delivery, including poetry reading and the recital of the liturgy, the rhythm appears more marked than usual. This is probably due to adjustments to the intonation (such as narrowed pitch range, and tones narrowed to the point where they become level) that background the intonation and leave the rhythm more prominent.

In a *stress-timed* rhythm, timing is based on stressed syllables that occur at approximately regular (*isochronous*) intervals: that is, the unit of rhythm known as the *foot* has about the same duration irrespective of the number of syllables it contains. According to this view, in the phrase ||*dozens off old*/ *photographs*||, *dozens of* takes about the same time to say as *old*. In practice, such languages are not strictly isochronous, but rather tend towards it: the syllables of polysyllabic feet are compressed, and monosyllabic feet lengthened. A second feature of such languages is the reduction of unstressed syllables. This applies to the weak syllables of words and unstressed words. In a *syllable-timed* rhythm, timing is based on the syllable. This does not mean, however, that all syllables are equal in duration: they vary according to the vowels and consonants they contain. Syllable-timed languages lack the rhythmical properties of stress-timing: syllables are not compressed between stresses, and unstressed syllables are not reduced. Although syllable-timing is not used in native-speaker English (except occasionally for comic purposes), it is common in the kind of English spoken by people whose first language is syllable-timed, as is usual in Africa. The consequent lack of reduction might superficially appear to make speech clearer, but by obscuring the stress pattern it reduces the information normally carried by stress and reduces intelligibility. See LINGUISTIC TYPOLOGY, SCHWA, WEAK VOWEL.

**ROGET'S THESAURUS**, full title *Roget's Thesaurus of English Words and Phrases*. A work of REFERENCE by the English physician, taxonomist, librarian, and inventor Peter Mark Roget (1779–1869), published in 1852 by Longman. Its aim was to supply, with respect to the English language, a desideratum hitherto unsupplied in any language; namely, a collection of the words it contains and of the idiomatic combinations peculiar to it, arranged, not in alphabetical order as they are in a Dictionary, but according to the *ideas* which they express' (original introduction). The *Thesaurus* has been revised many times, has sold over 30m copies worldwide in different editions, and has become an institution of the language. The words in *Roget* are arranged in listed sets like the genera and species of biology. The intention has not been to define or discriminate them, but to arrange them in synonymous and antonymous groups; it serves as both a word-finder and a prompter of the memory regarding words one knows but could not recall to mind.

The *Thesaurus* was sustained by the Roget family for three generations: Roget himself brought out several revisions before his death in 1869, after which his son John Lewis Roget, a lawyer, continued the work (adding a word-index, which greatly aided use of the book, and a major revision in 1879) until his death in 1908, when his son Samuel Romilly Roget, an engineer, took over, providing a major revision in 1936. During Samuel's time as editor, the boom for crossword puzzles developed, creating a demand for the word-finder that neither his father nor grandfather could have predicted. He sold the rights to Longman in 1952, the year before he died. Since then there have been three revisions: by Robert A. Dutch (1962), Susan M. Lloyd (1982), and Betty Kirkpatrick (1987). There have been many changes between 1852 and 1987, but Roget's basic structure survives in the Longman work, whose latest edition is entitled *The Original Roget's Thesaurus* to distinguish it from various adaptations by other publishers, especially alphabetic versions in the US.

The classification of the *Thesaurus* is hierarchical, with six major headings: *Abstract Relations*, *Space*, *Matter*, *Intellect*, *Volition*, *Affec-*tions. In the 1982 and 1987 editions, *Affections* has been replaced by *Emotion*, *religion*, *and morality*. Each of these headings is further divided, *Abstract Relations* for example into: *Existence*, *Relation*, *Quantity*, *Order*, *Number*, *Time*, *Change*, *Causation*. Each subheading is further subdivided, *Existence* for example into: *Existence*, *Inexistence*, *Substantiality*, *Unsubstantiality*, *Intrinsicality*, *Extrinsicality*, *State*, *Circumstance*. At this third level come the specific sets of words, among which are italicized keywords preceded by numbers. These keywords, which were introduced by Dutch, serve as cross-references to sets elsewhere in the book. The following is the content and layout of part of set no. 1 in the 1987 edition:

> *existence*, being, entity; absolute being, the absolute 965 *divineness*; aseity, self-existence; monad, a being, an entity, ens, essence, quiddity; Platonic idea, universal; subsistence 360 *life*; survival, eternity 115 *perpetuity*; preexistence 119 *priority*; this life 121 *present time*; existence in space, prevalence 189 *presence*; entelechy, realization, becoming, evolution 147 *conversion*; creation 164 *production*; potentiality 469 *possibility*; ontology, metaphysics; realism, materialism, idealism, existentialism 449 *philosophy*.

In addition to such thematic sets, which make up the bulk of the present-day book, a detailed index shows where a listed word may be found: for example, *existence* is shown as appearing not only in *existence* 1, but also in *presence* 189, *materiality* 319, and *life* 360. Longman claim that over 1.25m words are covered in the 1987 Kirkpatrick edition. Also in 1987, Bloomsbury (London) brought out a facsimile edition of the original *Thesaurus*, with an introduction by Laurence Urdang. See LEXICOGRAPHY, THESAURUS.

**ROMAN. 1.** Both with and without an initial capital: relating to the upright style of typeface that dominates texts in English (of which this volume is an example) and many other languages, and that derives from the LETTER shapes used in ancient Rome; Roman type or lettering: *a text printed in Times Roman*; *a mixture of Roman and Gothic*; *substituting italic for roman*. **2.** The Roman ALPHABET: *Malay can be written in both Roman and Arabic*. When the characters of another WRITING system are transliterated into

Roman, they are said to be *Romanized* or, more commonly, *romanized*. Systems of romanization include *Wade–Giles* and *Pinyin* ('classifying sound') for Chinese and *Hepburn* and *romaji* ('Roman letters') for Japanese. See CHINA, JAPAN, TRANSLITERATION.

# ■ ROMANCE LANGUAGES ──── ■

[From Medieval Latin *romancium/romancia* a Latin vernacular language, from *Romanicus* of Roman origin], sometimes *Romanic languages*. *Languages* descended from the LATIN of the Roman Empire, such as FRENCH and SPANISH.

**Identifying the languages**. The number of Romance languages varies according to the criteria used to establish them, such as: (1) Status as a national language, in which case there are five (French, ITALIAN, PORTUGUESE, Romanian, and Spanish/Castilian) or six if Romansch or Rhaeto-Romanic (a language of Switzerland) is included. (2) Possession of a literary tradition, in which case there are nine (the above, plus Catalan, Gallego (in Spain), and Occitan (including Provençal), in France). (3) Geographical or other distinctness, in which case there are 15 (the above, plus Andalusian (Spain), Friulian, Ladin (northern Italy), Sardinian and Sicilian (southern Italy), and Judeo-Spanish, also called Judezmo and Ladino (the Romance equivalent of Yiddish)). Extinct Romance varieties include Dalmatian (Yugoslavia) and Mozarabic (the language of Christians in Moorish Spain). There are also a number of Romance PIDGINS and CREOLES, including Haitian Creole French and Papiamentu, a mixed Portuguese–Spanish creole in the Netherlands Antilles. Romance languages are spoken by nearly 400m people and their creoles by nearly 6m more.

**Origins and development**. With the disintegration of the western Roman Empire (3–5c), forms of Vulgar or Popular Latin developed as the languages of many successor nations. In Italy, the transition was relatively straightforward, post-Latin varieties supplanting their closely related Italic predecessors, but elsewhere the success of the early Romance languages was largely at the expense of Celtic languages especially in Spain and France. Germanic invaders of Italy, Spain, and France did not retain their own languages, and even as late as the 10c,

Scandinavian invaders gave up Norse in favour of French when they settled what came to be known as Normandy. No Romance language developed in the Roman provinces of Britain, probably because Popular Latin was not so firmly established there, Celtic continued to be strong, and the language of the Anglo-Saxon settlers was little exposed to Latin influence before or after they left their homes on the north-western European coast. However, the many Latin loanwords in Welsh suggest that a Romance language might have developed in southern Britain if conditions had been more like those of Gaul and Spain.

**Romance in English**. The Germanic language of Britain developed largely free of Latin and of Romance influence until the 11c, when the Conquest of 1066 took Norman French across the Channel. For at least two centuries thereafter, a Romance language dominated social, political, and cultural life in much of the British Isles and had such an impact on the vocabulary and writing of English that, like Albanian and Maltese, English has been called a *semi-Romance language*; as Owen Barfield observed, 'the English language has been facetiously described as "French badly pronounced" ' (*History in English Words*, 1962, p. 59). Because of the French connection and the associated influence of Neo-Latin, English shares with the romance languages a vast reservoir of lexis, concepts, allusions, and conventions. The accompanying table (which could be greatly expanded) lists 20 everyday English words and their equivalents in French, Spanish, Italian, and Portuguese. It shows not only the similarity (even visual identity) of many items, but also, roughly in proportion to the various vocabularies, certain patterns of dissimilarity. Three English words of non-Romance origin (*bed, garden, oak*) are included, one of which (*garden*) is an example of how, on occasion, Germanic words have been adopted into Romance. See BORROWING, EUROPEAN LANGUAGES, LINGUA FRANCA, POLARI, SABIR.

**ROMANI**, also **Romany**. **1.** A member of the Romani community, *c.*6–10m worldwide. **2.** The originally Indo-Aryan language of the Gypsies, whose *c.*60 dialects vary greatly because of the community's wide dispersal and the impact of such languages as Persian, Greek, Hungarian, and English in places where Gypsies live or have

## SOME EVERYDAY WORDS IN ENGLISH AND FOUR ROMANCE LANGUAGES

| English | French | Spanish | Italian | Portuguese |
|---------|--------|---------|---------|------------|
| art | art | arte | arte | arte |
| bandage | bandage | venda | fasciatura | venda |
| bed | lit | cama | letto | cama |
| date (fruit) | date | dátil | dattero | tâmara |
| eagle | aigle | águila | aquila | águia |
| garden | jardin | jardin | giardino | jardim |
| January | janvier | enero | gennaio | janeiro |
| February | février | febrero | febbraio | fevereiro |
| legal | légal | legal | legale | legal |
| magic | magie | magia | magia | mágico |
| mountain | montagne | montaña | montagna | montanha |
| oak | chêne | roble | quercia | carvalho |
| parcel | paquet | paquete | pacco | pacote |
| poor | pauvre | pobre | povero | pobre |
| price | prix | precio | prezzo | preço |
| question | question | pregunta | domanda | pergunta |
| round | rond | redondo | rotondo | redondo |
| solution | solution | solución | soluzione | solução |
| value | valeur | valor | valore | valor |
| war | guerre | guerra | guerra | guerra |

lived. Most of the estimated 250,000 speakers of Romani are at least bilingual. In recent years, efforts have been made to create a standard written form for this largely non-literate language, in part so as to promote a stronger sense of ethnic identity among the Rom people. In Britain, there is a continuum of usage from a conservative inflected form called *Romnimos*, spoken by some 500 people mainly in Wales, to *Anglo-Romani*, *Angloromani*, *Anglo-Romany*, or *Romani English*, spoken by some 80,000 around the country, not all of them ethnic Gypsies. Anglo-Romani may contain more Romnimos or more English, depending on circumstances, and has often been regarded as a Travellers' argot. An excerpt from the New Testament in Anglo-Romani runs:

There was a rich mush with kushti-dicking purple togs. Every divvus his hobben was kushti. By his jigger suttied a poor mush called Lazarus. Lazarus dicked wafedi, riffly as a juk. He was ready to scran anything he could get his vasters on or kur it from the rich mush's

table (The Gospel According to Luke, 16: 19–21, in *More Kushti Lavs*, the Bible Society, 1981) [*mush* man, *kushti* good, *dick* look, *divvus* day, *hobben* food, *jigger* door, *sutty* sleep, *wafedi* bad, *riffly* dirty, *juk* dog, *scran* eat, *vaster* hand, *kur* steal, *lavs* news].

Words from Romani borrowed into English tend to be slangy or informal; they include *mush* ('moosh': BrE slang) a friend, buddy, *nark* a (police) informer or spy (from *nāk* nose), and *pal* a friend. See BORROWING, COCKNEY, POLARI, SHELTA.

**ROOT. 1.** Also sometimes *radical*. In traditional GRAMMAR and PHILOLOGY, the element, often monosyllabic, left after all affixes have been removed from a complex WORD: *-ceive* in *receive*, *help* in *unhelpfully*, *act* in *reactivation*. A root may or may not be a word, and may have several forms and meanings the further back it is traced in a language or languages. Compare BASE. **2.** Also *ROOT-WORD*. A word that is ancestral to a present-day word: the Latin verb *decidere*, the root of the English verb *decide* and the French verb *décider*. Compare ETYMON. The classical elements in the vocabulary of English have often been listed and discussed, especially in textbooks and dictionaries, as 'LATIN and GREEK roots', sometimes in the first sense given here, sometimes in the second sense, sometimes as a mix of the two.

In LINGUISTICS, a distinction is generally made not only between the two senses of *root* (above) but also between the terms *root* and *base*. The Latin *nescius* is the root or source of English *nice*, but is not a root in the philological sense. Rather, it consists of two elements, *ne* not, *scius* knowing. Its form cannot be detected anywhere 'inside' or 'under' present-day *nice*, which serves as a base for the formations *nicety* and *niceness*. *Ne* is a particle that also appears in *neuter*, and *scius* is made up of a linguistic root *sci* and an inflectional ending *-us*. *Sci* is present in the Latin *scientia* and its English derivative *science*; it is ancient, being the Latin 'descendant' of the Indo-European root *\*skei* to cut, split. This 'deep' primoridial root also appears to underlie Old English *scinu* (Modern English *shin*), Old High German *scina* needle, Old Irish *scian* knife, Greek *schizein* to split, and Latin *scindere* to cut. See INDO-EUROPEAN ROOTS, ROOT-CREATION, WORD-FORMATION.

**ROOT-CREATION**. A term in WORD-FORMATION for the creation of a new ROOT, BASE, or simple WORD. The process is rare compared with compounding and derivation, and is divided into *motivated root-creation* and *ex nihilo root-creation*. By and large, motivated root-creation (in which a reason can be given for the formation of an item) is ad hoc and echoic, the new form resembling one or more pre-existing forms. As with *cuckoo*, the new form may represent a real or imagined sound: *zap* the noise made by a ray-gun, *vroom* the sound of a powerful engine. By retaining the consonants and varying the vowel, a word like *splash* can be adapted to *splish*, *splosh*, *sploosh*, *splush*. In addition, a new form may be a reversal, an anagram, or some other adaptation of a pre-existing form. In ex-nihilo root-creation, however, there appears to be no lexicological way of accounting for the formation of a word: it has no known precursors, as with the trade name *Kodak* (invented in the US in 1888 by George Eastman) and the number

*googol* (invented on request by a 9-year-old boy).

Although rare in general usage, ex-nihilo forms are common in fiction, and especially fantasy, in which writers often seek to escape the bonds of their language: Robert A. Heinlein's Martian word *grok* suggests empathy and understanding: 'the ungrokkable vastness of ocean' (*Stranger in a Strange Land*, 1961). When sets of words are coined in a fantasy, however, escape from some degree of motivation is unlikely: for example, in Edgar Rice Burroughs's adventure novel *Tarzan at the Earth's Core* (1929), the inner world of Pellucidar is peopled by such creatures as the anagrammatic *tarag* and *jalok* (variants of *tiger* and *jackal*), the *thag* (a primeval ox, echoing *stag*), the *sagoth* (a gorilla-like hominid, echoing and perhaps blending *savage* and *Goth*), and the clipped *horib* (a snake-like being overtly referred to as *horrid* and *horrible*). The limits of actual or apparent root-creation are hard to establish, because it shades into such conventional processes of word-formation as turning names into words (*Hoover* becoming *to hoover a rug*), blending (*smog* from *smoke* and *fog*), and abbreviation (*mob* from *mobile vulgus*). A classic clipping is *tawdry*, from *tawdrie lace* (16c), in turn from *Seynt Audries lace*, as sold at St Audrey's Fair at Ely in East Anglia (*Audrey* in turn being a Normanization of Anglo-Saxon *Etheldreda*). Such creations can reasonably be identified as 'roots' because they can and often do become the foundations of more complex forms, such as *Hoovermatic*, *Kodachrome*, *mobster*, *smog-bound*, and *tawdriness*. See ECHOISM, NEOLOGISM, ONOMATOPOEIA, PHONAESTHESIA.

**ROOT-WORD**, also **root word**. A term in WORD-FORMATION for a WORD, usually monosyllabic, that is prior or ancestral to one or more other words: *blood* the root-word of *bloody*, *bloodily*, *bloodhound*, *bloodthirsty*, *bloodthirstiness*, *cold-blooded*, *cold-bloodedly*, *bleed*, *bleeds*, *bleeding*, *nose bleed*. The term belongs in a group of related and sometimes overlapping terms with *ROOT*, *BASE*, and *simple word*, and implies that every language has a certain number or range of basic words and word elements, often presumed to be known by every user and listed somewhere. However, no one knows all the root forms of English or can easily decide whether certain freshly encountered items are new, old, meaningful, or meaningless. Such items as *grise*, *quetch*, and *smidge* conform to a pattern of what English words are like, in terms of syllable, sound, and spelling. Items like *\*tleen*, *\*pwrg*, and *\*xacs* do not. However, as loans like *axolotl* from Nahuatl and *cwm* from Welsh indicate, alien structure is no bar to entry into English. See ROOT-CREATION, VOCABULARY CONTROL.

**ROYAL SOCIETY**, full name *Royal Society of London for the Promotion of Natural Knowledge*. The oldest continuously functioning scientific society in Britain and the world. It was founded in 1660 as the *Royal Society for the Advancement of Experimental Philosophy*, and granted royal charters in 1662 and 1663, when it acquired its present name. In its early years, the Society showed a brief inclination to 'improve the English tongue, paricularly for philosophic purposes', setting up in 1664 a committee with that end in view. Among its 22 members were the poets John Dryden and Edmund Waller, Bishop Thomas Sprat, and the diarist John Evelyn. However, the committee met only a few times and achieved nothing, despite considering a GRAMMAR of English and the omission of superfluous letters from the orthography. In his *History of the Royal Society* (1667), Sprat continued the discussion by arguing that the Society should require of its members 'a close, naked, natural way of speaking; positive expressions; clear senses; a native easiness; bringing all things as near the mathematical plainness as they can; and preferring the language of artisans, countrymen, and merchants, before that of wits and scholars'. The Society took such matters no further, however, and this limited exercise was as close as England came to forming anything like the Académie française.

**R-SOUNDS**. No other CONSONANT of English is as variable as that represented by the letter *R*. Although /r/ is one phoneme in English, there are six ways in which it is pronounced: (1) *A post-alveolar approximant*. This is made by raising the tip of the tongue behind, but without touching, the ALVEOLAR ridge, the lips usually rounded, the lower lip brought close to the upper teeth. It is dominant in EngE and common in AusE and NZE. If the tongue movement is omitted, the result is a sound like /w/, suggested by (often facetious) spellings using *w*

instead of *r*: *wound and wound the wugged wocks the wagged wascal wan*. This usage has been noted in EngE variously: as an aristocratic shibboleth, an affectation, and a speech defect. (2) *A retroflex*. If the tip of the tongue is raised further and curled back towards the palate, the result is a RETROFLEX *r*. It is dominant in the US. Canada, Ireland, and in the south-west of England, and gaining ground in Scotland. (3) *An alveolar flap*. If the tongue strikes the alveolar ridge as the tip is lowered, the result is a flapped *r*. This usage is characteristic of some varieties of IndE. (4) *An alveolar tap*. If the tongue strikes the ridge as the tip is raised, the result is a tapped *r*. This usage is dominant in ScoE, common among older speakers of RP in England, and typical of speakers of English in South Africa of Afrikaans background. When used by RP speakers in phrases like 'very American', Americans report hearing *Veddy Ameddican*. (5) *An alveolar trill or roll*. If the tongue is held in such a position that the air-stream causes it to vibrate against the alveolar ridge, the result is a trill or roll, a usage marked in Spanish by a double *r* (contrasting *pero*, 'but', with *perro*, 'dog'). It is widely regarded as a typically Scottish 'rolled r', and is so promoted in stage and jocular stereotypes. (6) *A uvular* /r/. If the tongue is pulled backwards towards the uvula, three kinds of *r* can be made: a uvular approximant, a uvulur fricative, and a uvular trill (as in Parisian-French). Small numbers of speakers with a uvular *r* can be found in various parts of northern Britain, such as north-east England (the *Durham* or *Northumberland BURR*) and south-east Scotland (the *Berwickshire burr*). See GEORDIE, INTRUSIVE *R*, LINKING *R*, LIQUID, *L*-SOUNDS, R, RHOTIC AND NON-RHOTIC.

**RULE**. **1.** A principle that contributes to the organization and control of a group, activity, system, etc., and has the backing of some kind of authority. **2.** In LANGUAGE TEACHING and learning, a formal statement about the use of an aspect of a language, such as REGULAR and IRREGULAR verbs in French. Traditionally, such rules have often been learned by heart. They are both prescriptive and proscriptive. See DESCRIPTIVE AND PRESCRIPTIVE GRAMMAR. **3.** In LINGUISTICS, a formal statement of the relationship between structures or units, such as the rules for forming plurals in English. Such rules are intended to be descriptive: explicit statements of how a language works (or may work), representing procedures applied by native speakers without conscious reflection when they talk to each other. It is not always easy to keep the first and second senses of the term distinct from the third sense. See DESCRIPTIVISM AND PRESCRIPTIVISM. **4.** In PRINTING, a thin strip of metal or its equivalent, used for printing a solid or decorative line or lines. Such a line has the length of an em is an *em rule*, of an en, an *en rule*; such rules are used in punctuation as longer or shorter DASHES.

**RUNE.** A character in an ancient script of 24 angular LETTERS, usually cut on wood or carved in stone, and known as either *the runic alphabet* or *Futhark/Futhorc* (with or without an initial capital: from the names of its first six letters, regarded as equivalents of *f*, *u*, *th*, *a* or *o*, *r*, and *k* or *c*). The origin of the script is uncertain; most probably it was adapted by the Goths from the Etruscan ALPHABET and later influenced by Roman. It was used from the 3c to the 16/17c, especially in Scandinavia, Iceland, and Britain, to write GERMANIC LANGUAGES. Runes, long regarded as magical, have been used on monuments, in charms, in fortune-telling (*casting the runes*), and as decorative motifs. Each has a mnemonic name beginning with the sound of the letter, such as *feoh* (property) and *ūr* (bison) for the *f* and *u* symbols. The letters *THORN* (thorn) and *WYNN* (joy) were added to the Roman alphabet for writing OLD ENGLISH, and the runic name *æsc* (ASH) was given to the digraph æ. Runic writings survive in *c*.4,000 inscriptions and some manuscripts.

■ **RUSSIAN** ————————————— ■

The major language of the Slavonic branch of the INDO-EUROPEAN language family, the language of the Russian people and the state language of the former Soviet Union, written in Cyrillic script. It has *c*.150m native speakers, and at least another 50m inhabitants of the ex-Soviet territories, and others, use it as a second language. Although the vast majority of its speakers live in the successor States of the USSR, Russian is used internationally in economic, scientific, and military contexts, and in the UNITED NATIONS Organization, where it is one of the six official languages. A thousand years or more ago, a relatively undiversified

East Slavonic dialect, generally known as *Old Russian*, was spoken in and around the approximate area of present-day Western European Russia, the Ukraine, and Byelorussia. Out of it emerged the Russian, Ukrainian, and Byelorussian languages. An early form of standard modern Russian developed in the 16c, centred on the educated speech of Moscow, and was influenced from the 17c onward by other EUROPEAN LANGUAGES, especially Dutch and French. It gained international status in the 19c because of the power of Imperial Russia and the achievements of such writers as Pushkin and Tolstoy. The Revolution of 1917, which led to the creation of the Soviet Union, associated the language closely with the maintenance and spread of Communism.

**Russian in English.** The impact of Russian on English has been slight in comparison with that of French or Spanish, but many of its loanwords stand out because of their exotic spellings and connotations. BORROWINGS fall into two broad categories: (1) Traditional cultural expressions: *bors(c)h* a soup based on beetroot, *borzoi* (swift) a kind of hound, *czar/tsar* (from Russian *tsar'*, from Latin *caesar*) emperor, king, *dros(h)ky* (from *drozhki*) an open, four-wheeled carriage, *r(o)uble* the unit of Russian currency, *steppe* (from *setp'* lowland) a prairie, *troíka* (three-some) a carriage drawn by three horses side by side, a group of three acting together, a triumvirate, *vodka* (diminutive of *voda* water) an alcoholic drink. (2) Soviet and Communist usage: *gulag* (acronym of *Glávnoe upravlénie ispravítel'no-trudovŷkh lagereĭ* Main Directorate of Corrective Labour Camps) a labour camp, especially for political prisoners, *kolkhoz* (from *kollektívnoe khozyáĭstvo* collective household) a collective farm. This group contains many expressions, including acronyms, coined in Russian from Latin and Greek: *commissar* (from *komissár*) a political officer; *agitprop* political agitation and propaganda (from the organization title *Agitpropbyuro*, from *agitatsiya* and *propaganda*), *apparat* party organization, *Comintern/Komintern* (from *Kommunistícheskiĭ Internatsionál*) the Communist International organization (1919–43), *cosmonaut* (from *kosmonávt* 'universe sailor') a Soviet astronaut, *intelligentisia* intellectuals considered as a group or class.

**English in Russian.** The impact of English on Russian has been largely lexical, especially in the following areas, and has been increasing in recent years: (1) Sport and entertainment, etc.: *basketbol, chempion, futbol, kemping, khobbi* (hobby), *khokkey, kloun, klub, match, nokaut, ralli, rekord, sport, sportsmen, sprinter, striptiz, tent, yumor.* (2) Politics, management, etc.: *boykot, interv'yu, lider, miting, pamflet.* (3) Food and drink: *bifshteks, dzhin,* *grog, keks, puding.* (4) Transport, commerce, and travel: *konteyner, motel', tanker, tonnel'* or *tunnel', trauler, trolleybus.* (5) Culture and technology: *bitnik* (beatnik), *detektiv* (meaning also *detective novel*), *komfort, komp'yuter, lift, poni, radar, servis, toster.* See INDO-EUROPEAN LANGUAGES, SLAV(ON)IC LANGUAGES.

# S

[Called 'ess']. The 19th LETTER of the Roman ALPHABET as used for English. It originated as the Phoenician symbol for a voiceless sibilant. The Greeks adopted it as the letter *sigma* (Σ), with lower-case variants according to its position in a word: medial (σ) and final (ς). The Etruscans and then the Romans further adapted the form to create S. A straightened lower-case variant (ʃ), known as LONG S was used in script and (except in final position) in printing until the 18c.

**Sound values: voiceless and voiced**. (1) In English, the letter *s* represents a sibilant alveolar fricative, both voiceless /s/ and voiced /z/, that is sometimes palatalized. (2) Initial *s* is normally voiceless, and precedes vowels (*sat, sail, set, seat, sit, site, soon, soil, south*) and consonants (*scare, skill, slip, smith, snip, sphere, spit, squeal, still, svelte, swing*). (3) Final *s* in monosyllables is voiced in *as, has, his, is, was*, but not in *gas, yes, this*, nor in most accents after *u*: *us, bus, pus, thus*. Final double *s* is always voiceless: contrast *his/hiss*. (4) Certain common *s*-endings of Romance or GREEK origin are voiceless (*-as* as in *atlas, -is* as in *cannabis, -os* as in *rhinoceros, -ous* as in *famous, -us* as in *terminus*), but final *-es* is typically voiced (*species, theses, Hercules*). (5) The Romance prefix *dis-* varies, with voicing in *disaster, disease* but not in *disagreeable, disgrace*. (6) The Germanic prefix *mis-* never has voiced *s*: *misadventure, mischance, misgovern, mishap, misspell*. (7) Between vowels, *s* is normally voiced: *bosom, busy, cousin, easy, feasible, hesitate, misery, peasant, poison, position, present, prison, reason, rosy, visit, weasel* (contrast *admissible, blossom, gossip, lesson, possible*). (8) Intervocalic *s* is voiceless in *basin, mason, sausage* (derived from earlier French *c*: compare Modern FRENCH *bassin, maçon, saucisse*), and usually also in *-osity* (*curiosity, luminosity*). (9) Greek-derived words commonly have voiceless medial *s*: *analysis, asylum, basalt, crisis, dose, episode, thesis* (but not *music, physics*). (10) After medial consonants *s* is usually voiceless: *balsam, arsenal, gipsy* but note *clumsy, crimson, damsel*. There is variation after *n*: *answer, ransom*, but *Kansas, pansy*. It is usually voiceless before voiceless medial consonants (*asphalt, basket, hospital, sister, whistle*), but otherwise voiced (*husband, wisdom, muslin, spasm, dismal*).

**-CE, -SE, -ZE**. (1) A final *e* sometimes distinguishes voiced and voiceless *s* (*tens/tense*), but the distinction is rarely reliable (contrast *chase/phase*) compared with voiceless *-ce* (*hens/hence, advise/advice*) and voiced *-ze* (*dose/doze*). *Lens* is unusual: a voiced singular without final *e*. The cluster *-nse* usually has voiceless *s* as in *tense/dense*, but note *cleanse*. The ambiguity of *-se* is not removed by contrasting forms with *-ce, -ze*: *since/rinse* both have voiceless /s/, while *fleece/freeze* are distinct. The dominant pattern of voiced or voiceless *-se* varies according to preceding vowel, but uncertainty is high after the long *e*-sound, as in *lease/please, geese/cheese*. (2) The pronunciation of *grease* (noun and verb) varies from accent to accent: /s/ in RP, /z/ commonly in ScoE, and regionally varied in AmE. (3) In *lose/loose* it is the consonant sounds that differ but the vowel spellings that vary. (4) Some words vary /s, z/ according to grammatical category, as in *close* (adjective and verb) and *house, use* (noun and verb) (*closest/closed, house/houses/housed* and *useful/useable*), sometimes using *c* for the voiceless alternative or *z* for the voiced, as in *advise/advice, glass/glaze*. (5) AmE sometimes prefers *-se* for BrE *-ce*: AmE *defense, offense, pretense, practise, license, vise* (the tool), BrE *defence, offence, pretence, practice, licence, vice*. (6) *Erase, eraser, erasure* are normally voiced in BrE but voiceless in AmE.

**Palatalized S**. (1) Before *i* or *u*, there are some common patterns of palatalization, with *s* pronounced *sh*, or, if voiced, *zh*. This arises by assimilation of a following *y*-sound, represented either by *i* or by *u* pronounced with an initial *y*-sound, as in *puce, pure*. Sometimes assimilation is incomplete, with *s* kept unpalatalized in careful speech: for example, /s/ in *issue* and /z/ in *casual*. Conversely, palatalization is sometimes extended to words like *assume* ('ashoom'). (2) Initial palatalized *s* is confined to *sugar, sure* (and the derivatives *assurance, insurance*), but palatalization is common before final *un-*

stressed vowels: geographical terms such as *Asia, Persia* are heard with both voiced and voiceless palatalized *s*. (3) Before final *-ion, s* is palatalized and voiceless after *l* or *n* (*impulsion, tension*), but has optional voicing after *r* (*version, immersion*, but not *torsion*), and regular voicing after vowels (*invasion, lesion, vision, erosion, fusion*). (4) Voiceless palatalized *s* after vowels is doubled: *passion, session, mission, concussion*: compare *Russian*, but unpalatalized *ss* in *hessian*. (5) Other endings preceded by palatalized *s* are *-ual, -ure*, voiced as in *casual, visual, usual, measure, leisure*, but voiceless in *fissure, censure, tonsure, sensual*. The list does not include *-ial*, before which the sibilant is written as *c* (facial) or *t* (spatial), for historical reasons.

**Silent S.** (1) Postvocalic *s* is often silent in French-derived words (*isle, apropos, chamois, chassis, corps, debris, fracas, precis, viscount, Grosvenor, Illinois*), or where inserted by false analogy with French: *island*, unrelated to *isle* (MIDDLE ENGLISH *yland*, etc.); *aisle* (compare French *aile*), which probably acquired its *s* by confusion with *isle*; *demesne*, cognate with *domain*. (2) Silent final *s* in French-derived words (*corps, fracas*) is often pronounced in the plural (*two army corps, frequent fracas*).

**Double S.** (1) *Ss* is normally voiceless (*pass, assess, dismiss*; *message, passage, possible*), but it is sometimes voiced in medial position (*brassiere, dessert, dissolve, hussar, scissors, possess*), and optionally in *hussy*. (2) In final position, *ss* typically occurs in monosyllables (*press, miss, loss, fuss, pass*), less often in polysyllables (*compass, embarrass, morass*), but commonly in the suffixes *-less* (*hopeless*) and *-ness* (*kindness*), derived from Germanic sources, and the suffix *-ess* (*hostess, princess*), derived from Romance sources. (3) The Latin prefix *ad-* becomes *as-* when assimilated to roots beginning with *s*: *assault, assemble, assimilate, assume*. (4) The prefixes *dis-, mis-* similarly produce *ss* when the following syllable begins with *s* (*misspell, dissatisfy*), but the *s* of *dis-* is assimilated into the digraph *sh* in *dishevelled* (formerly *discheveled*, etc.). (5) Some words optionally have double final *s* in their inflected forms: *biased/biassed, buses/busses, focusing/focussing, gased/gassed*. (6) *Ss* after a long vowel, as in *bass, gross* is rare, forms such as *face, dose* being more usual.

**SC and SCH.** The letter *s* occurs frequently with various values in conjunction with *c*

and *ch*: *effervesce, schedule, scheme, scent, schism, schist*. See C.

**SH.** (1) The digraph *sh* represents a distinct English phoneme, a voiceless alveolar fricative /ʃ/, which mostly arose from palatalization of early *s*, whether in OLD ENGLISH or Old French. (2) Old English used *sc* rather than *sh*, *ship* being written *scip*, and *sh* only became general after c.1450, probably by analogy with other *-h* digraphs such as *ch*, *th*, *wh*. The evolution is demonstrated by such Old English and MIDDLE ENGLISH forms as *Englisc, Englisch, Englissche, Englisshe*. Nevertheless *sh* is most typically found in words of Old English origin: *shadow, shall, shape, shed, ship, shoot, shot, shut, fish*. (3) A French-derived palatalized *s* was frequently changed to *sh* as in *abash, anguish, ashet, brush, bushel, cash, cushion, fashion, leash, parish*, and verbs ending in *-ish* (*abolish, famish, finish, punish*).

**ST.** (1) The sequence *st* is sometimes pronounced as /s/, *ss/st* having the same value in *hassle/castle*, and *st* having different values in *whistle, pistol*. (2) The /s/ value of *st* occurs mainly before *-en* (*fasten, listen, moisten*) and *-le* (*castle, wrestle, thistle, jostle, rustle*), although elision of /t/ before *m* in *Christmas, postman* has the same effect.

**Inflectional S.** (1) Final *s* is commonly an inflection, as in the plural of most nouns (*year/years*), the third-person singular of the present tense of most verbs (*eat/eats, need/needs*), and in possessive forms with apostrophe (*my uncle's house*). (2) Inflectional *s* is normally voiced, as after all vowels and voiced consonants (*rays, skis, skies, rows, rues, bananas, purrs, paws, ploys, ploughs, ribs, rods, rugs, ridges, rolls, rims, runs, roars, races, roses, rushes, wreathes, arrives, boxes, razes*), but not after voiceless non-sibilant consonants (*tics, tiffs, treks, tips, cliques, sits, myths*). (3) Possessive *s* is similarly voiced, as in the pronouns *his, hers, ours, yours, theirs, whose*, but not *its* after *t*, and *is* is similarly devoiced in the contraction *it's*. (4) The use of the possessive apostrophe raises uncertainties when a noun ends in *s*. Personal names ending in *s* may add only an apostrophe (*Achilles'*), but *'s* is also common (*Achilles's*), while in set phrases the apostrophe may be dropped (*Achilles tendon*). The *OED* gives various conventions in plant names, such as *Venus's flytrap, Venus' hair, Venus looking-glass*. Fowler has suggested using only an apostrophe before *sake*, producing *for goodness' sake*, and even *for conscience's sake*, but the practice is rare.

**Singulars and plurals**. (1) Noun plurals and verbs ending in a sibilant generally add *-es*: *lenses, buzzes, masses, foxes, wishes, touches, witches. Riches*, though a plural form, derives from singular French *richesse*. (2) Some names of diseases (*mumps, measles*) may be treated as plural, but *pox* (*smallpox, chicken-pox*, etc.) functions as singular rather than as the plural of *pock* (its ultimate origin). (3) *Forceps, gallows*, and BrE *innings* may be singular or plural, although *gallows* was formerly plural. FOWLER's *Modern English Usage* (1983) has recommended the plural *gallowses* if needed, and gives *inningses* as a BrE alternative to *innings* (compare AmE singular *inning*; plural *innings*, in baseball). (4) Tools with two arms (*pincers, pliers, scissors, shears, tweezers*) and garments with two legs (BrE *pyjamas*, AmE *pajamas, shorts, tights, trousers*) are grammatically plural, but semantically singular; plurality is expressed by preceding *pair of*, and *-es* is never added: no *\*scissorses*. (5) Family names of WELSH provenance, such as *Jones* and *Williams*, add *-es* for their plural, but are sometimes written with an apostrophe even when not possessive: *the Williams'*. (6) PLURALS are widely misspelt as possessives: for example, the so-called greengrocer's APOSTROPHE: *\*6 apple's*. (7) For the pattern *half/halves*, see F. (8) For plurals of words ending in *o*, as in *potatoes, pianos*, see O. (9) or changing *y to ies*, as in *pony/ponies*, see I.

**S/T variation**. (1) Some variations of *s* and *t* have arisen in such related forms as *pretension/pretentious, torsion/distortion*. (2) S/t variation with corresponding changed pronunciation occurs in the endings *-sis/-tic* in sets of related words from Greek: *analysis/analytic(al), neurosis/neurotic, psychosis/psychotic, synthesis/synthetic*. (3) The *-gloss/-glot* variation in *diglossia/glossary/glottal/polyglot* derives from dialect differences in ancient Greek. (4) Different derivational paths have been followed from LATIN and/or French to English in the doublets *poison/potion, reason/ration*.

**-IZE, ISE**. (1) Variation occurs between *s* and *z* in such words as *organise/organize, systematise/systematize*. Here the *-ize* ending reflects Greek origin, while *-ise* reflects the adaptation of some of these words during their passage through French, as in the verbs *organiser, systématiser*. (2) The *-ise* form

is widespread in BrE and virtually universal in AusE, whereas the *-ize* form is universal in AmE, favoured in CanE, and is employed by some British publishers, such as Oxford University Press. (3) In BrE *-ize* is not used in some two dozen verbs based on Latin roots, such as *advise, advertise, compromise, surprise*. In verbs with base nouns in *-lysis* (*analysis, paralysis*), BrE has *-lyse* (*analyse, paralyse*) and AmE *-lyze* (*analyze, paralyze*).

**Lost letters**. (1) An initial *s* in the Latin roots of some words has been assimilated by the prefix *ex-*, but appears after other prefixes, as in *exert/insert, exist/consist, expect/respect, expire/perspire, extinguish/distinguish, exult/result*. S has been similarly assimilated in *expatiate, exude*. (2) X has assimilated *s* from the now archaic forms *bucksome, cockscomb, pocks in* present day *buxom, coxcomb, pox*. (3) Some words that now begin with *s* have lost a preceding vowel by aphesis, although it may survive in cognates: *sample* from *example, squire* from *esquire, state* from *estate, story* from *history*. See APHESIS, ESH, PALATE.

**SABIR** [From Portuguese *sabir* to know]. A name for the original LINGUA FRANCA, the earliest known PIDGIN based on a European language. Its vocabulary is drawn mainly from the southern ROMANCE LANGUAGES, and it was used from the time of the Crusades (11–13c) until the beginning of the 20c for communication among Europeans, Turks, Arabs, and others in the Levant, and is believed by some scholars to have served as a base for the development of Atlantic and other pidgin languages first used by Portuguese sailors and traders and later by the British, Dutch, French, and Spanish.

**SAINT CHRISTOPHER AND NEVIS**, also **St Christopher-Nevis, St Kitts and Nevis, St Kitts-Nevis**. A Caribbean country and member of the COMMONWEALTH, consisting of St Christopher/Kitts, Nevis, and Sombrero. Languages: English, CREOLE. St Kitts became the first English colony in the Caribbean. Britain and France disputed control of the islands until in 1783 they became British under the Treaty of Versailles. They were united by the Federal Act of 1882 along with Anguilla. In 1980, Anguilla chose to remain a British dependency and in 1983 the other islands became independent. See CARIBBEAN ENGLISH.

**SAINT HELENA**, commonly written **St Helena**. A British dependency in the South Atlantic. Sole language: English. When the Portuguese navigator João da Nova Castella discovered the island on 21 May 1502, he named it after the mother of the Roman emperor Constantine, the saint of the Eastern Church whose feast day it was. St Helena was a port of call for ships travelling to the East Indies, may have been occupied by the Dutch in the mid-17c, and was annexed and occupied by the East India Company in 1659. In 1873, nearly half the population was imported slaves. Its remoteness made it the choice for Napoleon's exile, 1815–21. By the later 1830s, the island was under direct British rule. In 1922, Ascension Island was made a dependency, and in 1966 St Helena received a measure of autonomy. Local pronunciation includes: (1) Substitution of /w/ for /v/, so that *very* is pronounced 'werry'. (2) Replacement of /θ/ and /ð/ by /f/ and /d/, so that for example *bath* is pronounced 'baf', and *the* is 'de'. (3) Use of /ɔɪ/ for /aɪ/, so that *the island* is 'de oiland'. Special vocabulary includes: (1) Names for indigenous plants and animals, such as *gum wood*, *hog fish*, *old-father-live-forever*, *wire bird* (a small plover, the only native land bird). (2) Such usages as *jug up* to arrange flowers in a vase; *mug* a jug or pitcher for pouring; *make free with yourself* to take risks. See TRISTAN DA CUNHA.

**SAINT KITTS**. See SAINT CHRISTOPHER AND NEVIS.

**SAINT LUCIA**, commonly written **St Lucia**. A Caribbean country and member of the COMMONWEALTH. Languages: English (official), French Creole. Columbus may have landed in 1502, and in 1605 and 1638 the English made attempts to colonize the island. In 1650, St Lucia, Grenada, and Martinique were purchased by two Frenchmen, after which ownership of St Lucia was disputed by England and France until in 1814 it became British by the Treaty of Paris. The island became independent in 1979. See CARIBBEAN ENGLISH.

**SAINT VINCENT AND THE GRENADINES**, commonly written **St Vincent and the Grenadines**. A Caribbean country and member of the COMMONWEALTH, including the islands of St Vincent, Balliceau, Bequia, Canouan, Isle D'Quatre, and Mus-

tique. Languages: English (official), French Creole. Columbus visited the area in 1498. Europeans could only settle in St Vincent after making treaties with the local Caribs. The British and French competed for the island until 1763, when it became British by the Treaty of Paris. In 1773, the Caribs agreed to divide the island with the British, but grew resentful and with French help rebelled in 1795. Most were deported in 1796 to islands in the Gulf of Honduras. St Vincent became part of the Windward Island colony in 1871 and the group became independent in 1979. See CARIBBEAN ENGLISH.

**SAMOA**. See WESTERN SAMOA.

■ **SANSKRIT** ─────────────── ■

Also, especially formerly, **Sanscrit** [From Sanskrit *saṃskṛta* put together, well-formed, perfected]. The dominant classical and scholarly language of the Indian subcontinent, the sacred language of Hinduism (with Pali), a scriptural language of Buddhism, and the oldest known member of the Indo-European language family. It is usually written in the Devanagari script, which runs from left to right. Much as Latin influenced European languages, Sanskrit has influenced many languages in South and South-East Asia. Since the 19c, it has also provided loans to European languages including English and French. The most apparent of these loans relate to religion, philosophy, and culture, such as *ahimsa*, *chakra*, *guru*, *karma*, *kundalini*, *mahatma*, *pundit*, *swami*, and *yoga/yogi*, but less direct loanwords in English (borrowed through other languages) include *carmine*, *cheetah*, *chintz*, *chutney*, *juggernaut*, *jungle*, and *jute*.

All major modern Indian languages (both Indo-Aryan and Dravidian) have a Sanskritized register, used in religious and secular contexts. Indian English, especially when concerned with Hindu religion and philosophy, also freely uses Sanskrit terms, and Indian literature in English makes use of such conventions from Sanskrit as repetition of main themes in paragraphs and an abundance of compounds and embedded clauses. Sanskrit words appear in English texts in two forms: fully Anglicized, as with the variants *pundit* and *pandit* (through Hindi *pandit*); or, in scholarly writings, with various diacritics, following the conventions for transliterating Sanskrit into the

Roman alphabet, as with *pandita*. A representative scholarly text using full transliterations is:

> In the *Brhad-āranyaka Upanisad* (3.9.1) we are told that, when Sākalya asked the sage Yājñavalkya what was the number of the gods, the sage gave a cryptic answer (Alain Daniélou, *Hindu Polytheism*, 1964).

Differences in meaning and use often match the different styles: for example, *pandita* means a learned *brahmin* (or *brahman*, or *brāhmana*); *pandit* may have the same meaning and is used as a title for such a person, as in *Pandit Nehru*; *pundit* may have the same meaning and use, but is more fully integrated into English, in which it commonly refers to an expert; as in *political pundits*. Comparably, the term *guru* may refer to a Hindu teacher, a venerable spiritual leader, or any expert, as in the phrases *management guru* and *usage guru*. The extended non-Hindu senses of *pundit* and *guru* are often used to suggest that there is something suspect about the persons so described, whereas such terms as Gandhi's *ahimsa* and *satyagraha* have positive implications. See BORROWING, CLASSICAL LANGUAGE, INDIAN ENGLISH, INDO-EUROPEAN LANGUAGES.

**SARAMACCAN**. A CREOLE of SURINAM whose vocabulary derives partly from PORTUGUESE, partly from English; generally considered the oldest creole of Surinam and currently spoken by the *Central Bush Negroes* (the Saramaccans and the Matuari). It developed among 17c runaway slaves who may have spoken a Portuguese PIDGIN in addition to their West African languages, and who came into brief contact with English in the plantations. See NDJUKA, SRANAN.

**SAXON**. **1.** A member of a Germanic people that once lived near the mouth of the Elbe, and in Roman times spread across Germany from Schleswig to the Rhine. Some (*the Anglo-Saxons*: that is, those who joined the Angles) migrated in the 5–6c to Britain; others (*the Ealdseaxe, Old Saxons*) became the founding people of *Saxony*, the name of a German territory that has changed its location and political standing several times over the centuries. **2.** The DIALECTS spoken by the Saxons in southern England, in *Essex* (home of the East Saxons), *Middlesex* (the Middle Saxons), *Sussex* (the South Saxons). and *Wessex* (the West Saxons). The term has sometimes been used instead of OLD ENGLISH and ANGLO-SAXON, as the name of the language carried to Britain by the Angles and Saxons. **3.** A native of Saxony. **4.** The Low German dialect of Saxony. **5.** An English man or woman, especially in medieval times, in contrast to *Norman*, and sometimes in more recent times in contrast to *Latin* and *Celt*. **6.** Also *Saxon English, Saxon language*. Formerly, a name for native or VERNACULAR English in contrast to French and Latinate usage: 'Our vulgar Saxon English standing most vpon wordes monsillable' (George Puttenham, *The Arte of English Poesie*, 1589). **7.** Relating to any of the above: *Saxon traditions*.

**SAXON GENITIVE**. A term for the forms of the possessive associated with the APOSTROPHE (*boy's, boys'*), so called because, along with the plural ending, they are the only noun inflections surviving from Old English or Anglo-Saxon. This genitive is often described as a case form, but as it can be attached to phrases (*The King of Thailand's visit; somebody else's seat*), some grammarians argue against this view. The same meaning when expressed by an *of*-phrase is sometimes called the *of*-genitive: *the top of the hill*. The Saxon genitive can be used alone with a place reference: *See you at Tom's; I got it at the grocer's this morning*. Other usages include the *subjective genitive* (*the man's statement*, where the man made the statement); the *objective genitive* (*the group's leader*, where someone leads the group); and the *descriptive genitive* (*a moment's thought, a ladies' hairdresser, ship's biscuits, Parkinson's disease*), which shares some features with attribution and compound words. See GENITIVE CASE, POSSESSION.

**SAXONISM**, also **Anglo-Saxonism**. A semi-technical term for: (1) The use of, and preference for, expressions of ANGLO-SAXON origin. (2) A word or other expression of Anglo-Saxon origin or formed on an Anglo-Saxon or Germanic model, often contrasted with *classicism*, as in *foreword* with *preface*, *folkwain* with *omnibus*. Saxonisms are generally the out-come of a purist and nativist approach to the language. The aim behind many deliberately created forms has been to create compounds and derivatives to replace foreign borrowings; the device is rooted in the OLD ENGLISH practice of loan-translating LATIN words: *benevolentia* as *wel-willedness* (well-willingness); *trinitas* as *thrines* (threeness). LOAN TRANSLATION was standard before the Norman Conquest, but was limited from the mid-11c by the predominance of French. Since the decline of French influence in the 14c, Saxonism has resurfaced only occasionally. In the 16c, it was a reaction to INKHORN TERMS; in his translation of the BIBLE, John Cheke used *hundreder* and *gainrising* instead of *centurion* and *resurrection*. In the 19c, it was prompted by comparative PHILOLOGY, when *folklore* and *foreword* (modelled on German *Vorwort*) were coined, *handbook* was revived to compete with *manual*, and *leechcraft* was preferred by Walter SCOTT to *medicine*. DICKENS eulogized Anglo-Saxon times, when 'a pure Teutonic was spoken' (*Household Words* 18, 1858). The most enthusiastic 19c Saxonizer was William BARNES, who wished to turn English back into a properly Germanic language. Some of his coinages were structurally acceptable (*bendsome* for *flexible*, *folkwain* for *omnibus*), but others were awkward (*markword of suchness* for *adjective*). His work is now largely forgotten and where remembered is usually seen as quaint and unrealistic.

Currently, Saxonism occurs directly as a literary conceit and indirectly in campaigns for simpler English. In humorous writing, vernacular alternatives to established Romance words are coined and used for effect. In the magazine *Punch* in 1966, to celebrate the 900th anniversary of the Battle of Hastings, the humorist Paul Jennings wrote 'anent the ninehundredth yearday of the Clash of Hastings', and rendered Hamlet's most famous soliloquy into 'Anglish', beginning with:

> To be, or not to be: that is the ask-thing:
> Is't higher-thinking in the brain to bear
> The slings and arrows of outrageous dooming
> Or take up weapons 'gainst a sea of bothers
> And by againstwork end them?

In the word list of BASIC ENGLISH, C. K. Ogden showed a marked preference for vernacular over Romance and classical words. Campaigners for PLAIN ENGLISH often urge people to avoid polysyllables and keep to everyday language, implicitly proposing a kind of Saxonism. In such movements, however, the main criterion is not linguistic pedigree but ease of communication.

## ■ SCANDINAVIAN LANGUAGES ■

A group of languages in northern Europe. Strictly speaking, *Scandinavian* relates only to the peninsula of Scandinavia (Norway and Sweden), but the term usually includes Denmark and sometimes Finland. The languages spoken in this area are the GERMANIC LANGUAGES Norwegian, DANISH, and Swedish and the Finno-Ugric languages Lappish and Finnish. In LINGUISTICS, the terms *Scandinavian* and *North Germanic* both refer to a subgroup of the Germanic language family. The languages of this subgroup are Danish (in Denmark, the Faroe Islands, and Greenland), Faroese (in the Faroe Islands), Icelandic (in Iceland), Norwegian (in Norway), and Swedish (in Sweden and Finland). The Scandinavian language NORN was spoken in Scotland until the 17–18c. Originally, there was little variation in Scandinavian, the common language of the Viking raiders and settlers of the 9–11c. At the present time, in Norway, Sweden, and Denmark, educated people seldom have difficulty in communicating across frontiers, speakers using their own languages. Icelandic and Faroese, however, are no longer immediately intelligible to other Scandinavians, even though they retain many features of original Scandinavian. The justification for regarding Danish and Swedish as distinct languages lies largely in their separate literary traditions, dating from the 16c. The distance between them is like that between STANDARD ENGLISH and Lowland SCOTS. The situation in Norway is more complex, but can also be compared to the linguistic situation in Scotland.

**Scandinavian and English**. During the early Middle Ages, the Viking invasions led to settlements in Britain and Ireland: in the Northern and Western Isles, the northern and western coasts of Scotland, parts of Ireland (including DUBLIN), the ISLE OF MAN, and large parts of England, resulting in the DANELAW. As a consequence, Scandinavian was for several centuries a major language of Britain and Ireland, competing with GAELIC and English, on both of which it had a powerful impact. By 1200, however, Scandinavian (also referred to as Danish, Old Danish, NORSE, Old Norse) had ceased to be spoken in England, but survived elsewhere: for example, as Norn in Orkney and Shetland. In England, the long period of contact and ultimate fusion between the Anglo-Saxon and Danish populations, especially north of a line between London and Chester, had a profound effect on English. More recently, Scandinavian influence has been slight and sporadic, in such loans as *ombudsman, ski, smorgasbord, tungsten*.

**English and Scandinavian**. English influence, for centuries slight, began to increase from *c*.1750, and in the 20c, especially since the Second World War, has become extensive in such fields as journalism, computer technology, and aviation, as well as in areas of life where American influence has been predominant: youth culture, leisure activities, sport, business, advertising. The influence is particularly noticeable in journalism. The impact of English includes: (1) LOANWORDS: nouns are the largest group, followed by verbs and adjectives. Before *c*.1900, borrowings usually conformed to local conventions (English *strike* became Danish *strejke*, Norwegian *streike*, Swedish *strejk*), but recent loans generally undergo little or no modification. (2) LOAN TRANSLATIONS: *blood bank* has become *blodbank*; *self-service* has become Danish and Norwegian *selvbetjening*, Swedish *självbetjäning*. Phrasal verbs are a feature of Scandinavian as well as English and loan translations have been increasing: Danish *tone ned* (tone down); Danish *ende op med*, Norwegian *ende opp med* (end up with). In addition, idioms like *drag one's feet* and *conspiracy of silence* have entered Scandinavian usage in TRANSLATION. (3) Loan constructions: usages of the type *wall-to-wall carpets* and *lovely 20-year-old So-and-So* are no longer foreign to Scandinavian usage, although older people may object. (4) Semantic borrowing: the word for 'to sell' used in the sense ' to convince people of the worth of (a product, idea, etc.)'. (5) VOGUE WORDS from English competing with adequate existing terms: while *personlighed* or *personlighet* is usual, an advert for a new car might claim instead that it has *personality*. (6) Many existing BORROWINGS from LATIN have gained in frequency under the influence of their use in English: *status*; Danish and Swedish *kommunikation*, Norwegian *kommunikasjon*.

The above remarks apply to Denmark, Norway, and Sweden. In Iceland, English influence is felt on the colloquial level, but a purist tradition has kept the written language unaffected, neologisms being Icelandicized: *hamborgan* a hamburger.

Recently, however, some authors have broken with the more extreme form of purism and English is making inroads in television. The Faroese situation is comparable. In Scandinavia proper, emphasis is placed on the teaching of modern languages and English is compulsory in all schools. Scholarly and scientific publications are often in English. University regulations usually allow doctoral theses to be submitted in English, GERMAN, or FRENCH as an alternative to a Scandinavian language, and English is a frequent choice. See INDO-EUROPEAN LANGUAGES, ORKNEY AND SHETLAND DIALECTS.

**SCHWA** [From German *schwa*, from Hebrew *shwā*, from *shāw'*, emptiness. Hebrew grammarians traditionally mark consonants with signs referred to in Roman lettering as *sheva* or *shewa*. These signs indicate either no following VOWEL sound (*quiescent or movable sheva*). There was nothing comparable in alphabets derived from Roman until the development of the International Phonetic Alphabet in the late 19c, when an inverted e was introduced to serve the same purpose as vocal sheva]. Also **shwa**, **neutral vowel**, **obscure vowel**. A term in PHONETICS for a central vowel sound represented by the symbol /ə/. To make a schwa in isolation, the tongue is neither pushed forward nor pulled back, neither raised nor lowered, and the lips are neither spread nor rounded: hence the term 'neutral'. Although not represented in the conventional alphabet, schwa is the commonest vowel sound in English. It typically occurs in unstressed syllables, and in the following list is shown for illustrative purposes as if it were an everyday letter: əbove, əgain, səppose, photəgraph, scenəry, sofə. It is often an ill-defined voice gap between consonants: for example, in *today* it is formed as the tongue moves away from the alveolar ridge on the release of /t/ and returns to form /d/ (t'day). Many languages do not have a neutral vowel, and this causes problems for foreign speakers of English from such backgrounds. However, another vowel may replace it: for example, the short /a/ of North Indian languages (as in the first vowel of *Punjab*) is used as a schwa in IndE, or the /a/ in many kinds of AfrE: *speaker* /spika/. Learners who have not had access to native-speaker English tend not to attempt a schwa at all, but to pronounce words more or less according to the vowel letters of the spelling. Their speech is therefore likely to be SYLLABLE-timed rather than stress-timed. See VOWEL QUANTITY, WEAK VOWEL, and the letter entries A, E, I, O, R, U.

**SCOTCH-IRISH**. The name of that part of the population of northern Ireland descended from the Scottish Presbyterian settlers of the 17c and later. From the 18c, it has been applied to the people of this background who migrated in large numbers to Pennsylvania and neighbouring regions of the US and later to Ontario and other parts of Canada. Since around 1950, it has also been applied by linguists to the variety of SCOTS spoken in northern and northeastern Ireland, especially in Donegal, Derry, Antrim, and Down. The recent form *Scots-Irish* runs parallel with the increasing preference for *Scots* over *Scotch*. See APPALACHIAN ENGLISH, DIALECT IN AMERICA, ULSTER SCOTS.

# ■ SCOTS

**1.** Relating to or characteristic of Scotland, its people, languages, culture, institutions, etc.: *Scots traditions, the Scots language*. Although in certain uses (*Scots law, Scots thistle, a Scots mile, a pound Scots*) the adjective has never gone out of favour, in other uses its popularity declined after the mid-18c in competition with *Scottish* and *Scotch*, reviving when *Scotch* fell into disfavour in the 19–20c. **2.** A name for both GAELIC and the form of NORTHERN ENGLISH used in Scotland. The forms *Scottis, Scotis* and the LATIN adjectives *Scotticus, Scoticus* down to the 15c applied only to Gaelic and its speakers and have occasionally been so used since. From 1494, the term was increasingly applied to the Lowland speech, previously known as INGLIS, so as to distinguish it from the language of England. From then on, this was the regular application of the term, and until the early 18c *SCOTS* and *INGLIS* or *English* were more or less interchangeable: 'They decided not to disjoin but to continue the Scots or English classe in the gramer school as formerly' (Stirling Burgh Records, 23 Aug. 1718).

**The status of Scots**. Scholars and other interested persons have difficulty agreeing on the linguistic, historical, and social status of Scots. Generally, it is seen as one of

the ancient DIALECTS of English, yet it has distinct and ancient dialects of its own. Sometimes it has been little more than an overspill noted in the discussion of English as part of the story of England. Sometimes it has been called the English of Scotland, part of GENERAL ENGLISH yet often in contrast with it, and different from the STANDARD ENGLISH taught in Scottish schools. Sometimes, it has been called a Germanic language in its own right, considered as distinct from its sister in England in the same way that Swedish is distinct from DANISH. In addition, in its subordinate relationship with the English of England, its position has been compared to FRISIAN in the Netherlands (dominated by Dutch) and Norwegian (once dominated by Danish). In *The Languages of Britain* (1984), Glanville Price notes:

> In planning and writing this book, I have changed my mind four times, and, in the end, I devote a separate chapter to Scots not because I necessarily accept that it is a 'language' rather than a 'dialect' but because it has proved to be more convenient to handle it thus than include some treatment of it in the chapter on English.

Scots has since the beginning of the 18c been the object of scholarly investigation and those scholars who have specialized in its study divide its history into three periods: *Old English* (to 1100); *Older Scots* (1100–1700), divided into *Early Scots* (1100–1450) and *Middle Scots* (1450–1700); *Modern Scots* (1700 onwards).

**The King's Scots**. The first source of Scots dates from the 7c. It was the Old English of the kingdom of Bernicia, part of which lay in what is now southern Scotland: see NORTHUMBRIA. The second source was the Scandinavian-influenced English of immigrants from Northern and Midland England in the 12–13c, who travelled north at the invitation of the Anglo-Normanized kings of Scots. By the 14c, the variety of Northern English which had crystallized out of these sources (known to its speakers as *Inglis*) had supplanted Gaelic and CUMBRIC, languages formerly spoken in much of what is now Lowland Scotland. In Caithness, Orkney, and Shetland, however, the form of Norse known as *NORN* continued in use for some time. From the late 14c also, Latin began to be overtaken by Scots as the language of record and literature, a process well advanced by the early 16c, by which time it had become the national language of Stewart Scotland.

**Anglicization**. By the mid-16c, Scots had begun to undergo *Anglicization*, southern English word forms and spellings progressively invading written and later spoken Scots. Among the conditions favouring this trend was Protestant reliance (before and after the Reformation of 1560) on Bibles in English. By the late 16c, all Scots writing was in a mixed dialect, in which native Scots spellings and spelling symbols co-occurred with English borrowings: *aith/oath*, *ony/any*, *gude/good*, *quh-/wh-*, *sch-/sh-*, Scots *ei*, English *ee*, *ea*, with the English forms gradually gaining in popularity. Scots elements virtually disappeared from published writings in Scotland before the end of the 17c, except for VERNACULAR literature. The elimination of Scots from unpublished writings like local records took some decades longer. Early in the 18c, Sir Robert Sibbald distinguished three sorts of Scottish speech: 'that Language we call BROAD Scots, which is yet used by the Vulgar . . . in distinction to the *Highlanders* Language, and the refined Language of the Gentry, which the more Polite People among us do use'. That 'refined language', however, was no longer Scots but the ancestor of SCOTTISH ENGLISH.

**Scotticisms**. According to the Augustan ideals of good taste and propriety, shared by cultivated people in the 18c in both England and Scotland, the residue of Scots in the English of Scottish people was deplored as 'provincial' and 'unrefined'. This led many of the gentry and intelligentsia to try to rid themselves of all traces of their former national tongue by attending lectures on English elocution held in Edinburgh from 1748. In addition, from the late 17c they made great efforts to eradicate Scotticism from their writing and speech. Not all educated 18c Scots, however, accepted these propositions. From early in the century, a new literary Scots, which unlike most literary Middle Scots was based on up-to-date colloquial speech, burgeoned in the writings of Allan Ramsay (1686–1758) and some of his contemporaries, and such successors as Robert BURNS. This stream of vernacular literature in Scots was accompanied early in the 19c by a revival of interest in and approval of Modern Scots among the middle and upper classes, inspired to some extent by John Jamieson's *Etymological Dictionary of the Scottish Language* (1808). Scots was now generally accepted as a rich and expressive tongue and recognized as the 'national language', albeit (as had been repeatedly stated since 1763 or earlier) 'going out as a spoken tongue every year'.

**Revival and survival**. The need was now felt to record the old language before it was too late, as in Jamieson's dictionary, or to undertake the preservation or even restoration of Scots. In the 20c, this has manifested itself *inter alia* in the creation of LALLANS or Synthetic Scots by the Scottish Renaissance writers from *c*.1920, and in a sustained output in recent decades of narrative, expository, and even some transactional prose in Scots, notably in the Scots Language Society's journal *Lallans* (1973– ). From the early 18c to the present day, appeals in English prose or Scots verse have been made to Scots to speak their own language rather than Southron. Such activity has helped maintain the Scottish people's linguistic loyalty to their 'own dying language' (Robert Louis Stevenson, 1887) and has helped to slow the drift away from native Scots elements at all levels of speech. But it could not reverse the trend which favours English as the language of power and prestige or restore the full Scots of a dwindling minority of rural speakers to its former central position. Even after its 20c renaissance, Scots remains restricted to a narrow sphere of literary uses and it makes only a marginal appearance in the media, in comic strips, cartoons, jokes and columns in the popular and local press. None the less, although English is dominant, it remains permeated with features from Scots.

**Pronunciation**. (1) Like other Northern dialects, Scots displays the results of many early divergences from the Midland and Southern dialects of MIDDLE ENGLISH: *hame*, *stane*, *sair*, *gae* as against *home*, *stone*, *sore*, *go*; *hoose*, *oot*, *doon*, *coo* as against *house*, *out*, *down*, *cow*; *baw*, *saut* against *ball*, *salt*; *gowd*, *gowf* as against *gold*, *golf*; *mouter* as against *multure*; *fou* as against *full*; and *buit*, *guid*, *muin*, *puir*, *dui* (or with some other front vowel, depending on dialect) as against *boot*, *good*, *moon*, *poor*, *do*: see DIALECT IN SCOTLAND. (2) Of the features largely exclusive to Scots (in Scotland and Ulster), the most pervasive is the Scottish vowel length rule, the most striking result of which is the split of Early Scots /i:/ into two phonemes in Scots and ScoE: /aɪ/ in *ay* (yes), *buy*, *alive*, *rise*, *tied*, and /əɪ/ in *aye* (always), *life*, *rice*, *bite*, *tide*. (3) The consonant system retains the OLD ENGLISH voiceless velar fricative /x/ in *teuch*, *heich* (equivalents of *tough*, *high*) and many other words (including such Gaelic loans as *clarsach*, *loch*, *pibroch*), and the cluster /xt/ in *dochter*, *nicht* (*daughter*, *night*). Such forms were once universal in English and have only become obsolete in Northern England in recent decades.

**Spelling**. By the late 14c, Older Scots was developing its own distinctive orthography, marked by such features as *quh-* (English *wh-*), *-ch* (English *-gh*), *sch-* (English *sh-*), and the use of *i/y* as in *ai/ay*, *ei/ey* to identify certain vowels: compare Scots *quheyll*, *heych*, *scheip*, *heid*, *heyd* with English *wheel*, *high*, *sheep*, *heed*, *head*. Following the Anglicization of the 16–17c, the literary Scots of Allan Ramsay and his contemporaries and successors in the 18c had discarded some of these forms but retained others, including *ei* as in *heid* (head), *ui* or *u–e* as in *guid/gude* (good), and *ch* as in *loch*, *thocht* (loch, thought). This orthography, however, was in the main an adaptation of English orthography to represent Scots, as is shown by the free use of apostrophes to mark 'missing' letters. Unlike English, but like Older Scots, it is tolerant of spelling variation; attempts to regulate this, notably through the *Scots Style Sheet* of the Makars' Club (1947), have had only limited success. The *Concise Scots Dictionary* records many spelling variants such as *breid*, *brede*, *bread*, *braid* (bread), and *heuk*, *huke*, *hook* (hook), and the larger Scots dictionaries record very many more.

**Morphology**. (1) The regular past form of the verb is *-it* or *-t/(e)d*, according to the preceding consonant or vowel: *hurtit*, *skelpit* smacked, *mendit*, *kent/kenned* knew/known, *cleant/cleaned*, *tellt/tauld* told, *deed* died. (2) Some verbs have distinctive principal parts: *greet/grat/grutten* weep/wept, *fesh/fuish/fuishen* fetch/fetched, *lauch/leuch/lauchen* laugh/laughed, *gae/gaed/gane* go/went, *gie/gied/gien* give/gave/given. (3) A set of irregular noun plurals: *eye/een* eye/eyes, *cauf/caur* calf/calves, *horse/horse* horse/horses, *coo/kye* cow/cows (compare archaic English *kine*), *shoe*, *shae*, *shee/shuin*, *sheen* shoe/shoes (compare archaic English *shoon*). (4) Nouns of measure and quantity unchanged in the plural: *four fuit*

*foot*, *twa mile*, *five pund* pound, *three hunderwecht* hundredweight. (5) A third deictic adjective/adverb *yon/yonder*, *thon/thonder* (that and those there, at some distance): *D'ye see yon/thon hoose ower yonder/thonder?* (6) Ordinal numbers ending in *-t*: *fourt*, *fift*, *saxt/sixt*, etc. (7) Adverbs in *-s*, *-lies*, *-lin(g)s*, *gate(s)*, and *way(s)*, *-wye*, *-wey(s)*: *whiles* at times, *maybes* perhaps, *brawlies* splendidly, *geylies* pretty well, *aiblins* perhaps, *arselins* backwards, *halfins* partly, *hidlins* secretly, *maistlins* almost, *a'gates* always, everywhere, *ilka gate* everywhere, *onygate* anyhow, *ilkawye* everywhere, *onyway(s)* anyhow, anywhere, *endweys* straight ahead, *whit wey* how, why. (8) Diminutives and associated forms: in *-ie/y* (*burnie* small burn brook, *feardie/feartie* frightened person, coward, *gamie* gamekeeper, *kiltie* kilted soldier, *postie* postman, *wifie* wife, *rhodie* rhododendron), in *-ock* (*bittock* little bit, *playock* toy, plaything, *sourock* sorrel) and chiefly Northern *-ag* (*bairnag* little *bairn* child, *Cheordag* Geordie), *-ockie*, *-ickie* (*hoosickie* small house, *wifeockie* little wife). Note the five times diminished *a little wee bit lassockie*.

**Syntax and idiom**. (1) Verbs in the present tense are as in English when a single personal pronoun is next to the verb; otherwise, they end in *-s* in all persons and numbers: *They say he's owre auld*, *Thaim that says he's owre auld*, *Thir laddies says he's owre auld* They say he's too old, etc.; *They're comin as weel* but *Five o them's comin*; *The laddies?— They've went* but *Ma brakes has went*. (2) *Was* or *wis* may replace *were*, but not conversely as in some Northern English dialects: *You were/wis there*. (3) The MODAL VERBS *may*, *ocht to* ought to, and (except in Orkney and Shetland) *sall* shall, are rare or absent in informal speech, but occur in literary Scots. They are replaced respectively by *can*, *should*, and *will*. *May* and *shall* are similarly missing from most ScoE. (4) Scots, like NORTHERN ENGLISH, employs double modal constructions: *He'll no can come the day* He won't be able to come today, *Ah micht could come the morn* I might be able to come tomorrow, *Ah used tae could dae it*, *but no noo* I could do it once, but not now. (5) There are progressive uses of certain verbs: *He wis thinkin he wid tell her*; *He wis wantin tae tell her*. (6) Verbless subordinate clauses that express surprise or indignation are introduced by *and*: *She had tae walk the hale lenth o the road and her seeven month pregnant*; *He tellt me tae run and me wi ma sair leg* (and me with my sore leg). (7) Negation is mostly as in English, either by the adverb *no* (North-East *nae*), as in *Ah'm no comin* I'm not coming, or by the enclitic *-na/nae* (depending on dialect, and equivalent to *-n't*), as in *Ah dinna ken* I don't know, *They canna come* They can't come, *We couldna hae tellt him* We couldn't have told him, and *Ah huvna seen her* I haven't seen her. With auxiliary verbs which can be contracted, however, such as *-ve* for *have* and *-ll* for *will*, or in *yes–no* questions with any auxiliary, Scots strongly prefers the usage with the adverb to that with the enclitic: *He'll no come* rather than *He winna come*, and *Did he no come?* to the virtual exclusion of *Didna he come?* (8) The relative pronoun is *that* for all persons and numbers, and may be elided: *There's no mony folk (that) lives in that glen* There aren't many people who live in that glen. The forms *wha*, *wham*, *whase*, *whilk* (who, whom, whose, which) are literary, the last of these used only after a statement: *He said he'd lost it, whilk wis no whit we wantit tae hear. That* is made possessive by *'s* or appending an appropriate pronoun: *The man that's hoose got burnt*; *the wumman that her dochter got mairrit*; *the crew that thair boat wis lost.* (9) Verbs of motion may be dropped before an adverb or adverbial phrase of motion: *Ah'm awa tae ma bed*; *That's me awa hame*; *Ah'll intae the hoose and see him.* (10) Like Northern English, Scots prefers the order *He turned oot the licht* to *He turned the light out* and *Gie me it* to *Give it me.*

**Vocabulary**. The vocabularies of Scots and English overlap, but Scots contains words that are absent from the standard language, either shared with the dialects of Northern England, or unique to Scotland. The sources of the distinctive elements of Scots vocabulary include Old English, Old NORSE, FRENCH, DUTCH, and Gaelic.

*Old English*. (1) Not now shared with any dialect of England are such forms as: *but an ben* a two-room cottage, *but* the outer room, *ben* the inner room, *cleuch* a gorge, *haffet* the cheek, *skeich* (of a horse) apt to shy, *swick* to cheat. (2) Shared with (especially Northern) dialects of England: *bairn* a child, *bide* to stay or live (in a place), *dicht* to clean, *dwam* a stupor, *hauch* a riverside meadow, *heuch* a steep hill, *rax* to stretch, *snell* (of weather) bitter, severe, *speir* to ask, *thole* to endure. (3) Now in general or literary English: *bannock, eldritch, fey, gloaming, raid, wee, weird, wizened. Weird* and *fey* also have the original senses 'destiny' and 'fated to die'. *To dree yir ain*

*weird* means 'to endure what is destined for you'.

*Norse*. The Scandinavian element, introduced by 12–13c immigrants from Northern England, is generally shared with the Northern dialects, but some words that are obsolete there survive in Scots and ScoE: *ain* own (*ma ain* my own), *aye* always, *big* to build, *blae* blue (whence *blaeberry*), *blether* to chatter, *brae* slope of a hill, *cleg* a gadfly, *eident* diligent, *ferlie* a wonder, *gate* a road (also in street names: *Gallowgate*, in Glasgow), *gowk* a cuckoo, *graith* equip, equipment, *kirk* church, *lass* a girl, *lowp* to jump, *lug* ear. This element includes the auxiliary verbs *gar* to make or cause to do (*It wad gar ye greet* It would make you weep) and *maun* must (*Ah maun find her* I must find her, and the proverb *He that will tae Cupar maun tae Cupar* Scots equivalent of 'A wilful man must have his way'). Most of this is also shared by the dialects of Shetland, Orkney, and Caithness, which have in addition their own distinct vocabulary descended from Norn.

*French*. Influence from French was first through the Anglo-Norman baronage of 12–13c Scotland and the Frenchified literary and fashionable culture of medieval Britain, then partly as a result of the *Auld Alliance* (Franco-Scottish Alliance, 1296–1560), and partly from Scots travelling and living in France and Switzerland in medieval and later times: (1) Shared with early English but surviving only in Scots: *causey* the paved part of a street (cognate with *causeway*), *cowp* to capsize or upset (from *couper* to cut, strike) *cummer* a godmother (from *commère*), *douce* (originally of a woman or manners) sweet (from *doux/douce*), *houlet* owl (from *hulotte*), *leal* (a doublet of *loyal* and *legal*), *tass/tassie* cup (from *tasse*). (2) Virtually exclusively Scots: *ashet* a serving dish (from *assiette*), *disjune* breakfast (from *desjun*, now *dejeuner*), *fash* to bother (from *fâcher*), *Hogmanay* (from Old French *aguillanneuf* a New Year's gift), *sybow/sybie* the spring onion (from Old French *ciboule*), *vennel* an alley (from Old French *venelle*). (3) Shared from the 17c with English: *caddie, croup* (the disease), *pony*.

*Dutch*. The population of medieval Scotland included Flemish landowners in the countryside, wool merchants, weavers, and other craftsmen in the burghs, and trade with The Netherlands dates from the same period. Borrowings from medieval Dutch or Flemish include: *callan* a lad, *coft* bought, *cowk* to retch, *cuit* an ankle, *groff* coarse in grain or quality, *howf* a favourite haunt, public house (from *hof* a courtyard), *loun* ('loon') a lad, *mutch* a kind of woman's cap, *mutchkin* a quarter of a Scots pint, *pinkie* the little finger (passed on to AmE), *trauchle* to overburden, harass. The words *croon, golf, scone* have been passed on to English at large.

***Gaelic***. (1) Early borrowings, from around the 12c to the 17c, many of which have passed on into English: *bog, cairn* a pile of stones as a landmark, *capercailzie* the wood grouse, *clachan* a hamlet, *clan, clarsach* the Highland harp, *cranreuch* hoar frost, *glen, ingle* a hearth-fire, *loch, partan* the common crab, *ptarmigan* an Arctic grouse, *slogan* originally a war cry, *sonse* plenty, prosperity (whence *sonsy* hearty, comely, buxom), *strath* a wide valley, *tocher* a dowry. (2) From the 17c onward, also often passing into English: *ben* a mountain, *brogue* a Highlander's shoe, *claymore* a Highland sword, *corrie* a cirque or circular hollow on a mountainside, *gillie* a hunting attendant, *golach* an earwig, *pibroch* solo bagpipe music, *sporran* a purse worn in front of a kilt, *whisky*. (3) From the late 19c onward: *ceilidh* ('cayly') an informal musical party, *Gaidhealtachd* the area where Gaelic is spoken, *slàinte* ('slanch') health and *slàinte-mhath* ('slanche-va') good health (said as a toast).

***Latin***. The distinctive vocabularies of education, the Church, and especially law in Scotland are largely Latin: see SCOTTISH ENGLISH. From the classroom a little schoolboy Latin has trickled into Scots since the 15c or earlier: *dominie* schoolmaster, *dux* best pupil in a school or a class, *fugie* a runaway, truant, *janitor* a school caretaker, *pandie* a stroke on the palm with a cane, etc. (from Latin *pande manum* stretch out your hand: also *palmie*), *vacance* vacation, holiday, *vaig* and *stravaig* wander aimlessly.

***Echoisms, reduplications, and others***. (1) Words of uncertain origin but with a distinct onomatopoeic element include: *birl* to whirl, *daud* a thump or lump, *dunt* a thump, *sclaff* to slap, *skrauch* and *skreich* to shriek, *wheech* to move in a rush, *yatter* to chatter. (2) Scots has many widely used reduplicative words, such as *clishclash* and *clishmaclaver* idle talk, gossip, *easy-osy* easy-going, *eeksie-peeksie* six and half a dozen, *the hale jingbang*

the whole caboodle, *joukerie-pawkerie* trickery, *mixter-maxter* all mixed up. (3) Combinations and fanciful formations: *bletherskate* an incessant talker, *camshauchle* distorted, *carnaptious* quarrelsome, *carfuffle* a commotion (passed into English), *collieshangie* a noisy squabble, *sculduddery* fornication (whence AmE *skullduggery*), *tapsalteerie* topsy-turvy, and *whigmaleerie* a trifle, whim.

***Iteratives, intensives, and others***. (1) Iteratives and intensives: *donner* to daze (whence *donnert* stupid), *scunner* to disgust, and someone or something disgusting (from the root of *shun*: also Northern English), *scowder* to scorch (cognate with *scald*), *shauchle* to shuffle, *shoogle* to joggle or shake. (2) Common words of various derivations, some obscure: *bogle* a ghost (perhaps of Celtic origin: note *tattie-bogle* 'a potato bogle', a scare-crow), *bonny* or *bonnie* handsome, beautiful (perhaps from French *bon* good), *braw* fine, excellent (perhaps a variant of *brave*), *collie* a sheepdog (now in general use in English), *couthy* homely/homey, congenial (from *couth* known: compare *uncouth*), *eerie* fearful, ghostly (now general), *glaikit* foolish (from *glaik* trick, deceit, flash), *glamour* a spell (now general, for a special kind of magic: a doublet of *grammar*), *gowkit* or *gukkit* foolish (perhaps from the *guk-guk* call of the *gowk* or cuckoo), *glaur* mud, *glower* to stare (now general), *gomerel* a fook, *gumption* get-up-and-go, guts (now general). (3) Recent creations: *bangshoot* caboodle (compare *jingbang*, above), *bletheration* foolish talk (see *blether*, above), *duffie/yuffie* a water closet, *fantoosh* flashy (probably a play on *fancy* and *fantastic*), *gallus* mischievous, *heidbanger* a madman, *high-heid-yin* ('high-head-one') boss, manager, *laldie* a thrashing, *multy* a multi-storey tenement, *sapsy* soppy, effeminate, *scheme* (clipping 'housing scheme') a local-authority housing estate, *skoosh* to gush, fizzy drink, *squeegee* askew.

**Literary Scots**. Already in Middle Scots, literary and official prose had grown archaic in comparison with contemporary speech, and spoken innovations therefore largely fail to appear in writing, apart from comic verse and passages of quoted dialogue in law-court records. These last show novel forms such as *fow* for *full, mow* for *mouth, ha* and *gie* (later *hae* and *gie*) for *have* and *give*, and such new coinages as *glower* (to stare) and *glaikit* (foolish). The following passage illustrates polished 16c literary prose:

The samyn tyme happynnit ane
wounderfull thing. Quhen Makbeth and
Banquho war passand to Fores, quhair
King Duncan wes for the tyme, thai mett
be the gaitt thre weird sisteris or wiches,
quhilk come to thame with elrege
clething (from John Bellenden's
translation, c.1531 of Hector Boece's
Latin *Chronicles of Scotland*, 1527).

[Translation: At that time a wonderful
thing happened. When Macbeth and
Banquo were on their way to Forres,
where King Duncan was at the time,
they met by the roadside three 'sisters of
fate' or witches, who approached them
in unearthly (eldritch) garments.]

In the 20c, literary Scots of the variety that
includes Lallans and the language of W. L.
Lorimer's *The New Testament in Scots* similarly
differs from colloquial varieties. It draws
its typical word forms, vocabulary, and
grammar from an archaic, more or less
non-local, variety of Central Scots, retaining
for example obsolete or obsolescent uses
of modal verbs and negatives and such
archaisms as *aiblins* perhaps, *descryve* describe, *leed/leid* a language, *lift* sky, *swith*
quickly, and *virr* strength. It also sometimes
employs a stilted, non-colloquial, English-
like syntax. Occasionally, false analogies
produce forms and usages that have no
Scots pedigree: *ainer* an owner, *aipen* open,
*raim* to roam, *delicht* delight, *tae* too (whose
Scots equivalent is *owre*).

The following passages exemplify Modern
Scots since the 18c, in works of wide currency within 'English literature':

O! 'tis a pleasant thing to be a bride;
Syne whindging getts about your ingle-
    side,
Yelping for this or that with fasheous
    din,
To mak them brats then ye maun toil
    and spin.
                (Allan Ramsay, from the *The Gentle
                           Shepherd*, 1725)

'Weel, weel,' and Mr. Jarvie, 'bluid's
thicker than water; and it liesna in kith,
kin and ally, to see motes in ilk other's
een if other een see them no. It wad be
sair news to the auld wife below the Ben
of Stuckavrallachan, that you, ye Hieland
limmer, had knockit out my harns, or
that I had kilted you up in a tow'
                (Walter Scott, from *Rob Roy*, 1817).

Faith, when it came there was more to
remember in Segget that year than
Armistice only. There was better kittle in
the story of what happened to Jim the
Sourock on Armistice Eve. He was aye
sore troubled with his stomach, Jim,
he'd twist his face as he'd hand you a
dram, and a man would nearly lose
nerve as he looked—had you given the
creature a bad shilling or what? But syne
he would rub his hand slow on his
wame, *It's the pains in my breast that I've
gotten again*; and he said that they were
fair awful sometimes, like a meikle
worm moving and wriggling in there
(Lewis Grassic Gibbon, from *Cloud Howe*,
second in the trilogy *A Scots Quair*,
1932–4).

**Conclusion**. A wide linguistic distance lies
between Scots and standard English, the
poles of speech in most of Scotland. By and
large, spoken and written Scots are difficult
for non-speakers, and require an investment of effort. As a result, use of Scots in
mixed company can make 'monolingual'
English speakers feel excluded. In the larger
European context, the situation of Scots resembles that of FRISIAN in the Netherlands,
Nynorsk in Norwegian, Occitan in relation
to French in France, and Catalan in relation
to Spanish in Spain. Scots is the SUBSTRA-
TUM of general English in Scotland; most
Scots use mixed varieties, and 'full' traditional Scots is now spoken by only a few
rural people. None the less, despite stigma-
tization in school, neglect by officialdom,
and marginalization in the media, people
of all backgrounds have since the 16c insisted on regarding *the guid Scots tongue* as
their national language. See BORROWING,
DORIC, EDINBURGH, GLASGOW, GUTTER SCOTS,
HIGHLAND ENGLISH, ORKNEY AND SHETLAND
DIALECTS, ULSTER SCOTS, Z.

**SCOTT, Sir Walter** [1771–1832]. Scottish
poet, novelist, collector of ballads, and historian. Born in Edinburgh, he was partly
brought up in the Borders, whose history
and traditions were a fundamental influence. He was educated at the High School
and U. in Edinburgh, and after training as a
lawyer was appointed Sheriff-Depute of
Selkirkshire in 1799. His first important
published work was *Minstrelsy of the Scottish
Border* (1802–3), an edited collection in three
volumes of over 70 ballads. The tone and

quality of ballad poetry influenced his series of narrative poems on Scottish historical themes. However, his reputation rests mainly on his novels, of which many are set in 17–18c Scotland, but others have settings from various periods in the history of England and France.

By virtually inventing the historical and regional novel as genres, Scott exerted a profound influence on the subsequent course of literature throughout the world. His successors include not only English regional novelists such as the Brontë sisters and Thomas HARDY, but James Fenimore Cooper and Mark Twain, for example, in the US, and others in Australia, Canada, India, and elsewhere. His use of SCOTS for dialogue encouraged others to experiment with non-standard forms of English and to provide them with more or less consistent orthographies. His English vocabulary is ornamented not only with words taken from Scots but with a large number of ARCHAISMS from Spenser and SHAKESPEARE, particularly in such fields as warfare, weaponry, horsemanship, and medieval architecture. His Scots dialogue is realistic and expressive, but most of his Scots-speaking characters belong to the lower orders or are associated with an age that was gone or passing when he wrote.

**SCOTTICISM**. A feature of English peculiar to Scotland; a word or usage from SCOTS or related to Scotland that occurs in English at large or in any other language. The term has often been pejorative, especially in Scotland itself, where since the late 17c it has served to indicate a usage to be avoided for reasons of refinement at home and ease of communication abroad. As the Anglicization of Scots proceeded after the Union of the Crowns in 1603, Scottish writers began apologizing for, vindicating, or seeking English help in eradicating the Scots expression which occurred in their writings. Published collections such as James Beattie's *Scoticisms arranged in Alphabetical Order, designed to correct Improprieties of Speech and Writing* (Edinburgh, 1787, 115 pp., *c*.500 entries) began appearing in 1752, continuing to the 20c. The general response to these collections has been mixed: (1) Some of the expressions warned against were eliminated from ScoE: *to come/sit into the fire*; the French-derived verb *evite* (to avoid). (2) Some have become (and may always have been) part of general

English: *burial* for *funeral*; *come here* (18c refined usage in England preferred *come hither*); *close the door* (*shut* was preferred); *liberate* (*set at liberty* was preferred). (3) Many continue in present-day ScoE. With the return of Scots to respectability in the 19c, Scotticisms have lost much of their former odium, except for the SHIBBOLETHS of *Gutter Scots*.

## ■ SCOTTISH ENGLISH ─────── ■

Short forms *ScoE, ScE*. The English language as used in Scotland, taken by some to include and by others to exclude SCOTS, or to include or exclude SCOTS as appropriate to particular discussions. When included, Scots is taken to be a northern dialect of English and part of the range of English found in Scotland. When excluded, Scots is taken to be a distinct language, still intact in LITERATURE and in the SPEECH of some rural people, but otherwise now mixed with English from England. Although for many the relationship between English and Scots is not clear-cut, most people are fully aware of the great differences at the poles of the continuum between them. Whatever the case, the traditional Scots usage of the Lowlands is distinct from *HIGHLAND ENGLISH*, the English typically acquired by GAELIC-speakers in the Highlands and Islands. If Scots is excluded, ScoE can be defined as the mother tongue of a large minority of native-educated Scots (mainly the middle classes and those who have received a higher education) and the public language of most of the remainder (mainly the working class of the Lowlands). While most of its VOCABULARY and GRAMMAR belong to GENERAL ENGLISH, ScoE has many features of Scots.

**Pronunciation**. In many ways, the conservative ScoE accent is phonologically close to Scots, while in others it has departed from it.

*Scots-based phonology*. (1) The ScoE accent is rhotic, and all the vowels and diphthongs appear unchanged before /r/: *beard* /bird/, *laird* /lerd/, *lard* /lard/, *moored* /murd/, *bird* /bɪrd/, *word* /wʌrd/, *heard* /herd/, *herd* /hɜrd/, *cord* /kɔrd/, *hoard* /hord/. A distinction is made between the vowels in such words as *sword* /sɔrd/ and *soared* /sord/. Scots are widely supposed to trill the /r/, and many do, but majority usage is the alveolar tap in some phonetic environments and a frica-

# SCOTTISH PLACE-NAMES

The place-names of Scotland reflect mixed linguistic origins over more than 2,000 years: Pre-Celtic, Celtic (Cumbric, Pictish, and Gaelic), Germanic (Anglian, Norse, Scots, and English), and some French, together with both the Scotticization and Anglicization of older names and considerable hybridization.

**1. Pre-Celtic, Cumbric, and Pictish**. Many of the most ancient names label rivers, whether these remain unexplained (as with *Spey, Ettrick,* and *Tweed*), are Pre-Celtic (as with *Ayr* and *Nairn*), or are Celtic (as with *Avon, Clyde, Dee,* and *Don*). The Britons of Strathclyde, whose Cumbric speech was similar to Old Welsh, have bequeathed such names as *Cramond* ('fort on the river Almond'), *Glasgow* ('green hollow'), *Linlithgow* ('lake in the moist hollow'), *Melrose* ('bare moor') and *Penicuik* ('headland of the cuckoo'). Pictish has provided relatively few names, but one name element, *pett* ('parcel of land') occurs in some 300 names, such as *Pittenweem* and *Pitlochry*. Also Pictish is *aber* ('river mouth, confluence'), as in *Aberdeen* and *Aberfoyle*, contrasting with both the Gaelic *inver*, as in *Inverness* and *Inveraray*, and the Scots/English *mouth*, as in *Lossiemouth*.

**2. Gaelic**. The most pervasive of the place-naming languages. Common elements are: *achadh* ('field'), Scotticized in the Lowlands as *ach-* and *auch-*, as in *Auchmithie, Auchendinny,* and *Achnasheen*; *baile* ('farm'), Scotticized as *bal* as in *Balerno, Balfour,* and *Balmaha*; and *cill* ('church'), Scotticized as *kil* as in *Kilbride, Kilmarnock,* and *Kilmartin*. In the Highlands, Gaelic often has exotic spellings that breach the rules of both Gaelic and Scots, as in *Ardrishaig* ('height of briars'), *Drumnadrochit* ('ridge of the bridge'), and *Tighnabruaich* ('house on the bank'). The names of mountains and other natural features, however, tend to conform to Gaelic rules: *Sgurr Domhnall* (hill + Donald, 'Donald's hill'), *Rubha Mor* (headland + big, 'big headland'), and *Loch an Eilean* ('loch/lake of the island').

**3. Anglian, Norse, Scots, and English**. The Germanic language complex in Scotland has produced a variety of forms. **1.** Many names in the south-east are of Anglian (northern Anglo-Saxon) provenance, such as *Haddington* ('farm of Hadda's people') and *Whittinghame* ('homestead of Hwita's people'), or are hybrid Anglo-Celtic, as in *Jedburgh* ('fort on the Jed': ?twisting river) and *Edinburgh* (adapting Cumbric *Din-Eidyn*, 'Eidyn's fort', the original of both Gaelicized *Dun-eideann* and Anglicized *Dunedin*. **2.** Scandinavian names in Shetland, Orkney, Caithness, and parts of the Western Isles (Hebrides) and north-western Highlands, include *Dingwall, Isbister, Kirkwall, Lybster, Papa Westray, Scalloway, Scapa Flow,* and *Sullom Voe*. Gaelicized versions of *vik* ('bay', as in *Viking* and the town names *Wick* ansd *Lerwick*) survive in *Uig* and *Mallaig*, and the Gaelicized *Duirinish* and *Fishnish* are close parallels to the more transparently Norse *Durness* and *Stromness* (in all of which *nish* or *ness* means 'headland'). **3.** Names in Scots generally derive from Anglian, and include *Broomielaw, Canonbie, Dyke, Lamington, Neilston, Newbigging, Skinfasthaven, Staneycroft, Stewarton,* and *Windygates*. Such names are cognate in structure with many place-names in England and in recent times many have acquired Anglicized pronunciations, as with 'head' rather than 'heid' in such forms as *Fairmilehead* in Edinburgh. **4.** The Scots cognate for English *-borough* and *-bury* ('fort') is *-burgh*, as in *Edinburgh* and *Fraserburgh*. **5.** In naming settlements at the head of Highland *lochs* (lakes and arms of the sea), there has been a degree of competition between wholly Gaelic and Gaelic-with-English: contrast *Kinlochleven* ('head of Loch Leven') with *Lochearnhead* ('head of Loch Earn'); these might as easily have been *\*Lochlevenhead* and *Kinlochearn*.

tive or frictionless continuant in others. There is a minority uvular r (see BURR) and retroflex r appears to be gaining ground in the middle class. (2) There are distinct phonemes in such words as *rise* and *rice*. The /aɪ/ diphthong occurs in *rise, tie/tied, sly, why* while the /əɪ/ diphthong occurs in *rice, tide, slide, while*, as well as in such borrowings from Scots as *ay(e)* always, *gey* very, *gyte* mad. (3) ScoE operates the Scottish vowel length rule. (4) There is no distinction between *cam* and *calm*, both having /a/, between *cot* and *caught*, both having /ɔ/, and between *full* and *fool*, both having /u/. (5) There is a monophthong in most regions for /i, e, o, u/ as in *steel, stale, stole, stool*. (6) The monophthongs and diphthongs total 14 vowel sounds, perhaps the smallest vowel system of any long-established variety of English. (7) ScoE retains from Scots the voiceless velar fricative /x/: for example, in such names as *Brechin* and *MacLachlan*, such Gaelicisms as *loch* and *pibroch*, such Scotticisms as *dreich* and *sough*, and for some speakers such words of Greek provenance as *patriarch* and *technical*. (8) The *wh-* in such words as *whale, what, why* is pronounced /hw/ and such pairs as *which/witch* are sharply distinguished. (9) In some speakers, initial /p, t, k/ are unaspirated.

***Phonological options***. (1) Vowels: *lodge* and *lodger* with /ʌ/ and not /ɔ/; *there* and *where* with /e/ and not /ɛ/. (2) Consonants: *length* and *strength* with /n/ and not /ŋ/; *fifth* and *sixth* with final /t/ and not /θ/; *raspberry* with /s/ and not /z/, *December* with /z/ and not /s/, *luxury* with /gʒ/ and not /kʃ/; *Wednesday* retains medial /d/. (3) Stress patterns: *tortoise* and *porpoise* with spelling pronunciation and equal syllabic stress; many words with distinctive stressing, such as *advertise, baptize, realize, recognize* and *adjudicate, harass, reconcile, soiree, survey* with the main stress on the final syllable, and *lamentable* and *preferably* on the second.

**Hybrid accents**. The conservative accent just described is not the only accent of ScoE: (1) Especially in Edinburgh, in the group which includes lawyers, accountants, and architects, there exists a range of accents that to varying degrees incline towards RP. They date from the early 20c or earlier and their Scottishness is reduced by these main features: the addition of an RP-like /ɑ:/ in such words as *calm, gather, value* contrasting with /a/ in *cam, bad, pal*, and /ɔ:/ in *caught* be-

side /ɔ/ in *cot*; the merging of some of all of /ɪ, ʌ, ɛ, ɛ̃/ before /r/, in such words as *bird, word, heard*, and *herd* or *birth, worth, Perth*, and *earth*, usually with *r*-colouring; the sporadic or consistent merging of /əɪ/ and /aɪ/ under /aɪ/ in *tied/tide*; diphthongal realizations of /e/ as [eɪ] in *came*, and /o/ as [ou] in *home*; and sporadic or consistent loss of pre-consonantal /r/ in such words as *farm, form, hard*. (2) Another hybrid, strongly stigmatized in the population at large, is a middle-class variety associated with both EDINBURGH and GLASGOW: see MORNINGSIDE AND KELVINSIDE. (3) Speakers of Highland English form a distinct community whose accents are influenced by Gaelic, including a tendency to lengthen vowels and devoice voiced consonants and aspirate voiceless ones, *just* sounding like 'chust', *big* like 'pick': see HIGHLAND ENGLISH.

**Grammar**. Features of present-day Scots grammar are carried over into ScoE: (1) *Modal verbs*. Many speakers do not use *shall* and *may* in informal speech, using *will* as in *Will I see you again?* and *can* for permission as in *Can I come as well?* and *might* or *will maybe* for possibility, as in *He might come later/He'll maybe come later*. *Must* expresses logical necessity as in *He must have forgotten, He mustn't have seen us*, but not compulsion, for which *have (got) to* are used, as in *You've (got) to pay*. Both *should* and *ought to* express moral obligation or advice, as in *You should/ought to try and see it*, but otherwise *would* is used where other BrE has *should*, as in *I would, if I was you* (not *I should, if I were you*). *Need to, use to*, and *dare to* operate as main verbs rather than auxiliaries: *He didn't need to do that; I didn't use to do that; She doesn't dare to talk back*. (2) *Passives*. The passive may be expressed by *get*: *I got told off*. (3) Certain verbs are used progressively, contrary to other BrE practice: *He was thinking he'd get paid twice; I was hoping to see here; They were meaning to come*. (4) *Negatives*. As with Scots *no* and *-nae*, ScoE *not* is favoured over *-n't*: *He'll not come* in preference to *He won't come, You're not wanted* to *You aren't wanted*, and similarly *Is he not coming? Can you not come? Do you not want it? Did he not come? Not* may negate a main verb as well as an auxiliary: *He isn't still not working?; Nobody would dream of not obeying*. (5) Verbs of motion elide before adverbs of motion in some contexts: *I'll away home then; The cat wants out*. (6) *The* is used as in Scots in, for example, *to take the cold, to get sent to the hospital, to go to the church*. (7) Pronouns in *-self* may be used non-reflexively: *How's yourself today? Is himself in?* (Is the man of the house at home?). (8) *Anybody, everybody, nobody, somebody* are preferred to *anyone, everyone, no one, someone.* (9) *Amn't I?* is used virtually to the exclusion of *aren't I?*: *I'm expected too, amn't I?*

**Vocabulary and idiom**. There is a continuum of ScoE lexical usage, from the most to the least international: (1) Words of original Scottish provenance used in the language at large for so long that few people think of them as ScoE: *caddie, collie, cosy, croon, eerie, forebear, glamour, golf, gumption, lilt,* (*golf*) *links, pony, raid, rampage, scone, uncanny, weird, wizened, wraith.* (2) Words widely used or known and generally perceived to be Scottish: *bannock, cairn, ceilidh, clan, clarsach, corrie, first-foot, glengarry, gloaming, haggis, kilt, pibroch, sporran, Tam o' Shanter, wee, whisky.* (3) Words that have some external currency but are used more in Scotland than elsewhere: *bairn, bonnie, brae, burn, canny, douce, hogmanay, kirk, peewit* (the lapwing), *pinkie, skirl.* (4) General words that have uses special to ScoE and Scots: *close* an entry passage in a tenement building, *stair* a group of flats served by a single close in a tenement, *stay* to reside, *uplift* to collect (rent, a parcel, etc.). (5) Scottish technical usages, many of Latin origin, especially in law, religion, education, and official terminology: *advocate* a courtroom lawyer (in England *barrister*), *convener* a chairman of a committee, *induction* of an ordained minister to a ministerial charge, *janitor* caretaker of a school, *jus relicti/relictae* the relict's share of a deceased's movable property, *leet* a list of selected candidates for a post, *procurator-fiscal* an official combining the offices of coroner and public prosecutor, *provost* a mayor, *timeous* timely. (6) Colloquial words used and understood by all manner of Scots and by the middle class as overt Scotticisms: *ach* a dismissive interjection, *braw* fine, good-looking, *chuckiestane* a pebble, *footer* to mess about, *gillie* a hunting attendant, *girn* to whine, *glaikit* stupid, *haar* a cold sea-fog, *howf* a public house, *och* an interjection, *pernickety* fussy, *scunnered* sickened, *wabbit* tired out, *wannert* ('wandered': mad). (7) Traditional, sometimes recondite and literary, Scots words occasionally introduced into standard English contexts in the media, and known to minorities: *bogle* a phantom, *dominie* a schoolmaster, *eident* diligent, *forfochen* exhausted, *furth of* and *outwith* outside of, *gardyloo* the cry formerly used in Edin-

burgh before throwing slops from a high window, *hochmagandie* fornication, *leid* a language, *makar* a poet, *owerset* to translate, *Sassenach* an Englishman, a Lowlander, *southron* English, *yestreen* yesterday evening.

See BRITISH ENGLISH, DIALECT IN SCOTLAND, GUTTER SCOTS, L-SOUNDS, NORTHERN ENGLISH, R-SOUNDS, SCOTTICISM, SCOTTISH LANGUAGES.

**SCOTTISH GAELIC**. The Celtic language of the West Highlands and Western Isles of Scotland. GAELIC-speaking Scots arrived from Ireland on the west coast of what is now Scotland in 3–5c AD. As they gradually gained power, their language spread throughout the country, though not the whole population; in the south-east, for example, it was probably used mainly among the ruling classes. With the increased influence of NORTHERN ENGLISH, the use and prestige of Gaelic began to decline and since the 12c there has been a gradual retraction. Political factors, social pressures, and educational policies have combined to threaten the language with extinction. In the later 20c, more positive attitudes have developed and efforts are being made to sustain Gaelic, encourage bilingual policies, and give it a valued place in school and preschool education. Many, however, fear that these measures are too little too late. Gaelic is now used as a community language virtually only in the Western Isles. At the 1981 census, there were little over 80,000 speakers, with only a few hundred under the age of five and there are few monoglot speakers above this age.

Scottish Gaelic has an ancient literary tradition and paradoxically its literature flourishes in the 20c, with such poets as Sorley MacLean, Derick Thomson, and Iain Crichton Smith (also a novelist in English). Public performance and composition in Gaelic are encouraged by the *National Mod*, an annual competitive festival of music and poetry organized by *An Comunn Gaidhealach/The Highland Association*, founded in 1891 to support the Gaelic language and culture and the Highland way of life. *Comunn na Gàidhlig* (the Gaelic Association) was set up in 1984 with the more specific aim of promoting the language.

Gaelic BORROWINGS from English and SCOTS are numerous and increasing, especially in technical and administrative fields: for example, *teilebhisean* television, *rèidio* radio, and *briogais* trousers (from Scots *breeks*). The influence of English on Gaelic syntax is considerable and rapidly extending, now that virtually all adult speakers are bilingual. Pronunciation has been less affected, but phonemic changes based on English or Scots are noticeable in the speech of children of Gaelic-speaking immigrants to the cities. More of these children now speak Gaelic, because of a recent increase in Gaelic playgroups and schools. The language is taught in three of the Scottish universities, two of which (Edinburgh and Glasgow) have a chair of Celtic. See CELTIC LANGUAGES, HIGHLAND ENGLISH, IRISH, SCOTTISH ENGLISH.

# ■ SCOUSE ────────────── ■

[From 18c *lobscouse*, a sailor's dish of stewed meat, vegetables, and ship's biscuit, not unlike Irish stew. *Lobscouser* was a slang name for a sailor. The terms *Scouse* and *Scouser* for someone from Liverpool seem to be recent, and probably arose because the city is a port and stew was a feature of the diet. The *OED* cites the *Southern Daily Echo* (1945), in which 'a scouse' is explained as 'a native of Liverpool where they eat "scouse" ']. **1.** Also *Scouser*. A person born in the city of Liverpool, on the River Mersey, especially if from the working class. **2.** The often stigmatized working-class speech of Merseyside. The ACCENT combines features of LANCASHIRE with varieties of English from Ireland and to a lesser extent from Wales, brought in by 19–20c immigration. Accents range from broad Scouse though modifications towards RP and RP itself in the middle and upper classes. Among the distinctive expressions in Scouse are *the Pool*, a nickname for Liverpool, and *Liverpudlian* (the correct name for someone born in Liverpool, substituting *puddle* for *pool*). Non-Scousers, especially from north of the city, are sometimes called *woollybacks* (sheep), a nickname suggesting rusticity and lack of wits.

**Pronunciation**. Of the following features, 1–5 are widely regarded as SHIBBOLETHS, especially when several occur together: (1) A merger of the vowels in such pairs as *fair*/*fur* and *spare*/*spur*, realized as an /eː/ or /ɜː/. (2) As in other parts of the north-west of England, syllable-final *-ng* is pronounced /ŋg/, as in 'long-g' for *long* and 'sing-ging-g' for *singing*. (3) The vowel in such words as *pin* and *sing* is pronounced /i/, so that they

sound close to 'peen' and 'seengg'. (4) The sound /r/ may be either an alveolar continuant or an alveolar tap that is particularly distinct initially (*rabbit*, *run*), after stops and fricatives (*breathe*, *grass*, *three*), and between vowels (*carry*, *ferry*). (5) A /t/ between vowels is often replaced by /r/, sometimes shown in print as *rr*, as in 'marra' for *matter*: *What's the marra with you then?* In a publicity drive for the Liverpool clean streets campaign, litter was described as 'norra lorra fun'. (6) Some speakers, especially working-class Catholics of Irish background, replace /θ, ð/ with /t, d/, as in 'dese tree' for *these three*. *Month* may be pronounced 'muntth'. (7) In syllable-initial and syllable-final positions, a fricative can follow a stop, as in 'k/x/ing' for *king* (where /x/ represents the fricative in ScoE *loch*), 'me d/z/ad' for *my dad*, 'back/x/' for *back*, and 'bad/z/' for *bad*. (8) Scouse is often described as having a flat intonation, in effect a rise with a level tail where RP has a fall: in the statement *I don't like it*, it goes up on *like* then runs level, whereas RP starts going down on *like* and keeps going down. There is also a kind of fall in *yes–no* questions where RP would have a rise, so that in the question *Are you from Birkenhead?*, Scouse falls on *Birk* where RP rises. (9) Until recently it was possible to distinguish the speech of Irish Catholics from Protestant English through the pronunciation of some words: a double advertisement on local buses in the 1960s read on one side of the bus 'Treat us furly, travel early', on the other 'Treat us fairly, travel airly' (the latter denoting Irish-derived usage).

**Adenoidal speech**. The voice quality of speakers of Scouse has often been described as adenoidal, and phoneticians have speculated about the origins of such a feature. David Abercrombie, noting that children may acquire a quality of voice from others who have a problem, observes: 'A striking example . . . is afforded by some urban slum communities where adenoids, due doubtless to malnutrition and lack of sunlight, are prevalent, with their consequent effect on voice quality, but where people can be found with adenoidal voice quality who do not have adenoids—they have learnt the quality from the large number who do have them, so that they conform to what, for that community, has become the norm. . . . The accent of Liverpool seems to have had its origin in such circumstances' (*Elements of General Phonetics*, 1967). Gerald O. Knowles adds: 'In Scouse, the centre of gravity of the tongue is brought backwards and upwards, the pillars of the fauces are narrowed, the pharynx is tightened, and the larynx is displaced upwards.... The main auditory effect of this setting is the "adenoidal" quality of Scouse, which is produced even if the speaker's nasal passages are unobstructed' (in P. Trudgill (ed.), *Sociolinguistic Patterns in British English*, 1978). The effect is primarily achieved by the sustained closure of the velum or soft, palate. See DIALECT IN ENGLAND.

**SEASPEAK**, also **English for maritime communications**. The English of merchant shipping, a RESTRICTED LANGUAGE adopted in 1988 by the *International Maritime Organization (IMO)* of the United Nations for use in ship-to-ship and ship-to-shore communications as a necessary consequence of vastly increased shipping during the 1960s–70s. The need for regularization of practices in one language and the training of officers in its use was agreed, and English, already the language of civil aviation, was chosen by the IMO.

In 1982–3, Seaspeak was created by specialists in maritime communications and applied linguistics, working in Plymouth and Cambridge and funded by the UK government and Pergamon Press. It was made as concise and unambiguous as possible, was restricted to no more than two propositions in any message, allowed for constant checkback and confirmation, and made as few changes as possible to existing practice. The *SEASPEAK Reference Manual* by Weeks, Glover, Strevens, and Johnson (Oxford: Pergamon, 1984) was published after worldwide sea trials. Apart from special-format messages (as in stereotyped weather forecasts), all messages begin with a *message marker* that indicates the nature of what follows, such as advice, information, instruction, intention, question, request, warning, or a response to one of these. Below is a typical exchange, in which a ship called *Sun Dragon* calls up Land's End Coastguard in England, to inform them of a change of plan:

Ship. Land's End Coastguard, Land's End Coastguard. This is Sun Dragon, Sun Dragon. Over.

Coastguard. Sun Dragon. This is Land's End Coastguard. Switch to VHF channel one-one. Over.

Ship. Land's End Coastguard. This is Sun Dragon. Agree VHF channel one-one. Over.

Coastguard. Sun Dragon. This is Land's End Coastguard on channel one-one. Over.

Ship. Land's End Coastguard. This is Sun Dragon. Information: I am returning to Mount's Bay. Reason: north-west gale and very heavy seas. Over.

Coastguard. Sun Dragon. This is Land's End Coastguard. Information received: you are returning to Mount's Bay. Reason: north-west gale and very heavy seas. Question: do you require assistance? Over.

Ship. Land's End Coastguard. This is Sun Dragon. Answer: no assistance required, thank you. Nothing more. Over.

Coastguard. Sun Dragon. This is Land's End Coastguard. Nothing more. Out.

Compare AIRSPEAK. See ESP, -SPEAK.

**SEMANTIC CHANGE**, also **semantic shift**. Change in the meanings of words, especially with the passage of time, the study of which is *historical semantics*. Investigators of changes in meaning have established a set of semantic categories, such as GENERALIZATION, in which the meaning and reference of a word widen over the years ( *pigeon* once meant a young dove and now means all members of the family Columbidae), and SPECIALIZATION, in which the meaning of a word narrows over the years (*deer* once meant any four-legged beast and now means only members of the family Cervidae). Such categories are not always sharply distinguishable; one may shade into another or develop from another. For example, before it meant a young dove, *pigeon* meant a young bird; it therefore specialized from young bird to young dove, then generalized from young dove to all dove-like birds. For scholarly convenience, the processes of semantic change are often described as if each operates alone, the 'story' of a word being told without bringing in too many other words. Such stories, however, are often complex and disseminate across whole networks of words. When a part of such a network is considered (such as the set of all barnyard fowls), many processes can be seen working together: the reference of one word widens while narrowing another (*chicken* generalizing to include the meaning of *hen*), the reference widens in one period and narrows in another, sometimes establishing regional preferences (*cock* in BrE, *rooster* in AmE), and the reference extends figuratively (*chick* coming to mean a young woman) or idiomatically (*no spring chicken*), permitting a special use in one place but not another (in ScoE, *hen* as a term of endearment for women in and around Glasgow, comparable to *duck(s)* in parts of England). It has proved useful, therefore, to discuss semantic change in terms of webs of shifting forms and relationships rather than words on their own.

See BACK-FORMATION, CATACHRESIS, COMPUTER USAGE, CONVERSION, DERIVATION, DETERIORATION, EPONYM, ETYMOLOGY, EUPHEMISM, FIGURATIVE EXTENSION, FIGURATIVE LANGUAGE, HOMOGRAPH, HOMONYM, HOMOPHONE, JANUS WORD, LOCALISM, MELIORATION, METAPHOR METONYMY, PEJORATION, POLYSEMY, RADIATION.

# ■ SEMANTICS ──────────── ■

The study of MEANING. The term has at least five linked senses: (1) Sometimes *semasiology*. In LINGUISTICS, the study of the meaning of words and sentences, their denotations, connotations, implications, and ambiguities. The three levels or components of a common model of language are phonology, syntax, and semantics. (2) In philosophy, the study of logical expression and of the principles that determine the truth or falsehood of sentences. (3) In SEMIOTICS, the study of signs and what they refer to, and of responses to those signs. (4) In general usage, interest in the meanings of words, including their denotations, connotations, implications, and ambiguities. (5) Informally and often pejoratively, the making of (pedantic and impractical) distinctions about the meaning and use of words.

**Background**. The attempt to formulate a science of signs dates from the late 19c, when the French linguist Michel Bréal published *Essai de sémantique* (1897). He was interested in the influence of usage on the evolution of words and wished to extend the philological study of language (largely based on text and form) to include meaning. The historical study of meaning, however, is not currently central to the work of semanticists: see SEMANTIC CHANGE. Present-day semantic theory has developed largely from the later theories of the Swiss linguist Ferdinand de Saussure, who emphasized

synchronic system and not diachronic evolution. Post-Saussurean semantics is the study of meaning as a branch of linguistics, like GRAMMAR and phonology. In its widest sense, it is concerned both with relations within language (*sense*) and relations between language and the world (*reference*). Generally, sense relations are associated with the word or *lexical item/lexeme* and with a lexical structure; their study is known as *structural* or *lexical semantics*. REFERENCE is concerned with the meaning of words, sentences, etc., in terms of the world of experience: the situations to which they refer or in which they occur.

**Semantic fields**. One approach has been the theory of *semantic fields*, developed by J. Trier and W. Porzig in 1934. It attempts to deal with words as related and contrasting members of a set: for example, the meaning of English colour words like *red* and *blue*, which can be stated in terms of their relations in the colour spectrum, which in turn can be compared with the colour words of other languages. Thus, there is no precise equivalent of *blue* in Russian, which has two terms, *goluboy* and *siniy*, usually translated as 'light blue' and 'dark blue'. In Russian, these are treated as distinct colours and not shades of one colour, as users of English might suppose from their translation.

**Sense relations**. In addition to semantic fields and lexical sets, a number of different types of SENSE *relation* have been identified, some traditional, some recent: (1) *Hyponymy*. Inclusion or class membership: *tulip* and *rose* are HYPONYMS of *flower*, which is their *hyperonym* or *superordinate* term. In its turn, *flower* is a hyponym of *plant*. In ordinary language, however, words can seldom be arranged within the kinds of strict classification found in zoology or botany. For example, there are arguments about whether rhubarb is a vegetable or a fruit, and whether the tomato is a fruit or a vegetable. (2) SYNONYMY. Sameness of meaning: *large* is a SYNONYM of *big*. It is often maintained that there are no true synonyms in a language, but always some difference, of variety (AmE *fall*, BrE *autumn*), style (polite *gentleman*, colloquial BrE *chap*), emotive meaning (general *politician*, appreciative *statesman*), collocation (*rancid* modifying only *bacon* or *butter*). Partial or near synonymy is common, as with *adult*, *ripe*, and *mature*. (3) *Antonymy*. Oppositeness of meaning. There are, however, several types of opposite: *wide/narrow* and *old/young* are gradable both explicitly (X is wider than Y, A is older than B) and implicitly (a wide band is narrower than a narrow road). Such pairs allow for intermediate stages (neither wide nor narrow) and are ANTONYMS proper. *Male/female* and *alive/dead* are not usually gradable and allow for no intermediate stage, except in expressions such as *more dead than alive*. Such pairs are *complementaries*. *Buy/sell* and *husband/wife* are relational opposites (X sells to Y and Y buys from X; only a husband can have a wife, and vice versa). Such pairs are *converses*. (4) POLYSEMY or *multiple meaning*. The existence of two or more meanings or senses to one word: for example, *flight* defined in at least six different ways: the power of flying; the act of flying; an air journey; a series (of steps); fleeing; a unit in an air force. (5) *Homonymy*. Words different in meaning but identical in form: *mail* armour, *mail* post. It is not always easy to distinguish homonymy and polysemy, and dictionaries rely partly on etymology to help maintain the distinction. *Ear* (of corn) and *ear* (the organ) are examples of homonymy, because etymologically the former derives from Old English *éar* (husk) while the latter derives from Old English *éare* (ear). See HOMONYM, -ONYM.

**Componential analysis**. An approach which makes use of semantic components was first used by anthropologists in the analysis of kinship terms. Componential analysis seeks to deal with sense relations by means of a single set of constructs. Lexical items are analysed in terms of *semantic features* or *sense components*: for example, such sets as *man/woman*, *bull/cow*, *ram/ewe* have the proportional relationships *man : woman :: bull : cow :: ram : ewe*. Here, the components [male]/[female], and [human]/[bovine]/[ovine] may account for all the differences of meaning. Generally, components are treated as binary opposites distinguished by pluses and minuses: for example, [+male]/[−male] or [+female]/[−female] rather than simply [male]/[female]. It has been argued that *projection rules* can combine the semantic features of individual words to generate the meaning of an entire sentence, and to account for ambiguity (as in *The bill is large*) and anomaly (as in *He painted the walls with silent paint*). There are complexities where the features are not simply additive but arranged in

hierarchical structure: for example, in the proposal to analyse *kill* as [cause] [to become] [not alive]. It is controversial whether there is a finite set of such universal semantic components accounting for all languages and whether the components have conceptual reality.

**Semantics and grammar**. The meaning of a sentence is generally assumed to be derived from the meaning of its words, but it can be argued that we usually interpret whole sentences and that the sentence, not the word, is the basic unit of meaning, the meaning of words being derived from the meaning of sentences. This view is implicit in the referential theories of meaning discussed below. A distinction has been made by the British linguist John Lyons between *sentence meaning* and *utterance meaning*: sentence meaning is concerned with 'literal' meaning determined by the grammatical and lexical elements, unaffected by the context or what the speaker 'meant' to say.

Utterance meaning includes: (1) *Presupposition*. The statement *The king of France is bald* presupposes that there is a king of France, and the statement *I regret that Mary came* presupposes that Mary did come, but *I believe that Mary came* does not. What is presupposed in this sense is not asserted by the speaker but is nevertheless understood by the hearer. (2) *Implicature*. A term associated with H. P. Grice. The statement *It's hot in here* may imply the need to open a window, *I tried to telephone John yesterday* would normally suggest that I failed, and *I've finished my homework* (as a reply to *Have you finished your homework and put your books away?*) would suggest that the books have not been put away. Implicature is concerned with the various inferences we can make without actually being told, and includes presupposition. (3) *Prosodic features*. The use of stress and tone, as when *He SAW Mary this morning* means that he did not avoid her or telephone her, in contrast with *He saw MARY this morning*, rather than or in addition to anyone else. (4) *Speech acts*. Associated with J. L. Austin (*How to do Things with Words*, 1962). When a ship is launched with the words *I name this ship . . .* , the usage is not a statement of fact but an action. Similarly, *I declare this meeting closed* is the act of closing that meeting. Such speech acts, called *performatives*, cannot be said to be true or false. The notion of speech act can be extended to more common types of speech function:

questions, orders, requests, statements, etc., and it is instructive to note that what appears to be a question may actually be a request: for example, *Can you pass the salt?*, where it would be inappropriate, though true, to reply *Yes, of course I can* without taking any action.

**Reference**. The place of reference in semantics is controversial. A problem with word meaning in terms of reference is that though words for objects may seem to denote, or refer to, objects (as with *stone* and *house*), other words (abstract nouns, verbs, and prepositions, etc.) do not seem to refer to anything. Many words are quite vague in their reference, with no clear dividing line between them (*hill/mountain, river/stream/brook*), and may be used for sets of objects that are very different in appearance (*dog* and *table* covering a wide range of animals and pieces of furniture). Referential meaning (usually of words but also of sentences) is sometimes known as *cognitive meaning*, as opposed to *emotive* or *evaluative meaning*. In traditional terms, this is the difference between *denotation* and *connotation*. Since there are theoretical problems with the concept of referential meaning (which seems inapplicable to abstract nouns, verbs, etc.), some scholars prefer the terms *cognitive* and *affective*. Thus, the pairs *horse/steed, statesman/politician*, and *hide/conceal* may be said to have the same cognitive meanings, but different affective meanings.

**Approaches to meaning**. The American linguist Leonard Bloomfield regarded meaning as a weak point in language study and believed that it could be wholly stated in behaviourist terms. Following the Polish anthropologist Bronisław Malinowski, the British linguist J. R. Firth argued that *context of situation* was an important level of linguistic analysis alongside syntax, collocation, morphology, phonology, and phonetics, all making a contribution to linguistic meaning in a very wide sense. However, there have been few attempts to make practical use of that concept. Many scholars have therefore, excluded reference from semantics. Thus, in transformational-generative grammar, the semantic component is entirely stated in terms of sense or semantic components, as described above in terms of componential analysis. Others have argued for a *truth-conditional* approach to semantics, in which the meaning of *bachelor* as 'unmar-

ried man' is shown by the fact that if *X is an unmarried man* is true, then *X is a bachelor* is also true.

**Pragmatics**. Every aspect of meaning which cannot be stated in truth-conditional terms is PRAGMATICS; the distinction is close to that of sentence and utterance meaning. But there are problems with this distinction and with the exclusion of reference. Thus, such deictic relationships as *here/there* and *this/that*, and words such as *today* and the personal pronouns, appear to contribute to sentence meaning, yet depend for their interpretation on reference, which varies according to the identity of speaker and hearer and the time and place of the utterance.

**Conclusion**. There can be no single, simple approach to the study of semantics, because there are many aspects of meaning both within language and in the relation between language and the world. The complexity of semantics reflects the complexity of the use of human language.

See AMBIGUITY, COMMUNICATION, CONNOTATION AND DENOTATION, CONTEXT, LANGUAGE CHANGE, LEVEL OF LANGUAGE, LEXICOGRAPHY, LOGIC, SIGN, SLANG, STRESS, SYMBOL, TONE.

**SEMICOLON**, also **semi-colon**. The PUNCTUATION mark (;). Its main roles are: (1) To link statements that are closely associated or that complement or parallel each other in some way: *We will stay here; you may go*. In this role, it can link clauses (*they were poor; they had few clothes; they were often in despair*) or phrases or a mixture of phrases and clauses (*they had no money; nor any clothes; nor could they find work*). It marks antithesis, often with a word such as *and, but,* or *yet* to emphasize this: *They were poor; and yet they were happy*. Words such as *however, nonetheless/none the less,* and *moreover* are usually preceded by a semicolon when they begin a new statement; *books are cheap; moreover, they last a lifetime*. (2) To mark a stronger division in a sentence that is already punctuated with commas (*several people were still waiting, impatiently shuffling their feet, looking bored; but none of them, in spite of this, seemed willing to speak*). The semicolon is often avoided in ordinary writing, or replaced with a dash, because many users lack confidence in it. It is most often found in print. See COLON.

**SEMIOTICS**. The study and analysis of SIGNS and SYMBOLS as part of COMMUNICATION as for example in LANGUAGE, gesture, clothing, and behaviour. Present-day semiotics arises from the independent work of two linguistic researchers, one in the US, the other in Switzerland. Charles S. Peirce (1834–1914) used the term to describe the study of signs and symbolic systems from a philosophical perspective, while Ferdinand de Saussure (1857–1913) coined *semiology* as part of his interest in language as a system of signs. The terms have generally been regarded as synonymous, and *semiotics* is better known, especially in the English-speaking world.

Almost anything can be a sign: clothes, hairstyles, type of house or car owned, accent, and body language. All send messages about such things as age, class, and politics. Sign systems, however, are not peculiar to human beings: the study of animal communication by gesture, noise, smell, dancing, etc., is termed *zoosemiotics*, while the study of technical systems of signals such as Morse code and traffic lights is *communication theory*. In semiotics, the term *CODE* refers loosely to any set of signs and their conventions of meaning. Language represents a rich set of such codes, both *verbal* (in language proper) and *non-verbal* (in the paralanguage of facial expressions, body movements, and such vocal activities as snorts and giggles). The media provide visual and aural signals in photographs, radio and television programmes, advertisements, and theatrical performances. Literature is seen as a particularly rich semiotic field with such sub-disciplines as *literary* and *narrative semiotics*. Critical attention has come to focus not only on the codes themselves, but on the process of *encoding* and *decoding*. Readers, it is argued, do not simply decode messages, but actively create meanings: that is, they *re-code* as they read.

Peirce and Saussure were interested in the relationship between sign and *referent* (what a sign refers to). Although they both stressed that this relationship was essentially arbitrary, Peirce argued that different types of sign had different degrees of both *arbitrariness* and *motivation*. What he terms an *icon* is a highly motivated sign, since it visually resembles what it represents: for example, a photograph or hologram. His *index* is partly motivated to the extent that there is a connection, usually of causality, between sign and referent: spots indexical of a disease like measles; smoke indexical of fire. Peirce's *symbol* is the most arbitrary kind of sign: the word in language, the formula in mathematics, or the rose representing love in literary tradition. See LINGUISTIC SIGN, SEMANTICS.

**SEMI-VOWEL**. See CONSONANT, GLIDE, VOWEL.

**SENSE**. A term whose meanings range from physical faculties (such as *the sense of sight*) through analogous faculties of mind or spirit (*a sense of humour*), intelligence (*Show some sense!*), and what is logical and proper (the opposite of *nonsense*) to MEANING (*the sense of a text*) and the idea that many words have submeanings (*X used in the sense of Y; the various senses of the word 'mark'*). Although people agree that words may have different 'senses', there is no agreed means of establishing just how many senses many *polysemous* (many-sensed) words have. The boundaries between senses are not always clear: a sense may be precise and restricted or vague and diffuse, and may be susceptible to analysis into more or less easily delineated *subsenses*. Identifying a sense may depend on knowledge and experience, social and situational context, the reason for analysing a word, the policy used by compilers of a particular dictionary, the method of displaying words in that dictionary, the amount of detail to be provided, and different theories about what words are and of how they should be discussed and defined. As the accompanying table shows, dictionaries can differ considerably as to the main sense divisions of such words as *walk* and *crane*.

| Dictionary | Number of senses of: | | | |
| | walk | | crane | |
| | noun | verb | noun | verb |
| --- | --- | --- | --- | --- |
| *CoED* (1986) | 15 | 11 | 4 | 3 |
| *LDEL* (1984) | 5 | 12 | 3 | 2 |
| *AHD* (1985) | 7 | 4 | 4 | 2 |
| *ChED* (1988) | 25 | 20 | 4 | 4 |

*Key: CoED* Collins English Dictionary, *LDEL* Longman Dictionary of the English Language, *AHD* American Heritage Dictionary, *ChED* Chambers English Dictionary.

See HOMONYM, POLYSEMY.

# ■ SENTENCE ───────── ■

The largest structural unit normally treated in GRAMMAR. The sentence is notoriously difficult to define; numerous definitions have been offered and found wanting. The classical definition, that a sentence expresses a complete thought, dates from the first Western treatise on grammar, by Dionysius Thrax (c.100 BC), whose interest lay primarily in analysing, using, and teaching written Greek. This traditional notional definition, however, only solves the problem by transferring it: how does one define a complete thought? Linguists and anthropologists in the 19–20c, trained in the Greco-Latin grammatical tradition and faced with the analysis of previously unwritten Amerindian languages, have often noted how difficult it is to establish the boundaries between what might be words and what might be sentences in some of those languages. Because of this, the sentence as understood in the Western linguistic tradition has not yet been unequivocally established as a universal of language.

**The syntactic sentence**. Formal definitions usually refer to the structural independence of the sentence: that it is not included in a lager structural unit by such devices as coordination and subordination. However, dependence is relative: what are generally recognized as sentences may be dependent to some extent on other sentences through such devices as pronoun substitution and connective ADVERBIALS: *therefore*, *however*, *yet*. Elliptical sentences such as *Tomorrow* (in answer to *When is your birthday?*) are clearly dependent in some sense on linguistic context. There are also problems in deciding the status of formulaic utterances such as *Yes* or *Good morning*, which in dialogue are complete in themselves. Formal definitions may also refer to the internal structures of sentences. Indeed, it is possible to recognize as canonical sentences those that conform in their structure to the normal clause patterns, such as subject–verb–direct object. Other constructions would then be considered irregular or minor, and some (such as *Yes*) perhaps not sentences at all.

**The orthographic sentence**. In written language, sentence status is signalled by punctuation, primarily through the PERIOD (especially AmE) or *full stop* (especially BrE),

but the orthographic sentence is not necessarily identical with the syntactic sentence: CLAUSES separated by SEMICOLONS or COLONS might well be analysed as independent sentences, the punctuation reflecting the writer's feeling that the sentences to linked are closer semantically than the surrounding sentences. In addition, in the prose of publicists and advertisers, traditional conventions for the organization of written sentences are routinely abandoned, in order to highlight certain points:

> Have a little pick-me-up before you get back to work. Iberia's Business Class always welcomes you with a glass of sherry. A taste of Spanish sunshine to whet your appetite for the delicious meal ahead. And afterwards relax and take advantage of our unique, multilingual, on-board library. Efficient and professional but warm and hospitable. That's how we think business should be (advertisement, 1990).

**The phonological sentence**. Contemporary linguists tend not to worry over the definition of a sentence. They assume that they can recognize sentences, implicitly relying on their familiarity with their orthographic forms. The spoken language, however, does not signal sentence boundaries. The syntax of speech, particularly in spontaneous conversation, differs considerably from the regularities of the written (particularly printed) language in ways that have yet to be fully investigated. Everyday conversation exhibits abundant hesitations, shifts in sentence construction, apparently incomplete structures, and interconnections that are odd by the norms of the written language. Most grammarians focus on structures in the written language (and their analogues in more or less formal speech) for the data they use in constructing their grammars, and if they turn their attention at all to samples of speech tend to derive spoken structures from what they consider to be fuller forms normal in written texts. What constitutes a sentence in the language should be (but does not appear to be) of particular concern to generative grammarians who view the goal of their grammar as accounting for all and only the sentences of the language.

**Sentence structures**. If the sentence is to constitute a grammatical unit for the language as a whole, then the orthographic sentence cannot serve as that unit: speech signals do not correspond to sentence punctuation, and punctuation only crudely signals some elements of speech, such as possible points for pausing or changing one's tone. Instead, reference can be made to the relative independence of the unit and its internal structure. A sentence may be viewed as a clause complex, in which the parts are clauses linked to each other by co-ordination and subordination. From this viewpoint, the traditional SIMPLE SENTENCE is indeed simple, because it consists of only one clause, as in: *The governor of the prison negotiated with the prisoners throughout the day*. A COMPOUND SENTENCE involves the coordination of two or more *main clauses* (each of which could constitute a simple sentence), linked by the coordinators *and*, *or*, *but*, as in: *The governor of the prison negotiated with the prisoners throughout the day and talks were continued into the night*. A COMPLEX SENTENCE consists of one main clause within which there are one or more subordinate clauses: *The governor of the prison negotiated with the prisoners after police had seized control of the kitchen and food-store area*. The subordinate clause, here introduced by the subordinator *after*, can be moved to the front of the sentence, a typical property of subordinate clauses.

Further complexities are quite usual. A COMPOUND-COMPLEX SENTENCE resembles the simple sentence in having more than one main clause, but in addition one or more of the main clauses contains one or more subordinate clauses: *A police officer said that the prison authorities could not confirm that there were bodies inside the prison, but he believed that there had been some deaths*. Here, the two main clauses are coordinated by *but*, the first main clause has a *that*-clause within which is embedded another *that*-clause, and the second main clause also contains a *that*-clause. It is further possible to recognize a *complex-compound* sentence (though the term is not often used), in which the one main clause contains two or more subordinate clauses that are coordinated: *The Home Secretary said that nine prisoners had been forcibly injected with drugs and that eight others had taken drugs voluntarily*. In this example, the two subordinate *that*-clauses are coordinated by *and*. The subordinate clause may be embedded in a PHRASE rather than directly in another clause, as in this example of a relative clause (introduced by *who*) that is embedded in a noun phrase: *Twelve prison officers who received minor injuries during the riot have all been discharged from hospital*.

All the examples of subordinate clauses given above have been *finite clauses*, but subordination may be effected through *non-finite clauses* and *verbless clauses*. In the next example, two coordinated participle clauses (which follow the comma) are subordinate to the main clause in this complex sentence: *The rioters have destroyed most of the ten wings of the prison, systematically smashing cells and setting fire to buildings*. In the example that follows, the *if*-clause is verbless: *If possible, prisoners will be moved to other prisons*.

**Constituents of clauses**. This structured account of sentences assumes the recognition of clauses. A clause consists of central and peripheral constituents, the first usually obligatory, the second optional. The central constituents are the *subject* (though generally omitted in imperative sentences) and the *verb*, as in *Nobody moved*. Other central constituents are *complements* of the verb: that is, elements that complete its meaning, such as the direct object *my typewriter* in *Somebody has taken my typewriter*, the indirect object *me* in *Derek gave me some books*, the subject complement *hungry* in *Jane is hungry*, the object complement *strong* in *I like my tea strong*, the adverbial complement *in the garage* in *The car is in the garage* and in *I put the car in the garage*. The peripheral or marginal constituents are mainly adverbials such as *incidentally*, *also*, and *last week* in *Incidentally, Derek also gave me some books last week*, and vocatives such as *Natalie* in *I like my tea strong, Natalie*.

**Irregular structures**. Some constructions are irregular in some respect, but are generally considered sentences or (if attached to a sentence) parts of sentences: (1) Certain types of subordinate clauses constitute independent exclamations: *That we should come to this! To think that I once helped him! If it isn't my old friend Jeremy! If only you had listened to me!* (2) Questions in which the phrases or subordinate clauses are introduced by interrogative words: *How about a kiss? Why all the fuss? What if they don't come? How come you're not ready yet?* (3) Such headings as *How to get help in an emergency*; *Where you should eat in Paris*. (4) Elliptical constructions such as *Serves you right* and *Never fails, does it?*, and elements of dialogue such as *A: Where are you?*

B: *In the kitchen*. (5) Problematic sequences that cannot easily be analysed into clausal constituents appear in such contexts as labels, titles, warnings, and greetings: *Baked beans*; *The Department of English*; *Good morning*; *The police!*; *Thanks*; *Yes*. Conversations often contain such sequences as *That one. The big one. No, the one over there. Higher up. Yes. Beside the green jug*, which might as easily be written *That one—the big one—no—the one over there—higher up—yes—beside the green jug*, orthographically sidestepping the problem of deciding the status of the phrases in question. Such uncertain sequences are often referred to as *sentence fragments*.

**Functional and syntactic categories**. Sentences were categorized above by degree of internal complexity: *simple*, *compound*, *complex*, *compound-complex*, *complex-compound*. They are also commonly classified according to dominant function in discourse, as *declarative*, *interrogative*, *imperative*, and *exclamatory*. These functions are reflected in the four corresponding sentence types *statement*, *question*, *directive* (or *command*), and *exclamation*. In addition, sentences can be classified according to syntactic features that affect the sentence as a whole: *mood* (indicative, imperative, subjunctive), *voice* (active, passive), and *polarity* (positive, negative). Finally, they can be classified by the patterns of the central or kernel constituents that they exhibit: for example, *Subject–Verb–Direct Object* (SVDO); *Subject–Verb–Subject Complement* (SVSC).

See COMMA, COMPARATIVE SENTENCE, COMPLEMENT, EXISTENTIAL SENTENCE, OBJECT, PARTICIPLE, PART OF SPEECH, PERIODIC SENTENCE, PREDICATE, PUNCTUATION, SENTENCE WORD, STRESS, STYLE, SUBJECT, TAG, VERB, VERBLESS SENTENCE, VOICE, WRITING.

**SENTENCE WORD**. An occasional term in WORD-FORMATION for a SENTENCE which serves as a WORD or part of a word, such as *never say die*, attributively in 'a *never-say-die* attitude', suffixed in *never-say-die-ism*, or as an often allegorical name: *Captain Never-Say-Die*, *She-Who-Must-Be-Obeyed*. The attributive use is the commonest. In writing and print, the constituents are often linked by hyphens: *an aren't-I-just-the-cutest-thing* smile; her *I-don't-understand-you-look*. However, they may also come between quotation marks (*a Toyota 'Drop Everything' Sales Event*), be capitalized (*the I Did It My Way approach*), or mix hyphens

and capitals (*the great Support-Your-Local-Hostage binge*). Sentence words often begin with verbs in the imperative mood: *a Rent-a-Car contract*; *a get-up-and-go Britain in place of a sit-back-and-wait-for-it culture*. Compare PHRASE WORD.

## ■ SEXISM ──────────── ■

A term used in feminist critiques of society and in general usage for: (1) Attitudes and behaviour based on traditional assumptions about, and stereotypes of, sexual roles in society and some GENDER usages in language. (2) Discrimination or disparagement based on a person's sex, especially when directed by men or society at large against women. In terms of language, sexism refers to a bias through which patterns and references of male usage are taken to be normative, superordinate, and positive and those of women are taken to be deviant, subordinate, and negative. Usage typically challenged as sexist includes: (1) *Man* used to refer to the human race in general (book title: *The Ascent of Man*) and to individuals (*What does the average man in the street think?*). Such neutral forms as *humankind* and *person* have been recommended in its place. (2) *Girl* used to refer to adult women (considered to be as demeaning as the use of *boy* for adult non-white males) and used attributively in such expressions as *girl athlete*, *girl reporter*. The use of such phrases appears to have declined in recent years. (3) *Lady* used to indicate a woman professional, as in *lady doctor* and *lady lawyer*, a genteelism that dates from a time when women were rare in such professions and the few who did exist came from the upper and middle classes. (4) Naming that does not equally represent men and women, such as: *Professors Eliot, Goldstein, and Barbara Smith*. Many manuals of style now recommend strict parallelism: *Professors Eliot, Goldstein, and Smith* or *Professors Edgar Eliot, Sol Goldstein, and Barbara Smith*.

**Non-sexist usage**. Since the 1960s there has been strong social pressure from feminist and other groups, especially in North America, to make the use of English and other languages less biased against women. Some of these attempts have met with fairly widespread acceptance, while others have been resisted and appear to be regarded as too radical, or awkward, or unnecessary. An early change in the US (*c*.1970) was the coining of the abbreviated title *Ms* parallel to *Mr* in that it identifies gender but not marital status. This term is often used in public (such as in newspapers and the mail) in the way intended by feminists, but it has also often been used as a replacement of *Miss*, to designate an unmarried woman, while *Mrs* continues to designate a married woman (often because women and men wish to retain some such distinction). During the 1980s, increasing pressure against sexual discrimination in areas such as job advertisements and academic journals led to the development of guidelines for non-sexist usage, intended to help people avoid both explicit and implicit sexism in language. One such set of guidelines is *The Handbook of Nonsexist Writing* by Casey Miller and Kate Swift (Harper & Row, 1988). They cover such issues as not assuming that a doctor or other professional is always *he*, dropping such derivatives as *authoress*, *executrix*, and *usherette*, using neutral terms such as *draughter* for *draughtsman*, *chair* for *chairman*, *flight attendant* for *steward* and *stewardess*, and using *women* rather than *girls* for adults.

**Radical coinages and adaptations**. Many feminists consider that radical changes in the form of certain everyday words have psychological value, as with the conversion
argue, presents a new perspective on and analysis of life and the processes with which the original words have generally been associated. The forms *womyn* and *wimmin* are seen as more detached from *man*, the origin of *woman* being *wifman*, meaning 'female human being' but easily interpretable as 'wife of a man'. Equally radical is the *reclamation* or *positive reinterpretation* of negative words for kinds of women, such as *crone*, *hag*, *witch*.

**Generic male usages**. Despite traditional assertions that such generics as *man* and *he* include *woman* and *she*, in practice the gender for many words is often specifically male, as in *refugees and their wives* (who are also refugees). Both the *man in the street* and the *man of letters* are supposedly general, but the unacceptability of *\*She was a leading man of letters* and the non-use (or rarity) of *She was a leading woman of letters* demonstrate a primary and abiding male reference. A widely approved alternative to generic *he* (*Ask anyone and he'll tell you*) has not yet developed. The most common appears to be singular

*they*, which has a long history of usage: *Ask anyone and they'll tell you*. *He or she* and to a less extent in writing *s/he* (*s)he* occur, and sometimes *she and he*, but commentators generally recommend avoidance strategies, such as a shift to plural constructions.

**Use of *person***. The neutral use of *person* in its own right and in compounds has become more common: *chairperson*, *layperson*, *spokesperson*, with the occasional successful plural *-people*: *business people*, *lay people*, *sales people*, *working people*. However, the usage is often mocked (*clergyperson*, *fisherperson*), and remains an uneasy term for many people. In two cases, especially in North America, the first element alone has had some success: *anchor*, *chair*. The term *layman* is widely used, especially in such phrases as *in layman's language*, but neutral *layperson/lay person* appear to have caught on for both religious and professional reference: plural *lay people*, religious collective *the laity*. For many people, however, *person* remains an awkwardly formal and unwelcome intrusion in their lives, and of all the words associated with discussions of inclusive language has provoked the most jokes, as with *personhole covers and to person an assembly line*.

**Lexical asymmetry**. Male/female pairs of words are often asymmetrical: *governor* refers to a man with great power and position, *governess* to a woman employee with limited authority over children; *master* generally refers to a man who controls things (but may sometimes be a woman: *She's a master of the subject*), while *mistress* may refer to a powerful woman in charge of a house or college, but more often means a married man's kept lover (negative echoes from this sense often affecting the other). In some areas, however, female terms have not emerged, symmetrical or otherwise: the degrees of *Bachelor of Arts* and *Master of Arts*, once conferred only on men, are now conferred on both men and women without any such contrasts as *\*Spinster of Arts* or *\*Mistress of Arts*. In addition, although terms like *lady lawyer/doctor* are widely used, there has been no general move towards such forms as *doctorette*, *lawyeress*, instances of which are jocular and/or pejorative. The relative position of male and female in binomial phrases (such as *he or she*, *host and hostess*, *male or female*, *man and wife*, *men and women*, *men and girls*, *men and ladies*, *boys and girls*) gives primary status to males, the only exceptions being the chivalric *ladies and gentlemen* and the informal *mum/mom and dad*. Asymmetrical pairs are also common, with female terms as lower in status, as in *men and girls*, *men and ladies*. It is often also the case that pejorative terms are stronger when applied to women: *bitch* is seldom a compliment, whereas *bastard* (especially *old bastard*) can under some circumstances be intended as a term of respect or affection. Of similar positive status when masculine is *dog* (as in *you old dog!*, admiring a roué); when feminine in reference in AmE it means an ugly woman. *Witch* is almost always pejorative, whereas *wizard* is often a compliment.

**Marked suffixes**. In common with other European languages, English has traditionally indicated femaleness by the use of certain suffixes, indicating that the nouns to which they attach have traditionally been taken to refer only to men. The suffixes are (1) *-ess*, as used in *actress*, *authoress*, *sculptress*, *waitress*. It is sometimes said to highlight women's accomplishments, but is often linked to roles presented as less significant than those of men, such as *manageress*, *poetess*. *Actress*, however, is widely used at the same time as the inclusive use of *actor* has gained ground, especially in the theatre. *Hostess* continues to be widely used, but because of its occurrence in such phrases as *bar hostess* it may decline, making way for inclusive *host*. *Jewess*, *Negress* are dismissive additions to often disparaging usages of *Jew*, *Negro*. (2) *-ette* has three depreciative senses: small size (as in *cigarette*, *kitchenette*), artificiality (*leatherette*), femaleness and auxiliary status (*usherette*). The term *suffragette* is widely used to refer to activists at the turn of the 19–20c who sought votes for women. These women, however, called themselves *suffragists*. (3) *-trix*, as in the now rare *aviatrix*, has a limited use in legal language (for example, *executrix*, *testatrix*), and in the sadomasochistic term *dominatrix*. Such usages, however, mark females in these roles as unusual.

**Inclusive usage**. The possibility of eliminating sexism from language involves the Whorfian hypothesis: not just that language is a reflection of the society which uses it, but that society is in part shaped by its language. If this is so, language change may bring about social change: children hearing constant references to *the doctor* . . .

*he* may well assume that all physicians are or should be male. A consistent use of non-sexist and INCLUSIVE LANGUAGE might help change this perception. Male-based words appear to be increasingly challenged by both women and men. In many cases, they have been formally replaced by neutral terms: *chairman* by *chair*, *forefather* by *ancestor*, *headmaster* and *headmistress* by *head teacher*. Asymmetrical words such as *mistress* in the sexual sense are being replaced by neutral terms such as *lover*. The replacement of *mother/father* by *parent*, unless gender-specific roles are involved, reflects some breakdown in socially stereotyping according to gender. In the case of *housewife*, on the other hand, the male-oriented *househusband* seems to be integrated (sometimes mockingly) into both AmE and BrE, while *homemaker* appears to remain feminine in reference, and *home manager* has not gained acceptance. Common work terms can generally be neutralized without much difficulty: *manpower* can be changed to *personnel*, *work force*, or *workers*, and *man hours* to *operator hours*. Suffixes like *-er* in job titles such as *steelworker* and *bookkeeper* can be used to modify *longshoreman* to *longshoreworker* and *fisherman* to *fisher*, but often meet with ridicule. See FEMININE, FEMINISM, GENERIC, GENERIC PRONOUN, MASCULINE, POLITICALLY CORRECT.

**SEYCHELLES**. A country of the western Indian Ocean and member of the COMMONWEALTH, made up of over 100 islands. Languages: CREOLE or Seychellois (French-based and spoken by around 95% of the population), English, and FRENCH (all official). The islands were a French colony from 1768, a British colony from 1814, and became independent in 1976. The Seychellois are largely descended from French colonists and their freed African slaves, with smaller numbers of British, Chinese, and Indians.

■ **SHAKESPEARE, William** ——— ■

[1564–1616]. English poet and playwright, the foremost figure in ENGLISH LITERATURE and a primary influence on the development of especially the literary language. Knowledge of his life comes chiefly from documents unrelated to his career: records of his property transactions, his taxes, his occasional involvement in lawsuits. Other 'knowledge' derives from anecdotes, many set down long after his death, and biographical inferences from his writing. No record of his education survives. The tradition, first set down in the early 18c, that says he attended the Stratford 'free school' appears to be borne out by the knowledge of LATIN language and literature evident in his plays and poems. The same tradition says that his father's declining fortunes forced Shakespeare to quit school before he finished. He received special permission to marry Anne Hathaway in November 1582, when he was 18 and she was 26. Their daughter Susanna was born in May 1583; twins Hamnet and Judith were born in 1585.

**Career**. In 1592, the playwright Robert Greene alluded to another writer who 'with his *Tygers hart wrapt in a Players hide* . . . is in his owne conceit the onely Shake-scene in a countrey'. The allusion to *3 Henry VI* (1. 4. 137) and the PUN on his name make it clear that Shakespeare was already in 1592 a prominent, if controversial, figure on the London theatrical scene. Within a few years, his pre-eminence was beyond controversy: in 1598, Francis Meres gave Shakespeare pride of place among the English dramatists he listed in *Palladis Tamia*, praising the 'sugred' sonnets and naming twelve plays composed in 'Shakespeares fine filed phrase'.

The plague forced the closing of London theatres from 1592 to 1594, years in which Shakespeare's non-dramatic *Venus and Adonis* and *The Rape of Lucrece* appeared. When the theatres reopened, Shakespeare wrote new plays, acted in some of Ben Jonson's, and, according to some traditions, in several of his own. He also became a part-owner of his theatrical troupe, the Lord Chamberlain's company. In the five years or so following, according to the conventional chronology, Shakespeare wrote eleven plays, the early sonnets, and *The Lover's Complaint*. His increasing success enabled him to buy Stratford's second-largest house in 1597, when he was 33, and he continued to buy property in the town and in London as well until at least 1613.

Shakespeare's company opened the Globe theatre in 1599. Queen Elizabeth died in 1603, and her successor James I pronounced Shakespeare's troupe his servants under the name the King's Men. The company often performed at court and, in 1608, took over the Blackfriars, a private indoor theatre.

Shakespeare had written fewer plays since 1601, and seems to have stopped acting after 1607, perhaps because he was spending more time in Stratford. In 1613, he wrote his last play, probably in collaboration with Fletcher; in the same year, the Globe theatre burned down.

**Works**. Shakespeare's works do not survive in manuscript, and the copies that printers used were apparently not always his: some came from actors' reconstructions, some from the theatre company's prompt-books. Both scribes and printing-house compositors made occasional further alterations in the course of transmitting Shakespeare's text, including linguistic details such as punctuation, spelling, and grammatical inflections. Many of his works appeared in small separate editions known as 'quartos' during his lifetime; dates on the title page, or in the Stationers' Register, along with lists like Meres's, outline the chronology of Shakespeare's career. Some at least of the sonnets were already in circulation when Meres mentioned them over a decade before their 1609 publication, and some of the plays may likewise have been written and presented earlier than their publication. Several of the plays did not appear until the posthumous collected Folio edition of 1623, so the following chronology, though it reflects the preponderance of modern opinion, remains uncertain:

(1) Early works written before Shakespeare joined the Lord Chamberlain's company in 1594: *1 Henry VI*, *2 Henry VI*, *3 Henry VI*, *Richard III*, *Titus Andronicus*, *The Taming of the Shrew*, *Venus and Adonis*, *The Rape of Lucrece*.

(2) Works written between 1594 and the opening of the Globe in 1599: *Two Gentlemen of Verona*, *Love's Labour's Lost*, *Romeo and Juliet*, *Richard II*, *Midsummer Night's Dream*, *King John*, *Merchant of Venice*, *1 Henry IV*, *2 Henry IV*, *Much Ado About Nothing*, *Henry V*, the early sonnets, and *The Lover's Complaint*.

(3) Works written between 1599 and the acquisition of Blackfriars in 1608: *As You like It*, *Twelfth Night*, *Julius Caesar*, *Hamlet*, *The Merry Wives of Windsor*, *Troilus and Cressida*, *All's Well That End's Well*, *Measure for Measure*, *Othello*, *King Lear*, *Macbeth*, *Antony and Cleopatra*, *Coriolanus*, *Timon of Athens*, the later sonnets, and *The Phoenix and the Turtle*.

(4) The last plays, written between 1608 and the burning of the Globe in 1613: *Pericles*,

*Cymbeline*, *A Winter's Tale*, *The Tempest*, *Henry VIII*.

**Language**. The phrase 'Shakespeare's language' has come to mean both the state of English around 1600 and Shakespeare's use of it. Both are topics in the following discussion of orthography, pronunciation and rhyme, syntactic structure, vocabulary and word-formation, linguistic variety, rhetoric, and pragmatics. In it, all the citations are from *Richard II* in the Quarto first edition (Q) of 1597, and comparisons with the Folio (F) of 1623. This concentration of examples from one play makes it easier to follow the passages cited, and gives an idea of the frequency of the features. Though no play embodies the full range of Shakespeare's linguistic ideas and practices, *Richard II* is notably concerned with the powers, limits, and dangers of language.

**Orthography**. The original editions of Shakespeare's works look very different from present-day orthography. They used no apostrophe for possessives; the occasional capitals on common nouns were more frequent in F than Q (for example, *violl* Q, *Vyall* F); and the letters *v* and *u* varied according to position rather than sound: *v* stood for both the *v*- and *u*-sounds when initial, and *u* stood for both when medial. Similarly, *i* stood for both *i* and *j* initially (*Iohn*). Other non-substantive variants included silent final *-e* (*robbes* 1. 3. 173 Q, *robs* F); this *-e* remains in conservative spellings like the surname *Clarke*.

**Pronunciation and rhyme**. The printed page best preserves features of vocabulary and structure; it preserves features of sound worst. Early editions of Shakespeare spelled the vowel in *band* and *bond* (5. 2. 65, 67) indifferently, and made no distinction between the consonants in words like *Murders* (1. 2. 21) and *Murthers* (3. 2. 40). Presumably, the spellings represented indistinguishable pronunciations. Q has *my owne* (1. 1. 133) but *thine owne* (1. 2. 35); where Q has *my honour* (1. 1. 191) and *thy oth* (1. 3. 14), F has *mine honour* and *thine oth*. The changes show that the matter of this historical *-n* before a vowel received editorial attention, but variations within Q indicate that the attention was not uniform. However, *sit* (1: 2. 47) in F differs from *set* in Q because the two words were commonly confused in the late 16c.

A rhyme such as John of Gaunt's *when/againe* (1. 1. 162–3) contrasts with the Duchess of York's *againe/twaine* (5. 3. 131–2), perhaps opportunistically making use of two current pronunciations, both still heard today. But the rhymes *teare* (verb)/*feare* (1. 1. 192–3) and *beare/heere* (5. 5. 117–18) reflect consistent pronunciation in both cases, as does *pierce/rehearse* (5. 3. 125–6) in Q, where F has the spelling *pearce* (from Old French *percer*) and the *-ea-* in *rehearse* looks back to a time when it was pronounced like the *-ea-* in *bear*. So too *happie hauens* (1. 3. 276) is a pun depending on a pronunciation of *heavens* implied by the *-ea-* spelling as in *bear*. Much of the variation in spelling concerns the long vowels, which the Great Vowel Shift had left uncertain: for *yeeres* (1. 3. 159) in Q, F has *yeares*; but both have *yeeres* in line 171.

**Syntactic structure**. The structure of Shakespeare's EARLY MODERN ENGLISH is unlike present-day English. It seems familiar, however, because it is often studied, so its older features are overlooked, at least until they begin to cause difficulty. These features are, notably: word order; the polarity of adjectives and verbs; transitivity; subject–verb concord; negation and the use of *do*; relative pronouns and conjunctions; verb inflection; personal pronouns; and strong and weak verbs.

***Word order***. The sentence *My natiue English now I must forgo* (1. 3. 159–60) inverts typical English subject–verb–object word order from SVO to OSV, but is not ambiguous, because *I* is clearly the subject. However, there is structural ambiguity in *The last leaue of thee takes my weeping eie* (1. 2. 74): is *leaue* or *eie* the subject of *takes*? Shakespeare sometimes used the VS(O) order with the subjunctive verb for conditional clauses: *Holde out my horse* (2. 1. 300) means *If my horse holds out*, and *Put we our quarrell* (1. 2. 6) is a hortative order equivalent to *Let us put our quarrel to the will of heauen . . .*

***Polarity***. *It bootes thee not to be compassionate* (1. 3. 174) seems odd in part because *compassionate* now means *showing compassion*; for Shakespeare, it meant *seeking compassion*, and so the sentence translates as 'It won't help you to seek pity'. Similar instances of change in syntactic polarity are *pittiful* = *showing pity* (5. 2. 103), *fall* = *let fall* (3. 4. 104), *remember* (1. 3. 269) = *remind*, and *learne* (4. 1. 120) = *teach*.

***Transitivity***. A related feature is change in transitivity: *inhabit* (4. 1. 143) and *frequent* (5.

3. 6) are intransitive, while *Staies* for 'awaits' (1. 3. 3) and *part* for 'part from' (3. 1. 3) are transitive. The construction *Me thinkes* is impersonal, but Shakespeare could also write *I bethinke me* and *I had thought*.

**Concord**. His management of subject–verb agreement sometimes varied because the subject might be construed as either singular or plural; *this newes, these newes* (3. 4. 82, 100). Hence, *Reproch and dissolution hangeth ouer him* (2. 1. 258) is a singular verb following a double subject conceived of as a single entity.

**Negation and the use of 'do'**. Negatives like *I slewe him not* (1. 1. 133) avoid *do*, while *we do not vnderstand* (5. 3. 122) employs it; both are common in Shakespeare. The same is true of negative imperatives: *Call it not patience* (1. 2. 29), but *doe not so quickly go* (1. 2. 64). Multiple negations that retain negative sense are also common, though the Folio 'corrects' some of these: *Nor neuer looke vpon each others face, / Nor neuer write, regreete, nor reconcile* (1. 3. 185–6) Q becomes *Nor euer looke ... Nor euer write ... or reconcile* in F. Like negatives, questions can be formed with or without *do: Why dost thou say* (3. 4. 77), *what saist thou* (1. 1. 110).

Do also has an abundance of other uses: manage (*How shal we do for money*: 2. 2. 104); verb substitute (*let vs share thy thoughts as thou dost ours*: 2. 1. 273); idiomatically with *right* or *wrong* (*to do him right*: 2. 3. 137); idiomatically with *have* (*I haue to do with death*: 1. 3. 65); finish (*my life is done*: 1. 1. 183); with emphatic stress (*Yes ... It doth containe a King*: 3. 3. 24–5).

**Relative pronouns**. Shakespeare will omit a relative pronoun for the subject of the clause where modern English omits it only for the object: *neare the hate of those loue not the King* (2. 2. 127), or use intricate subordination: *Hath causd his death, the which if wrongfully, / Let heauen reuenge* (1. 2. 39–40). He was no stickler for the use of *that* and *which* in restrictive and non-restrictive clauses, respectively: *the hollow crowne / That roundes* but *this flesh which wals about* (3. 2. 160–1, 167). He also used a variety of subordinating conjunctions: *for* (1. 1. 132) meaning 'as for', *for that* meaning 'because' (1. 1. 129) and 'in order that' (1. 3. 125), *for-because* (5. 5. 3) and *for why* (5. 1. 46), both meaning 'because'.

**The endings -s and -th**. The third-person singular indicative ending in Shakespeare's verbs could be either -s, as now, or the older -th. No meaning attached to the choice, so one line might include both: *Greefe boundeth where it falls* (1. 2. 58) F. But the forms of *do* and *have* were almost invariably *doth* and *hath*. The subjunctive mood, marked in the third-person singular present by the absence of a -s or -th ending, is often used in place of an auxiliary like *may* or *let*, and sometimes in combination with them: *O set my husbands wronges on Herefords speare, / That it may enter butcher Mowbraies breast: / Or if misfortune misse the first carier, / Be Mowbraies sinnes so heauy in his bosome / That they may breake his foming coursers backe* (1. 2. 47–51).

**Pronouns**. Shakespeare's English included the second-person pronouns *you* or *ye* and *thou*. Historically, they were plural and singular respectively, but *you* had come to be used as a formal or honorific alternative for the singular. In *Richard II*, some usages conform to this pattern: the Queen calls the gardener *thou* in 3. 4 and he calls her *you* in her presence; after she leaves he changes to a compassionately familiar *thou*. Likewise, the King regularly calls the disputants, his subjects, *thou* in the singular and *you* in the plural. Generally, they call him the respectful *you*, as Mowbray does at the beginning of his 'protest' speech (1. 3. 154–73); but by the end of the speech he has switched to *thou*. The change could arise from Mowbray's growing anguish, but other alternations between the two forms occur: in 1. 2, John of Gaunt usually calls the Duchess of Gloucester *you* (but *thee*: 1. 2. 57), while she consistently calls him *thou*; in 5. 5, the Groom calls the King *thou*, but the Keeper uses *you*.

Shakespeare's English lacked the possessive *its*; he sometimes used the uninflected *it*, sometimes the historical neuter possessive *his: what a Face I haue, / Since it is Bankrupt of his Maiestie* (4. 1. 266–7) F.

**Strong and weak verbs**. Among Shakespeare's weak verbs, the spelling often shows that the suffix -ed is not syllabic: *learnt* 1. 3. 159, *casde* 1. 3. 163. The suffix after *t* or *d* is, however, regularly syllabic: *blotted*. Both pronunciations accord with modern practice; unlike it, however, are words like *fostered*, which had three syllables. His strong verbs occasionally take unfamiliar forms in the past: for example, *spake* (5. 2. 12). Some forms of strong past participles are identical with the simple past: *broke* (5. 5. 43–8) F (*broken* 2. 2. 59 Q is extra-metrical, and F has *broke*), *shooke* (4. 1. 163) F, *spoke*

(1. 1. 77) Q (*spoken* F). Others are archaic: *holp* (5. 5. 62), *eate* (5. 5. 85), *writ* (4. 1. 275) F.

**Vocabulary and word-formation**. Shakespeare's vocabulary is sometimes estimated at *c*.20,000 words. For it, he drew on Renaissance technical terms, derivations, compounds, archaisms, polysemy, etymological meanings, and idioms. *Richard II* abounds in technical terms, often words with specialized meanings distinct from their everyday use: in *That knowes no touch to tune the harmonie* (1. 3. 165) *touch* means 'fingering' and *to tune* means 'to play'. Suitably to the subject of the play, many technical terms are from the law or chivalry.

**Conversion**. Shakespeare is noted for verbal conversion such as *grace me no grace, nor vnckle me no vnckle* (2. 3. 86). Other examples include the verbs converted from nouns *refuge* (5. 5. 26), *twaine* (5. 3. 132), *priuiledge* (1. 1. 120), and *dog them at the heeles* (5. 3. 137).

**Derivation**. Shakespeare was also fecund with derviations, words created by the addition of a suffix, often in a new part of speech: the verb 'partialize' (1. 1. 120), from the adjective 'partial', a Shakespeare original as a transitive verb. In addition, every Shakespeare play makes concentrated use of some lexical field. Whereas in *Coriolanus* it is a lexical set centring on 'breath', 'voice', and 'vote', in *Richard II* it is a morphological set centring on privatives beginning with *un-*, like *vnfurnisht wals, / Vnpeopled offices, vntrodden stones* (1. 2. 68–9). Some of these appear nowhere else in Shakespeare, like *vndeafe, vnhappied,* and *vnkingd*.

**Compounding**. Lines like *My oile-dried lampe, and time bewasted light* (1. 3. 221) show Shakespeare's fondness for compounds: here, compounds formed on past participles. They are most often nouns, like *beggar-feare* (1. 1. 189), or adjectives, like the cluster *Egle-winged pride / Of skie-aspiring and ambitious thoughts, / With riuall-hating enuy* (1. 3. 129–31).

**Rhetoric**. Shakespeare was familiar with paradox and other figures of traditional rhetoric, for example *chiasmus* in *Banisht this fraile sepulchre of our flesh, / As now our flesh is banisht* (1. 3. 196–7); *the last taste of sweetes is sweetest last* (2. 1. 13); *Deposing thee before thou wert possest, / Which art possest now to depose thy self* (2. 1. 107–8). The last example also contains *paronomasia*; here, the pun is on *possessed* meaning both *having come into pos-*

*session* and *unreasonably determined*. Richard comments on Gaunt's onomastic word-play, *Can sicke men play so nicely with their names?* (2. 1. 84), but Gaunt has already juggled *inspire* and *expire* (2. 1. 31–2), and urged his son to *Call it a trauaile that thou takst for pleasure* (1. 3. 262), playing on *travel* and *travail*. Even in prison, Richard replies to the salutation *Haile roiall Prince* with *Thankes noble peare: / The cheapest of vs is ten grotes too deare* (5. 5. 67–8), the royal being a coin worth ten groats more than a noble.

See AUREATE DICTION, DIALOGUE, KRIO, LYLY, MULCASTER, PROSE, QUOTATION, RHETORICAL QUESTION.

■ **SHAW, George Bernard** ──── ■

[1856–1950]. Irish dramatist and critic. Born in DUBLIN. Educated at Wesley Connexional School. He moved to London in 1876, where he wrote five novels that had little success, was a music, art, and drama critic, and an early member of the Fabian Society. He found the contemporary English theatre trivial and remote from serious issues, and admired the Norwegian dramatist Henrik Ibsen's treatment of social problems; his first play, *Widowers' Houses* (1893), was an indictment of the profits made by slum landlords. Shaw began a long career as a playwright, controversial about specific issues and challenging the basic assumptions of his contemporaries, which sometimes brought conflict with theatrical censorship. Although polemical, his plays established him as the leading dramatist of his time by their humour, lively dialogue, and strong characterization. Shaw believed that, in order to survive, the human race must become more rational and better organized. He developed a philosophy of Creative Evolution, requiring cooperation with the Life Force, and against the mechanistic theory of Darwin he urged the power of human choice. His ideas on this subject appear in *Man and Superman* (1903), which emphasizes his belief in the creative strength of women, and *Back to Methuselah* (1921). Other plays are *Caesar and Cleopatra* (1898, the film 1945), *The Devil's Disciple* (1905), *Major Barbara* (1905, the film 1941), *Pygmalion* (1913, the film 1938), *Heartbreak House* (1919), *Saint Joan* (1923, the film 1956), and *The Apple Cart* (1929).

**Shaw and language**. In *Pygmalion*, the phonetician Henry Higgins teaches a COCKNEY girl to speak with an upper-class accent and adopt some social graces, then introduces her to smart society. Despite dramatic exaggeration, the play makes the point that in the stratified society of England powerful judgements of worth and suitability attached to accent and usage. Shaw's knowledge of phonetics and views on literacy led him to demand a rational system of spelling which would follow the sounds of English and reduce time wasted by traditional orthography. Having campaigned for SPELLING REFORM, he left a bequest for the establishment of a suitable new alphabet reflecting 'pronunciation to resemble that recorded of His Majesty our late King George V and sometimes described as Northern English'. A system was devised into which the play *Androcles and the Lion* (1912) was transcribed (published in 1962), but the project has had no further success.

**Innovations**. In his own work, Shaw adopted three innovations: (1) Some simplified spellings of the North American type, such as *cigaret, program, vigor*. (2) Omission of the APOSTROPHE in contractions, as in *didnt*. (3) Spacing between letters for emphasis (*m u s t*). He complained that dialect speech could not be shown in writing without a phonetic system, but none the less used non-standard spelling for the purpose, as in: 'Aw knaow. Me an maw few shillins is not good enaff for you. Youre an earl's grandorter, you are. Nathink less than a anderd pahnd for you' (from *Major Barbara*) [*maw* my, *grandorter* grand-daughter, *nathink* nothing, *anderd pahnd* hundred pounds]. Shaw was impatient of insistence on formal grammar and believed that a form of Pidgin English could become a world medium of communication.

**SHELTA**, also **Shelter, Shelteroch, Sheldru**. An ARGOT, derived from IRISH GAELIC, used by travelling people (*tinkers*) in Ireland and Britain. Many of its words are disguised through such techniques as BACK SLANG (such as *gop* kiss, from Irish *póg*) and altering the initial sounds of words (as in *gather* father, from Irish *athair*). The name appears not now to be used by its speakers, who call it *Gammon, Tarri*, or simple *the Cant* (compare CANT). It has also been referred to as *Bog Latin, Tinkers' Cant*, and *the Ould Thing*. There are two divisions, *Gaelic Shelta* (in Ireland and Scotland) and *English Shelta* (in England and Wales); although the influence of English in the latter is increasing, the varieties

share a common core of some 2,000–3,000 Irish-derived words. *American Travellers' Cant* was originally also Shelta but is now largely Anglicized. BrE slang may have absorbed from Shelta such words as *gammy* lame (from *gyamyath*, Irish *cam*) and *monicker* name (from *munnik*, Irish *ainm*). English Shelta uses Irish-derived words in English syntax (as in *I korbed him so hard I broke his pi* I hit him so hard I broke his head) with Irish syntactic influence shown in some constructions (such as *Have you the feen's dorah nyocked?* Did you take the man's bread?)

**SHETLANDIC**, also **Zetlandic**. Of or characteristic of Shetland. The term, in general use in Shetland since at least the mid-19c, has since *c*.1950 been used to mean *Shetland dialect*. See ORKNEY AND SHETLAND DIALECTS.

**SHIBBOLETH** [From Hebrew *shibbōleth*, meaning uncertain, perhaps either 'stream in flood' or 'ear of corn'. The English use originates in the Bible, in the Book of Judges 12: 5–6, where the Gileadites defeat the Ephraimites at the River Jordan: 'And the Gileadites tooke the passages of Iordan before the Ephraimites: and it was so that when those Ephraimites which were escaped saide, Let me go ouer, that the men of Gilead said vnto him, Art thou an Ephraimite? If he said, Nay: Then said they vnto him, Say now, Shibboleth: and he said, Sibboleth: for hee could not frame to pronounce it right. Then they tooke him, and slewe him at the passages of Iordan.' (Authorized Version, 1611)]. **1.** A peculiarity of pronunciation that indicates someone's regional and/or social origins, such as *toity-toid* thirty-third, serving to identify someone from Brooklyn. **2.** A style, expression, custom, or mannerism that identifies an enemy or someone disliked or different because of background, community, occupation, etc.: for example, extreme political slogans referred to as *Fascist/Commie shibboleths*. Usually, the disapproval runs one way, higher social Gileadites detecting and rejecting lower social Ephraimites, but the reverse is also possible, as when in Britain, in assessing the vowel sounds in *can't dance*, speakers who say 'cahn't dahnce' are often dismissed as toffs and snobs. See MARKED AND UNMARKED TERMS, STEREOTYPE.

**SHORTHAND**, also **stenography**. A method of WRITING rapidly by substituting special characters, symbols, and ABBREVIATIONS for letters, words, or phrases, and used for recording the proceedings of legislatures and testimony in courts of law, dictation for business correspondence, and note-taking by journalists and others. Cicero's orations, Luther's sermons, and Shakespeare's plays were all preserved by means of shorthand; Samuel Pepys used it to keep his diary, Charles Dickens used it as a reporter in the London law courts and Parliament, and Bernard Shaw wrote his plays in it. There are two basic systems of shorthand: *orthographic*, based on standard letters, and *phonetic*, seeking to represent speech sounds directly. Also involved are the use of arbitrary symbols and abbreviations to facilitate speed, comparable to the use of & for *and* and *etc.* for *etcetera* in longhand.

In 1837, in England, Isaac PITMAN launched his phonetic system, *Stenographic Sound-Hand*, which classified sounds in a scientific manner and introduced abbreviations for the sake of speed. Made up of 25 single consonants, 24 double consonants, and 16 vowel sounds, its principles include the use of the shortest signs for the shortest sounds, single strokes for single consonants, simple geometrical forms, and pairing consonants (one written more lightly, as for *f*, the other more heavily, as for *v*). Revised versions of this system are widely used throughout the English-speaking world and are predominant in Australia, New Zealand, and India. In 1888, John Robert Gregg published his *Light-Line Phonography*, a system that he took to the US, where it became the dominant medium, although Pitman's Shorthand is widely used there and is predominant in Canada. Gregg Shorthand is also phonetic, but the characters are based on elements of ordinary longhand, vowels are shown by circles and hooks, and curving motions are used throughout to ease movement. It also employs abbreviations, blended consonants, and affix forms to enable the writer to gain speed. Systems developed in the 20c use longhand symbols for most or all letters, and include: *Baine's Typed Shorthand* (1917), *Speedwriting* (1923, 1951), *HySpeed Longhand* (1932), *Abbreviatrix* (1945), *Quickhand* (1953), *Stenoscript* (1955), and *Carter Briefhand* (1957). The advantages of orthographic systems are relative ease of learning and transcription, the disadvantage loss of speed; the advantages of phonetic systems are speed and ease of transcription, the disadvantage difficulty of learning.

**SIBILANT**. In PHONETICS: (1) A CONSONANT characterized by a hissing sound, such as the /s/ in *hiss* and the /z/ in *his*. (2) Relating to such a consonant: *sibilant sounds*.

**SIERRA LEONE**. A country of West Africa and member of the COMMONWEALTH. Languages: English (official); KRIO (an English-based creole), Mende, and Temne widely spoken. The first Europeans to visit the area were Portuguese navigators and British slavers. In the 1780s, British philanthropists bought land from local chiefs to establish settlements for freed slaves, whence the name of the capital, *Freetown*. In 1808, the coastal settlements became a British colony, and in 1896 the hinterland became a protectorate. Sierra Leone became independent in 1961 and a republic in 1971. The English of Sierra Leone is a variety of WEST AFRICAN ENGLISH; it is distinct from KRIO, but the two shade into each other and into VERNACULAR usage. English is the language of all education, all newspapers and magazines, 95% of television and cinema, and the medium for documenting local history and culture. Its distinctive vocabulary includes: (1) Words derived from local languages: *agidi* a paste made from fermented cornflour, *bondo* a secret society for women, *fufu* grated and fermented cassava cooked into a paste and eaten with soup or sauce, *woreh* a cattle ranch. (2) Extensions of sense: *apprentice* a young man who loads and unloads vehicles, *bluff* to be elegantly dressed, to have a neat appearance ('She's bluffing today'), *cookery* cheap food eaten outside the home, *foolish* to make (someone) appear stupid ('The teacher was foolished'), *woman damage* money paid to a husband by another man as compensation for having a sexual relationship with his wife.

**SIGN**. Something that conveys meaning, such as an object, token, mark, image, movement, gesture, sound, event, or pattern. Signs may be directly representational (as when a drawing of a hand points in the direction to be taken) or symbolic (as when a cross denotes Christianity and not the Crucifixion alone), but are often entirely arbitrary (such as letters standing for speech sounds, or in mathematics a *plus sign* and a *minus sign*). If one thing *signifies* another, it serves as a sign for it: for example, the symbol + signifying 'plus' in arithmetic. The act of signifying is *signification*, a term that is often used synonymously with 'meaning' and 'sense', and occurs in the discussions of students of semantics and semiotics. See LINGUISTIC SIGN, SEMANTICS, SEMIOTICS, SIGN LANGUAGE, SYMBOL.

**SIGN LANGUAGE. 1.** A means of COMMUNICATION using gestures, usually between speakers of different languages: *Plains Indian sign language*. **2.** Also *sign*. A system of manual communication used by the deaf. The signs are conventional movements that represent a range of meanings similar to those expressed by speech (including abstract notions), and differing widely between communities. There are two main types: *concept-based systems* used as natural languages; *language-based systems* often used when teaching deaf children to communicate. There are rules governing the way signs are formed and there are many thousands of signs in the leading sign languages.

When a sign language becomes widely used, it develops varieties similar to those in spoken language. Several 'mixed' varieties exist, where people use signs that show the influence of the speech of the community to which the signer belongs. Not only is it impossible for French and English signers to understand each other (without one person learning the other's sign), but there is little mutual comprehension between signers of *American Sign Language* (short forms *Ameslan*, *ASL*) and *British Sign Language* (short from *BSL*), because the sign vocabulary is different. However, both sign languages can be traced to the early 19c work of two educators of the deaf, Thomas Gallaudet in the US and Laurent Clerc in France. The signs express a range of meanings and nuances comparable to those expressed by spoken or written language. For example, time relationships can be expressed by dividing the space in front of the body into zones, such as further forward for future time and further back for past time. Personal pronouns can be distinguished using different spatial areas: *you* is front-centre and various third-person forms are signed to the right and left. Use is made of repeated signs to convey such notions as plurality, degree, or emphasis. These signs are used simultaneously with other movements, such as facial expressions, eye movements, and shifts of the body: for example, questions can be signalled by a facial expression, such as raised eyebrows and a backwards head tilt. Fluent signing (between one and two signs per second) produces a conversational rate comparable to that of speech.

Sign languages within the community of English have been devised at various times to bring the signer into a close relationship with spoken or written English. These include: (1) *Finger spelling* (dating at least from the 19c), in which each letter of the alphabet has its own sign, using two hands in the British version and one hand in the American version. (2) *Cued Speech* (1966), a system of hand cues used alongside lip movements to draw attention to the phonemic contrasts in speech. (3) More complex systems that aim to reflect features of English grammar, including *Signed English* or *Sign English* (1966), *Seeing Essential English* (1969), *Manual English* (1972).

**SILENT LETTER.** A LETTER that is not pronounced, such as the *p* and *l* in *psalm*. See ALPHABET, B, D, E, G, H, K, L, M, N, P, R, S, SPELLING, T, W, X.

**SIMILE.** A FIGURE OF SPEECH, in which a more or less fanciful or unrealistic comparison is made, using *like* or *as*. *Some dogs are like wolves* is a realistic comparison and not a simile, but *The Assyrian came down like the wolf on the fold* (Byron) is a simile because neither savagery nor the Assyrian is physically like a wolf. Everyday usage is rich in similes, many of them idiomatic: (1) With *like*: *spread like wildfire*, *sell like hot cakes*, *like a fish out of water* (said of a person uneasy in an unfamiliar situation). (2) With *as . . . as*: as *thick as thieves* (of people cooperating closely), *as strong as an ox* (of someone very strong). See FIGURATIVE LANGUAGE, METAPHOR.

**SIMPLE SENTENCE.** A SENTENCE that consists of one main clause and does not contain a coordinate clause or a subordinate clause: *The storm blew down several of my trees.*

# ■ SIMPLIFIED SPELLING SOCIETY ─────── ■

Short form *SSS*. An association founded in Britain in 1908 with the aim of bringing about 'a reform of the spelling of English in the interests of ease of learning and economy of writing'. Its presidents have been predominantly philologists and linguists: W. W. Skeat (1908–11), Gilbert Murray (1911–46), Daniel Jones (1946–68), and Donald Scragg (from 1988). Others were the publisher and Member of Parliament Sir James Pitman (1968–72) and the psychologist John Downing (1972–87).

**A phonetic orthography**. Between about 1915 and 1924, the SSS issued reading books in a phonetic orthography for learners in schools, such as *Nerseri Rymz and Simpel Poëmz: A Ferst Reeder in Simplifyd Speling*. Considerable success was claimed for them as a means of teaching literacy quickly and effectively. In 1923, the SSS sought to persuade the Board of Education to set up a committee to examine the possibilities of reform, but without success. A second approach was made in 1933, supported by over 900 university figures from vice-chancellors to lecturers, 250 MPs, 20 bishops, and ten teachers' organizations, but it also had no success.

**New Spelling**. This failure led the SSS to concentrate on preparing a fully researched and revised version of the system it had previously advocated, a task undertaken by William Archer and Walter Ripman. The result was issued as *New Spelling*, a final edition (further revised by Daniel Jones and Harold Orton) appearing in 1948. Campaigning was renewed in Parliament by Mont Follick, an MP who twice promoted a Private Member's Bill (1949, 1953). Official opposition, however, led to a compromise in which the government undertook no more than to facilitate research into the use of simplified spelling in schools. By way of research, the U. of London Institute of Education, the National Foundation for Educational Research, and the Association of Education Committees were, at first tentatively, concerned with school experiments in the early 1950s.

**The initial teaching alphabet**. By the end of the 1950s Sir James PITMAN had evolved the INITIAL TEACHING ALPHABET (i.t.a), based on the Society's *New Spelling* system, but with new characters in place of digraphs. On his initiative and at his expense, i.t.a. was introduced in many hundreds of schools in the UK, US, Australia, and elsewhere. Its effects were researched by John Downing, who published his findings in *Evaluating the Initial Teaching Alphabet* (1967). Reformers argue that these findings confirmed previous experience: literacy skills were more successfully acquired in a phonographically regular system than in traditional orthography (t.o.). Organizational problems, however, led to rapid decline in the use of i.t.a in the 1980s. The i.t.a was controversial within the SSS, partly because of its unpopular new characters, and partly because it was a teaching medium and not the system for general use that the Society advocated.

**Recent developments**. In the 1970s–90s, the SSS broadened its interests and its worldwide links, initiating a series of international conferences and launching the *Journal of the Simplified Spelling Society*. In view of the non-acceptance of earlier reform proposals, the Society began to take up the ideas of Harry Lindgren in Australia and consider partial or staged reforms of t.o. as more practical and likely to overcome entrenched resistance. Three kinds of staged reform have so far been proposed: (1) The spelling of a single phoneme could be regularized, as with *e* in *eny, breth, frend*. (2) Problem graphemes such as *gh* could be regularized, producing forms such as *weit, dauter, tho, thru, cof*. (3) Redundant letters could be removed, as in *dout, principl, acomodate*, achieving far-reaching regularization with little disruption. See SPELLING REFORM.

## ■ SINGAPORE ENGLISH ────── ■

Informally **Singlish**. The English language as used in Singapore, where it is co-official with Mandarin Chinese, Malay, and Tamil. The English of Singapore serves as a means of uniting the country, an international medium, and a LINGUA FRANCA. In 1947, 31.6% of students in the colony were in English-medium schools; from 1987, English has been the sole medium of primary, secondary, and tertiary education in the republic. It is the main language of business and commerce, internally and externally, and has an influence extending well beyond the boundaries of the state. Educated Straits-born Chinese (locally known as the *Baba Chinese*) have traditionally used *Baba Malay* rather than a Chinese dialect, and currently tend to favour English over both Chinese and other languages. There are at least two forms of Singapore English:

the standard variety, based on educated BrE spoken with an RP accent (used in textbooks and by the *Singapore Broadcasting Corporation*), and a colloquial variety whose forms range from a 'low' BASILECT strongly influenced by Chinese and Malay to a 'high' ACROLECT that blends with the standard.

**Pronunciation**. (1) English in Singapore is non-RHOTIC and generally syllable-timed. It places more or less equal stress on all syllables, usually with the final syllable of a tone unit somewhat lengthened. (2) Its intonation, often described as 'SINGSONG', has many short tone groups; there is no contrastive stress. (3) Final consonants are often unreleased, resulting in glottal stops, as in /hɪʔ/ for *hit* and /stɛʔ/ for *step*. (4) Final consonant clusters are generally reduced to one spoken consonant, such as 'juss' for *just* and 'toll' for *told*. Often a Singaporean will say, for example, 'slep' or 'sle?', but write *slept*. Compare grammar point 1, below, on omission of *-s* and *-ed*. (5) The vowels in such words as *take*, *so*, and *dare* are often monophthongs: /tɛʔ/, /soʊ/, /dɛ/.

**Grammar**. (1) There is a tendency to omit the following: articles (*You have pen or not?*; *He went to office yesterday*); the plural inflection *-s* (*I got three sister and two brother*); the present-tense inflection *-s* (*This radio sound good*; *My mum, she come from China many year ago*); the past-tense inflection *-ed/-t* ('ask' for *asked*, 'slep' for *slept*; *He live there* for 'He lived there'); and the *be* before adjectives used predicatively (*This coffee house cheap*). (2) *Already* is used as a marker of completive aspect: *Eight years she work here already* She's been working here for eight years. (3) *Use to* occurs as a marker of habitual aspect: *My mother, she use to go to the market* My mother goes to the market. (4) *Would* is used for future events rather than *will/shall* or the present tense: *We hope this would meet your requirements* We hope this meets/will meet your requirements. (5) Direct and indirect objects are highlighted by being preposed: *This book we don't have*; *Me you don't give it to*. (6) The invariant tags *is it?*; and *isn't it?* are common: *You check out today, is it?*; *They come here often, isn't it?* (7) There is a preference for *also* over *too* and *as well*: *But we are supposed to learn Chinese also*. (8) There are various informal ways of checking that someone agrees or disagrees, or can or cannot do something. *Yes or not? Like it or not? Can or not? Enough or not? Got or not?* (9) Chinese particles, such

as *lah* and *aa*, are a common means of conveying emphasis and emotion, in effect replacing the intonational features of mainstream English: for example, *lah* as a token of informal intimacy (*Can you come tonight?—Can lah/Cannot lah*); *aa* in *yes–no* questions (*You wait me, aa?* Will you wait for me?; *I come tonight, aa?* Should I come tonight?; *You think I scared of you, aa?*).

**Vocabulary**. (1) Words borrowed from regional languages: (Malay) *makan* food, as in *Let's have some makan*; (Hokkien Chinese) *ang pow* a gift of money, traditionally in a red packet (the meaning of the Hokkien words). (2) Non-English interjections include: *ay yaah!* suggesting exasperation; *ay yōr!* suggesting pain, wonder, or both; *ay yēr!* indicating a reaction to something unpleasant and perhaps unexpected; *che!* expressing irritation or regret. (3) Words of English with adapted meanings: *send* in the sense of 'take' (*I will send you home*); *open* meaning 'put on' (*Open the light*); *take* suggesting 'eat, drink, like' (*Do you take hot food?* Do you like spicy food?); *off* and *on* as verbs (*to off/on the light*); *off* as a noun, for time off (*We had our offs changed to Thursdays*). (4) Reduplicating of a word so as to intensify or emphasize a point: *I like hot-hot curries*; *Do you speak English?—Broken-broken*. (5) Formal and informal registers are less marked off from one another than in BrE, with the result that the highly colloquial and highly formal may co-occur: *her deceased hubby* rather than *her dead husband*. See CHINA, MALAYSIAN ENGLISH, PHILIPPINE ENGLISH.

**SINGSONG**, also **sing-song**. A usually disparaging or condescending term for a rhythm or tone regarded as musical but monotonous and considered typical of certain ACCENTS, such as those of speakers of English in Wales and parts of Asia: 'A trace of Holyhead Welsh to his sing-song accent' (Ian Thomson, *Independent*, 29 Dec. 1990). See PHILIPPINE ENGLISH, SINGAPORE ENGLISH, WELSH ENGLISH.

**SINGULAR**. A term contrasting with PLURAL and *dual* in the number system of a language and referring to one person or thing. In English, the term is often used to include uncountable noun usages like *love* and *wine* because they take singular verb concord, even though in other ways such nouns are different from singular countable nouns like *horse* and *stone*.

# ■ SLANG ─────────────────── ■

An everchanging set of COLLOQUIAL words and phrases generally considered distinct from and socially lower than the standard language. Slang is used to establish or reinforce social identity and cohesiveness, especially within a group or with a trend or fashion in society at large. It occurs in all languages, and the existence of a short-lived vocabulary of this sort within a language is probably as old as language itself. In its earliest occurrences in the 18c, the word *slang* referred to the specialized vocabulary of underworld groups and was used fairly interchangeably with CANT, *flash*, ARGOT.

**Defining *slang***. The word is widely used without precision, especially to include informal usage and technical JARGON, and the social and psychological complexities captured in slang vocabulary make the term difficult to define. For linguistic purposes, slang must be distinguished from such other subsets of the lexicon as *regionalisms* or *dialect words, jargon, profanity* or *vulgarity*, COLLOQUIALISM, *cant*, and *argot*, although slang shares some characteristics with each of these. It is not geographically restricted (like BrE *lift*, AmE *elevator*), but is often regional (BrE *bloke*, AmE *guy*). It is not jargon (vocabulary used in carrying out a trade or profession), but it frequently arises inside groups united by their work.

Although slang synonyms abound in the taboo subjects of a culture, not all slang terms violate social propriety; *Mickey Mouse* meaning 'easy' and *dough* for 'money' may be inappropriate in some contexts, but they are not usually offensive. Slang belongs to the spoken part of language, but not all colloquial expressions are slang: *shut up* for 'be quiet' would rarely be written except in dialogue, but it is not slang, which is often the usage of the young, the alienated, and those who see themselves as distinct from the rest of society.

**Transience**. Despite the difficulty of defining the term, slang does have some consistent characteristics. Foremost, taken as a whole, the slang vocabulary of a language is ephemeral, bursting into existence and falling out of use at a much more rapid rate than items of the general vocabulary. This rapid change requires a constant supply of new words, sometimes replacing or adding to already established slang words, like a *waste case* for a 'drunk', and sometimes extending to new areas of meaning, like *jambox, ghetto blaster*, or *Brixton suitcase* for a portable stereo tape player. This makes novelty, or innovation, an often cited characteristic of slang and freshness a large part of its appeal. Yet some slang items have long lives. Thus, *bones* as slang for dice was used by Chaucer in the 14c and is still slang. But when such items remain in the language for years, they often lose their slang status: for example, *jeopardy* from gambling and *crestfallen* from cockfighting have even acquired a learned tinge.

**Sounds**. Although, for the most part, slang items conform to the general constraints on sound combinations that govern English, the venturesome spirit behind much slang includes playing with sounds. Onomatopoeia accounts for many slang terms, including these for 'vomit': *barf, ralph*. The American linguist Roger Wescott has noticed that some sounds appear to give words a slangier flavour, most noticeably: *z*, in words like *scuz* from 'scum', and *zap* from 'slap' or 'whap'; the replacement or addition of a vowel with *oo*, in words like *bazooms* from 'bosom' and *smasheroo* from 'smasher'. Rhyming, however, is the favourite sound effect of slang, as in *boob tube* television, *frat rat* member of a US college fraternity. The rhymers *par excellence* have been the Cockneys of London, who have developed an elaborate and colourful collection of slang terms based on rhyme, such as *trouble and strife* for 'wife' and *mince pies* for 'eyes'. See COCKNEY.

**Semantics**. The intricate interplay of exclusivity, faddishness, and flippancy which breeds and supports slang guarantees semantic and etymological complexity. Nevertheless, slang items often diverge from standard usage in predictable ways, especially by generalization and melioration. In generalization, a term acquires a wider range of referents: for example, in the 19c *dude* was 'a dapper man, a dandy' but in current US slang, via Black usage, it can be applied to any male. *Schiz out* is to have any kind of mental or emotional breakdown; it is not restricted to *schizophrenia*. Evaluative words in slang sometimes become so generalized in application that they lose specific meaning and retain only a value: for example, AmE *awesome, heavy, key*, and *solid*, BrE *ace, brill*, and *triff*, and *def* in both varieties, all mean 'worthy of approval'. Generalization often operates in conjunction with melioration, a process in which the connotations of a word become more favourable. Many words enter general slang from the taboo words of subcultures. Through increased use and broad application, they can lose their shock value and become more positive; the verb *jam* a century ago had specific sexual referents, but now means 'to dance, play music, have a good time, succeed'. Yet many words in slang remain negative, especially the large and constantly replenished set of epithets available at all time in slang: for example, the pejorative *boob, dork, dweeb, jerk, nerd, scuzbag, slimeball, wimp.*

Another characteristic of the semantics of slang is the tendency to name things indirectly and figuratively, especially through metaphor, metonymy, and irony. *Couch potato* one who lies around doing little except watch television, *coffin nail* a cigarette, are metaphors. *Brew* and *chill* (beer) take their meaning by association and are metonyms. Irony, in its simplest form, categorizes the tendency in slang for words to evoke opposite meanings: *bad, wicked, killer* can all mean 'good' when signalled with appropriate ironic intonation. The influence of semantic fields on productivity in slang is also important, as they provide an established framework to shape the form and meaning of new words. In English, the semantic field 'destruction' sets the pattern for the proliferation of terms for being drunk, such as *blitzed, bombed, fried, hammered, polluted, ripped, slammed, smashed, toasted, wasted.* Slang also often evokes meaning by drawing on the shared cultural knowledge of its users. The verb *bogart* (to take an unfair share, originally of a marijuana cigarette) alludes to the American actor Humphrey Bogart's tough-guy image in films.

**Functions**. The aim of using slang is seldom the exchange of information. More often, slang serves social purposes: to identify members of a group, to change the level of discourse in the direction of informality, to oppose established authority. Sharing and maintaining a constantly changing slang vocabulary aids group solidarity and serves to include and exclude members. Slang is the linguistic equivalent of fashion and serves much the same purpose. Like stylish clothing and modes of popular en-

tertainment, effective slang must be new, appealing, and able to gain acceptance in a group quickly. Nothing is more damaging to status in the group than using old slang. Counterculture or counter-establishment groups often find a common vocabulary unknown outside the group a useful way to keep information secret or mysterious. Slang is typically cultivated among people in society who have little real political power (like adolescents, college students, and enlisted personnel in the military) or who have reason to hide from people in authority what they know or do (like gamblers, drug addicts, and prisoners).

See BACK SLANG, COCKNEY, DICTIONARY OF SLANG AND UNCONVENTIONAL ENGLISH, PARTRIDGE, POLARI, RHYMING SLANG.

**SLANGUAGE** A non-technical term for SLANG usage or a variety of language dominated by slang. In *The Slanguage of Sex: A Dictionary of Modern Sexual Terms* (1984), Brigid McConville and John Shearlaw define a slanguage as 'an underground language' of simile, metaphor, euphemism, and innuendo. Compare ARGOT.

## ■ SLAV(ON)IC LANGUAGES ── ■

*BrE* **Slavonic**, *AmE* **Slavic**. A branch of the INDO-EUROPEAN language family spoken primarily by the Slav peoples of Central, Southern, and Eastern Europe. It is usually divided into *East Slavonic* (RUSSIAN, Ukrainian, Byelorussian), *West Slavonic* (Polish, Czech, Slovak, and Sorbian or Lusatian), and *South Slavonic* (Old Church Slavonic, Macedonian, Bulgarian, Serbo-Croat(ian), and Slovene). Slavonic languages also divide into those using the Roman alphabet (western and southern, including Polish, Czech, Slovak, and Slovene) and those using the Cyrillic alphabet (eastern and southern, including Russian, Ukrainian, and Bulgarian). Serbo-Croat uses both scripts, Serbs Cyrillic, Croats Roman. The impact of the group on English has been relatively slight. LOANWORDS include: *mammoth* (from 17c Russian *mamot*), *mazurka* (from Polish, after a regional name), *robot* (from Czech, from the base of *robota* compulsory labour, and *robotník* a peasant owing such labour), *samovar* (from Russian: 'self-boiling'), and *vampire* (through FRENCH from GERMAN from Serbo-Croat *vampir*). The especially AmE diminutive suffix *-nik* (mid-20c) is Slavonic in origin, and has entered English along two paths: from Russian, as in *sputnik* a space satellite, and through YIDDISH, which adopted it from its Slavonic neighbours in Eastern Europe, as in *kibbutznik* one who lives on a kibbutz. The suffix as used in English refers to a person who exemplifies or endorses a way of life or an idea, as in *beatnik*, *peacenik*, *refusenik*. It is often humorous or dismissive. Loans from English into the Slavonic languages have increased greatly in the late 20c, especially in such areas as sport (for example, Polish *faul* foul, *faulować* to cause a foul, *sprinter*, *tenis*) and high technology (Polish *bit*, *bajt*, *hardware* and *software*, and their adjectives *hardwarowy* and *softwarowy*. See BORROWING, CANADIAN ENGLISH, EUROPEAN LANGUAGES, INDO-EUROPEAN LANGUAGES.

**SLIP OF THE TONGUE.** An unintended MISTAKE made in speaking, sometimes trivial, sometimes amusing: *This hasn't solved any answers* (rather than *problems*, *questions*); *a great floating lunk* (blending *lump* and *hunk*). Normal speech contains a fairly large number of such slips, which mostly pass unnoticed. The errors fall into patterns, and can be divided into: *selection errors* and *as semblage errors*. Selection errors may involve: (1) Meaning: *crossword* instead of 'jigsaw'. (2) Sound: *cylinders* for 'syllables'. (3) Both of these: *badger* for 'beaver'. (4) Blends of two similar words: *torrible* for 'terrible' and 'horrible'. Of these, errors in sound, usually called *malapropisms*, are probably the best known. Such errors suggest that meaning and sound are only partially linked in the mind, and also that the linking up involves the activation of a number of words which are similar to the target (the word sought). Among assemblage errors, common patterns are: (1) Anticipations, with a word or sound coming in too soon: *crounty cricket* for 'county cricket'. (2) Perseverations, with a word or sound repeated: *beef needle soup* for 'beef noodle soup'. (3) Transpositions, with words or sounds transposed: *to gap the bridge* for 'to bridge the gap'; *hole of rostess* for 'role of hostess'. The best-known of these are the sound transpositions called *spoonerisms*. These errors indicate that chunks of speech are prepepared for utterance, possibly in a tone group (a group of words spoken within the same intonation pattern), and that the activated words are organized in accordance with a rhythmic principle. See FREUDIAN SLIP.

**SOCIETY FOR PURE ENGLISH, The.** A reforming society founded in England in 1913 by a number of writers and academics on the initiative of the poet Robert Bridges. The outbreak of the First World War impeded its development, but between 1919 and 1946 it carried on a campaign against what it regarded as degenerate tendencies within the language, mainly through a series of 66 *Tracts*, for many years printed and distributed by Oxford University Press. The terms *pure* and *tract* indicate the quasi-missionary approach adopted by Bridges and his associates. In Tract 21 (1925), which sets out the aims of the Society, Bridges indicated that by *pure* he did not intend *Teutonic* (that is, Germanic), an interpretation associated with the 19c reformer William BARNES, who had advocated a return to undiluted SAXONISM. *Pure* was deliberately adopted 'as an assertive protest against that misappropriation of the term which would condemn our historic practice'. Bridges considered that the spread of English throughout the world was 'a condition over which we have no control', but one that 'entails a vast responsibility and imposes on our humanity the duty to do what we can to make our current speech as good a means as possible for the intercommunication of ideas'.

Bridges argued that 'we are the inheritors of what may claim to be the finest living literature in the world', and that steps should therefore be taken to ensure that the everyday language does not 'grow out of touch with that literature . . . so that to an average Briton our Elizabethan heritage would come to be as much an obsolete language as Middle English is to us now'. He saw as a special peril the scattering of speakers of English among 'communities of other-speaking races, who . . . learn yet enough of ours to mutilate it, and establishing among themselves all kinds of blundering corruptions, through habitual intercourse infect therewith the neighbouring English'.

Although the Society had only a slender influence on users of English beyond literary and philological circles, many of the views expressed by Bridges and his fellow members continue to be widely endorsed, especially by older members of the middle classes throughout the English-speaking world. They are from time to time restated by pressure groups with similar interests, such as the *Queen's English Society* in England in the 1980s, under the presidency of the writer and retired BBC broadcaster Godfrey Talbot, who echoes Bridges in writing:

Accost me as The Old-Fashioned Anglo if you like, but it appears to me that the Mother Tongue which half the world now uses is a cause for concern because while in demand overseas it is in decay at home, where increasingly it is both taken for granted and tainted. Restoration and repair are needed. Rarely has a rich inheritance been so undervalued as English today ('Protecting the Queen's English', *English Today* 11, July 1987).

See BAD ENGLISH, GOOD ENGLISH, PLAIN, PROGRESS AND DECAY IN LANGUAGE.

**SOCIOLECT**. A social DIALECT or variety of speech used by a particular group, such as working-class or upper-class speech in the UK. See LECT.

■ **SOCIOLINGUISTICS** ─────── ■

The branch of knowledge which studies the social aspects of LANGUAGE, including how the use and norms of language vary from one society to another (in relation, for example, to ACCENT, DIALECT, and GRAMMAR), and the way in which attitudes influence perceptions of the characteristics and abilities of speakers. These attitudes are clearly social in origin: for example, speakers of the prestigious BrE accent known as RECEIVED PRONUNCIATION (RP) are often perceived to be more competent and intelligent than speakers with regional accents, this view arising from the high social status of RP. Similarly, some accents of English are regarded as being more or less aesthetically pleasing than others. This, too, can be shown to be the result of the social connotations that different accents have for listeners. Americans, for example, do not find the accent of the West Midlands of England ugly, as many British people do, which has much to do with the fact that they do not recognize these accents as being from the West Midlands.

**Accent, dialect, region, and class**. The relationship between accent and dialect, on the one hand, and social class background on the other, is an issue of considerable sociolinguistic importance. For example, dialects and accents of BrE vary both geographically and socially. The high status

of RP is traditionally associated with the British upper class and the public schools (a group of private boarding-schools), and, although often associated with southern England, it shows no regional variation. The further one goes down the social scale, however, the more regional differences come into play, with lower-class or 'broad' accents having many regional features. One of the major advances of modern sociolinguistics has been the introduction of quantitative techniques, following the lead of the American sociolinguist William Labov, which enables investigators to measure exactly and gain detailed insight into the nature of the relationship between language and social class.

In a sociolinguistic study in Bradford, Yorkshire, Malcolm Petyt showed that the percentage of *h*s 'dropped' by speakers correlated closely with social class as measured by factors such as occupation and income. While lower working-class speakers on average dropped 93% of all *h*s in words like *house*, upper working-class speakers dropped 67%, lower middle-class speakers 28%, and upper middle-class speakers only 12%. This study provides information about the source of some of the language attitudes mentioned above. *H-dropping* is widely regarded in Britain as 'wrong'. Teachers and parents have often tried to remove this feature from children's speech, sometimes claiming that since the *h* appears in the spelling it must be wrong to omit it in speech. This is obviously a rationalization: no one makes this claim about the *h* of *hour*, or the *k* of *knee*. The real reason for this condemnation of *h*-dropping is its correlation with social class and its low social status.

**Language change**. Such quantitative techniques enable linguists to investigate some of the processes involved in LANGUAGE CHANGE. Large amounts of tape-recorded data (obtained in such a way as to ensure as far as possible that speakers are speaking naturally) can be used to plot the spread of changes through the community and through the language. For example, Labov was able in the 1960s to show that in NEW YORK City the consonant *r* was being reintroduced in the pronunciation of words like *form* and *farm* by comparing the number of *r*s used by older speakers to the number used by younger speakers. He was also able to show that this change was being spearheaded by speakers from the lower middle class, probably because saying 'forrm' rather than 'fawm' is considered prestigious (and therefore 'correct') in US society, and because speakers from this class are more likely to be both socially ambitious and insecure about the worth of their dialects.

**Language planning**. Sociolinguistics can be concerned with observing the details of individual behaviour in, for example, face-to-face conversation. It can also be involved in the larger-scale investigation of linguistic behaviour in communities the size of New York City. It can furthermore be concerned with the relationship between language and society in even larger-scale units such as entire nations. Sociolinguists working in areas such as the sociology of language and LANGUAGE PLANNING are concerned with issues like the treatment of language minorities, and the selection and codification of languages in countries which have hitherto had no standard language. In nations such as Britain, Ireland, the US, Canada, Australia, and New Zealand, English is the majority language, in a relationship of dominance with numerically much smaller and officially much less well-supported languages, such as GAELIC and WELSH in Britain and Maori in New Zealand. Sociolinguists study such relationships and their implications for education. In the case of Britain, they also attempt to obtain information on more recently arrived languages such as Gujarati, Punjabi, Maltese, and Turkish. Elsewhere, they note that there are countries in which native speakers of English are in a minority, as in Nicaragua, Honduras, South Africa, and Zimbabwe.

**Switching languages and styles**. In multilingual situations, developments occur which are important for linguists, including the growth of pidgin and CREOLE languages. Sociolinguists study the behaviour of bilinguals, investigating the way in which they switch from one language to another depending on social context. Speakers in all human societies possess large verbal repertoires, which may include different languages, different dialects, and different (less or more formal) styles. Varieties of language will be selected from this repertoire depending on features of the social context, such as the formality of the situation and the topic of conversation. Stylistic variation occurs in all English-speaking communities, signalled for the most part by vocabulary: for example, one might say *somewhat foolish* or *rather silly* or *a bit daft* depending on who one is talking to, what one is talking about, the situation one is in, and the impression one wants to create. Some English-speaking communities, like many Scots and members of overseas Caribbean communities, are *bidialectal*, having access to more than one dialect as well as different styles.

**Conclusion**. Sociolinguistics of all types is concerned with language as a social phenomenon. Some aspects of this subject may be more sociological in emphasis, others may be more linguistic. It is characteristic of all work in sociolinguistics, however, that it focuses on English and other languages as they are used by ordinary people to communicate with one another and to develop and maintain social relationships. See CODE-MIXING AND CODESWITCHING, DIALECTOLOGY, LINGUISTICS.

**SOCIOLOGESE** [20c: from *sociology* and *-ese* as in *journalese*]. An informal, usually pejorative term for the STYLE and REGISTER of sociologists, especially when addressed to or used by non-sociologists. Fowler's *Modern English Usage* (1965, edited by Ernest Gowers) refers in the entry *sociologese* to 'the harm that is being done to the language' and adds:

> Sociology is a new science concerning itself not with esoteric matters outside the comprehension of the layman, as the older sciences do, but with the ordinary affairs of ordinary people. This seems to engender in those who write about it a feeling that the lack of any abstruseness in their subject demands a compensatory abstruseness in their language. Thus, in the field of industrial relations, what the ordinary man would call an informal talk may be described as *a relatively unstructured conversational interaction*.

Critics who condemn sociologese usually make a simultaneous plea for PLAIN LANGUAGE, especially in speeches and texts addressed to the general public. The issue appears to be the need to fit register to audience and be clear in what one says and writes rather than the invasion of the language at large by the jargon of sociology. See ACADEMIC USAGE, JARGON, TECHNOSPEAK.

**SOLECISM**, formerly **soloecism**. A traditional term for the violation of good grammar and manners, and any instance of this, such as saying *I didn't do nothin'* instead of *I didn't do anything* (especially if done by someone who 'ought to know better'). The term has often been used in tandem with BARBARISM, the perceived ABUSE of words.

**SOLOMON ISLANDS PIDGIN ENGLISH**, also commonly **Pijin** and technically **Neo-Solomonic**. A variety of MELANESIAN PIDGIN ENGLISH spoken in the Solomon Islands, a country in the south-western Pacific Ocean and member of the Commonwealth. It is closely related to Bislama in Vanuatu and TOK PISIN in Papua New Guinea. English is the official language of the Solomons, but Pijin is spoken by about half the population. In the early 1900s, copra plantations were established. The labourers employed there had also worked in Queensland and FIJI, where they had used pidgin English. The local variety stabilized early and several religious missions adopted it for use, though it never gained the status of Tok Pisin or BISLAMA. Throughout their post-colonial history, Solomon Islanders, unlike Papua New Guineans and Ni-Vanuatu, have never been in contact with any other European language but English. For this reason Pijin is closer than Tok Pisin to English and has less non-English vocabulary.

It is syntactically more elaborate than Tok Pisin, for example in having many more prepositions and a greater range of connectives, such as *so, bat, bikos* (so, but, because), as in: 'Mitufala jes marit nomoa ia so mitufala no garem eni pikinini iet. Mi traehad fo fosim haosben blong mi fo mitufala go long sip bat taem ia hemi had tumas fo faendem rum long sip bikos plande pipol wandem go-go hom fo Krismas tu' (from J. Holm, *Pidgin and Creole Languages*, volume 2, 1988, p. 536) [Translation: We've just got married only we haven't got any children yet. I tried hard to force my husband to go on the ship, but times were hard and we couldn't find room on board because plenty of people wanted to go home for Christmas too]. See AUSTRALIAN PIDGIN.

**SOMERSET**. The name of a south-western county of England and of its local speech, sometimes called *Somersetian* and occasionally referred to informally as *Zummerzet*.

Many of its features are common to the entire WEST COUNTRY, but the diphthongs in such words as *cow, house* and *tail, came* are closer to RP than elsewhere in the region. The use of the voiced initial fricative in words such as 'zum' for *some* and 'varm' for *farm* is becoming rare in the towns. Compare MUMMERSET.

**SOUND**. **1.** In technical terms, vibrations that travel through the air at some 1,087 feet (331 metres) per second at sea level and are heard through their stimulation of organs in the ear. **2.** A particular effect of such vibrations; *the sound of bells; a speech sound*. **3.** In PHONETICS, the audible result of an utterance: *the b-sound in 'big'*. Although the nouns *sound* and *noise* can often be used interchangeably (*What was that sound/noise?*), *sound* usually relates to regular and harmonious vibrations, *noise* to irregular and discordant vibrations. See SPEECH, TONE, VOICE.

## ■ SOUTH AFRICAN ENGLISH — ■

Short forms *SAfrE, SAE*. The English language as used in the Republic of South Africa, the first language of *c.* 10% (about 2.7m) of the total population of the RSA. About two-thirds of this 10% are white, and most of the rest Indian or 'Coloured' (mixed African and European descent). To a small but important African élite, English is a 'second first language', and it is spoken fluently by many Afrikaners. As a LINGUA FRANCA, it is used with varying degrees of proficiency by millions whose mother tongue is not English. Until 1994, with AFRIKAANS, it was one of the two official languages; in that year, nine indigenous languages became official: Ndebele, Pedi, Northern Sotho, Southern Sotho, Swati, Tsonga, Venda, Xhosa, and Zulu. In the following discussion, South African English focuses primarily on the usage of South Africans for whom English is their first language.

**History**. The Dutch settlement at the Cape dates from 1652. When the British seized the colony in 1795, they moved into a long-established DUTCH-speaking community with its own culture, administration, and patterns of relationship with the black and Khoisan peoples of the subcontinent. The Dutch community was already diglossic, for example using standard DUTCH for religious and governmental purposes and local varieties known variously as *Cape Dutch, colonial*

*Dutch, South African Dutch*, or simply *the taal* ('the language') as dialects of 'hearth and home'. These were later, between 1875 and 1925, standardized as *Afrikaans*. Since the end of the 18c, many speakers of English in southern Africa have been in close contact with Dutch/Afrikaans people (with many intermarriages), and less closely with speakers of BANTU and Khoisan languages. Competent bilinguals (for example, in English and Dutch, or Xhosa and English) have been numerous and influential, and conditions have favoured complex CODE-MIXING AND CODE-SWITCHING. There is also a large body of published English writings by non-English authors.

**Pronunciation**. (1) SAfrE is typically non-rhotic, but may become RHOTIC or partially so in speakers strongly influenced by

---

## SOUTH AFRICAN PLACE-NAMES

The place-names of South Africa reflect mixed linguistic origins over some 300 years, and are mainly of three kinds:

**1. *African***. The complex African heritage includes names from the earlier Khoisan (Bushman, Hottentot) languages (such as *Namib*, the name of a desert, providing the base for the Latinized *Namibia*, the neighbouring country formerly known as *South West Africa*) and the later and more widely distributed Bantu languages, including Zulu and Xhosa. Zulu names include *Amanzimtoti* ('sweet water'), *Khayelitsha* ('new home'), and *Majuba* ('doves'), also as a hybrid form *Majuba Hill*, the site of a battle between Zulus and British in 1882. The prefix *Kwa* ('place of') is common, as in *KwaZulu* ('place of the people of heaven', replacing the Anglo-hybrid *Zululand*) and *KwaMashu* ('Mashu's place'). The use of an internal capital letter in such names is distinctive; the prefix *Um* occurs with the names of rivers, as in *Umfolozi, Umhlanga*, and *Umkomazi*, but without such a capital. African-language town names include *Lusikisiki, Qumbu, Tabankulu, Tsolo*, and *Umtata*.

**2. *Afrikaans***. The Afrikaans language shares many place-name elements with Dutch, the European language from which it derives. These include *berg* as in *Drakensberg* ('dragon's mountain'), *burg* as in *Johannesburg* ('John's city'), *dorp* as in *Krugersdorp* ('Kruger's town'), *drift* ('ford') as in the hybrid *Rorke's Drift*, *kloof* as in *Groenkloof* ('green ravine'), *rand* as in *Witwatersrand* ('white water ridge') and *Randburg* ('ridge city'), and *stad* as in *Kaapstad* ('cape town'). Names of cities include those derived from Dutch and other European associations, as with *Frankfort* and *Utrecht*, and commemorating Afrikaner leaders, as with the Latin *Pretoria* (the South African capital, named for Andries Pretorius), *Pietermaritzburg* (after the Voortrekker leaders Piet Retief and Gerrit Maritz), and *Piet Retief*.

**3. *English***. Place-names in English are far outnumbered by those in both the regional African languages and Afrikaans, settlers from the British Isles having arrived at a point when a topographical naming system was largely in place. *Cape Town* is a direct translation of Afrikaans *Kaapstad*, and both forms are in regular everyday use, and distinctively English names follow the general pattern found elsewhere in territories formerly governed from Great Britain: transferred British names, often adapted, as with *Bedford, East London, Margate*, and *Sutherland*, and commemorative names, such as *Durban* (formerly *D'Urban*, after a governor of that name), *Ladysmith, Lambert's Bay, Marydale, Port Elizabeth, Grahamstown, George* (after King George III), *King Williams Town, Prince Albert Road*, and *Uniondale*. Hybridization occurs, between English and Zulu in *Mhlanga Rocks* and English and Afrikaans in *Fraserburg* (an Afrikaans adaptations of Scottish *Fraserburgh*).

AFRIKAANS ENGLISH. These may have final postvocalic /r/ and a medial /r/ as trill or tap. Lanham has observed an initial obstruent (fricative) /r/, in such phrases as *red, red rose*, in older speakers in the Eastern Cape. (2) Variations in ACCENT depend usually on education, social class, domicile (rural or urban), and accommodation to speakers of varieties different from one's own. (3) Conservative middle-class accents remain close to RP, though typically with the lowering and retraction (in certain phonetic contexts) of the vowel in RP *bit, pin* to a position approaching that of SCHWA /ə/, in varying degrees. The vowel of RP *goose* is often central rather than back. (4) Salient features of 'broader' accents include the following renderings: the vowel of RP *trap* as 'trep' (Afrikaans/Dutch and the southern Bantu languages lacking a vowel of the *trap* quality); the long back vowel of RP *car* in a higher and more rounded version as in the stereotype 'pork the car'; diphthong reductions as in *fair hair* as /fe: he:/, and the vowel of RP *price* in a glideless or nearly glideless version, so that *kite* may resemble *cart*. (5) In a class of LOANWORDS from Afrikaans, such as the interjection *ga* (/xa/) expressing disgust, and *gedoente* (fuss, bustle), most speakers use a borrowed velar or palatal fricative like the sound in ScoE *loch*. In another loan class, of words such as *bakkie* (light delivery van) and *pap* (porridge), there is a vowel between those of RP *but* and *hot*. The precise extent of Afrikaans influence on the sound system and other aspects of SAfrE is a matter of controversy. In many cases, such as the vowel of the *trap* class, there seem to have been convergent influences from English settler dialects, Dutch/Afrikaans, and in some cases African languages.

**Grammar**. The syntax of formal SAfrE is close to that of the international standard. Colloquial SAfrE, however, has many features, such as: (1) Sentence initiators such as affirmative *no*, as in *How are you?—No, I'm fine*, probably from Dutch/Afrikaans, and the emphatic *aikona* as in *Aikona fish* ('No fish today'), of Nguni (Bantu) origin. The common informal phrase *ja well no fine* (yes well no fine) has been adopted in solid written form as an affectionate expression of ridicule (*jawellnofine*) for broad SAfrE usage, and has served to name a South African television programme. (2) The suffixed phrase *and them*, as in *We saw Billy and them in town*

('Billy and the others'), a form found also in Caribbean varieties. (3) *Busy* as a progressive marker with stative verbs, as in *We were busy waiting for him*, and often with a nonanimate subject, as in *The rinderpest was busy decimating their herds*. (4) The all-purpose response *is it?*, as in *She had a baby last week.—Is it?*, heard also in Singapore and Malaysia, but closely parallel in use to Afrikaans *Is dit?* (5) Extensive use of Afrikaans 'modal adverbs', such as *sommer* ('just') in *We were sommer standing around*.

**Vocabulary**. SAfrE has borrowed freely. A rough estimate of source languages for distinctively South African words is: Dutch/Afrikaans 50%, English 30%, African languages 10%, other languages 10%. The most recent years show an increasing proportion of items of English or Africanlanguage origin. Most of the SAfrE items best known internationally, such as *Afrikaner, boer, trek*, and *veld*, are of Dutch/Afrikaans origin. An exception is *concentration camp*, coined by the British during the second Anglo-Boer War. In most domains, such as landscape and topography, there is likely to be: (1) A high proportion of 'common words' borrowed directly from Dutch/Afrikaans, such as *drift* ford (1795), *kloof* deep valley or ravine (1731), *land* a cultivated stretch, usually fenced (from Cape Dutch), and *veld* open country (1835). (2) A number of 'English' items translated or partially translated from Dutch or Afrikaans, such as *backveld* back country, outback, from Dutch *achterveld*. (3) Some words of English origin that have acquired new senses, such as *location*, originally, as in Australia, an area allocated to white settlers, later 'a district set aside for Blacks', and still later 'a segregated urban area for Blacks', typically with strongly unfavourable connotations (as in 'the usual mess, the location, of sacking and paraffin tins': Dan Jacobson). In this sense, *location* has largely given way to the equally euphemistic *township*. (4) A sprinkling of items of African-language origin: for example, *karroo* semi-desert (Khoi, 1776), *donga* an eroded watercourse, usually dry (Nguni). (5) A few words reflecting South Africa's cosmopolitanism, past and present, such as *kraal* an African or Khoikhoi village, an enclosure for cattle (probably from PORTUGUESE *curral*: compare SPANISH *corral*).

Most topic areas reflect the wide range of

peoples and cultures of past and present-day South Africa. Thus, among trees are the flowering *keurboom* (South African Dutch, 1731), the hardwoods *stinkwood* and *yellowwood* (translating Dutch *stinkhout* and *geolhout*) and *silver tree*, an English coinage dating from early travellers' accounts of the Cape (Dutch: *wittebome* white trees). Among living creatures are the antelopes *eland* (Dutch: elk), *kudu* (probably Khoisan), *impala* (Zulu), and *tssebe* (Tswana). Human types range from the *predikant* or *dominee* (Dutch/Afrikaans: minister of the Dutch Reformed Church) through the *sangoma* (Nguni: diviner) to the *ducktails* (Teddy boys) of the streets of the 1960s. Artefacts range from the traditional *kaross* (Khoisan via Afrikaans: skin blanket) through the *Cape cart* (mistranslating Afrikaans *kapkar* hooded cart) to the ubiquitous *bakkie* (from Afrikaans: basin or other container), a light truck, now a symbol of virile open-air life. Liquor ranges from traditional Nguni *tshwala* brewed with malted grain or maize (formerly *Kaffir beer*, now often *sorghum beer*) to *mampoer*, a brandy distilled from peaches and other soft fruits, possibly named after the Sotho chief Mampuru. *Mahog(a)* is brandy as served in township shebeens (many now legalized as *taverns*) and possibly from English *mahogany*. Foods include *boerewors* (Afrikaans: boer sausage), a centrepiece of a *braaivleis* (Afrikaans: barbecue), and *sosaties* (curried kebabs, probably from Malay). At outdoor parties, the focal dish may be *potjiekos* (Afrikaans), a stew with ingredients to taste, made in a three-legged pot over an open fire. African township culture has generated an enormous vocabulary that includes *matchbox* a small standardized dwelling, *spot* a shebeen or tavern, *boere* ('boers') the police, and *tsotsi* an African street thug (of uncertain origin). Much of the vast government vocabulary of apartheid remains in use, such as *group area* an area set apart for a particular racial group, and *resettlement*, sometimes forcible, of people into such areas. 'Resistance vocabulary' includes the rallying cry *Amandla* (*ngawethu*) 'Power (is ours)', from Nguni, and the more recent *Viva!*, perhaps from Portuguese-speaking Mozambique, *comrade* in the specialized sense of 'political activist, usually young', and *necklace* (execution by igniting a petrol-filled tyre hung round the victim's neck). Two items of special interest are *muti* and *larney*. The first, from Zulu,

originally designated traditional African medicines and other remedies, but has passed into general white colloquial use as in *The pharmacist gave me a special muti for this*. *Lahnee*, of unknown origin, appeared first in IndE in general colloquial use, usually as *larney*, meaning 'smart, pretentious', *as in a hell of a larney wedding*. See AFRICAN ENGLISH.

**SOUTH AFRICANISM**. A word or other expression that occurs in or is typical of the English of South Africa, such as the internationally known *laager* and *trek*, the local informal term *lekker* pleasant, excellent, delicious (as in *lekker sunshine* nice warm sunshine, and *the lekkerest ladies in London*). See ISM, SOUTH AFRICAN ENGLISH.

**SOUTH ASIAN ENGLISH**, short form *SAE*. The English language as used in BANGLADESH, Bhutan, India, the MALDIVES, NEPAL, Pakistan, and SRI LANKA. The combined populations of these countries, projected as 1,400m in the year 2000, constitute almost a quarter of the human race. English is their main link language, largely as a result of British commercial, colonial, and educational influence since the 17c. Only Nepal, Bhutan, and the Maldives remained outside the British Raj. All South Asian countries are linguistically and culturally diverse, with two major language families, Dravidian and Indo-Aryan, a shared cultural and political history, common literary and folk traditions, and pervasive strata of SANSKRIT, Persian, and English in language and literature. Three factors operated in favour of the spread of English: the work of Christian missionaries: demand from local leaders for education in English, to benefit from Western knowledge; and a decision by the government of India to make English the official medium of education. There is a general educated South Asian variety of English used for pan-regional and international purposes. Its use is influenced by three factors: level of education and proficiency; the user's first or dominant language (and the characteristics of the language family to which it belongs); and ethnic, religious, or other background. There is a continuum from this educated usage as an ACROLECT through various MESOLECTS to such BASILECTS as the BROKEN ENGLISH of servants, street vendors and beggars.

**SOUTH-EAST ASIAN ENGLISH.**
English as used in South-East Asia falls into
two broad types: second-language varieties
in countries that were formerly colonies or
protectorates of an English-speaking power
(Britain in the case of BRUNEI, Malaysia,
and Singapore; the US in the case of the
Philippines); and foreign-language varieties
in Cambodia/Kampuchea, Indonesia, Laos,
Thailand, and Vietnam. In the first group,
students in English-medium schools were
not only taught English but learned other
subjects through it; they were expected to
use English in the playground, and there
were often penalties for using anything
else. Such education began with the establishment of the Penang Free School in 1816
and the Singapore Free School in 1823.
English-medium education was the path
to better-paid employment and in some
cases to higher education leading to the
professions. As a consequence, English became a prestige language among the élite.
The greater the spread of English and the
more functions for which it could be used,
the more it became indigenized. This is
most apparent in Singapore where, since
1987, English has been the sole medium of
education, and there are now native speakers of SINGAPORE ENGLISH.

In formal situations, the English of educated Singaporeans is distinguishable
mainly by ACCENT, but in more informal
situations an innovative use of words is
noticeable, such as loans from Chinese and
Malay and modifications in the meaning
of English words. Grammatical structure
shows the influence of local languages, especially varieties of Chinese. In Malaysia, a
similar type of English developed. In colonial times, most of the students at English-
medium schools were Chinese, but since
independence in the 1950s Malay-medium
education has increased and Malay has become by far the main medium in primary
schools and the only medium in secondary
schools. English remains an important
compulsory subject but its functions have
greatly diminished. Brunei has a bilingual
Malay and English education policy, earlier
primary school classes beginning with
Malay alone, then an increasing use of English until in the senior secondary school
English is the medium for 80% of class time.

English-medium education began in the
Philippines in 1901 after the arrival of some
540 American teachers, not long after the
defeat by the US of the former colonial
power, Spain. English was made the language of education and with wider use
became indigenized by the inclusion of vocabulary from local languages, the adaptation of English words to suit local needs,
and the modification of pronunciation and
grammar to produce a distinctively PHILIP-
PINE ENGLISH. English was adopted for
newspapers and magazines the media, and
literary purposes. After independence in
1946, the national language Tagalog (later
called Pilipino) was made an official language along with English and Spanish.
With increasing nationalism, the role of
English diminished and in 1974 a bilingual
education policy was implemented, with
English as a school subject at primary level
but as the medium for science and mathematics at secondary level. At tertiary institutions it remains the main medium of
instruction. In the foreign-language countries, English has great importance as an
Asian and international lingua franca, in
tourism, a reading language for technical
subjects, and a token of modernity. See
MALAYSIAN ENGLISH.

**SOUTHERN ENGLISH**, also **Southern
American English** and **Southern**. A collective term for the geographic and social
varieties of English spoken in that part of
the US roughly coextensive with the former
slave-holding states. These varieties share
the inclusive plural personal pronoun *y'all*
(*Are y'all comin' tonight?*), the pronunciation
of *greasy* with /z/, and the use of double
modals like *might could* (*He might could come
Friday*). Two of the major US regional dialect
types, (*Coastal*) *Southern* and *South Midland*,
cut cross the vast territory in patterns following natural boundaries and settlement
routes: (1) (*Coastal*) *Southern* (also *Lowland
Southern*, *Plantation Southern*). Spoken along
the Atlantic seaboard and westward across
the lands of lower elevation with a predominantly agrarian economy once relying on
slave labour. In this area, white and black
speakers have traditionally shared many of
its characteristics: a non-rhotic accent, a
glide before /u/ in words like *news* and *Tuesday*, and the usages *tote* carry, *carry* escort,
and *snapbeans* string beans. (2) *South Midland*
(also *Appalachian*, *Hill Southern*, *Inland Southern*). Spoken in a region settled by the
Scotch-Irish and Germans coming from
Pennsylvania. It is rhotic, has a monoph-

thongal /a/ in *nice time* ('nahs tahm'), and the usages *skillet* frying-pan, *poke* paper sack, and *green beans* string beans. Not all varieties of English spoken in the South fit easily into types: for example, the relic area of Tangier Island in the Chesapeake Bay; the English influenced by the creole GULLAH around Charleston, South Carolina; and CAJUN English in Southern Louisiana. In addition, non-rhotic appears to be losing out to rhotic pronunciation among the younger generation. See AFRICAN-AMERICAN VERNACULAR ENGLISH, AMERICAN ENGLISH, APPALACHIAN ENGLISH, CHICANO ENGLISH, DIALECT (AMERICA), NEW ORLEANS, SPANGLISH, TEXAS, TEX-MEX.

**SOUTHERN ONTARIO**. Part of the Canadian province of Ontario considered as a dialect area that runs along the northern shore of the lower Great Lakes from Windsor on the Detroit River to Kingston at the eastern end of Lake Ontario. Because it is the most populous and wealthiest part of Canada, its usage preferences have generally been taken as normative for CANADIAN ENGLISH and treated not as a 'dialect' but as the 'language'. Originally known as the colony of *Upper Canada* (contrasted with *Lower Canada* below the rapids at Montreal), southern Ontario came to dominate British North America after 1815 when its border with the US was ascertained. Neighbouring border cities, connected by road bridges across the waterway, are linguistically distinct despite shared broadcast media and regular travel from one country to the other: Sarnia (Ontario) and Port Huron (Michigan), Windsor and Detroit (Michigan), Port Erie and Buffalo (New York), Kingston and Watertown (New York). The linguistic boundary is as sharp as the political one: for example, CanE merger of the vowels of *Don* and *dawn* is restricted to the northern shore. See DIALECT (CANADA).

**SPANGLISH**. An informal and often pejorative term, particularly common in North America, for any of several mixtures of SPANISH and English, ranging from extensive uses of LOANWORDS and LOAN TRANSLATIONS to CODE-SWITCHING among bilinguals. English-influenced Spanish is often referred to negatively in the US Southwest as *español mocho* (from *mochar* to cut limbs off trees) and *español pocho* (from Uto-Aztecan *potzi* short, tailless). The term often refers

broadly to non-standard Spanish which contains: (1) Loanwords from English, such as *wachar* to watch, *pushar* to push. (2) Loan senses attached to traditional Spanish words, such as *asistir* to assist, help, *atender* to attend (school). (3) CALQUES, such as *llamar pa(ra)* (*a*)*trás* to call back (on the telephone). (4) Code-switching, such as *Sácame los files for the new applicants de alla!* (Get out the files for the new applicants from over there). See CHICANO ENGLISH, PUERTO RICO, TEX-MEX.

■ **SPANISH** ────────────── ■

A Romance language of Western Europe, spoken by *c*.250m people worldwide: the official language of Spain (including the Balearic and Canary Islands), and most of the nations of Central and South America: Argentina, Bolivia, Chile, Colombia, Costa Rica, Cuba, Dominican Republic, Ecuador, El Salvador, Guatemala, Honduras, Mexico, Nicaragua, PANAMA, Paraguay, Peru, Uruguay, Venezuela. In Paraguay, official status is shared with Guarani, and in Peru, with Quechua, both Amerindian languages. Spanish is spoken in the US, especially in the Southwest (Arizona, California, New Mexico, Texas), Florida, parts of Louisiana, and such cosmopolitan cities as New York City and Chicago, as well as in the Commonwealth of PUERTO RICO. It has also been spoken on the Caribbean island of Trinidad and by Sephardic Jews in North Africa, Turkey, and the Balkans. In Africa, it is the official language of Equatorial Guinea and is spoken in parts of Morocco and in the Spanish COASTAL enclaves of Ceuta and Melilla. In Asia, it is spoken by a small minority in the Philippines. There have been Spanish CREOLES in Colombia, the Caribbean, and the Philippines.

**Origins**. Historically, Spanish evolved out of Late Vulgar Latin, with minor Germanic and major ARABIC influence. Its history is divided into three periods: Old Spanish (*c*.750–1500), Renaissance Spanish (1500 to 1808, the beginning of the Napoleonic Wars in Spain), and Modern Spanish (since 1808). At the close of the Roman period (early 5c), the Iberian Peninsula was overrun by the Vandals and Visigoths, Germanic invaders who contributed such war-related vocabulary as *brida* (bridle), *dardo* (dart), *guerra* (war), and *hacha* (axe). During the Muslim period (711–1492), when much of the peninsula was held by Moorish rules, ARABIC loanwords were absorbed into the local post-Latin dialects, such as *aceituna* an olive, *ahorrar* to save, *albóndiga* a meatball, *alfalfa*, *algebra*, *alquilar* rent, *cifra* a cipher, zero, *naranja* an orange, *ojala* may Allah grant, may it happen, if only, some hope. This influx appears to have been made easy by the Christians who lived in Moorish territories: they were known as *mozárabes*, from Arabic *musta'rib*, Arabicized. Many of them were probably bilingual, speaking Arabic and the now-extinct variety of Spanish known as Mozarabic. The national epic, *El poema/cantar de mío Cid* (the Poem/Song of My Lord), in which the word *cid* is of Arabic origin (*as-sīd* lord), is from the period of the Reconquest.

Works of literature first appeared in Spanish *c.*1150 and a literary language was firmly established by the 15c. Three pivotal events all occurred in 1492: (1) 'The Catholic kings', Ferdinand and Isabella of Castile and Aragon, completed the reconquest of Spain by taking Granada, the last Moorish kingdom. (2) Christopher Columbus, acting on their behalf, sailed west to find China and India and instead discovered the Americas. (3) The first grammar of a modern European language was published, Antonio de Nebrija's *Gramática de la lengua castellana* (Grammar of the Castilian Language), duly followed by his dictionary and orthography. Spain became a world power and the centre of a vast empire. The standard language of Spain and its empire was based on Castilian (the dialect of Castile), and for this reason continues to be referred to in Spanish as both *castellano* and *español*.

**Spanish in the United States**. Spanish has been spoken longer than English in what is now the US. Spanish settlement in San Agustin, Florida, dates from 1565, various areas in new Mexico were settled in 1598, and settlements in California were established from 1769 on. As the English-speaking US expanded, it incorporated territory originally held by Spain (Florida), France (the Louisiana Purchase), and Mexico (the Southwest, from Texas to California). Spanish was also incorporated into the US, by the addition of TEXAS in 1845 and the rest of the Southwest by the Mexican Cession in 1848. Although statehood for the Territory of New Mexico was delayed until 1912 at least partly because of a lack of

English-speaking citizens, Spanish was later granted legal status there along with English. Puerto Rico became associated with the US in 1898 and currently has Commonwealth status, with Puerto Ricans holding US citizenship.

In recent years, immigration from Latin America has made Spanish the second most widely spoken language in the US. The influx of Cubans into Florida beginning in 1960 turned the Miami-Dade County area into a centre of Hispanic language and culture. In the Southwest, immigration from Mexico increased during and shortly after the Mexican Revolution (1912–15), after World War II, and in the 1980s, Immigration from Central America also increased rapidly in the 1980s. The increasing Hispanic population has given some areas outside the Southwest and Florida a decidedly Hispanic flavour, including the cities of New York and Chicago. In all areas, bilingual education has been implemented as a method for bringing new immigrants to fluency in English in the shortest time. In reaction, however, many (including some Hispanics and members of other immigrant groups) have supported the appeals of the organization US English, which advocates a constitutional amendment to declare English the official language of the country and seeks the elimination of bilingual education.

**Spanish in English**. Because of the reintroduction of Greek learning to Europe by the Arabs in Spain and then the great wealth and power of the new empire, 16c Spain was a major centre of learning. Spanish was a language of high prestige throughout Europe, and in late 16c England was the subject of a number of linguistic treatises, including Richard Percivall's *Bibliotheca Hispanica, Containing a Grammar, with a Dictionarie in Spanish, English, and Latine* (1591). The *Real Academia* (Royal Academy) was founded in 1713, on the model of the French Academy (1637), in order to *limpia, fija, y da esplendor* ('purify, fix, and lend splendour') to the language, the motto on the great seal of the Academy that appears on the spine and title page of all volumes of the Academy's dictionary.

The influence of Spanish on English at large has extended over centuries and been primarily lexical. Phonological and grammatical influences have occurred relatively rarely and recently in the Americas, and have been limited to particular regions and varieties. English shares with Spanish a large vocabulary derived from Latin, due especially to the impact of Norman French after the 11c Norman Conquest of England. During the 16–17c, a time of rapid colonial expansion among the seafaring nations of Europe, Spain and England were competing to amass empires and influence, and Spanish had its first direct impact. Loan-words of the 16c include the orthographically unadapted words *armada*, *cargo*, *desperado*, *flotilla*, *mosquito*, *mulatto*, *negro*, *pec(c)adillo*, *sombrero* and the adapted *ambush*, *cannibal*, *cask*, *cigar*, *comrade*, *jennet*, *parade*, *renegade*, *sherry*. Other loans have entered the language since then, such as unadapted *albino*, *flotilla*, *hacienda*, *mesa*, *plaza*, *siesta*, adapted *barbecue*, *caramel*, *cockroach*, *corvette*, *doubloon*, *escapade*, *guitar*, *jade*, *lime*, *maroon*, *picaresque*, *quadroon*. Some Spanish loans have Arabic origins, such as *alfalfa* (Arabic *al-fasfasah*), *alcazar* (Arabic *al-qasr* the castle), *alcove* (through French *alcôve*, from Spanish *alcoba*, from Arabic *al-qubbah* the vault).

A wave of New World BORROWINGS occurred in the 19c, mainly in the Southwest of the US, such as the unadapted *arroyo*, *bronco*, *cantina*, *corral*, *gringo*, *mesa*, *patio*, *rodeo*, *tequila*, and the adapted *alligator*, *buckaroo*, *chaps*, *lariat*, *mustang*, *ranch*. Many items borrowed from Spanish were through Spanish from indigenous Amerindian languages, such as *avocado*, *chocolate*, *coyote*, *peyote*, from the Aztec language Nahuatl. In the 20c, there has been a second wave throughout the US, related to the increase in Latin American immigration; loans include *contras*, *guerrilla*, *jefe*, *macho/machismo*, as well as such culinary terms as *burrito*, *chiles rellenos*, *flautas*, *frijoles*, *frijoles refritos*, *nacho*, *pan dulce*, *salsa*, *taco*, *tortilla*.

**English in Spanish**. In recent decades, English has had a greater influence on Spanish than vice versa. This has happened wherever Spanish is spoken, but is particularly noticeable where Spanish- and English-speaking communities live as neighbours (such as along the US–Mexican border) and where communities of speakers of one language have migrated to the territory of another (such as Puerto Ricans in New York City: British expatriate communities and facilities for holiday-makers along the Mediterranean littoral of Spain). Close contact between the two languages has produced hybrid forms, for which casual names have arisen: SPANGLISH, a term covering all forms of English influenced by Spanish and Spanish influenced by English, and the more particular TEX-MEX or *Border Lingo* along the Texas–Mexican border.

In general, the influence is lexical, especially in the borrowing and adaptation of technical and sporting terms. Many of these borrowings are accepted only grudgingly or until more Hispanicized equivalents are coined. Not all are current in all dialects, but are clearly favoured in contact dialects. Some expressions are borrowings, either unadapted or adapted, while others are Anglicisms in a more general sense: loan shifts resulting from English influence in the usage of traditional Spanish words, often cognates of English Romance-derived words. Examples of borrowings are: (in sport) *boxeo* boxing, *boxear* to box, *nocaut* a knockout, *noquear* to knock out, *jonrón* a home run, *jonronear* to make a home run, *fútbol*, *criquet*, *basquetbol*; (culinary) *cake/queque* a cake, *pangqueques* pancakes, *(miel)maple* maple syrup, *bistec* a beefsteak, *cóctel* a cocktail, *hamburguesa*, a hamburger; (in politics) *agenda*, *boicot* a boycott, *boicotear* to boycott, *cartel*, *detective*; (in general usage) *bus*, *camuflaje*, *esmoking* a dinner jacket, *tuxedo*, *esnob* a snob, *esnobismo* snobbery, *jazz*, *jet*, *microchip*, *parquear* to park, *troca* a truck.

Loan shifts and translations may compete with established usages: the verbs *rentar* with *alquilar* (to rent) and *clarificar* with *aclarar* (to clarify); the nouns *elevador* with *acensor* a lift, elevator; *profesional* with *profesionista* a professional. They may also provide a new sense for a traditional word: *carácter*, in the theatre as opposed to *personaje*; *conductor*, of music as opposed to *director*; *década* for ten years as opposed to ten of anything; *educación* for schooling as opposed to manners. Sometimes they are entirely new: *perro caliente* a hot dog, *escuela alta* high school. Others, such as *filmoteca* a library of films, are loan blends.

See AMERICAN ENGLISH, CHICANO ENGLISH, DIALECT (AMERICA), ENGLISH LANGUAGE AMENDMENT, GIBRALTAR, PHILIPPINE ENGLISH, PORTUGUESE, ROMANCE LANGUAGES.

**-SPEAK, SPEAK** [From *Newspeak*, as coined by George Orwell]. Both a combining form and a word used informally (and often pejoratively or facetiously) for the style of a group or occupation, often regardless of whether it is spoken or written. In a compound that contains *-speak*, the first element indicates either the situation in which the style occurs (*adspeak*; advertising) or what the user thinks of it (*DOUBLESPEAK*: a jargon intended to mislead). There are three orthographic forms: (1) Solid: *Aussiespeak, computerspeak, Femspeak, healthspeak, lewdspeak, modernspeak, moneyspeak, nukespeak, pensionspeak, technospeak, tycoonspeak, unionspeak*. (2) Hyphenated: *gay-speak, golf-speak, management-speak, oblique-speak, Pentagon-speak*. (3) Open: *art speak, estate-agent speak, mandarin speak, political speak*. In terms of structure, there are two extremes: (1) The first element is monosyllabic like *new*, often a clipping of a longer word: *bizspeak, Russpeak*. (2) The first element is phrasal: *Hitch-Hiker's-Guide-to-the-Galaxy-speak, medical and social work 'speak'; Twentieth century era speak; Womenslibspeak*. Occasionally, blending occurs, as in *bureaucraspeak, litcritspeak, politspeak, Shakespeak*. Compare -ESE, -ISM, LINGO, TALK.

**SPECIALIZATION**. A process of SEMANTIC CHANGE in which narrowing occurs in the meaning of a word. In Middle English, *deer* meant a four-legged beast (compare Dutch *dier* and German *Tier*), but the early restriction to one kind of animal (the family Cervidae) has long since eclipsed the earlier meaning. Such specialization is slow and need not be complete; *fowl* is now usually restricted to the farmyard hen, but it retains its old meaning of 'bird' in expressions like *the fowls of the air* and *wild fowl* (compare Chaucer's 'Parlement of Fowles' and German *Vogel*).

## ■ SPEECH ──────────── ■

**1.** The primary form of LANGUAGE; oral COMMUNICATION in general and on any particular occasion: *Most people are more fluent in speech than in writing*. **2.** A usually formal occasion when a person addresses an audience, often with the help of notes or a prepared text. **3.** A way of speaking, often involving a judgement of some kind: *local speech, slovenly speech, standard speech*. **4.** The field of study associated with speaking and listening: *the science of speech*.

**Anatomy and physiology**. Speech is possible because of the development over millennia of an appropriate physical system: the diaphragm, lungs, throat, mouth, and nose, working together. All such organs pre-existed the evolution of language and have such prior purposes as breathing, eating, and drinking. With the advent of speech, they continued to perform these functions while becoming available for additional uses, so that two systems (maintenance of the body and systematic communication) exist side by side. Vocal sound becomes possible when a stream of air is breathed out from the lungs and passes through the larynx, then into and through the pharynx, mouth, and nose. This sound may be *voiced* or *voiceless*: that is, the larynx may vibrate or not. Different sounds are made in the mouth by moving the lips, tongue, and lower jaw to change the size and shape of the channel through which the air passes. A *CONSONANT* is made with a narrowing of the channel, and the point of maximum narrowing is the *place* (or *point*) of *articulation* for that consonant. The way in which this is done is the *manner of articulation*. A *VOWEL* typically has a wider channel than a consonant. Since it is difficult to be precise about the articulation of vowels, they are normally described by their auditory quality. In discussing articulation, phoneticians refer to an *articulator*, which may be *active* (as with the lips and tongue) or *passive* (as with the front teeth).

**Place of articulation**. For *bilabial* consonants, the narrowing is achieved by bringing the lips together. For *labio-dental* consonants, the active articulator is the lower lip. In other cases, the active articulator is part of the tongue, which is raised towards the passive articulator on the roof of the mouth: see table.

Sounds can be classified according to the active articulator, for example the tongue: *apical* sounds made with the tip (Latin *apex*); *laminal* sounds with the blade (Latin *lamina*); *dorsal* sounds with the back (Latin *dorsum*). *Retroflex* sounds are made with the tip of the tongue curled back behind the alveolar ridge towards the PALATE. However, the commonest classification is according to the passive articulator. This terminology assumes that the active articulator is the organ that lies opposite the passive articulator in the state of rest: for example, the passive articulator of a *dental* sound is the upper front teeth, and the active articulator is the tip of the tongue. If some other active articulator is used, it is specified explicitly: for example for /f, v/, the lower lip moves up

## THE ORGANS OF SPEECH

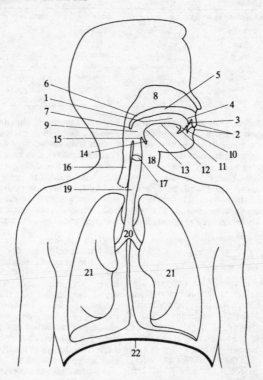

| | | |
|---|---|---|
| 1 mouth (oral or buccal cavity) | 9 pharynx (pharyngeal cavity) | 17 glottis |
| 2 lips | 10 tip (of the tongue) | 18 larynx and vocal |
| 3 teeth | 11 blade (of the tongue) |    cords/folds |
| 4 alveolar ridge | 12 front (of the tongue) | 19 trachea |
| 5 (hard) palate | 13 back (of the tongue) | 20 bronchi |
| 6 velum or soft palate | 14 root (of the tongue) | 21 lungs |
| 7 uvula | 15 epiglottis | 22 diaphragm |
| 8 nasal cavity | 16 *BrE* oesophagus, | |
| |    *AmE* esophagus | |

to the upper teeth, and these sounds are *labio-dental*: see table. The *ASPIRATE* /h/ is usually described as *glottal*. In English, /h/ is like a *voiceless vowel* in that there is no fricative-like narrowing in the mouth, so that the greatest point of narrowing is in the glottis. Most sounds have one place of articulation, but /w/ has a *double articulation*, being made by simultaneously rounding the lips and

raising the back of the tongue towards the VELUM. It is thus both bilabial and velar.

**Manner of articulation.** This refers mainly to the degree of narrowing at the place of articulation of a sound. If the air-stream is blocked completely, the result is a *STOP*, such as /b/, but if it is narrowed to the point where noise or *turbulence* is generated

| Articulator | | Description | Examples |
|---|---|---|---|
| Active | Passive | | |
| lower and upper lips | – | labial | /p, b, m/ |
| lower lip | front teeth | labio-dental | /f, v/ |
| tongue: | | | |
| tip | front teeth | dental | /θ, ð/ |
| tip | alveolar ridge | alveolar | /t, d, s, z, n, l, r/ |
| tip/blade | ridge/palate | palato-alveolar | /ʃ, ʒ, tʃ, dʒ/ |
| front | palate | palatal | /j/ |
| back | velum | velar | /k, g, ŋ/ |

as air passes through the gap, the resulting sound is a *FRICATIVE* /v/. In the case of an *AP-PROXIMANT* or *continuant*, the manner of articulation is more open, as with the /r/ of *rink* as compared to the /z/ of *zinc* (a voiced fricative). When a stop is released, the articulators move apart and necessarily pass through the degree of narrowing which produces fricative noise. A *PLOSIVE* is released quickly, whereas an *AFFRICATE* is released slowly:

| plosives | /p, b; t, d; k, g/ |
|---|---|
| affricates | /tʃ, dʒ/ |
| fricatives | /f, v; θ, ð; s, z; ʃ, ʒ; h/ |

There are several types of approximant. The velum is normally raised to prevent air from entering the nose: a *NASAL* is produced with the velum lowered. The airstream normally passes centrally through the mouth: in the case of a *lateral*, the air escapes at the sides. The tongue normally offers a convex surface to the roof of the mouth: for an *r-sound*, the tongue surface is often hollowed out and the tip raised. A *GLIDE* or *semi-vowel* is vowel-like and moves rapidly into the following vowel, and cannot be prolonged:

| nasals | /m, n, ŋ/ |
|---|---|
| lateral | /l/ |
| r-sound | /r/ |
| glides | /j, w/ |

Phoneticians conventionally describe consonants according to their articulation.

## ■ SPELLING ─────────── ■

The act, process, or system of relating speech sounds to LETTERS and to the written form of WORDS. The spelling system of an alphabetic language consists of the conventions by which its letters represent sounds and words (*E-G-G* spells *egg*) and the way(s) in which words are spelt/spelled (*How d'you spell 'accommodation'—one m or two?*). Phoneticians describe the ideal relationship

between sound and alphabetic WRITING as *phonographic*: letters indicate sounds and sounds indicate letters. As ALPHABETS have evolved, however, they have been adapted in different ways to different languages, and the relationship is sometimes indirect and far from ideal. In FRENCH and ENGLISH, whose orthographic traditions are ancient and intricate, the current situation is complex and often confused.

**English spelling**. The spelling of English has traditionally been discussed (and often taught) in terms of rules and exceptions. For example, the rule that the *ee* combination in *meet*, *sleep*, etc., stands for a single long /i/ sound, but the fact that the long /i/ sound can be represented in other ways, as in *be*, *sea*, *key*, *quay*, *ski*, *esprit*, *deceit*, *field*, *people*, *amoeba/ameba*, *aeon/eon*, *leave*, *these*. Similarly there is a rule that *c* before *a/o/u* is hard (*cat*, *cot*, *cut*) but before *e/i* is soft (*cent*, *cite*), with such exceptions as *façade* on the one hand and a common PRONUNCIATION of *Celtic* on the other. Word forms that conflict with the phonographic principle are common: (1) Those with aberrant letter values, such as the *a* in *any*, the *e* in *sew*, the *g* in BrE *gaol*, the *gh* in *laugh*, the *l* in *colonel*, the *o* in *woman* and *women*, the *s* in *sugar*, the *x* in *xenophobia*, and the *z* in *schizophrenia*. (2) Those with silent letters, such as the *a* in *head*, the *b* in *thumb*, the *c* in *indict*, the *e* in *height*, the *g* in *foreign*, the *h* in *honest*, the *k* in *knee*, the *n* in *column*, the *p* in *ptarmigan*, the *t* in *castle*, and the *w* in *write*. (3) Those that carry over all or something of their non-English spelling from other languages, such as the *aa* in *bazaar* (from Persian), the *c* in *cello* (from Italian), the *dd* in *eisteddfod* (from Welsh), the *ch* and *y* in *chrysanthemum* (from Latinized GREEK), the *chs* in *fuchsia* (from Latinized GERMAN), and the *j* in *marijuana* (from Spanish).

Although most of the letters of the alphabet have in isolation an unambiguous sound value, as represented in children's alphabet lists (*A is for Apple*, etc.) in the spelling of many words this correspondence does not apply (*A* is also for *above, all, and any*). Adult native speakers are often unsure how to pronounce such words as *algae, fungi, hegemony*, and *lichen*. Common misspellings include confusion over silent letters (for example, 'figth' for *fight*), doubled consonants ('supprise' for *surprise*, 'accomodate' for *accommodate*, 'commitee' for *committee*, 'dissapear' for *disappear*), and the representation of the weak vowel schwa ('assistent' for *assistant*, 'consistant' for *consistent*, 'burgler' for *burglar*, 'docter' for *doctor*).

**A hybrid system**. The major elements in the creation of the present-day spelling of English have been the adaptation of the Roman alphabet to serve English, outside influences on that language, and the GREAT VOWEL SHIFT. When the Roman alphabet was adopted for writing OLD ENGLISH, it was supplemented to cover sounds not present in Latin. The letters ASH, ETH, THORN, and WYNN (along with YOGH, a variant of Roman *g*) have not survived into Modern English, while the consonants *j*, *v*, *w* have been recent additions. Old English spelling appears to have represented pronunciation relatively consistently, but the Norman Conquest in 1066 introduced many Norman-French usages that conflicted with Old English tradition, such as the *qu-* in *queen* (Old English *cwēn*). Massive borrowing of LATIN and Greek words (often through French or French spelling conventions) as well as the adoption of words from many other languages created a great variety of often conflicting spelling patterns. Many small sets of words with their own inherited patterns of letters emerged, such as the *kn-* group representing Old English *cn-* (such as *knave, knife, know*), the *gu-* group from NORMAN FRENCH (such as *guard, guide, guise*), the *-ence* group from Latin through French (such as *sequence, diligence, residence*), and the group of silent *p-* words from Greek (*pneumonia, pterodactyl, psychology*). The spelling of early loans conforms to what are now traditional 'native' patterns (*beef* from Norman French *boef* is like *keep* from Old English *cēpan*), but later loans have tended to keep their foreign forms (*rendezvous* French, *spaghetti* ITALIAN, *yacht* Dutch). In the 15c the Great Vowel Shift changed the basic sound values of the

language (compare Chaucerian with Modern pronunciations) and such ancient Germanic consonant sounds as the *k* and *gh* of *knight* were lost. Spellings often did not change to reflect these phonological developments. At the same time, writers inserted letters in a number of words on erroneous grounds of etymology, such as the *s* in *island* and the *gh* in *delight* by analogy with *isle* and *light*.

**Fixed spellings**. Before the spread of printing, publishing, and education, spelling reflected differences in individual and regional usage. The *OED* records, from the 9c onward, the following spellings of one word, only the last of which is now accepted: *myrʒe, murʒe, myriʒe miriʒe, merʒe, meriʒe, murye, muri, murie, mury, miri, mirie, myry, miry, myrie, myri, mirrie, mirry, myrrie, myrry, mirre, meri, merey, merie, mery, merye, merrye, mere, meary, merrie, merry*. In 1586, Elizabeth of England wrote in a letter to James of Scotland *desiar* and *wold* and James in his reply wrote *desyre, desire* and *wolde, woulde*. As a consequence of the spread of printing and publishing (15c onward) and wider education in the VERNACULAR, most common words had acquired their present-day fixed spellings by the 19c, with minor variations between AmE and BrE. Samuel JOHNSON's *Dictionary of the English Language* (1755) served as an authoritative work of reference. Until the late 18c, when AmE and BrE usage began to diverge, both members of such pairs as *center/centre, color/colour, magic/magick, plow/plough* were in general use. AmE usage followed Noah WEBSTER's dictionary in 1829 in settling on the first in each of these cases. BrE usage, however, having favoured the second in each pair (as in Johnson's dictionary of 1755), continued with all but the *-ick* form as its standard practice, turning them into tokens of national distinctiveness. As a result, the most obtrusive differences between present-day American and British documents are their spellings.

**A system of systems**. Spellings became fixed in the 18c by a social consensus and not through the recommendation of an Academy or other institution. The result has been at the same time a lessening of variability and a fossilization of forms that came into existence in different times and places. These fossils occur, as it were, in orthographic strata: a vernacular SUBSTRATUM of ANGLO-SAXON, DANISH, and other Germanic material (and exotic material borrowed so early that it has come to look Germanic), a mid-stratum of Norman-French material, and a superstratum of nativized NEO-LATIN (Latin and Latinized Greek). The intricacies of this system of systems are so great that it is close to impossible to sort out its sets and subsets neatly, but literate users of English appear, by and large, to be aware (in functional, not etymological, terms) of the main patterns. These are amenable to several descriptions: a two-part contrast of Germanic and Romance (including Latinized Greek and ignoring the exotica); a five-part system of Germanic, French, Latin, Greek, and exotica; or a three-part system in line with the three major traditions of word-formation, Germanic, Latin, and Greek (Norman-French patterns variously affecting all three), representing a cline from the everyday to the highly technical. In addition to the core words that belong etymologically to each group there are many words that have crossed over from group to group or been drawn into a group from elsewhere, but what marks a group (among other things) is the distinctive pattern of its spellings, a limited selection of which are:

*A vernacular-style spelling.* (1) Syllable initial sets of consonants: *kn-* with silent *k* in *knave, knee, knife, know, knuckle*: *sk* in *skate, skill, skunk, sky*. (2) Syllable final sets of consonants: *-sh* in *bash, mesh, dish, slosh, gush*; *-tch* in *batch, ketch, ditch, splotch, hutch*; *-ck* in *back, deck, tick, mock, suck*; *-le* in *cattle, kettle, sizzle, bottle, nuzzle*; *-ckle* in *crackle, heckle, sickle, grockle, knuckle*; *-dge* in *badge, hedge, midge, dodge, nudge*. (3) Prefixes: *a-* in *ablaze, aglow, alive, asleep*; *be-* in *become, believe, belong*. (4) Suffixes: *-ly* in *brotherly, kindly, lordly, northerly*; *-ness* in *darkness, lordliness, slimness, wetness*; *-y* in *sandy, slimy, wishy-washy*.

*A Romance-style spelling.* (1) Soft *c* and *g* before *e* and *i*: *cell, gelatin, decision, ginger*. (2) Prefixes (unaltered or assimilated): *ad-* in *admit, adopt, advise, allege, apparent*; *con-* in *conclude, commensurate, collection*; locative *in-* in *inherent, innate, instinct, investigate*; negative *in-* in *indecisive, inconclusive, ignoble, illiterate, impossible, irreversible*; *post-* in *post-date, postpone*; *pre-* in *prescribe, prevent*; *pro-* in *progress, provide*. (3) Suffixes: *-ity* in *adversity, centrality*; *-ion* in *addition, admission, condition, eruption, propulsion, segregation*.

*A transliterated Greek-style spelling.* (1) *Ch* with the sound value /k/: *chaos, archetype, orchid, cholesterol, monarch*. (2) Word-initial silent *m* and *p*: *mnemonic, psychology, pterodactyl*. (3) Use of *y* rather than *i*: *analysis, psychology, synthetic, syzygy*. (4) Use of *ph* rather than *f*: *amphibious, pharmacy, philosophical*. (5) Initial *rh* and medial and final *rrh* as in *rhetoric, rhythm, diarrh(o)ea, h(a)emorrhage, catarrh*.

**Spelling and stress**. English is a stress-timed language, but its written form does not show where the stress falls in polysyllabic words. The noun and adjective *present*, which are stressed on the first syllable (*présent*), have the same spelling as the verb, which is stressed on the second syllable (*presént*). English can, however, indicate stress when an unstressed vowel is spelt with a syllabic consonant and not a vowel letter: *apple, acre, hadn't*, and *spasm* show that the first syllable, with the vowel *a*, carries the stress, and not the second syllable, in which no vowel letter figures. In the weak syllables of the language (initial in *about, conspire, decide, persuade, remove*, final in *anthem, beggar, metal, phantom, worker*), the vowel is reduced in speech to a central weak quality (schwa) or is represented by a syllabic consonant. Unless one already knows the spelling of such unstressed or weak syllables, it is not easy to guess what it might be: compare *anthem/fathom, medal/model, principal/principle*. In addition, patterns of stress associated with suffixes change the pronunciation of words without affecting spelling and without any indication of stress shift shown in writing, as in *átom/atómic, eléctric/electricity, nátional/nationálity, phótograph/photógrapher/photográphic*. Elsewhere, the stress shift is reflected in the spelling: *maintáin/máintenance, revéal/revelátion*.

**Homographs and heterographs**. Ambiguity of word form in English has three aspects: (1) HOMONYMS, words that have distinct meanings and are in origin unconnected, but have the same sound and spelling: *tender* as in *tender feelings, a locomotive tender*, and *to tender one's resignation*. In context, however, they seldom trouble the reader. (2) HOMOPHONES or HETERONYMS/*heterographs*, words that have the same pronunciations but are differently spelt, of which there are over 600 sets in English. Phonologically they are *homophones*, orthographically *heterographs*: *pair/pare/pear*, *right/rite/write/wright*, *cent/scent/sent*. Such forms are made possible by the many alternative sound–symbol correspondences in English. In reading, the different spellings prevent visual ambiguity, but for writing they require an effort of memorization and can lead to confusion, as when *flair* is written as *flare*. (3) HOMOGRAPHS or *heterophones*, words that have the same spelling but different pronunciations: *bow* for a violin, *bow* of a ship. These are ambiguous for readers but cause writers little trouble and are of two kinds: related and unrelated pairs. Related pairs include those that shift stress (*an ínsert/to insért*), introduce voicing (*a house/to house*), give an otherwise mute vowel full value (*aged, agèd*), and involve inflected forms (*bathing*, either from *bath or bathe*) and part-of-speech differences (*a live wire/to live nearby*). Unrelated pairs have usually resulted from accidental convergence: *axes* (plural of *ax(e)* or *axis*). Encounters with a member of such a pair can pose problems comparable to an optical illusion that can be interpreted in two ways: *bass, buffet, does, furrier, gill, lower, multiply, routed, sewer, skier, supply, tarry*. Such heterophones are not generally felt to constitute a problem, but some of the commoner pairs are easily misread: *lead, read, tear, wind, wound, bow, row, sow*.

**The psychology of literacy**. Because of the complexity of English spelling, psychologists, educationists, and linguists have long puzzled over the best way to teach it. It has become a widely held view that rather than seek sound–symbol correspondences, the spelling of words should be seen as forming a constellation of letters whose image is (or can be) more or less imprinted on the mind. Considered from this point of view, English spelling has been called *logographic*: not simply alphabetic, but with some of the qualities of Chinese writing; spellings such as *one* and *who* are read as wholes (gestalts), regardless of the implications of a letter-by-letter READING. Even a simple spelling such as *bad* triggers sound and meaning in a skilled reader's mind not by virtue of the letters alone but by global image, just like *one* and *who*. Proponents of such a 'look and say' approach to reading and writing consider that once these word-gestalts are imprinted on the mind, they can be read and written as easily as the spelling of a more directly phonographic language such as Spanish or Hungarian.

Proponents of a 'phonic' approach (relating individual letters to sounds) as well as spelling reformers argue that it is precisely the difficulty of acquiring a separate mental image of so many English spellings that prevents a large number of people from reaching a functional level of literacy. The 'look and say' approach teaches quick recognition of familiar words, but can leave users helpless in the face of unfamiliar words if they do not know how to relate sounds and letters. While it is relatively easy to learn to read and write by a system of regular sound–symbol correspondences, the irregularities of English spelling make it difficult for many to master the unpredictable conventions of the written language.

See entries for individual letters, A–Z, and also ABBREVIATION, ACCENT, DIACRITIC, DIGRAPH, EYE DIALECT, INITIAL, INITIAL TEACHING ALPHABET, INTERNATIONAL PHONETIC ALPHABET, LITERACY, NOTATION, ORTHOGRAPHY, PHONEME, PITMAN (I.), PITMAN (J.), PUNCTUATION, RESPELLING, SIMPLIFIED SPELLING SOCIETY.

**SPELLING PRONUNCIATION**. PRONUNCIATION based on the SPELLING of a word rather than on conventional speech, such as *often* pronounced with /t/. In a language such as Spanish, the patterns of whose speech and spelling correlate closely, the concept is unnecessary, but in English, in which correlations between spoken and written forms are often weak, the term labels a common, though often unevenly developed, phenomenon: for example, a number of English words that begin with *h*, such as *honour, honest, humble, human*, were borrowed from French with no /h/ in their pronunciation. While some, such as *honour* and *honest*, continue to be pronounced without /h/, others, such as *humble* and *human*, are now pronounced with /h/ to fit their spelling (except in such entirely aitchless varieties as COCKNEY); in standard BrE pronunciation, the /h/ is pronounced in *herb*; in AnE, it is not. In some cases, spelling pronunciation triumphs over erstwhile common pronunciations: in general usage, *waistcoat* is no longer pronounced 'weskit'. In others, when a word has been learnt only through reading, a spelling pronunciation may be used until the error is discovered: for example, that the *ch* of *archipelago* is pronounced /k/, not /tʃ/, and its closing syllables do not rhyme with *sago*. Spelling pronunciations can be invoked on an ad hoc basis, to contrast words that are otherwise homophones: for example, by saying 'stayshun-AH-ry' for *stationary* and 'stayshun-ER-y' for *stationery*.

# ■ SPELLING REFORM ─────── ■

The planned alteration of the established alphabetic WRITING system of a language so as to remove or reduce elements taken to be sources of confusion and difficulty in learning and using that system. Spelling reform does not usually include such changes as the substitution of one writing system for another (as, for example, in 1928, when Arabic script was replaced by Roman for the writing of Turkish), changes in systems of non-alphabetic signs (as with the reform of Chinese characters begun in the People's Republic of China in 1955), or the readoption of earlier individual spellings (such as, in English, the spelling *fantasy* after some three centuries of *phantasy*, there being no general substitution of *f* for *ph* throughout the language).

**Regulation and reform.** Before the advent of printing in the 15c, European spelling conventions were not usually rigid and often reflected writers' accents and preferences. The concept of 'correct writing' (*ORTHOGRAPHY*) emerged partly because printers sought uniformity and partly from a Renaissance interest in word forms, but it was only gradually, over centuries, that the availability and example of dictionaries and the pressures of formal systems of education led individuals to strive to observe the conventions of print. Systematic changes in spelling have generally been the responsibility of language academies or government departments. Academies have been founded for Italian (1582), French (1634), Spanish (1713), and various other languages (but excluding English), to act among other things as authorities on orthography, and have strongly influenced the orthographic development of the languages over which they have presided. For example, the 1740 edition of the dictionary of the Académie française altered the spelling of 36% of French words, chiefly replacing mute *s* by acute and circumflex accents: for example, *estoit* by *étoit*, *boiste* by *boîte*. Similarly, in 1959, the Real Academia de la Lengua Española issued its *Neuvas Normas de Ortografía* (*New Norms of Orthography*), recommending

that silent initial letters should be dropped; *psicología* could, for example, thenceforth be written *sicología*.

**Reforming English spelling**. Many linguists and educationists have been concerned with ways of systematizing written English. Although there could be no reform before spelling became more or less fixed, many of the ideas that have dominated the spelling-reform debate were already under discussion in the 16c. For example, in 1568, Sir Thomas Smith called for consistency within an extended alphabet, including letters and diacritical marks from Old English and Greek; in 1569, John Hart called for the spelling of words strictly by their sound; in 1582, Richard Mulcaster appealed for stability based on consistency, analogy, and custom, and the recollection that 'letters were inuented to expresse sounds'. However, the school-master Edmond Coote probably contributed most to the settling of English spelling in its present form through the 54 editions of his handbook *The English Schoolemaister* (from 1595 to 1737), which tended to avoid some of the redundant letters that were previously common.

Alexander Gil in 1619 and Charles Butler in 1633 advocated phonographic systems with the retention of Old English letters or the introduction of new letters (with some variation to mark etymology and distinguish homophones), but there was little serious advocacy or reform until 1768, when Benjamin Franklin assessed the needs of learners and poor spellers and devised an alphabet that did not use the letters *c, j, q, w, x, y* (which he considered superfluous) and introduced new characters for the vowels in *hot, up* and the consonants in *the, thin, -ing, she*. The scheme did not, however, receive much attention. A major 19c innovator was Isaac PITMAN, who moved from the invention of his phonetic shorthand to the development of an extended alphabet called *phonotype* or *phonotypy*. His emphasis on the need to encourage the education of the poor was echoed in Britain in the 1870 Education Act and led to a call by the National Union of Elementary Teachers in 1876 for a Royal Commission to consider spelling reform. The later 1870s saw the founding of spelling-reform associations on both sides of the Atlantic, whose members included Tennyson and Darwin. Such eminent philologists as Henry SWEET and Alexander Ellis in the UK and Francis March in the US experimented with reformed alphabets. In the 1880s, many students of the new science of phonetics were interested in the development of a phonetic alphabet not only for academic purposes but also as a possible precursor of a reformed spelling system for English.

**New Spelling**. At the beginning of the 20c, the cause of spelling reform was taken up for a time by the US President Theodore Roosevelt and sponsored by the industrialist and philanthropist Andrew Carnegie. In 1908, the British SIMPLIFIED SPELLING SOCIETY (SSS) was founded, chiefly with the aim of devising a reformed writing system based on the Roman alphabet, in the belief that such a development would stand a better chance of acceptance than a new alphabet. In 1948, the phonetician Daniel JONES and dialectologist Harold Orton published a system called *New Spelling*, the recommended orthography of the SSS, of which the following is a specimen:

> We rekwier dhe langgwej as an instroment; we mae aulsoe study its history. Dhe presens ov unpronounst leterz, three or for diferent waez ov reprezenting dhe saem sound, three or for uesez ov dhe same leter: aul dhis detrakts from dhe value ov a langgwej az an instrooment.

New Spelling was accepted in 1956, with small amendments, by the *American Simplified Spelling Association*, was further developed and computerized by Edward Rondthaler in New York (1986), and was revised in the 1980s, its most recent form being published in the Society's Pamphlet No. 12, *New Spelling* 90 (1991). It also provided the phonographic analysis on which Sir James PITMAN based his INITIAL TEACHING ALPHABET (*i.t.a.*) (1959). To date, however, the system has had little impact on the English-using world, and there appears currently to be little general interest in reform, and considerably less interest among language scholars than a century or even half a century ago.

**A new alphabet**. There have from time to time been attempts at radical change that go well beyond spelling reform proper into the creation and promotion of entirely new alphabets. Most prominently, a bequest from the dramatist and social reformer George Bernard SHAW financed a public competition in 1957–8 for the design of a new alphabet that would have at least 40 letters and no digraphs or diacritics. The winner of this competition, Kingsley Read (from Warwickshire in England), produced an alphabet that is utterly unlike Roman and has letters of four types: *tall* (those with ascenders) *deep* (those with descenders), *short* (those with neither ascenders nor descenders), and *compound* (combining basic symbols). In visual effect, the *Shaw Alphabet*, *Shaw's Alphabet*, or the *Shavian Alphabet*, as it is variously known, looks rather like the scripts used for the Dravidian languages of South India, with many gently curving characters. A bi-alphabetic edition of Shaw's play *Androcles and the Lion* was published by Penguin Books in 1962 to demonstrate the old and new orthographies side by side, the texts running parallel on facing pages. In it the Shaw Alphabet, though alien in its effect, proves markedly more compact and economical than the traditional system. To date, however, it has had no impact on the English-using world.

**The contemporary situation**. Recent thinking among spelling reformers stresses gradual rather than radical change, so as to ensure continuity of literacy, enable old and new to coexist, and limit the impact and scope of any one stage in reform: that is, evolution rather than revolution. Harry Lindgren in Australia, for example, proposes a multistage reform programme, each stage regularizing the spelling of a single phoneme. As a first stage, he suggests that the traditional short *-e* sound be written as *e*, as in *eny* 'any', *sed* 'said', *agenst* 'against', *bery* 'bury', *frend* 'friend', *hed* 'head'. Alternatively, rather than taking a rigid schema of sound–symbol correspondences as a starting-point, some reformers adopt a functional approach, asking what spellings would best suit the needs and abilities of users. One proposal suggests a first stage confined to removing the digraph *gh* in *though*, *caught*, etc. In addition, some reformers argue that by studying kinds of misspelling it is possible to identify the greatest difficulties among current spellings, and concentrate on regularizing them alone.

**Arguments about spelling reform**. The idea of reforming the spelling of English has long been controversial, with arguments about the relative value of tradition and literacy, the practicalities of introducing change, and the specific changes that might be made. Opponents of reform often describe the rich variety of present spellings as a heritage not to be lightly discarded, while reformers attach priority to the actual or perceived needs of contemporary users. Orthographic conservationists point out that present spellings often reflect the history of words and their links across groups of words and with words in other languages, while reformers present a counter-list of historically inconsistent spellings and cite arbitrary variations both within English and from the spellings of other European languages. Conservationists object that radically changed spellings would seem alien to the older generation, while texts in the old spelling would seem alien to the young; the change-over would also, they say, create uncertainty and cost a great deal. Reformers reply that the present system has already alienated many, that the spelling of earlier writers has in any case been updated in various ways, and reform could potentially save money. Anti-reformers fear that interfering with an ancient, delicately balanced system might make learning not easier but more difficult, while many who have taught regularized spelling (such as teachers of the *initial teaching alphabet*) have argued that a more regular system is easier to learn. Resistance to the idea of change is often provoked by the disturbingly unfamiliar appearance of radically reformed spellings, such as *kof* and *skool* for *cough* and *school*, which for many people are both aesthetically displeasing and suggest semi-literacy.

Among the practical objections to spelling reform is the problem of coordinating reform worldwide in so widely used a language as English, as well as the fact that there is no consensus among reformers on the system to be introduced. Anti-reformers argue in particular that, if English spelling is directly to represent pronunciation, there is no serious answer to the question: if reform is to be phonographic, on which accent of English should it be based? To these points reformers reply that the traditional orthography of English is quite simply out of date and is demonstrably difficult both to learn and to use. Literacy, they maintain, is a precondition for individual, national, and international prosperity, and the present spelling system of the world's foremost language hinders

the wider and fuller achievement of literacy in that language. As regards consensus and accent, they insist on the necessity of the major English-using communities getting together and discussing the problem, to find out what bases of agreement exist and to seek workable compromises, especially with regard to the phonemic analysis on which any international system might be built. Currently, there does not appear to be anything close to a meeting of minds in such matters.

**SPLIT INFINITIVE**. A prescriptive term for an INFINITIVE phrase such as *to cut* or *to enjoy* that has been opened up ('split', 'cleft') by the insertion of a word or phrase (especially an adverb), as in: '*to sharply cut* the federal deficit'; 'encouraging more people *to, for example, park* their cars'. Long a major bone of contention among teachers, grammarians, and commentators on style and usage, the split infinitive in the last two decades has become a matter of minor concern. For further discussion of the controversy, see USAGE GUIDANCE AND CRITICISM.

**SPOONERISM**. [From the name of the Reverend W. A. Spooner (1844–1930), Dean and Warden of New College, Oxford]. The transposition of the initial sounds of words, as in *ket of seas* (set of keys). The eponymous Spooner was reputed to make errors of this type, and a number of utterances are quoted as 'original spoonerisms': *a well-boiled icicle* (a well-oiled bicycle), *a scoop of Boy Trouts* (a troop of Boy Scouts), and *You have hissed all my mystery lectures and tasted a whole worm*. See SLIP OF THE TONGUE.

**SRANAN**, also **Sranan Tongo**, **Taki-Taki**. The major English-based creole of SURINAM in South America, used as a lingua franca by the coastal population and influential among speakers of Ndjuka and Saramaccan.

**SRI LANKA**. A country of South Asia, and member of the COMMONWEALTH. Languages: Sinhala, Tamil (both official, national languages), and English (often used in government and spoken by some 10% of the nation, including especially the Burghers). The first Europeans to visit the island were the Portuguese in 1505, who built a fort at Colombo. The Dutch forced them out in 1658, but failed to gain control of the whole island. The British defeated them in 1796 and established the colony of Ceylon in 1802, to which Tamil labourers were brought from south India to work on tea and coffee plantations. Ceylon became a Dominion of the British Empire in 1948 and the independent republic of Sri Lanka in 1972. Until about 1831, the teaching of English was in the hands of missionaries; when the government took control, there were 235 Protestant schools in the island, and until 1886 Christian schools and colleges predominated.

**English in Sri Lanka**. One result of the long-established tradition of such institutions was the emergence of two broad and at times hostile educated classes: an English-using and largely Christian minority and a Sinhala-educated majority, most of whom were Buddhists. Until 1948, three languages were used side by side, English, Sinhala, and Tamil. English served as the language of administration, the generally desired language of higher education, and a link language between the communities. In 1956, however, a socialist government replaced English with Sinhala, unleashing in the process social disturbance that has not yet come to an end. The Sinhala-only policy resulted in 'the sharp cleavage between Sinhalese and Tamils, most of whom are monolingual in their own tongues and therefore have no means of communication with members of the other community' (Rajiva Wijesinha, *An Anthology of Contemporary Sri Lankan Poetry in English*, Colombo, The British Council, 1988). In recent years, a three-language policy has been proposed that provides for equality among Sinhala, Tamil, and English, and to some extent seeks to restore the position of English, whose role in the community was greatly reduced from the 1960s to the 1980s. English in Sri Lanka, sometimes referred to as *Lankan English*, has a range of subvarieties based on proficiency in its use and the language background of its users. In general terms, it is a subvariety of SOUTH ASIAN ENGLISH sharing many features with INDIAN ENGLISH.

■ **STANDARD** ─────────────── ■

A prestigious and uniform variety of a LANGUAGE: *the literary standard, standard English*. The application of the term to language dates from the 18c, when the idea of standard shapes, sizes, and measures and of commercial and manufacturing standards began to develop. Since then, the concepts of a *standard language* (one with agreed norms and conventions) and a *language standard* (a level below which a 'cultivated' language should not fall) have been closely associated. For some, the expressions are two sides of the same linguistic coin: the standard is and should be the highest and best form of a language. For others, there is no necessary tie between the two: a standard language is an averaging-out of differences, neither higher nor better than any other variety of a language, and used with particular ends in mind. For others still, uncertainty may lead to ambivalence and confusion about the relative merit of standards and dialects. DIALECT, colloquial usage, and slang are often lumped together, with greater or less discrimination, as *nonstandard*, *SUBSTANDARD*, or *deviant* forms when judged against a dominant form that is taught in all schools and used by all major public and private institutions.

**Standards and languages**. In medieval times, the vernaculars of Europe were overshadowed by LATIN, the language of scriptural truth, learning, and debate: the gold standard, as it were, against which base VERNACULAR metal was judged. During the 12–16c, however, an accumulation of events and processes demoted Latin and promoted some vernaculars (such as Northern FRENCH over Occitan, the Romance language of southern France) and some varieties of some vernaculars (such as the East Midland dialect of English over other dialects). These events and processes were:

**1.** *Ethnic and cultural unification*. Many groups using the same languages began to develop a firmer sense of unity. If the unity lacked political cohesion, as in Italy and Germany, linguistic refinement was fostered in certain cities and courts and through certain literary styles. If the unity was accompanied by political centralization, as in France, Spain, and England, linguistic refinement was fostered by a capital where the court resided. Such forms as Parisian French, Castilian SPANISH, and the English of south-east England became the 'good' forms of those languages: that is, those drawn from or influenced by Latin. The presence of a strong, literate business class further enhanced the prestige and utility of metropolitan forms of speech and writing.

**2. *The growth of vernacular literatures***. New literatures developed as counter-points to Latin in such languages as Italian, Spanish, French, GERMAN, and English. They owed much to Latin and GREEK in terms of the genres, formulas, and allusions available to them, but differed from them in being widely understood. They were able to exploit, among other things, popular epic cycles such as the *Matter of Britain* (Arthur, the Round Table, the Holy Grail) and the *Matter of France* (Charlemagne and Roland).

**3. *The invention of movable type***. The use of PRINTING presses in the Rhineland from the mid-15c promoted standard letters, uniform formats and sizes of paper, and over time more regularized orthographies. The presses developed a greater influence over religious, literary, public, official, and educational language than scribes had ever had over the medieval and classical languages. In the case of English, Caxton and later printers, though at times anxious about their usages, built on a relatively stable written standard that had already been used for some decades by the clerks of Chancery when writing official documents.

**4. *The legacy of Latin***. During the Renaissance, the flow of elements of NEO-LATIN (Latin with admixtures of Greek) into the new 'high' forms of the vernaculars made them more effective as vehicles of learning and shed on them some of the lustre of the classics. This was particularly true of English, already receptive to the vocabulary of the Romance languages because of the impact of Norman French since the 11c.

**5. *Translating the Bible***. The questioning of the authority of the Pope and the Roman Catholic Church before, during, and after the Reformation also served to weaken the hold of Latin, the language of the Mass and of St Jerome's Vulgate Bible. In northern Europe in particular, the BIBLE in an élite ecclesiastical language ceased to be acceptable. When it was translated directly from the original HEBREW and Greek into such vernaculars as English, the variety used for the TRANSLATION became privileged by that use, much as Latin had been privileged before.

**Conclusion**. The development of vernaculars such as French and English and of high forms of those vernaculars such as educated Parisian French and educated south-eastern English depended therefore on the existence of a royal court, a literature associated with that court, laws and ordinances promulgated by court and parliament, the aspirations of a growing middle class, increasing literacy in writing and print, and schools inspired by Latin and the grammatical descriptions of Latin. Such forms benefited from the sense of an educated and refined minority set by Providence over an uneducated and unrefined majority in town and country, a sense that continued uninterrupted from the Middle Ages to at least the American and French Revolutions in the late 18c.

See BAD ENGLISH, CHANCERY STANDARD, CLASSICAL LANGUAGE, CULTIVATED, EDUCATED AND UNEDUCATED, GENERAL ENGLISH, GOOD ENGLISH, GRAMMATICALITY, HISTORY OF ENGLISH, NORM, NORMATIVE, PROPER, RECEIVED, RECEIVED PRONUNCIATION, RECEIVED STANDARD AND MODIFIED STANDARD, REFINED, U AND NON-U.

**STANDARD ACCENT**. An ACCENT that is (taken to be) STANDARD for a language or variety of a language: 'The standard accent—the one that is regionless rather than regional—is the accent of a minority . . . and those who speak it are associated with high status, socially, politically and economically' ( J. K. Chambers, in *In Search of the Standard in Canadian English*, 1986).

**STANDARD DIALECT**. A term in LINGUISTICS for a part of a language traditionally equated with the language itself, and seen as the product of such 'refining' forces as use at a royal court, by the middle classes, and in LITERATURE, PRINTING, publishing, and education. Because the standard has generally been set apart from and above *DIALECT*, the phrase *standard dialect* is sometimes used to indicate that, in linguistic terms, it too can be regarded as a dialect, despite its special status. In popular terms, the expression may well appear to be a contradiction in terms.

■ **STANDARD ENGLISH** ───── ■

A widely used term that resists easy definition but is used as if most educated people nonetheless know precisely what it refers to. Some consider its meaning self-evident: it is both the usage and the ideal of 'good' or 'educated' users of English. A geographical limitation has, however, often been imposed on this definition, such as the usage of educated people in Britain alone, England alone, of southern England alone, or the usage of educated people in North America and Britain generally. Others still find STANDARD English at work throughout the English-speaking world. For some it is a monolith, with more or less strict rules and conventions; for others it is a range of overlapping varieties, so that standard AmE is distinct from but similar to standard BrE. Although for some the term is negative, for most it appears to be either neutral or positive, referring to something important: 'Standard English (by whatever name it is known) is the variety of English that is manifestly recognised in our society as the prestigious variety' (Sidney GREENBAUM, in *English Today* 18, Apr. 1989).

**A minority form**. Some commentators regard standard English as a convenient fiction, like the law; others see it as a thoroughly inconvenient fiction built on social élitism and educational privilege. Even the distinction in writing between *Standard English* with two capital letters and *standard English* with only one implies that the form may be viewed as more or less institutional. It is generally agreed that standard English contrasts (often strongly) with other kinds of English, but there is no consensus about the best way of describing and discussing this contrast: for example, as between 'standard' and 'dialect', 'standard' and 'nonstandard', or 'standard' and 'substandard', or some mix of these. It is also usually agreed that standard English is a minority form. Some consider that this has always been so and probably always will be so; others see standard English as a social and political good to which all citizens of English-speaking countries have a birthright and/or should aspire; others again are less certain, or are hostile to the concept. The precise proportion of users of standard English to users of other kinds is not known, and may not be knowable; it is also seldom discussed. Even so, however, there appears to be a consensus that such a form exists, and serves (or should serve) as the basis for public and private education in English-speaking countries and in English-medium schools elsewhere.

**A general definition**. In everyday usage, *standard English* is taken to be the variety most widely accepted and understood within an English-speaking country or throughout the English-speaking world. It is more or less free of regional, class, and other shibboleths, although the issue of a 'standard accent' often causes trouble and tension. It is sometimes presented as the 'common core' (what is left when all regional and other distinctions are stripped away), a view that remains controversial because of the difficulty of deciding where core ends and peripheries begin. Linguists generally agree on three things: (1) The standard is most easily identified in print, whose conventions are more or less uniform throughout the world, and some use the term *print standard* for that medium. (2) Standard forms are used by most presenters of news on most English-language radio and television networks, but with regional and other variations, particularly in accent. (3) Use of standard English relates to social class and level of education, often considered (explicitly or implicitly) to match the average level of attainment of students who have finished secondary-level schooling.

**A negative definition**. In 'What *is* Standard English?' (*RELC Journal*, Singapore, 1981), the British applied linguist and language teacher Peter Strevens sought to establish the nature of standard English by saying what it was not:

(i) It is not an arbitrary, *a priori* description of English, or of a form of English, devised by reference to standards of moral value, or literary merit, or supposed linguistic purity, or any other metaphysical yardstick—in short, 'Standard English' cannot be defined or described in terms such as 'the best English,' or 'literary English,' or 'Oxford English,' or 'BBC English.'

(ii) It is not defined by reference to the usage of any particular group of English-users, and especially not by reference to a social class—'Standard English' is *not* 'upper class English' and it is encountered across the whole social spectrum, though not necessarily in equivalent use by all members of all classes.

(iii) It is not statistically the most frequently occurring form of English, so that 'standard' here does not mean 'most often heard.'

(iv) It is not imposed upon those who use it. True, its use by an individual may be largely the result of a long process of education; but Standard English is neither the product of linguistic planning or philosophy (for example as exists for French in the deliberations of the Academie Francaise, or policies devised in similar terms for Hebrew, Irish, Welsh, Bahasa Malaysia, etc); nor is it a closely-defined norm whose use and maintenance is monitored by some quasi-official body, with penalties imposed for non-use or mis-use. Standard English evolved: it was not produced by conscious design.

**A standard accent**? In Strevens's view, the term *standard English* is valuable because it helps account for a range of distinctions and attitudes, offers a label for the gram-matical and lexical components of the core taught to all students of the language, and constitutes the unifying element within the enormous diversity of the language. He ar-gued strongly, however, that the standard applies to grammar, vocabulary, writing, and print, but not to accent (except as a pro-nunciation target in the teaching of English as a foreign language). However, although it is widespread among contemporary 'lib-eral' linguists, this view is relatively recent and is not universal. Use of the term to in-clude, and specifically identify, an accent (and most commonly the accent known as RECEIVED PRONUNCIATION) has long been common and continues in use: *US* 'The British version of standard English, RP, is the same for all speakers regardless of their place of origin' (W. Nelson Francis, *The Eng-lish Language: An Introduction*, 1967); *UK* 'Both CHAUCER and SHAKESPEARE rhymed *cut* with our present-day (southern) standard English *put*' (John Honey, *Does Accent Matter?*, 1989). See RECEIVED STANDARD ENGLISH. The ques-tion of whether *standard English* does, can, or ought to include norms of speech remains the most controversial of the many difficult issues associated with the term.

**An institutional definition**. The Kingman Report on the teaching of English in Eng-land and Wales, submitted to the British government in 1988, began with a state-ment defining standard English that pre-sented the variety as virtually limitless in its reach yet closely bound to one medium:

All of us can have only partial access to Standard English: the language itself exists like a great social bank on which we all draw and to which we all contribute. As we grow older, and encounter a wider range of experience, we encounter more of the language, but none of us is ever going to know and use all the words in the Oxford English Dictionary, which is itself being constantly up-dated, nor are we going to produce or to encounter all possible combinations of the structures which are permissible in English. . . . It is important to be clear about the nature of Standard English. It developed from one of the Middle English dialects (East Midlands—the dialect first printed by Caxton) to become the written form used by all writers of English, no matter which dialect area they come from. It is the fact of being the written form which establishes it as the standard. And it is the fact of being the written form which means that it is used not only in Britain but by all writers of English throughout the world, with remarkably little variation.

**Standards and the standard**. The figura-tive strength of the term *standard English* has been considerable. Just as there was at one time only one standard yard, kept in the capital as a measure against which all yards everywhere might be checked, so (by exten-sion in the 19c) there was only one standard language, 'kept' in or near London for the 'same' purpose. Even after a war established the US as a separate centre of English, years passed before the British (and indeed many Americans) began to accept that govern-ment, writers, and publishers had set up a second centre and with it a second yardstick for the language. Even after 200 years, old ways of talking about the language die hard: 'The British are quick to point out how different American English is from Standard English' (Mandy Loader, *EFL Gazette*, Apr. 1990). Despite the time lag and the confusion of terms, however, there ap-pears to be little doubt that since at least the early 19c two yardsticks have existed for English, and that in principle more are possible, if not already actual.

**A standard of standards**. Among the ob-jective indicators that a language or a vari-ety of a language has a standard form are such artefacts as GRAMMARS and DICTIONAR-IES and such cultural achievements as a literary canon. It was taken to be proof positive of the success of French as a national and international language that by the end of the 17c it had all three. English had only achieved this status by the time the American colonies declared their independence. By the middle of the 19c, the US also had its grammars, its dictionaries, and its literary canon, although it took until the early 20c for many Americans to feel sure that 'American English' and 'American literature' were firmly established. In more recent times, Australia and Canada have produced national dictionaries and style guides, and have begun to acknowledge the extent and vitality of their literatures in English. In this, they appear to be experiencing afresh what happened in Britain and America. Some commentators favour the development and acceptance of various national standards: an indefinite number of distinct centres of gravity for a vastly complex world language. Others see such a plurality of 'Standard Englishes' as disruptive and disturbing. The paradox of the 1990s is the possibility that there can be, at one and the same time, a range of national standards and a single broadly recognizable international standard that subsumes them: a standard of standards. Even more than in the past, it is a creature born of consensus. See CLASSICAL LANGUAGE.

**STANDARD LANGUAGE**. A term for the form of a language used, for example, in general publishing, the news media, education, government, such professions as law and medicine, and by especially the middle classes. See STANDARD.

**STANDARD VARIETY**. A term in LINGUISTICS for the STANDARD form of a language: 'The standard variety of British or American English would perhaps not have served this purpose. The language of Indian writing in English is the natural product of an alien medium in interaction and interference with native languages and native cultures' (R. R. Mehrotra, 'Indian Literature in English', in *English Across Cultures, Cultures Across English*, eds. Ofelia Garcia & Ricardo Otheguy, 1989).

**STATIVE VERB**. A category of VERB that contrasts with *dynamic verb* in the aspect system of a language, and relates to state and

not action: in English, such verbs as *belong*, *love*. Syntactically, these verbs are used in simple rather than progressive tenses and generally not in the imperative (not \**Belong!*, but occasionally *Love me!*). Semantically, stative verbs refer to states of affairs (*belong, know, own*) in contrast to dynamic verbs that refer to actions (*buy, learn, jump*). In practice, the boundary between stative and dynamic verbs is sometimes fuzzy, and it is generally more useful to talk of stative and dynamic meaning and usage. In most varieties of English, some verbs are normally stative (therefore not \**I am owning this car*, \**Know how to give first aid!*), but others are partly stative and partly dynamic (not \**She is liking to help people*, but *How are you liking your new job?*; not \**I am forgetting their address*, but *Forget it!*). Some verbs belong to both categories *have* in *She has red hair* and *She is having dinner*. In IndE, the stative/dynamic distinction described above is considered standard, but it is widely ignored, so that expressions like *I am owning this car* and *She is liking to help people* are commonplace.

**STEM**, also **theme**. A term in GRAMMAR and WORD-FORMATION for a ROOT plus the element that fits it into the flow of language. Stems are basic to such inflected languages as Latin and rare in analytic languages like English. In Latin, the root *am* (love) and a thematic vowel -*a*- make up the stem *ama*-, to which appropriate inflections are added: -*s* in *amas* thou lovest, -*t* in *amat* he/she/it loves. The only stems in present-day English are acquisitions from Latin and Greek. Such stems have no syntactic role, but often decide the spelling and sometimes the pronunciation of derivatives: because *negative* and *auditory* derive from Latin *negare* to deny, *audire* to listen, their stems are *negat*- and *audit*-. Spellings like \**negitive* and \**audatory* are therefore not possible. Whereas the rhythm of Latin makes the quality and quantity of all stem vowels clear, the rhythm of English often does not do so, reducing the vowels to a schwa and therefore limiting sound–spelling correspondences. See THEMATIC VOWEL.

**STEM FORMATIVE**. A term in LINGUISTICS for a word element that attaches to a ROOT or BASE so that a SUFFIX can be then added: the -*t*- added to *dogma* to produce the STEM *dogmat*- in *dogmatic, dogmatism*.

**STEREOTYPE**. A STOCK concept, image, or type: *racial, ethnic, and sexual stereotypes; a stereotypical mean Scotsman/drunken Irishman*.

**STOCK**. Available for exploitation in acting, speaking, and writing, especially as part of a stock-in-trade of topics, arguments, plots, jokes, expressions, etc. 'If Agatha Christie works almost entirely with what the critics call "stock responses", she knows how to take advantage of our responding in a stock way to stock situations' (*The Times*, 20 Sept. 1975). Compare CLICHÉ, HACKNEYED.

**STOP**. **1.** Also (*full*) *point, full stop, period*. The mark (.) at the end of a sentence. See PERIOD, POINT, PUNCTUATION. **2.** Also *stop consonant*. In phonetics, a CONSONANT sound made by momentarily blocking the airstream. The two kinds of stop in English speech are the *PLOSIVE* (as in the *b*-sound of *bad*) and the *AFFRICATE* (as in the *ch*-sound of *choose*). See GLOTTAL STOP.

■ **STRESS** —————————— ■

**1.** In general usage, a word associated with emphasis, significance, tension, and strain. **2.** Also *ACCENT*. In poetics and phonetics, a term for the property by means of which syllables and words become *prominent*: that is, they are made to stand out from their background.

**Phonetic prominence**. Stress is not a single phonetic feature, stressed syllables having different kinds of phonetic prominence: (1) *Prominence of pitch*. A syllable is made prominent by a pitch movement on the syllable or by a pitch discontinuity involving a jump from the immediately preceding pitch. (2) *Prominence of duration*. Stressed syllables have full duration and may be prolonged, whereas unstressed syllables are likely to be shortened. (3) *Prominence of vowel quality*. Stressed syllables retain full vowel quality, whereas unstressed syllables may have weak vowels. (4) *Prominence of loudness*. Stressed syllables are generally said to be loud (although this is probably the least important kind of prominence for the recognition of stress in English). Stressed syllables with pitch prominence are said to be *accented* and a pitch contour or tone is associated with each accent.

**Word stress**. A property which makes some syllables in a word stand out. In writing and print, a stressed syllable is conventionally marked with the stress mark (') placed immediately before the syllable in phonetics and most contemporary dictionaries (but placed after it in many older works). The word 'foreign* is stressed on the first syllable, and *de'scribe* on the second. Longer words may have two or more stresses, in which case the main stress is referred to as *primary stress* and others as *secondary stress*. Secondary stress is marked with the stress mark (ˌ). The word *pho'tography* has just one stress on the second syllable, but ˌphoto'graphic* has primary stress on the third syllable and secondary stress on the first, while 'photoˌgraph* has primary stress on the first syllable and secondary stress on the third.

It is rare for unrelated English words to be distinguished solely by stress, as in *be'low, 'billow*. More commonly, related disyllabic words are stressed on different syllables, and the unstressed syllables may be reduced, for example, the verb *construct* is /kənˈstrʌkt/ and the noun *construct* is /ˈkɒnstrʌkt/. When a word is pronounced in isolation, it is treated as a tone group. The primary stress is the nucleus, and in isolation it is given a falling tone: ↓foreign, de↓scribe*. A secondary stress before the primary stress is the onset, which normally takes a level tone: photo↓graphic*. A secondary stress after the primary stress is an unreduced syllable in the tail of the tone group. See TONE.

**Sentence stress**. The process whereby some words in an utterance are made prominent while others remain in the background, as in: *THAT is the END of the NEWS*. In strict phonetic terms, *sentence stress* is a misnomer, as the domain of these patterns is not the sentence but the tone group. In general, lexical words (nouns, verbs, adjectives, adverbs in *-ly*) have sentence stress, unless they refer to information already provided, in which case the resulting pattern is *contrastive stress*. Grammatical words are more likely to be unstressed, and may be reduced to weak forms.

**Contrastive stress**. The process by which stress is used to imply a contrast, as in *MARY can go* (not Susan) and *Mary CAN go* (she is free to do so). A fall–rise tone with a wide pitch range is often associated with contrast: *I can't go on ↗ MONday* leads to the implication 'but I can go some other day'.

Whole words can be contrasted in a similar way in many languages, but English is unusual in that parts of words can be contrasted: *I wouldn't say she's an emplo ⟋YEE she is actually an emplo YER*. In such cases, the normal pattern of word stress is overridden. The term is also used to refer to a stress pattern relating a sentence to its context: without preceding information, the sentence *Ram's got a motorbike* is likely to be stressed on the first and last words, *RAM'S got a MOTorbike*. On the other hand, *RAM'S got a motorbike* belongs to a context where possessing a motorbike is already under discussion and *motorbike* is not given sentence stress because it is not in contrast with anything else (*bicycle, car*).

**Stress and weak forms**. The RHYTHM of English leads to special reduced forms in some monosyllabic grammatical words in unstressed contexts: in isolation, the words *an, from, his* are pronounced /æn, frɔm, hɪz/, but in context are usually reduced to /ən, frəm, əz/. The process of reduction includes replacing the vowel with a weak vowel, usually schwa, and dropping an initial /h/. If the vowel is lost altogether, the result is a contraction, represented in informal writing by an apostrophe replacing the missing vowel: *she's here*. Although a consonant may also have been dropped (for example, the *h* of *has* in *She's arrived*), this is not normally indicated. Weak forms are natural in all native varieties of English, even in slow, careful speech. This also applies to the dropping of /h/ from weak forms, which is different from the dropping of *h* from accented syllables, which is not normal in some varieties, such as RP, and is widely stigmatized in BrE.

**Stress shift**. It is a common feature of English that when derivative words are formed by means of certain suffixes, the (primary) stress shifts from a particular syllable in the base word to a new syllable in the derived word: *átom/atómic, cómplex/compléxity, devélopment/developméntal* (with appropriate adaptations in the fullness or weakness of the vowels). Such *stress shift* or *accent shift* occurs only in words of French, Latin, and Greek background, in terms of particular suffixes, such as *-ic, -ity, -al*, and not in words of vernacular Germanic background.

**STRINE**. A non-technical word coined by Alistair Morrison, to represent an alleged Australian pronunciation of *Australian*. Writing under the pseudonym Afferbeck Lauder ('alphabetical order') and as Professor of Strine Studies at the University of Sinny (Sydney), Morrison published a series of humorous articles in the *Sydney Morning Herald*, some of which were later collected under the title *Let Stalk Strine* (Sydney, 1965). The series made much of such features as ELISION, ASSIMILATION, and METANALYSIS, as characteristic of Broad Australian: *Emma Chisit* How much is it?; *money* Monday; *ass prad* house proud; *tan cancel* town council. The term has had some local and international acceptance as a name for a stereotype of pronunciation and syntax (the 'style' of AUSTRALIAN ENGLISH). Examples like *Gloria Soame* (glorious home) indicate the importance of EYE DIALECT in achieving the desired effect.

**STRONG VERB**. A term in the description of GERMANIC LANGUAGES for a VERB that indicates such differences as tense by modifying its vowels: English *ring, rang, rung*. In contrast, WEAK VERBS add inflections: *play, played, played*. These terms are usually replaced in grammars of MODERN ENGLISH by *regular verb* (in place of *weak verb*) and *irregular verb* (in place of *strong verb*). In Old English, strong verbs could have as many as four different vowels, since the first- and third-person singular in the past differed from all the other past forms: compare *was* and *were* in the Modern English past of the verb *be*. An example from OLD ENGLISH is the verb *helpan*, with *e* in the present tense, but past *healp* (first- and third-person singular) and *hulpon*, and the past participle *holpen* (with the -*en* inflection found in some Modern English irregular verbs: *shaken, taken*). In Modern English, this verb has become weak (*help, helped*), a change that has affected many other strong verbs over the centuries, such as *climb, step, walk*. The strong verbs that have survived into Modern English seldom retain the original distinctions, and all (except the highly irregular *be*, with *was* and *were*) have lost the two forms for the past. In some Modern English verbs, the vowels of the past and the past participle have become identical (*sting, stung*), and in others all three forms are the same (*put*). Some originally strong verbs have regular variants (*swell, swelled*, or *swollen*). A few originally weak verbs have become strong, such as *wear, dig, fling*. Differences may occur between varieties: (1) *dive, dived* in BrE, but often *dive, dove* in AmE; (2) *sell, sold* and *tell, told* in standard English worldwide, but *sell, sellt* and *tell, tellt* in SCOTS. Occasionally, for facetious purposes, people play with strong forms: *I thunk very hard about it* and *Where were you brung up?* In general, new verbs in Modern English are regular; that is, formed on the pattern of weak verbs, the pronunciation of the *-ed* inflection as /(ə)d/ or /t/ varying systematically according to the immediately preceding sound. Verbs formed by prefixation or compounding usually take the same forms as the verbs on which they are based: *offset, babysit,* and (both regular and irregular) *deepfreeze.* Some phrasal verbs prefer a weak form (contrast *The car sped up the hill* and *The car speeded up*).

**STRUCTURALISM**. A theory or method which assumes that the elements of a field of study make up a structure in which their interrelationship is more important than any element considered in isolation. Structuralist principles have been applied since the beginning of the 20c, primarily by francophone theorists, to various fields of interest: in linguistics, it is associated with the work of Ferdinand de Saussure in Switzerland and Leonard Bloomfield in the US; in anthropology, with Claude Lévi-Strauss in France; in literature and semiotics, with Roland Barthes in France; and in studies of history with Michel Foucault in France. Generally, structuralists follow de Saussure in emphasizing the arbitrary nature of the relationship between a SIGN (*le signifiant* the signifier) and what it signifies (*le signifié* the signified), and in treating objects of study (whether phoneme inventories, kinship groups, or texts) as closed systems abstracted from their social and historical contexts. See LINGUISTIC SIGN, SEMANTICS, SEMIOTICS.

**STRUCTURAL LINGUISTICS**. An approach to LINGUISTICS which treats language as an interwoven structure, in which every item acquires identity and validity only in relation to the other items in the system. All linguistics in the 20c is structural in this sense, as opposed to much work in the 19c, when it was common to trace the history of individual words. Insight into the structural nature of language is due to the Swiss linguist Ferdinand de Saussure, who compared language to a

game of chess, noting that a chess piece in isolation has no value and that a move by any one piece has repercussions on all the others. An item's role in a structure can be discovered by examining those items which occur alongside it and those which can be substituted for it. The structural approach developed in a strong form in the US in the second quarter of the century, when the prime concern of American linguists was to produce a catalogue of the linguistic elements of a language, and a statement of the positions in which they could occur, ideally without reference to meaning. Leonard BLOOMFIELD was the pioneer among these structuralists, attempting to lay down a rigorous methodology for the analysis of any language. Various Bloomfieldians continued to refine and experiment with this approach until the 1960s, but from the late 1950s onwards, *structural linguistics* has sometimes been used pejoratively, because supporters of *generative linguistics* (initiated by Noam CHOMSKY) have regarded the work of the American structuralists as too narrow in conception. They have argued that it is necessary to go beyond a description of the location of items to produce a grammar which mirrors a native speaker's intuitive knowledge of language.

**STUNT WORD**. An informal term for a WORD created and used to produce a special effect or attract attention, as if it were part of the performance of a stunt man or a conjuror. Stunt words used to exhibit and practise spelling patterns are a feature of the children's books of Theodor Seuss Geisel (Dr Seuss): 'Did you ever have the feeling, / there's a WASKET in your BASKET? / . . . Or a NUREAU in your BUREAU? / . . . Or a WOSET in your CLOSET?' (from *There's a Wocket in my Pocket!*, 1974). The preceding example derives from the work of an individual. Many stunt formations can, however, be the outcome of group effort, as for example forms based on the letters *y–p* (standing for 'young professional'), particularly fashionable in marketing and media circles in the 1980s, such as: *yuppie* (young urban professional), *yumpie* (young upwardly mobile professional), *yap* (young aspiring professional), *mumpie* (Malaysian yumpie), *McYuppie* (Scottish yuppie), and *yuckie* (a yuppie who makes you sick). Compare BUZZ WORD, NEOLOGISM, NONCE WORD, NONSENSE.

# ■ STYLE ─────────────── ■

A general term that primarily means a way of doing things, with additional senses such as doing them appropriately, doing them well or badly, doing them in a distinctive way, or doing them in one of a number of ways.

**Linguistic style.** Someone may write in an *ornate style*, speak in a *laconic style*, and have an *aggressive style* when arguing. In all such cases, the way in which people do things can be seen to vary: from one medium to another (speech to writing), from one situation to another (formal to informal, legal to journalistic), and from one period or genre to another (Elizabethan to Romantic, prose to poetry, sonnet to ode). *Yours faithfully* is recognizably a formula of writing, *He's kicked the bucket* is a slangy equivalent of the euphemism *He's passed away*. Although stylistic variation can be discussed in terms of groups, generations, movements, and the like, it is most apparent in terms of individuals. No two people have the same style in writing or playing a game; as Sir Thomas Browne put it in the 16c, *stylus arguit hominem* (style maketh the man). In the same way, for such 20c structural linguists as Ferdinand de Saussure, style in language was a matter of *parole* (individual performance) rather than *langue* (the collective system). Readers recognize distinctive authorial styles (the loose sentence structures and grotesque metaphors of Charles Dickens, the periodic sentences and abstract diction of Henry James) and also differences between the styles of writers at different points in their careers (the play of sound in Shakespeare's 'early style' in his comedies as distinct from the richly figurative style in his last plays).

**Appropriateness.** The definition of lingusitic *style* as a 'way' or 'manner' implies distinctiveness, that there are phonetic, grammatical, and lexical features which mark out a text, register, genre, or situation: for example, legalisms like the BrE *m'lud* (my lord: said to a judge); the often ambiguous ellipses of headlinese (*Defence cuts off agenda*); and the ways in which a secretary on the telephone handles different callers. In the study of literature, style is a matter principally of design and theme, but in the works of writers of usage manuals and style guides, it is a matter principally of layout and the physical appearance of a manuscript, typescript, or printed text. In both areas, however, a sense of *appropriateness* or *appropriacy* is crucial: that choices have been made or must be made that take into account situation, occasion, subject matter, and audience (readers, listeners, viewers).

The idea of appropriateness has its origins in the canon of classical rhetoric known as *elocutio*. The three ways of speaking or writing were the *high* or *grand style*, the *middle style*, and *plain* or *low style*, all three of which were carried over into the European vernaculars. The grand declamatory style was associated with epic poetry and had Homer and Virgil as its models; it is well illustrated in English by Milton's *Paradise Lost* (1667). The restrained middle style was used in the main for education and edification; it was the basis of the English tradition of sermons from Aelfric in the 10c to Sir Thomas More in the 16c. The plain or low style was close to colloquial speech, used relatively simple vocabulary and syntax, and was the medium of popular entertainment in ballads and folk-tales. By and large, in both classical and English literature and oratory, the three styles have been points of reference rather than dogmatic categories, allowing for what 20c linguists call *style-switching*.

**Good style, bad style.** Jonathan Swift's definition of style as 'proper words in proper places' suggests approval, that styles can be evaluated, prescribed, and proscribed. In the 18c, the leaders of literate opinion were interested in elevating the literary language and promoting elegant and refined everyday usage among the upper and middle classes. They were by and large prescriptive, laying the foundation of attitudes to grammar, style, and usage which were not significantly questioned, particularly in educational institutions, until after the Second World War. Style in the evaluative sense tends to fall into two broad groups: 'good', 'rich', 'elegant', 'refined', 'careful', and 'precise' style and usage on the one hand, and 'bad', 'poor', 'crude', 'vulgar', 'sloppy', and 'slovenly' style and usage on the other. The latter has tended to be associated with colloquial, especially dialect, speech.

To be said to have 'style' is a high compliment similar to having 'class'; to be said to have 'no style (at all)' is a serious adverse judgement. The precise social, cultural, and psychological bases for such assessments of speech and writing (especially if part of a consensus) are by no means clear. They appear, however, to involve a mixture of criteria associated with *status* (usually educational, often social, sometimes economic), *ability* (in such matters as selection, structure, clarity, delivery, and wit), and AES-THETICS (in such matters as balance, elegance, and euphony). Literary and other critics of the use of language generally agree that 'good style' is difficult to describe and by no means a matter of general agreement, yet there is often something on which wide agreement is possible, with regard to the style and success of a writer or speaker, just as there is often a consensus about the style and success of an athlete or musician.

**STYLISTICS**. The branch of LINGUISTICS that studies STYLE in language and especially in works of LITERATURE. It is less oriented towards writer (or speaker) than is literary (and dramatic) criticism and more towards TEXT, reader, and linguistic form. The advent of the computer has given rise to *computational stylistics*, which seeks to establish the distinctive patterns within texts and has been used to help establish the authorship of texts.

■ **SUBJECT** ────────────── ■

A traditional term for a major constituent of the SENTENCE. In a binary analysis derived from logic, the sentence is divided into *subject* and *predicate*, as in *Alan* (subject) *has married Nita* (predicate). In declarative sentences, the subject typically precedes the verb: *Alan* (subject) *has married* (verb) *Nita* (direct OBJECT). In interrogative sentences, it typically follows the first or only part of the verb: *Did* (verb) *Alan* (subject) *marry* (verb) *Nita* (direct object)? The subject can generally be elicited in response to a question that puts *who* or *what* before the verb: *Who has married Nita?—Alan*. Where concord is relevant, the subject determines the number and person of the verb: *The student is complaining/The students are complaining*; *I am tired/He is tired*. Many languages have special CASE forms for words in the subject, such as the *nominative* in Latin; and in English the subject requires a particular form (the *subjective*) in certain pronouns: *I* (subject) *like her, and she* (subject) *likes me*.

**Kinds of subject**. A distinction is sometimes made between the grammatical subject (as characterized above), the psychological subject, and the logical subject: (1) The *psychological subject* is the theme or topic of the sentence, what the sentence is about, and the predicate is what is said about the topic. The grammatical and psychological subjects typically coincide, though the identification of the sentence topic is not always clear: *Labour and Conservative MPs clashed angrily yesterday over the poll tax*. Is the topic of the sentence the MPs or the poll tax? (2) The *logical subject* refers to the agent of the action; *our children* is the logical subject in both these sentences, although it is the grammatical subject in only the first: *Our children planted the oak sapling*; *The oak sapling was planted by our children*. Many sentences, however, have no agent: *Stanley has back trouble*; *Sheila is a conscientious student*; *Jenny likes jazz*; *There's no alternative*; *It's raining*.

**Pseudo-subjects**. The last sentence also illustrates the absence of a psychological subject, since *it* is obviously not the topic of the sentence. This so-called 'prop *it*' is a dummy subject, serving merely to fill a structural need in English for a subject in a sentence. In this respect, English contrasts with languages such as Latin, which can omit the subject, as in *Veni, vidi, vici* (I came, I saw, I conquered: with no need for the Latin pronoun *ego*, I). Like prop *it*, 'existential *there*' in *There's no alternative* is the grammatical subject of the sentence, but introduces neither the topic nor (since there is no action) the agent.

**Non-typical subjects**. Subjects are typically noun phrases, but they may also be finite and non-finite clauses: *'That nobody understands me* is obvious'; *'To accuse them of negligence* was a serious mistake'; *'Looking after the garden* takes me several hours a week in the summer.' In such instances, finite and infinitive clauses are commonly postposed and anticipatory *it* takes their place in subject position: *'It is obvious that nobody understands me'*; *'It was a serious mistake to accuse them of negligence.'* Occasionally, prepositional phrases and adverbs function as subjects: *'After lunch* is best for me'; *'Gently does it.'*

**Subjectless sentences**. Subjects are usually omitted in imperatives, as in *Come here* rather than *You come here*. They are often absent from non-finite clauses (*'Identifying* *the rioters* may take us some time') and from verbless clauses ('New filters will be sent to you *when available*'), and may be omitted in certain contexts, especially in informal notes (*Hope to see you soon*) and in coordination (*The telescope is 43 ft long, weighs almost 11 tonnes, and is more than six years late*). See ANTICIPATORY IT, WORD ORDER.

## ■ SUBJUNCTIVE ─────── ■

A grammatical category that contrasts particularly with INDICATIVE in the MOOD system of verbs in various languages, and expresses uncertainty or non-factuality. Some languages have a range of subjunctive tenses: Latin (*Caveat emptor*: Let the buyer beware); French (*Je veux que tu travailles*, literally 'I want that you should work', I would like you to work). There was such a system in Old English (*Ne hē ealu ne drince opp wīn*: Nor shall he drink ale or wine), but in Modern English there are few distinctive subjunctive forms and the use of the term is controversial. Grammarians have traditionally described English as if it had a subjunctive system comparable to Latin and French, with present and past subjunctive tenses. This approach poses problems, because the 'present' subjunctive is used in subordinate clauses referring to both present and past time: *They are demanding that we pay now* and *They demanded that we pay there and then*. In form, this subjunctive is identical with the base of the verb (the bare infinitive), which means that, when the reference is to present time, it only differs from the indicative (except with the verb *be*) in the third-person singular: *We suggest that he leave soon* as against *They say he leaves at dawn tomorrow*. With past reference, the difference from the indicative is noticeable for all persons, as in *We suggested he leave*.

This subjunctive has three uses: (1) *Mandative*. Mainly in subordinate clauses, following a verb, adjective, or noun expressing a past or present command, suggestion, or other theoretical possibility: *I insist that she disband the team*; *It is essential that it be disbanded*; *She ignored his request that she disband the team*. When a negative is used with this subjunctive, it precedes the verb: *He requested that she not embarrass him*, except with *be* when *not be* and *be not* are both possible: *He was anxious that his name be not/not be brought into disrepute*. The mandative subjunctive is commoner in AmE than BrE, but

appears to be on the increase in BrE. In both, but especially in BrE, it can be replaced by a *should-* construction or an indicative: *He requested that she should not embarrass him*; *He was anxious that his name was not brought into disrepute*. (2) *Conditional and concessive*. Sometimes formally in subordinate clauses of condition or concession: *If music be the food of love, play on . . .* ; *Whether that be the case or not . . .* ; *Though he ask a thousand times, the answer is still NO*. The alternatives are an indicative or a *should*-phrase: *If music is . . .* ; *Though he should ask . . .* This usage does not extend to past time. (3) *Formulaic*. In independent clauses mainly in set expressions. Some follow normal subject–verb word order (*God save the Queen! Heaven forbid!*), while others have inversion of main verb and subject (*Long live the Queen!*; *Far be it from me to interfere*). *Come* plus a subject introduces a subordinate clause: *Come the end of the month, (and) there'll be more bills to pay*.

The 'past' subjunctive is now often called the *were*-subjunctive, because this is the only form in which there is a distinction from the indicative, and then only in the first- and third-person singular: *If I were you . . . as* opposed to *If I was you*. It is used with present and future (not past) reference in various hypothetical clauses, including condition: *If only I were young again*; *If he were asked, he might help*; *This feels as if it were wool*; *I wish she were here now*; *Suppose this were discovered*; *I'd rather it were concealed*. In popular and non-formal speech and writing, the *were*-subjunctive is often replaced by the indicative *was*, which brings this verb into line with other verbs, where the past tense is similarly used for hypotheses about the present and future: *If only I knew how*; *I'd rather you said nothing*. *Were* is, however, widely preferred in *If I were you . . .* In the fixed phrase *as it were* (*He's captain of the ship, as it were*), *were* cannot be replaced by *was*. The use of *were* instead of *was* to refer to a real past possibility is generally considered an over-correction: *\*If I were present on that occasion, I remember nothing of it*. This contrasts with the purely hypothetical past, *If I had been present . . .* , which strongly implies *but I was not*.

**SUBORDINATE CLAUSE**, also **dependent clause**. A CLAUSE that cannot normally function independently as a SENTENCE.

# ■ SUBORDINATION ─────── ■

In grammatical theory, a relationship between two units in which one is a constituent of the other or dependent on it. The subordinate unit is commonly a subordinate clause organized 'under' a superordinate clause. Such organization can be described in two ways: the subordinate unit as a constituent of the superordinate unit, and the subordinate unit as dependent on but distinct from the superordinate unit. In the SENTENCE, *They did it when they got home,* the subordinate *when*-clause may be either a constituent of its superordinate main CLAUSE, which begins with *They* and is coextensive with the entire sentence, or dependent on a more limited main clause *They did it.* There is in principle no limit (apart from comprehensibility and practicality) to the subordination of clauses one under another. In the sentence, *They saw that I was wondering who had won the competition,* the subordinate *who*-clause is a constituent of or dependent on its superordinate *that*-clause (which ends with *the competition*), while the *that*-clause is also a subordinate clause, in turn a constituent of or dependent on its superordinate clause beginning with *They.* Subordinate clauses may also be constituents of or dependent on phrases: in *What's the name of the woman who's winning the competition?,* the *who*-clause modifies the noun *woman.*

**Form.** Traditionally, part of a sentence can only be classed as a subordinate clause if it contains either an identifiable or an 'understood' finite verb. In contemporary grammatical analysis, however, subordinate clauses may be classed as: finite ('I think *that nobody is in*'); nonfinite ('He used to be shy, *staying on the fringes at parties*'); verbless ('She will help you, *if at all possible*'). Traditionally, the second category would be classed as a participial phrase and the third as a clause with the verb 'understood' (*it is*). Finite subordinate clauses are usually marked as subordinate either by an initial subordinating conjunction (*after* in *He got angry after I started to beat him at table-tennis*) or by an initial *wh*-word that also functions within the clause (*who* in *Most Iranians are Indo-Europeans who speak Persian,* where *who* is the subject of the subordinate clause). These subordination markers sometimes introduce nonfinite clauses (*while* in *I listened to the music while re-*

*vising my report*), and verbless clauses (*if* in *If necessary, I'll phone you.*'

**Function.** Subordinate clauses fall into four functional classes: *nominal, relative, adverbial, comparative.* Nominal or noun clauses function to a large extent like noun phrases: they can be subject of the sentence ('*That he was losing his hearing* did not worry him unduly') or direct object ('He knew *that he was losing his hearing*'). Relative or adjective/adjectival clauses modify nouns: the *that*-clause modifies *star* in 'She saw a star *that she had not seen before.*' Adverbial or adverb clauses function to a large extent like adverbs: the adverb *there* could replace the *where*-clause in 'You should put it back *where you found it.*' Comparative clauses are used in comparison and are commonly introduced by *than* or *as*: 'The weather is better *than it was yesterday*'; 'The weather is just as nice *as* it was yesterday.'

All such clauses occur in complex sentences. Subordination contrasts with COORDINATION, in which the units, commonly the clauses of a compound sentence, have equal status: the clauses joined by *but* in *We wanted to visit the cathedral first, but the children wanted to see the castle straight away.* Sentences in which both subordinate and coordinate clauses occur are compound-complex sentences: with *before* and *but* in *We wanted to visit the cathedral before we did anything else, but the children wanted to see the castle straight away.*

**SUBSTANDARD,** also **sub-standard.** A semi-technical term for usage that is not STANDARD or CORRECT, such as *He ain't done nothin'.* A variety of speech may also be so labelled: 'St. Mary's Lane, Lewes, is called "Simmery Lane" in local sub-standard speech' (*English Studies* 45, 1964). The term has often been used academically, without necessarily intending a negative judgement: 'In such communities the non-standard language can be divided, roughly, to be sure, and without a sharp demarcation, into *substandard speech,* intelligible at least, though not uniform, throughout the country, and *local dialect*' (Leonard Bloomfield, *Language*, 1933). Many linguists and teachers nowadays object to this use, arguing that in such phrases as *substandard housing* the term means 'of poor or low quality' and that usage referred to in the same way is perceived in the same way. They consequently prefer the term NONSTANDARD. Compare DEVIANT.

**SUBSTANTIVE**. A grammatical term that in the Middle Ages included both NOUN and adjective, but later meant noun exclusively. It is not usually found in later 20c English grammars. In such languages as Latin and French, the equivalent terms serve to distinguish the use of LATIN *nomen*, French *nom* (etc.) as 'name' from the grammatical use as 'noun', a distinction which is unnecessary in English. However, the term has been used to refer to nouns and any other parts of speech serving as nouns ('the substantive in English'). The adjective *local* is used substantively in the sentence *He had a drink at the local before going home* (that is, the local public house).

**SUBSTRATE**, also **substratum**. A LANGUAGE or aspect of a language which affects another usually more dominant language, often where the speech of a colonized people influences the superimposed language of the conquering group: for example, the syntax of GAELIC providing the model for the IrE construction *I am after eating my dinner* (I have eaten my dinner) in the English of bilingual English/Gaelic-speakers and of some unilingual English-speakers. Compare SUPERSTRATE.

**SUDAN**, also **the Sudan**. A country of north-eastern Africa. Languages: ARABIC (official), Nubian, and other indigenous languages. In the early 19c, the northern Sudan was controlled by Egypt. In 1899, the entire region became a condominium of Britain and Egypt (the *Anglo-Egyptian Sudan*), and in 1956, it became independent. The division between Arab and Nubian Muslims in the north and pagan and Christian societies in the south has been an on-going source of unrest. English was widely used in the 19c and earlier 20c, but currently has no official status. Of all the African nations colonially associated with Britain and English, Sudan has had least interest in maintaining the language, although English is more attractive to the non-Muslim south than to the Arabic-using north.

■ **SUFFIX** ——————————————————— ■

An AFFIX added at the end of a WORD, BASE, or ROOT to form a new word: *-ness* added to

*dark* to form *darkness*; *-al* added to *leg* to form *legal*. Two distinctions are usually made: (1) Between a derivational suffix proper, such as *-ness* and *-al*, which creates derivative words, and an inflectional *ending*, such as *-s* added to form the plurals of nouns, which changes the inflection of a word. (2) Between a *productive suffix*, which actively forms words (*-ness: darkness, newness, quaintness, wordiness*) and a *non-productive suffix*, which does not (*-ledge: knowledge*). There is a continuum from the highly through the mildly and rarely productive to the dormant and dead, and usage can vary according to time and place: the suffix *-y* has generally been added to vernacular nouns to form ADJECTIVES (*ease/easy, oil/oily, rain/rainy*) with some disyllabic bases (*paper/papery, powder/powdery*). In the 20c, however, *-y* has increasingly been added casually and often for nonce purposes to longer bases (sometimes with idiosyncratic or debatable spellings), including compounds and classical words: *chocolat(e)y, dry-biscuity, gardeny, linguisticky, statusy, teenagey, uppercrusty*.

**Origins**. In 1882, the philologist Walter W. Skeat noted: 'The number of suffixes in MODERN ENGLISH is so great, and the forms of several, especially in words derived through the FRENCH from LATIN, are so variable that an attempt to exhibit them all would tend to confusion' (*Etymological Dictionary of the English Language*). The diversity of the backgrounds from which the suffixes of English have been drawn, the different periods in which they have entered the language, and the different processes involved all contribute to the complexity of the subject. Most suffixes, however, fall into one of three groups:

**1. *Vernacular***. Suffixes in the main from OLD ENGLISH and other GERMANIC LANGUAGES: *-ish* as in *childish* is from Old English *an* is cognate with GERMAN *-isch* as in *kindisch*.

**2. *Romance***. Suffixes that have come especially from Old French and Latin: *-al* as in *legal* and *natural* derives either directly or through Old French from Latin *-alis* as in *legalis* and *naturalis*, and is cognate with the Modern French forms *-al* in *légal* and *-el* in *naturel*.

**3. *Greek***. Suffixes that have come mainly through NEO-LATIN and French: *-oid* as in *anthropoid* and *steroid* is from the combining

## THEMATIC GROUPS OF SUFFIXES

The major semantic groups of suffixes and suffix-like elements are listed, with examples of their use, in the groups below. The same element or a variant of an element may appear in more than one group, because many elements have more than one meaning and use. No attempt is made to signal the degree of productivity of any suffix listed.

**Forming agents, people, instruments** (feminine forms marked with an asterisk). *-ad\** naiad, *-aire* legionnaire, *-al* general, *-an* human, Cuban, sacristan, *-ant* claimant, *-ar* beggar, *-ard* sluggard, *-ary* fritillary, legionary, *-ast* enthusiast, *-aster* usageaster, *-ate* affiliate, magistrate, *-ator* aviator, *-atrix\** aviatrix, *-ean* epicurean, *-ee* employee, *-eer* engineer, *-ener* sharpener, *-ent* resident, *-er* mixer, runner, *-ess\** hostess, *-ete* athlete, *-ette\** usherette, *-i* Pakistani, *-ian* Australian, electrician, historian, simian, *-ic* cleric, stigmatic, herpetic, syphilitic, *-id* aphid, druid, *-ier* soldier, fusilier, *-iff* plaintiff, *-ifier* humidifier, *-ile* hostile, *-ine\** actorine, *-ion* hellion, *-ist* cyclist, mentalist, semanticist, *-ister* chorister, *-ite* ammonite, Hittite, Thatcherite, *-ive* captive, *-izer/iser* atomizer, *-oid* anthropoid, *-oon* octoroon, *-or* actor, *-ot* pilot, *-ote* zygote, *-ster* youngster, *-yst* analyst.

**Forming objects, items, concepts, substances** (scientific usages marked with an asterisk). *-a\** lava, ammonia, *-ad\** monad, *-ade* fusillade, lemonade, *-al\** methylal, *-alia\** mammalia, *-ane\** methane, *-ar\** pulsar, *-ary* capillary, *-ase\** oxidase, *-asm* orgasm, *-ate\** nitrate, *-eme\** phoneme, *-ene\** benzene, *-ese* manganese, *-iac* ammoniac, *-ian* obsidian, *-id* plasmid, *-ide* cyanide, *-il* fossil, *-in* insulin, protein, *-ine* caffeine, cocaine, plasticine, *-ino* neutrino, *-ism* organism, *-ite* dynamite, phosphite, *-ma* magma, *-mo* sixteenmo, *-ode\** electrode, nematode, *-oid* alkaloid, *-ol\** glycerol, *-oma\** carcinoma, *-ome\** genome, *-on\** photon, *-one* silicone, *-ose\** glucose, *-tron* cyclotron, *-um* platinum, *-us* phosphorus, *-yl\** methyl, *-yne\** alkyne, *-ysm* aneurysm.

**Forming states, conditions, situations, and instances**. *-acy* accuracy, *-age* baggage, blockage, wharfage, *-al* renewal, *-ale* morale, *-ance* clearance, *-ancy* occupancy, *-asm* enthusiasm, *-ation* communication, *-dom* kingdom, serfdom, *-efaction* liquefaction, *-ence* munificence, *-ency* consistency, *-erie* lingerie, *-ese* journalese, *-hood* adulthood, *-iasis* elephantiasis, *-ics* statistics, *-ie* bonhomie, *-ification* purification, *-ing* running, bridge-building, swimming pool, *-ion* junction, fusion, *-ism* Darwinism, euphemism, *-ition* tradition, *-itis* arthritis, telephonitis, *-ity* nudity, formality, humanity, ferocity, *-ization/isation* atomization, *-ledge* knowledge, *-ment* development, *-ness* darkness, *-or/our* color, labour, *-osis* osmosis, psychosis, *-red* hatred, *-ship* chieftainship, hardship, *-sis* synthesis, *-sy$^1$* minstrelsy, *-sy$^2$* epilepsy, *-th* warmth, *-tude* magnitude, *-ure* debenture, departure, *-ution* distribution, *-y* infamy.

**Forming groups, collections and classifications**. *-a* arthropoda, *-acea* cetacea, *-aceae* rosaceae, *-age* assemblage, *-alia* marginalia, *-ana* Americana, Shakespeari-

*Continued opposite*

form *-(o)eidḗs* as in *anthrōpoeidḗs* (human-like), and is cognate with French *-oïde* as in *anthropoïde* and Spanish *-oide(o)* as in both *antropoide* (adjective) and *antropoideo* (noun).

Some suffixes fall into more or less parallel sets according to use and background; for example, three suffixes for causative and

inceptive verbs: vernacular *-en* (*harden* to make or become hard), Latinate *-ify* (*purify* to make or become pure), and GREEK *-ize* (*systematize* to make or become systematic). The conditions for using such suffixes are strictly circumscribed: no *\*hardize*, *\*puren*, *\*systemify* (although the third is conceiv-

## THEMATIC GROUPS OF SUFFIXES *continued*

ana, *-aria* filaria, *-ata* chordata, *-dom* Christendom, *-hood* brotherhood, *-ia* amphibia, bacteria, *-iana* Darwiniana, *-idae* Formicidae, *-ilia* reptilia, *-ish* the British, *-kind* humankind, *-oidea* Crinoidea, *-ry* circuitry, peasantry, *-ship* readership.

**Forming places, lands, locations, and institutions**. *-a* Cuba, Java, hacienda, veranda, *-ada* Nevada, *-ades* the Cyclades, *-aea* Judaea, *-age* hermitage, vicarage, *-ain* Britain, *-aine* Aquitaine, *-alia* Australia, *-an* the Vatican, *-ana* Montana, *-ania* Romania, *-any* Brittany, *-arium* aquarium, *-ary* aviary, formicary, *-ate* caliphate, emirate, *-ea* Judea, *-ery* monastery, nunnery, rookery, *-ia* India, Somalia, *-iana* Louisiana, *-ides* the Hebrides, *-ory* dormitory, priory, observatory, *-um* asylum, mausoleum, Elysium, *-y* county, Italy.

**Forming national and ethnic types and associations**. *-ad* nomad, *-al* Oriental, Vandal, *-alian* Australian, *-an* American, Cuban, Moroccan, *-ard* Savoyard, *-arian* Bavarian, *-ch* French, *-ck* Canuck, Polack, *-ean* Galilean, *-ee* Chinee, Maccabee, Shawnee, Yankee, *-er* Londoner, Icelander, islander, villager, westerner, *-ese* Chinese, Japanese, Viennese, Congolese, *-i* Iraqi, Pakistani, *-ian* Brazilian, Canadian, Romanian, *-ic* Asiatic, *-ie* Scottie, townie, *-ish* British, Yiddish, *-ite* Hittite, Manhattanite, *-ot* Cypriot, Epirot, *-s(e)* Erse, Scots, *-tch* Dutch, *-wegian* Glaswegian, Norwegian, *-x* Manx, *-y* gypsy, Romany, Taffy.

**Forming adjectives**. *-able* teachable, *-aire* doctrinaire, *-al* doctrinal, ducal, incremental, royal, *-alian* Episcopalian, *-alic* vocalic, *-an* human, *-ane* humane, *-ant* concomitant, radiant, *-ar* solar, *-arian* vegetarian, *-aric* velaric, *-ary* arbitrary, *-astic* enthusiastic, *-atic* dramatic, phlegmatic, *-eal* laryngeal, *-ean* subterranean, *-en* brazen, golden, drunken, priest-ridden, *-ent* current, nascent, *-erly* southerly, *-ern* southern, *-ernal* fraternal, *-ernmost* southernmost, *-esque* Bunyanesque, grotesque, *-e(u)tic* phonetic, therapeutic, *-iac* cardiac, *-iacal* maniacal, *-ial* circumstantial, colonial, residential, *-ian* draconian, *-iar* peculiar, *-ible* tangible, *-ic* civic, comic, *-ical* ethical, heretical, *-id* horrid, *-il* civil, *-ile* fertile, *-ine* adamantine, feminine, *-ique* oblique, *-ish* owlish, sevenish, greenish-yellow, *-itic* arthritic, *-ly* princely, yearly, *-mental* incremental, developmental, *-oidal* adenoidal, *-ory* inflammatory, *-sy* cutesy, tricksy, *-uble* voluble, *-ular* granular, molecular, *-y* naughty, sandy, tidy, worthy.

**Forming verbs of causation and inception**. *-ate* accentuate, *-efy* liquefy, *-en* harden, *-esce* effervesce, *-ify* purify, *-ize/ise* atomize.

**Forming diminutives and hypocorisms**. *-cle* tabernacle, icicle, *er(s)* champers, rugger, soccer, *-ette* cigarette, *-ie* Jackie, lassie, *-ikin(s)* mannikin, sleepikins, *-ipoo* drinkipoo, *-let* leaflet, *-ling* darling. duckling, *-nik* beatnik, peacenik, *-o* arvo, cheapo, journo, reffo, *-ock* hillock, *-ola* granola, payola, *-ula* uvula, *-ule* granule, molecule, *-ulus* cumulus, *-y* Molly, Tommy.

---

able, on the model of *humidify*). Great variation is possible in a single form or group of related forms, as with the Latin form whose masculine is *-arius*, feminine *-aria*, neuter *-arium*. This has entered English in at least four ways: original forms unchanged, as ? in *denarius*, *urticaria*, *aquarium*; as the genderless *-ary* in *aviary*, *honorary*, *primary*, *salary*; as French *-aire* (contrast *legionnaire/legionary*, *commissionaire/commissioner*); in the complex forms *-arian* in *disciplinarian*, *-arious* in *hilarious*. In Latin, *-arius* was close to *-aris* (as in *similaris*, English *similar*); many words, especially from French, that contain the element *-ar-* derive from either *-arius* or *-aris*. In addition, a part of a word may look as though it contains a member of the *-ar-* group but does not, as with *barbarian*, whose division is *barbar/ian*, not *\*barb/arian*.

**Functions**. The functions of a suffix are: to form a noun, adjective, or verb from another noun, adjective, or verb, in such patterns as noun from verb and verb from adjective; to provide a more or less clear-cut element of meaning in the complex word so formed: when -*y* is added to *rock*, an adjective is formed from a noun and the meaning of the phrase *a rocky coastline* can be paraphrased as 'a coastline made up of rocks/covered with rocks/with a rock-like aspect'. Some suffixes function in isolation (for example, -*ard* in such words as *communard*, *drunkard*); no other element attaches to these words except the plural -*s* (but note *bastardy*). Others belong in sets, both associatively (-*ist*, -*ism*, -*ize*) and cumulatively (-*ist*, -*istic*, -*istical*, -*istically*). Such a cumulative set forms a *derivational paradigm*, a pattern

---

## SUFFIXES AND STRESS

Many suffixes of Latin and Greek origin trigger a shift in STRESS (technically, *stress shift* or *accent shift*) when added to polysyllabic bases: for example, -*ity* attracts stress to the syllable preceding it (*cómplex/compléxity*). No vernacular suffixes cause stress shift, nor do all classical suffixes do so: for example, there is no shift in the vernacular set *shárp/shárpen/shárpener*, nor in the Romance set *devélop/devélopment*, but a shift occurs when this set is extended with -*al*: *devélopment/developméntal*. In terms of stress shift, there are three groups of suffixes:

**1. *Vernacular: no shift*** Suffixes and compounding elements which do *not* cause stress shift: -*dom* kingdom, -*ed* salted, red-haired, -*en* darken, -*er* writer, -*erly* easterly, -*ern* northern, -*erner* westerner, -*ernmost* southernmost, -*ful* hopeful, -*fulness* truthfulness, -*hood* adulthood, -*iness* dirtiness, -*ing* startling, soap-making, -*ish* roundish, -*ishness* reddishness, -*less* useless, -*lessness* meaninglessness, -*let* leaflet, -*like* stone-like, -*liness* loneliness, -*ling* hireling, -*ly* womanly, -*ness* darkness, -*ship* readership, -*y* sandy.

**2. *Romance and classical: no shift*** Suffixes and compounding elements which do *not* cause stress shift: -*able* breakable, -*age* marriage, -*al* renewal, -*ant* dependant, -*ar* similar, -*ary* legionary, -*cy* accuracy, normalcy, -*ible* incorrigible, -*ion* attention, -*ism* Darwinism, -*ist* socialist, -*ite* meteorite, -*ive* suggestive, -*ment* development, -*or* dictator, -*ure* fixture. Although they do not themselves affect stress, they may occur in composites which do, such as -*ability*, in which the -*ity* attracts the stress to the syllable preceding it: *téachable/teachabílity*.

**3. *Classical: causing shift*** The lists indicate the form which the shift takes when the words containing the suffixes are pronounced in isolation. Minor changes relating to primary or secondary stress may occur in the flow of longer utterances. When the suffix is attached, stress falls: (*a*) on the only syllable of the suffix: -*ee* referée, refugée, -*eer* auctionéer, enginéer, -*ese* Japanése, Vietnamése, -*esque* picturésque, Junoésque, -*ette* cigarétte, usherétte. (*b*) on the first syllable of a composite suffix with two syllables: -*ation* commendátion, degradátion, transformátion, -*ition* compositíon, definítion, edítion, -*ution* dissolútion, revolútion, -*atic* dogmátic, systemátic, -*etic* energétic pathétic, -*iety* sobríety, socíety -*mental* developméntal, experiméntal, -*ental* continéntal, -*ential* presidéntial. (*c*) one syllable before the (composite) suffix: -*an* subúrban, -*ian* Canádian, -*ial* torréntial, -*eal* larýngeal, -*ual* resídual, -*ify* humídify, -*ic* económic, históric, -*ical* económical, histórical, -*ity* compléxity, informálity. (*d*) two syllables before the suffix: -*al* colónial, indústrial, -*ar* molécular, rectángular, -*ize* decéntralize, réalize, -*ous* censórious, labórious.

whose potential can be exploited as needed. There are some 14 patterns of cumulative suffixation in English. Of these, four are vernacular and ten Neo-Latin, sometimes blending Latin and Greek. The VERNACULAR paradigms belong to the language at large, while the Neo-Latin PARADIGMS tend to be limited to educational, technical, and scientific registers. Such paradigms indicate a higher level of regularity in English suffixation than is often supposed to exist, but for every more or less regular system there are many incomplete or idiosyncratic arrangements in all areas and levels in which suffixes are involved. For example:

**1. Vernacular**. The nouns *sand*, *milk* provide the usually literal *sandy* and *milky*, but the nouns *brain*, *hand* provide *brainy* and *handy*, which are figurative and do not refer directly to brain or hand.

**2. Latinate**. The noun *nation* is the base of the adjective *national*. The noun *nationality* is formed from it, but not usually the noun *nationalness*. Compare the noun *use*, the etymological base of the adjective *usual*, which has little to do with using things. From it, *usualness* is formed, but not *\*usuality*.

**3. Greek**. The adjective *syllogistic* derives from the noun *syllogism*, not from *\*syllogy*, but *eulogistic* currently derives from the noun *eulogy*, not *eulogism*. Where *biology* begets *biological* and not *\*biologistic*, *eulogy* begets *eulogistic* and not in present-day English *\*eulogical*.

**Gradations of meaning and use**. Suffixes display all kinds of relationships between form, meaning, and function. Some are rare and have only vague meanings, as with the *-een* in *velveteen*. Some have just enough uses to suggest a meaning, as with *-iff* in *bailiff*, *plaintiff*, suggesting someone involved with the law, and *-ain* in *captain*, *suzerain*, suggesting someone with power. Some may be rare and apparently inert, yet come to life when needed: the Greek suffix *-ad* marks a nymph (*dryad*, *oread*), a number group (*monad*, *triad*), an epic (*Iliad*, *Dunciad*), and an activity occurring on an epic scale (*Olympiad*). Few nymphs and number groups are now created, but the recent *Asiad* as the name for pan-Asian games indicates that *-ad* is still available for epic events, at least in the context of athletics. See ABBREVIATION, CAUSATIVE VERB, COMPLEX WORD, DIMINUTIVE.

**SUPERLATIVE (DEGREE)**. In grammatical theory, the third DEGREE of an ADJECTIVE or ADVERB. This is usually formed either by adding *-est* to the uninflected positive or absolute form of shorter words (*kindest*, *fastest*) or by putting *most* before longer words and adverbs (*most extraordinary*, *most quickly*). Irregular superlatives include *best* and *worst*. See COMPARATIVE DEGREE.

**SUPERORDINATE CLAUSE**. In grammatical analysis, a term for a CLAUSE that contains another clause. In *It was raining when I left home*, the sentence constitutes a superordinate clause, since it contains a subordinate *when*-clause. In *I think it was raining when I left home*, the clause beginning with *it* remains superordinate to the *when*-clause, but is at the same time subordinate to the superordinate clause that constitutes the sentence. See SUBORDINATION.

**SUPERSTRATE**. Also **superstratum**. A LANGUAGE or aspect of a language which affects another less prestigious or socially and culturally dominated language: for example, LATIN or FRENCH influencing Old and MIDDLE ENGLISH; English influencing many of the indigenous languages of Africa and Asia. Compare SUBSTRATE.

**SUPPLETION**. A term in LINGUISTICS for a situation in which a form in a grammatical paradigm bears no family resemblance to the base from: for example, *went* in *go/goes/going/went/gone* and *better* and *best* in *good/better/best*. Suppletive forms are common in irregular usage in many languages.

**SURINAM**, also **Suriname**. A state of the Caribbean coast of South America. Languages: DUTCH (official), Sranan and other CREOLES, English, HINDI, Javanese. The first European settlers in the area were British from Barbados in 1651, but the Dutch gained the territory in 1667 in a swap that gave Nieuw Amsterdam (to become New York) to Britain. After this, the colony became *Dutch Guiana*. The British held it again (1799–1818) during the Napoleonic wars. The colony became independent as Surinam in 1975. It is remarkable for its variety of English-based creoles: NDJUKA, SARAMACCAN, and SRANAN or *Taki-Taki*. See CARIBBEAN ENGLISH CREOLE.

**SURVEY OF ENGLISH USAGE**. Short form SEU. A survey founded in 1959 by Randolph QUIRK at the U. of Durham, England, and which he took with him when he moved to U. College London (UCL) in 1960. Quirk remained its director until 1981, after which his successor to the Quain professorship of English, Sidney GREENBAUM, was its director from 1983 until his death in 1996. The aim of the SEU has been to provide resources for the accurate description of the GRAMMAR available to, and used by, adult educated native speakers of BrE. It is assumed that grammarians cannot rely simply on their own knowledge to provide the grammatical data at the disposal of speakers of English in a range of stylistic contexts. The major activity of the Survey has therefore been the collection and analysis of representative samples of spoken and written/printed BrE. A subsidiary activity has been the development and administration of experiments eliciting use and judgement among native speakers. The elicitation tests have supplemented corpus data on features in divided use or found to be infrequent in the corpus, such as: the choice of the subjunctive; the *should*-construction; the indicative after verbs such as *demand* and *recommend*; the normal positions of different types of adverbials.

**Content and analysis**. The CORPUS consists of 200 samples ('texts'), each of 5,000 words, for a total of 1m words. The TEXTS cover a wide range of subject matter, situations, and degrees of formality. The 100 spoken texts comprise: face-to-face conversations and telephone coversations; discussions; interviews; broadcast commentaries; lectures; demonstrations; sermons; committee meetings; and dictations. The 100 written/printed texts comprise: scripted material that was read aloud, such as drama and news broadcasts; manuscript material, such as social and business letters; printed publications, such as learned and popular books on various topics, fiction, news reports, and legal and administrative documents. The original Corpus is in photocopied booklets and slips, each slip (6 × 4 inches) containing 17 lines, including four lines of overlap with preceding and following slips to provide context. For each collected feature there is one slip that is marked for that item. The Survey has collected: 65 grammatical features (such as adverbs, names, negation, direct speech);

over 400 specified words or phrases that were felt to have grammatical significance (such as *a, is could, not, and, in spite of*); for spoken texts, about 100 prosodic features (such as rising and falling tones) and paralinguistic features (such as laughing, sobbing); for written texts, all punctuation marks. Scholars from many parts of the world have visited UCL to consult the files.

**Survey publications**. Numerous books and articles have drawn on data from the Corpus (including its computerized spoken texts in the LONDON-LUND CORPUS) and from the results of experiments conducted at the Survey or by its associates. Prominent among them are two major reference works: *A Grammar of Contemporary English* (Longman, 1972) and *A Comprehensive Grammar of the English Language* (Longman, 1985), both by Randolph Quirk, Sidney Greenbaum, Geoffrey Leech, and Jan Svartvik. Two advanced-level textbooks based on the 1972 reference grammar are used in universities and colleges worldwide: *A University Grammar of English*, by Quirk and Greenbaum (Longman, 1973; US title *A Concise Grammar of Contemporary English*, Harcourt Brace Jovanovich, 1973) and *A Communicative Grammar of English*, by Leech and Svartvik (Longman, 1975, 1994). An advanced-level textbook based on the 1985 reference grammar has also been published: *A Student's Grammar of the English Language*, by Greenbaum and Quirk (Longman, 1990). See INTERNATIONAL CORPUS OF ENGLISH.

**SWAHILI**, also **Kiswahili**, **KiSwahili**. A BANTU language spoken as a mother tongue or a second language in the East African mainland and islands, from Lamu Island in KENYA in the north to the southern border of TANZANIA, and west to Congo. It may have arisen from a Bantu language pidginized through contact with ARABIC. As a language of trade, it spread inland from the coast during the 19c. It is the official language of Kenya and Tanzania and a LINGUA FRANCA in UGANDA and Grgo (Zaire). Arabic has provided many LOANWORDS, and the earliest Swahili literature, from the 18c, is in Arabic script. The British colonial administration in the 1930s encouraged the development of STANDARD Swahili. Swahili nouns are divided into classes according to the grammatical prefixes they take. Such PREFIXES also bring verbs, adjectives, demonstratives, and possessives into concord with the subject of a sentence: for example, in *Watu wetu wale wakubwa wamekuja* (Those big people of ours have come), *watu* is the plural of *mtu* (person), and other words harmonize by beginning with *wa*. Comparably, *mbenzi* is a rich person (who owns a Mercedes-Benz), plural *wabenzi*. Swahili is one of the few indigenous African rivals to English. Because it is used over such a wide area, it tends to be ethnically neutral. See AFRICAN ENGLISH, EAST AFRICAN ENGLISH, WORD.

**SWAZILAND**. A country in southern Africa, between South Africa and Mozambique, and a member of the COMMONWEALTH. Languages: Siswati or SiSwati (also known as Swazi, the Zulu form of the name) and English (both official). The Swazi occupied the territory in the early 19c, in competition with the Boers. Their autonomy was guaranteed by Britain, but the territory was administered by the Boer province of Transvaal until 1903, when it came under the British governor of Transvaal, then a province of the Union of South Africa. Independence was gained in 1968.

**SWEARING**. A term that refers to both taking an OATH and using language that is regarded as foul, abusive, and profane. When people in a Christian culture swear on the Bible to tell the truth in court, they assume that God will punish anyone who then lies, quite apart from the legal consequences of 'being forsworn' (*perjury*). When people swear something or swear to do something, for example on their honour, they pledge that honour as a security to be forfeited if forsworn. Oaths sworn to a god or God are solemn matters, but over the centuries have passed from being ritual formulas to being exclamations. The negative aspect of oath-swearing (retribution) allows other kinds of negatively charged language to be called *oaths*, and their exclamatory use to

notions from *By God!* through *Hell!* and *Shit!* to *You son of a bitch!* is striking but not surprising; the last three can be called both *oaths* and *curses*, and the activity in general can be called *cursing and swearing*. The notion of CURSING has undergone a similar development: solemn cursing invokes supernatural retribution on someone or something the curser holds odious. See ABUSE, ANGLO-SAXON, AUSTRALIAN, AUSTRALIAN LANGUAGE, BAD LANGUAGE, BLAS-

PHEMY, DEROGATORY, EUPHEMISM, EXPLETIVE, FOUL LANGUAGE, FOUR-LETTER WORD, INFIX, OBSCENITY, PARTRIDGE, PLAIN ENGLISH, SLANG, SWEARWORD, TABOO, VULGAR, VULGARISM.

**SWEARWORD**. A non-technical term for a WORD or PHRASE that is obscene, abusive, and socially offensive. Swearwords are usually associated with the genitals and sexual activity (*cunt, fuck, prick*), excrement (*crap, shit*), or religion (*Jesus Christ!*), and may combine elements from each area (*fucking shit, fucking hell*). Conceptions of what is or is not, should or should not be, a swearword have varied over the years. In the 19c, *damn* was widely regarded as a swearword, but is nowadays generally considered mild because, by and large, religious topics such as heaven and hell are no longer taken as seriously as in the past. See SWEARING.

■ **SWEET, Henry** ─────── ■

[1845–1912]. English philologist, phonetician, and grammarian. Born in London, and educated at King's College School, London, he matriculated in 1864 at the U. of Heidelberg. In 1871, while still an undergraduate, he edited King ALFRED's translation of the *Cura Pastoralis* for the Early English Text Society, his commentary laying the foundation of OLD ENGLISH dialectology. Further works on Old English include: *An ANGLO-SAXON Reader* (1876); *The Oldest English Texts* (1885); *A Student's Dictionary of Anglo-Saxon* (1896). In 1877, he had published *A Handbook of PHONETICS*, which attracted attention among scholars and teachers of English on the Continent. He followed it with *Elementarbuch des gesprochenen Englisch* (1885), adapted as *A Primer of Spoken English* (1890). This was the first scientific description of educated London speech, the ACCENT later known as RECEIVED PRONUNCIATION. Sweet used phonetic script throughout this work, including specimens of connected speech in transcription. By emphasizing the spoken language and the use of phonetics he was a pioneer in LANGUAGE TEACHING. His views on the subject were set out in *The Practical Study of Languages* (1899). His last book on English PRONUNCIATION was *The Sounds of English* (1908). Bernard SHAW, who regarded Sweet as a man of genius, writes in the preface of *Pygmalion* about his 'Satanic contempt for all academic dignitaries and persons in general who thought more of Greek than of phonetics'. The play's Professor Higgins, he says, is not a portrait of Sweet: 'With Higgins's physique and temperament Sweet might have set the Thames on fire.' There are, however, 'touches of Sweet in the play'.

**SWUNG DASH**. A name for the tilde (~) when used in dictionaries as a space-saving device: in an entry for *house*, *~boat* stands for *houseboat* and *~style* for *house style*; in an entry for *hero*, *~es* stands for *heroes*. The device is common in bilingual dictionaries, when it is generally called a *tilde*, and has been extensively used in Oxford dictionaries, but has been disappearing from recent editions. See DASH.

**SYLLABICATION**, also **syllabification**. The division of a word into SYLLABLES: either phonologically, in terms of speech sounds, or orthographically, in terms of letters. In orthographic syllabication, there may be correspondences with spoken syllables (*na·tive* into *na·tive*) and/or with elements of morphological and etymological significance (*nat·ive* from Latin *natus* born, and -*ive*). The two kinds of division do not always correspond. Neither syllable boundaries in speech nor morphological/etymological elements are always clear-cut, and the fact that the same word may be pronounced differently in different varieties of English can mean a different number of syllables and different syllable boundaries: *medicine* generally pronounced with two syllables in BrE and three in AmE. Nevertheless, orthographic syllabication is straightforward in many words, as with the division of *postman* into *post·man*, which satisfies phonetic, morphological, and etymological criteria in both BrE and AmE. Such a word as *structure* is more problematic: both BrE and AmE phonology dictate *struc·ture*, while morphology and etymology require *struct·ure*. It has been claimed that when such a conflict occurs, AmE favours the phonetic and BrE the morphological and etymological. Rules for syllabication are given in various style manuals: for BrE, *Hart's Rules for Compositors and Readers at the University Press Oxford* (1893; 39th edition, 1983); for AmE, *The Chicago Manual of Style* (13th edition, 1982). See HYPHEN.

**SYLLABIC CONSONANT**. See SYLLABLE, and the letter entries L, M, N, R.

**SYLLABLE**. The smallest unit of SPEECH that normally occurs in isolation, consisting of either a vowel alone (as in the pronunciation of *ah*) or a combination of vowel and consonant(s) (as in the pronunciation of *no*, *on*, and *non*). Some consonants can be pronounced alone (*mmm*, *zzz*), and may or may not be regarded as syllables, but they normally accompany vowels, which tend to occupy the central position in a syllable (the *syllabic position*), as in *pap*, *pep*, *pip*, *pop*, *pup*. Consonants occupy the margins of the syllable, as with *p* in the examples just given. A vowel in the syllable margin is often referred to as a *glide*, as in *ebb* and *bay*. *Syllabic consonants* occur in the second syllables of words like *middle* and *midden*, replacing a sequence of schwa plus consonant; here, the time needed to pronounce the SCHWA is transferred to the following consonant: for example, in the pronunciation /'mɪdl̩/ for *middle* and /'mɪdn̩/ for *midden*. As the examples show, a syllabic consonant is marked phonetically with a subscript vertical dash (ˌ). See L, M, N, R.

A syllable standing alone is a *monosyllable*, and may be a word in its own right, as with *a*, *an*, *big*, *cat*, *no*, *the*, *yes*. A word containing many syllables is a *polysyllable* or *polysyllabic word*, such as *selectivity* and *utilitarianism*. A *disyllable* or *disyllabic word* has two syllables, a *trisyllable* or *trisyllabic word* has three. See BREVE, HYPHEN, MACRON, RHYTHM, ROOT-WORD, TONE.

**SYLLABLE WORD**. An occasional term in WORD-FORMATION for a word formed from SYLLABLES or syllable-like elements drawn from two or more other words: *sial* from the first syllables in *silicon* and *alumin(i)um*. Compare ACRONYM, LETTER WORD, MONOSYLLABLE.

**SYMBOL**. 1. Something that represents something else, such as a drawing of a heart pierced by an arrow, standing for romantic love. In principle, anything can symbolize anything else, temporarily or permanently, especially something concrete or material used to represent something abstract or non-material, if an association can be formed between them: for example, a river symbolizing the flow of life; a circle symbolizing completion; a light symbolizing God. A word, phrase, image, character in a story, etc., may, in addition to its immediate nature and purpose, have symbolic status:

for example, in ORWELL's allegory *Animal Farm* (1945), the dogs symbolize the police in a repressive state. In the discussion of art, literature, language, etc., the term *symbolism* may refer to symbolic meaning as a whole, to the use of symbols, or to the disposition to invest things with symbolic meaning. **2.** A mark, figure, character, etc., alone or in combination, that serves to designate something else, such as in the chemical formula *O*, representing oxygen. Compare SIGN. See NOTATION, SEMIOTICS.

**SYNCOPE** [Stress: 'SING-ko-py']. A traditional term for CONTRACTION in the middle of a word through the loss of a sound or letter, commonly marked (especially in verse) by an apostrophe: *ever* reduced to *e'er*, *even* to *e'en*, *taken* to *ta'en*. The process or act of making such a contraction is *syncopation*. See ELISION, STRINE.

**SYNECDOCHE** [Stress: 'sin-EK-doh-ky']. In RHETORIC, a figure of speech concerned with parts and wholes: (1) Where the part represents the whole: 'All *hands* on deck' (the members of a ship's crew represented by their hands alone). (2) Where the whole represents the part: '*England* lost to *Australia* in the last Test Match' (the countries standing for the teams representing them and taking a plural verb). See METONYMY.

**SYNONYM**. A WORD that means the same as another, such as *male* and *masculine*. Linguists and many writers agree that there is 'no such thing as a synonym', though the reasons for their opinions may differ. Linguists maintain that no two words have the same distribution, frequency, connotation, or language level; the reasons given by others are often vague, but in essence focus on differences in connotation, or reactions evoked in the reader or hearer by alternative words for the same thing. It is therefore perhaps best to say that a synonym is a word that shares the same denotation with another word. Notwithstanding disputes over the validity of the concept, there is a substantial body of published information containing synonym lists and studies, and it has become standard practice among dictionary publishers to include some of that information in general dictionaries. See ANTONYM, BISOCIATION, BOOK OF COMMON PRAYER, SEMANTICS, SYNONYMY, THESAURUS.

**SYNONYMY**. **1.** Equivalence in meaning, as with *enormous* and *immense*, both having the general sense 'very big'. Such equivalence may be precise, as is generally the case with these adjectives, or may be relative, as with *big* and *large*: the phrases *a big house* and *a large house* may communicate the same idea of size, but in *That was a big help* and *He was in large part to blame for what happened*, the two words are not interchangeable. **2.** A set, list, system, or book of synonyms. There have been many such works since the 18c, including books that seek through short essays to make discriminations among the members of sets of words. One of the earliest of these in English was Hester Thrale Piozzi's *The British Synonymy* (1794), which set the style for later works of the same kind. George Crabb brought out in 1816 a detailed work entitled *English Synonyms Explained in Alphabetic Order*, containing etymologies, citations, and discursive personal comment, and in 1851 Elizabeth Jane Whately published *A Selection of English Synonyms*, arguing that words in need of discrimination are not synonyms as such but 'pseudo-synonyms'. Since the mid-19c, alphabetically ordered synonymies are usually called dictionaries, and include Richard Soule's *A Dictionary of English Synonyms* (1871, revised by A. D. Sheffield, 1937: lists only), *Webster's New Dictionary of Synonyms* (ed. Rose Egan, 1968: largely with discriminating statements and described on the cover as a 'thesaurus'), and the *Longman Synonym Dictionary* (ed. Laurence Urdang, 1979: without discriminations but with usage labels). See THESAURUS.

**SYNTAX**. A term in general use and in LINGUISTICS for the study of the ways in which words combine into such units as PHRASE, CLAUSE, and SENTENCE. The sequences that result from the combinations are referred to in linguistics as *syntactic structures*. The ways in which components of words are combined into words are studied in MORPHOLOGY, and syntax and morphology together are generally regarded as the major constituents of *grammar*, although in one of its uses, *grammar* is strictly synonymous with *syntax* and excludes morphology. In models of language description that are divided into levels of analysis or components, the syntactic level or component is contrasted with the phonological and semantic levels or components. Syntactic descriptions do not usually go beyond the level of the sentence, though they may deal with relationships between sentences such as are signalled by a pronoun (*it, them*) or a conjunct (*therefore*). See LEVEL OF LANGUAGE, LINGUISTIC TYPOLOGY.

posed out of two or more grammatical units, as in Latin *amabamus* (we loved), which combines 'love', *past, first person, plural*. English has such synthetic words as *unfindable* (unfind-able) and *repainted* (re-paint-ed). See LINGUISTIC TYPOLOGY.

**SYNTHETIC**. A term in LINGUISTICS for a language in which words tend to be com-

**SYSTEMIC GRAMMAR/LINGUISTICS**. See HALLIDAY.

# T

[Called 'tee']. The 20th LETTER of the Roman ALPHABET as used for English. It originated as the Phoenician symbol *taw*, which the Greeks adopted and adapted as *tau* (τ), which was in turn adopted by the Etruscans and then the Romans as T.

**Sound value**. In English, the letter *t* represents a voiceless alveolar plosive stop, produced by the release of breath blocked by the tongue being placed against the roof of the mouth behind the front teeth. The aspiration of /t/ is slight after *s*, the *t* in *stub* being less forceful than in *tub* and rather resembling /d/. Before another stop, or *m*, or in syllable-final position, *t* may occasion no audible release of breath, as in *hatpin*, *atmosphere*, *Wait*! Before syllabic *l*, *n*, and (in rhotic accents) *r* the breath may be released nasally (*bitten*) or past the sides of the tongue (*little*) or its tip (*falter*).

**Glottalized *T***. In some accents, especially in Britain, the tongue may not touch the roof of the mouth, the *t* being spoken as a GLOTTAL STOP, as for example in London and Glasgow working-class pronunciations of *a bit of butter*.

**Voiced *T***. The letter *t* may be voiced almost as /d/ following a stressed vowel and before a second vowel. This pronunciation is typical of AmE and AusE, making virtual homophones of such pairs as *atom/Adam*, *latter/ladder*, *waiting/wading*, *writing/riding*. It is also heard sporadically in BrE, especially in certain rapid colloquial expressions, such as *I'd better go*, *get out*, and *not a hope*.

**Palatalized *T***. (1) When *t* is palatalized before *u*, it represents the affricate otherwise spelt *ch* as in *church*: before *-ure* (*capture*, *culture*, *fracture*, *legislature*, *picture*, *temperature*), before *-ual* (*actual*, *intellectual*, *perpetual*), and in some other environments (*century*, *fortune*, *statue*, *virtue*). Compare palatalized *d*, *s*, *z* in *verdure*, *closure*, *seizure*. (2) This affricate value also occurs before *i* in the ending *-stion* (*question*, *digestion*, *combustion*) and in *Christian*, and before *e* in *righteous*. However, in precise, conservative speech, the value of *t* in such words may be /t/ followed by a *y*-sound rather than /tʃ/. (3) Elsewhere, when followed by unstressed *i* and another vowel, *t* is commonly palatalized to produce the voiceless palato-alveolar fricative *sh*- sound. This value of *ti* is found in such words as *inertia*, *patient*, *ratio*, *nasturtium*, and the proper names *Domitian*, *Horatio*, *Titian*, but particularly in the endings *-tial* (*palatial*, *essential*, *initial*, *partial*, *potential*, *presidential*, *substantial*), *-tious* (*conscientious*, *superstitious*, *vexatious*), and the hundreds of *-tion* words (*association*, *completion*, *discretion*, *ignition*, *motion*, *solution*). Some of these also have a preceding consonant: *action*, *infarction*, *mention*, *adoption*. In words ending in *-tiate*, etc., the *i* usually remains syllabic: *negotiate*, *substantiate*. (4) Uniquely, *equation* may be heard with *zh*, rhyming with *invasion*. Occasionally, some of these words are pronounced carefully with non-palatalized *t* heard as /s/: *inertia*, *negotiate*.

**Double *T***. (1) Syllables containing a stressed short vowel double a final *t* before a suffix that begins with a vowel: *mat/matted/matting*, *bet/betting*, *fit/fitted/fitter/fittest*, *rot/rotted/rotting*, *cut/cutting/cutter*, *regret/regretted/regretting* (contrast *wait/waited/waiting*, *visit/visited/visiting*). *Format* commonly has *formatted/formatting*, while *benefit* is found with *benefited/benefiting* and, less commonly, *benefitted/benefitting*. (2) Disyllables commonly have medial *tt* following a stressed short vowel: *batter*, *better*, *bitten*, *bottle*, *butter*. (3) *T* is doubled when the Latin prefix *ad-* is assimilated to a stem beginning with *t*: *attain*, *attend*, *attract*. (4) Some cognate words vary in their doubling: *Britain/Brittany*, *catty/caterwaul*, *letter/literate*, *matter/material*. (5) Few words other than proper names end in *tt*: *watt* originated in the proper name *Watt*; *matt*, *nett* are alternatives for *mat* (not shiny), *net* (not gross); *mitt* is a clipped form of *mitten*; *putt* originated as a Scottish variant of *put*; *butt* (noun) may have retained double *t* so as to be distinguished from *but*.

**Inflectional *T***. (1) Regular verbs form their past tense with *-(e)d*, but many irregular verbs use *t*: *deal/dealt*, *feel/felt*. (2) Some have alternative forms, especially in BrE (*burnt/burned*, *learnt/learned*, *spoilt/spoiled*), the t-versions often being favoured as adjectival forms (*burnt papers, badly learnt lines, spoilt food*). (3) Some reduce a doubled consonant before t: *smelt/smelled, spelt/spelled, spilt/spilled,* and formerly also *past/passed*. (4) Some shorten their stem vowel (but not its spelling) before t: *dreamt/dreamed, leant/leaned, leapt/leaped*. (5) Many shorten sound and spelling before t: *cleave/cleft, creep/crept, feel/felt, keep/kept, kneel/knelt, leave/left, lose/lost, shoot/shot, sleep/slept, sweep/swept, weep/wept*. (6) Some substitute -*t* for final -*d* in their root: *bend/bent, build/built, gild/gilt* (also *gilded*), *gird/girt* (also *girded*), *lend/lent, rend/rent, send/sent, spend/spent*. (7) Some make more substantial changes to the vowel and/or final consonant of the stem in adding -*aught* or -*ought*: *beseech/besought, bring/brought, buy/bought, catch/caught, seek/sought, teach/taught, think/thought*. (8) Some have stems with final -*t* which is preserved without inflection in all tenses: *burst, cast, cost, cut, hit, hurt, let, put, quit, set, shut, slit, split, thrust*. (9) Some change their stem-vowel, but not final t: *fight/fought, light/lit, meet/met*.

**Epenthetic *T***. (1) The letter *t* and sound /t/ have sometimes intruded in words originally without them: *peasant, tapestry* (from French *paysan, tapisserie*). (2) In *against, amidst, amongst, betwixt, whilst*, t has arisen parasitically, perhaps by analogy with the superlative inflection of adjectives.

**Silent *T***. (1) In word- and syllable-final position in loans from French, both early and recent: *ballet, beret, bouquet, buffet, cabaret, chalet, crochet, croquet, depot, mortgage, parquet, potpourri, trait, valet*. (2) Elided after *s* following a stressed vowel: before /l/, especially in the terminal syllable -*le*, in *castle, nestle, pestle, trestle, wrestle, bristle, epistle, gristle, mistletoe, thistle, whistle, apostle, jostle, throstle, bustle, hustle, rustle*; before /n/, especially the terminal element -*en*, in *chasten, hasten, fasten, christen, glisten, listen, moisten*; and in isolated words such as *Christmas, postman, waistcoat*. (3) Elided after *f* in *soften* and often in *often*. (4) In *boatswain*, the elision is reflected in such alternative spellings as *bo 's'n, bosun*. (5) The historical function of *t* before *ch*, typically after short vowels as in *match, fetch, pitch, botch, hutch*, is the equivalent of doubling a simple letter, but is in present-day English redundant. The redundancy is particularly apparent in *ditch/rich, hutch/much*.

**Variations**. Some variation occurs between *t* and other letters in related words, as between *benefit/beneficial, space/spatial, extent/extend/extension* (contrast *retention*).

***TH***. This digraph is regularly used to represent a common, characteristically English phoneme, the dental fricative, both voiced /ð/ as in *this* and voiceless /θ/ as in *thin*. Sometimes related forms vary: voiceless *smith*, but voiced *smithy*. In OLD ENGLISH, the sounds were represented interchangeably by the runic letter *THORN* (þ) and *ETH* (ð), a modification of the letter *d*. A relic of thorn occurs in the form *Ye* for *the* in 'old' inn and shop signs, such as *Ye Olde English Tea Shoppe*, the *y* being a corruption of handwritten þ. English borrowed the digraph *th* from LATIN, where it served to transliterate GREEK *theta* (θ); *th* superseded other symbols for the dental fricative following the advent of printing. In MODERN ENGLISH *th* occurs in common words of Old English origin and in many, usually technical, words of Greek origin. The *h* is ignored in the pronunciation of a small number of words: *thyme, Thomas*, in BrE but not necessarily in AmE in *Thames* (for example, the Thames River in Connecticut has a spelling pronunciation), and usually in *Anthony, Esther*. *Th* may be silent in *asthma, isthmus, clothes*. *Th* in *north, south* is commonly omitted in nautical language: *nor' nor' east, sou'wester*. The form *good-bye* also arose from the omission of *th*, being a clipping of *God be with ye*.

**Voiced *TH***. (1) Initially in many grammatical words: *than, that, the, thee, their, them, then, thence, there, these, they, thine, this, thou, though, thus, thy*, but contrast *through*, in which the following *r* may have prevented the voicing of the *th*. (2) Medially: *bother, brother, father, further, gather, hither, leather, mother, northern, rather, smithy, southern, weather, wether, whether, whither, wither, withy, worthy*, but contrast *brothel* and the derived forms *healthy, wealthy*. (3) Some nouns voice final *th* in the plural (*baths, mouths, truths, youths*) but not in the corresponding inflected BrE verb *baths*. (4) A following final *e* indicates a voiced *th*, a long preceding vowel, and usually a verb form (contrast *breath/breathe*): *bathe, clothe, lathe, lithe, loathe, seethe, sheathe, soothe, swathe, teethe, wreathe, writhe*, but *to mouth, to smooth* lack final *e*.

**Voiceless *TH***. (1) Initially, in lexical words: *thank, thatch, theft*. (2) Finally, in both lexical and grammatical words: *bath*, *birth*, *both*, but contrast voiced *smooth*, and *booth* with either pronunciation. *Th* is voiced in the derivatives *mouths*, *northerly*, *southerly*. The word *with* is variable. (3) In Greek-derived words: *antithesis*, *epithalamium*, *hyacinth*, *pathos*, *theatre/theater*, *theme*, *theory*, *Theseus*, but not in *rhythm*.

**Morphological *TH***. The ending *-th* was formerly a present-tense verb inflection (for example, *maketh* for Modern English *makes*), and occurs as the ordinal ending for numerals (*fourth*, *fifth*, *twentieth*, *hundredth*, *thousandth*, but with written assimilation of preceding *t* in *eighth*, from *eight*). It creates abstract nouns from several common adjectives often suggesting measurement: *breadth*, *depth*, *length*, *strength*, *warmth*, *width* (but only *t* after *gh* in *drought*, *height*, *sight*).

**TABOO**. In language terms, something taboo is not to be mentioned, because it is ineffably holy or unspeakably vulgar. English Puritanism caused such words as *God* to be banned on the stage during the early 17c and references to *Hell* have also often been reproved. Sex and excrement are, or have been, taboo topics in English and other languages, and many of the words relating to these topics have been stigmatized as *bad language*, *foul language*, or *four-letter words*. They have been in effect banned in polite conversation, in writing, and especially in print; though occasionally recorded in earlier dictionaries, they were not entered in such works *c.*1760–1960. When taboo subjects must be broached, the techniques for doing so include:

**Truncation**. Taboo words can be amended both in writing (by a dash as in *G–d* and asterisks as in *f\*\*k*) and in speech (by using the letter *p*, usually spelt *pee*, for *piss*).

**Adaptation**. Because of a combination of the sense of taboo and the need for expletives, taboo words when used as exclamations have been adapted and softened so as to be less direct, sacrilegious, and offensive: *(by) God!* becomes *(by) Gosh! Jesus!* is shortened to *Gee! Christ!* becomes *Crikey!*, *Jesus Christ!* becomes *Jeepers Creepers! Damn (it)!* becomes *Darn (it)!*, *Damnation!* becomes *Tarnation!*, *Hell!* becomes *Heck!*, and *Fucking hell!* becomes *Flipping heck!* See MINCED OATH.

**Substitution**. Taboo expressions can be replaced with other words through EU-

PHEMISM, as with *make love* for 'have sex', and through the use of elevated technical terms, such as *coitus/coition* and *sexual intercourse*. In dealing with smuttier topics, users of English often find that there is no neutral phraseology available. Furthermore, the substitute for a taboo word can itself become socially awkward if its referent remains taboo: *intercourse* is avoided by some people in any of its other uses because of its sexual use. See ELLIPSIS, SWEARING.

**TAG**. A term in LINGUISTICS for several types of structure in which one or more words are tagged on to a clause or sentence, including: (1) *Continuation tags*. Words and phrases used as shorthand at the end of a list: *etc.*; *and so on*; *and so forth*. (2) *Questioning and commenting tags*. Questions, questioning words, and commenting words that can be added to statements are common in formal conversation: 'She's pretty, *don't you think?*'; 'You'll pay me back tomorrow, *OK?*'; 'It's difficult, *I suppose*'; '*You know*, it can't be easy for her.' Such forms can usually be re-arranged as standard questions and statements: *Don't you think she's pretty?*; *I suppose (that) it's difficult*. (3) *Focusing and emphasizing tags*. These usually restate the subject and sometimes the verb: 'She's amazing, *(is) my grandmother*'; '*My grandmother*, she's amazing'; 'She's amazing, *she is*'; 'She comes here often, *does Joan*' (a usage common in the North of England). See LATIN TAG, QUESTION TAG, TAG QUESTION.

**TAGALOG** [Stress: 'ta-GA-log']. A Malayo-Polynesian language of the Philippines, one of the major indigenous languages, the mother tongue of some 10m Filipinos, and the basis of the official and national language referred to as both *FILIPINO* or *Pilipino*. See TAGLISH.

**TAGLISH**, also **Mix-Mix**. An informal name for a mixture of TAGALOG and English, as used in the Philippines and particularly in Manila and the island of Luzon: 'Pwede kayong magbayad three months after arrival. Pwede pang i-extend up to two years payment. At sa pinakamababang interest rate pa' (quoted by Lily V. Kapili, *English Today* 16, Oct. 1988) [Translation: 'It is possible to pay three months after arrival. It is possible to extend payment up to two years. And the interest rate is the lowest.' *Pwede* is from Spanish *puede* it is possible].

The Philippine continuum between full English and full Tagalog is covered by the terms *English, Taglish, Engalog, Tagalog*. See PHILIPPINE ENGLISH.

**TAG QUESTION**. A grammatical term for a statement with a *QUESTION TAG* added at the end, turning it into an actual or apparent question: *They're coming here next week, aren't they? You really shouldn't do that, should you?* See NEGATION, TAG.

**TALK**. **1**. A way of talking or speaking, usually embracing what one talks about: *TEACHER TALK* the usage of teachers in the classroom; *chalk and talk* an informal term for teaching methods that do not use complex technology; *small talk* trivial news and gossip. The term is informal in such forms as *country talk* and *local talk*, and pejorative in such forms as *nigger talk*. **2**. A VARIETY or DIALECT, especially if not taken too seriously or low in prestige: *Bungo Talk* 'country bumpkin' speech in Jamaica; *Creole Talk of Trinidad and Tobago* (title of a book, 1980). This sense has long been associated with English-based PIDGINS and CREOLES; the word has been adopted and adapted, usually in the written form *tok*, in various names, such as *KAMTOK* in Cameroon and *TOK PISIN* in Papua New Guinea. It may also occur in such pidgin and creole usages as *tumantok* ('two-man talk') a tête-à-tête. **3**. Sound that approximates to SPEECH, whether produced by an animal, an infant, or a machine: *BABY TALK*. Compare -ESE, LINGO, -SPEAK. See AKU, DOUBLE TALK, FOREIGNER TALK, RASTA TALK, TECHNOBABBLE.

**TANZANIA** [A blend of *Tanganyika* and *Zanzibar*, with -*ia*. Usual stress: 'Tan-zan-EE-a']. A country of East Africa and member of the COMMONWEALTH. Languages: Swahili (official), English, and indigenous languages. The Germans colonized Tanganyika from the late 19c until in 1920 it became a League of Nations mandate and later a UNITED NATIONS trust territory administered by the British. Zanzibar was a British protectorate from 1890 to 1963. The territories united on independence in 1964. English was a joint official language with SWAHILI until 1967. This political empowerment of Swahili improved its prestige in relation to English and other indigenous languages. English continues to be important for higher education, media, and inter-

national relations, while Swahili has taken over roles in precollege-level education and internal government and business.

Tanzanian English shares many features with Zambian English. Devoicing of word-final /b, v/ is common ('laf' for *love*), and *f*/*v* may alternate ('lavin' for *laughing*). Mass or singular nouns may be construed as plurals (*behaviours, breads*). BORROWINGS from indigenous languages are frequent, and may become standardized as marking the Tanzanian variety: *sufuria* cook-pot, *pole* (an expression of sympathy), *foforu car* fancy car. Some typical local usages are: *Thank you for your postcard extended to us recently*; *We were happy to learn* (hear) *from you*; *Please inquire if she had the mails* (got the letters); *I decided to mail* (write) *you*. CODE-MIXING, particularly Swahili/English, is common: *Ile accident ilitokea alipo-lose control na aka-overturn and landed in a ditch* The accident occurred when he lost control and overturned and landed in a ditch. Here, mixing includes putting Swahili prefixes on English stems, as with *alipo-lose*. See EAST AFRICAN ENGLISH.

**TAUTOLOGY**, also *PLEONASM*. A term in RHETORIC for unnecessary and ineffective REPETITION, usually with words that add nothing new: *She was alone by herself.* Many tautological (or tautologous) expressions occur in everyday usage. The tautology in some is immediately apparent: *all well and good*; *cool, calm, and collected*; *free, gratis, and for nothing*. In others, it is less obvious, because they contain archaic elements: *by hook or by crook*; *a hue and cry*; *not a jot or tittle*; *null and void*; *rack and ruin*. Compare CIRCUMLOCUTION, REDUNDANCY.

**TEACHER TALK**. A semi-technical term in educational research and applied linguistics for the characteristic (often simplified) style of SPEECH of teachers. In general terms, this may be prompted by the social setting of the classroom, with repetition, rephrasing for the sake of clarity, and patterns of stereotyped interaction with learners, such as question, response, and evaluation. For teachers of English as a foreign language, speech may be slower and clearer than is usual, avoiding and minimizing elided usages such as *must've/musta* and *'sno good y'-know*, repeating the same thing in several ways, and using expressions particularly associated with education, classrooms, and textbooks. See TALK.

# ■ TEACHING ENGLISH ─────── ■

Also **the teaching of English** and **English teaching**. General, non-technical terms for the work of teachers of ENGLISH, whether with children, adolescents, or adults, and whether as a first, second, foreign, or additional language. However organized, whatever the aim, and whatever the methods used, such teaching currently proceeds on a scale well beyond that of any other language past or present, and approached only (in a more restricted geographical area) by Putonghua in the People's Republic of China. In LANGUAGE TEACHING and APPLIED LINGUISTICS, and increasingly in EDUCATION generally, the teaching of English is divided into five categories, each with its own tradition, terminology, perspective, theory, practice, publications, organizations, and conferences. They are:

**1. *Teaching English as a Native Language.*** Also *Teaching English as a Mother Tongue* and *Teaching English as a First Language.* In the English-speaking world, the teaching of children, adolescents, and adults in institutions of primary (elementary), secondary, and tertiary (higher) education, and of adults in continuing education, including literacy programmes. *English* is often used as a shorthand (but sometimes ambiguous) term for the teaching and study of both language and literature, being understood as meaning mainly language at the primary level, both at the secondary level, and at the tertiary level literature (perhaps with traditional philology), language (usually the modern language), or sometimes both. In recent years, however, there has been a tendency in secondary schools, universities, and other institutions to reduce the possibility of ambiguity by distinguishing 'English Language' and 'English Literature' clearly as the names of the courses, the subjects of degrees, and subjects for examination. The term *ENL countries* ('ee-en-ell': English as a Native Language) refers to those territories in which English is the first, and for many the only significant, language, such as Australia, anglophone Canada, Britain, the Irish Republic, New Zealand, and the US.

**2. *Teaching English as a Second Language.*** Short form *TESL* ('tessle'). (1) The teaching of English in countries where the language is not a mother tongue but has long been part of the fabric of society, usu-ally for imperial and colonial reasons in the relatively recent past, either as a lingua franca or a medium of education, or both. The term *ESL countries* ('ee-ess-ell') refers to those territories in which English has a statutory role such as (co-)official language or medium of education, but is not generally used in the home, such as India, Nigeria, and Singapore. (2) The teaching of non-English-speaking immigrants to ENL countries. The comparable term *TESOL* ('tee-sol': *Teaching English to Speakers of Other Languages*), originally used in North America primarily for the teaching of immigrants, is now used worldwide in both senses. See TESOL.

**3. *Teaching English as a Foreign Language.*** Short form *TEFL* ('teffle'). (1) The teaching of English in countries where it is of interest and/or importance but is not or has not been until recently a local medium of communication or instruction, such as Japan, Saudi Arabia, and Sweden. In the late 20c, the term *EFL countries* ('ee-eff-ell') refers in effect to the rest of the world. (2) Providing courses in ENL countries for visiting students from EFL countries. Another term used principally for this category, especially in Britain, is *English language teaching* or, more commonly, *ELT* ('ee-ell-tee').

**4. *Teaching English as an International Language.*** Short form *TEIL* ('teel', 'tee-ee-eye-ell'). Teaching English as a global lingua franca, making people aware in the process of the worldwide role of the language and the problems that derive from or are related to that role. EIL ('ee-eye-ell') embraces all countries, learners, and users (ENL, ESL, and EFL), its proponents arguing that native users of English need as much consciousness-raising with regard to an adequate international use of the language as those who learn it as a second or foreign language. They also argue that the more English becomes institutionalized as the world's main medium of international expression the more native and non-native users will need to learn to acclimatize to each other's ways of using it.

**5. *Teaching English as a Second Dialect.*** Short form *TESD* ('tezd', 'tee-ee-ess-dee'). Teaching the standard language to speakers of non-standard varieties of English, such as a dialect (Scouse in the UK, Appalachian in the US) or a creole (Nation Language in Jamaica or any Caribbean

Creole in the UK). Here, the term *English* is restricted to a use traditionally given to it (usually implicitly) by many educationists and grammarians: the language of professional and business people educated to college level or its equivalent and of the major media: that is, the standard language, dialect, or variety. Both term and abbreviation have been modelled on the labels of the preceding three categories. To make their standpoint clear, however, some proponents of TESD use the term *Standard English as a Second Dialect* (short form *SESD*) to present standard English as one dialect among many, and not as a specially prestigious entity in its own right.

**Mother-tongue English teaching**. In all ENL countries, the educational profession in general and a significant part of the interested public regard good English teaching (whatever 'good' is taken to mean) as fundamental to all schooling at all levels, and as an essential underpinning for students' later lives. Despite the often acrimonious debate that follows from close concern for the language and how it is taught, it is widely accepted that the roles of the people teaching English are so different at the three educational levels that in fact there is no such thing as a 'typical' teacher of English for all seasons:

(1) In primary schools, because of the nature of the work, most teachers teach English along with everything else that the children learn. Such teachers are not so much English specialists as educational generalists who integrate the key elements of elementary English teaching (such as listening, speaking, reading, and writing) into the whole fabric of the child's experience at school.

(2) In secondary schools, again because of the nature of the work, most teachers are (at least ideally) specialists in different subjects or groups of subjects. However, while English specialists have an obviously central role, the others are also in a serious sense teachers of English (whether they wish to see themselves in that light or not), because the language is the medium through which they work. When for example science teachers introduce new terms, indicate how the notes of an experiment should be kept, or discuss relevant texts, they are providing instruction in the register of scientific and technical English, some-thing that is not usually the concern of the English specialist.

(3) In tertiary institutions, teachers are not only (at least ideally) 'general' specialists in 'English', but also teachers and researchers in sub-specialities of their own, such as the Victorian novel, Creole Studies, Media Studies, or aspects of grammatical and literary theory. As a result, the precise nature of a degree course in English often rests not only on an understanding among the teachers and administrators of what must or should be covered as a foundation, but also on a supplement of courses arising from the special interests and inclinations of the staff available at any time a department.

**The secondary-school teacher of English**. Although it is relatively easy to specify what is going on at the primary and tertiary stages, it is difficult to be clear about the precise nature and aims of the work done in the middle years. As a result, the secondary level tends to receive more critical attention from the public than the others. The two professional comments that follow, on the nature of the teacher's work at this level, demonstrate the burden that English-speaking societies have long placed on the secondary specialist. The first quotation is from the US in 1965, the second from the UK in 1991, both periods of vigorous and controversial debate:

*The United States, 1965*. Like any other professional person, the professional English teacher is one who has been trained or has trained himself, to do competent work. For him professional competence should mean, at the minimum: a college major in English or a strong minor, preparation sufficient to qualify him to begin graduate study in English; systematic postcollegiate study, carried on privately or in a graduate school; a reading command of at least one foreign language, ancient or modern; a deep interest in literature, old and new, and a solid set of critical skills; the ability to write well and the habit of writing, whether for publication or not; a knowledge of the development of the English language and familiarity with recent work in linguistics; a desire not simply to know but to impart knowledge; skill in the handling of instructional problems and knowledge of the research concerning them; an unflagging interest in the processes by which the young learn to use language effectively and richly (from *Freedom and Discipline in English*, the Report of the Commission on English, chaired by Harold C. Martin of Harvard University, College Entrance Examination Board, New York, 1965).

*The United Kingdom, 1991*. English teachers are asked to cover a wide spectrum. In addition to the fundamentals of reading, writing, listening, speaking and spelling required by the National Curriculum [for England and Wales, 1987 onward], they usually teach drama and media studies and are expected to show greater interest in the whole child than many other subject specialists. Most children probably write more prose, and certainly compose more poetry in school than many of their parents. Hence the joke: 'Don't look out of the window or she'll make you write a poem about it.' Both science and English are important subjects in the curriculum, but if something goes amiss in adult life, then it is more likely that blame will be attached to English teachers than to science teachers. In the Sixties, Andrew Wilkinson drew attention to this wide role when he described several models of English teaching, ranging from 'proof reader', which involved meticulous correction of every spelling and punctuation error, to 'Grendel's mother, guardian of the word-hoard', the person with the awesome responsibility of keeping alive and enhancing the nation's cultural heritage. Fortunately, English teachers are among the best qualified academically to undertake such an assignment. Analysis of graduate recruits to teaching shows that English, history and modern languages entrants have more firsts and upper seconds than in any other subject (from 'Peace in the Civil English War', Schools Report, *Observer*, 22 Sept. 1991, by Ted Wragg, head of the School of Education, Exeter University, England).

**Society and the teacher**. In the last analysis, however, all teachers involved in English, primary or secondary, are regarded as responsible for the quality of the language skills of young people when they leave school. If employers and politicians, among others, complain (rightly or wrongly) about falling standards, the spotlight is turned on these teachers and their trainers, and on the theories that underpin their practices. It often seems to the professional English teacher that in public discussions of English teaching everyone has a view of how things should be done, where there might be caution in the expression of opinions about the teaching of mathematics or science, or about the work of lawyers and doctors. In public debate, there is often an elemental polarization: between conservatives who consider that changes in ways of teaching grammar and spelling (among other things) are symptomatic of a more general social decay, and radicals who consider that progress will never be made until the outdated methods favoured by the conservatives are utterly uprooted. As is often the case in other areas, most teachers are located at neither end of the spectrum, but are somewhere in the middle, where efforts can be made to unite, as judiciously as possible, the most effective aspects of the old and the new.

See BULLOCK REPORT, CLAUSE ANALYSIS, COX REPORT, ELT, EXAMINING IN ENGLISH, KINGMAN REPORT, LANGUAGE AWARENESS, LANGUAGE LEARNING, NEWBOLT REPORT, PARSING.

**TECHNOBABBLE**. An informal term for the use or overuse of technical JARGON. John A. Barry in the introduction to *Technobabble* (MIT Press, 1991) says that 'the word connotes meaningless chatter about technology' but 'is also a form of communication among people in the rapidly advancing, computer and other high-technological industries'. As an example he gives: *This paper-based, productized module is designed to support the robust implementation of a friendly, context-driven interface between the developer and the end-user* (a facetious description of his own book). In his glossary, he provides five near synonyms for the term: *compuspeak, computalk, tech speak, techno-talk,* and *technojive*. Compare COMPUTERESE, PSYCHOBABBLE, TECHNOSPEAK.

**TECHNOSPEAK**. An informal term for a PROSE style used by high-technology industries, their associated media, and the marketing and publicity groups that surround them, as in: 'LISA lookalike systems, such as

VisiCorp's VisiOn software, require a massive 256K bytes of Random Access Memory and a 5 megabyte hard disc capable of storing five million characters of information' (*Observer*, 7 Aug. 1983); 'Elegant, innovative and Inphone at its most ingenious, the Versatel features press-button dialling incorporated in the sleek lines of the handset' (*Inphone Info*, 1980s ad, British Telecom). There are at least ten identifying features: (1) The use of LETTER symbols, INITIALISMS, and ACRONYMS: *K*, *LISA* (local integrated software architecture). (2) Number-and-letter groups: 256K. (3) BLENDS: *SELECTaCOM*, *Versatel*. (4) VOGUE usages: *info*, *mega*. (5) Compounds: *lookalike*, *pressbutton*. (6) Fixed phrases: *hard disc*, *Random Access*. (7) Wordplay: *LISA lookalike*, *VisiOn*. (8) Novel orthography: *SELECTaCOM*, *VisiCorp*. (9) Heavy pre-modification: *Advanced Videotech Bike-to-Bike Intercom*, *LISA lookalike systems*. (10) A generally dense presentation. See COMBINING FORM, COMPUTERESE, INTERFIX, TECHNOBABBLE.

## ■ TEFL ■

**Short for *Teaching English as a Foreign Language***. Also *EFL* alone. The teaching of English to learners in or from countries where it has not been traditionally used. The terms (T)EFL, (T)ESL, and TESOL all emerged after the Second World War, and in Britain, no distinction was made between (T)EFL and (T)ESL before 1950, both being subsumed under *ELT* (*English Language Teaching*). *EFL* and *TEFL* are usually pronounced 'ee-eff-ell' and 'teffle'. Informally, someone engaged in TEFL is a *TEFLer*.

**Background**. The teaching of English as a foreign language has been common since at least the mid-19c, and for most of that time was comparable to the teaching of any other foreign language. However, with the explosion in the importance of English since the Second World War, teaching it to foreign learners has been so institutionalized that it has acquired a distinct name and acronym. Traditionally, such teaching has been mainly in the care of local teachers at the secondary and tertiary levels in such countries as France and Germany. It has been primarily cultural, more or less on a par with learning a musical instrument. In EFL, however, the teaching has mainly social and economic importance, and such cultural aspects as literature have a sec-

ondary role. The focus of (T)EFL is largely on everyday communication, business, and access to English-medium education. In such work, the place of native-speaking teachers has become significant, particularly in privately run schools and colleges. Currently, in Britain, EFL is largely a private, often entrepreneurial activity, ranging from well-established and respected institutions to 'cowboy' outfits. Rates of pay for teachers are generally low, conditions of service vary, and the quality of teaching varies with them.

**Current situation**. Between 1960 and 1990, as demand for courses in Britain steadily increased, TEFL became a significant earner of foreign currency. Some 1,000 private language schools, mainly in southern England, provide short courses for some 250,000 students a year, mostly young adults. A wide range of course materials, published and unpublished, has been produced to cater to this demand and the needs of learners elsewhere. There has been a great increase in radio and TV courses and the provision of examinations and certificates of attainment. The British Council is closely involved in EFL, providing scholarships for foreign students to attend courses or obtain higher degrees in applied linguistics and EFL/ESL. Organizations include the *Association of Registered English Language Schools* (1960) and the *International Association of Teachers of English as a Foreign Language* (*IATEFL*) (1971). Associated publications include the *ELT Journal* and *EFL Gazette*. Teachers at British language schools were at first mainly graduates in English Literature, usually without training as language teachers. In the 1970s–80s, however, there has been a move towards professionalization. Centres for research and development in applied linguistic and EFL/ESL have been established in such universities as Edinburgh, Lancaster, and Reading, strengthening the academic base of the profession and helping to provide teachers with an awareness of the theory and practice of foreign language teaching.

**Principles**. EFL, as represented by the major language schools and the universities in Britain, generally aims at a working command of the spoken and written language. Methods tend to be eclectic and the range of materials wide, generally emphasizing fluency and accuracy. Features of grammar are explained after rather than before being used. The explicit teaching of grammar is not dominant and most teachers do not consider that command of the language is a consequence of knowing a set of rules. The four skills of listening, speaking, reading, and writing are by and large taught in an integrated way. Classroom activity varies, and pair work, group work, tasks, and projects are all favoured. Reading and writing tend to be taught with practical aims in mind: letters, reports, notes, instructions, stories. Many teachers create their own materials as a supplement to, or a substitute for, published courses, which are available in great variety. By and large, teaching techniques are flexible, varying according to a student's level of attainment (beginner, intermediate, advanced) as well as the aims of the course and students' hopes and expectations.

See EXAMINING IN ENGLISH, LANGUAGE LEARNING, LANGUAGE TEACHING, TEACHING ENGLISH.

■ **TEIL** ───────────────────────── ■

Short for *Teaching English as an International Language*. Also *EIL* alone. A term in LANGUAGE TEACHING and APPLIED LINGUISTICS for teaching the use of English between or among speakers from different nations. Such persons may be native speakers (such as Americans and Britons who may not always understand each other well), non-native speakers (such as Thais dealing with Arabs or Mexicans dealing with Japanese), or native speakers and non-native speakers (such as Americans dealing with Hungarians, or Ethiopians dealing with Australians). The term differs from both *TEFL* and *TESL* in that native speakers are also seen as needing help in cross-national and cross-cultural communication, rather than as representing the norm at which non-natives should aim. It is assumed in TEIL that English belongs to all of its users (whether in its standard or any other form), and that ways of speaking and patterns of discourse are different across nations.

**Communication and miscommunication**. Problems of interpretation are especially likely to occur when native and non-native users are communicating, or when one non-native is communicating with another. In many instances, miscommunication is often linked to two mistaken

and often unconsidered assumptions: (1) Someone with a native or native-like control of pronunciation, grammar, and vocabulary has no cross-national communication problems, or should not have such problems. (2) The ways of speaking and patterns of discourse of all fluent speakers of English are similar. TEIL stresses that a good command of English is helpful for efficient international communication but is not enough, because information and argument are structured differently in different nations, and topics of conversation, speech acts, expressions of politeness and respect, irony, understatement and overstatement, and even uses of silence are different in different nations. People using English in an international context could benefit from knowing more about such things.

**Englishes**. Practitioners of EIL argue that international communication in English cannot be reduced to the limited range of material and communication patterns that characterize ESL and EFL, nor do they usually claim that more people should use English or that if everyone used the same language, the world would be a better place. The term *Englishes* is often used when discussing EIL, because it describes the functional and formal variation in the language and its acculturation in Africa, Asia, the Caribbean, and Oceania, as well as its traditions in the UK, the US, Ireland, Australia, Canada, and New Zealand.

**Teaching**. The goal of TEIL is to increase proficiency when using English across nations. Its students are both native and non-native speakers of English, and its concerns are intelligibility, comprehensibility, and interpretability. These concerns are not speaker- or listener-centred, but are shared by both speaker and listener; international communication is interactional, and meaning must be negotiated. Students are exposed to varieties of English from many different parts of the world and are encouraged where appropriate to become proficient users of their own country's educated variety. Cultural information is not limited to native English-using countries, but is given for countries in all three of Braj B. Kachru's English-using circles: the *Inner Circle* (the traditional English-speaking countries), the *Outer Circle* (the countries where English is developing new varieties), and the *Expanding Circle* (countries in which the use of English is increasing). See ENGLISHES, INTERNATIONAL LANGUAGE, TEACHING ENGLISH.

**TELEGRAPHESE**. An informal term for the concise expression achieved in telegraphic messages: *Arriving Monday 1800 Heathrow Sheila*, which condenses *I will be arriving on Monday at 1800 hours at Heathrow Airport, London: (this note is from) Sheila*. Such concision risks ambiguity and even wilful misinterpretation: a cable is said to have been sent by a movie agent who wanted to know Cary Grant's date of birth: it read HOW OLD CARY GRANT, and received the reply from Grant himself OLD CARY GRANT FINE HOW YOU.

**TELESCOPING**. The contraction of a phrase, word, or part of a word, on the analogy of a telescope being closed: *biodegradable* for *biologically degradable*; *sitcom* for *situation comedy*. There are two main processes: (1) Adapting classical combining forms through reducing the first word in a compound or fixed phrase: when *biologically degradable* is telescoped to *biodegradable*, *bio-* refers not to life alone but to biology; when *telephone communications* is reduced to *telecommunications*, *tele-* refers to the whole technology of remote communication. (2) Creating syllabic ACRONYMS like *sitcom* and blends like *smog*. The reduction of a series of words to some of their component syllables (or syllable-like elements) creates such new usages as *sitrep* for *situation report*, *Saceur* for *Supreme Allied Commander Europe*, and *NAVFORKOR* for *Naval Forces Korea*. Such forms are common in military, industrial, and technical usage. See ABBREVIATION.

# ■ TENSE ■

The grammatical category, expressed in forms of the VERB, that locates a situation in time. In English, tense must be expressed in all finite verb phrases. It is marked by the choice of the first or only verb in the verb phrase: *play* versus *played*; *has played* versus *had played*; *will play* versus *would play*; *is playing* versus *was playing*. Since contrasts in number and person, where they apply, are also marked on the first or only verb, these choices combine with tense: present *I/They play* versus present *She plays*; present *I am/She is* versus present *We/They are*; past *I/She was* versus past *We/They were*. By definition, non-

finite verb phrases do not have tense marking. There is also no tense choice for the imperative ('*Play* harder') or the subjunctive ('We insisted that he *play* harder').

**Tense in English**. In terms of morphology, English has only two tenses, the present or non-past (*take/takes*) and the past (*took*). The paradigm is extended by the use of the auxiliaries *be* and *have*: *be* followed by the present participle forms the progressive or continuous (*is taking*); *have* followed by the past participle forms the perfect (*has taken*). Although these are traditionally known as tenses, recent terminology refers to them as *aspects* (such as progressive aspect) and (for the perfect) *phase*. All three features can be combined: *had been taking* is past, progressive, and perfect. The passive voice is formed within the same paradigm, by *be* followed by the past participle, but is not a tense. The sequence of the auxiliaries is fixed: *have* + *be* + present participle, *be* + past participle, with the full verb in final position and a *MODAL VERB* preceding all other auxiliaries: *may have been taken*.

**The simple present**. With dynamic verbs, this tense expresses habitual activity and 'timeless truths': *He goes to London every day*; *Water boils at 100 Celsius*. In commentaries, demonstrations, and performatives, it serves to report events simultaneous with the speech event: *He passes the ball to Smith, and Smith scores*; *I take three eggs and beat them in this basin*; *I name this ship 'Fearless'*. With static verbs, it refers to a present or timeless state: *It contains sugar*; *Air consists of oxygen and other gases*. With private verbs (of sensation, mental processes, etc.) it expresses how things are: *I smell something burning*; *I think he'll come*. In statements about the future, it shows that events have been arranged: *We fly to Paris tomorrow*. In literature and conversation, as the *historic present*, it reports past events dramatically and dynamically: *He comes up to me and says . . .* With verbs of communication, it states or informs: *The Bible says . . .*; *John tells me that he is going to Spain*.

**The simple past**. Generally, this tense refers to events, habitual activities, and states in the past: *I talked to my brother this morning*; *The Normans conquered England in 1066*; *He went to London every day*; *It contained sugar*. In the 'sequence of tenses' rule in reported speech, it restates the present tense of the original utterance: 'He likes chocolate' as reported in *She said he liked chocolate*. However, the present tense may be retained if the state of affairs being reported is covered by the time of speaking: *John said he likes chocolate*. It is used to express unreality, especially in unreal conditional sentences (*If John came, Mary would leave*; compare *If John comes, Mary will leave*), with wishes and recommendations, etc. (*I wish I knew*; *It's time we went*), and for tentativeness or politeness (*Did you want to talk to me?*). This accounts for some of the uses of the modal forms *might*, *could*, and *would*, as in: *Might they want to see her?*; *Would you like us to come?*

**The progressive**. The present progressive is most commonly used to indicate an event in progress at the time of speaking: *He's reading a book*. With the past progressive, the time of the continuous event is often explicitly shown to overlap a point of time or another briefer event: *I was reading at ten o'clock/when he arrived*. In contrast, the simple past would suggest that the event was subsequent to the point of time or other event: *When he arrived, I left*. In standard English, static and private verbs are non-progressive, in that they do not usually occur in the progressive, the simple present being used instead (not *\*I am loving you*, not *\*I'm thinking he will come*, although such usages occur in varieties of IndE and PakE). There are a number of verbs with inherent duration which may be used in the non-progressive form, even if the duration is clearly indicated: *I worked all morning*; *She slept for eight hours*. The progressive may indicate: (1) Incompletion: *I was painting the house this morning* versus *I painted the house this morning*. (2) Simple futurity, especially with verbs of motion: *I'm flying to Paris tomorrow*. (3) Limited duration of habitual activities or with non-progressive verbs: *We're eating more meat now*; *We're living in London these days* (compare *We live in London*). (4) Sporadic repetition: *My car's always breaking down* versus *My car always breaks down when I forget to service it*.

**The perfect**. The non-progressive perfect refers to an event in the past with current relevance: *I've broken the window* indicates that I broke the window and that the window is probably still broken; *I've seen John* might suggest that I have told him what I intended to, or that he is now nearby. It is also used with *just* for events in the immediate past: *I've just seen him*. The progressive perfect relates to activity beginning in the past

and continuing up to the present, or, for past-tense forms, to a point of time in the past: *I've been reading for two hours*; *I'd been reading for two hours when he arrived*. It may also indicate continuous activity in the past with current relevance: *Someone's been moving my books—they are no longer where I left them*. The present perfect is not normally used with past-time adverbials: not *\*I've broken the window yesterday*. The simple past is often used in AmE where BrE uses the perfect: (1) BrE *Have you washed your hands?*, AmE *Did you wash your hands?* (2) BrE *Have you done it yet?*, AmE *Did you do it yet?* There is, however, wide variation in the use or non-use of the perfect in AmE.

**The future**. Traditionally, grammarians have taught that English has a future tense formed with *shall* and *will*, *shall* being used with first-person subjects (*I shall be happy to see her*) and *will* with the others (*She will be happy to come*). However, *will* is also commonly used with first person subjects (*I will be happy to see her*) to indicate futurity, though conversely *shall* is not used in the same way with the other persons (not *\*She shall be happy to come*). The view that *will* and *shall* mark the future tense is widely held and often strongly asserted, but there are three arguments against it: (1) Morphologically, there are only two tenses, present and past; to talk about the future tense is to confuse time marking with grammatical tense. (2) *Will* and *shall* are formally modal verbs, and should be handled in the modal system, not the tense system. (3) *Be going to* is as good a candidate for the marker of the future tense as *will* and *shall*.

In the majority of instances, *will* and *shall* express a conditional future and are the forms used in the apodosis of future conditionals (the part without *if*): *If you ask them, they will do it*. *Be going to* indicates an envisaged progression towards a future event: *It'll cost me a lot of money* may imply 'if I buy it', whereas *It's going to cost me a lot of money* suggests that the decision to buy has been made. There are two arguments in favour of treating *will* and *shall* as markers of the future tense: (1) Future tenses in other languages also often express conditional futures. This is not unexpected, since the future is not factually known as the present and past are, and it is not surprising, therefore, if the future tense in English is marked by modal-type verbs. (2) *Will* and *shall* function in some ways more like tense markers than modal verbs, particularly in that they cannot be marked independently from the main verb for negation, as most modal verbs can. Thus, there is only one negative of *You will see him tomorrow* (*You will not/won't see him tomorrow*), as there is only one negative of *You saw him yesterday* (*You did not/didn't see him yesterday*), but there are two negatives of *He may be in his office*: (1) *He can't be in his office* (It is not possible that he is in his office). (2) *He may not be in his office* (It is possible that he is not in his office).

## ■ TESD ────────────── ■

Short for ***Teaching English as a Second Dialect***. Also *SESD* (*Standard English as a Second Dialect*). The teaching of national or international standard English to speakers of non-standard dialects or varieties, on the principle that the standard will be additional to, rather than a replacement of, the kind of English already used. There are four kinds of non-standard variety: (1) Regional and class dialects, such as Cockney and New Yorkese. (2) Varieties influenced by other languages, such as Hispanic English and Malaysian English. (3) Creoles, such as Krio in Sierra Leone and Jamaican Creole English. (4) Vernaculars with distinctive histories, such as Hawaiian English and Black English. Such varieties have traditionally been regarded as bad or broken English, often by their own speakers as well as others; they tend to be associated with lower-class and/or lower-prestige ethnic, racial, political, and economic groups. Speakers of these varieties have been and often still are assessed at school as deficient in verbal and cognitive skills, as deaf, as learning-disabled, and as educationally or psychologically disturbed, whereas the significant difference lies in a use of language with which their teachers may be unfamiliar and for which they have not been prepared.

**Britain, Canada, and the United States**. In Britain and Canada, the movement against ethnic and linguistic prejudice has focused in the main on immigrant Afro- and Indo-Caribbean students. In the US, the focus has largely been on students of African-American background, and to a much lesser extent students of Hispanic background. In Canada and the US, some attention has been given to students in Native communities as well. In Britain, an important catalyst for change was a book by Bernard Coard in 1971 (*How the West Indian Child is Made Educationally Sub-Normal in the British School System*), together with rising linguistic nationalism in the Caribbean, and increasing tolerance for and interest in regional and class dialects. In North America, such sociolinguists as William Labov, William Stewart, and J. L. Dillard claimed both social and linguistic validity for these language varieties. Feeling towards their own language usage was often positive within the communities concerned, but parents and teachers also stressed the need for students to succeed in the kind of English (the standard variety) recognized as prestigious and useful by schools, business, and the community at large.

**The TESD approach**. The approach is based on an acceptance of language variation of all types, as exemplified in Mike Raleigh's *The Languages Book* (1981) and the Open University packet *Every Child's Language* (Open University, Milton Keynes, 1985). It is often contrastive, examining the grammar and vocabulary of different varieties, emphasizing variation and situational appropriateness in language, and using culturally and linguistically appropriate materials. Unlike ESL students, ESD students generally have a high comprehension and even production of standard English; similarities and overlaps yield positive progress in the beginning, but ESD students reach humps or plateaux which involve core differences between varieties. For example, in standard English *She does wait for the bus*, the auxiliary *does* indicates emphasis; in Trinidadian usage, however, *does* shows habitual action (she waits every day). Throughout the Caribbean, *hand* refers to the whole physical area covered by standard *hand* and *arm*. In Black English, the 'invariant *be*' denotes habitual or ongoing action (*We be playing after school* We play after school every day), and *it* denotes presence (*It ain't nobody there* There isn't anyone/anybody there).

Features such as different vocabulary and pronunciation are generally recognized, even if they are not understood, but differences in prosodic features, such as intonation and stress patterns, may be neither recognized nor understood. Features of discourse, such as patterns of turn-taking in conversation, are not commonly recognized as legitimate differences among varieties of English. For example, children who speak Black English, Caribbean Creole, or Hawaiian English tend to categorize many questions from adults as 'scolding', to which the proper response is silence, while not looking directly at the questioner; in standard English, such questions may indicate adult interest, but always require a verbal response while looking directly at the questioner's face. All such linguistic and social differences may cause confusion for teacher and student, with the result that responses to difficulties may be misinterpreted as misbehaviour or stupidity. Students may also have low motivation; many perceive themselves as already speaking English, and some may not want to identify with mainstream English and its speakers.

**General issues**. Current issues in TESD are linguistic, social, and political. There continues to be a widespread opposition to overtly anti-racist education and to devoting special attention to groups perceived as educationally and socially marginal. There is also often a lack of awareness of teaching methods that can be helpful with such students. Some educators consider that the particular difficulties for learners who already know some kind of English are unimportant or too subtle; there have always been such problems and in many generations of dialect speakers and immigrants many people have overcome them. Even where teachers and administrators are sympathetic to the principles involved, they may see TESD as legitimating 'substandard forms' and delaying students' progress, a view also held by some parents of these students and the community groups with which they identify. Some observers feel that the language issue is used as a smokescreen to avoid dealing with such larger and more important issues as low socioeconomic status, minority racial status, and the need to upgrade academic skills in both teachers and students. See TEACHING ENGLISH, TEFL, TESL, TESOL.

■ **TESL** ──────────────────── ■

Short for *Teaching English as a Second Language*. Also *ESL* alone. The teaching of English to non-native learners in countries where it has an established role, such as India, Nigeria, and Singapore, and to immigrants to English-speaking countries, such as Australia, Canada, the UK, and the US.

The terms (T)EFL, (T)ESL, TESOL emerged after the Second World War, and in Britain, no distinction was made between (T)ESL and (T)EFL before 1950, both being subsumed under *ELT* (*English Language Teaching*). *ESL* and *TESL* are usually pronounced 'ee-ess-ell' and 'tessel'. The terms apply in particular to two types of teaching that overlap but are in many ways distinct: *Commonwealth ESL* and *Immigrant ESL*.

**Commonwealth ESL**. In this sense, ESL is a major activity in many non-white countries of the Commonwealth, especially where English is official and/or a language of higher education and professional opportunity. It has been largely confined to school-age pupils, often in English-medium schools, and methods have been influenced by developments in language education and methodology generally, especially since the Second World War. It relates in the main to work undertaken not in Britain itself (apart from courses for teacher trainers), but in such countries as India, Nigeria, and Singapore. It assumes that the learners will encounter English outside the classroom and expects to achieve adequate levels of ability. By and large, emphasis on the acquisition of BrE Received Pronunciation has declined and an educated local accent and pronunciation are often the acknowledged target. An English-language examination is usually part of the school-leaving qualifications and teacher training is usually the responsibility of departments and colleges of education. Most teachers have a degree, and the emphasis in their training is on classroom techniques rather than linguistic theory. British EFL and Commonwealth ESL have much in common.

**Immigrant ESL in North America**. The teaching of ESL for immigrants to the US and Canada has a different tradition. It is concerned principally with adults and the need for learners to be integrated into local life. Waves of immigrants since 1945, especially from Asia and Latin America, have created a great demand. Local communities, particularly in the larger cities, offer adult courses and make provision for non-English-speaking children in schools. Many universities have instituted MA courses in related subjects and created centres for teaching and for research and development. In addition, many countries have looked to the US and Canada for assistance with teacher training. Some universities have therefore set up links with centres in other countries, and a number of in-country projects in English-language training and teacher education have been undertaken in such countries as Peru, the Philippines, and Thailand, with help from such bodies as the Ford Foundation or with government sponsorship. Because many US immigrants are refugees, their ESL teacher may be the only representative of society they can relate to without arousing their fears of authority. This gives a quality of social service to much North American ESL, especially in larger cities, and has led to characteristics not found elsewhere: (1) A sense among teachers that their students need special care because of past or present experiences, resulting in efforts to establish warm relationships in the classroom. (2) The promotion by some teachers of holistic methods that link a concern for the student as a whole person to the teaching of ESL. Such teachers typically have an MA degree in which linguistics and research figure prominently. While practical training is included, classroom methodology is usually secondary to academic content.

**Immigrant ESL in Britain**. Immigrants to the UK are in the main from Commonwealth countries, principally the West Indies and West Africa (where English and English-based creoles are spoken), Uganda (mainly South Asian traders), South Asia (Bangladesh, India, Pakistan, Sri Lanka), and Hong Kong, where English is widely used in the community. ESL work includes both school-age children and adults, including literacy for women. ESL teachers are mainly teachers of the mother tongue who have received special in-service training. How much and how effective this training is depends on where they work; the London and Birmingham areas currently provide the most thorough training. Because many people of West Indian background speak standard West Indian English in addition to English-based creoles, they have been classified as speakers of English rather than as second-language learners, a factor that can lead to the disregarding of language issues in schools where standard English is the expected norm. Until the mid-1980s, ESL was often taught in separate classes or language centres (where the numbers justified such provision). However, this

procedure came to be widely regarded as divisive, even racist, as it cut ESL learners off from the rest of the curriculum. After a court case by the Commission for Racial Equality in 1986, integrated classes became the norm, requiring ESL to become an element in the training of all teachers rather than the concern of only a few. ESL classes are also provided for adults in further education colleges, and by a range of voluntary groups providing individual home-based teaching. Increasingly, ESL teachers have concerned themselves with political issues arising from the status of many learners. In the 1980s, activists from minority groups became increasingly involved, determined to associate LANGUAGE LEARNING more strongly with minority rights. The successive renamings of one association from *Association for Teaching of English to People of Overseas Origin (ATEPO)* to *National Association for Multiracial Education* to *National Anti-Racist Movement in Education* (both *NAME*) illustrate this shift. See ENGLISH TEACHING, LANGUAGE TEACHING, TEIL, TESD.

**TESOL**, short for *Teaching English to Speakers of Other Languages*. A professional association for teachers of English as a second language, founded in the US in 1966, and the especially US name for TEACHING ENGLISH as a second or additional language, especially to immigrants in English-speaking countries. The organization was at first focused on North America, but in the 1970s–80s became increasingly international. Its core membership at June 1990 was some 16,000 individuals, but as an association of associations, with 70 affiliates worldwide, it represents an additional 26,000 English-teaching professionals. Its stated aim is 'to strengthen the effective teaching and learning of English around the world while respecting individuals' language rights. To this end, TESOL, as an international professional association: supports and seeks to inspire those involved in English language teaching, teacher education, administration and management, curriculum and materials design, and research; provides leadership and direction through the dissemination and exchange of information and resources; and encourages access to and standards for English language instruction, professional preparation, and employment.' TESOL is governed by an Executive Board elected by the membership to represent the affiliates, the 16 special-interest sections, and the membership at large. The Board is headed by a President who holds office for one year.

TESOL's major public activities are an annual conference of about 6,000 participants, usually held in March in either the US or Canada, and a Summer Institute of six to eight weeks, usually in North America but occasionally in Europe. In addition to books and policy statements, publications include *TESOL Quarterly* (a journal presenting mainly research papers), *TESOL Matters* (a bimonthly medium for news of the organization and the profession at large), and *TESOL Journal* (a quarterly featuring practical concerns). Its headquarters are at 1600 Cameron Street, Suite 300, Alexandria, Virginia, USA. See ENGLISH TEACHING, LANGUAGE LEARNING, LANGUAGE TEACHING.

**TEXAS**. A state of the US Southwest, bordering on Mexico to the south. Its first European colonizers, in the 18c, were speakers of Spanish, and until 1836 the region was part of Mexico. The terms *Texas English*, *Texas*, and *Texian* refer to English as used in the state. The variety is Southern is slightly nasal, and vowels are elongated into diphthongs which can be shown in eye dialect as *hee-ut* hit, *ray-ud* red. Some diphthongs, however, are rendered as single vowels, so that *the oil business* sounds like 'the awl bidness' and *barbed wire* like 'bob war'. Texas English is not homogeneous and shows some variety between East Texas (where phonology and lexicon show greater affinity with Southern usage) and West Texas (where they are somewhat more Midlands and Western). See DIALECT (AMERICA), SOUTHERN ENGLISH.

**TEX-MEX**. An informal and occasionally pejorative term for: (1) Anything considered to be a combination of Texan and Mexican, most commonly in food, cultural traditions, and language, especially along the common 1,200-mile border. (2) Anything of Mexican origin found in TEXAS or along the border. Tex-Mex food includes *enchiladas, frijoles refritos* with *salsa picante* (refried beans with a piquant sauce), and *tacos*, prepared in the Northern Mexican style. In language, the term refers to any of several varieties of SPANISH (also sometimes referred to as *Border Lingo*) that may

or may not show English influence, including code-mixing with English by Spanish-speakers:

> *Husband. ¿Que necesitamos? Wife.* Hay que comprar pan, con thin slices. [to sales clerk] ¿Donde está el thin-sliced bread? *Clerk.* Está en aisle three, sobre el second shelf, en el wrapper rojo. *Wife.* No lo encuentro. *Clerk.* Tal vez out of it (from Lorraine Goldman, 'Tex-Mex', *English Today* 5, Jan. 1986) [Translation: *H.* What do we need? *W.* We have to buy bread, with thin slices. Where's the thin-sliced bread? *C.* It's in aisle three, on the second shelf, in the red wrapper. *W.* I can't find it. *C.* Maybe we're out of it].

See SPANGLISH.

**TEXT. 1.** A continuous piece of WRITING, such as the entirety of a letter, poem, or novel, conceived originally as produced like cloth on a loom. **2.** The main written or printed part of a letter, manuscript, typescript, book, newspaper, etc., excluding any titles, headings, illustrations, notes, appendices, indexes, etc. **3.** The precise wording of anything written or printed: *the definitive text of James Joyce's 'Ulysses'.* **4.** A book prescribed as part of a course of study; a textbook: *the prescribed texts for the exam.* **5.** In PRINTING, type as opposed to white space, illustrations, etc. Traditionally, *text* as a concept has suggested something fixed and with a quality of authority about it not unlike scripture. Electronic and laser technology, however, has made the concept more fluid. See CONTEXT, PARAGRAPH, PROSE.

**THEMATIC VOWEL**, also **thematic**. In an inflected language like Greek or Latin, the VOWEL which adheres to a root or base, to form its stem or theme. This vowel then usually controls the inflectional and derivational affixes attaching to it: for example, in the Latin verb *amare* (to love), the base is *am*, the thematic vowel *-a-*, and the STEM *ama-*. The vowel appears in all or most of the other inflected forms and derivatives of a thematic group; for the *amare* group (the first conjugation of Latin verbs), *a* appears throughout the imperfect tense: *amabam, amabas, amabat, amabamus, amabatis, amabant.* A selection of Latin words formed by means of thematic *-i-* is shown in the accompanying table.

| Base | Thematic vowel | Addition | Outcome |
|------|---------|----------|---------|
| *aud* (hear) | -*i*- | *o* | *audio* (I hear) |
| | | *ens* | *audiens* (hearing) |
| | | *tor* | *auditor* (hearer) |
| *agr* (field) | -*i*- | *cola* | *agricola* (field-tender) |
| | | *ultura* | *agricultura* (field-tending) |
| *hort* (garden) | -*i*- | *cultura* | *horticultura* (garden-tending) |

Thematic vowels from Greek and Latin are common in English, often serving to mark sets or families of words: (1) *Latin*, -*a*- as in dict*a*te/dict*a*tor, negoti*a*te/negoti*a*tor/negoti*a*ble, aud*a*cious/aud*a*city, ten*a*cious/ten*a*city; -*e*- as in compl*e*te/compl*e*tion, conveni*e*nt/conveni*e*nce, Ven*e*real, larynx/laryng*e*al; -*i*- as in aud*i*t/aud*i*ence/aud*i*tion, agr*i*culture/hort*i*culture, minister/minister*i*al, president/president*i*al, space/spat*i*al; -*o*- as in atr*o*cious/atr*o*city, fer*o*cious/fer*o*city; -*u*- as in resid*u*e/resid*u*al, use/us*u*al, vacu*u*ous/vacu*u*ity, ambigu*u*ous/ambigu*u*ity, acu*u*puncture/acu*u*pressure; -*y*/*i*- as in colon*y*/colon*i*al, Ital*y*/Ital*i*an/Ital*i*anate, auditor*y*/auditor*i*um. (2) *Greek*, -*a*- as in dogm*a*/dogm*a*tism, theme/them*a*tic; -*e*- as in frenz*y*/fren*e*tic, phon*e*tic/phon*e*mic; -*eu*- as in herm*eu*neutic/pharmac*eu*tical; -*i*- as in arthr*i*tis/arthr*i*tic, bas*i*s/bas*i*c, cris*i*s/crit*i*c criticism; -*o*- as in astr*o*physics/astr*o*physicist, biograph*y*/biograph*i*cal, hypn*o*sis/hypn*o*tism, neur*o*sis/neur*o*tic. See COMBINING FORM, INTERFIX.

**THESAURUS** [Plurals: traditionally *thesauri*, more recently and less formally *thesauruses*]. **1.** A work of REFERENCE presented as a treasure house (Greek *thēsaurós*) of information about words, such as Thomas Cooper's bilingual dictionary, the *Thesaurus Linguae Romanae et Britannicae* ('Thesaurus of the Roman and British Languages', 1565). **2.** A work of reference containing lists of associated, usually undefined, words (such as synonyms) arranged thematically, in the style of *ROGET'S THESAURUS of English Words and Phrases* (1852). **3.** A work of reference containing such lists but presented alphabetically, such as *The New Roget's Thesaurus in Dictionary Form* (Putnam's, 1961) and *The Oxford Thesaurus* (1991). **4.** In information technology, an alphabetic index list of key terms, through which information of a spe-

cialist nature can be retrieved from a database. **5.** In word processing, a stored list of synonyms and antonyms, to be consulted in the preparation of texts, and provided as a service comparable to a spelling checker.

**THORN**. The name of a runic LETTER and its manuscript and printed form þ, used in OLD ENGLISH and MIDDLE ENGLISH for voiced and voiceless *th*. In late medieval times, its form became similar to, and in some handwriting identical with, *y*, with the result that *ye*, *yis*, *yat*, etc., were used (well into modern times) as variants of *the*, *this*, *that*, etc.: the origin of *ye* for *the* in such phrases and names as *Ye Olde Englishe Tea Shoppe* (often facetiously pronounced 'ye oldy Englishy tea shoppy'). See ETH, RUNE, T.

**THORNDIKE, Edward L(ee)** [1874–1949]. American psychologist and lexicographer, born in Williamsburg, Massachusetts, and educated at Wesleyan U., Connecticut, and Harvard. He won a fellowship to Columbia, where he studied with the psychologist James McKeen Cattell and the anthropologist Franz Boas, from whom he acquired a lifelong interest in the quantitative treatment of psychological data. Thorndike's research on stimulus-response and transfer of learning had a major impact on English-language instruction in US schools for both native and second-language speakers. He suggested that conditioned responses account, in part, for word meaning in everyday life and maintained that words which occur frequently in contiguity come to be associated with each other and function as a class. The meaning of a word could therefore be described as a 'habit bond'. To demonstrate his contention that the frequency of a word's usage was related to the recognition of its meaning on the part of the learner, Thorndike prepared with Irving Lorge several lists of the most commonly used English words (published as *The Teacher's Word Book* series, 1921, 1931, 1944) which were used by editors of elementary school readers and ESL texts to select vocabulary for their publications. Applying the results of his research on language and learning, Thorndike influenced the design, order, and writing style of *The Thorndike Junior Dictionary* (1935) and *The Thorndike Senior Dictionary* (1941), on which he collaborated with Clarence Barnhart. The definitions and illustrative sentences in these dictionaries emphasized what he held to be the ultimate aims in education: happiness, appreciation of beauty, utility, and service. Although many of his opinions were controversial, his influence was widespread. He produced more than 500 works, including *Reading Scales* (1919), *The Thorndike Test of Word Knowledge* (1922), and *Teaching English Suffixes* (1941), and served as president of the New York Academy of Sciences and the American Psychological Association.

**TIMESPEAK.** An informal term for the STYLE of the writers of *Time Magazine* and similar news-magazines. Often pejorative, it identifies a homogenized, racy, digest-like prose in which the following often overlapping features are prominent: (1) Heavy pre-modification, in such phrases as 'Surgeon Barnard's cardiologist colleagues', 'Black Power Proselyter [*sic*] Stokely Carmichael'. (2) A wide-ranging, often whimsical vocabulary that uses such recherché terms as *bravura* and *quondam*, such slang terms as *glitz(y)*, *miffed*, *natty*, and *wacky* (often in formal contexts), such neologisms as *shopaholic*, *sweetspeak*, *hippiedom*, and such phrase words as 'Johnson's *close-to-the-vest* method' and 'the ebullient, inexhaustible, *larger-than-life* campaigner'. (3) Word-play, again common in headlines: 'Call it Politics Lite, with lots of froth and little annoying substance'; 'Once and Future Champ'; 'Tressed to the Nines'. (4) Current, catchphrases and buzz words worked into the copy, often in adapted form, as when the name of the popular film *Fatal Attraction* was exploited in a feature on European road safety entitled 'A New Summer of Fatal Traction' (15 Aug. 1988). (5) An enthusiasm for sharp images: 'Ambulances scream to multiple pileups', 'vacationers of the white-knuckle variety'. See JOURNALESE.

**TMESIS.** The insertion of one WORD into another: for example *bloody* and *blooming* for emphasis in *every-bloody-where* and *abso-blooming-lutely*. See INFIX.

■ **TOK PISIN** ───────────────── ■

[From English *Talk Pidgin*. Pronounced 'tock pizzin'] Also **Tok Boi**, **Pidgin**; technically, **Papua New Guinea Pidgin**, and, especially formally, **Neo-Melanesian**, **Neomelanesian**, **Melanesian pidgin**. Names for

the English-based LINGUA FRANCA of PAPUA NEW GUINEA (PNG), officially named *Tok Pisin* in 1981. It descends from varieties of pacific jargon English spoken over much of the Pacific during the 19c and used as a lingua franca between English-speaking Europeans and Pacific Islanders. It was learned by Papua New Guineans on plantations in Queensland, Samoa, Fiji, and in PNG itself. Typically, male workers learned the PIDGIN and took it back to the villages, where it was passed on to younger boys. Tok Pisin crystallized in the New Guinea islands and spread to the mainland *c*.1880. Although a by-product of and sustained by colonialism, it quickly became more than a means of communication between the local people and their European colonizers. It has become the most important lingua franca for PNG and is now being acquired by children as a first language. In sociolinguistic terms, Tok Pisin is an expanded pidgin currently undergoing creolization. It now has more than 20,000 native speakers and some 44% of the population of 3.5 m claim to speak it. There has been considerable discussion as to whether it should become the national language of PNG. Currently, it has official status with English and another pidgin, Hiri Motu, which is largely restricted to the Papua area, and only about 9% of the population speak it.

**Grammar.** Many structural traits have been transferred from indigenous languages. Even where items derived from English are used to express grammatical categories, their patterns and meanings often follow structures in the substrate languages. For example, in most if not all of the Melanesian languages and in Tok Pisin, but not in English, there is a distinction between inclusive and exclusive first-person plural pronouns. The speaker of Tok Pisin distinguishes between *we* (speaker and person or persons addressed), and *we* (speaker and another or others, excluding anyone addressed). Where English has only *we*, Tok Pisin has inclusive *yumi* (from *you* and *me*) and exclusive *mipela* (from *me* and *fellow*). Although the lexical material used to make the distinction is from English, the meanings derive from categories in Melanesian languages. The element *-pela* (fellow) serves additional grammatical ends as a suffix marking attributives: *gutpela man* a good man; *naispela haus* a nice house; *wanpela meri* a woman. In the pronoun system, it appears as a formative in the first- and second-person plural, *mipela* (*we* exclusive) and *yupela* (*you* plural).

**Vocabulary**. There are five sources of words: (1) English, which makes up most of the approximately 2,500 basic words: *mi* I, *yu* you (singular), *askim* a question, to ask, *lukautim* to take care of. (2) German, because of the German administration of the northern part of New Guinea (1884–1914): *rausim* to get rid of, *beten* to pray. (3) Spanish and Portuguese words are widely found in European-based pidgin and creole languages and also occur in Tok Pisin: *save* to know (from *sabir/saber*), *pikinini* a small child (from *pequeño*, small). (4) Polynesian languages: *kaikai* food, *tambu* taboo (from *tabu*). (5) Indigenous PNG languages: *kiau* an egg (from Kuanua, a language of East New Britain, which played an important part as a substrate language). In some cases, Tok Pisin expressions have been borrowed into the varieties of English used by expatriates in PNG: *going finish* (from *go pinis*), as in *going finish sale* a sale of household goods held when people leave for good.

Traditionally, Europeans have regarded Tok Pisin as a bastardized form of English. In it, some everyday vulgar words have taken on different and socially neutral meanings: *baksait* (from *backside*) the back rather than the buttocks; *as* (from *arse*) the buttocks, but extended to refer to the base or foundation of anything, as in *as bilong diwai* (the base or foot of a tree) and *as bilong lo* (the reason or cause of a law); *bagarap* (from *bugger up*) used as noun and verb, as in *Em kisim bagarap* (He had an accident) and *Pik i bagarapim gaden* (The pig ruined the garden); *sit* (from *shit*), as in *sit bilong paia* (shit belonging to fire: ashes); *bulsitim* (from *bullshit*) to deceive. The Tok Pisin word for excrement is locally derived: *pekpek*. Tok Pisin has other terms of abuse often quite different from or completely unrelated to English: *puslama* (sea slug) for a lazy person; *tu kina meri* (where *kina* is a unit of currency and *meri* means 'woman') for a prostitute.

**Status and functions**. Tok Pisin has undergone structural and functional expansion. Although English is the official medium of education, Tok Pisin is used in a variety of public domains, not only in political debates in the House of Assembly (where it is the preferred medium), but also in broadcasting and journalism, and for all its new functions it has drawn heavily on English. So much English has been borrowed into the language, particularly by educated urban speakers, that there are now two main varieties: urban pidgin and rural or bush pidgin. Most of the printed material in Tok Pisin until recently has been religious, centred on a translation of the Bible. Since 1970, there has been a weekly newspaper in Tok Pisin called *Wantok* (one talk: one language), a word used to refer to members of one's own clan group. The use of Tok Pisin for literary purposes is becoming more common. See ENGLISH.

## ■ TONE ■

A term used generally for musical and vocal PITCH and quality, and in phonetics and linguistics for a level or contour of *pitch*, the quality or choice of which is known as *tonality*. Specifically, tone is a *pitch contour* that begins on an accented SYLLABLE and continues to the end of a *tone group*: that is, up to but not including the next stressed syllable. Simple tones move only in one direction: *fall* and *rise*. In English, these tones suggest finality, the fall frequently occurring at the end of a statement, the rise at the end of a *yes–no* question. The compound tones *fall-rise* and *rise-fall* are non-final, suggesting that the speaker has not yet finished (see below).

**Tone group and breath group**. Normal speech does not consist of unorganized strings of words, but stretches of words in the utterance of which breath and tone are integral parts. The *breath group* is a group of words uttered on a single breath, after which the speaker either stops speaking or draws breath to continue. This group may or may not correspond to phrases and sentences as recorded in writing or print, and will consist of one or more further groups of words organized in terms of tone. Such a further group is a *tone group* or *tone unit*. Major tone groups correspond more or less closely to sentences of prose, while minor tone groups (those which phoneticians have analysed in particular detail) are phrasal or lexical. The division of tone groups in SPEECH is analogous to punctuation in writing, and in historical terms the conventions of PUNCTUATION have by and large arisen as attempts to reflect on a surface such aspects of speech as tones and pauses for breath or effect. Where a punctuation mark like a period or a comma is appropriate in writing, a tone-group boundary is usually appropriate in speech. However, the reverse is not true: if a spoken text is written down, the position of many tone-group boundaries cannot be marked by punctuation.

**The constituents of the tone group**. The nature of the tone group relates to the natural RHYTHM, stress, and intonation of English. Each group contains one or more stressed syllables known as the *nucleus*, the *tonic syllable(s)*, or the *tonic(s)*: for example, the capitalized syllables in *YES* and in *OH YES it is*. The nucleus is often assumed to be the most prominent syllable in the tone group, but this is not always the case. Any syllables following the nucleus form the *tail*: for example, *it is* in *Yes it is*, *-shire* in *YORK-shire*. If there is more than one stressed syllable, the first is referred to as the *onset*: the *OH* in *OH YES it is*, the *NEW* in *NEW YORK is big*. The term *head* is used for a group of syllables beginning with the onset up to but not including the nucleus. Any weak syllables preceding the onset are generally known as the *prehead*: for example, *she* in *she WON'T*. A combination of prehead, nucleus, and tail occurs in *TasM Ania*. The end of a major tone group is typically marked by a pattern indicating finality: for example, a fall in pitch to close a statement. Nonfinal minor tone groups are often marked by levelling off in the pitch contour, or by a rise in pitch: for example, in a list-like series, with a fall on the closing item.

**Individual tones**. There are five tones in English: the falling tone or fall, the rising tone or rise, the rise–fall, the fall–rise, and the level tone: (1) The *fall* moves from a higher to a lower pitch, and there are two subtypes. A *low fall* is used to end statements, give orders, ask non-emphatic *wh*-questions, and ask emphatic and rhetorical *yes–no* questions. The *high fall* is used in contrastive stress: for example, in *John loves Mary* it is on *John* if he is being contrasted with *Bill*, on *loves* if it is contrasted with *hates*, and on *Mary* if she is contrasted with *Helen*. (2) The *rise* moves from a lower to a higher pitch, and there are two subtypes. The *low rise* is used for incomplete statements (often signalling an intention to continue speaking), in listing (until the end, when the tone falls), for requests, and in expressions of po-

liteness and interest. The *high rise* occurs in asking non-emphatic *yes–no* questions, echo questions, and emphatic *why*–questions. (3) The *rise–fall* moves from a lower to a higher pitch, then back. It is like the fall, but more emphatic or exclamatory, and may also express disagreement and irony. It is rare in RP, but common in some other varieties, such as WelshE, IrE, and IndE. In varieties which do not use it much, its actual or apparent overuse can suggest naïvety, unwarranted enthusiasm, and a patronizing attitude. (4) The *fall-rise* moves from a higher to a lower pitch, then back. It may express assertion and contradiction. (5) The *level tone* is one in which the 'slope' of the pitch movement is not enough for it to be classed as a rise or a fall. Its functions are similar to those of the rise. See INTONATION.

**TONGA**. A country in Oceania and member of the COMMONWEALTH, consisting of 170 islands due south of Western Samoa. Languages: Tongan, English (both official). Tonga was a British protectorate from 1900 until independence in 1970.

**TONGUE**. A flexible mass of tissue attached to the lower back of the mouth of most vertebrate animals; an aid to chewing and swallowing, the organ of taste, and an important component in the articulation of SPEECH. Words for 'tongue' in many languages stand for speech itself. English has a number of words and phrases of different origin which do this: *language*, through French *langue*, from Latin *lingua*, tongue; *linguistics*, directly from Latin; *polyglot* and *isogloss*, from the Greek *glõssa*, tongue; the phrases *mother tongue*, *foreign tongue*, and the Biblical *gift of tongues*; such idioms as *Has the cat got your tongue?* (said to someone who will not speak), *to bite one's tongue* (to remain silent despite provocation), *it's on the tip of my tongue* (I know it but I can't quite recall it), *Hold your tongue* (Be quiet).

In terms of anatomy and PHONETICS, the tongue has five parts: the *tip* (*of the tongue*), the *blade* (*of the tongue*), the *front* (*of the tongue*), the *back* (*of the tongue*), and the *root*, which lies not in the mouth but in the pharynx. Sounds made at the tip (the 'apex' of the tongue) are *apical*. The blade is immediately behind the tip, lies opposite the alveolar ridge of the upper mouth when the tongue is in a state of rest, and sounds made with the blade (Latin *lamina*) are *laminal*. The area behind the blade is the front, which lies opposite the hard palate when the tongue is in a state of rest, and sounds made with the front are *palatal*. The back of the tongue lies opposite the soft palate or velum when the tongue is in a state of rest, and sounds made with the back include *velar consonants* and *back vowels*.

**TONGUE-TWISTER**. A sentence, phrase, or rhyme that is difficult to pronounce, especially when said quickly. The difficulty is usually caused by ALLITERATION: the presence of similar-sounding consonants interspersed with a variety of vowels, as in *Peter Piper picked a peck of pickled pepper*. Such tongue-twisters may be accidental or deliberately used for especially comic effect. They became particularly popular in the 19c as rhymes designed to cause pronunciation problems and elocutionists used examples like *Truly rural* and *She sells sea-shells on the sea-shore* to improve enunciation.

**TRACHEA** [Stress: 'tra-KEE-a']. An anatomical term for the tube carrying air to and from the lungs, commonly known as the *windpipe*. See SPEECH.

**TRADE JARGON**, also **trade language**. A semi-technical term for a minimal language used by people with no common language, as a means of communication for trading purposes, such as *Chinook Jargon* and *Trader Navajo* in North America. Such languages do not generally stabilize and expand. See JARGON, PIDGIN.

**TRADEMARK**, also **trade mark**, **trademark**. **1.** A SIGN or NAME that is secured by legal registration or (in some countries) by established use, and serves to distinguish one product from similar brands sold by competitors: for example, the shell logo for *Shell*, the petroleum company, and the brand name *Jacuzzi* for one kind of whirlpool bath. Legal injunctions are often sought when companies consider that their sole right to such marks has been infringed; the makers of *Coke*, *Jeep*, *Jell-O*, *Kleenex*, *Scotch Tape*, and *Xerox* have all gone to court in defence of their brand (or proprietary) names. Although companies complain when their trademarks begin to be used as GENERIC terms in the media or elsewhere, their own marketing has often, paradoxically, caused the problem.

There is in practice a vague area between generic terms proper, trademarks that have become somewhat generic, and trademarks that are recognized as such. The situation is complicated by different usages in different countries: for example, *Monopoly* and *Thermos* are trademarks in the UK but generics in the US. Product wrappers and business documents often indicate that a trademark is registered by adding *TM* (for 'trademark') or *R* (for 'registered') in a superscript circle after the term, as with *English Today*™, *Sellotape*.® The term usually differs from *trade name* by designating a specific product and not a business, service, or class of goods, articles, or substances: but some trademarks and trade names may happen to be the same. Everyday words of English that were once trademarks (some now universal, some more common in one variety of English than another, some dated, all commonly written without an initial capital) include *aspirin*, *band-aid*, *cellophane*, *celluloid*, *cornflakes*, *dictaphone*, *escalator*, *granola*, *hoover*, *kerosene*, *lanolin*, *mimeograph*, *nylon*, *phonograph*, *shredded wheat*, *zipper*. Trademarks facing difficulties include *Astroturf*, *Dacron*, *Formica*, *Frisbee*, *Hovercraft*, *Jacuzzi*, *Laundromat*, *Mace*, *Muzak*, *Q-Tips*, *Scotch Tape*, *Styrofoam*, *Teflon*, *Vaseline*, *Xerox*. The inclusion of such names in dictionaries, even when marked 'trademark' or 'proprietary term', indicates that their status has begun to shift. Trademark names used as verbs are a further area of difficulty, both generally and in lexicography. One solution adopted by publishers of dictionaries is to regard the verb forms as generic, with a small initial letter: that is, *Xerox* (noun), but *xerox* (verb). **2.** A mark or feature characteristic of, or identified with, a person or thing: *That slow drawl is his trademark*.

**TRADITIONAL ORTHOGRAPHY**. Usual short form *t.o.* A term used especially by SPELLING reformers for the conventional ORTHOGRAPHY of standard English, usually in contrast to proposed replacements. See INITIAL TEACHING ALPHABET.

**TRANSFORMATIONAL-GENERATIVE GRAMMAR**, short form *TG*. In theoretical LINGUISTICS, a type of generative grammar first advocated by Noam CHOMSKY in *Syntactic Structures* (1957). Since then, there have been many changes in the descriptive apparatus of TG. Common to all versions is the view that some rules are transformational: that is, they change one structure into another according to such prescribed conventions as moving, inserting, deleting, and replacing items. From an early stage of its history, TG has stipulated two levels of syntactic structure: *deep structure* (an abstract underlying structure that incorporates all the syntactic information required for the interpretation of a given sentence) and *surface structure* (a structure that incorporates all the syntactic features of a sentence required to convert the sentence into a spoken or written version). *Transformations* link deep with surface structure. A typical transformation is the rule for forming questions, which requires that the normal subject–verb order is inverted so that the surface structure of *Can I see you later?* differs in order of elements from that of *I can see you later.* The theory postulates that the two sentences have the same order in deep structure, but the question transformation changes the order to that in surface structure. Sentences that are syntactically ambiguous have the same surface structures but different deep structures: for example, the sentence *Visiting relatives can be a nuisance* is ambiguous in that the subject *Visiting relatives* may correspond to *To visit relatives* or to *Relatives that visit.* The ambiguity is dissolved if the modal verb *can* is omitted, since the clausal subject requires a singular verb (*Visiting relatives is a nuisance*), whereas the phrasal subject requires the plural (*Visiting relatives are a nuisance*).

## TRANSITIVE AND INTRANSITIVE. A

transitive VERB (*enjoy, make, want*) is followed by an OBJECT (*We enjoyed the trip; They make toys; He's making progress*), or is preceded by its object, in such questions as *What do you want?* Such verbs are not normally found in the forms *We enjoyed, *They make/He's making, *Do you want? In this, they contrast with *intransitive* verbs, which do not have objects: *They shouted; He's fallen down; She hurried home.* Many verbs can, however, be both transitive and intransitive: *He is playing* (*football*); *She hurried* (*the children*) *home; He ran* (*a good race*). Some grammarians divide transitive verbs into: *monotransitive verbs*, which take one object (*She ate the apple*); *ditransitive verbs*, which take two objects (*Give a dog a bad name*); *complex transitive verbs*, which take an object and a complement (*Paint the town red*).

## ■ TRANSLATION ──────────── ■

The restatement of the forms of one LANGUAGE in another: the chief means of exchanging information between different language communities. Translation is a fundamental yet often overlooked element in life and has played a decisive part in the development of languages like English, especially by promoting the flow of ideas and the spread of the literary forms in which they have been expressed: for example, Homeric poetry from ancient Greece and the Bible translated from Hebrew and Greek. As the Canadian historian of translation Louis Kelly has observed, 'Western Europe owes its civilization to translators' (1979). Five distinctions are commonly made when discussing translation, none of which represent absolute positions, but rather end-points in an appropriate continuum:

**1. *Translating and interpreting*.** Written translation can be distinguished from oral translation or interpreting, which came first, as for example in military and diplomatic exchanges. However, because of its relative permanence and lasting influence on the transmission of culture and technology, written translation has traditionally been considered more important. Professional interpreting takes two forms: *simultaneous interpreting* (at international conferences, etc.) and *consecutive interpreting* (in court, at diplomatic gatherings, in business transactions, etc.).

**2. *Word-for-word and free translation*.** Languages do not match neatly in the way they form messages. Depending on the level at which translation equivalence can be established (word with word, phrase with phrase, word with phrase, etc.) translations can be more *literal* (that is, one-to-one at the level of words), or *free* (restatement of the message regardless of formal correspondence).

**3. *Literary and technical translation*.** Depending on the type of discourse translated, a distinction is often made between literary translation (of aesthetic, imaginative, fictional texts) and technical translation (of workaday, pragmatic, nonfictional texts). However, boundary lines between them are sometimes difficult to draw, as in the translation of the Bible (which is currently available in over 2,000 languages): for example, the drama of the Book of Job and the listing of laws in Leviticus.

**4. Professional and pedagogical translation.** A distinction can be made between translation as a vocation or trade (working for a client) and translation as an exercise in the process of language learning (working for a teacher). It has been argued that traditional grammar–translation tasks in school do not constitute a suitable training for translating as such.

**5. Human and machine translation.** The high cost of professional translating and interpreting has encouraged institutional investment in experiments with largescale electronic translation and dictionary systems. However, fully automatic translation of high quality still seems still to be a long way off.

**Translation and publishing.** Much of the world's publishing depends on translation, although the centrality of the translator's role is often only minimally indicated in the credits of particular works. Thousands of translators and interpreters around the world continue to perform essential tasks in often less-than-ideal conditions. By the early 1970s, close to half of the world's book production was made up of translations, the chief source languages being English, French, Russian, German, Spanish, and Italian, the chief target languages German, Russian, Spanish, English, Japanese, and French. Because of worldwide demand for translation of all kinds, the 20c has been referred to as 'the age of translation'.

**TRANSLATION EQUIVALENT.** An expression from a LANGUAGE which has the same meaning as, or can be used in a similar context to, one from another language, and can therefore be used to translate it: for example, English *I don't understand*, French *Je ne comprends pas*, Italian *Non capisco*, Modern Greek *Dhen katalaveno*, Japanese *Wakarimasen*. Achieving such correspondences involves special bilingual skills to cope with the tendency among languages to 'lack of fit' (technically, *non-isomorphism* or *anisomorphism*). Thus, the source-language expression may be a single word, a phrase, or a sentence within a text, but its target-language equivalent may have to be rendered at a different level: for example, the English idiom *It's pouring (with rain)* cannot be translated word-for-word into German,

but the meaning can be redistributed as *Es regnet in Strömen* (It rains in streams). Most bilingual speakers can supply examples of such equivalents, and bilingual dictionaries codify them in bulk, but it is the job especially of the translator and interpreter to decide whether a particular expression is a fitting match for a particular passage. A number of complex strategies are needed to find translation equivalents, ranging from literal procedures such as direct transfer, substitution, and loan translation to devices of free translation such as transposition, adaptation, and circumlocution (which aim to find the closest functional equivalent). The literal approach can work well when language pairs have a similar structure: for example English and German with *mother/Mutter*, *Mother's Day/Muttertag*: but see FAUX AMI. The free style, however, is demanded even in similar languages whenever anything close to idiom occurs: *mother-country/Heimat* (homeland), *necessity is the mother of invention/Not macht erfinderisch* (need makes inventive).

**TRANSLITERATION.** The action, process, or result of converting one set of signs to another, usually involving at least one set of alphabetic letters. Transliteration becomes necessary when two or more writing systems differ greatly. Such differences range along a continuum, from the somewhat similar (ROMAN and Cyrillic), through the significantly dissimilar (Roman ALPHABET, Arabic script), to the utterly different (Roman alphabet, Japanese syllabaries and ideograms). Transliteration became important in the 19c, when European scholars wished to find Roman equivalents for the writing systems of various 'exotic' languages. As a result, there are systems of Roman transliteration (each more or less standard for its purposes) for ARABIC, Chinese, GREEK, Japanese, Persian, Russian, SANSKRIT, and Tamil, among others. Conversion to Roman requires, in varying degrees, diacritics and special symbols for sounds or practices that have no equivalent in any prior Roman system.

**TRINIDAD AND TOBAGO.** A Caribbean country and member of the COMMONWEALTH, consisting of the two major islands at the southern end of the Lesser Antilles, close to the South American coast. Languages: English (official), English Creole,

## THE SPECTRUM OF TRANSLATION

At its widest, the process of restatement from one language into another can include both *transliteration* (transfer from one writing system to another) and the range of options from strict word-for-word literalism to free adaptation. The following excerpts, all from *The Bhagavad-Gita* (Book 2, verse 22) illustrate, more or less, the whole spectrum.

**1.  *The source*** The original Sanskrit verse, printed in the Devanagari script:

वासांसि जीर्णानि यथा विहाय
नवानि गृह्णाति नरोऽपराणि
तथा शरीराणि विहाय जीर्णा-
न्यन्यानि संयाति नवानि देही

**2.  *Transliteration*** The Sanskrit verse, printed in a variety of the Roman alphabet:

*vāsāṁsi jīrṇāni yathā vihāya*
   *navāni gṛhṇāti naro 'parāṇi*
*tathā śarīrāṇi vihāya jīrṇāny*
   *anyāni saṁyāti navāni dehī*

**3.  *Word-for-word literalism***

clothes worn-out just-as casting-off
new-ones takes a-man others
in-the-same-way bodies casting-off worn-out
different-ones takes-on new the-embodied.
                              (Tom McArthur, *Yoga and the Bhagavad-Gita*, Thorson, 1986)

**4.  *A close blank-verse translation***

As leaving aside worn-out garments
A man takes other, new ones,
So leaving aside worn-out bodies
To other, new ones goes the embodied (soul).
            (Franklin Edgerton, *The Bhagavad Gītā*, Harvard University Press, 1944)

**5.  *A close translation in prose***

As a man casts off his worn-out clothes and takes on other new ones, so does the embodied (self) cast off its worn-out bodies and enters other new ones.
            (R. C. Zaehner, *The Bhagavad-Gītā*, Oxford University Press, 1969)

**6.  *A freer translation in prose***

Just as a person casts off worn-out garments and puts on others that are new, even so does the embodied soul cast off worn-out bodies and take on others that are new.
                              (Sarvepalli Radhakrishnan with Charles A. Moore, in *Indian Philosophy*,
                              Princeton University Press, 1957)

For specimens of translations of two verses of the Bible over some six centuries of English, see BIBLE.

and some Bhojpuri, HINDI, FRENCH, and SPANISH. Both islands were visited by Columbus in 1498. The Spanish settled in Trinidad in the 16c and the island was periodically raided by the French, British, and Dutch. In 1802, it was ceded to the British under the Treaty of Amiens. Tobago, after being colonized by Dutch, British, and French settlers, became a British colony of the Windward Islands group in 1814. It was administratively linked with Trinidad in 1899 and the joint territory became independent in 1962.

The term *Trinidadian English* refers to the variety of English used for formal communication by educated speakers of Trinidad and Tobago. Its lexical distinctiveness derives from the use of Spanish and of a French-based CREOLE before the arrival of English speakers, as well as from the influence of East Indian languages dating from the earlier 19c. Its phonetic characteristics result from pressure from the Trinidadian and Tobagonian English-based creoles with which it coexists. See CARIBBEAN ENGLISH, CARIBBEAN ENGLISH CREOLE.

**TRISTAN DA CUNHA**, short form *Tristan*. A British dependency in the South Atlantic. Language: English. The Portuguese discovered SAINT HELENA and the Tristan Archipelago in 1506 and the British occupied Tristan in 1816 during the exile of Napoleon at St Helena. In 1961, the islanders were evacuated after a volcanic eruption, but returned in 1963. The people, among whom there are only seven surnames, number some 350. Distinctive features include: (1) An intrusive initial /h/: 'highland happle' for *island apple*. (2) Such words as *first*, *herb* pronounced 'farst', 'harb'. (3) Tense and possessive inflections often dropped and *is* often omitted. (4) Such usages as *plant in* (intransitive) to plant potatoes, *the sea put up bubbles* the sea grew (too) rough (for fishing), and *eastings* and *westings*, to indicate which way the island is circled. (5) The term *gulch* is common, as are such complex place-names as *Down-where-minister-pick-up-his-things*, *Ridge-where-the-goat-jump-off*, and *Blackinthehole Hill*.

**TROPE**, also **turn of phrase**. In RHETORIC, both an expression that deviates from the natural and literal through a change in meaning, often with a pleasing effect, and the device or technique that makes such a change possible. For the Roman rhetorician Quintilian, tropes were metaphors and metonyms, etc., and figures (*figurae*) were such forms of discourse as rhetorical questions, digression, repetition, antithesis, and periphrasis (also referred to as *schemes*). He noted that the two kinds of usage were often confused (a state of affairs that has continued to the present day). In the 18c, the term became associated with overornate style and fell into disrepute when a plainer style came to be preferred. As a result, what were once known as tropes and figures are now generally called *figures of speech* or, more broadly still, *rhetorical devices*. See FIGURATIVE LANGUAGE, FIGURE OF SPEECH.

**TURKS AND CAICOS ISLANDS**. A British Caribbean dependency, consisting of two groups of 30 islands and bays forming the south-east end of the Bahamian archipelago. Languages: English (official), CREOLE. In 1765, the islands were formally linked with the Bahamas, then in 1848 with Jamaica. When Jamaica became independent in 1962, the islands were again associated with the Bahamas, then in 1972 became a British colony by local choice.

**TUVALU**. A country of Oceania and member of the COMMONWEALTH. Languages: Tuvaluan, English (both official). Formerly known as the *Ellice Islands* and part of the British colony of the *Gilbert and Ellice Islands*, Tuvalu gained its independence in 1978. See KIRIBATI.

**TWANG**. **1.** Also *nasal twang*. A NASAL way of speaking attributed to English Puritans in the 16/17c: 'To make incoherent Stuff (seasoned with Twang and Tautology) pass for high Rhetorick' (Robert South, *Sermons*, 1661). **2.** A distinctive ACCENT or voice quality: 'You talk very good English, but you have a mighty Twang of the foreigner' (Farquhar, *The Beaux' Stratagem*, 1707). See CHEE-CHEE ENGLISH.

**TYNDALE, William** [*c*.1492–1536]. English cleric, BIBLE translator, and Protestant martyr. Born in Gloucestershire, he studied at Oxford, was ordained in 1521, and entered a Gloucestershire household as chaplain/tutor, where he resolved to translate the BIBLE and issued a challenge to a local priest: 'If God spare my life I will cause that the boy that drives the plough shall know more of the scripture than thou.' He preached and wrote in London before moving to Germany, where his New Testament was printed in Worms (1524–5), with a later revision printed in Antwerp (1534). Copies smuggled to England were rigidly suppressed. He also translated the Pentateuch and Jonah, and possibly other parts of the Old Testament, after contact with Jews at Worms in Germany. He was betrayed to officials of the Holy Roman Emperor in Antwerp and was strangled and burned as a heretic at Vilvorde, near Brussels. His biblical translation was deliberately homely and without pedantry, as in the phrases *for ever and ever, to die the death, a man after his own heart, apple of his eye*, which have passed into general English usage. The work fulfilled his aim of appealing to all classes in English society and formed a basis for most subsequent renderings, including the Authorized Version.

# U

## U, u

[Called 'you']. The 21st LETTER of the Roman ALPHABET as used for English. It originated in the Phoenician consonant symbol *waw*, the common ancestor of the letters *F, U, V, W, Y*. The Greeks adopted *waw* as upsilon (γ, lower case υ), which the Romans took from the Etruscans as *V*. The distinction in English between *u* as vowel and *v* as consonant was not made consistently in print until the 17c. Previously, the distinction tended to be positional, not phonological, with *v* used word-initially and *u* medially: *vnder, liue*. Until the 19c, some dictionaries listed *u* and *v* together rather than successively, or *v* before *u* in the alphabet. The use of *V* for *U* has survived into the 20c for some lapidary inscriptions: the BBC's *Bush House* in London has *BVSH HOVSE* carved over the entrance.

**Sound values**. (1) Formerly, the common feature in the pronunciation of *u, v, w*, was lip movement: lip-rounding is a feature of the back vowel in *put* and *truth* and the front vowel in French *tu*; /v/ is a labio-dental consonant; /w/ is a labial semi-vowel. In Modern English, French *u* has been Anglicized as a diphthong with a preceding *i*-glide (*music, argue*) and *u* commonly represents /w/ before a vowel after *g, q*, and *s* (*anguish, quiet, persuade*). (2) Beside these traditional values of *u*, most English accents have a further value. By the 17c, a vowel shift in southern England had changed the *put*-value of *u* in many words to a new sound, now heard in most accents, but not in the accents of the English Midlands and North. This is the value of *u* in *but* (except for the North of England), which today no longer rhymes with *put* and involves no lip-rounding. (3) In general pronunciation, the letter *u* spells four distinct vowel sounds, as in *but, put, truth, music*, as well as the /w/ in *quiet*, etc. The four vowel sounds will be referred to below as the values *but-u, put-u, truth-u, music-u*.

**Long and short U**. The four vowel values can be grouped into long and short pairs: *but-u* and *put-u* are short, *truth-u* and *music-u* are long. Like the long and short values of the other vowel letters, short and long *u* alternate in related words: *assumption/assume,* *humble/humility, judge/judicious, number/ numerous, punish/punitive, reduction/reduce, study/student.*

**Variation in values**. The four values are not consistently distinguished. ScoE typically does not distinguish *put-u* and *truth-u*, and AmE often gives a *truth-u* to words pronounced with *music-u* in RP: AmE *duty* rhyming with *booty*, RP *duty* rhyming with *beauty*. This change occurs only after alveolar consonants: /d, l, n, r, s, t/. Because the *but/put* split did not take place in the Midlands and North of England, *but/put* rhyme in the accents of these regions. This non-distinction of *but-u* and *put-u* has often been stigmatized as non-standard, while their occasional reversal (*butcher* being pronounced with *but-u* rather than *put-u*) is considered to be hypercorrection towards RP. Variation between *truth-u* and *music-u* is not always regional, the distinction generally being blurred after *l, s*, as when *lute/loot* may or may not be pronounced as homophones, and *sue/suit* may in BrE have either long value of *u*. Although four possible vowel values in many accents make *u* a complex letter (with division into short and long realizations, and with variation between these values), a particular value is generally apparent from the environment. *U* is normally short except syllable-finally, and *truth-u* only arises after certain consonants.

**Other spellings**. The values of *u* have common alternative spellings. As a result of vowel shifts or spelling changes, patterns have arisen with the sound values of *u* in *but, put, truth*, but using *o* (*son, wolf, do, move*), or *oe* (*does, shoes*), or *oo* (*blood, good, food*), or *ou* (*touch, could, youth*). Similarly the sound of long *u* is commonly spelt *ew* (*crew, dew, few, newt, pewter, steward*); arguably *w* should be seen here as a positional variant of *u* (compare *few/feud*).

**But-U (short)**. Short *u* occurs before final consonants and (usually multiple) medial consonants: initial *u* in words of Old English origin (*udder, ugly, under, up, us, utter*, and the negative prefix *un-* as in *unborn, uneventful*); before two consonants in some non-English words (*ulcer, ultimate, umbilical,* *umpire*); in monosyllables ending in a consonant letter (*tub, bud, cuff, mug, luck, cull, bulk, hum, sun, bunk, cup, bus, just, hut*); in short-vowel monosyllables ending in silent *e* (*budge, bulge, plunge*). A few monosyllables contain *put-u* (see below), and the *truth-u* in *truth* itself (and also in *Ruth*) is an exception. In polysyllables, *but-u* usually precedes two consonants, either doubled (*rubble, bucket, rudder, suffer, nugget, sullen, summer, supple, hurry, russet, butter*) or as a string (*publish, indulgent, number, abundant*). Words ending in *-ion* similarly have short *u* before two consonants: *percussion, convulsion, compunction, destruction, assumption*, but long *u* before a single consonant in *confusion, evolution*. Exceptions to these patterns include long *u* in *duplicate, lucrative, rubric* and as indicated by final magic *e* in *scruple* (contrast short *ou* in *couple*); short *u* before a single consonant in *study* (contrast *muddy, Judy*) and in *bunion* (contrast *trunnion, union*).

**Put-*U* (short)**. The lip-rounded *put-u* occurs in a few words, especially after the labial consonants *b, p,* and before *l*: *bull, bullet, bulletin, bullion, bully, bush, bushel, butcher, cuckoo, cushion, full, pudding, pull, pullet, pulley, pulpit, push, puss, put, sugar*. *Muslim* is heard with both *but-u* and *put-u*. *Put-u* is nevertheless not a rare sound in English, being also spelt *ou* in the common *could, would, should,* and frequently *oo,* as in *foot, good*.

**Truth-*U* and Music-*U* (long)**. Long *u* (whether, *truth-u* or *music-u*) occurs in polysyllables before a single consonant with following vowel: contrast *fundamental/funeral* and the patterns in *cucumber, undulate*. Long *u* occurs in: *alluvial, deputy, educate, fury, ludicrous, lunar, peculiar, refusal, ruby, rufous, ruminate, superb*. In final closed syllables, long *u* is usually shown by magic (lengthening) *e*: *amuse, flute, fume, huge, prelude, puce, puke, pure, refute, rude, rule, ruse, tube, tune*. In accordance with the above patterns, the monosyllabic prefix *sub-* has *but-u* (*subject*), but disyllabic *super-* has long *u*. In most circumstances, long *u* is *music-u*, the initial *i*-glide being assimilated to produce *truth-u* only after certain consonants. *Music-u* is therefore found word-initially before a single consonant, especially in derivations from the Latin root *unus* (one), as in *unicorn, unify, union, unity, universe*. Other cases include *ubiquitous, urine, use, utility*. *Music-u* follows consonants as in *ambulance, acute, confuse, coagulate, music, annual, compute, en-*

*thuse, revue,* and in RP but commonly not in AmE as in *duke, tube*. Both *music-u* and *truth-u* are heard after *l, s* (*lute, suit*). *Truth-u* occurs after *r, sh* (includingt the affricate *j*) and is explicit in *yu: truth, prune, Shute, chute, Schubert, June, jury, yule*. In an unstressed medial syllable, 'long' *music-u* tends in fact to be a rather short vowel: contrast *deputy, educate* with *dispute, duke*.

**Final *U***. Syllable-final *u* is pronounced long. Word-finally, it has an additional silent *e* in long-established English words (*argue, continue, due, rue*), although this commonly disappears before suffixes (*argue/argument, continue/continual, due/duty, true/truth*). Final *u* occurs without following *e*, particularly in recently formed or borrowed words: *emu, flu, guru, Hindu, jujitsu, menu*. Long *u* also arises syllable-finally before a vowel (contrast *annul, annual*): *dual, suet, fluid, fluoride, vacuum*.

***U* before *R***. Before *r* with no following vowel, RP gives *u* the same value as *e* or *i* before *r*: *fur, hurt, nurse, absurd, purchase, concur* (compare *her, sir*). When a vowel follows, *u* is long (*rural, bureau, during*), but is modified with the hint of an inserted schwa (*cure, pure, endure; rural, bureau, during*). Like other multiple consonants, *rr* normally induces a preceding *but-u*: *burrow, current, flurry, furrier* (noun): but the adjective *furry* retains the value of *u* of its base form *fur*, and its comparative *furrier* is then a homograph of the noun *furrier* with its *but-u*.

***U* and schwa**. Like all vowel letters in English, *u* when unstressed in fluent speech may lose distinctive value, being reduced to SCHWA: initially (*until, upon*), before a stressed syllable (*suggest, surround*), and after the main stress especially before *l, m, n, r, s* (medially, as in *faculty, calumny, voluntary, Saturday, industry,* and in final syllables *awful, difficult, autumn, album, minimum, museum, tedium, vacuum, murmur, injure, circus, radius*). In some words, *u* is reduced to schwa while retaining the preceding *i*-glide of *music-u: century, failure*. In *lettuce* and in the noun *minute, u* is commonly reduced to schwa, and in RP to the value of short *i*. The adjective *minute* has *music-u*.

**Assimilation**. Phonetically, *music-u* is a diphthong consisting of a glide *i*-sound followed by *truth-u,* but in fluent speech the glide often affects the value of a preceding consonant, sometimes being assimilated with it entirely, as when *duty, tune* are spoken as 'jooty', 'choon' (typically not in North America), and *casual, picture* are spoken as 'kazhel', 'pikcher'. Such assimilation is usual before the suffixes *-ual, -ure* after *d, s, t, z*: *gradual, casual, mutual; verdure, closure, picture, azure*. The assimilation with initial *s* in *sugar, sure* is of such long standing that the *s* is perceived as having an abnormal value. For some speakers, the tendency extends to *assume* and *presume* spoken as 'ashoom', 'prezhoom'.

**Semi-vowel U**. (1) vowel occurs commonly in words of FRENCH derivation and typically after *g* (*distinguish, guava, language, sanguine*), *q* (*quash, quail, quest, quit, quiet, quote, acquaint, equal, loquacious*), and *s* (*suave, suede, suite, persuade*). (2) In similar contexts, however, *u* may have its full vowel value: contrast *suite/suicide*. (3) Some words with initial *qu* are of OLD ENGLISH origin, having changed their spelling after the Norman Conquest from *cw-* to *qu-*: *cwen, cwic* now written *queen, quick*.

**Silent U**. (1) Especially in words of French derivation: after *g* (where it serves to distinguish hard and soft *g*: *page/vague*), as in *vague, fatigue, vogue, fugue*, and after *q*, as in *opaque, technique, mosquito*. (2) In initial *qu* (*quay, queue*) and in *conquer* and often *languor*, although pronounced /w/ in *conquest, languid*. (3) Elsewhere, *u* is inserted only to preserve the hard value of preceding *g*: *Portugal/Portuguese* (see G, Q). (4) Although apparently part of a digraph, *u* is effectively silent in *gauge, aunt, laugh*, BrE *draught* (compare AmE *draft*), *build, cough, trough, though*, BrE *mould, moult, smoulder* (compare AmE *mold, molt, smolder*), *boulder, shoulder, soul, buoy* (especially BrE), *buy*. Although *u* is silent in *biscuit, circuit*, it arguably indicates preceding hard *c* (contrast *explicit*). It is optionally silent in *conduit*.

**Digraphs**. *U* often has the secondary function of indicating a modified value for a preceding letter. For the digraph *au* (as in *taut*) and *ou* (as in *out*), see A, O respectively. *Eau* in *beauty* has the value of *music-u*. For final *eau* (*bureau*, etc.), see E. The main digraphs having one of the four sound values of *u* are:

*EU*. (1) The digraph *eu* regularly represents *music-u*, especially in words of GREEK derivation (*Europe, eulogy, pseudo-, neurotic*), but occasionally elsewhere (*feud*). (2) In

*sleuth*, the *eu* represents *truth-u*, as does *oeu* in BrE *manoeuvre* (AmE *maneuver*).

*OU*. (1) The digraph *ou* has one of the values of *u*, except when it is used as a standard digraph for the diphthong in *out* and for long *o* as in *soul*. See O. The spelling *ou* sometimes derives from French, and sometimes represents earlier pronunciation with a long vowel. (2) It represents *but-u* as in *country, couple, cousin, double, southern, touch, trouble, young*, with following /f/ spelt *-gh* in *enough, rough, tough*, and in BrE *courage, flourish, nourish*, AmE giving this *-our-* the value as in *journey*. (3) It represents *put-u* in *could, should, would* and *truth-u* in *ghoul, group, soup, through, uncouth, wound* (noun), *youth* and also in such recent French loans as *boulevard, bouquet, coup*, BrE *route* (in AmE often homophonous with *rout*), *souvenir, tour, trousseau*. (4) It represents modified *u* before *r*: *courteous, courtesy* (compare cognate *curts[e]y*), *journal* (cognate *diurnal*), *journey, scourge* (compare *urge*).

*UE, UI*. The combinations *ue* and *ui* usually indicate long *u*: *Tuesday, juice, sluice, bruise, nuisance, cruise, fruit, suit, pursuit, recruit*. The *i* is redundant when the word already ends in *e*: compare *reduce/juice, ruse/bruise*. In the verbs related to *suit, pursuit*, the *i* is replaced by *e*: *sue, pursue*.

**Variations**. (1) Historically, there has been variation of spelling and pronunciation, especially between *u* and *o*: in the cognates *custom/costume, ton/tun, tone/tune*. See O. One factor may have been a need to distinguish the vertical strokes or minims of *u* from the vertical strokes of adjacent letters in MIDDLE ENGLISH manuscripts; hence Middle English *sone* rather than *sune* for Old English *sunu* and Modern English *son*. (2) Similarly, *w* may sometimes have been used to avoid confusion of *u/v* (contrast *coward/cover* and French *couard*), or to distinguish homophones (*foul/fowl*), or even meanings of the 'same' word, such as the recent differentiation of *flour/flower*. (3) In general, *ou* occurs medially (*house, though*) and *ow* more often finally (*how, throw*), before vowels (*tower*), and before *l* (*howl, bowl*), *n* (*clown, sown*), and *d* (*crowd*). However, the choice between *ou, ow* is often arbitrary, as in the cognates *noun/renown*. (4) For AmE *-or*, BrE *-our*, see O. (5) The number *four* loses *u* in the derivative *forty*, though not in *fourteen*. See CLASSICAL ENDING, V, W.

**U AND NON-U**. Upper-class and non-upper-class usage, linguistic and social: terms first used by the philologist A. S. C. Ross for academic purposes and then popularized through inclusion in *Noblesse Oblige* (1956), edited by Nancy Mitford, a work whose lists of expressions that served as social clues inspired over the next few years a search for further U-isms and non-U-isms: '*Fault*, *also*, *Balkans* are pronounced by the U as if spelt *fawlt*, *awlso*, *Bawlkans*' (Ross, in *Noblesse Oblige*); ' "I don't think he's really U, though, do you?"—"Oh no. Shabby genteel, maybe" ' (Alison Lurie, *Love and Friendship*, 1962).

**UCLES,** short for **University of Cambridge Local Examination Syndicate**. Also informally *the Cambridge Syndicate*, *the Syndicate*. A local examining body based on the U. of Cambridge and established in 1858. It is responsible for schools examinations in England (as a member of the Midland Examining Group), for the *General Certificate of Secondary Education* (*GCSE*), and individually for the *General Certificate in Education at Advanced Level*. The strong involvement of UCLES in overseas examining dates from *c.*1870 with the *School Certificate* and examining in English as a foreign language from 1913, with the *Certificate of Proficiency in English*. See EXAMINING IN ENGLISH.

**UGANDA**. A country of East Africa and member of the COMMONWEALTH. Languages: English (official) SWAHILI, and Luganda and other indigenous, mainly BANTU, languages. English is the language of education, government, and the media. Uganda was visited by Arab traders in the 1830s, by the British explorer Captain John Speke in the 1860s, and in 1888 granted by the Crown to the Imperial British East Africa Company. In 1893, the Company withdrew and the territory was administered by a commissioner, the kingdom of Buganda becoming a British Protectorate in the same year. Between 1900 and 1903, treaties with the four Ugandan kingdoms resulted in the entire territory becoming a protectorate. Uganda gained its independence in 1962. The English of Uganda is a variety of EAST AFRICAN ENGLISH. It is non-rhotic and tends to be stress-timed. Because local Bantu languages generally have only two fricatives, /f, s/, the other English fricatives tend to be obscured: 'sooeh' for *sure*, 'ferry' for *very*. Many do not distinguish *r* and *l*: 'rorry', 'lolly',

and 'rolly' are all variants for *lorry*. There are fewer consonants in the vernaculars than in English and consonant clusters are managed by means of an epenthetic vowel ('sitring' for *string*) or by reducing the cluster (in various ways: for example, 'lents' or 'lenss' for *lengths*).

**ULSTER ENGLISH**. English as used in any part of the historic province of Ulster, which includes Northern Ireland and three counties of the Irish Republic. See NORTHERN IRISH ENGLISH.

**ULSTER SCOTS**. A variety of SCOTS spoken in the north of Ireland, mainly in parts of Antrim, Derry, Donegal, and Down, but influencing all varieties of speech in Northern Ireland and adjacent parts of the Irish Republic. The extent of Ulster Scots in a person's speech is related to region, education, and social position. The lower down the social ladder, the more likely is the speaker to roll the /r/ in words such as *war* and *work*; lose the postvocalic /l/ in words like *fall* and *full* (*fa,fu*); rhyme *die* with *me* ('dee'), *dead* with *bead* ('deed'), *home* with *name* ('hame'); *now* with *who* ('noo'); and use the voiceless velar fricative in the pronunciation of *Clogher*, *laugh*, *trough* (like ScoE *loch*). The phonological similarity between Ulster and Lowland Scots is reinforced by vocabulary, although many traditional words are in decline. Words shared by the two communities include *ava* at all, *bairn* a baby, child, *brae* a hill, steep slope, *firnenst* in front of, *greet* to cry, *ken* to know, *lum* a chimney, *message* an errand, *nor* than, *oxther* an armpit (Scots *oxter*), *peerie* a spinning-top, *tae* to. Two distinctive grammatical features are the negatives *no* (*We'll no be able to come*; *Do ye no ken who A mean?*) and *-nae/ny* added to auxiliary verbs (*A didnae think he would do it*; *Ye canny mean it*), and the demonstratives *thon* yon, *thonder* yonder (*Thon wee lassie's aye bonny*; *Thonder he is*). Ulster Scots has had a literary tradition since the 18c. See BELFAST, IRISH ENGLISH, NORTHERN IRISH ENGLISH, SCOTCH-IRISH.

**UNITED NATIONS**. Full form *United Nations Organization*. Short forms *UN*, *U.N.*, *UNO*, *U.N.O.* An international organization of nation-states set up in 1945 as successor to the League of Nations, with the aim of promoting peace, security, co-operation, and the self-determination of nations. Its headquarters are at the UN Building in New York. Its name originated as a cover term for the countries which fought against the Axis in the Second World War. When first constituted, there were 51 members; in 1995, there were 186 members (most of the sovereign nations of the world). The UN has a wide range of institutions (such as the General Assembly and Security Council) and agencies (such as the United Nations Children's Fund, UNICEF, and the Food and Agricultural Association, FAO). Its five official languages are English, French, Spanish, Russian, and Chinese; of these, English is the most widely used, notably in peacekeeping and aid projects. Official UN documents in English follow British print conventions; submissions by the US follow AmE print conventions, but any UN comments on them will be in the BrE style. In 1977, the US spacecraft Voyager One left Earth on a journey to Jupiter and beyond. On board was a recorded greeting on a golden disk to any sentient beings whom the craft might one day encounter in deep space. On it, Kurt Waldheim, an Austrian, spoke in English. He began: 'As the Secretary-General of the United Nations, an organization of a hundred and forth-seven member states who represent almost all of the human inhabitants of the planet Earth, I send greetings on behalf of the people of our planet.' This was followed by brief messages in 55 other languages.

**UNITED STATES ENGLISH**, also **US English**, **USE**. An alternative term for *AMERICAN ENGLISH*, the English language as used in the United States of America. The term is used especially by those who wish to make a clear distinction between US and Canadian usage or avoid the ambiguities inherent in the word *American*. The difficulty arose because the name *United States of America* has no simple and natural adjectival form; citizens of the land early solved the problem for their own purposes by adopting *American* from the last word of the country's name, an adjective already used for the western hemisphere and in colonial times for its English-speaking settlers.

**UPPER CASE**. A technical term for CAPITAL letters or majuscules (that is, letters larger in size and form than *LOWERCASE letters*).

**URDU**. An Indo-Aryan language of the Indian subcontinent, associated with the Moghul Empire, in which Persian was the court language. It is used especially by Muslims and written in a variant of the Perso-Arabic script. Closely related to Hindi, Urdu has a similar pronunciation and grammar but a more heavily Persianized and Arabicized vocabulary. It is the national language of Pakistan and is its co-official language with English. In India, it is the state language of the state of Jammu and Kashmir, and associate state language of the state of Uttar Pradesh. It is spoken as a first language by *c.*30m and as a second language by *c.*100m people in India and Pakistan, and some thousands of people of Indo-Pakistani origin in Fiji, Guyana, South Africa, the UK, and the US. See BANGLADESH, HINDI, HINDI-URDU, INDIAN ENGLISH, PAKISTANI ENGLISH.

■ **USAGE** ───────────────── ■

The way in which the elements of language are customarily used to produce meaning, including accent, pronunciation, spelling, punctuation, words, and idioms. The term occurs neutrally in *formal usage, disputed usage,* and *local usage,* and it has strong judgemental and prescriptive connotations in *bad usage, correct usage, usage and abusage,* and *usage controversies.*

**History**. The first citation of the term *usage* in the *OED* in a linguistic sense is from Daniel DEFOE in 1697, referring to the proposed English Academy to monitor the language, on the model of the Académie française: 'The voice of this society should be sufficient authority for the usage of words.' Before the 17c, the concept of usage or custom in English was hardly known: individuals spoke and wrote largely as they wished, and each printer had his own conventions. During the 17–18c, however, writers and leaders of society were concerned to codify the language in grammars and dictionaries, usually drawing on principles established in Latin and Greek. Defoe, Swift, Pope, and others held the view that usage should be monitored; but this notion failed along with the attempt to set up an Academy, and guidance about usage became largely the concern of teachers, publishers, and self-appointed usage guardians.

The present-day scholarly concept of usage as a social consensus based on the practices of the educated middle class has emerged only within the last century. For many people, however, the views and aims of the 17–18c fixers of the language continue to hold true: they consider that there ought to be a single authority capable of providing authoritative guidance about 'good' and 'bad' usage. For them, the model remains that of Greek and Latin, and they have welcomed arbiters of usage such as Henry Fowler who have based their prescriptions on this model. In spite of this, and although public opinion responds to arguments that the language is in decline, no nation in which English is a main language has yet set up an official institution to monitor and make rules about its usage. New words, and new senses and uses of words, are not sanctioned or rejected by the authority of any single body: they arise through regular use and, once established, are recorded in dictionaries and grammars. This means that, with the classical model of grammar in rapid decline, the users of English collectively set the standards and priorities that underlie all usage.

**Standard usage**. Guidance tends to centre on *standard English*, a form assumed to be shared, used, and accepted by educated speakers throughout the English-speaking world, despite great variety in accent, grammar, and vocabulary; it is based partly on intellectual argument and partly on received opinion. STANDARD usage is taught in schools on the assumption that students should speak and write English that is acceptable across a broad spectrum of society. The forms of standard usage correspond to the major national standards of English, such as those of BrE, AmE, and AusE. In Britain, and especially England, CORRECT usage has long been identified with the form of the language in use among the educated middle and upper classes in southern England, and surveys carried out in the US also suggest a class orientation. In both countries, a desire for guidance tends to predominate among the linguistically less secure, especially the lower-middle classes, while demands that 'good' usage be maintained may come from all levels of society, but particularly from those who feel secure in the prevailing standard forms and look to authorities on usage as much for reassurance and support as for guidance. Guidance is therefore based on what is thought to be acceptable to educated users of English, and

is often reinforced by the institutional authority associated with a famous scholar or publisher (Webster, Fowler, Merriam Webster, and the like).

**Criteria for criticism**. Criteria traditionally invoked in the criticism of usage include analogy (or precedent), logic, etymology (usually Greek and Latin, rarely Germanic), and questions of taste and social acceptability:

*Analogy*. Reference to ANALOGY is the most influential criterion, because analogy underlies the working of all language. Often, proponents of a particular usage tend to choose the analogies that suit their preference: for example, the stress patterns *conTROversy* and *forMIDable* are widely deplored and *CONtroversy* and *FORmidable* favoured, following the analogy of *MAtrimony* and *MANageable* rather than *orTHOgraphy* and *aMENable*. *KiLOmetre/kiLOmeter* follows the analogy of *speeDOMeter* rather than that of *KILogram* and *CENTimetre/CENTimeter*. Inflection also follows analogy: reference to two *Germanies* follows the example of *Ptolemies* and *Maries* and the behaviour of countable nouns in *-y* generally, but the form *Germanys* also occurs.

*Logic*. Appeals are regularly made to LOGIC: for example, in determining what a group of words ought to mean from its constituents. Such appeals work when logic and standard usage happen to coincide, but can often fail because the use of language is not always amenable to logic: for example, *Aren't I* as a TAG question is widely regarded in BrE as the proper form, and *Amn't I*, though eminently logical, is discounted as childish, while *ain't I* is considered either slovenly or archaic. The double negative, as in *I didn't do nothing*, has been condemned since the 18c solely on the ground that two negatives make a positive; before the 18c, the logic worked the other way in regarding the succession of negatives as cumulative in effect. Similarly, the grammatical treatment of collective nouns (*committee, government*, etc.), if based on logic, should require a singular verb, but usage often favours a plural verb to emphasize the collective sense of the word: *The committee have not yet reached agreement*.

*Etymology*. Appeals made to ETYMOLOGY to defend the language against change rarely satisfy by themselves, because they fail to recognize the independent development of words: for example, Latinate words such as *formula* and *stadium* have vernacular plurals *formulas*, *stadiums* that are often rejected by purists in favour of *formulae*, *stadia*, as if origin should be the predominant consideration. These are, however, adopted words, and may be treated on the analogy of words in English rather than Latin; *ultimatum* is so treated and few propose *ultimata* as a plural rather than *ultimatums*.

**Personal preference**. Criteria based on intuition, personal preference, or what one thinks educated users prefer, are common and may be supported by appeals to such further criteria as euphony ('*Biofeedback* sounds ugly and clumsy'), good taste ('No literate person says *irregardless* and *for free*'), and chauvinism ('Our language is rich enough; it doesn't need words like *chutzpah* and *shlep*'). Attitudes towards, and avoidance of, clichés such as *conspicuous by one's absence* and *at the present time* are a highly subjective matter that belongs in this category.

For all these reasons, it is difficult to evaluate usage objectively. In the view of linguists and lexicographers, evaluation must depend on sound evidence of what constitutes current established use; if not, it tends to become an argument for individual custom or preference. Establishing current majority usage is not as straightforward as it sounds, even in the age of mass media, because it rests on the need to be sure of what constitutes currency and majority. Until the development of databases, scholarly evidence consisted of collections of citations, generally from printed sources. Depending on the range of sources studied, the evidence has tended to have a literary or formal bias; usage criticism based on it does not therefore take adequate account of ordinary English spoken and written in everyday communication. Even computer corpora are collected mainly from the language in print, although conversational texts do exist, notably in the Survey of English Usage at U. College London, which aims at a million words available for on-line analysis. Grammars based on this kind of evidence have been published, but in general the traditional sources of usage prevail.

**Usage controversies**. There are always issues of special concern; these do not, however, remain constant. The SPLIT INFINITIVE

has been a controversial matter since the 18c, but is now of less importance; ending a sentence with a preposition was once considered a grave offence in formal writing, but is now generally accepted as a common feature of informal usage. Other controversies prove to be ephemeral, usually overwhelmed by the weight of actual usage: for example, *nice* was once strongly deplored in the now dominant sense 'agreeable', 'pleasant', in favour of the sense 'precise'. On the other hand, the double or multiple negative has long been deplored and is generally still regarded as uneducated, although it is used by many speakers of English throughout the world. A good example of the unpredictable and often capricious nature of usage controversies is the current issue of *hopefully* as a sentence adverb: *Hopefully, it won't rain tomorrow*. Well-established uses of other words as sentence adverbs, such as *Clearly, there is no case to answer*, and *Generally, the weather is fine in July*, are by contrast hardly noticed. So a particular use has been singled out for disapproval while others like it are passed over, and this is typical of many controversies. Usage controversies fall into several categories, with some overlap: *pronunciation*, including accent, stress, and the relationship of sound to spelling; *grammar*, including collocation, concord, and word order; *spelling and morphology*, including problems of inflection and confusable words; and *vocabulary*, especially with regard to the choice and meaning of words.

**Pronunciation**. Most pronunciation controversies concern *stress*, such as the examples *controversy* and *formidable* mentioned above. An older example is *abDOMen* (the second syllable stressed and pronounced like *dome*), now resolved in favour of *ABdomen*. Other current examples are *dispute* (where stress on the first syllable of the noun is deprecated but common), *harass* (where the same applies in BrE to stress on the second syllable; this however, is standard in AmE), and *kilometre*, which is pronounced in AmE and increasingly in BrE with stress on the second syllable, by (false) analogy with *speedometer* and related words. Problems also arise with vowel quality in words like *deity*, *spontaneity* and *homograph*, *homosexual*. In general preferences are based on what educated speakers are thought to prefer. The pronunciation of foreign words also causes difficulty, as with *garage* and *apartheid*. Recourse is often had to the pronunciation in the original language, but this can be a misleading criterion because the original pronunciation is usually based on rules and procedures that are inherently different from the phonology of English. Examples of loanwords now fully absorbed phonetically into English are *cadet* and *coupon*; sometimes a 'foreign' pronunciation is revived, as with *turquoise* and *valet*.

***Grammar***. Two grammatical categories account for a high proportion of disputes: COLLOCATION (the constructions with which words are assembled into phrases and sentences), and *CONCORD* (the way in which words of one part of speech agree with others). Among the most troublesome collocational issues is the word that follows *different*. In recent years, advice in usage guides has moved from prescribing *from* exclusively (as the traditionally preferred educated usage) to allowing and even advocating *from*, *to*, and *than*. The evidence suggests that *different than* is now the majority usage in North America, *different to* the majority usage in Britain, while *different from* retains a powerful influence on more conservative speakers and writers. This is because, with a classical model, *different* is seen as an extension of *differ*, and thought to require the same construction (*differ from*, and so *different from*). The same classical model applies to the construction required with *none*. Traditionally, *none* has been taken to represent *no(t) one* and should therefore be followed by a singular verb, as in *none of them is here* rather than *none of them are here*. This position is not, however, supported by actual usage over several centuries nor by many current usage guides, which advocate a choice of singular or plural according to sense: *none of them are here* when the sense is collective, *none of them is here* when the emphasis is on individuals.

Many grammatical problems have to be seen in the context of REGISTER or the kind of language being used. In formal English, especially in literature and official documents, grammar is usually given a higher value than idiom and ease of communication; in informal English, especially everyday speech, established custom is more predominant, because fluent and easy communication is the main consideration. None the less, the more prescriptive guidance on usage still tends to give insufficient weight to this factor. Especially relevant are

problems of word order, where there is less scope or need for precision in ordinary spoken English. The position of *only* has been the subject of much comment over many years. In formal and precise English the difference between *I only found them by chance* and *I found them only by chance* may be significant, but in speech it matters less, because intonation will usually clarify the sense.

***Spelling and morphology***. The role of usage in spelling is complex, and forms the basis on which dictionaries assess and record variants and stage preferences, as well as the basis of approved practice in matters such as inflection and hyphenation, where English is unpredictable. The 8th edition of the *Concise Oxford Dictionary* (1990) records many changes in hyphenation practice, including *benchmark*, *birdsong*, *figurehead*, *lawbreaker*, and *scriptwriter*, all previously hyphenated. These changes have been made on the basis of usage, and there is no theory of hyphenation beyond what is discernible in the evidence. This shows, in particular, that there is an increasing tendency to put two single-syllable elements together as single words, as with *benchmark* and *birdsong*. In other cases, practice varies and defies attempts at classification. The rules of *inflection* are also based on established practice, which is unpredictable, as in the matter of doubling a final consonant in forms such as *budgeted* and *travelled* (but *paralleled*). On the other hand, usage has to be critically assessed and tempered by considerations such as analogy and patterns of form. Variant spellings are not admitted in dictionaries simply on the grounds that they are known to be used; that would admit forms such as *\*accomodate* and *\*mischievious*, which are regarded as incorrect. They are rejected because they do not have sufficient authority in sources deemed to conform to standard English. On the other hand, Samuel Johnson's deviant spelling *despatch* for *dispatch* was established by its inclusion in his dictionary, and rapidly confirmed by usage afterwards. Borderline cases are *alright* (for *all right*; compare *altogether*, *almighty*), *nearby* (still resisted in its one-word form, especially as an adverb), and *onto* (resisted in printed BrE, despite its frequency in casual use, the analogy of *into*, and its standard use in AmE).

***Vocabulary***. There is a long-established, widespread belief that words have a 'true' meaning, usually based on etymology. If this were so, the earliest senses of all words would be the only proper senses: a *camera* would denote a room, not a machine, and a *doctor* would be a learned person, not a physician. Change in the meaning of words is the signal most clearly discernible to ordinary users that the language is changing. This is generally recognized and accepted as a historical phenomenon when the results are convenient to present-day users, but change as it happens is often resisted: *anticipate* in the sense 'expect', *aggravate* in the sense 'annoy', and *transpire* in the sense 'happen' (all disapproved of in current guidance on usage). Resistance is particularly strong where change occurs, or is perceived as occurring, in confusable words, such as *disinterested* (impartial) and *infer* (deduce). The senses just given are regarded as standard, while other senses (uninterested, imply) are often deprecated, despite equally sound historical credentials. Maintaining the distinctions between *disinterested* and *uninterested* and *infer* and *imply* is considered useful, in the same way as preserving the distinct senses of *childish* and *childlike*, *alternate* and *alternative*, and *regretful* and *regrettable* is useful. Usage guidance also deals with more accidental confusions of unrelated words, such as *sinecure/cynosure* and *prevaricate/procrastinate*. In all these cases, the purpose is to retain a distinction in the interests of clear meaning, and this is arguably the most sound basis on which any usage guidance relating to words can depend.

**Social and cultural factors in usage.** An important element of usage is the degree of social acceptability of certain terms and uses; these vary from age to age, and are matters of social or moral concern rather than of linguistic correctness. In the 16c, titles and forms of address such as *gentleman*, *master*, and *woman* had to be used with care because of the sensitivities arising from social status. *Chinaman*, once standard, is now regarded as offensive, as are *Eskimo* and *Mohammedan*. The preferred terms are now *Chinese*, *Inuit*, and *Muslim*. A far-reaching contemporary concern arises from the feminist movement and its wish to avoid the perpetuation of sex-based prejudice in language: for example, in the titles *Mrs*, *Miss*, relating to marital status. The neutral replacement *Ms* was originally based on the prescription of a social group on moral

grounds, was taken up by some style guides in the US, and came to be widely endorsed as socially convenient. Such prescription succeeds only rarely. Despite the invention of a variety of experimental forms, there is still no widely agreed gender-neutral third-person pronoun to replace generic *he* or stand for the often awkward *he or she*. In informal spoken English, and in some written English, the plural form *they* has emerged (or re-emerged, having been common though non-standard since the 16c) to fill the need, as in *If anyone calls, tell them to come back later*. Received opinion may regard this as bad grammar, but it shows that as grammar changes with usage a new model of grammar has to emerge.

See ACADEMIC USAGE, ACCEPTABILITY, AESTHETICS, AFFECTATION, APOSTROPHE[1], BAD ENGLISH, CANADIAN STYLE GUIDES, CATACHRESIS, CLICHÉ, COMPLETE PLAIN WORDS (THE), COMPUTER USAGE, DICTIONARY OF MODERN ENGLISH USAGE, DICTIONARY OF SLANG AND UNCONVENTIONAL ENGLISH, DIRECT AND INDIRECT SPEECH, DOUBLESPEAK, ELEMENTS OF STYLE, FOWLER, GENERIC PRONOUN, GOOD ENGLISH, GRAMMAR, JARGON, MISTAKE, NON-STANDARD, NORM, ORWELL, PARTICIPLE, PARTRIDGE, PASSIVE, PLAIN, PREPOSITION, QUOTATION MARKS, SOCIETY FOR PURE ENGLISH, SOLECISM, STYLE.

# ■ USAGE GUIDANCE AND CRITICISM ——————————— ■

The concept of USAGE and usage criticism in English dates from the 17c, when the first grammars of the language were written by William Bullokar (1586), Ben Jonson (1640), John Wallis (1658), and others. A more critical approach to the use of English emerged with literary figures such as John Dryden, Joseph Addison, Richard Steele, and Jonathan Swift. Bishop Robert Lowth's *Short Introduction to English Grammar* was published in 1762; it attempted to show that good use of language could be determined by the application of rules, and it became the largely unacknowledged source of the better-known work of Lindley Murray, an American grammarian who lived in England and wrote the school grammars *English Grammar*, *English Exercises*, and others, published from 1795 onwards. Robert Baker's *Reflections on the English Language* (1770) was one of the earliest works that would now be regarded as a usage book. The genre developed in the 19c, with Henry Alford (Dean of Canterbury) in Britain, author of *A Plea for the Queen's English* (1864), and Edward S. Gould (*Good English*, 1867), and Richard Grant White (*Words and Their Uses*, 1870) in America. Since the turn of the century, usage criticism in print has proliferated, in the form of reference books, usually arranged alphabetically as dictionaries, and columns on language in newspapers.

Another strand of usage criticism is represented by George ORWELL. Explicitly in a number of essays, and implicitly in his novel *Nineteen Eighty-Four* (1949), Orwell criticized language use that he saw as artificial and bureaucratic, and remote from the language of ordinary people. In his view, it had the effect of confusing and obscuring rather than communicating effectively, for example by writing 'in my opinion it is a not unjustifiable assumtion that . . .' instead of 'I think . . .'. He was not attempting to set standards of ordinary usage, but was condemning authoritarianism, seeing misuse of standard English as its instrument. This theme has also been pursued—though not with the same political implications—by Ernest Gowers and Ifor Evans (see below), and others, and in the work of scoieties promoting the cause of 'plain' or 'direct' English. See PLAIN ENGLISH, SOCIETY FOR PURE ENGLISH.

**British usage books**. The most famous and controversial British usage book is H. W. FOWLER'S *A DICTIONARY OF MODERN ENGLISH USAGE* (1926), in which he developed ideas presented earlier in the thematically organized *The KING'S ENGLISH* (1906). *MEU* is a blend of prescription, tolerance, and idiosyncrasy, and was the first usage book of its kind to be organized as a dictionary, thereby departing from the traditional codified grammar. It was also the first to include the name *usage* in its title. Fowler wrote about what he thought usage should be, not about what it was, and his evidence, as far as can be judged from the citations in the book, was selected to show where he thought users of English went wrong. None the less, it is to Fowler's credit that he avoided (especially misplaced) pedantry, as in his article on the *split infinitive*. The book was published in a 2nd edition in 1965 with revisions by Sir Ernest GOWERS, a senior civil servant who twenty years earlier had attempted to persuade the British Civil Service to avoid pretentious and often incomprehensible jargon in *Plain Words* (1948), in later editions *The COMPLETE PLAIN WORDS*. Other works on usage include Eric Partridge's *Usage and Abusage* (1942, with many revisions), B. Ifor Evans's *The Use of English* (1949), G. H. Vallins's *Good English* (1951) and *Better English* (1953), Logan Pearsall Smith's *Words and Idioms* (1925), A. P. Herbert's *What a Word* (1935), and Ivor Brown's *Words in Our Time* (1958) and other works. Current guides include Martin H. Manser's *Bloomsbury Good Word Guide* (1988), Sidney Greenbaum and Janet Whitcut's *Longman Guide to English Usage* (1988), *The Oxford Guide to English Usage* (1983), and John O. E. Clark's *Word Perfect* (Harrap, 1987).

Today, no major British reference publisher can afford to lack a usage guide, and some boast several, each with its own philosophy and style. In some cases, guidance is associated with a publisher's *house style*, as in *The Oxford Dictionary for Writers and Editors* (1981), a work largely concerned with spelling and hyphenation. Most current usage manuals are written by grammarians and lexicographers in alphabetical format and concentrate their advice on specific points, usually with made-up examples of use; an exception is *The Oxford Miniguide to English Usage* (1983), which organizes its material into thematic sections covering grammar, vocabulary, etc., and bases its advice on usage examplified by established writers, mostly of fiction. None of these, however, has attained the level of authority achieved by Fowler and by Partridge.

**American usage books**. Usage criticism in the US has tended to be in the conservative, prescriptive tradition of Lindley Murray, whose works remained in print to the end of the 19c. Standard works include Bergen and Cornelia Evans's *A Dictionary of Contemporary American Usage* (1957), Wilson Follett's *Modern American Usage* (1966), which derives its format and approach from Fowler and Fowler's US adaptation by M. Nicholson as *A Dictionary of American English Usage* (1957), and William and Mary Morris's *Harper Dictionary of Contemporary Usage* (1975, 1985), which drew on a usage panel of 166 consultants. A recent work that examines a wide range of issues, quoting extensively from printed sources, is *Webster's Dictionary of English Usage* (1989). H. W. Horwill's *Modern American Usage* (1935; 2nd edition, 1944) is primarily intended to help Britons with AmE, and Norman W.

## KINDS OF GUIDANCE

The nature, style, and content of the guidance provided by usage guides over the years is illustrated in the following sequence of advice and comment on a classic controversy, the *split infinitive*: 'to boldly go' as opposed to 'boldly to go' and 'to go boldly'. The comments range from 1851 to 1983.

Of the infinitive verb and its preposition *to*, some grammarians say that they must never be separated by an adverb. It is true, that the adverb is, in general, more elegantly placed before the preposition than after it; but, possibly, the latter position of it may sometimes contribute to perspicuity, which is more essential than elegance (Goold Brown, *The Grammar of English Grammars*, US 1851).

A correspondent states as his own usage, and defends, the insertion of an adverb between the sign of the infinitive mood and the verb. He gives as an instance, '*to scientifically illustrate*'. But surely this is a practice entirely unknown to English speakers and writers. It seems to me, that we ever regard the *to* of the infinitive as inseparable from its verb, and when we have a choice between two forms of expression, 'scientifically to illustrate', and 'to illustrate scientifically', there seems no good reason for flying in the face of common usage (Henry Alford, *A Plea for the Queen's English*, UK, 1864).

If you do not immediately suppress the person who takes it upon himself to lay down the law almost every day in your columns on the subject of literary composition, I will give up taking the *Chronicle*. . . . Your fatuous specialist . . . is now beginning to rebuke 'second-rate newspapers' for using such phrases as 'to suddenly go' and 'to boldly say'. I ask you, Sir, to put this man out . . . without, however, interfering with his perfect freedom of choice between 'to suddenly go', 'to go suddenly' and 'suddenly to go' (George Bernard Shaw, in a letter to the *Chronicle*, UK 2 Sept. 1892).

A constant and unguarded use of it is not to be encouraged. . . . On the other hand, it may be said that its occasional use is of advantage in circumstances where it is desired to avoid ambiguity (C. T. Onions, *An Advanced English Syntax*, UK 1904).

The English-speaking world may be divided into (1) those who neither know nor care what a split infinitive is; (2) those who do not know, but care very much; (3) those who know and condemn; (4) those who know and approve; and (5) those who know and distinguish. . . . Those upon whom the fear of infinitive-splitting sits heavy should remember that to give conclusive evidence, by distortions, of misconceiving the nature of the split infinitive is far more damaging to their literary pretensions than an actual lapse could be. . . . The attitude of those who know and distinguish is something like

*Continued opposite*

Schur's *British English A to Zed* (1987) is intended to help Americans with BrE.

**Usage criticism in newspapers**. Usage criticism and guidance is provided on a regular basis as a column in newspapers and other periodicals. The doyen of usage columnists in the US in the late 20c is William Safire of the *New York Times*, whose articles are widely syndicated. American journalism has also been the foundation of systematic usage and style guides, notably Theodore Bernstein's *The Careful Writer* (1965) and William Strunk Jr. and E. B.

## KINDS OF GUIDANCE *continued*

this: We admit that separation of *to* from its infinitive . . . is not in itself desirable, and we shall not gratuitously say either 'to mortally wound' or 'to mortally be wounded'; but we are not foolish enough to confuse the latter with 'to be mortally wounded', which is blameless English. . . . We will split infinitives sooner than be ambiguous or artificial; more than that, we will freely admit that sufficient recasting will get rid of any split infinitive without involving either of those faults, and yet reserve to ourselves the right of deciding in each case whether recasting is worth while (H. W. Fowler, *A Dictionary of Modern English Usage*, UK, 1926).

The name is misleading, for the preposition *to* no more belongs to the infinitive as a necessary part of it, than the definite article belongs to the substantive, and no one would think of calling 'the good man' a split substantive (Otto Jespersen, *Essentials of English Grammar*, UK 1933).

(1) There is no doubt that the rule [against the split infinitive] at present holds sway, and on my principle the official has no choice but to conform (Ernest Gowers, *Plain Words*, UK, 1941). (2) A friend whose opinion I value has reproached me for this. . . . I ought, he tells me, to have the courage of my convictions. I ought to say about the split infinitive . . . that is right for the official to give a lead in freeing writers from this fetish. . . . My friend may be right. Rebels will find themselves in good company (Ernest Gowers, *The Complete Plain Words*, UK, 1954).

Avoid the split infinitive wherever possible; but if it is the clearest and the most natural construction, use it boldly. The angels are on our side (Eric Partridge, *Usage and Abusage*, UK, 1947).

The temptation to split an infinitive is extremely rare in spoken English, because the voice supplies the stress needed by the unsplit form or conceals by a pause the awkwardness of the adverb placed before or after. It is in written work that splitting is called for, and desk sets should include small hatchets of silver or gold for the purpose (Wilson Follett, *Modern American Usage*, US, 1966).

The split infinitive is another trick of rhetoric in which the ear must be quicker than the handbook. Some infinitives seem to improve on being split, just as a stick of round stovewood does (Strunk & White, *The Elements of Style*, 3rd edition, US, 1979).

It is often said that an infinitive should never be split. This is an artificial rule that can produce unnecessarily contorted sentences. Rather, it is recommended that a split infinitive should be avoided by placing the adverb before or after the infinitive, unless this leads to clumsiness or ambiguity. If it does, one should either allow the split infinitive to stand, or recast the sentence (E. S. C. Weiner, *The Oxford Miniguide to English Usage*, UK, 1983).

White's *The ELEMENTS OF STYLE*, known affectionately as 'the little book' (3rd edition, 1979; earlier editions 1959, 1972). In Britain, Philip Howard in *The Times*, John Silverlight in *The Observer*, and Robert Burchfield in *The Sunday Times* have a more limited following, often seeming to entertain and inform the converted rather than advising the doubtful. A feature of some columns is a response to queries from readers, on which the columnists provide personal comment along with quotations from dictionaries and usage guides.

**Usage panels and usage notes**. Current general dictionaries of English often include usage notes attached to individual entries. The first such work to employ a team of advisers was the Random House *American College Dictionary* (1947). The practice was extended by Houghton Mifflin in the *American Heritage Dictionary* (1969), whose usage notes were compiled from replies to questionnaires from a panel of consultants including linguists, writers, journalists, and broadcasters. The results are often colourful and distinctive, as at *hopefully*: 'this usage is by now such a bugbear to traditionalists that it is best avoided on grounds of civility, if not logic' (2nd edition, 1982). The editor of the *AHD* was William Morris; with Mary Morris he took the panel approach further in the *Harper Dictionary of Contemporary Usage* (above), in which a range of controversies was treated with reference to the opinions of panellists, often quoted in full or given statistically. The panellists included writers, journalists, broadcasters, and academics, with many famous names among them, such as Isaac Asimov, W. H. Auden, Saul Bellow, Anthony Burgess, Alistair Cooke, Walter Cronkite, Jessica Mitford, and William Zinsser. The method affords flexibility, with different levels of usage distinguished. Panellists' comments are varied and colourful: 'The English language is the finest tool for communication ever invented. Since it is used indiscriminately by hundreds of millions, it is no wonder that it is badly misused so often' (Isaac Asimov); 'The English language began to curl up and die, instead of being regenerated, sometime after the Second World War, until now it has become like, wow!, you know' (Douglas Watt). The use of usage notes is now common in dictionaries on both sides of the Atlantic, for native speakers and foreign learners alike.

**Conclusion**. With the current proliferation of usage books publishers will need to strike a balance between two kinds of authority: that based on received opinion (backed up by their name and the names of their authors) and that derived from intellectual argument. This argument will in its turn depend on a model of English grammar that has yet to evolve.

**US ENGLISH**. **1.** An occasional term for the English language as used in the US. See AMERICAN ENGLISH, UNITED STATES ENGLISH. **2.** The name of an organization formed in 1983 to promote an amendment to the US constitution making English the official language of the republic. See ENGLISH LANGUAGE AMENDMENT.

**UVULA**. The anatomical term for the soft, fleshy protuberance at the back of the mouth, hanging down from the velum. The adjective *uvular* describes sounds made by raising and retracting the tongue towards the uvula: for example, the uvular fricative /r/, the *r grasseyé* of Parisian Franch. See *R*-SOUNDS, SPEECH.

**UVULAR *R***. See BURR, *R*-SOUNDS, UVULA.

# V

## ■ V, v ────────────── ■

[Called 'vee']. The 22nd LETTER of the Roman ALPHABET as used for English. It originated, along with *F, U, W, Y*, in the Phoenician consonant symbol *waw*, which the Greeks adopted first with the form V, then as Y (called *upsilon*: that is, Y-*psilón*, bare or simple Y). The Etruscans and then the Romans adopted the first symbol. In LATIN, V was a vowel letter, but in Romance languages such as French and Italian its value before a second vowel evolved to the modern consonantal pronunciation /v/. Until the 17c, *v* was ambiguous in English, capable of representing the sounds of both *u* and *v*. Further ambiguity arose with the introduction of the letter W, which originated as VV. This prevented the doubling of *v* in the same way as other consonants are doubled in English, except in such rare and recent forms as *revving/revved*.

**Sound value**. (1) In English, *v* nearly always represents a voiced labio-dental fricative. It occurs word-initially (*valley*), medially (*even*) and finally, usually supported by a following *e* (*active, drove*; *rev*). (2) Over centuries, there has been a tendency for medial *v* to become a vowel or disappear: *hawk* from OLD ENGLISH *heafoc*, the *f* pronounced /v/, *head* from Old English *heafod*, *curfew* from Anglo-Norman *coeverfu, kerchief* from French *cuevre-chef, lady* from Old English *hlæfdige, laundry* from Old French *lavandier, lord* from Old English *hlaford, manure* from Anglo-Norman *mainoverer, poor* from Middle English *povere*. (3) The once colloquial and now poetic forms *e'en, e'er, ne'er, o'er* mark the omitted *v* with an apostrophe.

**Word-initial V**. (1) In Old English, initial /v/ did not generally occur, and therefore *v* was not written word-initially. Latin *vannus* was for example respelt *fan*, and most words currently spelt with initial *v* are of later Romance derivation: for example, *vacant, vaccine, vague, vain, valley, value*. (2) Exceptions have arisen from dialects in which *f*-became *v* (*vane, vat, vixen*) or are exotic loans (*vaishya, Valhalla, Vanuatu, Viking, Vladimir, voltaic*). (3) V does not normally occur

syllable-initially before other consonants, *vroom* representing a conspicuous break with customary spelling patterns.

**Word-final V**. (1) Except for a few modern slang or clipped forms such as *lav, rev, spiv, gov, luv, v* does not occur as a final letter in English. (2) Where /v/ occurs as a final sound, as in *have, give, live, love*, the present spelling became fixed before the final *e* fell silent. Although final *e* may indicate a preceding long vowel (*save, eve, dive, rove*), that vowel value is often already indicated by a digraph (*waive, leave, sleeve, receive, believe, groove*), or a modified value is indicated by *r* (*starve, swerve, curve*), and the final *e* again serves simply to camouflage final *v*.

**Double V**. Medial *v* is found equally in words derived from Old English and Romance sources: *anvil, envy, heavy, marvel, over*. Because *vv* was already adopted as an early form of *w*, English did not double *v* even to indicate a preceding short vowel, as is common with other consonants (compare *comma/coma*), and ambiguity as to the length of a preceding vowel letter resulted. The spelling gives no indication of the differing vowel values in: *having/shaving, seven/even, driven/enliven, hover/rover, lover/mover*. More recently coined words not normally used in formal prose are under no such inhibition: *bovver, navvy, revving, skivvy* are all written with double *v*.

**Miscellaneous**. (1) V does not normally occur after *u*, since until *u* and *v* were regularly distinguished, the sequence *uv* could equally be read as *vu, vv, uu* (but note for example *uvular*). A preceding *u*-sound is therefore commonly written *o*, as in *dove, love, glove, cover, discovery*. However, a modern mock-spelling such as *luv* for *love* doubly flouts the conventions, with preceding *u* and final *v*. (2) In the 16c, *nevewe* was respelt *nephew*, and now usually has a spelling pronunciation with /f/ (but compare French *neveu*). Similarly, *Stephen/Steven* are variants, both with a /v/ pronunciation, and etymological variation between *b* and *v* occurs in *devil/diabolical*. (3) Oral variation between *v/w* formerly occurred in COCKNEY: Sam Weller in DICKENS's *Pickwick Papers* (1836–7) spells his name *Veller*, and his father refers to the letter *v* as *we*. See, F, U, W.

**VANUATU**. A country of Oceania and member of the COMMONWEALTH, consisting of twelve main islands and 70 islets. Languages: English, FRENCH, BISLAMA (all official), and ethnic languages. Until 1980 known as the *New Hebrides*, jointly administered since the late 19c by Britain and France. See BEACH LA MAR, MELANESIAN PIDGIN ENGLISH.

**VARIANT**. (1) Different in some aspects while the same or similar in others: *a variant reading of a text*; AmE *color* and BrE *colour* are *variant spellings* of the same word, each conforming to different national norms. (2) A similar but distinct form: the words *despatch* and *dispatch* are *spelling variants*, the first common in BrE, the second common in AmE; the Scots word *warsle* can be regarded as a variant of standard English *wrestle*.

**VARIETY**. A term in SOCIOLINGUISTICS for a distinct form of a language. Varieties fall into two types: (1) *User-related varieties*, associated with particular people and often places, such as *Black English* (English as used by blacks, however defined and wherever located, but especially African-Americans in the US) and *Canadian English* (English as used in Canada: either all such English or only the standard form). In this sense, the term *variety* is similar to but less likely to carry emotive and judgemental implications than *dialect*, *patois*, etc.: compare the phrases *speaking the local patois* and *speaking the local variety*. (2) *Use-related varieties*, associated with function, such as *legal English* (the language of courts, contracts, etc.) and *literary English* (the typical usage of literary texts, conversations, etc.). In this sense, the term *variety* is conceptually close to REGISTER and in practice is a synonym of USAGE, as in *legal usage*, *literary usage*.

Users and uses of English can be characterized in terms of variation in region, society, style, and medium. Regional variation is defined in terms of such characteristics as phonological, grammatical, and lexical features, as when *American English* is contrasted with *British English*: see AMERICAN ENGLISH AND BRITISH ENGLISH. Social variation represents differences of ethnicity, class, and caste, as in *BLACK ENGLISH* and *CHICANO ENGLISH* in the US, *ANGLO-INDIAN ENGLISH* in

India, and *HIBERNO-ENGLISH* in Ireland. Stylistic variation is defined in terms of situation and participants (such as formal versus informal usage, colloquial versus literary usage) and function (as with *business English* and the restricted variety known as *Seaspeak*). Variation according to medium is defined in terms of writing, speech, and the use of sign language for the deaf (where there are, for example, differences between American and British practices).

In discussing English at large, the term *variety* permits the identification of differences without pre-empting the argument in favour of one or other set of such differences: for example, standard usage is no more or less evidence of a 'variety' than non-standard usage, and non-standard forms need not be approached as 'deviations' from a norm. In order to describe regional varieties of English, the Indian scholar Braj B. Kachru has proposed a model consisting of three concentric circles: inner, outer, and expanding. The *Inner Circle* contains territories where English is the primary or *native* language. To it belong such varieties as *American English* and *New Zealand English*. The *Outer Circle* refers to territories colonized by Britain (such as India, Nigeria, and Singapore) and the US (such as the Philippines). In it can be found such institutionalized and increasingly autonomous *non-native* varieties as *Indian English* and *Philippine English*. The *Expanding Circle* contains those countries not colonized by Inner Circle nations: that is, the rest of the world. To it belong such *performance varieties* as *German English* and *Indonesian English*.

**VELUM**, also **soft palate**. The soft part of the roof of the mouth, behind the *hard palate*. There are two adjectives: *velar*, for the velum itself and sounds made by raising the back of the tongue towards the velum; *velaric*, referring to a stream of air. See ARTICULATION SPEECH.

## ■ VERB ───────────────── ■

A class of WORDS that serve to indicate the occurrence or performance of an action, or the existence of a state or condition: in English, such words (given here in the infinitive with *to*) as *to climb, to cultivate, to descend, to fish, to laugh, to realize, to walk*. Although many verbs in English have the same base form as nouns (*climb, fish, hound, love*, *walk*), they are morphologically and syntactically a distinct word class and one of the traditional parts of speech. There are two main types: *full verb*, AUXILIARY VERB. In terms of form, full verbs divide into REGULAR and IRREGULAR VERBS. Auxiliaries may be further divided into *primary auxiliaries* (*be*, *have*, *do*) and *modal auxiliaries* or *modal verbs* (*may*, *can*, *will*, *shall*, *must*, *ought to*, *need*, *dare*).

**The morphology of regular verbs**. Regular verbs have four forms used in the *verb phrase*: (1) The base form, for example *walk*, used for the PRESENT tense with all persons (except third-person singular) as subjects, for the IMPERATIVE, and (usually with *to*) for the INFINITIVE. (2) The *-s* form *walks*, used for the present tense with third-person singular subjects. (3) The *-ing* form, that is, the present or *-ing* PARTICIPLE, *walking*. (4) The *-ed* form, for both PAST tense and the past or *-ed* participle, *walked*. There are some spelling conventions associated with these forms, especially: (1) The doubling of the final consonants before *-ing* and *-ed* after a stressed syllable (*beg/begging/begged*) and, in BrE, of final *-l* and some other final consonants (*travel/travelling/travelled*, *worship/worshipping/worshipped*). (2) The dropping of final *-e* before *-ing* and *-ed* (*like/liking/liked*), except for the *-ing* forms of *dye* (*dyeing*), *hoe* (*hoeing*), some verbs ending in *-nge* (*singeing*), and optionally in *ag(e)ing*. (3) The addition of *e* before *-s* after sibilant consonants (*pass/passes*) and final *-o* (*go/goes*). (4) The change of *-y* to *-ie* before *-s* and to *-i* before *-ed* (*carries/carried*). The *-s* form is usually pronounced /z/ after sibilants (*miss/misses*) and voiced sounds (*tab/tabs*), and /s/ after all other voiceless sounds (*fit/fits*). The *-ing* form usually has its spelling pronunciation, but is also widely pronounced as if it were *-in* (sometimes shown with an apostrophe, as in *huntin'*, *shootin'*, and *fishin'*). The *-ed* form is pronounced as /ɪd/ or /əd/ after *d* and *t* (*pat/patted*), as /d/ after all other voiced sounds (*save/saved*), and as /t/ after all other voiceless sounds (*pack/packed*).

**The morphology of irregular verbs**. The *-s* forms and *-ing* forms are regular except that the *-s* form of *say* is usually pronounced 'sez'. Many irregular verbs distinguish the past tense and participle (*take/took/taken*), but others do not distinguish one (*come/came/come*) or both (*hit/hit/hit*) from the base form. Many have a vowel change in

either or both of the past tense or participle (*swim/swam/swum*), and may have an *-n* or *-en* ending for the past participle (*broken*, *driven*, *shaken*). There are seven main classes: (1) The past tense and participle are identical, but either the suffix is optionally devoiced and spelt with *-t* (as in *burn/burnt*: *burned*) or a final *-d* is changed to *-t* (as in *send/sent*). *Make/made* is idiosyncratic, but may be included here as it does not distinguish the two forms. (2) The past tense and participle are identical, the suffix usually devoiced, a vowel change occurring in the spoken form though not always shown in the spelling (as in *keep/kept*, *mean/meant*, *sell/sold*), but in BrE the forms *dreamt*, *leant*, *leapt* often occur, whereas in AmE only *dreamed*, *leaned*, *leaped* occur. Some forms are even more irregular with loss of final consonants (*teach/taught*). (3) The past participle has an *-(e)n* suffix (*show/showed/shown*) and in a few cases a vowel change (*shear/sheared/shorn*). (4) There are both an *-(e)n* suffix for the past participle and vowel changes of many kinds in either or both forms (*steal/stole/stolen*, *grow/grew/grown*, *bite/bit/bitten*). (5) Both forms are identical with the base form (*hit/hit/hit*). (6) There is a vowel change (not always shown in the spelling), no suffix, and the two forms are identical, but always pronounced and usually written differently from the base (*feed/fed/fed*, *read/read/ read*, *dig/dug/dug*, *shoot/shot /shot*). (7) There is vowel change, no suffix, and the two forms are different (*sing/sang /sung*). With a small number of verbs, the past participle is the same as the base form (*come/came/come*). See panel at IRREGULAR VERB.

**The morphology of auxiliaries**. *Be*, *have*, and *do* function not only as auxiliaries, but also as full verbs. The only morphological difference is that, except for *be*, the auxiliaries do not have the full range of non-finite forms (the infinitive and the participles). *Be* has eight different forms: in the present tense, *am* with first-person singular subjects; in the present tense, *is* with third-person singular subjects; in the present tense, *are* with the other pronouns; in the past tense, *was* with singular subjects; in the past tense, *were* with plural subjects and also with *you* when used in the singular; a present participle *being*; a past participle *been*; *be* itself, used as the infinitive and imperative. *Have* has an irregular *-s* form, *has*, and a past-tense *had*; the past participle *had* occurs only as a form of the full verb. *Do* has an irregular *-s* form in speech only (*does*), a past-tense form *did*, and a past participle *done*, but only the finite forms occur as auxiliaries. The present participles *being*, *having*, and *doing* are regular.

The modal auxiliaries have only one present-tense form, the base form (there is no *-s* form). Only *may*, *can*, *will*, *shall* have past-tense forms *might*, *could*, *would*, *should*, though these are not regularly used for the expression of past time: see MODAL VERB. Many of the auxiliaries have contracted forms: *'m* (*am*), *'s* (*is* or *has*), *'re* (*are*), *'d* (*had* or *would*), *'ll* (*will*). These are reflected in speech by 'weak' forms, but there are other weak forms not shown in the spelling, such as /wəz/ for *was*. Except for *am* and (usually) *may*, there is a full set of written contracted negative forms: *isn't*, *aren't*, *wasn't*, *weren't*, *can't*, *couldn't*, *mightn't*, *won't*, *wouldn't*, *shan't*, *shouldn't*, *mustn't*, *oughtn't*, *needn't*, *daren't*. These reflect speech, but not all the changes from the spoken forms are fully indicated by the spelling (for example, the omission of *t* in *mustn't*); especially in the English of England and of South Africa, the distinctive vowel of *can't*; the nasalized vowel and no /n/ in AmE *can't*.

**The syntax and semantics of auxiliaries**. The primary auxiliaries *be* and *have* mark aspect, phase, and voice (see TENSE) and the modal auxiliaries function in the modal system. A striking feature of the auxiliaries, which can be used as a criterion for recognizing them, is that there are four environments in which they alone of English verbs can occur: (1) Negation: *He isn't coming*, *He can't come*, but not \**He comesn't* or in contemporary English \**He comes not*. (2) Inversion of the subject: *Is he coming?*, *Can he come?* but not in contemporary English \**Comes he?* (3) In reduced clauses: *Yes, he is* and *Yes, he can* as replies, but not normally *Yes, he comes* as a reply to such a question as *Is he coming?* (4) Emphatic affirmation: *He IS coming*, *He CAN come* as confirmation of doubting questions or remarks. Where an auxiliary verb is not required by the semantics (to mark aspect, voice or modality), *do* is used, functioning as an 'empty verb': *He doesn't/didn't come*, *Does/did he come?*, *Yes he DOES/DID*, *He DOES/DID come*. However, *be* and *have*, even when used as full verbs, occur in these four environments without *do*: *He isn't very happy*, *Have you any money?—Yes, I HAVE*, *He IS very unhappy*, though *have* is also used with *do*, especially in AmE: *Do you have/Have you got any money?—No, I don't have any money*, *Do you have any money?—Yes, I do/I DO have some money*.

**Active and passive**. The PASSIVE is formed with *be* plus the past participle and involves placing the OBJECT of the active sentence in SUBJECT position and putting the subject after the verb, preceded by *by* (*John saw Mary* becoming *Mary was seen by John*). The function of the passive is to bring the object of the active sentence into focus, and not merely to remove the subject from focus, but frequently to omit it altogether, especially if it is unimportant or unknown. Constructions of the latter type are AGENTLESS PASSIVES: *Mary was seen*. The meaning is otherwise unchanged. With a small number of verbs it is the traditional indirect object that is placed in subject position (*The boy was given a book by the teacher*), but it can be argued that this is an interpretation derived from Latin. The corresponding active sentence is *The teacher gave the boy a book*, in which there is no formal evidence that *the boy* is an indirect rather than a direct object. Some prepositional objects are also placed in subject position: *The woman looked after the old man* becomes *The old man was looked after by the woman*; *No one has slept in the bed* becomes *The bed's not been slept in*. Here, *look after* and *sleep in* are treated as if they were single-word verbs. A few verbs appear not to be used in the passive, such as *resemble*, *have*, *hold* (in the sense of 'contain'), and *marry* (in the sense of 'wed': *Mary was married by John* is only possible if John is a priest or official and not the husband).

See ADVERB, ADVERBIAL, ASPECT, BARE INFINITIVE, CAUSATIVE VERB, CONCORD, COPULA, DECLARATIVE, FINITE VERB, FUTURE, GERUND, GRAMMAR, HELPING VERB, INDICATIVE, INTERROGATIVE, MODALITY, MOOD, NEGATION, NUMBER[2], PART OF SPEECH, PASSIVIZATION, PERFECT, PERFORMATIVE VERB, PERSON, PHRASAL VERB, PHRASE, PLUPERFECT, PREPOSITIONAL VERB, PRETERITE, PROGRESSIVE, REFLEXIVE, SENTENCE, SPLIT INFINITIVE, STATIVE VERB, STRONG VERB, SUBJUNCTIVE, TRANSITIVE AND INTRANSITIVE, VOICE, WEAK VERB.

**VERBAL NOUN**. A category of noncountable abstract NOUN derived from a verb, in English by adding the suffix *-ing*. Like the verb from which it derives, it refers to an action or state: *writing* in *The writing has taken too long*; *hearing* in *His hearing is defective*. Verbal nouns are frequently combined with the preposition *of* and a noun phrase that corresponds to the subject or object in a clause: *The grumbling of his neighbours met with no response* (compare *His neighbours grumbled*); *His acting of Hamlet won our admiration* (compare *He acted Hamlet*). Verbal nouns contrast with *deverbal nouns*, that is, other kinds of nouns derived from verbs, such as *attempt*, *destruction*, and including nouns ending in *-ing* that do not have verbal force: *building* in *The building was empty*. They also contrast with the GERUND, which also ends in *-ing*, but is syntactically a verb.

**VERBLESS SENTENCE.** A term in some grammatical descriptions for a construction that lacks a VERB but can be analysed as consisting of grammatical units functioning as subject, object, etc., as in: (1) Elliptical responses: *Who took my pencil?—Sam*; *Where did they go?—Straight home*. (2) Questions: *What about another drink?*; *Why no mail today?* (3) Commands: *Inside, everybody!* (4) Idiomatic usage: *The sooner, the better*. Subordinate verbless constructions, traditionally called phrases, often now called CLAUSES, are also common: 'I can help you *if necessary*'; '*Though in great pain*, they struggled on.'

**VERB PHRASE.** 1. Also *verbal phrase*. In traditional grammar, a term for the main VERB and any auxiliary or combination of auxiliaries that precedes it: *can spell*; *may have cried*; *should be paid*; *might have been transferred*. **2.** In generative grammar, a term roughly equivalent to the traditional *predicate*. It includes the traditional verb PHRASE with (at least) any complements of the verb, such as the non-bracketed parts of the following sentences: *(They) have understood his intention*; *(Susan) was very patient*. See NOUN.

**VERNACULAR. 1.** Occurring in the everyday language of a place and regarded as native or natural to it: *vernacular usage, expressions vernacular to English*. The term is used contrastively to compare the mainly or only oral expression of a people, a rural or urban community, or a lower social class (*a vernacular Indian language, a vernacular poet, vernacular Glasgow*) with languages and styles that are classical, literary, liturgical, or more socially and linguistically cultivated and prestigious (*a classical Indian language, Augustan English, standard English, polite Glasgow*). **2.** Such a language or variety: *speaking (in) the vernacular*; *written in the Yorkshire vernacular*. The term is used across the judgemental spectrum, from the warm approval of 'vernacularists' through the more or less neutral usage of linguists to a traditionally casual and dismissive attitude among many writers and teachers. **3.** Relating to the PLAIN standard style or variety of a language as opposed to more ornate, pedantic, classical, or complex styles and varieties; such a style or variety: *What's that in the vernacular?*

**VIRGIN ISLANDS.** Caribbean dependencies of Britain and the US in the Lesser Antilles. Their languages are English and CREOLE. The *British Virgin Islands* consist of four large islands (Tortola, Virgin Gorda, Anegada, Jost Van Dyke) and numerous small islands, with their capital Road Town on Tortola. The Dutch settled the islands in 1648 and gave way to British planters in 1666. They became part of the colony of the Leeward Islands in 1872 and a separate colony in 1956. The *US Virgin Islands* (official title *Virgin Islands of the United States*) consist of more than 50 neighbouring islands formerly known as the *Danish West Indies*, the three main islands being St Croix, St Thomas, and St John. In 1671, the Danish West Indies Company colonized St Thomas and St John and in 1733 bought St Croix from France. The islands were Danish for 200 years, with a short break in Napoleonic times. The US purchased them in 1917 as part of a strategic passage to the Panama Canal and they are an unincorporated territory of the US, with a republican-style democracy.

■ **VOCABULARY** ──────────── ■

[From Latin *vocabularium* a list of *vocabula* words. The medieval *vocabularium* was a list of Latin words to be learnt by clerical students. It was usually arranged thematically, with translation equivalents in a vernacular language]. A traditional term with a range of linked senses: (1) The WORDS of a language: *the vocabulary of Old English*. The general vocabulary of a language is sometimes called its *wordstock* and is generally referred to by linguists as its LEXICON or LEXIS. (2) The words available to or used by an individual: *a limited French vocabulary*. (3) The words appropriate to a subject or occupation: *the vocabulary of commerce*. (4) A word list developed for a particular purpose: *Use the vocabulary at the back of the book; a dictionary with a restricted defining vocabulary*.

## Specialized vocabularies in a language.

The vocabulary or lexicon of a language is a system rather than a list. Its elements interrelate and change subtly or massively from generation to generation. It increases through *borrowing* from other languages and through *word-formation* based on its own or borrowed patterns. It may decrease or increase in certain areas as interests change. Whole sets of items may vanish from general use and awareness, unless special activities serve to keep them alive. For example:

(1) *A vocabulary of carving*. There was in 16c England a set of verbs for carving kinds of game, fish, and poultry, which included *allaying a pheasant*, *barbing a lobster*, *chining a salmon*, *fracting a chicken*, *sculling a tench*, and *unbracing a mallard*.

(2) *A vocabulary of coaches*. In the 19c, there were many terms for horse-drawn vehicles, including *brougham*, *buckboard*, *buggy*, *cabriolet*, *carriage*, *chaise*, *coach*, *coupé*, *droshky*, *gig*, *hackney* (*carriage*), *hansom* (*cab*), *jaunting/jaunty car*, *landau*, *stagecoach*, *tonga*. The use of horse-drawn vehicles has steeply declined, but many such words are kept alive in historical novels and films, some refer to vehicles still in use in certain places, and some have moved into the vocabulary of rail travel and the automobile.

## Distinctive vocabularies across languages.

Just as the vocabulary of a language changes from age to age, so the vocabularies of different languages are distinct in their systems, uses, and references. There may be some close translation equivalents among several languages, but items and arrangements of items in one language may have no precise parallel elsewhere, because the culture in which the vocabulary has evolved rests on unique needs, interests, and experiences. As the American anthropologist Stephen Tyler has put it:

> The people of different cultures may not recognize the same kinds of material phenomena as relevant, even though from an outsider's point of view the same material phenomena may be present in every case. For example, we distinguish (in English) between dew, fog, ice, and snow, but the Koyas of South India do not. They call all of these *mancu*. Even though they can perceive

the differences among them if asked to do so, these differences are not significant to them. On the other hand, they recognize and name at least seven different kinds of bamboo, six more than I am accustomed to distinguish (*Cognitive Anthropology*, 1969).

**The vocabulary of English**. Historically, the word-store of English is a composite, drawn in the main from the Indo-European language family. There is a base of Germanic forms (mainly Old English and Old Norse) with a super-structure of Romance, mainly from French and Latin, with a technical stratum contributed by Greek (mainly through Latin and French): see BISOCIATION. In addition, there are many acquisitions from languages throughout the world. Because of such a complex background, and because dictionaries and other resources state that they list thousands of headwords and other items, the question often arises: *How many words are there in the English language?*

No easy answer is possible. In order to reach a credible total, there must be agreement about what to count as an item of vocabulary and also something physical to count or to serve as the basis for an estimate. Counting words (however defined) is wearisome, complex, and difficult, and experience suggests that no matter how well organized the count there can never be enough data to ensure completeness. There are at least five reasons for this: (1) There is no corpus available in a countable form which represents the whole language. (2) Even if there were, it would only indicate what was available at the time the count started. It would therefore be a static assessment of a dynamic process. (3) The result of the counting would consequently be out of date before the counting was completed. (4) Even with careful safeguards, the total reached would be different for each counter. In practice, counters tend to interpret instances differently and so count items in different ways. (5) The administrative work needed to homogenize the efforts of the counters would be formidable and time-consuming, making the survey even more out of date by the time it appeared.

Points 4 and 5 can be demonstrated by means of one example: the *-ing* form in *running* and *walking*. There are three ways to handle this suffix in a word count: (1) Count every item containing *-ing* as a distinct word. (2) Omit every item, treating *-ing* as an inflected form of the verb, like *runs* and *walks*, and therefore a matter of grammar, not lexis. (3) Count only some instances, like *clearing* and *drawing*, because these are used as distinct nouns with the plurals *clearings* and *drawings*, and ignore the rest. Whatever decision is taken significantly affects the outcome, because there are as many *-ing* forms as there are such verbs as *run* and *walk*. If solution 3 is chosen, it poses further problems, because in the corpus to be counted will appear citations like *rustlings and twitterings among the trees*. If *rustling* and *twittering* are taken as distinct words on this occasion, how will the counters handle the fact that many *-ing* forms can be so used, even if they are not recorded in the corpus?

In effect, the overall vocabulary of English is beyond strict statistical assessment. Nonetheless, limited counts take place and serve useful ends, and some rough indications can be given about the overall vocabulary. The *Oxford English Dictionary* (1989) defines over 500,000 items described as 'words' in a promotional press release. The average college, desk, or family dictionary defines over 100,000 such items. Specialist dictionaries contain vast lists of words and word-like items, such as the *Acronyms, Initialisms & Abbreviations Dictionary* (Gale, 1989), which contains over 450,000 accredited abbreviations. When printed material of this kind is taken into account, along with lists of geographical, zoological, botanical, and other usages, the crude but credible total for words and word-like forms in present-day English is somewhere over a million items.

**Individual vocabularies**. No one person can know, use, or imagine the entire available lexical resources of English. Many people are, however, curious about either how many words they or someone else knows, or what the 'average educated person' might be supposed to know and use. When such questions arise, they raise issues comparable to those of the vocabulary at large. Even in the case of writers whose texts are available for analysis, different totals emerge: the vocabulary of Shakespeare's works is variously listed as *c*.25,000 (Simeon Potter, *Our Language*, 1966), *c*.30,000 words (Robert McCrum *et al.*, *The Story of English*, book, 1986), and *c*.34,000 ( J. Barton, in McCrum *et al.*, *The Story of English*, TV series, episode 3, 1986). Such totals apparently depend on

what has been counted and the information passed on is a very rough approximation.

It is not unusual, however, to find assertions that the average person makes use of, for most purposes, fewer words than Shakespeare: perhaps 15,000 items. If, however, the count starts with the *c*.3,000 words in lists used for the early stages in the learning of English as a foreign language, such a total is soon exceeded simply by adding compounds, derivatives, phrasal verbs, abbreviations, and fixed phrases commonly associated with those *c*.3,000 words. For example, words formed on *run* alone include *runner, running, run in, run out, run on, run off, run up, run down, runway, gun-runner*, all with meanings and uses that qualify them as distinct words. All or most of such items are well within the range of most users of English educated to around 16–18 years of age. A crude extrapolation of $10 \times 3,000$ suggests that such people are familiar with some 30,000 such items, or twice the above estimate. Bringing in many everyday words not in the basic 3,000, and applying the same multiplier, soon takes the average person to double or treble this number without discomfort, every personal 'list' of words and wordlike items differing from every other.

**Active and passive vocabulary**. When teachers and linguists discuss the words people know, a distinction is commonly made between an *active* or *productive vocabulary* (what one can use) and a *passive* or *receptive vocabulary* (what one can recognize). The passive vocabulary is larger than the active, and the dividing line between the two is impossible to establish. All such terms and statements founder on the rock of what is meant by 'word' and 'vocabulary'. Lexical skills go well beyond the simplicities of printed words with white space on either side. These skills include knowledge of the *senses* of words. To take this knowledge into account would multiply what an individual knows many times over, because common words like *head* and *foot* have over a dozen important senses each, and many nuances. A person who 'knows' 50,000 'words', each with an average of five clear-cut senses, is actively or passively acquainted with 250,000 nuggets of lexical information. Such an estimate, however crude it may be, is decidedly impressive.

See: (1) FREQUENCY COUNT, VOCABULARY CONTROL. (2) The vocabulary sections of entries for major varieties of English, such as CANADIAN ENGLISH.

**VOCABULARY CONTROL**. A term in applied LINGUISTICS for the organization of WORDS into groups and levels, especially as the outcome of FREQUENCY COUNTS and in the form of word lists intended to help in writing, reading, and learning languages. Counting words and creating word lists is a complex task, and for useful results requires an initial conception of 'word' for the purpose in hand. Problems regarding what to count as a word include: (1) The orthographic problem of spelling variants such as *colour* and *color*. (2) The homonymic problem of identical forms such as *bear* (animal) and *bear* (carry). (3) The homographic problem of identical forms such as *wind* (air on the move) and *wind* (to turn, twist). (4) The phonological problem of statistics relating to spoken (and informally written) language (do items like *'ll* and *n't* count as *will* and *not*, are they special events to be counted on their own, or are they parts of units like *I'll* and *didn't*, to be counted separately?). (5) The morphological problem of the forms of *be* (are *be*, *am*, *art*, *is*, *are*, *was*, *were* different words or realizations of the same word?). (6) The lexical problems of counting COMPOUNDS and distinguishing them from ATTRIBUTIVE forms (is a *key decision* one word or two, in the same way that a *keyhole* or *key-hole* or *key hole* is one word?). (7) The statistical problem that, even granted that there is a utilitarian solution to the preceding problem, should the count include only agreed compounds or both compounds and their elements (so that for *keyhole* one counts *keyhole*, *key*, *hole*)? (8) The grammatical problem of particles and prefixes (does one count the *up* in *put up with* alongside the *up* in *up the hill*, and with the *up* in *uproot*?). (9) The onomastic problem of personal and place-names (are *Manchester*, *Manila*, and *Manitoba*, etc., to be counted as words simply because they appear in texts?). (10) The polysemic problem of deciding whether to count *fire* in a grate and *fire* at an artillery range as the same or a different word. (11) The lexicographical problem of how to describe and list the findings of any such survey, so that people of different experience can see and appreciate what has been counted. After all of these, there are two further problems: how to train the personnel and program the computer so

that such highly sophisticated work can be brought to a successful conclusion. See HOMONYM, POLYSEMY, VARIANT.

**VOCAL CORDS**, also **vocal chords**, **vocal folds**. Anatomical terms for folds inside the larynx, stretching from front to back, which control the flow of air from the trachea or windpipe into the pharynx, mouth, and nose. When muscular action pulls them apart a voiceless sound is produced, such as /s, t/. When they are held loosely together, air passing through forces them to vibrate, producing voiced sounds, such as /z, d/. See SPEECH.

**VOCAL TRACT**. A term in anatomy and PHONETICS for the area of the mouth and throat from the lips to the larynx, used in the production of SPEECH.

**VOGUE**, especially as used in **vogue word**. If something is *in vogue*, it is fashionable and widely used for a time. Linguistic usages can be as much in vogue as clothes or ideas: 'Pox on your Bourdeaux, Burgundie . . . no more of these vogue names . . . get me some ale' (Howard & Villiers, *Country Gentleman*, *c.*1669). *Vogue word* is a semi-technical term, and the terms *vogue name*, *vogue phrase*, *vogue term*, *vogue usage* all occur. When usages are taken up by journalists, publicists, and media celebrities, they quickly become fashionable and may prompt analogue forms: for example, *junk food* leading to *junk bonds*, *junk mail*, *junk fax*; *marathon* leading to *beg-a-thon*, *readathon*, *telethon*. Common sources of vogue expressions include: (1) Technology; *interface*, *input*, *downtime*. (2) Advertising and publicity: *bottom line*, *targeting*, *yuppie*. (3) Medicine, health care, social science, and accompanying social comment: *aerobic*, *executive stress*, *fitness freak*. Compare BUZZ WORD, KEYWORD, NONCE WORD.

**VOICE**. A term that refers to four aspects of language. The distinctions are illustrated in the phrases *a high-pitched voice* (general usage), *a voiceless consonant* (in phonetics), *the passive voice* (in grammar), and *narrative voice* (in literary theory).

**Voice as vocal sound**. The typical SOUND of someone speaking, the product of the vibration of the vocal cords, the resonant effect of the pharynx, mouth, nose, and tongue, the effect of rhythm and pitch, and such qualities as huskiness and throatiness.

Individual voices differ, but the voices of members of certain groups have common features: adult male voices are usually 'deeper' (have a lower pitch) than women's and children's voices; the voices of people from the same region and/or social group usually share features of a particular accent. Kinds of voice can be categorized according to musical register: *a tenor voice, a falsetto voice*.

**Voice in phonetics**. The buzzing sound made in the larynx by the vibration of the vocal cords or folds. In terms of this vibration, sounds are said to be *voiced* or *voiceless*. Voiced sounds such as /b, d, g, z/ are made by bringing the vocal folds close together so that the air stream forces them to vibrate as it passes through the glottis. The difference between voice and voicelessness can be checked by holding the larynx and saying *zzzz* and *ssss* in alternation, feeling vibration then lack of vibration. See ARTICULATION, DEVOICING, SPEECH, VOICE QUALITY.

**Voice in grammar**. A category that involves the relationship of subject and object in a sentence or clause. In English, the contrast is between *active voice* and *passive voice*, affecting both the structure of the sentence and the form of the verb: *Susan chose the furniture* is an active sentence whose corresponding passive is *The furniture was chosen by Susan*. The active object (*the furniture*) is identical with the passive subject, while the active subject is incorporated in a *by*-phrase (*by Susan*). The two sentences have the same truth value, though there are differences in style and emphasis, in that passives are usually more formal than actives and the end of a sentence or clause tends to have the greatest emphasis. The *by*-phrase is often omitted from the passive sentence, especially in technical writing, producing an *agentless passive*. See PASSIVIZATION.

**Narrative voice**. A term in literary criticism for the person who 'speaks' in a story, either a narrator who represents the author ('third person': the *implied author* or *omniscient narrator*), or who is represented by a character ('first person'). Within a narrative, other 'voices' may be heard in dialogue, in direct speech, and in some works of fiction several first-person voices may take up the same story from different perspectives. See DIRECT AND INDIRECT SPEECH.

**VOICE QUALITY**. The characteristic sound of the VOICE brought about by the mode of vibration of the vocal cords or folds. Differences in the degree and manner of glottal closure distinguish *modal voice* and *whisper*, and *breathy voice* and *whispery voice*. The quality of the voice also depends on the degree of tension in the larynx and pharynx, and on the vertical displacement of the larynx: a raised larynx produces a thin tense voice, and a lowered larynx a booming 'clergyman's' voice. Apart from distinguishing voiced and voiceless sounds, voice quality does not make linguistic contrasts, but conveys information about the speaker, such as language or dialect background, individuality, and emotional state. See ACCENT.

# ■ VOWEL ————————————————— ■

A term in general use and in phonetics for both a SPEECH sound that is distinct from a CONSONANT (also *vowel sound*) and the LETTER of the ALPHABET that represents such a speech sound (also *vowel letter*). In general usage, the distinction between vowels in speech and writing is not always clearly made, but linguists and phoneticians seek to keep the two kinds of vowel distinct.

**Vowel sounds**. Phonetically a vowel is a speech sound characterized by voicing (the vibration of the larynx) and by absence of obstruction or audible friction in the vocal tract, allowing the breath free passage. The quality of a vowel is chiefly determined by the position of the tongue and the lips: see VOWEL QUALITY. Vowel sounds divide into MONOPHTHONGS (single vowel sounds that may be long or short), DIPHTHONGS (double vowel sounds formed by gliding from one vowel position to another), and *triphthongs* (triple vowel sounds formed by gliding from one through another to a third vowel position). The human speech mechanism is capable of producing a wide range of simple and complex vowel sounds. As with consonants, however, in each language (or language variety) a particular range of vowels is used: for example, in standard Parisian French, there are 12 non-nasal and 4 nasal monophthongs (16 vowel sounds in all); in BrE, the basic vowel system of RP has 12 monophthongs and 8 diphthongs (20 vowel sounds in all) while the basic vowel system of ScoE has 10 monophthongs and 4 diphthongs (14 vowel sounds in all).

**Vowel letters**. The five classic vowel letters of the Roman alphabet are *A, E, I, O, U*, to which *Y* is usually added; apart from its syllable-initial role as a semi-vowel or semi-consonant in words like *year*, *y* functions in English largely as an alternative vowel symbol to *i*. Phonetically, the letters *w* (as in *win*) and *y* (as in *year*) are articulated similarly to vowels, but positionally they function as consonants, initiating syllables and introducing vowels: compare *wear/bear* and *year/fear*. Phonetically, too, the liquid consonants written as *l, r* and the nasal consonants written as *m, n* have some of the characteristics of vowels (such as continuous non-fricative voicing), and when used syllabically (as in the pronunciations of *apple, spasm, isn't, centre*) they in effect represent a preceding SCHWA vowel sound in addition to their own sound value.

Whereas the five classic vowel letters match the five vowel phonemes of a language like Spanish, they are insufficient to distinguish the much larger number of vowel phonemes of English. When unaccompanied by another vowel letter, the five letters usually have a basic 'short' sound value in medial position in English words (as in *pat, pet, pit, pot, putt/put*), but in some words (such as *yacht, pretty, son, busy*) their values are aberrant, and in certain environments, such as after /w/ and before /l, r/, they are commonly modified (as in *was, word, all, old, far, her, fir, for, fur*). For each of the short values there is a corresponding 'long' value which formerly (before the GREAT VOWEL SHIFT of the 15c) was close to the short value, but is today in varying degrees removed from it (and is not the 'long' value as understood in phonetics). The present-day long values are as heard in *mate, meet, might, moat, mute*. Native speakers perceive the long values as intimately associated with the short values; the two often alternate in related words (as in *sane/sanity, abbreviate/brevity, five/fifth, depose/deposit, student/study*) and the long values are heard as the names of the letters themselves (heard as *ay, ee, eye, oh, you*).

The spelling of the long values of the vowels is varied and unpredictable: for example, Edward Rondthaler and Edward J. Lias (*Dictionary of American Spelling*, 1986) list 114 alternative spellings for the five sounds. These include single graphemes (units of writing), as in *mind, post, truth*, DIGRAPHS as in *leave, sleeve, receive, believe*, and longer graphemes

as in *beau, queue*. Some of these longer graphemes include consonant letters (as in the *eigh* of *weigh* and the *et* of *ballet*) that are in effect constituents of vowels. Highly characteristic of English vowel spellings is the 'magic' *e* placed after a consonant, which has the effect in Modern English of showing the long value of a preceding vowel, as in *mate, mete, mite, mote, mute*. In addition to these parallel sets of short and long vowels corresponding to *a, e, i, o, u*, English also needs to spell several vowel sounds for which alternative pairs of digraphs are widely (but not consistently) used according to position: for example, initial and medial *au, eu, ou, ai, oi*, but final *aw, ew, ow, ay, oy* (contrast *fault/flaw, feud/few, count/cow, rain/ray, coil/coy*). A corollary of the many alternative spellings for the same vowel sound is the many alternative pronunciations that may be required for the same vowel letters: for example, *ea* is pronounced in nine different ways in *eat, threat, great, react, create, pear, hear, heart, hearse*.

See ABLAUT, ACCENT, APHESIS, DIACRITIC, DIAERESIS, ELISION, EPENTHESIS, LIGATURE, RECEIVED PRONUNCIATION, RHYTHM, SPELLING, STRESS, SYLLABLE, VOWEL QUANTITY, VOWEL SHIFT, WEAK VOWEL.

**VOWEL QUALITY**. A term in phonetics for the property that makes one VOWEL sound different from another: for example, /iː/ as in *sheep* from /ɪ/ as in *ship*. The quality of a vowel is determined by the position of the tongue, lips, and lower jaw, and the resulting size and shape of the mouth and pharynx. Vowels are classed as *close* or *open* (in British terminology) and *high* and *low* (in American terminology) according to whether the tongue is held close to the roof of the mouth or low in the mouth. They are classed *as front* or *back* in both terminologies according to whether the body of the tongue is pushed forward or pulled back. They are classed as *rounded* or *spread* according to the shape of the lips: for example, the /iː/ in *sheep* is a close front spread vowel, the /ɪ/ in *ship* a semihigh front unrounded vowel.

**Cardinal vowels**. While this general classification provides an approximate description of vowel quality, it is not sufficient to define all the vowels in a system such as English. Some vowels can only be defined in relation to other vowels: for example, /ɛ/ in

**VOWEL POSITIONS**

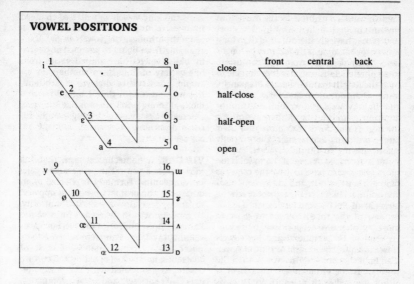

bet is intermediate between close /ɪ/ in *bit* and open /æ/ in *bat*. The most widespread method of dealing with relative vowel quality is based on the system of *cardinal vowels* devised by Daniel JONES. These vowels are used as reference qualities for the vowels of all languages.

Cardinal [i] is produced with the body of the tongue held forward in the mouth, and with the tongue surface as close as possible to the palate without generating turbulence (which would turn it into a consonant). Cardinal [ɑ] is produced with the body of the tongue held back in the mouth, and with the root of the tongue as close as possible to the back wall of the pharynx, again without generating turbulence. The remaining cardinal vowels are placed at equidistant points on the lines from [i] to [ɑ]. The system of cardinal vowels provides a means of describing vowel sounds.

Cardinal [i] has spread lips; from [i] to [ɑ] the vowels become less spread and progressively more lip neutral. From [ɑ] to [u] they are progressively more rounded, and [u] is fully rounded. For ease of reference, the cardinal vowels are numbered anti-clockwise (counter-clockwise) from 1 to 8. The statement 'a vowel in the region of cardinal 2' is equivalent to 'a vowel in the region of [e]'. Both refer to a 'half-close front spread

vowel'. Most vowels in most languages combine lip spreading with frontness, and rounding with backness, as in the primary cardinal vowels, but this is not always the case. *Secondary cardinal vowels* have the lip positions reversed from those of the primary cardinals, the first five being rounded and the last three spread. These cardinal vowels are numbered anti-clockwise from 9 to 16.

**VOWEL QUANTITY.** A term in phonetics and poetics for the length of a VOWEL, usually indicated in phonetic transcription by a LENGTH MARK [ː] or a colon [:] after a vowel, as in /aː/. Vowels so marked have in general greater duration than the same vowels with no such mark. Vowels so marked are described as *long*, and unmarked vowels are *short*, a distinction known as *vowel length*. However, the measurable duration of vowels depends also on at least two other factors: (1) Vowel height, in terms of the position of the tongue. Open vowels as in *ban* /ban/ or *balm* /bɑːm/ are longer than close vowels as in *bin* /bɪn/ or *beam* /biːm/. (2) Environment, in terms of preceding and following sounds. Vowels are shortened before some consonants and lengthened before others, for example /uː/ is longer in *move* /muːv/ than in *boot* /buːt/. These factors have different weightings in different varieties of

English, and contribute to the variety of rhythms in English. In many varieties, short vowels may have greater duration than long vowels: for example, /a/ in *jazz* may be longer than /i:/ in *sleep*. To avoid the confusion, some phoneticians consider it preferable to treat the length mark as a mark of quantity rather than duration, and refer to 'heavy' and 'light' vowels. If a vowel has sufficient duration, as in *halve* /ha:v/, there is time for the organs that form it to move into their target positions and remain there briefly before moving to the next target. Such a vowel is described as *tense*. If the vowel is too short, the organs have to leave the target as soon as they reach it, and in extreme cases (for example, in *six* /sɪks/) may not reach the target at all. Such a vowel is described as *lax*. In view of the time required to move to more peripheral vowel positions, tense vowels tend to be peripheral and lax vowels closer to *schwa*, the neutral or central vowel. If an English word ends in a vowel, then the vowel must be either heavy (that is, it is either marked with a length mark or is a diphthong) or reduced: for example, *me* /mi:/, *day* /deɪ/, *banana* /-nə/. See VOWEL QUALITY.

**VOWEL SHIFT**. A term in philology and phonetics for a process under which a set of VOWELs undergoes changes. The term GREAT VOWEL SHIFT is used for a number of long-term changes which affected the English VOWEL system during the 15c–17c. In this shift, the long vowels in *reed*, *rood* changed from [e:, o:] to [i:, u:], and close vowels became diphthongs, the vowels in *five*, *house* changing from [i:, u:] to [aɪ, aʊ]. The degree to which vowels have shifted varies from one variety of English to another: for example, conservative dialects of Scotland, Ireland, and the North of England retain a monophthong [e:, o:] in words like *raid*, *road*, whereas these vowels have generally become diphthongs elsewhere, as in RP [eɪ, əʊ]. See ABLAUT.

**VULGAR**. A nontechnical term that has moved from a neutral and general to a pejorative meaning. Formerly, it referred to ordinary life and ordinary people, as opposed to an upper-class or educated minority. *Vulgar Latin* was the everyday Latin of the Roman Empire and, until the 19c, European VERNACULAR languages were referred to as *vulgar tongues*. Concomitantly, a sense of coarseness and lack of breeding and culture developed, associated with the 'lowest orders' of society, and now dominates, particularly with reference to language: *a vulgar remark*. See PARTRIDGE, RECEIVED STANDARD AND MODIFIED STANDARD, SWEARING.

**VULGARISM**. A coarse expression, especially when used in elevated discourse or on formal occasions: for example, *fart* appearing in an academic treatise or *crap* said loudly at an elegant dinner party. See -ISM, VULGAR. Compare SWEARWORD.

# W

## ■ W, w ────────── ■

[Called 'double-you']. The 23rd LETTER of the modern Roman ALPHABET as used for English. The Romans had no letter suitable for representing the phoneme /w/, as in OLD ENGLISH, although phonetically the vowel represented by *v* (as in *veni, vidi, vici*) was close. In the 7c, scribes wrote *uu* for /w/, but from the 8c they commonly preferred for English the runic symbol *wynn* (*ƿ*). Meanwhile, *uu* was adopted for /w/ in continental Europe, and after the Norman Conquest in 1066 it was introduced to English as the ligatured *w*, which by 1300 had replaced *wynn*. Early printers sometimes used *vv* for lack of a *w* in their type. The name *double-u* for double *v* (French *double-v*) recalls the former identity of *u* and *v*, though that is also evident in the cognates *flour/flower*, *guard/ward*, *suede/Swede*, and the tendency for *u, w* to alternate in digraphs according to position: *maw/maul, now/noun*.

**Sound value**. In English, *w* normally represents a voiced bilabial semi-vowel, produced by rounding and then opening the lips before a full vowel, whose value may be affected.

**Vowel digraphs**. (1) The letter *w* commonly alternates with *u* in digraphs after *a, e, o* to represent three major phonemes. Forms with *u* typically precede a consonant, with *aw, ew, ow* preferred syllable finally: *law, saw, taut; dew, new, feud; cow, how loud*. (2) When the preceding vowel opens a monosyllable, silent *e* follows the *w*: *awe, ewe, owe* (but note *awful, ewer, owing*). (3) Word-finally, *w* is almost always preferred to *u* (*thou* is a rare exception), but *w* occurs medially quite often (*tawdry, newt, vowel, powder*), and the choice of letter may be arbitrary (compare *lour/lower, flour/flower, noun/renown*). (4) In some words, digraphs with *w* have non-standard values: *sew, knowledge, low*. Final *-ow* with its non-standard value in *low* occurs in nearly four times as many words as the standard value in *how*. (5) In the name *Cowper, ow* is uniquely pronounced as *oo* in *Cooper*. (6) Final *w* in many disyllables evolved from the Old English letter *yogh* (ʒ) for *g*, as in *gallows, hallow, tallow, bellows, fol-low, harrow, borrow, morrow, sorrow, furrow* (compare German *Galgen, heiligen, Talg, Balg, folgen, Harke, borgen, Morgen, Sorge, Furche*).

**WH**. (1) The digraph *wh* occurs wordinitially, and in ScoE, IrE, often in AmE, and among some RP speakers it has the once universal voiceless, aspirated pronunciation often represented as /hw/, sometimes as /ʍ/: *whale, wharf, what, wheat, wheel, wheeze, whelk, when, whelp, where, whet, whether, which, while, whimper, whip, whirl, whisker, whistle, white, whither, whorl*. Such forms were mostly spelt *hw* in Old English. The *h* in *whelk* appears to be a late insertion. (2) Several common parallel spellings without *h* are homophones for speakers who do not make the *w/wh* distinction: *whale/wail, where/ware, whet/wet, whether/weather, whey/way, which/witch, whig/wig, while/wile*. See WH-SOUND.

**Silent W**. (1)nitial *w* fell silent before *r* in the 17c, but is written in *wrack, wraith, wrangle, wrap, wrath, wreak, wreath, wreck, wren, wrench, wrest, wrestle, wretch, wriggle, wright, wring, wrinkle, wrist, writ, write, writhe, wrong, wrote, wroth, wreak, wrought, wrung, wry*. The form *awry* derives from *wry*. (2) The *w* in *two, who, whose, whom* is thought to have fallen silent under the rounding influence of the following *u*-sound, while the *w* in *whole* (cognate with *hale, heal*) and *whore* was added in the 15c under the influence of dialects in which a *w*-sound arose before the vowel *o* (as in the pronunciation of *one*). This was once the case with *whoop*, which now has the optional pronunciations 'hoop' and '(h)woop'. A modern instance of adding an etymologically inappropriate *w-* occurs when Greek-derived *holistic* (compare *holocaust, holograph*, from *hólos* entire) is spelt *wholistic*, on the assumption that it derives from *whole*. (3) Medial *w* has fallen silent after *s* in *answer, sword*, and after consonants when initiating unstressed final syllables in English placenames: *Chiswick* ('Chizzik'), *Norwich* ('Norritch', 'Norridge'), *Southwark* ('Suthark'), *Welwyn* ('Wellin'). This *w* has also fallen silent in nautical usage, with adapted spellings *bosun, bo's'n* for *boatswain*, and *gunnel* for *gunwale*. (4) In informal or nonstandard, often archaic, speech, *w* is elided in *allus* always, *forrad* forward, *ha'p'orth* half-pennyworth, *summat* something. (5) *Will*, *would* lose *w* when they assimilate to preceding pronouns, as in *he'll, I'll, it'll, he'd, I'd.*

**Variations**. (1) The sound /w/ has other spellings. Because lip-rounding is a feature of most pronunciations of *u*, /w/ is spelt *u* in some words, chiefly of FRENCH derivation, after *g*, *q*, and *s*, as in *languish, question, quiet, suite, persuade*. (2) Recent French loans may keep the French *oi* for the sound /wa/: *boudoir, memoir, repertoire, reservoir, soirée*, a pattern which may have influenced the re-spelling of *quire* as *choir* in the late 17c. (3) A change of pronunciation has given an unspelt initial /w/ to *one, once*, but not to their cognates *only, alone*. (4) *R* is sometimes spoken /w/. This has long been regarded as a SHIBBOLETH of some kinds of BrE upper-class accents and may occur in the speech of small children and in imitation of such speech (*Weally weally big!*), and in defective articulation. It is sometimes referred to as *rhotacism*. (5) Historically there has been some parallel development of Anglo-Norman spellings with *w* and French spellings with *g*: *ward/guard, warranty/ guarantee* (compare French *garde, garantie*), *reward/regard, -wise/guise*. See A, E, H, I, O, RHOTACISM.

**WEAK VERB**. In the traditional description of Germanic languages, a VERB that indicates such meaning differences as tense through the addition of inflections: Modern English *play, played*. In contrast, STRONG VERBS modify their vowels: *ring, rang, rung*. The terms are usually replaced in grammars of Modern English by *regular verbs* (in place of weak verbs) and *irregular verbs* (in place of strong verbs).

**WEAK VOWEL**. In phonetics, a VOWEL that normally occurs only in unstressed syllables. There are two weak vowels in English SCHWA /ə/, as in the unstressed syllables of *above* and *sofa*, and short *i* /ɪ/, as in the unstressed syllables in RP *example* and *Sophie*.

■ **WEBSTER, Noah** ─────── ■

[1758–1843]. American teacher, writer, editor, lexicographer, lecturer, and lobbyist, born in West Hartford, Connecticut, educated at Yale College (1778), and admitted to the bar (1781). His best-known works, *The*

*American Spelling Book* (the 'Blue-Back Spelling Book', 1783) and *An American Dictionary of the English Language* (1828), greatly contributed to lessening US dependence on British models of the standard language. His career as a schoolmaster led to the publication of *A Grammatical Institute of the English Language*, which included *The American Spelling Book* (1783), a grammar (1784), and a reader (1785). The speller was particularly popular, notably for its moral and patriotic flavour as opposed to the religious orientation of earlier texts. The grammar was less popular; it was criticized for being too advanced for schoolchildren and for overemphasizing elocution. Webster's achievement with *A Grammatical Institute* was in separating spelling, grammar, and reading into individual texts, a strategy which may have influenced other text-writers to stage the learning process for children. His vigorous lobbying to protect his work from piracy led to the institution of the first federal copyright laws in 1790.

Webster's lexicographical career began with the compilation of *A Compendious Dictionary* (1806), which was marked by innovations in spelling and by adherence to New England educated speech for pronunciation. Public criticism of the innovations eventually led to the 'dictionary wars' in which Joseph Emerson Worcester, who favoured BrE norms, led the opposition. Webster modified his stance in *An American Dictionary of the English Language* (1828, 1840), and considered its etymologies to be the most important aspect of his work. He adhered to the Biblical account of the origin of languages, claiming that all languages derived from 'Chaldee'. The inclusion of technical terms and an attempt at precision in definitions distinguished this dictionary, but few Americanisms were included.

Some of Webster's recommendations for spelling reform, suggested as early as his *Dissertations* (1789), survived modification in later editions of his texts. The principles behind his reforms were analogy, etymology, reason, and usage. He was most concerned about superfluous letters and indeterminate sounds and characters. Although most of his early suggestions were retracted, the US spelling of such words as *honor, center, defense, public* can be attributed to his choice of them rather than *honour, centre, defense, publick*. He recognized that language influences people and he sought to ensure that American texts reflected American values as he understood them.

**WEBSTER'S COLLEGIATE DICTIONARIES.** A line of best-selling desk dictionaries produced by Merriam–WEBSTER, Springfield, Massachusetts. The first *Collegiate* (1898) was compiled to be used by college students, taking its place in a series of abridgements intended to serve students from primary to university level. However, it was soon dubbed 'the busy man's dictionary', indicating its general usefulness. Subsequent editions appeared in 1910, 1916, 1931, 1936, 1946, 1963, 1973 (which sold over 11m copies) and 1983 (the 9th edition, with almost 160,000 entries based on a file of some 13m citations). The dictionaries, in addition to detailed coverage of pronunciations, spellings, word senses, and common synonyms, are known for their encyclopedic appendices, covering foreign words and phrases, biographical and geographical names, US and Canadian colleges and universities, signs and symbols, and a style manual. The 9th edition added the dates of first entry words into the language (where well substantiated) and usage notes at the ends of entries subject to controversy. The term *collegiate* is a proprietary registered trademark of Merriam–Webster though many similar desk dictionaries now exist. See DICTIONARY.

■ **WELSH** —————————— ■

**1.** An adjective relating to Wales, a principality in south–western Britain and part of the United Kingdom. It also relates to its people, and is used elliptically for the nation: *the Welsh*. **2.** The Celtic language of Wales, known to its speakers as *Cymraeg*. Welsh and Breton are the only surviving members of the ancient British or Brythonic subdivision of the Celtic language family. The original British language was highly inflected, but its descendant, Modern Welsh, has lost some of these inflections. Once the principal language of Wales and a literary language since the 6c, Welsh has been in decline since the accession of the partly Welsh Henry Tudor (Henry VII) to the English throne in 1485. There are now few monolingual speakers of Welsh, and some 500,000 of the people of Wales are bilingual: that is, 25% of the population.

The condition of Welsh at the end of the 20c is relatively stable, and it is being learnt by non-Welsh-speaking Welsh people and others, including immigrants from England. It is taught in all schools and is a medium of instruction in some. In the northern county of Gwynedd it is a language of local government and appears with English on road signs. Language activists, however, consider that much remains to be done.

The spoken language consists of several dialects, and has had a significant influence on the English language as used in Wales, but has had little impact on English at large. The most characteristic sounds of Welsh are the voiceless alveolar lateral fricative (spelt *ll* as in *Llanelli*), the voiceless alveolar roll /ɣ/ (spelt *rh* as in *Rhondda*), and the velar fricative (represented as in Scots and German by *ch*, as in *Llywarch*). As in all Celtic languages, grammatical mutations occur, as in the noun *ci* (dog), where the initial sound is affected by the modifier, as in *dy gi* your dog, *fy nghi* my dog, *ei chi* her dog, and *tri chi* three dogs. See BORROWING CELTIC LANGUAGES, CUMBRIC, WELSH ENGLISH.

■ **WELSH ENGLISH** —————— ■

The English language as used in Wales. The term is recent and controversial. English is, however, the majority language of Wales and, as in other parts of the English-speaking world, a concise term such as *Welsh English* (analogous to, among many others, *Canadian English* and *South African English*) appears unavoidable, however politically contentious. It is increasingly applied by sociolinguists to a continuum of usage that includes three groups of overlapping varieties of English: those influenced by the WELSH language; those influenced by dialects in adjacent counties of England; and those influenced by the standard language as taught in the schools and used in the media. The influence of Welsh is strongest in the northern counties (sometimes referred to as *Welsh Wales*), where Welsh/English bilingualism is most commonly found; it is weaker in mid-Wales, and weakest in the south, but even in such southern cities as Cardiff and Swansea the influence of Welsh is present.

**Origins**. It is not certain when speakers of an English dialect arrived in Wales, but it seems probable that Mercian settlers were in the Wye valley by the 8c. In the winter of 1108–9, Henry I established a group of Flemish settlers in Pembrokeshire and it is likely that there were English-speakers among that group. Other English settlements grew up in the 12–13c. Since most trade was in the hands of the English, the earliest regular Welsh users of English were almost certainly traders.

**Pronunciation**. Accent varies according to region, ethnicity, and education. RP is spoken mainly by English expatriates and its influence is strongest in the south-east. The following generalizations refer to native Welsh people: (1) Speakers of Welsh are often described as having a lilting or singsong intonation in their English, an effect created by three tendencies: a rise–fall tone at the end of statements (where RP has a fall); long vowels only in stressed syllables, the vowels in the second syllables of such words as 'increase and 'expert being short; reduced vowels avoided in polysyllabic words, speakers preferring, for example, /tɪkɛt/ for ticket and /kɔnɛkʃən/ for connection. (2) Welsh English is usually non-rhotic, but people who regularly speak Welsh are likely to have a postvocalic r (in such words as worker). (3) The accents of South Wales are generally aitchless. In North Wales, word-initial /h/ is not usually dropped, partly because it occurs in Welsh. (4) There is a tendency towards the monophthongs /e/ and /o/ and away from the diphthongs /eɪ/ and /əʊ/ in such words as late and hope. (5) The vowel /a/ is often used for both gas and glass. (6) Schwa is often preferred to /ʌ/ in such words as but and cut. (7) Diphthongs are often turned into two syllables with /biə/ for beer becoming /bijə/ and /puə/ for poor becoming /puwə/. (8) There is a preference for /u/ over /ju/ in such words as actually /aktuali/ and speculate /spɛkulət/. (9) The inventory of consonants is augmented from Welsh by the voiceless alveolar lateral fricative ɬ (spelt ll as in Llangollen), the voiceless alveolar roll /r̥/ (spelt rh as in Rhyl), and the voiceless velar fricative /x/ (spelt ch as in Pentyrch). (10) In many parts of the south, /l/ tends to be light and clear in such words as light and fall; in the north, it tends to be dark in both. (11) The voiced plosives /b, d, g/ are often aspirated in initial position, as with /bʰad/ for bad, often heard by non-Welsh people as 'pad'. The voiceless plosives /p, t, k/ are often aspirated in all positions, as with /pʰɪpʰ/ for pip. Consonants between

vowels are often lengthened, as in /mɪs:ɪn/ for missing, and /ap:iː/ for happy. (12) The -ing participle is often realized as /ɪn/, as in /dansɪn/ for dancing. (13) There is a tendency, especially in the north, to substitute /s/ and /ʃ/ for /z/ and /ʒ/, so that is becomes 'iss' and division 'divishon'. (14) The -y ending in words such as happy and lovely is realized by /iː/: 'appee', 'lovelee'.

**Grammar**. (1) Working-class users of English in Wales tend to use the following constructions, also found elsewhere in the UK: multiple negation (I 'aven't done nothin' to nobody, see?); them as a demonstrative adjective (them things); as as a relative pronoun (the one as played for Cardiff); non-standard verb forms (She catched it, The coat was all tore); 'isself for himself and theirselves for themselves ('E done it 'isself and they saw it for theirselves); the adverbial use of an adjective (We did it willin': that is, willingly); the addition of -like at the end of phrases and sentences ('E looked real 'appy-like); and the use of the -s verb ending with all subjects in the present (I goes to school an' they goes to work). (2) Non-standard forms reflecting an influence from Welsh include: do/did + verb, to indicate a regularly performed action (He do go to the rugby all the time; He did go regular-like); foregrounding for emphasis (Goin' down the mine 'e is He is going down the mine; Money they're not short of They aren't short of money); there and not how in exclamations (There's lovely you are!); untransformed embedded sentences, especially after verbs of saying and thinking (I'm not sure is 'e in I'm not sure if he's in); the over-generalization of the question tag isn't it? (We're goin' out now, isn't it?); occasional yes replacing a positive question tag (You're a teacher, yes?); will and not will be (I'm not quite ready, but I will soon); and too for either (I don't like it.—I don't like it too). (3) Look you (you see) is often regarded as a shibboleth of Welsh English in such sentences as Tried hard, look you, but earned nothin'. See is also often used: We were worried about 'im, see. The non-use of the subject pronoun is also characteristic of Welsh-influenced English: Saw 'im, bach. Saw 'im yesterday.

**Vocabulary**. (1) Words drawn from Welsh generally relate to culture and behaviour: carreg a stone, clennig a gift of money, eisteddfod (plural eisteddfodau) a cultural festival, glaster a drink of milk and water, iechyd da ('yachy da') good health (a salutation or toast, from iechyd health, da good); the use

## WELSH PLACE-NAMES

The place-names of Wales represent mixed linguistic origins over some 2,000 years: Welsh, Norse, Norman French, and English, together with the Anglicization of Welsh names and hybrids of Welsh and English.

**1. Welsh** The majority of place-names in Wales are from the Celtic language Welsh at various points in its history. Ten words commonly occurring in place-names are: (1) *aber* ('river mouth'), as in *Abergavenny* ('mouth of the Gefenni') and *Aberystwyth* ('mouth of the winding river', the Ystwyth); (2) *caer* ('fort'), as in *Caernarvon* ('fort in Arfon') and *Caerphilly* ('Ffili's fort'); (3) *cwm* ('valley'), as in *Cwmbran* ('valley of the river Bran') and *Cwmfelin* ('valley of the mill'); (4) *din* ('fort'), as in *Dinas Powys* ('fort of Powys') and *Dinefwr* ('fort of the yew'); (5) *llan* ('church'), as in *Llandaff* ('church on the river Taff) and *Llanfair* ('Mary's church'); (6) *llyn* ('lake'), as in *Llyn Vawr* ('big lake') and *Llyn Glas* ('green lake'); (7) *nant* ('stream'), as in *Nantgaredig* ('gentle stream') and *Nantyglo* ('stream of the coal'); (8) *pen* ('head, end'), as in *Penarth* ('head of the promontory') and *Penrhyndeudraeth* ('headland of the two beaches'); (9) *rhos* ('moor'), as in *Rhosgoch* ('red moor') and *Rhosllanerchrugog* ('moor of the heather glade'); (10) *tref* ('farm, homestead, town'), as in *Tregarth* ('ride farm') and *Tremadoc* ('Madoc's farm'). The forms *pont* ('bridge') as in *Pontnewydd* ('new port') and *porth* ('port'), as in *Porthcawl* ('harbour of the sea kale'), entered Welsh from French and come originally from Latin.

**2. Norse** Scandinavian raids in the 9–10c account for a number of largely Anglicized names around the coast, such as *Fishguard* ('fish yard'), *Milford Haven* ('harbour of the sandy inlet'), and *Swansea* ('Sveinn's sea'), as well as names ending in *-(e)y* ('island'), as in *Anglesey* ('Ongull's island'), *Bardsey* ('Bardr's island'), and *Caldy* ('cold island').

**3. Norman French** The Normans invaded Wales in the 11c and have left such names as *Beaumaris* ('beautiful marsh'), *Grosmont* ('big hill'), *Malpas* ('bad passage'), and *Montgomery* (the castle of Roger of Montgomery).

**4. English** The long-term interest of the English in Wales, the porous border between the two lands, and the English conquest in the 13c led to three types of place-name: (1) Old English names, as with *Chepstow* ('market place'), *Holyhead* ('holy headland', on Anglesey), *Knighton* ('knight's settlement'), and *Wrexham* (Wryhtel's pasture'); (2) Modern English names, such as *Newport* and *Welshpool*; (3) Anglicized Welsh names, such as *Cardiff* (adapting *Caerdydd*), *Carmarthen* (adapting *Caerfyrrdin*), *Denbigh* (adapting *Dinbych*), and *Lampeter* (adapting *Llanbedr*, 'Peter's church'). Because English has been spoken in the Gower Peninsula and south Pembrokeshire since the 12c, the area is known as 'Little England in Wales'; English names in the area include *Cheriton* ('church settlement'), *Middleton* ('middle settlement'), and *Newton* ('new settlement').

### Double names

Many places, especially towns, which are known throughout the United Kingdom by their non-Welsh names, have unrelated and much less widely known Welsh names, such as *Abergaun* ('mouth of the river') for *Fishguard*, *Abertawe* ('mouth of the river Tawe') for *Swansea*, *Caergybi* ('Cybi's fort') for *Holyhead*, *Trefaldwyn* ('Baldwin's homestead') for *Montgomery*, and *Yr Wyddfa* ('the cairn place') for *Snowdon* (from Old English: 'snow-covered hill'), the highest mountain in Wales.

of *bach* and *del* as terms of affection: *Like a drink, bach? Come near the fire, del.* (2) Words that are shared by Welsh English and dialects of England include: *askel* a newt, *dap* to bounce, *lumper* a young person, *pilm* dust, *sally* willow, *steam* a bread-bin. (3) General English words with local extensions of meaning include: *delight* a keen interest, as in *She's gettin' a delight in boys*; *lose* to miss, as in *'Urry or we'll lose the train*; *tidy* good, attractive, as in *Tidy 'ouse you've got, bach.* (4) The form *boyo*, from *boy*, is common as both a term of address and reference, and is sometimes negative: *Listen, boyo, I've somethin' to tell you; That boyo is not to be trusted.*

**Social issues**. Experiments reported in 1975 suggest that speakers of Welsh English are positively viewed in the principality. There is, however, considerable tension with regard to the use of the Welsh language, especially in schools and the media, and this can affect attitudes to English. Many consider that education should be bilingual, so that all Welsh people have access to Welsh as their 'national' language; others, however, including some parents originally from England, feel that bilingualism in schools puts an unnecessary strain on children, and do not necessarily regard Welsh as part of their patrimony. See BRITISH ENGLISH.

**WEST, Michael** [1888–1973]. English language teacher and lexicographer, educated at Oxford before joining the Indian Education Service. In 1923, he was commissioned to carry out a major examination of bilingualism that resulted in the *Bengal* (1926). Basing his argument on an analysis of the needs of learners, he concluded that reading should have a prominent place in bilingual education. The rest of his life was devoted to exploring the implications of that idea in materials and theoretical analysis. The *New Method Supplementary Readers*, based on controlled vocabulary, were produced by Longman under his editorship, and he convened the 1934 *Carnegie Conference on Vocabulary Selection* in New York which eventually led to *The General Service List of English Words* (1953), providing the ELT world with a minimum vocabulary based on frequency statistics. He also published widely in the teaching of oral language, writing, and methodology. See BASIC ENGLISH, FREQUENCY COUNT, GENERAL SERVICE LIST, LANGUAGE TEACHING.

**WEST AFRICAN ENGLISH**, short forms *WAfrE, WAE*. English as used in West Africa the official language of NIGERIA, GHANA, SIERRA LEONE, GAMBIA, and CAMEROON. It is typically acquired as a second, third, or fourth language, and the line between English as used by a small élite and the more general WEST AFRICAN PIDGIN ENGLISH is difficult to draw. Speakers in the five countries generally understand each other well, but there are differences inside and between countries. WAE is non-rhotic, and /r/ is often trilled. Intonation is influenced by the tonal systems of West African languages, and because there is a tendency towards syllable-timing, the schwa in unstressed syllables is usually replaced by a full vowel, as in 'stu-dent' and 'quiet-ness' for *student* and *quietness*. The consonants /θ, ð/ are generally realized as /t, d/, *three of these* being pronounced 'tree of dese'. Such words as *gush* and *fur* sound like *gosh* and *for*, and the vowel sounds of *bake* and *toe* are commonly the single vowels /e, o/, not diphthongs as in RP. Grammar is generally the same as standard BrE, but such constructions occur as *a country where you have never been there* and *He is an important somebody*. Regional vocabulary includes: loans from local languages, such as *buka* a food stand (from Hausa), and *danfo* a minibus (from Yoruba); compounds of English and vernacular words, such as *akara ball* a bean cake, and *juju music* a kind of music; loan translations and adaptations of local usages, such as *bush meat* game meat, and *father* and *mother* used for relatives, as in *He is staying with his fathers* (He is staying with relatives of his father); and local extensions of general English words, such as *corner* a curve in a road, *go slow* a traffic jam, to *wet plants* to water plants. See AFRICAN ENGLISH, AFRICAN LANGUAGES, CARIBBEAN ENGLISH, LIBERIA.

**WEST AFRICAN PIDGIN ENGLISH**, also **Pidgin English, pidgin**. Short form *WAPE*. A continuum of English-based pidgins and creoles from GAMBIA to CAMEROON, including enclaves in French- and Portuguese-speaking countries. Among its varieties are AKU in Gambia, KRIO in SIERRA LEONE, *Liberian Settler English* and *Liberian Pidgin English, Nigerian Pidgin English,* and KAMTOK or *Cameroon Pidgin English.* It originated in the 16c in contacts between West Africans and British sailors and traders. Its varieties are more or less mutually intelligible, and there is a complex continuum from constructions close to standard English to those far removed from it. WAPE is located midway between WEST AFRICAN ENGLISH and vernaculars spoken natively by those of its users for whom it is an additional language; some speakers, especially in cities, do not speak an African vernacular. Syntactic features of the variety furthest from standard English and with the lowest status (the basilect) are similar to those of the New World creoles, prompting researchers to speak of a family of 'Atlantic creoles' that includes WAPE, Gullah, Bahamian, Jamaican, Trinidadian, and Belizean. Tense and aspect are non-inflectional: *bin* denotes simple past or past perfect (*Meri bin lef* Mary left, Mary had left), *de/di* the progressive (*Meri de it* Mary is eating, Mary was eating), and *don* the perfective (*Meri don it* Mary has eaten, Mary had eaten). Depending on context, *Meri it* means 'Mary ate' or 'Mary has eaten' and *Meri laik Ed* means 'Mary likes Ed' or 'Mary liked Ed'. Adjectives are used without a copula when predicative: *Meri sik* Mary (is) sick. In *Meri de sik* Mary is falling sick, the progressive *de* marks transition into the condition of being sick. See AFRICAN ENGLISH, CREOLE, GHANA, LIBERIA NIGERIA.

■ **WEST COUNTRY** ———————— ■

Also **West of England, South-West**. A region of England with imprecise boundaries but generally agreed to centre on Avon, Devon, DORSET, Gloucestershire, and SOMERSET ('the cider counties'). Wiltshire and parts of Hampshire are sometimes included, as is Cornwall because of its location and despite its Celtic background, distinctive and controversial CORNISH language, and dialect of English influenced by Cornish. The range of accents in the West Country extends from broad in the working class and in rural areas through accents modified towards RP in the towns and the lower middle class to RP proper in the middle and upper classes. Local speech is rhotic, with a retroflex /r/ in such words as *rap*, *trip* and *r*-coloured vowels in such words as *car/cart*. Postvocalic /r/ is widely retained in such cities as Bristol and Exeter, despite the influence of RP, which is non-rhotic. In other cities, such as Plymouth and Bournemouth, rhoticity varies. Traces of variable *r*-pronunciation are found as close to London as Reading in Berkshire.

**Pronunciation**. For many people in Britain and elsewhere, traditional West Country has become stereotyped as rustic. Two particular shibboleths are associated with 'yokels' leaning on gates and sucking straws: a strong West Country burr, as in *Arrr, that it be* Yes, that's so; voiced initial fricatives, as in *The varmer zeez thik dhreevurrow plough* The farmer sees that three-furrow plough. Although the accent is now largely confined to the west and south-west, it was once common across England south of a line from the Severn to the Thames. West Country rhotic pronunciation is widely considered a survival of the /r/ of Old English. It turns preceding alveolar sounds into post-alveolars, resulting in a BURR that contrasts strongly with RP, and is often remarked on as a pleasing feature of West Country; it is similar to the Irish /r/ and that of many parts of the US. Another local feature is an initial /w/ in such words as *old* and *oak*, giving 'wold' and 'woak'. Before /ɔɪ/, a /w/ may also occur, as in 'bwoys' for *boys*. In a stretch of country from the Somerset coast to the sea in Dorset there is an *h*-sounding area; elsewhere in the West Country, initial *h* is not pronounced.

**Grammar**. Forms of grammar associated with traditional West Country speech are generally regarded as working-class and rural. They include: (1) The use of *thick* or *thicky* /ðɪk(ɪ)/ as a singular demonstrative, with *they* as plural: *thick man* that man, *they houses* those houses. (2) Present and past participles often preceded by *a-*, as in *a-goin*, *a-done*. (3) The use of periphrastic *do*, as in *He do go every week* He goes every week, *They do be ardworkin*. (4) The present tense of the verb *be* has been regularized to a single form that is still widely used: *I be, you be, he be, she be, we be, you be, they be*. (5) The negative *baint* is widely used: *I baint* I am not, *baint I* am I not, *ye baint* you aren't, *baint ye* aren't you, *they baint* they aren't, *baint they* aren't they.

**Vocabulary**. (1) Many West Country words are now restricted to part of only one county. Words formerly well known include: *fardel* a burden, *lew* dry, *mazzard* a black cherry, *truss* a bale (of hay), *tiddly* to do light housework. (2) In *The Grockles' Guide: An Illustrated Miscellany of Words and Phrases of Interest and Use to 'Voreigners' in Somerset* (Jeremy Warburg & Tessa Lorant, Thorn Press, 1985), the following are listed, among many others, as current: *anywhen* any time, *aps* a boil, *backalong* homeward (*I'll be doddlin backalong*), *brize* to bring pressure to bear on (*I'm goin to brize down on thik*), *caddle* a muddle or difficulty, *chammer* to chew noisily, chatter, *chatterbag* a gossip, *clumble-fisted* awkward with the hands, *combe* (pronounced 'coom') valley, *emmet* an ant, small fly, *gert* great, large, *jibber* a restless horse, *leary* hungry, tired, thin, empty, *mugget* the intestines of a young heifer or sheep, *pissabed* the dandelion, *quirk* to moan, whine, complain, *rafty* rancid, off, crafty, *randy* a party (*on the randy* out to enjoy oneself), *rozzum/ruzzum* a tall tale, *scrumpy* farmhouse cider, *somewhen* some time, *teddy* a potato, *verdic* a viewpoint, opinion (compare *verdict*). The term *grockle* for a holiday-maker or tourist is recent, its first *OED* citation being 1964.

**Literary West Country**. Most admired among West Country writers is Thomas Hardy, who in numerous novels attempted to represent the speech of rural men and women. His written dialect varies according to the speaker. Tess, the heroine of *Tess of the d'Urbervilles* (1891), although a peasant, had received some education and so had a regional accent, some local words, but more or less standard grammar. Hardy himself says of her: 'The dialect was on her tongue to some extent, despite the village school: the characteristic intonation of that dialect for this district being the voicing approximately rendered by the syllable UR, probably as rich an utterance as any to be found in human speech.' The dairy maids, on the other hand, use such forms as *zid* (saw), *hwome* home, and *I be, so be you*. See BARNES, DIALECT IN ENGLAND, NEWFOUNDLAND ENGLISH.

**WESTERN SAMOA** (Now called Samoa). A country of Oceania, a monarchy, and member of the COMMONWEALTH. Languages: Samoan, English (both official). A German colony from late 19c, Western Samoa was a League of Nations mandate in 1920, and later a United Nations trust territory administered by New Zealand, gaining its independence in 1962.

**WEST INDIES, The**. An ambiguous traditional term used in its widest geographical sense to refer to the islands of the Greater and Lesser Antilles excluding the Bahamas, and more narrowly to cover ex-British possessions (excluding Guyana and Belize on the mainland). See CARIBBEAN ENGLISH.

**WH-SOUND**. In phonetic terms, the voiceless counterpart of /w/. The distinction between /hw/ and /w/ in such pairs as *whales/Wales* and *which/witch* was once universal in English and is currently a matter of controversy and sometimes confusion. In Old English, *h* could precede *l*, *n*, *r*, *w* as in *hlāf* loaf, *hnecca* neck, *hwa* who, and was pronounced in each case. Only the /hw/ now survives, normal in IrE and ScoE, widespread in AmE and CanE, and common among older speakers of RP. The Old English written sequence *hw* was reversed to *wh* in the Middle Ages to align it with the other *h*-patterns (*ph*, *th*, *ch*, *sh*). In the process, an anomalous *w* was added in such words as *whole* (Old English *hāl*), *whore* (Old English *hōre*), while *whelk* (Old English *weoloc*) acquired a superfluous *h*. In Older Scots and formerly in Northern English, the /hw/ sound was distinctively represented as *quh*: *quhat* what, *quhilk* which. In *who*, *whom*, *whose*, *w* rather than *h* has fallen silent. The presence of *wh* can cause spelling difficulties for speakers who do not distinguish /hw/ and /w/: *\*wen* for *when*, *\*wheather* for *weather*, *\*whent* for *went*. Some speakers in England use /hw/ as a self-consciously 'correct' pronunciation in which overcompensation produces, for example, *\*the Prince of Whales*. See DIALECT IN SCOTLAND, W.

■ **WORD** ────────────────── ■

A fundamental term in both the general and technical discussion of language. The following selection of primary definitions of *word* is drawn from two American and two British works:

(1) *Webster's Ninth New Collegiate Dictionary* (1984): 'a speech sound or series of speech sounds that symbolizes and communicates a meaning without being divisible into smaller units capable of independent use'.

(2) *American Heritage Dictionary* (1985): 'a sound or a combination of sounds, or its representation in writing or printing, that symbolizes and communicates a meaning and may consist of a single morpheme or of a combination of morphemes'.

(3) *Collins English Dictionary* (1986): 'one of the units of speech or writing that native speakers of a language usually regard as the smallest isolable meaningful element of the

language, although linguists would analyse these further into morphemes'.

(4) *Chambers English Dictionary* (1988): 'a unit of spoken language: a written sign representing such an utterance'.

**Literacy and the word**. In ancient Greece, word study was an inseparable part of the study of texts, which had been prompted by the invention of script. Prior to that, NAME was a more clearly delineated concept than *word*, which was rather imprecisely associated with *speech* (apparently the meaning of *\*wer*, the Indo-European root underlying Latin *verbum*, Sanskrit *vrátam*, and English *word*). In oral communities, there appears generally to be no great interest in separating out 'units' of language, a lack of delimitation carried over into the early stages of alphabetic writing, in which letters followed each other in lines without spaces to separate off what are now perceived as 'words'. Spaces between groups of letters became important as the conventions of writing evolved. In alphabetic systems, spaces are now universal and as a result literate people learn to recognize 'words' as visual rather than auditory units.

Children learn about words while learning to write, become more or less comfortable with 'the written word', and may later assume that words as they are written automatically have a place as theoretical units of both speech and script. Grammarians, philologists, and linguists, all the legatees of the Greeks, have tended to focus on words as visual entities even when analysing sound, for which phoneticians developed a special alphabet. The place of the word as an ultimate unit of language has not, however, been easy to find, with the result that many 20c linguists have found it necessary to look elsewhere for key units of language: 'below' the word among phonemes and MORPHEMES or 'above' it in sentence and discourse.

**The word in different languages**. The nature of words varies from language to language: *amaverunt* is one word in Latin, but cannot be translated into one word of English (in which it means either *they loved* or *they have loved* ). It is a verb with a root *am-*, a THEMATIC VOWEL *-a-*, a marker of the perfect tense *-v-*, and a complex inflectional ending *-erunt*. The English verbs that translate it have different tenses (simple past *they loved*, present perfect *they have loved*) and

bear not the slightest resemblance to the structure of their Latin equivalent. Different from both English and Latin, Swahili has a primary verb form such as *kuta* (meet). The forms *kutana* ('meet each other') and *kutanisha* ('cause to meet each other') may be conceived as either variations of *kuta* or as distinct words. In effect, the conception 'word' is determined afresh within the system of every language, and as a result the word-as-element-of-speech is language-specific, not language-universal. The various kinds of language have their own broadly similar words, but even so there is variation from language to language inside a category: for example, among Romance languages between French and Spanish.

**Nine kinds of word**. Despite such complications, however, certain features are more or less true for many if not all languages. Nine such features are fundamental to English and each has its own 'word'.

*The orthographic word*. The word understood in terms of alphabetic or syllabic writing systems: a visual sign with space around it. It may or may not have a canonical form: in the 14c, before print encouraged standardization, *merry* was also spelled *myry*, *myrie*, *murie*, and *mery*. On occasion, the orthographic word has canonical forms for different varieties within English: BrE *colour* and AmE *color* ('the same word' in two visual forms).

*The phonological word*. The word understood in terms of sound: a spoken signal that occurs more commonly as part of a longer utterance than in isolation and is subject to rhythm. Traditional spoken English is a series of stressed and unstressed syllables which behave in more or less predictable ways: where an experienced listener hears *It's no good at all* being pronounced in a relaxed, informal way, a foreigner may hear *Snow good a tall*. In the flow of speech, words do not have such distinct shapes as on paper, and syllable boundaries do not necessarily reflect grammatical boundaries: the phrases *a notion* and *an ocean* are usually homophonic and only context establishes which has in fact been said.

*The morphological word*. The word in terms of form lies behind both the orthographic and the phonological word: *big* has a spelt-out realization *b-i-g* and a spoken realization /big/, but is independent of both, because it can be expressed in either medium and also in sign language. This entity is capable of realization in different 'substances'; it is distinct from such spelt-out variants as *colour* and *color* as well as from the innumerable ways in which African, American, Australian, Caribbean, English, Irish, Scottish or other people may say 'colo(u)r'. However, all such users have it in common and it is the basis of such further forms as *colourful* and *discoloured*.

***The lexical word*** (also called a *full word*, *content word*, *lexeme*, *lexical item*). The word in terms of content relates to things, actions, and states in the world. It is usually realized by one or more morphological words, as when *do*, *does*, *doing*, *did*, *done* are taken to be five 'versions' of the one verb DO. Lexical words are generally fitted into the flow of language through such mechanisms as *affixation*, *suppletion*, *stress shift*, and *vowel change*, all of which have morphological and other effects. The set of such words is always open to new members, and in English embraces nouns, verbs, and adjectives, and other parts of speech when they behave like nouns, verbs, and adjectives, as in 'But me no buts'. Lexical words may be simple in structure (*cat*, *mouse*), or composite (*cold-bloodedness*, *incomprehensible*, *teapot*, *blackbird*, *Commonwealth*, *stamp collector*, *put up with*, *natural selection*, *Parkinson's disease*).

***The grammatical word*** (also called a *form word*, *function word*, *structure word*, and in some theories a subvariety of *morpheme*). The word in terms of syntactic function contrasts with the lexical word and is an element in the structural system of a language. It serves to link lexical words. In English, conjunctions, determiners, interjections, particles, and pronouns are grammatical words. They occur frequently and have their own semantic systems, as with such particles as *up* and *down*, which relate to position, direction, space, and time. In principle, such words are a closed set to which new items are seldom added. As lubricants, grammatical words are like affixes: the *out* in *throw out* is like the prefix *e-* in *eject*; the *before* in *before the war* means the same as *pre-* in *pre-war*. They can also function like affixes, as in *he-man* and *yes-man*.

***The onomastic word***. The word in terms of naming establishes special, often unique reference: the difference between *Napoleon* and *emperor*. It may be simple like *Smith* or

complex like *Smithsonian*. Names may be motivated, like *Sitting Bull* (a Sioux name derived from an omen involving a bull buffalo) or conventional, like *Smith* today (though not in the Middle Ages, when the name was occupation-based). Although such words are lexical, they are not usually listed in dictionaries and may or may not be relevant in encyclopedias. They are often regarded as apart from normal vocabulary, though they too have to be learned.

***The lexicographical word***. The word in terms of dictionaries is usually presented in an alphabetical setting. Many dictionaries have an entry *did* as the past of *do*, an entry *them* as the object form of *they*, and so on, with cross-references to the representative form. There are therefore two kinds of entry: anything the compilers think anyone might look up, and the *citation forms* under which definition proceeds. The conventional citation form for nouns is the singular (unless a word is always plural) and for the verb is the bare infinitive (unless the verb only occurs as a participle, or is a modal verb).

***The statistical word***. The word in terms of occurrences in texts is embodied in such instructions as 'Count all the words on the page': that is, count each letter or group of letters preceded and followed by a white space. This instruction may or may not include numbers, codes, names, and ABBREVI-ATIONS, all of which are not necessarily part of the everyday conception of 'word'. Whatever routine is followed, the counter deals in tokens or instances and as the count is being made the emerging list turns tokens into types: for example, there could be 42 tokens of the type *the* on a page, and 4 tokens of the type *dog*. Both the tokens and the types, however, are unreflectingly spoken of as words.

***The translinguistic word***. The word in terms of several distinct languages in which versions of the same form exist: for example, *realitas* in Latin, *réalité* in French, *realidad* in Spanish, and *reality* in English. In one sense, these are not the same: they are all words in separate languages. In another sense, however, and one which is well understood by teachers and travellers, they are all 'the same word'; that is, a high degree of textual continuity survives across linguistic divides. It is a feature of such words, however, that no single omni-representative form can be cited for any such word: all the embodiments are linguistically equal and, in their various ways, subtly or significantly different.

**Other 'words'.** In addition, there is a large number of more or less common expressions, some technical, some semi-technical, some general and casual, all specifying kinds of words and word-like units. They fall into overlapping groups that include: (1) Terms in which *word* appears, such as: BASE *word*, BUZZ WORD, COMPOUND WORD, LONG WORD, ROOT-WORD. (2) Terms based on the suffix *-ism*, such as: AMERICANISM, AUSTRALIANISM, BURGESSISM, MALAPROPISM. (3) Terms based on the combining form *-onym*, such as: ANTONYM, *aptronym*, *characternym*, EPONYM, HYPONYM, SYNONYM. (4) Terms that relate to form more than meaning, such as: *abbreviation*, ACRONYM, COMPLEX WORD, *compound word*, INITIALISM, *portmanteau word*. (5) Terms that relate to meaning more than form, such as: ANTONYM, *burgessism*, *eponym* HARD WORD. (6) Terms that relate to social usage, such as: ANAGRAM, *buzz word*, CONFUSIBLE, LOANWORD, MALAPROPISM, NONCE WORD, PALINDROME, STUNT WORD, VOGUE *word*. All such terms fit in various ways and at various levels into the model of the word presented above.

**Words as clusters.** Because of its many dimensions, the concept 'word' is more like a cluster than an atom. On the level of theory, the cluster contains the kinds of words discussed above. On the level of practical activity, people 'know a word' not simply when they can use and understand a single item but when they know a range of variation and practices associated with it: for example, to know the word *know* entails knowing how to say, hear, read, and write its various forms and extensions, fitting them into phrases and sentences (*knows, knowing, knew, known*), relating the simple to the complex (as in *knowledge, knowledgeable, unknowing, unknowable, unknowably, unknown*), relating these to such compounds as *knowhow* and *know-all*, managing idioms (*y'know, in the know, know the ropes, know what's what, know a thing or two*), using and grasping senses, expressions, and collocations (*knowing someone or something, knowing how to do something, knowing better*, and even *knowing 'in the Biblical sense'*). This cluster, with its clear centre and hazy periphery, shares semantic space with other clusters cited as the words *understand, perceive, grasp*, and *fathom*. All operate within a system whose size and complexity defy comprehensive description, but without being beyond the reach of the everyday user of the language.

**WORD CLASS**, also **grammatical category**. Terms in linguistics for a category of words that have been grouped together because they are similar in their inflection, meaning, functions, or a combination of these. Many linguists prefer the term to PART OF SPEECH, which has traditionally been used for a more limited set of classes that are less rigorously defined. Others use the three terms as synonyms.

**WORD DIVISION**, **word-division**. See HYPHEN.

■ **WORD-FORMATION** ─────── ■

The formation of longer, more complex words from shorter, simpler WORDS. In the West, the analysis of word form began in classical Greece and passed in due course to Rome. Philosophers including Plato and Aristotle and grammarians such as Dionysius Thrax and Terentius Varro developed the study of the ways in which words were formed as a part of GRAMMAR, founding a long and subtle tradition that was inherited and extended by 19c comparative philology and 20c linguistics. The classical study was based only on GREEK and LATIN words, and contrasted *simple word* and *complex word*. The simple word was discussed either in terms of its ROOT (a basic element without adaptations or inflections), such as Greek *log*, whose core meaning was 'speech', or as a *root word*, consisting of a root, stem, and inflection (in most cases cited in standard forms, such as the nominative singular for nouns), such as Greek *lógos* (speech, word) and Latin *verbum* (word, verb). The complex word was discussed in terms of two processes or categories: (1) *Derivation*, in which AFFIXES and inflections could be added to a root, as with *logikós*, an adjective formed from *lógos*, and *verbalis*, and adjective formed from *verbum*. (2) *Composition*, in which two or more roots could be combined, with appropriate affixes and inflections added, as with the nouns *biología* and *biologistés*, formed from *bíos* (life) and *lógos*, and *agricultura*, formed from *ager* (field) and *cultura* (cultivation).

**Contemporary terms**. The classical description was somewhat simplified when transferred to English. The concept *root* has continued in use, but in the 20c has been increasingly replaced by *BASE* when discussing non-historical processes. A *root word* is usually called either a *simple word* or a *simplex*. The classical 'complex' forms divide into *COMPLEX WORDS* and *COMPOUND WORDS*, the formation of complex words being *DERIVATION* and of compound words being formerly called *composition* but now usually *compounding*. Derivation is the process by which the word *unfriendly* is built up from the simple word or free base *friend*, and *illegality* is built up from the bound base *-leg-* (from Latin, meaning 'law'). Compounding is the process by which the vernacular compound *teapot* is formed from the simple words *tea* and *pot* and the classical compound *biography* is formed from the combining forms *bio-* and *-graphy*. Although derivation and compounding account for a large number of the composite word forms of English and other languages, they do not cover everything. As a result, at various times further descriptive categories have been added, such as *conversion* or *functional shift*, *back-formation*, *phrasal verb*, *blend*, *abbreviation*, and *root-creation*. Sometimes, specific word-formational terms have lagged behind an awareness of the distinct forms actually occurring in a language: although, in English, verb forms like *put up* and *put up with* have been discussed since at least the 18c, the name *phrasal verb*, by which they are now most commonly known, was not applied to them until the early 20c.

In more detail, these categories are: (1) *CONVERSION or functional shift*, the process by which words extend their grammatical function: for example, from verb to noun (*run* in *go for a run*), and from noun to verb (*position* in *positioning people*). (2) *BACK-FORMATION*, the creation of a simpler or shorter form from a pre-existing more complex form: *edit* from *editor*, *intuit* from *intuition*. (3) *PHRASAL VERB*, a class of verb followed by an adverbial and/or prepositional particle: *put up* provide a bed for, *put up with* tolerate. (4) *BLEND*, the outcome of a process which collapses two words into one: *breakfast* and *lunch* into *brunch*; *electro-* and *execute* into *electrocute*. (5) *ABBREVIATION*, the shortening of words and phrases, in three basic forms: the *INITIALISM*, a set of letters pronounced as such and standing for

an idea, group, or institution (*BBC*, pronounced 'bee-bee-cee', for *British Broadcasting Corporation*); the *ACRONYM*, a set of letters pronounced as a word (*NATO*, pronounced 'Nay-toe', for *North Atlantic Treaty Organization*); the *CLIPPING*, a short form created by removing one or more syllables (*pro* for *professional*, *phone* for *telephone*, *flu* for *influenza*). Blends are often closely involved with the processes of abbreviation. (6) *ROOT-CREATION*, the formation of new roots or bases, which tend to be *echoic*, where a form resembles one or more pre-existing forms (*cuckoo*, *splish*: sounds of nature), or *onomastic*, deriving from names (*atlas* from the name of the mythical titan; *gin* from the city of Genoa). See *ECHOISM*.

**Word-formation clusters**. In accordance with need, social context, and formational patterns, clusters of derivatives, compounds, and other usages develop around words and bases. The noun *wolf*, for example, is the focus of a wide range of expressions: (1) Compounds like *prairie wolf* and *timber wolf* kinds of wolf, *wolf dog* the offspring of a wolf and a dog, *wolfhound* a dog that hunts wolves, *wolf-fish* a fish in some way like a wolf, *wolf spider* a spider that hunts its prey like a wolf, *wolfsbane* a poisonous plant, *wolf child* a child brought up by wolves, *wolfman* a man who can turn into a wolf, *wolf pack* a pack of wolves, *wolf note* a discordant note in music, *wolf whistle* a whistle of sexual admiration, *she-wolf* a female wolf, *werewolf* (from German) someone who can become a wolf. (2) Derivatives like *wolfer/wolver* a hunter of wolves, *wolf-like* and *wolfish* like a wolf, *wolfishly* its adverb, *wolfishness* the quality of being wolfish, *wolf down* to swallow food like a wolf, *wolverine* a large weasel-like animal with wolf-like attributes. (3) Fixed phrases like *Tasmanian wolf* a wolf-like animal in Tasmania, *lone wolf* a person who does things alone. (4) Idioms and sayings such as *cry wolf*, *keep the wolf from the door*, *be a wolf in sheep's clothing*, *throw someone to the wolves*.

Although the *wolf*-cluster exhibits the range of word-forming potential, it is an ancient and diffuse system whose members cover many contexts. As such, it does not illustrate the vigour of present-day word-formation, which can be seen in a recent more or less 'nonce' cluster based on the name *Tourette*. In 1885, the French neurologist Georges Gilles de la Tourette described a nervous condition marked by tics, jerks, grimaces, curses, mannerisms, imitative actions, and antic kinds of humour. This became known as *Gilles de la Tourette Syndrome*, then as *Tourette's syndrome*, often further shortened to *Tourette's*. When describing people with Tourette's, the American neurologist Oliver Sacks has used the following derivations, compounds, and other forms: (1) Nouns: *Tourettism* the syndrome and its effects, *motor Tourettism* the physical aspect of the syndrome, *mental Tourette's* the psychological aspect, *Tourette* a symptom of the syndrome, *Touretter* someone with the syndrome, *Tourette's Syndrome Association* a proper name, *TSA* its initialism, *Tourettoma* a figurative mind-tumour, *super-Tourette's* a powerfully destructive variety, *super-Touretter* one who has it, *Tourette psychosis* 'an identity frenzy', *Tourettesville* the nickname of the town of LaCrete in Alberta, Canada, many of whose Mennonite inhabitants have the syndrome, *Grandma Tourette* the nickname of a matriarch of the town. (2) Adjectives, adverbs: *Tourettic* (formal) pertaining to the syndrome, *Tourettically* its adverb, *Tourette-like* like the syndrome, *Touretty* (informal) showing symptoms, *Tourettish* (informal) relating to the syndrome, *Tourettishly* its adverb. (3) Verb forms: *Touretting* displaying the syndrome, *Tourettized* afflicted with the syndrome. (From Oliver Sacks, *The Man Who Mistook His Wife for a Hat*, 1985, and 'Being Moved by the Spirit', *Sunday Times*, 25 Sept. 1988.)

**Paradigms and paraphrases**. Although they often belong in clusters, complex words are usually formed one at a time in accordance with more or less established patterns. Such patterns or *paradigms* are built up analogically and differ for compounds and derivatives. Compound patterns involve a distinctive kind of stress on (the main syllable of) the first element, as in *TEApot* and *eMERgency plan*, and paraphrase formulas gloss the relationships between the bases in a compound: a *flower pot* is a 'pot for flowers' and so a *slop bucket* is interpretable as a 'bucket for slops'; a *goatskin* is 'the skin of a goat' and so an *iguana skin* is interpretable as 'the skin of an iguana'. Derivational paradigms are often cumulative, as in the set *form/formal/formality*, the paraphrases expressing relationships between base and other elements: *formality* is the condition of being *formal*, and *formal*

is the adjective that relates to *form*, and similar relations exist for the set *norm/normal/normality*, but not for *nature, natural,* *\*naturality*.

**The word-forming continuum**. Although much of English word-formation is regular, few patterns are neat and tidy and many forms blend their categories and mix their patterns. It is useful therefore to introduce the concept *HYBRID*: for example, compounds with derivational elements (*schoolboyish* and *mud-walled*) and abbreviations involved in attribution and compounding (*a NATO radar system* ), in derivation (*ex-IBMer*, someone who no longer works for International Business Machines), or in both (*an ex-CFL player*, someone who no longer plays for the Canadian Football League). It is likely that word-formation can be most usefully discussed in terms of both a continuum in which categories shade into each other and self-contained classical containers, each more or less insulated from the others. The fluidness of word-formation arises both from complex processes of change over centuries and from casual usage untouched by theories of language and norms of 'good' formation. The American linguist Dwight Bolinger, reflecting on 'the high informality of word-making in English', puts the matter as follows:

> Practically all words that are not imported bodily from some other language . . . are made up of old words and their parts. Sometimes those parts are pretty well standardized, like the suffix *-ness* and the prefix *un-*. Other times they are only broken pieces that some inventive speaker manages to re-fit . . . *Hamburger* yields *-burger*, which is reattached in *nutburger, Gainesburger,* and *cheeseburger*. *Cafeteria* yields *-teria*, which is reattached in *valeteria, groceteria,* and *washateria*. Trade names make easy use of almost any fragment, like the *-roni* of *macaroni* that is reattached in *Rice-a-Roni* and *Noodle-Roni*. The fabrication may re-use elements that have been re-used many times, or it may be a one-shot affair such as the punning reference to being a member of the *lowerarchy*, with *-archy* extracted from *hierarchy*. The principle is the same. Scientists and scholars may give themselves airs with high-bred affixes borrowed from classical languages, but they are

linguistically no more sophisticated than the common speakers who are satisfied with leftovers from the vernacular (*Aspects of Language*, 1968).

Word-formation in English operates among hundreds of millions of people, drawing on centuries of complex hybridization and prompting idiosyncrasy in forms and uses. As a result, even the most well-defined categories and patterns identify tendencies rather than absolutes that are thoughtlessly 'flouted' by the ignorant and insensitive. Around such focal points as compounding and affixation, with their relative certainties, swarm innumerable and unpredictable fringe formations, of longer or shorter duration, such as *lowerarchy*, *Rice-a-Roni* and *Grandma Tourette*.

See ASSIMILATION, BISOCIATION, BORROWING, BOUND AND FREE, CLASSICAL COMPOUND, CLASSICAL ENDING, COGNATE, COINAGE, COMBINING FORM, COMPLEX WORD, COMPUTERESE, COMPUTER USAGE, CONTRACTION, DERIVATIVE, DIMINUTIVE, DOUBLET, ELISION, -EME, ENDING, EPONYM, FORMATIVE, HARD WORD, INDO-EUROPEAN ROOTS, INITIAL, INITIALESE, INTERFIX, INTERNATIONAL SCIENTIFIC VOCABULARY, -ISM, ITERATIVE, LEXEME, LOAN, LONG WORD, MORPHEME, MORPHOLOGY, NEOLOGISM, NONCE WORD, NONSENSE, NOUN-INCORPORATION, ONOMATOPOEIA, PHONAESTHESIA, PLURAL, PREFIX, SHAKESPEARE, -SPEAK, STEM, STUNT WORD, SUFFIX, TELESCOPING, THEMATIC VOWEL, TMESIS, VOCABULARY.

**WORD ORDER**. A term for the order in which words appear in phrases and SENTENCES. In such highly inflected languages as Latin and Sanskrit, word order is relatively free, since the relations between words can be signalled by inflections, but it is relatively fixed in English: for example, an adjective generally precedes the noun it modifies (*tall woman*) and a preposition precedes its complement (*on my table*). The normal order of sentence elements in English is Subject–Verb–Object: *Tony wants an egg*.

**WORLD ENGLISH**. An increasingly common term for English as a world language: 'We may definitely recognize Australian English and New Zealand English as [forms] making their own special contribution to world English' (Robert D. Eagleson, in Bailey & Görlach (eds.), *English as a World Language*, 1982). Some scholars use the term cautiously or avoid it, because for them it

suggests global dominance by English and English-speaking countries, compare INTERNATIONAL ENGLISH.

**WORLD LANGUAGE**. **1.** A language used throughout the entire world. **2.** A language used in many parts of the world (such as Spanish and Portuguese), in specific large regions (such as the Latin of the Roman Empire, Arabic, Hindi, and Russian), and widely because of a special role (such as French for diplomatic purposes, especially in the 18–19c, and Sanskrit as the language of Hindu learning). See INTERNATIONAL LANGUAGE, LINGUA FRANCA.

**WORLD STANDARD ENGLISH**. Short form *WSE*. English in a standard form used as a (or *the*) world language: 'While *Congress* and *Parliament* originate in their respective countries, it is no longer very useful to call one AmE and the other BrE, from a linguistic point of view. They are now part of World Standard English (WSE)' (David Crystal, *The Cambridge Encyclopedia of the English Language*, 1995); 'Even if the new Englishes did become increasingly different, as years went by, the consequences for world English would not necessarily be fatal . . . A new form of English—let us think of it as "World Standard Spoken English" (WSSE)—would almost certainly arise. Indeed, the foundation for such a development is already being laid around us' (David Crystal, *English as a Global Language*, 1997). Compare INTERNATIONAL STANDARD ENGLISH.

**WORLD-WIDE WEB**. Short forms *WWW* and *the Web*. A global electronic system for organizing, making available and accessing documents on the INTERNET using a HYPERTEXT system. On Web menus, certain terms are numbered (on displays of characters) and underlined (in displays of graphics), indicating that they are links; when these are appropriately activated (usually by clicking on them with a mouse) they retrieve and display a document related to the one in which they occur.

■ **WRITING** ─────────────── ■

The term *writing* encompasses four pairs of linked senses. It may refer to: (1) An activity (*reading and writing*) or the product of that activity (*What illegible writing!*). (2) A concrete process (a *writing exercise*) or the concept behind that process (*Writing was invented over 5,000 years ago*). (3) Handwriting alone (*specimens of their writing*) or both handwriting and print (*Writing systems were extended by the invention of movable type*). (4) A general skill regarded as a social necessity (*Writing is part of everybody's education*) or a minority art form, occupation, hobby, and/or obsession (*This novel is the best example of her writing to date*).

Although written signs need not be permanent (as in writing on a blackboard or sky-writing from an aircraft), they are generally taken to be more or less durable. In the Germanic languages, as the etymology above indicates, the concept of writing related to cutting signs on wood or inscribing them on stone (see RUNE), but in principle the making of graphic signs is not restricted in either materials or methods: they may be cut with knife, chisel, drill, and other tools on stone, wood, plastic, and similar surfaces, or applied by pen, brush, type, and other instruments to surfaces such as paper, parchment, or cloth. The electromagnetic charges of the computer are also understood to be writing, whether temporary on screens or more permanently on disks and other devices for information storage and retrieval.

**A medium of language**. Each medium that carries language (such as speech, writing, or signing among the deaf) has its special features. All language is linear, but each medium has its distinctive units and marshals them differently: for example, an alphabetic letter, a dash, or the indenting of a paragraph has no equivalent in speech. Forms of writing and print have cultural resonances distinct from those of speech and song, as for example the contrast between capital and small letters, or between the use of roman or italic script. Although each medium of language can 'say' things about another, there is no way in which one medium can *be* another. In addition, many scholars consider that social systems such as religions and governments for which writing is a normal activity are quite different from those that depend on the more fluid and ephemeral processes of speech and memory: issues of morality become more abstract, reasoning more rigorous, and language more open to objective and logical analysis. With the help of writing, draft plans can be formulated and administrative routines can develop, and in the process the speech of such communities is also changed, becoming imbued with the styles and patterns of written language.

**Speech versus writing**. Since classical times, there have been two contradictory approaches to speech and writing: (1) The view that writing is the primary and speech the secondary medium, because writing is more culturally significant and lastingly valuable than speech. The term *grammar*, for example, derives from the Greek verb *gráphein* to write. The systematization of classical Greek GRAMMAR by such theorists and teachers as Dionysius Thrax, *c*.100 BC, was the first attempt at language description in the Western world, and unlike the early studies of language in India, which were soundbased, it rested entirely on writing. This tradition was extended to the study and teaching of many languages throughout the world with little change until the early 20c. (2) The view that speech is primary and writing secondary, because speech is prior to writing both historically and in terms of a child's acquisition of language. In the 4c BC, Aristotle said: 'Spoken sounds are symbols of affections of the soul, and written marks are symbols of spoken sounds' (*On Interpretation*, 16a 3–4). Comparably, but long afterwards, the Swiss philologist Ferdinand de Saussure observed: 'Speech and writing are two separate systems of signs; the sole purpose of the second is to represent the first' (1916: translated from *Cours de linguistique générale*, ed. Tullio de Mauro, Payot, Paris, 1978, Introduction, ch. 6). When Saussure made this comment, he was reacting against centuries of scholarship and education in which the text had been regarded as fundamental.

**Writing systems**. A major feature of writing is that it can operate over distance and time. Memorized and stylized speech that passes from person to person has some of this capacity, but has no existence apart from the performance of one speaker at one time. There is also no guarantee that an oral message will be the same after several stages of transmission, whereas a written document can be read at different times by different people and remain stable, unless overwritten. Although people may interpret such a document differently, they agree that it is an invariant object, and may accept it as incontrovertible evidence in a court of law. The signs on a well-kept 4,000-year-old clay tablet are virtually as legible and perhaps as intelligible today as at the time of writing, save that some shades of meaning and implications of context are likely to have been lost. There was nothing comparably durable for spoken language until the invention of the phonograph in the late 19c, but even so audio-recording remains distinct from text in its effect, its usefulness, and its technologies.

The first known system of writing was not a re-expression of spoken language. It was pictorial in origin, creating two-dimensional analogues of three-dimensional things in the world; only much later did writing systems acquire the capacity to 'reflect' or run parallel to the words and sounds of speech. The first writing was invented in West Asia 5,000–6,000 years ago, in Sumer in southern Mesopotamia. Since that time, writing systems have used a variety of symbolic forms, sometimes as relatively 'pure' systems of one kind of sign, but more commonly in combinations of the following two broad categories of signs:

***Picture-based signs***. The longer-established variety of sign is representational and analogous, as with early Sumerian. Scholars generally identify three types that are not always easy to set off one from another: (1) *Pictograms*, that directly represent things in the world, such as animals, people, houses, and geographical features, often in stylized and simplified outline forms such as a wavy line for water. (2) *Ideograms* (in effect 'idea grams'), that represent concepts, such as the numerals *I*, *II*, *III* or *1*, *2*, *3*, usually arising from the further stylizing and simplifying of pictograms. (3) *Logograms*, that represent words proper, such as the icons used in international airports: a drawing of a telephone directly standing for *telephone*, a man and a woman side by side indirectly standing for *toilets* (or their equivalents in different languages). The early writing systems of Sumer and Egypt and the writing of China belong almost wholly in the picture-based group, which deals directly in meanings and not in sounds.

***Sound-based signs***. The somewhat younger variety of sign is *phonographic*, relating sound to symbol. Two types can usually be kept distinct (but see ALPHABET): (1) *Syllabograms*, representing individual syllables, as in the *kana* systems of Japanese (see JAPAN). (2) *Phonograms*, or as they are more commonly known, *letters*, signs that represent individual sounds. Such signs have over the centuries often become detached from the specific language in which they were first used, as demonstrated by the many variants of the Roman alphabet (for English, French, German, Polish, etc.), and may therefore represent different sounds in different systems, as for example the letter *c* as used in English and Italian. Phonographic writing systems deal in sounds, not meanings.

**Writing technologies**. The development of technologies of writing is contingent on time, place, and environment. The Sumerian system, for example, developed in marshy terrain, where its inventors used a cut reed to impose wedge-like (*cuneiform*) marks on a soft clay tablet (the reed held in one hand, the tablet in the other). The inscribed clay was then left to dry in the hot sun, or for greater permanence was baked in an oven. Their system was an integrated technology of stylus, clay, and cuneiform that was at first pictographic and became in due course ideographic and syllabographic. The Egyptians, also a riverine people, did not develop clay but concentrated on plants, using a reed brush to paint their signs on papyrus stems that were pressed together to form sheets held in place by their own gum. Theirs was a technology of brush, papyrus, and hieroglyph that later developed phonographic elements. Both Sumerian and Egyptian writing methods were also applied successfully to large vertical surfaces, such as walls and pillars. In medieval Europe, scribes used trimmed feathers from the wings of large birds and various inks to mark a set of alphabetic letters on parchment skins. Theirs was a technology that combined pen, parchment, and alphabet. At the end of the 20c, as a sum of all the operations of the past throughout the world, a vast array of calligraphic and typographic options is available, for example word-processing, for the preparation of texts of many kinds on surfaces of many kinds.

**Writing implements**. The *pen* (a 13c term from Latin *penna* feather) is the oldest writing implement in general use. It has its origins in both the Sumerian reed and the medieval feather. Vast flocks of geese were once kept in Europe to provide quill pens that were sold in bunches. The writing ends of the goose quill feathers were cut and split with a *pen knife*, after which they could be dipped in *ink-wells* or *ink-horns* and put to use, the ink flowing down the split while one wrote until it was used up. Pens with metal nibs are an industrial-age adaptation of by reed or quill have thick and thin strokes, a feature that influenced the shapes given to letters in printing. The *fountain pen*, equipped with a reusable cartridge for holding a large supply of ink to be steadily fed to the nib, was a late 19c advance on the basic metal-nibbed pen. After the Second World War, however, all such pens were generally replaced by the cheap, easily disposable *ballpoint* (*pen*) or *biro* (named after László Biró, its Hungarian inventor). The present-day *pencil* (a 14c term from Latin *penicillum* a painter's brush, ultimately from *penis* a tail) is more recent than the pen. It consists of a stick of graphite (often erroneously called 'lead', as in *lead pencil*), protected by a machined sheath of wood. It developed as a variation of the markers that medieval scribes used to draw lines in manuscripts. The late 20c *felt-tip pen* (BrE) or *marker* (AmE) is a variation on the ancient reed brush, its ink supply stored in its stem like a biro.

**Pen and print**. Generally, documents written in ink have had both a higher social cachet and greater physical permanence than documents written in pencil, while texts in print have had still higher prestige and greater permanence (depending on the quality of paper used). Because documents written in pencil and pen are no longer widely circulated, there is less pressure on students to cultivate clear handwriting. Writing by hand continues to be basic to education while at the same time its value has declined in occupational terms. It is useful in note-taking, note-writing, and personal letters, but there are fewer and fewer clerical careers that require no more than the making of handwritten entries in books and ledgers. Handwriting and handwritten documents have become as a result increasingly demotic and spelling and grammar in personal letters appear to be increasingly seen as personal matters.

**Type and word-processing**. In 20c public life, writing by hand has long been displaced by typing. In recent years, the word-processing *personal computer* (the *PC*: whether desktop, laptop, or palmtop) has adopted and adapted many features from the typewriter, particularly the format of the keyboard, while advanced or 'smart' typewriters have come more and more to resemble PCs. With its battery of word-processing software, spelling and style checkers, dictionaries, thesauruses, and other built-in aids, the PC is, however, as different from the typewriter as the typewriter from the traditional printing press, and the press from the pen. Transmission systems known as *modems* (short for 'modulator demodulators') can send and receive texts electronically over distance, and scanners capable of *optical character recognition* (*OCR*) can read printed documents and transcribe them directly on to disk with ever greater accuracy. In addition, large computers routinely direct typesetting machinery in the production of books and periodicals. As a consequence, computers used for language work are changing many aspects of, and attitudes towards, traditional written and printed language.

**Learning to write**. All writing systems demand long periods of apprenticeship in which the student memorizes and learns to use the inventory of signs and the tools associated with them. Over the last two centuries, more and more societies have grown to expect more and more of their members to be able to write. Universal LITERACY became an aim in most industrialized nation-states over a century ago, but the concept of an adequately literate society remains unclear, and changes over time. There is also ongoing controversy over the teaching and acquisition of styles and skills in handwriting, and in learning how to spell and read adequately in languages with complex orthographies, such as English and French: see READING, SPELLING, SPELLING REFORM.

***Handwriting***. Basically, methods of teaching children to write have not changed greatly over the centuries. The principal procedure remains an introduction to the elements of the writing system. Models are then provided for copying and developing in various ways: usually the teacher's own handwriting and specimens in copybooks. For English, as with other languages originating in Europe, a cardinal feature in learning to write is learning to join letters as opposed to leaving them in an unjoined form known as *print script*. The ability to link separate letters by means of connecting lines is highly valued as proof of a child's success in learning to write. A significant subsidiary feature is the ability to move from large early letters formed with great care to smaller letters in a maturer 'hand' that stays within an acceptable size range. Once this is achieved, individuals are free to develop their own handwriting, descriptions of which include such evaluative terms as *generous* or *cramped*, *neat* or *untidy*, *rounded* or *spiky*, *legible* or *illegible*. In educational terms, such matters as a steady reduction in the size of letters relate to stages in children's neuromuscular development and physical coordination.

***Aids to learning***. Analogies and mnemonic devices continue to be common in helping young children write individual letter forms. Such devices are often reminiscent of past or different kinds of writing, as with the pictorial analogy: 'Letter *S* is a swan who holds her head up high' (Ruth Fagg, *Everyday Writing*, University of London Press, 1963). The visual system developed by Lyn Wendon uses animal and other shapes as templates for the child to work with (*Pictograms*, Barton, Cambridge, 1973/84). One of her pictographic examples is the character Dippy Duck, used to teach the direction and flow necessary when forming small *d*: '*Stroke* Dippy's back. Go *round* his tum. Go *up* his neck. Then *down* you come!'

***Factors in learning***. Teaching people to write includes such factors as: (1) Eliminating tension, especially in very young learners, through preliminary relaxing exercises. (2) Checking writing postures and hand grips. (3) Ensuring good writing conditions, such as a suitable seat, desk surface, and lighting. (4) Determining hand dominance and ensuring that left-handers in a society dominated by right-handers are not directly or indirectly penalized or neglected. (5) Providing adequate graded pattern exercises, such as the angular diagonal patterns that underlie the writing of capital M and the rounded equivalents for *m*. (6) Helping learners to achieve rhythm, fluency, and reasonable speed. (7) Constructively working on faults (such as wrong pencil grips, ill-formed letters, and inefficient directionality in the shaping of letters). (8) In due course allowing the learner to develop a confident individual hand.

**WYCLIFFE, John**, also **Wyclif**, **Wiclif**, and others [*c*.1320–1384]. English reformer and Bible translator, born at Wycliffe in Yorkshire, and Master of Balliol College, Oxford (*c*. 1356–*c*.1382). His role in the Lollard movement and the politics of the Reformation have tended to overshadow his significant contribution to the language. His translations (with collaborators) of the Vulgate BIBLE were the first complete Bible in English and existed in two forms, the Early Version (*c*.1380–2) and the Late Version (*c*.1382–8), the second being more idiomatic, less archaic, and freer from Latinisms and generally more highly regarded. Wycliffe was a friend of Geoffrey Chaucer, who may have used him as the model for the Poor Parson in *The Canterbury Tales*. He did for Middle English prose what Chaucer did for poetry, making English a competitor with French and Latin; his sermons were written when London usage was coming together with the East Midlands dialect, to form a standard language accessible to all, and he included scientific references, such as to chemistry and optics. His style influenced Reformation and later nonconformist writing, and John Milton was among his admirers. More than 300 of his discourses survive, with some 170 manuscript copies of his Bible, circulated from Lutterworth, where he was rector (1374–84). Its opening words are: 'In the firste made God of nought heuene and erthe. The erthe forsothe was veyn withynne and void, and derknessis weren upon the face of the see.' Wycliffe's own share in the translations bearing his name is uncertain, but was probably considerable.

**WYNN**, also **wyn**, **wen**. The name of a runic LETTER and its manuscript and printed form *Ᵽ*, used in Old and early Middle English for *w*, as in *snaᏢ* snow, *hᏢit* white. See RUNE.

# X

## ■ X, x ■

[Called 'eks']. The 24th LETTER of the Roman ALPHABET as used for English. It was adapted from the Greek letter *chi/khi* (X) by the Romans, with the value /ks/.

**Sound value**. Phonetically, *x* as used in English is redundant, its standard value /ks/ being equally represented by *cc* in *vaccine*, *ks* in *treks*, *cs* in *tocsin*, and *cks* in *socks*, allowing such homophones as *lax/lacks* and *cox/cocks*. However, *x* is not always pronounced as *ks*, different environments inducing the alternatives /gz/ in *example* and /z/ in *xenophobia*.

**Initial *X* and EX-**. (1) No vernacular English word begins with the sound /ks/, and the pronunciation is /z/ for initial *x* is such GREEK-derived bases as *xantho-* yellow, *xeno-* foreign, *xero-* dry, *xylo-* wood, and such names as *Xanthippe* and *Xerxes*. (2) Older SPANISH *x* as in *Mexico*, *Texas* is kept, with English pronunciation in Spain these are today written *Méjico*, *Tejas*, and pronounced with a velar fricative /x/, as in ScoE *loch*. (3) When initial *x* stands for the letter *x* (*Xmas*, *X-ray*), it is pronounced 'eks'. (4) *X* in the LATIN prefix *ex-* may be pronounced voiceless as /ks/ (typically when stressed, as in *export*, *extra*) or voiced as /gz/ (typically before a stressed vowel, as in *exact*, *exist*). In practice, however, voicing is often inconsistent, both realizations being heard in *exit*. The *c* in initial *exc-* (*excel*, *excite*) is assimilated into the voiceless value of *x*, while following *h* is usually assimilated into the voiced realization (*exhaust*, *exhibit*, but voicelessly in *exhibition*). A following root beginning with *s* loses the *s* (*ex + sert* becomes *exert*) and the *x* is voiced.

**Medial *X***. (1) In medial position, *x* is typically voiceless (*maxim*, *vexatious*, *elixir*, *toxin*, *approximate*, *buxom*, *axle*, *sexton*), but when an *i*-glide follows (whether represented by *i* with a following vowel, or by *u* with the value in *music*), the glide may be assimilated and *x* sounded as *ksh* (*noxious*, *luxury*, *sexual*), a palatalizing effect paralleled in other spelling patterns such as *fractious*, *actual*. (2) Voicing of this sound may occur medially before a stressed syllable, 'gzh' rather than 'ksh' being often heard in *luxurious*. (3) *Anxious* parallels *noxious* (though with the preceding *n* velarized as 'ng'), but in the noun *anxiety* the *i* is not assimilated, the *n* remains velarized, and *x* is voiced but loses its /k/, being pronounced /z/. (4) English usually retains *x* as derived from Latin, as in *exit* from *exitus* and *crucifixion* from *crucifixio/crucifixionis*, but, since the 17c, *connexion*, *inflexion* (the etymologically appropriate spellings) have increasingly been written *connection* and *inflection*, probably by analogy with *direction*. *Complexion* and *fluxion* do not have alternative forms.

**Final and silent *X***. (1) Final *x* is common and except in recent loans has the value /ks/, usually after a short vowel (BrE *axe*, AmE *ax*, *flax*, *relax*, *climax*, *wax*, *index*, *flex*, *complex*, *sex*, *vex*, *fix*, *mix*, *six*, *executrix*, *phalanx*, *jinx*, *ox*, *box*, *fox*, *pox*, *flux*, *crux*), but in *coax*, *hoax* after a long vowel. Final /ks/ is normally spelt *x* in English, except when the /s/ is an inflection: contrast *tax/tacks*. (2) In French loans, final *x* is typically silent (*choux*, *prix*, *Montreux*) or pronounced /z/ if a plural inflection (*tableaux*). *Sioux* is modelled on French with silent *x*, although Amerindian in origin. (3) Latin morphology sometimes affects final *x*. When the plural of *appendix*, *index*, *matrix*, *vortex* follows Latin, *x* becomes *c* in *appendices*, *indices*, *matrices*, *vortices*. However, regular English pluralizing with *-es* (*appendixes*, *indexes*, *matrixes*) is common, though sometimes implying a distinct sense of the word concerned: for example, *appendices* in books, *appendixes* in the body. (4) Similarly, the Latin feminine suffix *-trix* is occasionally used as a counterpart to masculine *-tor* rather than the commoner French-derived *-tress*, as in *dominatrix*, *executrix*, *victrix*, as against *actress*, *benefactress*.

**Miscellaneous**. (1) *X* sometimes alternates with *sk* by metathesis: *Manx* for earlier *Mansk*; *piskey* as a variant of *pixie*; *ax* as a dialect form of *ask*. (2) *Buxom* was formerly *bucksome* and *pox* derives from the plural of *pock*. Comparably, a recent tendency in commercial spelling reduces the morphologically distinct *cs*, *cks* to *x*: *fax* for *facts* and *facsimile*, *pix* for *pictures*, *sox* for *socks*, *trux* for *trucks*. (3) Disyllables ending in *x* include technical terms from Latin (*helix*, *vortex*) and, apparently as a consequence, many commercial and trade names (*Kleenex*, *Tampax*, *Xerox*). See C, K.

# Y

## Y, y

[Called 'wy', rhyming with *high*]. The 25th LETTER of the Roman ALPHABET as used for English. It originated as one of two letters derived by the Greeks from the Phoenician consonant symbol *waw*. The GREEK letter *upsilon* (γ, lower case υ) had a value like *u*, which LATIN wrote as *V*. Only later did the Romans adopt the form Y as a separate letter specifically to transliterate Greek *upsilon*, adding it to the end of the alphabet (*z* being a later addition still). Many European languages indicate the Greek origin in their name for *y*: FRENCH *i-grec*, SPANISH *i-griega* (Greek *i*), GERMAN *Ypsilon*. The French and Spanish names imply that the letter is an alternative for *i*.

**Origins and early uses**. The name *wy* may derive (with changes in pronunciation) from the sound the letter represented in OLD ENGLISH: a fronted *u* as in French *tu* and the value of *y* in German and the INTERNATIONAL PHONETIC ALPHABET. In Middle English, this sound typically merged with that of short *i*. In medieval times, *y* was commonly written with a superimposed dot to distinguish it from the similar forms of the OLD ENGLISH letters THORN and WYNN. After the Norman Conquest in 1066, fronted *u* was increasingly spelt in the French fashion as *u*, making *y* available as the alternative to *i*, which may have been useful for breaking up a series of vertical strokes, so that *min* (*mine*) might be more legibly written *myn*. There was, however, little consistency in the use of either *i* or *y*.

In addition, in MIDDLE ENGLISH, *y* often served to represent the Old English letter YOGH (3), especially word-initially. As this sound lost its velar quality, there emerged the semi-vowel value heard in *year*. This use was reinforced by its availability, unlike yogh, in printers' typefaces. A few words with initial yogh in Old English dropped it entirely, *enough*, *if*, *itch* now having no initial vowel. On the other hand, *you* has replaced an initial glide vowel with *y* (Old English *eow*). The similarity of the handwritten forms of *y* and thorn (þ) led to its occasional use as an alternative to *th*, the usual Roman equivalent of thorn, especially in *the*, *that*,

etc., so producing shorthand forms for these words as *yᵉ*, *yᵗ* which persisted in private use well into the Early Modern English period. The form *yᵉ* is currently used on pseudo-antique shop-signs such as *Ye Olde Englishe Tea Shoppe* (jocularly pronounced 'ye oldy Englishy tea shoppy'), in which the *ye* is generally not recognized as an alternative spelling for *the*.

**Sound values**. (1) In English, *y* is widely used as an alternative letter for the sounds represented by *i*, sometimes interchangeably, but often with a different positional distribution: word-initially as a semi-vowel (*year*, *yes*, *you*); word-finally in VERNACULAR words (*caddy*, *hilly*, *sorry*). (2) Like *i*, *y* commonly softens a preceding *c* or *g* (*cypress*, *gypsum*, *fancy*, *bulgy*), but there are exceptions and options in the pronunciation of words derived from Greek: in *Cythera* usually hard, in *gynecology* generally hard but sometimes soft, and in *demagogy* both hard and soft. (3) The letter *y* alternates with *a* in *scallywag/scalawag*, and in the spellings BrE *pyjamas*, AmE *pajamas*.

**Greek short Y**. Short *y* has the value of short *i* in many words derived from Greek (transliterating upsilon), often borrowed through Latin and French: *analysis*, *anonymous*, *chrysanthemum*, *crypt*, *cylinder*, *cynic*, *cyst*, *dynasty*, *dyslexia*, *Egypt*, *etymology*, *gymnasium*, *hymn*, *hypnosis*, *hypocrite*, *idyllic*, *lyric*, *martyr*, *methylated*, *myriad*, *myrrh*, *myrtle*, *mystery*, *myth*, *oxygen*, *physic*, *polygon*, *polyp*, *pterodactyl*, *pyramid*, *rhythm*, *syllable*, *sympathy*, *synagogue*, *system*, *zephyr*. Some words in short *i* may look Greek, but are not, and often have variants in *i*: for example, *syllabub/sillabub*, *sylvan/silvan*, *syrup/sirup*. However, *gypsy/gipsy* and *pygmy/pigmy* are Greek in origin.

**Word-final short Y**. The short *i*-sound in which many native English words end in most accents is always spelt *y*: contrast traditional words with loans, as in *jetty/spaghetti*, *windy/Hindi*, *juicy/sushi*. In some accents, however, this vowel has the same value /ɪ/ as medial short *y*; in others, it is lengthened to /iː/: for example, older RP has the value of medial short *y*, while more recent RP has a quality similar to that in *see*. These endings commonly change *y* to *ie* in inflected forms (*pity/pities/pitied*), and in Elizabethan times the base words were often spelt -*ie* (*citie*, *pitie*). Word-final *y* occurs in several common patterns: (1) Disyllabic concrete nouns: *baby, jetty, city ivy, body, study*. (2) Disyllabic nouns (mainly concrete) in -*ey*: *abbey, alley, chimney, donkey, hockey, honey, jersey, journey, medley, money, monkey, parsley, spinney, turkey, valley*. (3) Adjectives: *happy, holy, merry, pretty, silly, tidy*. This -*y* is often a suffix added to another word: *crazy, catty, easy, fiery*. (4) Abstract nouns, such as those based on an adjective ending in -*ous* (*curiosity, pomposity, notoriety*), on a word ending in *t* (*difficulty, pregnancy, prophecy*), or otherwise (*facility, necessity, opportunity*). They include many Greek-derived words: *biology, economy, hierarchy, liturgy*. (5) Adverbs in which the suffix -*ly* has been added to an adjective: *grandly, hurriedly, slowly, stupidly*; sometimes some assimilation takes place with the root: *wholly, happily, ably, incredibly, nobly, volubly, simply*. A few adjectives are formed by the addition of -*ly* to a base: *brotherly, friendly, kindly*. (6) Verbs; as *carry, marry, vary, pity, worry, hurry*. In some words, such as *bogey, bogy, caddy, pixy, stymy*, final -(*e*)*y* is alternatively spelt -*ie*.

**Long Y**. The letter *y* often represents the sound of long stressed *i*: *by, lyre*. Some related words alternate long and short values: *lyre/lyric, paralyse/paralysis*. Long *y* occurs: (1) In monosyllables, typically of Old English origin, in final position: *buy, by, cry, fry, guy, my, ply, sty, thy, why, wry*. A silent *e* is added to avoid spelling a non-grammatical word with just two letters: *bye, dye, eye, rye*. (2) In verbs, in final position, such as *ally, defy, deny, modify, multiply, occupy, prophesy, qualify, satisfy, specify, supply*. Y in *multiply, supply* is short when these words are adverbs derived from *multiple, supple*. (3) As the dominant pronunciation of Greek-derived bases and prefixes such as *cycl-, dyn-, gyr-, hydro-, hyper-, hypo-* (but not *hypocrite*), *pyro-* and such words as *hyacinth, hyena, hygiene, hymen, hyphen, lyre, papyrus, type, tyrant*. In some words of non-Greek origin, medial long *y* is interchangeable with *i*: *cyder, cypher, dyke, gybe, tyro*. (4) In such words as *rhyme* (see entry), *style* (see entry), *typhoon*, and BrE *tyre* (AmE *tire*).

**Semi-vowel Y**. (1) In medial positions, there is no clear phonetic distinction between the semi-vowel *y* and an *i*-glide. In the alternative spellings *lanyard/laniard* they are identical in pronunciation. (2) Semi-vowel *y* occurs in initial position in words mostly of Old English origin, formerly often spelt with yogh: *yard, yarn, year, yeast, yellow, yeoman, yes, yesterday, yew, yield, yoke, you, young, your, youth*. (3) Most other words beginning with *y* are more recent, and often loanwords: *yacht, yak, yam, yank, yodel, yoga*. (4) Medial *y* with a semi-vowel value as in *lawyer* is uncommon. (5) The semi-vowel value is also represented in the letter *u* (*cure, pure*) and the digraphs, *eu, ew* (*eureka, spew*). The semi-vowel is normally so spelt after a consonant: *fuse, few, feud*. (6) Word-initially, *u* commonly has the sound of *you* (*union, use*), as do *eu, ew; ewe* and *yew* are homophones.

**Digraphs**. Like *i*, *y* serves as the second letter in digraphs after other vowel letters, *y* usually word-finally, with *i* medially. (1) The digraph *ay* occurs in common monosyllables. This *ay* has the value of long *a* like *ai* as in *rain*: *bray, clay, day, flay, fray, gay, may, pay, play, pray, ray, say, slay, spray, stay, tray, way*. When -*r* (syllabic or with preceding schwa) is added, the value of *ay* may be modified: *layer, prayer, mayor, Ayr*. Exceptionally, the two forms *ay, aye* have the value of long *i*, while *ay* in *quay* has the value of long *e*. (2) The digraph *ey*, as opposed to the -*ey* ending of *abbey*, occurs in a few monosyllables and disyllables with the value of *ei* in *vein* and *ay* in *day*: *prey, they, whey, convey, obey, survey*, with modification before *r* in the name *Eyre*. Exceptionally, *ey* has the value of long *e* as in *me* in *key, geyser, Seymour*, and of short *e* as in *men* in *Reynolds*. (3) The word-final digraph *oy* parallels medial *oi* (*boy/boil*), and represents a diphthong typically deriving from French (*employ*: compare Modern French *emploi*). It occurs in the monosyllables *boy, buoy, cloy, coy, joy, ploy, toy* and the disyllables *alloy, annoy, convoy, decoy, deploy, destroy, employ, enjoy, viceroy*, between vowels in *loyal, royal, voyage*, and medially before a consonant in *oyster*. See I, U.

**YIDDISH**. The language used by Jews of Eastern and Central Europe and their descendants, spoken for nearly a thousand years and until World War II the most widely used Jewish language of modern times, with over 11m speakers. Currently, there are about 4m speakers worldwide, mostly in North and South America, Israel, and the Soviet Union. Yiddish is a Germanic language akin to English, but with a distinctive lexical component of about 18% HEBREW–Aramaic and 16% Slavic (Czech, Polish, Russian, Ukrainian) as well as Romance elements from Old French and Old Italian. It is the only Germanic language to be written in a non-Roman alphabet: like other Jewish languages, Yiddish is written in the Hebrew alphabet, and words of Hebrew or Aramaic origin retain their original spellings, while those of Germanic or other origin are spelled according to phonetic rules. Scholars divide Yiddish historically into four phases: *Earliest Yiddish* from *c*.1000, *Old Yiddish* from 1250, *Middle Yiddish* from 1500, and *Modern Yiddish* from 1700. Of the two major dialect groups, *Western* and *Eastern*, only the latter survives; Western Yiddish (Germany, Switzerland, The Netherlands, Alsace-Lorraine) went into decline after 1700. The chief dialects of Eastern Yiddish are *North-Eastern* (Lithuania, Latvia, Byelorussia), *South-Eastern* (Ukraine, Romania, eastern Galicia), and *Central* (Poland, western Galicia). *Standard Yiddish* is closest to the North-Eastern dialect in pronunciation, and generally closest in grammar to Central Yiddish. In the US, colloquial Yiddish became heavily influenced by AmE. Many words were replaced by Americanisms, some embodying distinctly US concepts, others reflecting the everyday dominance of English. A number of American Yiddish innovations, such as *allrightnik* and *boychik*, have found their way into colloquial AmE. See DIALECT IN AMERICA, JEWISH ENGLISH.

**YIDDISHISM**. An expression or construction typical of the YIDDISH language, especially when found in another language. Yiddishisms occur in such languages as Dutch, English, French, German, Hebrew, and Spanish. The earliest recorded Yiddishisms in English either refer to items of the Jewish religion (such as *kosher* ritually fit, and its antonym *treyf*, both first recorded in 1851) or were part of the argot of criminals (such as *ganef* a thief, *goy* a non-Jew, both first recorded in the 1830s). With the immigration of Eastern European Jews into the UK and US during the 1880s Yiddishisms began entering English in great numbers. The centrality of LONDON and NEW YORK City, where most of the immigrants settled, played a major role in disseminating such usages as *Yid, Yiddish, shnorrer, shlemiel, gefilte fish, shul, bar mitzva*. Through-

out the 20c, Yiddishisms have continued to make their way into English, increasingly as slang. The chief medium of transfer remains the Yiddish-influenced variety of English used by Jews of Eastern European origin or descent. See JEWISH ENGLISH.

**YINGLISH**. An informal and often facetious term for: (1) English that contains many YIDDISH words and expressions. It is an informal synonym of *JEWISH ENGLISH* (of the Ashkenazic or Eastern European variety). (2) Yiddish words and expressions that have become part of colloquial English, an informal collective term for *Yiddishisms*. (3) Words and expressions that blend Yiddish and English, such as *borscht circuit, fancy-shmancy, a whole megillah, a hearty mazel tov*. The term is viewed by scholars of Yiddish as slangy and disparaging. See -GLISH AND -LISH.

**YOGH**. The LETTER ȝ, a loosely written form of the letter g in Old English script. In Middle English, it became a distinct letter, having the values /j/ initially and medially, as in *ȝok* yoke, *beȝonde* beyond, /ɣ/ medially, as in *oȝen* own, *eȝe* eye, and /x/ medially and finally, as in *riȝt* right, *plouȝ* plough. In later Middle English, yogh was replaced by *y* and *gh*. See Y, Z.

■ **YORKSHIRE** ━━━━━━━━━ ■

Historically, the largest county of England, administered from the city of York, now the counties of East, West, and North Yorkshire, with some territory contributed to the county of Humberside. The name *Yorkshire* continues in informal use, however, for the area of the former county. Used attributively, the term refers to anything in or from the old county: *Yorkshire DIALECT, roast beef and Yorkshire pudding*. Used elliptically, it refers to the Yorkshire dialect: *talking broad Yorkshire*.

**Yorkshire dialect**. The dialects of the region derive from the northern dialect of Old English known as *Anglian* or *Anglic*; an early text is the song of Caedmon, a lay brother at the monastery of Whitby (*c*.670). Scandinavian influence, from invasions and occupations from the 9c to 1066, had its most immediate influence on the non-literate in the area. However, a Danish element from the north entered the standard southern language in such words as *sky* and *outlaw*. Some MIDDLE ENGLISH writers can be identified as writing a northern English representing Yorkshire speech: for example, Richard Rolle, author of *The Ayenbite of Inwit* (Modern: *The Prick of Conscience*, written *c*.1340), and the authors of the Miracles or Mystery Plays from York and Wakefield. A feature of northern Middle English orthography was *quh* rather than *wh*, as in *quhilk* for the more southern *hwich* (which): compare SCOTS; see Q. Although English as used in Yorkshire is often taken to be a single homogeneous dialect, it is not in fact so. There are many kinds of Yorkshire usage, some of which are mutually unintelligible. The two main varieties are derived from the two groups of speakers in the county, and are divided by the boundary between the Midland and Northern groups of dialects.

**Pronunciation**. (1) Yorkshire accents are non-rhotic, with the exception of East Yorkshire, where a postvocalic alveolar *r* is occasionally heard in stressed syllables and final unstressed syllables, the word *farmer* having two such *r*-sounds. (2) The *a*-sound before *s*, *f*, and voiceless *th* is regularly short, as in *fast*, *staff*, and *path*. Yorkshire-speakers use a short /a/ vowel in *my aunt can't dance*. In southern England, the vowel is nasalized and long. (3) Some, mainly rural, speakers in the North and East Ridings have preserved something of the northern vowels of Middle English in the ungrounded vowel of such words as /naː/ and /saː/ for *know* and *saw*, in /swan/ for *swan* and /kwari/ for *quarry*, and in an unchanged long vowel giving /huːs/ for *house* and /duːn/ for *down*. (4) The pronunciation or non-pronunciation of *the* is a well-known Yorkshire shibboleth. It varies from complete absence in the East, through a kind of suspended *t* in the central areas (often represented as *t' book*, *t' man*), to *d'* in the North before voiced consonants and *t'* before voiceless consonants (*d' book*, *t' packet*), and in the extreme West a *th'* before vowels and *t'* before consonants (*th' old man*, *t' book*). (5) Traditional short *u* in Yorkshire and throughout the north has the same sound in such words as *up*, *come* as in standard *wool*, *put*, but -*ook* words have remained long: /buːk/ and /kuːk/ for *book* and *cook*. (6) Regional variations often contrast greatly, especially between West on the one hand and North and East on the other: for example, *soon*, *road*, *stone* in the West sound like 'sooin', 'rooad', 'stooan', and in the North and East like 'see-en', 'reead', 'steean' (with 'sioon' for *soon* in the North-West).

**Grammar**. (1) The second-person singular *thou* survives in various forms, with /ðuː/ for *thou* in the East and North, and /ðaː/ in the West. In the West, *thou* can appear as /tə/, as in /wat duz tə want/ (What do you want?). The accusative form *thee* also survives, as in *Ah'll gi it thee* I'll give it to you. (2) *Happen* is widely used rather than *perhaps*, as in *Happen he'll come* Perhaps he'll come. (3) The form *summat* (somewhat), as in *There's summat up* and *I've summat to tell thee*, corresponds in use to *something*. (4) There is a common intransitive progressive use of the verb *like* in the question *Are you liking?* (Do you like it here?). (5) *Aye* and *nay* (yes and no) are widely used, especially in rural areas. (6) *While* is often used instead of *until*, as in *I'll stay here while eight*, a usage that occasionally causes confusion, as in the ambiguous *Wait while the light is green*. (7) The use of an echoic tag is common, usually *is that*, as in *It's a good buy, is that!* and *That's right nice, is that*.

**Vocabulary**. (1)The Scandinavian element is strong in rural and especially in agricultural usage that is obsolescent along with the objects it refers to: *flaycrow* scarecrow, *stoops* gateposts, *stower* rung (of a *stee* ladder), *lea* scythe, *flake* hurdle, *pike* small stack of hay. Most of such words were common to much of the north of England. (2) Many items in common use descend from Old Norse, and include: *addle* to earn, *beck* stream, brook, *cleg* horse-fly (shared with ScoE), *lake* or *laik* to play, *spaining* or *speaning* weaning (animals), and *ted* to spread hay. (3) The West Yorkshire form of the northern and Scots verb *thole* (permit, endure, tolerate) is *thoil*, which carries the Old English sense of *suffer*. It is applied mostly to spending money on something desirable but too expensive, as in *Nay, I couldn't thoil ten pound for that*. (4) The northern and ScoE term *bairn* (child) is common, as is the distinctive northern *childer*, plural of *child*, which descends from Middle English *childre* and *childer*, from late Old English *cildru* and *cildra*. The southern and standard *children* was assimilated to a now obsolete -*en* plural, as in *house/housen*. The cognate Scots *chiel(d)* (child, lad) has the regular plural *chiel(d)s*. Typical also, as part of northern English generally, are such usages as *lad* and *lass* (as in *We have a little lass*: a small daughter) and love, pronounced /lʊv/, as a form of address (as in *It's time to go, love*).

**Literary Yorkshire**. Yorkshire dialect began to be written for literary purposes in the 17c with the publication of an anonymous poem, possibly from the Northallerton area, entitled *A Yorkshire Dialogue between an Awd Wife, a Lass and a Butcher* (printed at York, 1673). It opens with the Old Wife saying:

> Pretha now lass, gang into t'hurn
> An' fetch me heame a skeel o' burn.
> Na pretha, barn, mak heeaste an' gang,
> I's mar my deagh, thou stays sae lang.

> [Prithee now, girl, go into the corner of the field / And fetch me home a bucket of water. / Now prithee, child, make haste and go, / I'll spoil my dough, you stay so long.]

This language would not at the time, nor would it now, be accepted over the whole area as Yorkshire dialect, but would be well understood, especially in parts of the North. Perhaps the most famous representation of Yorkshire dialect in literature is that by Emily Brontë in *Wuthering Heights* (1847), as in the following excerpt from Chapter 9, when the old servant Joseph says:

> Yon lad gets wur na' wur! . . . He's left th' yate ut t'full swing and miss's pony has trodden dahn two rigs uh corn, un plottered through, raight o'r intuh t'meadow!

> [That boy gets worse and worse. . . . He's left the gate wide open and the young lady's pony has pressed down two ridges of corn and floundered through right over into the meadow!

This kind of prose continues in many Yorkshire newspapers.

**Yorkshire Dialect Society**. The first group concerned with the dialect came together in 1894 as a Yorkshire Committee of the ENGLISH DIALECT SOCIETY, to assist in the preparation of Joseph Wright's *English Dialect Dictionary*. After the disbandment of the EDS in 1896, the committee reformed in 1897 as the Yorkshire Dialect Society, which publishes *The Transactions of the Yorkshire Dialect Society*. The society combines the scholarly study of local speech with the publication of prose and poetry in various forms of local dialect. It meets at colleges and university premises throughout the three Yorkshires as well as at industrial and folk museums, and promotes joint meetings with other groups. Papers on place-names and studies of local vocabularies are given as well as readings and recitations by dialect speakers. See DIALECT IN ENGLAND, ENGLISH IN ENGLAND, NORTHERN ENGLISH.

# Z

## ■ Z, z ■

[In BrE called 'zed', in AmE 'zee']. The 26th and last LETTER of the Roman ALPHABET as used for English. It originated as the 7th letter of the Phoenician alphabet and became the 7th letter of the Hebrew and Greek alphabets. The Greeks called it *zeta* (Z, ζ), probably first pronouncing it /dz/, then /z/. The Romans adopted Z later than the rest of the alphabet, since /z/ was not a native Latin sound, adding it at the end of their list of letters and using it rarely. They did not always use it to transliterate *zeta*. Old English did not normally use *z*, the name *Elizabeth* being an exception. The use of *zed* as a term of ABUSE in SHAKESPEARE's *King Lear* ('Thou whoreson zed! Thou unnecessary letter!', 2. 2) suggests that although it was then being increasingly written it was held in low esteem. The modification of BrE *zed* (from Old FRENCH *zede*, through LATIN, from GREEK *zeta*) to *zee* in AmE appears to have been by ANALOGY with *bee*, *dee*, *vee*, etc.

### Sound values and double Z. (1) In VERNACULAR English, *z* represents a voiced alveolar fricative, pairing with *s* as its voiceless equivalent. It occurs initially, medially, and finally, sometimes doubled: *zebra*, *horizon*, *dazzle*, *daze*, *buzz*. (2) Before the ending *-ure*, the initial *i*-glide of the *u* is commonly assimilated to the *z*, producing the sound 'zh': *azure*, *seizure* (compare *measure*). (3) The sound /z/ is more frequently represented by *s* than *z*. (4) Some possibly echoic monosyllables have *zz* (*buzz*, *fizz*, *fuzz*, *jazz*, *whiz(z)*), as have disyllables with the iterative suffix *-le* (*dazzle*, *razzle*, *fizzle*, *sizzle*, *guzzle*). (5) Monosyllables ending in single *z* after a short vowel (*fez*, *quiz*) inflect with *zz*: *fez/fezzes*, *quiz/quizzing*. (6) Final *y* requires preceding *zz* if the preceding vowel is short (*dizzy*, *muzzy*), but only *z* if long (*lazy*, *crazy*, *dozy*).

### Voiced and voiceless Z. The voiced/voiceless distinction of /s, z/ in OLD ENGLISH was predictable and did not need to be shown in spelling; medial *s* was voiced, as is still largely the case (*busy*, *weasel*), but French influence after the Norman Conquest in 1066 led to the writing of medial voiced *s* as *z* or *zz* in some words of Old English or Old

Norse derivation: *adz(e)*, *amaze*, *blaze*, *craze*, *daze*, *dazzle*, *dizzy*, *doze*, *drizzle*, *freeze*, *furze*, *gaze*, *hazel*, *ooze*, *sneeze*, *squeeze*, *wheeze*, *wizen*. Some related nouns have voiceless *s* (*brazen/brass*, *frozen/frost*, *glaze/glass*, *graze/grass*), others voiced *s* (*nuzzle/nose*, *wizard/ wise*). Words of Old English origin were not spelt with final *z*: *sneeze*, *booze*, not *\*sneez*, *\*booz*.

### English Z, *French S*. Many FRENCH-derived words contain *z* or *zz*, sometimes where French has or had *s*: English *breeze* (French *brise*), *buzzard*, *citizen*, *embezzle*, *frenzy* (French *frénésie*), *frieze* (French *frise*), *gizzard*, *grizzle* (French *grisailler*), *hazard* (French *hasard*), *lozenge* (French *losange*), *mizzen*, *muzzle* (French *museau*), *razor* (French *rasoir*), *seize* (French *saisir*). *Prize* corresponds to French *prix* and *size*, a clipping of *assize*, is derived from French *assise*. *Baize* appears to have been a misinterpretation of the French plural *baies*. Elsewhere, English *z* matches French *z*: *bizarre*, *bronze*, *dozen*, *gauze*, *lizard*.

### Exotic Z. (1) Initial *z* was used from the 14c in new words derived from French or Latin, often originating in other languages such as ARABIC, SPANISH, and Greek: *zeal*, *zebra*, *zenith*, *zero*, *zest*, *zeugma*, *zither*, *zodiac*, *zone*, *zoology*. GERMAN was the source of *zigzag*, *zinc*, while *zombie* originated in Africa. (2) Medial *z* occurs in more recent loans: Persian *bazaar*, Spanish *bonanza*, *maize*, Kongo *chimpanzee*, Greek *horizon*, German (from Italian) *marzipan*, Polish *mazurka*, Arabic *muezzin*, ITALIAN *stanza*, French (through Latin from Greek) *trapeze*. (3) In recent loans, *z* usually retains the value given to it in the source language: /ts/ in German *Alzheimer's disease*, *Nazi*, *Zeitgeist* and Italian *pizzicato* (*mezzo-soprano* has /dz/ in Italian). Older German loans may have a preceding *t*: *quartz*, *waltz* (compare modern German *Quarz*, *Walzer*). (4) In the *tz* combination, the *t* induces devoicing of a following *z*, as in *blitz*, *chintz*. *Quartz* and *quarts* are homophones. (5) Silent *z* occurs in recent French loans: *laissez-faire*, *rendezvous*, *répondez s'il vous plaît*. (6) Because of German influence, in the Greek combining form *schizo-* (as in *schizophrenia*), *z* is pronounced as a voiceless affricate, /ts/. (7) In the word *Czech*, the

digraph *cz* has the value of English *ch*, but in *czar* the initial *c* is silent and *z* has its normal value, as also in the alternative (and etymologically more accurate) spelling *tsar*. (8) Of unknown but recent origin are *bamboozle*, *blizzard*, *puzzle*.

**Archaic Scots Z**. In ScoE, some words, including names, have a silent *z* (*capercailzie* pronounced 'capercailie', *Dalrulzion* 'Dalrullion', *Dalziel* 'Deyell', *gaberlunzie* 'gabberloonie') or a digraph *nz* pronounced /ŋ/, as in the name *Menzies*, traditionally pronounced 'Mingis' (*ng* as in *singer*). Here *z* is an adaptation of the Old English letter YOGH (ȝ) rather than etymological *z*.

**British and American differences**. Some alternative *s/z* spellings are found, the most widespread the Greek-derived suffix *-ise/ize* (*regularise/regularize*), where *z* is universal in AmE, and *s* is widely used in BrE and preferred in AusE. This variation also occurs in AmE *cozy*, *cognizant*, BrE *cosy*, *cognisant*. See S, X.

**ZAMBIA**. A country of southern Africa and member of the COMMONWEALTH. Languages: English (official); seven indigenous languages recognized, including Bemba, Nyanja, and Tonga. The British colony of *Northern Rhodesia* gained its independence as *Zambia* in 1964. It is one of the most urbanized of East African countries, and the mix of languages in urban areas emphasizes the need for a link language. English is used exclusively in education from the first year and is important in the media. Zambian English is one of the most divergent forms of AFRICAN ENGLISH, with a good deal of borrowing from local languages, even to the extent of adding BANTU affixes to English roots: *maolanges* oranges (where *ma-* is a plural prefix and *l* replaces *r*); *cipoto* a pot (where *ci-* is a Bemba nominal prefix); *awashes* he or she washes, *adriver* he or she drives (where *a-* is a subject prefix). Examples of local innovations in the use of adverbial particles are illustrated by the omission of *up* in *I'll come to pick you at half eight*, its addition in *cope up with*, and a reassignment in its use in *I'm fed up* (I'm full). Lexical innovation includes *movious* always on the move. Cultural influences are evidenced in the questions: *How have you stayed the day?* How have things gone since this morning?; *How*

*are you suffering?* as a greeting to one who has suffered a misfortune. See EAST AFRICAN ENGLISH.

**ZEUGMA**. **1.** Also *syllepsis*. In RHETORIC, a phrase in which a word, usually a verb, is followed by two or more other words that commonly collocate with it, but not together: 'The morning brought misty sunshine and the nurse' (Mary Stewart, *Wildfire at Midnight*, 1956). A figurative use usually precedes a literal use; in Pope's *Rape of the Lock* (1714), the heroine might 'stain her Honour, or her new Brocade' and 'lose her Heart, or Neck-lace, at a Ball'. **2.** A form of ellipsis regarded as poor style: *X is as big if not bigger than Y*, from which the *\*X is as big than Y* can be extracted. The balanced form is *X is as big as, if not bigger than, Y*.

**ZIMBABWE**. A country of southern Africa and member of the COMMONWEALTH. Languages: English (official); the indigenous languages Shona and Ndebele, which may be used in the Senate. Zimbabwe, formerly the British colony of *Southern Rhodesia*, took its present form in 1980. English was introduced into the region toward the end of the 19c in colonial commerce (the ventures of Cecil Rhodes) and in missionary education. The English of Zimbabwe is non-rhotic. There is some blending of vowels into a five-vowel system and simplification of consonant structures, features shared with other varieties of East and South AFRICAN ENGLISH: 'men' the pronunciation of both *man* and *men*, 'fit' of both *fit* and *feet*. Syntactic structures are often attributable to transfer from local languages: *He (has) grown up in my eyes* I saw him grow up; *when the rain is in the nose* when the rainy season approaches. There are loans from local languages in the vocabulary, such as *shimiyaan* home-made liquor made from treacle, and *muti* medicine, as well as words of various origins common in southern Africa, such as *kraal* village, *veld* high open grassland, *commando* military unit, *trek* a journey (originally by ox-wagon). Local usages include *headring* a marker of elder or high status, *love-muti* a love charm, *now-now girl* a modern young woman. See EAST AFRICAN ENGLISH.

**ZUMMERZET**.          See          MUMMERSET, SOMERSET.

# Appendix 1:
# A chronology of English

A selection of dates associated with the history and spread of the English language from Roman times to 1998.

| | |
|---|---|
| **55 BC** | Roman military expedition to Britain by Julius Caesar. |
| **AD 43** | Roman invasion under the emperor Claudius, beginning 400 years of control over much of the island. |
| **150** | From around this date, with Roman permission, small numbers of settlers arrive from the coastlands of Germany, speaking dialects ancestral to English. |
| **297** | First mention of the Picts of Caledonia, tribes beyond Roman control, well to the north of Hadrian's Wall. |
| **410** | The Goths sack Rome. |
| **436** | The end of a period of gradual Roman withdrawal. Britons south of the Wall are attacked by the Picts and by Scots from Ireland. Angles, Saxons, and other Germanic settlers come first as mercenaries to help the Britons, then take over more and more territory. |
| **449** | The traditional date for the beginning of Anglo-Saxon settlements. |
| **450–80** | The first surviving Old English inscriptions, in runic letters. |
| **495** | The Saxon kingdom of Wessex established. |
| **500** | The kingdom of Dalriada established in Argyll by Scots from Ireland. |
| **527** | The Saxon kingdoms of Essex and Middlesex established. |
| **550** | The Angle kingdoms of Mercia, East Anglia, and Northumbria established. |
| **557** | At the battle of Deorham, the West Saxons drive a wedge between the Britons of Wales and Cornwall. |
| **597** | Aethelberht, king of Kent, welcomes Augustine, and the conversion of the Anglo-Saxons begins. |
| **613** | At the battle of Chester, the Angles of Northumbria drive a wedge between the Britons of Wales and Cumbria. |
| **638** | Edwin of Northumbria takes Lothian from the Britons. |
| **700** | The first manuscript records of Old English from about this time. |
| **792** | Scandinavians begin to raid and settle in Britain, Ireland, and France. In 793, they sack the monastery of Lindisfarne, the centre of Northumbrian scholarship. |
| **795** | The Danes settle in parts of Ireland. |
| **815** | Egbert of Wessex defeats the south-western Britons of Cornwall and incorporates Cornwall into his kingdom. |
| **828** | Egbert of Wessex is hailed as *bretwalda* (lord of Britain), overlord of the Seven Kingdoms of the Angles and Saxons (the Heptarchy). England begins to emerge. |
| **834** | The Danes raid England. |
| **843** | Kenneth MacAlpin, King of Scots, gains the throne of Pictland. |

| | |
|---|---|
| **865** | The Danes occupy Northumbria, establish a kingdom at York, and Danish begins to influence English. |
| **871** | Alfred becomes king of Wessex, translates works of Latin into English, and establishes the writing of prose in English. |
| **886** | The boundaries of the Danelaw are settled. |
| **911** | Charles II of France grants lands on the lower Seine to the Viking (Norman = Northman) chief Hrolf the Ganger (Rollo the Rover). The beginnings of Normandy and Norman French. |
| **954** | The expulsion of Eric Blood-axe, last Danish king of York. |
| **965** | The English invade the northern Welsh kingdom of Gwynedd. |
| **973** | Edgar of England cedes Lothian to Kenneth II, King of Scots. Scotland multilingual: Gaelic dominant, Norse in the north, Cumbric in the south-west, English in the south-east, Latin for church and law. |
| **992** | A treaty between Ethelred of England and the Normans. |
| **1000** | The approximate date of the only surviving manuscript of the Old English epic poem *Beowulf*. |
| **1007** | Ethelred the Unready pays *danegeld* to stop the Danes attacking England. In 1013, however, they take the country and Ethelred flees to Normandy. |
| **1014** | The end of Danish rule in Ireland. |
| **1016–42** | The reigns of Canute/Knut and his sons over Denmark, Norway, and England. |
| **1051** | Edward the Confessor, King of England, impressed by the Normans and with French-speaking counsellors at his court, names as his heir William, Duke of Normandy, but reneges on his promise before his death. |
| **1066** | The Norman Conquest. William defeats Harold Godwin at Hastings, and sets in train the Normanization of the upper classes of the Britain Isles. England multilingual: English the majority language, Danish in the north, Cornish in the far south-west, Welsh on the border with Wales, Norman French at court and in the courts, and Latin in church and school. |
| **1150** | The first surviving texts of Middle English. |
| **1167** | The closure of the University of Paris to students from England accelerates the development of a university at Oxford. |
| **1171** | Henry II invades Ireland and declares himself its overlord, introducing English and Norman French into the island. |
| **1204** | King John loses the Duchy of Normandy to France. |
| **1209** | The exodus of a number of students from Oxford leads to the establishment of a second university in Cambridge. |
| **1272–1307** | The reign of Edward I, who consolidates royal authority in England, and extends it permanently to Wales and temporarily to Scotland. |
| **1282** | Death of Llewelyn, last native prince of Wales. In 1301, Edward of England's son and heir is invested as Prince of Wales. |
| **1284** | The Statute of Rhuddlan establishes the law of England in Wales (in French and Latin), but retains the legal use of Welsh. |
| **1314** | Robert Bruce re-asserts Scottish independence by defeating Edward II at Bannockburn, an achievement later celebrated in an epic written in Scots. |
| **1337** | The outbreak of the Hundred Years War between England and France, which ends with the loss of all England's French possessions save the Channel Islands. |

**1343?–1400**    The life of Geoffrey Chaucer.

**1348**    English replaces Latin as medium of instruction in schools, but not at Oxford and Cambridge.
The worst year of the Black Death.

**1362**    Through the Statute of Pleading, written in French, English replaces French as the language of law in England, but the records continue to be kept in Latin.
English is used for the first time in Parliament.

**1384**    The publication of John Wycliffe's English translation of the Latin Bible.

**1385**    The scholar John of Trevisa notes that 'in all the gramere scoles of Engelond, children leveth Frensche and construeth and lerneth in Englische.'

**1400**    By this date the Great Vowel Shift has begun.

**1450**    Printing by movable type invented in the Rhineland.

**1476**    The first English book printed: *The Recuyell of the Historyes of Troye*, translated from French by William Caxton, who printed it at Bruges in Flanders. Caxton sets up the first printing press in England, at Westminster. In 1478, he publishes Chaucer's *Canterbury Tales.*

**1485**    The Battle of Bosworth, after which the part-Welsh Henry Tudor becomes King of England. Welsh nobles follow him to London.

**1492**    Christopher Columbus discovers the New World.

**1497**    Giovanni Caboto (anglicized as 'John Cabot'), in a ship from Bristol, lands on the Atlantic coast of North America.

**1499**    The publication of *Thesaurus linguae romanae et britannicae* (Treasury of the Roman and British Tongues), the first English-to-Latin wordbook, the work of Galfridus Grammaticus (Geoffrey the Grammarian).

**1504**    The settlement of St John's on Newfoundland as a shore base for English fisheries.

**1507**    The German geographer Martin Waldseemüller puts the name *America* on his map of the world.

**1525**    The publication of William Tyndale's translation of the New Testament of the Bible.

**1534**    Jacques Cartier lands on the Gaspé Peninsula in North America and claims it for France.

**1536, 1542**    The Statute of Wales (Acts of Union) unites England and Wales, excluding Welsh from official use.

**1542**    Henry VIII of England proclaims himself King of Ireland.

**1549**    The publication of the first version of the Book of Common Prayer of the Church of England, the work in the main of Thomas Cranmer.

**1558–1603**    The reign of Elizabeth I.

**1560–1620**    The plantation of Ireland, first by English settlers and after 1603 also by Scots, establishing English throughout the island and Scots in Ulster.

**1564–1616**    The life of William Shakespeare.

**1583**    Sir Humphrey Gilbert establishes Newfoundland as England's first colony beyond the British Isles.

**1584**    The settlement on Roanoke Island by colonists led by Sir Walter Raleigh. In 1587, Virginia Dare born at Roanoke, first child of English parents in North America. In 1590, the settlers of Roanoke disappear without trace.

**1588**   The publication of Bishop Morgan's translation of the Bible into Welsh, serving as a focus for the survival of the language.

**1600**   English traders establish the East India Company.

**1603**   The Union of the Crowns under James VI of Scots, I of England.

**1604**   The publication of Robert Cawdrey's *Table Alphabeticall*, the first dictionary of English.

**1606**   The Dutch explore northern New Holland (Terra Australis).

**1607**   The Jamestown colony in Virginia, the first permanent English settlement and the first representative assembly in the New World.

**1608**   Samuel Champlain founds the city of Quebec in New France.

**1611**   The publication of the Authorized or King James Version of the Bible, intended for use in the Protestant services of England, Scotland, and Ireland. A major influence on the written language and in adapting Scots towards English.

**1612**   Bermuda colonized under the charter of the Virginia Company.
          Traders of the East India Company establish themselves in Gujarat, India.

**1614**   King James writes in English to the Moghul Emperor Jehangir, in order to encourage trade with the Orientall Indies'.

**1619**   At the Jamestown colony in America, the first African slaves arrive on a Dutch ship.

**1620**   The *Mayflower* arrives in the New World and the Pilgrim Fathers set up Plimoth Plantation in Massachusetts. English is now in competition as a colonial language in the Americas with Dutch, French, Spanish, and Portuguese.

**1622**   Publication in London of the first English newspaper, *Weekly News*.

**1623**   Publication in London of the First Folio of Shakespeare's plays.

**1627**   An English colony established on Barbados in the Caribbean.

**1637**   English traders arrive on the coast of China.
          The Académie française founded.

**1640**   An English trading factory established at Madras.

**1647**   The Bahamas colonized by settlers from Bermuda.

**1652**   The first Dutch settlers arrive in southern Africa.

**1655**   England acquires Jamaica from Spain.

**1659**   The East India Company annexes St Helena in the south Atlantic.

**1660**   John Dryden expresses his admiration for the Académie française and its work in 'fixing' French and wishes for something similar to serve English.

**1662**   The Royal Society of London receives its charter from Charles II. In 1664, it appoints a committee to consider ways of improving English as a language of science.

**1670**   The Hudson's Bay Company founded for fur trading in northern America.

**1674**   Charles II receives Bombay from the Portuguese in the dowry of Catherine of Braganza and gives it to the East India Company.

**1687**   Isaac Newton writes *Principia Mathematica* in Latin: see 1704.

**1688**   The publication of *Oronooko, or the History of the Royal Slave*, by Aphra Behn: one of the first novels in English, by the first woman novelist in English, based on personal experience of a slave revolt in Surinam.

**1690**   A trading factory established at Calcutta in Bengal.

**1696**   British and French colonists in North America in open conflict.

| | |
|---|---|
| **1697** | The Boston clergyman Cotton Mather applies the term *American* to English-speaking settlers in the New World. |
| **1702** | Publication in London of the first regular daily newspaper in English, *The Daily Courant*. |
| **1704** | Isaac Newton writes his second major work, *Opticks*, in English: see 1687. |
| **1707** | The Act of Union, uniting the Parliaments of England and Scotland, creating the United Kingdom of Great Britain, but keeping separate the state religions, educational systems, and laws of the two kingdoms. |
| **1712** | Jonathan Swift in Dublin proposes an English Academy to 'fix' the language and compete adequately with French.<br>In India, the Moghul Empire begins to decline. |
| **1713** | At the Treaty of Utrecht, France surrenders Hudson's Bay, Acadia, and Newfoundland to the British.<br>Gibraltar is ceded to Britain by Spain. |
| **1731** | The abolition of Law French in England. |
| **1746** | The Wales and Berwick Act, by which England is deemed to include Wales and the Scottish town of Berwick is incorporated into England. |
| **1755** | The publication of Samuel Johnson's *Dictionary of the English Language*. |
| **1757** | The East India Company becomes the power behind the government of Bengal. |
| **1759** | General James Wolfe takes Quebec for the British. |
| **1759–96** | The life of Robert Burns. |
| **1762** | The publication of Robert Lowth's *Short Introduction to English Grammar*. |
| **1763** | The French cede New France to Britain, retaining only St Pierre and Miquelon (islands off Newfoundland). |
| **1768–71** | The partwork publication in Edinburgh of *The Encyclopaedia Britannica*. |
| **1770** | Captain James Cook takes possession of the Australian continent for Britain. |
| **1770–1850** | The life of William Wordsworth. |
| **1771–1832** | The life of Sir Walter Scott. |
| **1774** | The Quebec Act creates the British province of Quebec, extending to the Ohio and Mississippi.<br>The Regulating Act places Bombay and Madras under the control of Bengal and the East India Company becomes a kind of state. |
| **1776** | The Declaration of Independence by thirteen British colonies in North America and the start of the American War of Independence (1776–83) which created the United States of America, the first nation outside the British Isles with English as its principal language. |
| **1778** | Captain James Cook visits and names the Sandwich Islands (Hawaii). |
| **1780–1800** | British Empire loyalists move from the United States to Canada. |
| **1785** | In London, the newspaper *The Daily Universal Register* founded. Renamed *The Times* in 1788. |
| **1786** | Lord Cornwallis is appointed first Governor-General of British India.<br>A British penal colony is established at Botany Bay in Australia. In 1788, the first convicts arrive there. |
| **1791** | The British colonies of Upper Canada (Ontario) and Lower Canada (Quebec) are established.<br>In London, the newspaper *The Observer* is founded, the oldest national Sunday newspaper in Britain. |

| | |
|---|---|
| **1792** | The first Europeans settle in New Zealand. |
| **1794** | The publication of Lindley Murray's *English Grammar*. |
| **1802** | The establishment of the British colonies of Ceylon and Trinidad. |
| **1803** | The Act of Union incorporating Ireland into Britain, as the United Kingdom of Great Britain and Ireland.<br>The Louisiana Purchase, by which the United States buys from France its remaining North American territories, and doubles its size. |
| **1806** | The British take control of Cape Colony in southern Africa. |
| **1808** | The establishment of the British colony of Sierra Leone. |
| **1814** | The British annex Cape Colony.<br>France cedes to Britain Malta, Mauritius, St Lucia, and Tobago. |
| **1816** | The establishment of the British colony of Bathurst (the Gambia). |
| **1819** | The establishment of the British colony of Singapore.<br>The United States purchases Florida from Spain. |
| **1820** | Christian missionaries from the United States visit Hawaii. |
| **1821** | American settlers arrive in the Mexican territory of Texas. |
| **1828** | The publication of Noah *Webster's American Dictionary of the English Language*. |
| **1829** | Australia becomes a British dependency. |
| **1831** | The establishment of the colony of British Guiana. |
| **1833** | The abolition of slavery in the British Empire.<br>St Helena becomes a British colony. |
| **1835** | Thomas Macaulay writes the Minute on Education whereby the British rulers of India endorse English as a language of education for Indians. |
| **1835–1910** | The life of Sam Clemens (Mark Twain). |
| **1836** | Texas declares its independence from Mexico. |
| **1839** | The first Boer Republic is established in Natal, South Africa, after the Great Trek from the Cape. |
| **1840** | The Treaty of Waitangi, by which the Maori of New Zealand cede all rights and powers of government to Britain.<br>The transportation of convicts to Eastern Australia is ended. |
| **1841** | Upper and Lower Canada are brought together as British North America.<br>New Zealand becomes a British colony.<br>In London, the founding of the weekly magazine *Punch*. |
| **1842** | The opening of Chinese ports other than Canton to Western traders, after the defeat of China in the Opium War. Hong Kong is ceded by China to Britain as a Crown Colony.<br>The Philological Society is formed in London. |
| **1845** | Texas becomes a state of the United States. |
| **1846** | The British annex Natal but recognize the Transvaal and the Orange Free State as autonomous Boer republics. |
| **1848** | In the Treaty of Guadalupe Hidalgo, Mexico cedes vast western territories to the US. |
| **1850** | Britain takes control of the Bay Islands of Honduras, an English-speaking enclave in Central America.<br>Legislative councils are established in Australia by British Act of Parliament. |
| **1852** | The publication of *Roget's Thesaurus*. |

| | |
|---|---|
| **1853** | Japan is forced by Commander Matthew Perry of the US Navy to open its harbours to Western trade.<br>The transportation of convicts to Tasmania is ended. |
| **1855** | The Government to the colony of New South Wales is established. |
| **1856** | The Governments of the colonies of Tasmania and Victoria are established. |
| **1856–1950** | The life of George Bernard Shaw. |
| **1857** | The Sepoy Rebellion (War of Independence, Indian Mutiny) in India leads to the transfer of British India from the East India Company to the Crown. |
| **1858** | The Philological Society passes a resolution calling for a new dictionary of English on historical principles.<br>Britain cedes the Bay Islands to Honduras. |
| **1861** | The establishment of the British colony of Lagos (Nigeria). |
| **1862** | The establishment of the colony of British Honduras. |
| **1863** | The establishment of the Cambridge Overseas Examinations. |
| **1865** | The abolition of slavery in the US, at the end of the Civil War. At the outbreak of the war there were over 4m slaves. |
| **1867** | The Dominion of Canada is created, consisting of Quebec, Ontario, Nova Scotia, and New Brunswick.<br>Alaska is purchased from Russia by the US. |
| **1868** | Transportation of convicts to Western Australia is ended.<br>In the US, Christopher Latham Sholes and colleagues patent the first successful typewriter. |
| **1869** | Rupert's Land and the Northwest Territories are bought by Canada from the Hudson's Bay Company.<br>Basutoland becomes a British protectorate. |
| **1870** | Manitoba becomes a province of Canada. |
| **1871** | British Columbia becomes a province of Canada. |
| **1873** | The formation of the English Dialect Society (dissolved in 1896).<br>Prince Edward Island becomes a province of Canada. |
| **1874** | The establishment of the British colony of the Gold Coast in West Africa. |
| **1879** | James A. H. Murray begins editing the Philological Society's *New English Dictionary on Historical Principles*. |
| **1882–1941** | The life of James Joyce. |
| **1884** | The Berlin Conference, in which European powers begin 'the scramble for Africa'.<br>Britain declares a protectorate over South East New Guinea.<br>The French, Germans, and British attempt to annex what shortly becomes the German colony of Kamerun.<br>Publication of the first fascicle, *A-Ant*, of Murray's dictionary (the *OED*). |
| **1886** | The annexation of Burma into British India and the abolition of the Burmese monarchy. |
| **1888–94** | The establishment of British protectorates in Kenya, Uganda, and Zanzibar. |
| **1895** | The establishment of the British East African Protectorate, open to white settlers. |
| **1898** | The annexation of Hawaii by the US. In 1900, it becomes a US territory.<br>Spain cedes the Philippines and Puerto Rico to the United States.<br>Yukon Territory comes under Canadian government control. |
| **1901** | The establishment of the Commonwealth of Australia as a dominion of the British Empire. |

The first wireless telegraphy messages sent across the Atlantic by Guglielmo Marconi (Cornwall to Newfoundland).
The first film-show in an arcade opened in Los Angeles, California.

**1903**    A message from US President Theodore Roosevelt circles the world in less than 10 minutes by Pacific Cable.

**1903–50** The life of George Orwell.

**1905**    Alberta and Saskatchewan become provinces of Canada.
The first cartoon strip, 'Little Nemo', appears in *The New York Herald*.

**1906**    The formation of the English Association.
The first full-length motion picture, *The Story of the Kelly Gang*.
The publication of the Fowler brothers' *The Kings' English*.

**1907**    The establishment of New Zealand as a dominion of the British Empire.
The first regular studio-based radio broadcasts by the De Forest Radio Telephone Company in the US.
The foundation of Hollywood as a film-making centre.

**1910**    The establishment of the Union of South Africa as a dominion of the British Empire.
The first radio receivers made in kit form for sale in the US.

**1911**    The publication of the Fowler brothers' *Concise Oxford Dictionary*.

**1913**    The formation of the Society for Pure English.
The first crossword puzzle published, in the *New York World*.

**1914**    A third Home Rule Bill for Ireland passed by the British Parliament, but prevented from coming into operation by the outbreak of the First World War.
The German colony of Kamerun invaded by French and British.

**1915**    The death of Sir James A. H. Murray, aged 78, having finished the section *Trink–Turndown* in the *OED*.

**1916**    The Easter Rising in Dublin, an unsuccessful armed rebellion against the British, during which an Irish Republic is proclaimed.
The technicolor process is first used in the film *The Gulf Between*, in the US.

**1917**    The publication of Daniel Jones's *English Pronouncing Dictionary*.

**1918**    The formation of the English-Speaking Union.
The US War Industries Board declares moving pictures an essential industry.

**1919**    The German colony of Tanganyika ceded to Britain.
The German colony of Kamerun divided between France (Cameroun) and Britain (Cameroon).
The publication of H. L. Mencken's *The American Language*.

**1920**    The Partition of Ireland.
Kenya becomes a British colony.
The first public radio station set up by Marconi in the US.

**1921**    A treaty between the United Kingdom and the Irish Free State, which accepts dominion status within the British Empire.
The first full-length 'talkie' *Dream Street* produced by United Artists, in the US.

**1922**    The establishment of the British Broadcasting Company, renamed in 1927 the British Broadcasting Corporation (BBC).
The founding in the US of the monthly magazine *The Reader's Digest*.

**1923**    The founding of *Time* magazine in the US.

**1925**    The borders of the Republic of Ireland and Northern Ireland established.
Afrikaans gains official status in South Africa.
The founding of the weekly magazine *The New Yorker*.

**1926**     The publication of Henry W. Fowler's *Dictionary of Modern English Usage*.

**1927**     Fox's Movietone News, the first sound newsfilm, released in the US.
The first film with dialogue, *They're Coming to Get Me*, released in the US.

**1928**     The publication of Murray's Dictionary as *The Oxford English Dictionary*, 70 years
after Trench's proposal to the Philological Society.

**1930**     C. K. Ogden launches Basic English.
The first television programme with synchronized sight and sound broadcast
by the BBC.

**1931**     The British Commonwealth of Nations formed.
South Africa becomes a dominion of the British Empire.
The Cambridge Proficiency Examination held outside Britain for the first
time.

**1933**     The publication of a supplement to *The Oxford English Dictionary*.

**1934**     The British Council created as an arm of British cultural diplomacy and a
focus for teaching English as a foreign language.

**1935**     The Philippines become a self-governing Commonwealth in association with
the US.
The publication of the first ten Penguin paperback titles.

**1936**     The Republic of Ireland severs all constitutional links with Great Britain.

**1937**     Burma is separated from British India and granted a constitution and limited
self-rule.
In Wales, a new constitution for the National Eisteddfod makes Welsh as its
official language.

**1938**     Photocopying invented.

**1942**     The publication in Japan of *The Idiomatic and Syntactic Dictionary of English*,
prepared before the war by A. S. Hornby, E. V. Gatenby, and H. Wakefield.

**1945**     Japan is occupied by the Americans on behalf of the Allies.

**1946**     The Philippines gain their independence from the United States.
The French colony of Cameroun and the British colony of Cameroon become
United Nations trusteeships.

**1947**     British India is partitioned, and India and Pakistan become independent
states.
New Zealand gains its independence from Britain.

**1948**     Burma and Ceylon gain their independence from Britain.
The dictionary of Hornby *et al.* is brought out by Oxford University Press as *A
Learner's Dictionary of Current English*.

**1949**     Newfoundland becomes a province of Canada.
Two New Guinea territories are combined by the United Nations as an
Australian mandate: the United Nations Trust Territory of Papua and New
Guinea.

**1951**     The launch of the first two working business computers: the LED in the UK
and the UNIVAC in the US.

**1952**     Puerto Rico becomes a Commonwealth in association with the US.

**1957**     The Gold Coast becomes independent from Britain as the Republic of Ghana.
Robert W. Burchfield is appointed editor of a Supplement to *The Oxford English
Dictionary*.

**1957–63**  The British colonies of Malaya and Borneo become independent and unite as
Malaysia.

**1959**     Alaska and Hawaii become states of the US.

**1960**    Nigeria and French Cameroun become independent.

**1961**    South Africa becomes a republic, does not remain in the Commonwealth, and adopts Afrikaans and English as its two official languages.
The British colony of Cameroon divides, part joining Nigeria, part joining the ex-French colony to become the Republic of Cameroon.
Sierra Leone and Cyprus gain their independence from Britain.
The publication of *Webster's Third International Dictionary*.

**1962**    Jamaica, Trinidad and Tobago, and Uganda gain their independence from Britain.

**1963**    Kenya gains its independence from Britain.
The first protests in Wales by the Cymdeithas yr Iaith Gymraeg/Welsh Language Society, aimed at achieving fuller use of Welsh.

**1964**    Malta, Nyasaland (as Malawi), Tanganyika and Zanzibar (as Tanzania), and Northern Rhodesia (as Zambia) gain their independence from Britain.
The publication in Paris of René Etiemble's *Parlez-vous franglais?*

**1965**    Gambia and Singapore gain their independence from Britain.

**1966**    Barbados, Basutoland (as Lesotho), Bechuanaland (as Botswana), and British Guiana (as Guyana) gain their independence from Britain.

**1967**    The Welsh Language Act gives Welsh equal validity with English in Wales, and Wales is no longer deemed to be a part of England.

**1968**    Mauritius, Swaziland, and Nauru gain their independence from Britain.

**1969**    Canada becomes officially bilingual, with a commitment to federal services in English and French.

**1972**    East Pakistan secedes and becomes the Republic of Bangladesh.
Two feminist magazines launched: *Ms* in the US and *Spare Rib* in the UK.

**1973**    The Bahamas gain their independence from Britain.

**1974-9**  Cyngor yr Iaith Gymraeg/Council for the Welsh Language set up to advise the Secretary of State for Wales on matters concerning the language.

**1975**    Papua New Guinea gains its independence from Australia.
The Bas-Lauriol law is passed in France, requiring the use solely of French in advertising and commerce.

**1977**    The spacecraft *Voyager* travels into deep space, its main message to any extra-terrestrials recorded in English by the Secretary-General of the United Nations, Kurt Waldheim, an Austrian.
In Quebec, Loi 101/Bill 101 is passed, making French the sole official language of the province, limiting access to English-medium schools, and banning public signs in other languages.

**1978**    The Government of Northern Territory in Australia is established.

**1980**    The British government averts a fast to the death by Gwynfor Evans, leader of Plaid Cymru (Welsh National Party), by honouring election pledges to provide a fourth television channel using both Welsh and English.

**1981**    British Honduras gains its independence as Belize.

**1982**    The patriation from Great Britain of Canada's constitution. The Canada Act is the last act of the British Parliament concerning Canadian affairs.

**1983**    The publication by Penguin of *The New Testament in Scots*, a translation by William L. Lorimer.

**1984**    The launch of the Apple Macintosh personal (desktop) computer.

**1985**    The publication by Longman of *A Comprehensive Grammar of the English Language*.
The publication by Belknap Press of the first volume of the *Dictionary of American Regional English*.

The launch by Cambridge University Press of the quarterly journal *English Today: The International Review of the English Language*.

**1986** The showing by the BBC in the UK and public television in the US of *The Story of English*, a television series with both British and American backers, accompanied by a book of the same name, and followed by a radio version on BBC World Service.

**1989** The publication of the 2nd edition of *The Oxford English Dictionary*, blending the first edition and its supplements.

**1992** The publication of *The Oxford Companion to the English Language* by Oxford University Press.

**1995** The publication of *The Cambridge Encyclopedia of The English Language* by Cambridge University Press.

**1996** The publication of *The Oxford English Grammar* by Oxford University Press.

**1997** Hong Kong ceases to be a British colony and becomes a Special Autonomous Region of China.
The Scots vote by a strong majority for a devolved parliament to be set up in Edinburgh.
The Welsh vote by a slim margin for a Welsh Assembly to be set up.
Publication of the report *The Future of English?* by the British Council as part of its consciousness-raising campaign entitled *English 2000*.

# Appendix 2: Bibliography

A selection of titles over the last twenty years relating to major areas in the study of English and other languages.

## The English language: overviews

Blake, N. F., and Moorhead, Jean. 1993. *Introduction to the English Language*. Basingstoke: Macmillan.

Bryson, Bill. 1990. *Mother Tongue: The English Language*. London: Hamish Hamilton; New York: William Morrow.

Crowley, Tony. 1991. *Proper English? Readings in Language, History and Cultural Identity*. London: Routledge.

Crystal, David. 1995. *The Cambridge Encyclopedia of the English Language*. Cambridge: University Press.

—— 1997. *English as a Global Language*. Cambridge: University Press.

Görlach, Manfred. 1991. *English: Studies in Varieties of English 1984–1988*. Amsterdam and Philadelphia: John Benjamins.

Graddol, David. 1997. *The Future of English?* London: The British Council.

——Leith, Dick, and Swann, Joan, eds. 1996. *English: History, Diversity and Change*. Milton Keynes: Open University Press; London: Routledge.

Hayhoe, Mike, and Parker, Stephen. 1994. *Who Owns English?* Buckingham and Philadelphia: Open University Press.

McArthur, Tom, ed. 1992. *The Oxford Companion to the English Language*. Oxford: University Press. Abridged edn., 1996.

—— 1998. *The English Languages*. Cambridge: University Press.

Ricks, Christopher, and Michaels, Leonard, eds. 1990. *The State of the Language*. Berkeley and Los Angeles: California University Press (with the English Speaking Union of San Francisco); London: Faber & Faber.

Trudgill, Peter, and Chambers, J. K., eds. 1991. *Dialects of English: Studies in Grammatical Variation*: London and New York: Longman.

## The English language: history

Bailey, Richard W. 1991/92. *Images of English: A Cultural History of the Language*. Ann Arbor: Michigan University Press (1991); Cambridge: University Press (1992).

—— 1997. *Nineteenth-Century English*. Ann Arbor: University of Michigan Press.

Bauer, Laurie. 1994. *Watching English Change: An Introduction to the Study of Linguistic Change in Standard Englishes in the Twentieth Century*. London: Longman.

Baugh, Albert C., and Cable, Thomas. 1993. *A History of the English Language*, 4th edn. Englewood Cliffs: Prentice-Hall. London: Routledge.

Blake, N. F. 1992. *The Cambridge History of the English Language, ii. 1066–1476*. Cambridge: University Press.

—— 1996. *A History of the English Language*. Basingstoke and London: Macmillan.

Burchfield, Robert, ed. 1994. *The Cambridge History of the English Language, v. English in Britain and Overseas, Origins and Developments*. Cambridge: University Press.

Burnley, David. 1992. *The History of the English Language: A Source Book*. London: Longman.

Görlach, Manfred. 1990. *Studies in the History of the English Language*. Heidelberg: Carl Winter Universitätsverlag.

Görlach, Manfred. 1991. *Introduction to Early Modern English*. Cambridge: University Press.

Hogg, Richard M., ed. 1992. *The Cambridge History of the English Language, i. The Beginnings to 1066*. Cambridge: University Press.

Honey, John. 1997. *Language is Power: The Story of Standard English and Its Enemies*. London and Boston: Faber & Faber.

Knowles, Gerry. 1997. *A Cultural History of the English Language*. London: Arnold.

Lass, Roger. 1994. *Old English: A Historical Linguistic Companion*. Cambridge: University Press.

Leith, Dick. 1997. *A Social History of English*, 2nd edn. London: Routledge.

McCrum, Robert, Cran, William, and MacNeil, Robert. 1986. *The Story of English*. London: Faber; New York: Viking.

Mitchell, Bruce, and Robinson, Fred C. 1989. *A Guide to Old English*, 4th edn. Oxford: Basil Blackwell.

Mitchell, Bruce. 1994. *An Invitation to Old English and Anglo-Saxon England*. Oxford: Blackwell.

Smith, Jeremy. 1996. *An Historical Study of English: Function, Form and Change*. London: Routledge.

Barber, Charles. 1976. *Early Modern English*. London: André Deutsch.

## The English language: worldwide

Bailey, Richard W., and Görlach, Manfred, eds. 1982/1984. *English as a World Language*. 1982: Ann Arbor: Michigan University Press (1983); Cambridge: University Press (1984).

Cheshire, Jenny, ed. 1991. *English Around the World: Sociolinguistic Perspectives*. Cambridge: University Press.

Freeborn, Dennis, with Peter French and David Langford. 1993. *Varieties of English: An Introduction to the Study of Language*, 2nd edn. Basingstoke: Macmillan.

García, O., and Otheguy, R., eds. 1989. *English across Cultures, Cultures across English*. Berlin and New York: Mouton de Gruyter.

Glauser, Beate, Schneider, Edgar, and Görlach, Manfred, eds. 1993. *A New Bibliography of Writings on Varieties of English 1984–1992/93* (Varieties of English around the World series). Amsterdam and Philadelphia: John Benjamins.

Görlach, Manfred. 1991. *Englishes: Studies in Varieties of English*. Amsterdam and Philadelphia: John Benjamins.

Schneider, Edgar W. 1997. *Englishes around the World. i. General Studies, British Isles, North America. ii. Caribbean, Africa, Asia, Australasia*. Amsterdam and Philadelphia: John Benjamins.

Trudgill, Peter, and Hannah, Jean. 1994. *International English: A Guide to the Varieties of Standard English*, 3rd edn. London: Edward Arnold.

Viereck, Wolfgang, Schneider, Edgar, and Görlach, Manfred, eds. 1984. *A Bibliography of Writings on Varieties of English, 1965–1983*. Amsterdam and Philadelphia: John Benjamins.

## American English

Adams, Karen L., and Brink, Daniel T., eds. 1990. *Perspectives on Official English: The Campaign of English as the Official Language of the USA*. Berlin and New York: Mouton de Gruyter.

Baron, Dennis. 1990. *The English-Only Question: An Official Language for Americans?* New Haven: Yale University Press.

Bernstein, Cynthia, Nunnally, Thomas, and Sabino, Robin, eds. 1997. *Language Variety in the South Revisited*. Tuscaloosa and London: University of Alabama Press.

Daniels, Harvey A., ed. 1990. *NOT Only English: Affirming America's Multilingual Heritage*. Urbana, Ill.: National Council of Teachers of English.

Dillard, J. L. 1992. *A History of American English*. London and New York: Longman.

Grossman, John, ed. 1993. *The Chicago Manual of Style*, 14th edn. Chicago and London: University of Chicago Press.

Hendrickson, Robert. 1993. *Whistlin' Dxie: A Dictionary of Southern Expressions, vol. i of a Dictionary of American Regional Expressions*. New York: Facts on File.

Holloway, Joseph E., and Vass, Winifred K. 1993. *The African Heritage of American English*. Bloomington and Indianapolis: Indiana University Press.

Mencken, H. L. 1963. *The American Language*, revised by Raven I. McDavid, Jr. New York: Knopf.

Schneider, Edgar W., ed. 1996. *Focus on the USA* (Varieties of English Around the World series). Amsterdam and Philadelphia: John Benjamins.

Sutcliffe, David, and Figueroa, John. 1992. *System in Black Language*. Clevedon and Philadelphia: Multilingual Matters.

Wilson, Kenneth G. 1993. *The Columbia Guide to Standard American English*. New York: Columbia University Press.

## Australian English

Baker, S. J. 1945. *The Australian Language*, revised edn. 1966. Sydney: Currawong Press.

Collins, P., and Blair, D., eds. 1989. *Australian English: The Language of a New Society*. Brisbane: University of Queensland Press.

Hudson, Nicholas. 1993. *Modern Australian Usage*. Melbourne: Oxford University Press.

Murray-Smith, S. 1989. *Right Words: A Guide to English Usage in Australia*, revised edn. Ringwood, Victoria: Viking.

Peters, Pam, ed. 1995. *Cambridge Australian Style Guide*. Melbourne: Cambridge University Press.

Purchase, S., ed. 1990. *Australian Writers' and Editors' Guide*. Melbourne: Oxford University Press.

## British English (England, Scotland, Wales)

Aitken, A. J., and McArthur, Tom, eds. 1979. *Languages of Scotland*. Edinburgh: Chambers.

Barltrop, Robert, and Wolveridge, Jim. 1980. *The Muvver Tongue*. London: Journeyman.

Coupland, Nikolas, ed. 1990. *English in Wales: Diversity, Conflict and Change*. Clevedon and Philadelphia: Multilingual Matters.

Kay, Billy. 1986. *The Mither Tongue*. Edinburgh: Mainstream.

Kellett, Arnold. 1994. *The Yorkshire Dictionary of Dialect, Tradition and Folklore*. Otley: Smith Settle.

McClure, J. Derrick. 1995. *Scots and Its Literature* (Varieties of English around the World series). Amsterdam and Philadelphia: John Benjamins.

MacLeod, Iseabail, and Cairns, Pauline, eds. 1993. *The Concise English-Scots Dictionary*. Edinburgh: Chambers Harrap/Scottish National Dictionary Association.

Price, Glanville. 1984. *The Languages of Britain*. London: Edward Arnold.

Sebba, Mark. 1993. *London Jamaica: Language Systems in Interaction*. London: Longman.

Trudgill, Peter, ed. 1984. *Language in the British Isles*. Cambridge: University Press.

Viereck, Wolfgang. 1985. *Focus on: England and Wales*. (Varieties of English Around the World series). Amsterdam and Philadelphia: John Benjamins.

Wakelin, Martyn F. 1986. *The Southwest of England* (Varieties of English Around the World series). Amsterdam and Philadelphia: John Benjamins.

## Canadian English

Clarke, Sandra, ed. 1993. *Focus on Canada*. Amsterdam and Philadelphia: John Benjamins.

Fee, Margery, and McAlpine, Janice, eds. 1997. *Guide to Canadian English Usage*. Toronto: Oxford University Press.

Lougheed, W. C., ed. 1985. *In Search of the Standard in Canadian English*. Kingston, Ontario: Strathy Language Unit, Queen's University.

McArthur, Tom. 1989. *The English Language as Used in Quebec: A Survey*. Kingston, Ontario: Strathy Language Unit, Queen's University.

## Caribbean English

Allsopp, Richard, ed. 1996. *Dictionary of Caribbean English Usage*. Oxford: University Press.

Görlach, M., and Holm, J. A., eds. 1986. *Focus on: The Caribbean* (Varieties of English around the World series). Amsterdam and Philadelphia: John Benjamins.

Roberts, P. A. 1988. *West Indians and their Language*. Cambridge: University Press.

## Irish English

Dolan, T. P., ed. 1990. *The English of the Irish*. Special issue, *Irish University Review: A Journal of Irish Studies*. Dublin: University College.

Macafee, Caroline, ed. 1996. *The Concise Ulster Dictionary*. Oxford: University Press.

O Muirithe, Diarmaid. 1977. *The English Language in Ireland*. Cork and Dublin: Mercier Press.

Todd, Loreto. 1989. *The Language of Irish Literature*. London: Macmillan.

## New Zealand English

Bell, Allan, and Holmes, Janet, eds. 1990. *New Zealand Ways of Speaking English*. Clevedon and Philadelphia: Multilingual Matters.

Deverson, Tony. 1989. *Finding a New Zealand Voice: Attitudes Towards English Used in New Zealand*. Auckland: New House.

Gordon, Elizabeth, and Deverson, Tony. 1985. *New Zealand English: An Introduction to New Zealand Speech and Usage*. Auckland: Heinemann.

## Singapore English

Foley, J., ed. 1988. *The New Englishes: The Case of Singapore*. Singapore: University Press.

Fraser Gupta, Anthea. 1994. *The Step-Tongue: Children's English in Singapore*. Clevedon and Philadelphia: Multilingual Matters.

Ho, Mian Lian, and Platt, John. 1991. *Dynamics of a Contact Continuum: Singapore English*. Oxford: University Press.

## South African English

Branford, Jean. 1991. *A Dictionary of South African English*, 4th edn. Cape Town: Oxford University Press.

de Klerk, Vivian, ed. 1996. *Focus on South Africa* (Varieties of English Around the World series). Amsterdam and Philadelphia: John Benjamins.

Gray, Stephen. 1979. *South African Literature: An Introduction*. Cape Town: David Philip.

Silva, Penny M., ed. 1997. *A Dictionary of South African English on Historical Principles*. Oxford: University Press.

## South Asian English (India and Pakistan)

Baumgardner, Robert J., ed. 1993. *The English Language in Pakistan*. Oxford: University Press.

Kachru, Braj B. 1983. *The Indianization of English: The English Language in India*. Delhi: Oxford University Press.

Lewis, Ivor. 1991. *Sahibs, Nabobs and Boxwallahs: A Dictionary of the Words of Anglo-India*. Bombay: Oxford University Press.

Nihalani, P., Tongue, R. K., and Hosali, P. 1970. *Indian and British English: A Handbook of Usage and Pronunciation*. Delhi: Oxford University Press.

Rahman, Tariq. 1990. *Pakistani English: The Linguistic Description of a Non-Native Variety of English*. Islamabad: National Institute of Pakistan Studies, Qaid-i-Azam University.

## Communication

Barnow, Erik, ed. 1989. *International Encyclopedia of Communications*, 4 vols. New York: Oxford University Press.

Corner, John, ed., with Jeremy Hawthorn. 1993. *Communication Studies: An Introductory Reader*, 4th edn. London: Edward Arnold.

Mellor, D. H., ed. 1990. *Ways of Communicating*. Cambridge: University Press.

Watson, James, and Hill, Anne, eds. 1997. *A Dictionary of Communication and Media Studies*, 4th edn. London: Arnold.

Weiner, Richard, ed. 1996. *Webster's New World Dictionary of Media and Communications*. New York: Macmillan.


## Language and languages

Aitchison, Jean. 1996. *The Seeds of Speech: Language Origin and Evolution*. Cambridge: University Press.

—— 1997. *The Language Web: The Power and Problem of Words*. Cambridge: University Press.

Cameron, Deborah. 1995. *Verbal Hygiene*. London and New York: Routledge.

Campbell, George L. 1991. *Compendium of the World's Languages*, 2 vols. London and New York: Routledge.

Crystal, David, 1992. *An Encyclopedic Dictionary of Language and Languages*. Oxford: Blackwell.

—— 1997. *The Cambridge Encyclopedia of Language*, 2nd edn. Cambridge: University Press.

Mengham, Rod. 1993. *The Descent of Language*. London: Bloomsbury.

Milroy, James, and Milroy, Lesley. 1985. *Authority in Language*. London: Routledge.

Pinker, Steven. 1994. *The Language Instinct: How the Mind Creates Language*. New York: William Morrow; Harmondsworth: Penguin.

Trask, R. L. 1997. *A Student's Dictionary of Language and Linguistics*. London: Arnold.


## Language and literature

Benson, Eugene, and Conolly, L. W., eds. 1994. *Encyclopedia of Post-Colonial Literatures in English*, 2 vols. London: Routledge.

Blake, N. F. 1983. *Shakespeare's Language: An Introduction*. London: Macmillan.

—— 1990. *An Introduction to the Language of Literature*. London: Macmillan.

Bolton, W. F. 1992. *Shakespeare's English: Language in the History Plays*. Oxford: Basil Blackwell.

Chapman, Raymond. 1982. *The Language of English Literature*. London: Arnold.

Hussey, S. S. 1982. *The Literary Language of Shakespeare*. London: Longman.

Salmon, Vivian, and Burness, Edwina, eds. 1987. *A Reader in the Language of Shakespearean Drama*. Amsterdam and Philadelphia: John Benjamins.

Tambling, J. 1988. *What is Literary Language?* Milton Keynes: Open University Press.


## Language learning and teaching

Bennet-Kastor, T. 1988. *Analysing Children's Language*. Oxford: Blackwell.

Brumfit, C. J., and Johnson, K., eds. 1979. *The Communicative Approach to Language Teaching*. Oxford: University Press.

Crystal, D. 1986. *Listen to your Child*. London: Penguin.

Harmer, Jeremy. 1983. *The Practice of English Language Teaching*. London and New York: Longman. (EFL)

Howatt, A. P. R. 1984. *A History of English Language Teaching*. Oxford: University Press. (EFL)

Ellis, Rod. 1997. *Second Language Acquisition*. Oxford: University Press.

Mercer, Neil, and Swann, Joan. 1996. *Learning English: Development and Diversity*. Milton Keynes: Open University Press; London: Routledge.

Murphy, Edna, ed. 1990. *ESL: A Handbook for Teachers and Administrators in International Schools*. Clevedon and Philadelphia: Multilingual Matters.

Spolsky, Bernard. 1989. *Conditions for Second Language Learning: Introduction to General Theory*. Oxford: University Press.

Stern, H. H. 1983. *Fundamental Concepts in Language Teaching*. Oxford: University Press.

Widdowson, H. G. 1990. *Aspects of Language Teaching*. Oxford: University Press. (EFL)

## Pronunciation, accent, and dialect

Chambers, J. K., and Trudgill, P. 1980. *Dialectology*. Cambridge: University Press.

Cheshire, Jenny. 1982. *Variation in English Dialect: A Sociological Study*. Cambridge: University Press.

—— Edwards, Viv, Münstermann, Henk, and Weltens, Bert, eds. 1989. *Dialect and Education: Some European Perspectives*. Clevedon and Philadelphia: Multilingual Matters.

Honey, John. 1989. *Does Accent Matter? The Pygmalion Factor*. London: Faber.

Hughes, A., and Trudgill, P. 1979/87. *English Accents and Dialects: An Introduction to Social and Regional Varieties of British English*. London: Edward Arnold.

Jones, Daniel. 1997. *English Pronouncing Dictionary*, 15th edn., Peter Roach and James Hartman, eds. Cambridge: University Press (1st edn., 1917, London: Dent).

Wells, John C. 1982. *Accents of English*, 3 vols.: i. *An Introduction*, ii. *The British Isles*, iii. *Beyond the British Isles*. With cassette. Cambridge: University Press.

—— 1990. *Longman Pronunciation Dictionary*. Harlow: Longman.

## Grammar

Chalker, Sylvia, and Weiner, Edmund, eds. 1994. *The Oxford Dictionary of English Grammar*. Oxford: University Press.

Eastwood, John. 1994. *Oxford Guide to English Grammar*. Oxford: University Press.

Greenbaum, Sidney. 1991. *An Introduction to English Grammar*. London: Longman.

—— 1996. *The Oxford English Grammar*. Oxford: University Press.

Halliday, M. A. K. 1994. *An Introduction to Functional Grammar*, 2nd edn. London: Edward Arnold.

Jackson, Howard. 1990. *Grammar and Meaning: A Semantic Approach to English Grammar*. London: Longman.

Quirk, R., Greenbaum, S., Leech, G., and Svartvik, J. 1985. *A Comprehensive Grammar of the English Language*. London: Longman.

Palmer, F. R. 1988. *The English Verb*, 2nd edn. London: Longman.

## Vocabulary and lexicography

Bailey, Richard W., ed. 1987. *Dictionaries of English: Prospects for the Record of Our Language*. Ann Arbor: University of Michigan Press.

Barnhart, Robert K., ed. 1987. *The Barnhart Dictionary of Etymology*. New York: H. W. Wilson.

Bauer, Laurie. 1983. *English Word-Formation*. Cambridge: University Press.

Green, Jonathon. 1996. *Chasing the Sun: Dictionary-Makers and the Dictionaries they Made*. London: Jonathan Cape.

Hartmann, R. R. K., ed. 1986. *The History of Lexicography*. Amsterdam and Philadelphia: John Benjamins.

Hoad, T. F. 1993. *The Concise Oxford Dictionary of English Etymology*. Oxford: University Press (1st publ. 1986).

Landau, Sidney I. 1984/89. *Dictionaries: The Art and Craft of Lexicography*. New York: Charles Scribner's Sons. (1984); Cambridge: University Press (1989).

Lipka, Leonhard. 1990. *An Outline of English Lexicology: Lexical Structure, Word Semantics, and Word-Formation*. Tübingen: Niemeyer.

McArthur, Tom. 1986. *Worlds of Reference: Lexicography, Learning and Language from the Clay Tablet to the Computer*. Cambridge: University Press.

Morton, Herbert C. 1994. *The Story of Webster's Third: Philip Gove's Controversial Dictionary and Its Critics.* Cambridge: University Press.

Svensen, Bo. 1993. *Practical Lexicography: Principles and Methods of Dictionary-Making.* Oxford: University Press.

Willinsky, John. 1994. *The Empire of Words: The Reign of the OED.* Princeton: University Press.

## Linguistics and phonetics

Aitchison, Jean. 1987. *Linguistics*, 3rd edn. London: Hodder & Stoughton.

—— 1989. *The Articulate Mammal: An Introduction to Psycholinguistics*, 3rd edn. London: Unwin Hyman.

Clark, J., and Yallop, C. 1990. *An Introduction to Phonetics and Phonology.* Oxford: Blackwell.

Crystal, David, ed. 1997. *A Dictionary of Linguistics and Phonetics*, 4th edn. Oxford: Blackwell.

Malmkjær, Kirsten, ed. 1991. *The Linguistics Encyclopedia.* London: Routledge.

Milroy, James, and Milroy, Lesley. 1993. *Real English: The Grammar of English Dialects in the British Isles.* London: Longman.

Preston, Dennis R., ed. 1993. *American Dialect Research.* Amsterdam and Philadelphia: John Benjamins.

Pullum, Geoffrey K., and Ladusaw, William A. 1996. *Phonetic Symbol Guide*, 2nd edn. Chicago: University of Chicago Press.

Thomas, Alan R., ed. 1988. *Methods in Dialectology.* Clevedon and Philadelphia: Multilingual Matters.

Trudgill, Peter. 1990. *The Dialects of England.* Oxford: Basil Blackwell.

—— and Chambers, J. K., eds. 1991. *Dialects of English: Studies in Grammatical Variation.* London: Longman.

Upton, Clive, and Widdowson, J. D. A., eds. 1996. *An Atlas of English Dialects.* Oxford: University Press.

Widdowson, H. G. 1996. *Linguistics.* Oxford: University Press.

Yule, George. 1996. *The Study of Language*, 2nd edn. Cambridge: University Press.

## Rhetoric, style, and usage

Ayto, John. 1993. *Euphemisms: Over 3,000 Ways to Avoid Being Rude or Giving Offence.* London: Bloomsbury.

Burchfield, R. W., ed. 1996. *The New Fowler's Modern English Usage.* Oxford: University Press.

Cutts, Martin. 1995. *The Plain English Guide: How to Write Clearly and Communicate Better.* Oxford: University Press.

Fowler, Henry W., ed. Sir Ernest Gowers. 1965. *A Dictionary of Modern English Usage*, 2nd edn. Oxford: University Press.

Gilman, E. Ward, ed. 1989. *Webster's Dictionary of English Usage.* Springfield, Mass.: Merriam Webster.

Gowers, Sir Ernest. 1954. *The Complete Plain Words.* London: HMSO; Pelican edn. 1962; 2nd edn. 1973; 3rd edn 1986, revised by Sidney Greenbaum and Janet Whitcut; Penguin edn. 1987.

Hale, Constance. 1996. *Wired Style: Principles of English Usage in the Digital Age.* San Francisco: HardWired.

Haynes, John. 1995. *Style.* London: Routledge.

Holder, R. W. 1995. *A Dictionary of Euphemisms.* Oxford: University Press.

Nash, Walter. 1989. *Rhetoric: The Wit of Persuasion.* Oxford: Basil Blackwell.

—— 1993. *Jargon: Its Uses and Abuses.* Oxford: Blackwell.

Rees, Nigel. 1993. *The Politically Correct Phrasebook.* London: Bloomsbury.

Roberts, Philip Davies. 1987. *Plain English: A User's Guide.* Harmondsworth: Penguin.

Todd, Loreto, and Hancock, Ian. 1986. *International English Usage*. London: Croom Helm.

Wales, Katie. 1989. *A Dictionary of Stylistics*. London: Longman.

## Feminism and sexism

Cameron, Deborah, ed. 1990. *The Feminist Critique of Language: A Reader*. London and New York: Routledge.

Coates, J. 1986. *Women, Men and Language*. London: Longman.

Miller, Casey, and Swift, Kate. 1988. *The Handbook of Nonsexist Writing: For Writers, Editors and Speakers*. New York: Harper & Row.

Spender, Dale. 1980. *Man Made Language*. London: Routledge.

## Place-names

Cameron, Kenneth. 1988. *English Place-names*, revised edn. London: Batsford.

Hamilton, William B. 1978. *The Macmillan Book of Canadian Place Names*. Toronto: Macmillan.

Matthews, Constance M. 1972. *Place Names of the English-Speaking World*. London: Weidenfeld & Nicolson. New York: Scribner's.

Mills, David. 1991. *A Dictionary of English Place-Names*. Oxford: University Press.

Nicolaisen, W. F. H. 1976. *Scottish Place-Names*. London: Batsford.

Room, Adrian. 1986. *A Dictionary of Irish Place-Names*. Belfast: Appletree Press.

—— 1988. *Dictionary of Place-Names in the British Isles*. London: Bloomsbury.

—— 1989. *Dictionary of World Place Names Derived from British Names*. London: Routledge.

## Reading, writing, and spelling

Bailey, Richard W., and Fosheim, Robin Melanie. 1983. *Literacy for Life: The Demand for Reading and Writing*. New York: Modern Language Association.

Coulmas, F. 1989. *The Writing Systems of the World*. Oxford: Basil Blackwell.

Crowder, Robert G. 1982. *The Psychology of Reading*. New York: Oxford University Press.

Cummings, D. W. 1988. *American English Spelling*. Baltimore and London: Johns Hopkins University Press.

Davis, Philip. 1992. *The Experience of Reading*. London and New York: Routledge.

Edelsky, Carole. 1996. *With Literacy and Justice for All: Rethinking the Social in Language and Education*. London and Bristol, Pa. Taylor & Francis.

Eisenstein, Elizabeth. 1993. *The Printing Revolution in Early Modern Europe*. Cambridge: University Press. (1st publ. 1983).

Harris, Roy. 1986. *The Origin of Writing*. London: Duckworth.

Hooker, J. T. 1990. *Reading the Past: Ancient Writing from Cuneiform to the Alphabet*. London: British Museum Publications.

Scragg, D. G. 1974. *A History of English Spelling*. Manchester: University Press.

## Computing

Barry, John A. 1991. *Technobabble*. Cambridge, Mass., and London: MIT Press.

Butler, Christopher S., ed. 1992. *Computers and Written Texts*. Oxford: Blackwell.

Heim, Michael. 1987. *Electric Language: A Philosophical Study of Word Processing*. New Haven and London: Yale University Press.

Lanham, Richard A. 1993. *The Electronic Word: Democracy, Technology, and the Arts*. Chicago: University of Chicago Press.

Miall, David S., ed. 1990. *Humanities and the Computer*. Oxford: Clarendon Press.

Raymond, Eric, ed. 1991. *The New Hacker's Dictionary*. Cambridge, Mass., and London: MIT Press.

OXFORD

## MORE OXFORD PAPERBACKS

This book is just one of nearly 1000 Oxford Paperbacks currently in print. If you would like details of other Oxford Paperbacks, including titles in the World's Classics, Oxford Reference, Oxford Books, OPUS, Past Masters, Oxford Authors, and Oxford Shakespeare series, please write to:

**UK and Europe:** Oxford Paperbacks Publicity Manager, Arts and Reference Publicity Department, Oxford University Press, Walton Street, Oxford OX2 6DP.

Customers in UK and Europe will find Oxford Paperbacks available in all good bookshops. But in case of difficulty please send orders to the Cash-with-Order Department, Oxford University Press Distribution Services, Saxon Way West, Corby, Northants NN18 9ES. Tel: 01536 741519; Fax: 01536 746337. Please send a cheque for the total cost of the books, plus £1.75 postage and packing for orders under £20; £2.75 for orders over £20. Customers outside the UK should add 10% of the cost of the books for postage and packing.

**USA:** Oxford Paperbacks Marketing Manager, Oxford University Press, Inc., 200 Madison Avenue, New York, N.Y. 10016.

**Canada:** Trade Department, Oxford University Press, 70 Wynford Drive, Don Mills, Ontario M3C 1J9.

**Australia:** Trade Marketing Manager, Oxford University Press, G.P.O. Box 2784Y, Melbourne 3001, Victoria.

**South Africa:** Oxford University Press, P.O. Box 1141, Cape Town 8000.

**Oxford Paperback Reference**

## OXFORD PAPERBACK REFERENCE

From *Art and Artists* to *Zoology*, the Oxford Paperback Reference series offers the very best subject reference books at the most affordable prices.

Authoritative, accessible, and up to date, the series features dictionaries in key student areas, as well as a range of fascinating books for a general readership. Included are such well-established titles as Fowler's *Modern English Usage*, Margaret Drabble's *Concise Companion to English Literature*, and the bestselling science and medical dictionaries.

The series has now been relaunched in handsome new covers. Highlights include new editions of some of the most popular titles, as well as brand new paperback reference books on *Politics*, *Philosophy*, and *Twentieth-Century Poetry*.

With new titles being constantly added, and existing titles regularly updated, Oxford Paperback Reference is unrivalled in its breadth of coverage and expansive publishing programme. New dictionaries of *Film*, *Economics*, *Linguistics*, *Architecture*, *Archaeology*, *Astronomy*, and *The Bible* are just a few of those coming in the future.

# THE CONCISE OXFORD COMPANION
## TO ENGLISH LITERATURE

*Edited by Margaret Drabble and
Jenny Stringer*

Derived from the acclaimed *Oxford Companion to
English Literature*, the concise maintains the wide
coverage of its parent volume. It is an indispens-
able, compact guide to all aspects of English literature. For this revised edition, existing entries have
been fully updated and revised with 60 new entries
added on contemporary writers.

* Over 5,000 entries on the lives and works of
  authors, poets and playwrights

* The most comprehensive and authoritative
  paperback guide to English literature

* New entries include Peter Ackroyd, Martin
  Amis, Toni Morrison, and Jeanette Winterson

* New appendices list major literary prize-
  winners

From the reviews of its parent volume:

'It earns its place at the head of the best sellers: every
home should have one'
*Sunday Times*

# WORLD'S CLASSICS SHAKESPEARE

*'not simply a better text but a new conception of Shakespeare. This is a major achievement of twentieth-century scholarship.'* Times Literary Supplement

Hamlet
Macbeth
The Merchant of Venice
As You Like It
Henry IV Part I
Henry V
Measure for Measure
The Tempest
Much Ado About Nothing
All's Well that Ends Well
Love's Labours Lost
The Merry Wives of Windsor
The Taming of the Shrew
Titus Andronicus
Troilus & Cressida
The Two Noble Kinsmen
King John
Julius Caesar
Coriolanus
Anthony & Cleopatra